This New Ocean

NASA SP-4201

This New Ocean

A History of Project Mercury

Loyd S. Swenson, Jr.
James M. Grimwood
Charles C. Alexander

The NASA History Series

National Aeronautics and Space Administration
NASA History Office
Office of Policy and Plans
Washington, DC 20546
1998

We set sail on this new sea because there is new knowledge to be gained, and new rights to be won, and they must be won and used for the progress of all people. For space science, like nuclear science and all technology, has no conscience of its own.

Whether it will become a force for good or ill depends on man, and only if the United States occupies a position of pre-eminence can we help decide whether this new ocean will be a sea of peace or a new, terrifying theater of war.

John F. Kennedy
Rice University Stadium
Houston^ Texas
September 12, 1962

NASA SP-4201

FOREWORD

WHEN the Congress created the National Aeronautics and Space Administration in 1958, it charged NASA with the responsibility "to contribute materially to . . . the expansion of human knowledge of phenomena in the atmosphere and space" and "provide for the widest practicable and appropriate dissemination of information concerning its activities and the results thereof." NASA wisely interpreted this mandate to include responsibility for documenting the epochal progress of which it is the focus. The result has been the development of a historical program by NASA as unprecedented as the task of extending man's mobility beyond his planet. This volume is not only NASA's accounting of its obligation to disseminate information to our current generation of Americans. It also fulfills, as do all of NASA's future-oriented scientific-technological activities, the further obligation to document the present as the heritage of the future.

The wide-ranging NASA history program includes chronicles of day-to-day space activities; specialized studies of particular fields within space science and technology; accounts of NASA's efforts in organization and management, where its innovations, while less known to the public than its more spectacular space shots, have also been of great significance; narratives of the growth and expansion of the space centers throughout the country, which represent in microcosm many aspects of NASA's total effort; program histories, tracing the successes— and failures—of the various projects that mark man's progress into the Space Age; and a history of NASA itself, incorporating in general terms the major problems and challenges, and the responses thereto, of our entire civilian space effort. The volume presented here is a program history, the first in a series telling of NASA's pioneering steps into the Space Age. It deals with the first American manned-spaceflight program: Project Mercury.

Although some academicians might protest that this is "official" history, it is official only in the fact that it has been prepared and published with the support and cooperation of NASA. It is not "official" history in the sense of presenting a point of view supposedly that of NASA officialdom—if anyone could determine what *the* "point of view" of such a complex organism might be. Certainly, the authors were allowed to pursue their task with the fullest freedom and in accordance with the highest scholarly standards of the history profession. They were permitted unrestricted access to source materials and participants. Furthermore, they have with humility and some courage attempted to document what emerges as a complex accounting of the purposes of science, technology, and public funding in a challenging new area of human endeavor.

Some classical historians may deplore the short lapse of time between the actual events and the historical narration of them. Others may boggle at the mass of full documentary sources with which the Project Mercury historians have had to cope. There are offsetting advantages, however. The very freshness of the events and accessibility of their participants have made possible the writing of a most useful treatise of lasting historical value. Future historians may rewrite this history of Project Mercury for their own age, but they will indeed be thankful to their predecessors of the NASA historical program for providing them with the basic data as well as the view of what this pioneering venture in the Space Age meant to its participants and to contemporary historians.

MELVIN KRANZBERG
Case Institute of Technology
Chairman, NASA Historical
Advisory Committee

Members:

Lloyd V. Berkner, *Graduate Research Center of the Southwest*
James L. Cate, *University of Chicago*
A. Hunter Dupree, *University of California at Berkeley*
Wood Gray, *George Washington University*
Lawrence Kavanau, *North American Aviation, Inc.*
Marvin W. McFarland, *Library of Congress*
Paul P. Van Riper, *Cornell University*
Alan T. Waterman, *National Academy of Sciences*

VI

CONTENTS

List of Illustrations

All photographs and illustrations are U.S. Government ones except as credited on this list. People in photographs are identified in the captions and referenced in the Index.

LIST OF ILLUSTRATIONS

PREFACE

MANKIND in the past few years has sailed on one of its greatest adventures, the exploration of near space. Men have cast off their physical and mental moorings to Earth, and a few have learned to live in balance with their gravisphere and above their atmosphere. Transgressing old laws of terrestrial navigation and amending newer laws of aerodynamics, man has combined the experience gained from aviation and rocket technology with the science of celestial mechanics, thus to accomplish for the first time manned orbital circumnavigation. The initial American voyages in this new epic of exploration and discovery were products of Project Mercury, an intensive national program mobilizing creative science and technology to orbit and retrieve a manned Earth satellite.

This book is an attempt to describe the origins, preparation, and nature of America's first achievements in manned space flight. Neither a history of the National Aeronautics and Space Administration (NASA) nor a comparative study of the competition in space between the United States and the Soviet Union, this narrative spans the basic events in the managerial and technological history of Project Mercury.

The authors have no illusions that this single volume is complete or "definitive" (if any work of history ever can be). Writing only a few years after the events described, we inescapably suffer from short perspective, but perhaps our scholarly myopia is balanced by our having had access to a multitude of still-dustless documents and to most of the main participants in Project Mercury. Within obvious limitations of chronology and the sensitivities of persons still active in the conquest of space, we have tried to make this narrative as comprehensive and accurate as possible in one volume.

Already Project Mercury has come to be regarded as a single episode in the history of flight and of the United States. Rather, it was many episodes, many people, many days of inspiration, frustration, and elation. Journalists and other contemporary observers have written millions of words, taken thousands of photographs, and produced hundreds of reports, official and otherwise, on the origins, development, failures, successes, and significance of this country's first efforts in the manned exploration of space. The foremost image of Mercury emerging from its mountainous publicity was that of seven selected test pilots called "astronauts." Central as were their roles and critical as were their risks in the individual manned flights, the astronauts themselves did not design, develop, or decide the means and ends of the overall program. Thousands of engineers, scientists, technicians, and administrators, as well as the seven astronauts, cooperated to fulfill Mercury's goals, and this program history tries to blend and balance the personal, social, and technical facets of the project as it progressed.

Endeavoring to keep fickle human memories accurate in an age that moves incredibly fast in too many directions, we have sought to answer unanswered questions, to answer some questions that had not been asked, and even perhaps to pose some questions that cannot be answered yet. Written under sponsorship of NASA at its Manned Spacecraft Center (MSC) with principal reliance on a contract with the University of Houston, this study is, in the legal sense of the Space Act of 1958, an "official" history of Project Mercury. But NASA and its Historical Advisory Committee have wisely recognized that history should be written, taught, and finally judged by historians, and that the ultimate responsibility for historical generalizations and interpretations should rest with the authors. Accordingly, while we have trod circumspectly in places, we have been encouraged to arrive at historical judgments judiciously and independently. Thus there actually is no "official" NASA or MSC viewpoint on what happened. More details and acknowledgments on the historiography behind this work are to be found in the Note on Sources and Selected Bibliography at the end of the volume.

The organization and division of labor imposed on the narrative conforms to its chronology, to three genres of historical literature, and to the thesis that Project Mercury, from its inception in the fall of 1958, was preeminently an engineering, rather than a scientific, enterprise.

Part One, entitled "Research," could be called "origins" or "antecedents." This section on the long and complex "prehistory" of Project Mercury follows essentially a topical organization and might be seen as part of the external history of applied science. Emphasizing the contributions of individual minds and small groups of experimentalists, Part One recounts primarily progress in rocketry and research in space medicine, aerodynamics, and thermodynamics from the end of the Second World War to the inception of the first United States manned satellite project. The focus is on the evolutionary roles of the military services and the National Advisory Committee for Aeronautics, organizational nucleus of NASA.

Part Two, "Development," assumes with reason that all of the basic and most of the applied research necessary for undertaking a manned ballistic satellite project had been completed by October 1958. Thus the so-called research and development, or "R and D," phase of Mercury is mostly, if not entirely, "D" and corresponds to a relatively new professional interest, the history of technology. Part Two is a study of corporate technology in the crowded period during which the concurrent teamwork of previously diverse organizations drove toward placing a man in orbit around Earth.

For most people directly involved in Mercury, the dramatic "space race" aspect of the project was secondary to the accomplishment of an almost incredibly complex managerial and technological endeavor. Yet the historian cannot ignore the broadly political and social context surrounding all of the organizing, contracting, innovating, manufacturing, training, and testing before the time in 1961 when men first rocketed into space. Costs, schedules, and "quality control"—the range of procedures designed to ensure reliability during space vehicle manufacturing and preparation for flight—were far less dramatic than the flights themselves. But the NASA Space Task Group, primarily responsible for the development of Mercury, had an exciting life of its own as it evolved into the Manned Spacecraft Center. The Mercury team was much larger than the Space Task Group, or even than NASA, but the focus in Part Two on the field managers of the project should be meaningful for anyone wishing insight into the enormity and intricacy of modern government-managed technological programs.

Part Three, entitled "Operations," describes the fulfillment of Project Mercury and the only part of the program witnessed by most contemporary observers. This section begins with the successful suborbital flight of Astronaut Alan B. Shepard, Jr., in May 1961; proceeds through the completion of the orbital qualification of the Mercury spacecraft and the Atlas rocket; and ends with the four manned orbital missions, stretching from three to 22 circuits of Earth, in 1962 and 1963. Part Three is allied with a heroic tradition, the history of exploration and discovery.

Cosmonaut Yuri A. Gagarin first made a space flight around Earth on April 12, 1961, and four months later Gherman Titov's 17-orbit flight pushed the U.S.S.R. still further ahead in the cold war space competition. With American technological prestige damaged in the court of world opinion, the United States responded after Shepard's suborbital ride, when President John F. Kennedy proposed and an eager Congress agreed to make Mercury the first phase of an epochal national venture in the manned exploration of the Earth-Moon system.

Although the Soviet Union succeeded in orbiting more space travelers, for longer periods, and sooner than the United States, Project Mercury still appears magnificently successful. It cost more money and took more time than originally expected, but no precaution was overlooked and no astronaut was lost. And as the "space race" broadened into the "space olympics," Mercury evolved from a "dead-end" endeavor, pointed solely at achieving orbital flight and recovery, into a prerequisite course in what was needed to reach and return from the Moon.

If Mercury was not all that it might have been, it was certainly more than it originally was supposed to be. Less than three and a half years after its inception, its prime objectives were attained with the three-orbit flight of Astronaut John H. Glenn, Jr. In all, the Mercury astronauts flew two ballistic, parabolic flights into space and four orbital missions. Each flight went almost as well as planned, thereby substantially enlarging man's knowledge of near space, of his psychophysiological behavior beyond Earth's atmosphere, and of the impending requirements for cislunar travel. By June 12, 1963, when James E. Webb, the second NASA Administrator, announced its termination, Project Mercury had become the focal point of the American people's vicarious journey into space, the first rung on a ladder leading to the Moon, and perhaps beyond.

This volume, therefore, represents an effort to lift out of anonymity, where so much of mankind's technological progress lies buried, the odyssey of the men who developed the means for escaping our age-old habitat. We hope to enlarge man's knowledge of himself by recording who did what, when, and where to achieve the confidence and provide the machines for space flight. We have aimed to supply a reference to the past, a benchmark for the present, and a source for future scholarship. Later historians will write about Gemini and Apollo, and about Ranger, Mariner, and other projects in space exploration by men of our times. But like students of Mercury, present and future, they must begin with an accurate record of technological achievement. In time, perhaps, Project Mercury may deserve more, because it was both an effect of and a cause for the faith, vision, and prowess necessary to explore space.

ṻ ṻ ṻ ṻ ṻ ṻ ṻ ṻ ṻ

This history of Project Mercury is, in more than the usual sense, drawn from the memory of many of the primary participants in the program. They provided much of the documentation upon which this narrative is based, and some 150 of them have commented upon all or parts of a review edition before publication. They are not responsible, however, for the selection, organization, or interpretations of facts as here presented. If errors persist in this account, the fault lies solely with the authors.

A different emphasis might have been pursued in this history—perhaps, for instance, more on the management of manned space programs. But Project Mercury per se is the focus herein, and as history it is meant to be read consecutively. In the launching of this history, the endorsement and support of the late Hugh L. Dryden, Deputy Administrator of NASA (1958–1965); Chancellor George L. Simpson of the University of Georgia System, former Assistant Deputy Administrator (1962–1965); and Robert R. Gilruth, Director of the Manned Spacecraft Center, proved instrumental. Whatever value this volume may have in reflecting the broader concerns of NASA Headquarters results largely from the contributions of Eugene M. Emme, the NASA Historian, and Frank W. Anderson, the Deputy NASA Historian. They have minutely read and criticized the draft manuscripts and coordinated the details of publication.

Paul E. Purser, Special Assistant to the Director, Manned Spacecraft Center, and Allen J. Going, Chairman, Department of History, University of Houston, have read various phases of the draft work and suggested improvements at every step. Sigman Byrd and Pamela C. Johnson worked with the authors as editorial and research assistants in its formative stages. Ivan D. Ertel made the final index and basic selection of illustrations. Sally D. Gates made many invaluable editorial suggestions and comments, typed several "final" drafts, and administratively coordinated the review edition with the numerous readers. Geri A. Vanderoef typed many of the early manuscripts in the constant revision process.

Among those NASA field center historians and monitors who have been most helpful are David S. Akens of the Marshall Space Flight Center; Alfred Rosenthal of the Goddard Space Flight Center; Robert A. Lindemann and Francis E. Jarrett, Jr., of the Kennedy Space Center; Manley Hood and John B. Talmadge of the Ames Research Center; Lyndell L. Manley of the Lewis Research Center; and Robert W. Mulac of the Langley Research Center.

Government—particularly Air Force—and industrial historians, librarians, and archivists too numerous to mention offered courteous assistance on many aspects of Project Mercury. William D. Putnam, Office of Manned Space Flight and formerly of the Air Force Space Systems Division; Max Rosenberg of the Air Force Historical Liaison Office; Charles V. Eppley, Air Force Flight Test Center; Marvin E. Hintz, Air Force Arnold Engineering Development Center; Green Peyton of the Air Force School of Aerospace Medicine; Michael Witunski of the McDonnell Aircraft Corporation; Ralph B. Oakley of North American Aviation; and Louis Canter of General Dynamics/Astronautics deserve special mention and thanks.

At the Manned Spacecraft Center, the Public Affairs Office, under Paul P. Haney and Albert M. Chop, provided documentation, contract support, and many hours of critical reading; the Technical Library, through the efforts of Retha Shirkey, furnished literature; and the Technical Information Division's Robert W. Fricke helped immeasurably in securing documentation.

Countless others also should be mentioned for their aid on specific questions, but most of them have been credited in the citations.

L.S.S.
J.M.G.
C.C.A.

January 1966

Part One

RESEARCH

I

The Lure, the Lock, the Key

(TO 1958)

THE yearning of men to escape the confines of their Earth and to travel to
the heavens is older than the history of mankind itself. Religion, mythology,
and literature reaching back thousands of years are sprinkled with references to
magic carpets, flying horses, flaming aerial chariots, and winged gods.[1] Although
"science fiction" is a descriptive term of recent vintage, the fictional literature of
space travel dates at least from the second century A.D. Around the year 160 the
Greek savant Lucian of Samosata wrote satirically about an imaginary journey
to the Moon, "a great countrie in the aire, like to a shining island," as Elizabethan
scholars translated his description 1500 years later. Carried to the Moon by a
giant waterspout, Menippus, Lucian's hero, returns to Earth in an equally distinctive manner: The angry gods simply have Mercury take hold of his right ear and
deposit him on the ground. Lucian established a tradition of space-travel fiction,
and generations of later storytellers spawned numerous fantasies in which by some
miraculous means—such as a flight of wild lunar swans in a seventeenth-century
tale by Francis Godwin or a cannon shot in Jules Verne's classic account of a
Moon voyage (1865–1870)—earthlings are transported beyond the confines of
their world and into space.[2]

But apparently the first suggestion, fictional or otherwise, for an artificial
manned satellite of Earth is to be found in a short novel called "The Brick Moon,"
written in 1869 by the American Edward Everett Hale and originally serialized
in the *Atlantic Monthly*. Although, like most of his contemporaries, Hale had
only a vague notion of where Earth's atmosphere ended and where space began,
he did realize that somewhere the "aire" became the "aether," and he also understood the mechanics of putting a satellite into an Earth orbit:

> If from the surface of the earth, by a gigantic peashooter, you could shoot a pea
> upward . . . ; if you drove it so fast and far that when its power of ascent
> was exhausted, and it should fall, it should clear the earth . . . ; if you had
> given it sufficient power to get it half way round the earth without touching,
> that pea would clear the earth forever. It would continue to rotate . . . with
> the impulse with which it had first cleared our atmosphere and attraction.

3

Doré's mid-19th century illustration, "A Voyage to the Moon," captured man's age-old dream of lifting himself off Earth and venturing out toward our celestial neighbors, the Moon, the Sun, the planets, and even the stars.

The action of centripetal forces as advanced by Isaac Newton: "That by means of centripetal forces the planets may be retained in certain orbits, we may easily understand, if we consider the motions of projectiles; for a stone that is projected is by the pressure of its own weight forced out of the rectilinear path, which by the initial projection alone it should have pursued, and made to describe a curved line in the air; and through that crooked way is at last brought down to the ground; and the greater the velocity is with which it is projected, the farther it goes before it falls to the earth. We may therefore suppose the velocity to be so increased, that it would describe an arc of 1, 2, 5, 10, 100, 1,000 miles before it arrived at earth, till at last, exceeding the limits of the earth, it should pass into space without touching it."

In Hale's story a group of industrious New Englanders construct a 200-foot-diameter brick sphere, which, carrying 37 people, is prematurely hurled into an orbit 4000 miles from Earth by two huge flywheels.[3] Less than a hundred years later, Hale's own country would undertake a more modest and more practicable scheme for a manned satellite in Project Mercury.

Centuries before Hale wrote about an orbiting manned sphere, Nicolaus Copernicus, Johannes Kepler, Galileo Galilei, and other astronomers had helped put the solar system in order, with the Sun in the center and the various planets, spherical and of different sizes, orbiting elliptically around it. Isaac Newton had established the basic principles of gravitation and mechanics governing reaction propulsion and spatial navigation.[4] Thus it was possible for Hale and his fellow-fictionists to think at least half seriously about, and to describe in fairly accurate detail, such adventures as orbiting Earth and its Moon and voyaging to Venus.

Most flight enthusiasts in the nineteenth century, however, were absorbed with the problems of flight within the atmosphere, with conveyance from one place to another on Earth. This preoccupation with atmospheric transport, which would continue until the mid-twentieth century, in many ways retarded interest in rocketry and space travel. But the development and refinement of aeronautics in the twentieth century was both a product of and a stimulant to man's determination to fly ever higher and faster, to travel as far from his Earth as he could. Atmospheric flight, in terms of both motivation and technology, was a necessary prelude to the exploration of near and outer space. In a sense, therefore, man's journey along the highway to space, leading to such astronautical achievements as Project Mercury, began in the dense forest of his atmosphere, with feats in aeronautics.

Conquest of the Air

Man first ventured aloft in balloons in the 1780s, and in the next century gliders also bore human passengers on the air. By 1900 a host of theoreticians and inventors in Europe and the United States were steadily expanding their knowledge and capability beyond the flying of balloons and gliders and into the complexities of machineborne flight. The essentials of the airplane—wings, rudders, engine, and propeller—already were well known, but what had not been done was to balance and steer a heavier-than-air flying machine.

On December 8, 1903, Samuel Pierpont Langley, a renowned astrophysicist and Secretary of the Smithsonian Institution, tried for the second time to fly his manned "aerodrome," a glider fitted with a small internal combustion engine, by catapulting it from a houseboat on the Potomac River. The much-publicized experiment, financed largely by the United States War Department, ended in failure when the machine plunged, with pilot-engineer Charles M. Manley, into the cold water.[5] The undeserved wave of ridicule and charges of waste that followed Langley's failure obscured what happened nine days later at Kitty Hawk, North Carolina. There two erstwhile bicycle mechanics from Dayton,

Ohio, Wilbur and Orville Wright, carried out "the first [flight] in the history of the world in which a machine carrying a man had raised itself by its own power into the air in full flight, had sailed forward without reduction of speed, and had finally landed at a point as high as that from which it started."[6] Although few people realized it at the time, practicable heavier-than-air flight had become a reality.

The United States Army purchased the first military airplane, a Wright Flyer, in 1908. But when Europe plunged into general war in 1914, competitive nationalism—drawing on the talents of scientists like Ernst Mach in Vienna, Ludwig Prandtl in Germany, and Osborne Reynolds in Great Britain, and of inventors like the Frenchmen Louis Bleriot and Gabriel Voisin—had accelerated European flight technology well beyond that of the United States.[7] In 1915, after several years of agitation for a Government-financed "national aeronautical laboratory" like those already set up in the major European countries, Congress took the first step to regain the leadership in aeronautics that the United States had lost after 1908. By an amendment attached to a naval appropriation bill, Congress established an Advisory Committee for Aeronautics "to supervise and direct the scientific study of the problems of flight, with a view to their practical solution." President Woodrow Wilson, who at first had feared that the creation of such an organization might reflect on official American neutrality, appointed the stipulated 12 unsalaried members to the "Main Committee," as the policymaking body of the new organization came to be called. At its first meeting, the Main Committee changed the name of the organization to National Advisory Committee for Aeronautics, and shortly "NACA" began making surveys of the state of aeronautical research and facilities in the country. During the First World War it aided significantly in the formulation of national policy on such critical problems as the cross-licensing of patents and aircraft production. NACA did not have its own research facilities, however, until 1920, when it opened the Langley Memorial Aeronautical Laboratory, named after the "aerodrome" pioneer, at Langley Field, Virginia.[8]

In the 1920s and 1930s aeronautical science and aviation technology continued to advance, as the various cross-country flights, around-the-world flights, and the most celebrated of all aerial voyages, Charles A. Lindbergh's nonstop flight in 1927 from New York to Paris, demonstrated. During these decades NACA brought the United States worldwide leadership in aeronautical science. Concentrating its research in aerodynamics and aerodynamic loads, with lesser attention to structural materials and powerplants, NACA worked closely with the Army and Navy laboratories, with the National Bureau of Standards, and with the young and struggling aircraft industry to enlarge the theory and technology of flight.[9] The reputation for originality and thorough research that NACA quietly built in the interwar period would continue to grow until 1958, when the organization would metamorphose into a glamorous new space agency, the likes of which might have frightened the early NACA stalwarts.

6

Early
Aviation

Man's liberation from the surface of Earth began at Kitty Hawk, N.C., on December 17, 1903, when Orville and Wilbur Wright made the world's first controlled, powered flights in a heavier-than-air machine (above). At last it was within man's grasp to use Earth's atmosphere as a means of transportation. There was much to learn; in the United States the National Advisory Committee for Aeronautics pioneered aeronautical research in the 1920s. Early wind tunnel research at Langley Memorial Aeronautical Laboratory (right) culminated in the famous NACA cowling and the family of NACA wing shapes that would dominate several generations of aircraft from the 1920s into the 1940s. And aviation finally came of age in world opinion with the epochal solo flight from New York to Paris by Charles E. Lindbergh, May 20–21, 1927. Lindbergh and his plane, the "Spirit of St. Louis," are shown (below, right) visiting the Washington Navy Yard on June 11, 1927.

7

Over the years NACA acquired a highly competent staff of "research engineers" and technicians at its Langley laboratory.[10] Young aeronautical and mechanical engineers just leaving college were drawn to NACA by the intellectual independence characterizing the agency, by the opportunity to do important work and see their names on regularly published technical papers, and by the superior wind tunnels and other research equipment increasingly available at the Virginia site. NACA experimenters made discoveries leading to such major innovations in aircraft design as the smooth cowling for radial engines, wing fillets to cut down on wing-fuselage interference, engine nacelles mounted in the wings of multi-engine craft, and retractable landing gear. This and other research led to the continual reduction of aerodynamic drag on aircraft shapes and consequent increases in speed and overall performance.[11]

The steady improvement of aircraft design and performance benefited commercial as well as military aviation. Airlines for passenger, mail, and freight transport, established in the previous decade both in the United States and Europe, expanded rapidly in the depression years of the thirties. In the year 1937 more than a million passengers flew on airlines in the United States alone.[12] At the same time, advances in speed, altitude, and distance, together with numerous innovations in flight engineering and instrumentation, presaged the arrival of the airplane as a decisive military weapon.[13]

Yet NACA remained small and inconspicuous; as late as the summer of 1939 its total complement was 523 people, of whom only 278 were engaged in research activities. Its budget for that fiscal year was $4,600,000.[14] The prevailing mood of the American public throughout the thirties was reflected in the neutrality legislation passed in the last half of the decade, in niggardly defense appropriations, and in the preoccupation of the Roosevelt administration with the domestic aspects of the Great Depression. Without greatly increased appropriations from Congress, the military was held back in its efforts to acquire more and better aerial weapons. Without a military market for its products, the American aircraft industry proceeded cautiously and slowly in the design and manufacture of airframes and powerplants. And in the face of the restricted needs of industry and the armed services and severly limited appropriations, NACA kept its efforts focused where it could acquire the greatest quantity of knowledge for the smallest expenditure of funds and manpower—in aerodynamics.

As Europe moved nearer to war, however, the Roosevelt administration, Congress, and the public at large showed more interest in an expanded military establishment, including military aviation. Leading figures like Lindbergh and Vannevar Bush, president of the Carnegie Institution and chairman of the Main Committee, warned of the remarkable gains in aviation being made in other countries, especially in Nazi Germany.[15] While the United States may have retained its aerodynamics research lead, the Germans, drawing, in part from the published findings of NACA, by 1939 had temporarily outstripped this country in aeronautical development.

After the outbreak of war in Europe, NACA eventually secured authorization and funding to increase its program across the board, including a much enlarged effort in propulsion and structural materials research. A new aeronautical laboratory, named after physicist Joseph S. Ames of Johns Hopkins University, former chairman of the Main Committee, was constructed beginning in 1940 on land adjacent to the Navy installation at Moffett Field, California, 40 miles south of San Francisco. The next year, on a site next to the municipal airport at Cleveland, NACA broke ground for still another laboratory, to be devoted primarily to engine research. In later years the Cleveland facility would be named the Lewis Flight Propulsion Laboratory, after George W. Lewis, for 28 years NACA's Director of Research.[16]

Some nine months before Pearl Harbor, Chairman Bush of NACA appointed a Special Committee on Jet Propulsion, headed by former Main Committeeman William F. Durand of Stanford University, and including such leaders in aeronautical science as Theodore von Kármán of the California Institute of Technology and Hugh L. Dryden of the National Bureau of Standards.[17] Until then NACA, the military services, and the aircraft industry had given little attention to jet propulsion. There had been little active disagreement with the conclusion reached in 1923 by Edgar Buckingham of the Bureau of Standards: "Propulsion by the reaction of a simple jet cannot complete, in any respect, with air screw propulsion at such flying speeds as are now in prospect."[18] By 1941, however, Germany had flown turbojets, and her researchers were working intensively on the development of an operational jet-propelled interceptor. In Britain the propulsion scientist Frank Whittle had designed and built a gas-turbine engine and had flown a turbojet-powered aircraft.

Faced with the prospect of European-developed aircraft that could reach flight regimes in excess of 400 miles per hour and operational altitudes of about 40,000 feet, NACA gradually authorized more and more research on jet powerplants for the Army Air Forces and the Navy. Most of the NACA research effort during the war, however, went to "quick fixes," improving or "cleaning up" military aircraft already produced by aircraft companies, rather than to the more fundamental problems of aircraft design, construction, and propulsion.[19] So, understandably and predictably, during the Second World War, Germany was first to put into operation military aircraft driven by jet powerplants, as well as rocket-powered interceptors that could fly at 590 miles per hour and climb to 40,000 feet in two and a half minutes.[20] The German jets and rocket planes came into the war too late to have any effect on its outcome, but the new aircraft caused consternation among American aeronautical scientists and military planners.

The Second World War saw, in the words of NACA Chairman Jerome C. Hunsaker, "the end to the development of the airplane as conceived by Wilbur and Orville Wright."[21] Propeller-driven aircraft advanced far beyond their original reconnaissance and tactical uses and became integral instruments of strategic warfare. The development of the atomic bomb meant a multifold

9

increase in the firepower of aircraft, but well before the single B–29 dropped the single five-ton bomb on Hiroshima, long-range bomber fleets carrying conventional TNT explosives and incendiaries had radically altered the nature of war.[22]

The frantic race in military technology developing in the postwar years between the United States and the Soviet Union produced a remarkable acceleration in the evolution of the airplane. Jet-propelled interceptors, increasingly rakish in appearance by comparison with their staid propeller-driven ancestors, flew ever faster, higher, and farther.[23] Following the recommendations of a series of blue-ribbon scientific advisory groups, the Defense Department and the newly independent Air Force made the Strategic Air Command, with its thousands of huge manned bombers, the first line of American defense in the late forties and early fifties.[24] To many people the intercontinental bomber, carrying fission and (after 1954) hydrogen-fusion weapons, capable of circumnavigating the globe nonstop with mid-air refueling, looked like the "ultimate weapon" men had sought since the beginning of human conflict.

Working under the incessant demands of the cold-war years, NACA continued to pioneer in applied aeronautical research. By 1946 the NACA staff had grown to about 6800, its annual budget was in the vicinity of $40 million, and its facilities were valued at more than $200 million. Although Chairman Hunsaker and others on the Main Committee felt that NACA's principal mission should be inquiry into the fundamentals of aeronautics, the military services and the aircraft industry continued to rely on NACA as a problem-solving agency. The pressure for "quick fixes" persisted as the Korean War intensified requirements for work on specific aircraft problems.[25]

The outstanding general impediment to aeronautical progress, however, continued to be the so-called "sonic barrier," a region near the speed of sound (approximately 750 miles per hour at sea level, 660 miles per hour above 40,000 feet) wherein an aircraft encounters compressibility phenomena in fluid dynamics, or the "piling up" of air molecules. A serious technical obstacle to high-speed research in the postwar years was the choking effect experienced in wind tunnels during attempts to simulate flight conditions in the transonic range (600–800 miles per hour). A wind tunnel constructed at Langley employing the slotted-throat principle to overcome the choking phenomenon did not begin operation until 1951, and a series of NACA and Air Force supersonic tunnels, authorized by Congress under the Unitary Plan Act of 1949, was not completed until the mid-fifties.[26] NACA investigators had to use other methods for extensive transonic research. One was a falling-body technique, in which airplane models equipped with radio-telemetry apparatus were dropped from bombers at high altitudes. Another was the firing of small solid-propellant rockets to gather data on various aerodynamic shapes accelerated past mach 1, the speed of sound. Many of these tests supported military missile studies. The rocket firings were carried out at the Pilotless Aircraft Research Station, a facility set up by the Langley laboratory on Wallops Island, off the Virginia coast, in the spring of 1945. The Pilotless Aircraft Research Division at Langley, until the early fifties headed by Robert R. Gilruth, conducted the NACA program of aerodynamic research with rocket-launched models.[27]

The most celebrated part of the postwar aeronautical research effort in the United States, however, was the NACA-military work with rocket-propelled aircraft. In 1943, Langley aerodynamicist John Stack and Robert J. Woods of the Bell Aircraft Corporation, realizing that propeller-driven aircraft had about reached their performance limits, suggested the development of a special airplane for research in the problems of transonic and supersonic flight. The next year, the Army Air Forces, the Navy, and NACA inaugurated a program for the construction and operation of such an airplane, to be propelled by a liquid-fueled rocket engine. Built by Bell and eventually known as the X–1, the plane was powered by a 6000-pound-thrust rocket burning liquid oxygen and a mixture of alcohol and distilled water. On October 14, 1947, above Edwards Air Force Base in southern California, the X–1 dropped from the underside of its B–29 carrier plane at 35,000 feet and began climbing. A few seconds later the pilot of the small, bullet-shaped craft, Air Force Captain Charles E. Yeager, became the first man officially to fly faster than the speed of sound in level or climbing flight.[28]

The X–1 was the first of a line of generally successful rocket research airplanes. In November 1953 the Navy's D–558–II, built by the Douglas Aircraft Company and piloted by A. Scott Crossfield of NACA, broke mach 2, twice sonic speed; but this record stood only until the next month, when Yeager flew the new Bell X–1A to mach 2.5, or approximately 1612 miles per hour. The following summer Major Arthur Murray of the Air Force pushed the X–1A to a new altitude record of 90,000 feet above the Mojave Desert test complex consisting of Edwards Air Force Base and NACA's High Speed Flight Station. These spectacular research flights, besides banishing the myth that aircraft could not fly past the "sonic barrier," affected the design and performance of tactical military aircraft.[29] In the early fifties, the Air Force and the aircraft industry, profiting from the mountain of NACA research data, were preparing to inaugurate the new "century series" of supersonic jet interceptors.[30] And representatives of NACA, the Air Force, and the Navy Bureau of Aeronautics already were planning a new experimental rocket plane, the X–15, to employ the most powerful rocket aircraft motor ever developed and to fly to an altitude of 50 miles, the very edge of space.

Thus less than a decade after the end of the Second World War, airplanes—jet-powered and rocket-propelled—had virtually finished exploring the sensible atmosphere, the region below 80,000 or 90,000 feet. Much work remained for aeronautical scientists and engineers in such areas as airflow, turbulence, engines, and fuels, but researchers in NACA, the military, and the aircraft industry approached the thorniest problems in aeronautics with a confidence grounded in 50 years of progress. Man's facility in atmospheric flight and his adjustment to the airplane seemed complete. Pilots had mastered some of the most complex moving machines ever contrived, and passengers sat comfortably and safely in

11

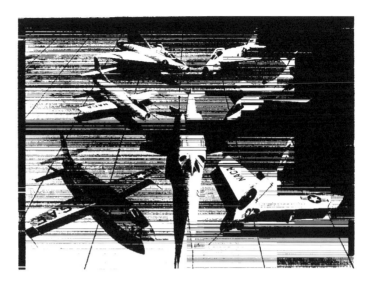

The famous research aircraft series is shown above: in the center, the Douglas X–3; lower left, the Bell X–1A; continuing left to right, the Douglas D–558–I, the Convair XF–92A, the Bell X–5, the Douglas D–558–II, and the Northrop X–4. In the photo below, the X–15 is shown as it drops away from its mother B–52 and starts its own 57,000-lb.-thrust engine to begin another of its highly successful research flights.

pressurized cabins on high-altitude airliners featuring an unprecedented combination of speed and luxury. It appeared that man at last had accomplished what the ancients had dreamed of—conquest of the air.

THE HIGHWAY TO SPACE

Space flight, however, was something else. While in one sense atmospheric flight was the first step toward space flight, extra-atmospheric transport involves much more than a logical extension of aviation technology. The airplane, powered either by a reciprocating or a jet engine, is a creature and a captive of the atmosphere, because either powerplant depends on air—more properly, oxygen— for its operation, and in space there is no air. But the rocket, unlike the gas turbine, pulsejet, ramjet, or piston engine, needs no air. It carries everything needed for propulsion within itself—its own fuel and some form of oxidizer, commonly liquid oxygen, to burn the fuel. So the rocket engine operates independently of its environment; in fact, its efficiency increases as it climbs away from the frictional density of the lower atmosphere to the thin air of the stratosphere and into the airlessness of space.[31]

Yet even the rocket research airplanes were a long way from spacecraft. Although some of these vehicles provided data on the use of reaction controls for steering in the near vacuum of the upper atmosphere, they were designed to produce considerable aerodynamic lift for control within the lower atmosphere; and, in terms of the mass to be accelerated, their powerplants burned too briefly and produced too little thrust to counterbalance the oppressive force of gravity. Fulfillment of the age-old desire to travel to the heavens, even realization of Hale's nineteenth-century concept of a manned sphere circling Earth in lower space, would have to await the development of rockets big enough to boost thousands of pounds and to break the lock of gravity.

Although black-powder rockets, invented by the Chinese, had been used for centuries for festive and military purposes, not until the late nineteenth and early twentieth centuries did imaginative individuals in various parts of the world begin seriously to consider the liquid-fueled rocket as a vehicle for spatial conveyance. The history of liquid-fueled rocketry, and thus of manned space flight, is closely linked to the pioneering careers of three men—the Russian Konstantin Eduardovich Tsiolkovsky (1857–1935), the American Robert Hutchings Goddard (1882–1945), and the German-Romanian Hermann Oberth (1894–   ).

Tsiolkovsky, for most of his life an obscure teacher of mathematics, authored a series of remarkable technical essays on such subjects as reaction propulsion with liquid-propellant rockets, attainable velocities, fuel compositions, and oxygen supply and air purification for space travelers. He also wrote what apparently was the first technical discussion of an artificial Earth satellite.[32] Although virtually unknown in the West at the time of his death, in 1935, Tsiolkovsky was honored by the Soviets and had helped establish a long Russian tradition of

13

astronautics. This tradition helps to account for the U.S.S.R.'s advances with rocket-assisted airplane takeoffs and small meteorological rockets of the 1930s and her space achievements of the 1950s and 1960s.[33]

In terms of experimentation, Goddard, professor of physics at Clark University, was by far the most important of the rocket pioneers.[34] As early as 1914 he secured a patent for a small liquid-fueled rocket engine. Six years later he published a highly technical paper on the potential uses of a rocket with such an engine for studying atmospheric conditions at altitudes from 20 to 50 miles. Toward the end of the paper he mentioned the possibility of firing a rocket containing a powder charge that could be exploded on the Moon. "It remains only to perform certain necessary preliminary experiments before an apparatus can be constructed that will carry recording instruments to any desired altitude," he concluded.[35]

Goddard's life for the next 20 years was devoted to making those "necessary preliminary experiments." Working in the 1920s in Massachusetts with financial support from various sources and in the New Mexico desert with Guggenheim Foundation funds during the succeeding decade, Goddard compiled an amazing list of "firsts" in rocketry. Among other things, he carried out the first recorded launching of a liquid-propellant rocket (March 16, 1926), adapted the gyroscope to guide rockets, installed movable deflector vanes in a rocket exhaust nozzle for stability and steering, patented a design for a multistage rocket, developed fuel pumps for liquid-rocket motors, experimented with self-cooling and variable-thrust motors, and developed automatically deployed parachutes for recovering his instrumented rockets. Finally, he was the first of the early rocket enthusiasts to go beyond theory and design into the realm of "systems engineering"—the complex and hand-dirtying business of making airframes, fuel pumps, valves, and guidance devices compatible, and of doing all the other things necessary to make a rocket fly. Goddard put rocket theory into practice, as his 214 patents attest.[36]

Goddard clearly deserves the fame that has attached to his name in recent years, but in many ways he was more inventor than scientist. He deliberately worked in lonely obscurity, jealously patented virtually all of his innovations, and usually refused to share his findings with others. Consequently his work was not as valuable as it might have been to such of his contemporaries as the young rocket buffs who formed the American Rocket Society in the early thirties and vainly sought his counsel.[37]

Goddard's disdain for team research prompted his refusal to work with the California Institute of Technology Rocket Research Project, instigated in 1936 by the renowned von Kármán, then director of the Guggenheim Aeronautical Laboratory at CalTech. The CalTech group undertook research in the fundamentals of high-altitude sounding rockets, including thermodynamics, the principles of reaction, fuels, thrust measurements, and nozzle shapes. Beginning in 1939 the Guggenheim Laboratory, under the first Federal contract for rocket

From theory through laboratory demonstration through design, construction, test flight, and use of payload, Robert H. Goddard must rank as the U.S. pioneer in modern rocketry. The famous photo at the right shows Goddard beside his first successful liquid-fuel rocket, flown March 16, 1926. Years later, in the spring of 1941, he had progressed to larger, more complex models, like the one shown below in his workshop at Mescalero Ranch, Roswell, N. Mex., with his assistants. In December 1944, Goddard sent this photo to his long-time benefactor Harry F. Guggenheim with the comment, "It is practically identical with the German V–2 rocket."

research, carried out studies and experiments for the Army Air Forces, especially on rocket-assisted takeoffs for aircraft. These takeoff rockets were called JATO (for "Jet-Assisted Take-Off") units, because, as one of the CalTech scientists recalled, "the word 'rocket' was of such bad repute that [we] felt it advisable to drop the use of the word. It did not return to our vocabulary until several years later . . . ." [38] In 1944, with the Guggenheim Laboratory working intently on Army and Navy contracts for JATO units and small bombardment rockets, the Rocket Research Project was reorganized as the Jet Propulsion Laboratory.[39]

In the 1920s and 1930s interest in rocketry and space exploration became firmly rooted in Europe, although the rapid expansion of aviation technology occupied the attention of most flight-minded Europeans. Societies of rocket theorists and experimenters, mostly privately sponsored, were established in several European countries.[40] The most important of these groups was the Society for Space Travel (*Verein für Raumschiffahrt*), founded in Germany but having members in other countries. The "VfR," as its founders called it, gained much of its impetus from the writings of Oberth, who in 1923, as a young mathematician, published his classic treatise on space travel, *The Rocket into Interplanetary Space*. A substantial portion of this small book was devoted to a detailed description of the mechanics of putting into orbit a satellite of Earth.[41]

Spurred by Oberth's theoretical arguments, the Germans in the *VfR* in the early thirties conducted numerous static firings of rocket engines and launched a number of small rockets. Meanwhile the German Army, on the assumption that rocketry could become an extension of long-range artillery and because the construction of rockets was not prohibited by the Treaty of Versailles, had inaugurated a modest rocket development program in 1931, employing several of the *VfR* members. One of these was a 21-year-old engineer named Wernher von Braun, who later became the civilian head of the army's rocket research group. In 1933 the new Nazi regime placed all rocket experimentation, including that being done by the rest of the *VfR*, under strict government control.[42]

The story of German achievements in military rocketry during the late thirties and early forties at Peenemuende, the vast military research installation on the Baltic Sea, is well known.[43] Knowing Goddard's work only through his published findings, the German experimenters contrived and elaborated on nearly all of the American's patented technical innovations, including gyroscopic controls, parachutes for rocket recovery, and movable deflector vanes in the exhaust. The rocket specialists at Peenemuende were trying to create the first large, long-range military rocket. By 1943, after numerous frustrations, they had their "big rocket," 46 feet long by $11\frac{1}{2}$ feet in diameter, weighing 34,000 pounds when fueled, and producing 69,100 pounds of thrust from a single engine consuming liquid oxygen and a mixture of alcohol and water. Called "Assembly-4" (A-4) by the Peenemuende group, the rocket had a range of nearly 200 miles and a maximum velocity of about 3500 miles per hour, and was controlled by its gyroscope and exhaust deflector vanes, sometimes supplemented by radio control.[44] When Major General Walter Dornberger, commander of the army works at Peenemuende, pronounced the A-4 operational in 1944, Joseph Goebbels' propaganda machine christened it *Vergeltungswaffe zwei* (Vengeance Weapon No. 2), or "V-2."[45] But for the space-travel devotees at Peenemuende the rocket remained the A-4, a step in the climb toward space.

Although the total military effect of the 3745 V-2s fired at targets on the Continent and in England was slight, this supersonic ballistic missile threw a long shadow over the future of human society. As the Western Allies and the Soviets swept into Germany, they both sought to confiscate the elements of the German rocket program in the form of records, hardware, and people. Peenemuende was within the Russian zone of occupation, but before the arrival of the Soviet forces von Braun and most of the other engineers and technicians fled westward with a portion of their technical data. The Americans also captured the underground V-2 factory in the Harz Mountains; 100 partially assembled V-2s were quickly dismantled and sent to the United States. Ultimately von Braun and about 125 other German rocket specialists reached this country under "Project Paperclip," carried out by the United States Army.[46]

The Soviets captured no more than a handful of top Peenemuende engineers and administrators. "This is absolutely intolerable," protested Josef Stalin to

Hermann Oberth with key officials of the Army Ballistic Missile Agency at Huntsville, Ala., in 1956. Counterclockwise from the left: Maj. Gen. H. N. Toftoy, commanding general of ABMA, who organized Project Paperclip; Ernst Stuhlinger; Oberth; Werner von Braun, Director, Development Operations Division; and Eberhard Rees, Deputy Director, Development Operations Division.

17

Lieutenant Colonel G. A. Tokaty, one of his rocket experts. "We defeated the Nazi armies; we occupied Berlin and Peenemuende; but the Americans got the rocket engineers."[47] The Russians did obtain a windfall, however, in the form of hundreds of technicians and rank-and-file engineers, the Peenemuende laboratories and assembly plant, and lists of component suppliers. From those suppliers located in the Russian zone the Soviets secured enough parts to reactivate the manufacture of V–2s. The captured technicians and engineers were transported to the Soviet Union, where the Russian rocket specialists systematically drained them of the technical information they possessed but did not permit them to participate directly in the burgeoning postwar Soviet rocket development program.[48]

During the war Russian rocket developers, like their American counterparts, had concentrated on JATO and small bombardment rockets. "Backward though they were often said to be in matters of technology," observed James Phinney Baxter right after the war, "it was the Russians who in 1941 first employed rockets on a major scale. They achieved a notable success, and made more use of the rocket as a ground-to-ground weapon than any other combatant."[49] In the postwar years the Soviets quickly turned to the development of large liquid-propellant rockets. Lacking an armada of intercontinental bombers carrying atomic warheads, such as the United States possessed, they envisioned "trans-Atlantic rockets" as "an effective straightjacket for that noisy shopkeeper Harry Truman," to use Stalin's words.[50] Consequently the U.S.S.R. undertook to build a long-range military rocket years before nuclear weaponry actually became practicable for rockets; indeed, even before the Soviets had perfected an atomic device for delivery by aircraft.

The U.S.S.R. began exploration of the upper atmosphere with captured V–2s in the fall of 1947. Within two years, however, Soviet production was underway on a single-stage rocket called the T–1, an improved version of the V–2. The first rocket divisions of the Soviet Armed Forces were instituted in 1950 or 1951. Probably in 1954, development work began on a multistage rocket to be used both as a weapon and as a vehicle for space exploration. And in the spring of 1956 Communist Party Chairman Nikita Khrushchev warned that "soon" Russian rockets carrying thermonuclear warheads would be able to hit any target on Earth.[51]

POSTWAR AMERICAN ROCKETRY

Meanwhile the United States, convinced of the long-term superiority of her intercontinental bombers, pursued national security by means of airpower. The extremely heavy weight of atomic warheads meant that they would have to be delivered by large bombers, or by a much bigger rocket than anyone in the military was willing to ask Congress to fund. Despite the early postwar warnings of General Henry H. Arnold and others, for whom the V–2 experience was prophetic, the Truman administration and Congress listened to conservative military men and civilian scientists who felt that until at least 1965 manned bombers, supplemented by air-breathing guided missiles evolving from the German V–1, should be the principal American "deterrent force." [52] Just after the war former NACA Chairman Bush, then Director of the Office of Scientific Research and Development, had expressed the prevailing mood in a much-quoted (and perhaps much-regretted) piece of testimony before a Congressional committee: "There has been a great deal said about a 3000-mile high-angle rocket. In my opinion, such a thing is impossible today and will be impossible for many years . . . . I wish the American public would leave that out of their thinking." [53]

The United States developed guided missiles for air-to-air, air-to-surface, and surface-to-air interception uses and as tactical surface-to-surface weapons. Rocket motors, using both liquid and solid fuels, gradually replaced jet propulsion systems, but short-range defensive missiles remained advanced enough for most tastes until the late 1950s.[54]

As for scientific research in the upper atmosphere, the backlog of V–2s put together by the United States Army from captured components would do in the early postwar years. From April 1946 to October 1951, 66 V–2s were fired at the Army's White Sands Proving Grounds, New Mexico, in the most extensive rocket and upper-atmospheric research program to that time. The Army Ordnance Department, the Air Force, the Air Force Cambridge Research Center, the General Electric Company, various scientific institutions, universities, and government agencies, and the Naval Research Laboratory participated in the White Sands V–2 program. Virtually all the rockets were heavily instrumented, and many of them carried plant life and animals. V–2s carried monkeys aloft on four occasions; telemetry data transmitted from the rockets showed no ill effects on the primates until each was killed in the crash. The most memorable launching at White Sands, however, came on February 24, 1949, when a V–2 boosted a WAC Corporal rocket developed by the Jet Propulsion Laboratory 244 miles into space and to a speed of 5510 miles per hour, the greatest altitude and velocity yet attained by a man-made object. A year and a half later, a V–2—WAC Corporal combination rose from Cape Canaveral, Florida, in the first launch at the Air Force's newly activated Long Range Proving Ground.[55]

By the late forties, with the supply of V–2s rapidly disappearing, work had begun on more reliable and efficient research rockets. The most durable of these indigenous projectiles proved to be the Aerobee, designed as a sounding rocket by the Applied Physics Laboratory of Johns Hopkins University and financed by the Office of Naval Research. With a peak altitude of about 80 miles, the Aerobee served as a reliable tool for upper-atmospheric research until the late 1950s.[56] The Naval Research Laboratory designed the Viking, a long, slim high-altitude sounding rocket, manufactured by the Glenn L. Martin Company of Baltimore. In August 1951 the Viking bettered its own altitude record for a single-stage rocket, reaching 136 miles from a White Sands launch. In the fifties, instrumenta-

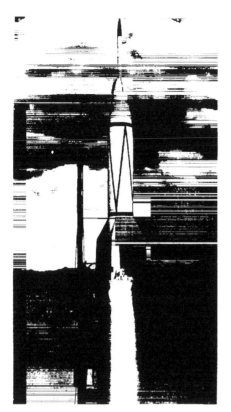

Launch of the record-setting U.S. Army–Jet Propulsion Laboratory Bumper WAC (V–2 first stage and WAC/Corporal second stage) from White Sands Proving Ground, N. Mex. The first Bumper-WAC launch occurred on May 13, 1948. On February 24, 1949, the two-stage rocket reached its record altitude of 244 miles and speed of 5150 miles per hour.

tion carried in Aerobees and Vikings extended knowledge of the atmosphere to 150 miles, provided photographs of Earth's curvature and cloud cover, and gave some information on the Sun and cosmic radiation.[57]

In 1955 the Viking was chosen as the first stage and an improved Aerobee as the second stage for a new, three-stage rocket to be used in Project Vanguard, which was to orbit an instrumented research satellite as part of the American contribution to the International Geophysical Year. The decision to use the Viking and the "Aerobee-Hi" in this country's first effort to launch an unmanned scientific satellite illustrates the basic dichotomy in thought and practice governing postwar rocket development in the United States: After the expenditure of the V–2s, scientific activity should employ relatively inexpensive sounding rockets with small thrusts. Larger, higher-thrust, and more expensive rockets to be used as space launchers must await a specific military requirement. Such a policy meant that the Soviet Union, early fostering the ballistic missile as an intercontinental delivery system, might have a proven long-range rocket before the United States; the Soviets might also, if they chose, launch larger satellites sooner than this country.

By 1951, three sizable military rockets were under development in the United

States.   One, an Air Force project for an intercontinental ramjet-booster rocket combination called the Navaho, took many twists and turns before ending in mid-1957.   After 11 years and $680 million, the Air Force, lacking funds for further development, canceled the Navaho enterprise.   Technologically, however, Navaho proved a worthwhile investment; its booster-engine configuration, for example, became the basic design later used in various rockets.[58]   The two other rocket projects being financed by the military in the early fifties were ultimately successful, both as weapons systems and as space boosters.

REDSTONE AND ATLAS

After the creation of a separate Air Force in 1947, the Army had continued rocket development, operating on the same assumption behind the German Army's research in the 1930s—that rocketry was basically an extension of artillery.   In June 1950, Army Ordnance moved its team of 130 German rocket scientists and engineers from Fort Bliss at El Paso to the Army's Redstone Arsenal at Huntsville, Alabama, along with some 800 military and General Electric employees.   Headed by Wernher von Braun, who later became chief of the Guided Missile Development Division at Redstone Arsenal, the Army group began design studies on a liquid-fueled battlefield missile called the Hermes C1, a modified V–2.   Soon the Huntsville engineers changed the design of the Hermes, which had been planned for a 500-mile range, to a 200-mile rocket capable of high mobility for field deployment.   The Rocketdyne Division of North American Aviation modified the Navaho booster engine for the new weapon, and in 1952 the Army bombardment rocket was officially named "Redstone." [59]

Always the favorite of the von Braun group working for the Army, the Redstone was a direct descendant of the V–2.   The Redstone's liquid-fueled engine burned alcohol and liquid oxygen and produced about 75,000 pounds of thrust. Nearly 70 feet long and slightly under 6 feet in diameter, the battlefield missile had a speed at burnout, the point of propellant exhaustion, of 3800 miles per hour. For guidance it utilized an all-inertial system featuring a gyroscopically stabilized platform, computers, a programmed flight path taped into the rocket before launch, and the activation of the steering mechanism by signals in flight.   For control during powered ascent the Redstone depended on tail fins with movable rudders and refractory carbon vanes mounted in the rocket exhaust.   The prime contract for the manufacture of Redstone test rockets went to the Chrysler Corporation.   In August 1953 a Redstone fabricated at the Huntsville arsenal made a partially successful maiden flight of only 8000 yards from the military's missile range at Cape Canaveral, Florida.   During the next five years, 37 Redstones were fired to test structure, engine performance, guidance and control, tracking, and telemetry.[60]

The second successful military rocket being developed in 1951 was an Air Force project, the Atlas.   The long history of the Atlas, the first American intercontinental ballistic missile (ICBM),[61] began early in 1946, when the Air Materiel Command of the Army Air Forces awarded a study contract for a long-range missile to Consolidated Vultee Aircraft Corporation (Convair), of San Diego. By mid-year a team of Convair engineers, headed by Karel J. Bossart, had completed a design for "a sort of Americanized V–2," called "HIROC," or Project MX–774. Bossart and associates proposed a technique basically new to American rocketry (although patented by Goddard and tried on some German V–2s)—controlling the rocket by swiveling the engines, using hydraulic actuators responding to commands from the autopilot and gyroscope. This technique was the precursor of the gimbaled engine method employed to control the Atlas and other later rockets. In 1947, the Truman administration and the equally economy-minded Republican 80th Congress confronted the Air Force with the choice of having funds slashed for its intercontinental manned bombers and interceptors or cutting back on some of its advanced weapons designs. Just as the first MX–774 test vehicle was nearing completion, the Air Force notified Convair that the project was canceled. The Convair engineers used the remainder of their contract funds for static firings at Point Loma, California, and for three partially successful test launches at White Sands, the last on December 2, 1948.[62]

From 1947 until early 1951 there was no American project for an intercontinental ballistic missile. The Soviet Union exploded her first atomic device in 1949, ending the United States' postwar monopoly on nuclear weapons. President Harry S. Truman quickly ordered the development of hydrogen-fusion warheads on a priority basis. The coming of the war in Korea the next year shook American self-confidence still further. The economy program instituted by Secretary of Defense Louis Johnson ended, and the military budget, including appropriations for weapons research, zoomed upward. The Army began its work leading to the Redstone, while the Air Force resumed its efforts to develop an intercontinental military rocket. In January 1951 the Air Materiel Command awarded Convair a new contract for Project MX–1593, to which Karel Bossart and his engineering group gave the name "Project Atlas."[63] Yet the pace of the military rocket program remained deliberate, its funding conservative.

A series of events beginning in late 1952 altered this cautious approach. On November 1, at Eniwetok Atoll in the Pacific, the Atomic Energy Commission detonated the world's first thermonuclear explosion, the harbinger of the hydrogen bomb. The device weighed about 60,000 pounds, certainly a much greater weight than was practicable for a ballistic missile payload. The next year, however, as a result of a recommendation by a Department of Defense study group, Trevor Gardner, assistant to the Secretary of the Air Force, set up a Strategic Missiles Evaluation Committee to investigate the status of Air Force long-range missiles. The committee, composed of nuclear scientists and missile experts, was headed by the famous mathematician John von Neumann. Specifically, Gardner asked the committee to make a prediction regarding weight as opposed to yield in nuclear payloads for some six or seven years hence. The evaluation group, familiarly known as the "Teapot Committee," concluded that shortly it would be possible to build smaller, lighter, and more powerful hydrogen-fusion warheads. This in turn would make it possible to reduce the size of rocket nose cones and propellant loads and, with a vastly greater yield from the thermonuclear explosion, to eliminate the need for precise missile accuracy.[64] In February 1954 both the Strategic Missiles Evaluation Committee and the Rand Corporation, the Air Force-sponsored research agency, submitted formal reports predicting smaller nuclear warheads and urging that the Air Force give its highest priority to work on long-range ballistic missiles.

Between 1945 and 1953 the yield of heavy fission weapons had increased substantially from the 20-kiloton bomb dropped on Hiroshima. Now, according to the Air Force's scientific advisers, lighter, more compact, and much more powerful hydrogen warheads could soon be realized. These judgments "completely changed the picture regarding the ballistic missile," explained General Bernard A. Schriever, who later came to head the Air Force ballistic missile development program, "because from then on we could consider a relatively low weight package for payload purposes."[65] This was the fateful "thermonuclear breakthrough."

Late in March 1964 the Air Research and Development Command organized a special missile command agency, originally called the Western Development Division but renamed Air Force Ballistic Missile Division on June 1, 1957. Its first headquarters was in Inglewood, California; its first commander, Brigadier General Schriever. The Convair big rocket project gained new life in the winter of 1954–55, when the Western Development Division awarded its first long-term contract for fabrication of an ICBM. The awarding of the contract came in an atmosphere of mounting crisis and urgency. The Soviets had exploded their own thermonuclear device in 1953, and intelligence data from various sources indicated that they also were working on ICBMs to carry uranium and hydrogen warheads. Thus the Atlas project became a highest-priority "crash" program, with the Air Force and its contractors and subcontractors working against the fearsome possibility of thermonuclear blackmail.[66]

Rejecting the Army-arsenal concept, whereby research and development and some fabrication took place in Government facilities, the Air Force left the great bulk of the engineering task to Convair and its associate contractors.[67] For close technical and administrative direction the Air Force turned to the newly formed Ramo-Wooldridge Corporation, a private missile research firm, which established a subsidiary initially called the Guided Missiles Research Division, later Space Technology Laboratories (STL). With headquarters in Los Angeles, the firm was to oversee the systems engineering of the Air Force ICBM program.[68]

In November 1955, STL's directional responsibilities broadened to include work on a new Air Force rocket, the intermediate-range (1800-mile) Thor, hastily designed by the Douglas Aircraft Company to serve as a stopgap nuclear deterrent until the intercontinental Atlas became operational. At the same time

23

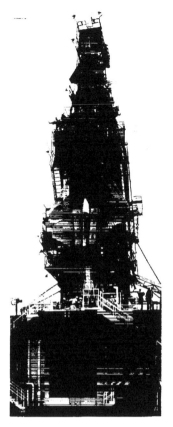

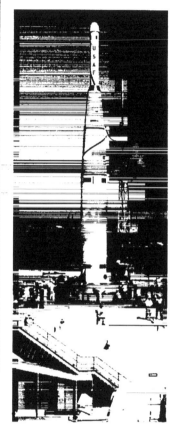

Military missiles of the 1950s provided both the technology and the first-generation boosters for the nascent space program. The Air Force's Navaho (left) was a long-range cruise missile overtaken by the onrush of technology; though it was canceled as a project, it had pioneered the development of large rocket engines and guidance systems. The Atlas missile (center) had a hectic on-and-off career in the early 1950s but became the first operational ICBM and the major "large" boost vehicle for manned and unmanned space missions in the first decade of the space age. Thor (right), the sturdy, reliable baby of the Atlas technology, served an interim military role as an operational IRBM and a longer and more illustrious role as the workhorse booster of the first decade of payloads for military and nonmilitary space projects. Shown here with an Able second stage, it accepted a variety of second stages and payloads.

24

Charles E. Wilson, Secretary of Defense in the Eisenhower administration, gave the Army and Navy joint responsibility for developing the Jupiter, another intermediate-range ballistic missile (IRBM), the engineering task for which went to the Army rocketmen at Redstone Arsenal. To expedite Jupiter development, the Army on February 1, 1956, established at Huntsville a Ballistic Missile Agency, to which Wernher von Braun and his Guided Missile Development Division were transferred. Later that year Wilson issued his controversial "roles and missions" memorandum, confirming Air Force jurisdiction over the operational deployment of intercontinental missiles, assigning to the Air Force sole jurisdiction over land-based intermediate-range weapons, restricting Army operations to weapons with ranges of up to 200 miles, and assigning ship-based IRBM's to the Navy. Partly as a result of this directive, but mainly because of the difficulty of handling liquid propellants at sea, the Navy withdrew from the Jupiter program and focused its interest on the Polaris, a solid-propellant rocket designed for launching from a submarine.[69]

As it developed after 1954, the Air Force ballistic missile development program, proceeding under the highest national priority and the pressure of Soviet missilery, featured a departure from customary progressive practice in weapons management. The label for the new, self-conscious management technique adopted by the Air Force Ballistic Missile Division–Space Technology Laboratories team was "concurrency." Translated simply, concurrency meant "the simultaneous completion of all necessary actions to produce and deploy a weapon system."[70] But in practice the management task—involving parallel advances in research, design, testing, and manufacture of vehicles and components, design and construction of test facilities, testing of components and systems, expansion and creation of industrial facilities, and the building of launch sites—seemed overwhelmingly complex. At the beginning of 1956 the job of contriving one ICBM, the Atlas, was complicated by the decision to begin work on the Thor and on the Titan I, a longer-range, higher-thrust, "second generation" ICBM.[71]

The basic problem areas in the development of the Atlas included structure, propulsion, guidance, and thermodynamics. Convair attacked the structural problem by coming up with an entirely different kind of airframe. The Atlas airframe principle, nicknamed the "gas bag," entailed using stainless steel sections thinner than paper as the structural material, with rigidity achieved through helium pressurization to a differential of between 25 and 60 pounds per square inch. The pressurized tank innovation led to a substantial reduction in the ratio between structure and total weight; the empty weight of the Atlas airframe was less than two percent of the propellant weight. Yet the Atlas, like an automobile tire or a football, could absorb very heavy structural loads.[72]

For the Atlas powerplant the Air Force contracted with the Rocketdyne Division of North American Aviation. The thermonuclear breakthrough meant that the original five-engine configuration planned for the Atlas could be scrapped in favor of a smaller, three-engine design. Thus Rocketdyne could contrive a unique side-by-side arrangement for the two booster and one sustainer engines conceived by Convair, making it possible to fire simultaneously all three engines, plus the small vernier engines mounted on the airframe, at takeoff. The technique of igniting the boosters and sustainer on the ground gave the Atlas two distinct advantages: ignition of the second stage in the upper atmosphere was avoided, and firing the sustainer at takeoff meant that smaller engines could be used. The booster engines produced 154,000 pounds of thrust each; the sustainer engine, 57,000 pounds; and the two verniers, 1000 pounds each. The propellant for the boosters, sustainer, and verniers consisted of liquid oxygen and a hydrocarbon mixture called RP–1. The basic fuel and oxidizer were brought together by an intricate network of lines, valves, and often-troublesome turbopumps, which fed the propellant into the Atlas combustion chambers at a rate of about 1500 pounds per second. The thrust of the "one and one-half stage" Atlas powerplant, over 360,000 pounds, was equivalent to about five times the horsepower generated by the turbines of Hoover Dam or the pull of 1600 steam locomotives.[73]

The Atlas looked rather fat alongside the Army Redstone, the Thor, or the more powerful Titan. The length of the Atlas with its original Mark II blunt nose cone was nearly 76 feet; its diameter at the fuel-tank section was 10 feet, at its base, 16 feet. Its weight when fueled was around 260,000 pounds. Its speed at burnout was in the vicinity of 16,000 miles per hour, and it had an original design range of 6300 miles, later increased to 9000 miles.[74]

The prototype Atlas "A" had no operating guidance system. The Atlases "B" through "D" employed a radio-inertial guidance system, wherein transmitters on the rocket sensed aerodynamic forces acting on the missile and sent radio readings to a computer on the ground, which calculated the Atlas' position, speed, and direction. Radio signals were then sent to the rocket and fed through its inertial autopilot to gimbal the booster and sustainer engines and establish the Atlas' correct trajectory. After the jettisoning of the outboard booster engines, the sustainer carried the Atlas to the desired velocity before cutting off, while the vernier engines continued in operation to maintain precise direction and velocity. At vernier cutoff the missile began its unguided ballistic trajectory. A few moments later the nose cone separated from the rest of the rocket and continued on a high arc before plunging into the atmosphere. Radio-inertial guidance, the system used on the Atlas D and in Project Mercury, had the advantage of employing a ground computer that could be as big as desired, thus removing part of the nagging Atlas weight problem.[75]

By the mid-1950s the smaller thermonuclear warhead predicted by the Teapot Committee was imminent, so that the 360,000-pound thrust of the Atlas was plenty of energy to boost a payload of a ton and a half, over the 6300-mile range. But while nose-cone size ceased to be a problem, the dilemma of how to keep the ICBM's destructive package from burning up as it dropped into the ever-thickening atmosphere at 25 times the speed of sound remained. At such speeds even the thin atmosphere 60 to 80 miles up generates tremendous frictional heat, which increases rapidly as an object penetrates the denser lower air. The temperature in front of the nose-cone surface ultimately may become hotter than the surface of the Sun. The atmospheric entry temperatures of the intermediate-range Thor, Jupiter, and Polaris were lower than those of the Atlas, but even for these smaller-thrust vehicles the matter of payload protection was acute.[76]

In the mid-fifties the "reentry problem" looked like the hardest puzzle to solve and the farthest from solution, not only for the missile experts but also for those who dreamed of sending a man into space and bringing him back. As von Kármán observed in his partially autobiographical history of aerodynamic thought, published in 1954:

> Any rocket returning from space travel enters the atmosphere with tremendous speed. At such speeds, probably even in the thinnest air, the surface would be heated beyond the temperature endurable by any known material. This problem of the temperature barrier is much more formidable than the problem of the sonic barrier.[77]

Years of concerted research by the military services, NACA, the Jet Propulsion Laboratory, and other organizations would be necessary before crews at Cape Canaveral, either preparing a missile shot or the launching of a manned spacecraft, could confidently expect to get their payload back through the atmosphere unharmed.

The American ballistic missile program of the 1950s produced some remarkable managerial and engineering achievements. Eventually the United States would deploy reliable ICBMs in larger numbers than the Soviet Union. Yet the fact remains that the Russians first developed such an awesome weapon, first tested it successfully, and first converted their larger ICBM for space uses.[78] Thus American missile developers fell short of what had to be their immediate goal—keeping ahead or at least abreast of the Soviets in advanced weaponry. Bureaucratic delays, proliferation of committees, divided responsibility, interservice rivalry, sacrificial attachment to a balanced budget, excessive waste and duplication, even for a "crash" program—these were some of the criticisms that missile contractors, military men, scientists, and knowledgeable politicians lodged against the Defense Department and the Truman and Eisenhower administrations. From 1953 to 1957, Secretaries of Defense Wilson and Neil H. McElroy presided over 11 major organizational changes pertaining directly to the missile program.[79] "It was just like putting a nickel in a slot machine," recalled J. H. Kindelberger, chairman of the board of North American Aviation, on the difficulty of getting a decision from the plethora of Pentagon committees. "You pull the handle and you get a lemon and you put another one in. You have to get three or four of them in a row and hold them there long enough for them to say 'Yes.' It takes a lot of nickels and a lot of time." [80] And even Schriever, certainly not one to be critical of the pace of missile development, admitted that "in retrospect you might say that we could have moved a little faster." [81]

27

SPUTNIKS AND SOUL-SEARCHING

On August 26, 1957, Tass, the official Soviet news agency, announced that the U.S.S.R. had successfully launched over its full design range a "super long distance intercontinental multistage ballistic rocket," probably a vehicle employing the improved V–2, the T–1, as an upper stage and a booster rocket with a thrust of over 400,000 pounds the T–3.[82] In the furor in the West following the Russian announcement an American general allegedly exclaimed, "We captured the wrong Germans." [83]

Then, on October 4, the Soviets used apparently the same ICBM to blast into orbit the first artificial Earth satellite, a bundle of instruments weighing about 184 pounds called *Sputnik*, a combination of words meaning "fellow-traveler of the Earth." A month later Soviet scientists and rocket engineers sent into high elliptical orbit a heavily instrumented capsule, *Sputnik II*, weighing some 1120 pounds and carrying a dog named Laika.

The Russian ICBM shot in August had given new urgency to the missile competition and had prompted journalists to begin talking about the "missile gap." The Sputnik launches of the fall opened up a new phase of the Soviet-American technological and ideological struggle, and caused more chagrin, consternation, and indignant soul-searching in the United States than any episode since Pearl Harbor. Now there was a "space race" in addition to an "arms race," and it was manifest that at least for the time being there was a "space lag" to add to the ostensible missile gap.

After the first Sputnik went into orbit, President Dwight D. Eisenhower reminded the critics of his administration that, unlike ballistic missile development, "our satellite program has never been conducted as a race with other nations." [84] As far as the Soviet Union was concerned, however, there had been a satellite race for at least two and perhaps four years before the Sputniks. There was probably a Soviet parallel to the highly secret studies carried out in the immediate postwar years by the Rand Corporation for the Air Force and by the Navy Bureau of Aeronautics on the feasibility and military applicability of instrumented Earth satellites.[85] As late as 1952, however, Albert E. Lombard, scientific adviser in the Department of the Air Force, reported that "intelligence information on Soviet progress, although fragmentary, has given no indication on Soviet activity in this field." [86] Late the next year, President A. N. Nesmeyanov of the Soviet Academy of Sciences proclaimed that "Science has reached a state when it is feasible to send a stratoplane to the Moon, to create an artificial satellite of the Earth."[87] A torrent of Soviet books and articles on rockets, satellites, and interplanetary travel followed the Nesmeyanov statement.

In August 1955, a few days after the White House announced that the United States would launch a series of "small, unmanned, earth-circling satellites" during the 18-month International Geophysical Year, beginning July 1, 1957, Soviet aeronautical and astronautical expert Leonid Sedov remarked that the U.S.S.R.

would also send up satellites and that they would be larger than the announced American scientific payloads. Most Americans complacently tossed off Sedov's claim as another example of Russian braggadocio.[88] The formal announcement of the Russian space intentions came at the Barcelona Geophysical Year Conference in 1956. And in June 1957 the Soviet press advertised the radio frequency on which the first Russian satellite would transmit signals. By the end of the summer a few American Sovietologists were predicting freely that the U.S.S.R. would attempt a satellite launching soon, and they were somewhat surprised that the shot did not occur on September 17, 1957, the centennial of the birth of Tsiolkovsky.[89]

American embarrassment reached its apex and American technological prestige its nadir just over a month after *Sputnik II*. As the Senate Preparedness Subcommittee, headed by Lyndon B. Johnson, began an investigation of the nation's satellite and missile activities, Americans turned their attention to Cape Canaveral. There, according to White House Press Secretary James C. Hagerty, scientists and engineers from the Naval Research Laboratory and its industrial contractors would attempt to put in orbit a grapefruit-sized package of instruments as part of Project Vanguard, the American International Geophysical Year satellite effort. In reality the Vanguard group was planning only to use a test satellite in the first launch of all three active stages of the research rocket. To their dismay swarms of newsmen descended on Cape Canaveral to watch what the public regarded as this country's effort to get into the space race. On December 6, before a national television audience, the Vanguard first stage exploded and the rest of the rocket collapsed into the wet sand surrounding the launch stand.[90]

In the face of the fact that "they" orbited satellites before "we" did, together with the apparent complacency of official Washington, the Vanguard blowup took on disastrous proportions. McElroy had become Secretary of Defense on October 9, after Wilson's resignation. In mid-November he had authorized the Army Ballistic Missile Agency at Redstone Arsenal to revive "Project Orbiter." This was a scheme for using a Redstone with upper stages to orbit an instrumented satellite. It had been proposed jointly by the Office of Naval Research and the Army in 1954–1955 but overruled in the Defense Department in favor of the Naval Research Laboratory's Vanguard proposal, based on the Viking and Aerobee.[91] Now Wernher von Braun and company hurriedly converted their Jupiter C reentry test vehicle, an elongated Redstone topped by clustered solid-propellant upper stages developed by the Jet Propulsion Laboratory, into a satellite launcher.[92]

On January 31, 1958, just 84 days after McElroy's go-ahead signal, and carrying satellite instruments developed for Project Vanguard by University of Iowa physicist James A. Van Allen, a Jupiter C (renamed Juno I by the von Braun team) boosted into orbit *Explorer I*, the first American satellite. The total weight of the pencil-shaped payload was about 31 pounds, 18 pounds of which consisted of instruments. Following a high elliptical orbit, *Explorer I* transmitted data revealing the existence of a deep zone of radiation girdling

29

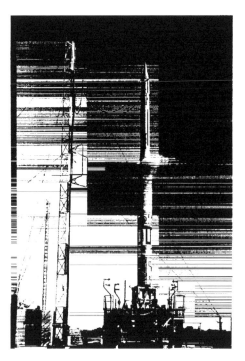

Vanguard was the one nonmilitary launch vehicle of the early space program. More or less a descendant of the Viking rocket, the Vanguard rocket was important in its own right and for its legacy of contributions to NASA's Delta launch vehicle that would follow. Also the program built the Minitrack tracking network, which was to have a long, fruitful part to play in the space program.

Earth, dubbed the "Van Allen belt." The following March 17, the much-maligned Vanguard finally accomplished its purpose, lifting a scientific payload weighing a little over 3 pounds into an orbit that was expected to keep the satellite up from 200 to 1000 years. *Vanguard I* proved what geophysicists had long suspected, that Earth is not a perfect sphere but is slightly pear-shaped, bulging in the aqueous southern hemisphere. *Explorer III*, with an instrumented weight of 18½ pounds, was fired into orbit by a Jupiter C nine days later. But in May a mammoth Soviet rocket launched a satellite with the then staggering weight of nearly 3000 pounds, some 56 times as heavy as the combined weight of the three American satellite payloads.[93]

Clearly, rockets that could accelerate such bulky unmanned satellites to orbital velocity could also send a man into space. And it seemed safe to assume that the Soviet politicians, scientists, and military leaders, capitalizing on their lead in propulsion systems, had precisely such a feat in mind. When the one-and-one-half-ton *Sputnik III* shot into orbit, the Atlas, star of the American missile drive, viewed not only as the preeminent weapon of the next decade but also as a highly promising space rocket, was still in its qualification flight program. Plagued by turbopump problems and fuel sloshing, so far it had made only two successful test flights, out of four attempts.[91]

Yet American military planners remained confident that the Atlas finally would become a reliable missile. It must if the United States was not to fall perilously behind in the frenzied competition with the Soviets, if the missile gap was not to widen. And what of the advocates of manned space flight, the ambitious individuals on the fringes of the scientific community, NACA, and the military services—people who saw the Atlas, not the frail Vanguard or the Jupiter C, as holding the key to space? They also kept their hopes high.

II

Exploring the Human Factor

(1948–1958)

THE development of the large liquid-fueled rocket made the dazzling prospect of manned flight beyond Earth's atmosphere and into the vacuum of space increasingly feasible from the standpoint of propulsion. By 1950, however, only instrumented sounding rockets, fired to ever higher altitudes in both the United States and the Soviet Union, had reached into space before falling earthward. Although a number of these experimental shots carried living organisms—everything from fungus spores to monkeys in the United States, mainly dogs in the U.S.S.R.—the data acquired from telemetry and from occasional recovery of rocket nose cones had not shown conclusively how long organisms could live in space, or indeed whether man could survive at all outside the protective confines of his atmosphere. Scientists still were hesitant to predict how a human being would behave under conditions to be encountered in space flight. Thus while space flight became technologically practicable, physiologically and psychologically it remained an enigma.

In the early 1950s an acceleration of efforts in upper-atmospheric and space medical research accompanied the quickened pace of rocket development in this country and in the Soviet Union. During the next few years medical specialists, profiting from substantial progress in telemetering clinical data, learned a great deal about what a man could expect when he went into the forbidding arena of space.[1] Much of the confidence with which the engineers of Project Mercury in 1958 approached the job of putting a man into orbit and recovering him stemmed from the findings of hundreds of studies made in previous years on the human factors in space flight.

Since the National Advisory Committee for Aeronautics was interested almost exclusively in the technology of flight, research in the medical problems of space flight, like aviation medicine in previous decades, was the province primarily of the military services and of some civilian research organizations receiving funds from the military. Of the three services, the United States Air Force, rich in background in aeromedical research and assuming that space medicine was but an extension of aviation medicine, undertook most of the early inquiry into the psycho-physiological problems of extra-atmospheric flight.

BEGINNINGS OF SPACE MEDICINE

After the Second World War the Air Force acquired the talents of a number of scientists who had done much remarkable research on the medical aspects of high-speed, high-altitude airplane flight for Germany's Luftwaffe.[2] Most of these German physicians, physiologists, and psychologists were brought to the expanding Aeromedical Laboratory at Wright-Patterson Air Force Base, near Dayton, Ohio. Six of the more prominent German aeromedical specialists, Hubertus Strughold, Hans-Georg Clamann, Konrad Buettner, Siegfried J. Gerathewohl, and the brothers Fritz and Heinz Haber, were assigned as research physicians to the Air Force School of Aviation Medicine, located on the scrub prairies of south central Texas at Randolph Air Force Base, outside San Antonio. The commandant of the school was Colonel Harry G. Armstrong, author of the classic text in aviation medicine.[3] While heavily instrumented V–2s lumbered upward from White Sands and plastic research balloons lifted seeds, mice, hamsters, fruit flies, and other specimens into the upper atmosphere, Armstrong and his associates were already considering the medical implications of flight by man into the hostile space environment.

In November 1948, Armstrong organized at Randolph a panel discussion on the "Aeromedical Problems of Space Travel." Featuring papers by Strughold and Heinz Haber and commentary by six well-known scientists from universities and the military, the symposium perhaps marked the beginning of formal, academic inquiry into the medical hazards of extra-atmospheric flight. Before this epochal gathering ended, Strughold had resolved the contradiction inherent in the title of the symposium by emphatically using the term "space medicine."[4]

The following February, Armstrong set up the world's first Department of Space Medicine, headed by Strughold and including the Habers and Konrad Buettner.[5] In November 1951, at San Antonio, the School of Aviation Medicine and the privately financed Lovelace Foundation for Medical Research at Albuquerque, New Mexico, sponsored a symposium discreetly entitled "Physics and Medicine of the Upper Atmosphere." It was still not respectable to speak plainly of space flight within the Air Force, which only that year had cautiously reactivated its intercontinental ballistic missile project and remained sensitive to "Buck Rogers" epithets from members of Congress and the taxpaying public. A good portion of the material presented by the 44 speakers at the 1951 symposium, however, covered the nature of space, the mechanics of space flight, and the medical difficulties of sending a man beyond the sensible and breathable atmosphere.[6]

It was at this meeting that Strughold, later to acquire a reputation as the "father of space medicine," put forth what is perhaps his most notable contribution—the concept of "aeropause," a region of "space-equivalent conditions" or

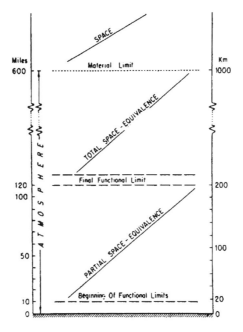

An important bridge from aviation medicine to space medicine was this chart by Hubertus Strughold in 1951. It related altitudes at which human functional borders occur with the altitudes at which the various physical characteristics of space occur.

"atmospheric space equivalence." Strughold pointed out that while many astronomers, astrophysicists, and meteorologists set the boundary between the atmosphere and space at about 600 miles from Earth, the biological conditions of space begin much lower, at about 50,000 feet. Anoxia is encountered at 50,000 feet, the boiling point of body fluids at 63,000 feet, the necessity for carrying all respiratory oxygen within a manned compartment at 80,000 feet, meteoroids at 75 miles, and the darkness of the space "void" at 100 miles. Above 100 miles the atmosphere is imperceptible to the flyer. "What we call upper atmosphere in the physical sense," said Strughold, "must be considered—in terms of biology—as space in its total form." Hence manned ballistic or orbital flight at an altitude of 100 miles would be, for all practical purposes, space flight.[7]

The rocket-powered research airplanes of the postwar years, beginning with the X–1, the first manned vehicle to surpass the speed of sound, took American test pilots well into the region of space equivalence. On August 26, 1954, when Major Arthur Murray of the Air Force pushed the Bell X–1A to an altitude of

90,000 feet, he was above 90 percent of the sensible atmosphere. Two years later, in the more powerful Bell X–2, Air Force Captain Iven Kincheloe climbed to 126,000 feet, "a space-equivalent flight to a very high degree." [8] The X–15, still on the drawing boards in the mid-fifties, was being designed to rocket its pilot to an altitude of 50 miles at nearly seven times the speed of sound. And human-factors research in the X–15 project, involving the development and testing of a new full-pressure flying suit, centrifuge conditioning to high acceleration forces, and telemetering a wide range of physiological data in flight, would contribute substantially to medical planning for space travel.[9]

Zero G

At peak speed and altitude an X–15 flight was supposed to afford about five minutes of "weightlessness" or "zero g." This is the effect created when a vehicle is balanced between centrifugal and centripetal forces—when the gravitational pull of Earth and other heavenly bodies is exactly balanced by the inertial character of the vehicle's motion. Weightlessness is undoubtedly the most fascinating medical characteristic of space flight, and it aroused the most speculation among aviation physicians in the late forties and early fifties. To be sure, approximations of zero g were not totally new human experiences; a common illustration of the sensation is the sudden partial lightening of the body in a rapidly descending elevator. But the necessity to function at zero g—to eat and drink, to eliminate body wastes, to operate the spacecraft controls—was a new requirement and presented new problems for the aeromedical teams.

Flight physicians were almost unanimous in expressing forebodings about the effect of weightlessness on man's physical and mental performance. Some feared that the body organs depended on sustained gravity and would not function if deprived of the customary gravitational force. Others worried over the combined effects of acceleration, weightlessness, and the heavy deceleration during atmospheric entry. Still other experts were concerned especially about perception and equilibrium. For example, Heinz Haber and Otto Gauer, another émigré German physician who joined the Air Force aeromedical program, noted that the brain receives signals on the position, direction, and support of the body from four mechanisms—pressure on the nerves and organs, muscle tone, posture, and the labyrinth of the inner ear. They theorized that these four mechanisms might give conflicting signals in the weightless state and that such disturbances "may deeply affect the autonomic nervous functions and ultimately produce a very severe sensation of succumbence associated with an absolute incapacity to act." [10]

The basic difficulty retarding the study of weightlessness was the impossibility of duplicating the exact condition on Earth. The X–15, considered by many in the mid-fifties to be the penultimate step to manned orbital flight, progressed slowly and would fly too late to shed much light on the problem of zero g for Project Mercury. By the fall of 1958, however, when the newly formed National

Aeronautics and Space Administration undertook to orbit a manned satellite, American aeromedical researchers had been studying the gravity-free condition intensively for some eight years.

The best but most expensive device for zero-g experimentation was the sounding rocket. For several years, beginning with the V-2 firings from White Sands, parachutes for nose cones containing rocket-launched animals invariably failed to open and the subjects were killed on impact. The first successful recovery came in September 1951, when an instrumented monkey and 11 mice survived an Aerobee launch to 236,000 feet from Holloman Air Force Base, New Mexico. The last of three Aerobee shots at Holloman, in May 1952, like the previous experiments, carried a camera on board to photograph two mice and two monkeys under acceleration, weightlessness, and deceleration. An Air Force aeromedical team, headed by James P. Henry, a physician who later would direct the Mercury animal program, and young Captain David G. Simons, found no adverse effects on the animals.[11]

For the next six years the priority military ballistic missile program almost monopolized rocket development in the United States. Medical experimentation employing live test subjects launched to high altitudes by rockets came to a virtual standstill. By contrast, during the same period from 1952 to 1957, researchers in the Soviet Union carried out numerous animal rocket flights, with dogs of the Pavlovian sort being their favorite passengers. By late 1957, when the Soviets sent the dog Laika into orbit aboard *Sputnik II*, the peak altitude of their vertical launches of animals was nearly 300 miles, and the Russian scientists had perfected a technique for catapulting animals from nose cones and recovering them with parachutes. Apparently the Russians also were able to measure a wider range of physiological reactions than their American counterparts.[12]

During the six-year hiatus in animal rocket experimentation in this country, investigators had to resort to the aircraft, "the oldest aeromedical laboratory," for studying the weightless phenomenon.[13] In 1950, Fritz and Heinz Haber, of the Air Force School of Aviation Medicine, had considered various ways of simulating zero g for medical experiments. Discarding the free fall and the elevator ride, the Habers concluded that the best technique involved an airplane flight along a vertical parabola, or "Keplerian trajectory." If properly executed, such a maneuver could provide as much as 35 seconds of zero g and a somewhat longer period of subgravity, a condition wherein the body is under only partial gravitational stress.[14] During the summer and fall of 1951 test pilots A. Scott Crossfield of NACA and Charles E. Yeager of the Air Force tried out the technique, flying a number of Keplerian trajectories in jet interceptors. Up to 20 seconds of weightlessness resulted from some of these flights. Crossfield reported initial "befuddlement" during zero g but no serious loss of muscle coordination, while Yeager described a sensation of falling and in one instance of spinning and feeling "lost in space." The latter sensation the physicians and psychologists called "disorientation."[15]

The Habers' technique and these early experiments with it represented a promising beginning, but as one Air Force aeromedical specialist pointed out, "The results of these flights were inconclusive in many respects." [16] An enormous amount of work remained before students of weightlessness could do much generalizing about this greatest anomaly of space flight.

In 1953 a small group comprising the Space Biology Branch of the Aeromedical Field Laboratory at Holloman Air Force Base inaugurated an ambitious program of parabolic flights to continue the investigations of weightless flight that had halted with the termination of the Aerobee animal launches in the spring of 1952. Supervised by Major David G. Simons, a physician who acted as test subject on many occasions, the Holloman studies for two years utilized T–33 and F–89 jet aircraft. Late in 1955, after Captain Grover J. D. Schock came to the field laboratory as task scientist, the standard tool for zero g research became the F–94C, which offered a longer parabola than other aircraft and thus a longer period of weightlessness. In the summer of 1958 the Air Force canceled all zero-g research at Holloman, and the coterie of scientists broke up. Colonel John P. Stapp, head of the field laboratory, and Simons went elsewhere, while Schock turned his attention to other research projects. [17]

For three years before the termination of the Holloman flight program, students of zero g at the School of Aviation Medicine had duplicated and even surpassed the investigations being carried out in New Mexico. Although sponsored by the Department of Space Medicine, the program carried out at Randolph Air Force Base was actually directed by Siegfried Gerathewohl, who was not a member of the department. Gerathewohl and his colleagues began their studies with the T–33 jet trainer, but like their counterparts in New Mexico, they soon turned to the superior F–94C. Major Herbert D. Stallings, a Randolph physician, estimated that by April 1958 he had flown more than 4000 zero-g trajectories and compiled about 37 hours of weightless flight. [18]

Gerathewohl, Simons, Schock, and the other scientists at Randolph and Holloman tried to get as great a variety of information as possible during the 30 to 40 seconds of weightlessness and subgravity produced by the F–94C flights. They carried out numerous eye-hand coordination tests, for example, wherein a subject tried to make crosses in a pattern or hit a target with a metal stylus. Subjects usually missed their mark in the first moments of zero g or subgravity, but most of them improved their performance with their cumulative experience. The Air Force scientists also studied eating and drinking, bladder function, and disorientation after awakening during weightlessness; the functions at zero g of various animals, especially cats, whose vestibular organs had been removed; and the phenomenon called the "oculo-agravic illusion," wherein luminous objects seen in the dark appear to move upward during weightlessness. [19]

At the Wright Air Development Center, in Ohio, a team of researchers headed by Major Edward L. Brown picked up the experimental program discontinued at Holloman in mid-1958, except that they used the relatively slow, propeller-driven

C–131 transport in their studies. A parabola in a C–131 gave only 10 to 15 seconds of weightlessness, but the spacious interior of the cargo carrier made it possible to observe the reactions of several subjects simultaneously, including their coordination and locomotion and even their ability to walk along the ceiling while wearing shoes with magnetic soles.[20]

In general the aeromedical specialists at Randolph, Holloman, and Wright-Patterson— as well as those in more modest programs at the Navy School of Aviation Medicine, Pensacola, Florida, and at the NACA Lewis Flight Propulsion Laboratory in Cleveland—found that the principal problems of weightless flight seemed solvable. Eating and drinking at zero g were not troublesome when squeeze bottles and tubes were used, and urination presented no real difficulty. Some subjects suffered nausea, disorientation, loss of coordination, and other disturbances, but the majority reported that after they adjusted to the condition they found it "pleasant" and had a feeling of "well-being." [21] As early as 1955, Simons concluded that weightlessness produced no abnormalities with regard to heart rate and arterial and venous blood pressure, while Henry, Simons' colleague in the Aerobee animal experiments, prophesied, "In the skilled pilot weightlessness will probably have very little significance." [22] And in 1959, about a year after Project Mercury got underway, Gerathewohl remarked that "the majority of flying personnel enjoy the exposure to the subgravity state in our controlled experiments. We have reason to believe that even longer periods of absolute weightlessness can be tolerated if the crew is properly conditioned and equipped." [23]

MULTIPLE G

Another problem perplexing aeromedical experts as the era of space flight neared was the effect on the human body of the heavy acceleration and deceleration forces, called "g loads," building up during rocket-propelled flights into space at speeds far greater than those yet experienced by man. Many fighter pilots in the Second World War had suffered momentary pain and blurred vision during "redout," when blood pooled in the head and eyes during an outside loop, or "blackout," when the heart suddenly could not pump enough blood to the head region as an airplane pulled out of a steep dive. Acceleration of a vehicle into space and the deceleration accompanying its return to the atmosphere would subject a man to g loads several times the normal accelerative force of gravity. In other words, for parts of a space mission a man would come to "weigh" several times what he normally did on Earth; a severe strain would be imposed on his body organs.

At the Aeromedical Field Laboratory in New Mexico, Harald J. von Beckh, a physician who had immigrated from Germany by way of the Instituto Nacional de Medicina Aeronáutica in Buenos Aires, was especially concerned about the ability of a space traveler to tolerate the high deceleration forces of atmospheric entry after several hours of weightlessness. In the last few months before such research ended at Holloman, von Beckh inquired into the relationship between zero g and the multiplication of g. He added a steep downward spiral to the level, weightless portion of the Keplerian trajectory in order to impose heavy g loads on a test subject immediately after a half minute or so of weightlessness. After a number of these parabolic-spiral flights, he reported pessimistically, "Alternation of weightlessness and acceleration results in a decrease of acceleration tolerance and of the efficiency of physiologic recovery mechanisms . . . Because there is a decreased acceleration tolerance," he warned, "every effort must be made to reduce G loads to a minimum." [21]

Throughout the 1950s a substantial number of aeromedical experts concerned themselves with acceleration-deceleration loads per se, not necessarily in connection with the gravity-free state. Research on g forces reached back for decades, to the primitive period of aviation medicine. The state of knowledge with regard to the physiology of acceleration-deceleration was still hazy and fluid in the early fifties, although for at least 25 years aviation physicians in Europe and the United States had been studying blackout, redout, impact forces, and other effects of high g in aircraft.[25] The V–2 and Aerobee animal rocket shots also had added to research data on the problem. But until the X–15 was ready, researchers had about exhausted the airplane as a tool for studying g loads, and from 1952 to 1958 experimentation with animal-carrying rockets was suspended in the United States. Consequently American scientists had to turn to two devices on the ground— the rocket-powered impact sled, used for studying the immediate onset of g loads, and the centrifuge, where the slower buildup of g could be simulated— to enlarge what they knew about the limits of human endurance of heavy acceleration and deceleration.

On December 10, 1954, Lieutenant Colonel John P. Stapp of the Aeromedical Field Laboratory gave an amazing demonstration of a man's ability to withstand immediate impact forces. Stapp rode a rocket-driven impact sled on the 3550-foot Holloman research track to a velocity of 937 feet per second and received an impact force of 35 to 40 g for a fraction of a second as the sled slammed to a halt in a water trough.[26] In February 1957 a chimpanzee rocketed down the track, now 5000 feet long, braked to a stop, and survived a load of some 247 g for a millisecond, with a rate of onset of 16,000 g per second. And 15 months later, on the 120-foot "daisy track" at Holloman, Captain Eli L. Beeding, seated upright and facing backward, experienced the highest deceleration peak yet recorded on a human being— -83 g for .04 of a second, with 3826 g per second as the calculated rate of onset. Afterward Beeding, recovering from shock and various minor injuries, judged that 83 g represented about the limit of human tolerance for deceleration.[27]

Such studies of deceleration were not directed primarily toward space missions but rather toward the problem of survival after ejection from or crashes in high-performance aircraft. The Holloman sled runs of the fifties, however, did broaden considerably the available data on the absolute limits of man's ability

40

to endure multiples of g. And, perhaps more important, the New Mexico experiments in biodynamics were directly applicable to the problem of high g forces resulting from the uncushioned impact of a spacecraft on water or land. Stapp reasoned that a properly restrained, aft-facing human being could withstand a land impact of some 80 knots (135 feet per second) in a spacecraft if the g forces were applied transversely, or through the body, and if the spacecraft did not collapse on him.[28]

The centrifuge, the other laboratory tool used by students of acceleration-deceleration patterns, became increasingly useful in the fifties. The basic feature of the centrifuge was a large mechanical arm with a man-carrying gondola or platform mounted on the end, within which a test subject would be rotated at high angular velocities. Centrifuge experiments had more immediate pertinence to space medicine than impact sled tests, because on the "wheel" investigators could duplicate the relatively gradual buildup of g forces encountered during the launch and reentry portions of ballistic, orbital, or interplanetary flight. In the fifties, centrifuges existed at several places in the United States. The best-known and most used were at the Navy's Aviation Medical Acceleration Laboratory, Johnsville, Pennsylvania, and at the Aeromedical Laboratory at Wright-Patterson Air Force Base. During the decade, researchers at Johnsville, Wright-Patterson, and elsewhere simulated a wide variety of acceleration and deceleration profiles, using an almost equally wide variety of body positions and support systems, to compile an impressive quantity of data on the reactions of potential space pilots to heavy g forces.[29]

Just after the Second World War, Otto Gauer and Heinz Haber, who had conducted centrifuge experiments for the German Air Force, proposed a series of acceleration patterns, ranging from 3 g for 9½ minutes to 10 g for 2 minutes, all of which would be tolerable for a space pilot.[30] Then, in 1952, E. R. Ballinger, leader of the research program at Wright-Patterson, conducted one of the earliest series of centrifuge tests directed expressly toward the problem of g forces in space flight. Ballinger found that 3 g applied transversely would be the ideal takeoff pattern from the physiological standpoint, but he realized that the rocket burning time and velocity for such a pattern would be insufficient to propel a spacecraft out of the atmosphere. Consequently he and his associates subjected men to gradually increasing g loads, building to peaks of 10 g for something over two minutes. Chest pain, shortness of breath, and occasional loss of consciousness were the symptoms of those subjected to the higher g loads. The tests led Ballinger to the conclusion that 8 g represented the acceleration safety limit for a space passenger.[31]

Data gained from the first Soviet and American instrumented satellites of late 1957 and early 1958 showed that the atmosphere reached considerably farther out than scientists previously had realized. Until these disclosures aeromedical experts had assumed that the deceleration, or backward acceleration, forces of reentry, producing what was graphically described as an "eyeballs out" sensation, would be much greater than the acceleration during the ascent, or "eyeballs in," phase of the mission. Proceeding on this assumption, a team of physiologists from the Army, Navy, and Air Force had used the 50-foot centrifuge at the Navy's Johnsville installation to study the anticipated high reentry g buildup, exposing five chimpanzees to a peak of 40 g for one minute. Post-run examinations of the primates showed internal injuries, including heart malfunctions. It appeared that prolonged subjection to high g might be severely injurious or perhaps even fatal to a man.[32]

The tests conducted by Ballinger at Wright-Patterson and the interservice experiments with the chimpanzees on the Navy centrifuge featured frontward (eyeballs-in) application of g loads during the launch profile, backward application (eyeballs-out) during the reentry simulation, and the use of rather elaborate restraint straps and basic aircraft bucket seats as a support system. The problem of determining optimum body position and support was vigorously attacked by biodynamicists during 1957 and 1958. A series of especially careful studies on the Wright Air Development Center centrifuge indicated that when the subject was positioned so that the g forces were applied transversely and backward to the center of rotation, breathing became easier. Acceleration-deceleration patterns of 12 g for 4 seconds, 8 g for 41 seconds, and 5 g for 2 minutes were endured without great difficulty by practically all the volunteer subjects, some having even higher tolerance limits. Results of runs on the Johnsville centrifuge with the subjects in an aft-facing position for both acceleration and deceleration patterns also appeared favorable.[33]

The students of g forces tried various support devices in the late fifties in their search for ways to increase human tolerance to acceleration and deceleration loads. One specialist in the Wright-Patterson centrifuge group came up with a suit of interwoven nylon and cotton material, reinforced by nylon belting, and attached to the pilot seat at six places to absorb the g loads and distribute them more evenly over the entire body. Later, Wright-Patterson scientists using a nylon netting arrangement in conjunction with a contour couch were able to expose several men to a peak of 16.5 g for several seconds without any discoverable adverse effects. Other Air Force specialists experimented with subjects partially enclosed in a "rigid envelope," actually a plaster cast, as protection against both g-load buildup and impact forces. And von Beckh, whose concern with the weightlessness-deceleration puzzle led him to experiment with anti-g techniques, developed a device called "multi-directional g protection," a compartment that turned automatically to ensure that the g forces were always applied transversely on its occupant. Von Beckh's invention was used to protect a rat that went along on Beeding's record sled run in 1958, and a modified compartment carried three mice on a Thor-Able rocket launch the same year. Results in both experiments were encouraging.[34]

Navy scientists were especially interested in water immersion as a means of minimizing g loads. Researchers in Germany, Canada, and the United States had experimented with water-lined flying suits and submersion in water tanks, beginning in the 1930s. Specialists had carried out sporadic biodynamic tests with immersed rabbits and mice in the late forties at the Navy School of Aviation Medicine and, after the giant centrifuge began operation in 1952, in Johnsville.[35]

In 1956, R. Flanagan Gray, a physician at the Johnsville laboratory, designed an aluminum centrifuge capsule that could be filled with water and was large enough to hold a man. After some initial troubles installing the contraption on the centrifuge and perfecting an emergency automatic flushing mechanism, the "Iron Maiden," as it was rather inaccurately nicknamed, went into use. In March 1958, Gray, immersed to his ribs in a bathtub-like device developed at the Mayo Clinic during the Second World War, had endured 16 g of headward (head to feet) acceleration. Then, the next year, Gray enclosed himself in the Iron Maiden and, positioned backward to the center of rotation and immersed in water above the top of his head, held his breath during the 25-second pattern to withstand a peak of 31 g transverse acceleration for five seconds. This performance with the water-filled aluminum capsule established a new record for tolerance of centrifuge g loads.[36]

Nylon netting, multidirectional positioning, and water immersion were all promising methods for combating g forces and expanding human endurance limits. But netting had a troublesome tendency to bounce the subject forward as the g forces diminished, while directional positioning and water-immersion apparatus required more space and weight than would be available in a small, relatively light spacecraft.[37] And considering the thrust limitations of the Thor, the Atlas, or the somewhat larger Titan ICBM, a small spacecraft was the only feasible design for an American manned satellite in 1958.

At the inception of the NASA manned satellite project, in the fall of 1958, the apparent solution to the problem of body support was an anti-g contrivance developed not by biodynamicists but by a group of practicing aerodynamicists in NACA's Pilotless Aircraft Research Division, part of the Langley Aeronautical Laboratory in Virginia. Maxime A. Faget, William M. Bland, Jr., Jack C. Heberlig, and a few other NACA engineers had designed an extremely strong and lightweight couch, made of fiber glass, which could be contoured to fit the body dimensions of a particular man. In the spring of 1958, technicians and shopmen at Langley molded the first of a series of test-model contour couches. The following July a group from Langley went to the Aviation Medical Acceleration Laboratory at Johnsville to try out their couch on the Navy's big centrifuge.[38]

The Navy biodynamicists and the NACA engineers experimented with the couch and various body positions in an effort to amplify a g-load tolerance. The couch made at Langley had been molded to fit the physical dimensions of Robert A. Champine, one of the foremost NACA test pilots. Champine rode the Johnsville centrifuge to a peak of 12 g on July 29, then departed for a conference on the Pacific Coast. The next day Navy Lieutenant Carter C. Collins volunteered to test the couch. Since his frame was smaller than Champine's, the Johnsville

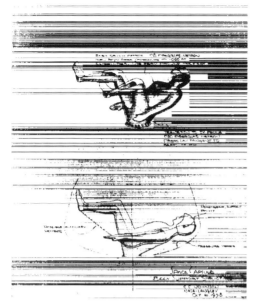

Mercury

One of the most critical design and feasibility problems in the early days of Mercury was whether the astronaut could be safely restrained and supported through the succession of vibration levels, g forces, weightlessness, and more g forces that would occur in space flight. Langley laboratory engineers conceived the contour couch (left) in 1958, and refined it enough to try a model (below) in 1959.

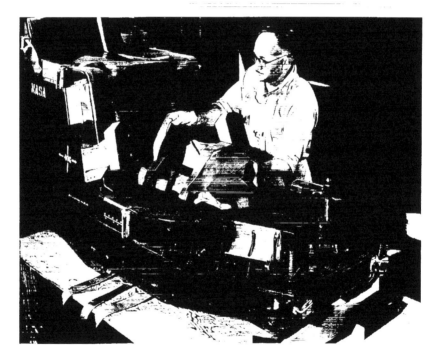

Couch

After the couch concept had been devised, there was the problem of a system to provide the contradictory combination of restraint, cushioning, and support. An early couch of nylon netting (right) was ruled out because it bounced the occupant forward as g forces diminished. The final choice was fiber glass cast to the contour of each astronaut (below) and equipped with restraining straps.

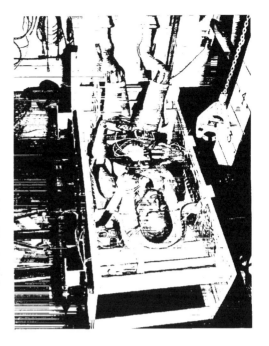

45

experts had to pack foam-rubber padding into the recesses of the fiber-glass bed. Collins then climbed into the centrifuge gondola and seated himself in the couch, the back angle of which was set forward 10 degrees. The 4000-horsepower centrifuge motor whirled the gondola progressively faster. On the first run the loads reached a peak of 12 g. Five more runs pushed the peak to 18 g. Then, on the sixth try, using a grunting technique to avoid blackout and chest pains, Collins withstood a peak of 20.7 g, applied transversely for a duration of six seconds. Later that day, Gray, inventor of the Iron Maiden, rode the centrifuge with the contour couch and also endured a 20-g peak. The acceleration patterns to which Collins and Gray were exposed corresponded to a reentry angle of 7.5 degrees. At that time the optimum reentry angle being considered for a manned satellite, 1.5 degrees, theoretically would expose the spacecraft passenger to only 9 g.[39]

The NACA engineers, already working overtime on designs for a manned orbital capsule, were elated. It seemed that they finally had an effective anti-g device that was small enough and light enough to fit into a one-ton ballistic capsule they had in mind for the initial manned space venture.[40] They had, in fact, made a major contribution to the protection of a space rider from sustained high g forces, although they did not fully realize as yet that body angles were more significant features of the couch than its contoured support.

The procedure ultimately used for protecting the Mercury astronauts from the g loads of acceleration to orbital velocity and deceleration during reentry represented a combination of the advantages gained from many experiments by military and other specialists in flight physiology, as well as from the ingenuity of the aeronautical engineers in NACA and NASA. Although the idea of using a hammock either for the basic support or in combination with the contour couch was perennially attractive to the human-factors experts in Project Mercury, all Mercury astronauts sat in essentially the same couch designed by Faget and his coworkers in the spring of 1958. But added to this basic technique were restraining straps, a semi-supine posture, frontward application of acceleration loads, and the reversal of the spacecraft attitude during orbit to permit frontward imposition of reentry loads as well. The final elements in the NACA–NASA campaign to minimize the effects of insertion-reentry g buildups was the use as astronauts of experienced test pilots provided by the military services. During the centrifuge experiments of the fifties such men had consistently proved capable of withstanding higher g forces than nonpilots.

ENVIRONMENTAL CONTROL

High-altitude atmospheric flight had necessitated much work related to two serious physiological problems of space flight—air supply and the pressure required for breathing in space. Research on these problems in the United States stretched back to 1918, when the Army began operation of a decompression chamber at Hazelhurst Field, Long Island. In the early 1930s the civilian aviator

Wiley Post wore a pressure suit, looking like a deep-sea diver's outfit, for high-altitude flying. By the early fifties the typical jet pilot breathed pure oxygen for hours in an artificially pressurized cabin while wearing a pressurized flying suit as an extra protection in case of cabin decompression.[41]

Air compression, however, is not practicable above 80,000 feet. Travel outside the breathable atmosphere, whether into space or to the bottom of the sea, necessitates living inside a hermetically sealed compartment, a completely airtight ecological system in which carbon dioxide exhaled by the traveler is constantly replaced by an onboard supply of pure oxygen or some combination approximating the nitrogen-oxygen composition at sea level. In this area of space flight research—space cabin environment—the Air Force achieved preeminence in the early fifties with the development of the first sealed space cabin.

The sealed space cabin had two essential precursors. One was the sealed gondola for stratospheric ballooning, used by the Swiss twins Auguste and Jean Piccard in several flights to altitudes of around 10 miles in the 1930s and in the *Explorer II* ascent of 1935, which carried Army experimenters Orvil A. Anderson and A. W. Stevens to 72,335 feet and set a record that stood for 20 years.[42] The other was the closed underwater environment of the bathysphere, used for many years in deep-sea exploration, and of the submarine. In the fifties, Air Force research on the sealed space cabin paralleled similar work by Navy scientists on an environmental control system for the new atomic-powered submarines, which were being designed to remain totally submerged for months.[43]

In 1952, Fritz Haber, of the Air Force School of Aviation Medicine, drew blueprints for a sealed chamber to be used for space medicine research; at the urging of Hubertus Strughold the Air Force let a contract for its construction. The Guardite Company of Chicago delivered a completed cabin in the summer of 1954.[44] "Nobody took notice of a 'sealed cabin,' " recalled Strughold. "We had to have a name that would attract attention to our work. So I named it the 'Space Cabin Simulator.' "[45]

The cabin provided about 100 cubic feet of living space, room enough for an ordinary aircraft seat and a panel of lights, switches, and displays to test the psychological reactions of the subject. It had systems for air conditioning, oxygen supply and carbon dioxide absorption, urine distillation, and the recycling of the distilled urine together with air moisture to provide water pure enough to drink. Cabin pressure was maintained constantly at a level equivalent to an altitude of 18,000 to 25,000 feet.[46]

The space cabin simulator received its first national publicity in March 1956, when Airman D. F. Smith spent 24 hours in the chamber at San Antonio, performing a number of tasks for psychological monitoring and wearing instrumentation to record his heart action, temperature, and respiration rate. During the next two years, Lieutenant Colonel George R. Steinkamp, Captain Julian Ward, and George T. Hauty, who had charge of the simulations, gradually increased the duration of the tests. On February 16, 1958, four and a half months after

Sputnik I and after seven days in the sealed chamber, Airman Donald F. Farrell stepped out to be greeted by a crowd of newsmen and by Senator Lyndon B. Johnson. In this, the most famous experiment ever run in the original space cabin simulator, Farrell had spent his week completely isolated in an environment that duplicated life inside a spacecraft in every respect except the weightless condition.[47]

The Farrell experiment provided no unexpected physiological data. But Hauty, chiefly interested in the psychological portion of the simulation, reported that the daily log kept by Farrell showed a deterioration from good spirits to "the seemingly abrupt onset of frank hostility." Farrell's mental condition "reached the point of becoming the single conceivable reason for a premature termination of the flight." Hauty noted that Farrell's proficiency at tasks assigned to him also deteriorated severely as the experiment progressed.[48]

The psychological data from the early space cabin simulator tests, as well as observation of subjects in the isolation chamber at Wright-Patterson Air Force Base, were not encouraging. Major Charles A. Berry, an Air Force physician who later would work closely with the astronauts in Project Mercury, perhaps expressed the consensus among space medicine investigators by 1958: "The psychological problems presented by the exposure of man to an isolated, uncomfortable void seem to be more formidable than the physiological problems."[49]

MATTER FROM SPACE

Even after enclosing himself in a sealed cabin and adjusting to prolonged isolation, the first man in space ran the danger of being killed by decompression if his cabin were punctured by one of the myriad meteoroids, ranging in size from less than a millimeter up to several meters, that constantly bombard Earth's atmosphere.[50] Impact with a meteoroid, even one the size of a BB shot, conceivably could put a hole in the structure of a spacecraft and cause death to its occupant through either gradual or explosive cabin decompression.

In the forties and early fifties scientists varied widely in their guesses as to the probability of meteoroid impact. Fletcher G. Watson, a Harvard University astronomer, predicted in 1946 that at least one of every 25 space ships going to the Moon would be destroyed by collision with a meteoroid. Two years later George Grimminger, a mathematician with the Rand Corporation, estimated that a spacecraft with an exposed area of 1000 square feet would be hit by a particle with a diameter of $\frac{1}{2}$ millimeter only about once every 15 years. As late as 1951, however, Fred L. Whipple of Harvard, one of the principal American authorities on meteoroids, was rather pessimistic about the chances of avoiding meteoroid penetration and suggested thick shielding on the spacecraft to guard against structural damage.[51]

The early instrumented satellites sent up by the Soviet Union and the United States did much to dispel the fears of the space flight enthusiasts about meteoroids.

The American satellite *Explorer I,* launched in January 1958, recorded only seven hits by micrometeoroids—particles considerably less than a millimeter in diameter—during the first month of its orbital life. Apparently none of these pieces of matter penetrated the satellite's outer skin. Data from the much larger Russian *Sputnik III,* sent into orbit in May 1958, indicated that an orbiting spacecraft with a surface of 1000 square meters (10,760 square feet) would be hit by a meteoroid weighing at least one gram only once every 14,000 hours. And *Explorer VI,* orbited by the United States in the late summer of 1959, encountered meteoroid dust particles only 28 times during the first two days it was in orbit.[52] These data prompted a human-factors specialist for one of the major aerospace firms to conclude that for low orbital missions in a manned spacecraft "the danger from meteorite [sic] penetration is minor to negligible in comparison to the other hazards of such flights."[53] Nevertheless, Project Mercury astronauts would wear a full-pressure suit, a closed ecological system in itself, so that if cabin decompression occurred each astronaut could live until his space capsule could be brought back to Earth.

SPACE RADIATION

In addition to weightlessness, g loads, air, water, and food supply, isolation, and meteoroids, the problems of space flight included protecting the passenger from different kinds of electromagnetic radiation found above the atmosphere. Of the varieties of radiations in space the most mysterious is cosmic radiation, the source of which presents one of the grandest puzzles in nuclear astrophysics. Some of this radiation possibly comes from the Sun, but the preponderance of the cosmic rays bombarding Earth's atmosphere evidently originates outside the solar system—thus the term "cosmic" radiation. High-energy cosmic ray primaries—subatomic particles, of which about 90 percent are protons of hydrogen and helium—slam into the atmosphere at velocities approaching the speed of light. Fifteen to 25 miles above Earth, the cosmic ray primaries collide with atoms and molecules in the thickening atmosphere, are broken up, and are converted into lower-energy rays called secondaries. Above 25 miles the atmosphere becomes too thin to absorb the cosmic ray primaries; since they are capable of penetrating a thick lead wall, it was futile to try to shield a spacecraft pilot completely. So in the early 1950s medical researchers, assuming that a space pilot would be exposed to some cosmic radiation, approached the problem primarily from the angle of establishing how large a dose a human being could tolerate.[54]

As with weightlessness and g-load research, the best postwar device for studying cosmic radiation was the instrumented sounding rocket. But the last of the rocket experiments with primates occurred in May 1952. From that time until animal rocket shots resumed in 1958, the only upper-atmospheric research rockets fired in the country were occasional Aerobees, launched by the Air Force to altitudes of about 150 miles.[55] These shots, carrying only instruments, brought back a modicum of data on cosmic rays. The prime instrument for cosmic ray research from 1952 to 1958 was the oldest vehicle for human flight, the balloon. The postwar development of sturdier, larger, polyethylene balloons to replace rubber aerostats made possible higher and higher ascents with increasingly heavier loads. At the same time the expansion of balloon technology, leading to an increasing number of giant, shiny spheres floating over the United States, multiplied reports of and popular interest in "Unidentified Flying Objects." [56]

In the balloon-borne space radiation experiments of the fifties, the Navy carried out some notable manned ascents into the stratosphere. On November 8, 1956, for example, Lieutenant Commanders Malcolm D. Ross and M. L. Lewis, as part of the Navy's Strato-Lab program of manned ascents from northern latitudes, reached 76,000 feet, then an altitude record. Less than a year later Ross and Lewis sat in their cramped sealed gondola as their huge polyethylene balloon ascended to nearly 86,000 feet. And in late June 1958 the same two Navy aerostation veterans remained in the 70,000-80,000-foot region for almost 35 hours.[57]

The Navy also pioneered in the use of balloon-launched rockets (rockoons). The first successful rockoon launch occurred in August 1952 when, from a ship off the coast of Greenland, a University of Iowa team headed by physicist James A. Van Allen sent up a balloon from which a rocket ignited at 70,000 feet and climbed to an altitude of nearly 40 miles. The Navy did most of its upper-atmospheric research, however, with instrumented balloon flights carrying small organisms and insects. In May 1954, for example, General Mills, Incorporated, under contract to the Office of Naval Research, launched a polyethylene balloon, with a capacity of 3 million cubic feet, that carried cosmic ray emulsions—plates designed for recording the tracks of ionizing particles—to an altitude of 115,000 feet. Five years later, from Sioux Falls, South Dakota, Raven Industries launched an Office of Naval Research balloon biological package to a record altitude of 148,000 feet.[58]

The center of Air Force balloon research in the early 1950s was the Aeromedical Field Laboratory in New Mexico. From July 21, 1950, when Air Force personnel launched the first polyethylene balloon at Holloman Air Force Base, to December 18, 1958, the scientists at the field laboratory sent up 1000 research balloons, although only a small number of these ascents were designed expressly for cosmic ray study. In 1953 the Holloman researchers moved most of their balloon experiments to the northern United States, in the higher geomagnetic latitudes, where they could obtain increased exposure to cosmic ray primaries. During the next year they sent aloft a collection of radish seeds on a series of flights, compiling some 251 hours of exposure of the seeds above 80,000 feet. Monkeys, mice, rats, hamsters, and rabbits also drifted upward in balloons launched by Winzen Research, Incorporated, as a Holloman contractor, from Sault Ste. Marie, Michigan. The most interesting effect observed among the various test subjects was a striking increase in the number of gray hairs on black mice exposed to the high altitudes.[59]

The first solo manned ascent into the stratosphere was also principally an undertaking of the field laboratory at Holloman.   In 1956 field laboratory experimenters inaugurated Project Manhigh, a series of flights from northern sites using Winzen balloons, to test man's ability to live for prolonged periods in a sealed-cabin environment like that inside a spacecraft and to gather new data on cosmic radiation.   David Simons, head of the Space Biology Branch at Holloman, was project officer for the Manhigh ascents.   The initial flight, from Fleming Field, Minnesota, took place on June 2, 1957.   Captain Joseph W. Kittinger stayed aloft inside his sealed gondola for nearly seven hours, breathing pure oxygen, making visual observations, and talking frequently with John P. Stapp, the flight surgeon, and other physicians on the ground.   Kittinger spent two hours above 92,000 feet; his maximum altitude during the flight was 96,000 feet.[60]

About nine weeks later Simons himself entered the space equivalent region, suspended in a sealed capsule below a 3-million-cubic-foot polyethylene balloon launched from an open-face mine near Crosby, Minnesota.   Simons exceeded Kittinger's mark for both duration and altitude, staying aloft 32 hours and remaining at 101,000 feet for about 5 hours.   Simons was the first man in history to see the Sun set and then rise again from the edge of space.   In the *Manhigh II* gondola he spent more time than anyone before him looking upward at the blackness of space and outward at the white and blue layers of the atmosphere.   "The capsule seemed like a welcome window permitting a fabulous view and precious opportunities, not a prison or an enclosure," he related after the flight.[61]

In October 1958 an excessive temperature rise in the capsule forced a premature termination of the third Manhigh flight, carrying Lieutenant Clifton M. McClure.[62]   Yet McClure's ascent, together with those of Kittinger and Simons, proved the workability of the sealed cabin for sustaining human life where "the environment is as hostile and very nearly as different in appearance as one would expect to observe from a satellite." [63]   The environmental control system of the Manhigh capsule and the instrumentation for physiological telemetering were strikingly similar to those later used in the Mercury spacecraft.

With regard to cosmic radiation, however, the Manhigh flights, like numerous rocket, balloon, and laboratory experiments of previous and succeeding years, returned data that were either negative or inconclusive.   During the *Manhigh II* ascent two containers of bread mold were attached to the underside of the capsule, and Simons wore emulsion plates on his arms and chest to measure cosmic ray penetration.   The plates did show indications of several hits by so-called "heavy" primaries—cosmic ray particles made up of nuclear particles heavier than are found in hydrogen or helium—but years later the skin in the area of the plates revealed no effects of radiation.[64]

All these experiments left most scientists as reluctant to speculate about the hazards from cosmic rays in flight as they had been in the early fifties.   Simons felt that in manned orbital flights following roughly equatorial orbits, where the spacecraft remained within the protective shielding of Earth's magnetic fields, the spacecraft pilot would be in no danger from cosmic radiation.   Yet he remained troubled by the possibility that a solar flare, a sudden burst of energy from the Sun, might precipitate a great increase in cosmic ray intensity during a space mission. About a twentyfold multiplication of cosmic radiation accompanied a solar flare of February 1956. Simons' concern with solar flares led him to the conclusion that continuous voice contact between ground stations and the space pilot would be essential, as well as stepped-up efforts to predict the flares.[65]

All proponents of manned space flight were alarmed when information transmitted from the first three Explorer satellites, launched during the first half of 1958, disclosed the existence of a huge envelope of radiation beyond the ionosphere. Evidently consisting of protons and electrons trapped in Earth's magnetic field, the radiation layer begins about 400 miles out in space and doubles in intensity about every 60 miles before tapering away about 1200 miles from Earth. This discovery was the first "Van Allen belt," named after James A. Van Allen, United States director of the International Geophysical Year radiation experiments. The *Pioneer III* probe, launched in December 1958, failed to reach escape velocity, but it did reveal that the radiation zone consisted not of one belt but of two at least—an inner belt of high-energy particles and an outer belt of less energetic particles. Two earlier Pioneer shots, in October and November, had shown that while the radiation zone was several thousand miles deep, it did not extend into space indefinitely.[66] Quite obviously, the doughnut-shaped Van Allen belts would pose a serious threat for manned travel in high orbits or interplanetary voyages. In the early manned ventures into space, however, a spacecraft could be placed in an orbit 100 to 150 miles from Earth, high enough to be free of atmospheric frictional drag, yet low enough to stay under the Van Allen radiation.[67]

The radiation hazards of space flight also include solar radiation. Solar heat, ultraviolet rays, and x-rays all become much more intense beyond the diffusive atmosphere of Earth, but they can be adequately counteracted by space cabin insulation, shielding, refractive paint, and other techniques. Advanced space missions may subject astronauts to dangers from other kinds of radiation, such as the radiation belts surrounding other planets or the radioactivity produced by a spacecraft with a nuclear powerplant.[68]

A Reason for Research

During 1958, scientists and engineers, both military and civilian, talked more openly than they had in previous years about radiation dosages, meteoroid penetration, weightlessness, and the other anomalies of space travel. They received a considerably more respectful hearing. What made members of the Congress and Americans in general responsive to such discussions and interested in past research and future plans for space exploration were the ever-larger scientific satellites launched by the Soviet Union, beginning October 4, 1957. In the midst of the nationalistic humiliation following the Sputniks, not only space rocketry but also medical research with rockets received an invaluable boost. In May 1958, Air Force physicians sent mice along on three reentry tests of the Able ablation nose cone for the Thor. Then, the following December and in May 1959, the Navy School of Aviation Medicine dispatched monkeys, sea-urchin eggs and sperm, molds, tissues, and seeds on two test firings of the Jupiter intermediate-range missile, carried out by the Army Ballistic Missile Agency.[63]

The new focus on space, the new curiosity about what went on beyond the atmosphere, the determination to "catch up" in the space race—these sentiments redounded to the benefit of those Americans who had been trying to solve the biological and technological puzzles of manned space flight long before there was a space race. Their principal stimulus was not international prestige or the drive for technological supremacy; it was a desire to discover the undiscovered, to probe into the unknown. And they believed that wherever man's instruments went, man should follow. The proponents of manned space flight in the United States could be found in several locations—in the military, in some universities, in the aerospace industry, even in the Congress. But an especially zealous contingent worked for NACA. Ultimately its members would become the engineering and managerial nucleus of the American program to rocket a man into orbit around Earth and bring him back.

Aeronautics to Astronautics: NACA Research

(1952–1957)

LITTLE known outside the military services and the aircraft industry, the National Advisory Committee for Aeronautics by the early 1950s had far outgrown its name and could look back on nearly four decades filled with landmark contributions to military and civilian aeronautics. NACA had matured much beyond its original "advisory" capacity, had established three national laboratories, and had become perhaps the world's foremost aeronautical research organization. Drag-reducing engine cowlings, wing fillets, retractable landing gear, thin swept wings, and new fuselage shapes for supersonic aircraft—these were only a few of the numerous innovations leading to improved airplane performance that were wholly or partially attributable to the agency. NACA had pioneered in institutionalized team research—"big science," as opposed to the "little science" of individual researchers working alone or in small academic groups—and over the years such activity had paid off handsomely for the Nation.[1] NACA's relative importance in the totality of American aeronautics had declined after the Second World War with the enormous increase in military research and development programs, but NACA did not exaggerate when it asserted that practically every airplane aloft reflected some aspect of its research achievements.

The contributions of NACA in aeronautics were spectacular, but regarding the inchoate discipline of astronautics, especially rocket propulsion research, the agency, like the rest of the country, was skeptical, conservative, reticent. The prevailing prewar attitude within NACA toward rocket technology was expressed in 1940 by Jerome C. Hunsaker, then a member and later chairman of NACA's Main Committee. Discussing an Army Air Corps contract with the California Institute of Technology for rocket research in relation to current NACA work on the deicing of aircraft windshields, Hunsaker said to Theodore von Kármán of CalTech, "You can have the Buck Rogers job."[2]

In the early postwar years the leaders of NACA viewed rocket experimentation, such as the program beginning in 1945 at the Pilotless Aircraft Research Sta-

55

tion, on Wallops Island, Virginia, as essentially a tool for aerodynamics research furthering the progress of supersonic flight within the atmosphere. NACA's annual report for 1948, for example, mentioned the heating rates generated on the noses of the V-2s then being fired at White Sands, but discussed the problem of structural heating only in the context of aircraft.[3]

At the request of the military services, the Langley, Lewis, and Ames laboratories did study the theoretical performance of missiles, the operation of rocket engines, the composition of rocket fuels, and automatic control arrangements for supersonic guided missiles and aircraft. But such research accounted for only a small percentage of the total NACA workload and budgetary allotments. The annual budget cuts suffered by NACA, beginning in 1949 and reaching a high point in 1954 when the agency received only a little more than half its request, perhaps intensified the scientific conservatism of the NACA leaders, while the Korean War once again shifted most NACA laboratory work to the "cleaning up" of military aircraft.[4] It was in this climate of declining support for flight research in 1953 that NACA Director Hugh L. Dryden, who less than ten years later would be helping manage a manned lunar-landing program, wrote, "I am reasonably sure that travel to the moon will not occur in my lifetime . . . ."[5]

NACA MOVES TOWARD SPACE

In the early 1950s, however, as a full-fledged program to develop large ballistic missiles got underway and as the rocket research airplanes reached higher into the stratosphere, NACA began to consider the prospect of space flight and what contributions the organization could make in this new area of inquiry. On June 24, 1952, the Committee on Aerodynamics, the most influential of NACA's various technical committees, met at Wallops Island. Toward the end of the meeting, committee member Robert J. Woods, the highly respected designer of "X" aircraft for the Bell Aircraft Corporation, suggested that since various groups and agencies were considering proposals for sending manned and unmanned vehicles into the upper atmosphere, NACA should set up a study group on "space flight and associated problems." To Woods, NACA was the logical agency to conduct research in spacecraft stability and control; such work would be a proper extension of current NACA activity. After some discussion the other members of the committee approved Woods' suggestion. They formally resolved that NACA should intensify its research on flight at altitudes between 12 and 50 miles and at speeds of mach 4 through 10, and "devote a modest effort to problems associated with unmanned and manned flight at altitudes from 50 miles to infinity and at speeds from Mach number 10 to the velocity of escape from the earth's gravity." On July 14 the NACA Executive Committee, the governing body of NACA, composed of practically all the members of the Main Committee, approved a slightly revised version of this resolution.[6]

Less than a month after the action of the Executive Committee, Henry J. E.

Reid, Director of the Langley Aeronautical Laboratory, appointed Clinton E. Brown, Charles H. Zimmerman, and William J. O'Sullivan, aeronautical engineers at the Virginia center, to work up a thorough proposal for research in upper-atmospheric and space flight. Specifically the Langley engineers were to suggest a suitable manned vehicle on which construction could be initiated within two years. Their proposal was to be reviewed by a board composed of representatives from the three NACA laboratories and NACA's High Speed Flight Station at Edwards Air Force Base, California.[7]

Throughout the next year and a half, the Langley study group, engineers at Ames and the flight station, and the review board worked on a plan for the new research instrument. There was wide divergence of opinion as to what should be the nature and objectives of the vehicle; some parties were even skeptical about the wisdom of any space-directed research. Reid, John Stack, and others at Langley favored modifying the X–2 research airplane, then under development by Bell Aircraft, to make it a device for manned flight above 12 miles.[8] Smith J. DeFrance, one of the early Langley engineers who had become Director of the Ames Aeronautical Laboratory when it opened in 1941, originally opposed Woods' idea for a study group on space flight because "it appears to verge on the developmental, and there is a question as to its importance. There are many more pressing and more realistic problems to be met and solved in the next ten years." DeFrance had concluded in the spring of 1952 that "a study group of any size is not warranted." [9]

In July 1954, however, representatives of NACA disclosed to the Air Force and the Navy their conclusions regarding the feasibility of an entirely new rocket-powered research airplane and suggested a tripartite program for the manned exploration of the upper atmosphere. NACA's views were based mainly on the findings and proposals of the Langley study group, which had been working on the problem since 1952 and had made a more detailed presentation than research teams from Ames and the High Speed Flight Station. NACA envisioned an aircraft that would fly as high as 50 miles and whose speed would reach perhaps mach 7 (approximately 5000 miles per hour). Such a craft would be especially valuable for studying the critical problems of aerodynamic heating, stability, and control at high altitudes and speeds. Data gathered on its flights "would contribute both to air-breathing supersonic aircraft . . . and to long-range high-altitude rocket-propelled vehicles operating at higher Mach numbers." Realizing that the temperatures generated on its return into the heavier atmosphere would be greater than on any previous airplane, NACA suggested as a structural metal Inconel–X, a new nickel-chrome alloy "capable of rapid heating to high temperatures (1200°F) without the development of high thermal stresses, or thermal buckling, and without appreciable loss of strength or stiffness." [10]

This long-range plan was shortly accepted by the Air Force and the Navy Bureau of Aeronautics and put into motion as the "X–15 project." In December 1954, NACA, the Air Force, and the Navy agreed to proceed with the project under operating arrangements roughly similar to the previous "X" aircraft ventures. The Air Force had responsibility for finding a contractor and supervising design and construction; both the Air Force and the Navy would provide financial support; and NACA would act as technical director.[11]

As prime contractor for the X-15, the Air Force picked North American Aviation of Los Angeles. The performance specifications of the X-15 called for a rocket engine consuming anhydrous ammonia and liquid oxygen and providing some 57,000 pounds of thrust for as long as six minutes. This powerplant would be four times as big as that of the X-2. A highly sensitive flight-data system, thick upper and lower vertical stabilizers for aerodynamic control, small reaction jets burning hydrogen peroxide for control in the near-vacuum of the upper atmosphere, and a new structural material—these were some of the novel characteristics of the stub-winged craft.[12]

The X-15 would not fulfill its original design objectives until 1962, long after NACA had become NASA and in the same year that Project Mercury achieved its basic goals. Even so, the X-15 was by far the most ambitious, expensive, and publicized research undertaking in which NACA ever participated. Its eventual success stemmed largely from the imagination and ingenuity of the NACA engineers who had started planning for an advanced aerodynamic vehicle in 1952.

In 1954, the year of Major Arthur Murray's climb to about 17 miles in the X-1A, the idea of manned rocket flight to an altitude of 50 miles seemed exceedingly visionary. Most people in NACA, the military, the aircraft industry, and elsewhere assumed that over the years vehicles with substantial lift/drag ratios would evolve to higher and higher speeds and altitudes until, by skipping in and out of the atmosphere like a flat rock across the surface of a pond, they could fly around the world. Even then, however, there were those within NACA who took the Executive Committee's mandate for "research in space flight and associated problems" literally and who felt that the X-15 concept did not go far enough. They looked to the second part of the resolution adopted by the Committee on Aerodynamics and approved by the Executive Committee, which sanctioned "a modest effort" on the "problems associated with flight at altitudes from 50 miles to infinity and at speeds from Mach number 10 to the velocity of escape from the earth's gravity."

Some of the most "far out" aeronautical engineers working for NACA in the early fifties were employed at the Ames laboratory. As early as the summer of 1952, Ames engineers, experimenting at the supersonic free-flight, 10-inch-by-14-inch, and 6-inch-by-6-inch wind tunnels at the California site, had examined the aerodynamic problems of five kinds of space vehicles—glide, skip, ballistic, satellite, and interplanetary. They knew that the aerodynamic forces acting on a vehicle above 50 miles were relatively minor, as were problems of stability and control at such altitudes. They concluded, however, that a space vehicle should probably be controllable at lower altitudes, although it "may not be optimum from the point of view of simplicity, etc. . . ."[13]

58

REENTRY: AERODYNAMICS TO THERMODYNAMICS

The Ames study had been specifically requested by NACA Headquarters, which in its initial prospectus on the new research airplane project had identified stability and control in high-speed, high-altitude flight as one of two areas needing much additional research. The other and far more critical area was aerodynamic heating, which becomes acute as an object knifes into the atmosphere from the airless environment of space and collides with atmospheric molecules of ever-increasing density. For several years NACA researchers had been studying aerodynamic heating, which begins to be troublesome at about twice sonic speed. The X-15 program was established largely to return data on heating generated up to mach 7. But such investigations of thermal stress hardly approached the heating problem faced by the military services and the missile industry in their efforts to produce a durable warhead for an intercontinental missile. In a typical ICBM flight with a peak altitude of 900 miles and a range of 6500 miles, the stagnation temperature in the shock wave at the front of the nose cone could reach 12,000 degrees F. This is some 2000 degrees hotter than the surface of the Sun and 10 times the maximum surface temperature that was calculated for an X-15 trajectory.[14] Of the myriad puzzles involved in designing, building, and flying the Atlas, the first American ICBM, the most difficult and most expensive to solve was reentry heating. The popular term "thermal barrier" to describe the reentry problem was coined as an analogy to the "sonic barrier" of the mid-1940s, although research in the fifties would reveal that the problem could have been described more accurately as a "thermal thicket."

During June 1952, in the same summer that NACA had decided to move toward space flight research and had proposed an advanced research aircraft, one of the scientist-engineers at Ames had made the first real breakthrough in the search for a way to surmount the thermal barrier. He was Harry Julian Allen, a senior aeronautical engineer at Ames and chief of the High-Speed Research Division since 1945. The burly Allen, who signs his technical papers "H. Julian" but who is known familiarly as "Harvey," was 42 years old in 1952 and looked more like a football coach than a scientist. Holder of a bachelor of arts degree in engineering from Stanford University, Allen in 1935 had left the Stanford Guggenheim Aeronautical Laboratory, where he had received the degree of aeronautical engineer, to join the NACA staff at the Langley laboratory. When Ames was opened in 1941, he went west with Smith DeFrance and others from Langley.[15]

At Ames, Allen had invented a technique of firing a gun-launched model upstream through a supersonic wind tunnel to study aerodynamic behavior at high mach numbers. This notion led to the construction of the Ames supersonic free-flight wind tunnel, opened in 1949. The tunnel had a test section 18 feet long, one foot wide, and two feet high. By forcing a draft through the tunnel at a speed of about mach 3 and by firing a model projectile upstream at a velocity

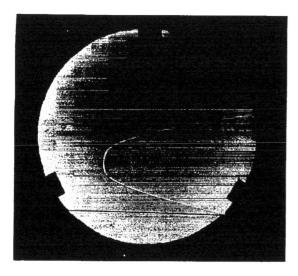

This shadowgraph of the Mercury reentry configuration was made in the Ames Supersonic Free-Flight Tunnel at a simulated speed of mach 10.

of 8000 feet per second, the Ames researchers could simulate a mach number of about 15. Schlieren cameras set up at seven stations along the test section, three on the side and four on the top, made shadowgraphs to show airflow characteristics over the model and thus determine the aerodynamic forces experienced. During the 1950s the facility, constructed at an original cost of only about $20,000, was to prove one of NACA's most valuable tools for hypersonic investigation.[16]

As a member of one of the panels of the Department of Defense Research and Development Board, a group charged with supervising weapons research, Allen was intimately familiar with the payload protection dilemma confronting the Air Force and Convair, the prime contractor for the difficult Atlas project.[17] In their designs the Convair engineers had already provided that at the peak of the Atlas' trajectory, its nose, containing a nuclear warhead, would separate from the sustainer rocket and fall freely toward its target. These exponents of the ICBM knew that without adequate thermal protection the nuclear payload would burn up during its descent through the atmosphere.

Fifty years of progress in aeronautics had produced more and more slender and streamlined aircraft shapes, the objective being to reduce aerodynamic drag and increase speed. In approaching the Atlas reentry enigma, the Convair group drew from the huge reservoir of knowledge accumulated over the years by aerodynamicists and structures experts dealing with airplanes, rockets, and air-breathing missiles. The men at Convair fed their data into a digital computer, which was supposed to help them calculate the optimum design for structural strength, resistance to heat, and free-flight stability in the separable nose section of a long-range rocket. The computer indicated that a long, needle-nosed configuration for the reentry body, similar to that of the rocket research airplanes, would be best for the ICBM. But tests of this configuration, using metal models in the supersonic wind tunnel at Ames and in rocket launches at Wallops Island, showed that so much heat would be transferred to the vehicle that the warhead would shortly vaporize as it plunged through the atmosphere. No protection system known at that time could prevent its destruction by aerodynamic heating.[18]

This disclosure evoked another spate of predictions that an intercontinental military rocket would not be feasible for many years. And while relatively few people were thinking seriously about manned space flight in the early fifties, those who were also understood that something radical would have to be done on the problem of reentry before it would be practicable to send a man into space and recover him.

The man who did something radical was Allen. As Allen put it, the Convair engineers "cut off their computer too soon." He took the sharpnosed Atlas reentry shape and began making mathematical calculations, using only a pad and pencil. Eventually he reached a conclusion that seemingly contradicted all the years of aeronautical research and streamlined aircraft design. For Allen's analysis showed that the best way to cut down reentry heating was to discard a great deal of one's thinking about orthodox aerodynamics and deliberately design a vehicle that was the opposite of streamlined. "Half the heat generated by friction was going into the missiles," recalled Allen. "I reasoned we had to deflect the heat into the air and let it dissipate. Therefore streamlined shapes were the worst possible; they had to be blunt." The Ames researcher determined that the amount of heat absorbed by an object descending into the atmosphere depended on the ratio between pressure drag and viscous or frictional drag. The designer of a reentry body, by shaping the body bluntly, could alter pressure drag and thus throw off much of the heat into the surrounding air. When the bluff body collided with stratospheric pressures at reentry speeds, it would produce a "strong bow shock wave" in front of, and thus detached from, the nose. The shock wave, the air itself, would absorb much of the kinetic energy transformed into heat as the object entered the atmosphere.[19]

Allen personally submitted his findings to select persons in the missile industry in September 1952. A secret NACA report memorandum embodying his conclusions on the blunt-nose design, coauthored by Alfred J. Eggers of Ames, went out to industrial firms and the military the next spring. The report bore the date April 28, 1953, but six years passed before the paper was declassified and published in the annual report of NACA.[20]

For his conception of the blunt-body configuration, Allen received the NACA Distinguished Service Medal in 1957. The award brought sharp criticism from H. H. Nininger, director of the American Meteorite Museum at Sedona, Arizona, who asserted that he had first proposed the blunt nose for reentry vehicles. In August 1952, Nininger, a recognized authority on meteorites, had suggested to the Ames laboratory that a blunt shape appeared promising for missile warheads. Nininger based his conclusion on his studies of tektites and meteorites, contending that the melting process experienced by a meteorite during its descent through the aerodynamic atmosphere furnished a lubricant enabling the object to overcome air resistance. Nininger's letter evidently came to Ames some weeks after Allen,

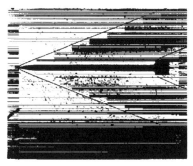

Initial missile concept

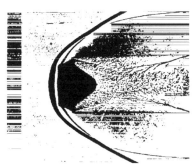

Missile nose cones, 1953–57

Blunt body concept, 1957

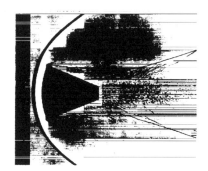

Manned capsule concept, 1957

Ten years of intensive aerodynamic research preceded the final determination of the reentry configuration for Project Mercury. Most of this was generated by the military development of ballistic missiles. As these schlieren photographs of wind tunnel tests indicate, the departure point of atmospheric aerodynamic configuration was to change drastically under the new heat and stability conditions imposed by Mercury's demanding sequence of atmospheric flight-spaceflight-reentry-atmospheric flight-landing.

assisted by Eggers, had completed his calculations on the relationship between warhead shape and heat convection. At any rate, what Allen wanted to do was exactly the reverse of Nininger's suggestion: deliberately to shape a reentry body bluntly in order to *increase* air resistance and dissipate a greater amount of the heat produced by the object into the atmosphere.[21]

Allen's high-drag, blunt-nose principle was of enormous interest and benefit to the missile designers. It led directly to the Mark I and Mark II nose cones developed by the General Electric Company for the Atlas and later for the Thor.

Years after the discovery, James H. Doolittle, chairman of NACA's Main Committee, pointed out that "every U.S. ballistic missile warhead is designed in accordance with his once radical precept." [22] In 1952 the problems of the missilemen were not of immediate concern to designers of manned flight systems, not even to those drawing up plans for the X-15, which would encounter a greater heating load than any previous airplane. Yet Allen's presentation of a new way to minimize the aerodynamic heating of reentry not only made possible an ICBM within a few years but "marked the potential beginning of manned space flight, with all of its attendant new structures and materials problems." [23]

The blunt-nose concept was just that—a concept. Succeeding years would see much experimentation with spheres, cylinders, blunted ogives, and even concave shapes at the supersonic free-flight tunnel, ballistic ranges, and various other facilities at Ames, at the 11-inch hypersonic tunnel at Langley, and at the Pilotless Aircraft Research Station on Wallops Island. [24] As aerodynamicists began thinking about space flight they would propose a variety of configurations for potential manned space vehicles, although all of the designs would feature some degree of bluntness. Finally, blunting a reentry body furnished only part of the solution to the heating problem. Allen's calculations presupposed that some kind of new thermal protection material would be used for the structure of a high-drag body. In 1952, aircraft designers and structures engineers were working mainly with aluminum, magnesium, and titanium, and were giving some attention to such heat-resistant alloys as Monel K, a nickel-and-steel metal used in the X-2, and Inconel-X, the basic alloy for the X-15. [25] But it would take much "hotter" materials to protect the payloads of the intercontinental and intermediate-range ballistic missiles—the Atlas, the Thor, the Jupiter, and later the Titan. Far more materials research was needed before the recovery of a manned spacecraft would be practicable.

Early in 1956, the Army Ballistic Missile Agency at Huntsville, Alabama, modified some of its medium-range Redstones in order to extend the studies of reentry thermodynamics that the Army had pursued at Redstone Arsenal since 1953. As modified, the Redstone became a multistage vehicle, which Wernher von Braun and his colleagues called the "Jupiter C" (for Composite Reentry Test Vehicle). Meanwhile the Air Force conducted its own investigations of reentry in conjunction with its nose-cone contractors, General Electric and the Avco Manufacturing Corporation, using a special multistage test rocket called the X-17, manufactured by the Lockheed Aircraft Corporation. [26]

Two principal techniques for protecting the interior of the nose cone offered themselves—"heat sink" and "ablation." The heat sink approach involved using a highly conductive metal such as copper or beryllium to absorb the reentry heat, thus storing it and providing a mass sufficient to keep the metal from melting. The major drawback of a heat sink was its heaviness, especially one made of copper. In the ablation method the nose cone was covered with some ceramic material, such as fiber glass, which vaporized or "ablated" during the period of reentry heating.   The vaporizing of the material, the conversion of a solid into a gas, dissipated or carried away the heat.   Thus the essence of the ablation technique was deliberately burning part of the exterior surface of the reentry body, but designing the body so that the surface would not burn through completely.[27]

Apparently no consensus existed among students of the reentry problem by late 1957.   The "first generation" ICBM nose cones produced by General Electric, the Mark I and Mark II, were blunt, heavy copper heat sinks, and the Air Force had decided to use the Mark II on its Thor intermediate-range missile.   But the Air Force's full-scale tests of the lighter, more sophisticated, but more difficult and less tidy ablation process had not begun yet.   Meanwhile, the Army and the Vitro Corporation, using the exhaust of liquid rocket motors as a heat source and the hybrid Redstone in reentry simulations, demonstrated to their own satisfaction the practicability of consuming part of the structural material during its use, the principle of ablation.   The Army's Jupiter-C shot of August 8, 1957, carrying a scale model Jupiter nose cone to an altitude of 600 miles and a range of 1200 miles, supposedly "proved the feasibility of the ablative-type nose cone" and "fulfilled the mission of the reentry test program." [28]   Yet the Ballistic Missile Agency engineers at Redstone Arsenal were working only on the intermediate-range Jupiter, not on an ICBM.   The question of whether an Atlas warhead or a manned reentry vehicle could best be protected by the heat-sink or ablation method, or by either, remained undetermined.   Much time and effort would be expended before the Army's claims for ablation would be fully verified and accepted.

NACA's official role in this accelerated program of materials research was that of tester and verifier.   Even so, the NACA experimenters greatly enlarged their knowledge of thermodynamics, became well grounded in the new technology of thermal protection, and prepared themselves to cope with the heating loads to be encountered in manned space flight.

At the request of the Air Force, the Army, and also the Navy (which was involved with the Polaris after 1956), NACA devoted an encreasing portion of its facilities and technical staff to tests of such metals as copper, tungsten, molybdenum, and later beryllium for heat sinks, and of ablating materials like teflon, nylon, and fiber glass.   During 1955–1956 the installation of several kinds of high-temperature jets at the Langley and Lewis laboratories greatly aided NACA thermodynamics research.   These included, at Langley, an acid-ammonia rocket jet providing a maximum temperature of 4100 degrees F and a gas stream velocity of 7000 feet per second, an ethylene-air jet yielding temperatures up to 3500 degrees F, and a pebble-bed heater, wherein a stream of hot air was passed through a bed of incandescent ceramic spheres.   Both Langley and Lewis had electric arc jet facilities, in which a high-intensity arc was used to give energy to compressed air and raise air pressure and temperatures.   The hot, high-pressure air then shot through a nozzle to produce a stream temperature of about 12,000 degrees F. NACA investigators used these high-temperature jets and other research tools, including the 11-inch hypersonic tunnel at Langley, to gather data eventually reinforcing the Army's contention that ablation was the most effective thermal protection method.[29]

Meanwhile Maxime A. Faget, Paul E. Purser, and other members of the Langley Pilotless Aircraft Research Division, working under the supervision of Robert R. Gilruth, used multistage, solid-propellant rockets for studying heat transfer on variations of Allen's basic blunt heatshield configuration. Robert O. Piland, for example, put together the first multistage vehicle to attain mach 10. Faget served as a regular NACA member and Purser was an alternate member of a Department of Defense panel called the Polaris Task Group, set up to give advice on the development of the Navy's intermediate-range, solid-fueled Polaris, which was to be launched from submerged submarines. NACA worked with the Atomic Energy Commission and the Lockheed Aircraft Corporation, prime contractor for the Polaris, in developing the heat-sink nose cone used on the early versions of the sea-based missile.[30]

Although there were some 30 different wind tunnels at Langley, the members of the Pilotless Aircraft Research Division (PARD) firmly believed in the superiority of their rocket-launch methods for acquiring information on heating loads and heat transfer, heat-resistant materials, and the aerodynamic behavior of bodies entering the atmosphere. As Faget said, "The PARD story shows how engineering experimentalists may triumph over theoreticians with preconceptions. Our rockets measured heat transfer that the tunnels couldn't touch at that time." Joseph A. Shortal, chief of PARD since 1951, recalled, "PARD made us more than aeronautical engineers and aerodynamicists. We became truly an astronautically oriented research and development team out at Wallops." [31]

The Ames experimenters, on the other hand, were just as firmly convinced that their wind tunnels and ballistic ranges represented the simplest, most economical, and most reliable tools for hypersonic research. To the Ames group, rocket shots were troublesome and expensive, and rocket telemetry was unreliable. As one Ames engineer put it, "You might get a lot of data but since you didn't control the experiment you didn't know exactly what it meant." [32]

The Ames devotion to laboratory techniques, the determination to do more and more in heating and materials research without resorting to rockets, furnished the impetus for a new test instrument devised by Alfred J. Eggers, Jr., in the mid-fifties. Eggers, born in 1922 in Omaha, had joined the research staff at Ames in the fall of 1944, after completing his bachelor of arts degree at the University of Omaha. He pursued graduate studies at Stanford University in nearby Palo Alto, where he received a Master of Science degree in aeronautical engineering in 1949 and a Ph.D. in 1956.[33] For years Eggers had worked with Allen and others at Ames on the aerodynamic and thermodynamic problems of hypervelocity flight, and as a conceptualizer at the California center he came to be regarded as second only to the originator of the blunt-nose reentry principle.

Eggers assumed that the major heating loads of reentry would be encountered within an altitude interval of 100,000 feet. So he designed a straight, trumpet-shaped supersonic nozzle with a maximum diameter of 20 inches and a length of 20 feet, which in terms of the model scale used was equivalent to 100,000 feet of thickening atmosphere. A hypervelocity gas gun launched a scale model upstream through the nozzle to a settling chamber. While in free flight through the nozzle to the chamber, the model passed through ever-denser air, thus closely approximating the flight history of a long-range ballistic missile. Since the apparatus simulated both motion and heating experiences, Eggers called the combination of hypervelocity gun and supersonic nozzle "an atmosphere entry simulator." [34]

Eggers calculated that using a model only .36 inch in diameter and weighing .005 pound, he could simulate the aerodynamic heating generated by an object three feet in diameter, weighing 5000 pounds, and having a range of 4000 miles. "In the simplest test," he said, "the simulator could provide with one photograph of a model rather substantial evidence as to whether or not the corresponding missile would remain essentially intact while traversing the atmosphere." The reentry research technique, proposed in 1955, went into operation during the next year. Construction of a larger version began in 1958. Eggers' atmosphere entry simulator proved especially useful in materials research at Ames. Like the high-temperature jets at Langley and Lewis, the rocket tests at Wallops Island, the Army's Jupiter-C shots from Cape Canaveral, and other experimental methods, it yielded data that later pointed toward ablation as the best method for protecting the interior of reentry bodies. [35]

Although the official focus of the NACA materials test program remained on missile warhead development, such activity was an obvious prerequisite to manned space flight. And the experience of men like Gilruth, Faget, Purser, and Shortal in the years before the Sputniks had a direct influence on their plans for shielding a human rider from the heat of atmospheric friction. Meanwhile other NACA engineers, especially at Langley and at the High Speed Flight Station, were working closely with the Navy, the Air Force, and North American Aviation on the X–15 project. At Cleveland, Lewis propulsion specialists were studying rocket powerplants and fuels as well as cooperating with Langley and Flight Station representatives in designing, operating, and studying reaction control systems for hypersonic aircraft and reentry vehicles.

A MOON FOR A MAN

Others in NACA, sensing the potential for manned space exploration that accompanied propulsion advances in military rocketry, began considering designs for a vehicle with which man could take his first step above the atmosphere. Early in 1954, Eggers, Julian Allen, and Stanford E. Neice of Ames put together a classic theoretical discussion of different space flight configurations in a paper entitled "A Comparative Analysis of the Performance of Long-Range Hypervelocity Vehicles." The research engineers examined the relative advantages, in terms of range and the ratio between payload and total weight, of three kinds

Alfred J. Eggers, Jr., stands beside the Atmospheric Entry Simulator he invented in 1958 as a laboratory means of studying the problems of aerodynamic heating and thermal stresses during reentry. The tubular tank in the foreground held air under high pressure. When a valve was opened, the air flowed through the test section (the dark area under the high-voltage signs) into the chimneylike vacuum tank. As the airstream moved, a high-velocity gun fired a test model through the chamber in a right-to-left direction. Instruments photographed the model in flight, timed the flight, and studied the nature of the incandescence generated by the aerodynamic heating.

of manned hypersonic vehicles: ballistic, a blunt non-lifting, high-drag projectile; skip; and glide, the last two designs also having fairly blunt noses but possessing some lifting ability. For satellite missions all three vehicles might be boosted to orbital velocity by a rocket and could then separate from the rocket and go into free flight, or orbit.

Eggers, Allen, and Neice found that the skip vehicle, which would return to Earth by performing an intricate series of progressively steeper dips into the atmosphere, would need an extremely powerful boost to circumnavigate the globe, and also would encounter a prohibitively large amount of aerodynamic heating.[36] By contrast, the glider, although heavy, would require less boost and would keep the g forces imposed on the pilot during reentry at a quite acceptable level. Like the skip craft, the glider would provide the advantage of pilot control during the landing phase. It would radiate heat well, but since its thermodynamic loads still would be high, the glider might experience dangerous interior heating during a "global" (satellite) mission. So the authors suggested a high-lift glider; like the high-lift-over-drag glider, it would have a delta-wing configuration but also would feature thick, rounded sides and bottom to minimize interior heating. It would enter the atmosphere at a high angle of attack, then level off at lower altitudes to increase the lift/drag ratio.

The ballistic vehicle, the simplest approach of the three, could not be controlled aerodynamically, but its blunt shape provided superior thermal protection, and its relatively light weight gave it a longer range. If it entered the atmosphere at a low angle, deceleration forces could be kept at or below 10 g, with 5 g lasting for 1 minute and 2 g for not over 3 minutes. Therefore the three NACA researchers concluded that "the ballistic vehicle appears to be a practical man-carrying machine, provided extreme care is exercised in supporting the man during atmospheric entry." [37]

As time passed, Eggers personally became convinced of the overall desirability of the manned satellite glider as opposed to the ballistic satellite. He revealed his preference in a modified version of the earlier paper done with Allen and Neice, which he read before the annual meeting of the American Rocket Society in San Francisco, in June 1957. Eggers was skeptical about the relatively high heating loads and the deceleration forces characteristic of ballistic reentry, even at a small entry angle. He warned that "the g's are sufficiently high to require that extreme care be given to the support of an occupant of a ballistic vehicle during atmospheric reentry," and pointed out that such an object, entering the atmosphere along a shallow trajectory so as to hold deceleration down to 7.5 g, would generate a surface temperature of at least 2500 degrees F. Thus, in Eggers' judgment, "the glide vehicle is generally better suited than the ballistic vehicle for manned flight at hypersonic velocities." [38]

Eggers realized that his glider design, if actually built, would be too heavy for the military rockets then under development. At the same time he remained concerned about the deceleration loads imposed on the space pilot and the heating loads on the spacecraft structure. He also saw the difficulty of recovering a ballistic satellite, which since it was noncontrollable in the atmosphere, would have to land somewhere in a target area of several thousand square miles. As a consequence of these apprehensions, during the last half of 1957 he sketched a semiballistic device for manned orbital flight, blunt but having a certain amount of aerodynamic lift, with a nearly flat top and a round, deep bottom for heat protection. This design, which Eggers called the "M–1," fell about halfway between the high-lift glider and the ballistic vehicle discussed in his 1954 NACA study with Allen and Neice. About 10 feet wide and nearly seven feet long, the M–1 from above looked like an isosceles triangle rounded at its apex.[39] A more graphic description was offered by Paul Purser, who called it a "¼ egg lifting shape."[40] The M–1's limited amount of lift would give it about 200 miles of lateral maneuverability during its descent through the atmosphere and about 800 miles of longitudinal discretion over its landing point. Eggers' calculations indicated that skillful piloting could keep reentry deceleration at about 2 g.[41]

AIR FORCE PROVIDES A NEED

The work of Eggers and others on designs for man-carrying space vehicles had been stimulated not only by general progress in long-range rocketry but also by the growing interest of the Air Force in manned space flight. Eggers knew that ever since the war the Air Force, through the Rand Corporation, had been considering the military potential of space technology, and that since early 1956 the service had been proceeding cautiously with contract feasibility studies of manned satellites.

The impetus for these feasibility studies came from a staff meeting at the headquarters of the Air Research and Development Command (ARDC) at Baltimore, on February 15, 1956. During the course of the meeting, General Thomas S. Power, Commander of ARDC, expressed impatience with the failure of his "idea men" to propose any advanced flight systems that could be undertaken after the X–15. Work should begin now, he declared, on two or three separate approaches beyond the X–15, including a vehicle that would operate outside the atmosphere without wings. He suggested that a manned ballistic rocket might be "eventually capable of useful intercontinental military and commercial transport and cargo operation." But the main benefit of having an advanced research project underway, Power pointed out, was that the Air Force could more easily acquire funds for the "general technical work needed."[42]

Thus prodded into action, Power's staff quickly proposed two separate research projects. The first called for a "Manned Glide Rocket Research System"— a rocket-launched glider that would operate initially at an altitude of about 400,000 feet and a speed of mach 21. The other, termed "Manned Ballistic Rocket Research System," would be a separable manned nose cone, or capsule, the final stage of an ICBM. Such a vehicle could lead to the "quick reaction delivery of high priority logistics to any place on Earth," as suggested by Power, or to a manned satellite. Power's staff argued that the manned ballistic concept offered the greater promise, because the solution to the outstanding technical problems, the most critical of which was aerodynamic heating, would result from current ICBM research and development; because existing ICBMs would furnish the booster system, so that efforts could be concentrated on the capsule; and because the ballistic vehicle possibly could be developed by 1960. Either program, however, should be pushed rapidly so that the Air Force could protect its own interests in the field of space flight.[43]

In March 1956, ARDC established two research projects, one for the glide rocket system, the other, known as Task 27544, for the manned ballistic capsule. ARDC planners shortly held briefings on the two proposed systems for its missile-oriented Western Development Division, in California, and for its pilot-oriented Wright Air Development Center, in Ohio. Other briefings were held for NACA representatives and for aircraft and missile contractors. Then, in October, Major George D. Colchagoff of Power's staff described the basic aspects of the two advanced systems to a classified session of the American Rocket Society's annual meeting in Los Angeles.[44]

Since the Weapons Systems Plans Office of ARDC Headquarters never received the $200,000 it had requested for its own feasibility studies, the command had to content itself with encouraging privately financed contractor research.[45] In particular Avco, then trying to develop serviceable nose cones for the Thor and Atlas missiles, was urged to study the manned ballistic capsule. In November 1956, Avco submitted to the Research and Development Command a preliminary study embodying its conclusions on the ballistic approach to manned space flight. ARDC still was short of funds, so Avco and other corporations continued to use their own money for further investigations.[46]

While ARDC promoted these systems studies and sponsored extensive research in human factors at the School of Aviation Medicine in Texas, at the Aeromedical Field Laboratory in New Mexico, and at the Aeromedical Laboratory in Ohio, it also sought to gain acceptance for its ideas within the Air Force organizational structure. On July 29, 1957, the Ad Hoc Committee of the Air Force Scientific Advisory Board, meeting at the Rand Corporation's offices in Santa Monica, California, heard presentations from the Ballistic Missile Division on ballistic missiles for Earth-orbital and lunar flights, and from ARDC Headquarters on the two advanced flight systems then under study. Brigadier General Don D. Flickinger, ARDC's Director of Human Factors, stated that from a medical standpoint sufficient knowledge and expertise already existed to support a manned space venture.[47]

Although the industrial firms investigated mainly the manned ballistic capsule, NACA, following the traditional approach of building up to higher and higher flight regimes, centered its efforts on the glide-rocket concept for most of 1957. Since late the previous year, when NACA had agreed in principle to an ARDC invitation to cooperate on the Manned Glide Rocket Research System, as they were doing for the X–15, small teams of engineers at the Langley, Lewis, and Ames laboratories had carried on feasibility and design studies.[48] In January 1957 the Ames group reported its conclusions on a new rocket-powered vehicle for "efficient hypersonic flight," featuring a flat-top, round-bottom configuration. Interestingly enough, the Ames document contained as an appendix a minority report written by Langley aerodynamicists- mostly from the Flight Research, Instrument Research, and Pilotless Aircraft Research Divisions––recommending that a nonlifting spherical capsule be considered for global flight before a glide rocket.[49] "The appendix was widely read and discussed at Langley at the time," recalled Hartley A. Soulé, a Langley senior engineer, "but there was little interest expressed in work on the proposal." He continued:

> . . . aside from the environment that limited the NACA mission to terrestrial transportation, the proposal was criticized on technical grounds. The report suggested that landings be made in the western half of the United States, not a very small area. The spherical shape was suggested so that the attitude would not be important during reentry. The shape was specifically criticized because the weight of material to completely shield the surface from the reentry heat would probably preclude the launching with programmed ICBM boosters. Further, the lack of [body] orientation might result in harm to the occupant during the deceleration period.[50]

NACA study groups continued their investigations of manned glide rocket concepts through the spring and summer. In September 1957 a formal "Study of the Feasibility of a Hypersonic Research Airplane" appeared, bearing the imprimatur of the whole NACA but influenced primarily by Langley proponents of a raised-top, flat-bottom glider configuration.[51]

A few days later, on October 4, *Sputnik I* shot into orbit and forcibly opened the Space Age. The spectacular Russian achievement wrought a remarkable alteration in practically everyone's thinking about space exploration, especially about the need for a serious, concerted effort to achieve manned space flight. New urgency attended the opening of a long-planned NACA conference beginning October 15 at Ames, which was to bring together representatives from the various NACA laboratories in an effort to resolve the conflict in aerodynamic thinking between advocates of round and flat bottoms for the proposed hypervelocity glider. Termed the "Round Three Conference," the Ames meeting produced the fundamental concept for what would become the X–20 or Dyna-Soar (for dynamic soaring) project- a delta-wing, flat-bottom, rocket-propelled glider capable of reaching a velocity of mach 17.5, almost 13,000 miles per hour, and a peak altitude of perhaps 75 miles.[52]

Although they had been working mainly on the hypersonic glider, as requested by the Air Force, the research engineers of PARD, in tidewater Virginia, also had been spending more and more time thinking about how to transmute missile reentry bodies into machines for carrying man in low Earth orbit. Their advocacy, along with that of other Langley workers, of a spherical capsule early that year had indicated their growing interest in making the quantum jump from hypersonic, upper-atmospheric, lift/drag flight to orbital space flight in a nonlifting vehicle. At the Round Three Conference, Faget and Purser compared notes with Eggers, perhaps the leading hypervelocity theoretician in NACA. Eggers related his own conclusions: for orbital flight the design giving the highest proportion of payload to total weight was the compact, low lift/drag vehicle, having little or no wings, and embodying Allen's blunt-nose principle. He discussed the analytical studies of his semiballistic M–1, which had some lift but would, he estimated, weigh from 4000 to 7500 pounds. Eggers cautioned his NACA colleagues that a nonlifting, or pure ballistic, vehicle might subject the passenger to excessive deceleration forces.[53]

Faget and Purser returned to Langley convinced that a maximum concentration of effort to achieve manned orbital flight as quickly as possible was imperative.[54] Obviously this meant that in the months ahead their research should focus on the ballistic-capsule approach to orbiting a man. Both the hypersonic glider, which called for progressing to ever higher speeds and altitudes, and Eggers' M–1, also too heavy for any existing booster system, would take too long to develop. The manned ballistic vehicle combined a maximum of simplicity and heat protection with a minimum weight and offered the best chance of getting a man into space in a hurry. Henceforth the aerodynamicists in PARD, and space enthusiasts in other units of the Langley laboratory, turned from NACA's historic preoccupation with winged, aerodynamically controllable vehicles and devoted themselves to the study of "a man in a can on an ICBM," as some in the Air Force called it.[55]

After *Sputnik I*, the aircraft and missile corporations also stepped up their research on the ballistic capsule; throughout November and December their design studies and proposals flowed into ARDC Headquarters. The most active of the firms considering how to put a man on a missile still was Avco. On November 20, 1957, it submitted to ARDC its second and more detailed study of systems for manned space flight, entitled "Minimum Manned Satellite." The Avco document concluded that "a pure drag reentry vehicle is greatly superior in satisfying the overall system requirements," and that the best available rocket for boosting a manned satellite into an orbit about 127 miles from Earth was the Atlas. Still unproven, the Atlas was to make its first successful short-range flight (500 miles) on December 17, 1957. An Atlas-launched satellite, according to the Avco idea, would be a manned spherical capsule that would reenter the atmosphere on a stainless-steel-cloth parachute. Shaped like a shuttlecock, the parachute was supposed to brake the capsule through reentry. Then air pressure would expand the parachute to a diameter of 36 feet, and the capsule would land at a rate of 35 feet per second.

Avco requested $500,000 to cover the expense of a three-month study and the construction of a "mockup," or full-scale model, of the capsule containing some of its internal systems. But because the Ballistic Missile Division was skeptical about the drag-brake apparatus, and because ARDC was uncertain about Air Force plans in general, a contract was not awarded. Avco engineers, believing that the limiting factor in putting a man in orbit was not the capsule but the development of a reliable booster, focused on the Atlas and began holding discussions with representatives of Convair, builder of the Atlas.[56]

JOCKEYING FOR POSITION

On October 9, only five days after *Sputnik I*, the Ad Hoc Committee of the Air Force Scientific Advisory Board urged the development of "second generation" ICBMs that could be used as space boosters, proposed the eventual accomplishment of manned lunar missions by the Air Force, and recommended the launching of Air Force satellites for reconnaissance, communications, and weather prediction purposes as soon as possible. A few days later, Secretary of the Air Force James H. Douglas appointed a committee of 56 academic and corporate scientists and Air Force officers, headed by the eminent but controversial nuclear physicist Edward N. Teller, to "propose a line of positive action" for the Air Force in space exploration. Not surprisingly, the Teller Committee in its report of October 28 recommended a unified space program under Air Force leadership.[57]

Then, on December 10, 1957, Lieutenant General Donald L. Putt, Air Force Deputy Chief of Staff, Development, set up a "Directorate of Astronautics" for the Air Force. Brigadier General Homer A. Boushey, who sixteen years earlier had piloted the first rocket-assisted aircraft takeoff in this country, became head of the new office. The move quickly met opposition from Secretary of Defense Neil H. McElroy, who was chary about any of the services using the term "astronautics," and from William M. Holaday, newly appointed Defense Department Director of Guided Missiles, whom the *New York Times* quoted as charging that the Air Force wanted to "see if it can grab the limelight and establish a position." The furor within the Defense Department caused Putt to cancel the astronautics directorate on December 13, only three days after its establishment.[58]

Sputnik II, the dismayingly large, dog-carrying Soviet satellite, had gone into orbit on November 3. As the mood of national confusion intensified in the last weeks of 1957, Headquarters USAF ordered the Air Research and Development Command to prepare a comprehensive "astronautics program," including estimates of funding and projected advances in space technology over the next five years. ARDC, which had been working on its own 15-year plan for Air Force research and development in astronautics, now boiled its findings down to a five-year prospectus. ARDC's report went to Headquarters USAF on December 30, and at the end of the year of the Sputniks the five-year plan was under consideration in the Pentagon.[59]

In any Air Force push into astronautics, NACA presumably would play a key role as supplier of needed research data. The agency had done this for nearly four decades in aeronautics. Proceeding on this premise, Putt wrote NACA

Director Dryden on January 31, 1958, formally inviting NACA's participation in a man-in-space program with the Air Force, including both the boost-glide research airplane, soon to be dubbed Dyna-Soar, and "a manned one-orbit flight in a vehicle capable only of a satellite orbit. . . ." [60] Dryden promptly approved NACA cooperation on the first approach, although the research agency and the Air Force would not sign their formal agreement on the subject until the following May. [61] Regarding the satellite project offer, however, Dryden informed Putt that NACA was working on its own designs for a manned space capsule and would "coordinate" with the Air Force late in March, when NACA completed its studies. [62]

Behind NACA's apparent reluctance to follow the Air Force lead into manned satellite development was a conviction, held by some people at NACA Headquarters, but mainly by administrators and engineers of the Langley and Lewis laboratories, that the agency should broaden its activities as well as its outlook Moving into astronautics, NACA should leave behind its historic preoccupation with research and expand into systems development and flight operations— into the uncertain world of large contracts, full-scale flight operations, and public relations. NACA should, in short, assume the leadership of a new, broad-based national space program, having as one of its principal objectives to demonstrate the practicability of manned space flight.

So in the 10 months between the first Sputnik and the establishment of a manned space program under a new agency, NACA would follow a rather ambivalent course. On one hand it would continue its traditional research and consultative capacity, counseling the Air Force on space flight proposals and imparting its findings to industrial firms. But at the same time ambitious teams of engineers here and there in the NACA establishment would be preparing their organization and themselves to take a dominant role in the Nation's efforts in space.

IV

From NACA to NASA

(NOVEMBER 1957–SEPTEMBER 1958)

SPUTNIK II, carrying its canine passenger into orbit on November 3, 1957, made clear what the first Sputnik had only implied: the U.S.S.R. would eventually try to put a man in orbit. Americans read of this latest Soviet achievement and wondered how soon the West might be able to restore the technological and ideological balance. Throughout the United States, individuals and organizations were doing an uncommon amount of introspection. It was time for some rethinking and reexamination, for an inquiry into the nature, meaning, and direction of American government and society in the Space Age.

One of the most introspective Government agencies in the post-Sputnik period was the National Advisory Committee for Aeronautics. To most people in NACA it was obvious that the organization had reached a crisis in its proud but rather obscure history; unless NACA moved rapidly and adroitly it might very well be overwhelmed in the national clamor for radical departures. New guidelines for its future clearly were in order. On November 18, 19, and 20, 1957, aboard the carrier *Forrestal* off the eastern coast of Florida, NACA's key Committee on Aerodynamics held another of its periodic meetings. Carried on in a mood of patriotic concern and challenge created by the Sputniks, these discussions reinforced the growing conviction that NACA should do more in astronautics. Among the 22 representatives of industry, the military, and academic aeronautics making up the committee, a consensus emerged that "NACA should act now to avoid being ruled out of the field of space flight research," and that "increased emphasis should be placed on research on the problems of true space flight over extended periods of time." The committee then adopted a resolution calling for "an aggressive program . . . for increased NACA participation in upper atmosphere and space flight research." [1]

Two days after the Committee on Aerodynamics adjourned, the Main Committee of NACA met and voted to establish a Special Committee on Space Technology. H. Guyford Stever, a physicist and dean of the Massachusetts Institute of Technology, took charge of the heterogeneous group. The special committee was the first established by NACA to concern itself expressly and exclusively with space matters. It was "to survey the whole problem of space technology from the point of view of needed research and development and advise the National Advisory Committee for Aeronautics with respect to actions which the NACA should take." [2]   Appointed to the new committee were such diverse leaders in space science and technology as James A. Van Allen, Wernher von Braun, William H. Pickering, and W. Randolph Lovelace II. [3]

As apprehensive Americans watched the failure of the Vanguard test vehicle in December and the successful Jupiter-C launch of *Explorer I* in January, NACA continued to assess its potential role in the Space Age.   Shortly after the Sputniks, NACA Director Hugh L. Dryden; Chairman James H. Doolittle; John F. Victory, the venerable executive secretary of NACA; and others at Headquarters in Washington had decided on the course NACA should follow in succeeding months. Assuming that now a unified space program would come into being, the NACA leaders wanted to ensure their organization a place in such a national enterprise. To Dryden, who largely guided the formulation of its strategy, NACA should proceed cautiously toward its minimum and yet most important objective— extension of its traditional preeminence as an aeronautical research organization into the higher realm of astronautics.   This would involve a continuation of NACA's traditional function as planner, innovator, tester, and data-gatherer for the Defense Department and the missile and aircraft industry.   While a larger role, entailing responsibilities for development, management, and flight operations in addition to research, very possibly could come to NACA in a national astronautics effort, publicly NACA should play down whatever ambitions for such a role individuals and groups within the agency might have. [4]

In keeping with this "soft-sell" philosophy and plan of attack, the Main Committee, at its regular meeting of January 16, 1958, resolved that any national undertaking in astronautics should combine the talents and facilities of the Defense Department, NACA, the National Academy of Sciences, and the National Science Foundation.   In other words, national space activities should follow roughly the pattern of Project Vanguard.   NACA, while taking part in the launching of space vehicles and acquiring more authority to let research contracts, should continue to function primarily as a research institution. [5]   Dryden essentially reiterated this viewpoint in a speech which Victory read for him nine days later before the Institute of the Aeronautical Sciences in New York.   The NACA Director proposed that the current division of labor among the military, industry, and NACA be perpetuated in a national space program, with NACA doing research and providing technical assistance and the military contracting with industry for hardware development. [6]

Then, the next month, the Main Committee considered and circulated a prospectus inspired by Abe Silverstein, Associate Director of the Lewis Aeronautical Laboratory, and written mainly by his senior engineers.   Entitled "A Program for Expansion of NACA Research in Space Flight Technology," it called for a "major expansion" of NACA activity to "provide basic research in support of the development of manned satellites and the travel of man to the moon and nearby planets." The Lewis group proposed an enlargement of NACA's existing laboratories and

76

a new, separate installation for nuclear powerplant research. The cost of the expansion of the program, including the expense of contracted research, was estimated at $200 million. Nothing was said about giving NACA added development, management, and operational tasks in manned space flight programs.[7]

So by early February 1958, as the Eisenhower administration began wrestling with the complexities of formulating a national program for space exploration, NACA had taken the official position that with regard to space it neither wanted nor expected more than its historic niche in Government-financed science and engineering. While NACA should become a substantially bigger instrument for research, it should remain essentially a producer of data for use by others.

Missiles to Manned Ballistic Satellites

The circumspect approach of NACA Headquarters to a national space program was only one of several being suggested formally in the winter of 1957–1958. Various other proposals came from the scientific community. In mid-October the American Rocket Society had called for a civilian space research and development agency. In November the National Academy of Sciences endorsed an idea for a National Space Establishment under civilian leadership. By April 1958 a total of 29 bills and resolutions relating to the organization of the Nation's space efforts would be introduced by members of the Congress. Almost everyone assumed that some sort of thorough-going reform legislation, probably creating an entirely new agency, was needed if the United States was to overcome the Soviet lead in space technology. On January 23, 1958, the Senate Preparedness Investigating Committee under Senator Lyndon B. Johnson had summarized its findings in 17 specific recommendations, including the establishment of an independent space agency.[8] During these months of debate and indecision, the military services continued their planning of space programs, both in hope of achieving a special role for themselves in space and in knowledge that U.S. planning could not simply stop during the months it took to settle the organizational problem.

Of the three military services the Air Force moved most rapidly with plans for advanced projects and programs. Responding to a request sent by the Office of the Secretary of Defense to the three military services, Headquarters USAF by mid-January 1958 had completed its review of the comprehensive five-year astronautics program submitted the previous month by the Air Research and Development Command. On January 24 the Air Force submitted the plan to William M. Holaday, Director of Guided Missiles in the Department of Defense. The five-year outline envisaged the development of reconnaissance, communications, and weather satellites; recoverable data capsules; a "manned capsule test system"; then manned space stations; and an eventual manned base on the Moon. The Air Force estimated that funding requirements for beginning such a long-range program in fiscal year 1959 would total more than $1.7 billion.[9]

The ambitious five-year plan, with its astronomical estimate of costs for the

77

coming fiscal year, had remained in Holaday's office. The Air Force pressed ahead with its astronautics plans, including the placing of a manned capsule in orbit. On January 29, 30, and 31, 1958, ARDC held a closed conference at Wright-Patterson Air Force Base near Dayton, Ohio, where 11 aircraft and missile firms outlined for Air Force and NACA observers the various classified proposals for a manned satellite vehicle that they had submitted to ARDC during November and December 1957. The industry presentations appear to have varied considerably in thoroughness and complexity. The Northrop Corporation, for example, simply reviewed the boost-glide concept suggested by NACA at the Round Three Conference the previous October and already adopted by the Air Force for its Dyna-Soar project. By contrast, the Avco Manufacturing Corporation, the McDonnell Aircraft Corporation, Republic Aviation, and North American Aviation made detailed presentations, including estimates of the minimum amount of time required to put a man in orbit. Like Avco and other firms, McDonnell of St. Louis had been working on designs for a "minimum" satellite vehicle, employing a pure ballistic shape, since the spring of 1956, when the Air Force had first briefed industry representatives on its original Manned Ballistic Rocket Research proposal. Republic sketched a triangular planform arrangement modeled on the vehicle suggested the previous year by Antonio Ferri and others at the Gruen Applied Science Laboratories.[10] The "Ferri sled," as the Republic device was called, was one of two approaches wherein the pilot would parachute after being ejected from the spacecraft, the vehicle itself not being recovered. The other company advocating an expendable spacecraft was North American; an X-15, although designed to land conventionally on skids as a rocket research aircraft, would orbit and then impact minus its parachuting pilot.[11]

After the Wright-Patterson conference, the Air Force stepped up the pace of its manned-satellite studies. On January 31, ARDC directed the Wright Air Development Center to focus on the quickest means of getting a man in orbit. The center was to receive advice from the Air Force Ballistic Missile Division in Los Angeles on selection of a booster system. A few weeks later the center issued a purchase request, valued at nearly $445,000, for a study of an internal ecological system that could sustain a man for 24 hours in an orbiting capsule.[12]

On February 27, ARDC officers briefed General Curtis E. LeMay, Air Force Vice Chief of Staff, on three alternative approaches to manned orbital flight: developing an advanced version of the X-15 that could reach orbital velocity; speeding up the Dyna-Soar project, which eventually was supposed to put a hypersonic glider in orbit; or boosting a relatively simple, nonlifting ballistic capsule into orbit with an existing missile system, as proposed by Avco, McDonnell, and other companies. LeMay instructed ARDC to make a choice and submit a detailed plan for an Air Force man-in-space program as soon as possible.[13]

While the Air Force pushed its manned satellite investigations and its development work on the Thor, Atlas, and Titan, the Army and the Navy initiated manned space studies of their own in addition to accelerating their ballistic missile efforts with the Jupiter and the Polaris, respectively. Flushed with the success of the *Explorer I* satellite launching in January, the Army reached the apex of its astronautical prestige. Proud of the prowess of von Braun's rocket team at its Army Ballistic Missile Agency, Huntsville, Alabama, the Army sought a major role in military space technology. Since the Army already had lost operational responsibility for its Jupiter intermediate-range ballistic missile to the Air Force, a space mission was vitally important to its future in astronautics. Central to the Army's space plans was securing authorization, priority, and abundant financing from the Defense Department for one of von Braun's pet ideas, a clustered-engine booster vehicle with more than a million pounds of thrust.[14]

On February 7, 1958, Secretary of Defense Neil H. McElroy, acting on President Eisenhower's instructions, ordered the creation of an Advanced Research Project Agency (ARPA) to manage all existing space projects. Roy W. Johnson, a vice-president of General Electric, took over the directorship of this new office; Director of Guided Missiles Holaday transferred some of his responsibilities to the agency.[15]

Three weeks after the establishment of ARPA, Johnson acknowledged publicly that "the Air Force has a long term development responsibility for manned space flight capability with the primary objective of accomplishing satellite flight as soon as technology permits." The statement was reiterated on March 5 by a spokesman for McElroy. The Defense Department also authorized the Air Force to develop its "117L" system—an Atlas or Thor topped by a liquid-propellant upper stage (later named Agena) as a booster combination, together with an instrumented nose cone—"under the highest national priority in order to attain an initial operational capability at the earliest possible date." The 117L system, designed originally to orbit reconnaissance satellites, would now also be used for orbiting recoverable biological payloads, including primates.[16]

In response to Vice Chief of Staff LeMay's instructions of February 27 and the apparent receptiveness of Defense Department officials to the Air Force's astronautical plans, the Air Research and Development Command moved to "firm up" its plans for manned space flight. On March 8, the Ballistic Missile Division proposed an 11-step program aimed at the ultimate objective of "Manned Space Flight to the Moon and Return." The steps included instrumented and animal-carrying orbital missions, a manned orbit of Earth, circumnavigation of the Moon with instruments and then animals, instrumented hard and soft landings on the Moon, an animal landing on the Moon, manned lunar circumnavigation, and a manned landing on the lunar surface. Then, on March 10, 11, and 12, ARDC staged a large conference at the offices of its Ballistic Missile Division in Los Angeles. On hand were more than 80 rocket, aircraft, and human-factors specialists from the Air Force, industry, and NACA. Although the space sights of the Ballistic Missile Division, under Major General Bernard A. Schriever, were set on the

79

distant "man on the Moon" goal, the basic objective of the Los Angeles man-in-space working conference was to hammer out an "abbreviated development plan" for getting a man in Earth orbit as quickly and as easily as possible.[17]

The conference focused on what some Air Force speakers called a "quick and dirty" approach—orbital flight and recovery using a simple ballistic capsule and parachutes for a water landing in the vicinity of the Bahamas. The ballistic vehicle would weigh between 2700 and 3000 pounds, and would be about six feet in diameter and eight feet long. Its "life support," or internal ecological, system would be designed to sustain a man in orbit for as long as 48 hours. Because there was no real certainty that man could function under the various stresses of space flight, all systems in the capsule would be fully automatic.[18]

The human passenger would be essentially a rider rather than a pilot, although for experimental purposes he would try to perform certain tasks. The body support arrangement—showing the influence of Harold J. von Beckh of ARDC's Aeromedical Field Laboratory—would have the spaceman supine on a couch that could be rotated according to the direction of the g forces building up during launch and reentry. The rotatable couch was regarded as necessary because the capsule would both exit and enter the atmosphere front-end forward. Maximum reentry loads on the occupant of the Air Force machine were expected to be about 9 g; the interior temperature during reentry was not supposed to exceed 150 degrees. An ablative nose cone would provide thermal protection. Small retrograde rockets would brake the vehicle enough to allow the pull of gravity to effect a reentry.[19]

Among the most fervent Air Force champions of a man-in-space project at the Los Angeles conference were the human-factors experts, some of whom had been studying the medical problems of upper- and extra-atmospheric flight for more than a decade. But predictably they were also the most cautious people in assessing the psychophysiological limits of human tolerance under the conditions of flight into space. Air Force medical personnel generally agreed that 15 or more launches of primates and smaller biological payloads should precede the first manned orbital shot. Colonel John P. Stapp of the Aeromedical Field Laboratory felt that the first human space passengers should have both engineering and medical training, that they should go through at least six months of selection, testing, and preparation, and that from a medical standpoint a television camera was an essential piece of equipment in the manned capsule. Major David G. Simons, Stapp's colleague, believed that continuous medical monitoring of the man, including voice contact throughout the orbital mission, should be mandatory.[20]

The Air Force flight physicians knew that German centrifuge experiments during the Second World War had proved that men could withstand as much as 17 g for as long as 2 minutes without losing consciousness.[21] Nevertheless, numerous centrifuge runs at Wright-Patterson and at Johnsville, Pennsylvania, and calculations of the angle of entry from an orbital altitude of about 170 miles had convinced them that a 12-g maximum was a good ground rule for designing the capsule body-support system. With a continuously accelerating single-stage booster following a steep launch trajectory, an aborted flight and subsequent re-entry might subject the rider to as much as 20 g. Consequently the Air Force specialists assumed that a two-stage launch rocket would be necessary to provide a shallower reentry path and lower forces.[22]

In retrospect, there were two striking aspects of the Los Angeles man-in-space presentation. The first was that the Air Force, historically devoted to piloted, fully controllable aircraft, was thinking in terms of a completely automatic orbital capsule, virtually without aerodynamic controls, whose passenger would do little more than observe and carry out physiological exercises. The other was that no attention was given to using the Atlas alone as a booster system for a manned satel-lite. Indeed hardly anyone advocated putting an upper stage on the Atlas to constitute the desired two-stage launch vehicle. Spokesmen for Space Technology Laboratories, technical overseer of the Air Force ballistic missile program, went so far as to declare that a more dependable booster than the Atlas would have to be developed. They favored adapting the intermediate-range Thor and combining it with a second stage powered by a new fluorine-hydrazine engine developing some 15,000 pounds of thrust. By the time the conference adjourned on March 12, the conferees were in fairly general agreement that about 30 Thors and 20 fluorine-hydrazine second-stage rockets would be needed for a manned satellite project. Some 8 to 12 Vanguard second stages would also be needed, to be mated with Thors for orbiting smaller, animal-bearing capsules.[23]

While the "abbreviated development plan" was emerging from the Los Angeles gathering, a NACA steering committee met at the Ames laboratory. Its members were Hartley A. Soulé and John V. Becker of Langley, Alfred J. Eggers of Ames, and Walter C. Williams of the High Speed Flight Station. They had been appointed by NACA Assistant Director Ira H. Abbott to suggest a course of action on the January 31 proposal by Lieutenant General Donald L. Putt, Air Force Deputy Chief of Staff, Development, to NACA Director Dryden for formal NACA-Air Force cooperation in a manned satellite venture.[24] The steering committee agreed that the zero-lift approach—the ballistic capsule—offered the best promise for an early orbital mission. Soulé, Becker, Eggers, and Williams recommended that "NACA accept the Air Force invitation to participate in a joint development of a manned orbital vehicle on an expedited basis," and that "the ballistic type of vehicle should be developed." [25]

On March 14, a month and a half after Putt's letter to Dryden, NACA officially informed Headquarters USAF that it would cooperate in drawing up a detailed manned satellite development plan. On April 11, Dryden sent to Gen-eral Thomas D. White, Chief of Staff of the Air Force, a proposed memorandum of understanding declaring an intention to set up a "joint project for a recoverable manned satellite test vehicle." Before a final agreement was actually signed, however, NACA Assistant Director for Research Management Clotaire Wood, at Dryden's direction, suggested to Colonel Donald H. Heaton of Headquarters USAF that the NACA-Air Force arrangement "should be put aside for the time being." Heaton agreed, and in mid-May the joint Air Force-NACA manned space undertaking was tabled indefinitely.[26]

NACA's Metamorphosis Begins

The explanation for Wood's action and for the general prudence of NACA in dealing with the Air Force on space matters in the spring of 1958 lay in the contents of the space bill sent by the Eisenhower administration to Capitol Hill on April 14 and then being debated in Congress. This proposal appeared likely to transform NACA into the focal point of the nation's efforts in space.

From the initial discussions in 1954 of a United States International Geophysical Year satellite project, President Eisenhower's position had been that space activities should be conducted solely for peaceful purposes. The nature and objectives of Project Vanguard had reflected this policy. He summed up his feelings in a letter to Soviet Premier Nikolai Bulganin, dated January 12, 1958. Describing the demilitarization of space as "the most important problem which faces the world today," he proposed that—

> . . . outer space should be used only for peaceful purposes. . . . can we not stop the production of such weapons which would use or, more accurately, misuse, outer space, now for the first time opening up as a field for man's exploration? Should not outer space be dedicated to the peaceful uses of mankind and denied to the purposes of war? . . .[27]

Consistent with this "space for peace" policy, the concentration on February 7, 1958, of Federal space activities in the Advanced Research Projects Agency of the Defense Department had been only an interim measure pending establishment of a new, civilian-controlled space management organization. Shortly before the creation of ARPA, Eisenhower had turned to his newly appointed, 18-member President's Scientific Advisory Committee (PSAC), chaired by President James R. Killian, Jr., of the Massachusetts Institute of Technology and including among its members NACA Chairman Doolittle. Eisenhower instructed the Committee to draw up two documents: a broad policy statement familiarizing Americans with space and justifying Government-financed astronautical ventures, and a recommendation for organizing a national program in space science. The "Killian committee," as the early PSAC was called, chose two subcommittees. One, on policy, was headed by Edward H. Purcell, a physicist and executive vice-president of Bell Telephone Laboratories; the other, on organization, was led by Harvard University physicist James B. Fisk.

The Fisk subcommittee on organization finished its work first. After talking with Doolittle and NACA Director Dryden, Fisk and his colleagues made a crucial report to PSAC late in February. A new agency built around NACA should be created to carry out a comprehensive national program in astronautics, emphasizing peaceful, civilian-controlled research and development. The White House Advisory Committee on Government Organization, consisting of Nelson B. Rockefeller, Killian, and Maurice H. Stans, Director of the Bureau of the Budget, used this PSAC subcommittee report as the basis for a formal recommendation on a national space organization, which Eisenhower received and approved on March 5. Five months after *Sputnik I*, the administration began drawing up proposed legislation for consideration by the Congress. As Dryden later observed, NACA's cautious post-Sputnik strategy had "paid off, in the long run."

PSAC's rationale for space exploration, entitled "Introduction to Outer Space," was issued on March 26. This statement proclaimed that "the compelling urge of man to explore and to discover," "the defense objective," "national prestige," and "new opportunities for scientific observation and experiment" were "four factors which give importance, urgency, and inevitability to the advancement of space technology." [28]

On April 2, Eisenhower sent his formal message on space matters to Congress. The document again indicated the President's intense conviction that space should be primarily reserved for scientific exploration, not military exploitation. It called for the establishment of a "National Aeronautical and Space Agency," which would absorb NACA and assume responsibility for all "space activities . . . except . . . those projects primarily associated with military requirements." The executive authority in the new organization would be exercised by one person, a director, who would be advised by a 17-member "National Aeronautical and Space Board." The proposal for a loose advisory board represented little more than an extension of the NACA Main Committee. The idea for a single executive, however, stemmed mainly from the opinions of Eisenhower's legislative experts and the officials of the Bureau of the Budget. They wanted authority in the new agency to be centralized, not diffused in a committee as was the case with NACA and the Atomic Energy Commission. The second and more critical departure from NACA history was Eisenhower's stipulation that the proposed organization would have not only research but development, managerial, and flight operational responsibilities. Unlike NACA, then, it would possess extensive authority for contracting research and development projects.[29]

Twelve days later, on April 14, the Eisenhower administration sent to the Democratic-controlled Congress its bill to create such an agency, drafted largely by the Bureau of the Budget.[30] In the House of Representatives and the Senate, special committees began hearings on the bill. The measure would undergo extensive amendment and reworking at the hands of the legislators. But it soon was apparent that a new agency would come into being, that NACA would constitute its nucleus, and that it would undertake large-scale development and operational activities in addition to research. The odds were better than good that a manned satellite project would fall within the domain of the civilian organization.

Proceeding on this assumption, engineers working at all of the NACA installations—at the ranges and wind tunnels at Langley and Ames, in the high-temperature jet facilities and rocket-test chambers at Lewis and Langley, at the

83

NACA witnesses testify before the Senate Special Committee on Space and Astro-nautics, on May 6, 1958, with regard to bill S. 3609, "a bill to provide for research into problems of flight within and outside the earth's atmosphere, and for other pur-poses." The legislative end product would be the National Aeronautics and Space Act of 1958, which created NASA. NACA witnesses shown here: left to right, Paul G. Dembling, NACA Legal Adviser; James H. Doolittle, Chairman, NACA; and Abe Silverstein, Associate Director of NACA Lewis Flight Propulsion Laboratory.

rocket launch pads and control panels on Wallops Island, and in the flight hangars at the High Speed Flight Station— stepped up their research in materials, aerody-namics, and control.[31] By early 1958, according to Preston R. Bassett, chairman of NACA's renamed Committee on Aircraft, Missile, and Spacecraft Aerody-namics, approximately 55 percent of all NACA activity was already applicable to space flight.[32] According to another set of NACA statistics, the Pilotless Air-craft Research Division (PARD) was expending 90 percent of its effort on space and missile research; the rest of the Langley laboratory, 40 percent; Ames, 29 per-cent; and Lewis, 36 percent.[33] Virtually every member of NACA's technical staff eagerly anticipated a national program of space exploration. Since the raison d'être of NACA always had been to improve the performance of piloted aircraft, most NACA engineers viewed manned space flight as an even more challenging and rewarding form of activity.

Not everyone in the NACA laboratories, however, was convinced that the agency's destiny lay in developing hardware, managing programs, and carrying out satellite launchings. Many scientist-engineers subscribed wholeheartedly to the official NACA position enunciated by Headquarters in January and February: While NACA ought to labor mightily in the furtherance of space science, it should continue to solve problems posed by other agencies engaged in development and operations, not handle programs itself. The "research-minded" element within the NACA technical staff probably was strongest at Ames. Most of the Ames complement had gone to work for NACA because of the nature of the organization. Its quasi-academic focus on research, its receptiveness to new and sometimes radical concepts, its relative obscurity and freedom from politics appealed to them. At the California institution the prospect of managing programs, which entailed fighting for appropriations, wrangling with industrial contractors, and perhaps competing with the military, seemed exceedingly distasteful.[34]

This attitude was not so prevalent at the two other laboratories or at the High Speed Flight Station. The years of direct participation with Air Force, Navy, and contract personnel in the research aircraft projects had given Walter Williams and his staff at the Flight Station a rather clear operational orientation, albeit with airplanes and not with space rockets and satellites. The Lewis and Langley staffs included a sizable number of research workers who, while enjoying the intellectual liberty of NACA, felt it would be quite a challenge to carry out a program of their own instead of simply providing advice for the military and industry. They looked on approvingly as the Eisenhower administration sent to Congress a measure substantially embodying their ideas.

The academic approach to aeronautics and astronautics pervaded much of Langley, the oldest and in some ways the most tradition-minded of the NACA laboratories. The commitment to basic research and the devotion to theoretical calculations and wind tunnels as the most efficacious means of gathering aerodynamic data were as strong among some Langley engineers as among the Ames investigators. But in the Flight Research, Instrument Research, and Pilotless Aircraft Research Divisions at Langley; at the semiautonomous Pilotless Aircraft Research Station on Wallops Island, 70 miles away across Chesapeake Bay; and in the Flight Research Division at Lewis, there were people who had gained the bulk of their experience by working with airfoils mounted on the wings of airplanes in flight and from air-launched and ground-launched scale models propelled by rockets. For years they had been close to "development" and "operations" in their research activities, but they had turned their telemetered findings over to someone else for practical application. Now it seemed that the Soviet artificial moons might have given these ambitious aeronautical engineers a chance to put their imagination and technical experience to use in a manned space flight program. As Paul E. Purser, then head of the High Temperature Branch of PARD, put it, "In early 1958 we simply assumed we would get the manned satellite project. So we started to work."[35]

Over the years the PARD specialists had perfected their techniques of launch, guidance, automatic control, and telemetry on small rockets, and had steadily added to the mountain of experimental data on hypervelocity performance and aerodynamic heating. Their rockets, while remaining small in thrust and payload, had become more and more sophisticated. During 1957, by firing five-stage research rockets, they had been able to achieve a final-stage velocity of mach 16.[36] And they already were doing conceptual work on a new and larger multistage research rocket, designed to boost scale models in their own stability and heat-transfer studies and to send up small instrumented satellites and space probes for the Air Force. Later called the Scout, this four- or five-stage, solid-propellant configuration could fire its stages sequentially to place either a 150-pound payload in a 300-mile orbit, 100 pounds in a 5000-to-10,000-mile orbit, or 30 pounds in an orbit more than 22,000 miles from Earth.[37]

In the hectic weeks and months following the Soviet satellite launchings, the advocates of manned space flight at Langley, realizing that their experience in nose-cone research was directly transferable to the design of manned satellite vehicles, turned their attention to spacecraft design as never before. NACA's initial agreement of March 14, 1958, to collaborate with the Air Force in drawing up plans for a manned orbital project gave official sanction to research they already had been doing largely on their own time. Theoretically this work still was in support of the Air Force and industrial manned-satellite studies. As it turned out, the Langley engineers were doing the early development work for their own enterprise, later to become Project Mercury.

The sparkplug behind much of this activity was Maxime A. Faget, head of the Performance Aerodynamics Branch in PARD. Thirty-seven years old in 1958, Faget had been born in British Honduras, the son of an honored physician in the United States Public Health Service. In 1943, when his father was developing sulfone drugs for the National Leprosarium in Carville, Louisiana, the diminutive Faget received a bachelor of science degree in mechanical engineering from Louisiana State University. After his discharge from the Navy's submarine service in 1946, he joined the staff at Langley. He soon devised choking inlets for ramjets, a flight mach number meter, and several mathematical formulas for deriving data from Richard T. Whitcomb's area rule.[38] Like Robert R. Gilruth and others before him at Langley, Faget preferred to enlarge his knowledge in aerodynamics and thermodynamics not in wind tunnels but by observing and telemetering data from vehicles in free flight.

In mid-March, less than a week after the conclusion of the Air Force man-in-space working conference in Los Angeles, Gilruth, as Assistant Director of Langley, called Faget and his other top engineers together to determine what should be the "Langley position" on optimum spacecraft configurations at the NACA Conference on High-Speed Aerodynamics, to be held at the Ames laboratory beginning March 18. The consensus of the meeting was that the Langley-PARD representatives should present a united front at Ames behind a ballistic concept.[39]

The Conference on High-Speed Aerodynamics, the last in a long line of full-dress symposiums held by NACA, attracted most of the luminaries in the organization, including Dryden, Silverstein, Eggers, H. Julian Allen, Walter Williams, and the members of the Committee on Aircraft, Missile, and Spacecraft Aerodynamics. Military personnel and representatives of most of the aircraft and missile firms also attended this forum. The 46 papers read at the conference, dealing with hypersonic, satellite, and interplanetary flight, represented the most advanced thinking in aerodynamics within NACA. Taken together, the papers demonstrated how far some NACA engineers trained in aeronautics had pushed their research into the new discipline of astronautics.[40]

Much interest centered around three presentations proposing alternative configurations for manned orbital flight. The first of these papers was authored by Faget, Benjamine J. Garland, and James J. Buglia. Faget presented it as the orbital configuration regarded most favorably by PARD personnel—the wingless, nonlifting vehicle. Faget and his associates pointed out several advantages of this simple ballistic approach. In the first place, ballistic missile research, development, and production experience was directly applicable to the design and construction of such a vehicle. The fact that it would be fired along a ballistic path meant that automatic stabilization, guidance, and control equipment could be kept at a minimum, thus saving weight and diminishing the likelihood of a malfunction.

The nonlifting vehicle simplified return from orbit because the only necessary maneuver was the firing of retrograde rockets—"retrorockets"—to decelerate the spacecraft, deflecting it from orbit and subjecting it to atmospheric drag. And even that maneuver need not be too precise for the accomplishment of a safe recovery. After retrofire, successful entry depended solely on the inherent stability and structural soundness of the ballistic vehicle. Faget, Garland, and Buglia acknowledged that the pure-drag device necessitated landing in a large and imprecisely defined area, using a parachute, and dispensing with lifting and braking controls to correct the rate of descent, the direction, or the impact force. Rather severe oscillations might occur during descent. But Faget and his associates noted that tests with model ballistic capsules in the 20-foot-diameter, free-spinning tunnel at Langley had shown that attitude control jets, such as those used on the X–1B, X–2, and X–15 rocketplanes, could provide rate damping and help correct the oscillations, while a small drogue parachute should give still more stability.

The three Langley engineers went so far as to propose a specific, if rudimentary, ballistic configuration—a nearly flat-faced cone angled about 15 degrees from the vertical, 11 feet long and 7 feet in diameter, using a heat sink rather than an ablative covering for thermal protection. Although the space passenger would lie supine against the heatshield at all times, during orbital flight the capsule would reverse its attitude so that the deceleration loads of reentry would be imposed from front to back through the man's body, the same as under

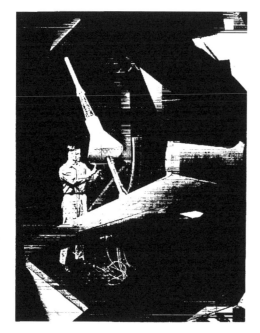

Once the basic Mercury space-craft configuration had been decided, aerodynamic research turned to the further problems generated by associated equipment, such as the escape tower and the landing parachute. At left is a model of the spacecraft with launch escape tower being prepared for test in the free-flight tunnel at Langley in 1959. Another scale model was fitted with a drogue parachute (below) and tested for stability during descent in Langley's vertical wind tunnel.

acceleration. The authors concluded that "as far as reentry and recovery is concerned [sic], the state-of-the-art is sufficiently advanced so that it is possible to proceed confidently with a manned satellite project based upon the ballistic reentry type of vehicle." [41]

One dissenter from the Langley consensus favoring a manned projectile was John Becker, of the Langley Compressibility Research Division and a veteran of X–15 development, who read a paper at the conference on possible winged satellite configurations. Becker's main concern was the reentry heating problem in conjunction with some maneuverability within the atmosphere. Combining his theoretical findings with those of Charles W. Mathews of Langley, Becker suggested a glider-like configuration. Instead of entering the atmosphere at a low angle of attack and using lift to return to Earth, it would deliberately come in at a high angle of attack, employing its lower wing surface as a heatshield. Deceleration loads still could be held at a little over 1 g in this fashion. The gross weight of such a low-lift, high-drag vehicle would be only about 3060 pounds. "Thus . . . the minimum winged satellite vehicle is not prohibitively heavier than the drag type," concluded Becker. "The weight is sufficiently low to permit launching by booster systems similar to that for the drag vehicle described in a previous paper by Maxime A. Faget, Benjamin J. Garland, and James J. Buglia." [42]

What some Langley researchers had come to regard as the "Ames position" on manned satellites was described in a paper by Thomas J. Wong, Charles A. Hermach, John O. Reller, and Bruce E. Tinling, four aeronautical engineers who had worked with Eggers. They presented a polished, more detailed version of the blunt, semilifting M–1 configuration conceived by Eggers the previous summer. For such a vehicle a lift/drag ratio of $\frac{1}{2}$ could be effected simply by removing the upper portion of a pure ballistic shape, making the body somewhat deeper than that of a half-cone, and adding trailing edge flaps for longitudinal and lateral control. Maximum deceleration forces would be only 2 g, low enough to permit a pilot to remain in control of his vehicle. Blunting would reduce heat conduction; the vehicle would be stable and controllable down to subsonic speeds and would provide substantial maneuverability; and structural weight would remain relatively low. Thus "it appears that a high-lift, high-drag configuration of the type discussed has attractive possibilities for the reentry of a satellite vehicle." [43]

The Ames engineers' presentation was not in the form of a spacecraft design challenge to the Langley-PARD aerodynamicists. Eggers and various others at Ames remained convinced of the overall superiority of the lifting body for manned satellite missions. But as Eggers explained, "Ames was not enthusiastic in 1958 to participate in an operational program for building and launching spacecraft of any kind, manned or unmanned." [44] While some Ames people were rather avidly pushing the M–1 concept, their avidity did not stem from any desire for operational dominance in a civilian space program. The California NACA scientists were quite willing to leave the business of building prototypes, carrying out full-scale tests, and then managing a program to their more "hardware-oriented" colleagues across the continent.

To Faget, Purser, and Gilruth the choice between the semilifting configuration favored by the Ames group and their nonlifting device really was an academic one. Given the assumption that a manned satellite should be fired into orbit as quickly as possible, then the Atlas ICBM, not the still untested Titan or a Thor-fluorine combination, should serve as the launch vehicle for a one-ton spacecraft. The Atlas was following a tortuous route toward status as a reliable operational rocket, but it was still the only ICBM anywhere near being ready. The criterion already adopted by Faget and his associates, that an attempt to orbit a man should follow the simplest, quickest, and most dependable approach, negated a heavier, semilifting vehicle; this would have required adding an extra stage to the Atlas or some other rocket. The same criterion even ruled out Becker's low-lift, high-drag proposal. If the first manned orbital project was to adhere to and profit from ballistic missile experience, then the capabilities of the Atlas should be the first consideration. Faget himself did not have detailed data on the Atlas' design performance before, during, or for some time after the Ames conference; such information was highly classified and he lacked an official "need to know." About two months after he delivered his paper he learned through conversations with Frank J. Dore, an engineer-executive of Convair, what he needed to design a manned ballistic payload.[45] In the weeks following the Ames conference, Faget's and other Langley-PARD research teams, centering their efforts on the basic ballistic shape, started working out the details of hurling a man-carrying projectile around the world.[46]

While the engineers at the NACA Virginia installations hurried their designs, tests, and plans, and while Congress received Eisenhower's space bill, the organizational transformation of NACA began. After the White House Advisory Committee on Government Organization recommended that a national civilian space program be built around NACA, Director Dryden and his subordinates in Washington began planning the revamping that would have to accompany the reorientation of NACA functions. Dryden called Abe Silverstein of Lewis to Washington to begin organizing a space flight development program. On April 2, as part of his space message to Congress, Eisenhower instructed NACA and the Defense Department to review the projects then under ARPA to determine which should be transferred to the new civilian space agency. NACA and Defense Department representatives, in consultation with Bureau of the Budget officials, reached tentative agreements on the disposition of practically all the projects and facilities in question, with the notable exception of manned space flight. In accordance with Eisenhower's directive that NACA "describe the internal organization, management structure, staff, facilities, and funds which will be required," NACA set up an ad hoc committee on organization under the chairmanship of Assistant Director Ira Abbott.[47]

90

Man in Space Soonest?

Officially NACA still was acting as consultant and tester for the Air Force and industry on spacecraft design and development. ARDC had sent its abbreviated development plan for a manned orbital capsule, based on conclusions reached at the Ballistic Missile Division conference, to Headquarters USAF on March 14. Five days later Air Force Under Secretary Marvin A. MacIntyre requested $133 million from ARPA for manned satellite development during fiscal year 1959. On the same day that Eisenhower proposed the civilian agency to Congress, General White, Air Force Chief of Staff, secured approval for a man-in-space project from the Joint Chiefs of Staff. Despite the introduction of the administration bill in Congress and the resultant tabling the next month of the proposed agreement between White and Hugh Dryden for a joint Air Force-NACA manned satellite project, NACA continued to furnish advice and information to the Air Force.[48]

Throughout most of April, representatives from the various offices within ARDC, forming a "Man-in-Space Task Force" at the Ballistic Missile Division, worked on an "Air Force Manned Military Space System Development Plan." The final goal was to "achieve an early capability to land a man on the moon and return him safely to earth." The first of four phases, called "Man-in-Space-Soonest," involved orbiting a ballistic capsule, first carrying instruments, then primates, and finally a man. In the second phase, "Man-in-Space-Sophisticated," a heavier capsule, capable of a 14-day flight, would be put in orbit. "Lunar Reconnaissance," the third phase, would soft-land on the Moon with instruments, including a television camera. The last phase was "Manned Lunar Landing and Return," wherein primates, then men, would be orbited around the Moon, landed on its surface, and returned safely. The whole undertaking was supposed to cost $1.5 billion, a level of financial support that should complete the program by the end of 1965. The Thor-Vanguard, the Thor with a fluorine upper stage, and a "Super Titan" topped by fluorine second and third stages would be the launch vehicles.[49]

The detailed designs and procedures for the Man-in-Space-Soonest portion of the long-range program went to Headquarters USAF on May 2. Based on Thor-117L, Thor-Vanguard, and Thor-fluorine booster combinations, the "Soonest" concept posited a manned orbit of Earth on the tenth launch of the Thor-fluorine system, in October 1960.[50]

Meanwhile, on April 30, the contractor team of Avco and Convair, which, since the Sputniks, had spent more time and money on manned satellite design than other industrial firms, presented to the Air Force a highly detailed proposal for development of a "minimum" vehicle. Featuring the "bare" Atlas, the basic "one and one-half stage" ICBM with no second stage, the Avco-Convair approach would orbit a man inside a sphere weighing 1500–2000 pounds. The steel-mesh drag brake, a metallic, inverted parachute, would be used for atmospheric entry.[51]

Specialists at the Ballistic Missile Division concluded that using the "bare" Atlas would save only three or four months of development time, that it would necessitate an undesirably low orbital altitude, that it ignored the prospect of dangerously high reentry g forces following an "abort" with what was essentially a single-stage booster, and that it presented little "growth potential," in contrast to the Thor-fluorine system.[52] As early as March, moreover, ARDC's advisers in NACA, led by Maxime Faget, had criticized the complex drag-brake apparatus as "poor policy that might interfere with the early completion of the program as well as being a totally unnecessary device." [53]

However, Air Force Vice Chief of Staff LeMay, whose directive back in February had accelerated the proposed military manned satellite project, now ordered a reevaluation of the Avco-Convair scheme. LeMay felt this was possibly a cheaper way to get a man into space than Man-in-Space-Soonest, which called for an expenditure of more than $100 million for fiscal 1959. On May 20, Lieutenant General Samuel E. Anderson, Commander of ARDC, replied that in view of a general lack of confidence within ARDC in the Avco metal shuttlecock device, the Air Force should pursue the Man-in-Space-Soonest approach. LeMay accepted this recommendation.[54] Henceforth, although there would be significant amendments to Man-in-Space-Soonest, the Air Force's own plan would encounter diminishing competition from would-be contractors' alternatives.

While Anderson was discouraging LeMay's interest in the Avco-Convair proposal, General Schriever, Commander of the Ballistic Missile Division, wrote Anderson that his office was ready to proceed with a manned orbital project; the selection of a capsule contractor awaited only allocation of sufficient funds. But ARDC still could not secure full authorization from the Advanced Research Projects Agency, under which the Air Force would have to fund a project to put a man in orbit. ARPA had sketched the Soonest plan before the National Security Council Planning Board, which supposedly had a "feeling of great urgency to achieve . . . Man-in-Space-Soonest at the earliest possible date." But ARPA Director Johnson still shrank from the initial $100-million-plus request contained in the program outline.[55]

The main trouble was the high cost of mating the intermediate-range Thor with 117L and Vanguard second stages, developing an entirely new rocket with a fluorine powerplant, and carrying out perhaps as many as 30 development flights before trying to orbit a manned capsule.[56] Late in May, Air Force Under Secretary MacIntyre and Assistant Secretary Richard E. Horner suggested that making the Atlas a carrier for manned flight might cut program costs below the $100 million mark. ARDC then had its Ballistic Missile Division prepare an alternative approach for Man-in-Space-Soonest. The BMD answer was that using the Atlas would mean reducing the orbital altitude of the 2000–3000-pound capsule from about 170 miles to about 115 miles. This in turn would mean that voice contact would be lost for long periods unless more orbital tracking stations were built around the globe. Despite these reservations, on June 15, the Ballistic

Missile Division sent to Washington a revised development plan for orbiting a man in an Atlas-boosted ballistic capsule by April 1960 at a total cost of $99.3 million. The next day ARPA gave its approval to the revised "Soonest" plan and authorized the Air Force to proceed with study contracts on the life support system of the proposed manned capsule. The Wright Air Development Center let two concurrent three-month study contracts, at $370,000 each, to North American Aviation and General Electric, which were to design the space cabin and ecological mechanisms and build "mockups"—full-scale working models— of the capsule interior.[57]

By late June, with the reworked version of the space bill proposed by the Eisenhower administration almost ready to be voted on in Congress, it was apparent that the Air Force was in much more of a hurry to hurl a man into orbit than was ARPA. The new Defense Department agency remained reluctant to commit heavy financing to a project that might well be abandoned or transferred when the civilian space organization proposed by Eisenhower came into existence. Throughout June and into July, an ARPA Man in Space Panel, headed by Samuel B. Batdorf, received briefings and proposals from the Air Force and in turn reported to Herbert F. York, chief scientist in ARPA. But during these weeks Faget, serving as the regular NACA representative on the ARPA panel, began to detect a definite change in the attitude of ARPA personnel toward NACA. The essence of this change, according to Faget, was the growing belief that now perhaps ARPA should give more advice to NACA on space technology than vice versa, as had been the case. For example, York recommended to Johnson that NACA Director Dryden's "personal concurrence" be obtained before any Air Force man-in-space program was formally approved by ARPA.[58]

On June 25 and 26, the ARPA Man in Space Panel sponsored a meeting in Washington for representatives from Headquarters ARDC, the Ballistic Missile Division, Convair, Lockheed, Space Technology Laboratories, and NACA. The meeting was called to resolve such outstanding questions as the relationship between payload weight and the lifting capabilities of various booster systems, booster reliability, and ablation versus heat sink thermal protection techniques. The gathering produced little specific technical agreement. Into July, ARPA continued to hold back adequate "go-ahead" funds for a full-fledged Air Force effort to send a manned vehicle into orbit.[59]

NACA MAKES READY

Throughout the spring and into the summer of 1958, as the administration bill made its way through Congress, NACA had given its full participation and support to the man-in-space planning sessions of ARPA and the Air Force. But at the same time the research engineers at Langley and on Wallops Island were pushing their own studies. They could see the opportunity to carry out a manned satellite project coming their way. By early spring all NACA laboratories were urgently engaged in basic studies in such areas as propulsion, spacecraft configuration, orbit and recovery, guidance and control, structures and materials, instrumentation, and aerodynamic heating. Ames and Langley researchers were conducting wind tunnel experiments and rocket launches with models of orbital vehicles.[60]

At the Langley laboratory, proponents and would-be managers of a manned space flight program studied the nonlifting approach to orbital circumnavigation, refined this concept, tested it, restudied it, and invented new ways to prove hardware feasibility and reliability. Floyd L. Thompson, Associate Director of Langley and Acting Director most of the time, gave Robert Gilruth the go-ahead for manned satellite work. In turn, Gilruth gave a free hand to PARD Chief Joseph A. Shortal, Faget, Purser, Charles Mathews, Alan B. Kehlet, Willard S. Blanchard, Jr., Carl A. Sandahl, and others at the Virginia laboratory.[61]

The search for better experimental methods in manned satellite research produced a concept by Purser and Faget for a new test rocket which would employ a cluster of four solid-propellant Sergeant rockets to provide a high initial thrust. Fired almost vertically and unguided except for large stabilizing aerodynamic fins, the rocket would be an inexpensive means of testing full-scale models of spacecraft in the most critical phases of an orbital mission—launch, abort, and escape at different speeds and under different stresses, parachute deployment, and recovery. Such a vehicle could also "toss" a man in a ballistic capsule to an altitude of perhaps 100 miles. Late in February, Purser and Faget received a job order and authorization to proceed with design work on the test rocket, which at that time they called "High Ride." [62]

Another experimental technique devised by the PARD engineers was a full-scale "capsule simulator." It was designed to test the practicability of controlling the attitude of a ballistic vehicle manually by activating air jets mounted on its body, similar to the method that would be used to control the X–15 at the peak of its trajectory. In March, Purser and several others in PARD put into operation a crude simulator rig featuring a small bed covered by a tent and attached to a pendulum. The pendulum permitted an oscillation period of two to four seconds, during which the "pilot" attempted to realign the simulator by firing the air jets. Throughout the spring Langley test pilot Robert A. Champine, Purser, and others took turns riding the simulator. Frequently modified and improved, it provided useful data on spacecraft reaction controls.[63]

Meanwhile Faget and his coworkers were steadily modifying the manned ballistic satellite design itself. Almost from the beginning of their design studies and tests, late in 1957, they had assumed that a ballistic vehicle should enter the atmosphere at an attitude 180 degrees from that of launch, so the g forces would be imposed on the front of the body under both acceleration and deceleration. The "tail" of the capsule when it went into orbit would become its "nose" during reentry. Their original capsule configuration—a squat, domed body with a nearly flat heatshield—resembled the Mark II missile warhead. The body was recessed slightly from the perimeter of the heatshield, leaving a narrow lip that theoretically would deflect the airflow in such a way as to minimize heat transfer to the after portion. But models of this configuration tested in the Langley free-spinning tunnel proved dynamically unstable at subsonic speeds. The Faget group then lengthened the capsule fuselage and eliminated the heatshield lip. By March 1958, the Langley ballistic vehicle, as described by Faget, Garland, and Buglia at the Ames Conference on High-Speed Aerodynamics, was an elongated cone. This design contrasted sharply with the configuration sketched earlier that month at the ARDC working conference in Los Angeles—a rather deep dome, the rounded front end of which was the heatshield.[64]

The elongated cone provided dynamic stability during the blazing period of reentry, but tests in the 11-inch hypersonic tunnel and other tunnels at Langley showed that too much heat would be transferred by turbulent convection to its afterbody. Besides thermodynamic considerations, the NACA planners could not figure out how to fit into the top part of the cone the two parachutes necessary for its recovery. The Virginia designers next tried a conical nose shape, then a rounded one with a short cylinder attached to it, but the problems of heat transfer from the heatshield and insufficient space for parachute packaging remained for both of these configurations. It was late summer 1958 before the Langley-PARD researchers had settled on a capsule design combining the advantages of maximum stability in a nonlifting body, relatively low afterbody heating, and a suitable parachute compartment. This was the shape that became the basis of the Mercury spacecraft—a blunt face, a frustum, or truncated cone, and a cylinder mounted atop the frustum. The completely flat heatshield had been discarded because it trapped too much heat, while a rounded face only increased heat transfer. The design ultimately chosen featured a heatshield with a diameter of 80 inches, a radius of curvature of 120 inches, and a ratio of 1.5 between the radius of the curve and the diameter of the shield.[65] This heatshield design, as worked out by William E. Stoney, Jr., of PARD at Langley, and confirmed by Alvin Seiff, Thomas N. Canning, and other members of the Vehicle Environment Division at Ames, got rid of a maximum amount of heat during reentry.[66]

Materials research continued at Langley throughout the spring and summer. In their man-in-space development plans, the Air Force experts initially had favored an ablation heatshield, but their NACA advisers generally felt that the ablation technique was not yet reliable enough for manned reentry. In March, two of the most respected engineers in the NACA establishment, Gilruth and Soulé of Langley, assisted by Clotaire Wood of Headquarters, had presented to the Air Research and Development Command NACA's design concepts for manned orbital flight, including use of the heat sink on a blunt body as the best thermal protection procedure. The question remained open, however. In June, the Wright Air Development Center, the Ballistic Missile Division, and NACA agreed to undertake joint investigation of heatshield materials, the objective being to compile a sufficient quantity of data for ARDC to make a decision between heat sink and ablation methods within three months.[67]

Considering the unreliability common in early ballistic missiles, and especially the widespread lack of confidence in the hard-pushed Atlas, some fast and almost foolproof means of escape would be essential to any launch system for manned space flight. The Air Force man-in-space designs had included an escape mechanism with many moving parts and a degree of complexity unacceptable to the NACA engineers. The Air Force plans envisioned a pusher rocket escape system, meaning that a rocket or rockets would fire at the base of the capsule to hurl it clear of the booster. The PARD rocket experts, again led by Faget, rejected this approach and began working on a solid-fueled tractor escape rocket. This would be mounted above the capsule and would pull it upward and away from a faulty launch vehicle. By the end of August 1958, Willard Blanchard and Sherwood Hoffman of PARD, working on plans and suggestions hurriedly made by Faget and Andre J. Meyer, Jr., had drawn designs for the escape rocket and tower, consisting of a slender rocket case and nozzle and three thin struts fastened to the cylinder of the capsule. The Wallops Island engineers already were planning a series of test firings of the awkward-looking escape mechanism, using "boilerplate" capsules, or full-scale metal models.[68]

The solid-fueled tractor rocket with a minimum of components reflected the Langley-PARD preoccupation with the easiest, most dependable way to get a manned spacecraft into orbit. There were certain interlocking aspects of the approach. The "bare" Atlas, the regular ICBM without an upper stage, should be the booster. With the ballistic capsule, acceleration forces during launch would be about 5 or 6 g; on a shallow reentry trajectory, deceleration loads should not exceed 8 or 9 g. But an abort and reentry after a launch following the steep trajectory and unbroken acceleration of a single-stage booster could impose as much as 20 times the force of gravity on the capsule passenger. Air Force planners had considered a two-stage booster and a flight profile with a more shallow trajectory, or a variable-drag device like the Avco metal parachute, to lessen the abort-reentry g loads—although by midsummer cost considerations were pushing the Air Force toward the bare Atlas.[69] For body support, the Air Force had thought in terms of some kind of rotational apparatus to maintain continuously optimum positioning in relation to the direction of acceleration.[70] This procedure, the NACA engineers felt, was too complicated and probably entailed too much weight.

As Man-in-Space-Soonest was taking shape in late spring, featuring a two-stage booster and either a rotatable interior cabin or a rotatable couch, Faget had another idea. Why not build a lightweight, stationary couch that a man would lie not on but in? This was the fundamental principle behind the contour couch designed by Faget, fabricated out of fiber glass at Langley, and tested on the big Navy centrifuge at Johnsville late in July.[71] There, in what Faget called "the only technical 'break-through' of the summer," Carter C. Collins and R. Flanagan

Gray of the Navy endured more than 20 g while riding in the contour couch. Then, said Faget, "we were able to disregard the USAF 'ground rule' (and a rather firmly established one in their minds) that 12 g was the reentry design limit." The bare Atlas could be used to hurl a man into orbit, and an abort need not impair his safety.[72]

BIRTH OF NASA

Even before the contour couch was demonstrated, the Air Force research and development planners also had about accepted the bare Atlas as a manned satellite booster, although they retained serious misgivings regarding abort and reentry g loads, orbital altitude, lifting ability, and reliability. But by early July 1958, there actually seemed to be an inverse relationship between the Air Force's progress on Man-in-Space-Soonest and the progress of the space bill through Congress. On July 10, Brigadier General Homer A. Boushey of Headquarters USAF informed the Air Research and Development Command that the Bureau of the Budget was firmly in favor of placing the space exploration program, including manned space flight, in the proposed civilian space organization. Nothing could be done to release further go-ahead funds from the Advanced Research Projects Agency.[73]

Only a little more than three months after the Eisenhower administration's draft legislation went to the Capitol, both houses of Congress on July 16 passed the National Aeronautics and Space Act of 1958, creating the National Aeronautics and Space Administration. Despite this long-expected action, there still seemed to be a chance for Man-in-Space-Soonest, provided it could be carried out at a relatively modest cost. So Roy Johnson and his subordinates in ARPA continued to admonish the Air Force to scale down its funding requests. The Ballistic Missile Division replied that a fiscal 1959 budgetary allotment of only $50 million, the latest figure suggested by ARPA, would delay the first manned orbital launch until late 1961 or early 1962. In its sixth development plan for Man-in-Space-Soonest, issued on July 24, BMD proposed orbiting a man by June 1960 with the bare Atlas, at a cost of $106.6 million. This was an increase of $7.3 million over the project cost estimate contained in the fifth development plan on June 15. Schriever personally wrote Anderson, Commander of ARDC, that the Ballistic Missile Division was already studying requirements for a worldwide tracking network, that the heat sink versus ablation question was under examination, that three companies were designing the 117L and the Vanguard second stage as possible backup systems for the bare Atlas, and that invitations for a briefing for prospective capsule contractors could be mailed within 24 hours. Schriever asked for immediate approval for Man-in-Space-Soonest at the $106.6 million level.[74]

In Washington, on July 24 and 25, Ballistic Missile Division specialists gave a series of briefings for ARDC, Secretary of the Air Force Douglas, the Air Staff, and ARPA. The ARPA briefing featured urgent appeals for full, immediate program approval to give the United States a real chance to be "soonest" with a

97

man in space.   ARPA Director Johnson flatly refused to give his go-ahead at that time.   President Eisenhower and his advisers, he explained, were convinced there was then no valid role for the military in manned space flight.   NACA, the nucleus of the civilian space program to be organized under the terms of the recently passed Space Act, already was planning its own manned satellite project, perhaps to be executed in conjunction with ARPA, at a cost of about $40 million for fiscal 1959.   Consequently, said Johnson, it was futile for the Air Force to expect more than $50 million for the current fiscal year for Man-in-Space-Soonest. The implication was the Air Force would be lucky to receive even that.[75]

Eisenhower signed the National Aeronautics and Space Act into law on July 29, 1958.   His action brought into being an organization to "plan, direct, and conduct aeronautical and space activities," to "arrange for participation by the scientific community in planning scientific measurements and observations," and to "provide for the widest practicable and appropriate dissemination of information concerning its activities and the results thereof"—in short, to guide the Nation into the Space Age.[76]   Space activities related to defense were to continue in the DOD.

There were certain basic differences between the final act and the bill that representatives of NACA, the Bureau of the Budget, and Eisenhower's other advisers had drafted and sent to Congress in April.   These changes were the product especially of the activities and influence of three men: Lyndon B. Johnson, Senate majority leader and chairman of the Preparedness Subcommittee of the Senate Committee on Armed Services and the Senate Special Committee on Space and Astronautics; John W. McCormack, House majority leader and chairman of the House Select Committee on Astronautics and Space Exploration; and Senate minority leader Styles Bridges of New Hampshire, ranking Republican on the Senate space committee.[77]

The large Space Board proposed by the administration to advise the head of the civilian agency gave way to a five-to-nine-member National Aeronautics and Space Council, charged with advising the President, who was to be its chairman.   The provision for a National Aeronautics and Space Administration, headed by an administrator and a deputy administrator, rather than a "Space Agency" headed by a single director was, according to two staff members of the House space committee, "a mighty promotion in Washington bureaucratic terms."[78]   Reflecting general concern in Congress over the relationship between space technology and national defense, the Space Act added a Civilian-Military Liaison Committee, appointed by the President, to ensure full interchange of information and data acquired in NASA and Defense Department programs. Other significant amendments pertained to patent procedures, authority to hire some 260 persons excepted from the civil service rating system, and NASA's obligation to cooperate with "other nations and groups of nations."[79]

Eisenhower, acting mainly on the advice of Killian, his chief scientific adviser, passed over the respected, apolitical Dryden, Director of NACA since 1949, and named T. Keith Glennan, president of the Case Institute of Technology in Cleveland, former member of the Atomic Energy Commission, and a staunch Republican, as the first Administrator of NASA. Dryden was appointed to the post of Deputy Administrator. Glennan would furnish the administrative leadership for the new entity, while Dryden would function as NASA's scientific and technical overseer. On August 15 the Senate voted its confirmation of Glennan and Dryden, and four days later the new Administrator met with the Abbott organization committee to review the proposed organization of NASA.[80]

The National Aeronautics and Space Administration, absorbing more than 8000 employees and an appropriation of over $100 million from NACA, was beginning to take shape. Under the terms of the Space Act, accompanying White House directives, and later agreements with the Defense Department, the fledgling agency acquired the Vanguard project from the Naval Research Laboratory; the Explorer project and other space activities at the Army Ballistic Missile Agency (but not the von Braun rocket group); the services of the Jet Propulsion Laboratory, hitherto an Army contractor; and an Air Force study contract with North American for a million-pound-thrust engine, plus other Air Force rocket engine projects and instrumented satellite studies. In addition, NASA was to receive $117 million in appropriations for space ventures from the Defense Department.[81] But the Space Act was silent regarding organizational responsibility for manned space flight.

OTHER MEANS TO THE SAME END

Besides Man-in-Space-Soonest of the Air Force, there were two other manned military space ventures seeking approval from ARPA in the summer of 1958. A rather heated competition was underway among the three armed services in the area of manned space flight. The Army's entry, much simpler than the Air Force approach, was supposed to lift a man into the space region "sooner" than Soonest. After the Sputniks, von Braun and his colleagues at Redstone Arsenal had had great success resuscitating their instrumented satellite project. Now they had unearthed one of their old proposals for using a modified Redstone to launch a man in a sealed capsule along a steep ballistic, or suborbital, trajectory. The manned capsule would reach an altitude of approximately 150 miles before splashing into the Atlantic about the same distance downrange from Cape Canaveral. The passive passenger would be housed in an ejectable cylindrical compartment about four feet wide by six feet long, which in turn would be housed in an inverted version of the kind of nose cone used on the Jupiter IRBM.[82]

The Army tried to justify the proposal partly as a step toward improving techniques of troop transportation. But, more important, such a ballistic shot supposedly could be carried out during 1959; this would recoup some of the prestige captured by the Soviet satellite launchings as well as furnish some much-needed medical information, especially regarding high g loading and the effect of about six minutes of weightlessness. Initially called "Man Very High," the project called for the support of all three services. The sealed compartment would be modeled closely on the Air Force Manhigh balloon gondola then being used in a series of record-breaking ascents. In April the Air Force, already overloaded with plans for its own Dyna-Soar and manned satellite projects, had decided not to participate. So the Army had renamed the plan "Project Adam" and had begun pushing it as an Army project, with Navy cooperation expected in the medical and recovery phases.[83]

The Adam proposal began the formal climb from the Army Ballistic Missile Agency through the Pentagon hierarchy to the office of the Secretary of the Army, then to ARPA. It came under very heavy criticism from sources both inside and outside the Defense Department. The ARPA Man in Space Panel unequivocally recommended that the proposal be turned down. Hugh Dryden of NACA told the House Space Committee that "tossing a man up in the air and letting him come back . . . is about the same technical value as the circus stunt of shooting a young lady from a cannon. . . ." And Arthur Kantrowitz of Avco, whose company was still trying to get the Air Force manned satellite contract, termed Adam "another project which is off the main track because I feel that weightlessness is not that great a problem." [84]

On July 11, ARPA Director Johnson notified Secretary of the Army Wilbur M. Brucker that ARPA did not consider Project Adam a practical proposal for manned space flight. Consequently the Army could not expect to receive the $10–12 million it requested for the "up-and-down" project. Early in August, Brucker, mentioning that the Central Intelligence Agency had expressed an interest in Adam, defended the approach as a potential "national political-psychological demonstration." Deputy Secretary of Defense Donald A. Quarles replied that in light of the Soviet achievement of orbiting an animal, the Air Force man-in-space project, and the creation of NASA, a decision on Project Adam would have to await "further study." In succeeding months the controversial "lady from a cannon" plan slipped quietly into the inactive category at Redstone Arsenal.[85]

Still a third military proposal for manned space flight came forth during the contentious first half of 1958. In April the Navy Bureau of Aeronautics presented to ARPA the results of its manned satellite study, cleverly acronymized "MER I" (for "Manned Earth Reconnaissance"). This approach called for an orbital mission in a novel vehicle—a cylinder with spherical ends. After being fired into orbit by a two-stage booster system, the ends would expand laterally along two structural, telescoping beams to make a delta-wing, inflated glider with a rigid nose section. The configuration met the principal MER I requirement: the vehicle would be controllable from booster burnout to landing on water. Fabric construction obviously implied a new departure in the design of reentry vehicles. At ARPA's direction the Bureau of Aeronautics undertook a second study (MER II), this one to be done jointly on contract by Convair, manufacturer of the Atlas, and the Goodyear Aircraft Corporation. The Convair-

Goodyear study group did not make its report until December. At that time it reasserted the feasibility of the lifting pneumatic vehicle but relegated the inflation of the craft to the postentry portion of the mission.[86] By December, however, Project Mercury already was moving ahead steadily under NASA. Funds for a MER III phase (model studies) were not forthcoming from the Defense Department, and the intriguing MER concept became a little-known aspect of the prehistory of manned orbital flight.

MER, sometimes referred to as "Project MER," was by far the most ambitious of the manned space flight proposals made by the military in 1958. Its emphasis on new hardware and new techniques meant it really had little chance for approval then. Conversely, Project Adam was not ambitious enough for the time and money involved. Of the three military proposals, Man-in-Space-Soonest came closest to full program approval. But by August the Air Force's hopes for putting a man into orbit sooner than the Soviet Union, or than any other agency in this country, were fading rapidly before the growing consensus that manned space flight should be the province of the civilian space administration.

NASA Gets the Job

After the passage of the Space Act on July 16, Killian had requested from Dryden a formal memorandum placing on record NACA's views regarding a manned satellite project. Two days later, a week and a half before Eisenhower signed the act, Dryden sent his memorandum to Killian. The NACA director sketched his organization's extensive research background in such pertinent areas as control systems for hypersonic vehicles, thermodynamics, heat-resistant structural materials, and the current X–15 project. Then, in his strongest official statement up to that time on development, operations, and managerial responsibilities, Dryden concluded, "The assignment of the direction of the manned satellite program to NASA would be consistent with the President's message to Congress and with the pertinent extracts from the National Aeronautics and Space Act of 1958. . . ."[87]

Like everyone else, including Air Force leaders, Dryden wanted to avert a potential conflict between NASA and the Air Force regarding manned space flight. On the same day that Eisenhower signed the Space Act, July 29, Dryden met with Roy Johnson and Secretary of Defense Neil H. McElroy to discuss the future management of manned space programs, but no agreement was reached. The conferees adjourned to await action from the White House.[88]

Some time between then and August 20, probably on August 18, Eisenhower made his decision. Again apparently acting on Killian's advice, he assigned to NASA specific responsibility for developing and carrying out the mission of manned space flight. This decision provided the coup de grace to the Air Force's plans for Man-in-Space-Soonest. Deputy Secretary of Defense Quarles decided the $53.8 million that had been set aside for various Air Force space projects, including Man-in-Space-Soonest (but not Dyna-Soar), would constitute part of the $117 million to be transferred from the Defense Department to NASA. LeMay, Air Force Vice Chief of Staff, then notified the Air Research and Development Command that he was transferring $10 million previously earmarked for the Soonest project. He added that Eisenhower's action obviously made impossible the immediate project approval Schriever had urged on July 24. A seventh and final manned satellite development plan, which the Ballistic Missile Division submitted to ARDC on September 11, significantly dropped the term "Soonest" from its descriptive title.[89]

The Air Force would proceed with its Dyna-Soar project in conjunction with NASA and later would inaugurate a "Discoverer biosatellite program" based on the 117L system. After August 1958, however, the project to rocket into orbit a man in a ballistic capsule was under undisputed civilian management, although it would draw heavily on all three services as well as industry and universities.

The National Aeronautics and Space Administration received authorization to carry out this primitive manned venture into lower space mainly because Eisenhower was wedded to a "space for peace" policy. He was joined by his closest advisers, most members of Congress, and perhaps a majority of politically conscious Americans. In 1958 there simply was no clear military justification for putting a man in orbit.[90] And while there is little evidence on this point, it may be assumed that the very ambitiousness of the Air Force planners, to whom the orbiting of a manned ballistic vehicle was only the first phase of a costly program aimed at putting a man on the Moon, discouraged the budget-conscious Eisenhower administration. Already enormous sums were being spent on ballistic missiles and other forms of advanced weapons technology.

Also helping to influence the President and his advisers, however, was the fact that NACA, around which NASA would be built, already had gone far in designing, testing, planning, and generally making itself ready for the execution of a manned satellite project. For months representatives from NACA Headquarters had conferred periodically with prospective contractors like Avco, Lockheed, and General Electric on such subjects as heatshield technology, environmental control systems, and communications requirements.[91] As early as March 1958, both before and after the Ames conference, Maxime Faget and Caldwell C. Johnson, working in PARD, together with Charles Mathews of the Langley Flight Research Division, had drawn up basic outlines for the manned ballistic satellite mission, the capsule configuration and internal equipment, heating loads and structural considerations, and weight limitations for a manned payload lifted into orbit by an Atlas. Throughout the spring and summer, Johnson, a self-made engineer attached to PARD from the Langley Engineering Services Division, continually modified his designs and specifications for the "can" to be mounted on the Atlas ICBM.[92]

By the end of the summer, experimenters operating in the 2000-foot towing tank at the Virginia laboratory already were using Langley-made scale models and

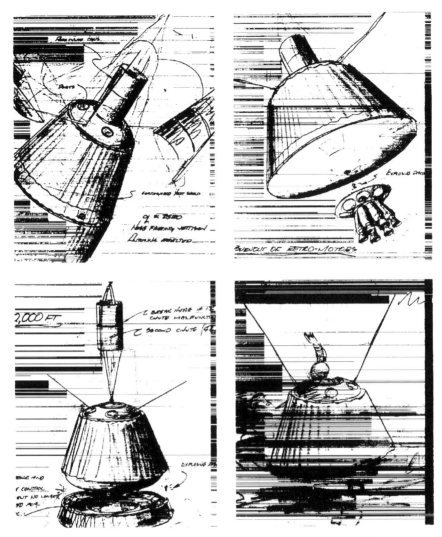

During the spring of 1958 engineers at Langley both researched and brainstormed the problems associated with a manned spacecraft. These engineering sketches were done in May 1958 by Caldwell C. Johnson. In the upper left, the spacecraft is still attached to the booster in powered ascent; the nose fairings have just jettisoned, exposing the parachute containers and permitting the antenna to deploy. Upper right, reentry has begun and the spent retrorockets are being jettisoned. Lower left, the parachutes are deploying and the heatshield is being jettisoned. And at lower right, the spacecraft has safely landed in the water and is now communicating.

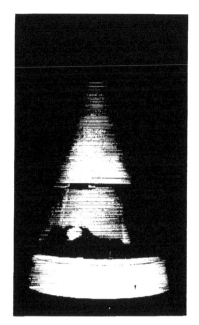

Two models of possible capsule configurations from early 1958. The cone shape was soon obsolete, while the rounded-end-with-cylinder configuration is clearly related to C. C. Johnson's engineering sketches. It is interesting that the couch configuration is the same in the two divergent capsule designs.

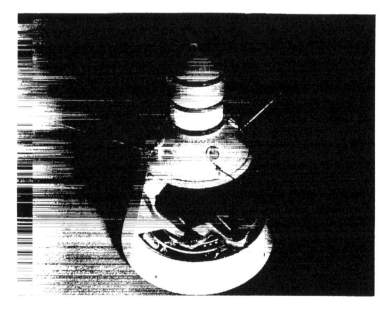

A water-drop test at the Langley laboratory is about to check the landing characteristics and flotation stability of the cone-shaped capsule configuration.

dummies of the ballistic capsule in water impact trials, while other engineers were carrying out air-drop tests of a boilerplate capsule parachute system over Chesapeake Bay. And a group from the Lewis laboratory was commuting regularly to Langley to participate in design discussions on all the orbital spacecraft systems, especially on thermal protection techniques and on the attitude control, separation (posigrade), and reentry (retrograde) rockets.[93]

Meanwhile Faget's and Paul Purser's proposal made early in the year for a clustered-rocket test booster to be used in payload design research and in manned vertical flights had undergone a politic modification. After Dryden publicly drew his analogy between the Army's Project Adam and the circus lady shot from a cannon, the PARD research team leaders dropped the name "High Ride" and shelved their ideas for using the rocket to fire a man into space. In August, Faget asked William M. Bland, Jr., and Ronald Kolenkiewicz of PARD to prepare precise specifications for a vehicle to launch full-scale and full-weight capsules to a maximum altitude of 100 miles. Only a year would pass before the experimental rocket went into operation. When it did, the former "High Ride" would have acquired the new nickname "Little Joe." [94]

Only three days after Eisenhower signed the Space Act and more than two weeks before he formally gave the manned satellite job to NASA, Dryden and several other representatives of the disappearing NACA had testified before the House space committee on their budget request for $30 million for fiscal 1959. Assistant Director Gilruth of Langley gave a hurriedly prepared presentation on plans for a manned ballistic satellite; his remarks amounted to the first open discussion of the technical aspects of what was soon to become Project Mercury. After exhibiting models of the contour couch and an outdated cone-shaped capsule, Gilruth turned to the proposed launch vehicle. Here he revealed the fears and hopes about the Atlas that would characterize NASA's efforts to orbit a man:

> The Atlas . . . has enough performance to put this in orbit and the guidance system is accurate enough, but there is the matter of reliability. You don't want to put a man in a device unless it has a very good chance of working every time.
> There are scheduled many Atlas firings in the next year and a half. Reliability is something that comes with practice. It is to be anticipated that this degree of reliability will occur as a result of just carrying out the national ballistic missile program.[95]

The Main Committee of NACA held its last meeting on August 21 and formally extended best wishes to NASA and Administrator Glennan, who attended the meeting.[96] In mid-September, Glennan and Roy Johnson of ARPA agreed that their two agencies should join in a "Man-in-Space program based on the 'capsule' technique." [97] They then established a joint NASA–ARPA Manned Satellite Panel to draw up specific recommendations and a basic procedural plan for the manned satellite project. Composed of Gilruth, who served as chairman, and Faget of Langley, Eggers of Ames, Williams of the Flight Station, and George M. Low and Warren J. North of Lewis, representing NASA, together with Robertson C. Youngquist and Samuel Batdorf of ARPA, the panel began holding meetings during the last week of September.[98]

On September 25, Glennan issued a proclamation declaring that "as of the close of business September 30, 1958, the National Aeronautics and Space Administration has been organized and is prepared to discharge the duties and exercise the powers conferred upon it." [99] In a message to all NACA personnel he added:

> One way of saying what will happen would be to quote from the legalistic language of the Space Act. . . . My preference is to state it in a quite different way—that what will happen . . . is a sign of metamorphosis. It is an indication of the changes that will occur as we develop our capacities to handle the bigger job that is ahead. We have one of the most challenging assignments that has ever been given to modern man.[100]

On Tuesday afternoon, September 30, more than 8000 people left work as employees of the 43-year-old NACA. The next morning almost all of them returned to their same jobs with NASA.

Part Two

DEVELOPMENT

V

Specifications for a Manned Satellite

(OCTOBER–DECEMBER 1958)

"All right.   Let's get on with it!"

These were the informal words of leadership that launched the development of the United States' first manned space flight program.   They were spoken by T. Keith Glennan, newly appointed first Administrator of the National Aeronautics and Space Administration, following a briefing by eight civil service aeronautical engineers who felt ready to become "astronautical engineers."   This was exactly a year and three days after national debate and preliminary planning had been precipitated by *Sputnik I*.   Glennan's words symbolized the firm resolution of the Congress, the Eisenhower administration, and the American people to accept the challenge of nature, technology, and the Soviet Union to explore the shallows of the universe.[1]

By the first anniversary of Earth's first artificial satellite, Americans generally seemed willing, if not eager, to accept the rationale of scientific experts and engineering enthusiasts that the new ocean of space could now and should now be explored by man in person.   The human and the physical energies necessary for man to venture beyond Earth's atmosphere had become, for the first time in the history of this planet, available in feasible form.   These energies only needed transformation by organization and development to transport man into the beyond.

If these were the articles of faith behind the first American manned satellite program, they had not been compelling enough to spark action toward space flight before the Sputniks.   Public furor was inspired primarily not by the promise of extending aeronautics and missilery into astronautics, but rather by the nationalistic fervor and punctured pride caused by the obviously spectacular Soviet achievements.   Faith, fervor, and even some fear were perhaps necessary if the

American democracy was to embark on a significant space program. But the people most directly concerned with mobilizing the men and the technology to accomplish manned orbital flight had first to organize themselves.

A MANNED SATELLITE PLAN

The establishment of an organization to carry through a manned space flight program depended upon gaining the national decision to create a space agency and then upon defining the objectives of the space agency as a whole and of its highest priority programs in particular. In July 1958 legislative debate had ended in the passage of the National Aeronautics and Space Act. In August administrative power struggles had abated with President Dwight D. Eisenhower's appointments and Senate confirmation of the administrative heads of the new space agency. By September the technical and jurisdictional questions remaining to be solved for an operational manned satellite program had been removed from the open forum by their assignment to the Joint NASA–ARPA Manned Satellite Panel. When Glennan proclaimed that the demise of NACA and the birth of NASA would take effect at the close of business on September 30, 1958, there was reason to suppose that a preliminary organization of the nation's space program was well in hand. But in Washington there was no clear commitment to the precise size or priority of the manned program within NASA, because NASA itself was as yet only a congeries of transferred people, facilities, and projects.[2]

Earlier attempts to coordinate interservice and interagency plans and procedures for putting a man in space had been ineffectual. During the middle of September, Glennan and Roy W. Johnson, Director of Advanced Research Projects Agency (ARPA), had come to agree on the bare outline of a joint program for a manned orbital vehicle based on the ballistic capsule idea. A month earlier, Hugh L. Dryden, the veteran Director of the NACA, and Robert R. Gilruth, Assistant Director of Langley Aeronautical Research Laboratory, had informed Congressional committees of their plans for a manned capsule and had requested $30 million to proceed with the work. But only when the Joint Manned Satellite Panel was established by executive agreement between NASA and ARPA in mid-September 1958 did plans and proposals begin to jell into a positive course of action.[3]

Of the eight members of this steering committee, only two were from ARPA. Six had come from NACA and were the principal policy makers who laid down the guidelines and objectives for the first manned space flight program. This group began to meet almost continuously in late September in an effort to establish preliminary plans and schedules for the manned satellite project. Thousands of scientists and engineers over past years made possible their outline report, entitled "Objectives and Basic Plan for the Manned Satellite Project." But technical liaison between military and civilian groups on the immediate working levels provided the specific data for the outline drawn up by this panel:[4]

I. OBJECTIVES

The objectives of the project are to achieve at the earliest practicable date orbital flight and successful recovery of a manned satellite, and to investigate the capabilities of man in this environment.

II. MISSION

To accomplish these objectives, the most reliable available boost system will be used. A nearly circular orbit will be established at an altitude sufficiently high to permit a 24-hour satellite lifetime; however, the number of orbital cycles is arbitrary. Descent from orbit will be initiated by the application of retro-thrust. Parachutes will be deployed after the vehicle has been slowed down by aerodynamic drag, and recovery on land or water will be possible.

III. CONFIGURATION

A. *Vehicle*

The vehicle will be a ballistic capsule with high aerodynamic drag. It should be statically stable over the mach number range corresponding to flight within the atmosphere. Structurally, the capsule will be designed to withstand any combination of acceleration, heat loads, and aerodynamic forces that might occur during boost and reentry of successful or aborted missions.

The document outlined generally the life support, attitude control, retrograde, recovery, and emergency systems and described the guidance and tracking, instrumentation, communications, ground support, and test program requirements.

In only two and one-half pages of typescript, the "Objectives and Basic Plan" for the manned satellite were laid out for the concurrence of the Director of ARPA and the Administrator of NASA during the first week of October 1958. Verbal elucidations of accompanying charts, tables, and diagrams, plus scale models brought along from Langley Field, successfully sold this approach for putting man into orbit. Although the Air Force, Army, and Navy, as well as numerous aviation industry research teams, also had plans that might have worked equally well, the Nation could afford only one such program. The simplest, quickest, least risky, and most promising plan seemed to be this one.[5]

The fact that the Joint Manned Satellite Panel was "loaded" six to two in favor of NASA reflected the White House decision that ARPA would assist NASA rather than comanage the project. The plans of the panel gave the appearance of unanimity among aeronautical engineers on how to accomplish manned orbital flight. Keith Glennan and Roy Johnson were impressed by this consensus but they refrained from making public their commitments for several more months. The tacit agreement among the panel members that no basic technical or scientific problems remained to be solved before moving into development and flight test would be tested by industrial response to the basic plan. If previous research had been sufficiently thorough to allow NASA to begin immediately applying engineering knowledge for the achievement of orbital flight, then the panel's judgment of

111

the state of the art should be confirmed by the aircraft companies. Only Alfred J. Eggers wished to be placed on record as favoring concurrent development of a lifting reentry vehicle.[6]

The panel recommended three types of flight testing programs. First, development tests should verify the components of the manned satellite vehicle "to the point where they consistently and reliably perform satisfactorily, and provide design criteria by measuring loads, heating, and aerodynamic stability derivatives during critical portions of the flight." Second, qualification flight tests should determine suitability of the complete vehicle to perform its specified missions. Third, training and pilot performance flight tests should validate man's "potential for the specified missions."

> In this program, all three types of tests will be made with full-scale articles. These tests will be initiated at low velocities, altitudes and loads. They will progress with a buildup in severity of these conditions until the maximum mission is reached. In general, development tests will be completed, followed by qualification tests, and pilot performance and training tests. However, there will be some overlap as the severity of conditions are built up in the flight test program. The number and type of pilot performance and training flights will be determined as the program develops.[7]

Although the conceptual design and the operating philosophy for the manned satellite program were remarkably firm at the time of authorization, specific technical difficulties in development could not be pinpointed in advance. The people who would have to solve them were only then being identified and appointed to their individual jobs. At NACA Headquarters in Washington, Hugh Dryden had presided during the summer over the metamorphosis of NACA into NASA. An established scientist and a proven technical executive, Dryden had been a logical choice if not for the Administrator, then for Deputy Administrator, the second highest position within the space agency. He must decide how many and who should move to Washington to manage the administrative side and to oversee the engineering work. What proportion of effort and funds should NASA spend on developing manned, as opposed to unmanned, spacecraft and rockets? On whom should the immediate responsibility for technical direction of the manned satellite program be put? Where should the locus for ground control of manned space flight operations be placed?

THE PEOPLE IN CHARGE

Glennan and Dryden decided many questions of appointment quite naturally by allowing informal working arrangements to become formal. Glennan's fellow Clevelander, Abe Silverstein, Associate Director of NACA's Lewis Flight Propulsion Laboratory, was appointed Director of Space Flight Development. Silverstein had been the technical director of research at Lewis since 1949 and had worked closely with Dryden since March and with Glennan since August in planning the early organization of NASA.[8] As reflected by his title, manned programs per se were supposed to occupy only about one-third of Silverstein's time. He brought with him from Cleveland three other scientist-administrators of demonstrated talents to handle most of his staff work concerning the manned satellite program, which then was a minor portion of Silverstein's responsibility compared with his concerns over propulsion development. Newell D. Sanders became Silverstein's Assistant Director for Advanced Technology. But the primary relations between Washington and the field activities for manned space flight development were to be handled by George M. Low, who eventually became chief of an Office of Manned Space Flight, and Warren J. North, a former NACA test pilot who at first headed an Office of Manned Satellites, then of Space Flight Programs. Dryden and Glennan depended heavily upon Silverstein and his aides for the technical review and supervision of the division of labor among the various NASA field centers. But the locus of manned space flight preparations remained with the small group of Langley and Lewis personnel under Gilruth, the group that had zealously researched, planned, and designed what was to become Project Mercury.

Dryden desired to conserve the character of the three primary NACA centers as national laboratories specializing as necessary in applied and advanced research for aeronautics and astronautics. Glennan agreed to assign the large new development and operational programs to distinct, or at least reorganized, groups of people. The directors of the Langley, Ames, and Lewis Research Centers should continue their aeronautical and missile work with a minimum of disturbance while expanding the proportion of their research devoted to space. NASA Headquarters personnel, temporarily located in the Dolley Madison House, across Lafayette Square from the White House, should be able to coordinate agency-wide activities without too much interference in the high degree of local autonomy at the research laboratories near airfields in Virginia, California, and Ohio.

With the birth of NASA all the former NACA laboratories had their names changed. Langley Memorial Aeronautical Laboratory, from 1920 until 1940 the first and only research lab for NACA, became on October 1, 1958, the Langley Research Center. Located on the Virginia peninsula, across Hampton Roads from Norfolk, the Langley laboratories flanked one side of old Langley Field, one of the pioneer U.S. military airfields; for 10 years now the Air Force had called it the Langley Air Force Base. NASA's 700 acres there contained buildings and hangars more permanent and other structures more unusual than were normally found at military airfields. On opposite edges of the runways, about 3000 civilians in 1958 worked at facilities worth more than $150 million. About 700 of these people were professional engineers and self-made scientists whose major tools were 30 different wind tunnels. Also they had experimental models, operating aircraft, shops, and laboratories for chemistry, physics, electronics, and hydrodynamics.[9]

As a national aeronautical laboratory Langley supported little if any "pure" or "basic" science, in the sense of independent individual investigations in pursuit of knowledge as opposed to utility. But it had long provided a world-renowned institutional setting for "applied science." Both research and development were carried on there without prejudice.[10]

Now that the "sky" was to be redefined in terms of "aerospace," man's mastery of dimensions at least five times higher than he had ever flown required radically new social as well as technological inventions. Silverstein was asked by Dryden to help Gilruth create an entirely new management organization, composed primarily of Langley personnel, without disrupting other work in progress. The Director of Langley Research Center, Henry J. E. Reid, was on the verge of retirement, and responsibility for administering Langley had devolved to Floyd L. Thompson. Neither Reid nor Thompson was close enough to the manned satellite working level, where events were moving so rapidly, to assume charge of the special organization taking shape there.

The project director of the manned satellite program should therefore be the man who had already directed it through its gestation period—Robert R. Gilruth. As Assistant Director of Langley and the former chief of the Pilotless Aircraft Research Division (PARD), he had long nurtured Maxime A. Faget and his associates, the conceptual designers of the NACA manned satellite. After the consolidation of professional consensus at Langley behind the Faget plan in March 1958, Dryden and his Washington associates Ira H. Abbott and John W. Crowley, Jr., had given Gilruth authority to get underway.[11]

Gilruth had come to Langley after earning his master's degree in aeronautical engineering at the University of Minnesota under Professor Jean Piccard in 1936. He had been a leader in research during the development of transonic and supersonic aircraft, becoming the man in charge of structures, dynamic loads, and pilotless aircraft studies at Langely in 1952. During the decade of guided missile development, Gilruth had served on some six scientific advisory committees for the military services and for NACA. His eminence was widely recognized both as a scientist-engineer and as a research administrator. Furthermore, he was eager to continue his leadership of the vigorous group of younger engineers working with Faget.[12]

As soon as Gilruth and Faget returned with Glennan's verbal approval "to implement the manned satellite project," Thompson, acting director of Langley, began making arrangements to establish in separate facilities at the Unitary Wind Tunnel Building the self-appointed group already working on space flight. Charles J. Donlan, Technical Assistant to the Director of Langley, was asked to serve as Assistant Project Manager. Under Gilruth and Donlan, 33 Langley personnel, 25 of these engineers (14 of them from PARD), were officially transferred on November 5, 1958, to form the nucleus of a separate organization to be called the Space Task Group.[13]

Although the new Task Group was responsible directly to Washington, its initial composition and actions were left largely to local initiative. The Langley group had anticipated by two months the official actions and had discussed organization of a "Manned Ballistic Satellite Task Group." Called by some of its secretaries the "Space Task Force," it had acquired 10 to 15 men from Lewis Research Center when Silverstein in July had directed them to commute to Langley to aid in working out detailed designs for structure, thermal protection, and instrumentation in the program. This informal Langley-Lewis working arrangement gradually integrated and expanded as the Space Task Group took shape through the following year.[14]

Gilruth's authorization gave him two hats: one as project manager of the Space Task Group, and the other—announced May 1, 1959—as assistant director of a new NASA "space projects center" to be located near Greenbelt, Maryland, about 15 miles northeast of the Nation's capital. In Washington, Dryden and Silverstein were making plans for this space development facility to accommodate the NASA inheritance of Project Vanguard and about 150 of its personnel, transferred from the Naval Research Laboratory. Such a facility might easily double as an operations control center. At this time the scientific and operational aspects of manned satellites appeared to complement the tracking network and instrumentation for the Vanguard satellites. So as soon as the building could be constructed on an agricultural experimental farm at Beltsville, Maryland, the Space Task Group would move there. In the interim Langley would continue to furnish lodging and logistic support while a space flight operations center was being built. All this was to change about two years later when it became apparent that the scope, size, and support for manned space endeavors called for an entirely separate center.[15]

Everyone connected with the Space Task Group in the first several months of its existence was too busy preparing and mailing specifications, briefing prospective contractors, and evaluating contractor proposals to take much interest in organization charts. A kind of executive committee, forming around Gilruth and Donlan during November and December, gradually organized itself along functional lines. Gilruth and Donlan, Faget and Paul E. Purser, Charles W. Mathews, and Charles H. Zimmerman formed the core of this first executive council. Other senior NACA engineers on the original STG personnel list, men like Aleck C. Bond, Christopher C. Kraft, Jr., Howard C. Kyle, George F. MacDougall, Jr., and Harry H. Ricker, Jr., also played important roles in the initial formulation of the technological plan of attack.

Of the 35 members of the original group from Langley, only eight provided administrative or clerical services. Thus, with the 10 additional people from the Lewis laboratory, Gilruth and Donlan had 35 scientist-engineers to assign to specific technical problems. Those 14 who came directly from PARD continued working on implementing their designs, as they had been doing for almost a year. Five men came from the Flight Research Division of Langley, two came from the Instrument Research Division, two from the Stability Research Division, and one each from the Dynamic Loads and Full-Scale Tunnel Research Divisions.

Some of these, men like William M. Bland, Jr., John P. Mayer, Robert G. Chilton, Jerome B. Hammack, Jack C. Heberlig, William T. Lauten, Jr., and Alan B. Kehlet, had made substantial professional investments in the space flight program at a time when this was still some risk to their careers. Being a Buck Rogers buff was not yet quite respectable.[16]

From Glennan's approval of the project until the formal establishment of the Space Task Group on November 5, and indeed for some months later, it was by no means certain how much support and what priority the manned satellite program might receive. Some NACA careerists were hesitant to join an operation that might easily prove abortive. So far Gilruth had no specified billets to fill nor any public, formal mandate from Headquarters. He and Silverstein worked together very closely through the shuttle service of George Low on Silverstein's staff, who divided his time between Washington and STG. The hectic early days, cluttered and confused, made the future of the Task Group appear less than certain. Although NASA Headquarters had received from ARPA and allocated to Langley the necessary funds to get started, NASA seemed to prefer the science programs it had inherited along with instrumented satellites. The Space Task Group wanted full and explicit support of the development engineering necessary for a manned satellite. But the members did not let lack of documented clarity from the policy level dampen their enthusiasm or activity. Throughout October, trips and conferences by key personnel verified at the working level and in the field what could and could not be done to implement policy planning in Washington. To many of the younger engineers under Gilruth, NASA's initial organizational confusion offered opportunity for initiative at the local level to accomplish more than directives from Headquarters in getting an American into orbit.[17]

In order to avoid the danger of converting the Langley Research Center into Langley "Research and Development" Center, Dryden insisted that the Space Task group should be separated from the mother institution and attached to the Beltsville Center. Some Langley engineers welcomed the opportunity to participate in a full-fledged development program; others, more research-oriented, abhorred the idea. In managing the Space Task Group, Gilruth had to reconcile these attitudes, to recruit talent and screen zeal, and to create an organization capable of developing into hardware what had been conceived in research.

"AEROSPACE" TECHNOLOGY

One of the scientific questions of the International Geophysical Year that had to be answered before the orbital mechanics of a manned satellite could be specified in detail was: where precisely does Earth's atmosphere end? By late 1958 the aeromedical fraternity, following Hubertus Strughold's lead, had accepted the conceptual outlines of "space-equivalent altitudes," with refined definitions of the "aeropause," as a general biological guide to answer a slightly different question:

where does space begin? But upper-atmospheric studies, based on the actual behavior of the six or eight known artificial satellites plus the data gained from a few rocket probes and about 100 comparable sounding rockets and balloons, were neither definite enough nor codified well enough to plan the precise height at which man should first orbit Earth.[18]

The NASA/ARPA mission specification of a circular orbit to be achieved by "the most reliable available boost system . . . at an altitude sufficiently high to permit a 24-hour satellite lifetime" (before the natural decay, or degradation, of the original orbit because of slight but effective upper-atmospheric friction) had carefully avoided a commitment to either a booster or an orbital altitude. The Space Task Group proceeded on the assumption that both apogee and perigee of the manned ballistic satellite should be within the rough limits of 100 ± 25 miles high. The Task Group chose 100 statute miles (87 nautical miles) as the nominal average altitude to ensure a full-Earth-day lifetime for the one-ton manned moonlet.

The outer limits of Earth's atmosphere, where it blends in equilibrium with the solar atmosphere or plasma, seemed around 2000 miles, and the "edge" of the outer ionospheric shell was thought to be perhaps 4000 miles above sea level, but these were irrelevant parameters for orbit selections. ICBM performance data at that time made it certain that the "most reliable available boost system" could not boost a 2200-pound ballistic capsule even to the 400-or-so-mile "floor" of the Van Allen belt.[19]

The Atlas ICBM was still "the most reliable available boost system"; there was as yet no viable alternative booster. All preliminary hardware planning had been based on the assumption that the Atlas would prove its power and prowess very soon. The NACA nucleus of NASA was composed for the most part of aeronautical engineers, airplane men not yet expert with missiles and rockets. Few of them at first fully realized how different were the flight regimes and requirements for the technology of flight without wings.

Since World War II winged guided missiles or pilotless drone airplanes had given way to rocket-propelled ballistic projectiles; by 1958 the industrial base and engineering competence for missilery had matured separately from and tangentially to the aviation industry.[20] If the manned satellite program were to become the first step for sustained manned space flight, a new synthesis between science and engineering and a new integration between the aircraft and missile industries would be necessary. "Space science" and "aerospace technology," terms already made popular by the Air Force, were now in the public domain, but their meanings were vague and ambiguous so long as they held so little operational content. Silverstein, Crowley, and Albert F. Siepert, the men who became the first executive directors of the top three "line offices" of NASA Headquarters, indubitably had their debates on programming operations for NASA and the Nation. But on the need for new syntheses and reintegrations of established disciplines and industries there could be no debate. NASA's legal mandate to coordinate and to contract for cooperative development "of the usefulness, performance, speed, safety, and efficiency of aeronautical and space vehicles" was second only to its first objective in the Space Act, expanding "human knowledge of phenomena in the atmosphere and space." [21]

The complex prehistory of NASA and the manned satellite program began to impinge on NASA policy. It affected project planners as soon as they set forth their intention to put a man into orbit. Industrial and military investments in feasibility studies to this same goal had been heavy. The Space Task Group decided in mid-October to withdraw from all contacts with industrial contractors while finishing its preliminary specifications for the manned satellite capsule. STG thus avoided any accusations of favoritism, but lost about two months in time before it was able to acquire the latest classified and proprietary studies and designs by other organizations.

Three most pertinent examples of industrial research going on concurrently with government research and leading up to seminal proposals for manned satellite specifications were those studies being conducted by the Convair/Astronautics Division (CV/A) of the General Dynamics Corporation in conjunction with the Avco Manufacturing Corporation, studies by the General Electric Company in conjunction with North American Aviation, Inc., and those by McDonnell Aircraft Corporation. The CV/A-Avco proposal to the Air Force in April 1958 for a spherical drag-braked manned satellite was followed by more reports by CV/A in June and November, and these proved that the builders of the Atlas were exploring every avenue for civilian uses of their booster rocket. Convair men like Karel J. Bossart, Mortimer Rosenbaum, Charles S. Ames, Frank J. Dore, Hans R. Friedrich, Byron G. MacNabb, F. A. Ford, Krafft A. Ehricke, and H. B. Steele had a continuing interest in seeing their fledgling weapons carrier converted into a launch vehicle for manned space flight, either with or without an upper stage.

At NASA Headquarters, Abe Silverstein decided early in November to formalize his earlier approval of Faget's plan for the "bare Atlas." On that basis a formal bidders' briefing for the capsule contract was planned for November 7. Only after mid-December, when all the proposals were in, did STG learn how great had been other industrial investments in research for a manned ballistic satellite.[22]

Although the Atlas airframe, design, and systems integration had all grown directly out of Convair engineering development, the liquid-fueled rocket engines for the Atlas, as well as for the Redstone, Jupiter, and Thor missiles, were all products of the Rocketdyne Division of North American Aviation, Inc. Hence North American, when teamed with another corporate giant, General Electric, appeared also to be a prime contender for the manned satellite contract. The Space Task Group was only dimly aware at this time of the specifications that had emerged from North American and General Electric as proposals for the Air Force's "Man-in-Space-Soonest" studies, but it did know at least that its own ballistic capsule plan was at variance with the "high lift over drag" thinking at North American.[23]

118

Back in May 1957, five months before *Sputnik I*, James S. McDonnell, Jr., the founder and president of a growing aircraft corporation bearing his name, gave an address at an engineering school commencement ceremony. He predicted a speculative timetable for astronautics that placed the achievement of the first manned Earth satellite, weighing four tons and costing one billion dollars, between the years 1990 and 2005 A.D. One year later, in a similar address, McDonnell sagaciously abandoned his timetable and said:

> I think it is fortunate that the Soviets have boldly challenged us in [space science and exploration] . . . . Their space challenge is a fair challenge. We should accept this challenge and help to turn it primarily into peaceful channels.
>
>   *   *   *
>
> So, fellow pilgrims, welcome to the wondrous age of astronautics. May serendipity be yours in the years to come as man stands on the earth as a footstool and reaches out to the moon, the planets, and the stars.[24]

Off and on since *Sputnik II*, McDonnell Aircraft Corporation's Advanced Planning Group had assigned first 20, then 40, and, from April through June 1958, some 70 men to work on preliminary designs for a manned satellite capsule. Led by Raymond A. Pepping, Lawrence M. Weeks, John F. Yardley, and Albert Utsch, these men had completed a thoroughgoing prospectus 427 pages in length by mid-October 1958. People at Langley had been aware of this work in some detail, but when NACA and PARD became part of NASA, a curtain of discretion fell between them and STG. The McDonnell proposal was repolished during November before it took its turn and its chances with all the rest of the bidders.[25]

While interested aerospace companies were endeavoring to fulfill the Government's plans and specifications for a manned satellite, a number of men in the institutional setting at Langley were busily engaged in final preparations for the bidders' conference. Craftsmen like Z. B. Truitt and Scott Curran, in the Langley shops, fabricated new models of both the couch and the capsule for demonstration purposes. Engineering designers like Caldwell C. Johnson and Russell E. Clickner, Jr., reworked multiple sets of mechanical drawings until Faget and the Task Group were satisfied that they had the architectonic engineering briefing materials ready for their prospective spacecraft manufacturing contractors. Gilruth, Donlan, Mathews, and Zimmerman meanwhile approved the block diagrams of systems as they evolved. They looked over their requirements for outside support in future launching operations, flight operations, trouble-shooting research, and crew selection and training. With everything going on at once among half a hundred men at most, there was no time now in STG for second thoughts or doubts about whether the "Faget concept" would work.[26]

Questions of policy and personnel at the time of the organization of NASA and during the birth of this nation's manned space flight program were affected significantly by a conflict then existing between the experts on men and the experts on missiles. In the eyes of the Space Task Group, the medical fraternity, particularly some Air Force physicians, was exceedingly cautious, whereas the Space

Task Group seemed overly confident to some Air Force medical men and some of their pilots. During the deliberations of the joint NASA-ARPA Manned Satellite Panel, the contrast between the technical aspects of the Air Force's "Man-in-Space-Soonest" proposal and the Faget plan sponsored by the Langley-PARD group had been resolved in favor of the latter. Air Force planners of the Air Research and Development Command early had accepted a basic ground rule specifying 12 g as the design limit for capsule reentry loads. They had opposed the so-called "bare Atlas" approach, which would carry the risk of imposing accelerations up to 20 g in case of a mid-launch abort. As a last resort they too had turned to the standard Atlas as the most feasible launch vehicle, even though, Faget believed, Air Force aeromedical experts had not accepted the significance of the physiological demonstrations by Carter C. Collins and R. Flanagan Gray on the Navy's centrifuge at Johnsville in July that man could sustain 20 g without lasting harmful effects. In calculating the risks in manned space flight, the group at Langley saw this event as having paramount importance.[27]

To ensure that NASA would have intelligent liaison and some expertise of its own in dealing with military aeromedical organizations, one of the early official actions of the NASA Administrator was the appointment on November 21 of a Special Committee on Life Sciences, headed by W. Randolph Lovelace II. This committee, composed of members from the Air Force, Army, Navy, Atomic Energy Commission, Department of Health, Education, and Welfare, and private life, should provide "objective" advice on the role of the human pilot and all considerations involving him. However, NASA and particularly STG would soon discover certain difficulties with this, as with other, review committees "having a certain amount of authority . . . yet no real responsibility" for seeing that the program worked properly.[28]

On a similar but lower plane, Gilruth asked for and received from the military services three professional consultants for an aeromedical staff. Lieutenant Colonel Stanley C. White from the Air Force and Captain William S. Augerson from the Army were physicians with considerable experience in aerospace medicine, and Lieutenant Robert B. Voas from the Navy held a Ph. D. in psychology. Thus both NASA and STG ensured the autonomy of their medical advice while at the same time they tapped, through White, the biomedical knowledge gained by the Air Force in its "Man-in-Space-Soonest" studies and, through Augerson, that gained by the Army and Navy through joint biosatellite planning.[29]

CALLING FOR A CAPSULE CONTRACTOR

The Space Task Group was ready by October 20, 1958, to initiate the formal quest for the best builder of a spacecraft. Silverstein, Gilruth, Donlan, Faget, Mathews, and Zimmerman had decided what they wanted; now the top-priority need was to decide which contractor would be most competent to construct, at maximum reliability and speed and with minimum cost and risk, the first manned spacecraft.

Preliminary specifications for capsule and subsystems were mailed by the Langley procurement office to more than 40 prospective firms on October 23, 1958. Thirty-eight of these companies responded by sending representatives to the bidders' conference at Langley Field on November 7. The briefing was conducted by Faget, Alan Kehlet, Aleck Bond, Andre Meyer, Jack Heberlig, and several others from STG and Langley. The verbal exchange of ideas at this meeting was preliminary to corporate expressions of interest expected by STG before mid-November. After that the Task Group would mail out formal specifications as the basis for bid proposals to be submitted before December 11, 1958. After his part of the briefing, Faget was asked by one of the representatives whether the retrorockets described could also be used for escape. Faget said no and explained why not. He then made it clear that any alternative capsule configurations would be considered "provided that you incorporate the retrorocket principle, the non-lifting principle, and the non-ablating heat sink principle." [30]

Nineteen of the companies present expressed interest in the competition; they were mailed copies of STG's 50-page "Specifications for Manned Space Capsule" on November 14, 1958. This document, officially numbered "S-6," formally described STG's expectations of the missions, configurations, stabilization and control, structural design, onboard equipment, instrumentation, and testing for manned orbital flight, but significantly it did not deal in detail with reliability, costs, or schedules for flight testing. [31]

By December 11, the deadline for bid proposals, the list of original competitors had narrowed to 11; there was a late starter in Winzen Research, Inc., whose proposal was incomplete. All but three of these manufacturers had been engaged for at least a year with feasibility studies related to the Air Force plans for a manned satellite. Of the 11, the eight corporations with deepest investments were Avco, Convair/Astronautics, Lockheed, Martin, McDonnell, North American, Northrop, and Republic. The three other bidders were the Douglas, Grumman, and Chance-Vought aircraft companies. Significantly perhaps, certain other major missile and aircraft companies, like Bell, Boeing, and United Aircraft, were not represented. Bell was preoccupied with the Dyna-Soar studies; Boeing also was working on Dyna-Soar and had obtained the prime contract for the Minuteman missile system; and United Aircraft sent its regrets to Reid that it was otherwise deeply committed. [32] Other military research and development contracts, such as those for the XB-70 "Valkyrie" and XF-108 were also competing for the attention of the aerospace industry.

The Space Task Group and NASA Headquarters meanwhile had worked out the procedures for technical assessment of these manufacturers' proposals and for contractual evaluations and negotiations. At Langley, a Technical Assessment Committee headed by Donlan was to appoint 11 component assessment teams to rate the contending companies in each of 11 technical areas. The classification system set up by the Space Task Group to evaluate these competitors for the space-craft contract illustrated the major areas of concern.

Between four and six research engineers sat on each of the following 11 components assessment teams: systems integration; load, structure, and heatshield; escape system; retrograde and landing system; attitude control systems; environmental systems; pilot support and restraint system; pilot displays and navigational aids; communications systems; instrumentation sensors, recorders, and telemeters; and power supplies. Each area was rated on a five-point scale ranging from excellent to unsatisfactory; the scores from these ratings were averaged to provide an overall technical order of preference.

All this had to be done over the Christmas holidays and while the Task Group was moving from the Unitary Wind Tunnel building on the west side of Langley Air Force Base to new quarters in an old NACA building on the east side. Early in January at NASA Headquarters a similar assessment team would gather to evaluate the competitors on their competence in management and cost accountability. MacDougall was to be the only Task Group representative on the "business evaluation" committee. Finally, a Source Selection Board, chaired by Silverstein at NASA Headquarters and including Zimmerman from STG, would review the grading, approve it, and make its final recommendation for the choice of the spacecraft contractor.[33]

Although virtually everyone in the Task Group participated in the process of selecting the capsule builder, there were other equally pressing tasks to be accomplished as soon as possible. Procurement of booster rockets, the detailed design and development of a smaller, cheaper test booster, and the problem of finding the best volunteers to man the finished product—these were seen as the major problems requiring a head start in the fall of 1958.

SHOPPING FOR THE BOOSTERS

Booster procurement was perhaps the most critical, if not the highest priority task to be initiated. Once the Hobson's choice had been made to gear a manned satellite project to the unproven design capabilities of the Atlas ICBM, the corollary decision to use the most reliable of the older generation of ballistic missiles for testing purposes followed ineluctably. While the intercontinental-range Atlas was still being flight-tested, the medium-range Redstone was the only trustworthy booster rocket in the American arsenal. For suborbital tests, the intermediate-range Jupiter and Thor bosters were possible launch vehicles, but as yet they were neither capable of achieving orbital velocities nor operationally reliable.[34]

Even while the Joint Manned Satellite Panel was briefing the administrators of ARPA and NASA during the first week in October, Purser, Faget, North, and Samuel Batdorf flew to Huntsville for a business conference with the Army Ballistic Missile Agency regarding procurement of launch vehicles. Wernher von Braun's people assured their NASA visitors that Redstone missiles could be made available on 12 to 14 months' notice and that the Army's Jupiters were far superior to the Thors of the Air Force. Although the Space Task Group had already consulted the Air Force Ballistic Missile Division, at Inglewood, California, and was considering the Thor for intermediate launchings, a careful reconsideration of the adaptability of each weapon system as a launch vehicle for a manned capsule was now evidently required. The so-called "old reliable" Redstones might have been ordered right away. But the question of the need for intermediate qualification and training flights along ballistic trajectories was not yet settled.[35] So more visitations to the Air Force and Army missile centers were arranged.

STG's wager on the Atlas was formalized by an order to the Air Force, placed on December 8, 1958, for first one, then nine of these Convair-made liquid-fueled rockets. The Air Force Ballistic Missile Division, heretofore the only customer for the Atlas, agreed to supply one Atlas, a C-model, within six months and the rest, all standard D-models, as needed over a period of several years. Faget was pleasantly surprised to know an Atlas-C could be furnished so soon. Having placed its first and primary order with the Air Force, the Space Task Group went on to decide a month later to buy eight Redstones and two Jupiter boosters from the Army Ordnance Missile Command. The decision to procure both medium- and intermediate-range boosters from the same source hinged largely on the fact that the Jupiter was basically an advanced Redstone. Both were Army-managed and developed and Chrysler-built. To adopt the Thor would have required another orientation and familiarization program for NASA engineers.[36]

Informed that the Atlas prime movers would cost approximately $2.5 million each and that even the Redstone would cost about $1 million per launching, the managers of the manned satellite project recognized from the start that the numerous early test flights would have to be accomplished by a far less expensive booster system. In fact, as early as January 1958 Faget and Purser had worked out in considerable detail on paper how to cluster four of the solid-fuel Sergeant rockets, in standard use by PARD at Wallops Island, to boost a manned nose cone above the stratosphere. Faget's short-lived "High Ride" proposal had suffered from comparisons with "Project Adam" at that time, but in August 1958 William Bland and Ronald Kolenkiewicz had returned to their preliminary designs for a cheap cluster of solid rockets to boost full-scale and full-weight model capsules above the atmosphere. As drop tests of boilerplate capsules provided new aerodynamic data on the dynamic stability of the configuration in free-fall, the need for comparable data quickly on the powered phase became apparent. So in October a team of Bland, Kolenkiewicz, Caldwell Johnson, Clarence T. Brown, and F. E. Mershon prepared new engineering layouts and estimates for the mechanical design of the booster structure and a suitable launcher.[37]

As the blueprints for this cluster of four rockets began to emerge from their drawing boards, the designers' nickname for their project gradually was adopted.

123

Since their first cross-section drawings showed four holes up, they called the project "Little Joe," from the crap-game throw of a double deuce on the dice. Although four smaller circles were added later to represent the addition of Recruit rocket motors, the original name stuck. The appearance on engineering drawings of the four large stabilizing fins protruding from its airframe also helped to perpetuate the name Little Joe had acquired.

The primary purpose of this relatively small and simple booster system was to save money—by allowing numerous test flights to qualify various solutions to the myriad problems associated with the development of manned space flight, especially the problem of escaping from an explosion midway through takeoff. Capsule aerodynamics under actual reentry conditions was another primary concern. To gain this kind of experience as soon as possible, its designers had to keep the clustered booster simple in concept; it should use solid fuel and existing proven equipment whenever possible, and should be free of any electronic guidance and control systems.[38]

The designers made the Little Joe booster assembly to approximate the same performance that the Army's Redstone booster would have with the capsule payload. But in addition to being flexible enough to perform a variety of missions, Little Joe could be made for about one-fifth the basic cost of the Redstone, would have much lower operating costs, and could be developed and delivered with much less time and effort. And, unlike the larger launch vehicles, Little Joe could be shot from the existing facilities at Wallops Island. It still might even be used to carry a man some day.

Twelve companies responded during November to the invitations for bids to construct the airframe of Little Joe. The technical evaluation of these proposals was carried on in much the same manner as for the spacecraft, except that Langley Research Center itself carried the bulk of the administrative load. H. H. Maxwell chaired the evaluation board, assisted by Roland D. English, Johnson, Mershon, and Bland of the Space Task Group. English later became Langley's Little Joe Project Engineer, Bland the STG Project Engineer, and Mershon the NASA representative at the airframe factory. The Missile Division of North American Aviation won the contract on December 29, 1958, and began work immediately at Downey, California, on its order for seven booster airframes and one mobile launcher.[39]

The primary mission objectives for Little Joe as seen in late 1958 (in addition to studying the capsule dynamics at progressively higher altitudes) were to test the capsule escape system at maximum dynamic pressure, to qualify the parachute system, and to verify search and retrieval methods. But since each group of specialists at work on the project sought to acquire firm empirical data as soon as possible, more exact priorities had to be established. The first flights were to secure measurements of inflight and impact forces on the capsule; later flights were to measure critical parameters at the progressively higher altitudes of 20,000, 250,000, and 500,000 feet. The minimum aims of each Little Joe shot could be supplemented from time to time with studies of noise levels, heat and pressure loads, heatshield separation, and the behavior of animal riders, so long as the measurements could be accomplished with minimum telemetry. Since all the capsules boosted by the Little Joe rockets were expected to be recovered, onboard recording techniques would also contribute to the simplicity of the system.[40]

Unique as the only booster system designed specifically and solely for manned capsule qualifications, Little Joe was also one of the pioneer operational launch vehicles using the rocket cluster principle. Since the four modified Sergeants (called either Castor or Pollux rockets, depending upon modification) and four supplemental Recruit rockets were arranged to fire in various sequences, the takeoff thrust varied greatly, but maximum design thrust was almost 230,000 pounds. Theoretically enough to lift a spacecraft of about 4000 pounds on a ballistic path over 100 miles high, the push of these clustered main engines should simulate the takeoff profile in the environment that the manned Atlas would experience. Furthermore, the additional powerful explosive pull of the tractor-rocket escape system could be demonstrated under the most severe takeoff conditions imaginable. The engineers who mothered Little Joe to maturity knew it was not much to look at, but they fondly hoped that their ungainly bastard would prove the legitimacy of most of the ballistic capsule design concepts, thereby earning its own honor.

Although Little Joe was designed to match the altitude-reaching capability of the Redstone booster system, and thus to validate the concepts for suborbital ballistic flights, it could not begin to match the burnout speed at orbiting altitude given by the Atlas system. Valuable preliminary data on the especially critical accelerations from aborts at intermediate speeds could be duplicated, but Little Joe could lift the capsule only to 100 miles, not put it at that altitude with a velocity approaching 18,000 miles per hour. For this task, a great deal more, some sort of Big Joe was needed. A Jupiter booster might simulate fairly closely the worst reentry heating conditions but ultimately only the Atlas itself could suffice.

Therefore, paralleling the planning of the Little Joe project at Langley, a counterpart test program was inaugurated by the Space Task Group with special assistance from the Lewis Research Center in Cleveland. Whereas Little Joe was a test booster conceived for many different demonstration flight tests, "Big Joe" was the name for a single test flight with a single overriding objective—to learn at the earliest practicable date what would happen when the "steel-balloon" rocket called Atlas powered a ballistic capsule on exit from Earth's atmosphere. Specifically, an experiment matching the velocity, angle of entry, time, and attitude at altitude for reentry from Earth orbit needed to be performed as soon and as exactly as possible by a powered ballistic test flight so that designs for thermal protection might be verified or modified. The Space Task Group was

125

most anxious about this; the whole manned satellite program was balanced tenuously on the stable thrust of the Atlas and the certain protection of the heatshield.

Public concern over whether the Nation possessed an intercontinental missile was alleviated on November 28, 1958, when an Atlas first flew its designed range—more than 6300 miles—down the Atlantic Missile Range toward Ascension Island. Three weeks later, on December 18, the Atlas scored again with a secretly prepared first launch into orbit of the entire Atlas vehicle (No. 10-B) as a communications relay satellite called "Project Score." Roy Johnson of ARPA claimed he was "sleeping more comfortably each night" after that.[41] In the midst of these demonstrations of the power of the prototype Atlas, NASA Headquarters and the Space Task Group planned to launch the first Atlas test for the space flight program in June or July 1959.

Gilruth appointed Aleck Bond, the former head of the Structural Dynamics Section at Langley, to take the reins as project engineer for Big Joe. Bond began to coordinate, with a real sense of urgency, the work of Langley and Lewis on the prototype capsule and of the Air Force Ballistic Missile Division and Convair/Astronautics on the Atlas propulsion system. Two Big Joe shots were arranged initially, but the second was to be merely insurance against the failure of the first. Although the Lewis laboratory traditionally had been most closely associated with propulsion problems and therefore was the logical center for NASA's first experience with large launch vehicles, neither Lewis direction nor Lewis propulsion experts were directly involved. NASA simply did not have time to learn the intricacies of launching the Atlas itself. Rather, Lewis contributed the expertise to design the electronic instrumentation and the automatic stabilization and control system for the boilerplate capsules being built jointly by the Lewis and Langley shops.

Bond recalled the initial rationale for Big Joe, alias the Atlas ablation test:

> At the time that the Big Joe flight test program was conceived, only limited experimental flight test data existed on the behavior of materials and the dynamics of bodies reentering the earth's atmosphere at high speeds. These data, which evolved from the ballistic missile program, were useful; however, they were not directly applicable to the manned satellite reentry case because of the vast differences in the reentry environment encountered and in the length of time the vehicles were subjected to the environment. There was considerable concern regarding the nature of the motions of a blunt body as it gradually penetrated the earth's atmosphere and began to decelerate. Of similar concern was the lack of after-body heating measurements and knowledge of integrity of ablation materials when exposed to the relatively low level, long duration heat pulse which is characteristic of the reentry of bodies with low ballistic parameters . . . entering the earth's atmosphere at shallow entry angles.[42]

Although for Big Joe the Task Group could center its attention on the capsule, whereas for Little Joe it had to develop the booster as well, the design and

126

development problems for Big Joe still were sufficient to cause slippage in the scheduled launch date from early to late summer in 1959. To launch and recover the capsule safely would require very extensive familiarization with new procedures. Central among the primary objectives for Big Joe were the twin needs to determine the performance of the thermal protection materials and to learn the flight dynamics of the spacecraft during reentry. Many critical decisions for the project depended upon early, reliable data on the heatshield, the afterbody radiative shingling, and the dynamic stability of the "raindrop" configuration during the craft's trajectory back through the atmosphere.[43]

Also necessary were evaluations of the aerodynamic and thermodynamic loads on the capsule all along its flight path and of the operation of its automatic attitude control system. But certainly nothing was more important in the fall of 1958 than the need to settle the technical controversy over the heat sink versus ablation principles for the heatshield. Whether to use absorbing or vaporizing materials to shield the astronaut from reentry heating was one of the few major problems remaining to be solved when the manned satellite project was established.

HEAT SINK VERSUS ABLATION

Since the peak heating rates for this blunt-body, high-drag configuration were expected to be one whole order of magnitude less than those experienced by ballistic missiles, no one competent to judge the issue now considered the "thermal barrier" problem insoluble. Rather, it had been proven to be no more than a "thermal thicket." Since the mid-fifties, various civilian and military experimental teams had studied the reentry problems for ballistic missile warheads, but only part of this research data was applicable to the different case of the spacecraft. Army and Vitro Corporation reentry experiments using ablation materials (such as graphite, teflon, nylon, or lucite) had already demonstrated that Jupiter nose cones worked quite well as ablators. But NACA preferred to rely on the successful prior experience of the Air Force with heat-sink metals, particularly copper, for early Thor nose cones. The results of these thermodynamic studies in materials science were contradictory, or at least inconclusive. So the manned satellite project began life officially in October without a commitment to either method of heat shielding, but with a definite preference for Faget's prejudice.[41]

Gilruth, Faget, and other members of the Space Task Group since March 1958 had been leaning toward the heat sink. A 600-pound metallic heat sponge might be a little heavier but it would be more reliable than a ceramic heat dissipator, for the simple reason that there was more industrial experience with fabricating refractory metals than with molding and bonding ablation materials. Some officials were convinced by the Navy's successful use of a lightweight beryllium heat sink on Polaris flight tests that beryllium was the answer. The heat sink method also was thought to have the considerable advantage over ablating materials of creating less of a "plasma sheath"—the envelope of ionized air generated by the friction of atmospheric braking. Telemetry and communications blackouts from this phenomenon might be troublesome. Pending further study, the Task Group and Silverstein decided to retain the original specification that a beryllium heatshield be provided by the capsule contractor. Requiring all the bidders to assume a beryllium shield should give a fairer evaluation of their proposals. Until Big Joe could test the ablation technique, no final decision would be made.[45]

Ablation technology, imprecise by nature, was neither well understood nor very highly sophisticated as yet, whereas the metallography of heat sink materials was straightforward, and the thermodynamics of metals was deducible. Faget believed there would be no intrinsic weight penalty for using a metal shield; the difficulty of ditching a hot shield without danger had yet to be solved. There was no disposition to ignore ablation in favor of heat sink. Big Joe was conceived to resolve the problem. By late November, when Aleck Bond took charge of it, his presumption was that Big Joe would provide the definitive test of an ablation heatshield.

Rocketry was not the only means considered for accomplishing high-altitude qualification tests at the beginning of the program. On their own initiative in the summer of 1958, Jerome Hammack, John B. Lee, Joe W. Dodson, and other Langley engineers had begun a modest program of parachute and stability trials by dropping boilerplate capsule models from C–130 transports provided by the Air Force. Balloon flights, however, seemed to promise even more effective and economical means of qualifying by "space-soaking" the complete capsule and its associated systems. From the Montgolfier brothers in the 1780s to David G. Simons' Manhigh ascents in 1957 and the contemporary Strato-Lab project of the Navy, ballooning had always been an attractive way to pierce the vertical dimension.[46]

Believing that the environmental conditions at extreme altitude could be experienced more easily than they could be simulated in vacuum chambers on Earth, the Space Task Group proceeded with plans to launch balloons carrying ballistic capsules as gondolas. Tests of instrumentation, retrorockets, drogue and main parachute systems, and recovery procedures, plus pilot orientation and training, might be done within a year's time by lighter-than-air ascents. Contracts were let to the Weather Bureau, the Office of Naval Research, and the Air Force Cambridge Research Center for planning this flight support program.[47]

No sooner had these feasibility studies been started than the Space Task Group discovered how intricate, vast, and expensive had become stratospheric sounding technology in recent years. The popular craze over Unidentified Flying Objects during the fifties had been caused partly by atmospheric and cosmic-ray research with floating objects, enormous Mylar plastic gas bags drifting around at high altitudes. Preliminary balloon flights for the manned satellite project threatened to become much more expensive than had been originally anticipated.[48]

Contract planning, booster procurement, and the need for specialized help

128

from the military services were central concerns of NASA and the Space Task Group during their first three months of existence. The possibility of friction in management relations between NASA and the Defense Department was also recognized as a potential problem. To facilitate coordinated work and plans, STG needed in-house representatives in uniform. Efficient administration demanded liaison officers to serve as single points of contact between STG and each of the military services. So in December orders were cut for Lieutenant Colonel Keith G. Lindell of the Air Force, Lieutenant Colonel Martin L. Raines of the Army, and Commander Paul L. Havenstein of the Navy to report to the Space Task Group for this function.

In general, relations between NASA and the Department of Defense had proceeded quite amicably since the drafting of a "Memorandum of Understanding" in September by the Joint Manned Satellite Panel.[49] However, with so much initiative being taken by the Space Task Group, there was danger that the concurrent actions of NASA Headquarters and STG might cause some frustrations and confusions in the Pentagon and among military contractors. NASA was still too young for its STG to be known. At this stage most of the planning for budgeting, procurement, tracking, and recovery operations had to be done in Washington; NASA Headquarters was carefully guarding its prerogative of conducting interagency business.[50] Cooperation between Defense and NASA, and between STG and its own Headquarters, was good, if not idyllic, during the first 100 days. Nowhere was this more obvious than in astronaut selection.

PROJECT ASTRONAUT?

Preliminary procedures for pilot selection had been worked out by the aeromedical consultants attached to the Space Task Group at Langley during November. Their plan called for a meeting with representatives from industry and the services to nominate a pool of 150 men from which 36 candidates would be selected for physical and psychological testing. From this group 12 would be chosen to go through a nine-month training and qualification program, after which six finally would be expected to qualify.[51]

On the basis of this plan, Donlan from Langley, and North in Washington, together with Allen O. Gamble, a psychologist on leave from the National Science Foundation, drafted civil service job specifications for individuals who wished to apply for the position of "Research Astronaut-Candidate." One of the early plans outlined very well the original expectations of NASA and STG on the type of man thought necessary. NASA Project A, announcement No. 1, dated December 22, 1958, was a draft invitation to apply for the civil service position of research astronaut-candidate "with minimum starting salary range of $8,330 to $12,770 (GS–12 to GS–15) depending upon qualifications." This document called the manned ballistic satellite program "Project Astronaut," and the first section described the duties of the astronaut:

Although the entire satellite operation will be possible, in the early phases, without the presence of man, the astronaut will play an important role during the flight. He will contribute by monitoring the cabin environment and by making necessary adjustments. He will have continuous displays of his position and attitude and other instrument readings, and will have the capability of operating the reaction controls, and of initiating the descent from orbit. He will contribute to the operation of the communications system. In addition, the astronaut will make research observations that cannot be made by instruments; these include physiological, astronomical and meteorological observations.[52]

Only males between 25 and 40 years of age, less than 5 feet 11 inches in height, and with at least bachelor's degrees were to be considered. Stringent professional experience or graduate study requirements specified five patterns of career histories most desirable. Candidates who had either three years of work in any of the physical, mathematical, biological, or psychological sciences, or who had three years of technical or engineering work in a research and development program or organization might apply. Or anyone with three years of operation of aircraft, balloons, or submarines, as commander, pilot, navigator, communications officer, engineer, or comparable technical position, would be eligible, as would persons who had completed all requirements for the Ph.D. degree in any appropriate field of science or engineering plus six months of professional work. In the case of medical doctors, six months of clinical or research work beyond the license and internship or residency would be required. Furthermore, the job qualifications required proof that applicants had demonstrated recently their "(a) willingness to accept hazards comparable to those encountered in modern research airplane flight; (b) capacity to tolerate rigorous and severe environmental conditions; and (c) ability to react adequately under conditions of stress or emergency." The announcement added:

These three characteristics may have been demonstrated in connection with certain professional occupations such as test pilot, crew member of experimental submarine or arctic or antarctic explorer. Or they may have been demonstrated during wartime combat or military training. Parachute jumping or mountain climbing or deep sea diving (including SCUBA) whether as occupation or sport, may have provided opportunities for demonstrating these characteristics, depending upon heights or depths obtained, frequency and duration, temperature and other environment conditions, and emergency episodes encountered. Or they may have been demonstrated by experience as an observer-under-test for extremes of environmental conditions such as acceleration, high or low atmospheric pressure, variation in carbon dioxide and oxygen concentration, high and low ambient temperatures, etc. Many other examples could be given. It is possible that the different characteristics may have been demonstrated by separate types of experience.

Finally, as a last check on ruling out the "lunatics" who might send in crank applications, this proposed plan for astronaut selection required that each applicant have the sponsorship of a responsible organization. A nomination form appended to this announcement would have required 17 multi-point evaluations of the nominee by some official of the sponsoring institution.

Clearly this astronaut selection plan was sober enough and stringent enough to ensure an exceptionally high quality applicant, but the plan itself was not approved and had to be abandoned. President Eisenhower during the 1958 Christmas holidays decided that the pool of military test pilots already in existence was quite sufficient a source from which to draw. Since certain classified aspects would inevitably be involved, military test pilots could most conveniently satisfy security considerations.[53]

Although some in NASA regretted the incongruity of allowing volunteers for the civilian manned space program to be drawn only from the military, the decision that the services would provide the candidates greatly simplified pilot selection procedures. A meeting held at NASA Headquarters during the first week of January brought together W. Randolph Lovelace II, Brigadier General Don D. Flickinger, Low, North, Gilruth, and several other members of the Space Task Group. There the elaborate civil service criteria for selection were boiled down to a seven-item formula:

1. Age—less than 40.
2. Height—less than 5 feet, 11 inches.
3. Excellent physical condition.
4. Bachelor's degree or equivalent.
5. Graduate of test pilot school.
6. 1500 hours total flying time.
7. Qualified jet pilot.

When these criteria were given to the Pentagon, service record checks revealed more than 100 men on active duty who appeared to be qualified. The military services were pleased to cooperate in further screening. NASA was relieved not to have to issue an open invitation, and STG was pleased to have Headquarters' aid in the selection.[54]

Contrary to the feeling expressed in some quarters, even among experimental test pilots, that the ballistic capsule pilot would be little more than "spam in a can," most members of STG believed from the beginning that their pilots would have to do some piloting. As George Low explained their views to Administrator Glennan, "These criteria were established because of the strong feeling that the success of the mission may well depend upon the actions of the pilot; either in his performance of primary functions or backup functions. A qualified jet test pilot appeared to be best suited for this task." [55] Exactly how much "piloting," in the traditional sense, man could do in orbit was precisely the point in issue.

The least technical task facing NASA and its Space Task Group in the fall of 1958 was choosing a name or short title for the manned satellite project. Customarily project names for aircraft and missiles were an administrative convenience best chosen early so as to guarantee general usage by contractors, press, and public. Langley had earlier suggested to Headquarters three possible emblems or seals for the use of NASA as a whole: one would have had Phaeton pulling Apollo across the sky; another would have used the Great Seal of the United States encompassed by three orbital tracks; and a third proposed a map of the globe circled by three orbits. These proposals, as well as the name suggested by Space Task Group for the manned satellite project, lost out to symbols considered more appropriate in Washington. "Project Astronaut," preferred at first by Gilruth to emphasize the man in the satellite, was overruled largely because it might lead to overemphasis on the personality of the man.[56]

Silverstein advocated a systemic name with allegorical overtones and neutral underpinnings: The Olympian messenger Mercury, denatured by chemistry, advertising, an automobile, and Christianity, was the most familiar of the gods in the Greek pantheon to Americans. Mercury, alias Hermes, the son of Zeus and grandson of Atlas, with his winged sandals and helmet and caduceus, was too rich in symbolic associations to be denied. The esteemed Theodore von Kármán had chosen to speak of Mercury, as had Lucian of Samosata, in terms of the "reentry" problem and the safe return of man to Earth.[57]

Had a mythologist been consulted, perhaps the additional associations of Mercury with masterful thievery, the patronage of traders, and the divinity of commerce would have proven too humorous. But "Mercury," Glennan and Dryden agreed on November 26, 1958, was the name most appropriate for the manned satellite enterprise.[58]

Greeks might worry about whether Mercury would function in his capacity as divine herald or as usher to the dead, but Americans, like the Romans, could be trusted not to worry. On Wright Brothers' Day, December 17, 1958, 55 years after the famous flights at Kitty Hawk, North Carolina, Glennan announced publicly in Washington that the manned satellite program would be called "Project Mercury." [59]

132

VI

From Design into Development

(JANUARY–JUNE 1959)

F ROM dreams into definitions and from design into development, the idea for a manned satellite was growing toward fruition.   During the first half of 1959, the Space Task Group (STG) guided the translation of its conceptual designs into detailed developmental plans for the molding of hardware.   Creating an engineering program, planning precisely the flight missions, organizing men, money, and material to fulfill those missions, and establishing technical policy and managerial responsibility were the prime necessities of the moment.   But this year began with the realization of a Russian "dream," *Mechta*.

On January 2, 1959, the Soviets announced they had successfully launched a rocket toward the Moon, the final stage of which weighed 3245 pounds, including almost 800 pounds of payload instrumentation inside its spherical shell. The Soviet *Mechta*, also popularly called *Lunik I*, was the first man-made object to attain the 25,000-mile-per-hour speed needed to break away from Earth's gravitational field.   By comparison the United States Moon probe *Pioneer III*, launched by a four-stage Jupiter called Juno II on December 6, 1958, had weighed 13 pounds and attained a velocity of 24,000 miles per hour.   And though it missed its target, *Lunik I* flashed past Earth's natural satellite to become the first successful "deep space" (i.e., translunar) probe and the first man-made artifact to become a solar satellite.[1]

While *Mechta* presumably went into solar orbit, and even while many incredulous Americans refused to accept this impressive claim, NASA mobilized for the national effort to catch up with the Soviets in propulsion and guidance, and in progress toward manned space flight.   The project named Mercury embodied the latter half of those hopes.

Robert R. Gilruth and his STG associates at Langley, together with Abe Silverstein and others in Washington, plunged knowingly into one of the greatest engineering adventures of all time.   Somewhat self-conscious in the role of men of action setting out to do what had never been done before, they tried to match means to their ends without too much introspection and by avoiding useless

133

worries over comparative scores in the space race. Like all good engineers, they were also professors of efficiency. They committed themselves to do their unique task as effectively, economically, and quickly as possible. But the inexorable conflict between the novelty of the experiment and the experience with novelty that alone can lead to efficiency they had to accept as an occupational hazard. Two of their ideals—to perform orbital flight safely and to perform it with economy—were embodied in preliminary designs for Project Mercury long before those same ideals became obligations during the development of the program. Their third ideal—timeliness—gradually became crushed between performance and cost considerations.

In the hectic three months of planning and procurement from September 1958 to January 1959, the original "objectives and basic plan" for Project Mercury gradually clarified by abbreviation to an itemized list. Continued reiteration throughout preliminary development (January through June 1959) finally reduced the aims, attitudes, and means of the Space Task Group to a set of nominative formulas used again and again as "Slide No. 1" in briefings:

Objectives
1. Orbital flight and recovery
2. Man's capabilities in environment

Basic Principles
1. Simplest and most reliable approach
2. Minimum of new developments
3. Progressive build-up of tests

Method
1. Drag vehicle
2. ICBM booster
3. Retrorocket
4. Parachute descent
5. Escape system

Reduced to this form by July 1959, the basic doctrine for Project Mercury remained essentially unchanged throughout the entire life of the program. Although the managers of Mercury found this a source of considerable pride, they were forced to make certain departures from their basic principles and to refine their methods continually.[2] The techniques and technology for landing, for example, were not specified this early. The efforts to ensure a safe touchdown, on water instead of land, became a critical concern over a year later.

BRICKBAT PRIORITY

From the beginning STG had sought to obtain the Nation's highest priority for the manned satellite program. But the White House, Congress, and NASA Headquarters at first regarded as equally important the development of a "10^6," or one-million-pound-thrust, booster engine, and the elaboration of space sciences through the continuation of instrumented satellite programs similar to Vanguard. Hugh L. Dryden initiated a request to the Department of Defense as early as November 14, 1958, to put the "manned satellite and the one-million-pound-thrust engine" in the DOD Master Urgency List alongside the Minuteman and Polaris weapon systems. But the National Aeronautics and Space Council (NASC) had deferred this request on December 3, pending a scheduled meeting the next week of the Civilian-Military Liaison Committee (CMLC). The Space Council did recommend that NASA assign its highest in-house priority to Project Mercury. When it met, the Liaison Committee recommended the "DX," or highest industrial procurement priority, for the manned satellite. They assumed that the Vanguard and Jupiter-C projects would be dropped from that category and that the million-pound-thrust engine would be assigned the next lower, or a "DO," priority.[3]

New additions to the DX list required the approval of the National Security Council, but earlier that body had delegated authority to the Secretary of Defense to decide on top priorities for satellite systems. Secretary Neil H. McElroy and the Joint Chiefs of Staff received the Liaison Committee's recommendations for a new Master Urgency List on December 17. NASA Administrator T. Keith Glennan protested to William M. Holaday, the Pentagon's Director of Guided Missiles and chairman of the Liaison Committee, that not only Mercury but the big new booster, to become known in February as the Saturn, should have top priority. McElroy therefore directed Holaday to review the entire DX category before deciding what to do about the dual NASA requests for the so-called "brickbat," or highest, priority rating.[4] Here matters stood at the end of the year.

For these reasons, financial allowances for extensive (and expensive) overtime work and the authorization for preferential acquisition of scarce materials were delayed well into 1959. Maxime A. Faget's optimistic belief before the program started that a man might possibly be placed in orbit within 18 months, or during the second quarter of the calendar year 1960, depended upon the immediate assignment of the Nation's highest priority to Mercury—and an enormous amount of the best possible luck! One of the first official estimates of the launch schedule for STG, made by Christopher C. Kraft, Jr., in early December for the Air Force Missile Test Center at Cape Canaveral predicted concurrent development, qualification, and manned orbital flights from April through September in 1960.[5] This "guesstimate" was likewise predicated on an immediate Defense Department order to allow Project Mercury to compete "on a non-interference basis" with the military missile programs in obtaining critical "off-the-shelf" components, particularly electronic and guidance items.

By the first of the new year, it was fairly clear that the large Saturn booster would be continued by the Army's Wernher von Braun team and that the Defense Department was not about to release von Braun and his associates to NASA. Glennan, Dryden, and Silverstein had given Project Mercury the highest priority within NASA itself, but among industrial suppliers and the Defense Department it ranked second to several more urgent and competing demands.   By March 1959, definite evidence of equipment and material supply shortages accumulated.   The new prime contractor warned of delivery schedule slippages resulting from Mercury's DO rating.   Holaday's reports were favorable toward Mercury, and Glennan compromised on the "10⁶-engines."   For the Advanced Research Projects Agency (ARPA) had directed the Army Ordnance Missile Command and the Air Force Ballistic Missile Division, respectively, to start independent development of both a clustered first-stage booster (the Saturn) and a single-chamber rocket engine (the F–1) able to generate about 1,500,000 pounds of thrust.[6]

So NASA finally presented a united front with the Defense Department to the President and Congressional committees.   On April 27, 1959, Eisenhower himself approved the request for the "brickbat" procurement rating for Mercury. The prime contract and most of the major subcontracts for the space capsule had been let well before May 4, when Mercury was officially listed in the topmost category on the Master Urgency List.[7]   But the attendant privilege of not having to seek the lowest bidder on every major item bought was probably less important to the development of the program than the added prestige and support the DX rating brought to Mercury within the aerospace industry and among the military services.

During the first quarter of 1959, confusion reigned in Washington aerospace circles as too many missile czars, too many space projects, and too many agencies clamored for more funds and support.   But journalists, scientists, and humanitarians applauded the successes of the Navy-NASA *Vanguard II,* a tiny weather satellite; of the Air Force's *Discoverer I,* first satellite in polar orbit; and of the Army-NASA *Pioneer IV,* which managed to duplicate *Mechta*'s escape velocity.   As a deep-space probe and the first U.S. solar satellite, *Pioneer IV,* launched March 3, was magnificently instrumental in expanding man's knowledge of the plurality of the Van Allen radiation belts and of the "solar winds," or radiation storms, that permeate interplanetary space.   Glennan had resolved to identify all NASA booster rockets with the name "United States" only, but other rocket agencies within the government were unlikely to follow suit.   In the midst of all this, Project Mercury seemed still an obscure conception to the public.   Roy W. Johnson of ARPA called it "very screwball" when first proposed; by the end of March he said, "It looks a little less screwball now." [8]

Meanwhile, within STG itself, the most urgent task in getting on with the program had already been accomplished by the end of 1958.   On December 29 the Task Group had completed its technical assessments of the industrial proposals for manufacturing the capsule and its subsystems.   Eleven complete proposals had been received.   The narrowing of the field of possible manufacturers was facilitated by the fact that so many alternate configurations were submitted.   Faget had invited the bidders "to submit alternate capsule and configuration designs if you so desire, provided that you incorporate the retrorocket principle, the nonlifting principle and the non-ablating heat sink principle. You are not limited to this particular approach only." [9] But some of the bidders had taken him altogether too literally in this statement.

AWARDING THE PRIME CONTRACT

During the first week in January, another group of men, led by Carl Schreiber at NASA Headquarters, evaluated the procurement aspects of the competitive proposals. This Management, Cost, and Production Assessment Committee was required to rank only eight companies, because four had been disqualified on purely technical grounds. By January 6, four companies were reported to the Source Selection Board as having outstanding management capabilities for the prime contract. But in the final analysis Abe Silverstein and the six members of his board had to decide between only two firms with substantially equal technical and managerial excellence: Grumman Aircraft Engineering Corporation and McDonnell Aircraft Corporation. The NASA Administrator himself eventually explained the principal reason for the final choice:

> The reason for choosing McDonnell over Grumman was the fact that Grumman was heavily loaded with Navy projects in the conceptual stage. It did not appear wise to select Grumman in view of its relatively tight manpower situation at the time, particularly since that situation might be reflected in a slow start on the capsule project regardless of priority. Moreover, serious disruption in scheduling Navy work might occur if the higher priority capsule project were awarded to Grumman.[10]

NASA informed McDonnell on January 12 that it had been chosen the prime contractor for the Mercury spacecraft. Contract negotiations began immediately; after three more weeks of working out the legal and technical details, the stickiest of which was the fee, the corporation's founder and president, James S. McDonnell, Jr., signed on February 5, 1959, three originals of a contract.[11] This document provided for an estimated cost of $18,300,000 and a fee of $1,150,000. At the time, it was a small part of McDonnell's business and a modest outlay of government funds, but it officially set in motion what eventually became one of the largest technical mobilizations in American peacetime history. Some 4000 suppliers, including 596 direct subcontractors from 25 states and over 1500 second-tier subcontractors, soon came in to assist in the supply of parts for the capsule alone.[12]

The prime contract was incompletely entitled "Research and Development Contract for Designing and Furnishing Manned Satellite Capsule." The omission of an article before the word "manned" and the lack of the plural form for the word "capsule" prefigured what was to happen within the next five months. The original contract began evolving with the program, so that instead of 12 capsules of identical design, as first specified, 20 spacecraft, each individually designed for a specific mission and each only superficially like the others, were produced by McDonnell. Contract change proposals, or "CCPs," as they were

137

known, quickly grew into supplemental agreements that were to overshadow the[··] prime contract itself.[13]

The relative roles of STG and McDonnell engineers in pushing the state of the art from design into construction are difficult to assess. Cross-fertilization of ideas and, after the contract was awarded, almost organically close teamwork in implementing them characterized the STG-McDonnell relationship. For a year before the company's selection as prime contractor, original design studies had been carried on with company funds. From a group of 12 engineers led by Raymond A. Pepping, Albert Utsch, Lawrence M. Weeks, and John F. Yardley in January 1958, the Advanced Design section at McDonnell grew to about 40 people by the time the company submitted its proposal to NASA. The proposal itself stated that the company already had invested 32 man-years of effort in the design for a manned satellite, and the elaborate three-volume prospectus amply substantiated the claim.[14]

In STG's 50-page set of final "Specifications for a Manned Space Capsule," drawn up in November, Faget and associates had described in remarkable detail their expectations of what the capsule and some 15 subsystems should be like. Now the McDonnell production engineers set about expanding the preliminary specifications, filling gaps in the basic design, preparing blueprints and specification control drawings, and retooling their factory for the translation of ideas into tangible hardware. Specification S-6 had enjoined the contractor to provide at his plant as soon as possible a mockup, or full-scale model made of plywood and cardboard, of the capsule system. With high expectations the Task Group awaited March 17, the date by which McDonnell had promised to have ready their detailed specifications and a dummy Mercury capsule and escape tower.[15] But the debut was not to be achieved easily.

Before the company could finish building the mockup, at least two technical questions affecting the configuration had to be resolved: one was the type of heatshield to be used; the other was the exact design for the escape system. A third detail, the shape of the antenna canister and drogue chute housing atop the cylindrical afterbody, was also tentative when STG and McDonnell engineers began to work together officially on January 12, 1959.[16]

HEATSHIELD RESOLUTION

To begin with, all capsule proposals had been evaluated on the basis of a beryllium heat sink, but the search for an ablating heatshield continued concurrently. George M. Low reported the tentative resolution of this conflict in late January:

At a meeting held at Langley Field on January 16 (attended by Drs. Dryden and Silverstein), it was decided to negotiate with McDonnell to design the capsule so that it can be fitted with either a beryllium heat sink or an ablation heat shield. It was further decided that McDonnell should supply a specified number (of the order of eight) ablation shields and a specified number (of the order of six) beryllium heat sinks. It is anticipated that flights with both types of heat protection will be made . . . . In case of a recovery on land, the capsule with a beryllium heat sink will require cooling; this is accomplished by circulating air either between the heat sink and the pressure vessel, or by ventilating the pressure vessel after impact.[17]

Regarding the escape system, McDonnell's proposal had carefully weighed the relative merits of STG's pylon, or tower, type of tractor rocket with the alternative idea, which used three sets of dual-pod pusher rockets, similar to JATO bottles, along either side of three fins at the base of the capsule. McDonnell chose the latter system for its design proposal, but the STG idea prevailed through the contract negotiations, because the Redstone was calculated to become aerodynamically unstable with the pod-type escape system, and the Atlas would likely be damaged by jettisoning the pod fins.[18] The escape system for an aborted launch was intimately interrelated with the problems of the heatshield and of the normal, or nominal, landing plans. By mid-March Robert F. Thompson's detailed proposals for a water landing helped clarify the nature of the test programs to be conducted.

While McDonnell agreed to design the capsule so that it could be fitted alternatively with either a beryllium heat sink or an ablation heatshield, the prime contractor farmed the fabrication of these elements to three subcontractors: Brush Beryllium Company of Cleveland was to forge six heat-sink heatshields; General Electric Company and Cincinnati Testing and Research Laboratory (CTL) were to fabricate 12 ablation shields. The Space Task Group relied on Andre J. Meyer, Jr., to monitor this critical and sensitive problem, the solution to which would constitute the foremost technological secret in the specifications for the manned capsule.

Meyer, one of the original STG members from Lewis in Cleveland, had been commuting to Langley for 10 months. He soon discovered a bottleneck in the industrial availability of beryllium. Only two suppliers were found in this country; only one of these, Brush, had as yet successfully forged ingots of acceptable purity. But ablation technology was equally primitive, so plans had to be made on dual tracks. Meyer had had much experience with laminated plastics for aircraft structures. He had previously learned, in consultations with the Cincinnati Testing Laboratory, how to design a "shingle layup" for fabrication of an ablation heatshield. While collecting all available information on both the ablative plastic and the beryllium industries, Meyer listened to the Big Joe project engineers, Aleck C. Bond and Edison M. Fields. They argued for ablation, specifically for a fiber glass-phenolic material, as the primary heat protection for the astronaut. Before moving to Virginia in February, Meyer consulted on weekends with Brush Beryllium in Cleveland, watching its pioneering progress in forging ever larger spherical sections of the exotic metal, which is closely akin to the precious gem emerald. But Meyer, along with Bond and Fields, grew more skeptical of the elegant theoretical deductions that supported the case for beryllium. Mercury would have a shallow angle of entry and consequently a long heat duration and high total heat; they worried about the possibility that any heat sink might "pressure cook" the occupant of the capsule. So Meyer, using CTL's shingle concept, perfected his designs for an ablative shield.[19]

There was something basically appealing about the less tidy ablation principle, something related to a basic principle in physics, where the heat necessary to change the state (from solid to liquid to gas) of a material is vastly greater than the heat absorbed by that material in raising its temperature by degrees. Meyer became convinced by March that beryllium would be twice as expensive and only half as safe. Consequently, Meyer and Fields concentrated their efforts on proving their well-grounded intuition that ablation technology could be brought to a workable state before the Big Joe shot in early summer.[20]

While lively technical discussions over ablation versus heat sink continued through the spring, the fact that Mercury officials had committed Big Joe to the proof-testing of an ablative shield also rather effectively squelched any further attempts at scientific comparisons. Whereas in January Paul E. Purser recorded that "we will procure both ablation and beryllium shields . . . and neither will be 'backup,' they will be 'alternates,' " by the end of April technological difficulties in manufacturing the prototype ablation shields became so acute as to monopolize the attention of cognizant STG engineers.[21]

Glennan and Silverstein in Headquarters therefore directed continuation of the heat sink development as insurance, while STG gradually consigned the alternative beryllium shield to the role of substitute even before the fiber glass-phenolic shield had proved its worth. By mid-year of 1959, apparently only the Brush Beryllium Company still felt confident that the metallic heat sponge was a viable alternative to the glass heat vaporizer in protecting the man in space from the fate of a meteor. The complicated glass-cloth fabricating and curing problems for the ablation shield were mostly conquered by July. John H. Winter, the heatshield project coordinator at the Cincinnati Testing Laboratory, delivered his first ablation shield to NASA in Cleveland on June 22 under heavy guard.[22]

The critical question of whether to jettison the heatshield was active early in 1959. If the shield were a heat sink, it would be so hot by the time it reached the lower atmosphere that to retain it after the main parachute had deployed would be hazardous to the pilot. Also in case of a dry landing such a hot sponge could easily start a prairie or forest fire. On the other hand, a detachable shield would add complexity to the system and increase the risk of its loss before performing its reentry job. In one of the early airdrops a jettisoned shield actually went into "a falling leaf pattern after detachment. It glided back and collided with the capsule, presenting an obvious potential hazard for the pilot in his vehicle late in the reentry cycle." [23] This incident prompted the decision that the heatshield would be retained, although it might very well be lowered in the final moments of the flight if it could help attenuate impact. The memory of this early collision after jettisoning continued to haunt STG engineers until they rejected the beryllium heat-sink shield altogether.

Although the heatshield problem was highly debatable at the inception of the project, there was consolation in the fact that at least two major development areas were virtually complete. The two items considered frozen at the end of January 1959 were the external configuration of the capsule, except for the antenna section, and the form-fitting couch in which the astronaut would be able to endure a force of 20 g or more, if it should come to that.[24] The Space Task Group was pleased to have something as accomplished fact when so many other areas were still full of uncertainties.

To George Low's ninth weekly status report for Administrator Glennan on STG's progress and plans for Project Mercury was appended a tabular flight test schedule that summarized the program and mission planning as envisioned in mid-March 1959. Five Little Joe flights, eight Redstone, two Jupiter, ten Atlas flights, and two balloon ascents were scheduled, the categories overlapping each other from July 1959 through January 1961. The first manned ballistic suborbital flight was designated Mercury-Redstone flight No. 3, or simply "MR-3," to be launched about April 26, 1960. And the first manned orbital flight, designated Mercury-Atlas No. 7, or "MA-7," was targeted for September 1, 1960. After that, STG hoped to fly several more, progressively longer orbital missions, leading finally to 18 orbits or a full day for man in space. Although merely a possible flight test plan, this schedule set a superhuman pace and formed the basis for NASA's earliest expectations.[25]

APPLIED RESEARCH

By March 1, Langley Research Center was formally supporting the Task Group in conducting five major programs of experimentation. The first was an airdrop study, begun the previous summer, to determine the aerodynamic behavior of the capsule in free fall and under restraint by various kinds of parachute suspension. By early January more than a hundred drops of drums filled with concrete and of model capsules had produced a sizable amount of evidence regarding spacecraft motion in free falls, spiraling and tumbling downward, with and without canopied brakes, to impacts on both sea and land.[26] But what specific kind of a parachute system to employ for the final letdown remained a separate and debatable question.

A second group of experiments sought to prove the workability of the escape system designs in shots at Wallops Island. On March 11 the first "pad abort," a full-scale escape-rocket test, ended in a disappointing failure. After a promising liftoff the Recruit tractor-rocket, jerking the boilerplate spacecraft skyward, suddenly nosed over, made two complete loops, and plunged into the surf.

So disappointing was this test that for several weeks the fin-stabilized pod rocket escape system was almost reinstituted.[27] Three Langley engineers, chagrined by this threat to their work, conducted a full postmortem following the recovery of the capsule. They blamed the erratic behavior on a graphite liner that had blown out of one of the three exhaust nozzles. Willard S. Blanchard, Jr., Sherwood Hoffman, and James R. Raper, working frantically for a month, were able to perfect and prove out their design of the escape rocket nozzles by mid-April. At the same time they improved the pitch-rate of the system by deliberately misaligning the pylon about one inch off the capsule's centerline.[28]

The third applied research program was a series of exhaustive wind-tunnel investigations at Langley and at the Ames Research Center to fill in data on previously unknown values in blunt-body stability at various speeds, altitudes, and angles of attack. Model Mercury capsules of all sizes, including some smaller than .22 rifle bullets, were tested for static-stability lift, drag, and pitch in tunnels. Larger models were put into free flight to determine dynamic-stability characteristics. Vibration and flutter tests were conducted also in tunnels. The variable location of the center of gravity was of critical interest here, as was also the shifting meta-center of buoyancy.[29]

Using the thunderous forced-draft wind tunnels at Langley and Ames, aeronautical research engineers pored over schlieren photographs of shock waves, windstreams, boundary layers, and vortexes. Most of the NASA tunnel scientists had long been airplane men, committed to "streamlined" thinking. Now that H. Julian Allen's blunt-body concept was to be used to bring a man back from 100 miles up and travelling about five miles per second, both thought and facilities had to be redirected toward making Mercury safe and stable.

Albin O. Pearson was one such airplane-tunnel investigator who was forced to change his way of thinking and his tools by the ever higher mach number research program for Mercury. Pearson worked at Langley coordinating all aerodynamic stability tests for Mercury with blunt models at trans-, super-, and hypersonic speeds. While exhausting the local facilities for his transonic static stability studies, Pearson arranged for Dennis F. Hasson, Steve Brown, Kenneth C. Weston, and other Langley, STG, and McDonnell aerodynamicists to use various Air Force tunnels at the Arnold Engineering Development Center, in Tullahoma, Tennessee. Beginning on April 9, 1959, a number of Mercury models and escape configurations were tested in the 16-foot propulsion wind tunnel and 40-inch (mach 22 capability) "Hot Shot" facility at Tullahoma. During the next 16 months a total of 103 investigations utilizing 28 different test facilities were made in the wind-tunnel program.[30]

A fourth experiment program concerned specifically the problem of landing impact. Ideally touchdown should occur at a speed of no more than 30 feet per second, but how to ensure this and how to guard against impacts in directions other than vertical were exasperating problems. Landing-loads tests in hydrodynamics laboratories for the alternative water landing had only begun. The anticipated possibility of a ground impact, which would be far more serious, demanded shock absorbers far better than any yet devised. Although there was still no assurance that the astronaut inside a floating capsule could crawl out through the throat without its capsizing, this egress problem was less demanding at the moment than the need for some sort of crushable material to absorb the brunt of a landing on land.

Through April and May, McDonnell engineers fitted a series of four Yorkshire pigs into contour couches for impact landing tests of the crushable aluminum honeycomb energy-absorption system. These supine swine sustained acceleration peaks from 38 to 58 g before minor internal injuries were noted. The "pig drop" tests were quite impressive, both to McDonnell employees who left their desks and lathes to watch them and to STG engineers who studied the documentary movies. But, still more significant, seeing the pigs get up and walk away from their forced fall and stunning impact vastly increased the confidence of the newly chosen astronauts that they could do the same. The McDonnell report on these experiments concluded, "Since neither the acceleration rates nor shock pulse amplitudes applied to the specimens resulted in permanent or disabling damage, the honeycomb energy absorption system of these experiments is considered suitable for controlling the landing shock applied to the Mercury capsule pilot." [31]

Fifth, and finally, other parachute experiments for spacecraft descent were of major concern in the spring of 1959, because neither the drogue chute for stabilization nor the main landing parachute was yet qualified for its task in Project Mercury. Curiously, little research had been done on parachute behavior at extremely high altitudes. Around 70,000 feet, where the drogue chute was at first designed to open, and down to about 10,000 feet, where the main landing chute should deploy, tests had to be carried out to measure "snatch" forces, shock forces, and stability parameters. Some peculiar phenomena—called "squidding," "breathing," and "rebound" in the trade—were soon discovered about parachute behavior at high altitude and speed. In March, one bad failure of an extended-skirt cargo chute to open fully prompted a thorough review of the parachute development program. Specialists from the Air Force, Langley, McDonnell, and Radioplane, a division of the Northrop Corporation, met together in April and decided to abandon the extended-skirt chute in favor of a newly proved, yet so far highly reliable, 63-foot-diameter ringsail canopy. The size, deployment, and reliability of the drogue chute remained highly debatable while STG sought outside help to acquire other parachute test facilities.[32] The status of most other major capsule systems was still flexible enough to accommodate knowledge and experience gained through ongoing tests.

Two other major problems on which Langley also worked with STG, while NASA Headquarters planned the role and functions of the new center in Beltsville, concerned the formulation of final landing and recovery procedures and the establishment of a worldwide tracking network. Mercury planners had assumed from the beginning that the Navy could play a primary role in locating and retrieving the capsule and its occupant after touchdown. But a parallel assumption that existing military and International Geophysical Year tracking

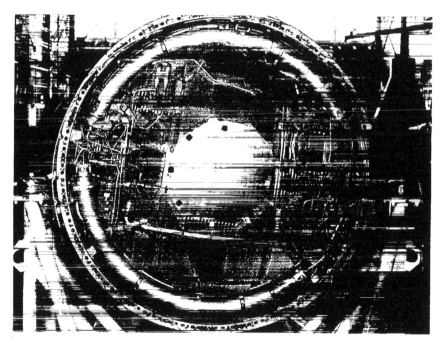

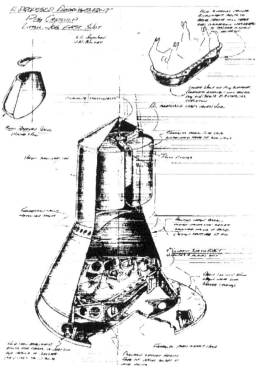

How to absorb the impact of landing without heavy weight penalties was a primary engineering problem. The solution: crushable aluminum honeycomb layered between the after pressure bulkhead and the heatshield (above); in the process of crushing, this material would absorb much of the shock of impact. The proof: pigs were dropped safely in a series of drop tests following the proposal in C. C. Johnson's sketch (left).

Parachute development and qualification was one of the areas that proved surprisingly time-consuming and troublesome, considering the long prior history of parachute use. The ring-sail parachute, shown at right in one of many test flights, was the type finally chosen to use as the capsule's main parachute.

and communications facilities could be utilized with relatively slight modifications had to be overhauled in the light of a more thorough analysis of Mercury requirements.

The Navy's experience with search and rescue operations at sea could be trusted to apply directly without much modification to retrieval of the Mercury capsule. But a multitude of safeguards had to be incorporated in the capsule to ensure its safety during and immediately after impact and to reduce the time required for recovery to a bare minimum. William C. Muhly, STG's shop planner and scheduler, was most worried about these recovery aids for the Big Joe tests.[33]

The most serious technical decision affecting the landing and recovery procedures concerned the feasibility of using an impact bag to cushion the sudden stop at the surface of Earth. Gilruth liked the idea of using a crushable honeycomb of metal foil between the shield and the pressure vessel to act as the primary shock absorber. But a pneumatic bag, perhaps a large inner tube or a torus made of fabric and extending below the capsule, either with or without the heatshield as its base, was still appealing. Associated with the recovery problem were innumerable other factors related to recovery operations. The seaworthiness of the capsule, its stability in a rough sea, the kinds of beacons and signaling devices to be used, and the provisions for the possibility of a dry landing were foremost among these worries.[34]

The second major area of uncertainty revealed in January 1959 came as something of a surprise to Task Group people. They had assumed that the world was fairly well covered with commercial, military, and scientific telecommunications networks that could be a basis for the Mercury tracking and communications grid. The Minitrack network established roughly north and south along the 75th meridian in the Western Hemisphere for Project Vanguard turned out to be practically inapplicable. On the other hand, the "Moonwatch" program and the optical tracking teams using Baker-Nunn cameras developed by the Smithsonian Institution Astrophysical Laboratory supplied invaluable data during 1958. Tracking of artificial satellites showed that all previous estimates of atmospheric density were on the low side.[35] Trajectory studies for equatorial orbits showed a remarkable lack of radio and cable installations along the projected track. Much depended upon the precise trajectory selections and orbital calculations for a Mercury-Atlas combination. New Atlas guidance equations that would convert the ballistic missile into an orbital launch vehicle had been assigned to the mathematicians of Space Technology Laboratories (STL) in Los Angeles. But whatever these turned out to be, it was becoming apparent that the world was far less well-wired around the middle and underside than had been thought. Furthermore the medical teams were insisting on continuous voice contact with the pilot. So by the end of February, Charles W. Mathews had convinced Abe Silverstein that STG should be relieved of the monumental tracking job, and NASA Headquarters drafted another contingent of Langley men to set up a brand-new communications girdle around the world.[36]

A large part of the Instrument Research Division at Langley, under the directorship of Hartley A. Soulé, provided the manpower. Soulé had previously laid out a timetable of 18 months for completion of a tracking network. Now he and the Langley Procurement Officer, Sherwood L. Butler, undertook to manage the design and procurement of material for its construction.[37] Ray W. Hooker accepted the supervision of the mechanical and architectural engineering, and G. Barry Graves began to direct the electronics engineering. By mid-March the problem of providing a tracking network for Mercury was on the shoulders of a special task unit that came to be known as the Tracking and Ground Instrumentation Unit, or by the barbarous acronym "TAGIU." Although by this time most of the other divisions at Langley were also acting partially in support of Mercury, the Tracking Unit held a special position in direct support of the Space Task Group. Indirectly it provided NASA with its first equatorial tracking web for all artificial satellites. Some 35 people in the unit went to work immediately on their biggest problem, described by Graves as "simply to decide what all had to be done." [38] By the end of April, Soulé had seen the imperative

146

The Rose Knot, *one of the two tracking ships used during Project Mercury, is pictured at Maryland Ship and Drydock, undergoing modifications and installation of new equipment. When completed, the ship would have a command transmitter as well as FPS-16 radar and other sophisticated tracking and electronic equipment. Below, activity in the communications support area of Goddard Space Flight Center just before a manned mission got underway. This was the relay point for all tracking network communications to and from the Mercury Control Center at Cape Canaveral.*

need for a high order of political as well as technical statesmanship to accomplish his task on time.   A detailed report to Silverstein outlined his operational plans.[39]

On March 17 and 18, 1959, at the McDonnell plant in St. Louis, the manufacturers presented to the Space Task Group for its review, inspection, and approval the first full-scale mockup of the complete Project Mercury manned satellite capsule.   This "Mockup Review Inspection" represented a rough dividing line between the design and development phases for the project.   The "Detail Specifications," 80 pages in length, provided a program for the customers.   Another McDonnell document provided a written description of the "crew station" procedures and capabilities.   And the mockup itself showed the configuration "exploded" into seven component parts: adapter ring, retrorocket package, heatshield bottom, pressure bulkhead, airframe, antenna canister, and escape rocket pylon.[40]

The chief designers, constructors, and managers of the program gathered around the capsule to watch demonstrations of pilot entry, pilot mobility, accessibility of controls, pylon removal, adapter separation, and pilot escape.   The board of inspection, chaired by Charles H. Zimmerman, then Chief of the Engineering and Contract Administration Division of STG, included Gilruth, Mathews, Faget, Low, Walter C. Williams, who was then still Chief of NASA's High Speed Flight Station, and E. M. Flesh, the engineering manager of Project Mercury for McDonnell.   In addition, eight official advisers of the board and 16 observers from various other interested groups attended the meeting.   The president of the corporation himself introduced his chief lieutenants: Logan T. MacMillan, company-wide project manager; John Yardley, chief project engineer; and Flesh. In consultation during the two days with some 40 McDonnell engineers, the Task Group recommended a total of 34 items for alteration or study.   Of these recommendations 25 were approved immediately by the board, and the rest were assigned to study groups.[41]

Among the significant changes approved at this meeting were the addition of a side escape hatch, window shades, steps or reinforced surfaces to be used as steps in climbing out of the throat of the capsule, and a camera for photographing the astronaut.   Robert A. Champine, a Langley test pilot who had ridden the centrifuge with Carter C. Collins and R. Flanagan Gray the previous summer to help prove the feasibility of the Faget couch concept, suggested more than 20 minor changes in instrumentation displays and the placement of switches, fuses, and other controls.   Also attending this mockup review were Brigadier General Don D. Flickinger; W. Randolph Lovelace II; Gordon Vaeth, the new representative of the Advanced Research Projects Agency; John P. Stapp, the Air Force physician who had proved that man could take deceleration impacts of up to 40 g; and a relatively obscure Marine test pilot from the Navy Bureau of Aeronautics by the name of John H. Glenn, Jr.

When they returned to Langley Field, Task Group officials were aware as never before of the magnitude of their tasks.   Conversations with more than 50

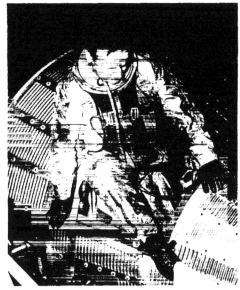

The Mockup Review Inspection in St. Louis, March 17–18, 1959, was a clear-cut intricacies of climbing out of the hatch of the Mercury mockup capsule (right). Faget, one of the principal conceptual engineers from STG, briefs on the concept (left), and Gilbert North, McDonnell test pilot, is suited up and demonstrating the intracacies of climbing out of the hatch of the Mercury mockup capsule (right).

McDonnell engineering group leaders had convinced them that more formal contract-monitoring arrangements were needed. Working committees and study groups had proliferated to such an extent that a capsule-coordination panel was needed. Gilruth appointed John H. Disher in mid-March to head the coordination temporarily. But by mid-June the panel was upgraded to an "office" and Disher was recalled to Washington by Silverstein to work with Low and Warren J. North.[42]

From a nucleus of 35 people assigned to STG in October 1958, the Group had grown to 150 by the end of January 1959. Six months later, in July, about 350 people were working in or with the Task Group, although some were still nominally attached to the research centers at Lewis or Langley.[43]

The rapid growth of STG, fully endorsed by Washington, was only one of the problems facing its management in the spring of 1959. Perhaps the most difficult lesson to learn in the first year of Project Mercury was the psychological reorientation required to meet new economic realities. Aeronautical research engineers who became administrators under NACA were still essentially group leaders of research teams. But when NACA became NASA and embarked on several large-scale development programs, those in development, and in STG in particular, became not primarily sellers of services but rather buyers of both services and products. To manage a development program required talents different from those required to manage a research program, if only because Government procurement policies and procedures are so complex as to necessitate corps of experts in supply and logistics. Senator Stuart Symington of Missouri, one of the knowledgeable observers watching the transition at this time, remarked, "The big difference between NACA and NASA is that NASA is a contracting agency." [44]

Costs and Cancellations

Trying to estimate what it should cost to develop hardware from their designs for a manned satellite, STG at first envisioned an expenditure of about $16 million to manufacture the program's spacecraft. But well before the contractor had been selected, Gilruth received a revised estimate based on new specifications, allowances for overtime, the fixed fee plus the estimated construction costs, and comparing capsule cost per pound with that of the X-15 and Dyna-Soar programs. George F. MacDougall, Jr., the aeronautical research scientist who signed this revised estimate, advised that the capsule costs should be raised to $22 million. Neither an economist nor a cost accountant, he did foresee the possibility "that the current estimated costs of $22,000,000 may be optimistically low." [45]

The contract negotiated with McDonnell had compromised between the company's bid of $17,583,717, which was far from the lowest, and the more liberal STG estimate, to settle on a price of $18,300,000 for manufacturing 12 capsules. In view of this compromise upward, NASA officials were unprepared for the sudden acceleration of costs that the contractor claimed was necessary for spare parts, ground support, and checkout equipment. Before the ink was dry on the prime contract, the scope of research and development work was found to have mushroomed. In March, when McDonnell advised NASA that spares and test equipment would more than double the total contract costs, Abe Silverstein applied counterpressure, saying indignantly, "I will not tolerate increases such as those above in the contract for any reasons—utterly unreasonable to increase an $18,000,000 contract to $41,000,000 by these devices." [46]

Meanwhile STG and McDonnell representatives held a meeting at the working level to consolidate and condense the requirements for spare parts and equipment. Savings effected here were eventually greatly overridden by costs arising elsewhere. No one could yet foresee that the basic contract for 12 spacecraft would have an evolutionary history of its own. [47] Cost accounting for a development program was recognized as a hazardous occupation, but just how hazardous and where to look for particular pitfalls took time to learn.

Whereas cynics might expect that the private-enterprise contractor for the capsule might have underbid to gain the contract, the civil servants in STG were more surprised to learn that the public enterprise of furnishing the Nation's ballistic missile defense systems should also have underestimated costs by approximately one third. Informed by the Air Force Ballistic Missile Division in January that each Atlas booster would cost $3.3 million instead of $2.5 million, George Low tried for two months to get a satisfactory explanation of this sudden inflation.[48]

When in May, however, the STG learned of an increase by $8 million in the amount the Army Ballistic Missile Agency proposed to charge for the Redstones and Jupiters, the time had come for a thoroughgoing review of cost effectiveness and program requirements. Gilruth and Purser learned by investigation that the Ballistic Missile Agency was billing NASA a "burden" surcharge for the benefit of laboratory overhead costs at Huntsville. Purser's considered reaction to this was to threaten cancellation of the Jupiter program. If NASA must pay for research and development at the Redstone Arsenal, he said, then NASA, and STG in particular, must be more frugal in the estimation of their needs.

The Jupiter rocket had been selected to boost a full-scale capsule to about 16,000 feet per second, a velocity midway between the capacities of Little Joe and Redstone (6000 feet per second), and of Atlas (25,000 feet per second). But rather than insist on this step, Purser argued that the Atlas should be harnessed to duplicate the mission of the Jupiter flights. Since "the cost now equals or exceeds the cost of an Atlas for the same mission" and the Jupiter system would not be a "true duplicate of the Mercury capsule system," Purser recommended that the two Jupiter shots be canceled.[49]

After further consideration and more negotiations, Purser's recommendation was adopted by NASA Headquarters; the Jupiter series was eliminated from the Mercury program. In the aftermath of this episode, Glennan made an official complaint to the Secretary of Defense about the necessity to curtail proposed launchings to control costs, describing the situation with some chagrin:

> Members of the staff who have visited Redstone Arsenal report that exceptionally high overhead rates apparently result from the necessity of supporting a large technical staff with a limited approved work program. The net result to us has been the increased costs of a Jupiter launching to more than that of an Atlas, whereas a Redstone launching is about $200,000 less than that of an Atlas. The prices being 2.7 and 2.9 million respectively.[50]

At the same time Mercury engineers who were looking for an alternative to the balloon flight program discovered that the altitude wind tunnel, the biggest physical installation at Lewis Research Center, could be used to simulate environmental conditions up to 80,000 feet. Therefore the balloon flight test program, primarily designed to "soak" the capsule at comparable altitudes, was in effect canceled by May. DeMarquis D. Wyatt and other NASA Headquarters staffers preparing the budget requests for fiscal year 1960 now had evidence of STG's cost consciousness. The cancellations of the Jupiter series and the balloon program greatly simplified the program buildup toward manned space flight. STG engineers were pleased by the resulting concentration of effort.[51]

One reason STG shed no tears over cancellation of Jupiter and the balloon tests was that the Little Joe program was making good progress. Blueprint work for the Little Joe airframe had begun early in 1959. North American had assigned A. L. Lawbaugh as project engineer; Langley Research Center had appointed Carl A. Sandahl as its representative for support of this test booster program; and William M. Bland, Jr., was managing Little Joe for the Space Task Group. Throughout the year 1959 these three men were primarily responsible for Little Joe.

Two significant design changes for Little Joe early in 1959 undoubtedly delayed the program slightly but contributed greatly to its eventual success. The first change, decided upon by Gilruth and Faget in January, required a switch from straight to canted nozzles on all the forward-thrusting rocket motors. Little Joe had no guidance system, and such a redesign would minimize any upset from unsymmetrical thrust conditions. The other departure from the original design was the addition of a so-called "booster destruct system." In the interest of range safety there should be some provision to terminate by command the thrust of the main motor units. Therefore Charles H. McFall and Samuel Sokol of Langley devised a booster blowout system, which North American and Thiokol Chemical Corporation, the manufacturers of the rocket motor components, added to the forward end of each rocket combustion chamber.[52]

By mid-February it was apparent that a development program for rocket hardware, even of such limited scope and relative simplicity as the Little Joe booster, demanded a far more sophisticated management organization than either Langley or the Task Group had envisioned. Although informal arrangements had sufficed to get the program started, funding allocations, personnel expansion, and contract monitoring problems began to weigh heavily. Carl Sandahl lamented in one weekly progress report that the transfer of Caldwell C. Johnson from Langley to the Space Task Group could "just about break up the Little Joe Project." Langley's loss was STG's gain in this respect, however, and cooperation continued to be encouraging. Indeed, in May, Bland reported that the delivery of the first Little Joe booster airframe could be expected approximately two weeks earlier than scheduled.[53]

Parallel to the development of the Little Joe test booster, STG and Langley engineers continued work on what now was called the Scout, the multistage, solid-propellant research rocket being designed since the previous year for sounding, probe, or small satellite missions. Langley had maintained its responsibility for designing the Scout for the Air Force after NACA became NASA; and early in 1959, Robert O. Piland and Joseph G. Thibodeaux came to work with William E. Stoney on the staging principles for the long, slim rocket. Although the Scout, as a Langley project, was not an integral part of STG's activities in Project Mercury, the Task Group held open the possibility of using this simple and relatively inexpensive rocket to launch scale models of the Mercury configuration and to probe for further critical data on heat transfer and stability. Thus the

Scout's capability could fill research gaps that might arise in the manned satellite project.[54]

Since January, when it had become apparent that the Army would not soon relinquish to NASA its rocket development team at Huntsville, NASA Headquarters had encouraged the Space Task Group to proceed full speed on personnel recruitment. The exact status of the organization and authority of STG was left unspecified, while Headquarters felt its way toward the establishment of the "space projects center" at Beltsville, just outside Washington. Although NASA had a "hunting license" as a result of its enabling legislation, STG's managers could not, without full support from President Eisenhower or Administrator Glennan, know how far or how hard to push the Space Task Group toward a permanent semi-autonomous establishment.[55]

STG's need for acquiring competent people without raiding established NASA research centers was met in large degree by a fortuitous accident that dramatized Anglo-European complaints about the "brain drain" of their scientific-technological manpower to the United States. A group of over 100 Canadian and British aeronautical engineers, who had been employed on a fighter-plane project for the British A. V. Roe (AVRO) Company near Toronto, Canada, were out of work. AVRO tried to find new jobs for them when the CF–105 Arrow project was canceled as a result of the Commonwealth's decision that the Bomarc missile made the Arrow obsolescent. Twenty-five of these engineers, led by James A. Chamberlin, a Canadian, were recruited by STG and immigrated to work at NASA's Virginia colony in mid-April. They were assigned jobs as individuals with the existing teams wherever each could be most useful, and they quickly proved themselves invaluable additions to making Mercury move.[56]

At the same time, the chief business administrator of the new NASA center at Beltsville, Michael J. Vaccaro, was planning to accommodate a complement of 425 people for fiscal year 1960 should Gilruth and his manned satellite team move to Maryland. On the first day of May 1959 the "space projects center," growing out of Naval Research Laboratory's Vanguard team, was renamed the Goddard Space Flight Center, and Gilruth's second hat, as the Center's Assistant Director for Manned Satellites, was reaffirmed. The Mercury program was specified as one of the six divisional offices at Goddard.[57]

While many questions of personnel, network management, and contract procedures for the capsule were still pending, Glennan made his first visit to the Space Task Group at Langley on May 18, 1959. He was impressed by the enormity of Project Mercury, by its working-level complexities, and by the extraordinarily fine morale in STG. Glennan returned to Washington resolved not to tamper with the esprit of STG. But he was also determined that NASA as a whole should not become a "space cadet" organization.[58] The Administrator's resolution that NASA must not be overwhelmed by the complexities of manned space flight led to a Headquarters policy of minimal interference with the Task Group. During the next year, however, the weight of pressure from

153

NASA Administrator T. Keith Glennan, right, arrives at Langley Field for his first visit to the Space Task Group. He is greeted by Robert R. Gilruth, left, Director of Space Task Group, and Floyd L. Thompson, Director of Langley Research Center.

the public press and the scope of intragovernmental coordination related to Mercury was to strain this policy.

Supporting Agencies and Industries

One of these complexities had been pointed up in the course of planning operational procedures for launching. Back in November 1958 the Air Force Missile Test Center had accepted Melvin N. Gough as director of NASA tests, but it was May 1959 before the Center made any allowance for the functioning of NASA's skeleton staff for the manned satellite program. When Herbert F. York, the Pentagon's Director of Defense Research and Engineering, testified before Congress early in June, he alluded to the coordination problem between the Department of Defense and NASA and admitted, "We haven't worked out exactly how to do that yet." B. Porter Brown, the first STG man to take up residence at the Cape, told his superior, Charles Mathews, that the administration of the launch complexes at the Atlantic Missile Range was as intricate as the technical equipment there.[59]

On May 1, 1959, when NASA set up its own liaison office at Canaveral, Brown and the STG were still trying to understand all the interrelationships existing between the Air Force (whose proprietorship stemmed from the establishment in 1950 of the Long Range Proving Ground), the Navy, and the Army. The Air Force Missile Test Center (AFMTC) was the steward operating the Atlantic Missile Range (AMR) for the Department of Defense. The Army had established its subsidiary Missile Firing Laboratory on the Cape as an integral part of its Ballistic Missile Agency. By the end of January 1959, Kurt H. Debus, director of the firing lab, had appointed a project engineer and coordinator for the Mercury-Redstone program, but the conversion of launch pads Nos. 5 and 6 into "Launch Complex No. 56" to meet the requirements for Mercury-Redstone launchings was less imperative than the need to prepare for the Fourth of July launch of Mercury's Big Joe by an Air Force Atlas.[60]

The palmetto-covered dunes at Canaveral had several dozen different kinds of launch pads, but they were still in short supply and under heavy demands. There were almost as many different military service and civilian contract organizations vying for them as there were pads. Proprietary interests were strongly vested, security restrictions were rigorous, and the newly constituted space agency was not yet accepted in the elite flight operations society there. Hangar S, in the industrial area of the Cape, had been tentatively assigned as "NASA space," but the former Naval Research Laboratory team that had built Hangar S and was still active with the Vanguard project was there first. Although now incorporated with NASA, the Vanguard team hoped to carry on with a new booster development program named Vega. Another group of half-NASA developers, the Jet Propulsion Laboratory, working with von Braun's people, were likewise seeking more room to convert Juno I (Jupiter-C) into Juno II (Jupiter IRBM) launch facilities for more Explorer satellite missions.[61]

With space for space (as opposed to defense) activities at such a premium, Porter Brown and his two advance-guard colleagues for STG at the Cape, Philip R. Maloney and Elmer H. Buller, pressed for a higher priority in Hangar S. But room was still scarce in early June when Scott H. Simpkinson with about 35 of his test operations engineers from Lewis Research Center arrived to set up a preflight checkout laboratory for Big Joe. They found a corner fourth of Hangar S roped off for their use, and instructions not to overstep these bounds.[62]

Another problem arose over the scheduled allocation of launch pad No. 14, which was one of only five available for Atlas launchings. Pad 14 was scheduled to be used for the Air Force MIDAS (Missile Defense Alarm Satellite) launchings throughout the same time period that the Mercury qualification flights were expected to be ready. Although admitting that firing schedules for both the Mercury-Redstone and the Mercury-Atlas programs were tentative, STG argued that the same pad assigned for the Big Joe shot should be continuously available for preparing all subsequent Mercury-Atlas launches.

The commander of the Air Force Missile Test Center disagreed. In the cause of maximum utilization of Cape facilities, Major General Donald N. Yates ordered switching of Mercury launches to various available launch stands. These initial conflicts of interests reached an impasse on June 24, when representatives of NASA and the Advanced Research Projects Agency of the Department of Defense met to decide whose shots to postpone. NASA was unable to obtain a concession: the urgency of ICBM and MIDAS development took precedence.[63]

The complexity of organizational problems at the Cape might have led space agency leaders to despair but for an auspicious space flight on May 28. On that date in 1959 an Army Jupiter intermediate range ballistic missile launched a nose cone carrying two primate passengers—Able, an American-born rhesus monkey, and Baker, a South American squirrel monkey—to a 300-mile altitude. At the end of 15 minutes and a 1500-mile trajectory, along which the cone reached a speed of about 10,000 miles an hour, the Navy recovered Able and Baker alive and healthy. The medical experiments were conducted by the Army Medical Service and the Army Ballistic Missile Agency with the cooperation of the Navy and Air Force Schools of Aviation Medicine. Not only was the flight a triumph for space medicine; it also demonstrated an organizational symbiosis of significant proportions for all of the services and branches involved.[64]

But the "interface" problems within NASA, and between NASA and other agencies, continued to exist, particularly at lower echelons in the planning of operational procedures for flight control. Mathews and his staff in the Flight Operations Division of STG were required to plan and replan mission profiles, schedules, countdown procedures, and mission directives while accommodating the procedures of other divisions and organizations contributing to the operation. By mid-spring these working relationships had become so involved that flight schedules had to undergo radical revision. It gradually became clear that the original schedules aimed at achieving a manned orbital flight early in April 1960 could not possibly be met.

On top of that, the production of spacecraft hardware and flight equipment began falling behind schedule. Only one month after the Mockup Review, it became evident that capsule and systems production slippages were going to become endemic. On April 17, 1959, Gilruth, speaking before the World Congress of Flight meeting at Las Vegas, announced casually, "The first manned orbital flight will not take place within the next two years." The first successful pad abort using the tower-rocket escape system had just been completed on April 12—two years to the day before Gagarin's orbital flight—but Gilruth cautiously refrained from pronouncing even the escape sequence firm. And he alluded to other areas of uncertainty:

> Although the Mercury concept is the simplest possible approach to manned flight in space, involving a minimum of new developments, as you can see, a great deal of research and development remains to be done. For flight within the atmosphere, the capsule must be stable over the widest speed range yet encountered by any vehicle—from satellite velocity to a very low impact speed. And in orbital flight, all of the systems must function properly in a weightless state. It must be compatible with the launch rocket and must be at home on the sea while awaiting recovery.[65]

156

In May 1959 the Mercury managers drew up a new functional organization chart dividing the supervisory activities of STG into five categories: capsules, boosters and launch, "R and D" support, range, and recovery operations. The design period for each of these areas having now evolved into developmental work, each area could more plainly be seen in terms of the contracts to be monitored by STG personnel. Capsules were divided into three categories, the first of which was the boilerplate models being built by Langley for the Little Joe program. For Big Joe, alias the Atlas ablation test, another boilerplate capsule was under construction jointly, with the STG at Langley responsible for the upper section and the STG at Lewis for the lower pressure-vessel section of the capsule. This meant that Langley in conjunction with Radioplane would perfect the recovery gear and parachute canister, while Lewis people would handle the automatic control system, the heatshield, sensors, and telemetry.[66]

For the production model capsule under McDonnell's aegis, a number of major subcontractors had long since been selected. Minneapolis-Honeywell Regulator Company was developing the automatic stabilization and control system; the reaction control system was being built by Bell Aerospace Corporation; some electronics and most radio gear were to be provided by Collins Radio Company; and the environmental control system, the periscope, and the horizon scanner were to be supplied by AiResearch, Perkin-Elmer Company, and Barnes Instrument Company, respectively. The alternative heatshields, as previously noted, were being provided by several different subcontractors; and the solid rockets for escape by Grand Central Rocket Company and for the retrothrust package by Thiokol Chemical Corporation.

With regard to boosters and launching, STG could rely on the extensive experience of the Ballistic Missile Division/Space Technology Laboratory/Convair complex for the Atlas, and on the Army Ballistic Missile Agency and the von Braun/Debus team for the Redstones. Only the Little Joe shots from Wallops Island would require extensive attention to launch problems because only Little Joe was exclusively a NASA booster. North American, the prime contractor, would provide whatever Langley could not for Little Joe.

Under the miscellaneous category "R and D support," however, Project Mercury would not only require the help of all the other NASA research centers—Langley, Ames, Lewis, and now Goddard—but also of the NASA stations for high-speed flight research at Edwards, California, and for pilotless aircraft research at Wallops Island, Virginia. At least 10 separate commands under the Air Force would be closely involved, and various facilities of the Navy Bureau of Aeronautics, especially the human centrifuge at Johnsville, Pennsylvania, would likewise be extensively used.

The range and tracking network requirements being supervised by the alter ego to STG, namely the Tracking Unit (TAGIU) or the Mercury network group at Langley, gradually became clear as contractors began to report on their feasibility and programming studies. The Lincoln Laboratory of the Massachusetts

The two major systems of Mercury flight hardware were of course the launch vehicle—the man-rated Atlas—being produced at General Dynamics/Astronautics plant in San Diego (left) and the Mercury spacecraft, being assembled at the McDonnell Aircraft Corporation plant in St. Louis (below).

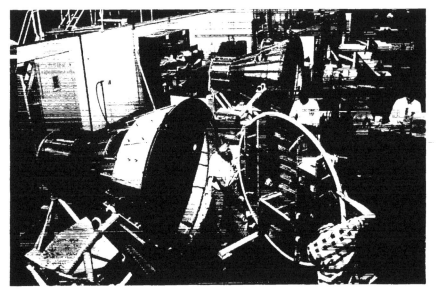

Institute of Technology, the Aeronutronics Division of the Ford Motor Company, Space Electronics Corporation, and the RCA Service Company held four study contracts to help Soulé decide on ground equipment, radar coverage, control center arrangements, and the exact specifications for various contracts. Although a preliminary bidders' briefing on the tracking, telemetry, and telecommunications plans for Project Mercury took place at Langley on April 1, the basic design document, "Specifications for Tracking and Ground Instrumentation System for Project Mercury," did not appear until May 21. Consequently NASA did not select the prime contractor for the tracking network until midsummer.[67]

Finally, regarding recovery operations, a NASA and Department of Defense working group decided on May 11 to make use of the investment already made by Grumman Aircraft Corporation in operations research for its spacecraft bid proposal on recovery requirements. Concurrently arrangements were being made with the Chief of Naval Operations, the Commander in Chief of the Atlantic Fleet, the Army Ballistic Missile Agency, the Strategic Air Command, the Atlantic Missile Range, the Marines, and the Coast Guard for the specific help each could render when the time should come for search and retrieval.

Although these relations appeared to have grown exceedingly complex, they had only just begun to multiply. Gilruth, however, was confident that by careful coordination and through the largely personal and informal working methods of STG, he and his men could handle the problems arising in the Mercury development program. As an encouraging example, the booster and launch coordination panels, established separately for the Atlas and the Redstone, had by mid-May already achieved impressive understandings on what had to be done. In the case of the Atlas, the coordination panel worked out the division of labor between NASA, McDonnell, the Ballistic Missile Division, Convair, and STG. Panel members simply discussed until they had resolved such key problems on their agenda as general launch operations procedures, trajectories and flight plans for the first two scheduled launches, general approach to an abort sensing system and procedures, range and pad safety procedures, general mechanical and electrical mating, blockhouse space requirements, general countdown and checkout procedures, and velocity cutoff in the event of overshooting the orbit insertion point. Six Redstone booster and launch panels, established at an important coordination meeting on February 11 with STG and McDonnell at Redstone Arsenal, likewise resolved in monthly meetings many such items.[68] For both boosters, many details remained outstanding, of course, but the fact that pending problems were being identified early and systematically in May 1959 gave the STG confidence that no further schedule slippages could be charged to the lack of intelligent planning.[69]

ASTRONAUT SELECTION

Now that the men had been chosen to serve as the focal points for all this effort, new spirits animated the Space Task Group. Indeed, the Nation as a whole began to participate vicariously in Project Mercury when, on April 9, 1959, at a press conference in Washington, Glennan introduced to the public the seven men chosen to be this Nation's nominees for the first human voyagers into space.[70]

They were to be called "astronauts," as the pioneers of ballooning had been called "aeronauts," and the legendary Greeks in search of the Golden Fleece were called "Argonauts," for they were to sail into a new, uncharted ocean. These personable pilots were introduced in civilian dress; many people in their audience forgot that they were volunteer test subjects and military officers. Their public comments did not class them with any elite intelligentsia. Rather they were a contingent of mature Americans, average in build and visage, family men all, college-educated as engineers, possessing excellent health, and professionally committed to flying advanced aircraft.

Compared with the average, white, middle-class American male, they enjoyed better health, both physically and psychologically, and they had far more experience among and above the clouds. Slightly short of average in stature, they were above average in seriousness of purpose. Otherwise these seven seemed almost random samples of average American manhood. Yet the names of Carpenter, Cooper, Glenn, Grissom, Schirra, Shepard, and Slayton were perhaps to become as familiar in American history as those of any actor, soldier, or athlete.

Despite the wishes of NASA Headquarters, and particularly of Dryden, Silverstein, and Gilruth, the fame of the astronauts quickly grew beyond all proportion to their current activities and their preflight mission assignments. Perhaps it was inevitable that the "crew-pool" members of STG were destined for premature adulation, what with the enormous public curiosity about them, the risk they would take in space flight, and their exotic training activities. But the power of commercial competition for publicity and the pressure for political prestige in the space race also whetted an insatiable public appetite for this new kind of celebrity. Walter T. Bonney, long a public information officer for NACA and now Glennan's adviser on these matters, foresaw the public and press attention, asked for an enlarged staff, and laid the guidelines for public affairs policy in close accord with that of other Government agencies.[71]

The astronauts were first and foremost test pilots, men accustomed to flying alone in the newest, most advanced, and most powerful vehicles this civilization had produced. They were talented specialists who loved to fly high-performance aircraft and who had survived the natural selection process in their profession. The demand for excellence in piloting skills, in physical health, and psychological adaptability becomes ever more stringent as one ascends the ladder toward the elite among military aviators, those senior test pilots with upwards of 1500 hours' total flying time.[72]

Eisenhower's decision that the military services could provide the pilots greatly simplified the astronaut selection procedure. From a total of 508 service records screened in January 1959 by Stanley C. White, Robert B. Voas, and William S. Augerson at the military personnel bureaus in Washington, 110 men were found to meet the minimum standards specified earlier. This list of names included five Marines, 47 Navy men, and 58 Air Force pilots. Several Army pilots' records had been screened earlier, but none was a graduate of a test pilot school. The selection process began while the possibility of manned Redstone flights late in 1959 still existed on paper.[73]

The evaluation committee at Headquarters, headed by the Assistant Director of STG, Charles J. Donlan, decided to divide the list of 110 arbitrarily into three groups and to issue invitations for the first group of 35 to come to Washington at the beginning of February for briefings and interviews. Donlan was pleased to learn from his staff, White, Voas, and Augerson, that 24 of the first group interviewed were happy with the prospects of participating in the Mercury program. Every one of the first 10 men interrogated on February 2 agreed to continue through the elimination process. The next week another group of possible pilot-candidates arrived in Washington. The high rate of volunteering made it unnecessary to extend the invitations to the third group. Justifying this action, George Low reported:

> During the briefings and interviews it became apparent that the final number of pilots should be smaller than the twelve originally planned for. The high rate of interest in the project indicates that few, if any, of the men will drop out during the training program. It would, therefore, not be fair to the men to carry along some who would not be able to participate in the flight program. Consequently, a recommendation has been made to name only six finalists.[74]

Sixty-nine men had reported to Washington in two groups by the middle of February. Of these, six were found to have grown too tall. Fifty-six test pilots took the initial battery of written tests, technical interviews, psychiatric interviews, and medical history reviews. Those who declined or were eliminated reduced the total at the beginning of March to 36 men. They were invited to undergo the extraordinary physical examinations planned for them at the Lovelace Clinic in Albuquerque. Thirty-two accepted and became candidates, knowing also that they were scheduled to pass through extreme mental and physical environmental tests at the Wright Air Development Center, in Dayton, Ohio, after being certified as physically qualified by the Lovelace Clinic. The 32 candidates were assured that the data derived from these special examinations in New Mexico and Ohio would not jeopardize their military careers, since none of the findings was to go into their service records.

Although the psychophysiological criteria for the selection of the best possible pilots for manned space flight had been under discussion for several years, the actual arrangement of the selection procedures for Mercury was directed by a NASA selection committee consisting of a senior management engineer, Donlan; a test pilot engineer, North; two flight surgeons, White and Augerson; two psychologists, Allen O. Gamble and Voas; and two psychiatrists, George E. Ruff and Edwin Z. Levy. These seven men had done the screening of records and the interviews and testing in Washington, constituting phases one and two of the selection program, before remanding their pool of 32 candidates to the medical examiners at the Lovelace Foundation.[75]

Individually each candidate arrived at Albuquerque to undergo approximately a week of medical evaluations under each of five different schedules. In this third phase of the program, over 30 different laboratory tests collected chemical, encephalographic, and cardiographic data. X-ray examinations thoroughly mapped each man's body. The ophthalmology section and the otolaryngology sections likewise learned almost everything about each candidate's eyes, and his ears, nose, and throat. Special physiological examinations included bicycle ergometer tests, a total-body radiation count, total-body water determination, and the specific gravity of the whole body. Heart specialists made complete cardiological examinations, and other clinicians worked out more complete medical histories on these men than probably had ever before been attempted on human beings. Nevertheless the selectees were so healthy that only one of the 32 was found to have a medical problem potentially serious enough to eliminate him from the subsequent tests at the Wright Aeromedical Laboratory.[76]

Phase four of the selection program was an amazingly elaborate set of environmental studies, physical endurance tests, anthropometric measurements, and psychiatric studies conducted at the Aeromedical Laboratory of the Wright Air Development Center. During March each of the 31 subjects spent another week experiencing a wide range of stressful conditions. Voas explained phases three and four: "While the purpose of the medical examinations at Lovelace Clinic had been to determine the general health status of the candidates, the purpose of the testing program at Wright Field was to determine the physical and psychological capability of the individual to respond effectively and appropriately to the various types of stresses associated with space missions." [77] In addition to pressure suit tests, acceleration tests, vibration tests, heat tests, and loud noise tests, each candidate had to prove his physical endurance on treadmills, tilt tables, with his feet in ice water, and by blowing up balloons until exhausted. Continuous psychiatric interviews, the necessity of living with two psychologists throughout the week, an extensive self-examination through a battery of 13 psychological tests for personality and motivation, and another dozen different tests on intellectual functions and special aptitudes—these were all part of the week of truth at Dayton.[78]

Two of the more interesting personality and motivation studies seemed like parlor games at first, until it became evident how profound an exercise in Socratic introspection was implied by conscientious answers to the test questions "Who am I?" and "Whom would you assign to the mission if you could not go yourself?" In the first case, by requiring the subject to write down 20 definitional identifications of himself, ranked in order of significance, and interpreted projectively, the psychologists elicited information on identity and perception of social roles. In the peer ratings, each candidate was asked which of the other members of the group of five accompanying him through this phase of the program he liked best, which one he would like to accompany him on a two-man mission, and whom he would substitute for himself. Candidates who had proceeded this far in the selection process all agreed with one who complained, "Nothing is sacred any more." [79]

Back at STG headquarters at Langley, late in March 1959, phase five began. The final evaluation of data was made by correlating clinical and statistical information from New Mexico and Ohio. Eighteen of the 31 candidates came recommended without medical reservations for final consideration by Donlan and North. According to Donlan, although the physicians, psychiatrists, psychologists, and physiologists had done their best to establish gradations, the attrition rate was too low. So the final criteria for selecting the candidates reverted to the technical qualifications of the men and the technical requirements of the program, as judged by Donlan, North, White, and finally Gilruth. "We looked for real men and valuable experience," said Donlan. The selection tests, as it turned out, were largely tests of tests, "conducted as much for the research value in trying to formulate the characteristics of astronauts as for determining any deficiencies of the group being examined." The verbal responses at the interviews, before and after the psychophysiological testing, therefore, seem to have been as important final determinants as the candidates' test scores.[80]

Sitting in judgment over 18 finalists, Donlan, White, and North pared down the final pool of selectees, choosing each to complement the rest of the group. The going was so difficult that they could not reach the magic number six, so Gilruth decided to recommend seven. Donlan then telephoned each of the seven individually to ask whether he was still willing to accept a position as a Mercury astronaut. Each one gladly volunteered again. The 24 who were passed over were notified and asked to reapply for reconsideration in some future program. Gilruth's endorsement of the final list was passed upward to Silverstein and Glennan for final review, and by mid-April the faces of America's original seven spacemen were shown to the world.

As the astronauts lost their private lives, Project Mercury found its first great public notice. An eighth military officer and pilot came aboard STG about the same time to manage the public information and press relations that were already threatening to intrude on the time and talent of STG. The eighth personality was an experienced Air Force pilot who had flown extensively in World War II, on the Berlin Airlift, and in Korea, and who also had proven himself as a public information officer after 1954, when he was charged with ameliorating public fears and complaints over jet noises, sonic booms, and the ballistic missile programs.[81] Lieutenant Colonel John A. Powers, USAF, came on board the STG staff in early April 1959. Thereafter the mellifluous voice and impish grin of "Shorty" Powers made his reputation as the primary buffer for STG in its relations with the press and the public. Throughout the Mercury program, he stood before the news media and the people of the world as the one living symbol of all the anonymous human effort behind the astronaut of the moment.

Powers propagated some oversimplified images in many instances, as it was his job to do, but no one man then or now could completely understand or communicate the complexity of the myriad research, development, and operations activities that lay behind a launch. Then, too, the caliber of the questions determined the quality of his answers, and all too often the questions asked were simple. What was an astronaut really like? What did he eat for breakfast? Which ones had been Boy Scouts? How did their wives take their commitment? Such questions provoked many to abandon asking how these seven came to be chosen and for what purpose they were entering training.

From the United States Marine Corps, Lieutenant Colonel John Herschel Glenn, Jr., received orders to report to the Space Task Group at Langley Field, on the first of May. He then found himself the senior astropilot in age and date of rank. From the Navy, Walter Marty Schirra, Jr., and Alan Bartlett Shepard, Jr., both lieutenant commanders, and Lieutenant Malcolm Scott Carpenter reported aboard STG. And the Air Force assigned three captains, Donald Kent Slayton, Leroy Gordon Cooper, Jr., and Virgil I. Grissom, to duty with NASA as test pilots, alias Mercury astronauts.

On May 28, 1959, the astronauts were brought before the House Committee on Science and Astronautics in executive session. They were asked to reassure the Congressmen that they were content with the orderliness, safety, and seriousness of Project Mercury. This they did vigorously, together and separately, before Schirra mentioned the "seven-sided coin" of competition over which one should get the first flight.[82]

The first seven American astronauts were an admirable group of individuals chosen to sit at the apex of a pyramid of human effort. In training to transcend

Project Mercury astronauts pose for an informal group portrait: From left to right, John H. Glenn, Jr.; Donald K. Slayton; M. Scott Carpenter, Jr.; Virgil I. Grissom; Walter M. Schirra, Jr.; Alan B. Shepard, Jr.; and L. Gordon Cooper, Jr.

gravity they became a team of personalities as well as a crew of pilots. They were lionized by laymen and adored by youth as heroes before their courage was truly tested. In volunteering to entrust their lives to Mercury's spirit and Atlas' strength to blaze a trail for man into the empyrean, they chose to lead by following the opportunity that chance, circumstance, technology, and history had prepared for them. Influential 20th-century philosophers as diverse as Bertrand Russell, Teilhard de Chardin, and Walter Kaufmann tell us that man's profoundest aspiration is to know himself and his universe and that life's deepest passion is a desire to become godlike. All men must balance their hubris with their humility, but, as one of those aspiring astronauts said, "How could anyone turn down a chance to be a part of something like this?" [83]

Shortly after the astronauts were introduced to the public, a literate layman asked directions of Mercury for mankind in general:

Which way will heaven be then?

Up?

Down?

Across?

Or far within? [84]

VII

Man-Rating the Machines

(JULY–DECEMBER 1959)

SADDLING ballistic missiles for manned space flight was in some respects like trying to ride Sinbad's roc: the bird was not built for a topside burden, and man was not meant for that sort of punishment. Once accepted in theory that this fabulous bird could be domesticated and that some men could tolerate, even enjoy, the strains and stresses of such a ride, practical questions of marrying the separate abilities of man and machine demanded immediate answers. Engineers in the Space Task Group and other NASA researchers at Langley, Lewis, and Ames were providing some of these answers; engineers and technicians in industry and in quasi-military organizations contributed equally important answers. The primary task of the Task Group managing Mercury was to ask the right questions and to insist on better answers from the industrial producers of the parts and from the academic, industrial, and military suppliers of services.

In the latter half of 1959, as STG monitored the gathering momentum of the various manufacturers, the urgent search for ways to reduce the ultimate risk of sending a man for a ride in an artificial moon lifted by a missile gradually became more systematic and better organized. The theme of this chapter is the quest for reliability in the automatic machinery developed for the Mercury mission. Making these devices safe enough for man took longer and exposed more doubts than STG had expected originally. During the curiously quiet first half of 1960, the flexibility of the Mercury astronaut complemented and speeded the symbiosis of man and missile, of astronaut and capsule. Technology, or hardware, and techniques, or procedures—sometimes called "software" by hardware engineers—both had to be developed. But because they were equally novel, reliability had to be built into the new tools before dexterity could be acquired in their use.[1]

At the beginning of 1959 NASA Headquarters had worried about three scientific unknowns needing resolution before actual attempts to conduct manned orbital flights. In their contribution to a House Committee Staff Report prognosticating for Congress on *The Next Ten Years in Space, 1959–1969,* Administrator T. Keith Glennan and the chief scientists at the helm of NASA in Washington listed these imperatives that must be investigated before man could go into space:

> The problems known to exist include (1) high-energy radiation, both primary and cosmic ray and the newer plasma type discovered in the IGY satellite series; (2) man's ability to withstand long periods of loneliness and strain while subjected to the strange environment of which weightlessness is the factor least evaluated; and (3) reentry into the atmosphere and safe landing. The reliability of the launching rocket must be increased before a manned capsule is used as a payload. Once these basic questions have been answered, then we can place a manned vehicle in orbit about the earth.[2]

By July 1959 the engineers in the Space Task Group were no longer concerned by the unknowns in each of these problematic areas. They had obviated the need for high-energy radiation shielding by selecting a circular orbit around the equatorial zone at an altitude between 80 and 120 miles, well above the stratosphere and well below the Van Allen belts. Loneliness would be no problem because the communications network would keep the astronaut in almost constant voice contact with ground crews. Weightlessness, to be sure, was the factor least evaluated, but by now this was the prime scientific variable that Project Mercury was designed to answer. The psychological outlook was good anyway, argued STG rhetorically, for does not everyone who has learned to swim enjoy the freedom and relatively "weightless" state when immersed in water? As to reentry, the strain of positive and negative acceleration forces had almost certainly been conquered; only a few questions remained unanswered about actual reentry and recovery stresses. Indeed, what Headquarters had left unnumbered in its presentation and therefore seemed to have regarded almost as an afterthought, the Task Group considered the paramount problem: the reliability of the rocket boosters must be increased before manned capsules could be attached to them.

The first major proof test of a critical part of the Mercury spacecraft design occurred on April 12, 1959. After a dismal failure a month before, the escape-tower rocket attached to a full-scale boilerplate model demonstrated its ability to lift both man and capsule away from a dangerous booster still on the ground. Giving first priority to providing an escape system in case of failure at launch was evidence of a pervading lack of confidence in the reliability of the big rockets. The men of the Space Task Group were not liquid-fuel propulsion experts; they had to rely on missile technicians and managers to convert weapon systems into launch vehicles for spacecraft. Since no one was expert in spacecraft engineering, STG had to rely on itself and on McDonnell Aircraft Corporation to gain as much experience as rapidly as possible with the capsule and its systems. This high adventure of learning how, specifically, to orbit a man safely was shared by a growing number of people supporting Project Mercury.

168

MERCURY TEAM TAKES SHAPE

Although Robert R. Gilruth's Space Task Group was growing rapidly, it remained small enough and intimate enough throughout 1959 to make everyone feel his worth. The creative engineering challenge of the project inspired an esprit that could be measured by the amount of voluntary overtime and vacation time relinquished by the members of STG. Gilruth's administrative assistant for staff services, 46-year-old Paul D. Taylor, died of a heart attack in May and was mourned by his colleagues as a martyr who overworked himself in the cause.[3]

According to its own estimates of present and future manpower requirements, the Task Group was hard pressed to meet all its commitments in mid-1959. At the beginning of the new fiscal year on July 1, NASA authorized the Task Group to hire another 100 persons, mostly recent college graduates. A total of 488 authorized positions was to be filled by the end of the calendar year. But STG argued that only one of its three major divisions at work on Mercury—Operations, under Charles W. Mathews—was fairly equal in numbers to the tasks at hand so far. The Flight Systems Division, under Maxime A. Faget, was called "greatly understaffed," and the Engineering and Contract Administration Division, now under the acting leadership of the Canadian James A. Chamberlin, was in "such urgent need" of more technical and administrative help that the Space Task Group requested 200 additional positions, to be filled within the next three months. Estimates of increased Langley and Lewis support activities for Project Mercury almost doubled this personnel request. The sheer size and immense scope of industrial and military personnel required to support Mercury stirred STG to a premonition of precarious control:

> In summary, a detailed study of staffing requirements for Project Mercury shows that the presently authorized complement of 388 should be increased by 330 positions during fiscal year 1960 in order to maintain the project schedules. This staff of 718 should be available by September of 1959, but orderly recruitment and integration of the additional staff would defer the filling of the complement until April of 1960. It is believed that everything practicable in the line of contracting on Project Mercury has been done without going to the extreme of effectively relinquishing control of the project. Failure to obtain the additional personnel shown must result in either major slippage of the schedule or in NASA effectively losing control of the project to the military or to industry.[4]

Because there was still no official commitment to manned space flight programs beyond Mercury and because hope was still high that manned orbital flight could be accomplished by the end of 1960, the Task Group accepted its temporary status and planned to phase out the people working on Project Mercury beginning in June 1961. Such plans were tentative, of course, and did not reckon with the technical and organizational problems that were to stretch out the program, nor with the astronautical and political events that were to change the course and expand the role of NASA's manned space flight efforts in 1961.

Nevertheless, by early August 1959, Gilruth was able to put his own field element of the Goddard Space Flight Center in much better order through a major reorganization.[5] His new title, Director of Project Mercury, was indicative of the expanded size and activity of the Task Group. The functions of "project manager" for engineering administration devolved upon Chamberlin, who also headed the new Capsule Coordination Committee. Addition of staff services and elaboration of branch and section working group leaders after August 3 made STG's organization charts much more detailed. But the block diagrams, while helpful to new recruits and to industrial visitors at the crowded old brick administration building at the eastern entrance to Langley Field, showed rather artificial separations of activity and authority within STG. The intimacy of the original group had suffered inevitable attrition as the result of an eightfold increase in size in less than a year, but the "inner circle" still operated personally rather than formally. Outside relationships, even those with Langley Research Center, on the other side of the airbase, were rapidly demanding more formality.

A partial solution to these problems, which in time grew to be one of the most important organizational decisions ever made for Project Mercury, was the informal agreement made in August 1959 between the Defense Department and NASA to select two men to act as "single points-of-contact." DOD appointed Major General Donald N. Yates, Commander of the Air Force Missile Test Center, to become in October its representative for military support activities for Project Mercury. The job of mobilizing and coordinating such diverse activities as Air Force prelaunch and launch support, Navy search and recovery operations, Army tracking and communications facilities, and joint service and bioastronautics resources demanded systematic, formal organization.[6] In turn, Hugh L. Dryden for NASA asked the chief of the High Speed Flight Station, Walter C. Williams, to join Gilruth to act as the contact point with Yates. Effective September 1, 1959, Williams and his colleagues Kenneth S. Kleinknecht and Martin A. Byrnes accepted transfers from NASA's High Speed Flight Station—shortly to be renamed the NASA Flight Research Center—to the Space Task Group. Having pioneered since 1945 in airborne launches of rocket research aircraft, Williams was a senior convert to the vertical ground launch cause of Mercury. Faget especially welcomed him. A personable and forceful leader, Williams took a position on a level with Charles J. Donlan. Each was an associate director for Project Mercury, Williams specializing in operations and Donlan in development. Williams had guided the NACA–NASA role in the flight operations of the X–15 rocket plane to a point just two days short of its first powered flight, on September 17, with North American Aviation's test pilot A. Scott Crossfield at the controls. When Williams, Kleinknecht, and Byrnes took up the higher national priority and professional challenge of working with spacecraft rather than aircraft, they brought to STG valuable operational and development experience with the highest-performance manned flight vehicles then in existence.[7]

Although there was pressure to get on with operations planning, engineering the Mercury capsule was still the primary task during these days. McDonnell and STG had swapped permanent field representatives during the spring in the persons of Frank G. Morgan and Wilbur H. Gray. Morgan came to live in a motel at Langley. Gray found a residence in St. Louis near the north side of Lambert Field, where the McDonnell plant was spread around the perimeter of the municipal airport. Though their technical liaison work was heavy, Morgan and Gray acted as hosts and guides as much as consultants, because visits by exchange delegations of engineers were so frequent. Just as the coordination of these meetings and trips for the development of the capsule became imperative among the aircraft and spacecraft designers and developers, so were closer, more orderly relations required with the developers of the ballistic missile boosters. Aerospace engineers often used one word to express the adaptation of systems, modules, organizations, and even technologies to one another: that word was "interface"; it connoted problems of integration, convergence, and synthesis of indeterminate magnitude.

Converging Technologies

The problem of man-rating the Redstone rocket was tackled with characteristic gusto by Joachim P. Kuettner, the man Wernher von Braun had called in 1958 to lead the Army's effort if Project Adam had been authorized. Kuettner had earned doctorates in law, physics, and meteorology before he became a flight engineer and test pilot for Messerschmitt during the Third Reich. Having been one of the first to test a manned version of the V–1 in 1944, Kuettner had made further use of his avocation as a jet aircraft and sailplane pilot for the U.S. Air Force Cambridge Research Center before joining the Army Ballistic Missile Agency (ABMA) at Huntsville.

In retrospect Kuettner has generalized about the problem of "Man-Rating Space Carrier Vehicles" in terms relating his experience with both aviation and missile technologies:

> While it is admittedly an oversimplification, the difference between the two technologies may be stated in the following general terms. From an aviation standpoint, man is not only the subject of transportation, and as such in need of protection as a passenger; but he is also a most important integral part of the machine over which he truly has control. His decisions in expected and unexpected situations are probably the greatest contributions to his own safety. Aviation, to the best of our knowledge, has never seen the necessity for a fully automatic initiation of emergency escape.
>
> In contrast, rocket technology has been for 20 years a missile technology governed by the requirements of target accuracy and maximum range. As such, it had to develop automatic controls. Unlike a human payload, a warhead has no use except on the target. Once the missile fails, it may as well destroy itself during flight. (For this reason, missilery has accepted aerodynamically unstable vehicles which, in case of loss of thrust, flip over and break apart,

destroying themselves in the air.) There has been no need to save the pay-load after a successful flight or in case of a catastrophe.

The development of manned space flight is not just a matter of replacing a warhead by a manned cabin. Suddenly, a switch is thrown between two parallel tracks, those of missile technology and those of aviation technology, and an attempt is made to move the precious human payload from one track to the other. As in all last-minute switchings, one has to be careful to assure that no derailment takes place.[8]

In the spring of 1959, while Kuettner was still signing himself the "Adam-NASA Project Engineer," he and his deputy, Earl M. Butler, began a series of triangular conferences, with Kurt H. Debus and Emil P. Bertram of ABMA's Missile Firing Laboratory at the Cape, in one corner, and Charles Mathews and Jerome B. Hammack, the Mercury-Redstone project engineer for STG, in the Langley corner. Between these informal discussions and six formal study panels inaugurated by von Braun, a consensus was supposed to arise on, among other things, the sort of emergency detection system necessary to warn of impending cataclysms in the booster and to trigger some sort of automatic ejection. Preliminary agreements on a design for an abort or safety system began early in good accord. But the uncertain reliability program, booster recovery proposal, capsule design changes, and electrical interface problems fouled the subsequent development of the Redstone abort-sensing system.[9] In this respect the Atlas was more nearly ready than the Redstone by the end of the year.

Many factors contributed to the slippage in the Mercury-Redstone schedule, but one significant cause for delay grew out of a subtle difference between ABMA and STG in their approach to pilot safety and reliability. The role of the astronaut was clearly at issue here longer than anywhere else. Conditioned by their designs for Project Adam, the Huntsville rocketmen thought of the astronaut throughout 1959 as merely an "occupant" or "passenger." The Adam proposal for an escape system during off-the-pad aborts would have ejected a biopack capsule laterally into a tank of water alongside the launch pad. Having less trust than STG in the reliability of "Old Reliable," the Redstone engineers insisted on putting safety first and making it fully automatic wherever possible. Reliability, they insisted, is only a concept and should be secondary to safety. This attitude was illustrated in the introductory paragraphs of the ABMA proposal for the Redstone emergency detection system. The author, Fred W. Brandner, began by saying that the use of missiles for transporting man would demand an automatic escape system to assure pilot safety:

> This system has to rely on emergency sensors. There are an enormous number of missile components which may conceivably fail. Obviously, it would be impractical and actually unsafe to clutter up the missile with emergency sensors. However, many malfunctions will lead to identical results, and, in sensing these results and selecting the proper quantities, one can reduce the number of sensors to a few basic types.[10]

172

The Mercury astronauts received their first detailed briefing on the Redstone booster at the Army Ballistic Missile Agency, Huntsville, Ala., in June 1959. Facing the briefer, Joachim P. Kuettner, the Mercury-Redstone project engineer under von Braun, are: left to right, Glenn, Shepard, Schirra, Carpenter, Slayton, Grissom, and Cooper. Kuettner touches the fin-stabilized Redstone model, explaining the purpose and construction of the carbon jet vanes barely visible below the single engine nozzle.

Brandner proposed to measure only three basic quantities: the control system attitude and angular velocity, the 60-volt control and 28-volt general electrical power supplies, and the chamber pressure of the propulsion system. To ensure "a high degree of passenger (pilot) safety" on the Mercury-Redstone rocket, if operational limits set on these sensors should ever be exceeded the capsule would eject from the booster and be lowered by parachute.

Brandner's modest proposal stated the issue but not the solution to the general question of man-machine relationships in Project Mercury. In 1959 the technical debate was still inextricably mixed up with previous attitudes toward the precise role of man in a manned satellite. Could the pilot test the vehicle or should the vehicle test the pilot? Mercury was NASA's program and STG's responsibility, but at this stage of development the military establishment and missile industries still knew, or thought they knew, more about the technological path for man's first climb into space than NASA–STG did.[11]

From the Pentagon, for example, Brigadier General Homer A. Boushey, Director of Advanced Technology for the Air Force, had predicted in January that the most important key to space flight in the next decade would be not simply manned but rather piloted spacecraft:

> By piloted spacecraft, I refer to a vehicle wherein the pilot operates controls and directs the vehicle. This is quite a different concept from the so-called man-in-space proposal which merely takes a human "along for the ride" to permit observation of his reactions and assess his capabilities. The high-speed flight experience of the NACA and the Air Force has shown that piloted craft return research data more effectively and more economically than do unmanned vehicles. While there is a place, certainly, for automatic, instrumented vehicles, I believe man himself will prove "the essential payload" to the full utilization of space. Orbital rendezvous, controlled landing after reentry, and space missions other than the simplest sensing and reporting type, will require man. If for no other reason than that of reliability, man will more than pay his way.[12]

Boushey's percipient remarks illustrated the persistent residue of misunderstanding remaining from interagency competition for the manned satellite project in the pre-NASA, pre-Mercury period. Task Group officials felt compelled to defend the distinctive nature of Mercury and to emphasize that NASA astronauts were never intended to be passive passengers. Rather, they were to prove their full potential as pilots, within limits prescribed by the mission requirements programmed into the automatic systems. Although there were long and hard arguments within STG as to whether man should be considered "in the loop" or "out of the loop" in performing various tasks, the preponderance of NACA-bred aeronautical engineers in STG usually voted for as active an astronaut as possible.

Outside pressures from scientists and missile engineers also helped unify and consolidate opinion within STG. The distinguished research chief of Bell Telephone Laboratories and one of the fathers of communication satellites, John R. Pierce, summed up the argument for automation: "All we need to louse things up completely is a skilled space pilot with his hands itching for the controls."[13]

The problem of man-rating the Atlas was preoccupying another task force of still larger proportions than the one concerned with the Redstone. The industrial and military engineers in southern California and at the Cape who were trying to make the Atlas meet its design specifications could and did mobilize more resources than either STG or ABMA could command. A few individuals stood out as leaders in the vast effort. Kuettner's counterpart for the Air Force was Bernhard A. Hohmann, another former test pilot at Peenemuende West, who had been project engineer on the first two models of the Messerschmitt–163, one of the first rocket-powered aircraft. In August 1959, Major General Osmond J. Ritland of the Air Force Ballistic Missile Division (BMD) assigned him the job of supervising the systems engineering at Space Technology Laboratories (STL) for a pilot safety and reliability program on the Mercury-Atlas series. As Brandner did for the Redstone, D. Richard White, an STL electronics engineer, made the preliminary designs for the Atlas emergency detection system. White was inspired, he said, "one Sunday in May when I imagined myself sitting atop that bird." Edward B. Doll, STL's Atlas project manager, could never imagine anyone foolish enough to sit on an Atlas, but he allowed Hohmann and White to proceed with their commitments.[14] STL performed an overall technical direction over the associate contractors for the Atlas similar to that performed by STG for NASA, but with significant differences. STL had not been involved in the original MX–774 design behind the Atlas, and although it became closely associated with conceptual development of Atlas as a weapon, ultimate responsibility remained with the Air Force Ballistic Missile Division. Both STL and STG were systems engineering organizations, but STG had a deeper background in research and was directly responsible for the development of the project it managed; STL had broader experience in systems engineering, missile development, and business management.

Hohmann and his assistant, Ernst R. Letsch, huddled closely with the reliability statisticians at STL, led by Harry R. Powell, and with BMD's Mercury project liaison officer, Lieutenant Colonel Robert H. Brundin, also appointed by Ritland in August 1959. But the main responsibility for detail design, development, and production work fell on the shoulders of the manufacturers, General Dynamics (formerly Convair)/Astronautics (GD/A or CV/A) of San Diego. The details, tooling, and implementation of the emergency detection or abort sensing system for the Atlas were guided by Charles E. Wilson, Tom E. Heinsheimer, and Frank Wendzel. Their boss, Philip E. Culbertson, the Mercury project manager for General Dynamics/Astronautics, conferred repeatedly and sometimes heatedly with Hohmann, Brundin, Doll, and his own factory production engineers, John Hopman, Gus Grossaint, Frank B. Kemper, and R. W. Keehn.[15]

Here, too, a triangular dialogue was going on during initial considerations for man-rating the Atlas. But STG engineers were far away, busy with other matters, and knew well how little they knew about the Atlas. NASA and the Air Force, like STG and the Army, informally had agreed to divide developmental responsibility and labor at the capsule-separation point in the trajectory. So STG was not directly involved in the tripartite workings of the so-called "BMD–STL–GD/A complex" in southern California.

Looking at Project Mercury from the West Coast in 1959 gave a set of very different perspectives on the prospects for accomplishing the program on time and in style. South of Los Angeles International Airport there was no consensus and precious little communication of the confidence felt across the continent on the coast of Virginia. But STL, Convair, and Air Force representatives at the Cape gradually diffused some of the contagious enthusiasm of STG while commuting between home and field operations. More important still, the sense of desperate military urgency to develop an operational ICBM still pervaded the factories and offices devoted to the Atlas in southern California. Motivation already mobilized might easily be transferred if only the Atlas could be proved by the end of the year. STG was more sanguine about this forthcoming proof than the Atlas people, and NASA Headquarters seemed even more optimistic.

Perhaps symbolic of the profound Air Force distrust of the "bare Atlas" approach and indicative of lingering doubts about the competence of the STG neophytes who had stolen the march on man in space was the acronymic name imposed by Air Force officers on the abort sensing system. White and Wilson wanted to call it simply the Atlas "abort sensing system." No, someone in authority insisted, let's make the name more appropriate to STG's plans to use the Atlas "as is." [16] So this play on words, "*Abort Sensing and Implementation System*," became the designator for the only part of the Atlas created solely for the purpose of man-rating that missile. Reliability was truly designed into the "ASIS"; once this component was proven and installed, the Atlas ICBM should, it was hoped, be electromechanically transformed into the Mercury-Atlas launch vehicle.

H. Julian Allen, Ames Research Center aerodynamicist who pioneered in hypersonic wind tunnel development and provided the concept of blunt reentry bodies, which was a major contribution to ballistic missile nose-cone technology and to the Mercury capsule, briefs a delegation from the National Aeronautics and Space Council visiting Ames on August 3, 1959. Visitors are, left to right, John T. Rettaliata, Alan T. Waterman, Executive Secretary Franklyn W. Phillips, William A. M. Burden, NASA Administrator T. Keith Glennan, and Center Director Smith DeFrance.

176

Astronaut Donald K. Slayton defended his prospective role and STG's stance on the issue of automation when he addressed his brethren in the Society of Experimental Test Pilots on October 9. By his own admission, these were some "stubborn, frank" words:

First, I would like to establish the requirement for the pilot. . . . Objections to the pilot range from the engineer, who semi-seriously notes that all problems of Mercury would be tremendously simplified if we didn't have to worry about the bloody astronaut, to the military man who wonders whether a college-trained chimpanzee or the village idiot might not do as well in space as an experienced test pilot. The latter is associating Mercury with the Air Force MISS or Army Adam programs which were essentially man in a barrel approaches. The answer to the engineer is obvious and simple. If you eliminate the astronaut, you can see man has no place in space. This answer doesn't satisfy the military skeptic, however, since he is not questioning the concept of a man in space but rather what type man. I hate to hear anyone contend that present day pilots have no place in the space age and that non-pilots can perform the space mission effectively. If this were true, the aircraft driver could count himself among the dinosaurs not too many years hence.

                    *   *   *

Not only a pilot, but a highly trained experimental test pilot is desirable . . . as in any scientific endeavor the individual who can collect maximum valid data in minimum time under adverse circumstances is highly desirable. The one group of men highly trained and experienced in operating, observing, and analyzing airborne vehicles is the body of experimental test pilots represented here today. Selection of any one for initial space flights who is not qualified to be a member of this organization would be equivalent to selecting a new flying school graduate for the first flight on the B-70, as an example. Too much is involved and the expense is too great.[17]

Slayton's defense of Mercury before his professional colleagues outside NASA was echoed time and again in the next two years by NASA spokesmen. But many critics remained skeptical because it was obvious that Mercury was being designed to fly first without man. Flight controllers and electronics engineers who had specialized in ground control of supersonic interceptors and who had confidence in the reliability of remote control of automatic weapon systems were the least enthusiastic about allowing the pilots to have manual overrides. Christopher C. Kraft, Jr., the chief flight director for STG, preceded Slayton on the same program at the meeting of the experimental test pilots. He reviewed the range network to be provided and the operational plan to be used for the Mercury orbital mission. At that time, Kraft circumspectly avoided any public indication of his personal views on the role the astronaut would play, but years later he confessed his bias:

The real knowledge of Mercury lies in the change of the basic philosophy of the program. At the beginning, the capabilities of Man were not known, so the systems had to be designed to function automatically. But with the addition of Man to the loop, this philosophy changed 180 degrees since primary success of the mission depended on man backing up automatic equipment that could fail.[13]

In public, the managers of NASA and of Mercury, who had to request funds and justify their actions before Congress and the people, appeared as optimistic as possible and pointed out what could be achieved with successful missions. Privately, they not only had doubts, they cultivated a group of professional pessimists whose job it was to consider every conceivable malevolent contingency. John P. Mayer, Carl R. Huss, and Howard W. Tindall, Jr., first led STG's Mission Analysis Branch and set a precedent for spending ten times as much effort on planning for abnormal missions as for normal ones.[19]

Although not always obvious to STG, there also were differences in attitudes within the space medicine fraternity. Since mid-1958, men like Siegfried J. Gerathewohl and George R. Steinkamp had led the school of thought that believed that man was more nearly machine-rated than machines were man-rated. Conversely, the chief of the space medicine division of the Air Force's School of Aviation Medicine, Colonel Paul A. Campbell, influentially asserted his belief that "in these past two or three years the situation has suddenly changed, and the machine capability has advanced far beyond man's capability."[20] Other biologists and medical college specialists also had doubts about the peculiar combination of stresses—from high to zero to high g loads—that the man in Mercury must endure. Whatever the majority medical opinion might have been, the Task Group felt itself beleaguered by bioastronautical specialists who wanted to "animal-rate" the space flight machines all the way from amoebas through primates before risking a man's life in orbit.

APPROACHES TO RELIABILITY

"Reliability" was a slippery word, connoting more than it denoted. Yet as an engineering concept it had basic utility and a recognized place in both aviation and missile technology. The quest for some means of predicting failures and thereby raising the odds toward success began modestly as a conscious effort among STG and McDonnell engineers only in mid-1959, after design and development work on major systems was well under way. Other engineering groups working in support of Project Mercury also began rather late to take special care to stimulate quality control and formal reliability programs for booster and capsule systems. Mercury would never have been undertaken in the first place if the general "state-of-the-art" had not been considered ready, but mathematical analyses of the word "reliability" both clarified its operational meaning and stirred resistance to the statistical approach to quality control.

The fifties had witnessed a remarkable growth in the application of statistical quality control to ensure the reliability of weapon systems and automatic machinery. The science of operations analysis and the art of quality management had emerged by the end of the decade as special vocations. Administrator Glennan himself, as president of Case Institute of Technology, had encouraged the development over the decade of one of the nation's foremost centers for operations research at Case.[21]   STG executive engineers studied an almost pedestrian example of these new methods for more scientific management of efficiency; it was one given by an automobile executive who compared the reliability of his corporation's product over 32 years before 1959:

> If the parts going into the 1959 car were of the same quality level as those that went into the 1927 car, chances would be even that the current model would not run.
>
> This does not mean that the 1927 car was no good. On the contrary, its quality was excellent for that time. But it was a relatively simple product, containing only 232 critical parts. The 1959 car has 688 such parts. The more the critical parts, the higher the quality level of each individual part must be if the end product is to be reliable.[22]

In view of the fact that estimates showed over 40,000 critical parts in the Atlas and 40,000 more in the capsule, the awesome scale and scope of a reliability program for Mercury made it difficult to decide where to begin.

To organize engineering design information and data on component performance, someone had first to classify, name, or define the "critical parts."   To create interrelated systems and to analyze them as separate entities at the same time was difficult.   The Space Task Group and McDonnell worked on creation at the expense of analysis through 1959.   Gradually NASA Headquarters and Air Force systems engineers steered attention to certain "semantic" problems in the primitive concepts being used for reliability analyses. For instance, what constitutes a "system"?   How should one define "failure"?   What indices or coefficients best "measure" overall system performance from subsystem data? [23]

These and other features of reliability prediction were so distasteful to creative engineers that many seriously questioned the validity and even the reliability of reliability predictions. "Reliability engineering," admitted one apologist in this field, "may seem to be more mysticism and black art than it is down-to-earth engineering. In particular, many engineers look on reliability prediction as a kind of space-age astrology in which failure rate tables have been substituted for the zodiac." [24]   Around STG this skeptical attitude was fairly representative. But at NASA Headquarters, Richard E. Horner, newly arrived in June 1959 as Associate Administrator and third man in command, had brought in a small staff of mathematicians and statisticians.   It was led by Nicholas E. Golovin, who transferred from the Air Force to NASA some of the mathematical techniques lending quantitative support to demands for qualitative assurance.   Theory-in-Washington versus practice-at-Langley were in conflict for a year until the nature of "reliability" for pilot safety on the one hand and for mission success on the other became more clearly understood by both parties.   The pressure exerted by Golovin and NASA Headquarters to get the Task Group and McDonnell to change its approach to raising reliability levels became a significant feature in redesign and reliability testing during 1960.[25]

Scientists, statisticians, and actuaries, working with large populations of entities or events, had long been able to achieve excellent predictions by defining reliability as a probability, but in so doing they sacrificed any claim to know what would happen in a unique instance. Engineers and managers responsible for a specific mission or project tended to ridicule probability theory and to call it invidiously "the numbers game." Being limited to a small set of events and forced by time to overlap design, development, test, and operations phases, they could not accept the statistical viewpoint. They demanded that reliability be redefined as an ability. The senior statistician at Space Technology Laboratories for the Atlas weapon system, Harry Powell, recognized and elaborated on this distinction while his colleagues became involved with man-rating the Atlas. His remarks indicated that STL and Convair/Astronautics faced the same divergence of opinion that NASA Headquarters and STG confronted:

> If reliability is to be truly understood and controlled, then it must be thought of as a device, a physical property which behaves in accordance with certain physical laws. In order to insure that a device will have these physical properties it is necessary to consider it first as a design parameter. In other words, reliability is a property of the equipment which must be designed into the equipment by the engineers. *Reliability cannot be tested into a device and it cannot be inspected into a device; it can only be achieved if it is first designed into a device.* Most design engineers are acutely aware that they are under several obligations—to meet schedules, to design their equipment with certain space and weight limitations, and to create a black box (a subsystem) which will give certain outputs when certain inputs are fed into it. It is imperative that they also be aware of their obligation to design a device which will in fact perform its required function under operation conditions whenever it is called upon to do so.[26]

There is a rule in probability theory that the reliability of a system is exactly equal to the product of the reliability of each of its subsystems in series. The obvious way to obviate untrustworthy black boxes was to connect two black boxes in parallel to perform the same function. In other words, redundancy was the technique most often used to ensure reliability.

After the cancellation of Mercury-Jupiter, Kuettner and others at ABMA set about a serious effort to develop a parachute system to recover the Redstone booster. They also began to concentrate on the simplifications necessary for the sake of reliability to custom-build a man-rated Redstone. Starting with the advanced, elongated version of the rocket, which had been renamed the "Jupiter-C" in 1956 for the Army's ablation research on reentry test vehicles, Kuettner called upon the expertise of all who could spare time from the Saturn program to help decide how to man-rate their stock. The fundamental change made to the Jupiter-C airframe was the elimination of its staging capability. Other modifications stripped it of its more sophisticated components while permitting it to retain greater performance characteristics than the original single-stage Redstone.[27]

The designers of the Redstone and Jupiter missile systems proposed an extensive list of basic modifications to adapt the vehicle to the Mercury capsule. The elongated fuel tanks of the Jupiter-C had to be retained for 20 extra seconds of engine burning time, especially since they decided to revert to alcohol for fuel rather than use the more powerful but more toxic hydyne that fueled the Jupiter-C. Another high-pressure nitrogen tank to pressurize the larger fuel tank and an auxiliary hydrogen peroxide fuel tank to power the engine turbopump also had to be added. To increase the reliability of the advanced Redstone, they had to simplify other parts of the Jupiter-C system. Instead of the sophisticated autopilot called ST–80, one of the first inertial guidance systems (the LEV–3) was reinstalled as the guidance mechanism. The after unit of the payload on the old Redstone, which had contained a pressurized instrument compartment, became the permanent forebody of the main tank assembly, there being no need to provide terminal guidance for the new payload. A spacecraft adapter ring likewise had to be designed to simplify interface coordination and to ensure clean separation between capsule and booster. At the other end of the launch vehicle it was necessary to use the most recent engine model, the A–7, to avoid a possible shortage of spare parts. Hans G. Paul and William E. Davidson, ABMA propulsion engineers, took the basic responsibility for "man-rating" this engine.[28]

Although STG engineers bought the Redstone in the first place because it was considered an "off-the-shelf" rocket, they gradually learned through Hammack's liaison with Butler that the Mercury-Redstone was in danger of being modified in about 800 particulars, enough to vitiate the record of reliability established by the earlier Redstones and Jupiter-Cs. Too much redesign also meant reopening the Pandora's box of engineering "trade-offs," the compromises between overdesign and underdesign. Von Braun's team tended in the former direction; Gilruth's in the latter. To use Kuettner's distinction, ABMA wanted "positive redundancy" to ensure aborts whenever required, whereas STG wanted more "negative redundancy" to avoid aborts unless absolutely essential.[29] This distinction was the crux of the dispute and the essence of the distinction between "pilot safety" and "mission success."

On July 22, 1959, STG engineers received a group of reliability experts from von Braun's Development Operations Division at Huntsville. Three decades of rocket experience had ingrained strongly held views among the 100 or so leaders of this organization about how to ensure successful missions. The ABMA representatives told STG that they did not play the "numbers game" but attacked reliability from an exhaustive engineering test viewpoint. Their experience had proved the adequacy of their own reliability program, carried out by a separate working group on a level with other engineering groups and staffed by persons from all departments in the Development Operations Division of ABMA. In conference with design engineers, ABMA reliability experts normally set up test specifications and environmental requirements for proving equipment compliance. STG felt sympathetic to this approach to reliability, but systems analysts at NASA Headquarters did not.

181

As for the prime contractor's reliability program, in the first major textbook studied by the astronauts, McDonnell's "Project Mercury Indoctrination" manual, distributed in May 1959, the pilots read these reassuring words:

> The problem of attaining a high degree of reliability for Project Mercury has received more attention than has any other previous missile or aircraft system. Reliability has been a primary design parameter since the inception of the project.[30]

Accompanying reliability diagrams showed over 60 separate redundancies designed into the various capsule systems, allowing alternate pilot actions in the event of equipment malfunctions during an orbital mission.

McDonnell specified three salient features of its reliability program in this preliminary indoctrination manual. First, by making reliability a design requirement and by allowing no more than a permissible number of failures before redesign and retesting were required, reliability was made a conscious goal from the beginning of manufacture. Second, five separate procedures were to implement the development program: evaluations, stress analyses, design reviews, failure reporting, and failure analysis. Third, reliability would be demonstrated finally by both qualification and reliability testing.

These assurances did not seem adequate; STG, as well as NASA-Washington, requested McDonnell to clarify its reliability policy in more detail and to hold a new symposium in mid-August to prove the claim that "reliability is everybody's business at McDonnell." McDonnell responded by changing its "design objective" approach to what may be called a "development objective" approach. The new program, drawn by Walter A. Harman and Eugene A. Kunznick, explicitly set forth mean times to failure and added more exhaustive demonstrations, or "life tests," for certain critical components. More fundamental assumptions were made explicit, such as: "the reliability of the crew is one (1.0)," and "the probability of a catastrophic explosion of the booster, of any of the rockets, of the reaction control system, or of the environmental control system is negligible." [31] McDonnell's presentation at this symposium stressed new quality control procedures and effectively satisfied STG for the moment. Golovin and his NASA Headquarters statisticians were pleased to note refinement in sophistication toward reliability prediction in the capsule contractor's figures for the ultimate 28-hour Mercury mission. At the August 1959 reliability symposium, McDonnell assigned impressively high percentage figures as reliability goals for both mission and safety success:

	Mission	Safety
Boost	.7917	.9963
Orbit	.9890	.9999
Retrograde	.9946	.9946
Reentry	.9992	.9992
Overall	.7781	.9914

To John C. French, who began the first reliability studies for Gilruth's group, this kind of table represented the "numbers game," mere gambling odds that might deceive the naive into believing that if not the fourth, then the third, decimal place was significant. French was an experienced systems engineer who recognized that numbers like these did mean something: obviously the authors felt the weakest link in the chain of events necessary to achieve mission success was the launch vehicle. McDonnell believed the safety of the astronaut would be ensured by the escape system, but the coefficient ".7917" diluted the confidence in overall mission success to ".7781." McDonnell and STG agreed that the onus was on the Atlas to prove its safety and reliability as a booster for the Mercury mission.

That point was not disputed by the men responsible for the Atlas. They professed even less confidence in their product for this purpose than the capsule contractor had. Not until November 13, 1959, did representatives of the Air Force Ballistic Missile Division and Space Technology Laboratories visit Langley to present in detail their case for a thoroughgoing plan to man-rate the Atlas as a Mercury booster. Harry Powell had prepared a carefully qualified chart that estimated that the reliability of the Mercury booster would reach approximately 75 percent only in mid-1961, and the first upbend (at about 86 percent) on that curve was to occur another year later.[32] Such pessimism might have been overwhelming to STG except that no abort-sensing system was yet computed as a factor in this extrapolation. Also STG and STL agreed never to entertain the idea of "random failure" as a viable explanation.

Because aircraft designers and missile experts held different opinions about which systems should be duplicated, redundancy itself was often a subject of dispute. Passenger aircraft were provided with many redundant features, including multiple engines and automatic, semi-automatic, and manual control systems, so that commercial flight safety had been made practically perfect. But in the military missile programs of 1959, redundancy to ensure mission success had been relegated to the duplication of the complete missile, "by making and launching enough to be sure that the required number will reach each target." [33] In the age of "overkill," one out of four, for instance, might be considered quite sufficient to accomplish the destructive mission of the ICBM. Both McDonnell and the Task Group placed more faith in quality control procedures and in redundant system development than in mathematical models for reliability prediction during design.

In the course of further symposia and conferences during the autumn, the Space Task Group, working with military systems analysts and industrial quality controllers, learned more than it taught about improving reliability programs. Abe Silverstein, whose Headquarters office was retitled Space Flight Programs (instead of Development) at the end of the year, was especially eager to see STG set up its own reliability program, with procedures for closer monitoring of subcontracts.[34]

But before STG could presume to teach, it had to learn much more about the mechanics of the Redstone and the Atlas. Mathews had his own mathematicians check the case histories for failures of every Redstone, Jupiter, and Atlas that had ever been launched. A statistical population of over 60 Redstone and about 30 Atlas launches yielded clinical diagnoses for generalizing about the most likely ways these boosters might fail. Gerald W. Brewer, Jack Cohen, and Stanley H. Cohn collected much of this work for STG, and then Mathews, Brandner of ABMA, White of STL, and others formulated some ground rules for the development of the two abort-sensing systems.

All the investigators were pleasantly surprised to find relatively few catastrophic conditions among the failures. Their biggest problem was not what to look for or when to allow the escape rocket to blast away but rather how to avoid "nuisance aborts." Such unnecessary or premature escapes would arise from overemphasis on pilot safety or "positive redundancy" at the expense of mission success. Long arguments ensued over several questions: How simple is safe? How redundant can you get and still have simplicity? How do you design a fail-safe abort-sensing system without overdesigning its sensitivity to situations less than catastrophic? [35]

Without trying to define every term, Mathews and his associates agreed that only imminent catastrophic failures were to be sensed, that reliability should be biased in favor of pilot protection, and that all signals from abort sensing should be displayed in the spacecraft. Application of these ground rules to the Redstone led to development of an automatic abort-sensing system (AASS) that sensed "downstream" or fairly gross parameters, each of which was representative of many different types of failures. Merely "critical," as opposed to "catastrophic," situations were not allowed to trigger the escape system automatically. Such merely "critical" situations as partial loss of thrust, a fire in the capsule, deviation from flight path, or loss of tank pressure might possibly be corrected or tolerated. But catastrophic situations were defined as existing where there were no seconds of time for intelligent decisions, corrective actions, or manual abort. The abort system for the Mercury-Redstone sensed and was activated by such typical catastrophic situations as excessive attitude deviations or turning rates (leading to high angles of attack during high dynamic pressures and resulting in a structural breakup), as sudden loss of tank or bulkhead differential pressure in pressure-stabilized structures, as loss of electrical power in the control and instrument system, and as loss of thrust immediately after liftoff.[36]

If any of these situations should arise, the automatic abort-sensing system was supposed to initiate an explosively rapid sequence of events. First, the engine of the Redstone would cut off (except during the initial moments over the launch site). Then the capsule would separate from the booster. And this would be followed by the ignition of the escape rocket, with acceleration up and away from the booster, and finally by the normal sequencing of events in the recovery phase of the launch profile.

During August, September, and October, the Task Group improved its understanding of the interrelated parts and procedures being developed for Mercury. New definitions were formulated in hardware and words. Some old worries—the heatshield, for instance—were abandoned as newer concerns replaced them. The success of Big Joe and the promise of Little Joe shots promoted confidence and sustained enthusiasm. At the end of this period optimistic forecasts were the rule, not only for booster readiness but also for firm operational schedules. The first Mercury-Redstone and Mercury-Atlas qualification flight tests were scheduled for launchings in May 1960. Even the final goal of Project Mercury, the achievement of manned orbital flight around Earth, still appeared possible by March 1961.[37]

But as autumn blended into winter in 1959, optimism cooled along with the weather. The job of keeping snow clear of its own drive was difficult enough, but heavier equipment than that possessed by the Task Group was necessary to plow aside the drifts that sometimes covered the streets of interagency cooperation. In particular, the Mercury-Redstone schedule began to look progressively more snowbound in the early winter of 1959, largely because the capsule and the Atlas commanded primary attention.

At the end of August, Gilruth had proposed to Major General John B. Medaris, commanding ABMA, that the first attempt at a Mercury-Redstone launch from the Cape be set for February 1, 1960. This proposal represented a slippage of about four months since February 1959, when the initial understanding between ABMA and STG had been reached. But the prospects for rapid accomplishments in the next six months were brighter at Langley than at Huntsville, St. Louis, or the Cape. Plans to use eight Mercury-Redstones for ballistic training flights between February and October 1960 were still in effect, and STG also hoped to complete six manned Redstone flights by March 1961 before launching the first of the manned Mercury-Atlas configurations. Such optimism was not entirely the result of youthful naivete or of underestimates of complexity. In large part, target dates were set deliberately at the nearest edge of possible completion periods to combat Parkinson's Law regarding bureaucratic administration, that work expands to fill the time allotted for its completion.[38]

Much of the fault for Redstone slippages must revert to STG for having canceled the Mercury-Jupiter series rather precipitously, thereby unceremoniously relegating the 4000 members of von Braun's division at Huntsville almost to "task element" status as far as Mercury was concerned. Although the Jupiter program per se was being phased out at ABMA, its sires, who sparked the entire Army Ordnance team, were sensitive to criticism of their strange love for space travel.[39] STG engineers should not have been surprised that the cancellation of the Mercury-Jupiter series would cause a reaction in Huntsville that would reverberate to the Cape and through Washington.[40]

Although NASA Headquarters had carefully coordinated STG's recommendation in this matter, many other factors contributed to the change in the Mercury

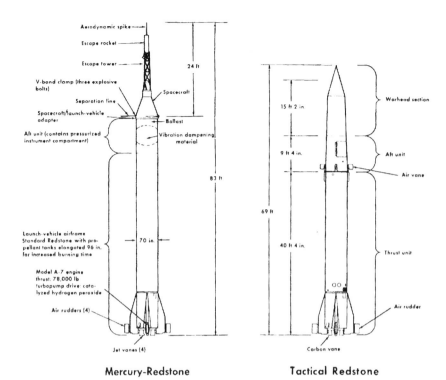

| Mercury-Redstone | Tactical Redstone |

Schematic of Mercury-Redstone.

program management plans that forecast the slip of MR–1 past MA–1 on the flight test schedule. There were at least three technical reasons for the Mercury-Redstone slippages as well as several other, perhaps more important, psychological and policy-planning reasons for this change in the "progressive buildup of tests" principle.

Foremost among all causes of delay was the fact that the pacing item, McDonnell's production model of the Mercury capsule, took longer to build than anyone supposed it would.[41] Because systems integration within the spacecraft was lagging by several months, every other area would be delayed also to some degree. Secondly, the design and development of the abort-sensing systems for the Redstone and Atlas were attacked separately and not cross-fertilized. The basic dispute over safety versus success, or positive versus negative redundancy, could be settled only with actual flight test experience.

A third technical reason for the fact that the Redstone team, with its ready and waiting boosters, failed to lead off the series of qualification flight tests was

186

related to the Teutonic approach to reliability. Long years of experience with rockets, together perhaps with some native cultural concern for meticulous craftsmanship, gave the von Braun group high confidence that most so-called "reliability" problems could be obviated by hard work, more flight tests, and intensive engineering attention to every detail. Elaborate operational checkouts were to be made at Huntsville and the Cape. STG agreed to these procedures in August, but by November time was clearly in contention between Huntsville and Langley. The Task Group wanted to launch its first three Redstones for Mercury during May and June 1960, but if this were possible, it was hardly advisable from ABMA's point of view.[42]

By then, however, this could be considered a family dispute among stepbrothers within NASA. On October 21, 1959, President Eisenhower announced his decision, pending congressional approval, to transfer the von Braun group and the Saturn project from ABMA to NASA. If this decision solved a morale problem among members of the Development Operations Division at ABMA, it undoubtedly complicated certain institutional and political problems. Jockeying for position probably intensified rather than abated, as plans for the future use of the Saturn launch vehicle overshadowed Mercury for the moment. Another five months were required to complete a transfer plan, and eight months would elapse before the official transfer was completed on July 1, 1960.[43]

Although the plans for the escape of a pilot from a malfunctioning Redstone were complex, plans for a similar emergency detection system on the Atlas were several times more complicated. Three engines, rather than one, with an overall range and thrust capability well over three times greater, and with guidance, gimbaling, and structural separation mechanisms far more complex than those to be used on the Redstone—these were some of the factors that put the problem of man-rating the Atlas on a higher plane of difficulty. · The Mercury capsule escape system was, of course, the same for both boosters, but the emergency detection systems had to be tailored to the differences between the launching vehicles. The single-stage Redstone was a piece of battlefield artillery that could stand on its own four fins, for example, whereas the fragile "gas-bag" Atlas would crumple if not pressurized. And in flight, the Atlas' outboard engines must stage properly and drop away from the central sustainer engine before the escape tower could be jettisoned.

While Charles Wilson and his crew at Convair in San Diego worked out the detailed design and hardware for ASIS, Richard White led Space Technology Laboratories through more detailed analytical studies and simulation tests at El Segundo. Their concurrent efforts ensured that the airborne emergency detection system for the Mercury-Atlas evolved, as Powell insisted it must, with the steadfast goal of reliability. Inspection and test programs were inaugurated separately by Hohmann, beginning in October, but reliability was designed into the ASIS black box from May onward. Wilson and White soon discovered that their biggest problem concerned the prevention of recontact between booster and capsule after

187

separation. Alan B. Kehlet and Bruce G. Jackson of STG had the primary responsibility to determine the proper thrust offset of the escape rocket and to ensure against recontact, but "Monte Carlo" probability analyses were done by both Convair and the Space Task Group.[44]

In addition to the ASIS, the Atlas D had to be modified in a number of other ways before it could carry a man. Because the Mercury-Atlas configuration was taller by approximately 20 feet than the Atlas D weapon system, the rate gyro package for the autopilot had to be installed 20 feet higher on the airframe, so it would sense more precisely the rate of change of booster attitude during launch. The Atlas would not need posigrade rockets to assist separation because the Mercury capsule would embody its own posigrade rockets inside its retrorocket package. Because the capsule's posigrade rockets could conceivably burn through the thin skin of the liquid-oxygen dome, a fiber-glass shield covering the entire dome was attached to the mating ring. The two small vernier rocket engines, which on the ICBM had thrust on after sustainer engine cutoff, or "SECO," for last-minute trajectory corrections, were regoverned to delete the "vernier solo" phase of operation, thus saving more weight and complexity. In addition to the use of older, more reliable types of valves and special lightweight telemetry, only one other major booster modification was considered at first. The man-rated Atlas D would use the so-called "wet start" instead of the newer, faster "dry start" method of ignition. A water pulse sent ahead of the fuel into the combustion chambers would effect slower and smoother initial thrust buildup, minimizing structural stress on the engine before liftoff. This change saved approximately 60 pounds, by enabling the use of a thinner skin gauge in the Atlas airframe. But the "thin-skinned" Atlas soon proved to be too thin-skinned, and the weight saved was lost again in 1961, when a thicker skin was found to be essential in the conical tank section just under the capsule. The longer, lighter spacecraft payload proved a cause of additional dynamic loads and buffeting problems, calling for more strength in the Atlas forebody.[45]

After additional study of the idiosyncracies of the Atlas missile, Mathews, Wilson of Convair, and White decided on the parameters most in need of monitoring for abort indications: (1) the liquid oxygen tank pressure, (2) the differential pressure across the intermediate bulkhead, (3) the booster attitude rates about all three axes, (4) rocket engine injector manifold pressures, (5) sustainer hydraulic pressure, and (6) primary electrical power.

Dual sensors gauging each of these catastrophic possibilities were fairly easily developed. If any one of these conditions should arise or any system should fail, the ASIS would by itself initiate the explosive escape sequence. But any one of four men with their fingers poised over pushbuttons also could abort the mission: the test conductor, the flight director in the control center, the range safety officer, or the astronaut with his left thumb would be able to decide if and when the escape rocket should be ignited. But these manual abort capabilities were only supplements, with built-in time delays, to the automatic abort sensing and implementation

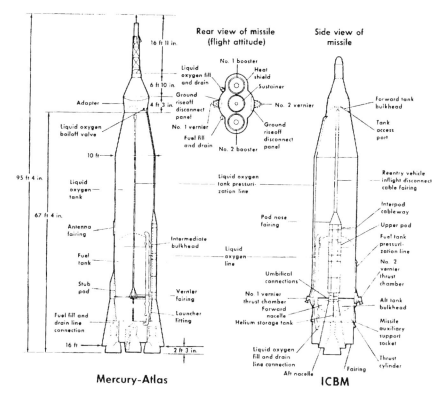

Mercury-Atlas

Rear view of missile (flight attitude)

Side view of missile

ICBM

Schematic of Mercury-Atlas D.

system. During the portion of the flight powered by the Atlas, human judgment was to be secondary to a transistorized watchdog autopilot. Their moral obligation to pilot safety made the Atlas redesigners reduce man-control to this minimum. Culbertson later explained, "While it was true that mission success provided pilot safety, provision for pilot safety did not always improve the probability of mission success." [46]

One of the most important analytical tasks in man-rating the Atlas was the careful and continuous study of the mathematical guidance equations for the launch phase of all the missions. Three men at Space Technology Laboratories shared this responsibility, C. L. Pittman, Robert M. Page, and Duncan McPherson. While Convair was learning that it cost approximately 40 percent more to build a man-rated Mercury-Atlas than a missile system, STL's mathematicians and systems engineers, like Hohmann and Letsch, were working out their differences on how to control quality and augment reliability. By the end of 1959, Hohmann had sold his plans for pilot safety. They were based on applying supercharged aircraft production techniques to industrial practices for military missile production. To live with the Atlas required no less and eventually much more.[47]

CRITICAL COMPONENTS OF THE CAPSULE

Basic as the boosters were for successful manned space flight, they were not the only machines that had to be certified for safety before a man's life could be entrusted to them. The capsule with all its systems and subsystems, designed to operate automatically on unmanned test flights at first, would also have to have reliable provisions for operation with a normal, or even with an incapacitated or unconscious, man aboard. Man-rating the spacecraft, therefore, involved the paradoxical process of dehumanizing it first for rehumanizing later.

When the seven Mercury astronauts first visited the McDonnell Aircraft Corporation laboratories and factory, for three days in May 1959, each was handed an indoctrination manual and given opportunities to inspect the mockup capsule and to review the requests for alterations made by the Mockup Review Board in March. Immediately they expressed some uneasiness about the poor visibility afforded by the two remotely placed portholes and about the difficulty of climbing out the bottleneck top of the capsule.[48] So, based on these and numerous other criticisms expressed by the men for whom these machines were being built, redesign studies were begun.

Just as Maxime Faget was the chief NACA–NASA designer of the capsule configuration and mission concept, so John F. Yardley, his closest counterpart in the McDonnell organization, was the chief developer of the Mercury capsule. Neither Faget nor Yardley was the nominal leader of the vast team within which each worked, but both animated the technical talents of their colleagues, from design through the final development stages of the Mercury hardware. John Yardley held a master's degree in applied mechanics, had worked for McDonnell since 1946 as a stress analyst, strength engineer, and project leader, and he was exceptionally talented in his capacity for work and for synthesizing technical knowledge. By telephone, teletype, and face to face, Faget and Yardley consulted each other about the multitude of detailed design and development decisions involved in production throughout 1959. But their bilateral agreements were restricted to details. Larger decisions regarding the development of systems or interaction between subsystems were reserved for the 17 different working groups in STG and the 10 or so at McDonnell. James Chamberlin instigated this capsule coordination system and gradually replaced Faget in relations with Yardley during the next year.[49]

In 1959 the McDonnell Aircraft Corporation became the 100th-largest industrial company in the United States, employing approximately 24,000 people to produce goods (primarily the F4H–1 Phantom twin-jet fighter for the Navy) and services (mainly computer time, electronic equipment, and systems engineering)

190

valued at $436 million. Within this corporate context, the contract with NASA for about $20 million to manufacture 12 or more spacecraft, requiring only 300 or 400 workers and representing less than five percent of McDonnell's annual sales volume, appeared rather minuscule. The president of the corporation, J. S. McDonnell, in September 1959 wrote for his twentieth annual report to stockholders that "there is no need to stampede away from the *air*craft business." [50]

When the prime contract for Mercury was awarded to McDonnell, the Corporation's vice-president for project management, David S. Lewis, assigned Logan T. MacMillan, a tall, tactful test pilot and mechanical engineer with a winning manner, to be companywide project manager with authority to mobilize the resources of the Corporation for the new venture. MacMillan, of the same age and rank as Faget, soon found it difficult to reconcile McDonnell's development and production phases with NASA's concurrent research and test phases. Time, cost, and quality control were interdependent, and now the astronauts and STG had called for major design changes in the window size and placement, the side entrance-exit hatch, the instrument panel, and switch accessibility. To his top management, MacMillan reported on July 18, 1959:

> The Space Task Group is a rather loosely knit organization of former Research Engineers. The Coordination Office is an attempt to channel and control information and requirements against MAC more closely and is a good move. It is clear, however, regardless of whether or not it succeeds, the NASA philosophy of investigation and approval of the smallest technical details will continue, and request for changes will also continue. We will continue to handle this by being responsive to requests for studies and recommendations and to be as flexible as we possibly can to incorporate changes. It is imperative that we continue to improve our capability to make these studies promptly, submit change proposals to cover the increased work as soon as possible, and evaluate the effect of changes on delivery schedules rapidly. [51]

A month later MacMillan complained by teletype message directly to Paul E. Purser that coordination meetings were being held too frequently for effective action on items from preceding meetings. He suggested that later meetings be scheduled "for one month from time minutes are received at MAC." But the pace did not slow significantly; the finish line simply moved farther away.

MacMillan and Yardley, together with Edward M. Flesh and William Dubusker, two older, more experienced production engineers, supervised the bulk of the load for McDonnell in tooling up, making jigs and fixtures, and organizing their craftsmen and procedures for production. Kendall Perkins, McDonnell's vice-president for engineering, had deliberately assigned Yardley and Flesh, combining youthful enthusiasm and experienced caution, to start the manufacture—literally the handmaking—of the first spaceframe. The subsequent design and technical development at McDonnell was carried out under their direction. [52]

By July 1959, Dubusker, the tooling superintendent, had completed McDonnell's first surgically clean "white room" for the later manufacturing phases, had taken on the job of manufacturing manager for Mercury, and had moved some

*White-room manufacturing stand-
ards typified the revolution in upgrading of precision and reliability
in manufacturing and checkout
techniques. At the McDonnell
plant, white-room conditions pre-
vail (left) as fabrication proceeds
on a spacecraft; (below) part of a
spacecraft's seven miles of wire is
installed on a breadboard; and
(below, left) a technician assem-
bles a compact spacecraft clock.*

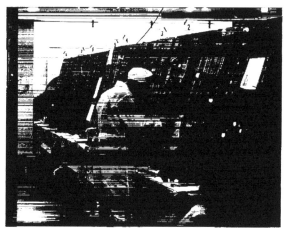

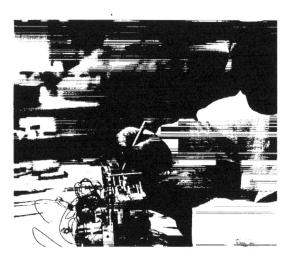

200 workmen onto the new production lines.   Learning to fusion-weld titanium .010-inch thin in an encapsulated argon atmosphere was his first challenge and proudest accomplishment.   But before the year was over, Dubusker had to contend with retooling for other unusual materials, with rising requirements for cleanliness, with stricter demands for machined tolerances, and with higher standards for quality control.

Flesh, the engineering manager, and Dubusker drew on all of McDonnell's experience with shingled-skin structures around jet afterburners for heat protection.   Their machinists had previously worked with the patented metal, René 41, a nickel-base steel alloy purchasable only from General Electric, but arc-jet tests of the afterbody shingles on the outer shell of the capsule showed a need for some ingenious new fabricating techniques.[53]

While Yardley and Flesh concentrated on developing the most critical components for the Mercury capsule, two other McDonnell employees began to play significant roles in man-rating this machinery.   The company was fortunate to have its own so-called "astronaut" in the person of Gilbert B. North, another testpilot engineer but one with a unique relationship for the NASA contract.   He was always being confused with his identical twin brother, Warren J. North, who served Silverstein and George M. Low in Washington as NASA Headquarters participant and monitor in astronaut training.   Gilbert North served McDonnell as chief human guinea pig in the St. Louis ground tests.   Warren and "Bert" North actively promoted the incorporation of test-pilot concerns in the Mercury program from two standpoints outside STG.

Most of the astronauts and test pilots, including the North twins, instinctively resented the "interference" of psychologists and psychiatrists in Project Mercury. Willing to wager their careers and perhaps their necks on the automatic systems of the capsule and booster, the pilots preferred to study the reliability of the machines and to assume themselves adaptable and self-reliant in any situation.   They were thus unprepared to discover that psychologists would be among their strongest allies in gaining a more active role for man during Mercury missions.   Throughout 1959, arguments over the necessity for the three-axis handcontroller, as opposed to the more traditional two-axis stick and one-axis pedal control system, demonstrated these pilots' confidence in themselves.   Distrusting what they regarded as tender-minded psychology and psychiatry, the astronauts-in-training studied hard to become more tough-minded electromechanical engineers.   And indeed their first complaints regarding spacecraft design resulted in changes adopted formally during September for later models of the capsule.[54]

John Yardley fortunately was not quite so tough-minded and recognized early an imbalance in detail design considerations.   He insisted on having the crossfertilization of parallel human engineering studies.   McDonnell hired in February a "human engineering" expert, Edward R. Jones, to conduct studies of pilot tasks and to analyze the various ways in which the man might fail his machines.   Proposing straightaway a thorough training regimen for the astronauts in procedures simulators, Jones went on to program a statistical computation of the human-factors implications of failures in the automatic systems in the Mercury capsule. By November 1959, Yardley and Jones together had convinced a majority of McDonnell engineers that man should more often be in the automatic loop than out of it.[55]

Part of the problem faced by Jones, Yardley, and the astronauts in regard to human factors and the "inhuman" automatic control systems was the initial position taken by seven members of a study group at the Minneapolis-Honeywell Regulator Company in March 1959. Assigned to recommend approaches to mission analysis and cockpit layout, this group, led by John W. Senders, James Bailey, and Leif Arneson, had reported to McDonnell that since "this vehicle does not behave like an airplane . . . . There is no apparent need for a complex, highly integrated display configuration at a sacrifice of reliability." [56] Jones studied the Minneapolis-Honeywell reports carefully and said they expressed a "wooden man" approach. Assuming pilot safety would be provided for, Jones believed more provisions should be made for the pilot to assure mission success. In August, Jones and a colleague, David T. Grober, wrote for Yardley a description of the quantifiable differences between flying this spacecraft and flying aircraft. They admitted: "Primary control is automatic. *For vehicle operation, man has been added to the system as a redundant component who can assume a number of functions at his discretion dependent upon his diagnosis of the state of the system.* Thus, manual control is secondary." [57] But Jones and Grober pointed to at least eight ways in which automation for reliability could interact with the autonomy of the astronaut to vary the chances both for pilot safety and for mission success. They warned McDonnell's reliability engineers against assuming, as they had in their latest formal reliability program given STG, that the reliability of the astronaut is unity:

> It has been assumed naively by those who are not familiar with the capsule that the operation of the systems will not be difficult because of the automatic programming of the normal mission and because of an assumed simplicity of the systems. However, preliminary analysis indicates that the operation of the capsule, considering the stringent mission requirements and the physiological environment, will be as difficult or probably more difficult than high performance aircraft. A vast number of different potential malfunctions may occur in the capsule's systems, and the isolation of these malfunctions can be extremely difficult. *Mission reliability determinations assume the astronaut can detect and operate these systems without error.*

Only three months later Jones read a paper before the American Rocket Society that, while not a reversal of primary and secondary control modes for the manned satellite, marked a symbolic shift from automation to monitored automatic flight. Man's function in space flight, argued Jones, should now be recognized as something more than secondary, if still less than primary:

> Serious discussions have advocated that man should be anesthetized or tranquillized or rendered passive in some other manner in order that he would not interfere with the operation of the vehicle . . . . As equipment becomes available, a more realistic approach evolves. It is now apparent with the Mercury capsule that man, beyond his scientific role, is an essential component who can add considerably to systems effectiveness when he is given adequate instruments, controls, and is trained. Thus an evolution has occurred . . . with increased emphasis now on the positive contribution the astronaut can make.[58]

Jones spoke, presumably, of the general attitudes prevailing around McDonnell. His fellow psychologist in STG, Robert B. Voas, supported his evaluation.

Nevertheless, until some Mercury missions were flown automatically to qualify the integration of all systems, man would not be allowed to fly one. Of all the critical systems in Mercury, therefore, the automatic controls, a part of which was the "autopilot," were most crucial for man-rating the capsule.

Guidance and control engineers in Project Mercury were often plagued by semantic confusions between the different electromechanical systems they designed and developed to stabilize, guide, control, or adjust relative motion. Their nomenclature helped confound confusion by the similarity of initials in official use to denote their orientation systems: ACS, ASCS, RCS, and RSCS all looked similar to men with other concerns, but some evolutionary reasons help explain the technical differences behind the initials. ACS, for Attitude Control System, applied specifically only to the Big Joe capsule, becoming a generic term in Mercury nomenclature after that launch in September 1959. In its place the redundant designation ASCS, for Attitude (or Automatic) Stabilization and Control System, grew up as a name for the autopilot, an airborne electronic computer that compared inputs of electronic sensory information with any deviation from preset reference points on gyroscopes or with the horizon. Outputs from the autopilot could then command small jets called thrusters to spew out small quantities of hot gas in order to maintain balance in space. These hydrogen peroxide jets, their fuel tanks, plumbing, and valves were called simply the RCS, or Reaction Control System.[59] The last of this quartet of initials, RSCS, requires a more thorough explanation.

In August and September 1959, the stabilization controls and drag-braking drogue chute were proving troublesome, and everyone in STG knew this. Provisions for the astronaut, or "human black box," in the control loop complicated every facet of the system, and yet the pilot had little choice over its operation. Robert G. Chilton, Thomas V. Chambers, and other STG controls engineers reconsidered the several different ways in which the Mercury capsule was being designed to act by chemical reflexes with complete self-control.

From the very beginning of controls design for a manned ballistic satellite, Honeywell had suggested using the same digital electronic system, for simplicity's sake, to control all Mercury flights. But this "simple" equipment was unnecessarily complicated for the first flight tests and could cause some unnecessary problems. Also, a direct mechanical linkage to a completely independent, completely redundant reaction control system had been provided to ensure that the pilot could adjust manually and proportionally his capsule's attitude in orbit. But this overweight and oversize manual redundancy, fundamental to the Mercury objective of testing man's capability as a pilot in space, was an exceedingly uneconomical part of the original design.

McDonnell and Honeywell controls engineers moved ahead with their development of the digital system while Chilton wrestled with the problem of raising the efficiency of the thirsty manual proportional thrusters. A wired jumper from the handcontroller to the jets for the ASCS should enable the astronaut to tilt or rotate his craft in its trajectory by electrically switching on and off the tiny solenoid valves that supplied hydrogen peroxide gas to the automatic thruster combustion chambers. Because this "fly-by-wire" system completely circumvented the autopilot, inserting the astronaut's senses and brain in its stead, it was not automatic. Rather, it operated semi-automatically; it would allow the pilot to aid or interfere with the automatic adjustment of rotation around his pitch, roll, and yaw axes. Thus in the autumn of 1959 the automatic attitude control system was already compromised by the addition of the semi-automatic fly-by-wire feature.

But this redundancy still seemed inadequate for mission success. Both McDonnell and STG controls engineers proposed various approaches to other attitude control systems for the Mercury capsule in the spring and summer, but Logan MacMillan resisted all such suggestions, awaiting NASA's formulation of a definite policy for judging the urgency of contract change proposals. Every change would invite inevitable delays, and the long leadtime for a new alternate control system (an AASCS!) made MacMillan, Yardley, and Flesh very skeptical of that approach.[60]

The fresh insight of one of the Canadians in STG's flight controls section, Richard R. Carley, helped Chilton to see the need for a second completely independent rate-command orientation system. Together they wrote a compromise proposal early in July that served as the midwife for a "rate damping" system for stabilization control:

> There is a natural reluctance to relinquish the mechanical linkage to the solenoid valves but the redundant fly-by-wire systems offer mechanical simplification with regard to plumbing and valving hydrogen peroxide so the overall reliability may not change appreciably. In fact, considering the controlability of the capsule as a factor in mission reliability, a net gain should result. Simulation tests indicate that manual control of the capsule attitude during retrograde firing will be a difficult task requiring much practice on the part of the pilot. By changing the command function from acceleration to rate, the task complexity will be greatly reduced and the developmental effort on display and controller characteristics can be reduced accordingly.[61]

Out of interminable meetings and proliferating technical committees, a compromise did finally emerge. Chilton's group, together with J. W. Twombly of McDonnell, worked out the design for a semi-automatic rate augmentation system. By connecting three more wires from the handcontroller to the three pairs of solenoid valves guarding the fuel flow to the manual reaction jets, the designers built a bench version of a rate-command control system that utilized the small rate gyros formerly supplying the references only for cockpit instruments. For the production model, rate command fuel would be taken only from the manual supply tank. By the end of October, Chilton's group and Minneapolis-Honeywell had completed preliminary designs of this rate orientation system, now officially sanctioned as contract change No. 61 and called the "RSCS." But the difficult electrical circuit for its independent rate logic system was only in the breadboard stage: wires had been stretched over the two-dimensional drawings as a preliminary test of the circuit designs.

The manual proportional method of slewing the capsule around required an extravagant use of fuel, but the rate mode relegated the manual to a last-ditch method of attitude control. Now with "rate command," essentially another fly-by-wire system superimposed on the manual reaction controls, the astronaut might control precisely his movements in pitch, yaw, and roll by small spurts of gas that would tip him up or down, right or left, and over on one side or the other. The exact attitude of the capsule at the critical time of retrograde firing could be held by this method, and the slow-roll stabilization of the capsule during reentry also could be accomplished by this system. Thus the quest for reliability led to four different methods of orienting the capsule by the end of 1959. Making both the automatic mode (through fly-by-wire provisions) and the manual mode (through the rate command, or RSCS) redundantly operable gave the astronaut three out of four options.

McDonnell and STG already were working with nine major subcontractors and 667 third-tier vendors, and the effort to man-rate all their products and all these subsystems—indeed each part from tiny diodes to the pressure vessel—required thawing out and refreezing the specification control drawings several times. When at the beginning of October NASA approved the funds for installation of an explosive side-egress hatch, a trapezoidal observation window, and another stabilization and control system, McDonnell engineers had already undertaken these and consequent redesign requirements. This independent advance action was evidence of a more advanced approach to the need for concurrent development and production.[62]

To save weight without sacrificing reliability, the electronic specialists—like all other Mercury design engineers—looked for microminiaturized, solid-state components. But they found less than they hoped. Miniature parts were evolving rapidly into microminiaturized parts, but the latter did not have good reliability records yet. Collins Radio Company, for example, holding the subcontract for capsule communications equipment, emphasized the conservative use of minia-turized but not superminiaturized components to achieve greater reliability.[63] Since the beginning of the development program the target of an effective capsule launch weight of 2700 pounds had been overshot continuously, primarily because of slight but cumulative increments in electrical circuitry weights. Vendors con-sistently seemed to underestimate the weights of the parts they supplied. At the beginning of October the effective capsule weight was estimated at 2859 pounds. This seemed likely to grow to 3000 pounds unless firm action was taken. A special coordination meeting in St. Louis at the beginning of October established a weight-reduction diet for the capsule development program and admonished NASA "all along the line to decide how much weight reduction should be sought and what items of capsule equipment should be sacrificed in order to achieve the desired reduction." [64]

At the time STG was considering the RSCS, it was also thinking of eliminating the 17.5-pound drogue parachute in the interest of weightsaving. The "fist-ribbon" drogue stabilizer, six feet in diameter and composed of concentric and radial strips of nylon, was being tested at Edwards Air Force Base and at the El Centro Naval Parachute Test Facility, at subsonic and transonic speeds and at altitudes down from 70,000 feet over the Salton Sea. One of the first canopies, released at a speed of mach 1.08 from an F–104 jet fighter at an altitude above 10 miles, plummeted into denser air whipping, fluttering, and spinning so badly that it disintegrated after a minute of this punishment. This test had put a special premium on development of the rate stabilization control system.

The recent decision to substitute a ring-sail for the extended-skirt main landing parachute made Gilruth fear that there might not be enough experience with big parachutes to determine whether they had similar bad characteristics. Gilruth and Donlan were so unsettled by the chute tests in general that they appealed to Washington for an expansion of applied research programs aimed at the development of more reliable parachute systems:

> It is apparent that the large load cargo type of parachute is far from as reliable as the personnel parachute that most people are familiar with. Part of this lack of reliability is due to unknown scale effects, perhaps. However, it is known that a great deal of this loss of reliability is due to the various fixes that are employed on large parachutes to attenuate the opening shock. Such fixes as extended skirts, slots, reefing, and other devices are designed to cause a para-chute to open more slowly. Therefore, it is not surprising that this tendency to open slower is also accompanied by a tendency not to open at all.[65]

Continued tests of the main parachute revealed few additional problems, but the drogue chute tests were getting worse. By the end of September the problem of drogue behavior at relatively high altitudes and barely supersonic speeds was so critical that the director of Langley thought it might be "easier to avoid than to solve." [66] All sorts of alternatives, including a flexible inflatable-wing glider proposed by Francis M. Rogallo of Langley, a string of discs trailing like a Chinese kite, and simple spherical balloons, were proposed as possible means of avoiding the instability of porous parachute canopies at high altitudes, where the air to inflate them is so rare.

Toward the end of 1959 still another lesson learned from studies of the aerodynamic stability of the capsule in the rarefied upper atmosphere added a slight refinement to the Mercury configuration. To break a possible "freeze" if the stable capsule should reenter the atmosphere small end forward, a spring-loaded destabilizing flap was installed under the escape pylon. Donlan and Purser asked George Low to explain around Washington why this "mousetrap" destabilizing flap was added to the antenna canister and why this innovation would require further wind tunnel tests:

> The Mercury exit configuration (antenna canister forward without escape tower) has been shown to be statically stable at mach numbers greater than four. This stability is undesirable because of the possibility of the capsule reentering the atmosphere antenna canister forward. Tunnel tests at a mach number of six have indicated that a destabilizing flap prevents this undesirable stability region. It is therefore necessary to know the effect of this destabilizing flap at subsonic and supersonic speeds.[67]

Continued poor performance of the fist-ribbon drogue convinced Faget, Chamberlin, and Yardley by the end of 1959 that the drogue chute should be eliminated altogether, but Gilruth and Purser, among others, saw as yet no cheaper insurance and no more workable alternative.[68] The mousetrap destabilization flap and the rate stabilization system would help to fill only the mid-portion of the gap in the reentry flight profile. It was still a long way down from 100,000 to 10,000 feet above sea level—roughly 17 miles as a rock might drop. But by this time, the big questions concerning the first part of the reentry profile had been answered by the Big Joe flight.

BIG JOE SHOT

On the same day, September 9, 1959, both the major preliminary flight test of Project Mercury and the final qualification flight test of the operational Atlas ICBM occurred, in separate launches from opposite sides of the United States. While NASA and STG were focusing their attention on the performance of Atlas booster No. 10–D, being launched from Cape Canaveral, most of the men behind the Atlas were watching missile No. 12–D being launched from Vandenberg Air Force Base in California. A novitiate crew of Strategic Air Command (SAC) officers and men had groomed No. 12–D for this critical test flight southwestward over the Pacific Missile Range. Likewise, neophytes from NASA stood by their payload on the Atlas 10–D, awaiting the results of its southeastward flight over the Atlantic Missile Range. If all went well this day, the Atlas would have proved itself capable both as an operational ICBM and as a launch vehicle for a Mercury ballistic flight. Reliability was something else again, but capability could be proved with one demonstration.

The men from Space Technology Laboratories; from Convair/Astronautics; Rocketdyne; General Electric; Pan American, who managed the "housekeeping" of the Atlantic Missile Range; and numerous other contractors supporting the Air Force development of the Atlas, deserved to be called experts. They had had experience in launching this rocket. By contrast, NASA personnel were even greener than the SAC crew going through the countdown at Vandenberg. NASA did not intend to learn to launch its own Atlases, but STG did hope to gain some expertise for living through its launches. The job of launching Big Joe belonged to the Air Force, supported by the Convair/Astronautics team at the Cape— Byron G. McNabb, Travis L. Maloy, Thomas J. O'Malley, C. A. Johnston, and others. Charles Mathews, the STG mission director, learned much about his operational requirements working with these men on Big Joe.

Few people outside the military-industrial teams working on the Atlas could have known what was happening in the ICBM program in mid-1959.[69] The fourth and supposedly standard version of the Atlas ICBM, designated the Atlas D, rapidly supplanted the third development version, called Atlas C, during the summer of 1959. Earlier A and B models, fired in 1957 and 1958, had phased through C and into D concurrently. The Air Force had committed itself in December 1958 to supply NASA with standard Atlas Ds for all Mercury missions. The first installment on this commitment came due in September, at the same time that the weapon system was to prove itself operational. Since April 14, 1959, when the first series-D missile exploded 30 seconds after liftoff, only four other Atlas Ds had been launched, the second and third of which were partial failures or partial successes, depending upon one's point of view.[70]

In July and August, however, the two successful Atlas-D launchings were supplemented by exceptionally encouraging flights of the last two series-C Atlases. Atlas 8–C had flown on July 21, bearing "RVX–2," or the first ablative reentry nose cone adapted to the Atlas. It was especially welcome to STG officials; both the flight and the recovery provided demonstrative evidence to reinforce STG's commitment to the ablation principle for the Mercury heatshield.[71]

Joe is a common name, but there was nothing common about the big Atlas missile and the Mercury payload that stood poised upright at launch complex 14 at Cape Canaveral on September 9, 1959. Some had hoped that Big Joe would skyrocket on July 4, but the launch date was postponed until mid-August by the Air Force because the booster did not check out perfectly at first. Then it was put off until early September by STG engineers, who were stymied by troubles in the sophisticated instrumentation and telemetry. Finally, on the evening of September 8, Atlas 10–D, the sixth of this model to be flight tested, stood on its launch pad at Cape Canaveral with a replica of the Mercury capsule (minus an escape tower) at its tip. All NASA waited for the countdown to begin at midnight. About a fourth of the Space Task Group members were at the Cape for the "Atlas ablation test." From this first full-scale, full-throttle simulation of the reentry problem, every member could expect further task definitions.

If Atlas 10–D should fail, if the boilerplate capsule should fail its test or be lost, then a backup shot, Big Joe II, would have to be made. But without proof that the ablation heatshield could actually protect a man from the intense frictional heat of reentry, and without dynamic evidence that the frustum-shaped spacecraft would actually align itself blunt-end-forward as it pierced the atmosphere, all the rest of the "R and D" invested in Faget's plan would avail little.[72]

The nose-cone-capsule for Big Joe, handcrafted by NASA machinists, had no retrorocket package. The inner structure held only a half-size instrumented pressure vessel instead of a pressurized cabin contoured to the outer configuration. Built in two segments, the lower half by Lewis and the upper by Langley craftsmen, the main body of the spacecraft replica was fabricated of such relatively thin sheets of corrugated Inconel alloy in monocoque construction that the appellation "boilerplate" capsule was especially ironic.[73]

For this model of the Mercury payload, more than a hundred thermocouples were installed around the capsule skin to register temperatures inside and under the heatshield, sides, and afterbody. Jacob Moser and a group of instrumentation specialists from Lewis had developed a multiplex system for transmitting data over a single telemetry link from all thermocouples plus 50 other instruments, including microphones, pressure gauges, and accelerometers.

Back in Cleveland, three controls engineers, Harold Gold, Robert R. Miller, and H. Warren Plohr, had designed a "cold-gas" attitude control system, using high-pressure nitrogen for fuel. They had worked directly with Minneapolis-Honeywell to devise the gyros, logic, and thrusters for the critical about-face maneuver after separation. It was essentially unique in its use of cold-gas nitrogen thrusters rather than the "hot-gas" hydrogen peroxide systems that Bell Aerosystems had developed for the X–15 program.[74]

To STG novices watching the launch preparations, the Atlas and the organization of people it required to get off the ground seemed incredibly complex. But they themselves were not well organized even for their sole responsibility with the payload. Big Joe had three bosses, all at work under Mathews. Aleck C. Bond, the Langley heat-transfer specialist, had accepted from Faget almost a year ago the responsibility for the overall mission success. B. Porter Brown, the Langley engineer first sent to pave the way for STG at the Cape, acted as STG's chief liaison with the Air Force-Convair team. And Scott H. Simpkinson, leading the group of about 45 test-operations people from Lewis, had been living with the capsule for Big Joe in a corner of Hangar S since the second week in June, when checkout and preflight operations tests began. The NASA-Goddard crew still held most of the hangar space in preparation for *Vanguard III*, their culminating launch, scheduled later in September.[75]

Porter Brown bore the title of NASA Atlas-Mercury Test Coordinator and worked—along with NASA Headquarters representative Melvin Gough—under nominal direction from the Missile Test Center. To fathom the complexity of launch operations and organizations at the Cape required expertise, tact, and

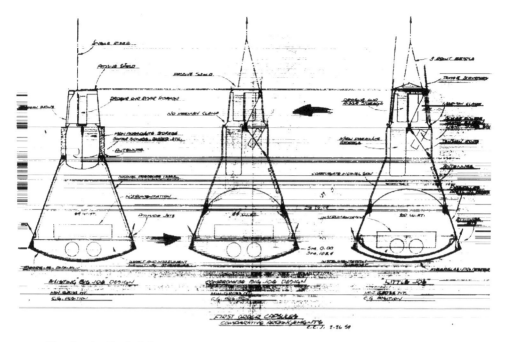

Sketches by C. C. Johnson of comparative boilerplate Mercury capsules used in Big Joe and Little Joe test flights. The sketches, dated February 26, 1959, show the transition from the original Big Joe capsule design (left) to the one actually used (center), which in turn would be a precursor of the capsules used in Little Joe launches.

drive. Security restrictions were so strict for the Atlas, and agencies and launch crews so compartmentalized, that horizontal or interpersonal communications in the lower echelons were virtually nonexistent. Brown had to keep vertical communications open and establish STG's "need-to-know" at every step.[76]

To launch a missile required a stack of documents almost as tall as a gantry. Documents called "preliminary requirements," "operations requirements," "operations directives," "test directives," and innumerable other coordinating catalogs had to be circulated and their orders followed before, during, and after getting a rocket off the ground. To active young engineers with a mission, this paperwork could only be frustrating, but Air Force experience had shown the value of the documentation system in imposing order on a chaotic situation.[77]

Atlas 10–D was programmed to rise, pitch over horizontally to the Atlantic before it reached its 100-mile peak altitude, then pitch down slightly before releasing its corrugated nose cone at a shallow angle barely below the horizontal.

202

In the near vacuum of space at that altitude, tiny automatic thrusters in the capsule should make it turn around for a shallow reentry into the stratosphere. The friction of the air, gradually braking the speed of the descent, would dissipate the kinetic energy imparted to the capsule by the Atlas. An incandescent cauldron of this transformed energy would envelop the capsule like a crucible as it penetrated denser air. It was hoped that enough of this heat would be deflected by the slip stream and boiled away into the turbulent boundary layer of the shock-wave to protect the capsule from vaporization. This flight should simulate closely what a man must ride through if he was to live to talk about an Atlas-boosted, Mercury-returned orbital flight around Earth.

About 2:30 a.m., a 19-minute hold in the countdown was called to investigate a peculiar indication from the Burroughs computer that was to guide the launch. A malfunction was found in the Azusa impact prediction beacon, a transponder in the booster. Since there were several redundant means, including an IBM machine that was part of the range safety system, for predicting the impact point, the trouble was ignored, the countdown resumed, and liftoff occurred at 3:19 a.m.[78]

It was a beautiful launch. The night sky lit up and the beach trembled with the roar of the Rocketdyne engines. For the first two minutes everyone was elated. Then suddenly oscillograph traces indicated that the two outboard booster engines had not separated from the centerline sustainer engine, as they were supposed to do when their fuel was exhausted. Flight controllers and test conductors in the blockhouse and control center began to worry about "BECO" (or booster engine cutoff) as contradictory signals appeared on their panels and computer readout rolls. Apparently all systems within the capsule were performing as planned, but the capsule seemed not to do its half-somersault. The added weight of the booster engines retarded velocity by 3000 feet per second. The Burroughs computer predicted an impact point about 500 miles short. All eight reaction control jets seemed to be working perfectly, yet the reentry attitude could not be verified before the telemetry blackout occurred as the capsule skidded back into the atmosphere.[79] No one could ascertain what had happened during that 20-minute flight unless the recovery forces downrange could retrieve the capsule and its onboard tape recordings.

Six ships of Destroyer Flotilla Four began racing uprange at flank speed. Patrol and tracking planes started flying their search patterns. Before dawn, tracking ships and downrange tracking stations detected the sofar bomb explosion underwater, and provided new coordinates for the point of impact. As the sun rose over the sea, a Navy P2V Neptune patrol plane, homing in on a sarah beacon signal, reported sighting the capsule bobbing in the water. It vectored the nearest destroyer, now still over 100 miles away, to the green-dyed area for retrieval. It was still too early to tell whether the primary objectives of Big Joe had been achieved. But as the morning progressed, more evidence from the range made it appear that all telemetry had functioned properly. If the capsule could be recovered before it sank, the most important objective, finding out how well the capsule's ablation shield had endured reentry, could be evaluated quickly.

While eager newsmen at the Cape were being cautioned to avoid erroneously identifying this custom-built prototype as the Mercury capsule, technicians were busily analyzing "quick-look" data that would give more information about booster and payload separation performance, the attitude control system, the internal and external temperature history of the model, noise and vibration levels, telemetry and tracking effectiveness, and acceleration and deceleration peaks.

About seven hours after launch, exultation swept over the Big Joe launch team at the Cape when the destroyer *Strong* reported that she had netted the precious capsule intact and secured it on deck. The terrestrial return trip by water and air required another 12 hours. As soon as the transferring cargo plane arrived at Patrick Air Force Base, the capsule was loaded onto a dolly, and a police escort cleared the way for the shrouded trailer bearing the tangible remains of the Big Joe mission along the 15 miles through Cocoa Beach to Cape Canaveral.

When the capsule arrived back home in Hangar S, about midnight, every NASA person at the launch site that day gathered around the capsule for a joyous autopsy. Gilruth, Faget, Mathews, Bond, Brown, and Simpkinson stood by as someone dropped the canvas veiling the secret heatshield. The group marveled at the superb condition of their archtype. Bond ran his fingers over the now cool glass beads on the face of the ablation shield, noticed that the afterbody was barely singed. Brown scratched the white-paint legend "United States" and found it hardly discolored. Although one of the afterbody recovery eyes was welded shut by reentry heating, a piece of masking tape, which Simpkinson had allowed to remain, was still intact inside the outer conical shell. A tired but happy crew unscrewed the two halves of the inner pressure vessel and handed to Gilruth a letter that had been sealed inside and signed by 53 people under Mathews in anticipation of this occasion:

> This note comes to you after being transported into space during the successful flight of the "Big Joe" capsule, the first full-scale flight operation associated with Project Mercury. The people who have worked on this project hereby send you greetings and congratulations.[50]

Within a week, data reduction made possible the reconstruction of the inflight history of Big Joe. As suspected, the outboard engines had failed to stage after booster engine cutoff, and the additional weight degraded the Atlas velocity about 3000 feet per second. This meant the trajectory of the flight path had been steeper and slightly lower than planned and that the sustainer engine had powered the capsule into a steeper downward course before burnout. Without a positive force to divide the two objects in free fall, the capsule had separated from the booster about 138 seconds late, after all of its high-pressure nitrogen fuel was expended in trying futilely to turn both booster and spacecraft around for reentry. When it finally broke loose from the launch vehicle at an altitude of 345,000 feet and at a space-fixed speed of almost 15,000 miles per hour, the capsule was an exhausted, passive, free-falling body. Yet by virtue of its configuration and center of gravity, the capsule turned itself around without the aid of either thrusters or damping controls and reentered the atmosphere successfully. The dynamic stability of the capsule configuration was so good that doubt of its ability to damp out its entry oscillations was also ended.

The heat pulse sustained in the actual Big Joe trajectory was shorter but considerably more severe than planned. If STG had been testing a beryllium heat sink shield, these untoward conditions would not have proved anything. For the ablation heatshield, the length of the heat pulse was sufficient to prove the value of the approach. The sequencing, structures, instrumentation, and cooling system had all worked well. The recovery of the capsule inspired so much confidence among STG leaders that Big Joe II, the backup launch, was canceled within three weeks.

The Mercury capsule Automatic Stabilization and Control System.

Cores and slices taken from the conservatively designed heatshield at many locations proved that the heating was uniform over its face and that its structural integrity had survived impact without compromise. The depth of ablation charring was shallow enough to leave at least two-thirds of the fiber-glass material in pristine condition. Bond and Andre J. Meyer were especially pleased with the large margin for error represented by the thickness of the heatshield remaining. Subsequently, they were able to reduce the thickness and the weight of the shield by almost one half.

One note of caution remained in all the jubilation following Big Joe. Leonard Rabb, the head of Faget's theoretical heat transfer section, signed a memo on October 7 demanding action to prove that the short heat pulse on Big Joe could be disregarded. "Calculations indicate," said Rabb, "that the present Mercury heatshield will *not* survive a reentry due to natural decay." If retrorockets should be lost or become inoperative and if the ablation shield in orbit should have to sustain and dissipate the long, slow building of the heat pulse over 24 hours or so, catastrophe would result, Rabb warned:

> Under no circumstances should the weight of the heat shield itself be shaved. Recent calculations cast doubt on the shield's performance, not only for natural decay reentry but for the one retro [rocket instead of three or two] case as well.[81]

By the end of October, the working papers giving the results of Big Joe were published, and gradually the lessons learned from this shot were incorporated in a number of major redesign decisions. The features that became standard for Project Mercury as a result of Big Joe have been summarized by Aleck Bond:

> (1) In view of the excellent performance of the ablation shield, the back-up beryllium heat sink shield was dropped from further consideration for Mercury orbital missions.
> (2) The basic heat shield fabrication techniques employed for the Big Joe shield were adopted for the Mercury heat shield.
> (3) The detailed temperature measurements made on the Big Joe shield provided for an efficient design thickness for the Mercury shield.
> (4) The afterbody heat transfer measurements indicated a need for heavier external thermal protection than had been provided for the Mercury spacecraft, and as a result the shingles on the conical afterbody were thickened and on the cylindrical afterbody the original René shingles were replaced with the thick beryllium shingles in order to handle the high heating loads in this region.

*   *   *

> The ability of the spacecraft to survive the severe test of reentry from near-orbital velocities in spite of its unprecedented release conditions, is certainly worthy of note. The heat shield performance was excellent and the results indicated that the original design concepts were sound. The spacecraft performance as a freebody reentry vehicle was exceptional. An important characteristic of the Mercury design was demonstrated; that the spacecraft could

Big Joe
Sept. 9, 1959

Big Joe was a critical flight in Mercury, combining a test of the reentry concept employing the ablating heatshield and a test of the as yet only half-tested launch vehicle, the Atlas D. At right, Big Joe on the launch pad at Cape Canaveral, being groomed for the big event. Below, Aleck C. Bond (left), Big Joe project engineer, and Scott H. Simpkinson, who had been in charge of capsule checkout at the Cape, kept track of their charge during the flight. Below right, the slightly singed but gloriously intact Big Joe capsule after its retrieval from the Atlantic.

reenter the atmosphere at high angles of attack and maintain the heat shield forward attitude without the aid of a control system! [82]

The elation of the Task Group over the dynamic proof of its passive design of Mercury was not shared by the Atlas people. Their booster 10–D, having failed to stage, performed only marginally and in fact was classed a failure by the Air Force and STL. But across the country, on the Pacific Coast, Atlas 12–D, launched by the SAC crew under the tutelage of Convair/Astronautics and STL, performed as a true ICBM on a 5200-mile flight to its target in the South Pacific. Immediately thereafter the Air Force announced the Atlas was now operational. Apparently the force-in-being totaled only the two missiles erected in training gantries at Vandenberg, but the delicate balance of power could not wait for the buildup of numbers. [83]

LITTLE JOE SERIES

While the results of the Big Joe launch were being studied, a five-man investigating committee at Langley was trying to learn why the first Little Joe shot, on August 21, 1959, had miscarried so badly. Out at Wallops Island that Friday morning several weeks earlier, the first Little Joe (LJ–1) had sat on its launcher, tilted toward the sea, with a full-sized model capsule and escape system on top. Its test mission was to determine how well the escape rocket would function under the most severe dynamic loading conditions anticipated during a Mercury-Atlas launching. At 35 minutes before launch, evacuation of the area had been proceeding on schedule, and the batteries for the programmer and destruct system in the test booster were being charged. Suddenly, half an hour before launchtime, an explosive flash and roar startled several photographers and crewmen into diving for cover.

No one was injured, but when the smoke cleared it was evident that only the capsule-and-tower combination had been launched, on a trajectory similar to an off-the-pad abort. The booster and adapter-clamp ring remained intact on the launcher. Near apogee, at about 2000 feet, the clamping ring that held tower to capsule released and the little pyro-rocket for jettisoning the tower fired. [84]

The accident report on LJ–1, issued on September 18, blamed the premature firing of the Grand Central escape rocket on an electrical leak, or what missile engineers were calling "transients," "ghost" voltages or currents, or simply a "glitch" in a relay circuit. The fault was found in a coil. It had been specially designed as a positive redundancy to protect biological specimens from too rapid an abort and as a negative redundancy to prevent inadvertent destruction of the test booster. Again the problem of upgrading the machines to provide safety for animal payloads as well as to ensure mission success had created unexpected problems. This first trial of the brand-new Little Joe test booster apparently had been too ambitious. Fortunately the momentum of the Little Joe test series was not disturbed by the debacle of the boilerplate payload on Little Joe No. 1.

North American Aviation finished and shipped on September 25, 1959, its sixth and last airframe for the Little Joe booster as promised. The Space Task Group therefore had available at the beginning of October all the Little Joe test boosters it had ordered. Designed primarily to man-rate the escape system operating from a Mercury-Atlas already in flight, the Little Joe booster also was committed to perform some biological research before fulfilling its primary mission.[85]

More by coincidence than by design, the next three Little Joe boosters were launched from Wallops Island exactly one month apart in the autumn of 1959. Still the primary aerodynamic test objectives remained unfulfilled. But the fourth shot, in January 1960, finally worked precisely as planned. STG was satisfied that its own pilot safety provisions were viable under the worst possible aerodynamic conditions. The same kind of test on McDonnell's finished product, rather than on boilerplate demonstration capsules, perhaps could be made the following summer.

On October 4, 1959, the same booster that had been jilted by the capsule and escape rocket in August was finally fired, this time with a double dummy—an uninstrumented boilerplate model fitted with an inert escape rocket system. After the fiasco of LJ-1, the more modest purpose of this test, which later became known as Little Joe 6 (LJ-6), was to prove the "reliability" of the whole booster propulsion cluster. All four Pollux motors, plus four smaller Recruit motors, were set to fire in sequence. Little Joe 6, 55 feet tall and weighing 20 tons at liftoff, blasted up to a peak altitude barely short of 40 miles; then it was intentionally destroyed after two and a half minutes of flight to prove the destruct system. Impact was over 70 miles from Wallops Island. All went well.[86]

Satisfied that Little Joe had proved itself as a booster, the supervisory team of NASA engineers, consisting of John C. Palmer from Wallops, and Roland English, James Mayo, Clifford Nelson, Charles McFall of Langley, and William M. Bland and Robert O. Piland of the Space Task Group, prepared for a new effort to check the correct operation of the abort escape system at maximum loading conditions. The region called "max q" (for maximum dynamic pressure) by aerodynamicists is the portion of the flight path at which relative speed between the vehicle and the atmosphere produces the greatest air resistance on the vehicle. Many variables were involved, but roughly both Little Joe and the Mercury-Atlas were expected to experience dynamic pressures of almost 1000 pounds per square foot at an approximate altitude of six miles after about one minute of flight time.

For the second attempt at this primary mission, Little Joe 1-A (LJ-1A) needed to propel another dummy capsule and pylon to the max q region. Both drogue and main parachute behavior were to be carefully studied on this flight. Surprised by the insistent demands from the news media to witness these developmental flight tests, STG gave the press a careful enumeration of situations that might call for a "hold" or a "scratch" of the shot.[87]

On November 4, 1959, when the second Little Joe booster was successfully launched, newspapermen could see nothing wrong. The flight looked straight and true until the rocket was out of sight. But the test engineers in the control center observed that the escape motor did not fire until 10 seconds after the point of maximum dynamic pressure. The parachutes and recovery operations performed well enough to fulfill secondary and tertiary objectives, but precisely why escape was too slow was never fully understood. Later analysis showed only that the delayed ignition of the escape rocket caused the separation of capsule from booster at a pressure only one-tenth of that programmed.[88] Because the next scheduled launch of a Little Joe booster was already committed to a test for certain aeromedical objectives and was now in a late stage of preparation, the primary aerodynamic test of the escape system was postponed until January, when a third try, to be called Little Joe 1–B, could be made.

Back in May, STG had begun planning with the Air Force School of Aviation Medicine to include some biological packages in later Little Joe flights. The booster designated No. 5 was reserved specifically to qualify all systems in the McDonnell capsule, carrying a chimpanzee occupant and escaping from a simulated Atlas explosion at the point of max q.[89]

After the disappointment of Little Joe 1–A, Donlan, Bland, and Piland decided to pull out the stops on Little Joe 2 and allow the aeromedical specialists to run all the experiments they wanted on a high-powered flight. The School of Aviation Medicine had made ready a biological package for its primate passenger, a small rhesus monkey named "Sam," after his alma mater. In addition to Sam's special capsule for rocket flight, the military physicians now prepared barley seeds, rat nerve cells, neurospora, tissue cultures, and insect packets to measure the effects of primary radiation, changes in appearance and capacity for reproduction, and ova and larvae responses to the space environment.

Little Joe 2 promised to be a spectacular flight if everything went as planned. The engineers could see how the capsule escape system would function under conditions of high mach number and low dynamic pressure; more important technically, they could measure the motions, aerodynamic loads, and aerodynamic heating experience of the capsule entering from the intermediate height of about 70 miles. The Air Force medical specialists might also learn about other things, but their chief interest was to see how well Sam himself would withstand weightlessness during the trip. This was also the chief interest of Alan B. Shepard and Virgil I. Grissom, who came to see this launch.[90]

On December 4, 1959, just before noon, the third Little Joe, LJ–2, ripped through the air under full power and burned out at an altitude of 100,000 feet. The tower and capsule separated as planned and the escape rocket gave an additional boost, throwing the capsule into a coasting trajectory that reached its zenith just short of 280,000 feet, or 53 miles. This peak height was about 100,000 feet lower than expected because of a serious windage error, so Sam experienced only three minutes of weightlessness instead of four. He survived the mild reentry, the not-so-mild impact, and six hours of confinement before he was recovered by a destroyer and liberated from his inner envelope.[91]

Little Joe 2
Dec. 4, 1959

A launch from Wallops Island was a quieter, simpler affair than at the Cape. This photo of LJ-2 being readied for launch shows the unpretentious gantry and service structure. The live payload for the flight, Sam, the rhesus monkey, is shown before the flight strapped into his miniature replica of the Mercury astronaut couch.

211

All preliminary indications reflected a highly successful flight. For the first time Little Joe had achieved full success on all three orders of its programmed test objectives. Congratulatory letters sped around the circuit among those responsible. It was a satisfying way to close out the year. But STG engineers knew that this full-performance test of the Little Joe was not the most crucial case for man-rating the Mercury escape system. They still had to prove that at max q, where everything conspired to produce failure, the escape system could be relied upon to save the life of any man who ventured into this region aboard an Atlas.

Later evaluations of Little Joe 2 were somewhat less sanguine. Biologists were disappointed: although results were better than on any previous biological space flight, they were still not good enough. STG engineers still awaited the more crucial test of the escape system under maximum aerodynamic stress. And the Mercury managers were disappointed at the way the news media had dramatized the animal experiments at the expense of the equally significant demonstration of technological progress.[92]

Public information officers John A. Powers of STG and E. Harry Kolcum of NASA Headquarters tried to correct the "misplaced emphasis" in the news stories before the fourth Little Joe shot, Little Joe 1–B, occurred in January. By this time, Gilruth wished the press would note "the relatively minor role of this particular task in the context of the total Mercury program."[93] But again, to the reporters the star of the event was "Miss Sam," the female counterpart to the occupant of LJ–2, whose life was at stake and whose nervous system was to be tested in psychomotor performance tasks during the short but severe flight. Some of the newsmen perhaps knew or divined that several of the astronauts wanted to ride one of the next Little Joes into space.

Finally, on January 21, 1960, with the fourth launching of the Little Joe series, the escape system performed as planned at the point of max q.[94] Propelled by two Pollux main motors, Little Joe 1–B blasted up to the nominal altitude of slightly less than nine miles and attained a maximum velocity slightly over 2000 miles per hour. Then the escape rocket kicked on the overdrive for an additional 250 feet in one second to "rescue" the Mercury replica from a simulated booster failure at that point. Over a range of 11.5 miles out to sea, Miss Sam, in her biopack prepared by medical technicians from Brooks Air Force Base and its School of Aviation Medicine, not only survived these severe g loads but also performed well (except for a 30-second lapse) at her business of watching for the light and pulling the lever. After 8.5 minutes of flight, during which the sequence system and capsule landing systems worked perfectly, Miss Sam touched down. She was recovered almost immediately by a Marine helicopter, and was returned in excellent condition to Wallops Station within 45 minutes after liftoff.[95]

For half a minute after the escape rocket fired, the little rhesus monkey had been badly shaken up and did not respond to stimuli, but otherwise Miss Sam acted the role of the perfectly trained primate automaton throughout the flight.

Evidence of nystagmus after escape rocket firing and after impact on the water did cause concern, for it suggested that an astronaut's effectiveness as a backup to the parachute system might be impaired. The internal noise level proved to be higher than expected, likewise causing some other worries over the provisions for communications and pilot comfort.[96]

To this point, the Little Joe series of five actual and attempted flights had expended four of the six test boosters North American had made for NASA and five prototype capsules made in the Langley shops. The primary test objectives for these solid-fuel-boosted models were an integral part of the development flight program conducted within NASA by the Space Task Group, with Langley and Wallops support. Now only two Little Joe boosters remained for the qualification flight tests. North American had manufactured seven Little Joe airframes, but one of these had been retained at the plant in Downey, California, for static loading tests. STG ordered the refurbishment of this seventh airframe so as to have three Little Joe boosters for the qualification flight program. The success of Little Joe 1–B in January 1960 meant that the next flight, the sixth, to be known as LJ–5, would be the first to fly a real Mercury capsule from the McDonnell production line.[97] In passing from development flight tests with boilerplate models to qualification flight tests with the "real McDonnell" capsule, the Space Task Group moved further away from research into development and toward operations.

One World Network

From the beginning of 1959, the United States' first manned space flight program was committed to manned ballistic suborbital flights as prerequisite to a manned orbital flight, and to a world-wide tracking and communications network as a safeguard for its man in orbit. Both of these distinguishing features were means of man-rating its machines. The second began to be implemented only in the latter half of 1959, after NASA Headquarters had relieved STG of the burden of the network.

Neither suborbital flight nor the tracking network for Mercury was established with any real notion of what the Soviets were doing toward a manned space flight program. But that the Soviets were doing something toward this end was made perfectly clear by Premier Nikita Khrushchev during his autumn tour of the United States. Having presented President Eisenhower with a medallion of the Soviet coat-of-arms borne by *Lunik II,* the first manmade object to hit the Moon, Khrushchev visited Hollywood, Iowa cornfields, and the Presidential retreat at Camp David. His departure coincided with press announcements that Soviet pilots were training for an assault on the cosmos. The first pictures of the back of the Moon, made by *Lunik III* on October 4, demonstrated impressive Soviet sophistication in guidance, control, and telemetry, if not in photography.[98]

If various American government agencies late in 1959 knew more than the public did about the probable speed and direction of the Soviet manned space program, this information was not passed down to the Space Task Group. Top administrators in Washington were undoubtedly accorded "need-to-know" briefings on Soviet progress, but at the working level around STG at Langley there was no such privileged information on the so-called "space race." In fact, not until mid-December did STG learn some of the operational details of Air Force programs then being conducted on the West Coast. Even the Dyna-Soar program, so heavily influenced by Hartley A. Soulé, John W. Becker, and others at Langley, seemed at times to be out of reach to Mercury engineers.[99]

In the "spirit of Camp David" the seven astronauts themselves proposed an exchange of visits and information with their Soviet counterparts, but to no avail. Proof that the United States and the Soviet Union could agree was shown in the Antarctic Treaty signed by 12 nations, including the two giants, on December 1, 1959. In the same spirit only a week later the NASA Administrator offered the services of the Mercury tracking network in support of any manned space flight the U.S.S.R. might care to undertake, but this offer also was stillborn. So sparse seemed available official information on Soviet manned space plans that Paul Purser, as special assistant to Gilruth, assumed an extra duty by beginning a scrapbook of published accounts relating to Soviet manned space flight plans.[100] It would have been "nice to know" in more detail what the Soviets were planning and how well they were proceeding, but STG's "need to know" was mainly psychological curiosity. Such information, if available, probably would have made little difference to the technological momentum of Project Mercury at the end of 1959. The impetus generated for the project by that time was truly formidable and still accelerating.

NASA Headquarters had relieved STG of developing the global range network in the spring of 1959, believing that the Tracking and Ground Instrumentation Unit (TAGIU) at Langley and the communications center at Goddard Space Flight Center together could develop radar and radio facilities more expeditiously. The wisdom of this assignment would prove itself; the communications network was never a cause for delay in Mercury operational schedules.

The decision to build an extensive new tracking network girdling the globe had derived largely from Langley studies of operational tracking requirements made by Edmond C. Buckley, Charles Mathews, Howard C. Kyle, Harry H. Ricker, and Clifford H. Nelson in the summer of 1958. Then followed four extensive and independent studies by Massachusetts Institute of Technology, Ford, Space Electronics, and Radio Corporation of America in the spring of 1959. Many interrelated technical, operational, and diplomatic considerations were involved in the evolution of the network, with pilot safety and limited capsule battery power setting the first standards.

Next to manufacturing the capsule itself, the Mercury network was the most expensive part of the entire program. But that network represented a capital investment in tracking and communications ability that NASA would also use effectively for scientific satellites and space probes. The full compass of the tracking range and communications network built for Project Mercury is beyond the scope of this volume, but salient features of the chain of tracking stations, of the communications grid, and of the ground instrumentation planned for Mercury set other basic parameters for the project. Hartley A. Soulé, the aeronautical scientist who directed Langley's part of the establishment, made a circumnavigation of the Earth to prepare the circumferential path for orbital overflights.[101]

When Christopher Kraft spoke to the Society of Experimental Test Pilots on October 9, 1959, he explained certain of the major criteria used to choose the orbital plane for Mercury and to select ground stations to monitor the man in orbit. "Since the first manned orbital flight will be a new type of operation involving many new experiences," Kraft said, "it would be desirable to keep the time in orbit as short as practical, while at the same time making an orbital flight." Emphasizing the necessity to secure an accurate and almost instantaneous determination of the potential orbit before actual insertion, as well as an exact retrofiring point and thereby a low-dispersion "footprint," or recovery area, Kraft explained how the first manned orbital mission should shoot for three rather than one or two orbits. He also listed four specific reasons why the best orbit inclination to the equatorial plane would be 32.5 degrees and the most desirable launching azimuth, or direction, would be 73 degrees true: (1) maximum use should be made of existing tracking stations and communications facilities; (2) the Atlantic Missile Range should be used for both the launching and the planned recovery area; (3) the orbital track should pass directly over the continental United States as much as possible to maximize unbroken tracking, especially during reentry; and (4) the orbital path should be planned to remain over friendly territory and temperate climatic zones.[102]

These criteria constrained the choice of both Mercury's orbital plane and its launching azimuth. East-northeast was an unusual firing direction from Cape Canaveral, where ballistic missiles were normally shot southeastward down the Atlantic range. Taking the sinusoidal track displaced for each orbit as it would look on a Mercator world projection, Soulé, Francis B. Smith, and G. Barry Graves of Langley, Mathews, Kraft, and Kyle in STG, and many others resolved the complex trades between the Atlas booster characteristics, capsule weight limitations, launch safety considerations, suitable recovery areas, existing Defense Department tracking and communications networks, and available land for locating instrument stations. Soulé and his Tracking Unit at Langley shouldered most of the responsibility for the compromises between what should and could be done with electronic communications and telemetry to promote pilot safety and ensure mission success.

While STG delegated such decisions as whether to select sites in Kenya or Guadalcanal, where to use C- or S-band radars, and whether to lay a cable or build a redundant control center on Bermuda, it kept tight control on all matters affecting control of the missions and especially of the decisions on orbital parameters. John Mayer and Carl Huss, leading STG's Mission Analysis Branch, had learned their celestial mechanics from the traditions established by Johannes Kepler, Sir Isaac Newton, and Forest R. Moulton, but from 1957 through 1959 more and more data from various artificial satellites continually refined their calculations. Keeping in close touch with STL on the improving Atlas perform- ance characteristics, Mayer's group sought to establish the ideal "launch window" or orbital insertion conditions. Not until May 1960 were these parameters established.[103]

John D. Hodge, another Anglo-Canadian, who helped Mathews learn how the Defense Department launching and tracking teams operated at the Atlantic and the Pacific missile ranges, explained how the major compromise on man-rating the worldwide network was achieved in 1959. Physicians like Lieutenant Colonel David G. Simons, of Project Manhigh fame; Major Stanley C. White, on loan to STG from the Air Force; and Colonel George M. Knauf, the staff surgeon at the Air Force Missile Test Center, had argued for continuous medical monitoring and complete voice and television coverage around the world. Physicist-engineers, like Soulé, Smith, and Graves, saw these demands as virtually impossible. The doctors were forced to retreat when asked what could possibly be done after diagnosis had been made on an ailing astronaut in orbit. Twenty minutes would be the absolute minimum time required to return him to Earth from orbital altitude after retrofiring. "Aeromedical clinicians finally had to agree late in 1959," said Hodge, "that they could do little if anything to help the astronaut until he was recovered." Once in orbit the pilot's safety primarily depended upon mission success. Mission success depended at this stage primarily upon positive control over reentry and recovery operations. The ground command and tracking systems were consequently more important than complete voice or telemetry coverage.[104]

Aside from the tight security surrounding the Atlas ICBM, perhaps the most closely guarded operational secret in Project Mercury was the ground control command frequencies established at strategic points around the Earth to enable flight controllers to retrieve capsule and astronaut from space in case of extreme necessity. Unlike the technological secret of the heatshield, this highly reliable command system was not classified as an industrial production secret, but rather to avoid any possible tampering or sabotage by electronic countermeasures.[105]

Once the specifications for the tracking and ground information systems for Project Mercury had been drawn up and distributed at a bidders' briefing on May 21, 1959, the Tracking Unit at Langley proceeded to select a prime con- tractor for the tracking network. In mid-June the organization, membership, and procedures for a technical evaluation board and source selection panel were specified. A month later the evaluation of industrial proposals was completed. The Western Electric Company, supplier of the parts and builder of the network for the American Telephone and Telegraph system, won the prime contract to build the Mercury network. After NASA sent Western Electric a letter of intent on July 30, 1959, Rod Goetchius and Paul Lein began organizing the resources of Western Electric for Project Mercury.[106]

Soulé arranged for six site survey teams chosen from his group at Langley to travel over Africa, Australia, various Pacific islands, and North America to choose locations for communications command posts. Much of the traveling Soulé did himself; he enjoyed both the technical intricacy and the scientific diplomacy of getting foreign scientists to urge their governments to cooperate for the tracking stations.[107]

Meanwhile NASA Headquarters acquired from the National Academy of Sciences Arnold W. Frutkin, who had had experience during the IGY in dealing with the State Department and foreign governments for international cooperation in scientific affairs. Beginning in September 1959, Frutkin laid the staff-work basis with the United Kingdom for Mercury tracking stations in Nigeria and Zanzibar. Zanzibar and Mexico in particular appeared reluctant to accept at face value the United States' good—that is, civilian—intentions for Mercury. The President's brother, Milton Eisenhower, personally obtained consent for full Mexican cooperation.[108]

By the end of November, preliminary designs for the Mercury tracking network were almost completed and a five-company industrial team was developing facilities. Western Electric had subcontracted to the Bendix Corporation for the search radars, telemetry equipment, and the unique display consoles for each site. Burns and Roe, Inc., took over the engineering and construction of the buildings, roads, towers, and other structural facilities at 14 sites. International Business Machines Corporation installed the computers at Goddard Space Flight Center, the Cape, and Bermuda, and supplied programming and operational services. Bell Telephone Laboratories, Inc., designed and developed the operations room of the Mercury Control Center at the Cape, and furnished a special procedures trainer for flight controllers as well as overall network systems analysis.

Eighteen gound stations were chosen for terminals in the communications network. Eleven of these sites, equipped with long-range precision radar equipment, would double for the tracking system. Sixteen of the stations were to have telemetry receivers, but only 8 of the 18 would be located on military missile ranges where existing radar and other facilities could be used. One new station (at Corpus Christi, Texas) would have to be established in the United States. Two stations were mobile, located on tracking ships at sea; seven were built in foreign countries. In November 1959, the total cost for the system was estimated at $41,000,000. The target dates for operational readiness were set as June 1, 1960, for suborbital Atlantic missions and as New Year's Day 1961 for worldwide operations.

The tracking and communications network for Project Mercury was a monumental enterprise that spanned three oceans and three continents by means of approximately 177,000 miles of hard-line communications circuitry. Although most of these wires were leased, the subtotals were likewise impressive: 102,000 miles of teletype, 60,000 miles of telephone, and over 15,000 miles of high-speed data circuits—plus the microwave radio telemetry and telecommunications circuits, which are not so easily described in linear distances. Although colossal in conception and execution, the Mercury tracking and communications network fell far short of 100-percent voice contact, telemetry contact, or tracking capability, not to speak of complete television coverage, which some aeromedical designers would have included.[109]

Despite NASA's boast about "real-time," or instantaneous, communications, the historical novelty of the Mercury communications network lay less in the temporal than in the spatial dimension. So-called "instantaneous" communications were born in the 19th century with the installation of "speed-of-light" wired communications—the telegraph, submarine cables, and the telephone. Neither radio nor radiotelephone of the 20th century brought strategic placement of telecommunications installations into such a unified network that the time of signals from antipodal sides of the world could be reduced to an "instant." Transoceanic telephone conversations between Hong Kong and Houston, for example, still delayed responses by enough time to give one the feeling of talking to oneself. Synchronous communications satellites supposedly would soon change all this, but surface communications used for Mercury operations cost some slight, but nonetheless real, time in transmission. The real innovation of the Mercury network lay in its combination of extremely rapid communications lines, linked and cross-linked around the world, culminating in digital data processing, which displayed its results in Florida virtually as soon as computed in Maryland.[110]

Only the development of digital electronic computers in recent decades made possible quick enough data digestion and display to allow communications engineers to speak of "real-time" presentations for Project Mercury. Telemetry grew more sophisticated separately in industrial and military circles until biomedical telemetry became by 1959 a recognized part of the margin of safety for manned space flight. But computer technology did not suffer this kind of bifurcated development. In fact, commercially sold digital computers were ready and actually operating under canvas tents while workmen were laying block and brick for the permanent building to surround them. No construction time could be lost if the communications and computing center was to be completed at the Goddard Center early in 1960.[111]

Harry J. Goett, formerly chief of Ames' Full Scale and Flight Research Division, took the reins as director of Goddard in September 1959. He found that the nucleus of some 150 Vanguard people had grown to approximately 500 employees. After *Vanguard III* finally terminated that program successfully on September 18, about one third of Goddard's complement turned to developing the facilities and teamwork for a space operations data control and reduction center. Actual direction of all Mercury computer programming was done from

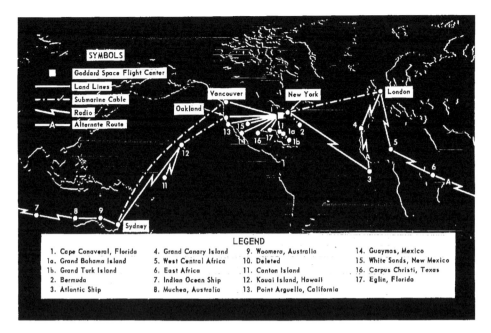

SYMBOLS
■ Goddard Space Flight Center
Land Lines
Submarine Cable
Radio
A Alternate Route

LEGEND

1. Cape Canaveral, Florida	4. Grand Canary Island	9. Woomera, Australia	14. Guaymas, Mexico
1a. Grand Bahama Island	5. West Central Africa	10. Deleted	15. White Sands, New Mexico
1b. Grand Turk Island	6. East Africa	11. Canton Island	16. Corpus Christi, Texas
2. Bermuda	7. Indian Ocean Ship	12. Kauai Island, Hawaii	17. Eglin, Florida
3. Atlantic Ship	8. Muchea, Australia	13. Point Arguello, California	

The worldwide Project Mercury tracking network was designed to provide the full range of communications objectives—tracking, data collection, command and control, and voice communication among ground points and with the capsule. If the Mercury Control Center at Cape Canaveral was the intellect of the Mercury flights, the Computing and Communications Center at Goddard Space Flight Center, Greenbelt, Md., was surely the nerve center. It acted as the communications link between the remote stations and Mercury Control Center. Its two IBM 7090 computers, operating in parallel, performed the continuous computation involved in determining powered-flight trajectory parameters, the smoothed present position of the spacecraft, continuous prediction of future spacecraft position, and constant data acquisition from all stations. Finally the computers calculated and transmitted to Mercury Control the quantities needed for instantaneous board display of the mission situation.

Langley by J. J. Donegan and H. W. Tindall, Jr., of the Tracking and Ground Instrumentation Unit. But in August 1959, John T. Mengel of Goddard conferred with Soulé; together with Edmond Buckley of NASA Headquarters they decided to assign about 14 senior engineers to specific Mercury problems. From October 1959 over the next 18 months this Goddard staff tripled in size and then doubled again when the Tracking Unit's responsibility and key men were transferred to Goddard.[112]

To raise the reliability of the computers and telemetry used in Project Mercury, redundancy and cybernetics were again incorporated in design. For example,

219

"real-time multi-programming" was the name for a technique and some hardware developed as digestive aids for Mercury data processing machines. M. J. Buist and G. M. Weinberg of Goddard tried to describe their efforts to achieve "real-time" data:

> The problem . . . is to develop a real-time computer system capable of receiving input arriving at asynchronous times and at different rates of transmission with minimum delay. It must be capable of performing mathematical computations while input is being received and edited. Simultaneously, it must send out information to numerous sites in varied formats and at varied speeds without human intervention.[113]

For this purpose two IBM 7090 transistorized computers were installed at Goddard, in Maryland. Two older model IBM 709 vacuum tube computers, one installed for NASA on Bermuda and the other an Air Force "IP" (impact predictor) for the Range Safety Officer at the Cape, were modified to handle a computer logic designed with equivalent alternative programs rather than with the usual subroutines. By means of special memory traps and automatic switching, the most critical data reduction operations were redundantly programmed into the IBM machines to ensure cross-checks on the man-rated machines in orbit.

Curiously, the difference between the IBM 709s and 7090s, so far as reliability was concerned in 1959, was the same difference the Mercury team encountered with miniaturization techniques. Although solid-state electronic devices like transistors, printed circuits, and molectronic capacitors promised tremendous savings in space, weight, and trouble-free operation, they were as yet so new that their reliability was not proved. The two 7090s at Goddard, therefore, were necessary redundancies for the heart or brain of the global tracking and target acquisition grid. The two independent and separate 709s at the Cape and Bermuda, amply stocked with spare parts, had the more limited but no less critical job of computing whether orbital launch conditions had been met. The two new transistorized computers at Goddard should man-rate the worldwide Mercury switchboard and data reduction. The older, more reliable vacuum-tube computers in the Mercury launch area should ensure nearly perfect orbital insertion conditions before the point of no return.[114]

That point of no return was first selected as insurance against landing in Africa. Later refinements to the "go/no go" decision point incorporated parameters from the standardized atmosphere, better drag coefficients, perturbation theory, preferred recovery areas, the improved Atlas booster, and the heavier Mercury capsule. These and many other intertwined considerations made the efforts of man-rating the machines for Mercury seem almost as limitless a task as space is a limitless continuum. They had the effect of canceling, for the time being, STG's hopes for an 18-orbit, or daylong, final Mercury mission.

By the end of 1959 Project Mercury was well under way on many different fronts. The American astronauts, supposedly shifting from academically oriented training to practical engineering and operational exercises, were widely known as men in training to challenge the impressive Soviet performances in space.   Most recently, *Lunik III* had photographed the unknown side of the Moon for the first time.   A few Soviet names and faces appeared in Western publications as challenging indications that the U.S.S.R. too was training pilots for space flghts. But the imagination and hopes of the American people were pinned on the seven of their own, each of whom had the chance of being the first human being to orbit Earth.   Publicized in accord with the law and in response to public demand, the plans and progress of Project Mercury were for the most part open knowledge.   NASA Headquarters was swamped with inquiries of all kinds from all sorts of people.   The field managers of Mercury had ruefully discovered that people, or at least reporters, were more interested in people than machines, so they allowed "Shorty" Powers to skew publicity toward machine-rating the men rather than man-rating the machines.[115]

VIII

Machine-Rating the Men

(JANUARY–JUNE 1960)

JUST as the safety of the pilot flying the Mercury mission depended primarily on the reliability of the boosters, so the overall success of the mission would depend primarily on the adaptability of the man inside the capsule. This proposition, recognizing man and machine as directly interdependent, had been far from evident at the beginning of the project. But by the middle of 1960 the developers of Mercury had encountered enough troubles with various automatic systems to dissipate much of their faith in automata. They began to believe that it might be simpler to train toward human perfection and safer to teach the operations team to act automatically than to try to make electromechanical systems operate faultlessly. If the gaps left after technologically man-rating the machines could be filled with techniques learned by machine-rating the men, then lack of experience need not jeopardize either the man or the mission.

Early in 1960 two peerless feats in hydronautics complemented mankind's first infantile steps toward astronautics. Two uncommon vessels named *Trieste* and *Triton,* sponsored by the United States Navy, made voyages probing the plenum of the seas only a year before men became able to venture upward into the near vacuum. While "space" was being defined popularly as the region above the atmosphere and below the ionosphere, man also conquered the aqueous seven-tenths of Earth's surface space between the atmosphere and the lithosphere for the first time in history. Demonstrating remarkable closed ecological systems and significant integrations of men and machines, the *Trieste* descended to the bottom of the deepest known point in the oceans and the *Triton* "orbited" the Earth underwater.[1]

The *Trieste* and *Triton* voyages symbolized an accelerating translation of science fiction into fact at the beginning of the sixth decade of the 20th century. These voyages not only dramatically demonstrated man's ability to explore and pioneer new frontiers but they also symbolized some complex interrelationships in the sociology of science, invention, innovation, and discovery. Project Mercury likewise promised to exhibit the social energy of a civilization intimately interlocked with industrial technology, governmental organization of manpower, and an

223

accumulation of usable knowledge. Motivationally, too, Mercury grew out of the curiosity, courage, and creativity of individual men who wanted to do "unnatural" deeds. An age-old question of humanistic inquiry—what is human nature?—seemed to become rhetorical, and, as preparations for manned space flight neared completion, inverted: what is *not* natural to man?

No one doubted at the beginning of 1960 that someone was going upward into space shortly, but precisely who, when, where, and even why were highly controversial questions. NASA Administrator T. Keith Glennan predicted the first Mercury suborbital flight within the year. Soviet spokesmen previewed their mid-January rocket tests over the Pacific as a preparation for placing man in space. Winds from conflicting opinions expressed by political, military, scientific, and industrial critics of American policy regarding space technology began to brew some squalls when NASA asked that almost $108 million of its total budget request of $802 million be appropriated for manned space flight development in fiscal 1961. Whether Mercury would finally cost $250 or $350 million, as was now variously estimated, it would still be a small fraction of the cost of the great Saturn rocket, not to mention other NASA projects.[2]

While the Eisenhower administration rejected the "space race" image attached to Mercury, Congress pressed for a greater sense of urgency, NASA Headquarters sought supplemental funds, and the Space Task Group concentrated on reconciling schedules with quality control. There was a detente in the cold war until the controversial U–2 incident in May 1960. But even during this thaw STG, as the technical coaching staff for the prime American contestant, became steadily more enmeshed in the confused competition between the United States and the Soviet Union to be first with its man in space. While Maxime A. Faget was being honored as one of the top 10 young men in government service for his designs of the Mercury capsule, couch, and escape concepts, Abe Silverstein stated publicly, "We feel no urgency to move the program unsafely." But the political pressure to produce would increase rapidly as 1960 wore on.[3]

At the end of January, Little Joe 1–B finally, with a boilerplate capsule, proved the basic aerodynamic viability of the Mercury abort concept. McDonnell Aircraft Corporation's first production hardware, which happened to be capsule No. 4, was delivered on demand only half-finished to Langley, where it was fitted with instruments like Big Joe's for the first flight to mate the Atlas booster with the "real McDonnell" head. As it turned out, the only other flight test for Mercury during this half year occurred at Wallops Island on May 9. There and then, McDonnell's Mercury capsule No. 1, so named because it had been first on the assembly line, was yanked by its escape rocket from the beach abort position to begin successfully the qualifying flights for the McDonnell capsule. It took only 14 months to build and deliver this first capsule with its most critical systems ready to be qualified for basic technical performance. Meanwhile qualification tests in laboratories began in earnest. No mechanisms were more difficult to qualify than those most intimately related to the human system.

224

CONTROLLING THE HOSTILE ENVIRONMENT

To replace the old warhead payloads with inhabitable cockpits on the missiles used to transport man into space required reliable, lightweight means of sustaining life beyond the atmosphere. When man ascends from the bottom of the ocean of air where life as we know it has evolved, he must stay inside a pressurized cell of air or die in the vacuum of space. Engineering the environmental cocoon to provide the basic metabolic needs of man became, through 1959 and 1960, one of the most complex and critical aspects in Mercury's development. Aristotle's classical anthropocentric elements—earth, water, air, and fire—correspond roughly to man's need for the gravisphere and atmospheric pressure, for hydration and waste disposal, for oxygen to breathe through lungs and skin, and for temperature and humidity control. Safety required that these life systems be redundant wherever feasible. The oxygen envelope, for instance, should be contained within the welded walls of the pressure vessel, but in case of leak, puncture, or blowout, the astronaut would wear a suit that was a second inner casing, fully capable of life support in a decompressed capsule.[4]

The environmental control system for Mercury, logically divided into the cabin and suit subsystems, grew directly out of previous aviation experience in maintaining men and machines at high altitudes. McDonnell had to seal hermetically the pressure vessel within prescribed limits; a subcontractor developed the dual air-conditioning system. Because the clothing needed for space travel turned out to be unavailable from the shelves of government issue, another subcontractor was called upon to make a full-pressure suit that would in effect be a secondary cabin.

When McDonnell and STG engineers first considered the problems of the pressurized cabin, they sought the experience of the foremost company of industrial specialists on the subject. AiResearch had grown since the 1930s into the Manufacturing Division of the Garrett Corporation, the Nation's primary supplier of the needs of the pressurized flight industry.[5] In January 1959 the three groups began to discuss the most realistic design criteria for ambient and partial gas pressures, air and water regeneration methods, thermostats, and heat exchangers. R. A. Fischer, Edward H. Olling, and Richard C. Nelson of Garrett, Herbert R. Greider, John R. Barton, and Earl A. Reed of McDonnell, and Stanley C. White and Richard S. Johnston of STG were the principal designers of this system.

While the process of fabricating the pressure-vessel shell by the fusion-welding techniques of William Dubusker and his production engineers was cut and tried on the factory floor, the important question of cabin atmosphere gas composition was being debated by physicians and physicists. Should the cabin air and pressure imitate "sea level" air mixtures of nitrogen and oxygen, or should the space cabin endorse the experience of aviation and use at highest altitude whatever would guarantee oxygenation?[6] Stanley White championed the latter position forcefully, in response to rather late outside criticism that "shirtsleeve" environ-

225

mental air might be preferable.   John F. Yardley and Barton, Faget and Johnston agreed emphatically that a five-pound-per-square-inch pressure of pure oxygen would be far more practical for saving weight, controlling leakage, and avoiding the extremely difficult problem of providing reliable oxygen partial-pressure sensors.   Faget explained STG's choice:

> The most important consideration in choice of a single gas atmosphere is reliability of operation.   If a mixed gas atmosphere were used, a major increase in complexity in the atmospheric control system and in monitoring and display instrumentation would have resulted.   Furthermore, the use of a mixed gas system would have precluded the use of simple mechanical systems for a great number of these functions which in itself would have decreased the reliability of performance.[7]

Reduced to practice, these designs had evolved into hardware for three spherical oxygen bottles, tested at 7500 pounds per square inch, with simple regulator valves, a lithium hydroxide canister to remove carbon dioxide and odors, an evaporator heat exchanger (its water would boil around 35 degrees F at a 100-mile altitude), and a simple pulsating-sponge water removal system, all to be located beneath the astronaut's legs.   Blowers, a fan, snorkels, and plumbing were also included to make the capsule livable under the extremely diverse conditions existing before, during, and after an orbital mission.   The most novel parts of this system were the high-pressure oxygen bottles, the use of lithium hydroxide, and the "sponge squeezer" to collect perspiration and respiration water vapor from the cabin atmosphere.   Cleanliness in the manufacture of these components was so important that AiResearch built the first "surgery," or "white room," for Mercury fabrication in the summer of 1959.[8]

McDonnell and AiResearch engineers consulted the voluminous literature on aeromedicine before imposing STG's specific requirements on top of the state of their art.   One of the best independent guides to that state was a report prepared in mid-1959 by A. B. Thompson of Chance Vought Astronautics, entitled "Physiological and Psychological Considerations for Manned Space Flight."   Thompson compiled a consensus on environmental parameters derived from a wide number of sources; then he presented these factors systematically in the order of their occurrence on a typical orbital mission.   Concerning the internal atmospheric environment, he drew heavily from submarine, as well as aviation, practice and expressed particular concern over abnormal toxicities peculiar to space conditions.   Regarding temperature tolerance, Thompson wrote:

> Man can exist and carry out simple tasks in environmental temperatures from −40° to 140° if suitable clothing is worn for the low, and if humidity is kept at 30-50% for the high.   Time of exposure to high temperatures should be well below man's tolerance limits.   Up to 160°F can be withstood for 20 minutes.   Such temperature highs are possible at reentry into atmosphere.   Insulation, double walls, cabin temperature and atmosphere cooling should limit the heat of cabin to less than 140°F even when skin temperature of the vehicle is much higher.[9]

Between John Barton of McDonnell and Edward Olling of AiResearch, the system specifications for environmental control began to emerge in mid-1959, subject to continuous reappraisal as other systems also took shape. Their original set of design parameters rather arbitrarily selected 400 British thermal units per hour for one man's average heat production rate over 28 hours, and an ambient pressure of 5 pounds per square inch circulating through the cabin, with a breathable supply of oxygen at the partial pressure of 3.8 pounds. An assumed oxygen consumption rate of 500 cubic centimeters per minute allowed a slight margin for suit leakage. Setting the average rate of perspiratory and respiratory water production at 6 pounds per day dictated the weight and size of their system's hardware.

Particularly knotty for the development of the active air-conditioning system and the passive insulation to control the cabin temperature was a problem that Barton described in terms of applied thermodynamics:

> Studies of launch, orbit and reentry heating effects disclosed that the insulation requirements for the cabin side-walls for the orbit and reentry phases were diametrically opposed. In orbit it is desirable to lose heat from the side-walls and during reentry it is necessary to prevent the entry of heat. The reentry phase, being more critical, dictated the side-wall insulation. In orbit, the insulation becomes an almost perfect heat barrier and dictates that the cabin cooling be primarily accomplished by the cabin heat exchanger.[10]

At the end of July 1959, Barton and Frank G. Morgan, Jr., met with 18 STG engineers, including all the astronauts, to describe the basic designs and developmental problems, especially leaky instrumentation fittings, for the system now known as "the ECS." Faget, White, William K. Douglas, William S. Augerson, and Robert B. Voas, and the ECS systems engineers, Richard Johnston, Frank H. Samonski, and Morton Schler, all warned that the design parameters were set too low. They demanded larger margins of at least 1000 British thermal units per hour for astronaut heat generation, at least 7 pounds per day assumed water production, and certainly no less oxygen pressure in the suit than in the cabin.[11] Greider and Barton warned the astronauts to learn early and thoroughly the symptoms of hypoxia in themselves so they could take action soon enough to ensure an emergency oxygen supply. Otherwise probe sensors of some sort in the nostrils or the lungs might be necessary.

McDonnell hurried the building of a "man-rating" environmental system test chamber through September 1959, so that a reliability test program for each subsystem could be conducted, complete systems tests could be scheduled, and astronaut familiarization training could begin as soon as possible. By the end of the month, Gilbert B. North, as McDonnell's test astronaut, had endured so many failures or inadequacies in the bench testing that STG sought the aid of physiologists from Duke University School of Medicine and from the Navy Air Crew Equipment Laboratory in Philadelphia to help speed the man-rating of the environmental control system. At the end of January 1960, neither the cabin nor the suit environmental control system had passed its test to operate as designed for 28 hours.

Richard Johnston reported that experience with the system was still "rather meager." He urged aeromedical investigators to provide more "realistic metabolic data" for his engineers to use in system redesign.[12]

Difficulties with the body ventilation and post-landing snorkel ventilation subsystems continued troublesome through 1960. Extensive testing at AiResearch and intensive manned tests at McDonnell beginning in June slowly eradicated most of the "bugs" plaguing the reliability of the environmental control system. A robot "crewman simulator," designed primarily by Charles F. Jahn and Eugene Wulfkehler at McDonnell, served to calibrate the physical parameters for average human inputs and outputs to this closed ecological system. Then, too, Gilbert North and Herbert Greider learned to outwit the peculiarities of the mechanisms to avoid hypoxia, dysbarism, and hyperventilation. The initial manned tests of the ECS hardware were endured by McDonnell volunteers; occasionally the Mercury astronauts would observe. Gas analysis problems delayed the accumulation of reliability records and the verification of certain operational procedures, such as ground purge and ground cooling, until early 1961.[13]

SUITING UP FOR SPACE

The pressure suit for Project Mercury was designed and first developed during 1959 as a compromise between the requirements for flexibility and adaptability. Learning to live and move within aluminum-coated nylon and rubber garments, pressurized at five pounds per square inch, was like trying to adapt to life within a pneumatic tire. Led by Walter M. Schirra, Jr., whose speciality assignment this was, the astronauts literally wrestled with the most elementary problem in becoming machine-rated—wearing the suit.

Back in February 1959, Maxime Faget and Stanley White became convinced that the so-called "pressure" suits being used by Air Force and Navy test pilots were rather "high-pressure" and partially anti-g flying suits. Ever since 1947 the Air Force and the Navy, by mutal agreement, had specialized in developing partial-pressure and full-pressure flying suits, respectively, but a decade later neither type was quite satisfactory for the newest definition of extreme altitude protection. Such suits would require extensive modifications, particularly in their air circulation systems, to meet the needs of the Mercury space pilots. The first suit conference on January 29, 1959, attended by more than 40 experts in the art of tailoring for men engaged in high-altitude flying, had recommended an extensive evaluation program.[14] Through the spring three primary competitors— the David Clark Company of Worcester, Massachusetts (a prime supplier for Air Force pressure suits), the International Latex Corporation of Dover, Delaware (a bidder on a number of government contracts involving rubberized material), and the B. F. Goodrich Company of Akron, Ohio (suppliers of most of the pressure suits used by the Navy)—competed to provide by the first of June their best products for a series of evaluation tests.

228

Few systems in the Mercury program were modified as frequently or as drastically as the space suit. Shown here are an early model worn by Slayton in 1960 (above) and the end-of-Mercury model worn by Cooper at the time of his flight in May 1963 (right). Cooper is followed by suit technician Al Rochford.

NASA had requested the Air Force Aeromedical Laboratory at Wright Air Development Center and the Navy Air Crew Equipment Laboratory in Philadelphia to plan and perform evaluations of the different test suits before mid-July. The Clark and Goodrich suits ranked highest in both evaluation programs, but predictably the Air Force favored the Clark suit and the Navy the Goodrich suit. After an evaluation conference on July 15 at Langley, the chairman, Richard Johnston, informed all parties of STG's decision to work with both the Clark and the Goodrich companies for several more months to allow further concurrent development and evaluation of various combinations of suits and ventilation systems.[15] By the end of August, William Augerson and Lee N. McMillion of STG recommended that "the suit should not be expected to cope with all the deficiencies of the Mercury capsule." The close interface between pressure suit and environmental control system caused enough problems to delay the formulation of suit specifications until October, but Goodrich was awarded the prime contract for the Mercury space suit on July 22, 1959.[16]

One of the most senior employees of the Goodrich Company was Russell M. Colley. In 1933, Wiley Post returned from the first solo flight around the world and wanted some kind of rubber suit that would enable him to fly his famous aircraft *Winnie Mae* above the record 47,000-foot altitude. Colley had designed an aluminum helmet resembling those used by marine divers and had stitched together on his wife's sewing machine the first crude space suit. The next year Colley and his company had designed and developed a more flexible flying suit for Wiley Post, with an off-center face plate to accommodate Post's one-eyed vision. In 1952, Colley had designed and helped develop swivel joints of air-tight bearings and fluted fittings for pressure suits fabricated by Goodrich for the Naval Bureau of Aeronautics. In 1959, Colley, along with Carl F. Effler, D. Ewing, and other Goodrich employees, was instrumental in modifying the famous Navy Mark IV pressure suit for NASA's needs in orbital flight.

Although the decision to let the capsule itself provide primary protection minimized the difference between corseted, pressurized g suits and a "space suit" for Project Mercury, the redundant suit environmental control system required complicated modifications and continual refittings.

The Task Group had discovered during 1959 that each Mercury capsule would have to be specially tailored to its own mission objectives. Pressure suits also were designed individually according to use—some for training, others for evaluation and development. Thirteen operational research suits first were ordered to fit astronauts Schirra and Glenn, their flight surgeon Douglas, the twins Gilbert and Warren J. North, at McDonnell and NASA Headquarters, respectively, and other astronauts and engineers to be specified later. A second order of eight suits supposedly would represent the final configuration and provide adequate protection for all flight conditions in the Mercury program.

The three major parts of the space suit—the torso coveralls, the helmet, and the gloves—were fabricated by techniques and procedures similar to those already in use in the manufacture of full-pressure flying suits. But the air system operation was unusual:

> The Mercury headpiece is a single cavity design with suit ventilation air exiting through the exhaust valve located in the right cheek area. This system is known as the "closed" or "single gas" system and utilized one air source for ventilation as well as breathing. This concept, which is desirable in space missions, permits simplicity of design and minimum weight of the ventilation and respiration equipment.[17]

According to Lee McMillion of STG's Life Systems Branch, the Big Joe reentry heating test in September 1959 allowed the developers of the pressure suit to remove much of the insulation previously thought necessary. This improved somewhat the mobility of the astronaut under full pressurization. By the end of the year McMillion, Colley, Schirra, and Glenn A. Shewmake, STG's "tailor," chose to modify the suit to facilitate mobility in the capsule rather than repattern for a more generally mobile suit. Schirra had felt many pressure points and was severely constricted in recent tests. His discomfort was traced to the design conservatism that had accepted the g suit and oxygen mask concepts used for the Navy Mark IV and Air Force X–15 flying suits. Furthermore, each time these prototype space suits were pressurized and worn, they stretched out of shape.[18]

Throughout the spring of 1960, fittings and tests with new textiles, different materials, and other human models continued until they finally solved the stretching problem. In mid-March a committee of eight members from STG, McDonnell, the Navy, and Goodrich decided on the final design features for the Mercury space suits. All kinds of minor troubles with zippers, the visor, the segmented shoulder, lacings, straps, snaps, seams, valves, underwear, gloves, microphones, and neck dams continued. But after a "gripe session" in mid-May 1960, the astronauts and their tailors essentially agreed on what the well-dressed man should wear into space.[19]

During an orbital flight, certain physiological limitations were expected to establish the requirements for matching man and machine in one smoothly functioning system.[20] In the area of noise and vibration, for example, research during the 1950s had led to the conclusion that 140 decibels, in the broad spectrum between 100 and 12,000 cycles per second, was the most that man could stand for durations of four or five seconds. Acceleration tolerances were rising, thanks to knowledge gained by centrifuge and rocket sled tests, but above 6 g pilots could breathe only by forcing abdominal constriction and could move effectively only their hands and fingers. An oxygen pressure inside the lungs corresponding to that of 100 millimeters of fluid mercury was judged necessary to preclude any symptom of hypoxia. To guard against the danger of "bends" (caisson disease or dysbarism), the cabin pressure should not be more than twice the suit emergency pressure of 180 millimeters of mercury. No more than two percent of carbon dioxide by volume at sea level should be permitted.[21] Other limitations, including extremes of temperature, humidity, radiation, and accumulating toxic gases from carbon monoxide, ozone, metal, and plastic fumes, also became "human parameters." Warning instruments in the capsule relied primarily on stimulating the astronaut's senses of sight and sound; psychologists also studied the feasibility of using his senses of touch and smell to aid him in diagnosing malfunctions.[22]

During the fifties academic and medical studies in sensory deprivation made an important, if indirect, contribution to the building of the spacecraft and the training of the astronauts. Made notorious by the experience of American prisoners of war who had been isolated and "brainwashed" in North Korean prison cells, the effects of isolation were attacked on many fronts. At McGill University, in Canada, at the University of Rochester in New York, and at the National Institute of Mental Health in Bethesda, Maryland, famous sensory deprivation experiments reduced all physical stimuli to near zero. Suspending people in water of body temperature in blacked-out, soundproof rooms at Bethesda revealed that normal men, regardless of their motivations, could hardly stay both conscious and sane if deprived of all sensory stimuli beyond three hours. Physicians and psychiatrists were warning in 1956 and 1957 that

> if one is alone enough and at levels of human and physical stimulation low enough, the human mind turns inward and projects outward its own contents and processes. . . . Man's mental state is dependent on adequate perceptual contact with the outside world. . . . Isolation produces an intense desire for extrinsic sensory stimuli and bodily motion, increased suggestibility, impairment of organized thinking, oppression and depression, and in extreme cases, hallucinations, delusions, and confusion.[23]

Such background studies strengthened aeromedical demands, originating outside NASA and STG, for continuous communications between the ground and an orbiting man, for increasing the number of meaningful cues to be given the man in space, and for accenting significant tasks to be performed by the man inside the capsule. There was room for controversy here, but STG and NASA believed the hypothetical risks did not justify the very large outlay of money, men, and time that a continuous communication network would have required.

If outside advice of this type was not always taken, there was still a conscious effort to solicit it. One of the most useful means of dialogue was the presenting of papers at meetings of professional societies. The size, lead time, and innovating nature of Project Mercury, together with the impetus from NASA's open information policy, all reinforced the normal professional obligation to inform and meet the judgment of one's colleagues. Thus it was that, on January 25, 1960, several leading engineers from the Space Task Group were in New York for the annual meeting of the Institute of Aeronautical Sciences and presented papers reviewing the scope and recent results of their research and development program.[24] In one of these, Charles W. Mathews set forth the operational plans for the orbital mission. He did not mention the role of the pilot until the end

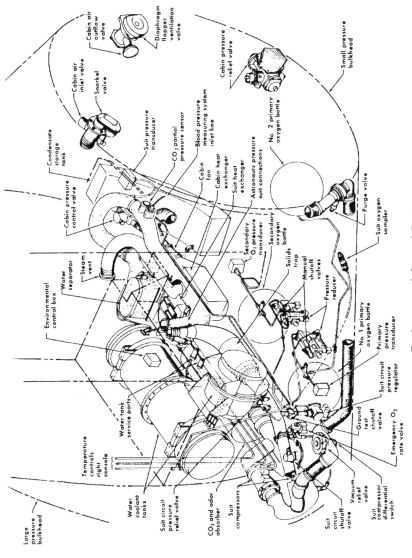

Large
pressure
bulkhead

Temperature
controls
right
console

Water
coolant
tanks

Suit circuit
pressure
relief valve

CO₂ and odor
absorber

Suit
compressors

Suit
circuit
shutoff
valve

Vacuum
relief
valve

Suit
compressor
differential
switch

Emergency O₂
rate valve

Ground
test
shutoff
valve

Suit circuit
pressure
regulator

No. 1 primary
oxygen bottle

Primary
pressure
transducer

Pressure
reducer

Manual
shutoff
valves

Solids
trap

Secondary
oxygen
bottle

Secondary
O₂ pressure
transducer

Astronauts pressure
suit connections

Suit heat
exchanger

Cabin heat
exchanger

Cabin
fan

Blood pressure
measuring system
inlet line

CO₂ partial
pressure sensor

Suit pressure
transducer

Water tank
service ports

Environmental
control box

Steam
vent

Water
separator

Cabin pressure
control valve

Condensate
storage
tank

Cabin air
inlet valve

Snorkel
valve

Cabin air
outflow
valve

Diaphragm
flapper
ventilation
valve

Cabin pressure
relief valve

No. 2 primary
oxygen bottle

Small pressure
bulkhead

Purge valve

Suit oxygen
sampler

Environmental Control System.

of his remarks. He then offered a summary list of eight activities to illustrate what the astronaut must be prepared to do: the Mercury pilot should communicate with ground stations, make scientific observations, monitor onboard equipment, control capsule attitude, navigate and fire retrorockets, initiate emergency procedures, activate escape system if necessary, and deploy landing parachute if required. Any one of these activities could conceivably save the mission.[25]

The degree of control over his own destiny that the astronaut might have during the first orbital flights steadily increased throughout 1959 by virtue of the development of two new semi-automatic control systems: fly-by-wire, interposed in the automatic stabilization and control system (ASCS), and the rate command system (rate stabilization control system, or RSCS), superimposed on the manual proportional control system. Further elaboration and sophistication of the hardware took account of man's flexibility by providing for the use of more than one system at a time. In addition to the "last resort," or manual-proportional, method of attitude control, other uses of the astronaut as a source of mechanical power were being incorporated to the mutual advantage of reliability and flexibility. Turnkey handles and pull rings were added to duplicate virtually every automatic function of the mission sequence.

In April 1960, Edward R. Jones, the chief psychologist at McDonnell, feeling that a vigorous offense is the best defense, argued in public that man in the Mercury capsule not only could act as an observer as well as the observed but should be considered an integral part of the system to increase the probability of mission success. Having just completed extensive studies of man's vision from the new centerline window, Jones supervised studies of other expected sensations during the Mercury orbital flight.[26] As the hardware and manned capsule systems tests progressed, Jones had more reason for his optimism about man's ability to perform effectively in space, once his life-support requirements were met. Concerning higher mental processes, Jones, speaking in a symposium at the Iowa Academy of Science, where James A. Van Allen represented the instrumentalists and John Paul Stapp represented the experimental physicians, maintained his positive approach:

> Most of the astronaut's tasks will involve complex mental activity even though some may be on a near reflex level as a result of constant practice. It is not expected that impairment of these functions will occur under normal vehicle operation. Stress and an abnormal atmospheric composition, if present, could cause some impairment of the higher mental functions.
>
> It should be apparent that the training of the astronaut in the operation of the space vehicle will be critical. Much of the physiological training and conditioning will be given on a part task basis in human centrifuges, and pressure and heat chambers. The operation of the vehicle can be practiced over and over again in a capsule simulator . . . built for Mercury. Overlearning far beyond the point that apparent progress stops seems to be the best guarantee that the astronaut will have developed response patterns that are least apt to deteriorate under the stresses of orbital flight.[27]

SEVEN ASTRONAUTS-IN-TRAINING

When the astronauts first had reported to the Task Group at the end of April 1959, they had been oriented with a series of lectures covering every aspect of STG's progress. After a welcoming general briefing by Paul E. Purser, Alan B. Kehlet delivered their first lecture on April 29, explaining the configuration and the escape system. Following two weeks of such lectures, the group began to visit contractor facilities for familiarization with mockups, hardware, and manufacturing processes. They went to the launch site at Cape Canaveral. At various military and medical centers, each man learned to know himself still better through training sessions in the pressure suit, in heat chambers, in heavy concentrations of carbon dioxide, and in parabolic flying. By July, Robert Voas, the astronauts' training officer, had prepared tentative curricula and schedules; during unscheduled times, each man was expected each week to fly for three hours, to spend six hours on his specialty area, and to exercise at least four hours in athletics. The primitive jury-rigged air-bearing platform trainer also was ridden by each astronaut for two hours per week at first.

During August 1959, each man spent approximately two weeks at Johnsville riding the centrifuge in "closeloop" (i.e., with man in the control circuit) simulation of the exit and reentry profiles. In September each man spent a week at McDonnell, another at the Cape for the Big Joe shot, and another at the Goodrich plant in Akron being fitted for his pressure suit. And in October 1959, the seven pilots, by now reluctant celebrities, traveled to Edwards and Vandenberg Air Force Bases, to the AiResearch and Convair factories, and to the Naval School of Aviation Medicine at Pensacola for different kinds of centrifuge runs and for training in survival, disorientation, and communications.[28]

Although everyone who read the news or looked at *Life* magazine knew that the Mercury astronauts had been assigned specialty areas befitting their profession as engineering test pilots, few could see the logic of those assignments.[29] M. Scott Carpenter accepted responsibility for communications and navigation because as a Navy lieutenant he had had special training in airborne electronics and celestial pathfinding. Virgil I. Grissom, who had earned a degree in mechanical engineering from Purdue University in 1950, became the expert for the group on the complicated electromechanical, automatic, and manual attitude-control systems. The senior man in age and date of rank, John H. Glenn, Jr., had the most experience in flying varieties of aircraft and could therefore make the best contribution to cockpit layout. Walter M. Schirra, Jr., born to a flying family and a graduate of the Naval Academy, took a special interest in life-support systems and the pressure suits. Alan B. Shepard, Jr., like Carpenter and Schirra, had the background training of the naval flier for specializing in tracking and recovery operations. L. Gordon Cooper, Jr., and Donald K. Slayton, both Air Force captains, accepted the jobs of astronaut liaison with the developers of the Redstone and the

Just as they did as military test pilots before they joined the Mercury program, each astronaut felt his first responsibility to be that of the engineer-test pilot responsible for knowing his spacecraft and its equipment so well that he could quickly and with certainty evaluate its performance. In these photos, Cooper (*left*) performs an engineering check on a spacecraft and Schirra (*below*) inspects a hatch in white room at the McDonnell Aircraft Corp. plant.

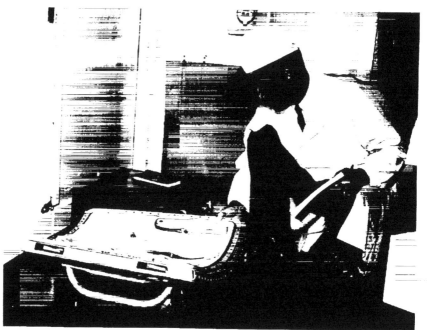

Atlas boosters, respectively. Cooper, the youngest of the group, had been dedicated to flying since childhood and had worked with performance engineering similar to what he would encounter at Redstone Arsenal. And Slayton, with a degree in aeronautical engineering from the University of Minnesota and having worked for two years with the Boeing Company in Seattle, was best fitted to report on the progress of the Atlas booster at Convair/Astronautics.

The astronauts' specialty assignments had some direct effect on the redesign of the Mercury suit, cockpit layout, and capsule hatch and window systems. More importantly, the assignments kept the crew informed in depth on the problems and progress in major areas of concern to all members. Carpenter and Shepard kept tabs on the progress of the Tracking Unit at Langley and of the Goddard Space Flight Center in preparing to operate the network. While Carpenter monitored the development of onboard navigation equipment, such as the Earth-path indicator and starfinder charts, Shepard paid special attention to recovery at sea and to problems of egress from the capsule and survival on Earth in inhospitable environments. Grissom studied the electromechanical worries of Robert G. Chilton, Thomas V. Chambers, and other controls engineers. Schirra worked closely with Richard Johnston and John Barton on the environmental system, and with Lee McMillion, Gilbert North, and the Goodrich people in preliminary fittings of the pressure suit. Cooper and Slayton spent much of their time traveling to Huntsville and southern California, respectively, attending meetings and offering suggestions from the pilot's viewpoint on how best to mate a manned capsule with the Redstone and Atlas missiles. Glenn, meanwhile, paid special attention to optimizing the cockpit and improving simulation training.[30]

Within months after joining the Space Task Group, the more eager than anxious astronauts found themselves barraged by questions regarding their emotional feelings about being catapulted into orbit. In answer to one such set of questions, posed in an author's questionnaire for a high-school textbook, Schirra perfunctorily replied that it was only natural for a test pilot to want to participate in the most advanced form of manned vehicular travel. Schirra's desire to "go higher, farther, and faster" than previously had been possible was to him neither mysterious nor worthy of introspection; it was simply the professional commitment of them all and of STG to want to expand the test pilot's "envelope." [31]

Partly because of this kind of natural public interest and partly because the civilian space agency had a statutory mandate to conduct educational publicity, NASA Headquarters, after investigation and decision, encouraged the astronauts to stay together and to accept the fringe benefits of a single private-enterprise publishing offer arranged in outline even before their selection. This precluded eventual competitive bidding for individual story rights. On August 5, 1959, the astronauts sold their "personal stories" to the highest bidder, Time-Life, Inc., for $500,000, an amount to be equally divided regardless of who might be chosen first to fly in space. This money was to be paid in installments throughout the program. The astronauts' wives also subscribed to the contract. Defense Department policy had been followed by the NASA decision because the astronauts were active-duty military officers.[32] There were similar precedents for test pilots, Presidents, and submarine captains. Many Congressmen approved this form of extra life insurance for the astronauts' wives.

A public furor, nevertheless, arose in the press over these exclusive rights to publish the memoirs of the seven. Few other peripheral policy decisions regarding Project Mercury were to become so controversial in the long run. As the waiting period before an astronaut flew in space stretched on, public interest grew; the competition among newsmen and media increased; the line between personal and public domains blurred. NASA and STG were forced to contend with no small amount of adverse and even spiteful publicity from indignant correspondents who were not of the favored few. Warren North, two days after this contract was signed, advised Silverstein about it and warned of other impending difficulties, including a loss of privacy to a degree the astronauts might not have anticipated.[33]

The agreement, arranged without fee by C. Leo DeOrsey, a prominent Washington lawyer and sportsman, assigned all magazine and book rights to Time-Life, Inc., for "non-official" feature stories on the astronauts and their families. Since it was cleared by NASA's legal and public relations chiefs, John Johnson and Walter T. Bonney, the astronauts and the Task Group had to adapt themselves to this policy. John A. "Shorty" Powers, at least, was relieved of one headache and was not displeased with the arrangements.[34]

Although Robert Voas at first had designed an orderly curriculum for the astronauts, their activities soon became so diverse and the group separated on sorties for their specialties so often that the academic approach became impossible. The coordination of astronaut training became his chief duty. Voas gathered and trained a team of training specialists. George C. Guthrie had responsibility for improving training aids, procedures, and simulation devices; Raymond G. Zedekar arranged the lecture series; Stanley Faber conducted the four-phase centrifuge training program on the Johnsville "wheel." By the end of 1959, each of the astronauts had trained for about 10 hours riding the gondola at Johnsville. Voas, meanwhile, turned his attention to an extensive astronaut task analysis, which paralleled the work of Edward Jones at McDonnell.[35] Just before Christmas 1959, John Glenn privately described his training experiences in a letter to a friend and fellow pilot:

> This past 8 or 9 months has really been a hectic program, to say the least, and by far the most interesting thing in which I have ever taken part, outside of combat.
>
> Following our selection in April, we were assigned to the Space Task Group portion of NASA at Langley Field, and that is where we are based when not traveling. The way it has worked out, we have spent so much time on the road that Langley has amounted to a spot to come back to get clean skivvies and shirts and that's about all. We have had additional sessions at Wright Field in which we did heat chamber, pressure chamber, and centrifuge work and spent a couple of weeks this fall doing additional centrifuge work up at

238

Johnsville. This was some program since we are running it in a laydown position similar to that which we will use in the capsule later on and we got up to as high as 16 g's. That's a batch in any attitude, laydown or not.

With the angles we were using, we found that even lying down at 16 g's it took just about every bit of strength and technique you could muster to retain consciousness. I found there was quite a bit more technique involved in taking this kind of g than we had thought. Our tolerances from beginning to end of runs during the period we worked up there went up considerably as we each developed our own technique for taking this high g. A few runs a day like that can really get to you. Some other stuff we did up there involved what we call tumble runs or going from a plus g in two seconds to a minus g and the most we did on this was in going from a plus 9 g to a minus 9 g. Obviously a delta of 18. . . . When we first talked about doing this, I didn't think it would be possible but in doing a careful buildup we happily discovered that this was not so horrible. At plus 9 g to minus 9 g we were bouncing around a bit but it was quite tolerable.

*   *   *

We just finished an interesting activity out at Edwards AFB doing some weightless flying in the F–100. This was in the two-place F–100 so that we could ride in the rear seat and try various things such as eating and drinking and mechanical procedures while going through the approximately 60 second ballistic parabola that you make with a TF–100. That started at about 40,000 feet, 30 degrees dive to 25,000, picking up about 1.3 to 1.4 mach number, pull out and get headed up hill again at 25,000 and about a 50 degree or 60 degree climb angle, at which point they get a zero-g parabola over the top to about 60 degrees downhill.

You can accomplish quite a bit in the full minute in those conditions and contrary to this being a problem, I think I have finally found the element in which I belong. We have done a little previous work floating around in the cabin of the C–131 they used at Wright Field. That is even more fun yet, because you are not strapped down and can float around in the cabin doing flips, walk on the ceiling or just come floating the full length of the cabin while going through the approximately 15 seconds of weightlessness that they can maintain on their shorter parabola. That was a real ball and we get some more sessions with this machine sometime after the first of the year.[36]

Seasoned rocket experts, especially in Wernher von Braun's group, were worried early in the program over the human tolerance to noise and vibration at the tip of a missile leaving Earth's atmosphere. Biomedical experimentation during the fifties had almost, but not quite, confirmed that a man literally can be shaken to death by sympathetic vibrations induced through various harmonics upon certain organs. No one was yet sure whether the 140-decibel noise limit would be attenuated enough by the double-walled capsule and the astronaut's helmet to keep him comfortable and able to communicate.[37] In February 1960, a representative from the Army Ballistic Missile Agency at Huntsville proposed a training project in which astronauts would experience controlled noise and vibration inside a simulated Mercury capsule mounted above a Jupiter engine being static-fired. The astronauts' personal physician, William Douglas, objected vehemently and saved the astronauts from this ordeal. Internal acoustic measurements in the capsules riding Big Joe and Little Joe 2, however, gave concern that aerodynamic noise at max q might blot out communications if it approached the 140-decibel limit. The astronauts decided to condition themselves to loud noises in other ways by occasionally stationing themselves near the blow-down exhausts of the wind tunnels around Langley. Carpenter, supported by the environmental control system in capsule No. 3, sat through these static noise tests and proved that communications remained satisfactory in spite of extremely loud outside noises.[38]

Other carefully controlled trials by ordeal were arranged to teach the astronauts how best to survive for a time anywhere on Earth beneath their planned orbital track. During the spring and summer of 1960, capsule egress training, and water, desert, and jungle survival courses were instituted for their benefit. So exotic and picturesque were these excursions that publicity photographs flooded the news media.[39]

Serious consideration was not given to the use of a personal parachute, with which the astronaut might bail out from his explosive side hatch, until May 1960, when Lee McMillion and Alan Shepard suggested the idea for the Mercury-Redstone flights at least. The exploits of the Air Force balloonist, Captain Joseph W. Kittinger, Jr., who had been making solo stratopheric ascents for the Air Force since 1957, were a significant factor in this reevaluation of the personal parachute. In Project Excelsior, Kittinger began a series of record-breaking sky dives. On November 16, 1959, he jumped from an open gondola at an altitude of 76,400 feet. Three weeks later, from *Excelsior II,* he bailed out at an altitude of 74,700 feet to establish a free-fall record of 55,000 feet before pulling his ripcord. STG knew of Kittinger's plans for *Excelsior III,* which he fulfilled on August 16, 1960, by diving from his balloon at 103,000 feet and falling 17 miles before opening his chute at 17,500 feet. If Kittinger could do it, so might the Mercury astronaut in case the escape tower would not jettison or both main parachutes failed on a Mercury-Redstone flight.[40]

Although supposedly the first phase of astronaut training through 1959 was to concentrate on academic studies in the eclectic new field of "space science," the astronauts did not relish book-learning at the expense of field trips, specialty assignments, and familiarization with the developing hardware. As soon as new training aids and partial simulators became available, they would make full use of them. Late in 1959, however, the only operable flight simulator was a crude "lash-up" of analog computers driving a cockpit panel display above a couch on an air-bearing floating platform at Langley. Gradually STG engineers Harold I. Johnson, Rodney F. Higgins, and George Guthrie built more sophistication into this special kind of Link trainer. By January 1960 they were calling it the Air Bearing Orbital Attitude Simulator. In use and development simultaneously through 1960, this machine slowly evolved into a major training aid called the ALFA (for "air lubricated free attitude" [or axis]) trainer. McDonnell provided a capsule shell as an egress trainer in mid-February 1960. But the most valuable and

240

elaborate training aids were the two McDonnell-built simulators called "procedures trainers." One for team training at the Cape and another at Langley were installed and in use by April 1960. Through long hours of practice in these procedures trainers, the astronauts "overlearned" their tasks, as Jones had recommended, so that they would act almost reflexively during their mission sequence.

During the first year of the astronaut training program, the seven pilots heard approximately 50 hours of space science lectures given primarily by senior members of the Langley Research Center. Elementary mechanics and aerodynamics made up 10 hours of this time. Formal presentations in space physics took up 12 hours. Other courses included principles of guidance and control (4 hours), navigation in space (6 hours), elements of communications (2 hours), and basic physiology (8 hours). Each astronaut spent approximately 8 hours at Morehead Planetarium at the University of North Carolina on star recognition and practicing celestial navigation.[41]

"Phase Two" of the training program, based on simulation training and engineering involvement, was to begin with the new year. But concurrent developments, individual study, and personal practice in various areas complicated the astronauts' training calendar. At the end of one full year of assignment to STG, each of the seven had spent approximately 10 days in St. Louis at the McDonnell plant; five days in San Diego at the Convair/Astronautics factory; and two days each at the Cape, at Huntsville, at Edwards Air Force Base, in El Segundo at Space Technology Laboratories and the Air Force Ballistic Missile Division, and at the Goodrich plant in Akron. Each also spent one day at the Rocketdyne factory of North American Aviation to see the engines being produced for the Atlas, another day at the AiResearch shops to meet the makers of their environmental control systems, and yet another at the Los Angeles plant of a subcontractor, Protection, Incorporated, where individual headgear was being molded.[42] These visits by the astronauts to the various industrial production lines were found to be so valuable in inspiring craftsmen and technicians at all levels to higher standards of workmanship that these personal contacts between producers and the astronaut-consumers became a regular feature of quality control programs. Grissom's simple remark on a visitation to Convair, "Do good work!" became a motto of incalculable value to every worker who heard it or shook his hand.

The astronauts also made many field trips to Government installations for familiarization with specific conditions of space flight. In addition to the training for high accelerations on the centrifuges at Johnsville, Dayton, and Pensacola, training for zero acceleration—weightlessness—was distilled from the short parabolic hops that were flown in C-131s at Wright-Patterson Air Force Base and in F-100 aircraft at the School of Aviation Medicine in San Antonio. Closer to their Langley home, the astronauts mastered scuba diving at the Naval Amphibious Base near Norfolk; at their home base swimming pool they practiced floating fully suited. Also immersions in a Langley test tank gave them the sensation of neutral buoyancy. Both at Dayton and Philadelphia the astronauts borrowed military

241

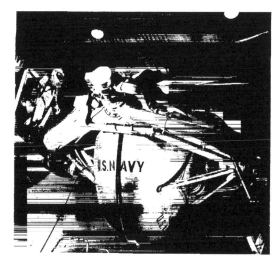

Johnsville centrifuge

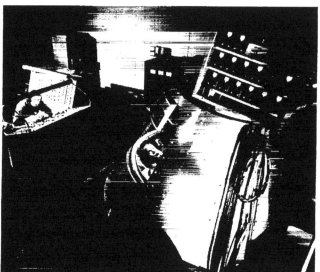

Procedures trainer

ALFA trainer

MASTIF trainer

Weightlessness in C–131

Weightlessness in F–100F

Trainers and simulators have for some years been part of all flight training. In the Mercury program the normal training requirement was intensified by the new areas of sensation and orientation that man had never before experienced. Hence the astronauts underwent centrifuge runs at Johnsville, Pa., for g-force training; procedures training at Langley; ALFA training at Langley for pilotage; MASTIF training at Lewis for acquaintance with space disorientation; movement training in weightless condition in C–131 flights at Wright Air Development Center; and piloting experience with weightlessness in supersonic flights at Edwards Air Force Base.

facilities to experience reduced ambient pressures in decompression chambers. For conditioning to withstand high heating rates, the astronauts were toasted in the Air Crew Equipment Laboratory ovens and in a "human calorimeter" at the National Institute of Mental Health at Bethesda. Two facilities at Pensacola, the "rotating room" and the "human disorientation device," provided some experience with induced vertigo. But for complex tumbling experiences, each astronaut spent some time at NASA's Lewis Center in Cleveland, in the curious test device called the "MASTIF." Finally, each man learned to know his own idiosyncrasy to high concentrations of carbon dioxide by experiments also done at Bethesda.

None of the mechanical aids for astronaut training could simulate more than a few of the conditions of space flight at a time. Even the seven Redstone ballistic flights, one planned for each astronaut, would be only partial simulations. Harold Johnson commented in February 1960 that the Redstone flights "may or may not be classified as training missions, depending on how sporting you may be." The astronauts were not only sporting in this regard, they were also chafing at delays. They suggested to Robert Gilruth that a rhesus monkey ride MR–1 so the schedule might be compressed enough to put the first chimp in orbit by the end of November.[43]

Perhaps the most impressive simulator, the whirligig called MASTIF (for Multiple Axis Space Test Inertia Facility), located at Lewis' cavernous altitude wind tunnel, was publicized far beyond its value as a training aid. Conceived in 1959 by David S. Gabriel of Lewis as a rig to test space equipment in three degrees of rotational and two degrees of linear freedom, the idea of concentric gimbaled cages was translated into hardware in the altitude wind tunnel early in 1959, when Lewis was assigned the job of testing Big Joe's attitude control system. Robert R. Miller directed the MASTIF project; Louis L. Corpas did the detail design work; and Frank Stenger developed the air-jet propulsion arrangement. Soon they had erected a tinker-toy-like rig 21 feet in diameter at its supporting yoke, capable of mounting a 3000-pound space capsule inside its three sets of gimbals, and able to turn and tumble the whole combination in three axes simultaneously at 60 noisy revolutions per minute. An early trial revved the outer cage from zero to 50 revolutions per minute in half a turn.[44]

James W. Useller, another mechanical engineer at Lewis, was first to see the potential in the MASTIF, if adapted, for astronaut training. Useller and a Lewis test pilot, Joseph S. Algranti, began taking cautious rides inside the MASTIF as soon as the controls engineers could spare it in mid-1959. They set up a formal test program for about 10 pilots and physiologists who wanted to see what rolling, pitching, and yawing at different speeds and for different lengths of time would do to a man. A thorough literature search revealed some similar late-19th-century German experiments, but Useller and Algranti proceeded to confirm a condition known as ocular nystagmus, an automatic flutter of the eyeballs induced by the acceleration of angular rotation. After extensive tests, they verified a rough limit of tolerance at about 30 revolutions per minute in three axes; beyond this limit, even the most experienced pilots could expect to get sick.[45]

Thus, in February 1960, when the first pair of astronauts, Grissom and Shepard, arrived in Cleveland for a week's stay to test the MASTIF and their reactions to it, extensive experience had already been accumulated by other pilots. After a hard night and a frustrating morning strapped in the seat while the MASTIF was being adjusted, Shepard again stepped inside the three large gimbal cages for his second sitting but first real ride in this machine. When MASTIF finally started to spin, Shepard turned green and pressed the red "chicken switch," sounding a claxon horn as a signal to stop. To control the nausea and vertigo induced by this maniacal carrousel required dogged determination. The next day Shepard—and before the end of March all the astronauts—took examination runs at 30 revolutions per minute in all three axes and quickly learned, by using the hand controller, to activate nitrogen reaction motor brakes, to halt their rotation and bring themselves to a stop while the cages continued to spin. The confidence gained from this experience was invaluable, but one series on the MASTIF was enough. Reporters who watched a demonstration by Carpenter were vivid in their descriptions of the piercing scream, multicolored cages, and extraordinary contortions of MASTIF, billing it the ultimate in wild carnival rides.[46]

Far more important and critical was the second phase of the Johnsville centrifuge program, which began in mid-April to test much of the McDonnell hardware, including the couch and hand controller, instrument panel and full pressure suit, and the astronauts' responses to the dynamic simulation of the g profiles. An STG status report for April listed eight multiplex objectives of the ongoing centrifuge training program: (1) to test the retention by the astronaut of the straining technique and other skills developed in the August program; (2) to familiarize the astronauts with straining under reduced pressure; (3) to familiarize the astronauts with performing at high g levels in an inflated pressure suit; (4) to evaluate the couch manufactured by McDonnell Aircraft; (5) to evaluate the handcontroller developed by McDonnell; (6) to test proposed voice procedures under acceleration and reduced pressure; (7) to rehearse and evaluate the feasibility of a two-hour countdown period following astronaut insertion; and (8) to provide initial experience with Redstone acceleration patterns.[47]

With over 120 controls at his glove tips, including about 55 electrical switches, 30 fuses, and 35 mechanical levers, the astronaut had to learn a great deal regarding the monitoring and operation of these points of contact with his machine. From the prime contractor came a series of operating and maintenance manuals entitled "Service Engineering Department Reports," or "SEDRs" (pronounced "cedars"). The indoctrination manual had been replaced by a familiarization manual in the fall of 1959, and this in turn was replaced at the beginning of 1960 by SEDR No. 109, called the "Astronauts' Handbook." Although the first capsule maintenance manual, SEDR No. 108, was not available until mid-year, it was not badly needed until the mass move to the Cape at that time.

The "Astronauts' Handbook" set forth operating procedures in three sections: normal, emergency, and trouble-shooting activities. The checklist for procedures envisioned in a normal orbital mission at that time included 130 items expected of the astronaut, 69 of which were part of an extensive preflight interior inspection. Under emergency operations procedures, 156 items were listed as possible pilot actions in case of equipment malfunctions. The five phases of the mission— launch, orbit, reentry, descent, and landing—each required special responses to emergencies arising during that portion of the mission. Finally, the mechanics of five major subsystems of the capsule were outlined in the trouble-shooting section and then condensed into checklists for the reaction and environmental control systems and for the electrical and communication systems. The attitude stabilization and control system checklist was promised but was not yet available.[48]

As McDonnell technical writers prepared and revised the "Astronauts' Handbook," STG's operational plans were becoming systematized through concurrent revisions of its "General Systems Information Document." Lewis R. Fisher, Donald D. Arabian, William M. Bland, Jr., and Sigurd A. Sjoberg first published this basic guide as "Project Mercury Working Paper No. 118" in March 1960 and revised it twice within the next year. They outlined the general plans for the Mercury-Atlas and Mercury-Redstone missions, including overall test objectives, flight plans, capsule design criteria, description of the capsule and systems, and the general operational plan from prelaunch phase through recovery. Specific mission directives were based on this format, and the authors of most later working papers presupposed a familiarity with "Working Paper No. 118." [49]

While John Glenn and Walter Schirra studied the interrelations of the pressurized suit and the cockpit layout, McDonnell design engineers rearranged the Mercury control panel to place all controls in a U-shaped pattern around either side and below the instruments. When an astronaut's suit was inflated, he could reach the right side and bottom of the panel with his right hand, and his left hand could reach the left side and bottom, but the center and top of the panel were inaccessible. Since Mercury gloves were thicker and heavier than those on flying suits, all controls had to be positive in operation, including guards for pushbuttons and with key handles and pull rings designed for a good grip and the application of considerable force, up to 50 pounds in some cases.

In their efforts to integrate man and machine, psychologists Jones and Voas, among others, had shown by late spring 1960 how the reliability of Mercury could be increased by the use of man's flexibility. Using the pilot as a trouble-shooter engineer in many cases could make the difference between mission failure and success. Conversely, as man's limitations became more precisely known in relation to the equipment to be used, correspondingly higher standards for the automatic systems, particularly the attitude stabilization controls, were introduced. Voas later expressed a new consensus when he said:

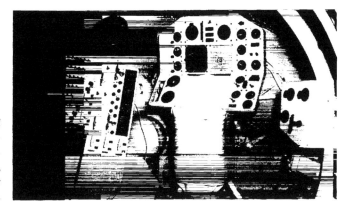

Contrast in Mercury panel and console arrangement: right, the instrument positions in early 1959; below, the panels as used in Glenn's orbital flight, Feb. 20, 1962.

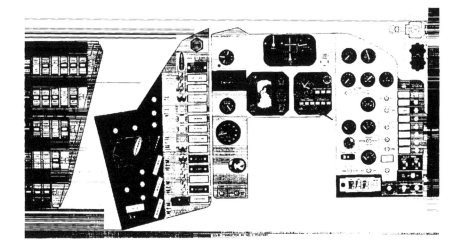

The astronaut's primary job is to control the vehicle. The astronaut is not a mere passenger, but an active controller of the vehicle who performs an important and complex task which is basic to the total reliability of the mission.

System flexibility is increased by provision for the use of more than one of these [attitude control mode] systems at a time. Since the automatic reaction jets and the manual reaction jets are completely independent, it is possible for the man to exercise control through the manual jets while the auto-pilot is exercising control through the automatic jets. One occasion for use of both control systems would be in maneuvering in orbit when the astronaut desires to let the autopilot control two axes such as roll and pitch while he takes control in yaw.[50]

Meanwhile Jones and the human factors engineers at McDonnell were determining more ways in which man could back up other automatic malfunctions through their "failure task analysis." Using the failure mode predictions from the design engineers' work on the reliability program, they elaborated "in detail the probable sensory output characteristics of the failure, the corrective responses required by the astronaut or ground monitor, and the failure effect." [51]

Jones' human-factors team worked closely with McDonnell's Mercury reliability experts, Walter A. Harmon and Eugene A. Kunznick. They in turn allied themselves with another McDonnell crew employed on a special check of the Mercury reliability program instigated by NASA Headquarters. Programmers at McDonnell coded on punch cards all probable systemic failures; by June 1960 they had assembled massive computer printouts that detailed corrective actions an astronaut could take in case the robots should go wrong. They found that over a third of such failures would not show up on instruments or through warning lights, but could be detected through symptoms presenting unusual sights, sounds, smells, or vibrations. As many as 18 different failures, however, might show the same set of multiple cues, so the work of categorizing and organizing these data required another full year. Preliminary results from these cooperative studies helped early to isolate malfunctions that needed new indicators, to rank the frequency of instrument use, and to shape the training program. Efforts to predict the total system reliability by this evaluation intensified the debate over the "numbers game." [52]

Looking Over Mercury and Beyond

In March and April 1960, NASA scored two spectacular triumphs by using the Air Force's Thor-Able booster combination to launch *Pioneer V* and *Tiros I*. The former was a highly successful instrumented probe to explore the space between the orbits of Earth and Venus. Launched on March 11, *Pioneer V* established a new telecommunications record of 22.5 million miles by the end of June and returned a bonanza of data on solar flares, particle energies and distribution, and magnetic field phenomena in translunar space. The initial Tiros weather satellite, sent up on April 1, transmitted the first global cloud-coverage photographs from a circular orbit 450 miles high, thereby inaugurating a new age for meteorology. The request for implementation of NASA's 10-year plan presented to Congress on January 20 seemed off to a good start. An extensive congressional "Review of the Space Program" put Mercury, even in the context of NASA's present programs, in perspective as a relatively minor part of the civilian space agency's activities. In terms of NASA's plans for the future or of the total military-civilian space program already in action, Project Mercury was hardly more than "an important first step in our manned exploration of space." [53]

Through the winter and spring of 1960, the big event toward which Mercury watchers looked with most anticipation was the launch of the first Atlas vehicle topped by a McDonnell capsule. Immediately after Big Joe, Gilruth had requested the Ballistic Missile Division to fly another Atlas along a Big Joe-type trajectory to qualify the McDonnell capsule for launch and reentry from a circular orbit roughly 105 miles high. At the beginning of 1960, it still had looked as though this could be accomplished by the end of May. A semifinal Defense Department operations plan outlining the support tasks of a dozen different military commands was under intensive study during this period. Serious reappraisals of schedule requirements and alternatives were underway in many areas, most of which threatened to delay the start of the qualification flight. By the end of January it was obvious that the payload, McDonnell's capsule No. 6, for the first Mercury-Atlas launch (MA–1) would not be ready soon enough.[54]

The bottleneck was the production line. Back in October 1959, when a letter amendment to the prime contract for six additional Mercury capsules was being processed, McDonnell had estimated it could deliver capsule No. 1 by the end of November. To be sure, this would be a stripped model suitable only for an off-the-pad or beach-abort mission, but at that time it looked as if the firing date for this first qualification test could be set for the last day of 1959. It then seemed that capsule No. 2, allocated to the first Mercury-Redstone flight, also could be delivered before the end of the year and shot about March 20, 1960. The sixth capsule, farther down McDonnell's production line, originally was allotted to the first Mercury-Atlas flight. It was barely framed, but McDonnell had hoped to deliver it by the end of February for a tentative launch date in mid-May. While STG was immersed in the Little Joe program, however, the production managers at McDonnell became aware that actual final assembly of the first capsules and equipment would take far more time than anticipated. On November 3, 1959, Sherwood L. Butler, the procurement officer at Langley, had notified NASA Headquarters that capsules Nos. 1 and 2 each would be delayed a month; No. 6 might be expected by the end of February.[55]

What, precisely, was causing these delays? Logan T. MacMillan, Edward M. Flesh, Yardley, and Dubusker of McDonnell felt constrained to answer as the pressure for delivery increased—as did certain conditions that obviously needed to be corrected. Incorporating the smallest changes during the final assembly of the first six capsules required many hours of disassembly, reassembly, and rechecking. Only one or two men at most could work in the confined space of the pressure vessel's interior, and rising standards of quality control imposed by McDonnell, STG, and resident Navy inspectors required much reworking.

For example, on the first shift on January 6, 1960, J. E. Miller, the McDonnell inspector on the floor at the time, logged in his record book a local cause of delay:

> Insp. discontinued all work on Cap. #1 this A.M. until the filthy condition of the capsule was cleaned up. A meeting of Prod. Supervision was called by Insp. & Engr., was asked to set [sic] in. Quality control was main subject & all agreed to extend more effort toward better quality control although Prod. did not think they could do much better than what was already being done.[56]

The next week at a capsule coordination meeting in St. Louis, Purser and

MacMillan, Yardley and Faget persuaded Robert Gilruth to save MA-1 by swapping capsule No. 6 for capsule No. 4, which had been scheduled for a static firing on the Redstone. Number 4 should be tidied up as quickly as possible and shipped to Langley by the end of the month. Only a structural shell, this first delivered piece of production hardware did include the exterior shingles, heatshield, landing and recovery gear, missile adapter-ring, retropackage and straps, with dummy retros and live posigrades. STG undertook to install Big Joe-type instrumentation and sequencing for its rescheduled use on the first Mercury-Atlas flight. The plan was to return the capsule to McDonnell by April 1 for final shingle fittings and adapter matings, then ship the completed capsule to the Cape by mid-April. At the same time it was decided to eliminate the flotation bags, which had proved to be too delicate to last long in the open ocean, from all capsules and to keep the configuration of capsules Nos. 5 and 7 unchanged in hope of making possible an earlier manned shot. Problems with the afterbody shingles and with the erosion of the window by the blast of the escape rocket were among a number left unsettled.[57]

As costs of solutions to these kinds of technological and training problems rose, NASA administrators appeared more frequently before Congressional committees and admitted their growing concern with manned space flight, as opposed to other space activities. T. Keith Glennan requested $23 million supplemental appropriation to the fiscal 1960 NASA budget of $500.6 million and justified $19 million of that extra sum on the basis of the urgent technological demands of Project Mercury. "It would be no exaggeration to say that the immediate focus of the U.S. space program is upon this project," stated Glennan.[58]

MANAGEMENT LEARNS ITS LIMITS

The astronauts were not alone in their need to become in some sense machine-rated. The managers of Mercury, both the civil servants and the contractors, had found truth in the maxim of industrial management that short-term estimates of accomplishment are nearly always overestimated. Mercury, like virtually all contractual development programs, entailed inherent technical and administrative difficulties impossible to foresee. A corollary to the rule of short-term estimates, namely that long-term predictions of accomplishments are very often underestimated, offered little solace at this stage of the development of Project Mercury. In its fifth status report at the end of January 1960, the Space Task Group related to Headquarters some of the lessons learned during its first year of contractual operations:

> A new capsule delivery schedule has recently been indicated by McDonnell to reflect a delay in delivery of over 3 months in the early capsules. This revision was made necessary by a realistic appraisal of progress to date. Although various proposals for improving the situation have been considered, there does not seem to be any practical avenue open at this time for effecting any worthwhile change.

Because of these delays and the fact that it has not been possible to sub-
stantiate the shingle structure adequately on the ground, it has been decided
to cancel the vibration program on capsule No. 4 and instead to fit this capsule
with an absolute minimum of equipment and instrumentation and to fire it on
an Atlas as MA–1 . . . at the earliest practicable date.[59]

Gilruth, Charles J. Donlan, and their younger associates in STG grew older
rapidly during their first 15 months as a contracting agency. Gradually attaining more autonomy, the Space Task Group still expected eventually to move to
Beltsville, Maryland. But in February NASA Headquarters made clear its intention not to move STG until Project Mercury was essentially completed. Relations with the Langley Research Center, STG's parent organization, improved
markedly with better organizational arrangements, such as job order procedures,
and with the growth of STG's own administrative staff. Close working exchanges
still prevailed in many areas, especially with the Langley shopmen under Jack A.
Kinzler providing technical services. But on STG's first birthday, only two out
of Langley's 12 applied research divisions could still say with regard to Mercury
that "there is as much to be done as has been done." [60]

The Pilotless Aircraft Research Division (PARD), renamed the Applied Materials and Physics Division at the end of 1959, and the Instrument Research Division
were still most actively supporting Mercury.

During STG's infant year, overall Langley support amounted to well over
100 separate preliminary data releases, contributed by more than 325 professional people, and costing approximately $1.9 million of Langley's own appropria-
tions. STG's personnel complement in January 1960 was climbing above 500;
the total cost of the prime contract with McDonnell, already modified in about
120 particulars, was approaching $70 million and rising. At the same time,
McDonnell estimated that more than half its total effort on Project Mercury was
still in engineering development; a third of its effort was on actual production;
and about 10 percent was on tooling. According to McDonnell's assistant contract manager, the overall weighted percentage of contract completion was just
below 60 percent.[61]

The magnitude of monitoring a contract of this size was reflected in another
reorganization of the Space Task Group in mid-January. Formalized in the new
block chart were the personnel office under Burney H. Goodwin, a budget and
finance office under J. P. Donovan, a procurement and supply office under Glenn
F. Bailey, and an administrative services office under Guy W. Boswick, Jr. STG
simplified its three line divisions by making James A. Chamberlin chief of its
"Engineering Division" instead of the "Engineering and Contract Administration
Division." Under Chamberlin, Andre J. Meyer, Jr., and Norman F. Smith served
as assistant chief and executive engineer, respectively. In Faget's Flight Systems
Division, Robert O. Piland and J. T. Markley were confirmed in their posts as
assistant chief and executive engineer.

At this time Faget unofficially set Robert Piland to work considering advanced vehicles suitable for a circumlunar space flight. This soft-spoken Virginian had turned from mathematics to aeronautical engineering in 1947 and had served as technical assistant to James T. Killian and the President's Science Advisory Committee during 1958. Technically able and politically experienced, Piland directed the circumlunar pilot studies for four months before authorization for an advanced vehicle team on May 25, 1960, formally added eight other senior STG engineers to look to the future beyond Mercury.[62]

Robert Piland also learned something from his older brother, Joseph V. Piland, assistant head of the contracts and scheduling office, who had evolved from a mechanical engineer into a contract administrator. Joseph Piland was instrumental in smoothing STG's formal relationships with its industrial contractors. His counterpart in McDonnell's organization was C. F. Picard, and together they had now to supervise over 50 subcontractors and over 5000 sub-subcontractors.

Charles Mathews' Operations Division was in a state of flux as he and Walter C. Williams shuffled men and positions in preparation for manned operations. Christopher C. Kraft, Jr., and Chris C. Critzos stayed put, while G. Merritt Preston went to the Cape and Scott H. Simpkinson was sent to St. Louis to help expedite matters at McDonnell. Other names on the STG organization chart of January 11, 1960, filled staff positions alongside Purser, Kenneth S. Kleinknecht, and Martin A. Byrnes. Another assistant to the director was Raymond L. Zavasky; heading the technical services liaison with Langley was Kinzler. The military officers originally assigned to STG as liaison remained aboard and active. They were Colonel Keith G. Lindell of the Air Force, who doubled as head of the astronaut and training section; Lieutenant Colonel Martin L. Raines of the Army; and Commander Paul L. Havenstein of the Navy. Even Langley Research Center, across the field, had its liaison man on STG's staff: W. Kemble Johnson.[63]

Beginning in January 1960, plans were made to integrate the astronaut with a flight-control team as well as with his machine. Team training of the remote-site ground crews required an extensive familiarization and orientation program. The initial proposal for training these teams began with an admonition:

> It is essential that the training of the flight control personnel be closely integrated with that of the astronaut's. As long as the astronaut is conscious all ground commands must be executed through or with the concurrence of the pilot. To be effective, the pilot and the ground crew must work as a closely knit team. An efficient system is dependent upon adequate team training and development of mutual confidence.[64]

In preparing to train and integrate the flight-control team for final operations, Walter Williams first discussed the problem with Kurt H. Debus, the Director of ABMA's Missile Firing Laboratory, and Major General Donald N. Yates, the Defense Department's representative and Commander of the Air Force Missile Test Center at Patrick Air Force Base, near Cape Canaveral. Manned missile operations were as new to them as to him, so on January 18, Williams wrote letters to each of these gentlemen formally proposing the establishment of new coordination committees for the upcoming flight tests. NASA Headquarters meanwhile had appointed another Air Force missile expert, Major General Don R. Ostrander, as Director of an Office of Launch Vehicles. His appointment, it was felt, would help interservice cooperation and relieve Silverstein of management responsibility for rocket development.[65]

In February Mathews and Williams organized a Launch Operations Branch within STG's Operations Division under Preston at the Cape. Then they specified the duties, organization, and responsibilities of the Mercury launch coordination office. Approaching a phase of heavy operational activity, different in kind as well as degree from Edwards and Wallops Island field operations, Williams and Mathews appointed Christopher Kraft as flight director, Stanley White as chief flight surgeon, Merritt Preston as launch operations manager, and Scott Simpkinson as capsule operations manager. By early March, 32 other position titles for ground operations—in the Mercury Control Center, in the blockhouse, at Atlantic Missile Range Central Control, and in the launch pad area—were specified. Capsule engineers at the Cape published quickly a thick "Manual for Launch Operations," which indicated their readiness to assume responsibility for launch operations. Williams also asked Destroyer Flotilla Four to plan for the recovery of MA–1 toward the end of May.[66]

If Debus and Yates were somewhat chagrined by the forceful speed and decision exhibited by Williams and Mathews in setting NASA firmly in control of launching operations, they were not alone in worrying about the future. Within other divisions of the Space Task Group there was also some worry lest the operations division should monopolize participation in the payoff phase of Project Mercury. William Bland, for instance, wrote a memo to Maxime Faget early in March urging that "the specialists who have matured with Project Mercury" not be diverted to advanced vehicular planning before getting a chance to prove in flight the systems they had designed:

> As Project Mercury matures, the total workload with the Space Task Group will increase with the greatest portion of the load carried by the operations division. This change in relative work does not mean that personnel of the flight systems division should decrease their participation in the project. Actually personnel of the flight systems division, at this particular time, have a much wider and deeper range of experience in preparations for launchings, in launchings of rocket vehicles, and in flight data analysis than the Mercury launch personnel (NASA and MAC). This experience in detailed knowledge which was collected during the Little Joe and Big Joe flight programs, the beach abort tests, the different system development programs (such as those conducted on escape motors, pyrotechnics, parachutes, drogue chutes, controls, etc.), and in the development of individual components which make up the capsule system, must be available to the Space Task Group organization conducting launch operations in order to insure direct approach to *successful launchings.*[67]

Bland expressed to Faget his concern about the possibility of being preempted from participation in Mercury operations. Faget, restlessly pursuing his first loves of conceptual design and initial development, first for Mercury and now for something soon to be called "Apollo," was in danger of losing the support of some of his lieutenants unless the Flight Systems Division got some role in the flying of their systems.

Part of this disaffection had been precipitated by a major meeting regarding the Mercury network, held on February 9 at Langley. Ostensibly this meeting was to discuss the operational organization, maintenance and operations training, and communications for the network. About 30 men from the Air Force, Navy, Western Electric, Bendix Radio, the oceanic missile ranges, and the Tracking Unit at Langley met with Williams, Mathews, Kraft, and John D. Hodge, but no representative of the Flight Systems Division was present. A week later Gilruth appointed the flight controllers and set C. Frederick Matthews, a Canadian whose name was often confused with that of his chief, Charles W. Mathews, in charge of coordinating the ground crew training programs. Walter Williams saw this as a full time job in itself. By the first of March flight controller indoctrination and training plans were underway, and Philco contractors and medical monitors were being briefed for a larger role at various ground sites whenever their training should warrant.[68]

In mid-March Faget confronted another problem in machine-rating his technicians when he received another technical complaint, this one from William A. Petynia, a conscientious engineer he had assigned to watch complete systems tests of capsule No. 1. Petynia had been working with McDonnell project engineer A. M. Paolini since June 1959, preparing capsule No. 1 for the beach-abort launch from Wallops. But the complicated, specialized knowledge required to do a faultless job seemed to Petynia to be overwhelming by the spring of 1960:

> To determine the "overall picture" is not difficult, but I found additional effort was required to be in a position to even partially understand capsule systems. I do not mean to become a specialist in each of the capsule systems, but I wanted to be able to recognize and understand problems and their relationship with the flight.
> The flight systems capsule engineer is the one person in the test organization who clearly understands the flight test objectives and the performance of the hardware in order to fulfill them. This I think is important! However, I think that due to the complexity of the capsule, the engineer cannot hope to become familiar with the hardware to any great degree in the short period before CST [Capsule Systems Test]. I believe that training classes for the engineers [should] be started immediately under MAC's supervision.[69]

Petynia's awareness of the necessity to machine-rate himself so he could do an adequate job of inspection was one individual manifestation within STG of the problem of getting all the million or so people involved to do a perfect job in order to man-rate all the machines. From the highest level to the lowest, supervisors sought better methods to inspire the men at work on Mercury to make the quest for reliability a personal matter.

One of the methods used to good effect was identification, both of parts and of workers in the project. The Redstone managers had adopted in 1959 a seal showing the anthropomorphic god Mercury in winged cap and boots bearing a missile and vaulting Earth. Atlas managers eventually selected the alchemical and astrological symbol for Mercury, enclosing a blue "R" for reliability, as their identifying label for Mercury-Atlas components and laborers. On personnel badges, these marks of distinction meant a record of highest performance, but on hardware these decals signified a test record that came closest to the nominal design desiderata. Machines or components that performed too well in certain respects were suspect as possible troublemakers in other respects for the future.[70]

The astronauts were now making periodic appearances along the production lines at McDonnell, Chrysler, Convair/Astronautics, and elsewhere to encourage the highest standards of craftsmanship among even apprentices or semiskilled workers handling or processing any components that bore the Mercury decal. Having shaken the hand of one of the pilots whose life depended on their work, the factory workers presumably would treat with the greatest care and tenderness the parts then still in their hands.

Credit for having first worked out the guidelines for a coherent plan to machine-rate everybody probably should go to Bernhard A. Hohmann and Ernst R. Letsch of Space Technology Laboratories (STL) and later of Aerospace Corporation. Together with Major General Osmond J. Ritland, former test pilot in command of the Air Force Ballistic Missile Division, Hohmann assured the astronauts that their interests would never be sacrificed. Hohmann's study of the "General Aspects of the Pilot Safety Program for Project Mercury Atlas Boosters" analyzed the differences between the ideas of reliability, quality control, and quality assurance before synthesizing them in a specific program adaptable to other areas of Mercury development. Hohmann combined the approaches of the mathematicians and systems engineers at STL with the viewpoints of production, inspection, and test engineers at Convair/Astronautics, Rocketdyne, and elsewhere.[71] But some of the compromises he recommended, such as choosing most nominal instead of highest performance parts to assure a higher level of final quality, were appropriated only gradually by NASA and STG.

Upgrading the intensity of quality control over raw materials, of inspections and tests of systems integration in the plant, and of the requirements for a complete vehicle at the time of the "factory rollout" were significant parts of the pilot safety program. In the final analysis for flight readiness, a Flight Safety Review Board, patterned on Air Force practice, should take the technical responsibility for certifying the booster to be man-rated.[72] Even after all these precautions there was always going to be an element of doubt. Procedural principles on paper would require two more years—and at least five flight experiments—to become realized in practice and working habits.

255

Is Perfect Reliability Possible?

At NASA Headquarters in Washington on February 29, 1960, the high-level debate over the meticulous versus the statistical approach to reliability was fervently renewed. NASA, STG, and McDonnell representatives that day met in conference to decide what weight to give the "numbers game" in their own confidential estimates of readiness. Gilruth, Donlan, and their chief of reliability, John C. French, defended STG's practical procedures against the theoretical approach of Nicholas E. Golovin, Landis S. Gephart, and Catherine D. Hock. The third revision of McDonnell's reliability program was delivered by Eugene Kunznick, who also outlined the particulars of the prime contractor's quality control measures. Walter Williams presented STG's latest views on operational flight safety, and STG generally endorsed McDonnell's reliability program review as its own. But neither Richard E. Horner nor Golovin was satisfied that the pains being taken by STG and McDonnell were sufficient or thorough enough.[73]

A new Division of Life Sciences Programs was created in March at NASA Headquarters, with Clark T. Randt, a neurosurgeon from Cleveland, as its director. Part of this division's purpose was to ensure machine-rated men for the future of manned space flights. Earlier in the year an Air Force aeromedical leader, Brigadier General Don D. Flickinger, reported to NASA and STG on his recent trip to Russia and on the opinions he had formed about Soviet progress toward manned space flight. Flickinger estimated that the Soviets would attempt without prior announcement to orbit a two-man laboratory about mid-year. The American astronauts were "anxious to do anything possible to speed things up."[74]

But the hardware was simply not yet hard enough or wearable enough for the insiders to get deeply excited about beating the Russians into space. Just after capsule No. 4 arrived at Langley, Purser went to look at it and reported to Gilruth:

> Although there are evidences of careless workmanship, I don't think it is too much worse than standard aircraft practice. Also, most of the bumps, patches, etc., seem to be on the unpressurized part of the structure. It was also mentioned by one of the boys that Capsule 4 was never intended as a flight vehicle, but only as a vibration-and-static test article; this can account for a lot of the errors. While many of the bad spots could be caught by inspection and corrected, a lot are non-fixable except by junking a capsule. These can only be avoided by inspiring in some way, better workmanship. I would suggest documenting the bad spots on Capsule 4 and then having a good inspection by STG people of the flight capsules now on the line. This could be repeated in 6 to 8 weeks to catch the next batch and probably would cure the troubles.[75]

After the late February meeting on reliability in Washington, a great deal of ferment was evident in systems testing, quality control, engineering inspection, and a new order of reliability testing. At the McDonnell factory, Robert L. Seat, who together with George Waldram had drawn up the first capsule systems test plan, began to clarify the differences between acceptable aircraft qualification test practices and spacecraft systems integration and reliability tests.

256

In early March, STG sent a delegation to Huntsville and Detroit for the latest word on reliability program upgrading at ABMA and at Chrysler. Joachim P. Kuettner, Eugene J. Buhmann, and von Braun's deputy, Eberhard F. M. Rees, conducted tours and arranged presentations for March 7 and 8. The next day at Chrysler's missile plant in Michigan, C. A. Brady, Bernard J. Meldrum, and L. L. Baker presented a similar review, which apparently satisfied their visitors from STG that the Redstones for Mercury could be trusted.[76]

Through March and April the pressure on McDonnell to deliver the goods unfinished and yet with perfect reliability records became so acute that James S. McDonnell and his board of directors in St. Louis appointed their factory manager, Walter F. Burke, to meet and satisfy that pressure. Burke, already a company vice-president, was named general manager for Project Mercury. Logan Mac-Millan remained as "company-wide project manager" for McDonnell, but the addition of Burke signified the scale of the growth in size and scope of the Mercury contract.[77]

McDonnell would have been remiss if it had not responded at the highest level to NASA's pressure. All the aerospace companies knew that Faget and Robert Piland were traveling around the country during April 1960 presenting their preliminary ideas and plans for "advanced vehicular" space flight programs to other members of the NASA family. Technical speculation was rife over how best to accomplish manned circumlunar flight. Other corporate giants, including Grumman and Convair/Astronautics, were competing for snippets of knowledge about what was going on in these confidential deliberations within NASA. But James Chamberlin, among others, was wondering, as he watched the difficulties in manufacturing and ground testing McDonnell's first capsules, difficulties particularly acute with the sequence and wiring systems, whether speculation about spacecraft ten years hence was legitimate, profitable, or even necessary.[78]

While uneasiness over reliability was interminable, there were limits—practical, political, and social—to the amount of time that could be sacrificed for quality assurance. Decisions had to be made and, after close calculation, risks taken. Abe Silverstein at NASA Headquarters intervened at this point, deciding to short-circuit a duplicate set of prelaunch checkout operations. On March 29, two weeks after President Eisenhower had ordered that the big new NASA facility at Huntsville should be called the George C. Marshall Space Flight Center, Silverstein wrote von Braun a lengthy letter of explanation:

> I have just completed an extensive reexamination of all Mercury schedules, from the point of view of expediting the entire Mercury program. As a result of this reexamination, I have arrived at the conclusion that it is of utmost importance to obtain flight performance data of certain critical components of the Mercury systems at the earliest possible time. More specifically, it is important to initiate the Mercury-Redstone flights as soon as possible in order to obtain inflight evaluations of the Mercury capsules at an early date.

*　　　*　　　*

257

A detailed study of the checkout programs at McDonnell, Huntsville, and Cape Canaveral has revealed that there exists a great deal of duplication; in particular all the booster capsule compatibility checks are performed both at Huntsville and at the Cape. The only unique tests scheduled to be made at Huntsville (on MR-1 only) is a vibration and noise test to be performed during the booster static firing.

* * *

In view of these facts, it appears that the capsule prelaunch operations at Huntsville are no longer required. I have therefore directed that the Mercury capsules assigned to the Redstone program be shipped from St. Louis directly to Cape Canaveral, thereby gaining approximately two months in the launch schedule. I suggest that all parties concerned meet at NASA headquarters in Washington in the near future to discuss detailed arrangements necessitated by this new procedure.[79]

But a week later Kuettner persuaded Silverstein to relent on this decision and to agree to a compromise: the capsule for MR-1 would be shipped to Huntsville for a much shorter period to test the mating and to check on problems of radio frequency and electrical compatibility. Silverstein now wrote von Braun a letter of appreciation for reducing the Huntsville checkout time "from 8 weeks to 16 days, so that the Mercury-Redstone program can proceed as rapidly as possible." Shortly thereafter, Silverstein also learned that the Air Force Chief of Staff, General Thomas D. White, was reaffirming in strong language to his troops that the Air Force should cooperate with NASA "to the very limit of our ability, and even beyond it to the extent of some risk to our own programs" if that were necessary.[80]

Scheduling problems continued, becoming acute toward the end of June, when the schedules for qualification flight tests were recognized to have slipped by at least six months. Complete capsule system testing seemed to require new organization, new procedures, and new ground test equipment. Purser filed a note for himself on a major meeting on June 27-28, attended by Silverstein and Director Harry J. Goett of Goddard, wherein the top technical managers of Mercury and STG began to admit that perfect reliability is indeed impossible. Quality control and reliability testing must be raised to a new level of effort, and not only man and machine but man-rating and machine-rating processes must be integrated, reflected Purser.

One of the major problems facing Mercury management is the conflict between a real desire to meet schedules and the feeling of need for extensive ground tests. The MAC capsule systems tests are not meeting this need since they were not intended for this purpose and since the pressure of time sometimes forces bypassing of some details (to be caught later at the Cape). Further, there has not been time available (or taken) on the part of MAC to study and update the CST procedures and SEDR's. It was concluded that a group (mostly MAC effort) should be set up to review and update the CST and SEDR procedures. It is also firm that no details will be bypassed in the Cape checkout without the express approval of STG management.

* * *

There was considerable discussion of a proposal to eliminate the unmanned orbital shots on the basis that the systems could be qualified in unmanned and manned ballistic shots and that the presence of the man would reduce the possibility of failure in the first orbital shots and thus reduce chances for a consequent delay in the program . . . *it was decided* to not change [sic] the program now but to keep the door open and reconsider when MA–5 and MA–6 are closer. Since the astronauts have expressed considerable interest in this proposal STG management is to discuss the above decision with them.[81]

Just before the reliability meeting in February, the Task Group had received welcome news of improving Atlas reliability as a result of more series-D firings since Big Joe. Already in mid-February STG had assigned a rough reliability coefficient of 75 percent, based on virtually perfect ignition and running of the engines and excellent performance from airborne and ground guidance systems in recent tests. Studies of the Abort Sensing and Implementation System for Mercury indicated that 13 of 43 series-D flights would have been aborted had the ASIS been aboard; only one of those 13 would have been terminated unnecessarily by the system's sensors.[82] Hopes were high, therefore, that whenever qualification flight tests should begin with Mercury-Atlas No. 1 (MA–1), they would follow each other rapidly at monthly intervals.

While Edison M. Fields and Sigurd A. Sjoberg of STG began the arrangements for adapting Atlas 50–D to capsule No. 4 for the MA–1 flight, Hohmann's engineers at STL, including James W. McCurry and Ernst Letsch, together with a reliability team supporting Philip E. Culbertson at Convair/Astronautics, were all warning of the consequences from the predicted increase in capsule weight. Guidance and trajectory equations, dependent upon moments of inertia, center of gravity, and a gross capsule weight now over 3750 pounds at launch, had to be recalculated.[83]

The first Mercury-Atlas test flight was to be virtually a repeat of Big Joe, with the significant difference that a McDonnell capsule was to be qualified rather than a NASA model demonstrated. The primary objectives for MA–1 were also similar to those for Big Joe: to determine the integrity and stability of the McDonnell-built structure and to measure heating rates on the afterbody shingles during a critical abort and reentry.

MA–2, scheduled for September, should test the integrity and flight dynamics of McDonnell capsule No. 6 during a simulated nominal reentry from orbit. Having decided to change the materials and increase the thickness of the outer shingles on both the conical and the cylindrical section of the capsule, STG had added 63 more pounds by specifying the use of René 41 nickel alloy .016-inch thick on the conical section and 12 beryllium panels .22-inch thick on the cylindrical afterbody. The reinstatement of the impact bag and the drogue chute, plus the addition of insulation, a super sarah beacon, and heavier batteries, raised the estimated weight of the orbital configuration of the capsule to 3000 pounds.[84]

Feverish, if not frantic, work and worry went into these decisions, beginning as soon as capsule No. 4 arrived at Langley. But Bond, Fields, and Meyer, taking up where they had left off with Big Joe, ran a taut project through mid-April; they "pessimistically and therefore," they believed, "realistically" estimated again that they would see this rocket's red glare on July 4, 1960. Caldwell C. Johnson and Jack Kinzler supervised the polishing of capsule No. 4 as they had for the Big Joe payload.

But summer arrived, and Chamberlin reported continual capsule delivery delays at the weekly STG capsule review board meetings. The slowdown and stretchout of the flight-test schedule became ever more vexing and costly. Meanwhile NASA Headquarters began to centralize and simplify its launch operations under Ostrander, leaving to Silverstein preflight worries and responsibility for Mercury boosters only. Warren North justified a $7 million overrun on the prime contract for which STG was seeking approval:

> This overrun was, of course, anticipated. A major factor involved in the McDonnell overrun is the high level of engineering required in support of the testing program. McDonnell previously planned to reduce their engineering effort in early 1960. However, because of the increased scope of the testing program and the capsule changes, these engineering reductions have not taken place; in fact, in their last monthly report, McDonnell shows their engineering head count at 913 and increasing. The procurement overrun is due primarily to subcontract overruns at Bell, AiResearch, Collins, Radioplane, and Perkin-Elmer.[85]

To try to speed things up and to keep safety paramount, Silverstein instituted biweekly meetings at NASA Headquarters with Walter Burke of McDonnell and Gilruth of STG. Both quality control and urgency militated against keeping cost ceilings permanent. They also militated against the schedule. Glennan had directed that no flight schedule changes should be made without his personal explicit approval. But the technological realities of ensuring highest technical performance and STG's priority concern for the orbital objectives of Mercury, rather than for suborbital man-in-space, allowed the first Mercury-Redstone flights to slip past, or at least alongside, the Mercury-Atlas qualification flights.

HEAD AND HANDS OF NASA

During March and April, Administrator Glennan called on the Space Task Group, as well as all of NASA, to conduct a self-appraisal of NASA's contracting policy and industrial relations. A firm of management consultants, McKinsey and Company, had entered into a contract with NASA on February 26, 1960, for a comprehensive study of how NASA should utilize industry and private institutions, how it could improve its utilization of its own research capability, and what the extent and manner of sharing responsibility and authority between Government and industry actually was.[86]

The Space Task Group responded with a self-analysis which listed the major elements of Project Mercury, gave an explanation of the major tasks involved, and discussed the reasons for performing each task within NASA or on contract. The preliminary draft of this information divided the tasks of the Task Group into three subsystems—the capsule, boosters, and tracking and communications—each of which was further subdivided into elements and tasks. When the representative of McKinsey and Company visited STG on April 19 to discuss the working methods used in the conduct of Project Mercury, he was briefed by Purser, Zavasky, Mathews, and Bond, and provided with documents tabulating the distribution of STG personnel man-years, associated costs, and "R and D" fundings. Although McKinsey's final report did not appear until October, the Task Group finished its part of the self-examination in May. STG learned from this exercise that it had shifted from research and development into almost exclusively development activities.[87]

At the highest level within NASA Glennan and associates recognized, as Robert Rosholt has described it, that the "opportunity to make comprehensive changes in NASA's organization and procedures would not exist too much longer, i.e., bureaucratic hardening of the arteries would make change more and more difficult as the agency became older and larger." The final McKinsey report appeared to endorse the "integrated project management team" approach used by STG. The Space Task Group, however, was still only a semi-independent subdivision of NASA's Goddard center and still closely related to the Langley center. The General Accounting Office and NASA had clashed recently over executive privilege in withholding certain documents relating to the selection of McDonnell as the prime contractor for Mercury. This furnished ammunition for some critics of NASA's industrial relations. But the decentralization policy of NASA was approved by McKinsey, with certain reservations taken in part from STG's experience.[88]

Through the winter and spring of 1960 the managers of Mercury both in Washington and in Virginia were learning to adjust to the limits imposed by a new technology and by the necessity to coordinate diverse, far-flung, and sometimes perverse human organizations of technicians and craftsmen. While they chafed at the slipping schedules, worried over technical details, swatted at gadfly reporters, and tried to anticipate every contingency in their planning for the missions ahead, Gilruth and his associates in management and systems engineering were just as surely learning to take their tumbles as were the astronauts in their centrifuge rides and in other exotic simulators.

McDonnell's capsule No. 1 finally arrived at Wallops Island on April 1, 1960, cleaned up but stripped of most of its subsystems, to be groomed for a test of its escape rocket, parachute recovery, and landing system. Petynia and Dennis F. Hasson had written a thick catalog of expectations, prescribed procedures, schematics, and checkoff lists for this "off-the-pad abort" test. While Alan Kehlet and Herbert G. Patterson worried over alignment and the abort sequence system, Wallops personnel prepared the canted pad and supplied logistical support

261

to the McDonnell and Task Group engineers for a month of preparation. Shake tests and sled tests were run first to ensure readiness before firing.[89]

Finally on May 9 the carefully weighed and balanced capsule pointed its pylon toward the sea. The ignition switch was closed and the escape rocket jerked the capsule away from the ground on its short flight, lasting one minute and 16 seconds but covering half a mile in an arc 2465 feet high. Recovery by a Marine Corps helicopter took only 17 minutes. The only significant defect noted from this test was a relatively poor separation distance when the tower jettisoned.[90]

The "beach abort" was a successful flight and a sterling qualification test, but it was hardly spectacular to the public. Certainly it was not all that STG had hoped to accomplish this long after the last of the development flights late in January. However, MA–1 was coming along nicely. It should be far more impressive in proving the "booster-capsule combination for exit flight and capsule for entry flight."[91] And spacecraft No. 2 was to be delivered to Huntsville at the end of June for static tests and compatibility adjustments with the first Redstone booster. Should it prove trouble-free, then presumably by the end of summer, if everyone worked hard enough and there were no interfering defense launch commitments, two more qualification flights on each of the big boosters should bring the day of the first manned space flight much closer.

On May 15, 1960, however, an event occurred that rekindled premonitions that the first manned space flight might be made by a Russian. In their only announced space launching during the first half of 1960, the Soviets orbited the first capsule large enough (10,011 pounds) to contain a human passenger. Called merely *Sputnik IV* by the Western press but more accurately named *Korabl Sputnik*, or *Cosmic Ship No. 1*, this vehicle failed four days later when its reaction control or attitude control system shot the ship containing its dummy astronaut the wrong way for recovery.[92] Perhaps, just perhaps, the United States might have better reaction and attitude controls than the Soviet Union.

IX

From Development into Qualification: Flight Tests

(JULY–DECEMBER 1960)

IN mid-1960, NASA and its Space Task Group hoped soon to begin launching a major qualification flight test for Project Mercury every six weeks. If all went well, these tests of the operational vehicles should permit a man to ride into space before the end of the year. But if Mercury's developmental experience to date was any guide, troubles could be expected to pyramid and might require more than six months to correct. Since the ultimate goal of Project Mercury was to achieve man-in-orbit rather than merely a sounding-rocket ride by a man into space, the Task Group would be running concurrent flight tests with the Little Joe, the Mercury-Redstone, and the Mercury-Atlas combinations. But attention and impetus were focused on the accomplishment of manned orbital circumnavigation.

NASA Administrator T. Keith Glennan sent a memorandum to his Director of Space Flight Programs, Abe Silverstein, on July 11, 1960, prompting him to make every effort to put forward to November the launch of MR–3, long designated the first manned suborbital flight. If that was not possible, Glennan urged Silverstein to hold fast the schedule for the first manned launching before the end of the year. Silverstein replied that the manned event had just been reset for the week of December 5. By mid-August 1960 the most realistic estimate of the earliest possible man-launching changed the program management plans once again and reset the MR–3 launching for mid-January 1961. As late as October 1960, this optimism prevailed while work on capsule No. 7 for MR–3 proceeded "somewhat better than expected." [1]

Having once called the Army's stillborn Project Adam a "circus stunt" because it proposed little more than shooting a man into space, Hugh L. Dryden, Deputy Administrator of NASA, had himself set a precedent for the criticisms of those influential scientists who came to regard Project Mercury as more of an exhibition than a demonstration. During 1959 few had raised their voices against NASA's plans and STG's development program for a manned satellite. But during this election year of 1960, many citizens scrutinized—and Eisenhower even established a commission to study—all national policies, goals, and ideals. This White

263

House-sanctioned introspection led to some criticism, not entirely constructive, of the civilian space agency, which all too often was equated with Project Mercury.[2]

Most Americans appeared to approve Mercury as a potentially stupendous adventure, and many Congressmen anxiously hoped that NASA would mobilize the Nation's vaunted technological know-how to put the first man above the atmosphere. Although Dryden, George M. Low, and other NASA officials recently had warned repeatedly that the Russians could and likely would achieve manned space flight first, no one in NASA seemed to wonder whether the Soviets would send men on ballistic suborbital missions before committing a man to orbital flight. Most citizens seemed to confuse their feelings of hurt pride with loss of prestige and were reluctant to accept Eisenhower's difficult rationalization that America should abjure any "space race" with Soviet Russia. But NASA followed Eisenhower's leadership in this matter and reinforced the official attitude by insisting that Mercury was an "R and D" program whose pace could not be forced.[3]

Glennan in his public statements appeared torn between the pressures of public sentiment expressed through Congress and the news media, on one hand, and the demands of loyalty to the Chief Executive and to technological realism, on the other. Aware of the Nation's late start in rocket propulsion development and yet of its amazingly rapid achievement of a workable ICBM, Glennan knew that the United States still did not have the weight-lifting prowess to join an avowed contest with the U.S.S.R. But Glennan also shared the aerospace community's satisfaction on May 20, 1960, when the Atlas first flew higher than 1000 miles and over 9014 miles downrange from Cape Canaveral into the Indian Ocean. By this time the Thor and Jupiter intermediate-range missiles were operationally deployed abroad. The Titan ICBM, in spite of some developmental failures, was emerging into a second-generation intercontinental missile.[4]

Mercury still was only a fractional part of NASA's total space effort, but publicity and public interest had reinforced each other until the manned program clearly had become the most promising hope of "beating" the Russians into space. When the Soviets orbited *Korabl Sputnik II* on August 19 and the next day recovered two dogs, Strelka and Belka, from it, grounds for complacency among Americans evaporated.[5] National phobias, stimulated by partisan criticism of the alleged "missile gap," were further distorted by technological chauvinism with respect to Soviet accomplishments in space. Popular attitudes were exacerbated after the "spirit of Camp David" was destroyed by the U–2 incident and after Khrushchev used the U–2 affair to destroy the summit conference in Paris.

Speculations on high policy and international relations were not the business of the field workers on the Mercury program. But as citizens they could not avoid being aware of some wondrous possibilities for the historic significance of their work. Both landlubbers and space lovers could find many excellent reasons to think that the ICBM and nuclear warheads might possibly become plowshares of peace rather than tools of terror if directed toward the exploration of space.

264

Peaceful coexistence and even international cooperation might be force-fed by the exorbitant economics of the competition to put men into orbit. Whatever one's particular brand of concern, there were motives aplenty to work on Project Mercury.

Toward the end of June 1960, the Space Task Group took another hard look at the status of Project Mercury. Having formalized three separate series of engineering inspections and tests—progressing from development through qualification into reliability phases—STG faced with increased confidence some criticism from technical associates. It felt it could gauge accurately the soft spots in the major systems for Mercury. Of the 17 nominal systems for the capsule, all but five or six by June were reported finished with qualification tests and almost done with reliability testing. The major unfinished items were the reaction control system, pyrotechnics, the retrograde and posigrade rockets, and the satellite clock.

Capsule system tests had revealed that certain pressure regulators, solenoid and relief valves, and thrust chambers for the reaction controls using corrosive hydrogen peroxide were going to be troublesome when operating in a high vacuum. On the other hand, the environmental system was progressing better than expected, with only five components still unqualified: the emergency oxygen bottle, a pressure reducer assembly, the odor and carbon dioxide absorber, a high-pressure oxygen transducer, and a suit-circuit water separator. The abort sensing and implementation system (ASIS) for the Atlas was 95 percent qualified, but its counterpart for the Redstone was not.[6]

The communications and tracking network faced four outstanding problems: no one had much experience with Atlas guidance and tracking at long ranges and low elevation angles; the reliability of the high-speed data links was unknown; capsule antenna patterns were erratic enough to make radar acquisition problematic; and control procedures and techniques as yet were untried.

Astronaut training, the Task Group believed, was virtually complete for disorientation, tumbling, and familiarization with high levels of carbon dioxide absorption. Adaptation to weightlessness and lectures on space sciences were 90 percent complete, but training in navigation and communications (at reduced pressures and with high heating, noise, and vibration rates) was less than a third finished. The training of ground crews in procedures for preparing, launching, and monitoring an astronaut in flight had only just begun. And NASA's planning for recovery operations in the summer of 1960 was grandiose, asking "virtually for the deployment of the whole Atlantic fleet." This requirement came down abruptly after NASA met with the Navy at the Pentagon and was shown that fleet operations of this scope might cost more than the entire Mercury program.[7]

The climax of the debate over reliability analyses came in early summer 1960, when NASA Headquarters decided to issue an independent contract with McDonnell for making assurance doubly sure. Associate Administrator Richard E. Horner and his deputy, Nicholas E. Golovin, the mathematical systems analyst who had come to NASA from the Advanced Research Projects Agency, achieved their first point on June 9, 1960, when a separate contract with McDonnell was signed for a reliability study of all Mercury capsule systems. Estimated to cost $52,892 with a fixed fee of $3,323 and planned to be administered by the Bureau of Naval Weapons representatives in St. Louis, this small contract was designed to provide Horner's office with the data it needed to analyze and evaluate the reliability efforts and achievements of McDonnell, of all 10 capsule subcontractors, of some 200 suppliers, and indirectly of STG's reliability monitoring and mission planning.[8]

Golovin's approach to a reliability prediction program was unusual to both the Space Task Group and to many of his professional colleagues. It reversed the common procedure of beginning with parts analysis and proceeding to the whole system. Golovin had recently explained his theoretical point of view before the American Society for Quality Control, citing other missile program precedents for inverting the crucial problem: "start with a definition of failure for the system, and then work back through subsystems and components to the data on parts failures." Glennan and Horner had approved this approach as an aid to fulfilling their desires for better "confidence coefficients" before accepting the readiness of the capsule for unmanned and manned suborbital and three-orbit missions. This kind of systems analysis used deduction and fully exploited "numbers game" techniques and data processing machines to check on the inductive systems engineering of STG and McDonnell. The experimentalists at the working levels, and many of the engineering managers, including STG's Director, Robert R. Gilruth, believed they saw a worthless expenditure of effort in this innovation.[9]

NASA Headquarters saw STG dragging its feet on this issue by the end of June. Glennan therefore tried another tack. He wrote directly to James S. McDonnell, shortly after a personal visit and briefing at the factory:

> As you know, during the last month there have been a number of discussions between my Office of Reliability and Systems Analysis and various members of your staff on the problem of Mercury capsule system reliability. These talks were the result of my having directed the Office of Reliability and Systems Analysis to prepare for me an objective quantitative evaluation of the anticipated mission and flight safety reliability of the Mercury capsule system. It has now been brought to my attention that discussions have not yet resulted in mutual agreement on getting this job seriously underway.
>
> I would appreciate it if you would give the matter your personal attention and have your staff responsively consider providing, as promptly as possible, the information detailed in the enclosed "Proposed Work Statements for McDonnell on Mercury Capsule System Reliability."
>
> If you foresee any serious problems in this connection, I would appreciate your bringing them directly to my attention, and I will be glad to set up a meeting in Washington to reach a full meeting of minds.[10]

The work statements enclosed in this letter, prepared by Golovin's assistants Landis S. Gephart, William Wolman, and Catherine D. Hock, called for precisely defined reliability definitions, assumptions, diagrams, equations, and estimates of each

266

subsystem design, together with all available test data from every source. The basic reasons for requesting this information were to allow NASA "to review and evaluate the techniques and the data employed by McDonnell" in its reliability report (No. 7007) issued almost a year earlier, and "to update and upgrade the reliability predictions and probability equations" for mission success in the light of uneven changes of component parts supplied to McDonnell:

> With all its subcontractors, McDonnell has established a reliability requirement for each major equipment. This requirement has been expressed either as a mean time between failures for a continuously operating device or as a probability of success for a single shot device, and has been incorporated as a firm contractual requirement in the appropriate McDonnell Specification Control Drawing. McDonnell also recognizes that "a requirement without a test to demonstrate compliance with it is meaningless." Accordingly, McDonnell has specified a variety of tests aimed at demonstration of the reliability requirements imposed on its subcontractors.

Golovin and associates wanted to examine all test plans and test results on every Mercury capsule component from pre-installation acceptance through systems, compatibility, qualification, and life tests. In short, they wanted virtually a whole library of files at McDonnell opened for their inspection promptly, within two weeks if possible. This was not quite possible, but the founder of McDonnell Aircraft did reply personally to Administrator Glennan in mid-July:

> I am happy to inform you that our company started work on 9 June 1960, the same day on which Dr. William Wolman made his first specific request, even though this request was only verbal [sic]. Our company is now at work on every one of the programs therein outlined even though we still have no contractual authorization for any of it.
>
>   *   *   *
>
> We are in full accord with providing as fast as humanly possible (without diluting other Project Mercury effort) whatever work is desired by NASA to assist in the reliability evaluations of Project Mercury. . . .[11]

A few days later Golovin's group, having requested Silverstein to show STG how invidious was its prejudice against the "numbers game," journeyed down to Langley Field and briefed the Task Group on how Headquarters proposed to raise quality by quantitative methods. Reliability goals for each major capsule system, progressive analyses, and periodic reviews, plus a new order of simulated mission-testing stringency, were proposed and accepted by STG. Since the last major reliability meeting at Headquarters on February 29, 1960, had been so acrimonious, STG was surprised to find how little difference there now appeared to be between Golovin's approach to reliability and its own. On July 21, Paul E. Purser logged this note for Gilruth: "Spent most of the day in the meeting with Dr. Golovin, et al. They sounded fairly reasonable. If we had held such a meeting several months ago, there would have been a lot less misunderstanding."[12]

Shortly after this rapprochement, Horner resigned from NASA to go to industry, Golovin resigned later to join the President's Science Advisory Committee staff, and Gephart and Hock obtained an expansion of the McDonnell reliability contract to cover the astronaut's task description and performance evaluation. Glennan meanwhile pressured Silverstein, who pressured Gilruth, to do something formal about taking into account contemporary mathematical techniques used in missile programs to enhance managerial confidence in reliability, hence in readiness before a launch. Gilruth in turn gave the job to John C. French, who proceeded to organize a "reliability and quality assurance office" in the Space Task Group. There was special significance in the word "assurance," because STG had by no means capitulated to the statistical approach nor to the mathematicians' belief in the efficacy of reliability prediction.[13]

Had the qualification flight tests actually started earlier, perhaps much of the debate over what to expect from Mercury launches would have been obviated. But while still standing on the threshold of the major flight test program after almost two years of virtually simultaneous work on detailed design, engineering, and manufacturing, the Mercury spacecraft developers had to talk out some of these difficulties before they could call for a vote. Far more significant than the formal reliability program in the long run were the test philosophy, test programs, and the test work in "space chambers" that could more realistically simulate the hot/cold vacuum of the exospheric environment.[14] To move in that direction required a move toward the "spaceport" at Cape Canaveral, Florida.

MOVING TO THE LAUNCH SITE

The imminent shift from development into the operational phase of Mercury was reflected in several different ways. Military and industrial relations at Cape Canaveral were undergoing rapid change as management and launch facilities were partially modified to accommodate the influx of a new team for manned space flight. Melvin N. Gough, the senior test pilot who had established NASA's basis for operations at the Cape, departed for a job with the Civil Aeronautics Board, and into his shoes stepped G. Merritt Preston for STG and Kurt H. Debus for Marshall's launch operations, now also a part of NASA. The Air Force also added more help for NASA support activities under Colonel Asa B. Gibbs and J. W. Rosenberry. Overcrowded facilities and overlapping checkout and launch schedules were causes for interminable official dickering but not for any program delay. Project Mercury eventually acquired Hangar S and launch complexes 56 for Mercury-Redstone and 14 for Mercury-Atlas.[15]

Although the rank and file of the Space Task Group were barely aware of the new liaison between NASA Headquarters and McDonnell reliability experts, the quest for quality control at the working level was entering a new phase. In the early summer of 1960, about 50 men from STG established residence in Florida. John F. Yardley, along with about 80 McDonnell technicians, set up shop in mobile-home trailers around Hangar S, in the industrial area within the fences of Cape Canaveral. By the end of the year the number of technicians working on the capsules for preflight checkout at the Cape had grown to more than 400, most of the increase made up by contract personnel.[16]

At the McDonnell factory in St. Louis, peak employment on Mercury systems had reached 880 in April 1960. After that, there was a gradual decline in Mercury production workers as Yardley's field team increased to 120 by summer's end. Because STG had called for the first four capsules from McDonnell's production line before they were entirely finished, the maximum of 427 workers on the factory floor in May 1960 declined with the buildup of preflight polishing activities at the Cape. Yardley and his crews soon became the center of attention for unofficial helpers and kibitzers from other organizations and contractors, many of whom were glad to provide materials and tools that were urgently needed and in short supply among McDonnell people at the Cape.[17]

Yardley, his assistants at the Cape—E. F. Peters and Robert L. Foster—and other working engineers knew little about the separate reliability contract between NASA Headquarters and McDonnell. Walter F. Burke, Logan T. MacMillan, and the quality manager, N. E. Covinsky, did know that this extra business was coming to their company through separate channels, but they and their production engineers were so busy trying to make each capsule work properly that they too could see little sense in the "numbers game." Each system and subsystem seemed to have its own personality. But to guard against overemphasizing these individual idiosyncrasies, capsule No. 10 was set aside as the standard test article at McDonnell. As preflight checkouts at the Cape uncovered more and more unique difficulties, the need for still more stringent quality control was made plain.

No one recognized this more than Yardley, who in the summer of 1960 urged his company to institute a new order of reliability tests. He did not insist on statistical performance data, but he did enjoin improvement of environmental-chamber reliability testing of components. Robert L. Seat, McDonnell's senior test engineer, was pressed by Silverstein in Washington, by Lewis R. Fisher of STG, and by Yardley from the Cape, as well as by the burgeoning number of test requests between McDonnell departments, to prepare specifications for an exhaustive environmental reliability testing program. On September 26, 1960, the project to flight-test a man in orbit was supplemented by an authorization to ground-test the capsule in a simulated mission through physical environments in a "space chamber." This simulated orbital test program gradually became known as "Project Orbit."[18]

The reaction control system on capsule No. 2 was giving Yardley headaches. In general the power and sequential systems on all capsules were full of "glitches," or minute transient voltages from inexplicable origins. Surely more problems could be expected from space operations. So the simulated mission test program, designed specifically to detect unknown anomalies arising from four and a half hours of continuous operation in a vacuum alternately hot and cold, like "day" and "night" for the manned satellite, was welcomed by all hands. Unfortunately it would take six months to build, install, test, and modify the new space chamber test facility at the McDonnell plant. Several smaller, less sophisticated "man-rating" vacuum chambers had already been used but none was capable of simulating the extremes of orbital conditions.

Prelaunch preparations at the launch site began in June 1960 with an understanding between STG and McDonnell that some rework would be performed there in addition to extravagant preflight checkout tests, but the extent of the last-minute work to be performed and the number of discrepancies to be corrected became so great that "preflight checkout" quickly came to be a misnomer. Under Preston at the Cape, John J. Williams eventually came to head the "Preflight Operations" division, instead of being simply "checkout" crew chief. Paul C. Donnelly, Archibald E. Morse, Jr., A. Martin Eiband, Walter J. Kapryan, and Jacob C. Moser gradually became involved with wholesale systems engineering as the thoroughgoing checkouts in Hangar S expanded.

Gilruth laid down the law "for what is perhaps the most important single requirement in our programs: that designs, procedures, and schedules must have the flexibility to absorb a steady stream of change generated by a continually increasing understanding of space problems." This policy of correcting every discovered deficiency and of modifying each spacecraft down to the finish line at launch time was what Gilruth meant by an "R and D" program; it sacrificed cost and schedules if necessary in the interest of quality or reliability as the experimentalists understood it.[19]

Through August 1960 "space chamber" ground testing for Mercury had consisted primarily of the capsule systems tests for integration and compatibility in a relatively mild vacuum and of the manned environmental control system tests simulating an altitude of 40,000 feet. McDonnell had detected many design deficiencies in these test programs. Now early development failures, arising from unanticipated interactions between parts and components and from errors in estimating the effects of environmental extremes, became most troublesome.

At St. Louis in mid-August, the "Development Engineering Inspection," a milestone meeting comparable to the Mockup Review, brought together for three days all the chief actors and participants in the hardware work on the capsule. Walter C. Williams and Kenneth S. Kleinknecht were eager to institute this old Air Force custom—the "D.E.I.," as they called it—as a basic check on systems integration and configuration control. When on August 18 the 30 members of the NASA inspection team departed, they were well assured that the Mercury capsule on display (No. 7) was safe for manned flight, but only for a suborbital mission. Orbital flight would require a higher order of precautions for reliability. "Project Orbit," taking advantage of recent advances in vacuum technology, promised to pioneer this new dimension in development engineering by bringing the space climate down to Earth. Capsule No. 10 was specifically set aside in September for environmental chamber testing at McDonnell for orbital conditions.[20]

270

While the Tenney Engineering Company of Union, New Jersey, was building the new vacuum chamber for man-rated environmental testing of the capsule at the Cape, and while McDonnell engineers were moving in to augment STG's preflight checkout group there, one NASA operations expert transferred back to tidewater Virginia to help Gilruth and French formulate policy and establish STG's competence to judge reliability and flight safety issues. F. John Bailey, Jr., was Gilruth's choice for the man most likely to reconcile the differences between reliability based on experience and on expertise. Bailey believed an engineer needed 15 or 20 years' experience in any specialty to be a proper judge of the state of his art; he also appreciated the value of mathematical models in the redesign stages of technological evolution. But he quickly became convinced, particularly by studying the carefully balanced engineering compromises between efforts to make the boosters perfect and to perfect the escape system, that Mercury dependability could hardly be improved except by flight testing.[21]

Everyone recognized dangers in the pragmatic experimental approach to pilotless spacecraft research, but each calculated the risks differently. Silverstein and the new Associate Administrator, Robert C. Seamans, Jr., who succeeded Horner at this post on September 1, 1960, were among those at Headquarters who justly feared that overemphasis on the uniqueness of each production capsule and on STG's policy of continuous rework might lead to so many "quick fixes" that a pyramid of unobtrusive changes could cover up the truth about whatever might go wrong.[22]

Perhaps the most pertinent of these difficulties with systems integration derived from NASA bench tests of the reaction control system. The manufacturer of the RCS, Bell Aerosystems Company, ran its qualification test program from August through October 1960 and reported all phases of the testing satisfactorily completed. Subsequent tests by McDonnell, STG, other NASA engineers, the preflight teams at the Cape, and eventually by the workers on Project Orbit revealed innumerable electrochemical and electromechanical problems in simulated environments that required small changes here and there and eventually everywhere. The thrust chambers, metering orifices, solenoid valves, expulsion bladder, and relief valves each presented developmental flaws that were "solved" more often by improvisations than by scientific redesign. Karl F. Greil, a thermodynamicist who was working for Grand Central Rocket Company in 1960 to perfect the escape pyrotechnology for Mercury, joined STG and its reaction controls test team in 1961 and tried in vain to apply the same perfectionistic standards to this vastly more complicated and inherently less reliable system of moving parts:

> This is the irony: the results that counted in Mercury's RCS were due to changes of the screen, heat barrier, and orifices, all of which were made upon simple first thought. On the other hand, the large amount of experimentation on the valve resulted merely in the assurance that nothing needed to be changed so far as valve design was concerned. This irony, that the simple approach

did the entire job while the sophisticated approach merely resulted in an "Amen", is indeed worthy of reflection, because it has in store both a risk and a lesson: a lesson because there is so much glamor cast on sophisticated pretense and so much disregard for the profane causes of all kinds of trouble; a risk because the simple remedy which did the job once without ever having become clear just how it really worked, such success without perspiration is likely to remain confined to its own historical case. But having established a precedent, it is bound to seduce us into relying on it, if it is not even bound to become a myth and a dogma.[23]

Fortunately neither the reaction system nor the environmental control system for the Mercury suborbital flight had to be so nearly perfected as the escape, structural, and landing systems. The development engineering inspection confirmed the faith of most project engineers, in spite of a spate of impatient criticism from outsiders, that capsule sequencing, electrical, communications, stabilization, environment, pyrotechnical, instrumentation, and landing and recovery systems were virtually ready to fly. McDonnell issued a revised set of detail specifications for capsule No. 7 soon afterward. The Aerospace Corporation, spawned from and now replacing Space Technology Laboratories (STL) for Air Force systems engineering activities, published in September its basic planning document, the "General Flight Plan: Atlas Boosters for Project Mercury."[24]

If Project Mercury were on the verge of technological bankruptcy, as some critics claimed, the problem was that man was still land-locked by inadequate boosters. The Redstone for Mercury was still not man-rated. The first Mercury-Atlas flight on July 29, 1960, not only did not qualify anything, it seemed actually to have disqualified an indispensable part of Mercury. It cast everything into doubt.

ATLAS-MERCURY ONE: A COMPLETE FAILURE

Late in February 1960 the Air Force Ballistic Missile Division (BMD) and Space Technology Laboratories (STL) had been hosts for a meeting in Los Angeles of people from Convair/Astronautics, McDonnell, and the Task Group who were to determine the final details of the ultimate booster-capsule system for Project Mercury. Already STG had decided unilaterally, as was its prerogative, to make the next shot split the difference between the Big Joe development mission and a full qualification flight test of the Mercury-Atlas configuration on a simulated reentry from orbit. To the Task Group, this configuration and mission had long since been known as "MA-1," but Air Force and Convair engineers usually transposed the names and spoke of "Atlas-Mercury" No. 1. As in many other particulars, which things should be first still was debatable. Maxime A. Faget recorded his impression of the central technical debate at the Mercury-Atlas meeting on February 26:

> STL/CVA representatives made an impassioned plea to use the escape tower on the MA-1 shot. Only with the escape tower on, can the Atlas people

determine the structural bending modes on the Atlas and, consequently, the adequacy of their control system to accommodate them. The writer explained that the tower was deleted from this flight only after a great deal of deliberation at the Space Task Group, that much water has gone over the dam since then, and to change now would be very difficult. Although I agreed to take back to the Space Task Group management their desires for further consideration, they were informed that there was virtually no chance that the change would be made.[25]

As the MA-1 launch date approached, the Langley outfitters of the Big Joe capsule installed inside the shell of McDonnell's capsule No. 4 another instrumentation package, built by Lewis Research Center and STG electronics technicians. Shipped to the Cape in mid-May, loaded with 200 pounds of sensing instruments—including two cameras, two tape recorders, and a 16-channel telemetry system—the MA-1 payload was equipped to measure some 50 temperatures (mostly on the afterbody); pitch, yaw, and roll rates; positive and negative accelerations; cabin and external pressures; and noise and vibration extremes. Besides the missing 1060-pound escape system, this payload also lacked the environmental control system, the astronaut couch and control panel, and the attitude-control and stabilization-control jets. An inert paste replaced the solid fuel in the retrorockets. For several months before the Atlas 50-D booster arrived at the Cape, Joseph M. Bobik, of the STG Launch Operations Branch, had work abundant as the inspector of the MA-1 capsule. Meanwhile Sigurd A. Sjoberg, John D. Hodge, Richard G. Arbic, John P. Mayer, and Robert E. McKann were hastily revising the mission directive, data acquisition plan, and general information on recovery requirements, landing area predictions, and a summary of calculated preflight trajectory data.[26] Robert F. Thompson, Christopher C. Kraft, Jr., and Charles W. Mathews listed in order of importance the test objectives of the MA-1 flight:

1. Recover the capsule.
2. Determine the structural integrity of the Mercury capsule structure and afterbody shingles under the maximum heating conditions which could be encountered from an orbital launching.
3. Determine Mercury capsule afterbody heating rates during reentry (for this purpose 51 thermocouples were installed).
4. Determine the flight dynamic characteristics of the Mercury capsule during reentry.
5. Determine the adequacy of the Mercury capsule recovery systems.
6. Familiarize Project Mercury operating personnel with launch and recovery operations.[27]

When capsule No. 4 actually arrived at Cape Canaveral on May 23, it was as complete as it was supposed to be except for flight instrumentation, parachutes, and pyrotechnic devices. Following a satisfactory test of the leakage rate of its pressure shell, the capsule's miles of wiring were verified while the instrumentation system was subjected to final bench tests. Minor difficulties with instruments and in using a new weight-and-balance fixture added two weeks to the work period. For integrated systems tests to verify the sequencing and monitoring during the reentry, the capsule was moved into the newly constructed clean room in Hangar S.

When every minor discrepancy had been corrected and the calibration curves for various units had been established, the spacecraft was moved out to launch complex 14 for the first mechanical mating of a Mercury capsule with an Atlas booster. The alignment was good; no rework was required for the umbilicals or for the complex wiring in blockhouse consoles. But mechanical problems with Freon lines and with some electrical contacts in the mating ring caused a delay. Taken back to Hangar S for dismantling to rework certain instrumentation and telemetry packages, the capsule again was transported to the pad and mated to the launch vehicle in preparation for the flight acceptance composite test, known by its acronym, FACT. From July 13 to 18 engineers stood on the bascule of the gantry, working to conclude the FACT satisfactorily.

Meanwhile the Atlas crews were checking out their vehicle. Friendly rivalry between the propulsion and payload people produced many wagers over which system would cause the next postponement, and whether the capsule or the booster would be first to report "all systems go." On July 21, the flight readiness firing, which was a dress-rehearsal static-firing test, tested the three Atlas engines and measured the vibrations and acceleration strains suffered by the capsule. Atlas partisans won a bet at this point; atop this particular capsule the short metal legs of the "stub tower" created some unique antenna and telemetry difficulties with power amplifiers, commutators, and a high voltage standing wave ratio. The purpose of the "stub tower" was to support a thermal fairing over the antenna and parachute canister. Again the spacecraft was returned to the hangar. The tape recorders and cameras were removed, reloaded, and reinstalled. The telemetry was checked. The recovery section equipment was removed, then reassembled with live pyrotechnics. The capsule again was balanced, weighed, and aligned optically before its final union with the booster.[28]

McDonnell's virgin spacecraft No. 4 moved to the seaside launch pad dressed in a polyethylene raincoat on July 24. This time it nestled nicely on top the Atlas, and the umbilical insertion and pull tests shortly certified readiness to begin the countdown. Wet weather made it difficult to keep the pyrotechnic connections dry, but otherwise preflight checkouts were completed on July 26, 1960. For the benefit of Administrator Glennan, George Low summarized the expectations for Mercury-Atlas 1: [29]

> The primary objective of this test is to determine the integrity of the Mercury capsule structure and afterbody shingles when subjected to the maximum heating conditions which could be encountered in any Mercury mission.
> Maximum velocity: 19,000 feet per second
> Maximum altitude: 98 nautical miles

274

Range: 1300 nautical miles
Peak deceleration: 16.3 g
Time of flight: 16 minutes

Heavy rain pelted the Cape early on Friday morning, July 29, 1960, but the cloud ceiling rose high enough to be considered acceptable for a launching. During the final 35 minutes of countdown before launch time (T), 48 minutes were accumulated by delays or "holds" because of bad weather; liquid oxygen tank-topping delays; and telemetry receiver difficulties. In the blockhouse Gilruth and Walter Burke watched Walter Williams direct operations and Aleck C. Bond, the project engineer, sweat away the minutes, while across the Cape at Central Control, other Air Force, Navy, and Convair officers and officials also watched and waited. Before their consoles in the blockhouse sat the Convair test conductors Kurt Johnston and William Williams; Scott H. Simpkinson, the payload test conductor; Harold G. Johnston, the ground instrumentation coordinator; Jacob Moser, the instrumentation engineer; B. Porter Brown, the launch coordinator; Richard Arbic, the range coordinator; and Donald C. Cheatham, the recovery coordinator. At 7:25 the weather looked cooperative in the impact area, where recovery aircraft and ships were reporting a visibility of five miles and a sea state of mild swells. So the gantry was ordered to back away, leaving MA–1 poised alone in the rain, ready for the final count. Intermittent holds for minor status checks left only 7 minutes of count at 9 o'clock.

Finally at 9:13 the man-made thunder clapped as the Rocketdyne engines spewed forth their reaction energy. The noise grew louder for several seconds as the Atlas pushed itself up on its fiery blast by inches, feet, and yards. Out of sight in seconds as it pierced the cloud cover, Atlas 50–D could still be heard roaring off in the distance. The initial phases of the launching appeared to be normal. Then everything went wrong:

> About one minute after liftoff all contact with the Atlas was lost. This included telemetry and all beacons and transponders. About one second before telemetry was lost, the pressure difference between the lox and fuel tanks suddenly went to zero. It is not known whether this caused the failure or was an effect of the failure. There was no progression of unusual events leading up to this pressure loss. During the remaining second of telemetry, the Atlas flight path appeared to be steady.

By telephone and teletype data links, Low in Washington pieced together the bad news on MA–1 and continued to dictate an immediate preliminary report for the administrator and his staff:

> As you know, the abort sensing system was flown open loop in this test. This system gave two signals to abort, apparently about the same time as the tank pressure differential was lost. These signals were monitoring missile electrical power and thrust; although the tank pressure differential was also monitored, no abort signal was received from this source. In the MA–1 mission, all of these signals were merely monitored, and were not connected to any of the capsule systems.

275

The current speculation is that the Atlas either exploded, or suffered a catastrophic structural failure. Some observers reported that they heard an explosion, but this is not verified. The failure occurred at the time of maximum dynamic pressure, at an altitude of about 32,000 feet, and a velocity of about 1400 feet per second.

The capsule separation systems were not to be armed until about three minutes after launch, and therefore the capsule remained attached to the Atlas or to pieces of the Atlas, until impact. Capsule telemetry continued to impact and indicated violent motions after the Atlas telemetry ceased. Temperatures and shingle vibrations flutter were recorded. Since all shingle thermocouples gave readings to splash, it is inferred that none of the shingles tore off. Impact occurred about seven miles off shore in an area where the water depth is roughly 40 feet. At the time of this writing, ships were still searching for debris.[30]

It was a sad day for Mercury. It was especially frustrating for those nearest to the Atlas-Mercury phase, for they knew only that MA–1, either Atlas 50–D or capsule No. 4, or both, exploded on its way through max q. They did not know precisely what had happened because the weather had been so bad as to prevent visual and photographic coverage. In Washington, at Langley, at the Cape, and in southern California, postmortems were held for two weeks, until a conference on August 11 marshalled the parties most interested in the MA–1 malfunction, along with all the flight records, telemetry, and tape recorder data. Salvage operations had been able to recover only small portions of the capsule, the adapter-ring, and the booster. Presiding at this meeting was Major General Leighton I. Davis, the new commander of the Air Force Missile Test Center, who had relieved Major General Donald N. Yates in June as the Department of Defense single-point-of-contact for support of Project Mercury. On August 22, Warren J. North summarized the "quick-look" opinions of NASA and STL but not of Convair/Astronautics:

> Both the NASA and STG localized the difficulty within the interface area between the capsule and the booster. A metallurgist from STL explained that it appeared the plumbing to the Atlas lox boiloff valve had failed due to fatigue. One would not ordinarily suspect a fatigue failure after such a short period of time, however, the NASA analysis showed that the lox valve plumbing could have failed if a 30 g oscillation existed at approximately 300 cycles per second. Culbertson (Convair) admitted that the lox valve was poorly supported and that 30 g was a feasible magnitude of acceleration. Vibration measurements show a two and one-half g vibration of the booster airframe, consequently a 12 g amplification factor would have been required at the lox valve.
>
> Jim Chamberlin, STG, has been appointed chairman of a joint committee to resolve the MA–1 incident and provide a fix prior to MA–2. Initial reaction of this committee would cause the establishment of a hardware mockup at McDonnell which would include the pressurized lox tank dome, lox valve, adapter, and capsule. This mockup will be vibrated in order to isolate resonance or amplification factors.[31]

276

MA-1
July 29, 1960

MA-1, a suborbital flight designed to check capsule structural integrity under maximum heating conditions, rose into the low rain clouds above Cape Canaveral (right) and mysteriously exploded one minute after lift-off. Pieces were meticulously collected (below) and painstakingly reassembled (below right). The engineering study delayed Mercury about 6 months but led to vastly improved interface between spacecraft and booster.

Two weeks later in San Diego, another committee of nine metallurgical engineers, a majority of whom were not from Convair, examined microscopically the hypothesis that MA-1 was destroyed by metal fatigue of the lox-vent valve elbow. "All conferees agreed finally that the factor at hand was not the primary one." [32] The official flight test report issued two months later concluded with these remarks:

> The Mercury Atlas No. 1 flight test was abruptly terminated approximately 58.5 seconds after launch by an in-flight failure of an undetermined nature. Solid cloud cover at the time of launch precluded the use of optical records in the investigation of this failure. The following conclusions are drawn regarding this flight test:
>
> a. None of the primary capsule test objectives were met.
> b. The structural integrity of the capsule was maintained throughout the flight until impact with the water. A substantial part of the adapter remained attached to the capsule to impact.
> c. The capsule onboard instrumentation performed in a highly satisfactory manner throughout the flight.
> d. The onboard instrumentation showed the presence of shingle vibration of a non-destructive nature.
> e. All Department of Defense support for the operation was very good. [33]

In mid-September one of the most important of the regular monthly meetings of the Mercury-Atlas coordination panel took place in the administration building at Patrick Air Force Base, Florida. Lieutenant Colonel Robert H. Brundin, Major Charles L. Gandy, and Captain I. B. Hanson were the BMD representatives, while Philip E. Culbertson and C. J. Holden represented Convair. Bernard A. Hohmann and Ernst R. Letsch were representing Aerospace Corporation, since STL was phasing out of Mercury. John Yardley, R. L. Foster, and J. T. Heard were present for McDonnell.

First and last on the agenda of this meeting were questions concerning better ways of inspecting and solving problems at the interface between the capsule and the booster. Charles Mathews, the chairman, began the meeting by insisting that in spite of the MA-1 failure, the overall Mercury-Atlas schedule could still be maintained. Hohmann suggested that a new seven-man joint capsule-booster interface inspection committee be established. This was done, and members representing all contributing organizations were named. Regarding the unsettled question of MA-1, Mathews briefly described several fruitless fact-finding activities and the need for additional instrumentation to determine the cause of failures like MA-1. No new hypothesis had yet emerged from the several test programs, so the 23 members of this coordination panel reexamined each other's previous answers to the enigma of MA-1. The 11 members from STG vetoed a proposal by the Air Force Ballistic Missile Division to establish still another "Mercury-Atlas interface panel." [34]

Although the MA-1 investigation was unsatisfying, the launch operations committee reported that MA-2 was so nearly ready for a November launching that there was little time for looking backward and no time for regret. Then on September 26, 1960, a lunar probe attempt by NASA, using Atlas-Able 5–A, also failed severely. This forced a wholesale review of the Atlas as a launch vehicle. Everybody responsible for MA–1 was trying to determine the cause of that failure, but each only discovered that there were too many other bodies, both organic and organizational, partly responsible.

Late in October, before the national elections and before another Mercury flight test had come to pass, Gilruth and Williams held another periodic press conference for the benefit of curious reporters. Inevitably the question was asked, "Are you satisfied that you have pinpointed the reason for the MA–1 failure?" "No," Gilruth answered. "We successfully salvaged the capsule and can account for all parts." His interrogator continued, "Do you believe that parts in the Atlas' upper stage caused the failure?" Gilruth replied, "We have explored this. We have answered all of the questions we have asked ourselves— but have we asked the right questions? We can't be sure. That is one of the reasons we are repeating the test. And on MA–2 the interface area will be heavily instrumented." [35]

When MA–2 finally became ready for launch, toward the end of February 1961, the managers of Mercury knew that a repetition of a total failure like MA–1 could easily cause abandonment of the project. The entire promise of the American manned space flight program seemed to hang in the balance. The technical aftermath of MA–1, during the politically sensitive period of the Presidential election and the lame-duck session of Congress, made interrelated technical and political considerations more acute than ever. To distinguish between the two soon became virtually impossible.

ELECTION YEAR APPRAISALS

The day that Mercury-Atlas 1 failed so badly, NASA Headquarters announced plans to follow Project Mercury with a manned space flight program called "Apollo"—a project conceived to carry three men either in sustained orbital flight or on circumlunar flight. Several days later, the X–15 set two new world records when NASA pilot Joseph A. Walker flew the manned rocket on partial power to a speed of 2196 miles per hour and when Major Robert M. White shot it up to a height of 136,000 feet over Nevada and California. [36]

In mid-August 1960, the Air Force accomplished two significant "firsts" within eight days when it managed to recover instrumented packages from the thirteenth and fourteenth attempts in its Thor-Agena-launched Discoverer series of satellites. *Discoverer XIII* dropped its 85-pound capsule into the Pacific off Hawaii on August 11 after 16 orbits; although a mid-air retrieval had failed, frogmen and helicopters from a naval vessel found and returned this, the first man-made object recovered intact from an orbital journey. On August 19, 1960, an Air Force C–119 cargo plane trailing a huge trapeze-like trawl succeeded in being at exactly

279

the right place at the right time to snare in mid-air the descending instruments from *Discoverer XIV*. That same day, however, the Soviets launched an ark, including the "muttniks" Strelka and Belka, and the next day they recovered the dogs and their live companions (rats, mice, flies, plants, fungi, and seeds) after 18 orbits above Earth's atmosphere. This marked the first successful recovery of living biological specimens from an orbital voyage. Three months later, on November 14, 1960, another C–119 aircraft succeeded in snatching the reentry capsule from *Discoverer XVII*, which carried human tissue, bacteria, spores, and film emulsions to an orbital apogee of 616 miles. For the moment, though, the Soviet achievement was overwhelming in its portents for manned space flight.[37]

On August 12, 1960, after an attempt that had failed in May, NASA's Project Echo succeeded in placing into orbit the first passive communications satellite, a 100-foot-diameter aluminized Mylar plastic balloon, which reflected radio signals beyond Earth's curvature. Launched by a Thor-Delta vehicle into an orbit roughly 1000 miles from Earth and inclined 47 degrees to the equator, *Echo I* was the first artificial moon that could be seen easily with the naked eye by all mankind. Although stargazing aborigines in neolithic cultures of New Guinea and Mozambique probably could see the Echo balloon with the unaided eye better than sophisticates in the smog and haze of urban-industrial centers from California to Kazakhstan, the new pinpoint of light in the heavens was a visible manifestation of the "space age." President Eisenhower's broadcast message reflected from this sphere circling Earth at 15,000 miles per hour proclaimed:

> It is a great personal satisfaction to participate in this first experiment in communications involving the use of a satellite balloon known as Echo. This is one more significant step in the United States program of space research and exploration. The program is being carried forward vigorously by the United States for peaceful purposes for the benefit of all mankind.
> The satellite balloon which has reflected these words may be used freely by any nation for similar experiments in its own interests. Information necessary to prepare for such participation was widely distributed some weeks ago.
> The United States will continue to make freely available to the world the scientific information acquired from this and other experiments in its program of space exploration.[38]

While the President was pointing to these and other achievements of the United States in the exploration and use of outer space, the Nation was in the midst of a highly contested presidential campaign and congressional elections. Four years earlier it had seemed sheer whimsy, but now the practical values of space exploration and policy decisions on space, missiles, and the Nation were being not only examined but reexamined. In September, a month after Strelka and Belka were orbited and recovered by the Soviet Union, Premier Khrushchev again came to the United States for some personal diplomacy and figurative sabotage in the United Nations General Assembly. Afterward he told reporters that his people were ready to launch a man into space but had not yet made any such attempt.[39] No longer could Khrushchev's brogan braggadocio be ignored.

Meeting at Barcelona, on October 7, 1960, the Fédération Aéronautique Internationale adopted the first set of rules to govern the award of official records for manned space flight. To be recognized under the "Code Sportif" that had been setting the rules for aeronautical records since 1905, the first flight into space must top at least 100 kilometers; later attempts to set records must exceed the existing record by at least 10 percent. Four categories of performance were set forth: duration of flight, altitude without orbiting Earth, altitude in orbit, and mass lifted above 100 kilometers. To be valid, all claims for records "must be supported by information on the date, time, place of takeoff and landing, identity of the vehicle commander, and any special apparatus used to assist liftoff, landing, or control." [40]

When in mid-October Soviet tracking ships deployed to stations in the Pacific, an alert went out to American forces to expect imminent Soviet attempts to fulfill Khrushchev's boast. In mid-August there had been much talk in the American press that the United States had "rejoined" the space race as a result of recent accomplishments. An Associated Press dispatch on August 8 reported that Abe Silverstein was not particularly dismayed by the MA–1 fiasco and believed that Project Mercury was "essentially along the same time schedule as was initially planned." Congressman Overton Brooks, Democrat from Louisiana and chairman of the House Committee on Science and Astronautics, waxed much more critical of the speed with which Project Mercury was moving. In September Glennan warned Americans to be prepared for new Soviet announcements of space spectaculars. The Mercury astronauts repeatedly were reported confident that one of them could ride a ballistic trajectory either in December or January.[41] In short, the dramatic race to be first to put a man in space made such colorful copy that news editors generally ran stories on the space contest second only to news about the political contest.

The news media both reflected and fostered a widespread restlessness over the apparent failure of American know-how to equal and surpass Soviet rocket technology. Back in October 1959, two years after *Sputnik I*, *Newsweek* had featured an article, "How to Lose the Space Race," itemizing blanket criticisms of all American space programs. To ensure that you have the losing ticket, advised *Newsweek,* simply "start late, downgrade Russian feats, fragment authority, pinch pennies, think small, shirk decisions." [42] At the beginning of 1960, Hanson W. Baldwin, the influential military affairs correspondent for the *New York Times,* had chided the Eisenhower administration for neglecting the power of intangible ideas and had advised the government to seek more advice from political rather than physical scientists: "It is not good enough to say that we have counted more free electrons in the ionosphere than the Russians have . . . we must achieve the obvious and the spectacular, as well as the erudite and the obscure." And in July 1960 one of the deans of space fiction and fact, Arthur C. Clarke, published a playful, widely viewed article that suggested that the United States had "already suffered a failure of nerve" and forfeited its future by failing to "rocket to the renaissance." [43]

Project Mercury specifically, as 1960 wore on without much to show for the taxpayers' millions, began to be criticized more minutely. Perhaps the most painful sting felt by the Mercury team came from adverse publicity in *Missiles and Rockets,* a weekly defense industry trade journal, on August 15, 1960. There, under the heading "Is Mercury Program Headed for Disaster?" writer James Barr excoriated Project Mercury:

> NASA's Mercury manned-satellite program appears to be plummeting the United States toward a new humiliating disaster in the East-West space race.
>
> This is the stark conclusion that looms in the minds of a growing number of eminent rocket scientists and engineers as the Mercury program continues to slip backward.
>
> These experts, many of whom are already calling Mercury a latter day Vanguard, contend:
>
> The program today is more than one year behind its original schedule and is expected to slip to two. Therefore, it no longer offers any realistic hope of beating Russia in launching the first man into orbit around the earth—much less serve as an early stepping stone for reaching the moon.
>
> Despite precautions and improvements, Mercury continues to be a technically marginal program that could easily end in flaming tragedy. Mercury, at best, is a technical stop-gap justifiable only as an expedient. It is no substitute for what is needed sooner or later, a maneuverable spacecraft similar to the Air Force's much hampered Dyna-Soar.
>
> Mercury originally had the supposed advantage of being cheap, an attribute that made it particularly attractive to the Administration. However, Mercury has proven to be a trip down a dead-end road that U.S. taxpayers are finding themselves paving in gold. Appropriations have reached a quarter-billion to date. They may double.[44]

Although Barr's animadversion could have been discounted in an election year as a plug for more encouragement and funding to the Air Force's Dyna-Soar program, the occasions for self-doubt inside Project Mercury indisputably were becoming more numerous. On September 16, 1960, Gilruth issued a memorandum for his staff that showed the effects of barbs like those from Barr on the morale of the Task Group. The subject of the memo was "Favorable Press Comments (for a change)":

> As most of you know, there have been some adverse comments in the press and trade publications about the progress, or lack of progress, being made in Project Mercury during recent weeks. A number of members of the Space Task Group have expressed concern about these articles.
>
> In any program as broad and complex and as important to our national stature as Project Mercury, it is inevitable that there will be people around us who either will not agree with us, period, or who tend to disagree in one element or another just to be disagreeable. At the same time, there are a number of people around our country who do understand how much work and how much blood and sweat go into an undertaking of this kind.

*   *   *

I am personally confident that the work that all of you are doing will bear fruit in the near future. In the interim, I urge all of you to put on your thickest hide, to continue your concerted efforts to make Project Mercury the kind of program it was designed to be, and to reflect with me upon our past accomplishments.[45]

At NASA Headquarters there was serious concern over how to answer public criticisms. On August 14 Warren North sent the Administrator some arguments filling in the contextual background of Mercury schedules:

Since the negotiation of the capsule contract, McDonnell personnel have averaged 14% overtime for an equivalent 56 hour week. McDonnell has assigned approximately 13,000 people in direct support of Project Mercury. In October 1959, production went on a 7-day week, three shifts per day. Since January 1960 capsule checkout personnel have worked three shifts per day seven days per week. McDonnell is also working three shifts at Cape Canaveral. During the past eighteen months, Space Task Group personnel have been using less than half their annual leave. Many have used essentially no annual leave since February 1959. Space Task Group personnel at Cape Canaveral worked approximately 50 hours a week preparing for flight operations. When the MA–1 capsule was delivered to the Cape on May 23, 1960, this group went on a 60-hour week. During the final month of MA–1 preparations, the launch operations crew was working a seventy-hour week. The forthcoming simultaneous operations with Atlas and Redstone will require a continuation of this type of effort.[46]

On September 9, 1960, George Low addressed a United Press International editors conference at a hotel in Washington on the subject of the progress made in Project Mercury to date. Low began by arguing against three common misconceptions about the project in the public press: Mercury was not, he said, "merely a stunt," not "designed only to win an important first in the space program," and should not "be terminated if the Soviets achieve manned orbital flight before we do." Firmly convinced that the Soviets now had the capability of achieving manned orbital flight, Low tried to persuade the opinion molders of the "fourth estate" to accept Mercury as an indispensable step toward Project Apollo, one which "must be carried out regardless of Russian achievement." This theme subsequently became official NASA policy. The urgency of Project Mercury was transferred onto the higher level of the urgency of manned space flight in general and for the future. "It has been a major engineering task," said Low, "to design a capsule that is small enough to do the mission, light enough to do the mission, and yet has reliable subsystems to accomplish the mission safely." [47]

Within the aerospace community of industrialists, technicians, and Government scientists and engineers, the context described by North and Low needed little explication. Experience with federally sponsored "R and D" programs since 1940 helped them understand the difference between a project rating the "DX," or highest industrial procurement priority, and one designated an all-out "crash" program. Mercury was never a "crash" project in the sense that the Atlas ICBM or the Manhattan Project had been, in which duplicative and parallel solutions were developed for its most difficult systems. The DX priority for materials, NASA's own first rating, and STG's high "sense of urgency" were tempered always by the rule of noninterference with priority defense programs. In mid-September NASA and the Defense Department agreed to aid each other to avoid duplication and waste by means of a new Aeronautics and Astronautics Coordinating Board, with Dryden and Herbert F. York as co-chairmen.[48]

But the citizenry, through the press, saw these problems in simpler terms. "Project Mercury: Race or Pure Science?" was a banner headline in a Norfolk newspaper of September 11. Richard M. Mansfield related therein how the United States "space fever" had fluctuated over the previous three years:

> Gilruth gets a little angry when people talk about Mercury lagging behind schedule. Some say it is behind as much as a year. Gilruth says this is pure nonsense, that no one can properly put a specific target date on a research program that explores "new frontiers," and is beset by such "detailed problems."
>
> *   *   *
>
> Gilruth gave assurance that extra money would not have cut time appreciably. He does not believe that a blank-check crash program would save much time even now.
> "I think we've done our optimum," he said. "It's just like having a baby. Maybe (with more money) we could have had a lot more of them, but you wouldn't have cut the time on any one of them."[49]

Reporter Mansfield went on to summarize the conflicting attitudes of scientists who "are never in a hurry," with Government employees, including scientists, who must respond to the demand of the electorate to "overtake the Soviets." The eagerness of the seven American astronauts to make their suborbital flights was tempered, he reported, by their recognition that the orbital venture into space had already slipped too far. "There is little doubt among them that the Russians will have been there first," said Mansfield.

Late in September members of the military and industrial community engaged in aerospace and defense business watched with interest for indications where best to invest their votes. The editors of *Missiles and Rockets* addressed an open letter to both the Republican and the Democratic candidates for the Presidency, inviting comments on a "modest proposal for survival." The journal sought specific commitments on the recognition as national policy of the strategic space race with Russia and on the endorsement of a bold long-range program for space projects during the next decade. Candidate John F. Kennedy responded immediately with his concurrence that "we are in a strategic space race with the Russians, and we have been losing. . . . if a man orbits earth this year his name will be Ivan." To this audience Kennedy also explained one meaning of his campaign slogans on "moving ahead" into the "new frontier": "This is the new age of exploration; space is our great new frontier." Vice-President Richard M. Nixon, seeing the issues of an alleged "missile gap" and of national prestige loom ever larger in the later stages of the campaign, at last replied by vigorously defending the record of the Eisenhower administration.[50] The issue of manned space flight was never clearly joined, here or in the television debates preceding the election. But after the first Tuesday in November, even though the popular vote barely showed a preference, it was clear that the next Chief Executive as well as the Congress would be Democratic and that this meant change.

Project Mercury, as one large and unproven part of NASA, could expect to be influenced by "the gathering storm over space" and some sharp changes in the Nation's defense and space programs.[51] The most forthright change to be expected with the new administration likely would be an honest and open admission of the competitive aspects of space technology. International negotiations on disarmament had failed to produce any further arms control measures since the 1958 Russian-American agreement to suspend atmospheric nuclear testing. Efforts in the United Nations to exempt space as an arena for international rivalries, following the example of the 1959 Antarctica treaty, had so far failed. It seemed purely sentimental to act as if coexistence would become any less competitive. Besides, recent successes of American missiles reinforced the United States' foreign policy of steadfast resistance to Communist encroachments. An Atlas ICBM had again flown 9000 miles for a bullseye in the Indian Ocean on September 19, 1960; the Thor was operational, and the Polaris and Titan weapon systems were in active test phases. A "booster gap" there admittedly was, but the "missile gap" appeared closed, at least to discussion, after the election. The new President would probably find it politic to move speedily but cautiously toward a more intensive national (in contrast to a scientific-international) space program. Kennedy was historically minded and could be trusted to see "the present in perspective," but whether he would consider, as one professional historian did, "manned space flight as the main object of Russo-American rivalry" was entirely moot.[52]

Congressional attitudes before and after the election of 1960 seemed to change less drastically because Congress was already Democratic and had been critical of the Republican "no-race" thesis for three years now. Some of those legislative representatives who felt a need to justify their loyal opposition to Eisenhower and their support for manned space exploration could do so by mailing their constituents a congressional staff report entitled "The Practical Values of Space Exploration." Philip B. Yeager, a staff member of the House Committee on Science and Astronautics, wrote this pamphlet "to explain to the taxpayer just why so many of his dollars are going into the American effort to explore space, and to indicate what he can expect in return which is of value to him." Two editions of this report, before and after the election, began with a quotation from a Russian workman who reportedly complained in a letter published on the front page of *Pravda* for June 12, 1960:

> What do Sputniks give to a person like me? . . . So much money is spent on Sputniks it makes people gasp. If there were no Sputniks the Government

285

could cut the cost of cloth for an overcoat in half and put a few electric flat-irons in the stores. Rockets, rockets, rockets. Who needs them now? [53]

Neither edition of Yeager's staff report spoke explicitly about Project Mercury, but both implicitly illustrated Mercury's motivation. The author delineated in lay language five categories of values served by national space programs. Intangible values came first and included scientific curiosity and the human urge to do as well as to know. National security was second, and included the argument for space rivalry as a substitute for war. Economic benefits, immediate and remote, were described in social terms for the third category. "Values for everyday living" described some of the technological and medical "fallout" or "spin-off" from space-related research. And finally this pamphlet pointed to long-range values and to possible interrelationships with the population explosion, water shortages, soil erosion, new leisure time, and the scientific and spiritual aspirations of humanity. In conclusion Yeager chose to quote a paragraph, from an editorial in the magazine *Industrial Research,* which "sober study indicates . . . may not be too 'far out' after all":

> Space technology is probably the fastest moving, typically free enterprise and democratic industry yet created. It puts a premium not on salesmanship, but on what it needs most—intellectual production, the research payoff. Unlike any other existing industry, space functions on hope and future possibilities, conquest of real estate unseen, of near vacuum unexplored. At once it obliterates the economic reason for war, the threat of overpopulation, or cultural stagnation; it offers to replace guesswork with the scientific method for archeological, philosophical, and religious themes. [54]

Technical Sprint for Man in Space

Although election year reexaminations and premonitions of the Soviet Vostoks were disconcerting, these were the least of the conscious worries of the men teamed in the technological harness to get a Mercury astronaut off the ground. They still had a plenitude of more prosaic problems of their own. The inexorable growth of the capsule weight, the marginal performance of the Atlas as a launch vehicle, interface wiring and structural problems, and the worrisome reaction and environmental controls for the capsule were outstanding. On the other hand, some problems, like thermal protection during atmospheric entry and the physiological effects of weightlessness for a short period, were assumed solved for the moment.

Benjamine J. Garland, one of Faget's fellow authors of the seminal 1958 NACA paper for Mercury, prepared a special report for Gilruth on the probability of damage to the capsule by micrometeoroids during an orbital flight. Garland advised that the danger to the capsule during an orbital flight from sporadic meteoroid activity was very small. He calculated probabilities of hits during a major meteoroid shower and found the danger was "still small but . . .

an order of magnitude greater than the danger due to the sporadic background. Since the periods of activity of the major showers are known, it is possible to avoid operations during these periods and would be advisable to do so." [55]

Because qualification and reliability tests on the retrograde and posigrade rocket systems proved disappointing in their later results, Gilruth's team called for help from the Ames and Lewis Research Centers. Robert R. Nunemaker led a group at Lewis, monitored by John B. Lee of STG, who found some serious difficulties with retrorocket alignment and escape tower separation. Among other things, they found that some igniters were faulty and that the jettisoning of the escape tower under certain conditions might permit a smashing recontact.

But the most serious problem with capsule systems at this time was the outside chance that one or more of the three retrograde braking rockets might fail. There was considerable margin for error in the design of the retropackage, but there was no emergency braking system. STG's mission analysis group under John P. Mayer had thoroughly investigated an inflatable balloon for this purpose, and Gilruth himself proposed an emergency brake that would have looked like a Chinese dragon kite trailing in the wake of the orbiting capsule. This auxiliary drag device to back up the retrosystem and to bring the capsule down sooner than in the 24 hours theoretically required for a normal decay of Mercury's orbit was independently appraised by Howard K. Larson and others at Ames. Meanwhile John Glenn and the other astronauts asked STG's mission analysts to study the effectiveness of a "fish-tailing" maneuver as a backup reentry mode of last resort. Both ideas were reported feasible, but the former was not pursued past the end of the year, when the reliability of the retrorockets and pyrotechnics began to rise appreciably. [56]

Among the number of unsolved problems regarding man-machine integration in late 1960, the complex final phase of the mission profile aroused much concern. If an astronaut could survive launch, insertion, orbiting, reentry, and the free-fall, nothing must jeopardize his chances to survive impact, exit from the capsule, and recovery. But as the capsule developed into flight hardware, the differences between its theoretical design and its measurable performance required constant restudy, redesign, and in some cases redevelopment. [57] While studying the Mercury capsule's stability in water, for example, Peter J. Armitage and E. N. Harrin of STG found that the deletion of the flotation bags and the addition of the impact skirts had seriously compromised the floating trim if not the seaworthiness of the capsule. [58]

After summarizing recent investigations by both McDonnell and STG engineers, Armitage and Harrin pointed out a number of unknowns and recommended close scrutiny of any changes to capsule center-of-gravity positions to keep the capsule within acceptable stability limits. While the model-makers at Langley were fabricating and testing 24 new impact skirts, Astronauts Shepard, Grissom, and Schirra practiced getting out of the capsule; it now listed at severe angles and sometimes even capsized. [59]

During September 1960 all the Mercury astronauts began to train more pointedly for the Mercury-Redstone mission. Early in October they gathered their personalized couches, pressure suits, and accessories for centrifuge runs at the Navy's Aviation Medical Acceleration Laboratory at Johnsville, Pennsylvania. Fitted with a production handcontroller assembly and environmental control system, the gondola of the centrifuge whirled each man as if he were experiencing the calculated acceleration profile of the MR–3 flight. At Johnsville the astronauts gained experience in attitude and rate control, monitored the normal sequencing functions, and learned to cope with emergency conditions like overacceleration and decompression. Alan Shepard, for instance, took 10 training "flights" during the October session.[60]

On September 8, 1960, Silverstein called to Washington NASA's and Mc-Donnell's chief engineers at work on Mercury to discuss plans for compressing the Mercury-Redstone schedule by expediting the capsule systems tests and checkout procedures for capsules Nos. 5 and 7, to be flown on MR–2 and MR–3, respectively. Once again Silverstein asked that McDonnell assign independent systems engineers to verify all hardware installations. Especially they were to improve the quality of capsule No. 7 before the formal systems testing period. This was done during October and November; for 43 days No. 7 underwent performance trials of all its systems except its reaction controls, automatic stabilization controls, and instrumentation and communications gear. McDonnell, Navy, and STG liaison inspectors tried hard to meet Silverstein's Cape delivery deadline of November 15, but two major discrepancies could not be allowed to pass. One problem had been perennial: overheating DC/AC inverters. Investigations disclosed that as long as the ambient temperature was kept below 165 degrees F they functioned properly. McDonnell attempted to cure this overheating problem by replacing the honeycombed inverter sockets with aluminum shelves that doubled as heat sinks.[61]

The second problem was new: tiny cracks were noticed in the outer titanium skin of the capsule pressure vessels. Samples of fractured material were sent to the Battelle Memorial Institute, an endowed foundation for applied scientific research, at Columbus, Ohio. Battelle found that the heated zones adjacent to the seam welds contained an excessive amount of precipitated hydrides, compounds of hydrogen and other elements. These impurities lowered the ductility of the skin of the pressure vessel, increased leakage rates, and increased the danger of structural collapse upon impact. But since capsule No. 7 had the best record of all in the capsule systems tests, it passed muster to begin its final factory shakedown tests on November 21, 1960. For later capsules, welding methods, vibration testing, and microscopic inspections were improved, but the long-standing "skin-cracking" problem required that the search be renewed for ways to eliminate hydride formations near the beads of fusion welds.[62]

On December 1, 1960, Jerome B. Hammack, the MR–3 project engineer for STG, and his assistant, James T. Rose, certified that capsule No. 7 was ready for

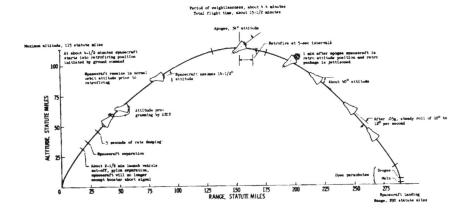

Normal sequence of events for Mercury-Redstone flight.

its manned mission, though some 20 days behind schedule. "The writers would like to stress that the majority of time spent during this period was spent on correction and rework rather than the actual CST and that every effort should be made in the future to achieve manufacturing perfection prior to the capsule entering CST." [63]

Meanwhile capsule No. 2, being readied for the first Mercury-Redstone flight, was delivered to the Cape at the beginning of August. This flight, MR–1, was then scheduled for launching early in October. Both McDonnell and STG preflight checkout crews in Hangar S worked around the clock to make ready the maze of systems in their capsule. Christopher Kraft talked over Mercury command functions with the Redstone launch team under Debus and with Air Force range safety officer Lieutenant Colonel R. D. Stephens early in September. They then decided to fly the MR–1 mission with the automatic abort system in the open-loop mode to lessen any possibility of a nuisance abort on this qualification flight.

On a trial basis, a smaller Flight Safety Review Board for the spacecraft (tailored after the Atlas boards by the same name), chaired by Walter Williams and consisting of Astronaut Cooper, F. J. Bailey, Jr., Kenneth S. Kleinknecht, and William M. Bland, Jr., was established at the Cape to pass final judgment during the week before the countdown on the readiness of the mission. During the first week in October, final preparations were made to launch MR–1, and on the morning of October 9, 1960, an unbroken countdown proceeded to within 22 minutes of launchtime before the shot was scrubbed because of a malfunction in the capsule reaction control system. [64]

By the first of November both LJ–5 and MR–1 appeared ready for launching on November 7, 1960. But both launches had to be postponed again (the day before the election) because of inclement weather at Wallops Island and because at the Cape a serious leak developed in the helium tank of capsule No. 2. Without helium to pressurize the hydrogen peroxide thrusters, the payload after posigrade release might not reorient itself properly for reentry. So heavy had the workload at the Cape become that Williams decreed a maximum of 12 hours' work for any one person in any one day.[65]

The possible political significance of these launches now was seen by the press and by the legislative staffs on Capitol Hill and at NASA Headquarters. George Low's routine report for James P. Gleason, Assistant Administrator for Congressional Relations, carefully explained the technical reasons first for delay and then for speedup on the launch schedules. Regarding Little Joe 5, Gleason informed the staff director of the Senate space committee that NASA Headquarters was keeping close tabs on MR–1 scheduling information because of the need to coordinate interagency activity, but that Little Joe missions "requiring no major coordination with non-NASA organizations" had always been handled on a less formal basis:

> You will notice that the launch target date was delayed from October 8, 1960, to November 11, 1960, at the time when it became apparent that the capsule delivery would be delayed until about August 1, 1960. Between August 17 and August 31, a large number of checkout difficulties was encountered in the noise and vibration test program. It was then expected that the capsule would not arrive at Wallops until October 5, and hence the launch date was moved to November 16.
>
> In the early part of September, the rate of progress at Langley picked up, and the capsule was actually shipped to Wallops on September 27th. Nevertheless, the projected launch date was not moved to an earlier date, since simultaneous experience with MR–1 at Cape Canaveral gave every indication that the prelaunch checkout would take longer than planned.
>
> In actual practice, the Wallops Island checkout ran very smoothly. Accordingly, a new target date of November 7 was established late in October. Barring difficulties during the final checkout period, and assuming that the weather will be clear and calm, the launching will take place on that date.
>
> . . . I feel that our project engineers have done an excellent job at predicting these dates; it is very seldom that actual dates on as complex a research and development program as this one have come out so close to the predicted dates as these have.[66]

Less out of sensitivity to the political winds than because the facts seemed to warrant it, the apolitical civil servants in the Task Group sent an encouraging status report on Project Mercury to their administrative superiors in Washington at the end of October 1960. There were a couple of negative items: the cause of the MA–1 failure was still unknown, and the checkout time at the Cape for capsule No. 2 for MR–1 was stretching interminably, it seemed. On the plus side, three capsules (Nos. 2, 5, and 6 for MR–1, MR–2, and MA–2, respectively) were on hand, and two more (Nos. 7 and 8 for MR–3 and MA–3) were expected at the Cape momentarily.   The Mercury Control Center, a command-post building trisecting the area between the two blockhouses beside the launching pads and the industrial hangars, was open and almost ready for operations.   Four preflight checkout trailers supplied by McDonnell were already in full use.   Procedures Trainer No. 2 was being wired to its computer banks, and the ground-test qualification program seemed almost complete.

The tracking and communications network was essentially finished, except for the stations at Kano, Nigeria, and on Zanzibar.   The Atlas ASIS was looking good, and with luck the first truly complete Mercury-Atlas configuration, MA–2, still might possibly be flown during the quarter.   Cost accounting for the program was still a black art, but according to STG's own estimates the summary of funds required to accomplish the Mercury mission as defined in October 1960 approached $110 million: [67]

Mercury capsules (20)	$48,720,000
Mercury boosters	25,429,000
Mercury network (incl. operations)	18,953,000
Mercury recovery (incl. operations)	10,573,000
Biological and human engineering	1,922,000
Development program	3,928,000
Total	$109,525,000

LITTLE JOE 5 VOTES NO

On Election Day, November 8, 1960, Space Task Group and McDonnell engineers at Wallops Island finally pulled the trigger on capsule No. 3, attached to Little Joe 5.   Having planned LJ–5 for over a year as the first qualification flight of a production capsule to sustain abort conditions at maximum dynamic pressure, the hard-working crews were especially chagrined to see the disintegration of all their plans only 16 seconds after liftoff.   At that time the escape rocket and the tower jettison rocket both prematurely ignited while the booster was still thrusting.   Therefore booster, capsule, and tower stayed mated together throughout their ballistic trajectory until impact shattered them to fragments.

Whether the limit switches at the clamp rings below or above the spacecraft were at fault, or whatever improper rigging, wiring, or voltage regulation was the cause, it was exceedingly hard to rationalize that something was learned from this flight failure.   Spacecraft and booster continued on their arc 10 miles high and 13 miles out to sea before being mangled on impact 2 minutes later.   Salvage operations in water 72 feet deep recovered 60 percent of the booster but only 40 percent of the capsule.[68]   Extensive tests on the clamp-ring problem were conducted on rocket sleds at the Naval Ordnance Test Station at Inyokern, California.

For well over a year Holloman Air Force Base personnel, led by Major John D.

291

Mosely, of the Aeromedical Field Laboratory, had prepared a packaged payload with a medium-sized chimpanzee to ride the LJ–5 qualification flight. As late as mid-July 1960, operational planning still included a first-order test objective to determine the effects of a simulated Atlas abort acceleration on a chimp. The delay in capsule delivery and a large number of checkout difficulties encountered in late August, especially with the booster-capsule clamp rings and pyrotechnics, led William Bland and Rodney G. Rose to persuade Gilruth to rule out the primate on Little Joe 5. Besides that, the second Mercury-Redstone now being groomed for a chimp flight represented a direct conflict in scheduling.

As disappointing as this decision was to aeromedical personnel, including James P. Henry, the physician who supervised the animal program for STG, the managers of the Task Group felt they could not afford to risk further delays. The structural integrity of McDonnell's Mercury capsule and the escape system during that most critical time in the region of highest dynamic pressure had to be demonstrated as soon as possible. By deliberately omitting the environmental control system and its problems, the Task Group had hoped to concentrate on hardware dynamics, taking extraordinary precautions "to minimize premature firing of any of the capsule pyrotechnics on the launching pad." [69] Obviously something—no one knew what—had been overlooked.

After the dismal failure of Little Joe 5, these bleak days for Project Mercury became even bleaker with the discovery that the helium leak in the capsule for MR–1 could not be fixed quickly; it would require the replacement of certain valves and the whole hydrogen peroxide tank. Furthermore a change in the MR–1 wiring was dictated by the poor sequence and circuitry design on Little Joe 5. NASA had one more Little Joe test booster on hand. One more airframe, the last one in existence, had recently been ordered as a backup to the next shot. On November 10, NASA Headquarters was reassured that a stripped capsule on the backup booster could fulfill the Little Joe 5 mission, "an essential one before manned flight," probably before the end of January. And both Mercury-Redstone 2 and Mercury-Atlas 2 still were considered "not beyond the realm of possibility" for launchings in December. [70]

There was precious little in Mercury to be thankful for during the Thanksgiving season of 1960, but there was more than enough work to keep everyone in STG preoccupied. Caldwell C. Johnson wrote Faget a summary memo concerning the capsule's weight growth and its effect upon Atlas performance and mission profiles. While McDonnell was conducting extensive tests of the impact skirt situation, Johnson and others were worried about whether it would ever work. In the light of later developments, the ferment over redesign at this time became significant, and Johnson's words grew in significance:

> We have been monitoring Mercury weight growth, McDonnell's airplane-weight history and the X–15 weight versus development phase and conclude that Mercury orbit weight by the time of manned flight will exceed 3000 pounds! Capsule weight during parachute opening mode will be 2600 pounds;

flotation weight is practically as great. These increases have a detrimental effect upon orbital insertion probability, retrograde action, parachute opening loads, and water stability. The only single action that will cure the problem is weight reduction in the capsule but its weight growth is inexorable. It appears that several separate actions are necessary.

J. Mayer calculates that at 3000 pounds the probability of orbit insertion is less than 96 percent even when based upon certain Atlas performance increases. Furthermore, the possibility of an African landing from an early abort is very real. He says there are some reasons to believe that Atlas weight can be further reduced and greater payload capacity realized but so far this is but speculation, and, in any case, doesn't do much for the African landing situation.

Some time ago increased retrograde capability was proposed but could not be justified at that time. There is little doubt that such a change is justified now—the question is whether posigrade impulse should likewise be increased to aid orbit insertion. It is tempting to combine posigrade and retrograde systems and to utilize the propellant as required by the particular flight situation. But, this is a rather drastic change.[71]

MR-1: THE FOUR-INCH FLIGHT

November 21, 1960, marked the absolute nadir of morale among all the men at work on Project Mercury. That was the day the MR-1 countdown reached zero, and when "all we did was to launch the escape tower."

Capsule No. 2 had been checked out at Huntsville on July 21 and shipped to the Cape the next day. The final standard trajectory was published on August 1, and the Redstone booster was delivered two days later. From July 23, when the capsule was airlifted to the Cape, until October 7, extensive internal reworking was required. Since this was the first complete capsule to be subjected to preflight checks, it was impossible to know precisely how long the checkout would take. Gleason of NASA Headquarters had explained these scheduling gymnastics to the Senate committee staff on November 3:

Between October 6 and October 31, 1960, the work proceeded exceedingly well. By October 24, for example, first mate had been completed. The rework had been accomplished and the simulated mission and servicing had been carried out. Not only had none of the contingency period been used up, but preparations were actually two days ahead of schedule! It was, therefore, hoped for the first time, that the working level target date might actually be met, assuming that some as yet unresolved electrical troubles would not cause any real delays.

On October 31, the final mating of the capsule and booster was accomplished. Still two days ahead of the target date established on October 7. Therefore, it became clear, upon examination of the remaining work, that the launching might take place on November 7. Accordingly, the Project Mercury operations director requested range clearance for November 7 and also requested support by Naval recovery forces for this date.

Because of the continuing great urgency of Project Mercury, and because each succeeding launching hinges critically on the dates of previous launchings, the selection of November 7 as a launch date for MR-1 was the only possible course of action to take for the operations director. In making this decision, he recognized that he was merely identifying the earliest possible launch date, and that this date might well be delayed if difficulties were to be encountered during the final checkout, or if bad weather was encountered. A later decision, on the other hand, would have been inexcusable for this might have caused unnecessary delays if all went well during the final checkout period.[72]

MR-1 was on the launch table on November 7, 1960, when the helium pressure dropped from 2250 pounds per square inch to 500 pounds in the capsule control system, and the mission was scrubbed again. The capsule was removed from its booster and the heat shield was removed from the capsule so that a helium relief valve and the toroidal hydrogen peroxide tank could be replaced. A wiring change was made to avoid a failure of the Little Joe variety, and electrical sequence checks were redone as reassembly proceeded. Then, on November 21, MR-1 was reassembled and the final countdown proceeded normally, with the exception of a one-hour hold to fix another leak in the capsule's hydrogen peroxide system. The Mercury Control Center was manned for the first time. At 9 a.m. Redstone ignition occurred precisely as scheduled.

The expected blast momentarily churned the air around launch complex No. 56. But then the roar stopped as suddenly as it had started. Watching by periscope from the blockhouse, the startled engineers saw the booster wobble slightly on its pedestal and settle back on its fins after, at the very most, a four-or-five-inch liftoff. The Rocketdyne A-7 engine shut down, and the escape pylon zipped up 4000 feet and landed about 400 yards away from the launch site. Three seconds after the escape rocket blew, the drogue package shot upward, and then the main chute spurted out of the top of the capsule followed by the reserve parachute, and both fluttered down alongside the Redstone.

Mercury-Redstone 1 was the most distressing, not to say embarrassing, failure so far in Project Mercury. Critics waxed unrestrained. Even the Redstone experts seemed disconcerted.[73] Technically it seemed inexplicable that the normal, instead of the abort ejection, sequence had followed engine shutdown. George Low later that day carried STG's report to the NASA Headquarters staff on what they thought had happened:

Apparently, sufficient thrust had developed to lift the booster at least $\frac{3}{32}$ inch, thereby activating all the systems. (This would require more than 85% of nominal thrust.) The booster settled back down on the pad, damaging the tail fins, and perhaps the structure as well (some wrinkles are visible in the shell). The reason for this shutdown is unknown—the only shutdown to the booster could have come from the booster programmer, at the end of the normal flight sequence. Just how this programmer malfunctioned cannot be determined without a detailed inspection.

The capsule sequence . . . was a normal one for the type of signal it received. A closed-loop abort sensing system would have given an abort signal under the conditions of this launching, carrying the capsule away in a regular off-the-pad abort sequence.

At the time of this writing, the booster destruct system is still armed, and

294

cannot be disarmed until the battery depletion during the morning of November 22. Capsule pyrotechnics (including posigrade and retrograde rocket) are also armed. The problem is further complicated by the fact that the main parachute is still hanging from the capsule; thus the booster could be blown over in a high-wind condition. Weather predictions, however, are good. It is planned to put the gantry around the booster in the morning, under the assumption that the Redstone has not shifted sufficiently to make this impossible. This will be followed by booster and capsule disarming and sequence checks to determine the cause of the failure.

The extent of damage to the capsule has not yet been assessed. Assuming a minimum of damage, it is planned to use the same capsule, together with the MR-3 booster, for the MR-1 firing. It will probably take a month before this launching can take place.[74]

MR-1
Nov. 21, 1960

Mercury-Redstone 1 has just "blown its stack" on the launch pad, seconds after ignition. After, at most, a four-or-five-inch liftoff, MR-1 launched its escape tower but not the capsule. Then followed the normal flight sequence of parachute deployment. The drogue chute is shown here deploying just after ejection of the antenna canister. A few seconds later would come the main and reserve main parachutes.

The day after the MR–1 attempt, Walter Burke of McDonnell volunteered to lead a squad of men to disarm the pyrotechnics and umbilical cable still hanging fire. Two days later, after intensive on-the-scene investigations of the puzzle presented by MR–1, Low reported a better consensus of expert opinion:

> The MR–1 failure is now believed to have been caused by a booster tail plug which is pulled out about one inch after liftoff.
>
> It has been determined that this two-prong plug is designed so that one prong disconnects about one-half inch before the second one does. This time interval between disconnect of the first and second prongs for MR–1 was 21 milliseconds.
>
> The booster circuitry is such that if one of these prongs is disconnected prior to the other and while the booster is not grounded, a relay will close giving a normal engine cutoff signal. The time interval between successive disconnects was apparently just sufficient to allow the relay to close.
>
> It is reasoned that Redstone missiles are somewhat lighter than the Mercury Redstone (with its extended tank), thereby giving higher initial acceleration and shorter time intervals between disconnects between the two prongs. This shorter time interval would be sufficient to allow the relay to close, thus having avoided this type of failure in the past.
>
> This relay behavior could not be detected during checkout procedures since it will only occur when the booster is not grounded.
>
> The above theory of failure was advanced by Marshall personnel at Cape Canaveral and has not been confirmed by Marshall-Huntsville. It is planned to continue tests at Huntsville using the Mercury-Redstone No. 2 booster to verify this hypothesis.[75]

Within a week, MR–1 was rescheduled for December 19, and MR–2 and MR–3 had been postponed until 1961. Low informed Silverstein that "The MR–1 capsule will be used as is, together with the escape tower from Capsule 8, and the antenna fairing from Capsule 10. The MR–3 booster will be used for this shot."[76] There was no longer any question that the mating of booster and spacecraft should be done at the Cape.

Physicists observing MR–1 might have expected someone among the 5000 members of the Marshall Center to have guarded against the relativity of simultaneity where electrical signals were concerned, but McDonnell and Task Group engineers dared not taunt their fellow workers on the Redstone about the cause of the "four-inch flight" of MR–1. They were happy that the sequence system on the capsule performed perfectly, but they too felt responsible for the failure of the MR–1 capsule to abort. Meanwhile Joachim P. Kuettner and Earl Butler at Huntsville, and Kurt Debus and Emil P. Bertram at the Cape, frantically drove the men of their respective Redstone-Mercury Office and Launch Operations Directorate to hasten preparations for MR–1A. By mid-December 1960, the Redstone team assured Washington that the repeat flight was almost ready:

> The November 21 type event will be avoided, in the future, by the addition of a ground cable sufficiently long to maintain a good ground connection until all umbilical plugs are pulled. In addition, the booster circuitry has been

modified so that a cutoff signal can only get to the capsule after 130 seconds of booster thrust (normal cutoff occurs at 140 seconds). Before that time, the capsule can only be released from the booster through an abort signal, manually given from the ground.[77]

Minor additional improvements were made to the capsule systems, a revised master operational schedule was issued, the Mercury ground control operations team was brought up to full strength, and Jerome Hammack, STG's Redstone project engineer, along with Paul C. Donnelly, the Mercury-Redstone test conductor in the blockhouse, worried through each day, hour, and minute before December 19.

MR–1A: SUBORBITAL QUALITY PROVEN

Early in the morning of December 19, winds of 150 knots aloft in the jet stream required a 40-minute hold. During the countdown another solenoid valve in the capsule's hydrogen peroxide system had to be replaced, necessitating a recycle of the count by one hour. So it was 45 minutes before noon when the dramatic final 10 seconds of countdown for MR–1A occurred. This time there were no fouls. The 83-foot Mercury-Redstone assembly was cheered on—"Go! Fly, bird! Go!"—as it lifted off, burning brightly for 143 seconds to a velocity (slightly high) of 7120 feet per second at cutoff. With this impetus, MR–1A coasted on up to 131 miles, its maximum altitude, then nosed over while the bolts in the mating-ring exploded as planned and the booster and its payload parted company. The capsule behaved perfectly in its attitude control and came down along its predestined trajectory to impact 235 miles from Cape Canaveral, 18 miles beyond the desired target impact point.

A P2V aircraft pilot saw the capsule descending on its parachute at 4000 feet, and about 35 minutes after launch a Marine helicopter from the aircraft carrier *Valley Forge* retrieved the capsule, and returned it secure to the flight deck of the carrier within 48 minutes from launch. This time Low elatedly reported to Glennan that "the launching was an unqualified success."[78]

The Goddard Space Flight Center computers, both men and machines, performed admirably in making their first "real-time" impact prediction. On the *Valley Forge* sailors crowded everywhere topside. Visual inspections of the capsule by a NASA recovery inspection team revealed no damage except a crack in one outer layer of glass in one capsule porthole.

Exuberance was obvious in the postlaunch reports of the various participants. Howard C. Kyle, the capsule communicator, said, "Except for a few minor discrepancies during the countdown, all equipment appeared to operate normally. Technical support was universally superb." Tecwyn Roberts, the flight dynamics officer, wrote, "All communications checked A. OK. Data selection loop had some noise, but intelligible communication was possible at all times." Henry E. Clements, a captain in the Air Force and network status monitor, reported all

297

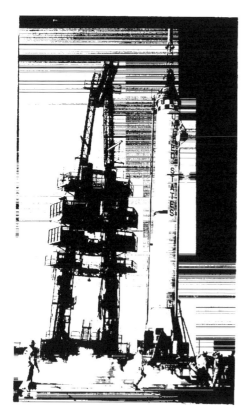

MR–1A
Dec. 19, 1960

Mercury-Redstone 1A, the repeat flight to Mercury-Redstone 1, was successfully undertaken 28 days later, on December 19, 1960. The electrical ground cable that had caused the failure of MR–1 had been lengthened. Here, during loxing for a flight readiness test, frost shows on the rocket and steam on the ground. Slight overacceleration of both this and the MR–2 booster caused an extra Redstone flight to be inserted in the Mercury schedule. The recovered spacecraft is shown below the day after the flight at the Cape being inspected by Charles J. Donlan (left), Robert Gilruth, and Maxime Faget; it came through the brief flight in excellent condition.

instrumentation "A. OK," with few discrepancies. One note of caution was entered by Stanley C. White, the Mercury Control Center flight surgeon:

> The acceleration associated with the reentry exceeded by at least 1 g the calculated value. If a similar overshoot occurs with the new profile being proposed on future MR flights, we are reaching the point where the astronaut has demonstrated inability to stay alert and to keep up with the events. The consequence of this aberration from predicted should be discussed before the new profile is accepted.[79]

Later, when the movies from the onboard camera were developed and shown, clean-room engineers and workers saw the necessity for still higher standards of cleanliness. Washers, nuts, and wire clippings came out from hidden niches and floated freely around the cabin during the weightless period. But otherwise, the Mercury team felt the pendulum of luck beginning to swing back in their favor at the end of 1960. They were proud of the Christmas gift represented by the demonstration of suborbital capability of the hardware in MR–1A.

Perhaps the most significant result of the Little Joe 5 and MR–1 failures was a profound reexamination among the managers of Project Mercury of their original design philosophy. Warren North reported to Silverstein at Headquarters on December 6 the results of a series of discussions among field hands on the subject of man-machine integration:

> During the week of November 27, Messrs. Gilruth, Williams, Mathews, Preston, Bland, Ricker, Fields, Roberts and others conducted a major review of the capsule and booster sequence logic in an effort to determine what improvements could be made to prevent incidents such as occurred during Little Joe 5 and MR–1. Also involved in the week long series of discussions at Cape Canaveral were key personnel from McDonnell (including Burke), Convair, Marshall, and Aerospace.
>
> As a result of operational experience, it was apparent that some of the original design philosophy should be changed, especially insofar as the role of the pilot is concerned. It has become obvious that the complexity of the capsule and booster automatic system is compounded during the integration of the systems. The desirability of avoiding, for manned missions, a direct link between capsule and booster systems, is therefore being studied. For example, the Little Joe-type failure would be averted by the use of an open loop manually controlled abort system. Similarly, the escape tower would not have jettisoned during the MR–1 launch attempt if this had been a manned flight with manual control over the escape rocket and capsule sequence system.[80]

Meanwhile the Atlas, the basic vehicle to propel Mercury into orbit, also was undergoing its most critical examination. A special ad hoc technical investigating committee, established on December 19, 1960, composed of both NASA and Air Force personnel, and headed by Richard V. Rhode of NASA Headquarters and Colonel Paul E. Worthman of the Ballistic Missile Division, was ordered to investigate the reasons why the Atlas had failed so often on NASA launches. Called the Rhode-Worthman Committee informally, the dozen members, representing all concerned organizations, looked carefully at three recent failures in the Atlas-Able series of lunar probes, at MA-1, and even at Big Joe, hoping to prevent another fiasco. Since the conferees at the last major coordination meeting, on November 16, had issued a test program summary reviewing MA-1 and subsequent action, the Rhode-Worthman group began with those inconclusive records and a set of 12 agreements on launch conditions for MA-2. Paul Purser and Robert E. Vale flew to Los Angeles the day after Christmas to defend STG's position on MA-1 and to expedite Convair's construction of a "quick-fix" solution for MA-2 and its fabrication of "thick-skin" Atlases for subsequent Mercury flights. Other members of the committee distrusted the original design for the "quick fix," which was in the form of a "belly band," or girdle, to strengthen the interface area around "station 502" on the Atlas booster, where the adapter ring for the capsule nested against the lox dome. Later the dissenting committee members supported a revised version of the fix after a number of their suggestions had been integrated. Both Chamberlin and Yardley had suggested the "belly band," but Hohmann disagreed. On December 31, 1960, Purser warned Charles Donlan, back at Langley Field, that STG and Convair might be overruled by Aerospace, STL, BMD, and NASA Headquarters representatives. As it turned out, on the second day of the new year Rhode sent a message to Seamans at NASA Headquarters that recommended great caution regarding the decision to incorporate the "quick fix," as many of the committee felt that it added uncertainty and possibly a new set of hazards. If so, MA-2 might have to wait three to six months more for a "thick-skin" Atlas from the factory.[81]

The year 1960 ended in suspense for the Mercury team. The Soviet attempt on December 1-2, 1960, to orbit and retrieve two more dogs from space had, as the Soviets admitted, ended in cremation for "Pchelka" and "Mushka" when their attitude control system failed at retrofire and their vehicle, *Korabl Sputnik III*, burned up on reentry from its rather too shallow orbit. To appraise the meaning of the flight of the Soviets' third man-sized spaceship from available information was exceedingly difficult. Obviously the Soviets were close to the day when they could put a man into orbit, but the similar failures of their first and third "cosmic ships," on May 19 and December 2, respectively, had made the question "How close?" highly debatable.[82]

On December 5, a member of the Soviet Academy of Science, G. Pokrovsky, had extolled the "socialist system," in spite of its failure to recover Pchelka and Mushka, and boasted that "we are on the threshold of manned space flight, and the first man to be in space will undoubtedly be a Soviet citizen." That same day, *Time* magazine had bemoaned "Lead-Footed Mercury" and ridiculed Wernher von Braun's calling MR-1 "a little mishap": "Project Mercury's latest failure, third in a row, just about evaporated the last faint wisp of hope that the U.S. might put a man into space before Russia does." A *New York Times* editorial agreed with that evaluation and advised the new President-elect to persevere: "The first man in space will not be the last, and after the tributes have been paid to that first man and those who made his feat possible the more important question will arise of what man can do in space that is worth the immense cost of putting him there." [83]

Although there was some exultation in the United States after the success of MR–1A on December 19, the public seemed to sense, without any deep understanding, a difference of several orders of magnitude between Soviet space flight tests and American qualification flight difficulties. Within the Space Task Group, NASA, and the Mercury team, technical understanding, sometimes divorced from political intuition, appeared to buttress the hope that an American manned ballistic flight into space might still precede the substantially more difficult manned orbital flight around Earth. Manned space flight was a name for a series of field events in the space olympics. Although the odds were with the Soviets to win the marathon of the first orbital circumnavigation, perhaps Mercury might win the suborbital sprint.

X

Tests Versus Time in the Race for Space

(JANUARY–APRIL 1961)

O N January 3, 1961, two years and three months after it was formed, the Space Task Group officially became a separate, autonomous NASA field element charged with the conduct of Project Mercury and any other manned space flight programs that might follow it. The Task Group, now composed of 667 people, was still located physically on the Hampton Roads side of the Langley Air Force Base and was supported by the Langley Research Center, but now the administrative marriage of STG with the Goddard Space Flight Center in Beltsville, Maryland, was annulled.[1] The Mercury team had not yet managed to launch a manned rocket, but neither apparently had their Russian counterparts. The United States still had a good chance to place the first man in space, at least for five minutes. The Soviet lead in orbital flight tests argued heavily against the first manned satellite being American, but to score first would still be some consolation.

In only three years and three months since *Sputnik I,* the Soviet Union and the United States had launched into space a total of 42 vehicles, 38 of which were Earth satellites, three were solar satellites, and one was a lunar probe. The box score in the "space race" between the United States and the Soviet Union was 33 to 9 in favor of the home team, as far as publicly successful space launchings were concerned. But with only nine acknowledged launchings the U.S.S.R. had hoisted some 87,000 pounds (as opposed to the U.S. total of 34,240 pounds), the Soviets had hit the Moon and photographed its backside, and they had recovered two dogs from one Earth orbital flight. Of the 33 American space launches, only three had been done by NASA launch vehicles and crews. Of the remainder, 24 had been launched by Air Force rockets, five by Army boosters, one by the Navy. In contrast to the responsibility for launching these 31 Earth satellites and two solar satellites, the credit for building the instrumented payloads was spread more widely; the Air Force counted 15 successes, the Army and Navy four each, and NASA 10 spacecraft. Already the complexity of accounting properly for mankind's successful satellite and space probe projects was reaching formidable proportions.[2]

303

On January 11, 1961, three Soviet tracking ships were reported moving into the central Pacific once again. The next day, in his final State of the Union address, President Eisenhower commended the young space administration for its "startling strides" and "real progress toward the goal of manned space flights." After listing all the successes of American instrumented payloads in space, Eisenhower said:

> These achievements make us unquestionably preeminent today in space exploration for the betterment of mankind. I believe the present organizational arrangements in this area, with the revisions proposed last year, are completely adequate for the tasks ahead.[3]

At this same time, President-elect John F. Kennedy announced that Jerome B. Wiesner of the Massachusetts Institute of Technology, who had chaired the Democratic science advisory committee for the campaign, would become the new Presidential special assistant for science and technology. And with this announcement Kennedy released most of a special report made to him by Wiesner's committee of nine campaign advisers on the state of the Nation's security and prestige. A political document, the "Wiesner Report" called for a sweeping reorganization of the national space program. It was critical of past leadership and direction, and it called for more effective use of the National Aeronautics and Space Council, better coordination with the Department of Defense, stronger technical management, and a closer partnership with industry. On top of all this came the uncorroborated news that an Army officer had told a seminar of almost 500 civilian and military participants that the United States had good evidence that at least one and probably two Soviet cosmonauts had been killed in unsuccessful attempts to orbit a man during Premier Khrushchev's visit to the United States in September 1960.[4]

INTERREGNUM

On January 16, 1961, President Eisenhower delivered his annual budget message to Congress, asking for amendments to the Space Act of 1958 and referring to Project Mercury with far less confidence than he had shown five days earlier:

> In the program for manned space flight, the reliability of complex booster, capsule, escape, and life-support components of the Mercury system is now being tested to assure a safe manned ballistic flight into space, and hopefully a manned orbital flight, in calendar year 1961. Further testing and experimentation will be necessary to establish whether there are any valid scientific reasons for extending manned spaceflight beyond the Mercury program.[5]

Members of the Space Task Group and of the Mercury team at large could take little comfort from the fact that this speaker was an outgoing President, for they also knew that the incoming President's scientific policy adviser had been quite critical of the "marginal" Mercury-Atlas program. Regarding "man-in-space," the Wiesner Committee had said:

304

We are rapidly approaching the time when the state of technology will make it possible for man to go out into space. It is sure that as soon as this possibility exists, man will be compelled to make use of it, by the same motives that have compelled him to travel to the poles and to climb the highest mountains of the earth. There are also dimly perceived military and scientific missions in space which may prove to be very important.

By having placed highest national priority on the Mercury program, we have strengthened the popular belief that man in space is the most important aim of our non-military space effort. The manner in which this program has been publicized in our press has further crystallized such belief. It exaggerates the value of that aspect of space activity where we are less likely to achieve success, and discounts those aspects in which we have already achieved great success and will probably reap further successes in the future.[6]

When the managers of NASA and of STG, a few days later, became aware of the earlier, longer, confidential version of the Wiesner report, they were reminded of Mercury's tenuous standing as an urgent, but not an indispensable, "crash" program. If they should fail on their first attempt to place a man in space, or to put him in orbit, or to recover him from orbit, they not only would sacrifice a human life but create a national humiliation. Mercury managers had always been acutely aware of these portents, but the low status of Mercury in real and rumored policy papers made these days darker than ever. Wiesner's Committee recommended that Kennedy not allow "the present Mercury program to continue unchanged for more than a very few months," and that he not "effectively endorse this program and take the blame for its possible failures." Above all else the Wiesner Committee recommended that:

We should stop advertising Mercury as our major objective in space activities. Indeed, we should make an effort to diminish the significance of this program to its proper proportion before the public, both at home and abroad. We should find effective means to make people appreciate the cultural, public service, and military importance of space activities other than space travel.[7]

Next to Mercury, the Wiesner group was most critical of the Nation's booster program, particularly of the inability of United States rockets to lift heavy payloads into space. Measured by rocket thrust, Russian superiority continued unchallenged. Profound criticism was levelled at the Atlas, which was now truly operational as a weapon system, but which had failed signally in its five most recent tests as a launch vehicle for NASA payloads. Wiesner's committee recommended vigorous study of the Titan missile as an alternative Mercury launcher, but STG had already studied and rejected the Titan as a launch vehicle.[8]

Whereas there seemed to be threats of cancellation or modification of Project Mercury from all sides, the Mercury teammates knew from their MR-1A experience of December 19, 1960, that nothing succeeds like success. While some of them carefully but hurriedly made ready for MR-2, others just as desperately sought to ensure the success of MA-2.

In moments of respite from its hectic pace, STG could see three essential tasks that had to be performed within a matter of weeks if the Task Group was to be kept together and functioning. First was the necessity to send a chimpanzee on a successful Redstone flight. Second was the need to qualify the McDonnell capsule and all its systems by a Little Joe flight under max q conditions similar to the worst possible Atlas abort. Third, but perhaps most important, was the imperative need to test and prove as soon as possible the Mercury-Atlas combination, even if only on an elementary ballistic flight.[9]

The admittedly "hasty" Wiesner report was received by the press with mixed reactions. According to the *Washington Post,* the study was tacitly adopted by the President-elect when he named Wiesner, simultaneously with its release, Chairman of the President's Science Advisory Committee (PSAC) for the new administration. *Aviation Week* said that Kennedy had rejected the committee's advice to revamp or scrap Mercury and that he had decided to risk receiving the blame if the first manned shot failed. To Roscoe Drummond, a syndicated columnist, the Wiesner report read like "a melange of observations based on superficial study." Drummond was highly critical of the entire political transition, noting that T. Keith Glennan had departed from Washington on Inauguration Day, January 20, 1961, leaving NASA headless, since no one had yet been named as his successor. Hugh L. Dryden, too, had resigned in accordance with protocol, but he remained on hand until he should be relieved. Drummond further charged that no Kennedy representative had consulted NASA to study the workings of the agency nor had any Kennedy official read or listened to briefings that had been prepared for the new leaders by outgoing Administrator Glennan and his staff.[10]

In this time of transition NASA officials expected a stronger challenge to the civilian space agency's sphere of influence from the military, perhaps supported by some defense industry contractors. Part of the "military-industrial complex" against which Eisenhower had warned in his farewell address seemed to be lobbying to shrink NASA's function to that of the former NACA—applied research and development engineering.[11] The retiring President also had warned against the domination of science by the needs of the Federal government and against the domination of public policy by a "scientific-technological elite." On the other hand, the editors of *Aviation Week* had expressed alarm several times over NASA's tendency toward enlargement of its own technical bureaucracy and assimilation of other space research organizations.[12] Whether or not there was actually any "power struggle" among the Air Force, Army, and Navy over the spoils from a stripped NASA, any such fears of the Pentagon were premature while the Mercury-Redstone attempt to fly and recover an "astrochimp" was still pending.

For some time, NASA had endured attacks from various eminent American men of science. The Wiesner report both reflected and encouraged such attitudes. Vannevar Bush, James R. Killian, and George B. Kistiakowsky were all long since on record as considering manned space flight a technological luxury that ought not to be allowed to eclipse more urgent scientific necessities. Even

306

within NASA, some scientists would have reallocated resources for manned space efforts beyond Mercury so as to give more funds and priority to instrumented, more purely scientific, research flights.[13]

Such political opinions of scientists to a large degree had been translated into official policy under the Eisenhower administration, whose last budget recommended a manned space flight research and development cut of $190.1 million from NASA's request for fiscal year 1962 of $1,109,600,000. The Bureau of the Budget in January allowed a total NASA request of $919.5 million, only $114 million of which was earmarked for manned space flight, including Project Mercury. Some $584 million was requested for military astronautics within the total $41.2 billion request for the Defense Department's budget.[14] Surely this contrast in funding carried significant meaning.

The criticisms of NASA and its struggle for money in Washington were serious enough, but of far greater concern to the civil servants, contractors, and servicemen working with NASA and STG was the problem of "Mercury-rating" the Atlas. Since the unsolved MA-1 disaster at the end of July 1960 had been blamed on, but never isolated in, the interface area where the capsule and booster were mated, both the Air Force and NASA shared uneasily the responsibility for finding preventive medicine before MA-2 could be launched.

The Wiesner Committee apparently had been unaware of the Rhode-Worthman Committee, established on December 19, 1960, four days after the explosion of the Atlas-Able 5-D Moon proble. NASA and the Air Force, acutely aware of Wiesner's activity, were pressuring the high-level investigating committee of seasoned engineers to find solutions to the interface problem. NASA Headquarters was very much concerned by the poor performance of the lighter-gauge Atlas modified for NASA launches and by the inability of STG and the Air Force complex to pinpoint the reason for the MA-1 failure. Richard V. Rhode, NASA Headquarters' senior structural engineer, was sent to California to press for a solution. The Air Force Ballistic Missile Division, under Major General O. J. Ritland and Brigadier General H. W. Powell, likewise had appointed a senior technical officer, Colonel Paul E. Worthman, to work with Rhode as co-chairman.

During the last week of December 1960 and the first week of January 1961, the 12 members of the Rhode-Worthman Committee met continuously at Convair/Astronautics in San Diego and at the Air Force Ballistic Missile Division in Los Angeles. One of the objectives of this meeting was to find a majority agreement on the diagnosis for MA-1 and the prognosis for MA-2. Paul E. Purser and Robert E. Vale, representing STG, with the aid of G. L. Armstrong of Convair, argued that a "quick-fix belly band" could be effectively used to reinforce the structural strength of the "thin-skinned" Atlas. Specifically they had in mind Atlas No. 67-D, which had been at the Cape since September, being prepared for mating with capsule No. 6 for the MA-2 launch. On the other hand, Bernhard A. Hohmann of Aerospace urged strengthening the adapter ring. James A. Chamberlin forthwith had redesigned the fillets and stringers in that casing also.

Because a "thick-skinned" Atlas—one whose upper conical sections would be made of stainless steel approximately .02 instead of .01 inch in thickness, costing thereby an extra 100 pounds in weight—could not be finished and shipped to the Cape before late March 1961, the Rhode-Worthman Committee finally, but not unanimously, agreed not to wait for a replacement booster. NASA assumed the risk of a messy technical and political situation in the event of failure, and the Air Force agreed to make every effort to push MA–2 through the region of maximum aerodynamic and political stress as soon as possible. But precisely how to do this still remained debatable.[15]

New band stiffeners in the adapter ring, some 20 extra accelerometers, strain gauges, pressure sensors, and mandatory operational restrictions for mild weather, winds, and complete photographic coverage, plus the use of the improvised truss or corset, called the "belly band," for MA–2, were all included in the interim report of the Rhode-Worthman Committee, issued on January 19, 1961. The joint team effort required for these decisions, said Purser to Rhode, "admittedly has not always been easy, but we believe it has worked. 'Resolution of conflicts of technical judgment' has been achieved by mutual discussion and education rather than by manager edicts."[16] The reluctance of Aerospace and STL representatives to accept the "belly band" truss was symbolized at first by their use of the invidious metaphor "horse collar" to describe it. So apt and fitting was the "horse collar" in distributing the load of max q over the Atlas airframe that all parties accepted the nickname and the hardware by mid-February. Meanwhile work proceeded frantically in laboratories and wind tunnels at Ames and at Tullahoma, Tennessee, to provide all the information possible through simulated conditions before subjecting this "quick-fix" to a flight test. But there was great drama and suspense in the technological preparations for the vitally important launching known as Mercury-Atlas 2.[17]

Now that Vice-President Lyndon B. Johnson, an early advocate of a strong space program and slated to become the new chairman of the strengthened Space Council, promised energetic leadership among the countervailing powers in Washington, the aerospace community waited impatiently to hear who would be named the new NASA Administrator. Kennedy assigned Johnson this task of selection. Considering Johnson's long-standing interest in space matters, many observers had supposed that the selection would be made soon after the election and that the designee might be a member of the Wiesner Committee.[18] But the case was not so simple. The problem seemed to be one of settling on qualifications and then finding a man who would agree to preside over an agency with an uncertain future. The risk of becoming a political scapegoat was great indeed. The Wiesner report stipulated that one of the prerequisites for a member of the Space Council was that he be technically well-informed, and this requirement would apply also to the NASA Administrator. But whereas a university scientist with engineering and executive experience might meet this qualification, Washington and management experience also was essential.[19]

Kennedy remarked at a press conference, five days after his inauguration, that the NASA Administrator should be chosen by the end of the week, thereby deflecting newsmen's attention to the Vice-President for the name of the new Administrator. Johnson, in turn, received suggestions from his former Congressional colleagues on the space committees, and Wiesner called to Washington the man who accepted the post. On February 2, 1961, Senator Robert S. Kerr, Democrat from Oklahoma and Johnson's successor as chairman of the Senate Committee on Aeronautical and Space Sciences, presided at the confirmation hearings on the nomination of James Edwin Webb.

An experienced business head of numerous corporations, a lawyer, Director of the Bureau of the Budget from 1946 to 1949, and Under Secretary of the Department of State from 1949 to 1951, James E. Webb also had been a director óf the McDonnell Aircraft Corporation and a reserve officer and pilot in the Marine Corps. Although his background was not that of a scientist, he was widely known in governmental and industrial circles for having worked with scientists on committees and with engineers as a director of such organizations as Educational Services, Incorporated; the Oak Ridge Institute of Nuclear Studies; Sperry Gyroscope Company; and as a trustee of George Washington University.[20]

Webb's appointment as NASA Administrator came as a surprise to those who expected one of the Wiesner Committee to be chosen. A few critics said that he lacked the technical background necessary to attract scientists and eminent engineers to NASA and that his nomination was a result of Senator Kerr's influence. But Wiesner supported and the Senate confirmed Webb's nomination after Webb severed all his business connections with McDonnell Aircraft. His active interest in science suggested that Webb would strive to keep a balance between science and technology in space activities. His governmental and executive experience promised that he could work well with the Bureau of the Budget and with the aerospace industries to promote NASA's interests. Webb's intellectual interests in public administration and international affairs indicated that he might become instrumental in achieving international agreements to prevent space from becoming a new theater for conflict in the cold war. Indeed, Webb's supporters felt certain that he actively would invite the Soviets to cooperate in American space exploration projects, a proposal that Kennedy had made notable in his inaugural address.[21]

With a vigorous new Administrator as its spokesman, and with the reconfirmation of Dryden as second in command, NASA quickly regained confidence regarding the scientific, budgetary, and military-industrial obstacles to its manned space flight program. In facing the military, Webb had the support of Representative Overton Brooks, chairman of the House Committee on Science and Astronautics. Early in 1961, Brooks became the first highly placed government official to lambaste the presumed campaign to build, at the expense of NASA, a stronger military space program.[22]

MR-2: HAM PAVES THE WAY

By the end of January 1961, the technical outlook for Project Mercury was much improved. The end of the qualification flight tests was in sight, if only the Little Joe, Redstone, and Atlas boosters would cooperate. First priority was to make sure the Mercury-Redstone combination was prepared for the first manned suborbital flights. Now, according to the progressive buildup plan, the reliability of the system required demonstration by the second Mercury-Redstone (MR-2) flight, with a chimpanzee aboard, as a final check to man-rate the capsule and launch vehicle.

Preparations for the MR-2 mission had begun long before the actual flight. Between manufacturing the capsule and flight readiness certification, several months of testing and reworking were necessary at the McDonnell plant, at Marshall Space Flight Center, and at Cape Canaveral. Capsule No. 5, designated for the MR-2 flight, had been near the end of its manufacturing phase in May 1960. When it was completed, inspectors from the Navy Bureau of Weapons stationed at St. Louis, in cooperation with STG's liaison personnel at McDonnell, watched it go through a specified series of tests, and the contractor corrected all detected deficiencies.[23] After capsule systems tests and factory acceptance tests, capsule No. 5 was loaded into an Air Force cargo plane and shipped to Marshall Space Flight Center on September 3, 1960. At Huntsville, Wernher von Braun's team hurried through its checkouts of the compatibility of capsule No. 5 with Redstone booster No. 2, and had finished well before its 16-day time limit.[24] On October 11, 1960, the capsule arrived by air at the Cape, where the first checkout inspections, under the direction of F. M. Crichton, uncovered more discrepancies, raising to 150 the total of minor rework jobs to be done. Because of the complexities of the stacked and interlaced seven miles of wiring and plumbing systems in the Mercury capsule, however, each minor discrepancy became a major cost in the time necessary for its correction. Checkout work in Hangar S required 50 days for systems tests and 60 days for rework. The capsule designated for the first manned space flight, No. 7, also had arrived at the Cape for preflight checkouts, but the launch vehicle for MR-2 was delivered to the Cape by air freight on December 20, 1960, the day after MR-1A was launched. It too had undergone exhaustive reliability testing in the shops and on the stands in the hills west of Huntsville, Alabama. When Joachim P. Kuettner, representing von Braun, transferred the MR-2 booster to Emil P. Bertram, representing Kurt H. Debus' Launch Operations Directorate, their confidence in this particular booster of the "Old Reliable" series was high but not towering.[25]

Using the "quick-look" evidence from the MR-1A flight, Marshall guidance engineers set about correcting the conditions that had made the trajectory too steep and accelerations too high. MR-1A had climbed to its programmed apogee of about 130 miles and landed 235 miles downrange, and high altitude winds had carried it too close to the range borders. Range safety restrictions dictated that a launch vehicle must get out and away from the Cape as soon as possible. For these reasons, Walter C. Williams, STG's Associate Director for Operations, agreed with H. F. Gruene and Kuettner that the MR-2 trajectory should be flattened. An apogee of 115 miles on a downrange distance of 290 miles should be well within the allowable safety limits. Gruene and others calculated that this trajectory would still provide almost five minutes of weightless flight and a reentry deceleration of 10 g. Since this g load was slightly less than that desired by STG, Williams had to use his best persuasion during a series of consultations on the reentry loads to get Marshall to match the 12-g median reentry load by moving the engine cutoff time ahead to assure such conditions. At the same time, the range safety officer felt that the designated 105-degree launching azimuth was uncomfortably close to the shoreline. Williams, Charles W. Mathews, and Christopher C. Kraft, Jr., held out against a requested change to a 100-degree azimuth, because they wanted to minimize pilot retrieval time in case of an abort. To this STG later acceded, in exchange for its point on the 12-g reentry load; Marshall added a timer switch that would cut off the ignition if the accelerometer cutoff signal should fail before fuel depletion.[26]

Capsule No. 5 contained several significant innovations. There were five new systems or components that had not been qualified in previous flights: the environmental control system, the attitude stabilization control system, the live retrorockets, the voice communications system, and the "closed loop" abort sensing system. Capsule No. 5 also was the first in the flight series to be fitted with a pneumatic landing bag. This plasticized fabric, accordion-like device was attached to the heatshield and the lower pressure bulkhead; after reentry and before landing the heatshield and porous bag were to drop down about four feet, filling with air to help cushion the impact. Once in the water, the bag and heatshield should act as a sort of sea anchor, helping the spacecraft to remain upright in the water. Chronic problems with wave-induced fatigue of the fabric bag led STG and McDonnell engineers to concentrate on the harness linkages inside. After the Big Joe ablation flight test in September 1959, STG had decided to use on the Redstone flights, simply because they were on hand, the expensive beryllium heatshields that had first been ordered for orbital reentry. Since the anticipated reentry temperature would reach only 1000 degrees F, the beryllium shields were not necessary as heat sinks, but they served as readymade impact bumpers. Temperatures on the conical portion of the spacecraft might approach 250 to 300 degrees F, but, compared with about 1000 to 2000 degrees for an orbital mission, the ballistic flights should be cool.[27]

Publicity once again focused on the biological subject in the MR-2 experiment. The living being chosen to validate the environmental control system before committing a man to flight was a trained chimpanzee about 44 months old. Intelligent and normally docile, the chimpanzee is a primate of sufficient size and sapience to provide a reasonable facsimile of human behavior. Its average response time to a given physical stimulus is .7 of a second, compared with man's average .5 second. Having the same organ placement and internal suspension as man, plus a long medical research background, the chimpanzee chosen to ride the Redstone and perform a lever-pulling chore throughout the mission should not only test out the life-support systems but prove that levers could be pulled during launch, weightlessness, and reentry.[28]

A colony of six chimpanzees (four female and two male), accompanied by 20 medical specialists and animal handlers from Holloman Air Force Base, where the "astrochimps" were stationed and trained, moved into quarters behind Hangar S on January 2, 1961. There the animals became acclimatized to the change from the 5000-feet altitude in New Mexico to their sea level surroundings at the Cape. Separated into two groups as a precaution against the spread of any contagion among the whole colony, the animals were led through exercises by their handlers. Mercury capsule mockups were installed in each of the compounds. In these, the animals worked daily at their psychomotor performance tasks. By the third week in January, 29 training sessions had made each of the six chimps a bored but well-fed expert at the job of lever-pulling. To condition the chimps to respond properly, they received banana pellets as rewards and mild electrical shocks as punishments.[29]

Although recovery procedures had worked well until now, recovery operations for MR-2, carrying life into space from the Cape rather than from Wallops Island, demanded extra care and attention. So STG provided the Navy with the detailed requirements, and the Navy again assigned Rear Admiral F. V. H. Hilles to command the recovery forces. Under Hilles were several task elements. One, located on the beach near the launch pad, consisted of numerous amphibious vehicles and several helicopters. Should an abort occur near the pad, these vehicles on the scene would pick up the pieces. Offshore the next recovery perimeter was covered by a small naval vessel, the *Opportune* (Auxiliary Recovery Ship 41). The largest recovery unit, the one in the anticipated landing area, consisted of six destroyers and a landing ship dock (LSD) with three helicopters on board. If the capsule were shot beyond the expected impact area, an air recovery unit consisting of four P2V aircraft from Jacksonville, Florida, would go into action.[30]

STG's man in charge of recovery operations was Robert F. Thompson, a Navy veteran who once had been first lieutenant of the deck crew aboard a destroyer and who by now had coordinated STG's recovery requirements for over two years. Through Walter Williams, Thompson asked the Navy to provide for the recovery personnel participating in the exercise and to take along photographers and public information people as well. Thompson assigned Donald C. Cheatham to brief the naval crews from Charleston, South Carolina, on postflight procedures for removing the biopack and primate from the spacecraft.[31]

According to the "Master Operational Schedule," a guidebook prepared by

Debus' experienced staff, a simulated or dress rehearsal flight must always be conducted three days before launch. For this exercise, the countdown started only 180 minutes before "launch," when Complex 56, Pad 5, the site of all the Mercury-Redstone launches, switched on the power to all systems in the Redstone. The team training of the launch crew, even for the old Redstone, required thousands of coordinated actions and easy familiarity by each of the 70 or so members of the blockhouse crew, by each of the 100 men in the Mission Control Center, and by each of another 100 people around the launch site to get a flight off the ground. While the booster was ready for mate with the capsule as scheduled in mid-January, the capsule was not ready, and the simulated flight test was carried out on January 27 for a "mission" that lasted 455 minutes.[32]

One of the procedural safeguards developed in the effort to man-rate the Redstone was the "split-count," with a built-in hold in the countdown checklist. The count began at 640 minutes before launch and stopped for a rest period 390 minutes short of liftoff time (T). At 640 minutes the complex went on critical power and the prescribed systems checks were started, the communication network readiness was verified, range equipment was checked, and the launch vehicle telemetry was tuned. At T minus 390 minutes all systems were secured for the standby period so that the crew could relax. This "split-count" became a standard part of manned preflight operations.

Before the second half of the count began, on the following day, the booster was again supplied its electrical power, the escape rocket igniter was installed but not connected, the liquid oxygen trailer truck was moved into position, weather forecast and range clearances were checked, and the booster guidance and control battery safety wires were installed. When the count was resumed at T minus 390, there were still at least 330 specific jobs to be performed or functions to be validated before liftoff.

The launch plan for the MR-2 mission followed closely all of the foregoing preparations, with each event preplanned and budgeted on the schedule. Many new systems were being qualified and, with the chimpanzee aboard, the control systems had to operate in the automatic mode. The operations directive for MR-2 specified that in case of an unduly long hold, the test would be canceled at high noon to avoid the risks of a recovery in darkness.[33]

Telemetry was to be all-important for the MR-2 mission. For that purpose two transmitters were installed in the capsule, providing eight channels of information to ground stations. These included three aeromedical channels to transmit pulse, respiration rate, and breath-depth information. The other channels carried information on structural heating, cabin temperatures, pressures, noise, and vibrations from 90 different points throughout the spacecraft.[34]

All six chimps in the colony were accorded equal treatment until the day before the flight, when James P. Henry of STG and John D. Mosely, the veterinarian from Holloman, had to choose the test subject and his substitute. First the animals were given a physical examination, and then they were each checked on sensors, the psychomotor programmer, and consoles for comparative ratings. The competition was fierce, but one of the males was exceptionally frisky and in good humor. A female was selected as his alternate. At nineteen hours before launch these two animals were put on low-residue diets, fitted with biosensors, and checked out in their pressurized couch-cabins. Seven and one-half hours before the flight a second physical examination was given, followed by more sensor and psychomotor tests. About four hours before launch, the two chimps were suited up, placed in their couches, and brought aboard the transfer van, where their environmental control equipment was attached. The trailer truck arrived at the gantry alongside MR–2, and there, an hour and a half before the scheduled launch time, the chimpanzee named "Ham," in honor of Holloman Aerospace Medical Center, still active and spirited although encased in his biopack, boarded the elevator to meet his destiny.[35]

At sunrise on January 31, 1961, feverish preparations were underway in the community around Launch Complex 56. Walter Williams was directing operations for the third time from the newly completed Mercury Control Center. Supporting him were some 500 men from NASA, the military services, and industrial contractors. Key supervisors included the recovery force commander, range commander, launch director, capsule test coordinator, flight director, Atlantic Missile Range coordinator, network status monitor, range safety observer, and director of medical operations.[36] About 5 o'clock systems checks were progressing well, and Tecwyn Roberts, flight dynamics officer, reported that the command checks were all working "A. OK."[37] Communications checks were the same, with the exception of the Goddard link from Mercury Control on the data selection loop, and trajectory checks and displays appeared to be in order. The broken link with Goddard, discovered well before the flight, was cleared and the data selection loop restored. Although the weather was threatening and five-foot waves were reported in the recovery area, the second half of the count-down began at 7:25 a.m. After the count had progressed 20 minutes, the first trouble of the morning appeared with a report that a tiny but important electronic inverter in the capsule automatic control system was overheating. Nevertheless, at 7:53 Ham was inserted into the spacecraft, and the clear-the-pad signal horn was sounded.

A few minutes after Ham went aboard, the inverter temperature began to rise again, causing several more holds. As the wait wore on, Christopher Kraft, the flight director, sought advice about Ham's ability to endure a long hold. William S. Augerson, medical monitor in the blockhouse, assured Kraft that the animal was all right. Ham's suit temperature remained in the comfortable mid-60s, while the inverter temperature was at least three times that hot. Eventually the inverter cooled to 150 degrees F, and the count was resumed at 10:45. As soon as the power was turned on again, the inverter temperature shot up again. So another cooling-off period was called until 20 minutes before noon, when it was decided that now or never was the time to go today. The countdown had been delayed almost four hours because of the hot inverter, but there were some other minor problems as well. The gantry elevator got stuck; too many people took too long to clear the pad area; checking the environmental control system required 20 minutes longer than planned; and the booster tail-plug cover flaps were jammed for a while.[38]

At last, five minutes before high noon on the last day of January 1961, MR-2 ignition occurred and liftoff of the Redstone followed in less than a second. As the launch vehicle rose, a transistorized television camera mounted externally near the top of the Redstone scanned the surface of the capsule and adapter ring to provide engineers with bird's-eye data on the flight behavior of the spacecraft when it blasted away from the launch vehicle. Computers sensed one minute after launch that the flight path angle was at least one degree high and rising. At two minutes, the computers predicted a 17-g load. Then, 137 seconds into the flight, the liquid oxygen supply became depleted, and in another half second the engine shut down according to the new timer-programmed plan. The closed-loop abort system on the Redstone sensed the change in engine chamber pressure upon depletion of the lox supply and fired the capsule escape system earlier than planned, within another half second. The abort properly signalled the expected Mayday message to the recovery forces, and they sped off toward a computed impact point farther downrange.[39]

The high flight angle, coupled with the early abort, added 52,000 pounds of thrust for one second, and yielded a maximum velocity of 7540 feet per second, against a planned 6465 feet. The retrorockets jettisoned prematurely when the tower aborted, which meant that the spacecraft on reentry would not be artificially slowed down and therefore would gain still more downrange mileage.[40]

An unexpected and nearly ultimate test of the chimpanzee's air circuit arose just before the abort, 2 minutes and 18 seconds into the flight, when cabin pressure dropped from 5.5 to 1 pound per square inch. This malfunction was traced later to the air inlet snorkel valve, a device that was spring-loaded to the closed position and held in place by a small detent pin. Apparently vibrations had loosened this pin and allowed the valve to open, as it was intended to do only after the main parachute opened on descent toward a water landing. Ham did not suffer, for although cabin pressure was lost, his couch pressure remained nominal, and suit temperature stayed well within the 60- to 80-degree optimum range. But the open valve caused problems after the capsule splashed.[41]

Because of overacceleration of the launch vehicle plus the added energy of the escape rocket, a speed of 5857 miles per hour was attained instead of the 4400 miles per hour planned, resulting in an apogee of 157 miles rather than the charted 115. At its zenith Ham's spacecraft was already 48 miles farther downrange than programmed, and Ham endured the weightless state for 1.7 minutes longer (6.6 minutes total) than the 4.9 minutes scheduled. He landed 422 miles downrange after a 16.5-minute flight; the preplanned figures called for 290 miles and 14.25 minutes. His peak reentry g was 14.7, almost 3 g greater than planned.[42]

How did Ham fare through all this? The physician in the blockhouse, William Augerson, reported that at liftoff he was stable and working his levers perfectly to avoid the punishment that came from inattention. At waist level in the chimpanzee's couch was a dashboard with two lights and two levers that required two pounds of effort to depress. Ham knew well how to stay comfortable by avoiding a series of electrical shocks. Each operation of his right-hand lever, cued by a white warning light, postponed the next scheduled shock for 15 seconds. At the same time, the animal had to push the left-hand lever within five seconds after a blue light flashed, about every two minutes, in order to avoid another series of shocks to the soles of his feet.

Ham performed these tasks well, pushing the continuous avoidance (right) lever about 50 times and receiving only two shocks for bad timing. On the discrete avoidance (left) lever, his score was perfect. Reaction time on the blue-light lever averaged .82 second, compared with a preflight performance of .8 second. Ham had gone from a heavy acceleration g load on exit through six minutes of weightlessness and to another heavy g load on reentry hardly missing a trick. Onboard cameras filming Ham's reaction to weightlessness also recorded a surprising amount of dust and debris floating around inside the capsule during its zenith. The cleanliness problem still was not licked.[43]

When Ham's capsule touched down, about 12:12 p.m., no human being was in sight. Some 12 minutes later, the first electronic recovery signal from the capsule was received, and quick triangulations showed that the capsule was about 60 miles from the nearest recovery ship, the destroyer *Ellison*. Some 27 minutes after landing, Technician G. T. Beldervack, aboard a P2V search plane, sighted the capsule floating upright alone in the Atlantic. Reckoning that the *Ellison* would require at least two hours to reach that point, STG officials decided to request the Navy to dispatch its helicopters from the next closest ship, the LSD *Donner*. When the helicopters arrived on the scene, they found the spacecraft on its side, taking on water, and submerging. Wave action after impact had apparently punished the capsule and its occupant severely. The beryllium heatshield upon impact had skipped on the water and bounced against the capsule bottom, punching two holes in the titanium pressure bulkhead. The plastic fabric in the landing bag had worn badly, and the heatshield was torn free from the spacecraft before recovery. After the craft capsized, the open cabin pressure relief valve let still more sea water enter the capsule. When the helicopter pilot, First Lieutenant John R. Hellriegel, and his copilot George F. Cox, finally latched onto and picked up Ham's spacecraft at 2:52 p.m., they estimated there was about 800 pounds of sea water aboard.[44] After a dangling flight back to the *Donner*, the spacecraft was lowered to the deck and nine minutes later Ham was out. He appeared to be in good condition and readily accepted an apple and

MR-2
Jan. 21, 1961

Mercury-Redstone 2, launched January 21, 1961, had the chimpanzee Ham as a passenger. At left, Ham contemplates the psychomotor test levers in his special "biopack" couch prior to the flight. At right, James Chamberlin (left) and Jerome Hammack look at the spacecraft upon its return to the Cape the following day. The landing bag (bottom) had been badly damaged and the heatshield torn free when the spacecraft was recovered by the helicopters of the U.S.S. Donner. Impact was probably responsible for the punctured pressure bulkhead, but the landing bag was more likely mangled by the fatigue of wave action as the capsule bobbed before pickup. This led to a great deal of last-minute redevelopment before the first manned mission.

317

half an orange.[45]   Ham had functioned like a normal chimpanzee in his flight into space.   Could homo sapiens do as well?

Ham's flight on MR-2 was a significant accomplishment on the American route toward manned space flight.   Now the Space Task Group knew that even with some hazardous malfunction it might reasonably hope to complete a manned ballistic mission successfully.   Ham's survival, despite a host of harrowing mis-chances over which he had no control, raised the confidence of the astronauts and the capsule engineers alike.   Except for an intensive effort to redesign the harness and impact attenuation system inside the landing bag, an exhausting final "quick-fix" led by Rodney G. Rose and Peter J. Armitage of STG, the Mercury capsule and all its systems seemed ready to carry man into space.   Since over-acceleration had occurred in both the MR-1A and MR-2 missions, however, the booster engineers responsible for "Old Reliable," Wernher von Braun and Joachim Kuettner, Kurt Debus and Emil Bertram, neither shared STG's optimism nor yet were satisfied that their launch vehicle was man-rated.[46]

MA-2: TRUSSED ATLAS QUALIFIES THE CAPSULE

So long and anguished had been the time since July 29, 1960, when the first Mercury-Atlas combination had exploded out of sight overhead, that members of the Mercury-Atlas launch team from STG were most eager to try to fly MA-2. Laboratory and wind tunnel tests of the "belly band," or "horse collar," in late January were practically prejudged as offering no ill omens.   On Inauguration Day, January 20, 1961, Robert R. Gilruth, Charles J. Donlan, Williams, Maxime A. Faget, Mathews, William M. Bland, Jr., and Purser had attended an important meeting of the STG senior staff to decide what to do about MA-2.   The pre-liminary recommendations of the Rhode-Worthman Committee were recon-sidered; after more technical talks STG decided to accept the risk and proceed with the trussed Atlas for MA-2 if top NASA management could be persuaded.   While a speedup of the flight schedule leading to the orbital mission and of plans for a program to follow after Mercury's manned 18-orbit mission were being discussed at length, the STG senior staff advised NASA Headquarters that MA-2 could wait no longer.[47]

A few days later the basic mission directive document appeared in its third revised edition; in turn it was superseded by a fourth edition and by a technical information summary.   At the end of January, Robert Seamans and Abe Silver-stein of Headquarters accepted Gilruth's STG recommendation to fly MA-2. Before the middle of February preparations were complete.   NASA had become convinced, but the Air Force was not sure MA-2 should fly yet.   This was a hazardous and complex decision, shared by a number of people in Washington, at Langley, St. Louis, Los Angeles, and San Diego.[48]   On February 17, Seamans called Rhode at Convair, asking his technical judgment as to MA-2's chances for success with its "belly-band fix."   Rhode replied that MA-2 was structurally

MA–2
Feb. 21, 1961

Mercury-Atlas 2 (right) featured the "horse collar" or "belly band," an 8-inch-wide steel corset to strengthen the interface area between this last of the thin-skinned Atlases and the adapter ring on the spacecraft. Below, McDonnell and NASA officials chat at the launch site: left to right, John Yardley, Walter Burke, and James S. McDonnell, Jr., all of McDonnell Aircraft Corporation; Wernher von Braun and Kurt Debus of NASA's Marshall Center.

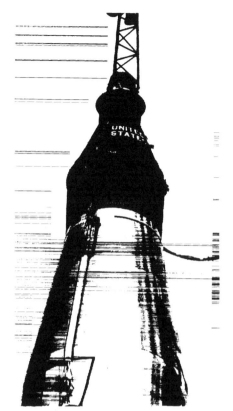

ready within acceptable wind velocities at launch.[49] George M. Low reported
to the new Administrator, James Webb, that MA-2 was scheduled for launch on
February 21 at 8 a.m.:

> Atlas 67-D will be the launch vehicle for this test. This is the last of the
> "thin-skinned" Atlases to be used in the Mercury program. It differs from the
> booster used in the MA-1 test in that the upper part of the Atlas has been
> strengthened by the addition of an 8-inch-wide stainless steel band. This band
> will markedly decrease the stresses of the weld located just below the adapter
> ring on top of the Atlas; the high stress region is shifted by about 8 inches,
> to a point where the allowable stresses are considerably higher. In addition to
> this strengthening of the top section of the Atlas, the bracing on the oxygen
> vent valve, which fits into the top of the Atlas tank, has been changed. The
> adapter between the Atlas and the capsule has also been stiffened.
>
> *   *   *
>
> The Atlas will be cut off prematurely at a velocity of about 18,000 feet per
> second. The resulting trajectory will yield the most severe reentry conditions
> that could occur during an abort in an orbital launching.[50]

Webb and Seamans, pressed by Air Force worries over the technical, political, and
public effects if MA-2 should fail, decided to trust the judgment of Rhode and
Gilruth and to back NASA's commitment to accept all the blame if the worst
should happen. Timely decisions by NASA had been required to permit deployment of the recovery forces to maintain the scheduled launch date.

There was so much concern over the Atlas-Mercury compatibility problem
that many people almost forgot the first of several first-order objectives for the
capsule and its booster. That was to test the integrity of the structure, ablation
shield, and afterbody shingles of the capsule for reentry from the most critical
abort situation. A second first-order objective required the Atlas abort sensing and implementation system (ASIS) to be operated "closed-loop" on the
Mercury-Atlas configuration for the first time. But because MA-2 had already
been made into a Federal test case, with the President, Congress, and top echelons
in the Pentagon and NASA Headquarters vitally interested in its outcome, the
engineers at the working levels were more anxious than ever to make this one
go. Its specific results were politically less important than its general appearance
of success.

The preflight checkouts had ticked off nicely the last several days before capsule No. 6 was to undergo its ordeal. And spirits were rising with the Sun on
the morning of February 21, 1961. The Mercury crew for launch operations
was much the same as that for MR-2, but just as Atlas was an entirely different
vehicle from the Redstone, so was its military/industrial launch operations crew
quite different. From the factory in San Diego had come most of the senior engineers in the Mercury booster program office, including Philip E. Culbertson,
Charles S. Ames, Howard Neumann, Joseph A. Moore, and Richard W. Keehn,
as well as the same machinists, welders, and test supervisors who had made the
"horse collar" work in bench and tunnel tests in California. At the Cape they

worked alongside the executive agent for Mercury-Atlas launchings, the 6555th Aerospace Test Wing of the Air Force, and with Thomas O'Malley and Calvin D. Fowler, who had the industrial responsibility for actual launch operations of the Atlas.   The Air Force Ballistic Missile Division representatives, Lieutenant Colonel R. H. Brundin and Major C. L. Gandy, together with Aerospace engineers Bernhard Hohmann and Ernst R. Letsch, were also on hand, watching final preparations to make this "bird" fly.   Their special concern with the design and implementation of the chief reliability component of the Atlas, namely the abort system or "ASIS," also brought Charles Wilson and J. W. Schaelchlin of Convair/Astronautics, and D. R. White of Space Technology Laboratories, into the blockhouse of Launch Complex 14 on this special morning.   John J. Williams was the Mercury-Atlas test conductor presiding there.

Engineers and workers at lower levels in the industrial and military hierarchy were beginning to call all these senior men "tigers" and to speak of them collectively as "tiger teams."   They were the senior designers and the old-line specialists on Atlas subsystems who came out to the launch site to help the field engineers actually doing the work of final preparation for a launch.[51]   Walter Williams and Christopher Kraft, in the Mercury Control Center about three miles southwest of the beach-side launch pad, watched the lights turn green one by one as the gantry backed away and "loxing" commenced about 7:30 a.m.   The weather was perfect at the Cape, but 1200 miles downrange in the recovery area there were scattered squalls, which delayed the launch for one hour.   Outside the Control Center that day stood Gilruth, Low, and Major General Ritland of the Air Force Ballistic Missile Division, waiting and watching for the liftoff. Each had prepared press releases in his pocket making this shot a NASA "overload" test in case of failure.

MA-2 roared off its pad at 9:12 a.m., and for the next 2 minutes the tiger teams and the managers of Mercury hardly dared breathe.   An audible sigh of relief spread through the Control Center and blockhouse about one minute after liftoff, when it was announced that the "horse-collared" booster had gone through max q intact and was accelerating.   At that point, said Low, "Gilruth became a young man again."   Telemetry verified "BECO" and the staging of the booster engines, escape tower separation, a good trajectory, capsule separation, capsule retrofire attitude, retrorocket firing, and retropackage jettison.[52] Capsule entry attitude looked excellent at the time tracking and telemetry were lost, because of extreme range, about 9:22 a.m.   Three minutes later, lookouts aboard the uprange destroyer *Greene* reported observing the reentry of both capsule No. 6 and Atlas booster No. 67-D.

> The capsule passed directly overhead and was lost in the sun at 09:37. Reentry was clearly visible and the capsule could be seen ahead of the booster tankage.   The capsule was not glowing but a distinct smoke trail was seen streaming behind it.   The booster tankage was glowing with an intense white glow.   Several fragments appeared to be traveling along with the tankage

321

and tumbling at a high rate. One of the ship's observers tracked the reentry on a gun mount and indicated a separation distance between the capsule and tankage of 50 mils when it passed overhead.[53]

The landing ship dock *Donner,* almost at the center of the 20-by-40-mile elliptical dispersion area, also sighted the reentry but lost sight over the horizon northeastward before the parachute descent. Within 10 minutes, however, radio signals from the sarah beacon pinpointed the floating capsule's location, and helicopters were dispatched to pick it up after only 24 minutes in the water. It was returned to the LSD less than one hour after launch.

MA–2 was a magnificent flight, "nominal in nearly every respect." This second mission followed a flight path essentially the same as that for MA–1. The Atlas-Mercury compatibility problem had been resolved, the sequence system for the booster-capsule combination had worked perfectly, and the tracking and real-time data transmission had given immediate and excellent impact prediction from the computers at Goddard to the control centers at the Cape and on Bermuda and to the recovery forces at sea. The capsule was in extremely good condition, its ablation heatshield being charred no worse than that for Big Joe, its afterbody shingles neither burned nor warped. The Space Task Group was pleasantly surprised to find the jettisoned antenna canister and to learn, even more surprisingly, that the "mousetrap" aerodynamic destabilizing flap had not, as expected, burned away.[54]

At a press conference later that day, Gilruth beamed as he announced that this was "a very successful test" that "gives us new confidence in the integrity of the system, although I would like to caution you all that there are still a number of critical tests that have to be made before we contemplate manned orbital flight." Asked if a man could have survived this flight, Gilruth said yes. When asked whether this flight also would aid the Mercury-Redstone program, Gilruth again gave an affirmative answer, stressing the identical nature of the capsule electrical, power, abort, and parachute systems. The Earth-fixed maximum velocity of the MA–2 capsule had been approximately 12,000 miles per hour, the highest velocity achieved by a Mercury launch since *Big Joe* had demonstrated the boilerplate model of the Mercury concept. As a capstone for this happy occasion, Gilruth read a statement announcing that three out of the seven astronauts, namely "Glenn, Grissom and Shepard, in alphabetical order," had been selected to begin concentrated preparations for the initial manned Mercury space flights. The nominees had known about and been in training for their missions since January, but most Mercury engineers did not know who was assigned to which flight.[55]

WHEN IS A VEHICLE MAN-RATED?

As soon as they had recovered from their jubilant celebration after the MA–2 flight, the men responsible for Project Mercury at NASA Headquarters and in the Space Task Group looked east and west to see where they stood in the race to

322

put the first man into space. The Soviets had announced, on February 4 and February 12, two more unsuccessful attempts, with heavy *Sputniks IV* and *V,* to launch interplanetary space probes to Venus. These were impressive attempts by instrumented vehicles to achieve scientific firsts, but they apparently had no direct relationship to any immediate manned space flight. It had been three months since the failure of *Sputnik Cosmic Ship No. 3* on December 2, 1960. At the end of February 1961, the Soviets' open record of two failures out of three attempts with their prototype manned spacecraft made it appear that they were having as many technical difficulties as the Americans were.

During the last week in February, therefore, the international space race seemed to have cooled. At home the reliability of the Redstone was very much at issue. It was at this juncture that the von Braun and Debus Mercury-Redstone teams presented to NASA Headquarters the results of three intensive reliability studies that they had made at Marshall since the overacceleration of MR-2 had given Ham such a rough ride. The first of these three separate probability studies was based on 69 Redstone and Jupiter flight histories; the second was based on a mathematical model using a reconstruction of the flight record of all components and subsystems of the Mercury-Redstone; and the third was a still more refined reliability study using adjusted values for the human factor and system design improvements. Together these studies yielded confidence figures that "led MSFC to the opinion that the Mercury-Redstone launch vehicle reliability was in the range of 88 percent to 98 percent probability for launch success and crew survival, respectively." [56] While President Kennedy, Defense Secretary Robert S. Mc-Namara, and Administrator Webb were learning their executive empires and were instituting a thorough review of the Nation's space program, Dryden, Seamans, Silverstein, and Gilruth accepted von Braun's insistence to postpone the first manned flight and to insert an extra Redstone booster test into the Mercury flight schedule. [57]

Whereas the Space Task Group had been elated with the performance of Ham in spite of difficulties with the capsule and the booster on the MR-2 flight the last day in January, the von Braun team at Marshall and the Cape had undergone an anguished period of reappraisal during the first two weeks in February as they tried once again to explain the "chatter" in the guidance system of their Redstone rocket. On February 6, Debus recorded in his daily journal his position with respect to the readiness status of the booster to be used for the first manned flight: "At least one unmanned shot must be obtained with flawless performance of the Mercury-Redstone mission booster flight, or at least no major shortcoming must be discovered in the vehicle system." Eberhard F. M. Rees, von Braun's Deputy Director for Research and Development, concurred and so informed von Braun. The next day Kuettner drew up an elaborate memo for internal use in deciding what should be Marshall's technical recommendation on whether to man the next Mercury-Redstone flight. In a covering note,

Kuettner explained the situation to von Braun,[58] and concluded that he personally would not advise calling a halt yet.

On Monday, February 13, 1961, Gilruth, Williams, Faget, Jerome B. Hammack, G. Merritt Preston, and Kenneth S. Kleinknecht of STG, along with John F. Yardley and R. L. Foster of McDonnell, met with the von Braun group at Huntsville to decide on "man or no man" for MR–3. By that date Debus had provided Kuettner with a list of 10 weak links, both in the hardware and in procedure, that needed correction before MR–3. The Marshall engineers incorporated their numerical guesswork into a "priority list of weak spots" that itemized seven major component problems, five minor component discrepancies, and six procedural difficulties still under study in mid-February.[59]

As Kuettner expected, political and medical considerations in the final decision to launch the first manned flight elevated the final choice to NASA Headquarters in Washington. Gilruth, his Redstone project engineer, Hammack, and the rest of STG were satisfied with the "quick fixes" made by Marshall and ground tested after MR–2. Certainly the seven astronauts felt impatiently ready to go. But von Braun and Debus reminded the Task Group of its own original ground rule for reliability: no manned flight would be undertaken until all parties responsible felt perfectly assured that everything was in readiness. Marshall engineers doubted that the difficulties encountered on the MR–1A and MR–2 missions would have endangered a human passenger. But they were committed to scrupulousness in their reliability program, too, and during the last week in February there were still seven significant modifications to the Redstone booster that seemed to require another unmanned flight test. So during this last week in February, Robert Seamans, Abe Silverstein, and Robert Gilruth acquiesced in the demands of Marshall Space Flight Center to insert one more Redstone flight into the Mercury schedule. The fateful decision was made to postpone MR–3, the first manned flight, until April 25 so something then called "MR–2A" could be inserted for a launch on March 28. On March 3 there seemed little question of the technical wisdom of this decision, although there was extreme sensitivity about the time set for the launch and about its possible public consequences.[60]

Marshall undertook to correct everything and asked STG only to provide the payload for the additional mission. Neither the Task Group nor McDonnell had an extra production capsule, so the boilerplate model that had been used on Little Joe–1B in January 1960 was refurbished and sent to Huntsville for the first mating with Redstone booster No. 5. Instead of the normal designation for the second try at an unfulfilled mission, MR–2A was renamed "MR–BD" (Mercury-Redstone Booster Development). Gilruth and company made no plans either to separate the capsule from the launch vehicle or to recover the remains. MR–BD was left primarily to von Braun and Debus, while STG turned most of its attention to Little Joe 5A. Only the operations team from STG would participate in manning the Control Center. As Marshall and the Cape made ready this flight with the booster that had formerly been designated for the third manned sub-orbital training flight (MR–5), they were unaware that the Soviet Union was making ready another series of heavy Sputniks.[61]

On March 9, 1961, the U.S.S.R. announced it had launched into orbit its fourth cosmic ship, or *Korabl Sputnik IV,* weighing some 4700 kilograms (10,364 pounds) and containing a dog passenger named Chernushka. When the dog was recovered, later that day, the Soviet recovery record suddenly became two out of four tries, and NASA saw the possible consequence of its MR–BD decision. Outside of NASA, the implications were by no means clear. The newspaper space race continued unabated.

In a highly publicized letter, Representative Overton Brooks wrote to President Kennedy on March 9, 1961, of his concern over military and trade journal reports that the space program might veer toward military control. Brooks thought the Wiesner report had implied this, and he knew of a special PSAC investigating committee of scientists, called the "Hornig panel" after its chairman, Donald F. Hornig. This group, charged with an overall review of the manned space program, had just finished spending the first four days of March traveling around investigating Project Mercury. Brooks reminded the new President that the intent of the Space Act of 1958 was to ensure that control of space research remain in civilian hands so that resulting information and technological applications would be open for the benefit of all enterprise, both private and public. Too much information would become classified, he said, if the military were preeminent in space research, development, and exploration. Brooks asked for and received Kennedy's reassurance that neither he nor Wiesner had considered subordinating NASA to the military.[62]

With Kennedy's affirmation of NASA's leadership role and its 10-year plan for space research, development, and exploration, Administrator Webb concentrated on the scientific criticisms and budgetary deficiencies of the agency. Program priorities and the funds necessary for them were taken up first. Webb found that most of his staff and field scientists were enthusiastic about getting on with advanced manned space exploration beyond Mercury. They wanted large booster development and manned spacecraft and space flight development leading to exploration of the Moon. Webb also learned that the scientific community outside of NASA was not so disenchanted with manned space flight as some had supposed. Lloyd V. Berkner, a geophysicist and chairman of the Space Science Board of the National Academy of Sciences, championed the cause of NASA programs. Berkner and Hugh Odishaw had just edited an anthology, *Science in Space,* attempting to garner the support of many disciplines for an expanded space program.[63]

On March 13 and 14, Administrator Webb and his chief lieutenants began a new series of annual presentations to Congress justifying their financial requests for the coming fiscal year 1962. Abe Silverstein, spurred several times by Chairman Brooks of the House Committee on Science and Astronautics, departed from his prepared text on the progress of Mercury to explain the MR–BD decision in connection with the imminent first manned mission into space:

> I don't know whether you heard our briefing here several weeks ago in which we pointed out that this Redstone booster traveled 400 miles out when it should have gone 293, and went to an altitude of about 150 miles, when it should have gone to 110. These were due to some booster malfunctions. We have tracked these down and we intend to go ahead and make changes in the booster so that we have better control of it. We are not about to operate with a booster that is as sloppy in performance as that.[64]

Several days later in a speech before the American Astronautical Society, Administrator Webb publicly stated that NASA's program should be expanded to include more scientific space exploration.[65] The effort of NASA management to get White House approval at this time for post-Mercury manned flight and basic funding for booster development was to prove of historical importance.[66] On March 22, President Kennedy called Webb, Dryden, and Seamans to meet with himself, the Vice-President, and key White House staff to review the need for supplementing the NASA fiscal 1962 budget. As a result a $125.76 million increase was approved for NASA.[67] In the mind of the general public, unaware of these deliberations on an accelerated space program, NASA was thoroughly identified with Project Mercury and attention was pointing toward the first manned mission in the near future.[68]

LJ–5A STILL PREMATURE

"The purpose of the Little Joe 5A," began the technical information summary document issued for this flight on March 6, 1961, "is to qualify the Mercury capsule, escape system, and other systems which must function during and after escape at the combination of dynamic pressure, mach number, and flight path angle that represent the most severe conditions that can be anticipated during an orbital launch on an Atlas booster." Using McDonnell's capsule No. 14, the Little Joe flight test engineers at Wallops Island were behind schedule and eager to improve on the Little Joe 5 test, which had failed on Election Day in 1960. The premature ignition of the escape rocket motor, followed by the failure of the capsule to separate from the booster, still remained unexplained. It had made the prevention of such a recurrence one of the unstated first-order test objectives of LJ–5A. Using another of the beryllium heat-sink heatshields, two Castor and four Recruit rocket motors in the booster, a special backup retrorocket system, and much better instrumentation, William Bland and his crew from STG, together with John C. Palmer, the Wallops Island range director, also hoped to get better data on the capsule's structural integrity and on its sequential, landing, and recovery systems.[69] The close simulation that Little Joe 5A should have with the Mercury-Atlas configuration was shown by the following table: [70]

	LJ–5A	Mercury-Atlas
Time (sec.)	34.4	60
Max. q (p.s.f.)	972	973
Mach number	1.52	1.58
Flight path angle (deg)	48.6°	56.4°
Altitude (ft)	30,960	34,300

On Saturday, March 18, 1961, after a four-hour delay caused by checkout problems, Little Joe 5A roared and soared up from the beach at Wallops Island at 11 minutes before noon. The takeoff looked good, but 20 seconds later and 14 seconds too early the capsule escape rocket again fired without the capsule. Warren North described this flight graphically:

> At 35 seconds the normal abort signal released the capsule clamp ring. A single retrorocket, which was installed as an emergency separation device, received a premature firing signal at 43 seconds. The dynamic pressure at this point was 400 psf—ten times as great as dynamic pressure at apogee where emergency capsule separation should have taken place. The capsule tumbled immediately upon separating and narrowly missed the booster as it decelerated. The retropack and escape tower were inadvertently jettisoned or torn off as the capsule tumbled. Apparently the centrifugal force and/or the escape tower removed the antenna canister, deploying both the main and reserve parachutes. The capsule descended on both parachutes which were only slightly damaged during high q deployment.[71]

Postflight analyses showed that both LJ–5 and LJ–5A had failed primarily because of structural deformations near the clamp rings that fouled the electromechanical separation systems.

The impact bag on Little Joe 5A was deployed by its barostat at 10,000 feet. The capsule drifted 10 miles on both its parachutes and finally splashed down 18 miles from the launch site, almost twice as far as planned. On top of that, the parachutes fell unreleased over the capsule as it floated in the water, thereby preventing helicopters from recovering it; a Navy salvage ship made the pickup an hour later. The capsule was in fairly good condition, with only one shingle damaged from its ordeal, and parachute loads six times higher than expected had caused no significant damage to its structure.

Spectacular but disappointing had been this test. The primary objective of qualifying a Mercury capsule during a maximum-q abort had to be rescheduled four weeks later, utilizing the last Little Joe booster. Capsule No. 14 was cleaned up, repaired where necessary, and furnished with another set of sensors, instrumentation, and telemetry for the reflight coming up, the seventh in the Little Joe series and for that reason called prematurely "LJ–7." The postlaunch report for LJ–5A summarized the reason for renaming the last Little Joe flight LJ–5B:

> Analysis of data show that the escape-rocket motor fired prematurely and prior to capsule release, thus precluding accomplishment of most of the first-order test objectives. The premature ignition was apparently caused by un-

scheduled closure of at least two of the capsule main clamp ring limit switches.

Operation of a capsule backup system by ground command separated the capsule from the booster and released the tower, making it possible for the parachutes to deploy. The main and reserve parachutes were deployed simultaneously under very severe flight conditions and enabled the capsule to make a safe landing. However, in spite of the descent rate of 60 percent less than normal, the heat shield caused some damage upon recontact. Examination of the recovered capsule showed that it did not sustain any structural damage sufficient to preclude its rapid refurbishment for another flight test.[72]

There was no time for more contingency planning if the United States hoped to orbit a man before the end of 1961. But for the moment the question in STG was not what could be done in nine months but what might be done in nine weeks.

MR–BD Is Not MR–3

In the midst of the restudies of Mercury-Redstone reliability in early February, Wernher von Braun talked with his chief of public information, Bart J. Slattery, Jr., about the way the public had been "conditioned" to believe that the Mercury astronaut would not be allowed to ride the vehicle until 100 percent assurance of his safe return was obtained from testing. "There isn't such a thing!" proclaimed von Braun, and he added that future publicity releases should emphasize that there "is a risk," perhaps greater than the traffic risks Americans take every day but possibly no greater than test pilots take with maiden flights of new jet aircraft.[73]

During the following month, while trying to reduce that risk to a minimum, the von Braun team represented by Slattery, the Space Task Group represented by John A. Powers, and NASA Headquarters represented by Paul P. Haney, agreed to plan the public information for MR–BD to avoid "over-emphasis or overly optimistic assumptions relating to future manned flights."[74]

Redstone engineers meanwhile quickly fixed the MR–BD launch vehicle, making their seven technical changes during the first two weeks in March 1961. The foremost cause of previous Redstone booster overaccelerations was a small servo control valve that had failed to regulate properly the flow of hydrogen peroxide to the steam generator, which in turn powered, and in the case of MR–1A and MR–2 overpowered, the fuel pumps. Modifications were made to the thrust regulator and velocity integrator, in hopes that MR–BD would be physically incapable of exceeding the speed limit again. Another technical difficulty had been some harmonic vibrations induced by aerodynamic stress in the topmost section of the elongated Redstone. Four stiffeners were added to the ballast section and 210 pounds of insulation was applied to the inner skin of the upper part of the instrument compartment. Although oscillations at the second bending mode frequencies were less on MR–2 than on MR–1A, several other electronic changes were made to reduce the dangers from noise and vibration.

MR–BD
Mar. 24, 1961

The boilerplate spacecraft used on the Mercury-Redstone-Booster Development flight on March 24 is lifted by crane to its place atop the Redstone. This was an extra flight inserted into the schedule at the request of von Braun to acquire further experience with the man-rated Redstone before a manned flight was actually attempted.

High winds aloft probably had added some extra stress in the former case, but in any event the next trajectory would smooth out the tilting maneuver in the region of high dynamic pressure, and 65 telemetry sensors were placed where the rocket's bending moments needed to be monitored. Finally, after a great deal of diagnostic study, five resettings were made to ensure that the booster engine cutoff time would not precede oxidizer depletion and hence cause another premature abort signal, as had happened with MR–2. All these changes proceeded smoothly while the boilerplate capsule was ballasted and corrugated to approximate the production model, McDonnell spacecraft No. 7, and fitted with an inert escape rocket. The capsule did not have a posi-retrorocket package.[75]

On the morning of March 24, 1961, the second half of the split countdown for MR–BD was in progress, and so far everything had proceeded without a hitch or a "glitch." To test procedures for the launch pad rescue crews, a manned M–113 armored personnel carrier was parked only 1000 feet southwest of the unmanned Redstone. The firemen in this vehicle were going to endure bone-jangling noise and vibration during the launch to see how much emergency rescue crews could stand. Closer still, an unmanned asbestos-covered truck was

329

parked 65 feet from the MR–BD blast deflector to simulate the position that the "cherry picker," or mobile egress tower, would occupy during the launch of a manned missile.

Liquid oxygen loading for MR–BD began only two hours before the scheduled launch time. During the automatically controlled loading process, winds of about 20 knots swayed the Redstone and produced sloshing during the "topoff" operation. The fuel temperature began to rise toward the boiling point, and soon an overflow bled out the booster standpipe and boil-off valve. This potentially dangerous situation was governed by a computer, which, when its electronic bias in the topping circuit was lowered, continued the "lox-topping" normally. No holds were called, and the countdown proceeded to launch without further incident.

At 12:30 p.m., MR–BD lifted off straight and smooth from Cape Canaveral on its programmed trajectory. The people in the armored vehicle on the ground watched it all without discomfort, and a truck driver later moved the simulated "cherry picker" away undamaged. Although the actual exit velocity was 89 feet per second higher than planned, there was in general, said Hammack in his report to STG, "hardly a plotting difference between the actual trajectory data computed . . . and the nominal trajectory published in NASA working paper 178." [76] The whole configuration impacted in the Atlantic 307 miles downrange (five miles short of the plan) and sank to the bottom, exploding a sofar bomb en route. MR–BD was highly successful; as George Low reported to Administrator Webb, it "demonstrated that all major booster problems have been eliminated." [77] Telemetry revealed that the Redstone still wriggled a bit with high vibrations in the instrument compartment, but all the "quick-fixes" had worked properly. MR–BD satisfied von Braun's team, Debus' crew, and all of NASA that the Redstone was now trustworthy enough to be called "man-rated." Enough experience was at hand to tackle the next step in Project Mercury, manned suborbital flight. [78]

But the very next day, March 25, the Soviets announced the successful launch and recovery of their fifth *Korabl Sputnik,* containing a dog named Zvesdochka, or Little Star. Three out of five was their record now for successful recovery of "cosmic ships" and dogs from orbit. Three days later, at a Soviet Academy of Science press conference in Moscow, six of Strelka's pups, as well as four other space dogs, were on exhibit as evidence and harbingers of the imminent flight of man into space. MR–BD might have been that first flight had it been "MR–3," as originally scheduled, but the decision of a month before froze the Mercury-Redstone schedule for at least two months afterward. And the Mercury team, aware of but not dominated by the space race, could only hope that the "Sputnik Spacecraft Team" was having comparable final checkout difficulties.

At the beginning of April 1961, Mercury-Redstone launch vehicle No. 7 was erected on its launch pedestal at pad No. 5 and made ready for the first mating of the man-rated capsule No. 7. Feverish activity pervaded Hangar S and the service structure, where another "white room" was being hastily rigged on the third level of the gantry at MR–3's capsule height. Rework on the capsule's reaction control system was completed during the first week in April, while the three chosen astronauts went through final procedures training and acceleration conditioning in centrifuge runs at Johnsville. The Space Task Group now believed that the development phase of the project was practically over. Symbolizing this shift, the Associate Director responsible for development, Charles Donlan, left STG formally on the first of April to return to Langley Research Center, leaving Walter Williams, the operations chief, as Gilruth's sole Associate Director.[79]

The Space Task Group nevertheless could not afford to become too preoccupied with the preparations for MR–3 because MA–3 and Little Joe 5B were scheduled first, and within two weeks, as prerequisites for the orbital objective. On April 10, foreign correspondents in Moscow reported rampant rumors sweeping the city that the U.S.S.R. had placed a man into space. That same day at Langley Field, Virginia, another rumor reached the attention of STG to the effect that the 10 members and four consultants of the President's Hornig panel were recommending at least 50 more chimpanzee runs before putting man in space. Gilruth remarked facetiously that if this were true, the Mercury program ought to move to Africa.[80]

This hearsay recommendation did not become a part of the "Report of the Ad Hoc Mercury Panel" or of the Hornig Committee, as it was more widely known, which was submitted on April 12, 1961. Having been delegated by President Kennedy and his scientific adviser, Wiesner, the panel visited the McDonnell plant, Cape Canaveral, and Langley Field and talked with representatives of supporting services and contractors. In its 18-page report it reviewed the accomplishments and failures of the Mercury program, assessed the risks and probability of success, and commented upon medical aspects of Project Mercury as a whole and medical readiness for manned suborbital flight in particular. It concluded with some reasonable medical reservations that a Redstone flight now would be "a high risk undertaking but not higher than we are accustomed to taking in other ventures," such as in the initial flights of the Wright Brothers, Lindbergh, and the X-series of research aircraft.[81]

In its reliability assessments, the Hornig panel graded the Mercury subsystems or components according to three classes of reliability percentages: Class 1, 95–100 percent; Class 2, 85–95 percent; Class 3, 70–85 percent. Eleven items were rated as Class 1: Capsule structure and reentry properties; separation mechanism and posigrade rocket; tower and abort rockets; voice communications; abort sensing instrumentation system; manual control system; retrorocket system; parachute landing system; ground environment system; recovery operation; and pilot training. Three items were rated in Class 2: Landing bag; environmental control system; and automatic stabilization and control system. The two items in the Class 3 category, booster (Redstone or Atlas) and telemetry, were explained as "not per se a cause for alarm" for pilot safety but only for mission success.[82]

Vostok Wins the First Lap

The first unofficial rumors out of Moscow were confirmed by an Associated Press dispatch on April 12 that translated an official Soviet news agency Tass announcement:

> The world's first space ship Vostok with a man on board, has been launched on April 12 in the Soviet Union on a round-the-earth orbit.
> The first space navigator is Soviet citizen pilot Maj. Yuri Alekseyevich Gagarin. Bilateral radio communication has been established and is maintained with Gagarin.

Aside from this assertion, the news out of Moscow and Turkestan on April 12 was neither crisp nor very detailed. For a few days a great deal of speculation over conflicting reports, fuzzy photographs, and the lack of eyewitnesses encouraged those disappointed Westerners who wished to believe that Gagarin's flight in *Vostok I* (meaning East) had not occurred. The danger that history might be made to order in a closed society was compounded by the rumors in the *London Daily Worker* and elsewhere since April 7. The propagandistic exploitation of this magnificent deed was evident from the fact that no confirmed announcement was made during the 108 minutes of flight—not until Yuri Gagarin landed intact near the Volga River, some 15 miles south of the city of Saratov. The present tense in the Tass dispatch above could easily have been doctored for control purposes, drama, or even for more serious reasons.[83]

Be that as it may, NASA officials from Webb and Dryden down to Gilruth and Powers, at least six months earlier, had planned their comments for this occasion, just in case. About 4 a.m., telephones began buzzing up and down the east coast of the United States as reporters demanded responses from NASA officials to the Tass dispatch. John A. "Shorty" Powers half-consciously replied to his first inquisitor, "We're all asleep down here." Some journalists ignored the fact that Gilruth had long since gone on record as saying he would not be surprised to be awakened some morning in this manner. Webb went on nation-wide network television at 7:45 a.m. to extend congratulations to the Soviets, to express NASA's disappointment, and to reassure the nation that Project Mercury would not be stampeded or panicked into a premature speedup of the Mercury timetable. The next morning Webb and Dryden were roasted before the verbal fire of the House space committee as they were asked to explain what had happened. All the information available to the United States government, said Dryden, and past experience with Soviet technical statements, tended to confirm the report of Gagarin's flight. Representatives James G. Fulton of Pennsylvania, J. Edgar Chenoweth of Colorado, Victor L. Anfuso of New York, and David S. King of Utah were especially disappointed that the name Gagarin would "go down in the history books." Webb and Dryden held up well under this heat, taking the position that this particular race was lost "before the space agency was founded." But Representative Joseph E. Karth, a Democrat from

332

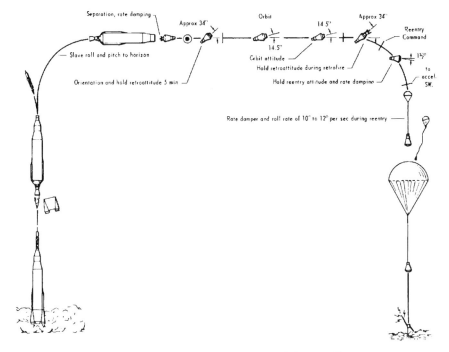

Project Mercury normal orbital mission profile.

Minnesota, gave the most popular rationale of why a Russian had won the first lap in the manned space race:

> The United States and the Soviet Union have proceeded along two different lines of attack. The Soviets have pretty much rifled their program, if I may use the word, as opposed to the United States shotgunning their effort. We have been interested in many programs and I think the Soviets have been interested primarily in putting a man in space.[84]

The flight of the first cosmonaut seemed remarkably similar in many respects to the plans for the first Mercury astronaut's orbital mission, but there were momentous differences as well—the single near-polar orbit, the lack of a worldwide tracking network, and the provisions for pilot ejection before impact.[85] According to the corrected and reduced data obtained from their measurements and published in *Pravda* on April 25, 1961, the twin module spaceship-satellite, or *Korabl Sputnik VI,* was renamed generically as the first in the Vostok series. Specifically its call sign was *Swallow.* The payload compartment, manned by 27-year-old, 154-pound Gagarin, weighed altogether 10,417 pounds, and attained

333

an apogee of 203 miles and a perigee of 112 miles, with an orbital inclination of 65 degrees to the equator. Cosmonaut Gagarin was probably launched by a two-stage booster from the Baikonur cosmodrome, east of the Aral Sea, south of the industrial district of Magnitogorsk, near Tyura Tam, a boom town comparable to Cocoa Beach, Florida. Apparently the Gagarin flight had not been preceded by a parabolic manned suborbital flight into space. The anonymous engineers behind him, mysteriously called "the chief designer" and "the chief engineer," evidently had developed a mixed-gas air supply at sea-level pressures for his life support system. *Vostok I* also had a separate and separable instrument section and retrorocket package for telemetry, television, and radio telephone communications during orbit and for braking the spacecraft velocity 5000 miles and 30 minutes before the desired impact point. Gagarin rode in a capsule almost three times the weight of the Mercury spacecraft and inside a spherical pressure vessel 7.5 feet in diameter, both of which were automatically controlled. Gagarin was the first person in history to attain an Earth-fixed speed of 17,400 miles per hour, and at this speed around his 25,000-mile course, as high as 203 miles from sea level, he was also the first man ever to endure 89 minutes of weightlessness.[86]

What the Soviets announced after the fact was indeed true:

> History's first flight in outer space, accomplished by the Soviet cosmonaut Yuri Gagarin in the space ship Vostok, has made it possible to draw the immensely important scientific conclusion that manned flights in space are practicable. It demonstrated that man can normally bear up against the conditions of a space flight, the placing of a ship in orbit, and the return to earth. This flight showed that in a state of weightlessness man fully retains his capacity for work, his coordination of movements, and his clarity of thought.[87]

And while it was hardly an overstatement to claim, as the Soviets did after the celebrations in Red Square were over, that "in the progress of science, the flight of a Soviet man in outer space pushed all other developments into the background," it must certainly have been an oversimplification that prompted Gagarin to say in retrospect: "I felt very well before the flight. I was fully confident of its successful outcome. Our machines and equipment are very reliable and I and all my comrades, the scientists, engineers and technicians, never doubted the success of the undertaking." [88]

Gagarin's flight, while not having the depressive impact of *Sputnik I* in October 1957, nonetheless came as a crushing disappointment to many Americans. The announcement was received in this country with a variety of reactions: admiration for the flight's purely scientific merits; disbelief, since various Russian accounts carried conflicting statements, at least in transliteration and at most in their technical secretiveness; and the feeling that the United States had lost face once again. The Associated Press conducted a poll in Miami, Detroit, Akron, Charlotte, Denver, Dallas, Minneapolis, Los Angeles, Oklahoma City, and Washington, D.C., by having its reporters call all the Joe Smiths in the telephone directories. The Joe Smiths registered a wide range of emotions, but perhaps the persons feeling the keenest disappointment were the American astronauts. They knew how close and yet how far they had come toward being first in space, if not in orbit. Of the four who made statements, Glenn was most articulate and magnanimous:

> The Russian accomplishment was a great one. It was apparently very successful and I am looking forward to seeing more detailed information. I am, naturally, disappointed that we did not make the first flight to open this new era. The important goals of Project Mercury, however, remain the same—ours is peaceful exploration of space. These first flights, whether Russian or American, will go a long way in determining the direction of future endeavors. There is certainly work for all to solve the tremendous problems involved. I hope the Russians have the same objectives and that we can proceed with mutual dissemination of information so that these goals which all mankind shares can be gained rapidly, safely, and on a progressive scientific basis.[89]

"News Will Be Worse Before It Is Better": MA-3 and LJ-5B

Although Project Mercury was not stampeded by the flight of *Vostok I,* Congress nearly was. As Mercury approached its goal, its ends became merely a means to the Moon. While the funding for Project Apollo was being discussed in Congress, the Gagarin flight provided a tremendous impetus to the desires of Americans, as mirrored in the lower house of their national legislature, to become first once again. In the chagrin of the moment, some Congressmen appeared willing to appropriate more money than NASA could spend. Robert Seamans, third in command of NASA as Associate Administrator and general manager, actually had difficulty restraining the House space committee's demands for an all-out crash program for a lunar landing. President Kennedy, consistent with one of his campaign promises, reacted to the Gagarin announcement by saying, "We are behind . . . the news will be worse before it is better, and it will be some time before we catch up." [90]

The President knew not how well he had prophesied the major Mercury events of the next two weeks. The time was up for Mercury to be first in space, but the qualification flight tests were still far from over. Mercury-Atlas 3, composed of "thick-skinned" Atlas 100–D and capsule No. 8, was, on April 10, 1961, standing on the pad at the Cape being groomed for a long ballistic flight over Bermuda and the Atlantic Ocean. A primary purpose of MA–3 was to test the dual abilities of the Cape and Bermuda to handle an abort about the time of orbital insertion. Walter Williams had already satisfied himself that this was no problem and that the MA–3 mission should be more ambitious. After Gagarin's flight the Mercury senior staff on April 14 decided it was technically feasible to change the MA–3 mission objectives to a full-scale one-orbit goal. When Warren North informed Silverstein of this change on April 17, he also noted that MA–4 should be a chimp-carrying orbital flight about mid-July.[91] However, Low,

335

MA-3
Apr. 25, 1961

Mercury-Atlas 3 (left) was launched from the Cape April 25, 1961. Its mission was upgraded from a suborbital to an orbital attempt only a few days before the flight. MA-3 was destroyed by the range safety officer after 40 seconds of flight, the inertial guidance system having failed to pitch the vehicle over toward the horizon. The spacecraft successfully aborted and was retrieved a short distance offshore. This was the last major flight failure in Mercury.

LJ-5B
Apr. 28, 1961

Little Joe-5B (right) was launched from Wallops Island April 28, 1961. Although not nominal in flight trajectory, LJ-5B did finally demonstrate the ability of the escape and sequence systems to function properly at max-q conditions equal to the worst a Mercury-Atlas could encounter.

336

acting for Silverstein, in direct consultation with Seamans, Gilruth, Williams, and others after Gagarin's flight, had already approved the speedup in the mission objectives for MA–3.

Carrying a "crewman simulator," an electronic mannequin that could "inhale" and "exhale" manlike quantities of gas, heat, and water vapor, MA–3 should test not only the capsule systems but also the reliability of this standard Mercury-Atlas. The critical tracking system and computer arrangement at Goddard, the Cape, and Bermuda must prove its ability to predict the "go/no go" decision before the danger of impacting in Africa. It was too late to change most of the documentation for MA–3, including the information summary and mission directive, but revised preflight trajectory data were hastily computed and disseminated. Computer programmers James J. Donegan of Goddard and John P. Mayer of STG worked their men through the eve of the flight checking the changed flight plan.[92]

MA–3 failed tactically, but strategically this orbital flight attempt probably did more than anything else in the Mercury program to implement the "gold-plating," or the real man-rating of the Atlas. It carried the last of the first series of capsules with the dual ports and without a landing impact bag. The capsule was to be inserted into orbit at an altitude of 100 miles and a slant range of 515 miles from Cape Canaveral. If the velocity of Atlas 100–D was not high enough, it could be aborted into any one of several preplanned recovery zones between Bermuda and the Canary Islands.

As it happened, the Atlas attempt to orbit a robot, made at 11:15 a.m. on April 25, 1961, was intentionally destroyed by the range safety officer only 40 seconds after launch when the autopilot programmer on the Atlas failed to roll and pitch the vehicle over toward the horizon. The mission having aborted, however, the entire Mercury escape system worked perfectly and the launch site recovery team responded exactly as if there had been a pilot's life at stake. The spacecraft was towed to a maximum altitude of 24,000 feet by the escape rocket and lowered gently by its main parachute a short distance offshore. The capsule came through this relatively easy abort with only minor damages and was quickly recovered and refurbished for reuse on MA–4.[93] Destroyed after its failure to initiate roll and pitch programs, booster 100–D left few artifacts as memorials of its existence. Before the official investigation board could complete its report two months later, however, a significant piece of the MA–3 autopilot, the programmer, was found buried in the mud near the beach, thereby leading to the corroboration of one of the prime hypotheses for this failure.[94]

Meanwhile, back at Wallops Island, the seventh and last booster in the Little Joe series was fitted with capsule No. 14 and made ready for a repeat of LJ–5 and LJ–5A in hopes that the third try would be charmed. This was to be an extremely critical test before MR–3. Gilruth, from Low's home in Washington, called William Bland at Wallops Island to encourage the launching if weather permitted. The preflight documentation was virtually identical to that of the previous Little Joe flight, as was the refurbished spacecraft. Still more instru-

337

mentation and even more careful checkout procedures to ensure that the abort would occur at the right time were instituted in addition to the redesigned clamp ring and limit switches. A steep trajectory up to about 45,000 feet was desired before tower separation and drogue chute deployment. The max-q punishment of about 990 pounds per square foot was desired to match the worst of the Atlas abort conditions.[95]

When on April 28, 1961, at 9:03 a.m., LJ–5B rammed upward, technical observers cringed when they saw immediately that one of the booster's Castor rocket motors failed to ignite for 5 seconds after liftoff. This resulted in a much lower trajectory than planned, giving a maximum altitude of only 14,600 feet, but the dynamic pressure, instead of 990 pounds per square foot, was about twice that amount, 1920 pounds. The abort was initiated about 33 seconds after launch as intended, and all events following the abort occurred as they should have. Recovery by helicopter was quick and clean, even though the low-flying capsule impacted two miles farther downrange after skidding through the atmosphere rather than vaulting through it. Lewis R. Fisher, Leo T. Chauvin, and Norman F. Smith of the STG Little Joe team were able therefore to wind up their program with a boast despite the erroneous trajectory:

> This launching successfully demonstrated the structural integrity of the Mercury capsule and escape system and sequential system under significantly more severe conditions than those expected to be encountered during a non-tumbling type of abort from an Atlas booster during a Mercury orbital launch . . . . Changes in circuitry and redesign of clamp-limit-switch installations in Capsule 14 for the Little Joe 5–B mission successfully eliminated the problem of premature ignition of the escape rocket motor.[96]

One by one the major obstacles to the growth of the manned space flight enterprise seemed to have dissolved. The opposition of some in the scientific community was not expected to become a factor in national policy. The so-called "military-industrial complex" had failed, if indeed it had ever tried, to reduce NASA. The White House and NASA administrators were determined to advance national capability in space technology. Political dangers were now neutralized. Except for the Atlas and the spacecraft's orbital capacities, all Mercury systems were qualified. Despite the embarrassment to American nationalism brought by Gagarin's flight, Mercury as a technological accomplishment was on the verge of sending a man to visit the edge of the black sea of space. And certainly this year of grace 1961 should also see an American citizen orbit the globe.[97]

Part Three

OPERATIONS

XI

Suborbital Flights into Space

AT 9:34 a.m. on May 5, 1961, about 45 million Americans sat tensely before their television screens and watched a slim black-and-white Redstone booster, capped with a Mercury spacecraft manned by Astronaut Alan B. Shepard, Jr., lift off its pad at Cape Canaveral and go roaring upward through blue sky toward black space.

At 2.3 seconds after launch, Shepard's voice came through clearly to Mercury Control; minutes later the millions heard the historic transmission:

> Ahh, Roger; lift-off and the clock is started . . . Yes, sir, reading you loud and clear. This is *Freedom 7*. The fuel is go; 1.2 g; cabin at 14 psi; oxygen is go . . . *Freedom 7* is still go!

America's first man in space was in flight only 15 minutes and 22 seconds and was weightless only a third of that time. *Freedom 7* rose to an altitude of 116.5 miles, attained a maximum speed of 5180 miles per hour, and landed 302 miles downrange from the Cape. Shepard experienced a peak stress of 6 g during booster acceleration and less than 12 g on reentry. Recovery operations went perfectly, the spacecraft was undamaged, and Shepard was in excellent and exuberant condition.[1]

In the light of later American space accomplishments, the flight of *Freedom 7* was impressive for its benchmark of technical excellence in the new technology of manned space flight and its hallmark of open media reporting. When compared, as it inevitably was, with the previous April 12 orbital flight of Yuri Gagarin, MR–3 was anticlimatic.

Ever since December 1958, when T. Keith Glennan, the NASA Administrator, had announced Project Mercury, the American public had awaited the first manned Mercury flight with fairly general misgivings. Many people whose expectations had been stimulated by publicity became impatient at the long delays and postponements. Some deplored the whole space program as wasteful and of doubtful value. A few still believed space travel was impossible for human beings.

341

Then, on February 22, 1961, the Space Task Group announced that Shepard, John H. Glenn, and Virgil I. Grissom had been chosen to begin special training for the MR–3 vault into space. More than a month before the public announcement, Robert R. Gilruth personally had made his choice, even to the exact flight order of the men selected. In early January, back at Langley, the day after he had bid outgoing Administrator Glennan goodbye in Washington, Gilruth had decided to inform the flight crewmen of their selection status. He drove over to the temporary building housing the astronaut offices, called the seven men together, and told them of his decision that Shepard would be the first flight astronaut.[2] And while the West awaited the next development, Gagarin made his 108-minute near-polar orbit of Earth aboard the five-ton *Vostok I* (meaning East) spacecraft.

Although some Americans professed disbelief in the Gagarin flight, a majority surely felt a twinge of nationalistic pain in admitting the Soviets had won the first honor in the two-nation race into space. When Shepard's flight took place, barely a month after Gagarin, even the skeptics appeared to derive consolation from the fact that the American launch and recovery had been made in the light of full publicity, with all world news media participating, whereas the Vostok flight had been veiled in official secrecy until after the fact.

Freedom 7, Shepard's capsule, missed what had been widely considered a "realistic" launch schedule by six months. When the capsule had finally been delivered to the Cape on December 9, 1960, some assumed the flight could be made at once. But 21 weeks of preparation—not all of it anticipated—were required by STG's Cape preflight checkout group and a host of McDonnell engineers based at the Florida site. Reaction control system checkout and rework were responsible for a launch schedule postponement to March 6, 1961. Replacement of damaged and corroded peroxide lines forced a further delay of eight days. Rerunning the simulated mission test and correcting structural and equipment defects were other time-consuming problems.[3]

Thus, technically, it was May 2 before the launch of capsule No. 7 might have been made. Then why not use capsule No. 8 or 9 or 11? Because capsule No. 7 had been selected in the summer and groomed since October 1960 as McDonnell's best product to date, the only porthole version of the capsule that had been or would be man-rated in all respects. By January 1961, after the MR–1A flight had used up Mercury-Redstone booster No. 3, the one originally intended for the first man-launch vehicle, it was clear that Redstone No. 7 would boost capsule No. 7. At the end of March, when booster No. 7 arrived at the Cape, Shepard already knew he was Robert R. Gilruth's prime choice to fly it. "There was no hope," said Shepard, "that a later model of the capsule incorporating our suggestions could be ready in time for MR–3." So capsule No. 7 on booster No. 7 should be the first combination of a series of at least seven flights to put Americans into space. "What better name or call-sign could I choose than *Freedom 7?*" asked Shepard.[4]

Although the delays were disheartening, there were compensatory benefits in the way of astronaut training. Some psychologists feared that this long time lapse before the flight actually took place might cause "over training" and staleness. But in the postflight debriefing, Shepard complimented the so-called "over training"; he remarked that the similarity of training conditions to actual flight conditions was a key factor in making the mission seem almost routine. In addition, new and better procedures were developed during repeated rehearsals of the mission, which might not have come to light had the training not been expanded a few weeks.

FINAL PREPARATION FOR MR–3

The Space Task Group had decided to train Shepard, Glenn, and Grissom especially for the MR–3 mission because the competitive field had to be narrowed for this particular mission to allow the remaining astronauts to prepare for ground support jobs and the Mercury-Atlas orbital missions. Shepard's activity chart for February 1961 shows that he spent 18 days at Cape Canaveral becoming oriented to spacecraft No. 7 and its peculiarities. Long before the final phases of pilot preparations came about, Shepard and Walter C. Williams had insisted that the designated astronaut must become an integral part of the preflight checkout activities. So, based on this procedure, Shepard and Glenn acquired the special feel of No. 7's attitude control system in hangar checkouts. When the capsule was placed in the altitude test chamber, Shepard went along for the "ride" and exercised the environmental control system.

The most valuable operational training the astronaut received before his mission came from sessions in two McDonnell-built, Link-type trainers, one at Langley and the other at the Cape. These devices were first called "procedures trainers" and later "Mercury simulators." Here the space pilot, supine in a mock-up capsule, rehearsed the flight plan for a specific mission. The trainer instruments were capable of being tied in with computers at the Mercury Control Center. Overall operations team practice welded ground controllers and astronaut into a unit. Although not devoted exclusively to the MR–3 mission, the simulators were in use 55 to 60 hours a week during the three months preceding the flight of *Freedom 7*. During the entire training period, Shepard "flew" 120 simulated Mercury-Redstone flights.[5]

For an eight-week period immediately preceding the flight, the rehearsals became even more exacting. In preparing for the altitude chamber runs at space equivalent altitudes, the astronaut was examined in preflight physicals, fitted with medical sensors, including a rectal thermometer, and helped into his 20-pound pressure suit. The pilot and his medical attendants then went through the mission as realistically as conditions would allow, conducting pressure and medical checks.

Another carefully rehearsed phase of the program consisted of the transfer

In the delay-filled weeks before the first U.S. manned spaceflight, Astronaut Alan B. Shepard, Jr., kept profitably busy with "over training," the rerunning of all phases and aspects of the flight to the point that response to them became reflexive.   Left, Shepard arrives in the white room at Pad 5 on April 21, 1961, ready for the full-scale simulation of the flight.   Below, he once more "flies" the mission in the procedures trainer at the Cape.   Below left, he leaves the altitude chamber in Hangar S following an altitude test.

MR–3
Preflight

of the pilot from his quarters on the balcony of Hangar S to the transfer van, the ride to the pad, and simulated flights with the astronaut sitting in the actual spacecraft. Countdowns were conducted while controllers manned their consoles. The first two rehearsal "flights," held on April 18 and 19, kept the service structure, or gantry, against the vehicle, and the capsule hatch was not closed. But the next day, on a third simulated mission, the hatch was closed, the gantry was pulled away, and the spacecraft was purged with oxygen as if an actual mission were in progress. Training like this and in the procedures trainer continued until two days before the scheduled flight.[6]

Three purposes were served by this extensive training program. The astronaut became intimately familiar with the role and voice of each person supporting the mission. He acquired more physical and mental familiarity with all of the associated hardware. And he was made even more aware of the day-to-day status leading to launch date. The operations team benefited by having the astronaut attend the team's technical briefings. These discussions covered both the spacecraft and the launch vehicle and included mission reviews held the week before launch.

On the eve of the launch, a briefing was conducted exclusively for the astronaut, with specialists in each system reporting on final readiness. Walter J. Kapryan presented the capsule and booster status; Robert B. Voas reviewed astronaut flight tasks; Christopher C. Kraft, Jr., briefed the astronaut on flight control and network status; Robert F. Thompson told him of recovery procedures; and Ernest A. Amman gave him the forecast on weather conditions. Next morning, L. Gordon Cooper, blockhouse communicator, obtained reports from key operations personnel and gave the astronaut his final ready-room briefing before he ascended the gantry. Plans for the postflight debriefing sessions, wherein the student astronaut would become the teacher of his preflight instructors, were also laid out in detail by the end of April.[7]

The planning of recovery operations was as important as any other phase of the mission. Rear Admiral F. V. H. Hilles, in command of the experienced flotilla of eight destroyers known as DesFlotFour, worked with another flag officer, G. P. Koch, aboard the carrier *Lake Champlain,* on the tactics for this mission. STG's primary strategy was to recover both man and capsule by using land-based Marine helicopters for launch-site abort situations within about 80 miles of the Cape and carrier-based helicopters in the primary recovery area, within a hundred-mile radius. Makeup of the recovery force was similar to that for MR-2, with tiered groups of men and equipment, beginning at Cape Canaveral, ready to cover all contingencies—abort, normal flight, or overflight. The main recovery force of ships was deployed in an elongated pattern 500 miles down along the range. It consisted of the carrier, eight destroyers, and one Atlantic Missile Range radar tracking ship. The helicopters again were manned by Marine Air Group 26, a veteran recovery unit.[8]

Some innovations were added to the recovery plans as a result of experience gained in the MR-2 chimpanzee flight. For one thing, there was still the possibility that *Freedom 7* might overshoot its landing target, in which case the time factor could be vital. Obviously a highly mobile unit was desirable. Walter Williams, operations director, requested an amphibian SA-16 aircraft with a pararescue team as an emergency rescue measure. Two such teams were provided, adding the support of the Air Rescue Service and Navy frogmen to Project Mercury.

A second change involved communications. When the spacecraft was near impact it passed below the radio horizon; Williams reminded the Air Force Missile Test Center commander that continuous voice communications with the astronaut in the final moments of flight and after impact required a communications relay plane. The Air Force assigned a communications aircraft, code-named Cardfile 23, to the mission.[9]

The helicopter recovery technique was perfected late during the astronaut preparation period. According to the original helicopter recovery procedures, the chopper would lift the spacecraft with the pilot inside and ferry both to the ship. John Glenn protested that the danger in this procedure to both astronaut and helicopter pilots was too great in case trouble developed during the operation. He strongly recommended further review. After much study and practice of procedures, STG decided at a conference on April 15, 1961, to use helicopters as the primary mode of recovery. The helicopter would arrive, hover over the spacecraft, and talk with the pilot by UHF. The helicopter copilot would snip off the capsule's high-frequency antenna, snare the capsule recovery loop, and raise the vehicle slightly out of the water. By this time the astronaut would be completely out of harness and the hatch would be clear of the water. Then the astronaut would open the side hatch, crawl through, and catch a second sling lowered from the helicopter. The helicopter would hoist both astronaut and spacecraft and carry them to the main recovery ship.[10]

Since a man was to be aboard this flight, another vital part of the planning activities involved weather reporting and surveillance. Beginning in June 1960, Francis W. Reichelderfer, chief of the United States Weather Bureau, had promised to Administrator Glennan and provided for the Space Task Group full meteorological support for Project Mercury. By mid-April 1961, a special weather support group, consisting of three units under Kenneth M. Nagler, was utilizing every resource of the Bureau (including the satellite *Tiros II*) to forecast the weather accurately for STG.[11]

Before MR-3, the seven-man Miami forecast unit, headed by Jesse R. Gulick, analyzed reconnaissance data on weather conditions for 200 miles beyond the planned launch and recovery areas. Weather Bureau aircraft from Miami overflew the area at altitudes of 5000 to 20,000 feet, then, three hours before launch, dipped down below 1500 feet. The flight plan followed a box pattern, with the amount of surveillance dictated by weather conditions at a particular point. The recovery ships were integrated into a weather-reporting mission, making reports at assigned times and providing special surface observations, such as sea state and wind velocity, at the critical time near launch. Weather observers at the launch site also kept a careful watch on air and seawater temperatures, relative humidity, cloud cover, and winds.[12]

As the flight date neared, STG personnel briefed the ship crews of the recovery force. Martin A. Byrnes, Robert Thompson, and Charles I. Tynan, Jr., of STG found the naval crews not wholly trained in the specifics of this particular mission. So they immediately initiated a brief education program, giving talks, providing reading material, and showing motion pictures of the MR–2 chimpanzee flight. Tynan also carefully briefed each man charged with capsule-handling duties on his particular role. To cradle the recovered capsule the Navy had constructed 20-by-25-foot dollies and topped them with old mattresses. Then aeromedical teams arrived, prepared sick bay areas, and briefed the ships' medical personnel. After one medical group found that two members of one of the destroyers had recently contracted hepatitis, the crew members of that ship were barred from donating blood, even in an emergency. Byrnes, who felt that the recovery-force briefings should become standard procedure for succeeding flights, said that the Navy was pleased with the pep talks.[13]

Last-Minute Qualms

While the entire NASA program was under review by the new Administration in Washington early in 1961, Project Mercury was nearing its manned space flight phase. During the first four months of the year the major discussion would center around a proposed acceleration of the entire United States' space program to include a lunar-landing mission. Conversely, the Mercury program in the same time frame came under direct scrutiny of the President's Science Advisory Committee (PSAC), which was charged with reviewing the scientific contents of all major Federal projects. Some members of PSAC were not fully satisfied that Project Mercury was all it should be, particularly with regard to the reliability of the Redstone and Atlas boosters and to the novel life-science hazards.

The Mercury-Atlas and Mercury-Redstone failures of the year before, as was made evident in the January 1961 report of the President-elect's Space Task Force under the leadership of Jerome B. Wiesner, had not helped build the confidence of physical and life scientists that Mercury was truly a man-rated program. An ad hoc Mercury panel was created by PSAC to delve into the scientific details and reliability of the overall Mercury system and advise the President if it appeared likely that the United States would be beset with another well-publicized but inexplicable failure. Basically, the PSAC panel sought to investigate the level of risk involved in Mercury before a man was to be committed to an actual space flight. This inquiry was penetrating. Panel members spent five days in March visiting McDonnell, Space Task Group, and Cape Canaveral, receiving a series of detailed briefings and interviews. Several medical uncertainties appeared outstanding and worrisome, although the panel had found the NASA presentations to be frank, competent, and impressive.

The scientific objective of Mercury in determining the effects of weightlessness upon man, some felt, might have been pursued in a more clinical manner. Before the first manned flight there might have been a greater number of animal flights progressing toward absolute physiological and psychological limits. Past Mercury flight tests appeared more systematic for hardware engineering than for medical problems. As a case in point, it was noted by the panel members that the MR-2 mission had demonstrated excessive vibration and overacceleration in the launch phase, so that an additional booster test flight (MR-BD) had been inserted to precede the first manned suborbital flight. Pilots in the X-15 rocket research airplane, as well as Ham, the "space chimp" aboard MR-2, had recorded surprisingly high pulse rates concurrently with low blood pressures, yet there were no plans to include a blood-pressure measuring device in the upcoming manned flight (efforts to develop such a device were as yet unsuccessful). In addition, the panel members learned that Ham had taken his turn on the centrifuge, but that the acceleration profiles had no precise correlation with stresses and forces of those predicted for the MR-2 mission.

Despite these gnawing medical doubts, in general the PSAC panel members felt that the Mercury hardware and its reliability had been developed with great care. They were especially impressed with the redundant systems of the spacecraft, as well as the procedures and devices that had been integrated to assure pilot safety during launch. In fact, several panel members stated at STG that it seemed everything necessary to assure pilot survival had been considered.

In their final analysis, the PSAC panel assessed all risks and agreed that Mercury was ready to fly a man. The scientific purpose indeed was to determine man's suitability for the stresses and weightlessness associated with space flight.[14]

The orbital flight of Yuri Gagarin on April 12 seems to have removed any lingering medical qualms about manned flight. Mercury Director Gilruth had full confidence in the Space Task Group physicians and their endorsement by the space medicine community long before *Vostok I*. W. Randolph Lovelace II, Brigadier General Don D. Flickinger, and others familiar with the medical stresses of flight likewise had been convinced that pilot safety was fully assured. Yet if the medical profession as a whole had voiced scientific opposition to manned flight in Mercury, or if *Vostok I* had not flown when it did, it would have been impossible to proceed with a man in MR-3 immediately.[15]

Centrifuge tests of the astronaut's couch continued to raise NASA confidence in the adequacy of Mercury systems to maintain an astronaut's safety under acceleration into and deceleration from the space environment. But the abrupt negative acceleration of the final impact on Earth remained a nagging worry, particularly in case of a land landing. The aluminum honeycomb shock-attenuation material under the couch had been bought as insurance, but was it enough? Continued experiments early in 1961 at Wright-Patterson Air Force Base, Ohio, were conducted to determine how rapidly one could stop, facing aft in the semi-supine position, without exceeding human tolerance. These tests showed that forces up to 35 times a person's weight could be endured for a fraction of a second. But the volunteers so tested were momentarily stunned. In theory, this meant that a spacecraft could land without an impact bag, but the idea of having a "slightly stunned" astronaut in what should be made a routine operation was unacceptable. So STG had reassigned the development of a suitable impact bag system to Jack A. Kinzler's technical services team and to Rodney G. Rose and Peter J. Armitage. These men worked around the clock in March and April trying to perfect a seaworthy shock-absorber. All other pilot-safety systems were ready for a safe and successful flight.[16]

Barely a month had passed after the three chosen astronauts began training for MR–3 when the press began speculating as to which one would make the flight. On March 25, John Glenn became the favorite contender, although one report added that there was plenty of betting on Grissom, since the Air Force had been designated by the Defense Department to manage and conduct military space missions. This intimation of service competition spread quickly. Some newspapers even implied that the Army and Navy strongly suspected the Air Force had leaked Glenn's name to embarrass NASA and reduce his chances.[17]

The astronauts themselves watched all these conjectures with amusement, keeping tight the secret knowledge of their order of succession. According to Voas, their psychologist and training officer, there was only one thing that terrified all seven: the fear that something might prevent one of them from flying his own mission when the time came.[18]

Speculation on the designated pilot abated shortly after Robert C. Seamans, Jr., third in command at NASA Headquarters, appeared before the House Science and Astronautics Committee and testified that each astronaut would have his flight training opportunity aboard a Mercury-Redstone at six-week intervals. Gilruth had, of course, long since decided on an order of preference among the three astronauts designated, and had informed them of it, but everyone kept the secret well because of the everpresent likelihood of unforeseen changes.[19]

Toward the end of April there was so much publicity that some Senators, among them Republican John J. Williams of Delaware and Democrat J. W. Fulbright of Arkansas, thought the flight should be postponed and then conducted in secret lest it become a well-publicized failure. This was not the general view in Congress, however. Most members, while aware of the danger of too much publicity, felt tradition required the press to have free access to events of such magnitude as the first American manned space flight. Besides, the Russians had received international criticism for conducting an ultra-secret space program.

While many highly placed officials, several close to President Kennedy, were apprehensive about the possibility of an overly publicized fiasco, others pressed to get the manned space flight program moving. On March 22, at a White House meeting, Hugh L. Dryden had explained to the President that no unwarranted risks would be involved in the first manned Mercury flight, and that the decision to "go" was that of the project management best qualified to assess the operational hazards. When the notion was raised in late April that MR–3 should be postponed until all possible hazards had been removed, Edward C. Welsh, Executive Secretary of the National Aeronautics and Space Council, observed to the President, "Why postpone a success?"

President Kennedy wanted to be assured of a much better than average chance for success and asked for these assurances almost until launch. On the day preceding the flight, the President's personal secretary, Evelyn Lincoln, called NASA Headquarters Public Information Officer Paul P. Haney at the MR–3 News Center in Cocoa Beach, Florida. She said the President wanted to review television coverage plans. Live coverage was to begin two minutes before launch. After some delay, Mrs. Lincoln said the President had asked Press Secretary Pierre Salinger to handle the call. Salinger said the President was concerned over the reliability of the escape system in the event of a Redstone malfunction. Haney reviewed the history of the launch escape system for the President's office and Salinger said the information should satisfy the President's inquiry.[20]

Cancellation of the flight on Tuesday, May 2, because of inclement weather, forced a recycle of the systems countdown for a 48-hour period. On Thursday unfavorable weather again prevented the launch. Countdown did begin, however, for a Friday launch.[21]

As it happened, the press and public learned the MR–3 astronaut's identity only after the countdown had been canceled, 2 hours and 20 minutes before launch, on May 2. Shepard had been waiting in Hangar S in his pressure suit ready to go for more than 3 hours. Gilruth reaffirmed his prime pilot decision a day before the scheduled launch, basing Shepard's selection on advice from his medical, training, and technical assistants.[22] But he had withheld his announcement because of the chance for a last-minute change.

The American public participated vicariously in the experiment. For the first time, the maiden flight of a revolutionary manned vehicle, climaxing years of research and development, was open wide to public view. Only a handful of spectators saw the Wright Brothers accomplish man's first powered flight in 1903. In many parts of the country and the world, people accepted that event only years afterward. But for the American taxpayers' first manned space flight, NASA arranged procedures well in advance to enable all domestic news media and foreign news services to view and report the events surrounding MR–3. By April 24, some 350 correspondents were registered. As a result of their activities, the dateline "Cape Canaveral" soon became familiar to all the world. Radio and television coverage was equally energetic; telecasts originating at the Cape, particularly on May 5, were enthralling.[23]

Starting at 8:30 p.m. on May 4, the countdown proceeded without a hitch. Around midnight a built-in hold was called for the purpose of installing the pyrotechnics, servicing the hydrogen peroxide system, and allowing the operations team some rest. The countdown was resumed in the early morning hours of May 5, and another intended hold occurred some two and a half hours before the 7 a.m. anticipated launch to assure that spacecraft checkout was complete before transporting the astronaut to the pad area.

Shepard, awakened at 1:10 a.m., began an unhurried but precise routine involving a shower and a shave. With his physician, William K. Douglas, his understudy, John Glenn, and a few other members of the operational team, he sat down to a breakfast consisting of orange juice, a filet mignon wrapped in bacon, and some scrambled eggs. Shepard had begun a low-residue diet three days before the anticipated launch. At 2:40 a.m. he received a physical examination. This was followed by the placement of biosensors at points indicated by tattoo marks on his body. He was now ready for Joe W. Schmitt, an STG suit technician, to assist him in donning the pressure suit.[21]

Shepard entered the transfer van at 3:55 a.m. In the van, on the way to the pad, he lay on a couch while technicians purged his suit with oxygen. When the van arrived at the pad, Schmitt began to attach the astronaut's gloves while Gordon Cooper briefed him on the launch status.

At 5:15 a.m. Shepard, carrying his portable air conditioner, ascended the gantry, and five minutes later he entered the spacecraft. If everything went well, he had two hours and five minutes to wait before liftoff. While Shepard was preparing to lower himself into the couch, his right foot slipped off the right elbow support. But he eased himself into position without further difficulty.

Schmitt fastened the harness and helped with the hose connections. Then he solemnly shook the spaceman's gloved hand. "Happy landings, Commander!" chorused the gantry crew.

For Alan Shepard, this was the most dramatic moment of his 37 years, a moment he would recall with the most acute poignancy for the rest of his life. Afterward he told how his heart quickened as the hatch was closed.

The sensation was brief; his heartbeat soon returned to normal. At 6:25 a.m. he began a denitrogenation procedure by breathing pure oxygen. This was to prevent aeroembolism, or decompression sickness, the airman's equivalent of the deep-sea diver's bends.[25]

Now the countdown resumed.

At 15 minutes before launch the sky became slightly overcast, so photographic conditions were below par. Weathermen said the conditions would clear in 35 to 40 minutes, and a hold was called. Shepard became resigned to this hold and relaxed by peering through the periscope. He was not uncomfortable, because he was able to shift his body in the couch. Telemetered biomedical data confirmed that his condition was good. While waiting for the clouds to clear away, a hold was called to replace a 115-volt, 400-cycle inverter in the electrical system of the launch vehicle. This hold lasted for 52 minutes, after which the count was recycled to 35 minutes before launch.

351

At the 15-minute point, one of the Goddard IBM 7090 computers in Maryland was found to be in error. Making this correction required a complete computer recheck-run. After a total hold time of two hours and 34 minutes, the count continued and progressed without more trouble. Shepard had been in the capsule four hours and 14 minutes when the final seconds ticked off to liftoff.[26]

Two minutes before the launch, voice communications between the astronaut and the operations team switched from Cooper in the blockhouse to Donald K. Slayton in the Mercury Control Center. From that point until launch, the "talk" was continuous as each panel monitor advised Slayton of his system's status for relay to Shepard. To the astronaut the monitors seemed slow in reporting the go condition, and this he attributed to his own eagerness to be off. Schirra was now circling above in his F–106 chase plane, waiting to follow the Redstone and Shepard as high as he could. Because of his excitement, Shepard said he failed to hear much of the closing countdown, with the exception of the firing command. During this period his pulse rate rose from 80 per minute to 126 at the liftoff signal. This rise caused no medical concern, for it was about the same as that of an automobile driver moving out from a service road to a freeway crowded with heavy traffic. Shepard was not alone in his excitement; he was joined by the operations team, the press corps at the Cape, and millions of people viewing the liftoff on television.[27]

Shepard's Ride

Shepard saw the umbilical cable supplying prelaunch electrical power to the Mercury-Redstone and its supporting boom fall away. He raised his hand to start the elapsed-time clock that ticked off the seconds of the flight. The onboard camera, clicking at six frames per second, confirmed his alertness as the MR–3 combination roared and began to climb. He was surprised by the smoothness of the liftoff and the clearness of Slayton's voice in Mercury Control. All his transmissions were acknowledged without requests for repeat. The ride continued smoothly for about 45 seconds; then the rocket, capsule, and astronaut began vibrating. Conditioned to these circumstances, Shepard realized that he was passing through the transonic speed zone, where turbulence built up. The buffeting became rugged at the point of maximum aerodynamic pressures, about 88 seconds after liftoff; Shepard's head and helmet were bouncing so hard that he could not read his panel dials. Sound levels were noticeably higher at that point but still not uncomfortable. Shortly thereafter both the noise and the vibration abated. Now enjoying a much smoother ride, Shepard told Slayton that the dial-scanning procedure he was supposed to follow was impractical. He had to omit reading the electrical power dials to pay more attention to his oxygen and hydrogen peroxide supply indicators.

The cabin pressure inside *Freedom 7* sealed off at 5.5 pounds per square inch,

352

as programmed. Pressed by 6 g at two minutes after launch, Shepard still was able to report "all systems go." The Redstone's engine shut down on schedule at 142 seconds, having accelerated the astronaut to a velocity of 5134 miles per hour, close to the nominal speed. The trajectory, similar to that of the MR–BD flight, was only one degree off course, which meant a variation of slightly more than a mile in peak altitude. After engine cutoff, Shepard heard the tower-jettison rocket fire and turned his head to peer out the port, hoping that he might see the smoke from the pyrotechnics. There was no smoke, but the green tower-jettison light on his panel assured him that the pylon was gone. Shepard strained in his couch under an acceleration that hit a peak g load of 6.3. Outside the capsule the shingle temperature reached 220 degrees F, but inside the cabin the temperature was only 91 degrees. The astronaut was hardly perspiring in his pressure suit at 75 degrees.

After tower separation, which occurred two minutes and 32 seconds after launch, Shepard disarmed the retrorocket-jettison switch and advised Slayton that his capsule was free from the booster. At three minutes the automatic attitude control system about-faced the capsule to a heatshield-forward position for the remainder of the flight. Momentary oscillations climaxed the turnaround maneuver, whereupon the automatic thrusters cut in for five seconds to steady, or "damp," the capsule into its proper attitude. Now almost at the top of his suborbital trajectory, Shepard went to work on his most important task, determining whether an astronaut could control his spacecraft's attitude.

He began to switch the control system to manual, one axis at a time. First he took over pitch, which he was able to adjust by moving the handcontroller in his right grip forward or backward to give the spacecraft the proper up or down attitude. His first action was to position the spacecraft in the retrofire attitude, tilted 34 degrees above a local horizontal mark. The pitch indicator on *Freedom 7* was scribed at 45 degrees, as earlier studies had proposed, but more recent investigations had indicated that 34 degrees was a better angle.

While Shepard was in control of pitch, the automatic system was controlling yaw, or left and right motion, and roll, or revolving motions. When Shepard assumed control of all three axes, he was pleased to find that the feel was about the same as in the procedures trainer, the Mercury simulator. Although he could control his ship well, he was unable to hear the spurting control jets above the noise of his radio. He encountered one small problem while using his hand-controller: when he moved his hand to yaw, the wrist seal bearing of his suit bumped into his personal parachute. To make the proper displacement, he had to push hard.[28]

When he tried to carry out another of his flight objectives, observing the scene below him, Shepard immediately noticed that the periscope had the medium gray filter in place. While waiting on the pad, he had used this filter to eliminate the glare of the intermittently bright sunlight and had planned to remove the filter when he retracted the periscope, just before launch. But being otherwise

*Sensors are attached
to Shepard by
William K. Douglas*

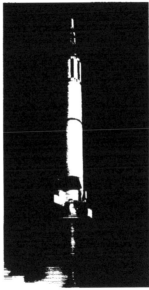

*Launch of
Freedom 7*

**Flight of
Freedom 7
May 5, 1961**

Astronaut recovery

*Astronaut and
spacecraft
safely aboard
the carrier*

occupied at the time, he had forgotten to make the change. During spacecraft turnaround he tried to remove the filter, but as he reached for the filter knob the pressure gauge on his left wrist banged into the abort handle. He carefully pulled his hand away. After that he forgot about the intensity filter and observed the wondrous sights below through the gray slide. He first tried to estimate the span of his terrestrial vision. The periscope, located two feet in front of him, had two settings, low and high magnification. On low at the 100-mile altitude, there theoretically should have been a field view of about 1900 miles in diameter, and on high, a segment 80 miles in diameter. Shepard was able to distinguish clearly the continental land masses from the cloud masses. He first reported seeing the outlines of the west coast of Florida and the Gulf of Mexico. He saw Lake Okeechobee, in the central part of Florida, but could not see any city. Andros Island and the Bahamas also appeared in the scope. Later Shepard would remark that Earth displays flashed before him in his air-lubricated free-axis trainer had been most valuable in helping him to distinguish land masses passing beneath the spacecraft.

As Shepard sped over the peak of his trajectory, now under fully automatic attitude control, he began to notice a slow pitch rate. At this point his flight plan dictated that he switch to the fly-by-wire mode of operation, wherein the astronaut operated the handcontroller to change the position of the capsule, using the hydrogen peroxide jets of the automatic system to effect the changes rather than those of the manual system. Thus Shepard would manually position *Freedom 7* for the retrofire that was scheduled to occur shortly after attaining the zenith of his trajectory at 116.5 miles. The astronaut switched to fly-by-wire, but as he started to make a yaw and roll maneuver he noticed that the spacecraft pitch position was low, being 20 to 25 degrees rather than the desired 34 degrees for retrofire attitude. Although he could not remember exactly whether he made a yaw or roll maneuver, he did immediately begin to work on his pitch problem. Then the retrorockets fired, creating a noise that was easily heard but was not as loud as the sound of the ALFA trainer jets. This provided what later astronauts on orbital missions described as "a comforting kick in the pants." Pieces of debris, including a restraining strap, flashed by the capsule portholes as the retropack was jettisoned. Glancing back to the control panel, Shepard saw no confirming sequence light, but Slayton radioed his telemetered knowledge of retropack jettison. So the astronaut pushed the manual override; finally the reluctant light appeared. This was the only failure of an event-sequence light during the MR–3 mission.

While riding down the reentry curve toward a water landing, Shepard again assumed the fly-by-wire mode of control. He later reported that the feel of fly-by-wire was very similar to that of the trainers. Although he had a tendency to overcontrol in the fly-by-wire mode, he had the pleasant feeling of being in full command, for a few minutes at least, of his spacecraft's attitude. Then Shepard allowed the automatic system to regain control and stabilize the spacecraft for reentry. The periscope automatically retracted when *Freedom 7* began its plummet into Earth's atmosphere.

On the way down, Shepard tried to look out the awkwardly placed ports to observe the stars. He saw nothing, not even the horizon. These futile attempts at star-finding got him behind in his work. As he commented later, this was the only time during the flight when he did not feel "on top" of the situation and ready for anything. The feeling of indecision passed quickly. He immediately reported when the .05-g light came on, the indication that the g-load buildup was about to commence. He was surprised that the light flashed and zero g ended about a minute ahead of the time he had come to expect from his simulated experience in the procedures trainer. As the reentry loads began to build up to a peak of 11.6 g, the oscillations also increased moderately. As soon as the highest g point had passed and the spacecraft had steadied, Shepard left fly-by-wire and cut in the automatic control system.

Shepard was supposed to give an altimeter reading between 80,000 and 90,000 feet, but since his rate of descent was faster than he expected, he became worried over the deployment of the drogue parachute and forgot to report his altitude. As the altimeter dial slipped past 40,000 feet, the astronaut braced and listened closely for the drogue mortar to fire. He gave the Cape a reading of 30,000 feet, and 9000 feet later the drogue snapped out without a kick. Once his fall was broken the periscope extended, giving a view of the trailing and reassuring drogue. The opening of the air-inlet snorkel valve to accept ambient air pressure at 15,000 feet struck Shepard as coming a trifle late. The antenna canister atop the spacecraft blew off as planned at 10,000 feet, pulling the main parachute with it. Shepard clearly saw and felt it in its initial reefed and partially unfurled condition, which prevented the lines from snapping. Within seconds it spread to its 63-foot diameter, giving the astronaut a reassuring jolt, but one considerably less violent than he had received in centrifuge simulated training. "I was delighted to see it," Shepard remarked with considerable understatement. And well he might be, for at that stage of the flight most of the critical moments had passed. *Freedom 7* had closely followed its assigned trajectory and the recovery forces were standing by for its pickup.

Falling toward the water at a rate of 35 feet per second, in contrast to the maximum rate of 6550 feet per second during the powered phase of the flight, Shepard pushed the switch to dump the remaining hydrogen peroxide fuel. Glancing at the dials, he noted another green light, indicating that the landing bag with its four-foot impact skirt had dropped down to cushion the water landing. He reported to the Cape that everything was in order before *Freedom 7* dropped below the radio horizon.

The astronaut used the brief remaining time before impact to remove his knee straps, open the faceplate shield, and remove the hose connections of his pressure suit. Then came the thud of water impact, comparable to landing an aircraft on a carrier. *Freedom 7* splashed and listed over into the water on the astronaut's right side, about 60 degrees from an upright position. The chutes cast loose automatically on impact to prevent dragging. As the water sloshed over the ports, the spaceman saw the fluorescein dye spreading over an ever-increasing area. Shepard quickly checked the spacecraft interior to see if any leaks had resulted from impact. There were none; it was dry. Now slowly *Freedom 7* came to an upright position, taking about a minute's time, and Shepard jubilantly reported to Cardfile 23, the communications airplane, that he was all right.

Helicopters of Marine Air Force Group 26 were waiting. Wayne E. Koons and George F. Cox, pilot and copilot, respectively, of the primary helicopter, had watched the spacecraft for about five minutes on its descent. After splashdown, Koons quickly maneuvered his chopper into position for the retrieval exercise. Glancing at *Freedom 7*, Cox noted that the high-frequency antenna was not in its correct position as he hooked the cable through the recovery loop. Koons maneuvered the helicopter to lift the spacecraft partially out of the water, awaiting pilot egress. All of a sudden the high-frequency antenna pronged upward, hit and dented the bottom of the helicopter, and broke off. But no damage was done; Shepard told Koons he would debark as soon as *Freedom 7*'s hatch cleared the water.

While Shepard worked himself into a sitting posture, Koons asked again if he was ready. Not yet, he replied; he was still removing his restraint harness and he could still see water against the ports. So the chopper raised the spacecraft further and Shepard unlocked the hatch.

The astronaut then wormed his way over the hatch sill and grappled for his "horse collar" hoisting sling. He soon grasped the line and fitted the sling under his arms. On the way up he brushed against the remainder of the high-frequency antenna, but it was flexible and did no harm. The hovering chopper had no difficulty getting Shepard aboard and in lifting *Freedom 7* from the water and transporting it to the carrier *Lake Champlain*. When Shepard finally stepped on the carrier's deck, only 11 minutes had elapsed since the water landing. About half an hour after he had begun his free-dictation report, Shepard was called to the flag bridge to answer an unexpected telephone call from President Kennedy, who had watched the launching and followed flight details closely via television and who now congratulated the astronaut on his flight into space.[29]

Aboard the *Lake Champlain*, the immediate task was determining what shape Shepard was in after that brief but awesome excursion through space, with its accompanying high acceleration load, weightlessness, and deceleration loads. Some physiologists had feared that even a few minutes of weightlessness could cause disorientation, while some psychologists were equally apprehensive about what would happen to a space passenger's mind. But Shepard reported that he found his five minutes of weightlessness quite pleasant. In fact, he said, he was already in the weightless state before he realized it. For evidence, he cited a washer that had floated beside his left ear. The weightless Shepard had grabbed for the weightless washer—and missed. Anticipating his debriefing, the astronaut had used an analogy from his professional experience to describe his sensations. The best comparison in his memory was riding in the back seat of an F–100F airplane. "It was painless," he said, "just a pleasant ride." As for any other effects of weightlessness and g stresses, Shepard had demonstrated by assuming direct pilot control that man was quite capable of functioning in space. He experienced no impairment of his faculties. He had reported to Mercury Control with perfect clarity regarding his and the spacecraft's status, and when two physicians, M. Jerome Strong and Robert Laning, made a preliminary postflight physical examination of Shepard aboard the carrier, they found him to be in excellent condition. From beginning to end the flight mission had been almost perfect. The jubilant but technically perfectionist engineers called it only an "unqualified success." [30]

Now there remained no possible doubt that man could function intelligently aboard the Mercury spacecraft and with relative safety in a true space environment for 15 minutes. What of the primitive spacecraft that he had inhabited? How well did it perform? The answer seemed to be, very well indeed. But could its systems be trusted to work under even more demanding conditions in orbital flights? Had all the flight preparations been adequate? These were only a few of the questions that the returning astronaut would have to answer, if only partially and indirectly, at the seemingly interminable debriefings.

BRIEFING THE BRIEFERS

The initial postflight period of debriefing, held aboard the recovery ship, included a medical examination and free dictation by the astronaut of his flight impressions. This was followed by a short debriefing questionnaire. From the ship, the astronaut was taken to Grand Bahama Island for an exhaustive two-day debriefing by medical and technical personnel. This session used a prepared list of questions. Interrogations were led by Carmault B. Jackson on medical matters, by Robert Voas on pilot activities and performance, and by Harold I. Johnson and Sigurd A. Sjoberg on systems performance. Some 32 specialists joined in the Grand Bahama debriefing, including program managers, operations physicians, engineers, photographers, and public relations personnel.

Astronaut Shepard arrives at Grand Bahama Island for medical and flight debriefing following his flight in Freedom 7. *He is flanked by (left to right) Slayton, Keith Lyndell, and Grissom.*

His pressure suit, Shepard said, was generally comfortable and allowed sufficient mobility, but the left wrist pressure gauge was difficult to see during acceleration. It should be moved, perhaps to the knee. And there was a circulation problem caused by the rubber cots at the ends of his gloved fingers, which meant he had to keep drawing his fingers back inside the gloves to maintain comfort. The helmet was satisfactory. Shepard had obtained an enlarged faceplate for his own helmet to gain better vision. He had no complaints against the couch or restraint harness. He remembered only minor pressure points from the couch while waiting on the pad. The straps around his shoulders had seemed tight at times before launch, but slight shrugs had relieved the tension and stimulated circulation.

The biosensors caused some skin irritation for Shepard, as they had for others in the Mercury program, both astronauts and test subjects. Better adhesives were promised. Throughout the mission the suit temperature and humidity had been quite comfortable, Shepard reported. During the hours while he was waiting on the pad he was able to maintain a suit reading of 75 degrees, although this rose to 77 degrees a minute or two before liftoff. His suit temperature dropped back to 74.5 degrees for most of the flight, with a brief rise to 82 degrees during reentry. Just before the loss of contact as the spacecraft dropped below the radio horizon, his suit temperature dropped to 77 degrees. Then, in the capsule awaiting pickup, Shepard experienced the hottest part of the mission. When Byrnes suggested that ventilation procedures should be improved, Shepard remarked that he could have obtained some relief by simply unzipping his suit.[31]

Other parts of the environmental control system also worked satisfactorily. The cabin temperature inside *Freedom 7* stayed within a tolerable range from 92 to 100 degrees. Only part of one of the two four-pound bottles of oxygen aboard had been needed. The drain on the coolant supply had been slight.

The engineers among the debriefing team quizzed Shepard about the whole of the spacecraft attitude control systems, but especially about the workings of manual control. According to the flight plan, Shepard was to exercise three modes of control—automatic, manual, and the fly-by-wire combination of the two. He reported that the manual mode was quite responsive and felt the same as the manual mode in the procedures trainers. There seemed to be a tendency for the spacecraft to roll slightly clockwise while in the manual control. Postflight inspectors found a small piece of debris lodged in the hydrogen peroxide tubing, which probably caused the jets to leak a tiny increment of thrust. Near the six-minute point in the flight, according to plan, Shepard was supposed to switch to the fly-by-wire mode of control. Apparently he forgot to turn off the manual valve, so the capsule's attitude control system sucked fuel from both manual and automatic tanks. The debriefing interrogators asked him whether he got more control than desired; he replied that rate changes seemed high but that he thought this was caused by microswitch positions rather than the addition of manual-proportional fuel. Shepard could not recall for certain whether he had turned off the manual valve; telemetry data monitoring the spacecraft movements and countermovements indicated that he had not.

The accessory rockets and pyrotechnics on the capsule performed adequately during the *Freedom 7* mission, each sequence firing on time and as designed. One exception was a secondary escape-tower jettison rocket, which was later disassembled and found to have ignited by manual pull-ring actuation. Since Shepard did not remember whether or not he pulled that ring, how the rocket fired remained a mystery. It was known that this backup component had not been used to separate the escape tower from the spacecraft. Otherwise the capsule rocketry had performed flawlessly. The posigrades effected spacecraft separation, the three retrograde rockets ripple-fired to provide a 510-feet-per-second velocity decrement, and the drogue parachute mortar discharged correctly. The green sequence lights appeared on Shepard's panel with heartwarming regularity except for the retropack jettison indicator.

At impact the landing bag had performed as designed to cushion the shock, but one heat sink stud did pierce the fiber-glass protective shield. While the pressure vessel was undamaged, recovery had been too rapid for the seaworthiness of the impact bag to be tested. Several rips observed in the impact skirt aboard the carrier apparently occurred during postflight handling rather than at impact or by bobbing in the water.

In general the radio communications during flight had been extremely clear. Slayton, the Mercury Control Center capsule communicator ("Cap Com"), said Shepard's voice transmissions were slightly garbled at liftoff but that seconds later the quality improved markedly. Using the ultra-high-frequency system, Slayton was able to maintain crisp contact with *Freedom 7*. Shepard and Slayton stayed on UHF, using the Cape antenna, but then as distance increased, voice communications deteriorated. In Mercury Control Center the communications technician monitoring the Grand Bahama Island antenna reception switched Slayton onto a relay from Bahama, and Shepard came in loud and clear once again. Slayton and Shepard communicated well with each other until main parachute deployment. The Mercury Control Center communicator then tried unsuccessfully to use Cardfile 23, the communications relay airplane. Having lost contact with Cap Com, Shepard had expected the recovery forces to garble the radio in competition to talk with him, but circuit discipline was businesslike both before and after countdown.[32]

PRECIPITATION FROM MR–3

The ¹"unqualified" success of the Shepard suborbital flight brought immense joy and satisfaction to the managers, engineers, associates, and astronauts of the Space Task Group. They had labored almost two and a half years for this first triumph. Flight failures, schedule slippages, press criticism, and most recently the U.S.S.R.'s attainment of the first orbital flight, all had tempered the pride of the Mercury team. But May 5, 1961, saw the Nation rejoice with relief and pleasure in the success and safety of Alan Shepard. President Kennedy's shore-to-ship radio telephone call to the astronaut was spontaneous, though difficult to link, and symbolic of the American mood that day. Although the seven-member corps of astronauts had combat records and test-pilot experience to their credit, one of them at last was truly a hero and not just a celebrity.

In the aftermath of the flight of *Freedom 7*, Gilruth once again published a morale memorandum for his staff. This time the subject was not a single favorable newspaper article, as had been the case of a story by Los Angeles newspaperman Marvin Miles the year before, but a compilation of formal congratulations to Alan Shepard from individuals in various walks of life, including the King of Morocco and a group of scientists in Peru.[33]

At the postflight press conference, Admiral Hilles quipped that the space race had turned into a world series played with a space ball, and that the Navy, naturally, had "caught the crucial fly." But the much more impressive Gagarin flight tempered everyone's pride but the Soviets'. What most enhanced the United States' prestige was not the technical prowess exhibited by MR–3 but the contrast between the open-door policy toward news coverage of its flight and the impenetrable secrecy surrounding the Soviet program.

One result of all this publicity was a widespread skepticism toward the space claims of the U.S.S.R. Many people around the world questioned whether a Red cosmonaut had flown at all. An Istanbul newspaper called *Millyet*, for example, reported that Turkish journalists, after viewing official films of both Shepard's and Gagarin's flights, asked of the Soviet consul general, "In the Shepard film we followed all phases of his flight, but in yours we followed only Khrushchev. Why don't you show us your space flight, too?" A Tass correspondent, replying for the consul general, was quoted as having explained, "We are mainly interested in the people's excitement and reaction. This is what we wanted you to see." [34] Premier Nikita Khrushchev was supposed to have been much chagrined because the "up and down" flight of Shepard gained such extensive media publicity even though Gagarin had long since orbited the world.

Although NASA had kept a few secrets—such as ground-control command frequencies and persisting classifications of old military data—the agency made reasonable efforts to cooperate with newsmen.

President Kennedy presents the NASA Distinguished Service Medal to Astronaut Shepard in the White House Rose Garden. They are flanked by the other astronauts and Administrator Webb.

The President awarded NASA's Distinguished Service Medal to Alan Shepard in a Rose Garden ceremony at the White House on May 8. Although little notice was given, crowds of people lined Pennsylvania Avenue, cheering the veteran Navy pilot and new spaceman as he rode to the Capitol for lunch and back. Here and abroad, millions of people later filed by an itinerant NASA display to inspect *Freedom 7* at close hand. Members of Congress sensed a formidable change in the public's attitude toward the space program. In place of widespread apathy or lack of understanding toward space exploration, many of their constitutents now seemed aware of the meaning of the adventures into the space void. Congressmen who had been reviewing manned space flight plans and proposals since early April began thinking about increased allocations of national resources, such as scientific manpower, for future manned space exploration.

On May 25, 1961, President Kennedy presented a special message to Congress on "urgent national needs." At one point he spoke of space and of Shepard:

> Now is the time to take longer strides—time for a great new American enterprise—time for this nation to take a clearly leading role in space achievement, which in many ways may hold the key to our future on earth.
>
> I believe we possess all the resources and talents necessary. But the facts of the matter are that we have never made the national decision or marshalled the national resources required for such leadership. We have never specified long-range goals on an urgent time schedule, or managed our resources and our time so as to insure their fulfillment.
>
> Recognizing the head start obtained by the Soviets with their large rocket engines . . . and recognizing the likelihood that they will exploit this lead for some time to come in still more impressive successes, we nevertheless are required to make new efforts on our own. For while we cannot guarantee that we shall one day be first, we can guarantee that any failure to make this effort will make us last. We take an additional risk by making it in full view of the world, but as shown by the feat of Astronaut Shepard, this very risk enhances our stature when we are successful. . . .
>
> I believe this nation should commit itself to achieving the goal, before this decade is out, of landing a man on the moon and returning him safely to the earth. No single space project in this period will be more impressive to mankind, or more important for the long-range exploration of space; and none will be so difficult or expensive to accomplish.[35]

The Congress, believing that the American people were also ready to support an expanded and ambitious long-term space exploration program, quickly endorsed these words of leadership from President Kennedy. Project Apollo shifted from a circumlunar expedition plan to a lunar landing endeavor, to be achieved before 1970, or "before this decade is out."

All through March, April, and May, members of the space committees of the Senate and the House busily quizzed James E. Webb, Dryden, Seamans, and other leaders of NASA about the implications of the Russian program and about how the planned time for the development of Apollo could be cut in half. But the appropriations debate was brief. By August 7, the Senators and Representatives had agreed on $1,671,750,000 for NASA's fiscal 1962 budget. This was the first time Congress had appropriated over a billion dollars for NASA's space program at one time. Only $113 million less than President Kennedy had requested, this billion and a half dollars was but an initial appropriation, for the legislators understood that NASA would ask for a supplement about January 1962.[36]

Thus American aspirations in space, personalized by Astronaut Shepard on May 5 and codified by President Kennedy's endorsement of NASA's follow-on plans on May 25, 1961, gained clear direction, ample funds, and official sanction. The national mood for space had definitely changed from what it had been at the uncertain beginning of the Kennedy administration. A goal of developing space technology for space exploration was a tangible means to "get the country moving again."

Industries born of the frantic missile race of the mid-fifties would turn more and more to space-related research and development. Unlike military technology, such products were not needed in quantity; reliable performance was their highest criterion. Whereas Project Mercury, toward the end of its manufacturing phase in June 1961, supposedly affected approximately one out of 90 people in the United States through industrial support of some 10,000 companies, Project Apollo as redefined by NASA and approved by the President would take far more of a national effort.[37] Kennedy had promised that expanded conquest of space would be difficult and costly. But so impressive and dramatic an enterprise was Apollo, so full of engineering and gadgetry, that the project seemed made to order for a new American destiny. To President Kennedy, the United States could win an open competition with the Soviet Union in space because of the inherent superiority of an open society.

Besides its portents, the President's decision had an immediate impact on the Space Task Group, an organization that had been studying the possibilities of advanced manned flight as early as 1959. In September 1960, the Apollo projects office formally appeared on the organization chart of the Space Task Group's Flight Systems Division, indicating the fulltime status of planners for Apollo. But the day after President Kennedy's speech of May 25, Wesley L. Hjornevik, formerly Glennan's administrative assistant and now Gilruth's, signed a notice to the Space Task Group that reassured the Mercury team of a future with Apollo. New funds and facilities, if approved by Congress as expected, would certainly affect the personal lives of the Space Task Group members by the necessity to reorganize and perhaps to relocate.[38]

NASA Headquarters had recognized for some time that a center was needed to survey the whole spectrum of manned space flight programs. On January 3, 1961, the Space Task Group had at last been designated an autonomous field element, no longer to be considered a part of the Goddard Space Flight Center. The Space Task Group's personnel strength had increased to a total of 794 people in mid-1961. Until Kennedy's lunar landing decision was endorsed by the Congress, the Space Task Group had had only one responsibility, Project Mercury, and no authorization to proceed with more ambitious endeavors. The end of Project Mercury could have meant the end of the Space Task Group.

But President Kennedy's clarion message to Congress verified a new course for the Space Task Group's civil servants. Back in February 1961, Gilruth had asked his second in command, Charles J. Donlan, to begin considering the most feasible programs to succeed Project Mercury. Whatever the future programs were, they would require new, separate, functional facilities. By May a draft study was completed on how such undertakings should be managed. Entitled "Organizational Concepts and Staffing Requirements" for a "Manned Spacecraft Development Center," the study declared in its preamble:

> One of the essential elements required to implement an agressive national effort for manned space exploration is a capability within government to conceive, manage, and technically monitor the development of large manned spacecraft and to operate the spacecraft and related ground support equipment. This portion of the total job is in itself one of the largest, if not the largest research and development job ever undertaken in war or peace.
>
> The nucleus of the capability now exists in the Space Task Group, which has handled, with industry and other government resources, the Mercury Program. However, a program of the much larger magnitude now contemplated would require a substantial expansion of staff and facilities and instituting an organizational and management concept consistent with the magnitude of the program. How—and how effective—the capability is organized will have a direct bearing on the success or failure of the total program.[39]

Only a few days had elapsed after President Kennedy's call to Congress for approval of the lunar landing program when the rank and file members of the Space Task Group began to read speculations in their local Virginia newspapers about where they might have to move. Few were eager to leave the Virginia peninsula. Many were glad to stop worrying about a move to Beltsville, Maryland, but no one knew what the alternative site would be. While wives and families fretted, the men and women of the Space Task Group were busier than ever before, because the group had just entered the final manned phase of the Mercury program. In August 1961, NASA Headquarters ordered John F. Parsons, Associate Director of the Ames Research Center, to head a survey team to recommend the permanent location for a manned spacecraft center. One of the members of the Parsons team, Martin Byrnes, was subsequently assigned to study relocation programs for STG's members.[40]

Responsibilities lay heavily upon STG. It had to accelerate the Mercury program to achieve its primary objective, manned orbital flight. It should start to recruit personnel and organize activities for the newly authorized Project Apollo. And, most immediately, it must carry out the second suborbital Mercury flight as scheduled. Once the next astronaut was recovered, the operations team in concert with the Space Task Group management would have to decide just how far to carry the Mercury-Redstone suborbital program. Many of the 30 or so who had attended Shepard's postflight debriefing felt that this phase had served its purpose and that now the manned orbital phase should be initiated. This point was discussed in June but not by any means decided. From Shepard's success, however, one thing seemed clear: it was certainly not necessary to train all the astronauts on suborbital flights before trying to duplicate or triplicate Gagarin's feat.

Second Suborbital Trial

Preparation for the second suborbital flight of man into space was essentially the same as that for Shepard and *Freedom 7*. Much of the astronaut and ground support training, spacecraft checkout, and booster preparation had been accomplished concurrently with the grooming of MR-3, since the anticipated six-week interval was too short to begin anew. Thus Air Force Captain Virgil I. Grissom, told by Gilruth in January 1961 that he would probably be the pilot for Mercury-Redstone 4, and John H. Glenn, Jr., once again the suborbital backup pilot, returned to work quickly after Shepard's flight. In April all three had undergone refresher centrifuge training at Johnsville, and now they were well fortified to endure the actual Redstone acceleration profile.

Most of their training period was spent at the Cape so that Grissom and Glenn could follow the technical progress of spacecraft and launch vehicle by participating in minute checkout operations. In Hangar S the astronauts exercised themselves and all their capsule systems in the simulated high-altitude chamber tests. Their physicians recorded metabolic data and refined physiological reactions. Communication checks, manual control system checks, sequence system verifications, and many simulated missions in the procedures trainer kept them busy. Twice Grissom and Glenn went back to Langley for sessions in the ALFA trainer. In all, each simulated about 100 Mercury-Redstone flights before the upcoming MR-4 launch, scheduled for July.[41]

Spacecraft No. 11, designated since October for the second manned Mercury flight, had come off the production line at McDonnell in May 1960. As the first operational capsule with a centerline window, No. 11 more nearly approximated the orbital version of the Mercury capsule than Shepard's *Freedom 7*, or spacecraft No. 7.[42]

Among other innovations in No. 11 for MR-4 was an explosive side hatch, whose evolution, encouraged by the astronaut corps, had begun early in the Mercury program. The original egress procedure had been to climb out through the antenna compartment, a difficult maneuver that required the removal of a small pressure bulkhead. Since all the astronauts had found it hard to snake out the top of the frustum and cylinder, the STG and McDonnell designers had concluded that removal of an injured astronaut would be even more precarious. Moreover, valuable time would be lost in such a rescue

365

At left, Grissom in spacecraft check. At right, Grissom (seated inside) tests space-craft on the gantry with Guenter Wendt of McDonnell Aircraft Corporation.

MR–4
Preflight

MR-4 Mission Review Conference at the Cape: left to right, Slayton, Grissom, Kenneth M. Nagler, Warren J. North, William K. Douglas, Glenn, Shepard, Charles W. Mathews, John D. Hodge, Stanley C. White, and Christopher C. Kraft, Jr.

operation; to open the hatch from the outside, someone had to remove several shingles and 70 bolts.

McDonnell engineers set to work on the problem and came up with two egress hatch models—one with a latch, which was used on Ham's MR-2 and Shepard's MR-3 missions, the other with an explosive hatch cover. The simple latch mechanism weighed 69 pounds, too much of a weight addition for incorporation in the orbital version of the spacecraft. The explosive hatch, on the other hand, utilized the 70 bolts of the original design; a .06-inch hole was bored into each of the quarter-inch titanium bolts to provide a weak point. When a mild detonating fuse, placed in a groove around each bolt, was energized, the bolts were sheared simultaneously and the hatch sprang open.

There were two ways to activate the explosive egress hatch during recovery. About six to eight inches from the astronaut's right arm, as he lay in his couch, was a knobbed plunger. The pilot would remove a pin and press the plunger with a fist-force of five or six pounds, detonating the small explosive charge and blasting the hatch 25 feet away in a second. If the pin was in place, a fist-force of 40 pounds was required. A rescuer outside the capsule could blow open the hatch simply by removing a small panel from the fuselage side and pulling a lanyard. This complete explosive hatch weighed only 23 pounds.[43]

The welcome new trapezoidal window assembly on spacecraft No. 11 replaced the two 10-inch side ports through which Shepard strained to see. The pilot now could look upward slightly and see directly outside. Visually the field covered 30 degrees in the horizontal plane and 33 degrees in the vertical. The Corning Glass Works of Corning, New York, designed and developed the multilayered panes. The outer pane was made of Vycor glass, .35-inch thick, and could withstand temperatures on the order of 1500 to 1800 degrees F. Three panels were bonded to make the inner pane, one a .17-inch-thick sheet of Vycor, the two others made of tempered glass. This fenestration was as strong as any part of the capsule pressure vessel.[41]

The manual controls for the second manned flight incorporated the new rate stabilization control system. With it the astronaut could control the rate of spacecraft attitude movements by small turns of his hand controller rather than by jockeying the device to attain the desired position. This rate damping or rate augmentation system, like power steering on an automobile, gave finer and easier handling qualities and another redundant means of driving the pitch, yaw, and roll thrusters.

By the time of the MR-4 flight, Lewis Research Center and Space Task Group engineers had analyzed the thrust rating of the posigrade rockets and had made a valuable discovery. Fired into the booster-spacecraft adapter, the posigrade rockets developed 78 percent greater thrust than when fired openly. Accordingly the capsule separation rockets when ignited inside the adapter, producing what the NASA testers called a "popgun effect," afforded an initial separation velocity of about 28.1 feet per second. This determination provided the engineers with the confidence that spacecraft-booster separation would occur with little likelihood of recontact.

STG's calculations indicated that the Redstone booster and the Mercury spacecraft should be about 4000 feet apart on their suborbital trajectory at retrofire. The unbraked booster would hit the water some 566.2 seconds after launch, while the longer and steeper trajectory of the spacecraft would keep it aloft 911.1 seconds. The booster would land about $16\frac{1}{2}$ miles beyond the spacecraft.[45] Because of the relatively short distance between the two impact points, STG was concerned enough to assign John P. Mayer and Ted H. Skopinski to study the problem, especially as related to possible recontact of the spacecraft and the booster after separation. As a result of the studies, Skopinski's recommendations for minor changes in the sequencing of retrofire were accepted as solutions to prevent recontact.

Other hardware changes involved attaching a redesigned fairing for the capsule adapter clamp-ring, rearranging the capsule instrument panel, and adding more foam padding to the head area of the contour couch. The fairing and some more insulation should overcome the vibration and consequent blurred vision Shepard had complained about, while the rearrangement of the instruments sought to improve the eye-scan pattern, which Shepard had found poor. These changes cost several more weeks' time. On July 15, 1961, Gilruth affirmed that Grissom would be the prime pilot for Mercury-Redstone No. 4 and that Glenn would be his stand-in. Grissom in turn announced that he had chosen the name *Liberty Bell 7* as the most appropriate call-sign for his bell-shaped capsule, because the name was to Americans almost synonymous with "freedom" and symbolic numerically of the continuous teamwork it represented.[46]

Modifications made on Grissom's pressure suit reflected the experiences of Shepard's flight. Nylon-sealed ball-bearing rings were fitted at the glove connections to allow full rotation of the wrists while the suit was pressurized. A new personal parachute harness was designed to keep the chute out of the way. On the chest of Grissom's suit was a convex mirror, called a "hero's medal" by the astronaut corps, that served simply to allow the pilot-observer camera to photograph instrument readings. Another welcome addition to the suit was a urine reservoir, fabricated the day before the flight. Although during his flight Grissom would find the contraption somewhat binding, it did work. Lastly, Grissom's helmet was equipped with new microphones that promised to filter out more noise and make transmission quality even better.[47]

Materials successfully used in other phases of the space program also became a part of the second manned flight. In the continuing quest for weight reduction, a lightweight, radar-reflective life raft was developed jointly by the Langley Research Center and the Space Task Group. Weighing three pounds and four ounces (45 percent lighter than the original version), this raft was constructed of Mylar and nylon, the same materials used in *Echo I,* the passive communication satellite balloon that began circling the globe in August 1960. The survival pack, with the raft inside, was secured on a shelf in the spacecraft conveniently near the astronaut's left arm.[48]

Grissom's flight plan was revised rapidly and altered substantially as a result of MR–3. Shepard had really been overloaded with activities during his five minutes of weightlessness. Now Grissom was given a chance to look through his new trapezoidal window to learn more about man's visual abilities in space. If he could recognize landmarks for flight reference, the pilot tasks for the Mercury orbital flights might be considerably simplified. Shepard had assumed manual control of only one axis of movement—yaw, pitch, or roll—at a time, whereas Grissom had instructions to assume complete manual control as soon as he could, to make three maneuvers in about one minute instead of Shepard's 12 minutes, and then to spend as much time as possible making exterior observations.

Mercury-Redstone booster No. 8 had arrived at Cape Canaveral on June 8. Kurt H. Debus' contingent of Wernher von Braun's team and G. Merritt Preston's capsule checkout team had proceeded with the mating of the launch vehicle and capsule and the checkout requirements. On July 13, the flight safety review was held and the spacecraft was pronounced ready for flight. Two days later Walter Williams heard the reports during the mission review; the Redstone and *Liberty Bell 7* were pronounced ready to go. The recovery ships, anticipating the launch date on Tuesday, July 18, moved into their assigned positions.

Essentially a repeat of MR–3, Grissom's flight was to reach an apogee of 116 miles, over a range of 299 miles, with the astronaut feeling a maximum acceleration load of 6.33 g and deceleration of 10.96 g. Only the launching azimuth, changed by three degrees to stay within range bounds, varied from Shepard's flight into space.[49]

On July 16 the news media received a weather bulletin predicting that the cloud cover in the launch area for the next 48 hours would be below average, but that the impact area would be slightly cloudier than usual. The mission was postponed early Tuesday, the 18th, in hope of better weather. Fortunately the frosty liquid oxygen had not been loaded so the launch delay was only 24, rather than 48, hours.

Early Wednesday, July 19, Grissom, asleep in his quarters on the balcony of Hangar S, was awakened by his physician, William Douglas, who told him that Walter Williams' operations team was pushing for a 7 a.m. launch to beat the weather. The launch day routine began again. By 5 a.m. Grissom was up in the gantry. He slid into his niche; the count resumed and continued unbroken until 10 minutes and 30 seconds before launch, when a hold was called to wait for a rift in the cloud cover. When no break appeared, the mission was scrubbed again. This time the liquid oxygen had been tanked, so a dreary 48-hour delay would be necessary.[50]

The weather conditions on July 21 were still not ideal. The view from an altitude of a hundred miles would show that all the northern portion of Florida was completely obscured by high cirrus and lower patches of cumulus clouds. Southern Florida and Cuba would be splotched by scattered cumulus. The operations team nevertheless decided that since the view was not essential to the success of the mission, the launch should come off as scheduled.[51]

Because Grissom had shaved and showered before going to bed rather than before his low-residue breakfast, and because Slayton, the blockhouse communicator, briefed the astronaut on the status of the capsule and booster during the van ride to the pad rather than just before gantry ascent, the routine was a bit less hurried. George E. Ruff, an Air Force psychiatrist, had time to interrogate Grissom about his feelings before he lay in his contour couch for MR–4's liftoff.[52]

Grissom was unruffled, calm, and poised as he entered *Liberty Bell 7* again. The count resumed and proceeded smoothly until 45 minutes before launch time, when a gantry technician discovered that one of the 70 hatch bolts was misaligned. A 30-minute hold was called, during which the McDonnell and STG supervisory engineers decided that the remaining 69 bolts were sufficient to hold and blow the hatch, so the misaligned bolt was not replaced. The countdown was resumed, but two more holds for minor reasons cost another hour's wait.[53]

Alone in his capsule awaiting liftoff, Grissom experienced a wide range of impressions. As the gantry, or service structure, moved back from the launch vehicle, he had the illusion that he was falling. His pulse rate ranged from 64 to 162 beats per minute, depending upon his feelings. His heart beat rose during the oxygen purge, fell while the hatch bolt repair decision was being made, rose again when the go decision was made, and finally doubled at launch. His liftoff was at 7:20 a.m.[54]

Liberty Bell Tolls

Grissom later admitted at the postflight debriefing that he was "a bit scared" at liftoff, but he added that he soon gained confidence along with the g buildup. Hearing the engine roar at the pedestal, he thought that his elapsed-time clock had started late. Like Shepard, he was amazed at the smooth quality of the liftoff, but then he noticed gradually more severe vibrations, never violent enough to impair his vision. To the watchers on the ground, the Redstone and the capsule appeared to rise slowly and to pass through a thin, broken cloud window. Then the rocket disappeared, leaving a contrail that was visible on the beach for about a minute. Grissom's cabin pressure sealed off at the proper altitude, about 27,000 feet, and he felt elated that the environmental control system was in good working order. The suit and cabin temperature, about 57.5 and 97 degrees F, respectively, were quite comfortable. Watching his instruments for the pitch rate of the Redstone, Grissom saw it follow directions as programmed, tilting over about one degree per second.

370

Under a 3-g load on the up-leg of his flight, Grissom noticed a sudden change in the color of the horizon from light blue to jet black. His attention was distracted by the noise of the tower-jettison rocket firing on schedule. The pilot felt the separation and watched the tower through the window as it drifted off, trailing smoke, to his right. At two minutes and 22 seconds after launch, the Redstone's Rocketdyne engine cut off after building a velocity of 6561 feet per second. Grissom had a strong sensation of tumbling during the transition from high to zero g, and, while he had become familiar with this sensation in centrifuge training, for a moment he lost his bearings.

The Redstone coasted for 10 seconds after its engine cut off; then a sharp report signaled that the posigrade rockets were popping the capsule loose from the booster. Although Grissom peered out his window throughout his ship's turnaround maneuver, he never caught sight of his launch vehicle. Angular motion was perceptible to Grissom only by watching the needle move on the dial or by seeing an Earth reference by chance. Another cue to the spacecraft's movement was the Sun's rays, which gradually moved up his torso toward his face, threatening temporary blindness. Grissom fretted over the automatic turnaround that should have reversed the capsule faster.

With turnaround accomplished, the Air Force jet pilot for the first time became a space pilot, assuming manual-proportional control. A constant urge to look out the window made concentrating on his control tasks difficult. He told Shepard back in Mercury Control that the panorama of Earth's horizon, presenting an 800-mile arc at peak altitude, was fascinating. His instruments rated a poor second to the spectacle below.

Turning reluctantly to his dials and control stick, Grissom made a pitch movement change but was past his desired mark. He jockeyed the handcontroller stick for position, trying to damp out all oscillations, then made a yaw movement and went too far in that direction. By the time the proper attitude was attained, the short time allocated for these maneuvers had been used, so he omitted the roll movement altogether. The manual controls impressed Grissom as very sluggish when compared to the Mercury procedures trainer. Then he switched to the new rate command control system and found perfect response, although fuel consumption was high.[55]

After the pitch and yaw maneuvers, Grissom made a roll-over movement so he could see the ground from his window. Some land beneath the clouds (later determined to be western Florida around the Apalachicola area) appeared in the hazy distance, but the pilot was unable to identify it. Suddenly Cape Canaveral came into view so clearly that Grissom found it hard to believe that his slant-range was over 150 miles.

He saw Merritt Island, the Banana River, the Indian River, and what appeared to be a large airport runway. South of Cape Canaveral, he saw what he believed to be West Palm Beach. He tried to report to Shepard on the high-frequency

371

communications circuit every landmark he saw, but his transmissions were not received.   These observations got Grissom behind in his work procedures, as he realized when he saw the periscope retract.

With *Liberty Bell 7* at an altitude of 118.26 miles, it was now time to position the spacecraft in its reentry attitude.   Grissom had initiated the retrorocket sequence and the capsule was arcing downward.   His pulse reached 171 beats per minute.   Retrofire gave him the distinct and peculiar feeling that he had reversed his backward flight through space and was actually moving face forward. As he plummeted downward, he saw what appeared to be two of the spent retro-rockets pass across the periscope view after the retrorocket package had been jettisoned.

Pitching the spacecraft over into a reentry attitude of 14 degrees from Earth-vertical, the pilot tried to see the stars out his observation window.   Instead the glare of sunlight filled his capsule, making it difficult to read the panel dials, particularly those with blue lights.   Grissom felt that he would not have noticed the .05-g light if he had not known it was about to flash on.

Reentry presented no problem.   Grissom could not feel the oscillations follow-ing the g buildup; he could only read them on the rate indicators.   Meanwhile he continued to report to the Mercury Control Center on his electric current reading, fuel quantity, g loads, and other instrument indications.   Condensation and smoke trailed off the heatshield at about 65,000 feet as *Liberty Bell 7* plunged back into the atmosphere.

The drogue parachute deployed on schedule at 21,000 feet.   Grissom said he saw the deployment and felt some resulting pulsating motion, but not enough to worry him.   Main parachute deployment occurred at 12,300 feet, which was about 1000 feet higher than the design nominal altitude.   Watching the main chute unfurl, Grissom spotted a six-inch L-shaped tear and another two-inch puncture in the canopy.   Although he worried about them, the holes grew no bigger and his rate of descent soon slowed to about 28 feet per second.   Dumping his peroxide control fuel, the pilot began transmitting his panel readings.

A "clunk" confirmed that the landing bag had dropped in preparation for impact.   Grissom then removed his oxygen hose and opened his visor but deliberately left the suit ventilation hose attached.   Impact was milder than he had expected, although the capsule heeled over in the water until Grissom was lying on his left side.   He thought he was facing downward.   The capsule gradually righted itself, and, as the window cleared the water, Grissom jettisoned the reserve parachute and activated the rescue aids switch.   *Liberty Bell 7* still appeared watertight, although it was rolling badly with the swells.

Preparing for recovery, he disconnected his helmet and checked himself for debarkation.   The neck dam did not unroll easily; Grissom tinkered with his suit collar to ensure his buoyancy if he had to get out of the spacecraft quickly. When the recovery helicopters, which had taken to the air at launch time and visually followed the contrails and parachute descent, were still about two miles from the impact point, which was only three miles beyond the bullseye, Lieutenant James L. Lewis, pilot of the primary recovery helicopter, radioed Grissom to ask if he was ready for pickup. He replied that he wanted them to wait five minutes while he recorded his cockpit panel data. Using a grease pencil with the pressure suit gloves was awkward, and several times the suit ventilation caused the neck dam to balloon, but the pilot simply placed his finger between neck and dam to allow the air to escape.

After logging the panel data, Grissom asked the helicopters to begin the approach for pickup. He removed the pin from the hatch-cover detonator and lay back in the dry couch. "I was lying there, minding my own business," he said afterward, "when I heard a dull thud." The hatch cover blew away, and salt water swished into the capsule as it bobbed in the ocean. The third man to return from space was faced with the first serious emergency; *Liberty Bell 7* was shipping water and sinking fast.

Grissom had difficulty recollecting his actions at this point, but he was certain that he had not touched the hatch-activation plunger. He doffed his helmet, grasped the instrument panel with his right hand, and scurried out the sloshing hatchway. Floating in the sea, he was thankful that he had unbuckled himself earlier from most of his harness, including the chest restraints. Otherwise he might not have been able to abandon ship.

Lieutenant John Reinhard, copilot of the nearest recovery helicopter, reported afterward that the choppers were making their final approach for pickup. He was preparing to cut the capsule's antenna whip (according to a new procedure) with a squib-actuated cutter at the end of a pole, when he saw the hatch cover fly off, strike the water at a distance of about five feet from the hatch, and then go skipping over the waves. Next he saw Grissom's head appear, and the astronaut began climbing through the hatch. Once out, the pressure-suited spaceman swam away.

Instead of turning his attention to Grissom, Lewis completed his approach to the sinking spacecraft, as both he and Reinhard were intent on capsule recovery. This action was a conditioned reflex based on past training experience. While training off the Virginia beaches the helicopter pilots had noted that the astronauts seemed at home in and to enjoy the water. So Reinhard quickly clipped the high-frequency antenna as soon as the helicopter reached *Liberty Bell 7*. Throwing aside the antenna cutting device, Reinhard picked up the shepherd's hook recovery pole and carefully threaded the crook through the recovery loop on top of the capsule. By this time Lewis had lowered the helicopter to assist Reinhard in his task to a point that the chopper's three wheels were in the water. *Liberty Bell 7* sank out of sight, but the pickup pole twanged as the attached cable went taut, indicating to the helicopter pilots that they had made their catch.

Reinhard immediately prepared to pass the floating astronaut the personnel hoist. But at that moment Lewis called a warning that a detector light had flashed on the instrument panel, indicating that metal chips were in the oil sump

Grissom is helped into Liberty Bell 7 *by backup pilot Glenn.*

Water-filled Liberty Bell 7 *denies the helicopter's lift.*

Flight of
Liberty Bell 7
July 21, 1961

374

because of engine strain. Considering the implication of impending engine failure, Lewis told Reinhard to retract the personnel hoist while he called the second chopper to retrieve the pilot.

Meanwhile Grissom, having made certain that he was not snared by any lines, noticed that the primary helicopter was having trouble raising the submerged spacecraft. He swam back to the capsule to see if he could assist but found the cable properly attached. When he looked up for the personnel line, he saw the helicopter start to move away.

Suddenly Grissom realized that he was not riding as high in the water as he had been. All the time he had been in the water he kept feeling air escape through the neck dam. The more air he lost, the less buoyancy he had. Moreover, he had forgotten to secure his suit inlet valve. Swimming was becoming difficult, and now with the second helicopter moving in he found the rotor wash between the two aircraft was making swimming more difficult. Bobbing under the waves, Grissom was scared, angry, and looking for a swimmer from one of the helicopters to help him tread water. Then he caught sight of a familiar face, that of George Cox, aboard the second helicopter. Cox was the copilot who had retrieved both the chimpanzee Ham and Astronaut Shepard. With his head barely above water, Grissom found the sight of Cox heartening.

Cox tossed the "horse-collar" lifeline straight to Grissom, who immediately wrapped himself into the sling backwards. Lack of orthodoxy mattered little to Grissom now, for he was on his way to the safety of the helicopter, even though swells dunked him twice more before he got aboard. His first thought was to get a life preserver on. Grissom had been either swimming or floating for a period of only four or five minutes, "although it seemed like an eternity to me," as he said afterward.

As the first helicopter moved away from Grissom, it struggled valiantly to raise the spacecraft high enough to drain the water from the impact bag. Once the capsule was almost clear of the water, but like an anchor it prevented the helicopter from moving forward. The flooded *Liberty Bell 7* weighed over 5000 pounds, a thousand pounds beyond the helicopter's lifting capacity. The pilot, watching his insistent red warning light, decided not to chance losing two craft in one day. He finally cast loose, allowing the spacecraft to sink swiftly. Martin Byrnes, aboard the carrier, suggested that a marker be placed at the point so that the capsule might be recovered later. Rear Admiral J. E. Clark advised Byrnes that in that area the depth was about 2800 fathoms.

On the carrier *Randolph*, examining physicians Strong and Laning, the same men who had gone over Shepard, found Grissom extremely tired. But the MR-4 astronaut elected to proceed with his preliminary debriefing before going on to Grand Bahama. The recovery finale, of course, continually intruded in the discussion. Grissom said he was extremely grateful to Walter Schirra for the developmental work he had done on the neck dam. He felt that this had saved his life, although later tests disclosed other difficulties. The debriefing sessions aboard the *Randolph* and at Grand Bahama centered on the need for more egress training (there had been none since April) and the formulation of specific emergency recovery procedures. Grissom said that he thought he should have been a little more precise in his attitude control functions. This was a moot point in view of the sluggishness he had encountered with the manual system and the apparent play in the control stick linkage. Other than this anomaly, the spacecraft had performed well; noises of the sequential events had provided good cues; vibrations had been minimal; the new window had been a delight and should prove useful on orbital flights; and the environmental control system had functioned well. But, said Grissom, there were too many couch restraint straps; the panel lights were too dim; the oxygen consumption rate was high; the urinal device needed further development; the high-frequency communication circuit was unsuccessful; and hydrogen peroxide fuel consumption proved to be high on the rate control system. The last item of that list caused little concern among the Space Task Group engineers, for they had decided that the rate command mode would be used primarily for reentry, when fuel economy was less important.

At Grand Bahama, Grissom rested and appeared to have suffered no abnormal effects from flight into space. The evaluators conceded, however, that the abnormal recovery experience would have made any such effects difficult to analyze or to attribute to flight causes. Further questioning of the astronaut followed the routine established in Shepard's debriefing.[56]

Obviously one of the major problems to be explained and resolved following the flight of *Liberty Bell 7* was the malfunction of the explosive egress hatch. Before the mission, Minneapolis-Honeywell had conducted environmental tests to qualify the hatch and igniter assembly. Although the tests had been run with the pin installed, conditions had been severe. The component had been subjected to low and high temperature ranges, a 100-g shock force, and salt-spray and water-immersion tests. After MR–4, the Space Task Group established a committee that included Astronaut Schirra to study the hatch problem. Tests were conducted in an environment even more severe than that used by the manufacturer, but no premature explosions occurred. Studies were made of individuals operating the panel switches on the side nearest the actuator; the clearance margin appeared to be adequate. According to Schirra, "There was only a very remote possibility that the plunger could have been actuated inadvertently by the pilot."

The mystery of Grissom's hatch was never solved to everyone's satisfaction. Among the favorite hypotheses were that the exterior lanyard might have become entangled with the landing bag straps; that the ring seal might have been omitted on the detonation plunger, reducing the pressure necessary to actuate it; or that static electricity generated by the helicopter had fired the hatch cover. But with the spacecraft and its onboard evidence lying 15,000 feet down on the bottom of the Atlantic Ocean, it was impossible to determine the true cause. The only solution was to draft a procedure that would preclude a recurrence: henceforth the astronaut would not touch the plunger pin until the helicopter hooked on and the line was taut. As it turned out, *Liberty Bell 7* was the last manned flight in Project Mercury in which helicopter retrieval of the spacecraft was planned. In addition, Grissom would be the only astronaut who used the hatch without receiving a slight hand injury. As he later reminded Glenn, Schirra, and Cooper, this helped prove he had not touched his hatch plunger.[57]

TITOV WIDENS THE GAP

Despite the loss of *Liberty Bell 7*, the Mercury-Redstone phase of the program had been so successful that there was little reason for keeping it alive. The termination of the manned suborbital flights had seemed predictable after Gagarin and certain after Shepard. A month and a half before Grissom flew, the Space Task Group had decided to cancel the fourth such flight, MR-6. Silverstein and Gilruth also had considered canceling the third flight, MR-5, to concentrate on Mercury-Atlas operations. But Silverstein believed that data obtained from Grissom's MR-4 should be appraised before deciding whether to bypass the MR-5.

Besides, at that time the subject was politically sensitive. Since three astronauts were training for the Mercury-Redstone missions, the public expectation, expressed in Congress and through the press, was that there would be at least three manned Redstone flights. But if Mercury-Atlas could be expedited, an astronaut making three orbits would eclipse the cosmonaut who had made one orbit.

On August 7, 1961, all such hopes were erased by the day-long, 17-orbit flight and successful recovery of Cosmonaut Gherman S. Titov. When the U.S.S.R. announced its spectacular second space flight, some Americans were filled with awe, some with admiration, and some even with fear, while a few expressed only scornful disbelief. At 9 a.m., Moscow time, on August 6, 1961, the Soviet pilot rocketed into orbit aboard *Vostok II*. The space voyage of this 26-year-old Russian covered 17.5 orbits and took 25 hours and 18 minutes.[58]

After the data gathered from the Grissom flight had been evaluated, NASA and Space Task Group managers decided that little could be gained from any further Mercury-Redstone missions. On August 14, Paul Purser drafted a termination recommendation for Gilruth's submittal to Silverstein. Purser pointed out that the Redstone had done well its job of qualifying the spacecraft, astronauts, and most other critical aspects of the operation. Mercury-Redstone also had validated the various training devices, and it had uncovered many technical problems, none of which appeared to be insoluble before an American orbital flight.[59] Now it was time to turn to the principal Mercury-Atlas problem areas, such as explosive hatch, inverter heating, oxygen usage rate, control system linkage, and egress training, and to cope with the more complex Atlas program. Four days later, on August 18, NASA Headquarters publicly announced that the objectives of the Mercury-Redstone program had been achieved, and that accordingly it was canceled. Six days later, Joachim P. Kuettner, Mercury-Redstone Project Chief at the George C. Marshall Space Flight Center, told his subordinates that the Redstone must now be retired after helping gain a toehold on space.[60]

Several accounts of the Soviet manned space feats indicated striking similarities in cosmonaut and astronaut selection and training. The Russians were chosen by a strenuous selection program, which was much like the American procedure, but their selection emphasized youth and stamina, rather than flight experience and engineering. Soviet training, like American, employed the human centrifuge, altitude chamber, isolation, technical systems study, and personal physical training. Also, three pilots trained in competition for the first flight, Titov being Gagarin's backup pilot on *Vostok I* of April 12. Gagarin's and Titov's accounts of liftoff and orbital flight described the same phenomena—g-load buildup, vibrations, and impressions of weightlessness.

Titov was reported to have exercised manual control. This transliteration was taken in some circles to mean that he changed his orbital plane, but the Mercury experts believed that Titov's manual control was for attitude only, like that exercised by Shepard and Grissom. Titov reported sleeping seven hours or more, and some translations indicated that he was awakened by his weightless arms floating. This last claim was too much for David Lawrence, a syndicated columnist, who suggested that the flight might have been a hoax. But the members of the Space Task Group never doubted the authenticity of either *Vostok I* or *Vostok II*. Too much was similar. Although only two or three people in the Space Task Group could read Russian, the reports translated from Soviet journals seemed to correspond to their own experience.

One of Titov's publicized problems caused concern among NASA and Space Task Group medical specialists. Before entering his rest period, Titov complained of feelings "akin to seasickness" and became nauseated. He had to be careful not to move his head too swiftly in any direction. After sleep, his nausea apparently abated; it finally disappeared completely when Titov began to feel reentry pressures. NASA aeromedical advisers suggested that the first American in orbital flight ought to guard against, watch for, and test out this peculiar physiological reaction reported by Titov and the Soviets.[61]

Psychologically, the Russian Vostok feats created some uneasiness in the United States. Many people admired the Soviet's technological proficiency but were concerned by the strategic implications. The fact that Titov's orbital track in a near-polar plane carried him over the United States three times was alarming to some people. In spite of the fact that the decision for the accelerated space program was confirmed, the term "space lag" began appearing more frequently in the press and in the statements of some Congressmen. Criticism of NASA, the departed Eisenhower administration, and even the Kennedy administration mounted. After the Gagarin flight, for example, Democratic Senator Stuart

Symington of Missouri caustically pointed to the years of indecision that had so long delayed the Saturn launch vehicle. After the Titov flight, John W. Finney, aerospace and science writer for the *New York Times,* pictured Washington officialdom as carping over NASA's "easy pace" in implementing the lunar landing program outlined by President Kennedy. No specifications for a lunar spacecraft yet were evident; no agreement on the route to take or on the necessary launch vehicle had been reached. But these were mostly NASA Headquarters worries; the primary task of the Space Task Group still lay ahead. Regardless of the fact that Mercury could now only duplicate the feats of the Vostoks, Project Apollo, the manned lunar-landing project, depended upon Mercury Mark II (later named Gemini), the two-man rendezvous and docking project; and Gemini depended upon the fulfillment of Mercury; in turn, that depended upon the strength and stability of Atlas. The day Titov came back to Earth, NASA's Space Task Group announced candidly, if not calmly, that the first try at putting an American in orbit might slip unavoidably into January 1962.[62]

XII

Final Rehearsals

WITH the 1961 Labor Day holiday passed, the Space Task Group buckled down to an exceptionally busy season, one that was to be climaxed with STG's own demise and phoenix-like resurrection. Its activities had become farflung. Dead ahead, at Cape Canaveral, loomed the first orbital flight test of a Mercury capsule, carrying a true "black box," called a "crewman simulator," instead of an astronaut. Then, too, plans long had been ripening for a multi-orbital Mercury-Scout flight to qualify the ground tracking and communications network. A second orbital flight carrying a chimpanzee in the spacecraft couch also had an early place in the program.

Meanwhile NASA agents had completed an extensive survey of potential sites for the new development and operations installation for manned space projects of the future. At its Langley Air Force Base domicile, STG was busy planning for its expanding role in manned space exploration. Its personnel were weighing persistent rumors that the new Manned Spacecraft Center might be located in Texas, somewhere near the booming city of Houston.

The first objective of all this simultaneous activity was Mercury-Atlas 4, the fifth flight of an Atlas-launched spacecraft. This mission had been planned and replanned many times before the unsuccessful launch of MA–3 back in April 1961, and the failure of that mission directly affected the MA–4 plans. During the early months of 1960, MA–3 had been scheduled for a suborbital flight, with a crewman simulator aboard. First plans called for the Atlas booster to be held 150 feet per second below orbital velocity, with capsule separation occurring at the normal 100-mile-orbital-insertion altitude. Forty seconds after separation, retrofire was to have produced a landing beyond the Canary Islands and about 100 miles short of the African coast. And when this test was completed successfully, MA–4 was to repeat MA–3, but with a chimpanzee in the cockpit. Spacecraft No. 9 was to be specially fitted for the MA–4 flight.

Toward the end of 1960, however, Walter C. Williams advised the commanding officer of the recovery force, Destroyer Flotilla Four, that MA–4 would try for three orbits with a crewman simulator aboard and that the targeted launch date was April 1, 1961. But the MA–3 launch, still scheduled for a suborbital flight with its "mechanical astronaut," slipped to April 25. While many Americans worried over the Soviet space coup represented by Yuri Gagarin's one-orbit flight on April 12, Robert R. Gilruth and Williams already had made the decision to change MA–3 to a one-orbit mission.[1]

April 25, 1961, came, but the day's recorded results were far from heartening. The MA–3 launch vehicle failed to program over into the proper trajectory; after 40 seconds of flight straight upward the Air Force range safety officer destroyed the Atlas booster. So it was necessary on MA–4 to strive for the same one-orbit objective and to delay still further the nominal three-orbit Mercury mission.

Meanwhile, for various reasons, production of the spacecraft and booster for MA–4 fell behind schedule. Atlas No. 88–D, allotted for MA–4, did not receive its factory rollout acceptance inspection until June 29–30, 1961, and it was July 15 before it was delivered to Cape Canaveral. And spacecraft No. 9 was not used, though originally planned. Instead No. 8 was fished from the Atlantic after its ill-fated flight in MA–3 and shipped back to McDonnell in St. Louis on April 27 for extensive overhauling. That meant cleaning, installing new insulation, replacing the external portion of the hydrogen peroxide control system, making spot-weld repairs in the large pressure bulkhead, and replacing the heatshield, antenna canister, escape tower, tower clamp ring, adapter, main clamp ring, and the inlet and outlet air snorkels. The overhauled spacecraft, redesignated 8–A, was returned to the Cape, but G. Merritt Preston's crew still had plenty of work. A leak had to be repaired in a reaction control system fuel tank; the environmental control system and the automatic stabilization and control system had to be reworked. A fairing to reduce launch vibration, like the one used on the Little Joe 5–B flight on April 28, 1961, and similar to that used on Virgil I. Grissom's suborbital mission in July, was added to the adapter clamp ring.[2]

Because of all this modification and overhaul, it was August 3 before the spacecraft for MA–4 was delivered to the pad and mated with the booster, supposedly to be launched on August 22. The day before the scheduled flight the Air Force's Space Systems Division in California called Cape Canaveral and reported that solder balls had been found in some transistors of the same brand that had been installed in the MA–4 booster. Coordination of this information among the various Mercury-Atlas teams at the Cape brought to light the fact that these types of transistors also had been used in the spacecraft. There was nothing left to do but postpone the launch and give both vehicles a thorough going-over to replace the defective transistors. On August 25 the spacecraft was returned to Hangar S, when it became apparent that this work might encompass several days. After these labors in the hangar, spacecraft 8–A was mated with the booster again on September 1. This time the engineers conducting the prelaunch checkouts found nothing wrong. Although 8–A was a secondhand capsule, its landing bag had not been installed, it had ports instead of the new window, and the explosive egress hatch had been omitted, it still passed inspection.[3]

Besides the problem with the defective transistors, the Mercury-Atlas booster had been proceeding along the same tortuous route as the capsule toward flight qualification. By September, the Atlas had undergone so many changes that had to be integrated into launch vehicle No. 88–D, and experienced so many setbacks, that a successful orbital mission was necessary for the sake of NASA and national morale and to forestall any new attacks on the Atlas as the Mercury launch vehicle. The year in which the Soviets had orbited a man now was in its ninth month, yet the United States was still preparing to orbit a box full of instruments. The Mercury-Atlas flight record had produced only one completely successful launch—the MA–2 reentry heating test—out of four tries.

This was scarcely an enviable record. Many hours, days, and months had been spent by special committees and working groups in ferreting out the sources of trouble. The STG, Space Technology Laboratories, Convair, and Air Force engineers who had reviewed the failure of MA–1 had concluded that the forward end of the Atlas was not designed to withstand the flight dynamic loads fed through the adapter section, that the adapter was too flexible, and that stiffeners were needed. MA–2 had confirmed the controversial "fix" of the adapter section. MA–4 would be the second of the "thick-skin" Atlases. Reviewing the MA–3 abort, the engineers assumed that the programmer's failure to pitch the booster into a proper trajectory was due to a transient voltage. Also, some two years previously, another anomaly caused the Big Joe Atlas to fail to stage, and even in MA–2 there had been some propellant sloshing in the booster. To correct the programmer problem, Convair modified the autopilot controls to give the gimbaling engines of the Atlas a preventive counteraction capability. One objective of MA–4, therefore, was to assess this innovation.[4] In September the NASA-Air Force-contractor engineering team that had been beset with Atlas problems for two years felt that the ICBM-turned-space-launcher was ready to do its part in Project Mercury. In the words of Scott H. Simpkinson, STG's liaison man at the Convair factory, "MA–4 just had to work."

Not only would a successful orbital mission on MA–4 provide the necessary data on the performance of systems and components, but the Mercury tracking network crews and Department of Defense recovery forces would receive valuable training for supporting a manned orbital circumnavigation by an American. Many components, elements, procedures, and flight maneuvers had to be watched and assessed before one of the "Mercury seven" could be committed to an orbital mission around Earth.

Of the manifold segments of an orbital flight, reentry was perhaps the most critical. As it dropped back into the heavy atmosphere, the capsule would be subjected to searing temperatures of about 2000 to 3000 degrees F for six or seven minutes, or about eight times longer than on the previous Mercury suborbital shots. Retrofire between Hawaii and Guaymas, Mexico, would bring about a gradual descent over the North American continent. About 345 miles east of Savannah, the first contact with atmospheric resistance would begin, at an altitude of 55 miles. At this point the appearance of the .05-g light on the panel would telemeter a signal that reentry was coming up. Peak aerodynamic heating would come when the spacecraft had descended to an altitude of 37 miles and was traveling at 15,000 miles per hour. Braking would be dramatic. Between 46 and 12 miles high, traveling over a slant range of 460 miles, the capsule's air speed would be reduced from about 17,000 to 1350 miles per hour. Aerodynamic stresses in this region would provide a severe test of the spacecraft's structural strength, particularly the heatshield and the afterbody shingles.

Perhaps the second most critical segment of the orbital mission would come during the powered phase of the flight. The Space Task Group, supported by the DOD and industry, would also monitor carefully the vibration levels to ascertain if they would be tolerable for an astronaut. Even more important as the capsule was rocketed toward orbit was a reliable escape system, to wrench the capsule clear if the launch vehicle failed to perform. Also it was necessary to judge the ability of the Atlas to release the spacecraft, to evaluate the abort sensing and implementation system, to determine if the launch vehicle could withstand the aerodynamic loads of max q, and to demonstrate the capability of the Mercury network to perform its intended flight-control and data-collection functions.[5] If all went well, MA-4 would provide data proving the validity of years of engineering calculations.

MA-4 would be launched from complex 14 at the Cape on a true azimuth heading of 72.51 degrees east of north. Following engine ignition, after being held to the pad for three seconds to ensure smooth combustion, the Atlas booster engines would propel the spacecraft within two minutes to a speed of about 6500 miles per hour and an altitude of 35 miles over a downrange distance of 45 miles. The sustainer engine would continue to burn. A gradual pitch program would begin to tilt the Atlas toward the sea about 20 seconds after liftoff. Seconds after booster engine cutoff (called "BECO" by the various Mercury-Atlas working teams at the Cape), or at about 41 miles' altitude and a slant range of 56 miles from the pad, the launch vehicle programmer would trigger a greater pitch-over maneuver to put the Mercury-Atlas combination on a course parallel to Earth's surface. At this time the escape tower would be jettisoned. After capsule separation, orbital insertion would occur about 498 miles downrange from the pad at an altitude of about 100 miles. The nominal inertial velocity at this point was supposed to be 25,695 feet per second, increased to 25,719 feet per second by the ignition of the posigrade rockets, which separated the spacecraft from the booster. Within 50 seconds, the spacecraft should have drifted some 790 feet from the booster. The Atlas, rather than falling away, would trail the orbiting spacecraft around Earth at an altitude of about 100 miles, and should complete each circle about once every 90 minutes for an estimated three days.[6]

Instrumentation affixed to the spacecraft would provide data from nearly every conceivable point about the capsule. Noise levels in the vicinity where an astronaut's head would rest would be measured and recorded on magnetic tape. Excess vibration, a problem during early Mercury-Redstone flights, would be monitored closely by seven strategically placed sensors, mostly in the area where capsule and adapter joined. To determine what radiation dosages a pilot would encounter, four standard and two special film packs would be carried. The standard packs were placed on the sides and at the top and bottom of the couch. Carrying a heavier emulsion, the two extra packs would measure the radiation spectrum—the range of all kinds of radiation to which the capsule would be exposed—as well as penetration levels. Flight data other than radiation would be transmitted by two separate telemetry links, each providing essentially the same information.

The flight would be well covered photographically. Located on the left side of the capsule cabin was the instrument panel camera, which would start operating at liftoff, provide about 20,000 frames of panel information during the mission, and cease five seconds after impact. Placed near the right-side port, the Earth-sky camera was loaded for about 600 frames of pictorial data, which would be exhausted somewhere over the Indian Ocean. A third camera, affixed to the periscope, was loaded with about 10,000 frames of film for the mission. This camera would provide especially useful information on the spacecraft's orbital attitude reference to Earth at points where landmarks were recognizable.

Five recorders aboard the spacecraft would tape most of the mission data. Three were seven-track systems to record all telemetry outputs, vibration levels, noise, and shingle strain. The two others were single-track recorders, to be operated in tandem and used to check the reliability of the tracking network communications system.[7]

Plans for spacecraft operations after the powered phase were essentially the same as those for the suborbital flights, only on a much larger scale. Retrofire was scheduled at 1 hour, 29 minutes, and 4 seconds after launch, with the three rockets firing at five-second intervals in order: top-left, bottom, top-right.[8] Recovery plans for orbital missions were considerably more complicated than they had been for the suborbital flights, since many more contingency areas, including abort and overshoot, had to be considered. Besides the nominal landing area off the coast of Bermuda, five secondary landing areas were selected. Providing that the launch was nominal and proceeded according to the preflight calculated trajectory, the abort recovery areas were spaced as follows: Area A began about 13 miles from the launch pad and continued along the track for 2200 miles. For the first 550 miles the coverage extended 30 miles to each side of the track. This area covered the first 72 seconds after launch, or through booster staging. The remainder of Area A, accounting for the period up to 298 seconds after launch, narrowed to about 15 miles on either side of the track. Areas B and C were small elliptical blips on the track, 4 and 8 degrees of longitude beyond A. These were designated for a possible abort at 298 or at 301 seconds, respectively. The third contingency site, Area D, was a longer ellipse (20 by 122 miles) beginning about 7 degrees of longitude past C. At this point the "go/no go" flight decision would be made. The last, Area E, an ellipse 24 by 231 miles along the track, covered aborts up to 304 seconds after the go/no go decision.[9]

The MA–4 capsule also was fitted with a number of aids to assist the DOD forces in their recovery task. Two one-pound sofar bombs, one set to eject upon main parachute deployment and the other set to detonate at 4000 feet of hydrostatic pressure if the spacecraft sank, were carried. A flashing light with a life of about 24 hours was set to activate upon impact. Fluorescein dye, ejected at touchdown, would be visible for about six hours. Navy recovery forces were asked to attempt the recovery of the drogue and main chutes and the spacecraft antenna canister. Balsa wood blocks and Styrofoam had been attached to these components for flotation.[10]

As the launch date of the Mercury-Atlas 4 combination neared, weather problems began to threaten this attempt to orbit a "mechanical astronaut." Not one but two hurricanes thrashed the Mercury tracking areas. "Carla" raked the Corpus Christi tracking station, while "Debbie" moved in a northerly direction on the day before the launch, menacing and causing the ships to get rather a "rough ride" in the prime recovery zone. The equipment at the Texas site withstood the storm without damage. The STG-Air Force-Navy recovery planners at the Cape felt that Weather Bureau support predictions had given them a sufficient margin of safety in the Atlantic to allow the mission to proceed.[11]

Mercury Orbits at Last

On launch day, September 13, the cloud coverage was scattered; visibility was 9 miles; the wind velocity was about 11 miles per hour; and the temperature was 78 degrees. Ninety minutes before launch time a half-hour hold was called to replace a broken screw in one of the afterbody shingles. The liquid oxygen was loaded by 8:30 a.m., and 5 minutes later the operations crew determined that all systems were go. At 8:57, however, the low-speed data timing was momentarily lost at the Bermuda tracking site, and the countdown was recycled to T minus 3 minutes and 30 seconds.

A little after 9:04 a.m. on September 13, 1961, MA–4 was launched on its one-orbit mission. During the first 20 seconds from liftoff, fairly severe booster vibrations were detected by the flight dynamics officer in the Control Center. The "thick-skin" Atlas passed its max-q test. At the 52-second point, a spacecraft inverter that was converting electrical power from direct to alternating current failed, but the standby inverter switched on automatically. Guidance data soon disclosed that the trajectory was .75-degree high; later, at engine cutoff, it was .14-degree low. Although booster engine cutoff occurred 2.5 seconds early, booster velocity was about 100 feet per second too high. Then the sustainer engine cut off 10 seconds early, so the desired velocity was essentially achieved.

Despite these dispersions, which were within design limits, perigee and apogee of the orbit were only slightly more than a mile and 12 miles, respectively, below plan. The Goddard computers instantly indicated a go for the mission. The powered phase, plus posigrade rocket increment, provided a peak velocity of 25,705 feet per second; g loads during the powered phase reached a peak of 7.6.[12]

Despite a slight disturbance in the roll, pitch, and yaw of the booster, separation occurred properly, and after a 5-second steadying or damping period the capsule began its turnaround maneuver. Soon, however, large attitude excursions were observed, and the spacecraft took 50 seconds to reverse its ends to heatshield forward, as opposed to a normal 20 seconds, using 9.5 pounds of hydrogen peroxide attitude control fuel against the 2.2 pounds supposedly required. Even with the abnormal turnaround, the spacecraft attitude gyros and scanners soon transmitted nominal readings, and there seemed no doubt that the mission would proceed to its orbital conclusion. The cause of these undue excursions later was found to be an open electrical connection in the pitch-rate gyro.[13]

A high oxygen usage rate like that on Grissom's suborbital mission cropped up early and continued throughout the flight. At the 27,000-foot point the system sealed off at 5.5 pounds per square inch; then an abrupt drop was indicated in the primary oxygen supply and a concurrent rise in cabin and suit pressure values to 6 pounds per square inch. "Primary oxygen going down fast," Paul E. Purser jotted in his notes as he listened to the communications circuit. "Zanzibar reported 30 percent of primary oxygen left," he later added. Toward the end of the mission, with the primary supply depleted, the system switched over to secondary. Usage from this source was so slight, however, that Walter Williams, commenting on the high usage problem in a press conference following the mission, said that the secondary supply was virtually untouched. Throughout the flight the crewman simulator continued to use oxygen to produce moisture and carbon dioxide, and to monitor the operations while recording heat and suit pressure changes.[14]

Despite the abnormalities with the oxygen supply, once the automated Mercury spacecraft was on its orbital course, the computers indicated that the mission could go for more than seven orbits. In general, the control systems operated well, although on three occasions the spacecraft dropped out of its 34-degree, Earth-reference mode, once just before the ignition of the retrorockets and twice just before the .05-g light telemetry signal. These attitude variations came from the failure of a one-pound yaw-positive thruster and a one-pound roll-negative thruster.

Communications between the capsule and the tracking stations were good, especially on high frequencies, which on the earlier suborbital flights had been virtually unsuccessful. In some cases radar tracking was not good, largely because a few of the operators lacked experience. Telemetry reception was excellent, with some 137 observations received by the various tracking stations during the flight.[15]

387

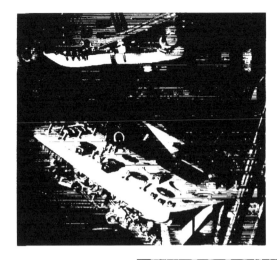

Crewman simulator checks space-craft conditions during the flight.

Flight monitors in the blockhouse: left to right, Ralph B. Gendielle of McDonnell, and Donald D. Arabian and Walter J. Kapryan of NASA's Space Task Group.

MA–4
Sept. 13, 1961

Inspecting the heatshield after the flight: kneeling, left to right, William C. Hayes, of STG; John F. Yardley, of McDonnell; and Charles W. Mathews, Samuel T. Beddingfield, G. Merritt Preston, all of STG.

One hour, 28 minutes, and 59 seconds after MA–4's liftoff, the first retrorocket fired in the vicinity of Hawaii. Monitors at the Guaymas station in Mexico indicated that retrofire, triggered by the spacecraft clock, had gone off as planned. Within the range of the Cape Canaveral control center, telemetry data disclosed that MA–4 was in the proper reentry attitude. Over the Atlantic the drogue parachute opened at 41,750 feet, and the main chute deployed at 10,050 feet. At 10:55 a.m. the capsule splashed down 176 miles east of Bermuda. After an hour and 22 minutes, the destroyer *Decatur*, which had been about 34 miles from the impact point, pulled alongside the spacecraft and hoisted it aboard. From there the capsule and its robot "astronaut" rode to Bermuda, whence they were airlifted to the Cape for an exhaustive examination.[16]

The cause of the oxygen supply malfunction was immediately attacked by the STG and McDonnell engineers. Onboard film, they found, disclosed that the oxygen supply emergency light had blinked on, which would have signaled an astronaut to take corrective action. The inspectors also learned that vibration had dislodged the rate handle from its detent, allowing a valve to crack open. But the flow rate had not been sufficient to trip the microswitch that would have given the Mercury Control Center a telemetry indication of an emergency rate actuation while the mission was in progress. Normally a force of from three to eight pounds was needed to break the handle free from the detent, whereas in this case the inspectors moved the handle with very little force. A new emergency rate handle with a positive latching mechanism was to be devised for later missions.[17]

Other postflight analyses by the engineers found the MA–4 spacecraft and its systems in good condition. There was no afterbody shingle buckling or warping, and the structural materials were only mildly discolored. The horizon scanner window was partially coated with a film of oxidized material caused by aerodynamic heating. Some internal debris, including solder balls and washers, had apparently escaped preflight tumbling and vacuum cleaning. Six buckled skin panels between the base ring and the lower pressure bulkhead indicated that the capsule landed with the heatshield edge striking the water first. Still the inspectors concluded that the structural damage was not enough to have endangered an astronaut. The center section of the heatshield was partially delaminated and the center plug was loose, conditions apparently caused by water impact and cooling. Two cracks were found on the shield in the vicinity of the water-impact point. The depth of the char on the ablation shield was very shallow.[18]

NASA officials showed their pleasure at the success of MA–4 at the press conference held at the Cape immediately after the flight. Gilruth pointed out that this had been the hardest test flight in the whole NASA program. He added that the Atlas had demonstrated that it was capable of boosting a man into orbit, as he, Maxime A. Faget, Purser, and others from NACA-Langley days had long believed. Without hesitation Gilruth concluded that a man would have survived the flight.

389

Above, architect's conception of the new NASA Manned Spacecraft Center, Houston, Texas, as of early 1962. Right, the Center under construction as of the end of Project Mercury, May 1963. The structure in the center is the administration building.

At that point a reporter asked whether a man would fly the next Mercury orbital mission. Walter Williams answered that a three-orbit circuit, either unmanned or carrying a chimpanzee, was still necessary. Then why was the upcoming Mercury-Scout mission necessary, asked a newsman. Again Williams affirmed his confidence in the wisdom of the agreed-upon schedule of flights.[19]

Space Task Group Gets a New Home and Name

Between flight planning and scheduling launches in August 1961, a NASA site survey team headed by John F. Parsons, Associate Director of Ames Research Center, had inspected a number of sites competing for the permanent location of a center for manned space flight projects. The new center had been approved in principle by President Kennedy in accordance with his strategic decision, endorsed by the Congress, to accelerate the space program. The team appraised the sites on 10 points, briefly stated as follows: availability of educational institutions and other facilities for advanced scientific study, electric power and other utilities, water supply, climate, housing, acreage, proximity to varied industrial enterprises, water transportation, air transportation, and local cultural and recreational resources. On September 19, 1961, NASA Administrator James E. Webb announced that the new Manned Spacecraft Center (MSC) would be established on a 1000-acre tract to be transferred to the Government by Rice University, near Houston. The site was in Harris County, Texas, on the edge of Clear Lake, an inlet of Galveston Bay on the Gulf of Mexico.[20]

Webb maintained that selection of the Houston site had been influenced by

390

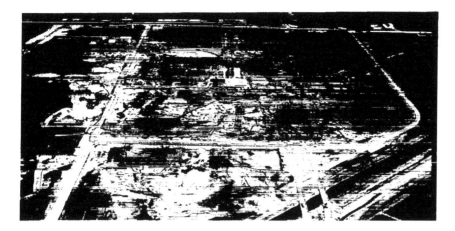

recent decisions to expand the launch complex at the Atlantic Missile Range and to establish a fabrication facility for large booster and space vehicle stages at the Michoud Plant, near New Orleans, where torpedo boats had been manufactured during World War II. The Manned Spacecraft Center, the Michoud Operations, and the Cape Canaveral complex would become a vast integrated enterprise coordinating the development, manufacture, and operation of the manned space flight program.

Not unexpectedly, there was some criticism of the Texas site chosen for the new development center. Charges of inordinate political influence involved the names of Vice-President Johnson, a Texan and chairman of the National Aeronautics and Space Council, and Democratic Representative Albert Thomas of Houston, Chairman of the House of Representatives Independent Offices Subcommittee of the Appropriations Committee. NASA spokesmen categorically denied that there had been any improper influence. Particularly crestfallen were the citizens of the Virginia peninsula, who realized they were losing some of the activities at the Langley Research Center and the Wallops Station. All through August, September, and October, the dailies of Newport News echoed this disappointment. To Houston, of course, this was "wonderful news," as the Chamber of Commerce proclaimed, and local business leaders dispatched representatives to brief the transferring NASA employees in Virginia on the advantages of the Texas coast.[21]

Less than a month after Webb's announcement, a Houston journalist went on an inspection tour of the site planned for the spacecraft center. He found cowboys driving herds of cattle to new pasture, a crew of surveyors from the Army Corps of Engineers mapping the prairie near Clear Lake and fighting snakes, and a lone wolf hunter with the carcass of a freshly slain wolf. The hunter said he had just seen several wild turkeys, a fox, and many deer tracks.[22]

Gilruth and other officials of the Space Task Group reacted quickly to the Webb announcement. The very next day they flew into Houston to begin a search for an estimated 100,000 square feet of temporary floor space. Moving began in October 1961, when Martin A. Byrnes, as the local manager, and a small cadre of center operations, procurement, and personnel employees opened offices in Houston's Gulfgate Shopping City. By mid-1962, when the move was completed, activities were scattered in 11 locations, occupying 295,996 square feet of leased office and laboratory space in the vicinity of Telephone Road and the Gulf Freeway. For both old and new employees, a street map was a necessity in the coordination of information among the various offices located in the dispersed buildings. Besides the leased quarters, NASA personnel liberally used surplus facilities available at nearby Ellington Air Force Base.[23]

By early October 1961, the Space Task Group had established an information relocation center in its Public Affairs Office to help personnel facing the move. Inquiries from the employees about schools and housing were numerous. Shortly thereafter, members of the Space Task Group received procedure directions for permanent change of duty station and then were advised on November 1, 1961, that "the Space Task Group is officially redesignated the Manned Spacecraft Center." The center was now a de facto NASA unit, a nerve center of the accelerated manned space flight program. It was several months, however, before the administration of projects was subdivided for management of the three major programs—Mercury, Gemini, and Apollo. NASA outlined its building requirements for the center on October 13, 1961, at which time two plans were under consideration, one with 13 major buildings and the other with 14, to accommodate 3151 people. The estimated cost was $60 million for the first year's construction.[24]

WIRES GET CROSSED: MERCURY-SCOUT I

Despite the flurry of activity at Hampton, Virginia, Houston, and elsewhere, generated by the impending move, STG did not pause in its scheduled Mercury flight test program. Plans had been in progress for several months and by the summer of 1961 were well developed for Mercury-Scout, whose flight was to provide a dynamic checkout of the Mercury tracking network.

Early in May, Purser and Williams of STG, Charles J. Donlan, who had returned to the Langley Research Center rolls in April, and Warren J. North of NASA Headquarters had met to discuss how the Mercury tracking network, completed at the end of March, could be exercised and evaluated. They agreed that the four-stage, solid-propellant Scout, originally designed at Langley and popularly called the "poor man's rocket," could perform this task economically. North briefed Abe Silverstein, NASA Director of Space Flight Programs, when he returned to Washington from Langley. In the meantime, William E. Stoney of STG had inquired of the Air Force, which also used the Scout, about the availability of a Scout launch vehicle. The planners proposed to use the Air Force and its contractors for payload design and construction and for vehicle assembly and launch. On May 11, Air Force officials replied that a Scout was available, but concurrently North reported that Silverstein was not interested in a Scout shot. Purser, relaying this information on to Gilruth, remarked that "you or Williams will have to talk to him [Silverstein] about it." Mercury-Scout mission planning, meanwhile, was already in progress, and Marion R. Franklin of STG was temporarily appointed as project engineer. This responsibility took on the aspects of a revolving door, with the assignment being shuffled among several Task Group engineers. James T. Rose was named to head the project a few days later; then Rose and Lewis R. Fisher had co-responsibility, until Rose was relieved to continue his work with James A. Chamberlin on what became the Gemini two-man spacecraft project proposals.[25]

Although Silverstein at Headquarters opposed such a test, those on the operations end of Mercury felt that a flight to train the operators and check the tracking stations was a necessity. On May 15, 1961, personnel of NASA Headquarters and several of its cognizant centers, including Harry J. Goett of Goddard, Williams and Purser of Space Task Group, Low from NASA Headquarters, and Thomas A. Harris, G. Barry Graves, and Paul Vavra from Langley, met to review the proposed Scout launch in view of Silverstein's reluctance. They still concluded that the Scout was the best booster for network checkout purposes. The problem was how to sell the idea to Silverstein.

Low and Graves saw Silverstein the next day. They told him that only a one-orbit flight, possibly carrying a chimpanzee, was scheduled for the next six months; moreover, the Air Force had a spare research and development Blue Scout booster. This readiness gave promise of a reasonably early launch date, which was necessary if the communications exercise were to be worthwhile. Silverstein tentatively acquiesced, but he demanded assurance that all the design problems, including payload and antennas, would be resolved before he gave final Headquarters approval. After that approval, he added, all effort should be made to meet an August 15, 1961, firing date.[26] This stipulation apparently was made so that the flight would precede the scheduled August 22 launch date of the MA-4 one-orbit flight.

With Silverstein's reluctant blessing, the planners wasted no time in getting the Scout enterprise rolling. At a meeting at Langley on May 17, attended by Williams, Purser, Merritt Preston, Franklin, and Chamberlin of STG; North of NASA Headquarters; and Graves, Virgil F. Gardner, and Elmer J. Wolff of Langley, responsibilities were assigned and some general requirements were outlined. As noted, Rose and Fisher were named project engineers. Rose was in Los Angeles discussing boosters for the two-man project at the time. He received a call from Chamberlin requesting him to go to Aeronutronic in Newport Beach, California, to talk about instrumentation for the payload. He was joined there by Earl Patton, communications expert from McDonnell Aircraft Corporation.

Graves asked the Goddard Space Flight Center to supply minitrack equipment and Goddard tentatively agreed to do so. The purpose of the minitrack equipment (used in the instrumented satellite programs) was to furnish data for comparison with that which would be transmitted by Mercury instrumentation. Mercury instrumentation was to include C- and S-band beacons, telemetry carriers, and either a command channel on the minitrack or a receiver operated by a command transmitter. Graves also planned to arrange with Goddard for minitrack drawings, and Chamberlin volunteered to contact McDonnell for the Mercury instrumentation drawings and hardware components. Some thought was briefly given to the possibility of using the Langley Research Center to instrument the payload; otherwise the Ford Motor Company's Aeronutronic Division, Air Force contractor for the Scout, probably would provide the instrumentation.[27]

On May 23, North in Washington telephoned Purser at Langley and reported that Silverstein "had bought the Scout." There was a qualification, however: planning could proceed, but money was not to be committed until Robert C. Seamans, Jr., NASA's "general manager," approved. Silverstein immediately sought Seamans' concurrence, offering the inducement that only the payload would require NASA funding ($130,000); the Air Force, using the operation to provide experience for its launch crews, would bear the cost of the launch vehicle and launch. Silverstein argued to Seamans that delays in the Mercury-Atlas program, with a reduction of the flights to be conducted before a manned orbital mission, made using the Scout to check out the network seem sensible. The proposed payload, he said, would be prepared by Ford Aeronutronic, using components from Mercury capsule No. 14, which had already flown in the Little Joe 5-B test of April 28, 1961. The STG planners estimated that the earliest possible launch date was sometime in July, but Silverstein told Seamans that an August date seemed more realistic. Seamans agreed and returned the formal STG request on May 26, stamped "approved." [28]

Now that the blessing was official, the Space Task Group made a sustained effort to launch in July. In June STG engineers considered the components that were to make up the 150-pound payload. Since Associate Administrator Seamans at NASA Headquarters had suggested in his approval document that a backup launch vehicle be obtained, STG secured the Air Force SSD's commitment to supply a second four-stage Scout. Seamans' suggestion proved to be prophetic; although no second Mercury-Scout mission was ever launched, the backup fourth stage had to be used in the first attempt.[29]

By early July, the trajectory data and mission directive for Mercury-Scout were completed. MS-1 would be launched at the Cape from complex No. 18-B, formerly the Project Vanguard launching site, on a true azimuth heading of 72.2 degrees east of north, aiming at an apogee of about 400 miles and a perigee of about 232 miles. Orbital insertion of the payload was to occur some 1100 miles from the Cape, at a speed of 25,458 feet per second and an altitude of

232 miles. A small rectangular box held the payload, which consisted of a C-and S-band beacon, two minitrack beacons, two command receivers, and two telemetry transmitters, all with antennas; a 1500 watt-hour battery; and the fourth-stage instrumentation package. The payload equipment was to function for 18½ hours in orbit. To conserve electrical power while in flight, the equipment would be turned off by a ground command after the first three orbits. During shutdown, the results would be analyzed, and the equipment would then be activated to make another three-orbit data collection. The planners felt that by repeating the shutdown and reactivation operation they could obtain data equivalent to three full missions, gather a wealth of information for comparison, and give the DOD and NASA trackers a good workout.[30]

The launch vehicle for the mission was a 70-foot, solid-propellant Scout rocket weighing 36,863 pounds at liftoff. The booster had four stages. Starting from the bottom, these included an Aerojet Algol engine with a steel case and steel nozzle, burning polyurethane fuel and guided by hydraulic exhaust vanes; a Thiokol Castor motor, also with steel case and nozzle, burning a polybutadiene-acrylic acid propellant, with a precision autopilot employing hydrogen peroxide reaction motors; an Allegheny Ballistic Laboratories Antares motor encased in filament-wound fiber impregnated with epoxy resin, propelled by nitrocellulose nitroglycerin, and guided by an autopilot identical to that in the Castor; and an Allegheny Altair engine of the same construction as stage 3, using the same propellant, but with a spin-stabilizing control mechanism.[31]

The Scout was erected on the pad on July 25 to await mating with the payload. Ford Aeronutronic had completed what turned out to be the initial packaging and had shipped the payload to the Cape on July 3. There the equipment underwent spin-ballast and operational checks and was mated with the booster. But trouble with faulty solid-state telemetry transmitters, developing during the pad checkout, caused such a delay that a July launching became impossible. At about that same time NASA Headquarters decided that the payload had not had sufficient vibration testing, so it was shipped to Aeronutronic at Newport Beach, California, for testing and repackaging. After it returned to the Cape, malfunctions appeared in the Scout's fourth stage, and the Cape engineers had to lift the fourth stage from the backup vehicle. The question in August was which would be ready first, the launch vehicle or the payload. Then on September 13, MA-4, carrying its mechanical astronaut, essentially preempted the Mercury-Scout by its orbital trek around Earth. The Scout payload reached the Cape on September 20, but all four Scout stages did not return to the pad until October 22. The anticlimactic Scout launch was supposed to take place on the 31st.[32]

On Halloween, 1961, a launch crew under the technical supervision of the Air Force launch director (who, in turn, was responsible to the NASA operations director) attempted the Mercury-Scout launch. The countdown proceeded well down to the moment of ignition—when nothing whatever happened. The

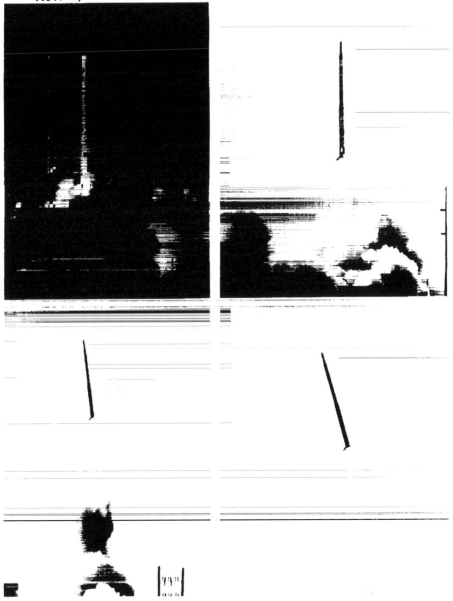

ignition circuits were rechecked and repaired and the next day, November 1, 1961, Mercury-Scout took off. Immediately after liftoff, the vehicle developed erratic motions, and after 28 seconds the booster began tearing apart. The range safety officer gave the destruct signal 43 seconds after launch. The failure, it was later determined, resulted simply from a personal error by a technician who had transposed the connectors between the pitch and yaw rate gyros, so that yaw rate error signals were transmitted to pitch control, and vice versa.[33] Six months of plans and labors had disintegrated in less than a minute.

Ambitions for a second Mercury-Scout, such as had been advocated earlier by Seamans, collided with the reality that another Scout rocket would not be ready before a Mercury-Atlas launch afforded a satisfactory and complete ground-tracking network checkout. The first stage of the backup Scout rocket failed its inspection tests, while the fourth stage had been used on the ill-fated Mercury-Scout 1 mission. Besides, Mercury-Atlas 5 was scheduled to go in mid-November, and the first manned orbital mission was set for December 19. Consequently, Low recommended the cancellation of the Mercury-Scout program to D. Brainerd Holmes, who had taken on manned space flight duties in NASA Headquarters.[34] So the Scout had a short but chaotic life as a member of the Mercury family of launch vehicles.

MAN OR CHIMPANZEE FOR MA-5?

From its unseemly beginning embodied in the Mercury-Scout failure on the first day of its formal existence, the newly titled Manned Spacecraft Center would go on in November to direct and record a resounding success, Mercury-Atlas 5. A curious atmosphere surrounded the approaching animal orbital mission, a sense of impatience, as though the Nation wanted to see it done quickly so the program could hurry forward to a manned orbital shot. The press clearly deplored any slip in MA-5 that would delay the manned flight. Putting an American into orbit before the end of 1961 was popularly regarded as something sorely needed for national prestige. NASA officials obviously were influenced by these pressures, and rank-and-filers in the space program were like members of a football team committed to a warmup game before a conference classic.[35]

Some NASA leaders flatly opposed the chimpanzee flight. Administrator Webb's office questioned MSC on the need for another unmanned Mercury mission in view of the successful orbital flights of Cosmonauts Gagarin and Titov. A Washington newsman suggested that the President's advisers feared another American animal flight would only invite Soviet ridicule. Paul P. Haney, a public-affairs spokesman at NASA Headquarters, finally cleared the air when he announced to the public, "The men in charge of Project Mercury have insisted on orbiting the chimpanzee as a necessary preliminary checkout of the entire Mercury program before risking a human astronaut." [36]

Other space-related events soon distracted public attention from the impending primate voyage on MA–5. One was the perfect launching of the mammoth Saturn I on its maiden flight. On the morning of October 27, the 163-foot-tall vehicle, with its 1.3 million pounds of thrust, rocketed 215 miles into space. The flight immediately triggered public discussion of whether a super-Saturn might be selected for launching the lunar mission spacecraft.[37] In Houston, the Manned Spacecraft Center, site for the direction of manned space projects of the future, captured the imagination of local citizens. A space-age tradition was born when H. T. Christman, a procurement officer, became the first member of the organization to buy a home in the Houston area, which was located in the Timber Cove residential development that was to become the neighborhood of several Mercury astronauts, near the site of the to-be-constructed Spacecraft Center.

Preparation for MA–5, initiated many months previously, continued without much fanfare. As early as January 1961, notes on the status of hardware for this mission had begun to appear in STG's quarterly progress reports to NASA Headquarters. Both booster and spacecraft then were being manufactured and tested. On February 24, spacecraft No. 9 had arrived at the Cape to begin a 40-week preflight preparation. This lengthy period, longest in the Mercury project, derived from the various flight program changes that required corresponding configuration changes. No. 9 had been configured initially for a ballistic instrumented flight, then for a ballistic primate flight, next for a three-orbit instrumented mission, and finally for a three-orbit chimpanzee flight.[38]

Another factor contributing to the long preparatory period was that the data obtained from the MA–4 mission demanded a number of modifications. For the environmental control system, a locking device was added to the oxygen emergency rate handle, while the inverters, one of which had failed during MA–4, were put through a severe vibration-test program. Since some unbonding had occurred on the heatshield of the MA–4 spacecraft, x-rays twice were made of the ablative layer to determine the soundness of the glue line. For the explosive side egress hatch, as yet untried on an orbital mission, thermocouples were added and a limit switch was installed to signal any premature hatch firing, an experience that cost the loss of a flight-tested spacecraft in MR–4. And the horizon scanner sensor system was modified to avoid the erroneous signals transmitted during the orbit of the "mechanical man." [39]

Thus the spacecraft mounted on Atlas No. 93–D for MA–5 differed considerably from that used on the September orbital flight. This was another reason Haney had said that "the men in charge of Project Mercury" wanted another qualifying round before a manned mission. Besides modifications already described, No. 9 had a landing bag installed and a large viewing window. Although the window had been used on MR–4 and had proved useful to Astronaut Grissom, it had not been subjected to the much greater reentry heat the MA–5 capsule would encounter. Aside from these new components, No. 9 had about the same equipment as carried in MA–4—tape recorders for gathering data and exercising the communications network, cameras, and radiation film packs. Of course, "Enos," the chimpanzee eventually selected from the colony in training, would need no simulator to do his breathing or perspiring. He had his own metal-plastic pressure couch, which was connected to the suit circuit of the environmental control system.[40]

The spacecraft operated in a fashion similar to the first orbital Mercury vehicle. Once again, as during MA-4, the hydrogen peroxide fuel supplies for the automatic and manual control systems were linked to provide a common reservoir. The automatic stabilization and control and rate stabilization control systems would be operated separately, so that the performance of each could be evaluated. The automatic system was programmed to exercise capsule attitude control until one minute after the .05-g light signal; then the rate system would take over for reentry, providing a constant-roll rate of about 7.5 degrees per second as well as damping motions in the yaw and pitch axes. The rate system would switch off at main parachute deployment.[41]

Recovery aids and operations, too, were about the same as for MA-4, including radar chaff, sofar bombs, a flashing light, and dye marker. The probable launch abort recovery areas were spaced and designated as before, although there were more contingency recovery areas because the mission was longer. For each of the three planned orbits about five contingency locations were selected. During the second orbit, for example, the emergency landing areas included the Atlantic Ocean near the west coast of Africa, the Indian Ocean near the east coast of Africa, the Indian Ocean near the west coast of Australia, and the Pacific Ocean either 440 miles southeast of Hawaii or 165 miles southwest of San Diego. The primary recovery zone shifted following the completion of each full orbit.[42]

Space Task Group officials expected delivery of the MA-5 launch vehicle, Atlas No. 93-D, about mid-August 1961, but it was decided by STG and the Air Force to delay shipment until the flight of MA-4. Then, when faulty transistors had delayed the MA-4 launch, intensive quality assurance inspections of the transistors had to be initiated. The electronic gear of the rocket was also modified, its 100-watt telemetry system was replaced by a 3-watt transistorized unit, and the autopilot circuitry was altered to alleviate the high vibrations experienced during the first orbital Mercury flight. These changes dragged the delivery date back to October 9, 1961. In Washington, George Low warned Seamans that the time needed to secure several components necessary for these modifications might affect the delivery date of Atlas No. 109-D, the booster scheduled to launch the first astronaut into orbit. No. 93-D was the third "thick skin" Atlas booster, employing a heavier gauge of metal in its forward tank.[43]

According to plans, which now were to approximate those for the manned orbital mission as nearly as possible, MA-5 would rise from complex 14 at Cape Canaveral on a heading 72.51 degrees east of north. Orbital insertion of the spacecraft should occur about 480 miles from the Cape at an altitude of 100 miles and at a speed of about 25,695 feet per second. Retrofire to initiate entry into the atmosphere was planned for 4 hours, 32 minutes, and 26 seconds after launch. Twenty-one minutes and 49 seconds later the spacecraft should hit the water in the Atlantic. Estimated temperatures during reentry should be about 3000 degrees F on the heatshield, 2000 degrees on the antenna housing, 1080 degrees on the cylindrical section, and 1260 degrees on the conical section. The STG operation planners estimated that the spent Atlas sustainer engine would reenter the atmosphere after 9⅓ orbits, a considerable change from their estimates for the descent of the MA–4 rocket.[44]

Training Primates and Men

For the all-important task of checking out the environmental control system on a long-duration flight, a chimpanzee was chosen to "stand in" for man. As in the preparation for Ham's suborbital mission on MR–2, two colonies of chimps traveled to the Cape about three weeks before the flight date. Again the military handlers from Holloman Air Force Base separated the colonies to prevent cross-infection. Training involved restraining the animals in a pressurized flight couch, with biosensors attached to their bodies at various points. And psychomotor training that had been started in New Mexico was continued at the Cape so that the animals' proficiency would not deteriorate.[45]

On October 29, 1961, three chimps and 12 medical specialists moved into their Cape quarters to join two other simians and eight persons already in flight preparation status. The name given to "Enos," the animal selected as the flight test subject, in Greek or Hebrew means "man," and the training and flight performance recorded by this chimpanzee proved the sobriquet to be well chosen. Captain Jerry Fineg, chief veterinarian for the mission, described Enos as "quite a cool guy and not the performing type at all." This "immigrant" from the French Cameroons had none of the tendencies of his circus-trained counterparts. Enos' backup "pilots," listed in order of their flight readiness ability, were "Duane," named for Duane Mitch, a veterinarian; "Jim," named for Major James Cook, of the same profession; "Rocky," named for a well-known pugilist (Graziano) because of his cauliflowered ear and pugnacious spirit; and "Ham," the astrochimp veteran. The ratings were made by Fineg and another Air Force officer Marvin Grunzke. Fineg later learned that when these same chimps had gone through their earlier launch and reentry training on the centrifuge at the University of Southern California, they had been rated in the same order.[46]

The psychomotor equipment used by Enos on the MA–5 mission was more complicated than that operated by Ham during the Mercury-Redstone 2 suborbital flight. Housed in the cover of his pressurized couch, Enos' package was rigged to present a four-problem cycle. The first would last for about 12 minutes, and the second followed six minutes of rest. The routine would proceed until the

400

cycle was completed, then the four problems would be repeated until the mission ended. Problem one would offer right- and left-hand levers that Enos could use to turn off lights, avoiding a mild shock in the left foot (the same as for Ham). The second problem planned was a delayed-response experiment. Twenty seconds after a green light would appear on the panel, Enos would have to press a lever to receive a drink of water. Although there would be no penalty for his failure to respond, if the chimpanzee should pull the lever too early the problem would simply recycle and he would receive nothing. The third, a fixed-ratio problem, would involve pulling a lever exactly 50 times to receive a banana pellet. This would also be voluntary and without penalty. Chimpanzee intelligence would be tested in the fourth. Three symbols—circles, triangles, and squares—would appear in various two-of-a-kind combinations, with the task being to pull a lever under the odd symbol to avoid a mild shock. Lack of response during rest periods would give the indication that the animal was well oriented to his spacecraft environment.[47]

Planning for this second trial of the Mercury worldwide tracking network was elaborate. Supporting the MA-5 mission were 18 stations, plus the Goddard Space Flight Center and the Mercury Control Center. Goddard and the Control Center furnished computer support and management of the overall operation, respectively.

Station	Type
Mercury Control Center	Launch
Cape Canaveral (AMR)	Launch
Grand Bahama Island (AMR)	Downrange tracking
Grand Turk	Downrange tracking
Bermuda	Computer
Atlantic Ocean Ship	Remote tracking
Canary Islands	Remote tracking
Kano, Nigeria	Remote tracking
Zanzibar, Africa	Remote tracking
Indian Ocean Ship	Remote tracking
Muchea, Australia	Command
Woomera, Australia	Remote tracking
Canton Island	Remote tracking
Kauai, Hawaii	Command
Point Arguello, California	Command
Guaymas, Mexico	Command
White Sands, New Mexico	Remote tracking
Corpus Christi, Texas	Remote tracking
Eglin Air Force Base, Florida	Remote tracking
Goddard Space Flight Center, Maryland	Computing and communications

With the exception of White Sands, all stations would receive "real time" telemetry data, consisting of magnetic tape recordings, Sanborn recorder displays, meter displays, and clock displays. The overall operation of this network was a vast cooperative undertaking of the Department of Defense, NASA, and industry.[48]

MA–5
Nov. 29, 1961

*Enos in his couch
prior to launch.*

*Enos returns to the Cape
following his space flight.*

Seventy-three key people assigned to the various stations received their final mission briefing on October 23. Once again the tracking teams included several Mercury astronauts. Shepard was assigned to Bermuda, Schirra to Australia, Slayton to Guaymas, and Cooper to Point Arguello, while at the Cape, Carpenter had a station in the blockhouse, Grissom was the capsule communicator in the Mercury Control Center, and Glenn served as backup capsule communicator in the center.[49]

CHIMPANZEE INTO ORBIT

By mid-October, reported George Low to NASA Headquarters, problems with capsule No. 9 and booster No. 93–D had forced STG to delay the launch from November 7 to November 14. On November 11, however, after the preflight checkout crew found a hydrogen peroxide leak in the fuel line of the capsule manual control system, the earliest possible launch date slipped to November 29.[50] Although NASA did not comment officially on the effect of the delay, chances for a manned orbital mission in 1961 now were dim.[51]

On November 28, 1961, an 11½-hour launch preparation count began for MA–5. The count stopped at T minus 390 minutes, to be resumed the next day. Some 11 hours before the launch, Enos, the 39-pound chimpanzee, underwent his final physical examination, stood still as his medical sensors were taped on, allowed himself to be secured in the specially constructed primate couch, and rode in the transfer van to the gantry. About 5 hours before launch the couch was inserted in the spacecraft. Thereafter Enos' condition was monitored by lines connected to his couch in the Mercury capsule and by radio telemetry. He was relaxed during countdown. His temperature ranged from 97.8 to 98.4 degrees, normal for the suit inlet temperature of about 65 degrees; his respiration averaged 14; and his pulse rate was 94. The only time Enos displayed agitation was when he was roused by the opening of the hatch during a countdown hold caused by a telemetry link failure at T minus 30 minutes. The gantry was hauled back to the spacecraft, the hatch was opened, and an off-and-on switch was correctly positioned. This hold lasted 85 minutes. Some members in the control center joked that Enos had turned the switch off because he had talked to Ham and did not want to go.[52]

In the Mercury Control Center the flight control monitors had manned their stations and were busily checking out their consoles. Tecwyn Roberts, serving as flight dynamics officer, noted the intermittent problems cropping up in the data-gathering and translating computers. A faulty transistor in the direct data receiver caused one hold, and when the replacement was also faulty, several more minutes were lost in repairing the computer. Morton Schler, the capsule environment monitor, reported that the environmental control system was working smoothly. The Freon flow rate, he reported, leveled at a comfortable 20 pounds per hour in the prelaunch period. From the oxygen partial-pressure transducer some erratic readings proved erroneous; Mercury Control teletyped the tracking stations to discount these readings as the spacecraft passed over.[53]

Holds during the countdown amounted to almost 2 hours and 38 minutes. Shortly after the hatch was bolted at T minus 90 minutes, the technicians discovered that they had failed to install some hatch cover heat insulation material. They took a little more than an hour to correct this oversight. Then, at T minus 30 minutes, the discovery of an improperly positioned switch necessitated the 85-minute hatch-opening hold. And finally, at T minus 15 minutes, a 4-minute hold was called to correct a data-link problem between Mercury Control and the General Electric ground command guidance equipment.

Walter Williams, the mission director, listened as the various difficulties arose and became somewhat agitated at the chain of events. Although his usual position during such times was at a console in the mission control center, he left the building and quickly drove the distance to pad 14 to personally express his expectations that things would proceed in a more orderly manner. As a member of Convair later said, "Williams was a master in imparting a need for orderly urgency."

Despite these holds, weather conditions remained favorable. Only a few thin cirrus clouds hung in the sky, visibility was 10 miles, and the surface wind velocity was at a moderate 11 miles per hour from the northwest. In the landing area the weather was even better.[54]

The Goddard computers received the liftoff signal 13 seconds before the booster actually rose from the pad, an error apparently caused by feedback between two recorders. Nor was this the last incorrect signal. The Goddard computers registered sustainer engine cutoff twice before that event happened, once shortly after liftoff and again two minutes after launch. In each case the Mercury Control Center had to switch to override the signal until the panel indicator cleared.[55] Liftoff came at 10:08 a.m. The powered phase of the flight went well, although there were minor discrepancies. Between liftoff and staging, the horizon-scanner signal was lost briefly. All spacecraft systems nevertheless appeared to be working normally, with the guidance system of the Atlas keeping the booster on an almost perfect insertion trajectory. Guidance system noise was only about half that recorded during MA-4, and vehicular vibration also was much lower. Four and a half minutes after launch, Christopher C. Kraft, Jr., unhesitatingly made the go-for-orbit decision. At sustainer engine cutoff, the velocity, flight angle, and altitude were nearly perfect. The Atlas hurled the spacecraft into an orbit with a perigee of about 99 miles and an apogee of 147 miles, .5 and 5.4 miles low, respectively.[56]

Spacecraft and booster separation occurred precisely as planned, while the turnaround maneuver took less than 30 seconds. The capsule's position excursions were very slight, which contrasted sharply with the erratic turnaround of MA-4. The spacecraft quickly dropped into its 34-degree orbit mode and began streaking over the oceans and continents. Of the 61.5 pounds of control fuel aboard, turnaround and damping had consumed 6 pounds, as opposed to 9.5 for MA-4. From that point and on through the first orbit the thrusters used only 1.5 pounds to maintain a correct position, with the automatic stabilization and control system functioning perfectly.

The environmental control system and the tracking and communications network performed in a satisfactory fashion. On this mission, for the first time, the primary and secondary oxygen bottles were pressurized at 7500 pounds per square inch (the design specification) rather than at 3000, as on previous flights. A functioning water separator also was used for the first time. Each tracking station's range on the ultra-high-frequency band lasted for about six minutes; on high frequency, overlap communications between stations were similar to that experienced during MA-4. The Goddard computers received valid telemetry data from all stations except Woomera, but there were instances when communications were momentarily lost at particular stations. Just before retrofire, for example, Point Arguello, the site giving the firing command, lost contact with the Cape. In each instance, as Walter Williams would point out at the postflight press conference, communications were reestablished whenever that particular station was needed.[57]

Enos, the orbiting chimpanzee, fared well. He withstood a peak of 6.8 g during booster-engine acceleration and 7.6 g with the rush of the sustainer engine. He had been performing his lever-pulling duties for some two minutes before the Atlas roared and rose from the pad. During his two orbits he made 29 pulls (divided among four sessions) on the continuous-avoidance and discrete-avoidance levers, receiving only one shock in each category. On his second problem, which required at least a 20-second delayed response to receive a drink of water, his average delay was about 33.8 seconds. For these labors he was rewarded with a total of 47 measures of water, or about a pint during the three-hour mission. For the fixed-ratio task, problem three, Enos pumped his lever and received 13 banana pellets during his four opportunities. On the first session of problem Four, Enos was correct for 18 out of 28 symbol presentations (64.2 percent), thus receiving 10 shocks as a result of his miscues. On the second session of problem four, however, the center lever malfunctioned, causing shocks even if he pulled the correct lever. He received 36 and 43 successive shocks on the third and fourth sessions, respectively, because a manmade device had failed. The shocked and frustrated chimpanzee nevertheless kept pulling the levers. As he was also trained to do, Enos remained at rest during the six-minute intervals between problems.[58]

Near the end of the first orbit, the tracking monitors noted that the capsule clock was about 18 seconds too fast and as it passed over the Cape a corrective command was dispatched to and accepted by the clock. At that time the Mercury Control Center display panels indicated that all spacecraft systems were in good order. Suddenly the Atlantic tracking ship reported that inverter temperatures were rising. The Canary Island trackers confirmed the environmental control system malfunction. Since abnormal heating had occurred on earlier flights and the inverters had continued working or had switched to standby, there was no alarm among members at Mercury Control. Then, across the world from the Cape, Muchea, Australia, detected high thruster signals and capsule motion excursions, although other data indicated that the 34-degree orbit mode was being maintained. The Woomera, Australia, tracking station failed to confirm this report, and it was discounted.[59]

By the time the MA-5 capsule reached the vicinity of the Canton Island station, the operations team realized that the attitude control system was allowing the vehicle to go out of its proper orbital mode. A metal chip in a fuel supply line (the postflight inspection would reveal) had cut off the propellant flow to one of the clockwise roll thrusters. This inactive thruster allowed the spacecraft to drift minus 30 degrees from its normal attitude, at which point the automatic stabilization and control system brought the spacecraft to zero in a normal roll-turn maneuver. Then the spacecraft swung briefly back into the nominal 34-degree orbital attitude, and the sequence started again. The spacecraft repeated this process of drift and correction nine times before retrofire and once more between retrofire and the receipt of the .05-g light telemetry signal. The still-active thrusters used about 9.5 pounds of control fuel working to keep the capsule properly aligned. Each loss of orbit mode cost a little over a pound of fuel compared with a first-orbit expenditure of only 1.5 pounds.[60]

The cooling equipment in the environmental control system also began to give trouble during the second orbit. Between the Canary Islands and Kano, the suit circuit temperature rose rapidly from 65 to 80 degrees, indicating a freezing condition in the heat exchanger. As water in the felt evaporator pad of the exchanger turned to ice, Enos' body temperature climbed to 99, then to 100 degrees. The medical observers began to worry, especially about the chimp's ability to handle his psychomotor test problems. Then, at 100.5 degrees, his body temperature appeared to stabilize, suggesting that the environmental system was ceasing to overheat. Their fears relieved, the physicians felt that the mission could continue. Although the cooling system had seemed to correct itself, Kraft, the flight director, later remarked that a deicing unit should be added to warm the troublesome unit, which had also caused a freeze-up on MA–4.[51] Although the medical monitors were willing to allow the mission to proceed through its scheduled third pass around the world, the operations team believed that the problem of the spacecraft's erratic attitude was too grave to live with. The engineers felt that there simply was not enough attitude fuel left to complete the circuit and then go through the reentry phase, in which, even under normal circumstances, fuel usage would be high.

After the attitude aberrations were first noted, Kraft had alerted the tracking unit in Hawaii for a possible clock change to initiate retrofire during the second orbit. Then he decided to continue the flight toward California and notified Gordon Cooper at Point Arguello that that station might have to initiate a ground command for retrofire. Meanwhile, the capsule continued to drift and swing in and out of the orbital mode, demonstrating that the attitude control system, unlike the environmental control system, would not solve its own problems. Twelve seconds before the retrofire point was reached for the normal second-orbit primary recovery point, Kraft decided to bring Enos back to Earth. Arnold Aldrich, MSC's chief flight controller at Point Arguello, correctly executed the command.[62]

With the exception of the one repeated variation in attitude position, caused by the dead roll thruster, reentry went according to plan. The destroyers *Stormes* and *Compton* and a P5M airplane began preparing for spacecraft retrieval in Station 8, the predicted impact point. Three hours and 13 minutes after launch and about nine minutes from water impact, the P5M spotted the descending spacecraft at an altitude of about 5000 feet and radioed the *Stormes* and the *Compton,* 30 miles away. All spacecraft recovery aids except the sarah beacon functioned properly. During the spacecraft's descent, the airplane circled and reported landing events, then remained in the area until the *Stormes* arrived, an hour and 15 minutes after the landing, and hauled Enos and his spacecraft aboard. Shortly thereafter the hatch was explosively released from outside the capsule by a pull on its lanyard, causing the chimp's "picture" window to crack.[63]

Aboard the *Stormes* and later at Cape Canaveral, Manned Spacecraft Center and McDonnell engineers gave the capsule the usual close scrutiny and happily found that it had held up well. Except for a slight discoloration caused by aerodynamic heating, the exterior showed no buckling or warping. The interior was in good shape, too, although the inspectors did find a small amount of salt water. Activation of the explosive hatch caused minor damage in the form of the cracked window, several bolts pulled from the skin, and a slight buckle. Thermodynamic effects on the ablation heatshield had produced several radial and circular cracks, none of which had been severe enough to threaten the capsule's structural integrity. The center plug of the heatshield was missing (it had only worked loose on MA-4), but close inspection of the opening showed that the plug had evidently been in place during reentry. Condition of the impact bag, which had survived its first orbital test, was fairly good, although several straps were broken and others were severely bent. Again the plastic bulkhead was pierced, probably by the heatshield, and the honeycomb material was crushed in several places. There was no damage to the tubing or wiring in this area.[64]

At the Cape postflight press conference the leaders of Project Mercury revealed no regrets over missing a third orbit. They seemed to regard the reprogramming operation, conducted in the middle of the mission, as a satisfying technical accomplishment. In view of the decisiveness with which the various potentially critical difficulties had been overcome or circumvented, MA-5 had to be termed an excellent operation, one that had achieved most of its objectives and that would become a milestone on the road into the unknown.

Enos had been weightless for 181 minutes and had performed his psychomotor duties with aplomb. Operations director Williams felt that an astronaut riding in the MA-5 spacecraft could have made the necessary corrections in flight to complete the three-orbit mission normally. On the spacecraft attitude control problem, for example, a man could simply have switched from automatic to manual mode, he said. At the same time, Williams was pleased that the automatic systems had worked well for over two hours. Equally significant, the vast network of NASA, military, and industry personnel had performed like veterans during the emergency. The spacecraft had reentered and landed without handing the Navy any unexpected recovery problems.

Now a Man in Orbit?

The press corps at the usual postflight press conference listened courteously to this technical postmortem, but their main concern was whether another test mission would be flown before a manned orbital flight. Williams and Gilruth cautiously replied that first the MA-5 data would have to be thoroughly evaluated. Then the reporters wanted to know who had been selected to make Mercury's first manned orbital flight. Gilruth was ready for that one; he announced the team members for the next two missions. John H. Glenn was the selected prime pilot for the first mission, with M. Scott Carpenter as his backup. Donald K. Slayton and Walter M. Schirra were pilot and backup, respectively, for the second mission.[65] This announcement represented a considerable change from the tighter news policy regarding crew selection that had prevailed in suborbital days.

Meanwhile Enos had his moment. After the urbane anthropoid came

407

aboard the *Stormes,* he ate two oranges and two apples, his first fresh food since he had gone on a low-residue pellet diet. The destroyer dropped Enos at the Kindley Air Force Base hospital in Bermuda, where Jerry Fineg took over. The chimp was walked in the corridors and appeared to be in good shape. His body temperature was 97.6 degrees; his respiratory rate was 16; and his pulse was 100. Apparently reentry, reaching a peak of 7.8 g, had not hurt him. His composure at his "press conference" surprised the correspondents. One reporter remarked that Enos, unlike Ham, did not become "unhinged" with the popping of the flash bulbs. On December 1, Enos reached the Cape for another round of physicals, and a week later he departed for his home station at Holloman, and well-deserved retirement.[66]

Enos' fame was short-lived. Public attention now turned to the supposedly imminent American manned orbital flight, although there still was no assurance that a spacecraft would next carry a man. Speculation mounted when Atlas 109–D was hauled into the Cape on the night of November 30. Newsmen immediately gathered around B. G. MacNabb, the Convair preparation chief, to ask when the checkout would start. "Tomorrow," he replied. When asked if there would be a crash effort in order to make the flight in 1961, Wil-

"We're a Little Behind the Russians and A Little Ahead of the Americans"

A humorous view of the implications of the "monkey flights" to the space race was offered by cartoonist John Fischetti of the Newspaper Enterprise Association.

liams said that three shifts were working a 168-hour week (all the hours possible), and that no special pressure would be applied. None of these statements dampened speculation by the press early in December. Signs, rumors, and portents cropped up daily. One correspondent, for example, noted that John Glenn had moved into special quarters at the Cape, adding that NASA had requested Atlantic Missile Range support beginning on December 20 and continuing to year's end.[67]

If NASA had ever been involved in a drive to put an American in orbit in the year of the Vostoks, that effort halted on December 7, the 20th anniversary of the Pearl Harbor attack. Almost casually Gilruth and Williams announced that the flight was now scheduled for early 1962. The decision, said MSC officials, had been influenced by "minor problems dealing with the cooling system and positioning devices in the Mercury capsule." The official press release did state that NASA considered the spacecraft, its systems, and the tracking network qualified for manned flight. It had been apparent to many NASA officials for some time that the manned orbital launch might have to be postponed until 1962. George Low, at NASA Headquarters, had recognized the probability soon after mid-October, when he wrote, "The pad conversion time between MA–5 and MA–6 is exceedingly short if MA–6 is to remain on schedule." On schedule meant December 19.

Hugh L. Dryden summed up his philosophy regarding adherence to schedules for manned flight when he said, "You like to have a man go with everything just as near perfect as possible. This business is risky. You can't avoid this, but you can take all the precautions you know about."[68]

Although there was regret that this country did not get a man into orbit before the Soviets, or at least in the same year, 1961 had recorded substantial progress toward making the United States a spacefaring nation. In contrast with the atmosphere of uneasiness marking the end of 1960, the Manned Spacecraft Center engineers now knew that they were on the brink on fulfilling Project Mercury's basic objectives. The rehearsals were over.

XIII

Mercury Mission Accomplished

PROSPECTS looked bright to the managers of Project Mercury at the beginning of 1962. In store was Mercury-Atlas 6, scheduled as a manned orbital flight and viewed by some as a salvage operation for America's space prestige. If one of its citizens, Marine pilot John Glenn, journeyed successfully through space on a multi-orbit global mission, the United States would at least begin matching the pace set by the Soviet Union. Although a 3-orbit trek would by no means equal the 17-orbit, day-long voyage of Gherman S. Titov, the imminence of the mission had helped to allay national uneasiness somewhat. The notion that the manned orbital launch should be made in 1961 to coincide with Russian feats in the history books subsided with the end of the old year; 1962 was now here. Whatever regrets the American people had harbored over the numerous delays in Project Mercury, they seemed reconciled to schedule slippages if safety demanded them.

But the new year was barely three days old when the news media learned that the announced launch date of January 16 had been postponed until January 23, at the earliest, because of technical problems in the booster fuel tanks. With each succeeding delay, and there would be several more, journalists and Congressmen became a little more critical and fidgety. Once again, as on several previous occasions, the press spoke of the "space gap," and doubts were raised by some writers that the Mercury undertaking would ever succeed. A senior member of the House Committee on Science and Astronautics, Republican James G. Fulton of Pennsylvania, apparently subscribed to this feeling when he remarked, after viewing a January 27 MA-6 launch attempt, that the Mercury spacecraft and Atlas booster could be described as "a Rube Goldberg device on top of a plumber's nightmare." President Kennedy disclosed at a news conference on February 14 that he too shared the general disappointment voiced about delays in the program, but he added that the decision to go or not to go should be left to the "group who are making the judgment." Moreover, he reaffirmed his faith in the NASA Mercury team: "I'm going to follow their judgment, even though we've had bad luck." [1]

Statements issued by the Manned Spacecraft Center's operations team after each postponement of the MA-6 mission were terse and technical, and their frankness in reporting the reasons for these delays prompted some favorable news comment. The *Wall Street Journal* commended NASA for its open information policy, and pointed out that anything but "Candor at Canaveral" could only hurt the "national image." In response to their persistent and sometimes annoying questions, reporters were quietly told that this mission had been in the planning processes for almost three years and that a few more days' or weeks' delay was of little consequence if confidence in its success could be raised another notch. This acceptance of the situation by the Cape launch crew and operations team stemmed from the program's composite flight test experience. John Glenn, knowing all of this, enjoined the press representatives covering the event not to worry: [2]

> This mission has been in preparation for a long time. I can't get particularly shook up about a couple of days' delay. As a matter of fact, I'm so happy to have been chosen to be the pilot for this mission that I'm not about to get panicky over these delays. I learned very early in the flight-test business that you have to control your emotions—you don't let these things throw you or affect your ability to perform the mission.

The Mercury team alone knew what had to be right to make it go.

Back in October 1959, the MA-6 flight, possibly carrying a chimpanzee in spacecraft No. 18, had been scheduled for launch in January 1961. But the fortunes or misfortunes of manufacture and the ensuing flight test program forced many schedule slippages, redesignation of flight order, and capsule configuration changes to meet altered test objectives. According to an April 1960 chart, the first manned orbital attempt (originally MA-7) was slated for a May 1961 launch. Six months later the planners moved the target date for this mission to July, and after a similar interval they foresaw October as the likely launch date. NASA Headquarters' approval of the proposal to add one-day missions to the Mercury flight series required further schedule alterations. Several spacecraft had to be modified for the flights of longer duration. Spacecraft No. 13 was allocated to the MA-6 mission, replacing No. 18, which now was entered into the modification cycle. In spite of all this shuffling, as late as October 1961 the program managers held hopefully to an anticipated manned orbital liftoff within 1961. MA-6, instead of MA-7, the managers indicated, would carry the first astronaut into orbit, providing the MA-5 chimpanzee flight succeeded in November. [3]

A host of manufacturing changes had delayed the progress of spacecraft No. 13 as it traveled through the McDonnell production and checkout line. Number 13, beginning to take form in May 1960, also met with the usual fabrication problems its predecessors had faced during assembly. On October 10, for example, McDonnell reported to the Space Task Group that a shortage of environmental control system components had completely halted work on the capsule's interior.   At the end of January 1961, however, the company had started a three-month test shakedown of the vehicle.   Shortly after the completion of this work the failure of the MA–3 mission on April 25 had forced a rearrangement of spacecraft allocations, and McDonnell had been told by the NASA planners to redesign No. 13 for the initial manned orbital mission.   The factory finished and delivered the spacecraft to the Cape on August 27.   Four months later, after a thorough checkout by the Manned Spacecraft Center's (formerly Space Task Group) Cape team, on January 2, 1962, it was mated to its launch vehicle, Atlas 109–D.[4]

These had been some of the trials that made planning and scheduling difficult occupations, especially in a program that had been so often under national scrutiny.   Therefore, the successive MA–6 launching delays logged in the early days of 1962 simply were noted and accepted, and the planners met to decide when they could be ready to try again.

PREPARING A MAN TO ORBIT

Of course, hardware was only part of the problem of readying MA–6.   What about the second half of the "spacecraft-man" combination?   Would the man be just a passenger-observer or a participating system?   By mid-September 1961, Robert B. Voas, the astronauts' training officer, had drawn up a number of basic specifications concerning the pilot's duties in MA–6 in answer to questions of this sort.   If some part of the automatic attitude control system should fail, for example, the pilot would need to control spacecraft attitude using the manual system.   Or if displayed information on the spacecraft's attitude position should malfunction, the pilot would have to take over and rely on his visual abilities for position reckoning by external references.   Voas had studied high-altitude photographs of the MA–4 flight and he knew that on the sunlit side of Earth the horizon should quickly provide an excellent capsule attitude reference, but the nightside might present problems unless there was bright moonlight.   Possibly known stars could serve as attitude reference points, he theorized.   Voas also felt that a comparison of window and periscope reference was needed.[5]

To measure man's potential as a spatial navigator, Voas wanted the astronaut to look for the smallest detectable landmark, to estimate the effects of weather conditions on visibility, and to judge precisely the occultation of the stars by Earth's atmosphere.   Theoretically, from the vantage point of the orbital flight trajectory an astronaut should see about a 900-mile arc of the horizon.   He should be able to determine how much of this was effective horizon in terms of his ability to recognize a landmark with the unaided eye.   One important facet of any later space exploration, Voas said, would be man's visual acuity in estimating spatial depth and distance; tracking an artificial object in a nearly identical orbit during a Mercury circumnavigation would partially test this ability.   The spent Atlas tankage trailing the capsule should offer an excellent opportunity in this respect.

413

Ever since the Soviet reports of Gherman Titov's sensations of dizziness and nausea caused by his head and body movements, some aeromedical specialists had worried that perhaps the prolonged absence of gravitational stress did adversely affect a space passenger or pilot. Voas, considering this subject, contended that it was impossible to say whether Titov had had a purely personal aversion to weightlessness or whether men in general would have similar troubles under zero g. Neither Alan Shepard nor Virgil Grissom had experienced vertigo during the two Mercury suborbital flights. Voas felt that if disorientation and nausea were in fact products of longer durations of weightlessness, as some physicians and physiologists believed, the symptoms could be remedied through preflight training, proper flight procedures, or, if necessary, by drugs.

Voas acquainted the astronauts with the probable effects of weightlessness on their sensory organs. The otoliths, the ear's angular accelerometers, should not be affected, he said. Muscle and skin sensory functions should be affected only slightly, but those muscles sensing the amount of gravity would lose their acuity completely. By and large, the general diminution of sensory perception accompanying space flight should be overcome by the astronaut's eyes and his memory. To test his theories, Voas prescribed an experiment to be conducted on the dark side of Earth. The pilot would touch certain panel dials with his eyes open and then with his eyes closed, after moving his head quickly to the right, left, and forward. Gordon Cooper expressed qualms felt by several people over Voas' "blind flying" test when he remarked, "You shouldn't be reaching over on this panel with your eyes shut."

Other tasks planned by Voas included taking pictures through the window and periscope with a hand-held camera, describing the cloud cover on the day side, and looking for lightning in squall lines as requested by the United States Weather Bureau. On the night side the pilot should repeat those tasks and observe the aurora and luminescence of Earth's clouds. Finally, he should scan the star fields, the Milky Way, and note the size and appearance of the Moon as well as describe a moonset.[6]

The September study by Voas included the initial efforts of the Space Task Group to foster a scientific inroad into the manned space flight program. After distributing his paper among the astronauts and receiving favorable comment from several, Voas then sought the assistance of NASA Headquarters to obtain a broader base for possible astronaut activities in space from the various scientific disciplines that were available. Homer E. Newell and Nancy G. Roman of that organization reacted by directing the formation of an ad hoc committee for astronomical tasks for the Mercury pilots, assigning Jocelyn R. Gill as the committee chairman. This group was an offshoot of the formal Astronomy Subcommittee, a part of NASA's Space Sciences Steering Committee.[7]

As a beginning Gill and Voas attended a meeting of the Astronomy Subcommittee held at the Grumman Aircraft Engineering Corporation, Bethpage, New York, on October 30–31, 1961. Voas reviewed the abilities of the astronauts

414

to assume some additional tasks, such as observations of astronomical phenomena. He also cautioned that any integration of scientific equipment inside the spacecraft would have to be severely restricted in weight. The Astronomy Subcommittee discussed the possibilities and then suggested 10 tasks that an astronaut might accomplish. A few of these were: observe the night airglow as to its intensity and structure, look for comets before sunset and after dawn, note the frequency of meteor flashes, look for the aurora and describe its intensity, sketch the zodiacal light relative to the star background, and observe the size and position relative to the star background of the gegenschein.[8]

Besides generally acquainting the Mercury astronauts with the spatial environment, their possible reactions, and what they might accomplish in the way of operations and scientific observations, Voas also had pressed forward with a plan for a specific training program to prepare the crewmen to operate and manage the spacecraft systems on orbital missions. He first compiled a list of proposed training activities, and then he called a meeting at Langley on September 26 to discuss his report. The STG officers present adopted the training proposal, which became a formal working paper on October 13. With slight subsequent amendments, this working paper, No. 206, spelled out the astronaut training and preparation procedures that would be followed for the rest of the Mercury program.[9]

The first stated prerequisite for the astronaut, as formulated by Raymond G. Zedekar of STG, was a thorough familiarity with the spacecraft and all its systems. He must know every mission detail, including every flight and ground rule; he would be expected to demonstrate peak performance in every task during the flight; and his skills must include making failure diagnoses and taking the proper corrective action.

Preparing the pilot for his role during an orbital mission, the astronaut training personnel obviously could draw heavily on Shepard's and Grissom's suborbital experiences. The nine separate checkouts of the spacecraft after it arrived at the Cape, they felt, would provide excellent familiarization and systems training for the prime pilot and his alternate, who would be assigned to take turns in the capsule's contour couch. Then, if any modifications to the hardware or change in methods should become necessary, either man would be fully prepared to give valuable advice as well as to learn how the component change or new procedure would affect the mission. But by all accounts, as particularly ascribed to by the Mercury suborbital pilots, the best training sesssions for practicing both normal and abnormal flight conditions in the Mercury program were those held in the procedures trainer. There all phases of a mission—prelaunch, countdown, launch, orbit, reentry, recovery, and emergency—could be simulated. The training planners decided that at least 30 hours of practice would be scheduled in this McDonnell-made trainer. On some occasions the simulation called for hooking the trainer in with the Mercury Control Center and the Bermuda tracking site, an exercise that also would help the flight controllers check, promulgate, or practice their communications and control procedures.

Voas and his colleagues scheduled numerous other training activities that would supposedly hone the astronauts to a fine edge. One such plan called for the pilot or his designated stand-in to attend the spacecraft scheduling meetings, operational planning sessions, and booster, spacecraft, and mission reviews. After the spacecraft had been mated with the booster, the astronaut would have a key role in the capsule systems test, sequential and abort exercises, and the simulated flight that accompanied each countdown launch simulation. With the astronaut sitting in the spacecraft, all countdown checks would be run up to the point of hatch installation. Voas' training document stipulated that even the exercise of slipping the pilot into his capsule should be practiced until the insertion crew had it down perfectly. Besides all this work at the Cape, preflight trips were planned to the Morehead Planetarium in North Carolina, so that the astronaut and his backup pilot could fix star patterns in their minds as an aid to their orbital celestial observations. To obtain a familiarity with angular motion, they would attend sessions in the Pensacola Naval Air Station's "rotating room" and on the human disorientation device. Egress training, the value of which Grissom vouched for after his harrowing recovery, was scheduled on the open water in the Atlantic. Finally, there were Morse code instruction, map study, and briefings by the Weather Bureau support team on observation procedures.[10]

All these varied tasks had to be scheduled in logical progression to bring about a status of "flight readiness." The original training directive specified that an intensive training program for an upcoming flight should begin with a comprehensive study of all capsule instrumentation about 81 days before the launch was scheduled. Nine days later, after the astronaut and his alternate had memorized everything they could about the capsule instrument panel, they would start spending at least three hours per week in the procedures trainer, making brief excursions to Langley for sessions on the air-lubricated, free-axis (ALFA) trainer. In the procedures trainer they would go through specific mission profiles. These included a normal one-orbit mission, lasting about 90 minutes, with the astronaut in casual clothes; five-hour sessions simulating three orbits, with the astronaut wearing a pressure suit on some occasions; and 30-minute abort simulations, including such hazards as the failure of the retropackage to jettison, failure of the spacecraft's main batteries shortly after orbital insertion, and many other malfunctions covering every conceivable contingency that the training officers could devise.[11]

By December 1961, after Glenn and Carpenter had been publicly named for the Mercury-Atlas 6 mission, training plans were expanded to include their medical evaluations. For the altitude chamber simulated flight conducted about 45 to 60 days before the anticipated launch, Glenn was examined, fitted with biosensors, suited, pressure-checked, and then loaded into the transfer van and medically observed during the trip to the altitude test chamber. After he seated himself in the couch, his biosensor data were checked, his electrocardiogram leads were monitored, and the newly fabricated blood pressure equipment was exercised. Also there was a checkout of the spacecraft's environmental control system.[12]

416

Glenn performs simulated flight in the procedures trainer; Robert B. Voas looks on during the training session.

MA–6
Preflight

Glenn undergoes disorientation test.

Carpenter practices egress from the neck of Glenn's spacecraft.

Glenn takes time in the pad white room to pose with Thomas J. O'Malley of General Dynamics and Paul C. Donnelly of STG.

Jocelyn Gill also began planning the scientific aspects that Glenn might attend to while he was in orbit, when she called the first meeting of the ad hoc committee in Washington on December 1, 1961. William K. Douglas, Voas, and John J. Van Bockel attended from the Manned Spacecraft Center. The main purpose of this gathering was to adjust the suggestions emanating from the earlier meeting of the Astronomy Subcommittee into a workable order to provide the astronauts with as much background as possible of what they might expect to see in space. The first piece of equipment for scientific purposes aboard the spacecraft discussed was a small filter planned for use in studying the irregularities of the night-sky illumination and aurorae. For later missions an ultraviolet camera was suggested for possible use in photographing the stellar spectra.[13]

Some eight days later Glenn, Carpenter, and Schirra accompanied Voas and Douglas to a second meeting called by Gill. Point by point the requested astronomical observations were explained to the three astronauts. Because of their evident interest, Gill was of the opinion that such briefings, perhaps with even more detailed information, should be provided at intervals as well as just before flight time.[14]

During the month before the MA-6 mission, Glenn underwent at the launch site a realistic test termed "Pad Rehearsal No. 1." This exercise started with biosensor and suiting-up preparations at the hangar, transportation to the pad, and insertion of the astronaut into the spacecraft. Both the blockhouse and the Mercury Control Center were tied into and participated in this exercise. Several days later this operation was carried out again, and this time the gantry was pulled away to make conditions more realistic. Then about three days before the scheduled flight, after he had already begun his low-residue diet, Glenn went through a simulated mission encompassing the entire flight plan.

Other preflight medical activities included a complete physical examination two days before the anticipated launch. The Mercury physicians issued Glenn a number of medications for his survival pack, including morphine for pain, mephentermine sulfate for shock, benzylamine hydrochloride for motion sickness, and racemic amphetamine sulfate (a common pep pill) for a stimulant. Radiation-measuring film packs were tucked inside the spacecraft.[15]

Glenn and Carpenter had completed most of their preflight training program by the end of January, but the continuing delay of the MA-6 launch forced them to go on with their crowded routine. Glenn spent 25 hours and 25 minutes in the spacecraft during the hangar and altitude test chamber checks and uncounted hours on the pad after the launch rocket and spacecraft were mated. On the procedures trainer between December 13, 1961, and February 17, 1962, he logged 59 hours and 45 minutes (far beyond the 30 required by the training directive) and worked through 70 simulated missions in the process, reacting to some 189 simulated system failures. Glenn and Carpenter, along with Donald Slayton and Walter Schirra, already picked for MA-7, participated in a two-day (December 11 and 13, 1961) recovery exercise on the Back River near Langley Air Force

Base, Virginia, easily making both top and side hatch exits. Later Glenn and Carpenter, wearing life vests, carried out a survival equipment exercise off the beach at Cape Canaveral.[16]

Not only the pilots but many others were training for the MA–6 mission. On January 15, 16, and 17, 1962, recovery team swimmers practiced jumping from helicopters and placing the new auxiliary flotation collar around a boilerplate capsule. The flight controllers who were to deploy to the remote tracking sites got their final briefing on January 3 and left for their respective stations, where they engaged in seven rather extensive network exercises. Mercury Control, Goddard, and the Bermuda site conducted tests to check the Control Center-Bermuda abort command sequence. On January 25, Eugene F. Kranz reported to Christopher C. Kraft, the flight director, that the network team was at its peak condition. He feared that motivation and performance might decline if the flight continued to be delayed.[17]

Although this was to be the first manned orbital flight in Project Mercury, earlier flights set many precedents in the planning process for such items as recovery requirements, mission rules, and test objectives, and consequently the mission planning for MA–6 was almost routine. The launch azimuth heading was to be the same that Enos had followed into orbit riding MA–5; the recovery forces, now thoroughly seasoned, although somewhat larger than for MA–5, were stationed to cover essentially the same landing areas; ignition procedures and range rules for the launch were about the same as on previous Mercury-Atlas missions.[18]

BUILDUP FOR THE SPACE OFFENSIVE

Again NASA invited the world's news media to send representatives to cover one of its launches. On December 5, 1961, Headquarters informed newspaper and magazine editors that NASA was planning to accommodate up to 400 accredited reporters. No exact flight date was mentioned, but the press was told that the launch would occur "either late this year or early the next." [19] All hopes for a 1961 shot were dashed two days later when NASA Headquarters announced the postponement of MA–6 until early 1962.

Work to assist the news media in covering the event had been proceeding at the Manned Spacecraft Center for some time. Several months before the MA–6 launch, its Public Affairs Office, then under the direction of Lieutenant Colonel John A. "Shorty" Powers, began preparing a "Public Information Operating Plan," giving the estimated dates on which particular phases of the mission plan would be carried out. Powers evaluated each segment of the plan and recommended to the press various training and hardware preparation activities that the reporters might be interested in covering, as well as arranging for the reporters to cover flight-day activities. News release handouts were prepared covering almost every conceivable phase of the flight, from what the pilot would have for breakfast to an intricate discussion of how a spacecraft attitude control system should work.

419

About five days before the anticipated launch date, Powers and his troupe established a news center at Cocoa Beach, Florida. Some of his men were assigned to pass out fact sheets, some were to record pictorial events surrounding the flight for use by the news media, some were to seek answers to the myriad technical queries posed by newsmen, and some were assigned to prepare advisories concerning mission progress status.

Correspondents accredited by NASA, many clad in colorful beach raiment, descended on the area. They avidly consumed the space agency's prepared information, interviewed key figures of the NASA-DOD-industry operations team, sunned on the beach, and pressed for more news and anecdotes after the evening meal. Some critics likened the atmosphere to that of a circus, but literally hundreds of thousands of words about every conceivable phase of the manned space program poured out for the edification of the tax-paying masses.[20] Surely in history no program that still essentially was in its research and development stage had ever been so open to the public through the eyes of the Fourth Estate.

The first "gathering on the beach" to view the MA-6 launch occurred on a cloudy Saturday morning, January 27, 1962, after bad weather had forced the launch to slip day-to-day from January 23, when the firing was first intended. The countdown ticked on but the overcast remained solid, and a general feeling swept through the crowd of faithful "bird watchers" that this still was not the day. Finally, at T minus 20 minutes Walter C. Williams, the mission director, canceled the shot. The overcast was so heavy that the necessary camera coverage of the early trajectory events would be impossible. "It was one of those days," said Williams later, "when nothing was wrong but nothing was just right either. I welcomed that overcast." [21] John Glenn had been in his spacecraft, *Friendship 7*, named in a contest by his own family, a little over five hours. The rescheduling of the launch for February 1, four days ahead, necessitated emptying and purging the Atlas of its propellants.

On January 30 the ground support crew once more began fueling Atlas 109-D. During preflight checkout, a mechanic discovered, by a routine opening of a drain plug, that there was fuel in the cavity between the structural bulkhead and an insulation bulkhead separating the fuel and oxidizer tanks. The launch vehicle team estimated that, since the insulation had to be removed, a maximum of 10 work days would be needed to correct the problem and to check out the systems. This delay would slip the launch date, and slipping the launch date caused problems for the recovery force. Some 24 ships, more than 60 aircraft, and a number of specialized units, manned by a combined total of 18,000 personnel around the world, had to consider whether they could remain at their stations for a new date that might very well slip again. When all the tallies from the widespread units were before the recovery force commander, Rear Admiral John L. Chew, February 13 seemed the earliest possible next try at MA-6.[22]

On January 31, amidst an audible groan from more than 600 news-media

Press site 2, Cape Canaveral, in the early morning hours of January 27, 1962. Friendship 7 is silhouetted against gray clouds that would postpone the mission.

representatives who had managed to become accredited, the new launch date two weeks ahead was announced. Two weeks more at the Cape was too much for most of the benumbed newsmen; the exodus from the Florida peninsula began immediately. Only the spacecraft and launch vehicle technicians were left to minister, as Walter Williams termed it, to the "sick bird." Glenn took several days off to spend some time with his family at home in Arlington, Virginia. On one occasion he crossed the Potomac River to the White House for a brief visit with President Kennedy, who asked him many semitechnical questions about plans and systems for the orbital flight.[23]

On February 9, as NASA personnel began to move back to the Cape, the weather was still foul. Evidently the newsmen felt there was little chance for a launching on the scheduled date; by the 13th only 200 had checked in at the motels in nearby Cocoa Beach. They received some grist for the journalistic mill at a press briefing arranged by NASA's Paul P. Haney and "Shorty" Powers. Robert L. Foster from McDonnell answered some questions about the spacecraft and Major Charles L. Gandy and Lieutenant Colonel Kenneth E. Grine of the Air Force answered others on the launch vehicle work and the general state of readiness for the flight.[24]

The turbulent February weather in Florida improved little in succeeding days, and the space pilot continued to train. On the 15th, for example, Glenn, learning upon awakening that the weather still held up the launch, slept until 9:30 a.m., had breakfast, spent two hours on the procedures trainer, and that afternoon studied the flight plan and technical documentation.

On February 19 the sky brightened; so did the spirits of the operations crew, who immediately began the 610-minute split countdown. During the afternoon the Department of Defense recovery force weather observers in the Atlantic reported to Williams that they had favorable weather conditions. At the Cape, however, the Weather Bureau personnel observed a frontal system moving across central Florida which, they surmised, could cause broken cloudiness over the Cape area on Tuesday morning (February 20). Williams, hoping for the best, decided to continue and ordered the launch crew to pick up the second half of the countdown at 11:30 p.m. on the evening of the 19th.[25]

Meanwhile Glenn restudied the detailed mission sequence, first reviewing the countdown progress and then looking over his flight plan and checking the equipment list. That afternoon he attended another "final" mission review meeting, called by Williams. Glenn believed an astronaut should study his spacecraft's systems until the last possible minute before a flight. Shortly before he went to bed that night he read a section in the flight controller's handbook on the automatic stabilization and control system.[26]

AN AMERICAN IN ORBIT

Glenn was awakened once again at 2:20 a.m. on February 20. After showering, he sat down to a breakfast of steak, scrambled eggs, toast, orange juice, and coffee. At 3:05 the astronauts' flight surgeon, William Douglas, gave him a brief physical examination.

Douglas, Glenn, and his suit technician, Joe W. Schmitt, were only three of a multitude hard at work on the cloudy February morning. In the Mercury Control Center procedures log, the flight control team noted at 3:40 that they were "up and at it." The team immediately conducted a radar check, and although ionospheric conditions made the results poor the controllers believed the situation would improve soon. So they went on to check booster telemetry and the Control Center's voice intercom system, both of which were in good order. Shortly thereafter they found a faulty communication link that was supposed to be obtaining information about the capsule's oxygen system, but within minutes they had corrected the problem.[27]

At 4:27 a.m. Christopher Kraft, sitting before his flight director's console, received word that the global tracking network had been checked out and was ready. In Hangar S, Douglas placed the biosensors on Glenn, and Joe Schmitt began helping the astronaut don his 20-pound pressure suit. At 5:01 the Mercury Control Center learned that the astronaut was in the van and on his way to the launch pad. The van moved slowly and arrived at 5:17, 20 minutes behind schedule. But the delay was of little consequence, for at 5:25 (T minus 120 minutes) trouble had cropped up in the booster's guidance system. Since this came during the built-in 90-minute hold part of the countdown for the astronaut insertion activity, the delay was not likely to halt the readying procedures for very long. The installation of a spare unit and an additional 45 minutes required for its checkout, however, made a total of 135 minutes lost.[28]

Because of overcast weather and the guidance problem in the Atlas, Glenn relaxed comfortably in the van until 5:58, when the sky began to clear. The capsule and booster validation checks were progressing normally as he emerged from the van, saluted the onlookers, and boarded the gantry elevator. At 6:03, the operations team noted in its procedures log, the astronaut "put a foot into the spacecraft." Once inside *Friendship 7,* Glenn noticed that the respiration sensor—a thermistor attached to the astronaut's microphone in the air stream of his breath—had shifted from where it had been fixed during the simulated flight. Stanley C. White pointed out to Williams that a correction could only be made by opening the suit, a very tricky operation atop the gantry. So the two officials decided to disregard the slipped thermistor, even though faulty data would result. White advised the range to ignore all respiratory transmissions.[29]

At last the technicians began to bolt the hatch onto the spacecraft, but at 7:10, with the countdown proceeding and most of the 70 bolts secured, a broken bolt was discovered. Although Grissom had flown in MR–4 with a broken hatch bolt, Williams, taking no chances this time, ordered removal and repair. Taking the hatch off and rebolting would require about 40 minutes, so the operations team took this opportunity to run still another check of the guidance system on Atlas 109–D. Glenn evidently maintained his composure during this hold, with his pulse ranging between 60 and 80 beats per minute. When a little more than half of the bolts had been secured, he peered through the periscope and remarked to Scott Carpenter and Alan Shepard in the Control Center, "Looks like the weather is breaking up." [30]

Minutes later the hatch installation was completed and the cabin purge was started. A check of the cabin oxygen leakage rate indicated 500 cubic centimeters per minute, well within design specifications. At 8:05, T minus 60 minutes, the countdown continued, but after 15 minutes a hold was called to add about 10 gallons of propellant to the booster's tanks. Glenn had been busily going over his capsule systems checklist. As the holds continued, he occupied his time and relieved the pressure at various points on his cramped body by pulling on the bungee-cord exercising device in front of his head in the capsule. The countdown resumed while the liquid oxygen was being pumped aboard the Atlas, but at T minus 22 minutes, 8:58, a fuel pump outlet valve stuck, causing still another hold.[31]

At that point in the countdown, Glenn, the blockhouse and Control Center crews, and workers scurrying around and climbing on the gantry were joined by some 100 million people watching television sets in about 40 million homes

Above, Glenn leaves Hangar S with Dr. William K. Douglas (center) and Joe W. Schmitt. The launch (above right). At right, Army Larc stands ready for emergency recovery. Below right, Mercury Control's big radar follows the launch trajectory.

**Flight of
Friendship 7
Feb. 20, 1962**

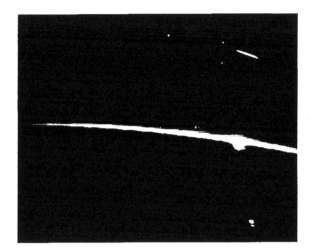

Glenn photographs the flattened sun of an orbital sunset.

Mercury Control mans its bank of flight monitoring consoles.

On Grand Turk Island, Glenn continues debriefing for, left to right, Kenneth S. Kleinknecht and John J. Williams of STG.

throughout the United States. Countless others huddled around radios in their homes or places of business and about 50,000 "bird watchers" stood on the beaches near Cape Canaveral, squinting toward the erect rocket gleaming in the distance. Some of the more hearty and sun-tanned spectators had been at the Cape since mid-January and had organized trailer towns, complete with "mayors." Mission announcer Powers, popularly known as "the voice of Mercury Control," who had been at his post in the Control Center since 5 o'clock that morning, went on the air to advise the waiting public of the status of the countdown and the cause for the present hold.

With the stuck valve cleared, the count picked up at 9:25, but another suspenseful moment came at $6\frac{1}{2}$ minutes before launch time, when the Bermuda tracking station experienced an electrical power failure. Although the breakdown was brief, it took several more minutes to steady the Bermuda computer.

At 9:47, after two hours and 17 minutes of holds and three hours and 44 minutes after Glenn entered his "office," *Friendship 7* was launched on its orbital journey. The Atlas, supported by its tail of fire, lifted off its pad, and Powers made the announcement that this country had waited three long years to hear: "Glenn reports all spacecraft systems go! Mercury Control is go!" As Atlas 109–D lunged spaceward, Glenn's pulse rate climbed to 110, as expected. The Atlas and its control systems telemetered signals that they were functioning perfectly.[32]

Half a minute after liftoff the General Electric-Burroughs guidance system locked onto a radio transponder in the booster to guide the vehicle until it was through the orbital insertion "window." The vibration at liftoff hardly bothered Glenn, but a hundred seconds later at max-q he reported, "It's a little bumpy about here." After the rocket plunged through the max-q region, the flight smoothed out; then two minutes and 14 seconds after launch, the outboard booster engines cut off and dropped away. Glenn saw a wisp of smoke and fleetingly thought the escape tower had jettisoned early, but that event occurred exactly on time, 20 seconds later.[33]

When the tower separated, the vehicle combination pitched over still further, giving Glenn his first view of the horizon, which he described as "a beautiful sight, looking eastward across the Atlantic." Vibration increased as the fuel supply spewed out the sustainer engine nozzle, then abruptly stopped when the sustainer shut down. The sustainer had accelerated the capsule to a velocity only seven feet per second below nominal and had put the Atlas into an orbital trajectory only .05 of a degree low. Joyously the operations team noted in the log, "9:52- - -We are through the gates." Glenn received word that he could make at least seven orbits with the orbital conditions MA–6 had achieved. To Goddard's computers in Maryland the orbital insertion conditions appeared good enough for almost 100 orbits.[34]

Although the posigrade rockets kicked the capsule loose from the booster at the correct instant, the five-second rate-damping operation started two and a half seconds late. This brief lapse caused a substantial initial roll error just as the

426

capsule began its turnaround. The attitude control system managed the deviation very well, but it was some 38 seconds before *Friendship 7* dropped into its proper orbital attitude. Turnaround spent 5.4 pounds of fuel from a total supply of 60.4 pounds (36 for automatic and 24.4 for manual control). Despite his slow automatic positioning maneuver, Glenn made his control checks with such ease that it seemed, he said, as if he were sitting in the procedures trainer. As Voas had asked him to do, the astronaut peered through the window at the tumbling Atlas tankage. It had come into view exactly as Ben F. McCreary of MSC had predicted it would. He could see the spent vehicle turning end over end, and he called out estimates of distances between the separating vehicles: "One hundred yards, two hundred yards." At one point Glenn's estimate matched the telemetry signal exactly. He visually tracked the sustainer intermittently for about eight minutes.[25]

Glenn, noticing the onset of weightlessness, settled into orbital free flight with an inertial velocity of 17,544 miles per hour and reported that zero g was wholly pleasant. Although he could move well and see much through his trapezoidal window, he wanted to see even more. "I guess I'd like a glass capsule," he later quipped. Weightlessness also helped him as he used the hand-held camera. When his attention was drawn to a panel switch or readout, he simply left the "weightless" camera suspended and reached for the switch. Dutifully carrying out all of the head and body movements requested by Voas, he experienced none of the sensations reported by Gherman Titov. While any Glenn-Titov comparison might be ruled invalid since Titov reportedly became nauseated on his sixth orbit and Glenn flew only three orbits, MA-6 at least was to demonstrate to the American medical community that there were no discernible adverse physiological effects from over four hours of weightlessness.[36]

The first orbit of *Friendship 7* began ticking off like clockwork with the Canary Islands reporting all capsule systems in perfect working order. Looking at the African coastline, and later the interior over Kano, Nigeria, Glenn told the tracking station team that he could see a dust storm. Kano flight communicators replied that the winds had been quite heavy for the past week.[37]

Glenn, completing his spacecraft systems checks over the Canaries, had commented that he was getting a little behind in his schedule but that all systems still were "go." Then, over Kano, he had commenced his own first major yaw adjustment, involving a complete turnaround of the capsule until he was facing his flight path. Glenn noted that the attitude indicators disagreed with what he could see were true spacecraft attitudes. Despite the incorrect panel readouts, he was pleased to be facing the direction his spacecraft was going.[38]

Over the Indian Ocean on his first orbit, Glenn became the first American to witness the sunset from above 100 miles. Awed but not poetically inclined, the astronaut described the moment of twilight simply as "beautiful." Space sky was very black, he said, with a thin band of blue along the horizon. He could see the cloud strata below, but the clouds in turn prevented his seeing a mortar flare fired by the Indian Ocean tracking ship. Glenn described the remarkable sunset: the sun went down fast but not quite as quickly as he had expected; for five or six minutes there was a slow but continuous reduction in light intensity; and brilliant orange and blue layers spread out 45 to 60 degrees on either side of the sun, tapering gradually toward the horizon.

On the nightside of Earth, nearing the Australian coastline, Glenn made his planned star, weather, and landmark observations. He failed to see the dim light phenomenon of the heavens called the zodiacal light; he thought his eyes had not had sufficient time to adapt to the darkness. Within voice radio range of the Muchea, Australia, tracking station, Glenn and Gordon Cooper began a long space-to-Earth conversation. The astronaut reported that he felt fine, that he had no problems, and that he could see a very bright light and what appeared to be the outline of a city. Cooper answered that he probably saw the lights of Perth and Rockingham. Glenn also said that he could see stars as he looked down toward the "real" horizon— as distinguished from the haze layer he estimated to be about seven or eight degrees above the horizon on the nightside—and clouds reflecting the moonlight. "That sure was a short day," he excitedly told Cooper. "That was about the shortest day I've ever run into." [29]

Moving onward above the Pacific over Canton Island, Glenn experienced an even shorter 45-minute night and prepared his periscope for viewing his first sunrise in orbit. As the day dawned over the island, he saw literally thousands of "little specks, brilliant specks, floating around outside the capsule." Glenn's first impression was that the spacecraft was tumbling or that he was looking into a star field, but a quick hard look out of the capsule window corrected this momentary illusion. He definitely thought the luminescent "fireflies," as he dubbed the specks, were streaming past his spacecraft from ahead. They seemed to flow leisurely but not to be originating from any part of the capsule. As *Friendship 7* sped over the Pacific expanse into brighter sunlight, the "fireflies" disappeared. [40]

The global circuit was proceeding without any major problems, and Glenn still was enjoying his extended encounter with zero g. He ran into some bothersome interference on his broadband HF radio when he tried to talk with the Hawaiian site at Kauai. An aircraft from the Pacific Missile Range tried unsuccessfully to locate the noise source. Other than the mystery of the "fireflies" and the intermittent HF interference, the mission was going fine, with the capsule attitude control system performing perfectly.

Then the tracking station at Guaymas, Mexico, informed the control center in Florida that a yaw reaction jet was giving Glenn an attitude control problem that, as he later recalled, "was to stick with me for the rest of the flight." This was disheartening news for those in the operations team, who remembered that a sticking fuel valve discovered during the second orbital pass of the chimpanzee Enos had caused the early termination of MA-5. If Glenn could overcome this control problem he would furnish confirmation for Williams' and others' contention that man was an essential element in the loop. If the psychologists' failure task analyses were correct, the flexibility of man should now demonstrate the way to augment the reliability of the machine.

Glenn first noticed the control trouble when the automatic stabilization and control system allowed the spacecraft to drift about a degree and a half per second to the right, much like an automobile with its front wheels well out of alignment. This drift initiated a signal in the system that called for a one-pound yaw-left thrust, but there was no rate response. Glenn immediately switched to his manual-proportional control mode and eased *Friendship 7* back to orbital attitude. Then, switching from mode to mode, he sought to determine how to maintain the correct attitude position with the least cost in fuel. He reported that fly-by-wire seemed most effective and economical. Mercury Control Center recommended that he stay with this control system. After about 20 minutes the malfunctioning thruster mysteriously began working again, and with the exception of a few weak responses it seemed to be working well by the time Glenn was over Texas. After only about a minute of automated flight, however, the opposing yaw-right thruster ceased to function. When similar trials and waiting did not restore the yaw-right jet, Glenn realized that he would have to live with the problem and become a full-time pilot responsible for his own well-being.[41]

To the operations team at the Cape and to the crews at the tracking sites, Glenn appeared to be coping with his attitude control problem well, even though he had to omit many of his observational assignments. But a still more serious problem bothered the Cape monitors as *Friendship 7* moved over them. An engineer at the telemetry control console, William Saunders, noted that "segment 51," an instrument providing data on the spacecraft landing system, was presenting a strange reading. According to the signal, the spacecraft heatshield and the compressed landing bag were no longer locked in position. If this was really the case, the all-important heatshield was being held on the capsule only by the straps of the retropackage. Almost immediately the Mercury Control Center ordered all tracking sites to monitor the instrumentation segment closely and, in their conversations with the pilot, to mention that the landing-bag deploy switch should be in the "off" position. Although Glenn was not immediately aware of his potential danger, he became suspicious when site after site consecutively asked him to make sure that the deploy switch was off. Meanwhile the operations team had to decide how to get the capsule and the astronaut back through the atmosphere with a loose heatshield. After huddling for several minutes, they decided that after retrofire the spent retropackage should be retained to keep the shield secure during reentry. William M. Bland, Jr., in the control center, hurriedly telephoned Maxime A. Faget, the chief designer of the Mercury spacecraft, in Houston, to ask if there were any special considerations they needed to know or to watch. Faget replied that everything should be all right, providing all the retrorockets fired. If they did not, the retropack would have to be jettisoned, because any unburned solid propellant would ignite during reentry.

heatshield correct? If so, would the straps on the retropack keep the heatshield in place long enough during reentry? And even if they did, was the thermal protection designed and developed into the Mercury spacecraft truly adequate? Would this, America's first manned orbital flight, end in the incineration of the astronaut? The whole Mercury team felt itself on trial and awaited its verdict.

Glenn and *Friendship 7* slowed down during their long reentry glide over the continental United States toward the hoped-for splashdown in the Atlantic. The Corpus Christi station told Glenn to retain the retropack until the g meter before him read 1.5. Busily involved with his control problems, Glenn reported over the Cape that he had been handling the capsule manually and would use the fly-by-wire control mode as a backup. Mercury Control then gave him the .05-g mark, and the pilot punched the override button, saying later that he seemed to be in the fringes of the g field before he pushed. Almost immediately Glenn heard noises that sounded like "small things brushing against the capsule." "That's a real fireball outside," he radioed the Cape, with a trace of anxiety perhaps evident in his tone. Then a strap from the retropackage swung around and fluttered over the window, and he saw smoke as the whole apparatus was consumed. Although his control system seemed to be holding well, his manual fuel supply was down to 15 percent, with the deceleration peak still to come. So he switched to fly-by-wire and the automatic tank supply.[45]

Friendship 7 came now to the most fearful and fateful point of its voyage. The terrific frictional heat of reentry enveloped the capsule, and Glenn experienced his worst emotional stress of the flight. "I thought the retropack had jettisoned and saw chunks coming off and flying by the window," he said later. He feared that the chunks were pieces of his ablation protection, that the heatshield might be disintegrating, but he knew there was nothing to gain from stopping work.[46]

Shortly after passing the peak g region, the spacecraft began oscillating so severely that Glenn could not control the ship manually. *Friendship 7* swung far past the "tolerable" 10 degrees on both sides of the zero-degree point. "I felt like a falling leaf," Glenn would recall. So he cut in the auxiliary damping system, which helped to stabilize the large yaw and roll rates to a more comfortable level. Fuel in the automatic tanks, however, was getting low. Obviously the heatshield had stayed in place; Glenn was still alive. But now he wondered whether his capsule would remain stable down to an altitude at which the drogue parachute could be deployed safely.

The pilot's fears proved real when both fuel supplies ran dry. Automatic fuel gave out at 111 seconds, and manual fuel depleted at 51 seconds, before the drogue deployment. The oscillations rapidly resumed, and at about 35,000 feet Glenn decided he had better try to deploy the drogue manually lest the spacecraft flip over into an antenna-downward instead of a heatshield-downward position. But just as he lifted his hand toward the switch, the drogue automatically shot out at 28,000 feet instead of the nominal 21,000. Suddenly the spacecraft straightened out and, as Glenn reported, "everything was in good shape."[47]

432

All systems in *Friendship 7* worked with precision for the remainder of the flight. At about 17,000 feet the periscope opened again for the pilot's use. Glenn, instead, glanced out the window, but it was coated with so much smoke and film that he could see very little. The spacecraft stabilized in its descent; the antenna section jettisoned; and Glenn, with immense relief, watched the main chute stream out, reef, and blossom. The Florida control center reminded Glenn to deploy the landing bag. He flipped the switch, saw the green light confirmation, and felt a comforting "clunk" as the shield and impact bag dropped into position four feet below the capsule. Glenn watched the ocean coming up to meet him and braced as the gap closed. Jolted by an impact that was more reassuring than stunning, he bobbed in the water, checked his watertight integrity, and relayed his elation that a successful MA-6 mission seemed assured.[48]

Friendship 7 had splashed into the Atlantic about 40 miles short of the predicted area, as retrofire calculations had not taken into account the spacecraft's weight loss in consumables. The *Noa,* a destroyer code-named Steelhead, had spotted the spacecraft during its descent. From a distance of about six miles the destroyer radioed Glenn that it could reach him shortly. Seventeen minutes later, the *Noa* cruised alongside; a sailor smartly cleared the spacecraft antenna; and Boatswain's Mate David Bell deftly attached a davit line for pickup. During the hoist upward the spacecraft bumped solidly against the side of the destroyer. Once *Friendship 7* was lowered to the mattress pallet, Glenn began removing paneling, intending to leave the capsule through the upper hatch. But it was too hot, and the operation was too slow for the already long day. So he told the ship's crew to stand clear, carefully removed the hatch detonator, and hit the plunger with the back of his hand. The plunger recoiled, cutting Glenn's knuckles slightly through his glove and giving him the only injury he received during the whole mission. A loud report indicated that the hatch was off. Eager hands pulled out the smiling astronaut, whose first words were "It was hot in there."

Lieutenant Commander Robert Mulin of the Navy and Captain Gene McIver of the Army, physicians assigned to the Mercury recovery team, described Glenn as being hot, sweating profusely, and fatigued. He was lucid but not loquacious, thirsty but not hungry. After drinking a glass of water and showering, he became more talkative. Asked if he felt any "stomach uneasiness" either during the flight or while he lolled the 17 minutes in the floating spacecraft waiting for pickup, Glenn admitted only to some "stomach awareness," beginning after he was down on the water. But there was no nausea, and the examining physicians assured themselves that Glenn's condition was caused by heat, humidity, and some dehydration. He had lost five pounds, five ounces from his preflight weight of 171 pounds, seven ounces. He had consumed the equivalent of only 94 cubic centimeters of water, in the form of applesauce puree, during the flight, while his urine output was 800 cubic centimeters. He also had perspired profusely while awaiting pickup.

Glenn's temperature an hour after landing was 99.2 degrees, or only a degree higher than his preflight reading, and by midnight he recorded a normal temperature. His blood pressure registered only a fraction higher than the preflight readings. The condition of his heart and lungs was normal before and after the mission, and there was nothing unusual about his skin except the superficial abrasions on the knuckles, caused by opening the hatch. By the time President Kennedy called his personal congratulations by radio telephone to Glenn aboard the *Noa*, the "wonderful trip—almost unbelievable" was over, Glenn was safe and sound, and 100 million American television viewers had happily ceased their vigil.

After recording on tape a "self-debriefing" aboard the *Noa*, Glenn was transferred to the carrier *Randolph*, where his chest was x-rayed, an electrocardiogram was made, and the initial phase of the technical debriefing was started. From there the astronaut was transported to Grand Turk Island, where a much more thorough physical began about 9:30 p.m., under the direction of Carmault B. Jackson, assistant to Flight Surgeon Douglas. February 20, 1962, proved to be "a long day at the office" for Glenn. After exhaustive tests and observations the attending physicians could find no adverse effects from Glenn's threefold circumnavigation in space. Technical debriefings continued for two days on the island and then moved to the Cape for another day's session.

The postflight analysis of Glenn's use of the three-axis handcontroller during reentry showed that about half of the thrust pulses he initiated opposed the direction of spacecraft motion, as they were supposed to. But the other half of the handcontroller movements either reinforced oscillating motions or had no net damping effect. The issue of "pilot-induced error" was picked up by some newsmen and reported as a controversy rather than a problem.

Now that the primary objectives of Project Mercury had been achieved at last in grand style, the drive for perfection in performance, so indispensable to manned space flight, still did not slow down.[49]

The Hero

The American reaction to this country's first manned orbital flight was a mixture of relief, pride, and exaltation. From the Rose Garden at the White House, President Kennedy echoed the sentiments of the Nation: [50]

> I know that I express the great happiness and thanksgiving of all of us that Colonel Glenn has completed his trip, and I know that this is particularly felt by Mrs. Glenn and his two children.
>
> I also want to say a word for all of those who participated with Colonel Glenn at Canaveral. They faced many disappointments and delays—the burdens upon them were great—but they kept their heads and they made a judgment, and I think their judgment has been vindicated.
>
> We have a long way to go in this space race. But this is the new ocean, and I believe the United States must sail on it and be in a position second to none.

Not only Americans but friendly foreigners hastened to add their praises for Glenn and Project Mercury. India's news media gave the flight top billing over an important national election. Most of the South American press viewed the space gap as already closed or being closed, while a sense of relief that a more favorable balance of power existed was evident in the African newspapers. Western Europeans were pleased with the openness of the undertaking, with the fact, frequently mentioned, that the United States had not used this momentous event to intimidate either opponent or neutral, and that the astronaut had kept his inflight remarks strictly apolitical. Numerous expressions of hope were voiced, as Khrushchev suggested and Kennedy repeated that Russians and Americans could enter into some sort of cooperative space program.[51]

The men of NASA, the Defense Department, and the aerospace industry viewed the feat more prosaically. They realized something of its impact on mankind, but most of their pride stemmed from the smooth-working demonstration of their space hardware and the recovery forces in action. And their interest quickly returned to the tasks of full exploitation of men and machines for Mercury.

Those who in the past had been the targets of technical kibitzing, domestic skepticism, and political pressure now were lauded by the American press for having "stuck by their guns." Periodicals praised Hugh L. Dryden, Robert R. Gilruth, Williams, Faget, Kraft, George M. Low, and Hartley A. Soulé, the "leaders of this technical team who did their work on civil service pay and sold no serial rights to national magazines. . . ."[52]

The MA-6 honors and celebrations consumed several days. Glenn, his family, Vice-President Johnson, and the Mercury entourage passed in review on February 26 before an estimated 250,000 people lining rainy streets in Washington, after which the astronaut gave a 20-minute informal report to a joint session of Congress. New York City proclaimed March 1 " John Glenn Day," and Mayor Robert Wagner presented medals to Glenn and Gilruth. The next day there was an informal reception in honor of the orbiting American at United Nations Headquarters. Glenn then journeyed to his home town, New Concord (population 2300), Ohio, where about 75,000 greeted him on March 3.

While everyone else feted Glenn, Mercury and contractor engineers at the Cape subjected his spaceship to a minute examination. Except for the usual discoloration, the interior and exterior of the capsule were in excellent condition. In several places where there were separations between the shingles, deposits of aluminum alloy had accumulated from the disintegration of the retrorocket package during reentry. A brownish film of undetermined origin covered the exterior surface of the window. Heatshield slices and cores showed about the same minor char depth found after the MA-4 and MA-5 missions; the center plug was sticking out about half an inch. There was also a wedge-shaped darker area on the shield, striated by several radial marks about four inches long, which the inspectors theorized was caused by the slipping retropack. The investigation

435

team also found that the rotary switch that was to be actuated by the heatshield deployment had a loose stem, causing the electrical contact to break when the stem was moved up and down. This, they believed, accounted for the false deploy signal that worried everyone so much during the flight. Although there were several tears in the landing bag, caused either by impact or retrieval handling, for the first time no cables or straps in the landing system were broken. And while the lower pressure bulkhead again was slightly damaged, the equipment there escaped harm.[53]

After this thorough postflight analysis, Glenn's spacecraft, McDonnell capsule No. 13, went on a global tour, popularly known as the "fourth orbit of *Friendship 7.*" Literally millions of people stood patiently in line to look inside the spacecraft as it was exhibited in 17 countries and Hawaii. By August 1962 *Friendship 7* had reached the "Century 21 Exposition" at Seattle. There, thousands more viewed the craft that had carried man on an orbital journey through space. Finally, on the first anniversary of its voyage, *Friendship 7* came officially to rest near the Wright Brothers' original airplane and Lindbergh's *Spirit of St. Louis* in the Smithsonian Institution.[54]

PROGRAM GROWTH

The dramatic series of events surrounding the MA-6 mission tended to obscure what was happening elsewhere in the national space program. While Project Mercury finally was fulfilling its prime objective, NASA picked the launch vehicle for its Apollo program. Headquarters announced on January 9, 1962, that a "Super Saturn" (also known as "Advanced Saturn" and "Saturn C-5") would be the Moon program rocket. The Saturn was then described as being as tall as a 27-story building generating 7.5 million pounds of thrust in its first stage, which would make it about 20 times more powerful than the Atlas. On January 25, the Marshall Space Flight Center received orders from NASA Headquarters to develop this booster that could support manned circumlunar flights and manned lunar landings. The Saturn was to place 120 tons in low-Earth orbit or send 45 tons of spacecraft toward the Moon. At the same time, the public got its first view of drawings of the Apollo and Gemini spacecraft.[55]

When the House Committee on Science and Astronautics opened its annual budget hearings on February 27, 1962, among the first witnesses to testify were John Glenn, Alan Shepard, and Virgil Grissom. Representative George P. Miller of California, chairman of the committee, introduced the three as "men who have been closest to the angels and still remain on Earth." All committee members expressed their satisfaction with the management of Project Mercury, and they reminded NASA that the agency was the committee's protege. Every tax dollar required to make Project Mercury and the rest of the civilian space program a success so far had resulted from the committee's study, approval, and authorization.[56]

Above, President Kennedy rides with Glenn and Gen. Leighton I. Davis at Cocoa Beach. At right, Glenn talks to a joint session of the Congress in Washington. Below right, Glenn, his wife, and Vice-President Lyndon B. Johnson are welcomed by 4 million in New York. Finally, in Washington (below), Friendship 7 is presented to the Smithsonian Institution. Shown here are Senator Clinton P. Anderson, Glenn, and NASA Deputy Administrator Hugh L. Dryden.

Astronauts Grissom, Shepard, and Glenn testify before House Committee on Science and Astronautics on February 28, 1962. Standing behind them are (left to right) Representatives Ken Hechler, Alphonzo Bell, and Perkins Bass, and Paul Dembling, Director, NASA Office of Legislative Affairs.

After the astronauts had made brief statements and answered some questions posed by the committee members, Administrator James E. Webb outlined the NASA budget request for fiscal year 1963. The total NASA request was for $3,787,276,000, of which $2.26 billion was earmarked for developing Gemini and Apollo and for further exploration with Mercury in manned space flight. Robert Gilruth testified about the Mercury portion of NASA's undertaking. By August 1962, when Congress passed the authorization bill, the NASA appropriation had been pruned to $3,644,115,000. This reduction included $90 million from research, development, and operational requests, and about $52.8 million asked for construction of new facilities. But the total NASA money bill, coupled with almost $1 billion that the Department of Defense received for its space projects, meant that the Nation was going to spend almost $5 billion annually on its space efforts.[57] The second phase of the Space Age seemed about to commence.

438

Constant communication of status information from one part of STG to another, from STG to NASA Hq. and other elements of the Government, and between STG and its contractors occupied much of the time of operating and staff personnel. At right is a typical preflight briefing, this one taking place at the Air Force Ballistic Missile Division for personnel of BMD, SSD, and Aerospace Corp.; involved in this particular discussion are, left to right, Christopher C. Kraft of STG, Byron G. McNabb of General Dynamics/Astronautics, and Bernhard A. Hohmann of Aerospace Corp. And in the tense atmosphere of Mercury Control during a flight, communication was at a premium. Below, in the front row of the VIP viewing room at Mercury Control, George Low of NASA Hq. leans forward to make notes for the report that he forwarded to the NASA Administrator immediately after every Mercury mission; next to him D. Brainerd Holmes, NASA Deputy Associate Administrator for Manned Space Flight, and Robert R. Gilruth, Director of STG, listen to the flight narration and watch the display board.

Meanwhile the Manned Spacecraft Center had been undergoing rapid changes, even though it was still located at the Langley Research Center pending the move to Houston. On January 15, 1962, the Mercury Project Office was established, reporting directly to Gilruth, together with the Gemini and Apollo management offices. Kenneth S. Kleinknecht, a former leader in NASA's X–15 project and technical assistant on Gilruth's staff since January 11, 1960, was picked to manage the completion of Mercury's program. Under its charter, the Mercury Project Office was "responsible for the technical direction of the McDonnell Aircraft Corporation and other industrial contractors assigned work on the Mercury Project." [58]

Project Office staffing and division of duties had been completed by the end of January. Kleinknecht chose William Bland, who had been associated with numerous engineering phases of the manned satellite enterprise since its inception, as his deputy. The internal labor divisions of the Office were: Project Engineering Office, Project Engineering Field Office (Cape), Engineering Operations Office, and Engineering and Data Measurements Office. At the outset, 42 people worked in the Project Office primarily on scheduling, procurement, and technical monitoring tasks. The similar management organizations set up for the Gemini and Apollo programs had James A. Chamberlin (manager of Mercury until the inception of Project Gemini) and Charles W. Frick as their managers, respectively. [59]

Moving MSC from tidewater Virginia to the Gulf Coast of Texas could have had adverse effects on its staffing. Quite a number of the employees had long years of service with NACA and its successor NASA, and had established deep personal roots at Langley and around Hampton, Virginia. Now they would be uprooted and transplanted some 1500 miles away in Texas. Many would face inconvenience and monetary and personal losses resulting from the transfer. Stuart H. Clarke, chief of the Personnel Office of MSC, polled the staff to determine how many favored the move. Of 1152 employees, only 84 indicated that they would not go. [60] Gilruth and Williams decided that while people, records, and equipment were being transferred, the operational and Mercury Project Office activities should remain at Langley to prevent the disruption of Project Mercury's flight planning. This meant that management in Mercury would be directed from Langley at least through Mercury-Atlas 7. [61]

THE SLAYTON CASE

Donald K. Slayton and Walter M. Schirra, pilot and backup, respectively, for Mercury-Atlas 7, had been in training side by side with Glenn and Carpenter since the team announcements were made after the MA–5 flight. On March 15, 1962, NASA announced that Slayton, because of an "erratic heart rate," had been replaced by Carpenter as the pilot for MA–7. The suddenness of this announcement surprised almost everyone, especially journalists who had begun turning out "human interest" copy about Slayton. The obvious question was: How could an astronaut, supposedly a perfect physical specimen, develop, of all things, a heart condition? The truth was that Slayton had been under close medical surveillance for over two years, and he and his fellow astronauts each knew how precarious a thing is perfect health.

The astronauts' physician, William Douglas, recognized that Slayton had a condition medically termed as idiopathic atrial fibrillation—occasional irregularity of a muscle at the top of the heart, caused by unknown factors—when the astronauts first rode the centrifuge in August 1959 at Johnsville. Douglas noted Slayton was performing his tasks in magnificent fashion, but he still thought it best to consult with the chief of cardiology service at the Philadelphia Navy Hospital. The consultant assured Slayton and Douglas that the condition was of no consequence and should not influence Slayton's eventual choice as a flight astronaut. The astronaut's physician did not accept this appraisal as a final diagnostic decision. He and Slayton visited the Air Force's School of Aviation Medicine in San Antonio, Texas, where a member of the internal medicine staff voiced the same opinion. Sometime later Douglas learned that this individual wrote to Administrator James E. Webb, making a recommendation that Slayton should not be assigned a flight.

After sojourns at various medical centers, Douglas informed Mercury Director Gilruth of Slayton's condition during the fall of 1959. Gilruth, in turn, briefed NASA Headquarters in Washington. Douglas also relayed the information to the Air Force Surgeon General's office and was advised to take no action. For some time thereafter the "Slayton file" lay dormant. The astronaut was selected as a pilot in November 1961 and began training for his flight.

Shortly after the beginning of the new year, NASA Administrator Webb, remembering the dissenting vote he had received from an Air Force physician, and, mindful of the fact that Slayton was an Air Force officer on loan, directed a complete reevaluation of the case. In response Douglas called together Stanley White, William S. Augerson, and James P. Henry, physicians assigned to the Mercury program, to study the matter in detail. Their considered recommendation was that Slayton should continue as the pilot for MA-7. From MSC, Douglas journeyed to Washington to brief Brigadier General Charles H. Roadman and Colonel George M. Knauf, Chief and Deputy Chief of the Office of Space Medicine in NASA Headquarters. These doctors also recommended that Slayton remain on space flight status. The reopening of the case was brought to the attention of the Air Force Surgeon General, who convened a board of eight flight surgeons to review the matter. The MSC physician appeared before that body, presenting it with every facet of the medical file. Slayton also appeared. The board judged Slayton to be "fully qualified as an Air Force pilot and as an astronaut."

Administrator Webb referred the case to a group of three nationally eminent cardiologists—Proctor Harvey, professor of cardiology, Georgetown University; Thomas Mattingly, heart specialist, Washington Hospital Center; and Eugene Braunwall, National Institutes of Health. Their consensus was that they were

441

unable to state conclusively whether Slayton's physiological performance would be jeopardized by his heart condition. Because of this unknown, they felt that if NASA had an available astronaut who did not "fibrillate," then he should be used rather than Slayton. Braunwall added that if there was sufficient time he would like to subject Slayton to some physiological tests.[62]

Asked several years later if he had known about his heart condition when he was chosen for Project Mercury, Slayton replied:[63]

> No, I didn't, but in the examinations prior to the August 1959 centrifuge program at AMAL the medics discovered that my heart skipped a beat now and then. I went ahead with the centrifuge runs and began to watch myself very closely, noticing that quite often after supper my pulse would be irregular. I would get out and run a mile and everything was normal again. I was terribly concerned over what in my diet might be causing it, but every hypothesis turned up wrong. Concern in STG and even NASA Headquarters got so great in 1960 that I was sent to all kinds of exhaustive examinations under the best heart specialists in the country—in Philadelphia, San Antonio, and New York City. I was examined by different groups of heart specialists who could find nothing wrong. Even Paul Dudley White, Ike's personal physician, gave me a clean bill of health but rendered an operational rather than a diagnostic decision, recommending that the unknown factor in my heart murmur not be added to all the other unknowns for manned space flight.

The Slayton decision was irrevocable, even though Gilruth and William Douglas disagreed with the high-level medical verdict. Slayton, they felt, had withstood greater stresses in the training program than he would have experienced had he been rocketed into orbit. On the other hand, Administrator Webb, because of the unknown elements, concurred with the cardiologists that it was neither safe nor politic to subject an individual who had a heart condition, however slight, to the stresses of orbital flight when there were other flight-trained astronauts available.

Shortly after the replacement, Douglas, having completed a three-year tour of detached duty with NASA, returned to his career service, the Air Force. Some newsmen were quick to conclude that this action suggested bitterness. They had not known that Douglas had been invited to the medical hearings but had known that Douglas had been outspoken in his opposition to Slayton's removal from flight status. Stanley White denied the charge in a news conference, maintaining that Douglas' return to the Air Force had been arranged for "better than six months."[64] Of the original team of astronauts, Slayton had been considered the professional test pilot par excellence, largely because of his overwhelming experience and flight time. He soon became the coordinator of astronaut activities. He never abandoned hope that he still might make a space flight. As late as December 1964, more than a year and a half after Project Mercury had completed its last flight and when Project Gemini was nearing its first manned flight, the unlucky astronaut remarked, "I've never been grounded and I'm not now. I still hope to get my chance to go beyond the atmosphere."

MA-7 PREPARATIONS

One would have expected, in keeping with the "backup" concept, that Schirra, the MA-7 alternate pilot, now would step in as prime astronaut. But in view of the numerous delays and consequent lengthy training preparations for MA-6, Williams, as the operations team leader, recommended to Gilruth that Carpenter, Glenn's backup pilot, was most primed for the upcoming mission. Carpenter had logged $79\frac{1}{2}$ hours of preflight checkout and training time in Glenn's *Friendship 7*, more than twice the $31\frac{1}{2}$ hours he would spend in his own *Aurora 7* for the same purposes.[65]

Although Glenn's mission had been highly successful, the Mercury operations team was still in the learning process. Experience with a component in the Mercury capsule or a flight procedure during the MA-6 orbital flight served to guide MA-7 mission planning. Glenn had shown that man definitely could be more than just a passenger, so the MSC planners adjusted the MA-7 flight plan to allow more pilot control of the mission. Combined yaw-roll maneuvers were scheduled to permit observation of the sunrise, as well as maneuvers to determine the use of day and night horizons, landmarks, and stars as navigation references. One of the more interesting planned innovations for Carpenter's voyage involved a period of inverted flight (head toward Earth) to determine the effect of Earth-up and sky-down on pilot orientation. Flight planners recognized the need for perceptual reorientation in space flight as well as for the motor skills that had been demonstrated so well by Glenn. The next Mercury mission ought to be as much of a scientific experiment as possible, not only to corroborate MA-6 but also to explore new possibilities with the manned Mercury spacecraft.[66]

Since Glenn had been able to respond to many of the scientific astronomical observation requests, Homer Newell, who had been Director of NASA's Office of Space Sciences since November 1, 1961, decided that the direction of the scientific portion of the manned space flight program should now become the responsibility of a formal committee. Jocelyn Gill again was chosen to serve as chairman of a group called the Ad Hoc Committee on Scientific Tasks and Training for Man-in-Space. Two days after receiving the mandate, Dr. Gill called a meeting of members, consisting of representatives from the various scientific disciplines, on March 16, 1962, to outline objectives, review past activities in this respect, present a preliminary analysis of the scientific debriefing of Glenn, and outline tasks and goals for the next meeting. One of the aims of the new committee was to devise a curriculum that would provide the astronauts with the best informational sources available about the spatial phenomena they might see. In addition to this, they proceeded to suggest several experiments to the Manned Spacecraft Center.[67]

So without jeopardizing either pilot safety or mission success, the MA-7 flight would be designed to yield as much scientific, as opposed to engineering, information as possible. Kleinknecht, head of the MSC Mercury Project Office, named Lewis R. Fisher chairman of the Mercury Scientific Experiments Panel, as a parallel to the NASA Headquarters unit, to manage and arrange for the experiments being suggested. Fisher and his associates were charged with reviewing all proposed experiments from an engineering feasibility standpoint in terms of their scientific value, relative priority, and suitability for orbital flight.[68]

The Fisher panel first met at Cape Canaveral on April 24, 1962, and decided to emphasize five suggested experiments: releasing a multi-colored balloon that would remain tethered to the capsule, observing the behavior of liquid in a weightless state inside a closed glass bottle, using a special light meter to determine the visibility of a ground flare, making weather photographs with hand-held cameras, and studying the airglow layer—for which Carpenter would receive special training. The tethered balloon was a 30-inch mylar inflatable sphere, which was folded, packaged, and housed with its gas expansion bottle in the antenna canister. The whole balloon package weighed two pounds. Divided into five sections of different colors—uncolored aluminum, yellow, orange, white, and a phosphorescent coating that appeared white by day and blue by night—the balloon was to be cast off near perigee after the first orbital pass to float freely at the end of a 100-foot nylon line. The purposes of the balloon experiment were to study the effects of space on the reflection properties of colored surfaces through visual observation and photographic studies and to obtain aerodynamic drag measurements by use of a strain gauge.[69]

Some experimentation on the effects of reduced gravity on liquids previously had been conducted at Holloman Air Force Base, at the Air Force School of Aviation Medicine in San Antonio, and at the Lewis Research Center. But the duration of these experiments, involving parabolic airplane flights and drop-tower tests, had been necessarily short. Results of an extended study would have both immediate and long-range implications in manned space flight operations. Already the problem of gas or fuel vapor ullage in space vehicles and in storage tanks was causing some difficulties, and later there would be related problems in orbital rendezvous fuel transfer. Before fuel tanks and pumps for extended use in space could be designed, the behavior of surface tension and capillary action of liquids in the weightless state had to be determined. For this experiment the Lewis Center provided a small glass sphere containing a capillary tube with tiny semicircular holes at the bottom of the open tube. The sphere, only 20 percent filled, contained 60 milliliters of a mixture of distilled water, green dye, aerosol solution, and silicone. The liquid had a surface tension of 32 dynes per centimeter on Earth.

The Massachusetts Institute of Technology requested photographs of the daylight horizon through blue and red filters to define more precisely the Earth-horizon limb as seen from above the atmosphere. These findings would be particularly valuable for navigation studies in the Apollo program. The Weather Bureau wanted information on the best wavelengths for meteorological satellite photography. John A. O'Keefe and Jocelyn Gill at the Goddard Space Flight

Center and NASA Headquarters, respectively, wanted a distance measurement of the airglow layer above the horizon, its angular width, and a description of its characteristics, and for this experiment Carpenter was provided with a photometer and trained to use it. Paul D. Lowman, also of Goddard, requested special photography of the North American and African land masses. Lowman's interest was based on his studies of planetary surfaces, particularly regarding meteoroid impact features.[70]

A number of technical changes based on MA–6 mission results were made for MA–7, mostly involving deletions of certain equipment from the spacecraft to reduce weight. Kleinknecht's office eliminated the sofar bombs and radar chaff recovery aids, which seemed unnecessary in view of the effectiveness that had been demonstrated by the sarah beacon and dye markers. Other deletions included the knee and chest straps on the couch, which had bothered Grissom; the red filter in the window; the moderately heavy Earth-path indicator; and the instrument panel camera, which had already gathered sufficient data.

Modifications made to improve spacecraft, network, and astronaut performance included a radio frequency change in the telemetry system to eradicate transmission interference like that experienced on Glenn's flight. The two landing-bag switches were rewired so that both had to be closed to activate the deploy signal. To correct temporarily the control problem experienced by Glenn, Karl F. Greil of the Mercury Project Office studied masses of data and concluded that the problem lay in the fuel line filters. So the dutch-weave filters in the fuel lines were replaced with platinum screens, and a stainless-steel fuel line was substituted. This was intended as an "interim fix," but it became permanent in the Mercury project for the later flights. Even the astronaut's attire underwent some modifications. Pockets were added on the upper sleeves and on the lower legs of the pressure suit for pencils, a handkerchief, and other small accessories. And the waterwing life vest, first carried by Glenn, was installed on the chest beneath the parabolic mirror. To add to Carpenter's comfort while he was waiting in his capsule on the launch pad, a new and more resilient liner was fitted in the couch.[71]

The three principal components of the MA–7 mission—spacecraft, launch rocket, and astronaut—were in preparation for several months. Spacecraft No. 18 was the first of these to reach the Cape, arriving on November 15, 1961. During its long checkout period by G. Merritt Preston's crew, this vehicle was reworked twice to incorporate lessons learned during MA–5 and MA–6. Some equipment and systems in the capsule had to be exchanged because what it had carried to Florida simply did not work properly. The original periscope, for example, failed to latch in the retracted position. Glenn's drogue parachute mortar supposedly had fired before the pilot triggered its button; the McDonnell engineers decided that a barostat in the recovery arming circuit should prevent another premature action. Since there still were questions concerning the temperature at different places on the capsule while it was in orbit, a device known as a "low-level commutator" was added, and temperature pickups were strategically located at 28 points on the spacecraft to record temperature data on a tape recorder carried on board.[72]

When in March he learned that he would fly spacecraft No. 18, Scott Carpenter named his capsule *Aurora 7*. He chose this name deliberately, "Because I think of Project Mercury and the open manner in which we are conducting it for the benefit of all as a light in the sky. Aurora also means dawn—in this case the dawn of a new age. The 7, of course, stands for the original seven astronauts." Coincidentally, the astronaut as a boy had lived at the corner of Aurora and Seventh Avenues in Boulder, Colorado.

The Atlas, the astronaut, and the ground support personnel entered into their final preparatory phase in March 1962. On March 8, six days after the Air Force accepted it at the rollout inspection at the Convair factory in San Diego, Atlas 107–D arrived at the Cape and was erected on the pad. Since the previous Atlas had performed well in boosting Glenn into orbit and since the MA–7 launch requirements were to duplicate those of MA–6, few changes were necessary for 107–D. One alteration was a slight reduction in the staging time, from 131.3 to 130.1 seconds after liftoff, to improve the launch vehicle's ability to reach the precise center of the insertion "window."[73] Intensive training for the astronaut, his backup, and the tracking teams on the MA–7 mission began on March 16. Mission simulations, flight controller training, and an exercise of the Defense Department recovery forces proceeded much as they had for MA–6. The Atlantic tracking ship, however, was not on station for MA–7 because she was at a Baltimore shipyard, being converted into a command ship to support the longer-duration Mercury missions.[74]

At the time of Glenn's flight, the launch of MA–7 had been scheduled for the second week in April, but the installation of new components, such as the temperature survey instrumentation and the barostat in the drogue parachute circuit, as well as other work, delayed the launching until May. Also contributing to the postponement was an Atlantic Fleet tactical exercise that required participation by the recovery ships and aircraft for several weeks. The week beginning May 20 looked the most feasible for sending a second American into orbit.[75]

FLIGHT OF *Aurora 7*

At 1:15 a.m., May 24, 1962, Scott Carpenter was awakened in his quarters in Hangar S at Cape Canaveral. He ate a breakfast of filet mignon, poached eggs, strained orange juice, toast, and coffee, prepared by his dietitian. During the next hour, starting about 2:15 a.m., he had a physical examination and stood patiently in his underwear as the sensors were attached at various spots on his lean body, and by 3:25 he had donned his silver suit and had it checked. Everything had gone so smoothly that Carpenter had time to relax in a contour chair while waiting to board the van.

At 3:45, Carpenter and his retinue, including Joe Schmitt and John Glenn, marched from the hangar and climbed aboard the vehicle for a slow ride to Pad 14, where *Aurora 7* sat atop the Atlas. Again there was a pause, during which a Weather Bureau representative presented a briefing to the astronaut-of-the-day, predicting a dispersal of the ground fog then hovering around the launch site. Finally, at 4:35, Carpenter received word from Mercury Control to ascend the gantry. Just before he boarded the elevator he stopped to swap greetings with and to thank the flight support crewmen. After the final checks in the gantry white room, the astronaut crawled into the capsule and got settled with only minor difficulties, and soon the capsule crew was bolting the hatch. This time all 70 bolts were aligned properly.[76]

Meanwhile the booster countdown was racing along. Christopher Kraft recalled that the countdown was "as near perfect as could be hoped for." The only thing complicating the prelaunch sequence was the persistent ground fog and broken cloudiness at dawn. Strapped in the contour couch, and finding the new couch liner comfortable, Carpenter was busy verifying his preflight checklist. Just 11 minutes before the scheduled launch time, the operations team decided that adequate camera coverage was not yet possible, and three consecutive 15-minute holds were called. Although Carpenter felt that he could continue in a hold status indefinitely, he was thirsty and drank some cold tea from his squeeze bottle supply. During the holds he talked with his wife Rene and their four children at the Cape, assuring them that all was well.[77]

The rising sun rapidly dispelled the ground fog. Then at 7:45 a.m., after the smoothest countdown of an American manned space mission to date, Mercury-Atlas 7, bearing *Aurora 7,* rose majestically off the pad while some 40 million people watched by television.[78]

Kraft, the flight director, described the powered phase of the flight as so "excellent" that the decision to "go-for-mission" was almost routine. Seventy-three seconds from launch, the booster's radio inertial guidance system locked on and directed the flight from staging until T plus 5:38 minutes. Actually this amounted to some 28 seconds after the Atlas sustainer engine had died, but no guidance inputs were possible after engine shutdown. Carpenter tried using the parabolic mirror on his chest to watch the booster's programming, but he could see only a reflection of the pitch attitude. At about 35,000 feet he noticed out his window a contrail, and then an airplane producing another contrail. The sky began to darken; it was not yet black, but it was no longer a light blue.

The booster performed much more quietly than Carpenter had expected from all its awesome power. Vibration had been slight at liftoff. Booster engine cutoff was smooth and gentle, but a few seconds later the noise accompanying maximum aerodynamic stress began to build up. A wisp of smoke that appeared out the window gave Carpenter the impression that the escape tower had jettisoned, but a glance showed that it was still there. Shortly thereafter, when the tower did separate from the capsule, Carpenter "felt a bigger jolt than at staging." He

447

watched the tower cartwheel lazily toward the horizon, smoke trailing from its three rocket nozzles.[79]

Sustainer engine cutoff came only as a gentle drop in acceleration. Two bangs were cues that the clamp-ring explosive bolts had fired and that the posigrade rockets had propelled the spacecraft clear of the booster. Now *Aurora 7* was on its own and in space. Becoming immediately aware that he was weightless, Carpenter elatedly reported that zero g was pleasant. Just as the capsule and booster separated, the astronaut had noticed that the capillary tube in his liquid-test apparatus seemed to fill. Then he averted his gaze; it was time to turn the spacecraft around to its normal backward flying orbital attitude. Since Glenn had left this maneuver to the automatic control system and the cost in fuel had been high, Carpenter used fly-by-wire. The spacecraft came smartly around at an expense of only 1.6 pounds of fuel, compared with over 5 pounds used on Glenn's MA–6 maneuver.[80]

As the capsule swung around from antenna-canister-forward to heatshield-forward, Carpenter was impressed by the fact that he felt absolutely no angular motion; his instruments provided the only evidence that the turnaround maneuver was being executed. Like Glenn, he was amazed that he felt no sensation of speed, although he knew he was traveling at orbital velocity (actually 17,549 miles per hour). Soon he had his first awe-inspiring view of the horizon—"an arresting sight," as he described it. Quickly checking his control systems, he found everything in order. Unknown to him, however, the horizon scanner optically sensing his spacecraft's pitch attitude was off by about 20 degrees. It was some time before he deduced this system was in error.

As Glenn had done, Carpenter peered out the window to track the spent Atlas sustainer engine. The tankage appeared to fall downward, as the engineers had predicted, and was tumbling away slowly. A trail of ice crystals two or three times longer than the launch vehicle streamed from its nozzle. Over the Canary Islands, Carpenter still could see the sustainer tagging along below the spacecraft. Meanwhile the astronaut continued to check the capsule systems and report his findings to the tracking sites. Over Kano, in mid-Nigeria, he said that he was getting behind in his flight plan because of difficulty in loading his camera with the special film to photograph the Earth-horizon limb. Before he moved beyond radio range of Kano, however, he managed to snap a few photographs. Although it was now almost dusk on his first "45-minute day," Carpenter was becoming increasingly warm and began adjusting his suit-temperature knob.[81]

Over the Indian Ocean on his first pass, Carpenter glanced down for a view through the periscope, which he found to be quite ineffective on the dark side of Earth. Concluding that the periscope seemed to be useless at night, he returned to the window for visual references. Even when the gyros were caged and he was not exactly sure of his attitude position, he felt absolutely no sensation of disorientation; it was a simple matter in the daylight to roll the spacecraft over and watch for a landmark to pop into view. Carpenter mentioned many recognizable landmarks, such as Lake Chad, Africa, the rain forests of that continent, and Madagascar. But he was a little surprised to find out that most of Earth when seen from orbit is covered by clouds the greater part of the time.[82]

While over the Indian Ocean, Carpenter discovered that his celestial observations were hampered by glare from light seepage around the satellite clock inside the capsule. The light from the rim of the clock, which should presumably have been screened, made it hard for him to adjust his eyes to night vision. To Slayton at the Muchea station, Carpenter reported that he could see no more stars from his vantage point in space than he could have seen on Earth. Also he said that the stars were not particularly useful in gaining heading information.[83]

Like his orbital predecessor, Carpenter failed to see the star-shell flares fired in an observation experiment. This time the flares shot up from the Great Victoria Desert near Woomera, Australia, rather than from the Indian Ocean ship. According to the plan, four flares of one-million candlepower were to be launched for Carpenter's benefit on his first orbit, and three more each on his second and third passes. On the first try the flares, each having a burning time of $1\frac{1}{2}$ minutes, were ignited at 60-second intervals. At this time most of the Woomera area was covered by clouds that hid the illumination of the flares; the astronaut consequently saw nothing and the experiment was discontinued on the succeeding two passes, as weather conditions did not improve.[84]

Out over the Pacific on its first circuit, *Aurora 7* performed nicely. The Canton Island station received the telemetered body temperature reading of 102 degrees and asked Carpenter if he was uncomfortable at that temperature. "No, I don't believe that's correct," Carpenter replied. "I can't imagine I'm that hot. I'm quite comfortable, but sweating some." The medical monitors accepted Carpenter's self-assessment and concluded that the feverish temperature reading resulted from an error in the equipment. For the rest of the journey, however, the elevated temperatures persisted, causing the various communicators to ask frequently about Carpenter's physical status.[85]

The food Carpenter carried on his voyage was different from Glenn's which was of the squeeze-tube, baby-food variety. For Carpenter the Pillsbury Company had prepared three kinds of snacks, composed of chocolate, figs, and dates with high-protein cereals; and the Nestlé Company had provided some "bonbons," composed of orange peel with almonds, high-protein cereals with almonds, and cereals with raisins. These foods were processed into particles about three-fourths of an inch square. Coated with an edible glaze, each piece was packaged separately and stored in an opaque plastic bag. As he passed over Canton he reported that he had eaten one bite of the inflight food, which was crumbling badly. Weightless crumbs drifting around in the cabin were not only bothersome but also potentially dangerous to his breathing. Though he had been able to eat one piece, his gloved hands made it awkward to get the food to his mouth around the helmet microphones.[86] Once in his mouth, however, the food was tasty enough and easy enough to eat.

449

During the second orbit, as he had on the first, Carpenter made frequent capsule maneuvers with the fly-by-wire and manual-proportional modes of attitude control. He slewed his ship around to make photographs; he pitched the capsule down 80 degrees in case the ground flares were fired over Woomera; he yawed around to observe and photograph the airglow phenomenon; and he rolled the capsule until Earth was "up" for the inverted flight experiment. Carpenter even stood the capsule on its antenna canister and found that the view was exhilarating. Although the manual control system worked well, the MA-7 pilot had some difficulty caging the attitutude gyros to zero before inverting the spacecraft. On two occasions he had to recycle the caging operation after the gyros tumbled beyond their responsive limits.

Working under his crowded experiment schedule and the heavy manual maneuver program, on six occasions Carpenter accidentally actuated the sensitive-to-the-touch, high-thrust attitude control jets, which brought about "double authority control," or the redundant operation of both the automatic and the manual systems. So by the end of the first two orbits Carpenter's control fuel supply had dipped to about 42 percent in the manual tanks and 45 percent in the automatic tanks. During his second orbit, ground capsule communicators at various tracking sites repeatedly reminded him to conserve his fuel.

Although his fuel usage was high during the second circumnavigation, Carpenter still managed to continue the experiments. Just as he passed over the Cape, for example, an hour and 38 minutes from launch, Carpenter deployed the multicolored balloon. For a few seconds he saw the confetti spray, signaling deployment. Then, as the line lazily played out, he realized that the balloon had not inflated properly; only two of the five colors—orange and dull aluminum— were visible, the orange clearly the more brilliant. Two small, earlike appendages about six to eight inches each, described as "sausages," emerged on the sides of the partially inflated sphere. The movement of the half-inflated balloon was erratic and unpredictable, but Carpenter managed to obtain a few drag resistance measurements. A little more than a half hour after the balloon was launched, Carpenter began some spacecraft maneuvers and the tether line twined to some extent about the capsule's antenna canister. Carpenter wanted to get rid of the balloon and attempted to release it going into the third orbit over the Cape, but the partially successful experimental device stayed doggedly near the spacecraft.[87]

As Carpenter entered the last orbit, both his automatic and manual control fuel tanks were less than half full. So *Aurora 7* began a long period of drifting flight. Short recess periods to conserve fuel had occurred earlier in the flight, but now Carpenter and his ship were to drift in orbit almost around the world. Although his rapidly depleting fuel supply had made the drift a necessity, this vehicle control relaxation maneuver, if successful, would be a valuable engineering experiment. The results would be most useful in planning the rest and sleep periods for an astronaut on a longer Mercury mission. Carpenter enjoyed his floating orbit, observing that it was a simple matter to start a roll rate of per-

Flight of Aurora 7
May 24, 1962

Mission Planning Conference (left), including, left to right, Kenneth S. Kleinknecht, Walter C. Williams, Christopher C. Kraft, Jr., Carpenter, and Robert D. Mercer. Carpenter ready to enter Aurora 7 (lower left). The launch (below).

Recovery by helicopter (left). Postflight checkup onboard the Intrepid (above).

haps one degree per second and let the capsule slowly revolve as long as desired. *Aurora 7* drifted gracefully through space for more than an hour, or almost until retrofire time.

While in his drifting flight, Carpenter used the Moon to check his capsule's attitude. John Glenn had reported some difficulty in obtaining and holding an absolute zero-degree heading. Carpenter, noting that the Moon appeared almost in the center of his window, oriented the spacecraft so that it held the Moon on the exact center mark and maintained the position with ease.[88]

During the third orbital pass, Carpenter caught on film the phenomenon of the flattened Sun at sunset. John O'Keefe and his fellow scientists at Goddard had taught Carpenter that the color layers at sunset might provide information on light transfusion characteristics of the upper atmosphere. Carpenter furnished a vivid description of the sunset to the capsule communicator on the Indian Ocean ship:

> The sunsets are most spectacular. The earth is black after the sun has set. . . . The first band close to the earth is red, the next is yellow, the next is blue, the next is green, and the next is sort of a—sort of a purple. It's almost like a very brilliant rainbow. These layers extend from at least 90 degrees either side of the sun at sunset. This bright horizon band extended at least 90 degrees north and south of the position at sunset.

He took some 19 pictures of the flattened Sun.[89]

As Carpenter drifted over oceans and land masses, he observed and reported on the haze layer, or airglow phenomenon, about which Glenn had marveled. Carpenter's brief moments of airglow study during the second orbit failed to match the expectations he had derived from Glenn's reports and the Goddard scientists' predictions on the phenomenon. Having more leisure on his third circuit, Carpenter described the airglow layer in detail to Slayton at the Muchea tracking site:

> . . . the haze layer is very bright. I would say about 8 to 10 degrees above the real horizon. And I would say that the haze layer is about twice as high above the horizon as the bright blue band at sunset is; it's twice as thick. A star—stars are occluded as we pass through this haze layer. I have a good set of stars to watch going through at this time. I'll try to get some photometer readings. . . . It is not twice as thick. It's thinner, but it is located at a distance about twice as far away as the top of the band at sunset. It's very narrow, and as bright as the horizon of the earth itself.

The single star, not stars, that Carpenter tracked was Phecda Ursae Majoris, in the Big Dipper or Great Bear constellation, with a magnitude of 2.5.[90]

With each sunrise, Carpenter also saw the "fireflies," or "Glenn effect," as the Russians were calling it. To him the particles looked more like snowflakes than fireflies, and they did not seem to be truly luminous, as Glenn had said. The particles varied in size, brightness, and color. Some were gray, some were white, and one in particular, said Carpenter, looked like a helical shaving from a lathe. Although they seemed to travel at different speeds, they did not move out and away from the spacecraft as the confetti had in the balloon experiment.

At dawn on the third pass Carpenter reached for a device known as a densitometer, that measured light intensity. Accidentally his gloved hand bumped against the capsule hatch, and suddenly a cloud of particles flew past the window. He yawed right to investigate, noting that the particles traveled across the front of the window from right to left. Another tap of the hand on the hatch sent off a second shower; a tap on the wall produced another. Since the exterior of the spacecraft evidently was covered with frost, Glenn's "fireflies" became Carpenter's "frostflies." [91]

Until *Aurora 7* reached the communication range of the Hawaiian station on the third pass, Christopher Kraft, directing the flight from the Florida control center, considered this mission the most successful to date; everything had gone perfectly except for some overexpenditure of hydrogen peroxide fuel. Carpenter had exercised his manual controls with ease in a number of spacecraft maneuvers and had made numerous and valuable observations in the interest of space science. Even though the control fuel usage had been excessive in the first two orbits, by the time he drifted near Hawaii on the third pass Carpenter had successfully maintained more than 40 percent of his fuel in both the automatic and the manual tanks. According to the mission rules, this ought to be quite enough hydrogen peroxide, reckoned Kraft, to thrust the capsule into the retrofire attitude, hold it, and then to reenter the atmosphere using either the automatic or the manual control system. [92]

The tracking site at Hawaii instructed Carpenter to start his preretrofire countdown and to shift from manual control to the automatic stabilization and control system. He explained to the ground station over which he was passing at five miles per second that he had gotten somewhat behind on the preretro checkoff list while verifying his hypothesis about the snowflake-like particles outside his window. Then as Carpenter began aligning the spacecraft and shifting control to the automatic mode, he suddenly found himself to be in trouble. The automatic stabilization system would not hold the 34-degree pitch and zero-degree yaw attitude. As he tried to determine what was wrong, he fell behind in his check of other items. When he hurriedly switched to the fly-by-wire control mode, he forgot to switch off the manual system. For about 10 minutes fuel from both systems was being used redundantly. [93]

Finally, Carpenter felt that he had managed to align the spacecraft for the retrofire sequence. The Hawaiian communicator urged him to complete as much of the checklist as possible before he passed out of that site's communications range. Now Alan Shepard's voice from the Arguello, California, station came in loud and clear, asking whether the *Aurora 7* pilot had bypassed the automatic retroattitude switch. Carpenter quickly acted on this timely reminder. Then the countdown for retrofire began. Because the automatic system was misbehaving, Carpenter was to push the button to ignite the solid-fuel retrorockets strapped to the heatshield. About three seconds after Shepard's call of "Mark! Fire One," the first rocket ignited and blew. Then the second and the third followed in reassuring succession. Carpenter saw wisps of smoke inside his cabin as the rockets braked him out of orbit.[94]

Carpenter's attitude error was more than he estimated when he reported his attitude nearly correct. Actually *Aurora 7* was canted at retrofire about 25 degrees to the right, and thus the reverse thrust vector was not in line with the flight path vector. This misalignment alone would have caused the spacecraft to over-shoot the planned impact point by about 175 miles. But the retrorockets began firing three seconds late, adding another 15 miles or so to the trajectory error. Later analyses also revealed a thrust decrement in the retrorockets that was about three percent below nominal, contributing 60 more miles to the overshoot. If Carpenter had not bypassed the automatic retroattitude switch and manually ignited the retrorockets he could have overshot his pickup point in the Atlantic by an even greater distance.[95]

Unlike Glenn, Carpenter had no illusion that he was being driven back to Hawaii at retrofire. Instead he had the feeling that *Aurora 7* had simply stopped and that if he looked toward Earth he would see it coming straight up. One glance out the window, however, and the "impression was washed away." [96] The completion of retrofire produced no changes the pilot could feel until his reentry began in earnest about 10 minutes later.

After the retrorockets had fired, Carpenter realized that the manual control system was still on. Quickly he turned off the fly-by-wire system, intending to check the manual controls. Although the manual fuel gauge read six percent left, there was, in fact, no fuel and consequently no manual control. So Carpenter switched back to fly-by-wire. At that time the automatic system supply read 15 percent, but the astronaut wondered how much really remained. Could it be only about 10 percent? With this gnawing doubt and realizing that it was still 10 minutes before .05-g time, Carpenter kept hands strictly off for most of his drifting glide. Whatever fuel there was left must be saved for the critical tumble. This 10-minute interval seemed like eternity to the pilot. The attitude indicators appeared to be useless, and there was little fuel to control attitude anyway. The only thing he trusted for reference was the view out of the window; using fly-by-wire sparingly he tried to keep the horizon in view. Although concerned about the fuel conservation problem, Carpenter gained some momentary relief from the fascinating vistas below: "I can make out very, very small—farm land, pasture land below. I see individual fields, rivers, lakes, roads, I think. I'll get back to reentry attitude." [97]

Finally, *Aurora 7* reached the .05-g acceleration point about 500 miles off the coast of Florida. As he began to feel his weight once again, Carpenter noted that the automatic fuel needle still read 15 percent. Within seconds the capsule began to oscillate badly. A quick switch to the auxiliary damping mode steadied the spacecraft. Grissom, the Cape communicator, reminded him to close his faceplate.[98]

454

Aurora 7 was now in the midst of its blazing return to Earth. Carpenter heard the hissing sounds reported by Glenn, the cues that his ship was running into aerodynamic resistance. Immediately the capsule began to roll slowly, as programmed, to minimize the landing point dispersion. Carpenter looked out the window for the bright orange glow, the "fireball," as Glenn had described it, but there was only a moderate increase in light intensity. Rather than an orange glow, Carpenter saw a light-green glow apparently surrounding the cylindrical section. Was this radiant portion of the spacecraft ablating? Was the trim angle correct? The evenness of the oscillations argued to Carpenter that the trim angle was good. All the way through this zone Carpenter kept talking. Gradually it became difficult to squeeze the words out; the heaviest deceleration load was coming. The peak g period lasted longer than he had expected, and it took forceful breath control to utter anything.[99]

The automatic fuel tank on *Aurora 7* was emptied between 80,000 and 70,000 feet. As the plasma sheath of ionized air enveloped his spacecraft, communication efforts with Carpenter became useless, but the telemetered signals received by the radar stations at the Cape and on San Salvador predicted a successful reentry. The oscillations were increasing as the capsule approached the 50,000-foot level. *Aurora 7* was swinging beyond the 10-degree "tolerable" limits. Carpenter strained upward to arm the drogue at 45,000 feet, but he forced himself to ride out still more severe oscillations before he fired the drogue parachute mortar at 25,000 feet. The chute pulsed out and vibrated like thin, quivering sheets of metal. At 15,000 feet Carpenter armed the main parachute switch, and at 9500 feet he deployed the chute manually. The fabric quivered, but the giant umbrella streamed, reefed, and unfurled as it should. The rate of descent was 30 feet per second, the exact design specification. The spacecraft landing bag deploy was on automatic. Carpenter listened for the "clunk," heard the heatshield fall into position, and waited to hit the water. *Aurora 7* seemed to be ready for the landing, and the recovery forces knew within a few miles the location of the spacecraft as radar tracking after retrofire had given and confirmed the landing point.[100]

Splashdown was noisy but less of a jolt than the spaceman had expected. The capsule, however, did not right itself within a minute as it was supposed to do. Carpenter, noticing some drops of water on his tape recorder, wondered if *Aurora 7* was about to meet the fate of *Liberty Bell 7,* and then sighed in relief when he could find no evidence of a leak. He waited a little longer for the spacecraft to straighten up, but it continued to list to his left. Grissom's last transmission from Mercury Control had told Carpenter that it would take the pararescue men about an hour to reach him, and the astronaut realized that he had evidently overshot the planned landing zone. When he failed to raise a response on his radio, he decided to get out of the cramped capsule. Then he saw that the capsule was floating rather deeply, which meant that it might be dangerous to remove the hatch. Sweating profusely in the 101-degree temperature of the cabin, he pulled off his helmet and began the job of egress as it had been originally planned. Carpenter wormed his way upward through the throat of the spacecraft, a hard, hot job made bearable by his leaving the suit circuit hose attached and not unrolling the neck dam. He struggled with the camera, packaged life raft, survival kit, and kinky hose before he finally got his head outside.

Half out of the top hatch, Carpenter rested on his elbows momentarily, released the suit hose but failed to deploy the neck dam and lock the hose inlet, and surveyed the sea. Lazy swells, some as high as six feet, did not look too forbidding. So he carefully laid his hand camera on top of the recovery compartment, squeezed out of the top, and carefully lowered himself into the water, tipping the listing spacecraft slightly in the process. Holding onto the capsule, he was able to easily inflate the life raft– upside down. By this time, feeling some water in his boots, he secured the hose inlet to the suit. He then held on to the spacecraft's side and managed to flip the raft upright. After crawling onto the yellow raft, he retrieved the camera, unrolled the suit neck dam, and prepared to wait for as long as it took the recovery searchers to find him. The recovery beacon was operating and the green dye pervaded the sea all around him.[101]

The status of Carpenter and *Aurora 7* was unknown to the public. Everyone following the flight by radio or television knew that the spacecraft must be down. But was the pilot safe? What the public did not know was that one P2V airplane had received the spacecraft's beacon signal from a distance of only 50 miles, while another plane had picked up the signal from 250 miles. *Aurora 7*'s position was well known to the recovery forces in the area. About eight minutes before the spacecraft landed, an SA–16 seaplane of the Air Force Air Rescue Service had taken off from Roosevelt Roads, Puerto Rico, for the radar-predicted landing point. Three ships—a Coast Guard cutter at St. Thomas Island, a merchantman 31 miles from the plotted point, and the destroyer *Farragut* about 75 miles away to the southwest—were in the vicinity of the impact point. But it would certainly take longer than an hour for any recovery unit to reach the site. Since Carpenter's raft had no radio, the drama was heightened. What exactly had happened to Carpenter after his landing was known only to the astronaut and perhaps to a few sea gulls and sea bass.[102]

Carpenter settled down on his raft and waited patiently for his rescuers. He mused over some seaweed floating nearby and "a black fish that was just as friendly as he could be—right down by the raft." In time, 36 minutes after splashdown, he saw two aircraft, a P2V and, unexpectedly, a Piper Apache. The astronaut watched the planes circle, saw that the Apache pilot was photographing the area, and knew that he had been found. Twenty minutes later several SC–54 aircraft arrived, and one dropped two frogmen, but Carpenter, watching other planes, did not see them bail out.[103]

Airman First Class John F. Heitsch, dropping from the SC–54 transport about an hour and seven minutes after Carpenter had first hit the water, missed the life raft by a considerable distance. Releasing his chute harness, he dove under

456

the waves and swam the distance to the side of Carpenter's raft. "Hey!" called the frogman to the spaceman. Carpenter turned and with complete surprise asked, "How did you get here?" Shortly thereafter a second pararescue man, Sergeant Ray McClure, swam alongside and clutched the astronaut's raft. The two frogmen quickly inflated two other rafts and locked them to the spacecraft. McClure and Heitsch later described the astronaut as smiling, happy, and not at all tired. The pilot broke out his survival rations and offered some to the two Air Force swimmers, who declined the space food but drank some space water.[104]

The three men, still without radio contact, perched on the three rafts and watched the planes circling above. One plane dropped the spacecraft flotation collar, which hit the water with a loud bang, breaking one of its compressed-air bottles. The swimmers retrieved and attached the flotation collar with only its top loop inflated and then crawled back onto their rafts. Shortly a parachute with a box at the end came floating lazily down some distance from the spacecraft. The men on the rafts supposed this was the needed radio, and one of the frogmen swam a considerable distance to get it. He returned with the container, opened it, and found that there was no radio inside, only a battery. Later Carpenter laughingly declined to repeat the swimmer's heated remarks.[105]

The Air Force SA–16 seaplane from Roosevelt Roads arrived at the scene about an hour and a half after the spacecraft landed in the Atlantic. To the SA–16 pilot the sea seemed calm enough to set his craft down upon and pick up the astronaut, but the Mercury Control Center directed the seaplane not to land. As later depicted by the news media and thoroughly discussed in Congress, this delay grew out of traditional rivalry between the Air Force and the Navy. Brigadier General Thomas J. Dubose, a former commander of the Air Rescue Service, wrote to Florida's United States Senator Spessard L. Holland, charging that Carpenter floated in the raft an hour and 20 minutes longer than was necessary. D. Brainerd Holmes, a NASA official, testified at the hearings that Admiral John L. Chew, commander of the Project Mercury recovery forces, feared the seaplane might break apart if it landed on the choppy waters. Because of this, according to Holmes, the decision had been made to proceed with helicopter and ship pickup as originally planned.[106]

After three hours of sitting on the sea in his raft, Carpenter was picked up by an HSS–2 helicopter, but either the rotorcraft settled as a swell arose or the winch operator accidentally lowered away, and the astronaut was dunked. Up went his arm and the hand holding the camera to keep the precious film dry. With nothing else amiss, Carpenter was hoisted aboard the helicopter, a drenched but happy astronaut. Richard A. Rink, a physician aboard, described Carpenter as exhilarated. The astronaut draped one leg out of the helicopter and, by cutting a hole in his sock, drained most of the water from his pressure suit. He then stood up and proceeded to pace around, sometimes settling in a seat, and intermittently talking about his flight. Carpenter arrived aboard the carrier *Intrepid* some four hours and 15 minutes after his return to Earth. The medical

Carpenter and his wife are greeted in big Denver parade.

Aurora 7
Aftermath

Following visit to White House, Carpenter (right) and Walter C. Williams (center) receive in New York at the Waldorf-Astoria, along with former Presidents Hoover and Truman.

examinations began immediately but were interrupted when the astronaut was called to the phone to receive what was by now President Kennedy's traditional congratulatory call. The President expressed his relief that Carpenter was safe and well, while Carpenter gave his "apologies for not having aimed a little better on reentry." From the *Intrepid* the astronaut was flown to Grand Turk Island, where, as Howard A. Minners, an Air Force physician assigned to Mercury, described it, Carpenter wanted to stay up late and talk.[107]

Aurora 7, picked up by the destroyer *Pierce*, was returned to Cape Canaveral the next day. When retrieved, the spacecraft was listing about 45 degrees compared to the normal 15 to 20 degrees, and it contained about 65 gallons of sea water, which would hamper the inspection and postflight analyses. Carpenter recalled two occasions on which the spacecraft had shipped small amounts of water, but he was unable to explain the larger amount found by the pickup crew. The exterior of the spacecraft showed the usual bluish and orange tinges on the shingles, several of which were slightly dented and scratched as after previous missions. Since there was no evidence of inflight damage, these slight scars presumably were the result of postflight handling. The spacecraft heatshield and main pressure bulkhead were in good condition except for a missing shield center plug, which had definitely been in place during reentry. Some of the honeycomb was crushed, resulting in minor deformation of the small tubing in that area. Heitsch and McClure, the pararescue men, had reported the landing bag in good condition, but when it was hauled out of the water most of the straps were broken, probably by wave action. All in all, *Aurora 7* was in good shape and had performed well for Project Mercury's second manned orbital flight.[108]

The postflight celebrations and honors followed the precedents and patterns established by Glenn's flight. Administrator Webb presented to Carpenter and Williams NASA Distinguished Service Medals in a ceremony at the Cape. Carpenter also learned of Soviet Premier Nikita Khrushchev's cabled congratulations. Then the astronaut's hometown, Boulder, Colorado, gave him a hero's welcome. After being awarded a degree by the University of Colorado, where he had lacked a credit in a heat-transfer course, the astronaut facetiously commented that the blazing MA–7 reentry surely qualified him as a master in the field of thermodynamics. Memorial Day found the pilot in Denver, where a crowd of 300,000 people cheered and honored him. The next day he returned to work at Langley, where exhaustive technical debriefings were held to glean all the knowledge possible from MA–7.[109]

In these postflight sessions the astronaut insisted that he knew what he wanted to do at all times, but that every task took a little longer than the time allotted by the flight plan. Some of the equipment, he said, was not easy to handle, particularly the special films that he had to load into a camera. As a consequence he had been unable to get all the pictures the Weather Bureau had requested for its satellite photography program. Moreover, the flight plan that had been available during training was only a tentative one, and the final plan had been completed only a short while before he suited up for the launch. Carpenter felt that the completed plan should be in the astronaut's hands at least two months before a scheduled flight and that the flight agenda should allow more time for the pilot to observe, evaluate, and record. When asked about fuel consumption by the high thrusters, Carpenter replied that the 24-pounders were unnecessary for the orbital phase of a flight.

The astronaut recommended that some method be devised for closing off the high thrusters while the automatic control system was in operation. He granted that on the fly-by-wire, low-thruster operation, the spacecraft changed its attitude slowly, as was shown by the needle movement, and that the pilot would have to wait momentarily to pick up the desired attitude change rate. For tracking tasks, however, the manual-proportional mode served well; attitude changes could be made with only a gentle touch of the handcontroller. Talking with newsmen after the flight, Carpenter assumed full responsibility for his high fuel consumption. He pointed out, however, that what he had learned would be valuable for longer Mercury missions.[110]

As mid-year 1962 approached, Project Mercury faced yet another crossroad. Had enough been learned during the two three-orbit flights to justify going on to longer missions? Joe W. Dodson, a Manned Spacecraft Center engineer, speaking before the Exchange Club of Hampton, Virginia, indicated that the MSC designers

459

and planners and the operations team were well pleased with the lessons derived from Glenn, from Carpenter, and from their spacecraft. They were pleased especially at how well the combination of man and machine had worked.

Shortly thereafter, the press began to speculate that NASA might try a one-day orbital flight before 1963. Administrator Webb, however, sought to scotch any premature guesswork until Gilruth and his MSC team could made a firm decision. He stated that there might well be another three-orbit mission, but added that consideration was being given to a flight of as many as six orbits with recovery in the Pacific. Robert C. Seamans, Jr., NASA's "general manager," told congressional leaders that if a decision had to be made on the day on which he was speaking, it would probably be for another flight such as Glenn and Carpenter had made. But many members of Congress wanted to drop a third triple-orbit mission in favor of a flight that would come closer to or even surpass Gherman Titov's 17-orbit experience.

On June 27, 1962, NASA Headquarters ended the speculation by announcing that Walter Schirra would pilot the next mission for as many as six orbits, possibly by the coming September, with L. Gordon Cooper as alternate pilot.[111] The original Mercury objectives had been met and passed; now it was time to proceed to new objectives—longer missions, different in quality as well as quantity of orbits. Project Mercury had twice accomplished the mission for which it was designed, but in so doing its end had become the means for further ends.

460

XIV

Climax of Project Mercury

WALTER M. Schirra, a naval aviator who had won the Distinguished Flying Cross for his combat missions over Korea, received his most important assignment to date on July 27, 1962. It was the flight plan for Mercury-Atlas 8, a six-orbit flight that was to qualify the spacecraft and man's endurance for an extended spatial mission. A new plan, revised slightly for yaw-reference experiments using the periscope, was delivered on August 8. This was almost 60 days before the mission, allowing the period for training that Scott Carpenter had recommended. Carpenter had received his MA–7 document late, and major revisions had been inserted almost until launch day. Although Schirra's flight plan was altered in September, it did escape a thorough last-minute rewrite.

MA–8 was to be an engineering flight, in contrast with the exploratory nature of Glenn's flight in MA–6 and the developmental and scientific nature of MA–7. Schirra was expected to concern himself largely with the management and operation of the spacecraft's systems to conserve hydrogen peroxide attitude control fuel and electrical power. The MSC planners had examined the minute-by-minute details from launch to recovery in the interest of spacecraft endurance and had programmed only a few experiments that would require fuel or electrical power. The pilot was to try to observe a ground xenon light of 140-million candlepower at Durban, South Africa, and four flares of 1-million candlepower each that would be launched near Woomera, Australia. The only other experiment requiring astronaut participation included some weather and terrestrial photography as the pilot sighted targets of opportunity. Besides these experiments, several passive test devices were superimposed on the spacecraft's exterior. Eight ablation panels, consisting of several types of material, were fused onto the afterbody's beryllium shingles, and a white paint patch was brushed on the capsule's side for still more evaluations of spatial thermal effects on various materials.[1]

Early in August, Schirra trained energetically for a targeted September launch; spacecraft No. 16 was almost ready for a simulated flight in Hangar S; and Atlas No. 113–D had arrived at the Cape. Then on August 11, the Soviet Union, without prior announcement, launched *Vostok III*.   NASA leaders, who had endured much needling on the space gap since Gherman S. Titov's 17-orbit flight, a little more than a year earlier, grimly read the press reports.   The five-ton Vostok spacecraft, with Major Andrian G. Nikolayev aboard, was in an orbit with a 156-mile apogee and a 113-mile perigee, inclined (as usual for Vostoks) at 65 degrees.

The "gap" seemed to become a "gulf" the following day, when *Vostok IV*, carrying Lieutenant Colonel Pavel R. Popovich, shot into an orbit with an apogee of 157 miles and a perigee of 112 miles.   Soon after the second launch, Nikolayev reported that he had sighted Popovich's spacecraft.   Western tracking stations variously reported that the two craft were as close as 3 and as far as 300 miles apart. Intercepted communications between Nikolayev (code-named Falcon) and Popovich (Golden Eagle) caused serious speculation that the Vostoks might try to rendezvous, but apparently no such attempt was made.

On August 15, Nikolayev landed after 64 orbits and more than 95 hours in space.   Popovich touched down six minutes later, after 48 orbits and more than 70 hours' flight.[2]   The U.S. decision to accelerate the space program called for by President Kennedy in May 1961 seemed more than validated to most critical observers.   Meanwhile engineers who were designing what became the Gemini vehicle for rendezvous with an orbiting Agena rocket studied the possibility of adding a space-maneuvering capability to Mercury.   On August 24, Kenneth S. Kleinknecht, the Project Office chief, reported that such an innovation would require at least 400 pounds of additional spacecraft hardware and fuel.   Upon hearing this, Christopher C. Kraft, Jr., the Mercury flight director, dourly observed that this added weight might dangerously degrade the capsule's chances of reaching orbit, but Robert R. Gilruth asked Kleinknecht to continue his studies.   A few days later the Mercury Project Office and the Flight Crew Operations Division handed the MSC director a joint proposal for maneuvering an orbiting Mercury spacecraft close to a passive Echo-type satellite.   But because of time, weight, and safety considerations, Gilruth and his management lieutenants rejected the proposal, abandoned the idea of a maneuverable Mercury spacecraft for the time being, and turned back to the more prosaic but essential business of preparing for the modest doubled-distance, six-orbit flight slated for Walter Schirra.[3]

LONGER LEGS FOR MERCURY

Specific planning for MA-8 had begun back in February during the technical debriefing of John Glenn following the MA-6 mission.   While attending the Grand Turk Island meetings, Kleinknecht and Donald K. Slayton had agreed that a flight of six or seven orbits seemed to be a logical intermediate step from the three-pass flight of Glenn toward an ultimate 18-orbit goal then under study. When Kleinknecht returned to his office (then at Langley) he put his staff to work in conjunction with John F. Yardley's group of McDonnell engineers on the changes necessary to accomplish a seven-orbit Mercury flight.[4]

The staff's problem was to appraise the spacecraft components' lifetime in terms of the ability of each system to perform two or three times longer than the operating limits originally built into them. Flight rules so far had specified an almost continuous operation of the automatic stabilization and control system, which caused a heavy drain on the spacecraft's electrical power supply. Also critical were oxygen reserves, reaction control fuel supplies, and increased recovery requirements. The tracking and communications network, built for three-orbit coverage, would require extensive modification if the tracking criteria applied to three orbits should apply to six or seven.

The three-orbit Mercury spacecraft, with all its electrically powered systems in action, consumed about 7080 watt-hours of battery power from a total of about 13,500 watt-hours available. Thus a seven-orbit mission, obeying previous flight rules, would consume about 11,190 watt-hours, leaving a reserve supply of only 6.7 percent. Mercury Project Office engineers insisted there should be at least a 10 percent postlanding reserve as a safety factor and suggested at least two conservation methods to attain and surpass this amount. One was drawn from an earlier recommendation presented by McDonnell designers and planners; they had outlined possibilities for an 18-orbit mission, proposing that some of the systems be turned off during a substantial portion of the flight. In addition to this, the MSC engineers recommended switching telemetry transmitter and radar beacon operations to ground command. These measures, they felt, would raise the reserve power levels to about 15 percent.

After studying the spacecraft's environmental control system, the project engineers at MSC concluded that about 4.4 pounds of oxygen would be consumed during a seven-orbit flight, taking pilot usage and cabin leakage rates into consideration. By prevailing mission rules, this would leave an insufficient supply to meet possible contingencies of abnormal recovery. A supply of 8.6 pounds would meet the requirement, but the system carried only two 4-pound capacity bottles. So, either the rules had to be relaxed or the system had to be modified. The MSC study group recommended the modification possibility, adding that a strenuous program to reduce cabin leakage rates to 600 cubic centimeters per minute should be started. Formerly up to 1000 cubic centimeters had been within design specifications. To cover the increase in carbon dioxide production from the longer flight, the project office planners pointed out that the canister carried in the three-orbit spacecraft could be filled with lithium hydroxide to its 5.4 pound capacity. This amount represented an increase from the 4.6 pounds that had been carried on the three-pass flights and should be sufficient extension of the CO_2 removal capability.

At the same time that these efforts were being made to provide the spacecraft systems with all the power they needed and the astronaut with enough breathable oxygen, some NASA and McDonnell engineers were wrestling with more advanced problems of tripling, quadrupling, and even raising by factors of six and eight the capabilities of the Mercury spacecraft to orbit Earth. But at this stage, planning for the day-long, 18-orbit mission depended heavily on some positive proof from MA–8 that man and machines could tolerate, over a longer period and with larger margins for pilot safety and mission success, the vacuous, weightless, hot-cold extremes of space.

The most critical problem in preparations for the extended mission was providing enough hydrogen peroxide fuel to power the capsule's reaction control system. A seven-orbit mission operating in the fully automatic control mode would consume about 28 pounds of fuel, providing the systems were functioning normally. The Mercury Project Office suggested alternating a combination of automatic and manual modes to provide safer fuel reserves at the end of the flight. Such a procedure would expend 23 pounds of automatic and 18 pounds of manual fuel, leaving reserves of 12 and 15 pounds, respectively. Then, in case of malfunction in one of the control modes, the astronaut would be assured of an adequate fuel supply in the other mode.

Recovery procedures changed considerably for the proposed seven-orbit mission. The fourth, fifth, sixth, and seventh sinusoidal curves of the orbital ground trace passed over geographical points that almost intersected, while the fifth and sixth orbits did intersect in the northern Pacific about 275 miles northeast of Midway Island. This pattern shifted to the Pacific Ocean the optimum recovery area that had been in the Atlantic for MA–4 through MA–7. Kleinknecht's staff pointed out that a once-an-orbit primary recovery capability could be maintained with only a slight increase in the recovery forces. The primary landing area during the seventh orbit could be covered easily by Navy vessels moving to the zone from their base at Pearl Harbor, but some of the aircraft staging bases for past contingency landing areas would have to be relocated.

Then Sigurd A. Sjoberg, Robert F. Thompson, and other mission and recovery planners discovered a slight flaw in the seven-orbit flight profile. A hard mission rule required a contingency recovery capability within 18 hours after landing. This requirement could be easily met for a six-orbit mission, but adding a seventh orbit required additional recovery forces to satisfy that mission rule. So NASA decided to make MA–8 a six-orbit flight.[5]

During August 1962 the MA–8 mission planners continued to wrestle with many other operational considerations. But within the month they were able to issue the mission rules, data acquisition plan, a slight revision to the flight plan, recovery requirements and procedures, and the mission directive, only to find on some occasions that closer study of engineering preparations revealed new constraints, requiring minor changes to most of their guidebooks.[6]

PREPARATIONS FOR MA–8

While the long-duration mission studies were in progress and the mission rules and directives were being prepared and issued, other personnel of the NASA-military-industry complex were readying the spacecraft, booster, and recovery forces. The astronaut and alternate pilot were in intensive training.

464

The Manned Spacecraft Center allocated spacecraft Nos. 16 and 19 for the six-orbit mission, with No. 16 as the preferred vehicle. No. 16 had arrived at Cape Canaveral in January 1962, while No. 19 had followed two months later. Rework to incorporate a six-orbit capability was done at the Cape by the MSC Preflight Operations Division with the help of McDonnell technicians. The work and testing began slowly but were well underway in April. In that month temperature surveys at the critical points on the capsule were completed, the environmental control system passed its altitude-chamber tests, and the reaction control system was exercised satisfactorily. Minor troubles cropped up, as usual. Emergency oxygen rate valves stuck. Water coolant flowed too freely. The cabin's oxygen leakage rate was too high. Each difficulty slowly was overcome, but it became evident that a hoped-for August launching might slip at least a month.[7]

The Mercury Project Office had pronounced 5.4 pounds of lithium hydroxide sufficient for oxygen purification for the MA–8 mission, but the MSC Life Systems Division personnel checking this theory found the absorbers unsatisfactory. Canisters containing 4.6 pounds of the mixture had been used in the three-orbit spacecraft and tests showed that this amount of the chemical functioned to keep the air breathable for 34.5 hours before carbon-dioxide levels rose too high. Then canisters supposedly containing 5.4 pounds of absorbent were tested, with both fixed and variable inputs of heat, water vapor, and carbon dioxide, and with a human subject breathing the oxygen. To the amazement of the testers, the lifetimes of these canisters averaged only slightly higher than those that were partly filled.

Then it occurred to somebody in the division to weigh the canisters. Each proved to have been packed about half a pound short. Finally the completely filled canisters were tested for as long as 71 hours before breaking down, demonstrating that the original design met the development demands, after all. Well-filled absorbers would qualify for a day-long mission as well as for six orbits.[8]

As the work continued at the Cape on spacecraft No. 16, Scott Carpenter made his fuel-thirsty, three-orbit flight on May 24. During *Aurora 7*'s postflight analysis MSC engineers, including G. Merritt Preston's checkout crew, took new and closer looks at the attitude and reaction control systems. They decided that attitude thrusters slightly different in design would have to be installed in the MA–8 spacecraft. While Preston's men were implementing this decision, they also managed to get No. 16's cabin oxygen leakage rate down to a highly satisfactory 460 cubic centimeters per minute, although in the weeks ahead this rate would rise slightly.[9]

Other results from MA–7, as recorded from telemetry data, as reported by Carpenter, and as revealed by examination of flight-tested *Aurora 7*, had intensified the flurry of activity all along the line to prepare No. 16 for its flight. Carpenter had many suggestions regarding spacecraft configuration. The heavy periscope, he said, was useless on Earth's nightside; the window alone could be used to find the spacecraft's attitude. The determined workers for spacecraft weight reduction were delighted to hear this assessment. But the MA-7 postflight inspection team reported that Carpenter's landing error had been caused by a faulty yaw attitude, largely because Carpenter had performed a final control systems check just prior to retrofire and had used the window mainly as his chief yaw reference. Could the window and the pilot be trusted? the Mercury team wondered. Would the periscope have assisted in correcting the attitude and the resultant overshoot? The only way to find out the answers was to fly the periscope again.[10]

So for MA-8 the periscope became, in a sense, an experimental instrument. Using both the periscope and the window for spacecraft attitude reference, Schirra would check the position of his capsule carefully on Earth's day and night sides. Then he would check his visual judgment to gauge attitude, comparing his ability against the scope and instrument readings.

Having decided to retain the periscope, the mission planners and Cape preparations team for MA-8 butted into fresh difficulties. The experiment schedule had called for an ultraviolet airglow spectrograph to be put in the periscope's well. This spectrograph had been developed through the intensive work of Albert Boggess, III, at the Goddard Space Flight Center upon the request of the NASA Headquarters Ad Hoc Committee on Scientific Tasks and Training for Man-in-Space. Now the decision to carry the periscope forced the withdrawal of the experiment, creating some disappointment among NASA's scientifically interested personnel. Even the implementation of this decision turned out to be somewhat of a problem. Preston's men tried to use the periscope from the alternate spacecraft (No. 19) but found it to be defective. By the end of August they managed to install a standard periscope, "cannibalized" from spacecraft No. 15.[11]

Carpenter, the second astronaut to land with empty fuel tanks in the manned orbital program, also suggested that a control-mode selector switch be integrated with the control system to seal off the high thrusters until they were needed for fast reaction maneuvers. The Project Office approved, and this fuel-saving switch was installed in the MA-8 spacecraft.[12]

Aside from these and other minor modifications spacecraft No. 16 was a duplicate of *Aurora 7*. Many of the technical changes were aimed at weight reduction, fuel conservation, and adding extra supplies for a longer mission. Deletions included the astronaut-observer camera, one of two redundant command receiver-decoders, and the high-frequency voice transceiver. To increase pilot comfort and save weight, the preflight preparations crew extracted the lower leg section of the couch and substituted toe, heel, and knee restraints. During the orbital phase of the mission, the knee restraints could be loosened. An extra 15 pounds of coolant water and an improved fastening technique for the heatshield center plug completed the list of additions.[13]

While the engineers were working, Astronaut Schirra proceeded through the most efficient flight training program yet undertaken. Except for added yaw-recognition displays, he used the same procedures trainers that his predecessors had used; having a definite flight plan, he could practice on his own specific mission profile. He was able to work through his simulated retrofire and reentry tasks in the Langley procedures trainer before the device was dismantled for shipment to Houston. And for personal physical conditioning, he often went swimming and water skiing.[14]

Late in July, Preston reported that the work schedule for spacecraft No. 16 was aimed at a September 18 launch date. When the flight preparation crews added a sixth day to their work week to compensate for various delays, the MSC managers remained optimistic.[15]

Some worry among the mission planners had been injected in July when Project Dominic, an Atomic Energy Commission (AEC) high-atmosphere nuclear test over the Pacific, had created a new zone of radiation, lower than the Van Allen belts. In the face of this possible threat to an orbiting man, AEC, NASA, and McDonnell carefully studied a number of satellite and probe launchings in August designed to explore the belt. After the solar batteries of several satellites failed—including *Ariel I,* the world's first international satellite project, which developed operational difficulties probably attributable to Dominic—the investigators reported that the new radiation circled Earth at the geomagnetic equator and was about 400 miles wide and 4000 miles deep. Sounding rockets by telemetry data indicated rapid and continuing decay of radioactivity in the corridors of the next Mercury mission. By the end of August the radiation hazards seemed negligible. The MSC engineers, distrusting the reports that all danger had disappeared, installed a radiation dosimeter on the spacecraft hatch, provided the pilot with a hand-held model, and attached four more to Schirra's pressure suit.[16] The hand-held model could provide real-time indications during the flight.

Besides some labor-management difficulties that momentarily hampered the activities of the aerospace industry at this time, the booster for MA-8 contributed its share of troubles. Atlas 113–D was to have been delivered to Cape Canaveral toward the end of July, but it failed its initial composite test at the San Diego factory. Finally it was shipped on August 8. Then the Air Force, revealing that its Atlas program had suffered four recent turbopump failures, advised the Manned Spacecraft Center that No. 113–D would be put through a flight-readiness static firing. Since the MA-8 launch vehicle would be the first one in the Mercury program not having the two-second post-ignition hold-down time, the Air Force felt the static firing to be an important requirement.

A one-week slippage was now added. But before the test could be made, the Air Force and Convair inspectors found a fuel leak in a seam weld on the booster. Calculating the time required for work to be done, on September 6 the Mercury-Atlas launch operations committee rescheduled the mechanical and electrical matings of spacecraft and booster and three planned simulated flights. These tests would continue through September 24, making October 3 the most likely day for the MA-8 launch.

**MA–8
Preflight**

*At the Cape, Schirra closely watches
the mating of spacecraft and booster.*

*Schirra checks his spacecraft
camera equipment with Paul
Backer of McDonnell, left,
and Roland Williams of RCA.*

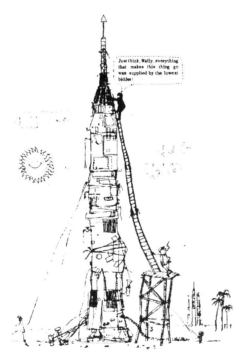

Just think, Wally, everything
that makes this thing go
was supplied by the lowest
bidder!

*Underscoring Schirra's test-pilot-like
concern for his equipment is this
Raytheon Corporation cartoon.*

Atlas 113–D actually differed little from its predecessors in the manned flight program. It incorporated a dozen or so technical changes from the 107–D configuration that had propelled Carpenter into orbit. The fuel tank insulation had been removed as a solution to some of the difficulties that had beset John Glenn's booster (Carpenter's launch vehicle had retained the insulation). More important, baffled fuel injectors (which had been found in static firing tests to virtually eliminate the possibility of combustion instability) and the accompanying hypergolic ignition (in which fuel and oxidizer ignite on contact) were added to 113–D. These innovations, therefore, eliminated the two-second hold-down at ignition, saved fuel, made for smoother initial combustion, and provided a safer liftoff.[17]

The tracking network for MA–8 was augmented by five airborne relay stations, in the form of five Air Force C–130s, to cover areas that otherwise would have been out of communications range of the ground sites. The C–130s, each equipped with ultra-high-frequency and very-high-frequency equipment for voice relay, were based at Patrick Air Force Base, Florida; Ramey Air Force Base, Puerto Rico; and Midway Island.[18] The mixed recovery force, deployed by the Department of Defense, included 19 ships in the Atlantic and nine in the Pacific. Aircraft numbering 134 of various types covered primary and secondary spacecraft landing areas. In all, about 17,000 men, including over 100 aeromedical monitors and specialists, made up the global MA–8 recovery forces.

Recovery commanders in the Pacific directed a training course in spacecraft and astronaut retrieval for appropriate teams, using boilerplate capsules, flotation collars, and other gear provided by MSC. Major General Leighton I. Davis and Walter C. Williams made an inspection tour to the Pacific to evaluate the training program and the overall recovery readiness picture. Later Kraft, reading their findings, reported that preparations and materials seemed "reasonably well" developed. But he was disappointed that NASA had been unable to enlist the support of another Navy radar ship equipped with FPS–16 equipment for C-band operation and thus had to rely on two S-band ships instead. Kraft felt that S-band radar, called "Verlort" for its 700-mile "very long range tracking" ability, was less reliable than the C-band.[19]

If recovery was to go smoothly, interservice misunderstandings like the one that had developed during Carpenter's rescue would have to be avoided. General Davis, the DOD military representative for Mercury support operations, had reported to Secretary of Defense Robert S. McNamara that the delay at Mercury Control in the decision to pick up Carpenter had stemmed partially from a lack of direct communication with the astronaut. To overcome this breakdown, the recovery room in the Control Center was modified to permit almost instantaneous communication between tracking stations and recovery forces; and Schirra's spacecraft was equipped with a long extension line, which would permit him to maintain voice contact even in the life raft. The extended period of suspense that climaxed Carpenter's mission should never happen again in Project Mercury.[20]

At this juncture, President Kennedy set out on a tour of the space centers of the South to inspect and show his interest not only in the preparations for MA-8 but also in the vast array of technological talents being mobilized for the accelerated space program, including the first lunar voyage. Kennedy flew down to Cape Canaveral to see the Merritt Island Launch Area that was being built for the huge Saturn V rockets. Then he went on to Houston to see the site for the management and control center on the Texas coastal prairie. Before a sweltering crowd half-filling the 72,000-seat Rice University stadium, the President spoke on September 12, 1962, in earnest defense of his proclaimed program for manned exploration of the Moon. "No man can fully grasp how far and how fast we have come," said Kennedy. "The exploration of space will go ahead, whether we join it or not. . . . It is one of the great adventures of all time, and no nation which expects to be the leader of other nations can expect to stay behind in the race for space. . . . We intend to be first. . . . to become the world's leading space-faring nation." The youthful President then addressed one of his memorable statements to those who had asked, "Why send a man to the Moon?"

> We set sail on this new sea because there is new knowledge to be gained and new rights to be won, and they must be won and used for the progress of all people. For space science, like nuclear science and all technology, has no conscience of its own. Whether it will become a force for good or ill depends on us, and only if the United States occupies a position of preeminence can we help decide whether this new ocean will be a sea of peace or a new, terrifying theater of war. . . . Space can be explored and mastered without feeding the fires of war, without repeating the mistake that man has made in extending his writ around this globe of ours.[21]

If President Kennedy's remarks in Houston, later at the McDonnell factory in St. Louis, and elsewhere, proved an accurate reflection of most Americans' sentiments about the space program, his words persuaded few of the vocal economic, political, and scientific conservatives who were watching costs soar along with the engineering effort. The NASA space budget alone for this fiscal year was over $5 billion, which represented a tax of about 40 cents on each American per week; but the Nation was prosperous, the economy seemed sound, and critics of the "space circus" were seldom heard.

Toward the end of September, all mission preparations, the astronaut, the spacecraft, and the launch vehicle reached a high state of readiness. The spacecraft and the booster mated well; the simulated tests before mission ticked off without further hitches; and October 3 thus remained a promising launch date.

Schirra, viewing the elaborate preparation effort, studying his flight plan, and knowing that his mission involved the evaluation of the capsule's ability to accomplish a day-long flight, recognized the immensity of the engineering effort behind him. In honor of these labors, he selected the name *Sigma 7* for his spacecraft. "Since this was to be an engineering evaluation," he explained, the name chosen for capsule No. 16 was that of an engineering symbol for summation, Sigma,

470

President John F. Kennedy, touring space facilities, spoke to 35,000 people in the stadium at Rice University, September 12, 1962: "We intend . . . to become the world's leading spacefaring nation."

with the number seven added to it for the seven-member Mercury astronaut team. "Thus," he said, "was derived the name and symbol that was painted on the spacecraft, Sigma 7." [22]

On the final lap toward launch day, Schirra began a controlled diet on September 21; nine days later physician Howard A. Minners placed him on his low-residue diet. Schirra complained mildly while adjusting to the low-residue food, but in every other respect he was primed and ready, mentally and physically.

As always when flight day neared, the Mercury operations team through the Weather Bureau support group kept a watchful eye on existing weather disturbances in both the Atlantic and Pacific areas. About 400 miles north by northeast of Puerto Rico, tropical storm Daisy churned the waters of the Atlantic, while three typhoons, Dinah, Emma, and Frieda, whipped Pacific waves. On October 1, Walter Williams told the news corps covering the flight at the Cape that except for the weather "all elements of the MA-8 flight are in a go condition as of this time." By 5 p.m. the following day, Williams was satisfied with the chances for success and decided to launch as planned. [23]

Notified by Williams that he had a 7 o'clock liftoff "appointment" the next morning, Schirra dined leisurely and retired early. Without any sleep-inducing medications, the pilot drifted into slumber shortly after 8 p.m. and got about five hours of sound rest. Minners roused Schirra at 1:40 a.m. to begin the precise readiness routine. The astronaut showered, shaved, and met with Gilruth, Williams, Slayton, and Minners for breakfast. He ate heartily the "astronaut launching breakfast," consisting of eggs, filet, dry toast, orange juice, and coffee, plus a portion of a bluefish that he had speared the day before. The major preflight physical having taken place two days earlier, Minners checked Schirra briefly, pronouncing him in excellent physical condition. After Minners applied the physiological sensors to the astronaut's body, Schirra signaled to Joe W. Schmitt to assist him in donning the silvery pressure suit. At a little past 4 o'clock, Schirra and his attending retinue emerged from Hangar S.

As Schirra headed for the transfer van, Alvin B. Webb, a veteran space-newsman assigned by the press pool to report activities in that area, observed that the astronaut seemed to be unusually relaxed and smiling, as compared to previous astronauts on their way to the launch pad. Seconds later, Schirra, carrying his portable air conditioner, climbed aboard the van for a leisurely ride toward the flood-lit spire in the distance. As the van reached the blockhouse and gantry complex, Byron G. MacNabb, representing the Convair-Atlas team, greeted Schirra and said: "On behalf of the crew of Pad 14, I wish you a successful flight and a happy landing." Acknowledging this salutation, Schirra boarded the elevator and moved up the gantry. At 4:41 a.m. the astronaut slid inside *Sigma 7*.[24]

THE TEXTBOOK FLIGHT

As October 3, 1962, dawned, television viewers and radio listeners in the United States faced the day with a spectacular doubleheader in store: in the new "world series" in space, the orbiting of a third American; in the older World Series on Earth, the opening baseball game between the New York Yankees and the San Francisco Giants. Many dials switched later in the day to the traditional nine-inning sports event, but two of the three major networks continued to compete for the attention of Americans with minute-by-minute coverage of *Sigma 7*'s six orbits.[25]

Schirra slipped into his capsule, buckled himself comfortably in the couch, and smiled when he saw an automobile ignition key hanging from the handcontroller safety latch. This represented a tension breaker provided by the ground crew. Then he began to inventory his gear inside the cabin—flight-plan bar charts neatly placed in a slot just below the instrument panel, star charts arranged in a rack to his side, cameras in place, and accessories stowed in his ditty bag. When he stuck his hand in the glove compartment, he found some crinkly plastic wrapped around a soft object that turned out to be a steak sandwich. Otherwise, everything was as it should be, and Schirra began his prelaunch checkout tests.[26]

Outside the spacecraft, technicians busily bolted on the side hatch, and every bolt sank neatly in its threads. From there on, the countdown proceeded rapidly until about 6:15 (T minus 45 minutes), when the Canary Island station reported a malfunction in one of its radar sets. Since this equipment would be critical in ascertaining the orbital parameters, Williams quickly called a hold in the countdown. The Canary radar required only 15 minutes to be fixed and for the next 45 minutes the countdown ticked off with precision.

At 7:15 a.m., the engines of Atlas 113–D roared and the big booster rose from the pad to rocket Schirra and *Sigma 7* on their journey through space. "I have the lift-off," Schirra shouted into his microphone to Slayton in the Mercury Control Center, "and she feels real nice." Ten seconds above the pad, however, No. 113–D telemetered signals showing an unexpected clockwise roll. Both primary and secondary sensors inside the launch vehicle, monitoring such movements to determine the seriousness of the situation, registered a rifling roll only 20 percent short of an abort condition. Then, to the relief of the capsule and booster monitors in the control center, the threatening twist suddenly smoothed out. Schirra began transmitting the status of his supplies and systems' operation. After a little more than a minute, he realized that he seemed to be talking to himself. Glancing around the cockpit, he noted that evidently the noise associated with max q had incorrectly operated the sound-activated radio microphone, and so he pushed the button to talk to Slayton. Surely something should be done to obviate this problem, he thought, because he needed to keep his hand on the abort handle, or "chicken switch," rather than having to press the "talk" button manually.

Schirra listened for booster engine cutoff; it came two seconds earlier than programmed. He saw a flash of light and smoke reflected from the booster engines at the time the aft section parted from the sustainer. Seconds later the escape tower jerked away from the top of *Sigma 7,* its rocket blast spreading a spotty film on the window. Sustainer engine acceleration seemed slow, Schirra mused, but since his escape tower had "really said 'sayonara,' " he could only wait and see if the sustainer would burn long enough to accelerate him into orbit. Acceleration seemed to drive on and on, the pilot said, and finally the sustainer engine cut off, about 10 seconds late. Data registered on the control panels at the Cape indicated a 15-foot-per-second overspeed that would send Schirra higher—176 miles—and faster—17,557 miles per hour—than any other astronaut had gone or would go during Project Mercury.[27]

When *Sigma 7* parted from its Atlas rocket, Schirra turned on the auxiliary damping controls to eliminate the spacecraft quivers produced by the blast of the posigrade rockets. Although he dearly wanted to look out the spacecraft window at the scene below, Schirra fixed his eyes on the instrument panel, flipped his attitude control to the fly-by-wire mode, and started a leisurely four-degree-per-second cartwheel movement to obtain his correct orbital attitude position. Turnaround, which was deliberately slow to conserve fuel, used only three-tenths of a pound from a total supply of almost 59 pounds of hydrogen peroxide. To Schirra the thruster jets operated as if they had been programmed by a computer, providing tiny single pulse spurts to obtain exactly the position he desired.[28]

Now he could look out the window to track the sustainer tankage. Peering at a prescribed spot, Schirra saw the spent vehicle come into view in the upper left corner of his "picture" window, just as his predecessors had said it should. Glenn and Carpenter had mentioned that their tankage appeared to be silvery in color; to Schirra, his looked almost black, "with a white belly band of frost." The spent launch vehicle seemed to have completed the same turnaround maneuver as the spacecraft, because Schirra looked down its nozzle. The *Sigma 7* pilot saw none of the ice crystals or contrails streaming from the tankage reported by Carpenter.

Schirra said that the fly-by-wire system that had been redesigned to use only the low thrusters, if desired, served well to adjust his attitude to track the spent sustainer. The thrusters responded crisply and cut off without residual reactions. Tracking the booster seemed even easier than following a target in an aircraft on an air-to-air gunnery problem. Schirra nevertheless knew that he had neither the attitude control and maneuvering thrust nor the computational ability to perform a rendezvous. There were simply too many conditions to be judged if he were to solve the orbital mechanics task so shortly after launching. Schirra later expressed the opinion that rendezvous with another vehicle in space appeared to be possible, but that he believed a pilot would have to have very precise attitude data to effect a coupling. He confirmed what students of celestial mechanics already knew, while providing them with a feel for the problems of perceiving relative motion. Differences in velocity of only 20 to 30 feet per second between two objects in space could be disastrous, he said.

As Schirra neared the Canary Islands, he turned aside from tracking the booster to check out the manual-proportional mode of spacecraft control. The pitching-up maneuver matched well with his experience on the procedures trainer. As Grissom had done before him in Mercury-Redstone 4, Schirra noted that he tended to overshoot his desired attitude position and that the manual mode of control seemed "sloppy" compared with the semi-automatic modes. Manual-proportional control clearly was not the best way to "park" the spacecraft in one attitude. A far better method, he learned, was to rely on fly-by-wire with low thrusters only.

Passing over Nigeria, Schirra transferred spacecraft control to the automatic stabilization and control system and busily monitored his panel dials. Minutes later he had traversed the African continent without yielding more than once to the temptation to watch the panorama passing beneath him. Moving toward Zanzibar, Schirra began to feel warm. He decided to devote full attention to this before somebody, as he said later in the postflight debriefing, started "jumping up and down in the control center" and yanked him out of orbit. Frank H. Samonski, the environmental control system monitor in the Mercury Control Center, had also watched the temperature rise. At Mercury Control the suit heat signal, creeping steadily upward, had indeed caused the ground controllers to think about terminating the mission after the first circuit. Samonski conferred with Charles A. Berry, who had relieved Stanley C. White as flight surgeon in the Control Center. Berry believed that the astronaut was in good condition. He advised trying a second orbit to see if the suit and its occupant could settle their temperature differences. Kraft, the flight director, listened to the two men and decided to give the go-ahead to Schirra for a second orbit. Wrestling with communications checks and with his suit temperature, he found himself halfway around the world before the Guaymas station relayed the official green light for his second orbit.

474

When the temperature problem first appeared, the control knob setting was at Position 4. Prior to the flight, Schirra had established a procedure for just this situation. Rather than rushing to a high setting, he slowly advanced the knob by half a mark at a time, then waited about 10 minutes to evaluate the change. Had the valve been advanced too quickly, the heat exchanger might have frozen and reduced its effectiveness even more. By the time Position 7 was reached, Schirra was much cooler and felt sure that his temperature problem was nearing resolution, but for good measure he turned to Position 8. Shortly he became a little cool, and Samonski recommended that he return to Position 3.5. Schirra, thinking that some kind of analysis had been performed in the Mercury Control Center, complied. Immediately noting that the temperature was rising again, he quickly returned the setting to 7.5 and left it alone for a while.

Rounding Muchea, Australia, on his first pass, Schirra had nosed the small end of *Sigma 7* down to watch for the first ground flare launch. He said that he saw the flare before realizing the flash was only lightning. Shortly thereafter, Woomera reported flare ignition; the pilot still saw lightning—but only as a big blob of light, never like the jagged streaks seen nearer Earth. Again, as on past missions, the flare launching area was cloaked by clouds. Minutes later, however, he reported seeing the outline of a city, which he guessed to be Brisbane, Australia.

With careful adjustments, Schirra peered into the periscope on his first night trip through space, endeavoring to prove its optical advantages. Very graphically, he finally reported, "I couldn't see schmatze through it. Schmatze translated means nothing." He, like Carpenter, found the periscope was excess baggage during the daytime and nearly useless at night. Reaching the morning side of Earth near Hawaii, he recoiled when the Sun, glaring through the scope, almost blinded him. Placing a chart over the scope, he commented that it "helps no end to cover up that blasted periscope."

Though he did not feel rushed in his few tasks, Schirra did notice a remarkable "speeding up of time" as distance flew by so rapidly. After crossing the Pacific, he reported to Scott Carpenter at Guaymas, Mexico, "I'm in chimp configuration," meaning that the capsule systems were all on automatic and working beautifully. Even the temperature range had now become more comfortable, and one more adjustment of the knob would end that problem. He then told Carpenter that he would soon start his first daytime yaw maneuver, using the window as a reference. Schirra said to Slayton, while sailing over the Cape, that the "reticle is working well for yaw, as well as for almost any other attitude." Any object that could be seen on Earth could be centered on the window reticle long enough to judge yaw misalignment. Always the most difficult of the three axes to judge precisely, as demonstrated during MA–7, yaw alignment with the flight path was a major control task to be tested by the MA–8 mission. Over areas of extreme cloudiness, there was no worry so long as rifts or thunderheads provided breaks in the blanket of cloud cover. By the end of his first circuit, Schirra felt he had become so adept in determining yaw attitude that he could estimate any yaw angle his ship happened to take away from the flight path.

The pilot for a second time carefully compared his visual ability, both with and without the periscope, to position the capsule's attitude correctly. He felt satisfied with the results. He conceded that by using the periscope on high magnification he could obtain the yaw attitude faster than with the window, but speed was unnecessary in most cases.

Schirra had to devote much of his time during the first orbit and a good portion of the second to correcting his suit temperature settings. Perspiration salted around his mouth as a result of suit inlet temperature reaching 82 degrees F; he became quite thirsty, but he resisted opening the visor so the suit could have every opportunity to settle in a more comfortable range. Despite the heat—which he described as comparable to what he had endured mowing his lawn in Texas on a summer's day—all other aspects of the flight were going well. *Sigma 7* had consumed 1.4 pounds of fuel on the first orbit, Schirra noted as he reported the status of the spacecraft systems. He saw the exterior particles first reported by Glenn and tapped the cabin wall to obtain the same shower effect Carpenter reported. Much of his conversation with the tracking sites involved the status of his suit circuit. He seemed to enjoy talking with the communicators during his first orbit, but later he would complain that this became a chore, especially when he was trying to concentrate on his work.

On Earth's nightside, Schirra reported that the Moon made an excellent yaw reference; after completing and reporting on the yaw maneuver, Schirra told Slayton in the Mercury Control Center that he had shifted back to the automatic system. By now the temperature had subsided enough to permit a quick drink of water. He took the opportunity during this respite to report that all systems were performing very well. So far he had felt only one unwanted spurt from a 24-pound thruster when he returned to fly-by-wire for a yaw-maneuver exercise. Becoming a little bored with automatic flight halfway around the world, Schirra shifted to the manual-proportional system and produced a similar moment of double authority. About two percent of the manual supply spat out in a pitch-down motion of the spacecraft. "It was my boo-boo," he confessed.

Over Muchea, Australia, on his second pass, Schirra began a more serious and considerably more difficult night-yaw experiment. He was to test his ability to use celestial navigation to align the spacecraft properly. Using star-finder charts, Schirra was supposed to orient himself by positioning *Sigma 7* in relation to known stars or planets and the Moon. Then he was to test his sense of facing to the right or left of his flight path by watching the apparent motions of heavenly bodies. The pilot found that the airglow layer was an excellent reference for pitch and roll. This belt, which appeared very thick above the horizon, could provide reference for these attitudes quite accurately. For experimentation with the airglow layer, he positioned *Sigma 7* so that it appeared to aim at the upper layer of the belt. The panel indicators then showed a zero reference in pitch.

Schirra conceded that night-yaw reference could be a bit of a problem. The field of view from the window did not make it easy to identify the constellations and find a known star. Preferring to obtain the correct yaw reference on the daylight side, Schirra seemed to lack confidence in his ability to effect the night maneuver. To some degree his difficulty stemmed from his star-finder charts, which had been fixed in their relationship to Earth for a period up to about 7:16 a.m. on October 3. Schirra, now deep into the second orbit, knew that his launch time had been 7:15. The difference in time, plus his restricted field of view, reduced the value of this night-yaw exercise; but as it turned out, telemetry data received at the Muchea tracking station showed his error to be only four degrees.

During the night-yaw maneuver, Schirra happened to notice one excellent celestial pattern that he could use to align the spacecraft in the retrofire position when it was time to reenter the atmosphere. Checking the panel indicators against his own observations, he determined that the correct retrofire attitude would place the planet Jupiter in the upper right-hand corner of the window, the double-star constellation Grus tracking in from the left side of the window, and the star Fomalhaut at the top of the window, near the center.

Across the Pacific, Schirra again placed the controls in the automatic, or "chimp configuration," mode. He chatted with Grissom at the Hawaiian site about how well the spacecraft's systems were working. Grissom had made some rather strong points concerning the manual-proportional control operation during his suborbital flight, and the two astronauts, in a space-to-Earth conversation, compared notes. Just as Hawaii lost his signal and California picked it up, Schirra called that the "fireflies" were coming into view. "I have a delightful report for one John Glenn," he told the California communicator. "I do see fireflies." Impressed by the view out of the window, even though much of the California coast was covered with clouds, Schirra remarked to Glenn, "It's kind of hard to describe all this, isn't it, John?" Suddenly, through rifts in the clouds, he could see San Clemente Island, off the coastline. Then, looking northeastward, he saw more of the coastal area come into view, followed by the Salton Sea, an excellent view of lower California, the ridges of Mount Whitney, and several roads in the Mojave Desert area.

Although Schirra flew higher than either Glenn or Carpenter, he was rather unimpressed by the height of his voyage. Psychologically he had prepared himself for space flight, knowing that he would be flying 10 times higher than he had ever flown before. But once in space, the number, size, and detail of the objects he could see with the unaided eye, such as roads and terrain changes, made him actually feel no higher than he had climbed in an aircraft. "Same old deal, nothing new," he remarked in debriefing, "might as well be in an airplane at 40- to 50-thousand feet altitude."

According to his flight plan, if the yaw-reference checks had been satisfactory *Sigma 7* would be phased into drifting flight during the third orbit. After giving

477

Slayton a systems status report, Schirra proceeded to cage the spacecraft's gyros, cut off its electrical power, and allow *Sigma 7* to drift through space. Schirra took this opportunity to make an old psychomotor experiment that Robert B. Voas a year earlier had asked to be performed. Choosing three dials on the control panel, he closed his eyes and attempted to touch the target points. In a total of nine trials, he made only three errors, the largest being a displacement of some two inches. The weightless state, he concluded, created no disorientation or new problems in blindly reaching for his controls.

After that test, Schirra drifted along, reporting his status again to the Canary station and enjoying a brief period of looking out the window. He mentioned that his outer pane was streaked with a pinkish-orange film and surmised that this had emanated from the exhaust gases of the launch escape rocket. According to his flight plan, he was supposed to eat and drink now; although he said, "I'm having a ball up here drifting," eat and drink he did—peaches and ground beef mush from squeeze tubes.

Out over the Indian Ocean, he informed the tracking ship in that vicinity that he had switched the electrical power back on and gone into fly-by-wire control to check systems operations after the "powered down," or free-flight, period. Excitedly, the Indian Ocean ship communicator told Schirra that some of the crew topside had actually caught sight of *Sigma 7* for five minutes and through nine degrees of tracking. Schirra, quite pleased, said, "I'll have to go by and say hello." The pilot then reported that powering up again presented no difficulty; all systems worked beautifully, with absolutely no responses from the high thrusters. Smoothly transferring into the automatic stabilization and control system, he began to look toward the heavens for familiar stars. When the Moon failed to show, he went to the fly-by-wire, low-thruster control to bring it into sight. He identified Cassiopeia during the process, then said, "There's our friend the Moon." Over Muchea again by this time, he told the communicator that he had locked the automatic system onto the disk of the Moon. Mercury Control had alerted the ground stations to pay particular attention to fuel usage by the thrusters. Canton Island and Kauai, Hawaii, rolled by underneath with everything working so well that Grissom, at the Hawaiian station, gave Schirra the official good news that he had a "go" for the full six orbits.

As *Sigma 7* came near the California tracking site on its third pass, Schirra told Glenn, "I'm going to shove off for a relaxation period," meaning he would cut his electrical power, cage his gyros, and start drifting again. Schirra's flight schedule now called for experimental observations and photography. He had to struggle getting the camera out of the ditty bag, but once out it was weightless, and Schirra easily snapped pictures from Baja California to Cuba as *Sigma 7* drifted along beautifully. Nearing the Cape, Slayton asked for a radiation reading from the hand-held dosimeter. Schirra replied that the value was so small that it was nearly unreadable. Then Kraft himself came on the air to compliment Schirra, to urge him to look for the giant Echo balloon-shaped satellite on his next pass over

Zanzibar, and to notify him that his voice would be broadcast live for two minutes during his next flight across North America. The enthusiastic pilot then exclaimed that he had just drifted into an inverted position (head to Earth) and "for some reason or another, you can tell that the bowl [spacecraft] is upside down." He saw the whole eastern coastline of the United States, took a picture of that, and then another of an interesting cloud formation. Still complaining that the camera was difficult to extract, he decided not to stow it in the case for a while. As for Echo, he never saw that (or any other) man-made satellite while in orbit.

Floating through space around the world on his fourth orbit, Schirra took pictures that struck his fancy, watched the nightfall, recognized several stars as they appeared, and looked at lightning in the thunderstorms covering portions of the Australian continent. As he came over the Pacific command ship, he facetiously reported to Shepard that his hydrogen peroxide had not evaporated and suggested that they should make some plans, the next time around, about retrofire countdown. Schirra then tuned on the radar ships *Huntsville* and *Watertown* for a communications check. As Hawaii was sliding by, he told Grissom that he was in inverted flight and that the impression was similar to "looking out a railroad train window. You see the terrain going by you." The yaw attitude of the spacecraft was clearly discernible against this background.

As he approached, head down and looking toward California on his fourth pass, Schirra joked with Glenn about his "real weird attitude" and transmitted another short status report. Then at 6 hours, 8 minutes, and 4 seconds elapsed time from launch, Schirra and Glenn began a dialogue heard by much of the western world via radio and television:

GLENN: Okay, Sigma 7. This is Cal Cap Com. You're at 6:08. Two minutes on live TV. Go ahead, Wally.

SCHIRRA: Roger, John. Just came out of a powered-down configuration where we had the ASCS inverter off. It came up in good shape and will stay on now for the rest of the flight. The amps and volts are reading properly. . . . I'm coming toward you inverted this time, which is an unusual way for any of us to approach California, I'll admit.

GLENN: Roger, Wally. You got anything to say to everyone watching you across the country on this thing? We're going out live on this.

SCHIRRA: That sounds like great sport. I can see why you and Scott like it. I'm having a trick now. I'm looking at the United States and starting to pitch up slightly with this drifting rate. And I see the moon, which I'm sure no one in the United States can see as well as I right now.

GLENN: I think you're probably right.

SCHIRRA: Ha-ha, I suppose an old song, "Drifting and Dreaming," would be apropos at this point, but at this point I don't have a chance to dream. I'm enjoying it too much.

GLENN: Things are looking real good from here, Wally.

SCHIRRA: Thank you, John. I guess that what I'm doing right now is sort of a couple of Immelmanns across the United States.

479

And here ended Schirra's epistle from space. Glenn continued the conversation in relative privacy, asking whether Schirra had noticed anything surprising about the haze layer. Schirra replied with another understatement—"It's quite fascinating"—but later he recalled that this phenomenon had been his biggest spatial surprise. Both Glenn and Carpenter had briefed him on the night view of the horizon from the heavens, but "it just never did sink in to me that it was as large in magnitude as it really was." Schirra remarked that the airglow layer covered about a quarter of his view out the window. When first sighted, he said, "I thought it was clouds, until stars appeared below." [29]

Halfway through the fourth orbit, liquid collected over the inner surface of his helmet faceplate, evidently from the water coolant circuit. Although Schirra was annoyed by this problem for the next two hours, he was thankful that the suit temperature remained reasonably comfortable. So long as his visor was sealed, he had to crane his head about inside the helmet to find a clear view out of the faceplate. He was still reluctant to disturb his suit temperature by opening his visor to wipe it clean.

Going into his fifth orbit, Schirra told Slayton by radio relay that the flight had been his first opportunity to relax since the previous December. His life had suddenly become so sedentary that he gladly used the bungee cord exerciser to tone up his muscles a bit. "Not exactly walking around," he said, "but a little bit of stretching." Because *Sigma 7* was now over the Yucatan Peninsula, communications with the Cape were a little strained, causing Slayton to quiz Schirra, "Did you say you'd like to get up and walk around?" The ground controllers cleared the matter by switching circuits to a relay communications aircraft.

Schirra now began another check of the manual-proportional attitude controls, recording a third brief instance of double authority control. Regarding this latest spew of fuel, he complained that he "really flotched it. It's much too easy to get into double authority, even with the tremendous logic you have working on all these systems." His check of all the axes of movement proved that the manual-proportional system was still in good working order. After this trial he returned to observing and photographing targets of opportunity.

As he prepared to look for the 140-million candlepower light near Durban, South Africa, Schirra reported "getting some lighted areas over the southern tip of Africa. . . . I definitely have a city in sight." Betting that this was Port Elizabeth, a city a little more than 300 miles to the southwest of Durban, Schirra did not seem surprised that Durban was being drenched with rain and its brilliant light was not visible on this pass.

Passing into its fifth revolution of Earth, *Sigma 7* still performed beautifully in all respects. Astronaut Schirra had little to tell the ground tracking station except to repeat how well the systems were working and how gorgeous were the sights. With each orbit, he was now moving farther from the beaten track nominal to a three-pass flight, and the periods of silence were longer. A lighted area appearing much like an airport showed up in what he surmised were the

Philippine Islands. "Possibly it's at Zamboanga," he guessed, a city on the southwest coast of Mindanao. Minutes later he talked with Alan B. Shepard aboard the Pacific command ship, reporting with pleasure that his fuel supply stood at 81 and 80 percent in the automatic and manual tanks, respectively. His oxygen supply was properly pressurized, and his suit temperature was at a comfortable 62 degrees. Shepard replied, "Well, I could say that you were definitely go." Quickly he checked in with the *Huntsville* and *Watertown,* presenting, as he put it, a "hunky dory" report. As the pilot came over the Kauai station, Grissom fed him the correct retrosequence time that he should use on his next, and final, pass. Checks with Glenn at Point Arguello and with Carpenter at Guaymas showed that communications should be good for checkoff and reentry during the sixth orbit. Schirra then bade farewell to South America with a "Buenos dias, you-all," to the Quito, Ecuador, communications relay station.

Going into the sixth orbit, Schirra almost regretfully began his preparations to return to Earth. On his last pass over South America, heavy cloud coverage obscured most of the hemisphere but he did catch sight of a large winding river. He reached for the slow-scan camera and pointed it downward at the surface of the window to capture the view, making a panoramic shot of the continent that he thought would aid the Weather Bureau in continental cloud analyses. Then he stowed the camera, rearranged the contents of the ditty bag and glove compartment, and began going down the checklist of actions to be accomplished before retrofire and reentry.

He shifted the control mode from the automatic system to the fly-by-wire, low-thrusters, and found his command of the system still worked well. He looked briefly out the window for the lights of Durban, but clouds still hid the glow of that huge lamp from sight. He closed the faceplate, found it fogging again, and opened it briefly to wipe the visor clean. The instrument panel showed that the inverter temperatures were in a good range, that the battery voltage checked out high, and that the oxygen pressure was holding its mark. Although quite comfortable, he decided to advance the suit-circuit knob "just a tad to increase the cooling for reentry," to Position 8. The checkoff proceeded so methodically that he had time to try another eyes-closed orientation test. He reached for the manual handle and felt it in his grasp. Then he reached for the emergency handle but brushed an adjacent radio box before touching it.

Down below, the Indian Ocean ship communicator asked if he needed any help in completing the pre-retrosequence checklist. "Negative," he replied. All was in readiness for the last-minute arming of the retrorocket squibs. He waited and watched until he came in range of Shepard aboard the Pacific command ship. In the darkness, he viewed a moonset, saw the proper star and planet pattern for his correctly aligned attitude swing into view, and noticed that one of his fingertip lights had burned out. Musing out loud for whoever could listen, he likened his situation once again to riding a train on celestial tracks leading back toward Earth. Listening to the humming of the systems, he was reminded also of a ship underway at sea.   As a pilot, Schirra curiously refused to compare his limited control of the spacecraft with his freedom of maneuver in aircraft.

When he came into range of the Pacific command ship, he glanced at the fuel levels: 78 percent in both the automatic and manual tanks, the meters read. Shepard asked him how he stood on the checklist.   Completed, with the exception of arming the rocket squibs, Schirra replied.   He told Shepard that his ship was holding well in the retroattitude mode on the automatic system, that the high thrusters were in good working order, and that he had the manual-proportional system in a standby position.   With everything set, Shepard gave the countdown to arm the squibs on the "Mark!"   Next came the retrosequence countdown. Eight hours and 52 minutes after *Sigma 7* lifted off from the Cape, the first retrorocket fired.   When Schirra punched the button for this action, the tiny instant of time before the firing "seemed agonizingly long."   As each retrorocket fired crisply at five-second intervals, Schirra was pleasantly amazed that the spacecraft appeared to hold as steady as a rock.   Quickly he checked this impression with a glance out of the window; the star pattern he could see did not even appear to quiver.   After retrofire he checked the automatic fuel gauge and found the needle hovering between 52 and 53 percent.

Then Schirra shifted gears to his favorite fly-by-wire, low-thruster mode of control.   He armed the retropack jettison switch and the spent unit spun away. Shortly after retrofire his attitude control felt "a little bit sloppy," and he felt himself wobble toward reentry.   Although this could have been corrected by using the low thrusters, he intentionally cut in the high thrusters to get into position quickly. Schirra pitched *Sigma 7* up to the 14-degree reentry attitude with no difficulty and cut in the automatic control mode to damp away undesirable motions.   Then, as the engineers had asked him to do, he turned on the fuel-gulping rate stabilization control system (RSCS).   His return to the atmosphere was "thrilling" to the astronaut.   He said the sky and Earth's surface really began to brighten, but, most surprisingly, the "bear" he rode felt "as stable as an airplane."

Schirra realized that he had heard none of the hissing noises reported by Glenn and Carpenter.   Possibly, he thought, his concentration on the rate control system caused him to miss the sounds.   Having conserved his hydrogen peroxide so well thus far, Schirra was quite perturbed with the rate system because he could see the fuel supply being dumped like water being flushed.   Resisting the temptation to switch to a more economical mode of control because the engineers wanted to evaluate this system once and for all, he pulled his eyes away from the gauge and looked out the window.   He could see the green glow from air friction that Carpenter had reported.   To him it looked limeade in color, almost chartreuse. Suddenly, as a three-foot strap flopped past the window, he exclaimed, "My gosh!" Then he remembered, "That's the same thing John saw."

Soon the barometric altimeter dial came into operation, and Schirra calmly waited for the needle to edge toward the 40,000-foot reading.   He punched the drogue button, heard a "strong thrumming," and then felt the drogue parachute pop open. What had felt like a smooth highway now seemed like turning off on "a bumpy road." As long as he could, the astronaut strained to watch "the drogue up there pounding away," but the window became virtually occluded by smoky deposits from reentry. Schirra then turned back and flipped on the fuel jettison switch.

At the 15,000-foot mark he ejected the main parachute and saw it stream and blossom at 10,500 feet. This event, as Schirra quipped, "sort of put the cap on the whole thing." As he started his descent to Earth, Schirra remarked to Shepard, "I think they're gonna put me on the number 3 elevator" of the carrier *Kearsarge*. *Sigma 7* missed this mark by a scant 4.5 miles downrange from the planned landing point, but the recovery force had the spacecraft well within its sights electronically and visually. The carrier made radar contact with *Sigma 7* at a slant-range of 202 miles; 90 miles uprange from the carrier, sailors of the destroyer *Renshaw* reported hearing a sonic boom. Men on the deck of the *Kearsarge* then saw a contrail, while a few of its crew claimed to see the drogue and others heard two successive sonic booms and saw the main chute unfurl. After nine hours and 13 minutes in flight, *Sigma 7* settled on the water, in full view of the ship's crew and the cameras of newsmen.

Sigma 7 hit the surface with a "plop," as Schirra described it, and "went way down" before it surfaced and floated. He waited patiently for 45 seconds and then broke off the main parachute and switched on the recovery aids. Inside, the spacecraft remained dry and the temperature range was very comfortable as *Sigma 7* rode the lazy ocean swells. This condition prompted the pilot to exaggerate in debriefing that he "could stay in there forever, if necessary." Through the window he could see the green dye permeating the water in a widening perimeter, and he knew that the whip antenna had telescoped out fully. Seeing the antenna pole deploy while *Sigma 7* was still submerged, Schirra later joked that he thought he might spear another bluefish. All was well, and so far as this test pilot could judge, the Mercury spacecraft "had gone to the top of the list," even over the F8F aircraft he liked so well.

Long before Schirra's splashdown, the *Kearsarge* had launched helicopters with swimmer teams, and soon three swimmers jumped into the dye beside the floating capsule. During the 30 seconds while he was keeled over in the water, Schirra had had some trepidation about his watertight integrity. He momentarily wished for the pressure regulator handle that had been deleted from *Sigma 7* to save another pound of weight. As the capsule righted itself and remained shipshape, he noticed that communications had been better with Hawaii than they were with the *Kearsarge*. The pararescue men then cut the whip antenna and attached the flotation collar around the heatshield. Since he was comfortable, he radioed a request to the helicopter pilot that he "would prefer to stay in and have a small boat come alongside" and tow him to the carrier's cranes. Five men piled into a motor whaleboat and within minutes had covered the half-mile to the bobbing *Sigma 7* and attached a tow line to it.

483

Some nine hours and 54 minutes after launch, the small space ship was hoisted aboard the huge carrier. Five minutes later Schirra whacked the plunger to blow the explosive hatch, incurring the same kind of superficial hand injury as Glenn before him. He stepped out onto the deck of the *Kearsarge* and paused to acknowledge the jubilant shouts and applause of the ship's crew. As he walked down to the ship's sick bay, Schirra looked tired and hot but happy. When reporters called out, "How do you feel, Wally?" he replied, "Fine," with a flip of the hand.

For the next three days, the *Kearsarge* was to be his home during the medical examinations and technical debriefings. While still in his space suit and sitting on a cot in the officers' sickroom, he received successive congratulatory telephone calls from President Kennedy, his wife Josephine Schirra, and Vice President Johnson.[30]

Richard A. Pollard of MSC, Commander Max Trummer of the Navy, and several other physicians began to check Schirra in every medical way possible. When his phone calls were completed, about 45 minutes after he came on board, the systematic examinations began. At first appearance, the spaceman showed no evidence that he was dizzy or required walking assistance. He told the physicians, "I feel fine. It was a textbook flight. The flight went just the way I wanted it to." Contrary to the impression of some newsmen, the physicians did not find Schirra overly fatigued. He talked easily and actively assisted in his postflight physical. Only after he had been strapped on a tilt table did several unusual symptoms begin to appear. For example, when lying supine his heartbeat averaged 70 a minute; standing, it rose to 100. Blood pressure readings, although not so pronounced in range, registered differently in standing, sitting, and prone positions. His legs and feet assumed a dusky, reddish-purple color when Schirra stood up, connoting that his veins were engorged. This condition persisted for about six hours, and then the astronaut was permitted to retire for the night. The next morning Schirra's heart and blood pressure readings were near normal, and there was no evidence of pooling of blood in his legs when he stood.

Other than this minor anomaly, and the small lesion on his hand, Schirra seemed none the worse for his lengthy weightless sojourn in space. Life-systems specialists in NASA, at McDonnell, and at AiResearch, however, had another question: What caused the elevated suit temperatures during the first two orbits? Postflight inspectors dug into the matter promptly. The technical ills of the spacecraft's systems were more easily determined than the subtleties of man's physiological system; as it turned out, the flow in the suit coolant circuit had been impeded by the silicone lubricant on a needle valve's having dried out and flaked.

Postflight inspection of *Sigma 7* found little else that seemed out of the ordinary. Circular cracks on the ablation shield were moderately larger than on Glenn's and Carpenter's spacecraft; also it appeared that the shield had banged into the fiber-glass protective bulkhead upon impact, causing several small holes. Once again the heatshield showed some delamination from the center, but it still

Flight of
***Sigma* 7**
Oct. 3, 1962

Schirra, assisted by Cooper, heads for elevator that will carry them to the top of Gantry 14 where Sigma 7 awaits her astronaut.

Six orbits and a landing later, the whaleboat from the Kearsarge *approaches* Sigma 7 *to help para-rescue men secure the capsule.*

Sigma 7 *is hauled aboard the principal recovery ship* Kearsarge.

appeared, as in past flights, that this occurred after reentry. Char depth on the shield, about a third of an inch, was quite nominal. The shield's center plug, which had been loose or missing after previous missions, stayed tightly in place. All in all, the inspectors found very few problems to analyze or to correct. The quality of the mission, of the hardware, of the software, of procedures, and of the pilot were all superb. In terminology the engineers agreed with Schirra that MA–8 was a "text book flight"—the best so far.

Walter Williams was especially jubilant over the MA–8 success; now he could confidently turn his operations team to the task of the day-long mission. Schirra's conservation of fuel and the excellent manner in which the spacecraft had performed, he said, made planning for MA–9, if not routine, at least considerably easier.[31]

Upon leaving the *Kearsarge*, Schirra received the leis of Hawaii and a tumultuous aloha. Then he flew back to Houston. In a press conference at Rice University, he reported about his spatial voyage to an American public that now was more conversant with the terminology of space technology. Thereafter, the hamlet of Oradell, New Jersey, greeted its most famous son, and from there Schirra went to Washington to receive the NASA Distinguished Service Medal from the President and, from the Chief of Naval Operations, the Navy's anchored version of the coveted astronaut's wings. Throughout the national hurrahs, however, the thoughts and words of participants in Project Mercury turned toward the advent of the day-long mission, another step toward reaching the lunar landing goal in the decade of the sixties.[32]

In mid-October 1962 the frightening Cuban missile crisis raised the spectre of nuclear holocaust. This dampened some of the postflight celebrations for Schirra. When President Kennedy appeared on nationwide television to explain his actions in blockading Cuba to force the Soviets to withdraw their ballistic missiles from Fidel Castro's island, Americans perhaps for the first time became acutely aware of the differences between medium-range (200–500-mile) "defensive" missiles and intermediate-range (1000–1500-mile) "offensive" rocket weapons. Neither the ICBM deterrent (defined as having an operational range of about 6000 miles) nor the success of Kennedy's confrontation of Khrushchev over Soviet IRBMs in Cuba could entirely relax the tension built up by this crisis. But it probably did more than any manned space flight had to educate the public on relative thrust capacities of rockets.

REDEVELOPMENT FOR MA–9

The flight of *Sigma 7* had been so nearly idyllic that some observers, whether from cynicism or a kind of parental possessiveness, believed Project Mercury should be concluded on Schirra's positive note. Any further attempt at manned satellite flight with this first-generation hardware might press the program's luck too far and end sourly, if not calamitously. To cancel Mercury now would ensure the reputation of the project. Others argued it would sacrifice the living potential, as well as the intense desire, of the Mercury team to test man in space for one full day.[33]

Among Manned Spacecraft Center officials, there was no real decision to be made here; Mercury had begun in earnest in 1959 with a vision of an ultimate 18-orbit mission. But by October 1959, the inexorable growth in capsule weight and power requirements and the limitations of the network had forced the Space Task Group to erase that vision. The 18-orbit mission for Mercury had been revived by the summer of 1961, in conjunction with serious planning for Project Apollo and for a "Mark II" ballistic capsule design. And when Project Gemini was publicly named on January 3, 1962, as an interim program to fill the void before Apollo could be developed, Mercury engineers were already driving headlong toward the revived 18-orbit, 27-hour mission.[34]

During the period from September 1961 to January 1962, the word "capsule" had been erased from Mercury vocabulary in favor of the word "spacecraft." It was then that the Space Task Group (STG) became Manned Spacecraft Center (MSC), and NASA Headquarters reorganized Abe Silverstein's Office of Space Flight Programs into an Office of Manned Space Flight under a new director, D. Brainerd Holmes. In the midst of all this confusion, one thing had been clear: a Mercury spacecraft would have to fill the gaps in space, time, and knowledge before a Project Gemini two-man capsule could be developed and qualified. Although the physiological effects of extended exposure to weightlessness were still of primary interest, the only local policy issue was whether to adopt another change in nomenclature. Should the day-long sustained space flight be called MA–9 or Manned One-Day Mission (MODM)?[35]

Throughout the spring and summer of 1962, Mercury engineers, both at NASA centers and in St. Louis, had studied various design proposals for advanced versions of the ballistic spacecraft. The first Gemini capsule mockup review had been held at the factory on March 29, about the same time that Lewis R. Fisher, James E. Bost, William M. Bland, Jr., Robert T. Everline, and others had completed the specifications for a Mercury spacecraft for the manned one-day flight. Not until September, however, were negotiations settled with McDonnell over configuration changes to the four capsules set aside for this purpose (Nos. 12, 15, 17, and 20). A week before the Schirra flight, NASA Headquarters announced a new plan to phase Mercury into Gemini more quickly, if MA–8 and MA–9 met all expectations.[36]

After Schirra, Atlas 113–D, and *Sigma 7* excelled those expectations in nearly every respect, the Manned Spacecraft Center forwarded its sixteenth quarterly status report to NASA Headquarters, claiming:

> This report will be the final in the series of Project MERCURY, as such, since the MA–8 flight was the last mission of Project MERCURY. Future reports, although they will continue with the following number (17), will be on the status of the Manned One-Day Mission (MODM) Project (MERCURY Spacecraft).

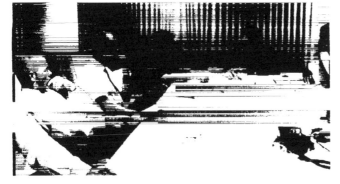

Following his MA–8 flight Schirra participated in the first shipboard technical debriefing of the Mercury program. Present were, left to right, Walter C. Williams, Glenn, Helmut A. Kuehnel, Robert Mercer, and Schirra.

Schirra at his postflight news conference, with Robert R. Gilruth at left and James E. Webb at right.

Schirra discusses his six-orbit space flight with Paul E. Purser (left), Wernher von Braun, and Robert R. Gilruth.

A technical review meeting at Space Systems Division in November 1962: left to right, Shepard, Christopher C. Kraft, Jr., Kenneth S. Kleinknecht, Walter C. Williams, Col. Robert Hoffman, Lt. Col. Toby Gandy, Bernhard A. Hohmann, and Cooper.

Robert Gilruth's team, now located in temporary quarters at 13 buildings scattered over southeast Houston, was planning on an April 1963 launch date for MA-9, using spacecraft No. 20. On November 9, 1962, MSC's senior staff decided to aim for 22 rather than 18 orbits (or 34 rather than 27 hours), if all went normally.[37]

Walter Williams, Christopher Kraft, and Kenneth Kleinknecht proceeded to coordinate the mission planning with the Defense Department. This flight would involve vastly expanded support, because MA-9 was to criss-cross virtually all of Earth's surface between latitudes 33 degrees north and south of the equator. L. Gordon Cooper was officially announced as the pilot and Alan Shepard was named alternate in mid-November. McDonnell had estimated that this mission alone would cost $17,879,834 to complete, but as yet the Air Force, Navy, and Army participants had not conferred with NASA about new needs for the recovery network and medical support.[38] Clearly the MA-9 operation would not be able to challenge the 64-orbit feat of Nikolayev in *Vostok III* nor the 48 orbits of Popovich in the tandem *Vostok IV*, but MA-9 should go well beyond Titov's 17 orbits in *Vostok II*.

Meanwhile NASA and the Manned Spacecraft Center took their cues from President Kennedy and Administrator James E. Webb to mobilize greater effort toward the longer-range goals symbolized by Project Apollo. Only 55 persons staffed Kleinknecht's Mercury Project Office specifically to coordinate the diverse preparations for MA-9. Of the 2500 people employed by MSC in January 1963, only 500 were working directly on Mercury. The Gemini and Apollo teams were rapidly taking shape. NASA had just honored a group of nine old-time engineers from the Space Task Group as the "Mercury Spacecraft Inventors." The list of innovators was headed by Maxime A. Faget, and included Andre J. Meyer, Jr., William Bland, Alan B. Kehlet, Willard S. Blanchard, Robert G. Chilton, Jerome B. Hammack, Caldwell C. Johnson, and Jack C. Heberlig. But of that group of designers and developers, only Bland still remained employed in the Mercury Project Office. The rest had gone to work on Gemini and Apollo.[39]

One of the more significant New Year's resolutions enacted by NASA in 1963 was the appointment of a Manned Space Science Planning Group and of a Panel on Inflight Scientific Experiments, known informally as POISE, chaired respectively by Eugene M. Shoemaker and John A. O'Keefe. These two new groups were established to replace the Ad Hoc Committee on Scientific Tasks and Training for Man-in-Space and to ensure closer coordination between the Manned Spacecraft Center and the NASA Office of Space Sciences. They were only temporary expedients, staffed by most of the same people who had served earlier as consultants, but at least the manned space science programs for Gemini would be born more respectably than those for Mercury.[40]

At the first MSC senior staff meeting in 1963, Walter Williams warned his colleagues that two recent failures in Atlas-F launchings by the Air Force were inexplicable, or so far, at least, unexplained. Unless investigating committees

489

could clear up these failures soon, absolving the Atlas-D from any guilt by association, the MA-9 schedule might suffer. After five years of developmental experience, the Atlas ICBM had approached but still not attained a reliability high enough for comfort. The Atlas, even as modified and "gold-plated" by the "man-rating" tests and procedures, was still basically a ballistic missile, only converted and not designed to launch men into space. After five consecutive Mercury-Atlas launches without a failure, it was all too easy to forget this fact.[41] When the 130-D, Cooper's "bird," was first rolled out of the factory in San Diego on January 30, it failed to pass inspection and was returned for some rewiring.

Amid some charges from impatient newsmen that NASA had "muzzled" Cooper, the prime pilot took time out on February 8 to hold a press conference in Houston that refuted such public speculation. Cooper forthrightly admitted what little he knew about the booster problem and answered in picturesque detail a host of questions about new developments for his space suit, his spacecraft, his mission. "This is going to practically be a flying camera," he said, explaining the new slow-scan television monitor, the 70-millimeter Hasselblad and its different film packs, the special zodiacal-light 35-millimeter camera, and a 16-millimeter, all-purpose moving-picture camera. Cooper had difficulty convincing some reporters that the duration of the MA-9 mission would depend on how well it went— for "as many as 22 orbits"--and that he was still "struggling" to find a suitable name for spacecraft No. 20. But otherwise he talked freely about the most significant differences between the MA-8 and MA-9 spacecraft, although obviously he could not name all 183 of the changes then underway at McDonnell's Canaveral shop.[42]

Weight growth had been the primary nemesis in preparing for every Mercury mission, and this was especially true for the day-long mission. As is characteristic perhaps of all American technology, and especially of advanced modifications to military aircraft, overweight accessories tended to compromise the vehicles' performance. In the case of the MODM spacecraft, heavier batteries for more electrical power, another 4-pound bottle of oxygen, 9 pounds of cooling and 4.5 pounds of drinking water, plus 15 more pounds of peroxide fuel were imperative additions. Experimental gear, a full load of consumables for life support systems, and various modified components were also judged necessary, though heavier, installations. In an effort to compensate for these added weights, the 12-pound Rate Stabilization Control System (RSCS), a 3-pound UHF and a 2-pound telemetry transmitter, both of which were true redundancies now; and, in particular, the 76-pound periscope were deleted. Manned Spacecraft Center engineers almost discarded the fiber-glass couch in favor of a new hammock to shave away 17 more pounds, but that change did not materialize because the engineers feared the material might stretch and the astronaut bounce. So the MA-9 payload continued, through 31 weeks of grooming, to grow into an estimated weight of 3026.3 pounds in orbit.[43]

Such weight increases had become expected, at the rate of about two pounds per week of preparation, and early in 1962 the Mercury managers had called for an extensive requalification program of the parachute and landing system. Known as Project Reef, these tests had effectively allayed all fears about the ring-sail parachutes' margin for error with heavier loads long before *Sigma 7* gave an even better demonstration. At the beginning of 1963, NASA scientists from other centers were pleased to gain some voting strength on the 20-man committee established nine months earlier to decide what in-flight scientific experiments should be conducted. But the majority voting strength of this panel still remained with MSC engineers, whose weight-consciousness and power-consciousness effectively stifled the transformation of MA–9 and spacecraft No. 20 into a more purely scientific orbital laboratory.[44]

Another ground test program behind the scenes, namely Project Orbit, which by the end of February 1963 had completed a 100-hour full-scale simulated mission in its thermo-cryogenic vacuum chamber, stirred up concern that the reaction control thrusters might get sluggish or freeze during long periods of inactivity in space. In all other respects, Project Orbit seemed to certify that the McDonnell spacecraft and all subcontracted systems were ready and reliable for a full day or more up there.[45]

Meanwhile, the tiger teams at work on Atlas 130–D were exceptionally pleased when, on March 15, 1963, the second factory rollout and flight-acceptance inspections on this booster were completed without a single minor discrepancy. Philip E. Culbertson, Gus Groissant, John P. Hopman, and David R. Archibald of General Dynamics/Astronautics flew across the country to deliver to their test conductor at the Cape, Calvin D. Fowler, what they believed to be their best bird yet. Bernhard A. Hohmann and helpers at Aerospace Corporation had defined an offset of the booster engines to counteract the threatening roll rate that Schirra had experienced at liftoff. And on April 22 spacecraft and rocket were mated.[46]

By the end of April, all plans and preparations had been well laid and revised in accord with the precedents and lessons of previous flights. The detailed flight plan, technical information summaries, calculated preflight trajectory data, public information directives, experiments guidebook, and documentation directives were all disseminated. The world was girdled by military and medical recovery personnel waiting for May 14 and the launch of Gordon Cooper. A total of 28 ships, 171 aircraft, and about 18,000 servicemen were assigned to support MA–9. These included 84 medical specialists, a reduction by half in the number of medical monitors and corpsmen since Glenn's flight. This was a token of the confidence the planners now had in Mercury and its men.[47]

But that confidence was not shared by everyone. While Cooper struggled to select the most appropriate name for his capsule, criticism of NASA and its implementation of national space goals swelled once again. Philip H. Abelson, editor of *Science,* the journal of the American Association for the Advancement of Science; Warren Weaver of the Alfred P. Sloan Foundation; and Senator J. William Fulbright from Arkansas raised voices in protest against the Moon race and against manned space flight in general. The costs of manned orbital flight,

491

the confusion regarding "science" and "technology," and urgent social and political problems deserving equal attention were to be widely debated.[48]

Against this context, when Cooper finally announced his choice of a call-sign— *Faith 7*, symbolizing "my trust in God, my country, and my teammates"—NASA public affairs officers were described by the *Washington Post* as worried:

> The naming of the bell-shaped capsule—a tradition accorded to the astronaut riding it—has given Cooper some bad moments. He has picked *"Faith 7,"* which has drawn some raised eyebrows in the "image" conscious space agency.
> "Suppose that, for some reason, we lost the capsule at sea," said one source. "Then it would come out reading something like, 'The United States today lost Faith. . . .' " [49]

So much had happened, so many things had changed in the four years since Project Mercury had become publicized by the selection of its seven astronauts, that the Manned One-Day Mission seemed an appropriate new name to symbolize the differences. Now there was a second class of nine more astronauts-in-training; there was the national goal of a lunar landing before 1970; there were new facilities, new administrators, and thoroughly reorganized procedures and policies to follow. *Mariner II*, in its magnificent survey of Venus in December 1962, was interpreted a few months later as having proved Venus to be one destination in planetary space that might as well be forgotten as a target for manned landings. Mars remained a mystery, and so also did Earth's Moon, for that matter, but the decision to try Project Apollo made Mercury already merely a demigod. While Project Ozma used radio telescopes in a search for evidence of intelligent life elsewhere in the universe, *Telstar II* was launched May 7, 1963, to renew the hope that Earthmen might exercise greater intelligence than they had in the past by establishing more intelligent communications with each other.[50]

In the midst of the heat of scientific and political criticism of both Department of Defense and NASA space priorities and costs, NASA and the Mercury managers had to decide what, if anything, should be the next mission after MA–9. If Walter Williams and others at MSC had their way, an MA–10 mission, planned for a three-day sojourn in space, would follow. But they were overruled, and Julian Scheer, the new NASA Deputy Assistant Administrator for Public Affairs, announced emphatically on May 11, "It is absolutely beyond question that if this shot is successful there will be no MA–10." [51]

So Astronaut Cooper knew, as he made the final preparations after four years of training, that his flight would mark the end of the beginning. A well-known life insurance company subscribed to Cooper's faith by underwriting the first commercial astronaut policies, including one for Cooper. The Mercury operations team gathered at the Cape the second week in May and found *Faith 7*, Atlas 130–D, and Cooper all ready to take off. Only the weatherman, Ernest A. Amman, voiced his doubts about the May 14 launch date.[52]

At 6:36 on the morning of May 14, Gordon Cooper was sealed inside his *Faith 7* spacecraft atop the steeple that was his Atlas. He checked off all his sys-

The worldwide interest and sense of identification with Project Mercury was always apparent. From Glenn's flight on, one country that particularly responded to the challenges of manned space flight was Australia. Shown here on April 21, 1963, is Premier of Western Australia David Brand (center) presenting the original painting, "Perth, the City of Lights," to Manned Spacecraft Center. Astronauts Schirra and Slayton accepted this commemoration of Perth's role in Project Mercury.

tems and awaited completion of the blockhouse and Control Center checkoffs, which should count down to ignition about 9 o'clock and lift him up to insertion about 9:05. A suction-cup force pump, the kind commonly called a "plumber's friend," had been Alan Shepard's parting gift to Cooper, but the instruction inscribed on the handle, "Remove before launch," had been obeyed. It would not make the long trip with Cooper.

While waiting, Cooper heard the secondary control center on Bermuda report that its basic C-band radar system was misbehaving both in azimuth and range. So he napped for a time during repairs. When Bermuda had corrected the difficulty, at about 8 o'clock, the countdown was resumed, and the gantry was ordered back. But the diesel engine failed to move the gantry, and engineers scurried around, looking for the proper plumber's helper to repair a fouled fuel injection

493

pump. More than two exasperating hours were lost on the "fail-safe" diesel locomotive before the count could resume.

At high noon, the gantry was driven back. But radar data from Bermuda, which was vital to the go/no go decision before the point of no return, now was intermittent. The launch was postponed. Cooper emerged from his capsule, saying, "I was just getting to the real fun part. . . . It was a very real simulation." Later that afternoon he went fishing, while checkout crews stayed at the pad, seeking out unsuspected trouble spots such as the diesel fuel pump.[53]

That night Mercury Operations Director Williams broadcast the word: "All systems are go, and the weather is good. Let's pick up the count and go." Cooper lay down to sleep, confident that his safety and the mission would keep until he should awake and take his place.

Next morning the countdown proceeded smoothly. Cooper had lain in the capsule only two and a half hours when he heard the final chant:

"T minus 10, 9, 8, 7, 6, 5, 4, 3, 2, 1. Ignition. Liftoff." [54]

Faith 7 FOR 22 ORBITS

Thirteen seconds past 8:04, range-zero time, on the morning of May 15, 1963, Mercury-Atlas 9 lumbered upward the two inches that defined liftoff and thundered on toward its keyhole in the sky. Inside MA–9, Astronaut Gordon Cooper felt the smooth but definite push intensify as *Faith 7* gained altitude faster each second. His clocks marking the moments in synchronization, Cooper shouted through the din of the afterburner behind him to Walter Schirra, his predecessor and now capsule communicator at the Cape, "Feels good, buddy. . . . All systems go." [55]

Sixty seconds upward, MA–9 initiated its pitch program, and Cooper felt the max-q vibrations grow, but the rate gyros sensed greater lateral oscillations than the pilot did. Six or seven swings from peg to peg on his instruments, and the flight smoothed out. Two minutes and 14 seconds upward Cooper heard "a loud 'glung' and then a sharp, crisp 'thud' for staging" as booster engines cut themselves out and off. Then away flew the needless escape tower, and at three minutes after launch cabin pressure sealed and held while Cooper reported, "*Faith Seven* is all go."

The Atlas sustainer engine continued to accelerate, and its guidance system performed perfectly for two more minutes before SECO. *Faith 7* and "*Sigma 7*" swapped remarks on the sweetness of the trajectory. Schirra, at the point of Cooper's orbital insertion and capsule separation, said, "Smack dab in the middle of the go plot. Beautiful." And Cooper replied, after turning around on the fly-by-wire, "Boy, oh, boy . . . working just like advertised!"

In full horizontal flight over Bermuda at 17,547 miles per hour, Cooper watched his booster lag and tumble for about eight minutes, then checked his temperatures and contingency recovery areas, and tried to adjust to the strange

494

new sensations and perspectives at a little more than 100 miles (near his perigee) above sea level. Floating higher in his couch, now that he was weightless, Cooper agreed with Carpenter's report that an astronaut's sense of the cockpit changes when he reaches zero g and no longer feels himself lying flat on his back. Status checks with the Canary Islands and Kano, Nigeria, came on so fast that Cooper could hardly believe he had crossed the Atlantic Ocean and half of Africa already.

Over Zanzibar, he learned that his orbital parameters looked good enough for at least 20 revolutions and that all *Faith 7*'s telemetry was working well. His suit temperature fluctuated somewhat erratically, but as he watched his first sunset from space over the Indian Ocean he forgot his discomfort while looking at the airglow, spotting the twinkleless stars, and observing sheet lightning in scattered thunderstorms "down under." He saw the lights of Perth, Australia, on schedule 55 minutes after liftoff, and over Canton Island, in the Polynesian Archipelago, just south of the equator, the Sun began to rise behind him (as he flew backward toward the sunrise), and Cooper reported observing Glenn's "fireflies," or Carpenter's "frostflies," drifting along with the spacecraft at five miles per second.

From Guaymas, Mexico, Grissom, acting as capsule communicator, officially relayed the computer-blessed "go for seven orbits." Cooper, audibly impressed with the perfection of the flight so far, said, "It's great. . . . quite a full night. . . . everything appears very nominal on board here." As Cooper passed over the launch site at Cape Canaveral, Schirra raised him on the radio circuits once again and complained, "You son-of-a-gun, I haven't got anything to talk about. . . . I'm still higher and faster, but I have an idea you're going to go farther." The manned one-day mission was off to an auspicious start. Alan Shepard, who had been Cooper's backup pilot and was now also talking to *Faith 7* from Mercury Control, coached Cooper into his second orbit, saying, "All of our monitors down here are overjoyed. Everything looks beautiful."

Cooper thought so, too. All his spacecraft and physiological systems performed perfectly on his first two orbits. His only complaint concerned an oily film on his "windshield" that seemed to be on the outside pane of the window. Between Zanzibar and Muchea on his second pass, Cooper dozed off for a four-minute nap and then drifted across the Pacific, observing storms while inverted and stars when facing spaceward.

Beginning with his third orbit, the astronaut checked over the 11 experiments in which he was to participate. He prepared to eject a six-inch-diameter sphere, equipped with polar xenon strobe lights, that was to test his ability to spot and track a flashing beacon in a tangential orbit. At three hours and 25 minutes elapsed time, Cooper clicked the squib switch and heard and felt the beacon kick away. But, try as he might, he could not see the flashing light in the dusk or on the nightside during this round. On the fourth orbit, however, he did spot the beacon at sunset and later saw it pulsing. So he knew he had indeed launched a satellite from his satellite. Cooper jubilantly reported to Carpenter on Kauai, "I was with the little rascal all night."

Subsequently, on his fifth and sixth orbits, Cooper saw the flashing xenon several more times, and likewise spotted the constant xenon ground light of 44,000 watts placed at Bloemfontein, a little horseshoe-shaped town in the Union of South Africa. Having eaten some bite-sized brownie and fruitcake foods and excreted periodic samples for urinalysis, Cooper also kept up with his calibrated exercises, took oral temperatures and blood pressure readings, and did other duties required for the highest priority experiments of the MA–9 mission, the aeromedical ones.

Also on his sixth orbit, after nine hours in space, the astronaut set his cameras, attitude, and switches to deploy a tethered balloon, similar to the one tried on MA–7, for aerodynamic studies of drag and for more visual experiments. The balloon, a 30-inch-diameter Mylar sphere painted fluorescent orange, was to be inflated with nitrogen and attached by a 100-foot nylon line to the spacecraft antenna canister; a strain gauge in the canister should be able to measure the differences in pull on the balloon at apogee (166 miles) and perigee (100 miles). Cooper carefully went through his checklist, then tried to eject the balloon package, but nothing happened. He tried again, and still nothing happened. Because the antenna canister was later lost, no one ever knew why the tethered balloon failed to eject. But the second failure of this experiment was more severely disappointing than the first.

When Cooper surpassed Schirra's record by moving into a seventh orbital pass, he was engaged with the radiation experiments and with the hydraulic work of transferring urine samples and condensate water from tank to tank. During the automatically recorded radiation measurements, he had to turn the recorders on and off precisely on time and estimate accurately, without benefit of gyros, his drifting spacecraft's attitude. The hydraulic work was more difficult, because the hypodermic-type syringes used to pump the liquid manually from one bag container to another were unwieldy and exasperatingly leaky. At 9:27 elapsed time, Cooper spoke into his tape recorder, "The thing about this pumping under zero g is not good. [Liquid] tends to stand in the pipes, and you have to actually forcibly force it through."

After 10 hours of the mission, Zanzibar officially informed Cooper that he had a go for 17 orbital passes. The tracking, communication, and computing facilities at Goddard Space Flight Center in Maryland had long since settled down to a routine in following *Faith 7* around the world. The actual orbital parameters for Cooper's flight were proving so close to those planned that the differences were measurable only in tenths of a mile and hundredths of a degree. MA–9 was circumnavigating Earth once every 88 minutes and 45 seconds at an inclination angle of 32.55 degrees to the equator. Soon, as Earth turned beneath Cooper, his orbital track would have shifted too much to keep him within range of most of the scattered tracking and communications sites in Mercury's worldwide network. Then, too, the word "orbit" would become confused, because passing over the same meridian on the rotating planet is not the same as passing through the space-fixed point of orbital insertion.

Cooper spent his last "orbit" before his scheduled rest period, on orbits 9 through 13, in extensive activity. He finished the radiation measurements; he ate his supper of powdered roast beef mush and gulped some water; he took pictures over India and Tibet; and he checked all his machinery for readiness to power down and drift and dream for the next seven hours or so. Passing from the Himalayas to Japan in less than five minutes, Cooper was aroused by John Glenn's second transmission from the tracking ship *Coastal Sentry*, located near Kyushu. Veteran spaceman Glenn assured Astronaut Cooper, "You're sure looking good. Everything couldn't be finer on this pass." Ten minutes later Cooper had traversed the Pacific lengthwise in a southeasterly direction and had come over the telemetry command ship *Rose Knot*, positioned near Pitcairn Island, at latitude 25 degrees south and 120 degrees west. There he gave a full report on all systems; the shipborne communicator advised him to "settle down for a long rest."

But Cooper was still too excited and fascinated to feel sleepy. Orbit 9 was to carry him again around South America, over Africa, northern India, and Tibet during daylight, and he resolved to record on film some of the remarkable things he could see while looking down at open terrain. On this circuit Cooper snapped most of his best photographs, demonstrating his contention that he could see roads, rivers, small villages, and even individual houses if the lighting and background conditions were right. High over the highest plateau on Earth, the Tibetan highlands, where the air is thin and visibility is seldom obscured by haze, Cooper thought he could even judge speed and direction of ground winds by the smoke from the house chimneys.

In their third radio contact, John Glenn, as "Coastal Sentry Quebec," advised Cooper, who had now been in space over 13 hours, 34 minutes, that he should "tell everyone to go away and leave you alone now." Cooper then relaxed and fell into a sound sleep. He awoke drowsily an hour later when his suit temperature got too high. Intermittently, for the next six hours, during orbital passes 10 through 13, Cooper napped, took more pictures, taped status reports occasionally, and cursed to himself over the bothersome body-heat exchanger that kept creeping away toward freezing or burning temperatures. At the end of his rest period, Cooper taped his surprise at having napped so soundly that neither floating arms nor weightless dreams had startled him into awareness of where he was when he woke. But he cautioned psychologists not to make too much of this:

Have a note to be added in for head-shrinkers. Enjoy the full drifting flights most of all, where you have really the feeling of freedom, and you aren't worried about the systems fouling up. You have everything turned off, and just drifting along lazily. However, I haven't encountered any of this so-called split-off phenomena. Still note that I am thinking very much about returning to Earth at the proper time and safely.

497

Cooper enters his spacecraft, assisted by suit technician Joe W. Schmitt.

Flight of *Faith* 7
May 15–16, 1963

Liftoff.

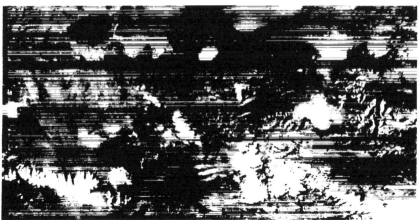

Cooper photographs the rugged Tibetan lake country (above).

Mercury Control relaxes after Faith 7; *left to right, Robert R. Gilruth, D. Brainerd Holmes, and Walter C. Williams.*

Coming around Muchea again, on his fourteenth pass, Cooper checked over all his systems, found his oxygen supply plentiful, and reported his peroxide fuel for attitude control showing 69 percent remaining in the automatic tank and 95 percent in the manual. He was in good shape, and all systems were still working "as advertised." At this point, Gordon Cooper spoke a prayer into his tape recorder aboard *Faith 7*, high in the heavens over the South Pacific. The MA-9 mission was well beyond its midpoint in time and space, and Cooper was humbly grateful that everything was still nominal. Physiologically his vision he knew was abnormally good. Philosophically the vision of this eighth man in history to orbit Earth in a manned satellite was bound to his culture, his times, and his origins in Oklahoma.[56]

Orbit 15 was consumed largely in calibration of equipment and synchronization of clocks, since by now Earthmen had experienced one more full 24-hour day of grace, whereas *Faith 7*'s elapsed time was faster by some 16 seconds than range-zero elapsed time. Orbit 16 brought Cooper back over Cape Canaveral and onward, virtually retracing his first shadow over Earth. The President of El Salvador had radioed greetings on pass 15, and on 16 Cooper sent a similar political greeting to African leaders meeting in Ethiopia. Then he buckled down immediately to another high-priority experiment requiring elaborate timing precautions.

As he entered Earth's shadow, or nightside, on this sixteenth orbit, Cooper caged and freed his gyros in such a manner as to allow his automatic attitude control system to torque the spacecraft slowly in pitch through the plane of the ecliptic. He could view, through his window, the mysterious phenomena of zodiacal light and night airglow layer. Together these two different objectives were called "dim light" phenomena, and the experimental photographs were designed to answer astrophysical questions about the origin, continuity, intensity, and reflectivity of visible electromagnetic spectra along the basic reference plane of the celestial sphere. They might also help answer some questions about solar energy conversion in the upper atmosphere. From Zanzibar, past the Canton Island station, Cooper called out the count as he clicked the series of astronomical photographs. Although the zodiacal light pictures turned out underexposed and the airglow shots overexposed, they were of usable quality and supplemented Carpenter's pictures from *Aurora 7* nicely.

Over Mexico, Cooper shifted to the next most important photographic task, that of snapping horizon-definition imprints in each quadrant around his local vertical position. Just as University of Minnesota scientists had prepared him for the zodiacal light task, so Massachusetts Institute of Technology researchers had arranged for these snapshots to aid in the design of a guidance and navigation system for Project Apollo. Cooper's horizon-definition pictures marked a significant advance beyond those from the MA-7 mission. In contact with the Cape once again, Cooper lightheartedly complained like a typical American tourist, "Man, all I do is take pictures, pictures, pictures!"

But he was not through yet. On orbits 17 and 18 he took infrared weather photographs of good quality and a few excellent moonset Earth-limb pictures. Meanwhile, he resumed the geiger counter measurements for radiation, continued his aeromedical duties, and adjusted his television monitor at the request of ground observers. The eighteenth pass over the United States, like the sixteenth, gave his extraordinary vistas of his country from southern California, across Dallas the first time and Houston the second, to the Florida peninsula. He sang during orbits 18 and 19, still surprised with every pass, still marveling at the greenery on Earth and on his instrument panel as he came toward his thirtieth hour in space.

Although "this fine plumbing they put in this thing" proved more troublesome later, Cooper had learned to adjust his suit temperatures for comfort and to eat and drink over the rim of his helmet fairly effectively, if awkwardly. Then on his nineteenth orbit, while checking his warning lights before a high-frequency antenna test over Hawaii, Cooper noticed the first potentially serious systems anomaly of his mission.

A small telelight lit up green, indicating that *Faith 7* was decelerating and that the centripetal force of gravity had overcome by .05 g the centrifugal force of the spacecraft's orbital moment of inertia. This had to be a false indication, reasoned Cooper, because he felt, and his loose gear still appeared, weightless. But were g forces building up imperceptibly? California confirmed no such indication. Mercury Control showed great concern over the implications of this little light for the attitude stabilization at retrofire. The fears of the flight controllers were realized on the next pass, when Cooper lost all attitude readings. Then, on the twenty-first orbit, a short-circuit occurred in a busbar serving the 250-volt main inverter, leaving the automatic stabilization and control system without electric power. The minor glitch had become a serious hitch.

Mercury Control Center was in a flurry of worried activity, cross-checking *Faith 7*'s problems and Cooper's diagnostic actions with identical equipment at the Cape and in St. Louis, then relaying to each communications site questions to ask and instructions to give. Cooper remained cool, if not calm, now that his alertness had been stimulated by a medically prescribed pill of dextroamphetamine.

On the twenty-first pass (over the tracking ship *Coastal Sentry*), John Glenn helped Cooper prepare a revised checklist for retrofire procedure during the next, and last, time around. Only Hawaii and Zanzibar were within voice radio range on this last circuit, but communications were good. When the ASCS inverter blew out, Cooper also noted that the carbon dioxide level was rising in both his suit and cabin. "Things are beginning to stack up a little" was his classic understatement to Carpenter, and then Zanzibar heard him say he would make a manual reentry.

Twenty-three minutes later Cooper came into contact with Glenn again, reporting himself in retroattitude, holding manually, and with checkoff list complete. Glenn gave the 10-second countdown, and Cooper, keeping his pitch down 34 degrees by his window reticle, shot his retrorockets manually on the "Mark!" Glenn reported: "Right on the old gazoo. . . . Dealer's choice on reentry here, fly-by-wire or manual . . . It's been a real fine flight, Gordo. Real beautiful all the way. Have a cool reentry, will you."

"Roger, John. Thank you."

And that he did. All the complicated, crowded events of the next 15 minutes occurred precisely as planned, while *Faith 7* plummeted down through the atmosphere. Four miles ahead of the prime recovery ship, again the carrier *Kearsarge,* just south of Midway Island, the canopied capsule containing Gordon Cooper broke through a mild overcast and landed on the lazy waves of the blue Pacific.

Splashdown came 34 hours and 20 minutes after liftoff. Cooper professed disappointment that he too had "missed that third elevator" aboard "Begonia," meaning the *Kearsarge.* The spacecraft floundered in the water for a moment, then righted itself, as hovering helicopters dropped their swimmers and relayed Cooper's request as an Air Force officer for permission to be hoisted aboard the Navy's carrier. Permission was granted, and 40 hot, humid minutes later the explosive hatch blew open at the command of MSC engineer John B. Graham, Jr. Physicians examined Cooper for eight more minutes while he lay in the couch. Then they helped him emerge and steadied him during a moment of dizziness until he regained his equilibrium. Away in triumph marched the one-man crew of the one-day Mercury mission.[57]

Like Schirra, Cooper went through arduous medical, technical, and operational debriefings aboard the *Kearsarge* and later back at the Manned Spacecraft Center. He, too, was found to be dehydrated and suffering from a slight case of orthostatic hypotension. He had lost seven pounds since suiting up, but after drinking "a few gallons of liquid," he was fine, ebullient both mentally and physically, and convinced that "we certainly can elongate this mission." Robert C. Seamans, Jr., Associate Administrator of NASA, and Robert Gilruth, Director of MSC, had different ideas about MA-10, but Cooper reiterated the proof that "man is a pretty good backup system to all these automatic systems, and I think the mission was conducted just like it was planned . . . in spite of . . . equipment breaking down."[58]

In addition to undergoing technical debriefings over the next several days, Cooper was honored by parades through Honolulu, Cocoa Beach, Washington—where he addressed a joint session of Congress—and New York City, where he was hailed by one of the largest tickertaped crowds ever to greet an individual. Other crowds in Houston and in his hometown of Shawnee, Oklahoma, also celebrated the return of the sixth Mercury astronaut from space.

The fact that Cooper, like Glenn, had had to take action to save his mission from a probable failure added luster and meaning to the glory he received. While postflight inspections, data reduction, and mission analyses proceeded through the following month to pinpoint the causes of the few electromechanical faults of the flight, Mercury systems engineers could find no fault with pilot performance. Physicians, however, were cautious about the implications for longer space missions of Cooper's hemodynamic response.

501

Faith 7
Aftermath

Members of the Project Mercury team were honored along with Cooper in ceremonies in the Rose Garden at the White House. Astronaut Cooper (left) and Christopher C. Kraft, Jr. (center), are shown with President Kennedy, Vice-President J o h n s o n , and NASA Administrator Webb. In addition to Cooper, those receiving the NASA Distinguished Service

Medal were G. Merritt Preston, chief of MSC's Cape Operations; Christopher C. Kraft, Jr., chief of the Flight Operations Division; Kenneth S. Kleinknecht, manager of Project Mercury; Floyd L. Thompson, Director of Langley Research Center; and Maj. Gen. Leighton I. Davis, Commander, Air Force Missile Test Center at Cape Canaveral. NASA Group Achievement Awards were made to Rear Admiral Harold G. Bowen, Jr., Commander of Destroyer-Flotilla 4, for the recovery forces, and to Maj. Gen. Ben I. Funk, Commander, Space Systems Division, for the Atlas program.

After speaking to a joint session of the Congress, Cooper left the Capitol: left to right, Mrs. Hattie Cooper, Vice-President Lyndon B. Johnson, Cooper and his wife Trudy, Speaker John McCormack, and Lady Bird Johnson.

Part of the 2900 tons of ticker tape and confetti that rained down on the official party as they rode along Broadway. Official estimate of this, the largest crowd in New York City history, was 4½ million.

Probably no other result of the MA-9 mission excited more interest than Cooper's claim to have seen from orbit objects on the ground as small as trucks and houses. Skepticism on this point abated after the astronaut explained in detail to representative scientists at the Cape on May 21 just where, when, and how he could see dust and smoke below, from 100 miles directly above—if the contrast was right. Also at this, the first and only "scientific debriefing" following a Mercury flight, the value of extensive questioning of the subject pilot was clearly demonstrated, when Cooper was asked whether he could see Earthshine on the Moon. "Well," he replied, "the Moon was fuller as it was setting than it was on the nightside. It was almost a full Moon. Gee, that's funny, I hadn't even realized that before. It seemed to be almost full as it was setting, whereas on the nightside it was only a third of a Moon." [59] This Moonshine was clearly Earthshine. Other postflight analyses added praise for the sunshine that blessed *Faith 7*. "The sun literally smiled on MA-9," wrote J. C. Jackson and Niles R. Heller in Goddard's report of the network radio performance. "It [MA-9] was favored with better than average radio frequency propagation conditions for the present phase of the solar sunspot cycle." [60]

WHITHER GEMINI?

On June 6 and 7, 1963, Brainerd Holmes, Gilruth, Walter Williams, and Kleinknecht met with Administrator Webb, Hugh L. Dryden, and Seamans in Washington to make a final decision on whether to fly an MA-10 mission. President Kennedy had clearly left the decision up to NASA. Webb listened thoughtfully to the presentations of each NASA official, and although both he and President Kennedy had heard the Mercury astronauts' plea for one more Mercury mission, Administrator Webb announced before the Senate space committee on June 12, 1963, that "we will not have another Mercury flight." [61] It was to be 22 months before another American manned space flight.

Project Gemini, designed in 1961 to double the volume while retaining the basic shape and systems of the McDonnell-Mercury spacecraft, now was well into the development and redesign phase of construction. And the Martin Company's mighty Titan II rocket, in spite of a recent explosion on launch, had a record of nine cleancut successes out of 16 launches. Another Mercury-Atlas flight would have been a relatively economical way to extend space technology and fill the time (then estimated at a year) before Gemini-Titan could be flight-tested. But now that Project Apollo, employing a concept called lunar orbital rendezvous (LOR) to land a man on the Moon and recover him, was the ultimate goal of the decade, space rendezvous and docking had to be perfected. Mercury had served far more than its original purpose, but it could hardly be maneuverable. And so Project Gemini was designed to fill these gaps. As people were asking whither and whether Gemini was taking them, Mercury died a natural death, while Apollo and Saturn were aborning.

Epilogue

PROJECT Mercury ended on the threshold of an era of exploration and discovery that staggers the imagination. Manned space flight of the most elementary sort had proved so successful that mankind seemed destined to embark on more ambitious celestial expeditions. The seventh decade of the 20th century also promised the logical extension of manned space flight technology beyond Earth's orbital corridor. Largely because of Project Mercury, which fostered Project Apollo and fathered Project Gemini, the United States had become committed to send men to explore the Moon only 350 years after Galileo first turned a telescope toward Earth's natural satellite.

Precedents set by Mercury were visible in many different ways to the taxpayers who watched the plans for NASA's Gemini and Apollo programs take shape. Most obvious was the configuration of the two-man spacecraft that McDonnell was building for launches by the Martin Company's Titan II missile. The Gemini spacecraft was to be a far more sophisticated vehicle, with modular components easily accessible, with a lift/drag ratio provided by an offset center of gravity, with a real, if limited, orbital maneuvering capability, and with ejection seats instead of an escape pylon. Except for its doubled size, its countersunk viewports, and its lack of the escape tower, however, Gemini looked much like the familiar Mercury capsule.[1]

Plans and boilerplate models of the Apollo spacecraft—rather, of the so-called "command module" that would house three men in a tubby pyramid during launch and return to Earth, via the Moon—were being tested by airdrops from airplanes, by a second Little Joe (II) booster series, and by pad aborts using a tractor-rocket escape pylon. These and other evidences of Mercury's influence on design, development, testing, and training for more advanced space flights showed that NASA's new Manned Spacecraft Center and its Marshall, Kennedy, and Goddard Space Flight Centers were managed and staffed by most of the same personnel who had formed the original Mercury team. Growth and thoroughgoing organizational changes affected many individuals adversely, but the core of the Mercury team moved forward in the mid-1960s toward further exploitation of "lessons learned" from Mercury for manned space flight at large.[2]

It was primarily to hasten concentration on the accelerated manned space program and to move away from the "egg-shell" Mercury package and toward

505

more nearly "first-class" spacecraft accommodations that James E. Webb, Hugh L. Dryden, and Robert C. Seamans had decided against a fifth manned Mercury-Atlas mission. NASA administrators wanted to concentrate their engineering talent as soon and as completely as possible on the next major step toward the Moon. They realized the political and psychological risks of a lengthy delay before Americans again went into space, but they took these in stride as necessary to the longer range goals.[3]

The week after Mercury was officially terminated, the Soviet Union launched into orbit *Vostok V*, carrying Valery F. Bykovsky, and two days later *Vostok VI*, with "cosmonette" Valentina V. Tereshkova aboard. Both flights ended on June 19, 1963, after 81 circuits by Bykovsky and 48 by Tereshkova. The flights followed slightly different orbital planes, exhibited no co-orbital maneuvers, and thus were similar to the tandem flights of Andrian Nikolayev and Pavel Popovich in August 1962. Tereshkova, trained as a parachutist and not as a pilot, became not only the first woman to go into space but also the first "layman," or non-pilot-engineer. When later she and Nikolayev were married and became parents, their healthy and normal baby seemed to indicate that fears about genetic damage from exposure to cosmic radiation were groundless.[4]

Most significantly, perhaps, *Vostok*s *V* and *VI* apparently signaled the end of the era of solo space flight. When the Soviets next sent men into space, on October 12, 1964, they began a new series with *Voskhod I*, which carried three men around Earth 16 times. And in 1965, the United States—taking what comfort it could, said one historian, from the fable of the tortoise and the hare—began its new Gemini series of twin-seated, maneuverable satellite missions, which were to make Mercury seem primitive indeed. When in March and June of that year Cosmonaut Alexei Leonov and Astronaut Edward H. White took their respective closely tethered "walks"—more nearly "swims"—in space, the fact that their command pilots were in the spacecraft to help in case of trouble seemed comforting.[5] Neither cosmonauts nor astronauts were ever again likely to go into space alone in their machines. In this sense only, therefore, man's heroic age of solo space exploration may be said to have ended in June 1963.

Almost four months after the passing of Mercury and the last Vostok flights, and only a few weeks before the national shock of President Kennedy's assassination, NASA and its Manned Spacecraft Center held their formal, public postmortem on the first American manned satellite program. Staged on October 3 and 4, 1963, at the Music Hall in Houston and attended by some 1300 people from NASA, the military, industry, and news media, this "Mercury Summary Conference" featured 20 papers on the overall program, with emphasis on Gordon Cooper's day-long MA-9 mission of May. Covering program management, booster performance, astronaut preparation, network operations, and MA-9 in-flight experiences and experiments, these papers constitute the best available technical overview of Project Mercury.[6]

The decorous proceedings were marred somewhat on the final day of the conference by the appearance in newspapers throughout the country of a controversial story built around three pages of one report.[7]   In a paper on "Spacecraft Preflight Preparation," four MSC engineers from Florida sketched the nature and evolution of the intricate and exhaustive checkout procedures followed at the Cape after McDonnell's delivery of one of its capsules to the launch site.   Discussing "quality assurance," the authors dwelled on the problem of component defects and malfunctions discovered by Mercury inspectors in industrial hardware. Inspections for MA–9 turned up 720 system or component discrepancies, 536 of which were attributed to faulty workmanship.   "In Project Mercury," concluded the MSC authors, "thousands of man-hours were expended in testing, calibration, assembly, and installation of a variety of hardware that later failed to meet performance specifications or that malfunctioned during systems tests in a simulated space environment."   And often these delays could have been avoided "if adequate attention to detail during manufacture or thorough inspection before delivery had been exercised."[8]

Although the import of this rather didactic engineering treatise was that the history of Mercury spacecraft prelaunch preparations presented a good object lesson in the rigorous demands for quality control and reliability testing before manned space flight--as opposed to missile, instrumented spacecraft, or even aircraft experience—journalists blew the implied criticism of McDonnell into a *cause célèbre*.   "NASA blasts industry" was the general tenor of the news dispatches coming out of Houston.   Coupled with the General Accounting Office's contemporaneous criticism of NASA and its contractors in the lagging Centaur program, the news coverage of the summary conference added some ammunition for attacks on the "great moondoggle."[9]

In a hurriedly called press conference in Houston and in hearings the next week before the House Committee on Science and Astronautics, NASA, MSC, and McDonnell leaders denied that any resentment or dissatisfaction existed because of anything in past or present NASA-McDonnell relations.[10]   Congress was satisfied, if the press was not, and this rather small tempest in a rather large teapot subsided quickly.   The furor did suggest, however, that one of the lessons the Mercury technical staff had not learned well enough was extreme prudence in all public references to relations between NASA and its contractors and other agencies.   Possibly the "candor at Canaveral" and elsewhere, for which the press had occasionally commended the Mercury team, would be the first casualty of the ongoing manned space effort.

In general, the authors of papers read at the Mercury Summary Conference, aware of the difficulty of making technological and administrative generalizations in the new and rapidly changing field of astronautics, offered only guarded conclusions about the significance of Mercury experiences for the Gemini and Apollo programs.   But indirectly there, and more directly elsewhere, they did assess the state of the art and science of manned space flight, ask what Mercury had taught that might benefit Gemini and Apollo, and even venture some answers.[11]

Project Mercury lasted 55 months, from authorization through the one-day mission, and while the earliest planned orbital mission slipped 22 months past its first scheduled launch time, Mercury achieved its original objectives with John Glenn's MA-6 flight only 40 months after formal project approval. Compared with either advanced missile or aircraft development programs, this was a good record; but many engineers denied the validity of such a comparison.

Mercury mobilized a dozen prime contractors, some 75 major subcontractors, and about 7200 third-tier sub-subcontractors, and vendors, all of whom together employed at most about two million persons who at one time or another had a direct hand in the project. In addition, the NASA complement on Mercury eventually reached 650 workers in the Space Task Group and Manned Spacecraft Center and 710 elsewhere in research and development support of the project. A conservative estimate of the maximum number of military servicemen and Defense Department personnel supporting an individual Mercury mission (both MA-6 and MA-9) counted 18,000 people, and another conservative estimate added 1169 persons from educational and other civilian institutions. Thus, if the estimate of 1,817,000 workers employed by the Mercury vendors was too liberal and unrealistic, the total peak manpower figure of 2,020,528 was probably as accurate a figure as could be obtained.[12]

"Quick look" total cost estimates given at the summary conference in October 1963 showed that Mercury had cost $384,131,000 throughout the program, of which 37 percent went for the spacecraft, 33 percent for the tracking network, and 24 percent for launch vehicle procurement. Flight operations and "R and D" costs made up the remainder, as then estimated, but the final cost accounting was complicated by the unsettled conditions of closing and disposition costs and the mingling of Mercury and Gemini costs during 1962 and 1963. Through Glenn's flight, however, Mercury had cost about $300 million.[13] Through Cooper's flight NASA estimated the grand total cost of Mercury at slightly more than $400 million (see Appendix F).

NASA engineers and physicians listed three primary "lessons learned" from their experience with Mercury for manned space flight. Their foremost medical objectives had been fulfilled, and the responses of two men in suborbit and four men in orbit had shown that human beings can function normally in space if adequately protected. Rather than acceleration g loads and weightlessness limiting man's capacity to fly in space, the men who flew Mercury seemed to adapt to "zero g" surprisingly well. The main medical problems were simple personal hygiene in flight, and the postflight readjustment symptom of orthostatic hypotension. Both appeared to be curable by technical developments rather than by preventive medicine.

Secondly, Mercury had proven that final launch preparations took far more time than anyone had anticipated in 1958 to ensure perfect readiness and reliability of the machines and men. NASA had had designed, therefore, an automated digital system for the future, called "ACE," for Acceptance Checkout Equipment, to reduce human error in environmental chamber testing and the length of time required on the flight line at the Florida spaceport. Thirdly, mission control requirements, integrating the astronaut with his flight monitors and directors around the world, had grown to encompass the fullest utilization of real-time telemetry, tracking, computing, and display data. Nothing less would suffice for future missions. Two more acronyms came into use, "MCC" for the new Mission Control Center at Houston, and "GOSS" for Ground Operational Support Systems, reflecting the degree of complex automation being installed for positive ground control of future space flights.

Studying how they could improve on their performance for succeeding programs, NASA officials and engineers listed several other valuable technological and managerial lessons from Mercury. In spacecraft design, problems had been encountered with safety margins, redundancy, accessibility, shelf-life of parts, interchangeability, and with materials whose behavior under unfamiliar environmental conditions had not been wholly predictable. Regarding qualification of systems and components, there should be more analysis in an effort to make techniques "conservative, complete, integrated, and functional." Fabrication and inspection standards carried over from development into manufacturing work should be made still more "rigorous, detailed, current, and enforced." Engineers working for the Manned Spacecraft Center, both in Houston and at the Cape, called for continuous upgrading of tests, inspections, and other validation procedures, particularly with respect to interface compatibilities between systems. In configuration control, NASA manned space flight developers recognized their perennial weight control problem and their need to become more responsive, more familiar in detail, and more aware of danger signals in the production and fabrication phases of their business. And the managers of Mercury now acknowledged that methods of management that had worked well enough in the first American manned space project would not suit Gemini and Apollo, already in motion. They had only begun to use the sophisticated Program Evaluation and Review Technique, called "PERT," which had evolved from the Navy's experience in its nuclear submarine and Polaris missile development programs. Now PERT and other management tools, such as the incentive contract, would have to be exploited to the fullest extent practicable.[14]

Perhaps the most significant lesson learned from Mercury was that man was still invaluable to the machine. Mercury saw the evolution of the astronaut from little more than a passenger in a fully automatic system to an integral and fully integrated element in the entire space flight organism. By the end of the project, the Mercury capsule, instead of simply being a machine with a man in it, had truly become a manned space vehicle. Mercury Flight Director Christopher C. Kraft, an engineer, spoke for all exponents of manned space flight, irrespective of discipline: "Man is the deciding element. . . . As long as Man is able to alter the decision of the machine, we will have a spacecraft that can perform under any known conditions, and that can probe into the unknown for new knowledge."[15]

509

By November 1963, Project Mercury was clearly relegated to an honorable niche in history. The resources that had fed Project Mercury were now reorganized and recommitted toward Projects Gemini and Apollo. That reorientation is underscored in this photograph from President Kennedy's visit to Cape Canaveral on November 16. As the charts and models show, the subject is not Mercury but Apollo. The place is Blockhouse 34. The briefer is George E. Mueller, successor to D. Brainerd Holmes as head of NASA's manned space flight program. The front row, left to right: George Low, Kurt Debus, Robert C. Seamans, Jr., James E. Webb, President Kennedy, Hugh L. Dryden, Wernher von Braun, Gen. Leighton I. Davis, and Sen. George Smathers.

Yet as Mercury faded farther into the past and Gemini and Apollo moved forward, some profound questions remained unanswered, and indeed usually not even asked.[16] In the democratic society of the United States, did the formal commitment to costly space exploration, and especially the increased emphasis on manned space flight beginning in the Kennedy administration, actually represent a consensus among the electorate? The pace and chances for success of this country's drive toward spacefaring preeminence depended, finally, on the continued willingness of the American taxpayer to pay the bills. However divergent may have been the appeals of the two political parties in the 1964 Presidential election, neither the Republicans nor Democrats seriously questioned the existence of such a consensus.

Many more mundane problems plagued the times, some seeming so overwhelming as to demand dramatic and drastic solutions like those widely presumed to issue from space technology. But the arrival of the so-called "space age," heralded by Mercury astronauts and Vostok cosmonauts, did capture most men's imagination and did seem to dwarf the petty quarrels of men and nations. Vague hopes for future peace and prosperity accompanied public support of preparations

510

for two- and three-man spacecraft, but fears about the population explosion, nuclear proliferation, and social disparities made many wonder whether the manned space flight enterprise was worth the effort and the price. Why send two or three men to the Moon when two or three billion others remained rooted in human turmoil? Questions similar to this found traditional answers in terms of national security, scientific curiosity, economic benefits, and technological by-products, but ultimately the national commitment was an act of faith.

Still, many Americans, both technically literate and illiterate, doubted the return from the $400 million spent on Project Mercury and the vastly greater expenditures being allocated for succeeding manned space projects. A substantial portion of the scientific community agreed with Alvin M. Weinberg, Director of the Atomic Energy Commission's Oak Ridge National Laboratory, who argued that "most Americans would prefer to belong to a society which first gave the world a cure for cancer than to the society which put the first astronaut on Mars."[17] Others deplored the fact that the American space effort was basically a "race to the Moon," having no nobler motivation than traditional nationalistic rivalry. Still others would confine the Nation's astronautical activities to unmanned instrumented space vehicles, thereby diminishing the cost of space exploration, as well as presumably avoiding the likely prospect that some day men would die in space.[18]

Nevertheless, whether most people in the United States approved or not, in the mid-1960s it seemed that not only American machines but selected and trained American citizens were in the space venture to stay. Project Mercury, leaving a legacy that perhaps was even more important psychologically than technologically, was already history. Hugh L. Dryden, only a few weeks before his death late in 1965, expressed his faith in manned space flight and offered a fitting epitaph for Project Mercury:

> Man is distinguished from other forms of life by his powers of reasoning and by his spiritual aspirations. Already the events of the last seven years have had profound impact on all human affairs throughout the world. Repercussions have been felt in science, industry, education, government, law, ethics, and religion. No area of human activity or thought has escaped. The toys of our children, the ambitions of our young men and women, the fortunes of industrialists, the daily tasks of diplomats, the careers of military officers, the pronouncements of high church officials—all have reflected the all-pervading influence of the beginning steps in space exploration. The impact can only be compared with those great developments of past history like the Copernican theory which placed the Sun, rather than the earth, at the center of our solar system; to the work of Sir Isaac Newton in relating the fall of an apple to the motion of the moon around the earth through the universal law of gravitation; to the industrial revolution; or to other great landmarks in the history of mankind.[19]

FOOTNOTES, SOURCES AND BIBLIOGRAPHY, APPENDIXES, AND INDEX

Footnotes

Chapter I

[1] See Gertrude and James Jobes, *Outer Space: Myths, Name Calendars, Meanings: From the Emergence of History to the Present Day* (New York, 1964).

[2] For the long history of space travel fiction see Marjorie Hope Nicolson, *Voyages to the Moon* (paperback ed., New York, 1960), and *Science and Imagination* (Ithaca, N.Y., 1965); Willy Ley, *Rockets, Missiles, and Space Travel* (Rev. ed., New York, 1957), 9–40; Arthur C. Clarke, "Space Travel in Fact and Fiction," *Journal of the British Interplanetary Society*, IX (Sept. 1950), 213–230; James O. Bailey, *Pilgrims Through Space and Time: Trends and Patterns in Scientific and Utopian Fiction* (New York, 1957); Roger L. Green, *Into Other Worlds: Space-Flight from Lucian to Lewis* (New York, 1958); Philip B. Gove, *The Imaginary Voyage in Prose and Fiction: A History of Its Criticism and a Guide to Its Study* . . . (New York, 1961); John Lear, *Kepler's Dream* (Berkeley, Calif., 1965); and W. R. Maxwell, "Some Aspects of the Origins and Early Development of Astronautics," *Journal of the British Interplanetary Society*, XVIII (Sept. 1962), 415–425.

[3] Edward Everett Hale, "The Brick Moon," *Atlantic Monthly*, XXIV (Oct., Nov., Dec., 1869), 451–460, 603–611, 679–688. Also published in Hale, *The Brick Moon and Other Stories* (New York, 1899). Hale is of course better known for another story, "The Man Without a Country."

[4] Good treatments of astronomical developments in the 16th, 17th, and 18th centuries are in A. R. Hall, *The Scientific Revolution, 1500–1800: The Foundation of the Modern Scientific Attitude* (Boston, 1954); and Alexandre Koyré, *From the Closed World to the Infinite Universe* (paperback ed., New York, 1958).

[5] Charles G. Abbot, *Great Inventions* (Washington, 1943), 227–229. On Langley's failure and the public reaction to it, see Mark Sullivan, *Our Times: The United States, 1900–1925*, Vol. II: *America Finding Herself* (New York, 1927), 562–564. In 1914, after numerous modifications and largely as an attempt to invalidate the Wright Brothers' patents, Glen H. Curtiss flew the Langley aerodrome successfully with pontoons. Fourteen years later the Smithsonian reconciled itself to the fact the Wrights' airplane of 1903 was the first successful flying machine, rather than Langley's aerodrome. See Abbot, "The Relations between the Smithsonian Institution and the Wright Brothers," *Smithsonian Miscellaneous Collections*, LXXXI (Sept. 29, 1928).

[6] Orville Wright, quoted in N. H. Randers-Pehrson, *History of Aviation* (New York, 1944), 36. For a description of the flight, see Elsbeth E. Freudenthal, *Flight into History: The Wright Brothers and the Air Age* (Norman, Okla., 1949), 3–90; Marvin W. McFarland, ed., *The Papers of Wilbur and Orville Wright* . . . (2 vols., New York, 1953), I, 395–397; and Charles H. Gibbs-Smith, "The Wright Brothers and Their Invention of the Practical Aeroplane," *Nature*, CXCVIII (June 1, 1963), 824–826.

[7] There are several reasonably good histories of aviation and aeronautical research, including M. J. B. Davy, *Interpretive History of Flight* (London, 1948); Charles H. Gibbs-Smith, *The History of Flying* (New York, 1954) and *The Aeroplane* (London, 1960); Lloyd Morris and Kendall Smith, *Ceiling Unlimited: The Story of American Aviation from Kitty Hawk to Supersonics* (New York, 1953); Theodore von Kármán, *Aerodynamics: Selected Topics in the Light of Their Historical Development* (Ithaca, N.Y., 1954); and R. Giacomelli, "Historical Sketch," in William F. Durand, ed., *Aerodynamic Theory: A General Review of Progress* (2 ed., 6 vols. in 3, New York, 1963), I, 304–394. See also Hunter Rouse and Simon Ince, *History of*

Hydraulics (Iowa City, Iowa, paperback ed., New York, 1963), 229–242.

[8] Jerome C. Hunsaker, "Forty Years of Aeronautical Research," *Report of the Smithsonian Institution for 1955* (Washington, 1956), 241–251; Arthur S. Levine, "United States Aeronautical Research Policy, 1915–1958: A Study of the Major Policy Decisions of the National Advisory Committee for Aeronautics," unpublished Ph. D. dissertation, Columbia University, 1963, 7–16; George W. Gray, *Frontiers of Flight: The Story of NACA Research* (New York, 1948), 9–15; A. Hunter Dupree, *Science in the Federal Government: A History of Policies and Activities to 1940* (Cambridge, Mass., 1957), 283–287; John F. Victory, "The NACA: Cradle of Research," *Flying*, LX (March 1957), 40–43. In 1921, NACA installed at Langley a pioneering variable-density wind tunnel, which featured the use of compressed air to produce an airflow over small models, thus closely simulating the flow over full-scale aircraft.

[9] Hunsaker, "Forty Years of Aeronautical Research," 251–254; Levine, "U.S. Aeronautical Research Policy," 7–41. The passage in 1926 of the Air Commerce Act, which made the Secretary of Commerce responsible for encouraging and regulating civil aviation, clarified the role of NACA and made possible the focus on aeronautical research.

[10] The great majority of the people who joined the research staff of NACA during the history of the organization, 1915–1958, held degrees in engineering rather than the physical sciences. Thus "research engineer" became the most common formal designation for those working in aeronautical science for NACA.

[11] Gray, *Frontiers of Flight,* 33–70; Hunsaker, "Forty Years of Aeronautical Research," 254–259. The classic text on subsonic aerodynamics is Richard von Mises, *Theory of Flight* (2 ed., New York, 1959).

[12] Elsbeth E. Freudenthal, *The Aviation Business: Kitty Hawk to Wall Street* (New York, 1940), 62–304; John B. Rae, "Financial Problems of the American Aircraft Industry," *Business History Review,* XXXIX (spring 1965), 99–114.

[13] By 1938 the altitude record set for aircraft, as established by an Italian aviator, had reached beyond 56,000 feet. Eugene M. Emme, *Aeronautics and Astronautics: An American Chronology of Science and Technology in the Exploration of Space, 1915–1960* (Washington, 1961), 162.

[14] Hunsaker, "Forty Years of Aeronautical Research," 262.

[15] Levine, "U.S. Aeronautical Research Policy," 74–79; *Twenty-third Annual Report of the National Advisory Committee for Aeronautics—1937* (Washington, 1938), 2. The NACA organizational structure, in addition to the 15-member Main Committee, which established the research policies of the agency, and the various field installations, eventually included four technical committees, charged with studying problems in particular areas of aeronautical science and recommending to the Main Committee changes in policy and practice. The membership of the various technical committees, like that of the Main Committee, came from the military, the aircraft industry, and the academic community. Each of the technical committees had subcommittees. In 1957 the technical committees were: Aerodynamics, Power Plants, Aircraft Construction, and Operating Problems. See *Forty-third Annual Report of NACA—1957* (Washington, 1957).

[16] Gray, *Frontiers of Flight,* 19–33; Hunsaker, "Forty Years of Aeronautical Research," 261–262.

[17] Nicholas J. Hoff and Walter G. Vincenti, eds., *Aeronautics and Astronautics: Proceedings of the Durand Centennial Conference Held at Stanford University, 5–8 August, 1959* (New York, 1960), 16.

[18] Edgar Buckingham, "Jet Propulsion for Airplanes," in NACA Report No. 159, in *Ninth Annual Report of NACA—1923* (Washington, 1924), 75–90.

[19] Hunsaker, "Forty Years of Aeronautical Research," 266–267; Levine, "U.S. Aeronautical Research Policy," 81–89.

[20] See Robert L. Perry, "The Antecedents of the X–1," paper, American Institute of Aeronautics and Astronautics, San Francisco, July 26–28, 1965, 2–17; and Ley, *Rockets, Missiles, and Space Travel,* 411–413.

[21] Hunsaker, "Forty Years of Aeronautical Research," 267. See also John B. Rae, "Science and Engineering in the History of Aviation," *Technology and Culture,* III (fall 1961), 391–399. Hunsaker, head of the Department of Aeronautical Engineering at the Massachusetts Institute of Technology and a member of the Main Committee since the 1930s, assumed the chairmanship of NACA in 1941 on Bush's resignation.

[22] On the role of air power in the Second World War, see Eugene M. Emme, "The Im-

pact of Air Power Upon History," *Air University Quarterly Review*, II (winter 1948), 3–13; Eugene M. Emme, ed., *The Impact of Air Power: National Security and World Politics* (Princeton, N.J., 1959), 209–294; and Wesley F. Craven and James L. Cate, eds., *History of the Army Air Forces in World War II* (7 vols., Chicago, 1948–1955).

[22] See C. Fayette Taylor, "Aircraft Propulsion: A Review of the Evolution of Aircraft Powerplants," *Report of the Smithsonian Institution for 1961* (Washington, 1962), 245–298.

[24] The best-known of these advisory groups was the so-called von Kármán Committee, established late in 1944 at the direction of Henry H. Arnold, Commanding General of the Army Air Forces, and headed by Theodore von Kármán, of the California Institute of Technology. After surveying wartime achievements in aeronautical science and rocketry, the panel of scientists published its findings in August 1945 and its recommendations in December. While giving full credit to the German accomplishments in rocketry, the von Kármán committee concluded that jet propulsion offered the key to "air supremacy," and that progress toward long-range ballistic missiles should come through the development of air-breathing pilotless aircraft. The philosophy embodied in these 14 reports was to guide Air Force thinking for almost 10 years. See Army Air Forces Scientific Advisory Group, *Toward New Horizons: A Report to General of the Army H. H. Arnold* (14 vols. [Washington], 1945). For a retrospect of the findings of the committee, see Hugh L. Dryden, "Toward the New Horizons of Tomorrow: First Annual ARS von Kármán Lecture," *Astronautics*, XII (Jan. 1963), 14–19. Dryden served as deputy scientific director to von Kármán on the committee.

[25] Levine, "U.S. Aeronautical Research Policy," 91–97; Hunsaker, "Forty Years of Aeronautical Research," 267–268.

[26] The unitary plan was designed to provide dispersed NACA-Air Force wind-tunnel facilities characterized by a minimum of overlap and a maximum of variety. Five new supersonic wind tunnels were constructed, one at each of the NACA laboratories and two at a new Air Force installation, the Arnold Engineering Development Center at Tullahoma, Tenn. See *Manual for Users of the Unitary Plan Wind Tunnel Facilities* (Washington, 1956); and Alan Pope, *Wind-Tunnel Testing* (2 ed., New York, 1954).

[27] Axel T. Mattson, interview, Houston, July 2, 1964; Gray, *Frontiers of Flight*, 330–359; Frank Waters, *Engineering Space Exploration: Robert R. Gilruth* (Chicago, 1963), 38–39; "History of NACA Transonic Research," Langley Aeronautical Laboratory, undated copy in Archives of the Manned Spacecraft Center (MSC), Houston. Unless otherwise indicated, originals or copies of all primary materials cited in this work are located in the MSC Archives.

The Langley engineers also pursued their transonic investigations with a method devised in 1944 by Gilruth, whereby small models of wings or complete aircraft were attached to the upper wing surface of an airplane, thus employing the accelerated airflow over the wing surface for studying the aerodynamic characteristics of the model at transonic speeds.

[28] Perry, "Antecedents of the X–1," 18–20; Kenneth S. Kleinknecht, "The Rocket Research Airplanes," in Eugene M. Emme, ed., *The History of Rocket Technology: Essays on Research, Development, and Utility* (Detroit, 1964), 193–198; Hunsaker, "Forty Years of Aeronautical Research," 268, 269; Gray, *Frontiers of Flight*, 334–336; Ley, *Rockets, Missiles, and Space Travel*, 419–432. Because of the fear that the X–1, operating with an entirely new rocket powerplant, might not be ready as early as planned, the NACA-Air Force-Navy group concurrently developed a jet-propelled research airplane, the Douglas D-558-1. This was also in keeping with NACA's original conviction, shared by the Navy, that the first research aircraft would be turbojet-powered.

[29] Kleinknecht, "Rocket Research Airplanes," 199–204; Ley, *Rockets, Missiles, and Space Travel*, 424–426; Charles V. Eppley, *The Rocket Research Aircraft Program, 1946–1962* (Edwards Air Force Base, Calif., 1962), 1–25; Hunsaker, "Forty Years of Aeronautical Research," 269; James A. Martin, "The Record-Setting Research Airplanes," *Aeronautical Engineering Review*, XXI (Dec. 1962), 49–54; Walter C. Williams and Hubert M. Drake, "The Research Airplane: Past, Present, and Future," *Aeronautical Engineering Review*, XVII (Jan. 1958), 36–41; Walter T. Bonney, "High-Speed Research Airplanes," *Scientific American*, CLXXXIX (Oct. 1953), 36–41. For the experiences of two rocket-airplane test pilots, as well as for useful treatments of the postwar research aircraft series, see A. Scott Crossfield and Clay Blair, *Always Another Dawn* (Cleveland, 1960); and William Bridgeman and Jacqueline Hazard, *The Lonely Sky* (New York, 1955).

 Probably the greatest NACA contribution to the century series (F–100, etc.) was a discovery made in 1951 by Richard T. Whitcomb, an aeronautical engineer working mainly in the recently opened 8-foot, slotted-throat tunnel at the Langley laboratory. Whitcomb collected data on the lengthwise distribution of fuselage and wing volume and suggested an airplane configuration that minimized drag at supersonic speeds. Whitcomb's findings, known as the "area rule," indicated that a coke-bottle, or wasp-waisted, shape would significantly increase the speed of jet-propelled airplanes. The importance of the area rule was reflected in the configuration of practically every jet interceptor designed and built for both the Air Force and the Navy in the mid-1950s. See Richard T. Whitcomb, "A Study of the Zero-Lift Drag-Rise Characteristics of Wing-Body Combinations Near the Speed of Sound," NACA Tech. Report 1273, *Forty-Second Annual Report of the NACA–1956* (Washington, 1957), 519–539.

[31] Discussions of the principles of rocketry can be found in many places, but some of the most lucid explanations from the layman's standpoint are in Ley, *Rockets, Missiles, and Space Travel,* 60–65; Erik Bergaust and Seabrook Hull, *Rocket to the Moon* (Princeton, N.J., 1958), 33–43; Ralph S. Cooper, "Rocket Propulsion," *Report of the Smithsonian Institution for 1962,* 299–313; and Andrew G. Haley, *Rocketry and Space Exploration* (Princeton, N.J., 1958), 33–43. See also NASA news release, unnumbered, "Liquid Propellant Rocket Engines," Jan. 1962. Equally informative as an introduction to rocketry but historically important as a spur to enthusiasts was G. Edward Pendray's *The Coming Age of Rocket Power* (New York, 1945), wherein rocket efficiency was pictured as opening "the way to an entire new world of velocities, altitudes, and powers which have hitherto been closed to us; and consequently to a whole new world of human experiences and possibilities" (p. 9).

[32] See A. A. Blagonravov, ed., *Collected Works of K. E. Tsiolkovsky,* Vol. II: *Reactive Flying Machines,* NASA TT F–237 (Washington, 1965).

[33] For biographical information on Tsiolkovsky, see A. Kosmodemyansky, *Konstantin Tsiolkovsky, His Life and Work,* trans. X. Danko (Moscow, 1956); Albert Parry, *Russia's Rockets and Missiles* (Garden City, N.Y., 1960), 94–104; Beryl Williams and Samuel Epstein, *The Rocket Pioneers on the Road to Space* (New York, 1955), 52–69; Heinz Gartmann, *The Men Behind the Space Rockets* (New York, 1956), 26–35; and K. E. Tsiolkovsky, "An Autobiography," trans. A. N. Petroff, *Astronautics,* IV (May 1959), 48–49, 63–64; V. N. Sokolskiy, "The Works of the Russian Scientist-Pioneers of Rocket Technology," in T. M. Melkumov, ed., *Pioneers of Rocket Technology* (Moscow, 1964), NASA TT F–9285 (Washington, 1965), 125–162.

[34] Biographical material on Goddard, little known outside of scientific circles until recent years, is accumulating rapidly. A valuable but not definitive biography is Milton Lehman, *This High Man: The Life of Robert H. Goddard* (New York, 1963). See also E. R. Hagemann, "Goddard and His Early Rockets: 1882–1930," *Journal of the Astronautical Sciences,* VII (Summer 1961), 51–59; Eugene M. Emme, "Yesterday's Dream—Today's Reality," *Air Power Historian,* VII (Oct., 1960), 216–221; G. Edward Pendray, "Pioneer Rocket Development in the United States," in Emme, *The History of Rocket Technology,* 19–23; also published in *Technology and Culture,* IV (Fall 1963), 384–388; Williams and Epstein, *Rocket Pioneers,* 70–110; Shirley Thomas, *Men of Space* (6 vols., Philadelphia, 1960–1963), I, 23–46; Gartmann, *Men Behind the Space Rockets;* and Emme, *A History of Space Flight* (New York, 1965), 85–87.

[35] Goddard's 1920 Smithsonian Institution report and a less famous report to the Smithsonian summarizing his findings to 1936 are in Robert H. Goddard, *Rockets, Comprising "A Method of Reaching Extreme Altitudes" and "Liquid-Propellant Rocket Development"* (New York, 1946). A condensation of Goddard's notebooks is Esther C. Goddard and G. Edward Pendray, eds., *Rocket Development: Liquid-Fuel Rocket Research, 1929–1941* (New York, 1961). The eastern daily newspapers seized on Goddard's "moon-rocket" reference in his first Smithsonian paper and blew it completely out of proportion. Some journals, having no conception of the mechanics of rocketry, even ridiculed the idea that a rocket could ascend into space, because in a vacuum it would have nothing to "react against." See, for example, the lead editorial in *New York Times,* Jan. 13, 1920. The storm of embarrassing publicity doubtless abetted the aversion to notoriety that characterized Goddard throughout his career.

[36] Pendray, "Pioneer Rocket Development in the United States," 21–23; Pendray, *The*

Coming of Age of Rocket Power, 35–43; Ley, *Rockets, Missiles, and Space Travel*, 443.

[37] Pendray, "Pioneer Rocket Development in the United States," 23–24; Pendray, "The First Quarter Century of the American Rocket Society," *Jet Propulsion*, XXV (Nov. 1955), 586–593.

[38] Frank J. Malina, "Origins and First Decade of the Jet Propulsion Laboratory," in Emme, ed., *History of Rocket Technology*, 52–54.

[39] *Ibid.*, 46–66; Haley; *Rocketry and Space Exploration*, 97–99; Ley, *Rockets, Missiles, and Space Travel*, 249–250, 436, 438; Perry, "Antecedents of the X–1," 20–23.

[40] An exception to the pattern of private sponsorship of rocket societies was the "Group for the Study of Rocket Propulsion Systems," known as GIRD, established under government auspices in the Soviet Union in 1931. House Committee on Science and Astronautics, 87 Cong., 1 sess. (1961), House Report No. 67, *A Chronology of Missile and Astronautic Events*, 3; G. A. Tokaty, "Soviet Rocket Technology," in Emme, ed., *History of Rocket Technology*, 275–276; also published in *Technology and Culture*, IV (Fall 1963), 520–521.

[41] On Oberth see Williams and Epstein, *Rocket Pioneers*, 111, 143; Gartmann, *Men Behind the Space Rockets*; Ley, *Rockets, Missiles, and Space Travel*, 108–130; William Meyer-Cords, "Introduction" to Hermann Oberth, *Man into Space: New Projects for Rocket and Space Travel*, trans. G. P. H. deFreville (New York, 1957), vii–xiv; Hermann Oberth, "From My Life," *Astronautics*, IV (June 1959), 38–39, 100–104; and G. V. E. Thompson, "Oberth—Doyen of Spaceflight Today," *Spaceflight*, I (Oct. 1957), 170–171.

[42] Ley, *Rockets, Missiles, and Space Travel*, 118–162, 197–201; Walter Dornberger, "The German V–2," in Emme, ed., *History of Rocket Technology*, 29–33; also published in *Technology and Culture*, IV (Fall 1963), 394–395. Williams and Epstein, *Rocket Pioneers*, 144–170. Von Braun received a doctorate in physics from the University of Berlin in 1934.

[43] See Walter Dornberger, *V–2* (New York, 1954); Dornberger, "The German V–2," 33–45; Williams and Epstein, *Rocket Pioneers*, 204–231; Ley, *Rockets, Missiles, and Space Travel*, 202–231; Dieter K. Huzel, *Peenemünde to Canaveral* (Englewood Cliffs, N.J., 1962); Leslie G. Simon, *German Research in World War II: An Analysis of the Conduct of Research* (New York, 1947), 33–35; and Theodore Benecke and A. W. Quick, eds., *History of German Guided Missiles* (Brunswick, Ger., 1957).

[44] Ley, *Rockets, Missiles, and Space Travel*, 212–217; Kurt H. Debus, "Evolution of Launch Concepts and Space Flight Operations," in Ernst Stuhlinger, Frederick I. Ordway III, Jerry C. McCall, and George C. Bucher, eds., *From Peenemünde to Outer Space: Commemorating the Fiftieth Birthday of Wernher von Braun* (Huntsville, Ala., 1962), 45. During the powered phase of its flight within the atmosphere the V–2 was stabilized by large aerodynamic fins.

[45] *Chronology of Missile and Astronautic Events*, 7; Dornberger, "The German V–2," 32–33. "Vengeance Weapon No. 1"— V–1—was a radio-controlled, subsonic guided missile powered by a pulsejet engine, developed by the German Air Force. Besides the A–4, the accomplishments of the Peenemünde rocket workers included the launching in the early part of 1945 of a winged A–4, called the A–9, which they had designed as the upper stage of a rocket to attack the United States. And by the end of the war Eugen Sänger, already well-known as an Austrian rocket scientist before going to work for the Luftwaffe, and Irene Bredt, a noted German physicist, had written an elaborate report containing a design for an antipodal rocket bomber that would skip in and out of the atmosphere to drop its payload and land halfway around the world. See also Eugen Sänger, *Rocket Flight Engineering*, NASA TT F–223 (Washington, 1965).

[46] Senate Preparedness Subcommittee of the Committee on Armed Services, 85 Cong., 1 and 2 sess. (1957–58), *Inquiry into Satellite and Missile Programs, Hearings*, testimony of Wernher von Braun, Part 1, 850; David S. Akens, *Historical Origins of the George C. Marshall Space Flight Center* (Huntsville, Ala., 1960), 24–29; Tokaty, "Soviet Rocket Technology," 278–279; James McGovern, *Crossbow and Overcast* (New York, 1964); Clarence G. Lasby, "German Scientists in America: Their Importation, Exploitation, and Assimilation, 1945–1952," unpublished Ph. D. dissertation, University of California at Los Angeles, 1962. All together, Paperclip brought nearly 500 aeronautical and rocket scientists, engineers, and technicians to the United States.

[47] Quoted in Tokaty, "Soviet Rocket Technology," 279.

[48] *Inquiry into Satellite and Missile Pro-*

grams, testimony of von Braun, Part 1, 581; Parry, *Russia's Rockets and Missiles,* 118–125.

⁴⁹ James P. Baxter, *Scientists Against Time* (Boston, 1946), 201.

⁵⁰ Quoted in Tokaty, "Soviet Rocket Technology," 281.

⁵¹ *Ibid.,* 282–283; Parry, *Russia's Rockets and Missiles,* 131–133; Frederick I. Ordway III, and Ronald C. Wakeford, *International Missile and Spacecraft Guide* (New York, 1960), 3–4; Donald J. Ritchie, "Soviet Rocket Propulsion," in Donald P. LeGalley, ed., *Ballistic Missile and Space Technology,* Vol. II: *Propulsion and Auxiliary Power Systems* (New York, 1960), 55–85; *Chronology of Missile and Astronautic Events,* 26; Charles S. Sheldon II, "The Challenge of International Competition," paper, Third American Institute of Aeronautics and Astronautics/NASA Manned Space Flight Meeting, Houston, Nov. 6, 1964.

⁵² Among the air-breathing guided missiles (a term that simply meant any pilotless flying craft) designed and developed by the Navy and the Air Force in the first decade after the war were the Gorgon, Plover, Regulus, Cobra, Bomarc, Snark, Matador, and Loon, the last being a Navy version of the German V-1. Of these weapons only the Snark was a genuinely long-range, or intercontinental, missile, and it was subsonic and thus vulnerable to radar-controlled antiaircraft rockets. See Ordway and Wakeford, *International Missile and Spacecraft Guide,* 3–5, 8–9, 15–16, 20–24, 26, 61.

⁵³ Quoted, among many other places, in *Inquiry into Satellite and Missile Programs,* Part I, 283. For a more lengthy argument against early attempts to develop intercontinental ballistic missiles, see Vannevar Bush, *Modern Arms and Free Men* (New York, 1949).

⁵⁴ See Kenneth W. Gatland, *Development of the Guided Missile* (London, 1954); and Nels A. Parsons, *Guided Missiles in War and Peace* (Cambridge, Mass., 1956), and *Missiles and the Revolution in Warfare* (Cambridge, Mass., 1962).

⁵⁵ On the postwar V-2 program at White Sands and Cape Canaveral, see U.S. Army Ordnance Corps/General Electric Co., *Hermes Guided Missile Research and Development Project, 1944-1954* (Sept. 25, 1959), 1–4; Ley, *Rockets, Missiles, and Space Travel,* 254–271; Akens, *Historical Origins of the Marshall Space Flight Center,* 28–35; Ernest Krause, "High Altitude Research with V-2 Rockets,"

Proceedings of the American Philosophical Society, XCI (1947), 430–446; and J. Gordon Vaeth, *200 Miles Up: The Conquest of the Upper Air* (2 ed., New York, 1956), 117–134. Unless otherwise indicated, all mileage figures used in this work refer to statute miles.

On Thanksgiving Day 1963, several months after Project Mercury officially ended, President Lyndon B. Johnson renamed Cape Canaveral, Cape Kennedy. Since that is beyond the historical context of this study, throughout the rest of this work Cape Canaveral will be used.

⁵⁶ *Ibid.,* 178-194; Homer E. Newell, *Sounding Rockets* (New York, 1959), 54–95; Emme, *Aeronautics and Astronautics,* 53–54, 58–59, 63, 67, 69–70, 77.

⁵⁷ On the Viking see Ley, *Rockets, Missiles, and Space Travel,* 271–276; Milton Rosen, *The Viking Rocket Story* (New York, 1955); John P. Hagen, "The Viking and the Vanguard," in Emme, ed., *History of Rocket Technology,* 123–125; also published in *Technology and Culture,* IV (Fall 1963), 436-437; Vaeth, *200 Miles Up,* 195–206; and Newell, *Sounding Rockets,* 235-242. The first Viking shot, fired in May 1950 from the deck of the *Norton Sound* in the Pacific, set a new single-stage altitude record, 106.6 miles.

⁵⁸ On the Navaho see Ordway and Wakeford, *International Missile and Spacecraft Guide,* 9–10; and Emme, *Aeronautics and Astronautics,* 64, 70, 72, 74, 76, 77, 86. Besides booster development, the technological heritage from the Navaho program included the airframe for the Hound Dog air-to-surface missile, progress in using titanium for structures, and the guidance system for nuclear-powered submarines.

⁵⁹ Akens, *Historical Origins of the Marshall Space Flight Center,* 36–37; Wernher von Braun, "The Redstone, Jupiter, and Juno," in Emme, ed., *History of Rocket Technology,* 108–109; also published in *Technology and Culture,* IV (Fall 1963), 452–455; A. A. McCool and Keith B. Chandler, "Development Trends in Liquid Propellant Engines," in Stuhlinger, Ordway, McCall, and Bucher, eds., *From Peenemünde to Outer Space,* 292; John W. Bullard, "History of the Redstone Missile System," Hist. Div., Army Missile Command, Oct. 1965, 135-151. The creation of the North Atlantic Treaty Organization in 1949 had provided a clear military need for a battlefield rocket.

⁶⁰ *Jane's All the World's Aircraft, 1962-1963* (London, 1963), 391–392; von Braun,

FOOTNOTES

"The Redstone, Jupiter, and Juno," 109–110; McCool and Chandler, "Development Trends in Liquid Propellant Engines," 292; Bullard. "History of the Redstone," 53–93.

[51] The term "ballistic missile" refers to a projectile fired along a ballistic, or high-arc, trajectory, reaching an altitude of several hundred miles before falling freely toward its target. Such a vehicle is to be distinguished from the jet-propelled guided missile, which is controlled throughout its flight, requires oxygen within the air for its propellant oxidizer, and can operate only within the atmosphere. Thus by definition a ballistic missile, which reaches well into space, is a rocket.

[52] John L. Chapman, *Atlas: The Story of a Missile* (New York, 1960), 30–54; *Inquiry into Satellite and Missile Programs*, testimony of James R. Dempsey, Part 2, 1871–1872.

[53] Chapman, *Atlas*, 60–62; *Inquiry into Satellite and Missile Programs*, testimony of Dempsey, Part 2, 1872; Robert L. Perry, "The Atlas, Thor, Titan, and Minuteman," in Emme, ed., *History of Rocket Technology*, 143; also published as "The Atlas, Thor, and Titan," in *Technology and Culture*, VI (Fall 1963), 467.

[54] House Select Committee on Astronautics and Space Exploration, 85 Cong., 2 sess. (1958), *Astronautics and Space Exploration, Hearings*, testimony of Bernard A. Schriever, 668; Chapman, *Atlas*, 70–74; Bernard A. Schriever, "The USAF Ballistic Missile Program," in Kenneth F. Gantz, ed., *The United States Air Force Report on the Ballistic Missile* (Garden City, N.Y., 1958), 2–28; House Committee on Government Operations, 86 Cong., 1 sess. (1959), House Report No. 1121, *Organization and Management of Missile Programs*, 70–71; Ernest G. Schwiebert, *A History of the U.S. Air Force Ballistic Missiles* (New York, 1965), 67–73.

[55] *Astronautics and Space Exploration*, testimony of Schriever, 668. See also, Herman Kahn, *On Thermonuclear War* (Princeton, N.J., 1961), and *Thinking about the Unthinkable* (New York, 1962).

[56] See Schwiebert, *Air Force Ballistic Missiles*, 75–95.

[57] On this point Schriever elaborated: "I think the Air Force philosophy of having industry do development and having the capability of planning for production simultaneously is a much better way. . . . The Air Force had quite a number of German scientists right after the war at Wright Field, and made, deliberately made, the decision not to try to retain that group of scientists as a group, similar to what they have done at Redstone, and . . . most of them have gone into American industry. . . . They are at Convair, they are at Bell, and a number of other companies, and . . . my feeling is that these people, distributed to American industry, are doing equally as good a job for the United States as this one small group that are still assembled at the Redstone Arsenal." *Inquiry into Satellite and Missile Programs*, Part 2, testimony of Schriever, 1637–1638.

[58] Chapman, *Atlas*, 74, 78; Schriever, "USAF Ballistic Missile Program," 28; Perry, "Atlas, Thor, Titan, and Minuteman," 144–148; *Organization and Management of Missile Programs*, 73–79; Thomas, *Men of Space*, II, 143–149. The Ramo-Wooldridge Corporation was established by Simon Ramo and Dean Wooldridge, missile experts who, as employees of the Hughes Aircraft Company, had served on the Teapot Committee. They left Hughes in 1953 to set up their missiles research and management firm. For a description of the role of Space Technology Laboratories in the American missile effort and a critique of the STL/Air Force arrangement, see *Organization and Management of Missile Programs*, 81–100. In 1958 the Ramo-Wooldridge Corporation merged completely with an initial financial backer, the Thompson Products Company of Cleveland, to form the Thompson Ramo Wooldridge Corporation. See Robert Sheehan, "Thompson Ramo Wooldridge: Two Wings in Space," *Fortune*, LXVII (Feb. 1963), 95–99ff.

[59] *Inquiry into Satellite and Missile Programs*, Part I, 471; Wyndam D. Miles, "The Polaris," in Emme, ed., *History of Rocket Technology*, 164–166; also published in *Technology and Culture*, VI (Fall 1963), 480–482. The competition deliberately established by the Defense Department between the Air Force and the Army over the Thor and the Jupiter, while perhaps necessary, proved intense, acrimonious, and apparently wasteful. The full story of the Thor-Jupiter rivalry in the period 1955–1958 is yet to be told, but some valuable insight can be gained from *Organization and Management of Missile Programs*, 101–116. An account heavily biased in favor of the Army is John B. Medaris, *Countdown for Decision* (New York, 1960), 86–150. The Air Force side of the story is presented in Julian Hartt, *The Mighty Thor: Missile in Readiness* (New York, 1961).

[60] Perry, "Atlas, Thor, Titan, and Minuteman," 148. On concurrency see also Schriever, "USAF Ballistic Missile Program," 30–39; and Osmond J. Ritland, "Concurrency," *Air*

University Quarterly Review, XII (Winter-Spring 1960–1961), 237–250. Parallel development of components had characterized numerous advances in 20th-century science and technology, of course, notably the Manhattan Project that produced the atomic bomb in the Second World War. (See Baxter, *Scientists Against Time,* 419–447; and Richard G. Hewlett and Oscar E. Anderson, *A History of the United States Atomic Energy Commission,* Vol. I: *The New World, 1939–1946* [University Park, Pa., 1962], 9–407.) But "concurrency" as a formal research and engineering management technique is properly credited to the Air Force ballistic missile program of the fifties.

[71] Perry, "Atlas, Thor, Titan, and Minuteman," 149–150. The Strategic Air Command assumed operational planning responsibility for all intermediate and intercontinental missiles in 1958.

[72] Chapman, *Atlas,* 88–89; *Jane's All the World's Aircraft, 1962–1963,* 394. On the intricacies involved in fabricating the extremely thin Atlas airframe, see Robert Sweeney, "Atlas Generates Fabrication Advances," *Aviation Week,* LXXII (Jan. 4, 1960), 38–49; and "Manufacturing the Atlas at Convair," *Interavia,* LXXI (1959), 810–811.

[73] Chapman, *Atlas,* 136–137; *Jane's All the World's Aircraft, 1962–1963,* 394; Ordway and Wakeford, *International Missile and Spacecraft Guide,* 1–3; NASA/MSC news release, "The Mercury-Atlas 8 Launch Vehicle," Oct. 1, 1962; C. L. Gandy and I. Hanson, "Mercury-Atlas Launch-Vehicle Development and Performance," in *Mercury Project Summary, Including Results of the Fourth Orbital Flight, May 15 and 16, 1963* (Washington, 1963), 84–91. On Rocketdyne's problems in developing the powerplant for the Atlas see Thomas F. Dixon, "Development Problems of Rocket Engines for Ballistic Missiles," *Interavia,* LXXI (1959), 818–821.

[74] Ordway and Wakeford, *International Missile and Spacecraft Guide,* 1–3; *Jane's All the World's Aircraft, 1962–1963,* 395.

[75] Chapman, *Atlas,* 81–82; Gandy and Hanson, "Mercury-Atlas Launch-Vehicle Development and Performance," 91–92; *Jane's All the World's Aircraft, 1962–1963,* 394–395; Ordway and Wakeford, *International Missile and Spacecraft Guide,* 2. Beginning in late 1960 with the "E" version, the guidance system of the Atlas became all-inertial, meaning that all guidance components were carried aboard the rocket. General Electric and Burroughs Corp. developed the radio-inertial guidance system for the Atlas, while the American Bosch Arma Corp. produced the all-inertial system.

[76] Atmospheric entry heating was not a critical problem for the medium-range (200-mile) Redstone, which did not develop the velocities of the intermediate and intercontinental rockets. Thus protecting the astronaut during the reentry phase of the suborbital (Redstone) flights in Project Mercury, while deserving attention, was not of acute concern.

[77] Von Kármán, *Aerodynamics,* 189. In view of the continually modifying nature of astronautical terminology, the authors throughout this work have used the terms "entry" and "reentry" interchangeably. They realize that some aerodynamicists make a distinction between the two.

[78] Colonel Oleg Penkovsky, the now-famous Russian "master spy" for the West in the Soviet intelligence system, supposedly wrote as late as the first part of 1962: "Only the smaller (IRBM) missiles are in production. . . . Right now we have a certain number of missiles with nuclear warheads capable of reaching the United States or South America; but these are single missiles, not in mass production, and they are far from perfect." (Frank Gibney, ed., *The Penkovsky Papers,* trans. Peter Deriabin [Garden City, N.Y., 1965], 331–348.) Thus while the Soviets may have been able to fire an ICBM over its design range before the United States and use it to launch relatively heavy satellites, they apparently had great troubles producing such a military rocket in quantity, as the United States was doing by 1962 with its Atlas, Titan, and Minuteman.

[79] House Committee on Science and Astronautics, 86 Cong., 2 sess. (1960), House Report No. 2092, *Space, Missiles, and the Nation,* 5–7; *Organization and Management of Missile Programs,* 108–109.

[80] *Inquiry into Satellite and Missile Programs,* testimony of J. H. Kindelberger, Part 1, 1280.

[81] *Astronautics and Space Exploration,* testimony of Schriever, 669.

[82] Parry, *Russia's Rockets and Missiles,* 141; Ordway and Wakeford, *International Missile and Spacecraft Guide,* 3–4; Ritchie, "Soviet Rocket Propulsion," 71; Alfred Z. Zaehringer, "Table of Soviet Missiles," in F. J. Krieger, ed., *A Casebook on Soviet Astronautics* (2 vols.,

Santa Monica, Calif., 1956–1959), I, 242.

[50] Quoted in Parry, *Russia's Rockets and Missiles*, 111.

[51] Quoted in Mary Stone Ambrose, "The National Space Program," unpublished M.A. thesis, 2 vols., American University, 1960–1961, I, 17. See also Dwight D. Eisenhower, *The White House Years: Waging Peace, 1956–1961* (Garden City, N.Y., 1965). A useful anthology of official reactions to the Soviet space coup is Richard L. Witkin, ed., *The Challenge of the Sputniks* (New York, 1958).

[52] See R. Cargill Hall, "Early U.S. Satellite Proposals," in Emme, ed., *History of Rocket Technology*, 67–93; also published in *Technology and Culture*, VI (Fall 1963), 410–434.

[53] Memo, Albert E. Lombard, Scientific Advisor, Directorate of Research and Development, Department of the Air Force, to Committee on Aerodynamics, NACA, "Upper Stratosphere, Ionosphere, and Space Flight," June 25, 1952.

[54] Quoted in Parry, *Russia's Rockets and Missiles*, 184; and Krieger, ed., *Casebook on Soviet Astronautics*, II, 1.

[55] Parry, *Russia's Rockets and Missiles*, 185–186; *Astronautics and Space Exploration*, testimony of Andrew G. Haley, 1462–1463.

[56] Krieger, ed., *Casebook on Soviet Astronautics*, II, 2–10; Parry, *Russia's Rockets and Missiles*, 186–188; *Astronautics and Space Exploration*, testimony of Haley, 1464.

[57] Hagen, "Viking and Vanguard," 137; John Lear, "The Moon That Refused to Be Eclipsed," *Saturday Review*, XLIII (March 5, 1963), 45–48; Kurt R. Stehling, *Project Vanguard* (Garden City, N.Y., 1961), 141–181.

[58] The controversial history of the decision to build a new satellite rocket based on the Viking and the Aerobee, as proposed by the Naval Research Laboratory, rather than to adapt the Redstone for the Geophysical Year satellite program, as proposed by the Office of Naval Research and the Army in Project Orbiter, is beyond the scope of this work. The Vanguard-Orbiter imbroglio is covered in von Braun, "Redstone, Jupiter, and Juno," 111–113; Carsbie C. Adams, *Space Flight* (New York, 1958), 112–113; E. Nelson Hayes, "The Smithsonian's Satellite Tracking Program: Its History and Organization," *Report of the Smithsonian Institution for 1961* (Washington, 1962), 275–322; *Astronautics and Space Exploration*, testimony of John T. Hayward, 293–294; *Inquiry into Satellite and Missile Programs*, testimony of James M. Gavin and J. B.

Medaris, Part 2, 1473–1475, 1633–1634; Hagen, "Viking and Vanguard," 125–127; Akens, *Historical Origins of the Marshall Space Flight Center*, 38–40; Jay Holmes, *America on the Moon: The Enterprise of the Sixties* (Philadelphia, 1962), 46–51; and R. Cargill Hall, "Origins and Development of the Vanguard and Explorer Satellite Programs," *Air Power Historian*, XI (Oct. 1964).

[59] After losing out in the satellite rocket competition, the Army engineers at Redstone Arsenal had stubbornly sought authorization to reactivate their satellite project. Rebuffed in the Defense Department, the Army group shrewdly renamed a modified Redstone, which they were preparing for tests of the Jupiter reentry nose cone, the Jupiter-C, in order to continue receiving funds for the satellite project. See von Braun, "Redstone, Jupiter, and Juno," 113–114; *Inquiry into Satellite and Missile Programs*, testimony of J. B. Medaris, Part 2, 1700–1701; Medaris, *Countdown for Decision*; James M. Gavin, *War and Peace in the Space Age* (New York, 1958); *Astronautics and Space Exploration*, testimony of Gavin, 183–184; Akens, *Historical Origins of the Marshall Space Flight Center*, 40–44; *Organization and Management of Missile Programs*, 130.

[60] Akens, *Historical Origins of the Marshall Space Flight Center*, 44–50; von Braun, "Redstone, Jupiter, and Juno," 114; Bullard, "History of the Redstone," 142–146; Lear, "Moon That Refused to Be Eclipsed," 47; Hagen, "Viking and Vanguard," 448–451; Stehling, *Project Vanguard*, 182–219; House Committee on Science and Astronautics, 86 Cong., 1 sess. (1959), *U.S. Aeronautics and Space Activities, Jan. 1 to Dec. 31, 1958: Message from the President of the United States*, 3–4. On March 5, 1958, an attempt to launch *Explorer II* failed when th Jupiter-C fourth stage did not ignite.

[61] These four shots were made with the Atlas A, a version with a dummy sustainer engine and nose cone, designed solely for test purposes. The first Atlas A went out of control and was destroyed after less than a minute of flight on June 11, 1957, and a second attempt, on Sept. 25, ended in the same fashion. Success came on Dec. 17, 1957, when an Atlas A impacted on its target about 500 miles downrange from Cape Canaveral. On April 5, 1958, the test rocket flew successfully 600 miles downrange from the Cape. Chapman, *Atlas*, 118–133; Perry, "Atlas, Thor, Titan, and Minuteman," 151; George Alexander, "Atlas Accuracy Improves as Test Program is

Completed," *Aviation Week*, LXXVIII (Feb. 25, 1963), 57-58.

Chapter II

[1] On advances in telemetry since the Second World War, see Wilfred J. Mayo-Wells, "The Origins of Space Telemetry," in Eugene M. Emme, ed., *The History of Rocket Technology: Essays on Research, Development, and Utility* (Detroit, 1964), 253-268; also published in *Technology and Culture*, IV (Fall 1963), 499-514.

[2] For the German work in aeromedicine during the 1930s and early 1940s, see U.S. Air Force, *German Aviation Medicine, World War II* (2 vols., Washington, 1950).

[3] Harry G. Armstrong, *Principles and Practices of Aviation Medicine* (3 ed., Baltimore, 1952). Armstrong later became a major general.

[4] Harry G. Armstrong, Heinz Haber, and Hubertus Strughold, "Aero Medical Problems of Space Travel, Panel Meeting, School of Aviation Medicine," *Journal of Aviation Medicine*, XIX (Dec. 1949), 383-417; Hubertus Strughold, interview, San Antonio, April 24, 1964. People interested in the physiology and psychology of extra-atmospheric flight have devised a number of terms to describe their field of investigation—biomedicine, space biology, astrobiology, bioastronautics, aerospace medicine. The most suitable single term seems to be that used by Strughold, "space medicine." It is used throughout this work except where more precise terminology, such as "biodynamics," appears appropriate.

[5] Shirley Thomas, *Men of Space* (6 vols., Philadelphia, 1960-1963), IV, 234-250; USAF Air Training Command, *History of the United States Air Force*, Pamphlet 190-1, Randolph Air Force Base, Tex., 1961, 19; Strughold interview. Siegfried J. Gerathewohl, a psychologist, and Hans-Georg Clamann, a physiologist, remained with the School of Aviation Medicine but did not become members of the Department of Space Medicine.

[6] Clayton S. White and Otis O. Benson, eds., *Physics and Medicine of the Upper Atmosphere: A Study of the Aeropause* (Albuquerque, 1952).

[7] Hubertus Strughold, "Basic Environmental Problems Relating Man and the Highest Regions of the Atmosphere as Seen by the Biologist," *ibid.*, 32. On the concept of space equivalence see also Strughold, Heinz Haber, Konrad Buettner, and Fritz Haber, "Where Does Space Begin? Functional Concept of the Boundaries between the Atmosphere and Space," *Journal of Aviation Medicine*, XXII (Oct., 1951), 342-357; Strughold, "Atmospheric Space Equivalence," *Journal of Aviation Medicine*, XXV (Aug., 1954), 420-424; Strughold, "The Medical Problems of Space Flight," *International Record of Medicine*, CLXVIII (1955), 570-575; and Strughold, "A Simple Classification of the Present and Future Stages of Manned Flight," *Journal of Aviation Medicine*, XXVII (Aug., 1956), 328-331.

[8] "Thirty-Five Years of Winged Rocket Flight," *Thiokol Magazine*, II (1963), 10; Hubertus Strughold, "Introduction," to Morton Alperin, M. Stern, and H. Wooster, eds., *Vistas in Astronautics: First Annual Astronautics Symposium* (London, 1958), 283.

[9] See Burt Rowen, "Human Factors Support of the X-15 Program," in Kenneth F. Gantz, ed., *Man in Space: The United States Air Force Program for Developing the Spacecraft Crews* (New York, 1959), 216-221; Stanley C. White, "Progress in Space Medicine," paper, Second World and Fourth European Aviation and Space Medicine Congress, Rome, Oct. 27-31, 1959; and Richard E. Day, "Training Aspects of the X-15 Program," in *The Training of Astronauts* (Washington, 1961), 5-14.

[10] Otto Gauer and Heinz Haber, "Man under Gravity-Free Conditions," in *German Aviation Medicine, World War II*, I, 641-643.

[11] David Bushnell, "History of Research in Subgravity and Zero-G at the Air Force Missile Development Center, 1948-1958," Air Force Missile Development Center, 1959, 3-7; David G. Simons, "Use of V-2 Rocket to Convey Primate to Upper Atmosphere," Air Force Tech. Report 5821, Air Materiel Command, Wright-Patterson Air Force Base, Ohio, May 1959; James P. Henry et al., "Animal Studies of the Subgravity State During Rocket Flight," *Journal of Aviation Medicine*, XXIII (Oct. 1952), 421-423; David G. Simons, interview, San Antonio, April 24, 1964. A breezy popular account of the Holloman shots with V-2s and Aerobees is Lloyd Mallan, *Men, Rockets, and Space Rats* (Rev. ed., New York, 1962), 84-116.

[12] Andrei G. Kousnetzov, "Some Results of Biological Experiments in Rockets and Sputnik II," *Journal of Aviation Medicine*, XXIX (Nov. 1958), 781-784; S. M. Polovskov and B. A. Mirtov, "Study of the Upper Atmosphere by Means of Rockets at the U.S.S.R. Academy of Sciences," and A. V. Pokrovskii, "Study of the Vital Activity of Animals during Rocket Flights in the Upper Atmosphere," in F. J.

FOOTNOTES

Kreiger, ed., *A Casebook on Soviet Astronautics* (2 vols., Santa Monica, Calif., 1956–1959), II, 151–172; Siegfried J. Gerathewohl, *Principles of Bioastronautics* (Englewood Cliffs, N.J., 1964), 91–95.

[13] Harald J. von Beckh, "Human Reactions during Flight to Acceleration Preceded by or Followed by Weightlessness," *Aerospace Medicine*, XXX (June 1959), 391.

[14] Fritz Haber and Heinz Haber, "Possible Methods of Producing the Gravity-Free State for Medical Research," *Journal of Aviation Medicine*, XXI (Oct. 1950), 395–400.

[15] Allen C. Fisher, "Aviation Medicine on the Threshold of Space," *National Geographic*, CVI (Aug. 1955), 257; Siegfried J. Gerathewohl, "Weightlessness," in Gantz, ed., *Man in Space*, 115.

[16] *Ibid.*

[17] Bushnell, "Research in Subgravity and Zero-G at the Air Force Missile Development Center," 12–17; James H. Hanrahan and David Bushnell, *Space Biology: The Human Factors in Space Flight* (New York, 1960), 137, 139–140; Green Peyton and Jean Evans, "History, Aerospace Medical Division, Air Force Systems Command: Reorganization, 1 November 1961–30 June 1962," Hist. Publication 62–180, Brooks Air Force Base, Tex., 1962, 93–97.

[18] Hanrahan and Bushnell, *Space Biology*, 139–140; "USAF School Simulates Living in Space," *Aviation Week*, LXVIII (Jan. 27, 1958), 49–51; Siegfried J. Gerathewohl, Oskar L. Ritter, and Herbert D. Stallings, "Producing the Weightless State in Jet Aircraft," Report 57–143, Air Force School of Aviation Medicine, Aug. 1957.

[19] Gerathewohl, *Principles of Bioastronautics*, 211–234; Siegfried J. Gerathewohl and Herbert D. Stallings, "Experiments during Weightlessness: A Study of the Oculo-Agravic Illusion," *Journal of Aviation Medicine*, XXIX (July 1958), 504–515; Julian E. Ward, Willard R. Hawkins, and Herbert D. Stallings, "Physiologic Response to Subgravity I: Mechanics of Nourishment and Deglutition of Solids and Liquids," *Journal of Aviation Medicine*, XXX (March 1959), 151–154, and "Physiologic Response to Subgravity II: Initiation of Micturition," *Aerospace Medicine*, XXX (Aug. 1959), 572–575.

[20] "They Float through the Air," *Astronautics*, IV (Feb. 1959), 42; Hanrahan and Bushnell, *Space Biology*, 147–148; William Leavitt, "The Weird World of Weightlessness," *Air Force*, XLII (April 1959), 113.

[21] Gerathewohl, "Weightlessness," 108–132. The Navy School of Aviation Medicine experiments also employed parabolic aircraft flights, while the Lewis studies featured use of a tall drop-tower.

[22] David G. Simons, "Review of Biological Effects of Subgravity and Weightlessness," *Jet Propulsion*, XXV (May 1955), 209–211; Fisher, "Aviation Medicine on the Threshold of Space," 257.

[23] Gerathewohl, "Weightlessness," 132. See also Oskar L. Ritter and Siegfried J. Gerathewohl, "The Concepts of Weight and Stress in Human Flight," paper no. 58–154, Air Force School of Aviation Medicine, June 26, 1958.

[24] Von Beckh, "Human Reactions during Flight to Acceleration Preceded by or Followed by Weightlessness," 391–406. After the termination of zero-g flights at Holloman and Randolph, weightless experiments in aircraft continued at Wright-Patterson and at the Air Force Flight Test Center, Edwards Air Force Base, Calif.

[25] See Mae M. Link and Hubert A. Coleman, *Medical Support of the Army Air Forces in World War II* (Washington, 1955).

[26] Hanrahan and Bushnell, *Space Biology*, 86–88; David Bushnell, "Major Achievements in Biodynamics: Escape Physiology at the Air Force Missile Development Center, 1953–1958," Air Force Missile Development Center, 1959, 10–13; Martin and Grace Caidin, *Aviation and Space Medicine* (New York, 1962), 199–203; Mallan, *Men, Rockets, and Space Rats*, 99–116. Stapp had taken his first rocket sled ride in 1947 at Edwards Air Force Base, Calif. He became Chief of the Aeromedical Field Laboratory in 1953 and made several more rides before his record run on Dec. 10, 1954. See John P. Stapp, "Tolerance to Abrupt Deceleration," in *Collected Papers on Aviation Medicine, Presented at Aeromedical Panel Meetings of the Advisory Group for Aeronautical Research and Development, North American Treaty Organization* (London, 1955), 122–169.

[27] Eli L. Beeding, Jr., and John D. Mosely, "Human Deceleration Tests," Air Force Missile Development Center, Jan. 1960; Hanrahan and Bushnell, *Space Biology*, 93–94. The "daisy track" was named for a popular make of air rifle, because it was originally designed as a compressed-air catapult system. From 1955 to 1959 it used a cartridge system.

[28] John P. Stapp, "Biodynamics of Space Flight," in Gantz, ed., *Man in Space*, 68.

[29] See William J. White, *A History of the Centrifuge in Aerospace Medicine* (Santa Monica, Calif., 1964).

[30] Gauer and Haber, "Man under Gravity-Free Conditions," 641–643.

[31] Hanrahan and Bushnell, *Space Biology,* 72.

[32] *Ibid.,* 75–76. The largest centrifuge in operation in the United States during the 1950s was the Navy's mechanical arm at Johnsonville, with a radius of 50 feet and a capability of 40 g. The Johnsville facility had a device allowing the gondola to be gimbaled to simulate buffetings and cross-currents. The Wright Air Development Center centrifuge, on the other hand, had a radius of 20 feet and a capability of 20 g. Instead of a gondola it featured an open platform, which could be whirled in one plane only.

[33] *Ibid.,* 77; John P. Stapp, "Acceleration: How Great a Problem?" *Astronautics,* IV (Feb. 1959), 38–39, 98–100.

[34] *Ibid.,* 77, 105–109; memo for files, Gerard J. Pesman, Human Factors Br., Space Task Group, "Present Status—Major Systems, Pilot Support and Restraint" [about Feb. 1959]; Harald J. von Beckh, "Multidirectional G-Protection in Space Vehicles," *Journal of the British Interplanetary Society,* XVI (Sept.–Oct. 1958), 531.

[35] Hanrahan and Bushnell, *Space Biology,* 96–98.

[36] Carl C. Clark and James D. Hardy, "Preparing Man for Space Flight," *Astronautics,* IV (Feb. 1959), 18–21, 88; Clark and R. Flanagan Gray, "A Discussion of Restraint and Protection of the Human Experiencing the Smooth and Oscillating Accelerations of Proposed Space Vehicles," U.S. Naval Air Development Center, Dec. 29, 1959, 26–46. During 1957–1958 scientists at the Wright Air Development Center also carried out water-immersion studies, using a coffin-like container. Peak accelerations on the limited Wright centrifuge were only about 16 g, but the durations of the acceleration patterns were longer.

[37] John P. Stapp, interview, San Antonio, April 24, 1964.

[38] Maxime A. Faget, interview, Houston, Jan. 3, 1964, and Aug. 24, 1964; Gerard J. Pesman, interview, Houston, March 17, 1964; James M. Grimwood, *Project Mercury: A Chronology,* NASA SP-4001 (Washington, 1963), 20. For USAF concept of rotating couch, see p. 96.

[39] Faget interview; Clark and Gray, "A Discussion of Restraint and Protection," 26; Pesman memo; John Dille, ed., *We Seven, by the Astronauts Themselves* (New York, 1962), 110–112.

[40] Clark and Gray, "A Discussion of Restraint and Protection," 26; Pesman memo. Faget and his men became even happier in December 1958, during the early days of Project Mercury, when a second Langley couch, its back angle raised 8 degrees, supported Lt. Carter C. Collins on the Navy centrifuge during a peak of 25 g for approximately 10 seconds.

[41] Stanley R. Mohler, "Wiley Post's Aerospace Achievements," *Airpower Historian,* XI (July 1964), 66–70; Frederick R. Ritzinger, Jr., and Ellis G. Aboud, "Pressure Suits—Their Evolution and Development," *Air University Review,* XVI (Jan.–Feb. 1965), 23–32.

[42] Caidin and Caidin, *Aviation and Space Medicine,* 49–54; Eugene M. Emme, *Aeronautics and Astronautics: An American Chronology of Science and Technology in the Exploration of Space, 1915–1960* (Washington, 1961), 26, 29, 30, 33, 160, 162; Auguste Piccard, *Between Earth and Sky,* trans. Claude Apcher (London, 1950), and *Earth, Sky, and Sea,* trans. Christina Stead (New York, 1956). For a useful survey of research in the physiology of high-altitude living, see *From the Mountains to the Moon: Some Historical Aspects of Survival at Great Heights* (undated microfilm, produced by Biomedical Laboratory, University of California at Los Angeles, NASA Historical Archives, Washington).

[43] Hubertus Strughold, "The U.S. Air Force Experimental Sealed Cabin," *Journal of Aviation Medicine,* XXVII (Feb. 1956), 50; Hanrahan and Bushnell, *Space Biology,* 24–26.

[44] Strughold, "Air Force Experimental Sealed Cabin," 50–51; Hans-Georg Clamann, interview, San Antonio, April 23, 1964.

[45] Strughold interview.

[46] "USAF School Simulates Living in Space," 49–55.

[47] Emme, *Aeronautics and Astronautics,* 81, 95; Strughold interview; George R. Steinkamp and Willard R. Hawkins, "Medical Experimentation in a Sealed Cabin Simulator," in Otis O. Benson and Hubertus Strughold, eds., *Physics and Medicine of the Atmosphere and Space* (New York, 1960), 370–376.

[48] George T. Hauty, "Human Performance in Space," in Gantz, ed., *Man in Space,* 84–108. Besides the aircraft weightless and sealed-cabin programs, the School of Aviation Medicine

carried on various other research activities in space medicine. As early as 1947 scientists at the school were studying the ecological conditions on other planets. From this and other research came Strughold's *The Green and Red Planet: A Physiological Study of the Possibility of Life on Mars* (Albuquerque, 1953). Throughout the 1950s and to the present the Department of Space Medicine at the school has done research on the atmospheric composition of other planets, photosynthesis as a means of air supply, and other subjects.

[49] Charles A. Berry, "The Environment of Space in Human Flight," *Aeronautical Engineering Review*, XVII (March 1958), 38; George E. Ruff, "Isolation," *Astronautics*, IV (Feb. 1959), 22–23, 110–111. After 1951 psychologists in several universities in the United States and Canada conducted sensory deprivation studies, laboratory experiments in which a subject was immersed in water in a blackened room and thus was deprived of his visual, auditory, and kinesthetic senses. The experiments indicated "a general loosening of the subject's ability to perceive reality and the weakening of the stable norms against which perception is evaluated." Later studies at the Navy Air Crew Equipment Laboratory in Philadelphia, the Air Force School of Medicine, and the Wright Air Development Center demonstrated, however, that stable, well-trained persons "can endure severe restrictions of their natural habitat for relatively long periods of time without significant degradation." Gerathewohl, *Principles of Bioastronautics*, 308, 311. See also D. Ewen Cameron et al., "Sensory Deprivation: Effects upon the Functioning Human in Space Systems," in Bernard E. Flaherty, ed., *Psychophysiological Aspects of Space Flight* (New York, 1961), 225–237.

[50] Among astronomers, astrophysicists, and space flight experts there is considerable variation in the uses and definitions of the terms "meteoroid," "meteorite," and "meteor." Throughout this study the authors have employed what is apparently standard NASA terminology: a meteoroid is a solid object larger that a molecule and smaller than an asteroid, moving in interplanetary space; a meteorite is such an object that reaches Earth's surface without completely vaporizing in the atmosphere; and a meteor is the light phenomenon resulting from a meteoroid's entrance into the atmosphere.

[51] Hanrahan and Bushnell, *Space Biology*,

31; George Grimminger, "Probability That a Meteorite Will Hit or Penetrate a Body Situated in the Vicinity of the Earth," *Journal of Applied Physics*, XIX (Oct. 1948), 947–956; Fred L. Whipple, "Meteoric Phenomena and Meteorites: The Conquest of Interplanetary Space," in White and Benson, eds., *Physics and Medicine of the Upper Atmosphere*, 137–170. On the meteoroid phenomenon see also Whipple, "Meteorite Material in Space," in Benson and Strughold, eds., *Physics and Medicine of the Atmosphere and Space*.

[52] Hanrahan and Bushnell, *Space Biology*, 31.

[53] A. B. Thompson, "Physiological and Psychological Considerations for Manned Space Flight," Report E9R–12349, Rev., Chance Vought Aircraft, Inc., Dallas, July 7, 1959, 115.

[54] On cosmic radiation see, for example, James A. Van Allen, "The Nature and Intensity of the Cosmic Radiation," in White and Benson, eds., *Physics and Medicine of the Upper Atmosphere*, 239–266; Joseph A. Connor, "Space Radiation Protection," NASA–MSC fact sheet No. 106; Hermann J. Schaefer, "Appraisal of Cosmic-Ray Hazards in Extra-Atmospheric Flight," in Alperin, Stern, and Wooster, eds., *Vistas in Astronautics*, 291–298; Gerathewohl, *Principles of Bioastronautics*, 133–138; and C. Frederick Hansen, "The Characteristics of the Upper Atmosphere Pertaining to Hypervelocity Flight," *Jet Propulsion*, XXVII (Nov. 1957), 1155–1156.

[55] Emme, *Aeronautics and Astronautics*, 77, 82.

[56] On Unidentified Flying Objects see several works by Donald E. Keyhoe, especially *Flying Saucers in Outer Space* (New York, 1953); and Donald H. Menzel, *Flying Saucers* (Cambridge, Mass., 1953).

[57] Malcolm D. Ross, "A Consideration of the U.S. Navy Strato-Lab Balloon Program and Its Contributions to Manned Space Flight," in *Proceedings of the Second National Conference on the Peaceful Uses of Space, Seattle, Washington, May 8–10, 1962*, NASA SP–8 (Washington, 1962), 261.

[58] Gerathewohl, *Principles of Bioastronautics*, 475–476.

[59] David G. Simons, "The 1954 Aeromedical Field Laboratory Balloon Flights: Physiological and Radiobiological Aspects," *Journal of Aviation Medicine*, XXVII (Apr. 1956), 100–110; Simons interview; Bushnell, "Major

527

Achievements in Space Biology at the Air Force Missile Development Center," 2-12.

[60] David G. Simons, "Psychophysiological Aspects of Manhigh," *Astronautics,* IV (Feb. 1959), 32-33; Bushnell, "Major Achievements in Space Biology at the Air Force Missile Development Center," 27-34.

[61] David G. Simons, "Manhigh II," Technical Report 59-28, Air Force Missile Development Center, Holloman Air Force Base, N. Mex., June 1959; Simons, "Psychophysiological Aspects of Manhigh," 33, 62; Simons, "Observations in High-Altitude, Sealed-Cabin Balloon Flight," in Gantz, ed., *Man in Space,* 133-160; Simons et al., "Personal Experiences in Space Equivalent Flight," in Flaherty, ed., *Psychophysiological Aspects of Space Flight,* 39-41; Bushnell, "Major Achievements in Space Biology at the Air Force Missile Development Center," 34-41; Simons, "Space Medicine—the Human Body in Space," monograph No. 6, *Journal of the Franklin Institute Series,* Dec. 1958, 169-178; Simons interview. For a popularly written personal account of the *Manhigh II* flight see David G. Simons and Don Schanche, *Man High* (Garden City, N.Y., 1960).

[62] "Manhigh III: USAF Manned Balloon Flight into the Stratosphere," Tech. Report 60-16, April 1961; Simons, "Psychophysiological Aspects of Manhigh," 63; Simons et al., "Personal Experiences in Space Equivalent Flight," 41-43.

[63] Simons, "Observations in High-Altitude, Sealed-Cabin Balloon Flight," 146. See also Simons, "Manhigh Balloon Flights in Perspective," in *Proceedings of the Second National Conference on the Peaceful Uses of Space,* 243-248. Simons' record for a manned ascent stood until May 4, 1961, when Cdr. Malcolm Ross and Lt. Cdr. Victor G. Prather reached 113,740 feet in an Office of Naval Research *Strato-Lab High V* balloon, launched from the carrier *Antietam.* Prather was killed during helicopter recovery when he stood up in the "horse collar" sling and fell into the ocean.

[64] Simons, "Manhigh II," 272-294; Hanrahan and Bushnell, *Space Biology,* 171-172; Simons interview.

[65] Simons, "Observations in High-Altitude, Sealed-Cabin Balloon Flight," 137; Simons, interview. On Air Force solar flare observatories, see David Bushnell, "The Sacramento Peak Observatory, 1947-1962," Air Force Office of Aerospace Research, 1962.

[66] Gerathewohl, *Principles of Bioastronautics,* 136-138; Hanrahan and Bushnell, *Space Biology,* 180-187; Connor, "Space Radiation Protection"; James A. Van Allen, "On the Radiation Hazards of Space Flight," in Benson and Strughold, eds., *Physics and Medicine of the Atmosphere and Space,* 2-11; House Committee on Science and Astronautics, 86 Cong., 1 sess. (1959), *U.S. Aeronautics and Space Activities, Jan. 1 to Dec. 31, 1958: Message from the President of the United States,* 3, 4.

[67] Simons, "Space Medicine—the Human Body in Space," 162.

[68] Connor, "Space Radiation Protection"; Hanrahan and Bushnell, *Space Biology,* 179-180, 187-188.

[69] F. L. Van der Wal and W. D. Young, "Project MIA (Mouse-In-Able), Experiments on Physiological Response to Space Flight," *Jet Propulsion,* XXXI (Oct. 1959), 716-720; Ashton Graybiel, et al., "An Account of Experiments in Which Two Monkeys Were Recovered Unharmed after Ballistic Space Flight," *Aerospace Medicine,* XXX (Dec. 1959), 871-931; House Committee on Science and Astronautics, 86 Cong., 1 sess. (1959), *Jupiter Missile Shot—Biomedical Experiments, Hearings;* David S. Akens, *Historical Origins of the George C. Marshall Space Flight Center* (Huntsville, Ala., 1960), 52, 54-56; Gerathewohl, *Principles of Bioastronautics,* 98-108; Mae M. Link, *Space Medicine in Project Mercury,* NASA SP-4003 (Washington, 1965), 27-28.

Chapter III

[1] See Derek J. de Solla Price, *Little Science, Big Science* (New York, 1963); and A. Hunter Dupree, *Science in the Federal Government: A History of Policies and Activities to 1940* (Cambridge, Mass., 1957), 1-2, 369-391.

[2] Quoted in Frank J. Malina, "Origins and First Decade of the Jet Propulsion Laboratory," in Eugene M. Emme, ed., *The History of Rocket Technology: Essays on Research, Development, and Utility* (Detroit, 1964), 52.

[3] *Thirty-Fourth Annual Report of the National Advisory Committee for Aeronautics— 1948* (Washington, 1951), 37.

[4] Hugh L. Dryden, "NACA: What It's Doing and Where It's Going," *Missiles and Rockets,* I (Oct. 1956), 44-46; *Thirty-Fifth Annual Report of the NACA—1949* (Washington, 1951), 19; *Thirty-Sixth Annual Report*

of the NACA—1950 (Washington, 1951), 33; Thirty-Seventh Annual Report of the NACA—1951 (Washington, 1952), 26; Thirty-Eighth Annual Report of the NACA—1952 (Washington, 1954), 38; Thirty-Ninth Annual Report of the NACA—1953 (Washington, 1955), 30–31; Arthur S. Levine, "U.S. Aeronautical Research Policy, 1915–1958: A Study of the Major Policy Decisions of the National Advisory Committee for Aeronautics," unpublished Ph. D. dissertation, Columbia University, 1963, 111–112. NACA's contribution to the International Geophysical Year's Project Vanguard was limited to the calculation of optimum satellite trajectories.

[5] Hugh L. Dryden, "Fact Finding for Tomorrow's Planes," National Geographic, CIV (Dec. 1953), 772. Dryden, a distinguished physicist with the National Bureau of Standards and a member of NACA's Committee on Aerodynamics since the 1930s, became the Director of NACA in 1949. Despite the tremendous acceleration of the space program in the 1960s, Dryden's words were prophetic for himself if not for his generation. He died in December 1965, two months before the first major launch in the Apollo program.

[6] Minutes, NACA Committee on Aerodynamics, Wallops Island, Va., June 24, 1952, 19–21; memo, M. B. Ames, Jr., Acting Asst. Dir. for Research, to Langley Aeronautical Laboratory, "Research on Space Flight and Associated Problems," July 10, 1952; memo, John W. Crowley, Assoc. Dir. for Research, to Ames Aeronautical Laboratory, "Research on Space Flight and Associated Problems," Aug. 26, 1952; memo, Crowley to Langley Aeronautical Laboratory, "Research on Space Flight and Associated Problems," Aug. 31, 1952; minutes, NACA Executive Committee, Moffett Field, Calif., July 14, 1952, 15, NASA Historical Archives, Washington.

[7] Memo, Henry J. E. Reid, Dir., Langley Aeronautical Laboratory, to NACA, "Research on Space Flight and Associated Problems," Aug. 5, 1952; NACA Research Authorization A73L95, Sept. 8, 1952.

[8] Memo, Reid to NACA, "Meeting of Committee on Aerodynamics at Wallops Island on June 24, 1952," May 26, 1952.

[9] Memo, Smith J. DeFrance, Dir., Ames Aeronautical Laboratory, to NACA, "Report on Research of Interest to Committee on Aerodynamics," May 29, 1952.

[10] "NACA Views Concerning a New Research Airplane," NACA, Washington, Aug. 1954. On the development of nickel for use in aircraft construction see F. B. Howard-White, Nickel: An Historical Review (New York, 1963), 249–258.

[11] Wendell H. Stilwell, X-15 Research Results (Washington, 1965), 11–16; Kenneth S. Kleinknecht, "The Rocket Research Airplanes," in Emme, ed., History of Rocket Technology, 205–208; Editors, Air University Quarterly Review, "The Spiral Toward Space," in Kenneth F. Gantz, ed., Man in Space: The United States Air Force Program for Developing the Spacecraft Crews (New York, 1959), 208–210; Myron E. Gubitz, Rocketship X-15 (New York, 1960); Jules Bergman, Ninety Seconds to Space: The Story of X-15 (New York, 1960). The X-2 was the last rocket-powered research airplane that flew before the X-15 went into operation, although the fifties also saw flights of jet-propelled research craft like the X-3, nicknamed the "Flying Stiletto," the X-4, and the variable-sweep X-5, as well as the rocket-powered X-1B, used by NACA for reaction-control and heating studies. X-15: Research at the Edge of Space, NASA EP-9 (Washington, 1964), 9.

[12] Stilwell, X-15 Research Results, 17–31; Editors, Air University Quarterly Review, "Spiral Toward Space," 210–212; X-15, 11–15; Charles V. Eppley, The Rocket Research Aircraft Program, 1946–1962 (Edwards Air Force Base, Calif., 1962), 25–30; Gubitz, Rocketship X-15, 61–74; John V. Becker, "The X-15 Project: Part I: Origins and Research Background," Astronautics and Aeronautics, II (Feb. 1964), 52–61.

[13] Memo, DeFrance to NACA, "Research on Space Flight and Associated Problems," Sept. 18, 1952.

[14] Mark Morton, "Progress in Reentry-Recovery Vehicle Development," pamphlet, Missile and Space Vehicle Dept., General Electric Co., Philadelphia, Jan. 2, 1961.

[15] Jacques Cattell, ed., American Men of Science: A Biographical Directory: The Physical and Biological Sciences (10 ed., Tempe, Ariz., 1960), 42; H. Julian Allen, biography sheet, NASA/Ames Research Center, Aug. 1963. Besides supporting the aeronautical laboratory at the California Institute of Technology, Guggenheim philanthropies also made possible the establishment of research institutions for aeronautics at Stanford and elsewhere.

[16] Ibid., Alvin Seiff, "A Free-Flight Wind Tunnel for Aerodynamic Testing at Hypersonic Speeds," NACA Tech. Report 1222, Forty-First Annual Report of the NACA—1955 (Wash-

ington, 1957), 381–398; Alvin Seiff and Thomas N. Canning, interviews, Moffett Field, Calif., April 22, 1964. The schlieren method was invented in the early 20th century by the Viennese physics professor and philosopher Ernst Mach, who also devised the unit of measurement representing the ratio of the speed of a body to the speed of sound in the surrounding air, i.e., mach 1. The schlieren technique involves training a beam of light perpendicular to the direction of the airflow to be investigated. A camera is placed behind the light. The camera then photographs a stationary or moving object in the light beam and the surrounding air-streaks, which have varying densities and refractive indices resulting from aerodynamic pressures. See Theodore von Kármán, *Aerodynamics: Selected Topics in the Light of Their Historical Development* (Ithaca, N.Y., 1954), 106–108; and Dr. W. Holder and R. S. North, "Optical Methods of Examining the Flow in High-Speed Wind Tunnels," Part I: "The Schlieren Method," North Atlantic Treaty Organization Advisory Group for Aeronautical Research and Development, Nov. 1956.

[17] H. Julian Allen, interview, Moffett Field, Calif., April 22, 1964.

[18] *Ibid.; Science News Letter,* LXXII (Dec. 21, 1957), 389.

[19] *Ibid.;* Allen C. Fisher, Jr., "Exploring Tomorrow with the Space Agency," *National Geographic,* CXVII (July 1960), 85; *Forty-Third Annual Report of the NACA—1957* (Washington, 1957), 5.

[20] H. Julian Allen and Alfred J. Eggers, Jr., "A Study of the Motion and Aerodynamic Heating of Ballistic Missiles Entering the Earth's Atmosphere at High Supersonic Speeds," NACA Tech. Report 1381, *Forty-Fourth Annual Report of the NACA—1958* (Washington, 1959), 1125–1140. Allen and Eggers pointed out that while the blunt shape was optimum for relatively lightweight reentry bodies, as warheads became heavier the total heat absorbed and the rate of heating would probably dictate longer, more slender shapes. Some blunting at the tip of the body, however, would continue to be desirable. This is precisely the evolution that has occurred over the years as rocket thrust has increased and warheads have grown heavier. See Herman H. Kurzweg, "Basic Research," in *Proceedings of the Second NASA-Industry Program Plans Conference,* NASA SP–29 (Washington, 1963), 127–130.

[21] Letters, H. H. Nininger to Ames Aero-

nautical Laboratory, Aug. 23, 1952; Daniel F. Wentz, Aeronautical Information Specialist, Ames, to Nininger, Sept. 18, 1952; Nininger to Wentz, Sept. 23, 1952; Nininger to Robert Nininger, July 5, 1957; Crowley to Nininger, July 12, 1957, in selected papers of H. H. Nininger 1935–1957, NASA Hist. Archives. Regarding Nininger's claims, Allen has commented: "It is rather ironical that Nininger's 'proof' that blunt bodies are optimum was based on observations of meteorites. All meteorites . . . enter the atmosphere in a speed range for which one can demonstrate that a body which is pointed at the stagnation point is the optimum and not the blunted body as proposed by Dr. Nininger." Letter, Allen to C.C.A., Aug. 17, 1964.

[22] *Forty-Fourth Annual Report,* 30. Doolittle, leader of the famous carrier-based raid of B-25s on Tokyo, succeeded Hunsaker as chairman of the NACA Main Committee in 1956.

[23] Richard V. Rhode, "Structures and Materials Aspect of Manned Flight Systems—Past and Present," NASA/MSC fact sheet, July 12, 1962.

[24] See, for example, David H. Crawford and William D. McCauley, "Investigation of the Laminar Aerodynamic Heat-Transfer Characteristics of the Hemisphere-Cylinder in the Langley 11-Inch Hypersonic Tunnel at a Mach Number of 6.8," NACA Tech. Report 1323, *Forty-Third Annual Report,* 1001–1021; and Jackson R. Stalder, "A Survey of Heat Transfer Problems Encountered by Hypersonic Aircraft," *Jet Propulsion,* XXVII (Nov. 1957), 1178–1184. Throughout the mid- and late fifties other laboratories also carried on research in reentry body configurations, especially the Jet Propulsion Laboratory at the California Institute of Technology, which did contract research for the Army. See Lester Lees, "Laminar Heat Transfer over Blunt-Nosed Bodies at Hypersonic Flight Speeds," *Jet Propulsion,* XXVI (April 1956), 259–269, and "Recent Developments in Hypersonic Flow," *Jet Propulsion,* XXVII (Nov. 1957), 1162–1178.

[25] Rhode, "Structures and Materials Aspects of Manned Flight Systems."

[26] Wernher von Braun, "The Redstone, Jupiter, and Juno," in Emme, ed., *History of Rocket Technology,* 110–111; John W. Bullard, "History of the Redstone Missile System," Hist. Div., Army Missile Command, Oct. 1965, 141–142; Frederick I. Ordway III and Ronald C. Wakeford, *International Missile and*

Spacecraft Guide (New York, 1960), 44–45, 53–54; House Committee on Government Operations, 86 Cong., 2 sess. (1959), House Report No. 1121, *Organization and Management of Missile Programs,* 108.

[26] General Electric Co., Missile and Space Vehicle Dept., *Reentry Vehicles—Man Made Meteors* (Philadelphia, undated).

[26] Von Braun, "Redstone, Jupiter, and Juno," 111; *Reentry Studies,* 2 vols., Vitro Corp. report No. 2331–25, Nov. 25, 1958. On the significance of the differing approaches to the reentry problem of the Air Force and the Army see *Organization and Management of Missile Programs,* 108–109. See also W. R. Lucas and J. E. Kingsbury, "The ABMA Reinforced Plastics Ablation Program," reprint from *Modern Plastics* (Oct. 1960).

[29] Message, John A. Powers, Public Affairs Officer, Space Task Group, to Eugene M. Emme, NASA Historian, July 5, 1960; *Forty-Third Annual Report,* 7; ' Leonard Roberts, "A Theoretical Study of Nose Ablation," and Aleck C. Bond, Bernard Rashis, and L. Ross Levin, "Experimental Nose Ablation," in "NACA Conference on High-Speed Aerodynamics, Ames Aeronautical Laboratory, Moffett Field, Calif., March 18, 19, and 20, 1958, A Compilation of the Papers Presented," 253–284.

[30] Paul E. Purser, log of administrative activities related to space and missile research, Jan. 4, 1956, to April 25, 1958. See also John R. Dawson, "Hydro-dynamic Characteristics of Missiles Launched Under Water," in "NACA Conference on High-Speed Aerodynamics," 177–184.

[31] Maxime A. Faget, interview, Houston, Jan. 9, 1964; Joseph A. Shortal, interview, Langley Field, Va., Jan. 7, 1964.

[32] Seiff and Canning interviews.

[33] Dr. Alfred J. Eggers, Jr., biography sheet, NASA/Ames Research Center, March 1963.

[34] Alfred J. Eggers, Jr., "A Method for Simulating the Atmospheric Entry of Long-Range Ballistic Missiles," NACA Tech. Report 1378, *Forty-Fourth Annual Report,* 1009–1015; *Forty-Third Annual Report,* 5.

[35] Eggers, "Method for Simulating the Atmospheric Entry of Long-Range Missiles," 1014; *Forty-Third Annual Report,* 6–7; Clarence V. Syvertson, interview, Moffett Field, Calif., April 22, 1964; letter, Eggers to C.C.A., June 24, 1964. For the kind of research done in the simulator, see Stanford E. Neice, "Preliminary Experimental Study of

Entry Heating Using the Atmospheric Entry Simulator," in "NACA Conference on High-Speed Aerodynamics," 285–312.

[36] The critical problem of aerodynamic heating on the skip vehicle was not considered in the theoretical work on an antipodal bomber done by Eugen Sänger and Irene Bredt for the Luftwaffe in World War II. See Eugen Sänger, *Rocket Flight Engineering,* NASA TT F-223 (Washington, 1965).

[37] Alfred J. Eggers, Jr., H. Julian Allen, and Stanford E. Neice, "A Comparative Analysis of the Performance of Long-Range Hypervelocity Vehicles," NACA Tech. Report 1382, *Forty-Fourth Annual Report,* 1141–1160. A modified version of this paper is Allen, "Hypersonic Flight and the Reentry Problem," *Journal of the Aeronautical Sciences,* XXV (April 1958), 217–230.

[38] Alfred J. Eggers, "Performance of Long Range Hypervelocity Vehicles," *Jet Propulsion,* XXVII (Nov. 1957), 1147–1151. Actually the peak temperatures on the heatshield of the Mercury spacecraft during its reentry from an orbital mission reached approximately 3000 degrees F.

[39] Eggers' design is sometimes erroneously referred to as the "sled," after the nickname for a quite similar proposal first made in 1957 by Antonio Ferri and two others at the Gruen Applied Science Laboratories, of Hempstead, New York. See Antonio Ferri, Lewis Feldman, and Walter Daskin, "The Use of Lift for Re-entry from Satellite Trajectories," *Jet Propulsion,* XXVII (Nov. 1957), 1184–1191. Ferri, Feldman, and Daskin described a high-drag configuration which by flying at a proper angle of attack could produce a comparable amount of lift. Their vehicle would have an open top surface, and in this open area would be located a bubble-canopy sealed cabin. Reentry would be along a phugoid skip trajectory, with the lower surface of the vehicle acting as a heat sink.

[40] Purser log.

[41] Eggers letter; Syvertson interview.

[42] Memo, Major George D. Colchagoff to Lt. Col. R. C. Anderson, "New Research Systems," Feb. 16, 1956; Colchagoff interview, Washington, December 3, 1964; "Chronology of Early USAF Man-in-Space Activity, 1945–1958," Air Force Systems Command, 3–4.

[43] Colchagoff memo. Since 1952 the Air Force had sponsored studies of the rocket-launched glider concept at the Bell Aircraft Corp. (Project Bomi). These studies had been instigated at Bell by Walter Dornberger.

who was intrigued by the antipodal rocket bomber proposed during the war in Germany by Sänger and Bredt. See Sänger, *Rocket Flight Engineering.*

[44] Letter, David Bushnell to J. M. G., Dec. 11, 1964; Colchagoff interview; "Chronology of Early USAF Man-in-Space Activity, 1945–1958," 4–5.

[45] "Chronology of Early Air Force Man-in-Space Activity, 1955–1960," Air Force Systems Command, 1.

[46] House Select Committee on Astronautics and Space Exploration, 85 Cong., 2 sess. (1958), *Astronautics and Space Exploration, Hearings,* testimony of Arthur Kantrowitz, 509.

[47] "Chronology of Early Air Force Man-in-Space Activity, 1955–1960," 2–6; Mae M. Link, *Space Medicine in Project Mercury,* NASA SP-4003 (Washington, 1965), 23–24; "Chronology of Early USAF Man-in-Space Activity, 1945–1958," 6. The Western Development Division was renamed the Ballistic Missile Division on June 1, 1957.

[48] Minutes, NACA Executive Committee, Washington, Feb. 21, 1957, 7–8, NASA Hist. Archives.

[49] "Preliminary Investigation of a New Research Airplane for Exploring the Problems of Efficient Hypersonic Flight," NACA/Ames Aeronautical Laboratory, Moffett Field, Calif., Jan. 18, 1957. This Ames proposal for a hypervelocity glider with a round bottom for heat protection should not be confused with Eggers' M-1 concept, which was planned as a much smaller manned satellite vehicle. The technical kinship between the two, however, is obvious.

[50] Letter, Hartley A. Soulé to J. M. G., Aug. 29, 1965.

[51] Letter, Crowley to Edward W. Sharp, Dir., Lewis, June 17, 1957; letter, Crowley to Reid, Langley, June 17, 1957; memo, Crowley to Ames, "Meeting of Round III Steering Committee to be held at NACA Headquarters, July 2, 1957," June 18, 1957; memo for Dir., Clotaire Wood, "Presentation to Air Force Headquarters on Round III," July 11, 1957; "Study of the Feasibility of a Hypersonic Research Airplane," NACA, Washington, Sept. 8, 1957.

[52] *Ibid.,* 6–24. The term "Round Three," as used by the NACA and Air Force, referred to the third phase of the research airplane program, the first beginning with the X-1 and extending through the X-2, the second being the X-15.

[53] Eggers letter; Paul Purser, interview,

Houston, Feb. 12, 1964; Faget, interview, Aug. 24, 1964.

[54] Hartley Soulé recalled that during the Round Three Conference, Faget asked for the floor and declared that NACA had misplaced its research emphasis, that he would spend no more effort on the Round Three concept, and that henceforth he would go to work on orbiting a man as fast as possible. "For me," said Soulé, "Project Mercury was born with Faget's remarks. . . ." Soulé letter.

[55] This was a phrase current in ARDC in 1956–1957, Colchagoff interview; Virgil I. Grissom, interview, Houston, April 12, 1965.

[56] *Astronautics and Space Exploration,* testimony of Kantrowitz, 510; "Chronology of Early Air Force Man-in-Space Activity, 1955–1960," 14–15; "Chronology of Early USAF Man-in-Space Activity, 1945–1958," 8.

[57] *Ibid.;* Link, *Space Medicine in Project Mercury,* 24.

[58] Chronology of Early Air Force Man-in-Space Activity, 1955–1960," 15; House Committee on Science and Astronautics, 87 Cong., 1 sess. (1961), House Report No. 67, *A Chronology of Missile and Astronautic Events,* 36; *New York Times,* Dec. 11, 14, 1957.

[59] "Chronology of Early Air Force Man-in-Space Activity, 1955–1960," 12, 18–19.

[60] Letter, Donald L. Putt, Deputy Chief of Staff, Development, United States Air Force, to Dryden, Director, NACA, Jan. 31, 1958.

[61] Memorandum of Understanding, "Principles for Participation of NACA in Development and Testing of the Air Force System 464L Hypersonic Boost Glide Vehicle (Dyna-Soar I)," May 20, 1958, NASA Hist. Archives. In July 1958 the Air Force awarded concurrent feasibility study contracts to two contractor teams headed by the Martin Company and the Boeing Company. Almost two years later, after Project Mercury was well underway, Martin was chosen to build the booster system and Boeing the hypersonic vehicle itself. By that time the Dyna-Soar concept called for a true satellite vehicle acting as a controllable glider in the atmosphere. After a complex and controversial history, Dyna-Soar finally fell victim to leapfrogging space technology, particularly the two-man Gemini program initiated by NASA. Economy drives in the Defense Department also played a part in this December 10, 1963, decision. After an expenditure of over $350 million without a single test flight, and in the face of a predicted total cost of around $800 million, Secretary of Defense Robert S. McNamara ordered the can-

cellation of the Dyna-Soar project. On the general characteristics of Dyna-Soar see, for example, Senate Committee on Aeronautical and Space Sciences, 87 Cong., 2 sess. (1962), *Manned Space Flight Program of the National Aeronautics and Space Administration: Projects Mercury, Gemini, and Apollo,* 151–154; Glenn L. Martin Co. advertisement, *Space/ Aeronautics,* XXX (Dec. 1958), 78; "Dyna-Soar's History Full of Re-examinations," *Aviation Week,* LXXVII (July 22, 1963), 233; and Martin Caidin, *Rendezvous in Space* (New York, 1962), 260–269.

[62] "Chronology of Early USAF Man-in-Space Activity, 1945–1958," 13; House Committee on Science and Astronautics, 86 Cong., 1 sess. (1960), *Project Mercury, First Interim Report,* 3.

Chapter IV

[1] Minutes, NACA Committee on Aerodynamics, *Forrestal,* Nov. 18–20, 1957, 17–18.

[2] Minutes, NACA Executive Committee, Washington, Nov. 21, 1957, 6–5, NASA Hist. Archives, Washington. Jerome C. Hunsaker, who only the previous year had resigned the chairmanship of the Main Committee, initially was offered the chairmanship of the Special Committee on Space Technology, but he declined.

[3] Minutes, NACA Executive Committee, Washington, Feb. 20, 1958, NASA Hist. Archives.

[4] Hugh L. Dryden, interview, Washington, Aug. 31, 1965; Paul G. Dembling, interview, Washington, Sept. 2, 1965.

[5] Minutes, NACA Executive Committee, Washington, Jan. 16, 1958, NASA Hist. Archives; Arthur S. Levine, "United States Aeronautical Research Policy, 1915–1958: A Study of the Major Policy Decisions of the National Advisory Committee for Aeronautics," unpublished Ph. D. dissertation, Columbia University, 1963, 146–147.

[6] The speech was published in somewhat revised form as "Space Technology and the NACA," *Aeronautical Engineering Review,* XVII (March 1958), 32–34, 44. See also Jay Holmes, *America on the Moon: The Enterprise of the Sixties* (Philadelphia, 1962), 72.

[7] NACA Lewis Staff, "A Program for Expansion of NACA Research in Space Flight Technology, with Estimates of the Staff and Facilities Required," Washington, Feb. 10, 1958.

[8] See *Historical Sketch of NASA,* SP-29

(Washington, 1965), 5–9.

[9] "Chronology of Early USAF Man-in-Space Activity, 1945–1958," Air Force Systems Command, 11–12; "Chronology of Early Air Force Man-in-Space Activity, 1955–1960," Air Force Systems Command, 24.

[10] See n. 39, chap. III.

[11] Memo, Clarence A. Syvertson to Dir., Ames Aeronautical Laboratory, "Visit to WADC, Wright-Patterson AFB, Ohio, to Attend Conference on January 29–31, Concerning Research Problems Associated with Placing a Man in a Satellite Vehicle," Feb. 18, 1958. For a more detailed rundown of the company proposals presented at the conference, see James M. Grimwood, *Project Mercury: A Chronology,* NASA SP-4001 (Washington, 1963), 14–15.

[12] "Chronology of Early USAF Man-in-Space Activity, 1945–1958," 13–15; "Chronology of Early Air Force Man-in-Space Activity, 1955–1960," 27–32.

[13] "Chronology of Early USAF Man-in-Space Activity, 1945–1958," 16; George D. Colchagoff, interview, Washington, Dec. 3, 1964.

[14] See John B. Medaris, *Countdown for Decision* (New York, 1960); and David S. Akens, *Historical Origins of the George C. Marshall Space Flight Center* (Huntsville, Ala., 1960).

[15] House Committee on Science and Astronautics, 86 Cong., 1 sess. (1959), *U.S. Aeronautics and Space Activities, Jan. 1 to Dec. 31, 1958: Message from the President of the United States,* 8; Mary Stone Ambrose, "The National Space Program," unpublished M.A. thesis, 2 vols., American University, 1960–1961, I, 51–53; Levine, "U.S. Aeronautical Research Policy," 149–150.

[16] "Chronology of Early USAF Man-in-Space Activity, 1945–1958," 16; "Chronology of Early Air Force Man-in-Space Activity, 1955–1960," 33–34. The first successful flight of the Atlas, as noted earlier, came on Dec. 17, 1957, when an Atlas-A, a test rocket minus the sustainer engine, impacted on its target about 500 miles downrange from Cape Canaveral. On Dec. 19, 1957, a Thor made its first fully guided flight with an all-inertial guidance system. See Julian Hartt, *The Mighty Thor: Missile in Readiness* (New York, 1961), 70–75.

[17] "Chronology of Early USAF Man-in-Space Activity, 1945–1958," 17–18; memo, Lawrence A. Clousing to Dir., Ames Aeronautical Laboratory, "Working Conference for the Air Force 'Man-in-Space Soonest' Program, held March 10-11-12, 1958, at the Air Force

Ballistic Missile Division Offices, Los Angeles," March 24, 1958.

[15] *Ibid.*

[17] *Ibid.*

[20] *Ibid.;* John P. Stapp and David G. Simons, interviews, San Antonio, April 24, 1964.

[21] See Otto Gauer, "The Physiological Effect of Prolonged Weightlessness," in U.S. Air Force, *German Aviation Medicine, World War II* (2 vols., Washington, 1950), I, 577.

[22] Clousing memo; "Chronology of Early USAF Man-in-Space Activity, 1945–1958," 11–12.

[23] *Ibid.*, "Chronology of Early Air Force Man-in-Space Activity, 1955–1960," 37–38; Clousing memo.

[24] See pp. 73–74.

[25] Memo, Ira H. Abbott, Asst. Dir. for Research, to Langley Aeronautical Laboratory, Ames Aeronautical Laboratory, Lewis Flight Propulsion Laboratory, and High Speed Flight Station, "Meeting of the Steering Committee for a New Research Vehicle," Feb. 19, 1958; memo, Hartley A. Soulé, "Meeting of the Steering Committee for a New Research Vehicle System at Ames Laboratory on March 11, 1958," March 12, 1958.

[26] Memo, John W. Crowley, Assoc. Dir. for Research, NACA, to Comdr., Air Research and Development Command, "Man-in-Space— NACA Participation in Preparing Abbreviated Development Plan," March 14, 1958; Proposed Memorandum of Understanding, "Principles for the Conduct by the NACA and the Air Force of a Joint Project for a Recoverable Manned Satellite Test Vehicle," April 11, 1958; memo, Clotaire Wood, Asst. Dir. for Research Management, to Dir. of Research and Development, Office of Deputy Chief of Staff, Development, Hq. USAF, "Transmittal of Copies of Proposed Memorandum of Understanding Between Air Force and NACA for Joint NACA-Air Force Project for a Recoverable Manned Satellite Test Vehicle," April 11, 1958; memo for files, Wood, "Tabling of Proposed Memorandum of Understanding Between Air Force and NACA for a Joint Project for a Recoverable Manned Satellite Test Vehicle," May 20, 1958. See also memo for historical files, Dryden, "The Signed Agreement of April 11, 1958, on a Recoverable Manned Satellite Test Vehicle," Sept. 8, 1965. The postponed joint NACA-Air Force manned satellite project should not be confused with the cooperative arrangement set up for Dyna-Soar, a formal agreement on which was signed by NACA and the Air Force in May 1958.

[27] Quoted in Senate Committee on Aeronautical and Space Sciences, 88 Cong., 1 sess. (1963), *Documents on International Aspects of the Exploration and Use of Outer Space, 1954–1962*, Staff Report No. 18, 52–53. See also Dwight D. Eisenhower, *The White House Years: Waging Peace, 1956–1961* (Garden City, N.Y., 1965).

[28] President's Scientific Advisory Committee, *Introduction to Outer Space,* in Senate Special Committee on Space and Astronautics, 85 Cong., 2 sess. (1958), *Compilation of Materials on Outer Space, No. 1,* 45–46. The foregoing account of the work of PSAC in the late winter of 1958 is taken mainly from interviews with Dryden, Wood, and Dembling, Washington, Aug. 31, Sept. 1 and 2, 1965; and memo, Dryden for Eugene M. Emme for NASA Historical Files, "The NACA–NASA Transition, October 1957 to October 1958," Sept. 8, 1965.

[29] Levine, "U.S. Aeronautical Research Policy," 151–156; Ambrose, "National Space Program," I, 79–87; Robert L. Rosholt, *An Administrative History of NASA, 1958–1963,* NASA SP–4101 (Washington, 1966), 6–12; Dryden interview. Eisenhower's message of April 2 is reprinted, among many other places, in House Select Committee on Astronautics and Space Exploration, 85 Cong., 2 sess. (1958), *Astronautics and Space Exploration, Hearings,* 820–821.

[30] The administration bill is reprinted, among other places, in *Astronautics and Space Exploration,* 11–15. The legislative history of the bill is discussed in detail in Alison E. Griffith, *The National Aeronautics and Space Act: A Study of Public Policy* (Washington, 1962).

[31] Indicative of the widespread and growing concern at Langley over the prospect of space flight was a special course in basic space technology, given by members of the Flight Research Division from Feb. to May 1958. The lectures covered such subjects as lunar orbits, rocket operation, aerodynamic heating of spacecraft, and the medical problems of space flight. See "Notes on Space Technology Compiled by the Flight Research Division," Langley Aeronautical Laboratory, Feb.–May 1958. One of the members of the Flight Research Division at the time has referred to these collected lectures as "essentially the first U.S. textbook in space flight technology." John P. Mayer, comments, Sept. 8, 1965.

[32] This estimate was broken down into 30 percent space research in aerodynamics, 20 percent in propulsion, and 5 percent in structures.

Minutes, NACA Committee on Aerodynamics, Moffett Field, Calif., March 21, 1958, 6.

[33] "National Advisory Committee for Aeronautics, Organization and Distribution of Effort Related to Space Research for the Fiscal Year 1958," chart in *Astronautics and Space Exploration,* 404–405.

[34] These generalizations are based on conversations with various senior members of the technical staff at what is now the NASA Ames Research Center, Moffett Field, Calif., April 22–23, 1964. During this visit mottoes such as "NACA Forever" and "NASA Go Home" were observed posted around the laboratories.

[35] Paul E. Purser, interview, Houston, Feb. 12, 1964.

[36] See Ms., anon., "NACA Research into Space," Washington, Dec. 1957; and William M. Bland, Jr., "The Design of Multistage Rocket Vehicles for Hypersonic Research," Langley, 1958.

[37] For the characteristics of the Scout see "Considerations Affecting Satellite and Space Probe Research with Emphasis on the 'Scout' as a Launch Vehicle," NASA Tech. Report R–97, Washington, 1961.

[38] Maxime A. Faget, biography sheet, NASA/MSC, May 1963.

[39] Charles W. Mathews, interview, Houston, Feb. 24, 1964; Faget, interview, Houston, Aug. 24, 1964; Purser, log of administrative activities related to space and missile research, Jan. 4, 1956, to April 25, 1958.

[40] "NACA Conference on High-Speed Aerodynamics, Ames Aeronautical Laboratory, Moffett Field, Calif., March 18, 19, and 20, 1958: A Compilation of the Papers Presented."

[41] Maxime A. Faget, Benjamine J. Garland, and James J. Buglia, "Preliminary Studies of Manned Satellites—Wingless Configurations: Nonlifting," *ibid.,* 9–34.

[42] John V. Becker, "Preliminary Studies of Manned Satellites—Winged Configurations," *ibid.,* 45–58.

[43] Thomas J. Wong, Charles A. Hermach, John O. Reller, Jr., and Bruce E. Tinling, "Preliminary Studies of Manned Satellites—Wingless Configurations: Lifting Body," *ibid.,* 35–40.

[44] Letter, Alfred J. Eggers to C. C. A., June 24, 1964.

[45] Faget interview.

[46] For the specific problems in launching and recovering a manned satellite being examined at Langley, see the outline "Manned Satellite Program, Prepared by the NACA staff, March 12, 1958."

[47] Rosholt, *Administrative History of NASA,* 37–40; memo, Warren J. North to NASA Administrator, "Background of Project Mercury Schedules," with enclosures, Aug. 14, 1960.

[48] "Chronology of Early USAF Man-in-Space Activity, 1945–1958," 19–20; "Chronology of Early Air Force Man-in-Space Activity, 1955–1960," 38–39. See pp. 81–82.

[49] "Chronology of Early Air Force Man-in-Space Activity, 1955–1960," 41, 43–44; "Chronology of Early USAF Man-in-Space Activity, 1945–1958," 21–22. See also Mae M. Link, *Space Medicine in Project Mercury,* NASA SP–4003 (Washington, 1965), 25.

[50] "Chronology of Early USAF Man-in-Space Activity, 1945–1958," 23.

[51] "Proposal for a Manned Satellite," Avco Manufacturing Corp., and Convair/Astronautics Div., General Dynamics Corp., April 30, 1958.

[52] "Chronology of Early USAF Man-in-Space Activity, 1945–1958," 22–23; "Chronology of Early Air Force Man-in-Space Activity, 1955–1960," 45–46.

[53] Memo for files, Faget, "Attendance at ARDC Briefing on 'Man in Space' Program," March 5, 1958. See also memo to NACA, Soulé, "Second Discussion of ARDC Briefing on 'Man in Space' Program," March 27, 1958.

[54] "Chronology of Early USAF Man-in-Space Activity, 1945–1958," 23–34; "Outline of History of USAF Man-in-Space Research and Development Program," Air Force information policy letter supplement No. 109, Aug., 1962, published in *Missiles and Rockets,* X (March 26, 1962), 148; memo, Crowley to Langley, Ames, Lewis Laboratories and High Speed Flight Station, "An AVCO-Convair Proposal for Manned Satellite," May 16, 1958.

[55] "Chronology of Early USAF Man-in-Space Activity, 1945–1958," 25.

[56] See memo, Herbert F. York, Chief Scientist, ARPA, to Roy W. Johnson, "Next Steps to be Taken in Formulating Man in Space Program," June 7, 1958.

[57] "Chronology of Early USAF Man-in-Space Activity, 1945–1958," 25–27; "Outline of History of USAF Man-in-Space Program," 148.

[58] Faget interview; memo, Faget to Dryden, "Faget Dealings with ARPA during the Past Several Weeks," June 5, 1958; York memo.

[59] "Outline of History of Man-in-Space Program," 149; "Chronology of Early USAF Man-in-Space Activity, 1945–1958," 26;

"Chronology of Early Air Force Man-in-Space Activity, 1955–1960," 53–54.

⁶⁰ See "Current NACA Aerodynamic Research Relating to Upper Atmosphere and Space Technology," NACA Hq., March 10, 1958; "NACA Research into Space," 6–15; memo, Purser to Robert R. Gilruth, "Langley Manned Satellite Program," April 11, 1958.

⁶¹ Purser interview.

⁶² Purser log; Grimwood, *Mercury Chronology*, 14; William M. Bland, Jr., "Project Mercury," in Eugene M. Emme, ed., *The History of Rocket Technology: Essays on Research, Development, and Utility* (Detroit, 1964), 212.

⁶³ Purser log; Purser memo.

⁶⁴ "How the Mercury Capsule Design Evolved," *Aviation Week*, LXX (Sept. 21, 1959), 52–53; letter, Alan B. Kehlet to L.S.S., July 2, 1964; Faget interview.

⁶⁵ "How Mercury Capsule Design Evolved," 53–54; Christopher C. Kraft, Jr., "A Review of Knowledge Acquired from the First Manned Satellite Program," NASA/MSC fact sheet No. 206.

⁶⁶ William E. Stoney, Jr., "Aerodynamic Heating of Blunt Nose Shapes at Mach Numbers Up to 14," in "NACA Conference on High-Speed Aerodynamics, Ames Aeronautical Laboratory, Moffett Field, Calif., March 18, 19, and 20, 1958, A Compilation of the Papers Presented," 227–244; Stoney, interview, Houston, Feb. 13, 1964; Alvin Seiff and Thomas N. Canning, interviews, Moffett Field, Calif., April 22, 1964.

⁶⁷ Wood, interview, Washington, Sept. 1, 1965; memo, Wood, "Background on WADC Letter to NASA of October 22, 1958, Covering 'Ablation/Heat Sink Investigation—Manned Reentry,'" Nov. 7, 1958. The Air Force and NACA investigators completed their tests in October 1958. ARDC had conducted tests at the Chicago Midway Laboratories, while the NACA engineers had worked in the hot jet facilities at Langley. Both groups devoted most of their time to studies of ablation. Memo, Lester J. Charnock, Tech. Dir., Deputy Chief of Staff for Plans and Operations, to Comdr., Air Research and Development Command, "Ablation/Heat Sink Investigation—Manned Reentry," Oct. 21, 1958.

⁶⁸ Memo, George M. Low to NASA Administrator, "House Committee Staff Report on Project Mercury," Jan. 26, 1960; "How Mercury Capsule Design Evolved," 55; Willard S. Blanchard, interview, Langley Field, Va., Jan. 6, 1964; Bland, "Project Mercury," 215.

⁶⁹ Besides fear of excessive g on the abort-reentry flight profile, the Air Force was reluctant to use the bare Atlas because of its unproven nature and because it supposedly would place a capsule in a lower orbit than the Thor-fluorine rocket, necessitating more tracking stations to maintain constant voice contact with the human passenger.

⁷⁰ Stanley C. White, interview, San Antonio, Aug. 18, 1965.

⁷¹ See pp. 43–46.

⁷² Faget, marginal notes on "Outline of History of Man-in-Space Program."

⁷³ "Outline of History of Man-in-Space Program," 149.

⁷⁴ "Chronology of Early USAF Man-in-Space Activity, 1945–1958," 28–29; "Chronology of Early USAF Man-in-Space Activity, 1955–1960," 58–60.

⁷⁵ Colchagoff interview; "Outline of History of Man-in-Space Program," 149; "Chronology of Early USAF Man-in-Space Activity, 1955–1960," 60–62; "Chronology of Early USAF Man-in-Space Activity, 1945–1958," 29–30. Some sense of the frustration felt by various Air Force leaders regarding man-in-space plans during this period can be gained from the biographical sketch on Brig. Gen. Don D. Flickinger in Shirley Thomas, *Men of Space* (6 vols., Philadelphia, 1960–1963), III, 77–79.

⁷⁶ Public Law 85–568, 85 Cong., 2 sess. (1958), H.R. 12575, *National Aeronautics and Space Act of 1958*, Sec. 203(a).

⁷⁷ Charles S. Sheldon II, interview, Washington, Sept. 2, 1965; Glen P. Wilson, interview, Washington, Sept. 2, 1965.

⁷⁸ Frank Gibney and George F. Feldman, *The Reluctant Space-Farers: A Study in the Discovery of Politics* (New York, 1965), 68.

⁷⁹ Rosholt, *Administrative History of NASA*, 13–15; Ambrose, "National Space Program," I, 92–152; Levine, "U.S. Aeronautical Research Policy," 172–180. The Space Council consisted of the Secretaries of State and Defense, the Administrator of NASA, the Chairman of the Atomic Energy Commission, and the President.

⁸⁰ Senate Special Committee on Space and Astronautics, 85 Cong., 2 sess. (1958), *Nominations, Hearings on the Nomination of T. Keith Glennan and Hugh L. Dryden.*

⁸¹ Rosholt, *Administrative History of NASA*, 40–42; memo for Dir., NACA, Ira H. Abbott, Ralph E. Cushman, Paul G. Dembling, Robert J. Lacklan, Ralph E. Ulmer, Clotaire Wood, "Submittal of Final Report of Ad Hoc Committee on NASA Organization based on the

National Aeronautics and Space Act of 1958," Aug. 12, 1958; memo for Dir., NACA, "Functions of Organizational Elements in NASA Headquarters," July 25, 1958.

[52] "Development Proposal for Project Adam," Army Ballistic Missile Agency, Redstone Arsenal, Ala., April 17, 1958. The Adam concept involved use of drag flaps to slow the nose cone's rate of descent and provide aerodynamic stability during reentry. At lower altitudes, parachutes would deploy to slow the capsule down still more. The development plan for Adam specified that several primate flights would precede the first manned shot. Unquestionably the most unusual technical aspect of Adam, and one that later produced considerable amusement among the engineers who directed Project Mercury, was the tank filled with water, into which the payload would be tossed by an automatic mechanism in case of booster malfunction on the launch pad.

[53] Message, John B. Medaris to August Schomburg, Chief of Ordnance, Dept. of the Army, Feb. 12, 1958; notes, "Project 'Man Very High' (MVH)," Feb. 17, 1958; message, J. A. Barclay to "Col. Coffin," Washington, "Proposed Project Adam," April 1958; Norman L. Baker, "Air Force Won't Support Project Adam," *Missiles and Rockets*, III (June 1958), 40–41; Link, *Space Medicine in Project Mercury*, 26–27.

[54] *Astronautics and Space Exploration*, testimony of Hugh Dryden and Arthur Kantrowitz, 117, 420, 516–517; Holmes, *America on the Moon*, 73–74. In August, Avco representatives presented a briefing to Brig. Gen. Homer A. Boushey, Director of Advanced Technology, Headquarters USAF. The Ballistic Missile Division still opposed the dragbrake device and advocated the Man-in-Space-Soonest approach. "Chronology of Early Air Force Man-in-Space Activity, 1955–1960," 66.

[55] Memo, Roy W. Johnson, ARPA Dir., to Secretary of the Army, "Project Adam," July 11, 1958; "Project Adam Chronology," Army Ballistic Missile Agency, undated; memo, Donald A. Quarles, Deputy Secretary of Defense, to Secretary of the Army, "Project Adam," Aug. 15, 1958; Link, *Space Medicine in Project Mercury*, 27.

[56] "MER II: Navy Manned Satellite Study, Summary," Convair Div., General Dynamics Corp., Dec. 1958; House Committee on Science and Astronautics, 86 Cong., 2 sess. (1960), *Project Mercury, First Interim Report*, 4.

[57] Memo, Hugh Dryden, NACA Dir., to James R. Killian, Jr., "Manned Satellite Program," July 18, 1958.

[58] "Chronology of Early Air Force Man-in-Space Activity, 1955–1960," 63.

[59] *Ibid.*, 68; "Chronology of USAF Man-in-Space Activity, 1945–1958," 31–32; "Outline of History of Man-in-Space Program," 149; Colchagoff interview.

[60] The pros and cons of the military's place in space have been debated almost incessantly since the immediate post-Sputnik days. For a treatment of the controversy, see, for example, Vernon Van Dyke, *Pride and Power: The Rationale of the Space Program* (Urbana, Ill., 1964). In retrospect, it seems proper to conclude that "the real issue within the Government was not whether to have a military or civilian space effort, but to create suitable arrangements for both." House Committee on Government Operations, 89 Cong., 1 sess. (1965), *Government Operations in Space*, Staff Report No. 445, 36.

[61] See memo for files, Hugh M. Henneberry, NACA Space Flight Office, "Briefing by General Electric Representatives on Studies Related to Man-in-Space Program," July 17, 1958; memo, Henneberry and G. C. Deutsch, to Assoc. Dir., "Discussions with Avco and Lockheed Representatives Concerning Materials for Thermal Protection of Satellite Reentry Vehicles, Washington, June 26–27, 1958," Sept. 8, 1958.

[62] "Specifications for a Manned Satellite Capsule," Langley Research Center, undated; C. C. Johnson, interview, Houston, Feb. 13, 1964; Mathews interview.

[63] Memo for files, Purser, "General Background Material on Project Mercury," March 23, 1959; *Project Mercury, First Interim Report*, 5.

[64] Purser, interview, July 18, 1965; North memo; Ms., William M. Bland, Jr., for Project Mercury Technical History Program, "The Birth of the Little Joe Booster," undated; Bland, interview, Houston, April 14, 1965.

[65] House Select Committee on Astronautics and Space Exploration, 85 Cong., 2 sess. (1958), *Authorizing Construction for the National Aeronautics and Space Administration, Hearings*, 17–18.

[66] Eugene M. Emme, *Aeronautics and Astronautics: An American Chronology of Science and Astronautics in the Exploration of Space, 1915–1960* (Washington, 1961), 101.

[67] Memo, Roy Johnson, ARPA Dir., to NASA Administrator, "Man-in-Space Pro-

537

gram," Sept. 18, 1958.

[98] *Project Mercury, First Interim Report,* 5; Gilruth, interview, Houston, March 18, 1964; minutes, Panel for Manned Space Flight, Warren J. North, secretary, Sept. 24 and 30, and Oct. 1, 1958.

[99] T. Keith Glennan, "Proclamation on Organization of the National Aeronautics and Space Administration," NASA General Directive No. 1, Sept. 25, 1958.

[100] Quoted in message to Langley Research Center, Sept. 25, 1958.

Chapter V

[1] T. Keith Glennan, in a letter to C. C. A. dated Dec. 18, 1963, said he could not recall precisely either the dates or the happenings at the meetings during his first official week in office. But he added, "It seemed the natural course for me to accept the recommendations of the only people who knew very much about the matter and initiate the program as soon as NASA became an operating agency. In short, I do not recall that President Eisenhower actually assigned the manned space flight program to NASA—I guess I just accepted the tasks which we would have to undertake." See also Clotaire Wood, interview, Washington, D.C., Sept. 1, 1965, for witness to the words to proceed.

[2] *NASA First Semiannual Report to Congress, Oct. 1, 1958-Mar. 31, 1959* (Washington, 1959); "Historical Sketch of NASA," NASA EP-29 (Washington, 1965).

[3] Memo, Roy W. Johnson to NASA Administrator, "Man-in-Space Program," Sept. 18, 1958; House Select Committee on Astronautics and Space Exploration, 85 Cong., 2 sess. (1958), *Authorizing Construction for the National Aeronautics and Space Administration,* 17–21; Senate Committee on Appropriations, 85 Cong., 2 sess. (1958), *The Supplemental Appropriations Bill, 1959, Hearings,* 801–806.

[4] Minutes, Panel for Manned Space Flight, Appendix A, 1, Warren J. North, secretary, Sept. 24 and 30, and Oct. 1, 1958. For membership of the committee, see p. 106.

[5] See Paul E. Purser, "History," in Purser, Maxime A. Faget, and Norman F. Smith, eds., *Manned Spacecraft: Engineering Design and Operation* (New York, 1964), 6, 8. Cf. articles by William Leavitt in John F. Loosbrock, ed., *Space Weapons: A Handbook of Military Astronautics* (New York, 1959), 107, 177.

[6] Alfred J. Eggers' advocacy of a higher

L/D vehicle is discussed on pp. 68–69.

[7] Minutes, "Panel for Manned Space Flight." The final report of the NACA Special Committee on Space Technology, chaired by H. Guyford Stever, was not published, but it did circulate as a 15-page endorsement by seven working groups generally favorable to these plans for manned space flight. See Ms. in NASA Hq. Hist. Archives, "Recommendations to the NASA Regarding a National Civil Space Program," No. VIII–C, Oct. 28, 1958.

[8] Abe Silverstein, interview, Cleveland, May 1, 1964. For details on the launching of NASA, see Robert L. Rosholt, *An Administrative History of NASA, 1958 to 1963* (Washington, 1966), Chap. 3. See also "Top Aides Named by Space Agency," *New York Times,* Oct. 5, 1958.

[9] "Background Information on Langley Research Center," Public Affairs Office, LRC, June 1960. The bulk of the professional staff consisted of "aeronautical research engineers." Since about 1954 some engineers, recruited from industry or from "accredited" schools of aeronautics, together with senior and most valuable members of the NACA laboratory teams, had been given more nearly competitive salaries and the title of "aeronautical research scientist." College accreditation and comparative evaluation were as problematical in this as in any other field, but institutions with high reputations for excellence in aeronautical engineering and aerodynamics included the California and Massachusetts Institutes of Technology, Stanford, Michigan State, and Cornell Universities, and many others certified by various professional societies.

[10] A few generalizations may be hazarded about Langley before 1959. Most of its professional staff came from the South and Midwest; few had been academically trained as aeronautical engineers; most held only bachelor's degrees, usually in mechanical or electrical engineering, often from Georgia Institute of Technology, Virginia Polytechnic Institute, or Auburn University. An esprit de corps based on many years of valuable service to aviation and to the nation seems to have been pervasive. And certainly the Langley professional people always would insist on their own experience and contributions as having proved the artificiality of invidious distinctions between science and engineering. Most helpful for understanding the nature of governmental management of applied science is David Novick, "What Do We Mean By Research and Development?" in *California*

Management Review (Spring 1960), 21, as quoted in Merton J. Peck and Frederick M. Scherer, *The Weapons Acquisition Process: An Economic Analysis* (Boston, 1962), 27, 28.

[11] Hugh L. Dryden, interview, Washington, Aug. 31, 1965; Robert R. Gilruth, interview, Houston, March 18, 1964.

[12] See the biography by Frank Waters, *Robert Gilruth: Engineering Space Exploration* (Chicago, 1963), 24–60.

[13] Memo, Gilruth to Assoc. Dir., "Space Task Group," Nov. 3, 1958; memo to all concerned, Floyd L. Thompson, "Space Task Group," Nov. 5, 1958. See memos, Charles H. Zimmerman to Procurement Officer, "Request for Authority to Negotiate a Contract for Manned Satellite Capsules," Nov. 3, 1958; Sherwood L. Butler to NASA Hq., "Request for Authority," Nov. 4, 1958.

[14] Ms. notes, Jerome B. Hammack, "Manned Ballistic Satellite Group," Aug. 19, 1958; letter, Purser to Mary S. Ambrose, undated, 2; Andre J. Meyer, Jr., interview, Houston, Feb. 24, 1964. For key management positions and progression, see James M. Grimwood, *Project Mercury: A Chronology*, NASA SP–4001 (Washington, 1963), Appendix 8.

[15] Alfred Rosenthal, *The Early Years: Goddard Space Flight Center Historical Origins and Activities through December 1962* (Washington, 1964), 17–20, 27.

[16] Besides those named in the text, the original list of Space Task Group members on Nov. 5, 1958, included Edison M. Fields, Claiborne R. Hicks, Jr., Ronald Kolenkiewicz, John B. Lee, Herbert G. Patterson, Frank C. Robert, William C. Muhly, and Paul D. Taylor, as professionals; Shirley J. Hatley, Norma L. Livesay, Nancy C. Lowe, Betsy F. Magin, Joseph J. Rollins, Ronelda F. Sartor, Jacquelyn B. Stearn, Julia R. Watkins, and Shirley P. Watkins, as clerical staff. The 10 members of the formal Lewis detachment were Elmer H. Buller, A. M. Busch, W. R. Dennis, M. J. Krasnican, Glynn S. Lunney, Andre J. Meyer, W. R. Meyer, W. J. Nesbitt, Gerard J. Pesman, and Leonard Rabb. Others from Lewis, like John H. Disher and Kenneth C. Weston, also commuted informally.

[17] George M. Low, interview, Houston, March 19, 1964; Gilruth, interview; Dryden, interviews, Washington, Sept. 11, 1964, and Aug. 31, 1965.

[18] John P. Mayer, interview, Houston, Oct. 19, 1964. For an overview of scientific expectation from the IGY, see D. R. Bates, ed., *The Earth and Its Atmosphere* (New York, 1957; Science Editions, Inc., 1961), 97–112. The difference between "sounding" and "probe" rocket flights was generally accepted by 1958 as being a matter of altitude, with the division point at a height of one Earth radius. Sounding rockets were those ascending to about 3900 miles; instrumented rockets going higher than that were called probes. On the word "aerospace" as used by the Air Force, see David Burnham, "The Air Force Coins a Word," *The Reporter,* XXVIII (June 6, 1963), 32–33.

[19] On the evolution of the standard atmosphere, see the works of Harry Wexler, Director of Meteorological Research of the United States Weather Bureau, and the foreword by Maurice Dubin, Norman Sissenwine, and Wexler to *U.S. Standard Atmosphere, 1962* (Washington, 1962), xiv–xv. Also a 1957 course of lectures sponsored by Space Technology Laboratories and the University of California at Los Angeles provided a comprehensive topical guide to the "state-of-the-art" of aerospace technology and achieved wider circulation when printed: Howard Seifert, ed., *Space Technology* (New York, 1959).

[20] Peck and Scherer, *The Weapons Acquisition Process,* 9, passim. See also article by H. Guyford Stever, "Outer Space: The Technical Prospects" in Lincoln P. Bloomfield, ed., *Outer Space: Prospects for Man and Society* (Englewood Cliffs, N.J., 1962). Comments by Manley J. Hood of Ames, Oct. 29, 1965, disagree with this general assessment, but the missile divisions of old aircraft corporations were more often than not semi-autonomous.

[21] *NASA First Semiannual Report to Congress,* 36, 37, 50. On this synthesis, see Hugh L. Dryden, "Scientific Bases of Airplane, Projectile and Missile Development," paper, American Ordnance Assn., New York City, Dec. 7, 1955, 2–3. Cf. John B. Rae, "Science and Engineering in the History of Aviation," *Technology and Culture,* II (Fall 1961), 391–399.

[22] The Convair/Astronautics-Avco Mfg. Corp. "Proposal for a Manned Satellite," No. ARL 03752, April 30, 1958, was an excellent introduction for STG to the men behind the Atlas as well as to their preliminary thinking. Cf. "Study for Manned Space Vehicle," Convair/ Astronautics, June 1958; and H. S. Gault and M. R. Tyson, "Study—Increased Capability of XSM–65 for Manned Space Flight Using 'Off-the-Shelf' Upper Stages," Convair/Astronautics, A2P–059, Nov. 5, 1958. Memo, Silverstein to Assoc. Dir., Lewis Research Center, "Request for Information on Atlas LOX Pump Performance," Nov. 14, 1958; Silverstein interview.

[23] Ms., R. B. Oakley, "History of North American Aviation, Inc.," undated [about June 1964], 9. For some insight into General Electric's contribution to the NAA/GE studies, see memo for files, Hugh M. Henneberry, "Briefing by General Electric Representatives on Studies Related to Man-in-Space Program," July 17, 1958.

[24] James S. McDonnell, Jr., "The Conquest of Space: A Creative Substitute for War," speech, Washington University, St. Louis, June 9, 1958. Cf. McDonnell, "The Challenge of Man's Future in the Golden Age of Engineers," speech, University of Missouri School of Mines and Metallurgy, Rolla, Mo., May 26, 1957.

[25] "Manned Orbital Flight," Report 6272, McDonnell Aircraft Corp., Oct. 10, 1958. Cf. "Manned Orbital Flight Planning Proposal," Report 6418, McDonnell Aircraft Corp., Oct. 15, 1958. Kendall Perkins, interview, St. Louis, Aug. 31, 1964; Raymond A. Pepping, interview, St. Louis, Sept. 1, 1964.

[26] "Briefing for Prospective Bidders for Manned Satellite Capsule," STG, Nov. 7, 1958; Ms., Jack A. Kinzler for Project Mercury Technical History Program, "Manufacturing by NASA for Project Mercury," Aug. 1963; E. M. Gregory, interview, Langley Field, Va., Jan. 7, 1964; Caldwell C. Johnson, "Specifications for a Manned Satellite Capsule," undated [about Oct. 20, 1958]; C. C. Johnson, interview, Houston, Feb. 13, 1964.

[27] Faget, marginal notes on "Outline of History of United States Air Force Man-in-Space Research and Development Program," anon., Aug. 1962; Wood, "Comments on Draft of Congress Staff Report on Mercury," Jan. 26, 1960. See also Mae M. Link, Space Medicine in Project Mercury (NASA SP-4003, 1965), 16, 67.

[28] Purser, "Project Mercury Background Material," March 23, 1959, 1; Purser, "Summary of Management, Design and Operational Philosophy," lecture, University of Houston, Spring 1963, 3. Cf. Purser, Faget, and Smith, eds., Manned Spacecraft, 492.

[29] Link, Space Medicine in Project Mercury, 28. One of the best broad assessments of the "state-of-the-art" of aerospace technology at this time was prepared by the Rand Corporation under the direction of Robert W. Buchheim, and reissued as a Congressional report: House Select Committee on Astronautics and Space Exploration, 86 Cong., 1 sess. (1959), Space Handbook: Astronautics and its Implications, 105, 166.

[30] "Questions and Answers from Bidders' Briefing for Manned Space Satellite," STG, Nov. 7, 1959, 3; George F. MacDougall, Jr., interview, Houston, Sept. 13, 1965.

[31] "Specifications for Manned Space Capsule," specification No. S-6, Nov. 14, 1958, passim.

[32] See letter, Boone T. Guyton, sales manager, Missile and Space Systems Div., United Aircraft Corp., to Henry J. E. Reid, Dir., Langley Research Center, Nov. 26, 1958; Ruben F. Mettler, Space Technology Laboratories, to Gilruth, Nov. 11, 1958. After the bidders' briefing, STG mailed additional material to prospective bidders. See letters, Gilruth to all bidders on prime contract for Mercury capsule, Nov. 25, 1958. Cf. letters, Reid to prospective bidders on Mercury capsule, Nov. 19, 1958. Back in the fall of 1954, the X-15 research airplane attracted nine companies to attend the bidders' briefing, and only four submitted bids. Walter C. Williams, interview, Houston, Aug. 23, 1965.

[33] Memo for files, Charles J. Donlan, "Procedures for Technical Assessment of Manufacturers' Proposal . . . on Specification S-6," Dec. 10, 1958; memo, Silverstein to NASA Administrator, "Schedule for Evaluation and Contractual Negotiations for Manned Satellite Capsule," Dec. 24, 1958. See p. 137. MacDougall, interview; memo, Low to NASA Administrator, "Status of Manned Satellite Project," Nov. 25, 1958. See also letter, Clarence A. Syvertson, Ames Aeronautical Laboratory, to Dir., Langley Aeronautical Laboatory, re conference at Wright-Patterson Air Force Base, Jan. 29-31, 1958, on research problems associated with orbiting a manned satellite, Feb. 18, 1958.

[34] See John W. Bullard, History of the Redstone Missile System, U.S. Army Missile Command, Historical Monograph AMC 23-M, Redstone Arsenal, Alabama, Oct. 15, 1965; anonymous booklet, This Is Redstone, Chrysler Corporation Missile Division [Detroit, ca. Oct. 1958].

[35] Memos, Purser to Gilruth, "Procurement of Ballistic Missiles for Use as NASA Satellite Boosters," Sept. 25, 1958; "Procurement of Ballistic Missiles for Use as Boosters in NASA Research Leading to Manned Space Flight," Oct. 8, 1958. See also memo, Purser and Faget to Silverstein, "Assignment of Responsibility for ABMA Participation in NASA Manned Satellite Project," Nov. 12, 1958; A. Richard Felix, "Static Stability and Drag Investigation of Jupiter C Boosted NASA

Manned Space Capsule," ABMA Technical Note No. 76–58, Dec. 5, 1958.

[36] Messages, Ralph E. Cushman to Commanding General, Army Ordnance Missile Command, Jan. 8 and 16, 1959; memo, North to Asst. Dir. for Advanced Technology, "Visit to ABMA Regarding Boosters," Dec. 4, 1958. See also "Development and Funding Plans for AOMC Support of NASA Manned Satellite Project," AOMC, Dec. 12, 1958; and Faget, interview, Houston, Aug. 23, 1965.

[37] Memo, North to NASA Administrator, "Background of Project Mercury Schedules," Aug. 14, 1960; Ms., William M. Bland, Jr., for Project Mercury Technical History Program, "The Birth of Little Joe Booster," undated; Bland, interview, Houston, April 14, 1965. Unknown to STG, a JATO-powered ship-to-air missile named "Little Joe" had been authorized at the end of World War II to combat the Japanese suicide rocket or Baka bomb. See Eugene M. Emme, *Aeronautics and Astronautics: An American Chronology of Science and Technology in the Exploration of Space, 1915–1960* (Washington, 1961), 50.

[38] See the description by Bland, "Project Mercury," in Eugene M. Emme, ed., *The History of Rocket Technology: Essays on Research, Development and Utility* (Detroit, 1964), 224–226.

[39] Memo, Carl A. Sandahl to Assoc. Dir., Langley Research Center, "Langley Participation in Little Joe Project," Dec. 9, 1958.

[40] Letter, Donlan to J. A. O. Stankevics, Avco-Everett Research Laboratory, May 5, 1960.

[41] See John L. Chapman, *Atlas: The Story of a Missile* (New York, 1960), Chap. I and 154–165, for a description of Project Score. Low, "Status Report No. 1—Manned Satellite Project," Dec. 9, 1958. Johnson's concurrence on the manned satellite booster was reported in "Atlas Seen as Vehicle to Put Man Into Space," *Washington Post*, Dec. 22, 1958. See also, Frank J. Dore, comments, Aug. 16, 1965.

[42] Ms., Aleck C. Bond for Project Mercury Technical History Program, "Big Joe," June 27, 1963, 5. A large part of the President's first annual report, required by the Space Act of 1958, was devoted to the problems of reentry, including aerodynamic heating. See House Committee on Science and Astronautics, 86 Cong., 1 sess. (1959), *U.S. Aeronautics and Space Activities, Jan. 1 to Dec. 31, 1958: Message from the President of the United States,* 2, 12, 20, 23.

[43] Initial efforts to develop a reliable landing and recovery system for the Big Joe payloads were begun by STG in conjunction with Norfolk Navy Yard personnel in December 1958.

[44] Message, Commanding Officer, Wright Air Dev. Center, to C.O., Air Research and Development Command, July 9, 1958. On Army Ballistic Missile Agency's successes with ablative Jupiter nosecones in 1957 and 1958, see *Reentry Studies,* 2 vols., Vitro Corp. report no. 2331–25, Nov. 25, 1958; Sarah S. Whitaker, "Bibliography—Jupiter Nose Cones," MSFC, Sept. 14, 1962; and W. R. Lucas and J. E. Kingsbury, "The ABMA Reinforced Plastics Ablation Program," reprinted from *Modern Plastics* (Oct. 1960).

[45] Memo, Wood to Office of Space Flight Development, "Background on Letter of October 22, 1958, Covering 'Ablation/Heat Sink Investigation—Manned Reentry,' " Nov. 7, 1958. Cf. memo, Low to Newell Saunders, Nov. 28, 1958; "Specifications for Manned Space Capsule"; Faget (interview) said "Ablation was ruled out as a material in the competition for the simple reason that it would prove to be too much of a 'wild card' in the technical assessment." In other words, said George Low, Oct. 5, 1965, "we wanted to select the best spacecraft manufacturer and not only the best heat shield inventor."

[46] Jack C. Heberlig, interview, Houston, Feb. 20, 1964; Hammack, interview, Houston, Feb. 13, 1964. See pp. 50–52. For a convenient overview of the Manhigh, Excelsior, and Strato-Lab projects, see "Report on Manned Space Flight," session VII of *Proceedings of the Second National Conference on the Peaceful Uses of Space, Seattle, Washington, May 8–10, 1962,* NASA SP-8 (Washington, 1962), 241–261.

[47] "Project Mercury Status Report No. 1 for Period Ending Jan. 31, 1959," STG. See also, Emme, *Aeronautics and Astronautics 1915–1960,* appendix C, 161–165.

[48] Careful study of the "half proposal" by Winzen Research, Inc., described in "Technical Proposal for NASA Man-in-Space Capsule Program," No. 1160-P, Dec. 8, 1958, for a balloon-hoisted sealed cabin similar to those used in the Air Force Project Manhigh and the Navy Strato-Lab continued within STG for several more months and was instrumental in determining that this kind of "space soak" would not justify its cost.

[49] Low, "Status Report No. 2—Manned Satellite Project," Dec. 17, 1958. The danger

of friction was probably greatest in the anomalous relationship between the Advanced Research Projects Agency of the Department of Defense and the military services' own advanced research groups. Memorandum of understanding, NASA–ARPA Manned Satellite Panel, "Principles for the Conduct by NASA and the Department of Defense of a Joint Program for a Manned Orbital Vehicle," Sept. 19, 1958. See also memo, Gilruth for all concerned, "Organization of Space Task Group," Jan. 26, 1959.

[49] Letter, Silverstein to Lt. Gen. Roscoe E. Wilson, U.S. Air Force, Nov. 20, 1958; NASA-Army joint news release, "NASA-Army Agreement," Dec. 3, 1958; DeMarquis Wyatt, interview, Washington, Sept. 1, 1965.

[51] "Status Report No. 1." See also Link, *Space Medicine in Project Mercury*, 44–59.

[52] "Invitation to Apply for Position of Research Astronaut-Candidate," announcement No. 1, NASA Project A, Dec. 22, 1958, 1. Succeeding quotations are from pages 3 and 4. Original plans for a maximum age of 35 were compromised by the requirements for extensive experience. Accumulating 1500 hours of flying time requires about 10 years. See letter, Robert B. Voas to John A. Walter, Syracuse University, April 1, 1960.

[52] Low, "Status Report No. 3 – Project Mercury," Dec. 27, 1958; letter, Emme to Link and Grimwood, March 23, 1964.

[54] Donlan, interview, Langley Field, Va., Jan. 7, 1964. Cf. Neil A. Armstrong, "I Decided to Get Aboard," *Life*, CV (Sept. 27, 1963), 84.

[55] Low, "Status Report No. 6—Project Mercury," Feb. 3, 1959; see also Donlan, comments, Sept. 3, 1965.

[56] Letter, Reid to NACA Dir., July 29, 1958; memo, Low to Silverstein, Dec. 12, 1959.

[57] Letter, Low to Grimwood, Nov. 13, 1963; Theodore von Kármán, *Aerodynamics: Selected Topics in the Light of Their Historical Development* (Ithaca, N.Y., 1954), 189. The famous Renaissance sculpture by Giovanni da Bologna of Mercury poised on a zephyr's head, ready to spring into space, is an "image of energy" and the "accepted symbol of victorious speed," according to Kenneth Clark, *The Nude: A Study in Ideal Form* (New York, 1959), 282.

[58] Edith Hamilton, *Mythology* (New York, 1958), 33; Thomas Bulfinch, *Mythology*, abridgement by Edmund Fuller (New York, 1959), 18; Emme, *Aeronautics and Astronautics, 1915-1960*.

[59] The announcement of the code name for NASA's man-in-space program was reported in a two-page edition of the strikebound *New York Times* as an incidental part of the main story: "Big Rocket Engine for Space Flights Is Ordered by U.S.," *New York Times*, Dec. 18, 1958. See also, Ms., Louise Dick, "Public Statements on Manned Space Flight and Project Mercury," Aug. 12, 1960, 4.

Chapter VI

[1] House Committee on Science and Astronautics, 87 Cong., 1 sess. (1961), *A Chronology of Missile and Astronautic Events*, 64–66; Eugene M. Emme, *Aeronautics and Astronautics: An American Chronology of Science and Technology in the Exploration of Space 1915-1960* (Washington, 1961), 106, 143. Cf. House Committee on Science and Astronautics, 86 Cong., 1 sess. (1959), *The First Soviet Moon Rocket*. On technological chauvinism, see the congressional furor aroused by Lloyd Mallan, "The Big Red Lie," a series of articles in *True* (April, May, June, July, 1959), which alleged Soviet space claims, especially *Mechta*, to be the "biggest hoax in history." House Committee on Science and Astronautics, 86 Cong., 1 sess. (1959), *Soviet Space Technology, Hearings*.

[2] "Project Mercury Discussion," brochure for press tour of Langley Research Center, STG, July 7, 1959, 1; Maxime A. Faget and Robert O. Piland, "Mercury Capsule and Its Flight Systems," paper, Institute of the Aeronautical Sciences, New York City, Jan. 25, 1960, 1–2; Ms., Paul E. Purser, "Project Mercury Technical History," June 12, 1963, intro., 5–6; Faget and Walter C. Williams, interviews, Houston, Aug. 23, 1965.

[3] T. Keith Glennan, "The Task of Government," in Lincoln P. Bloomfield, ed., *Outer Space: Prospects for Man and Society* (Englewood Cliffs, N.J., 1962), 65. For more of the background on engine and booster priority assignments, see Senate Committee on Aeronautical and Space Sciences, 87 Cong., 2 sess. (1962), Staff Report, *Manned Space Flight Program of the National Aeronautics and Space Administration: Projects Mercury, Gemini, and Apollo*, 160–168.

[4] Letter, Hugh L. Dryden to Robert R. Gilruth, March 23, 1959; memo, Clotaire Wood to NASA Administrator, "Priority for Project Mercury," March 12, 1959, Table D.

[5] Memo, Christopher C. Kraft to Gilruth, "Operational Program Estimate for AFMTC," Dec. 4, 1958.

[5] Letter, Lloyd Harrison to Charles H. Zimmerman, March 10, 1959; letter, C. F. Picard to Zimmerman, March 23, 1959; memo for files, R. L. Barber, "NASA Contract NAS 5–59 Manned Satellite Capsules," April 10, 1959; Senate Committee on Aeronautical and Space Sciences, 86 Cong., 1 sess. (1959), *Governmental Organization for Space Activities*, 42–43. For a different interpretation of the facts surrounding the DX priority for Mercury, Saturn, and the F-1 engine, see House Committee on Science and Astronautics, 86 Cong., 2 sess. (1960), *Space, Missiles, and the Nation*, 10–12. For details on the birth of the F-1 engine and the Saturn booster, see *Saturn Illustrated Chronology, April 1957–June 1964*, Marshall Space Flight Center, Aug. 10, 1964, 1–16.

[6] Memos, George M. Low to J. W. Gannon, "Priority for Project Mercury," April 25, 1959; Low to House Committee on Science and Astronautics, "Urgency of Project Mercury," April 27, 1959; House Committee on Science and Astronautics, 86 Cong., 1 sess. (1960), *1961 NASA Authorization*, 348.

[7] Roy W. Johnson, quoted by John W. Finney, "Space Ship Model Tested in Flight," *New York Times*, March 27, 1959. On rivalry and confusion in Washington, see Drew Pearson, "Too Many Czars in Space Work," *Washington Post*, Feb. 9, 1959; William Hines, "Policies of Washington Blamed for Missile Lag," *Washington Evening Star*, Feb. 17, 1959. For part of the furor over Project Argus, see Walter Sullivan, et al., *New York Times*, March 19, 20, 22, 1959. See also "Roy W. Johnson, Early Builder of U.S. Space Program, Dies," *New York Times*, July 23, 1965.

[8] See "Questions and Answers from Bidders' Briefing for Manned Space Satellite," STG, Nov. 7, 1958, 3; letter, Sherwood L. Butler to R. E. Cushman, "Proposals on Requisition S-6—Manned Satellite Capsule," Dec. 12, 1958.

[9] Glennan, "Statement of the Administrator on the Selection of McDonnell Aircraft Corporation to Design and Construct a Manned Satellite Capsule for Project Mercury," typescript, undated.

[10] NASA Contract No. NAS 5–59, "Cost-Plus-A-Fixed-Fee Research and Development Contract for Designing and Furnishing Manned [sic] Satellite Capsule." This document is officially dated Feb. 13, 1959, the date on which it was approved by Glennan. For an elaborate 37-page report on the contract nego-tiations, see memo for files, Willis A. Simons and George F. MacDougall, Jr., "Procurement of Manned Satellite Capsule (Project Mercury) (Requisition S-6)," Feb. 9, 1959.

[12] News release, "McDonnell Aircraft's Role as Prime Contractor for the Mercury Spacecraft," McDonnell Aircraft Corp., April 1962.

[13] Ms., Stephen A. Armstrong for Project Mercury Technical History Program, "The History of Project Mercury Contracts," April 8, 1963; Armstrong, interview, Houston, June 4, 1964.

[14] *Manned Satellite Proposal, Vol. I: Management Proposal; Vol. II: Technical Proposal; Vol. III: Cost Proposal*, Report 6483, McDonnell Aircraft Corp., Dec. 4, 1958.

[15] Prepared by L. M. Parker and approved by John F. Yardley, E. M. Flesh, and Albert Utsch of McDonnell, "Project Mercury Capsule Detail Specification," Report 6603, was first issued on March 12, 1959, and revised on April 10 and July 15, 1959. By the latter date McDonnell model designation "133K" had been assigned the Mercury capsule, indicating 11 significant drawing changes so far. Cf. "Specifications for Manned Spacecraft Capsule," Specification No. S-6, item 2.2.1.1, STG/Langley Research Center, Nov. 14, 1958.

[16] Low, "Status Report No. 4—Project Mercury," Jan. 12, 1959. Evidence that the earlier NASA capsule design continued to compete with the McDonnell configuration is found in studies of drogue parachute effectiveness in stabilizing the capsule at subsonic speeds. See memo, James S. Bowman, "Transmittal of Project Mercury Data to the Space Task Group," June 3, 1959. The precise shape of the "coolie hat" blast shield was still debated in late 1960. See letter, Purser to Walter F. Burke, "Progress Report on pylon jettison rockets test at NASA," Sept. 21, 1960.

[17] Low, "Status Report No. 5," Jan. 20, 1959. Cf. Low, "Status Report No. 3," Dec. 27, 1958.

[18] "Status Report No. 5"; *Manned Satellite Proposal, Vol. II: Technical Proposal*, 10.

[19] Andre J. Meyer, Jr., interview, Houston, Feb. 24, 1964, and comments, Sept. 1, 1965; Ms., Meyer for Project Mercury Technical History Program, "Mercury Heat Shield History," June 1963, regards the beryllium alternative as only a secondary solution from the beginning.

[20] Edison M. Fields, interview, Houston, June 18, 1964; Aleck C. Bond, interview, Houston, March 13, 1964.

[21] Purser, log for Gilruth, Jan. 14, 1959. Cf. "Specifications for Manned Spacecraft

Capsule." Memos, Fields to Chief, Flight Systems Div., "Visit to B. F. Goodrich Concerning Ablation Heat Shield for HS-24," April 20, 1959; and "Visit to C.T.L. Concerning Ablation Heat Shields for HS-24," April 21, 1959. General Electric Co. (Missile and Space Vehicle Dept., Philadelphia) had found it necessary to subcontract the large-scale development of its design process to the B. F. Goodrich Co., Akron. Big Joe flew a Goodrich heatshield.

[22] "Specification for Ablation Heat Shield," STG Specification No. S-19-B, April 28, 1959, a five-page revision by Fields of Specification No. S-19A, March 2, 1959. See also "Beryllium in Project Mercury," brochure, Brush Beryllium Co., undated [about June 1959]. For the techniques of ablation shield manufacture, see "Development of Reinforced Plastic Materials and Fabrication Procedures for Reentry Protection Shield for Capsule, Project Mercury," Cincinnati Testing and Research Laboratory, Reports Nos. 1 and 2 (final), May 1 and July 1, 1959.

[23] "How Mercury Capsule Design Evolved," *Aviation Week*, LXX (Sept. 21, 1959), 57.

[24] "Project Mercury Status Report No. 1 for Period Ending Jan. 31, 1959," STG/Langley Research Center, 2, 26. See also Ms. paper, Marvin S. Hochberg, "Design and Fabrication of the Project Mercury Astronaut Couch," an undated and unnumbered McDonnell Aircraft Corp. report received by STG June 20, 1963.

[25] Low, "Status Report No. 9—Project Mercury," March 21, 1959, 6. On this chart MA-1 stood for the flight that later became known as Big Joe. Hence all flights in the Atlas series dropped in numerical sequence; MA-7 became MA-6, but remained the first planned manned orbital flight.

[26] "Status Report on Project Mercury Development Program as of March 1, 1959," Public Affairs Office, Langley Research Center.

[27] Low, "Status Report No. 9—Project Mercury," 2, 4; W. C. Moseley, Jr., interview, Houston, Sept. 21, 1965.

[28] Willard S. Blanchard and Sherwood Hoffman, interview, Langley Field, Va., Jan. 6, 1964. Cf. their formal papers on configuration studies published after 18 months' lead time as TN D-223, "Effects of Nose Cone Radii, Afterbody Section Deflections, and a Drogue Chute on Subsonic Motions of Manned-Satellite Models in Reentry Configuration," March 1960; and as TM X-351, "Full-Scale Flight Test of a Proposed Abort-Escape System for a Manned Space Capsule from Sea Level," Aug. 1960; also Blanchard and James R. Raper,

TM X-422, "Full-Scale Flight Test from Sea Level of an Abort-Escape System for a Project Mercury Capsule." Blanchard's work with tow rockets and the first full-sized model of the Mercury configuration was publicized by *Aviation Week*, which featured his picture on the cover of its April 1959 issue. Alternative modifications of the escape rocket system were being tested by Herbert G. Patterson using $\frac{1}{4}$-scale boilerplate capsule-pylon systems in beach abort launches from Wallops Island.

[29] For a résumé of these activities at Langley, see memo, Carl A. Sandahl to Assoc. Dir., "Langley Presentation to the Space Task Group," May 19, 1959. Cf. memo, Abe Silverstein to Dir., Aeronautical and Space Research, "Langley and Ames Research Center Support for Project Mercury," March 6, 1959, with two enclosures. See also memo, Lloyd J. Fisher to Assoc. Dir., "Flotation Investigations in Support of Project Mercury," May 12, 1959.

[30] Albin O. Pearson, interview, Langley Field, Va., Jan. 7, 1964; memo, Pearson to Assoc. Dir., "Visit of NASA Personnel to Arnold Engineering Development Center, Tullahoma, Tenn.," March 5, 1959; memo, Moseley for files, "Summary of Project Mercury Wind Tunnel Program," Aug. 26, 1960. See also Marvin E. Hintz, *A Chronology of the Arnold Engineering Development Center*, Air Force Systems Command Historical Publication Series 62-101, June 30, 1963, 62.

[31] "Pilot Support System Development (Live Specimen Experiment)," Report 6875, McDonnell Aircraft Corp., June 1959. Cf. "Test Results Memorandum," McDonnell Aircraft Corp., June 9, 1959. John H. Glenn, interview, Houston, Aug. 3, 1964; memo, Wilbur E. Thompson to Chief, Flight Systems Div., "Status of Impact Test Program," June 9, 1959.

[32] Letter, Gilruth to Commanding Officer, Wright Air Development Center, March 26, 1959; Low, "Status Report No. 11," April 6, 1959. Cf. "Project Mercury Status Report No. 2 for Period Ending April 30, 1959," STG/Langley Research Center. On the history of parachute development for Mercury, see Joe W. Dodson, transcript of a taped discussion with Donald C. Cole, "Mercury Parachute History," September 1962.

[33] William C. Muhly, interview, Houston, Aug. 9, 1965; see also Muhly's draft Ms., "Planning and Scheduling," May 28, 1963, for the Mercury Technical History. Regarding STG's first plans for astronaut pickup, see STG, "Recovery Operations for Project Mercury," March 20, 1959.

[34] See Chapters IX and X, pp. 287 and 311 following. Lloyd Fisher of Langley worked on a torus landing bag for several months in 1959 before the honeycomb structures developed well enough to abandon the idea for a while. But reconsiderations of dry landing from an abort at the Cape or nearing Africa led Gerard Pesman, Faget, and Donlan to reinstate the pneumatic impact bag development late in 1960. Pesman, interview, Houston, Aug. 16, 1965.

[35] E. Nelson Hayes, "The Smithsonian's Satellite-Tracking Program: Its History and Organization," Parts I and II, Publications 4482 and 4574, respectively (Washington, 1962–1964), I, 318.

[36] Letter, J. W. Crowley to F. L. Thompson, "Request that LRC Assume Responsibility for Project Mercury Instrumentation Facilities," Feb. 20, 1959, with enclosure (Silverstein to Crowley, Feb. 16, 1959); Charles W. Mathews, interview, Houston, Sept. 23, 1965; and Low, comments, Oct. 5, 1965.

[37] Hartley A. Soulé, interview, Hampton, Va., Jan. 7, 1964. Soulé retired in 1962 to write histories of Langley and of the Mercury tracking network. Cf. memo, Soulé to Assoc. Dir., "Questions Concerning the Project Mercury Range . . .," April 13, 1959.

[38] G. Barry Graves, interview, Houston, Feb. 17, 1964. Cf. memo, Graves to Gilruth, "Progress on Range for Project Mercury . . .," Feb. 13, 1959.

[39] Letter, Henry J. E. Reid to Silverstein, April 27, 1959, with enclosure (Soulé, "Tentative Plan for Operation of Range for Project Mercury"). Cf. earlier plans in letter, Reid to Crowley, March 9, 1959.

[40] "Project Mercury Crew Station Description," Report 6710, McDonnell Aircraft Corp., March 16, 1959; "Model 133 Mockup Review Pictures," Report 6732, McDonnell Aircraft Corp., March 18, 1959. It is perhaps significant that a large sign behind the mockup in the McDonnell factory said, "When a change is not necessary, it is necessary not to change."

[41] Minutes, "Model 133 Mockup Review," McDonnell Aircraft Corp., March 18, 1959.

[42] Memos, Gilruth to STG/Langley Research Center, "Coordination of Meetings of Study Panels . . . ," March 20, 1959; and "Establishment of Capsule Coordination Office and Review Board," June 19, 1959: John H. Disher, interview, Washington, Sept. 2, 1965. For an overview of the nature and scope of Project Mercury as seen by STG at this time, see memo for files [and distribution among supporting groups], Purser, "General Background Material on Project Mercury," March 23, 1959.

[43] Ms., C. F. Bingman for Project Mercury Technical History Program, "Organization," June 3, 1963, 5, 14. See also STG/Langley, "Status Report No. 2."

[44] Senator Stuart Symington's remark is in *Governmental Organization for Space Activities*, 28. Cf. House Committee on Appropriations, 86 Cong., 1 sess. (1959), *National Aeronautics and Space Administration Appropriations, Hearings*, testimony of Hugh L. Dryden, 9. Faget recalled in interview the "family joke" of the symbols: NA¢A → NA$A.

[45] Memo, MacDougall to Project Manager, "Estimated Cost of Manned Space Capsule Contract," Dec. 15, 1958; MacDougall, interview, Feb. 5, 1965.

[46] Silverstein, marginal notes on memo, Low to Dir. for Space Flight Development, March 12, 1959; MacDougall, interview, Sept. 13, 1965.

[47] Memo for files, Meyer, "Visit of McDonnell Representatives to Discuss Spare Parts and Ground Support Equipment," March 10, 1959. See also Ms., G. F. Bailey and S. A. Armstrong for Project Mercury Technical History Program, "Outline of the History of the Mercury Contract," April 8, 1963.

[48] Low, "Status Report No. 8—Project Mercury," March 4, 1959. Cf. Low, "Status Report No. 4." The extent of redesign work to "man-rate" the Atlas was more quickly recognized by its fabricators than by its new customers; Williams interview.

[49] Memo, Purser to Gilruth, "Analysis of Army Ordnance Missile Command Revised Funding Estimate for Redstones and Jupiters," June 5, 1959.

[50] Letter, Glennan to Neil H. McElroy, July 14, 1959. Administrator Glennan began to keep a desk diary in December 1958 [not available to this author], which carefully noted each day's transactions thereafter.

[51] Low, "Status Report No. 14—Project Mercury," May 22, 1959. De Marquis Wyatt, interview, Washington, Sept. 1, 1965; Bond interview.

[52] Ms., William M. Bland, Jr., for Project Mercury Technical History Program, "The Birth of Little Joe Booster"; memo for files, Charles H. McFall, Jr., "Project Little Joe: Ground Instrumentation Required," April 15, 1959.

[53] Memo for files, Sandahl, "Progress on

Little Joe," Feb. 16, 1959; memo for files, Bland, "Results of Trip," May 19, 1959.

[51] Purser, log for Gilruth, Jan. 12, 1959; memo, Charles B. Rumsey to Assoc. Dir., "Meeting to Discuss Project Mercury Problems to Which PARD Rocket Firings Might Contribute Information at an Early Date," Feb. 24, 1959. William E. Stoney, interview, Houston, Feb. 13, 1964. For Scout's capabilities, see "Considerations Affecting Satellite and Space Probe Research with Emphasis on the 'Scout' as a Launch Vehicle," NASA Technical Report R–97, Washington, 1961.

[52] Purser log, Jan. 12, 1959. Cf. *NASA Appropriations, Hearings,* testimony of Dryden, 83–115. Wesley L. Hjornevik, interview, Houston, Feb. 17, 1964.

[56] "Canadian Personnel Chart: Duty Assignments, Need to Know, Travel Requirements," STG, April 1959; Purser, log for Gilruth, April 21, 1959. Bringing fresh insight and seasoned experience to aid STG, this group included two, John D. Hodge and Jack Cohen, of rank equivalent to civil-service rating GS–14. Several more Anglo-Canadian engineers later joined STG.

[57] Purser, log for Gilruth, April 27, 1959. See also documents signed by Glennan, Silverstein, and T. E. Jenkins, Administrative Officer of Goddard Space Flight Center, published as Exhibits 10, 11, and 12 of Appendix D in Alfred Rosenthal, *The Early Years: Goddard Space Flight Center, Historical Origins and Activities through December 1962* (Washington, 1964), 35.

[58] Glennan, interview with Eugene M. Emme, Cleveland, April 6, 1965; Purser, log for Gilruth, May 20, 1959.

[59] House Committee on Science and Astronautics, 86 Cong., 1 sess. (1959), *Basic Scientific and Astronautic Research in the Department of Defense,* testimony of Dr. Herbert F. York, June 4, 1959, 16; B. Porter Brown, interview, Cape Kennedy, April 30, 1964.

[60] Francis E. Jarrett, Jr., and Robert A. Lindemann, "Historical Origins of NASA's Launch Operations Center to July 1, 1962," Kennedy Space Center, Historical Monograph No. 1 (KHM–1), Oct. 1964. There is a dispute over proper nomenclature regarding the combination of launch complexes 5 and 6 into "No. 56." If the latter is a misnomer, it was so commonly used as to justify its use throughout this work.

[61] Memo for files, Emil P. Bertram, "NASA Space Requirements at MFL," April 7, 1959. For an account of the ill-fated Vega vehicle, see Evert Clark, "Vega Study Shows Early NASA Problems," *Aviation Week,* LXXII (June 27, 1960), 62–68.

[62] Scott H. Simpkinson, interview, Houston, June 2, 1964. Hangar S had been built by NRL for Project Vanguard in the face of earlier housing shortages for checkout facilities.

[63] Purser, logs for Gilruth, June 15 and 29, 1959.

[64] Ashton Graybiel, et al., "An Account of Experiments in Which Two Monkeys Were Recovered Unharmed After Ballistic Space Flight," *Aerospace Medicine,* XXX (Dec. 1959), 871–931. Cf. Siegfried J. Gerathewohl, *Principles of Bioastronautics* (Englewood Cliffs, N.J., 1963), 100–108. NASA press releases on primate flights always carried notice of the birthplaces of the subjects to avoid offending Hindus, who believe in transmigration of souls. Presumably 100 percent American monkeys were always 100 percent American. See also p. 53.

[65] Gilruth, speech, Space Age Conference, World Congress of Flight, Las Vegas, April 17, 1959.

[66] "Project Mercury Discussion," 50-page collection of graphic charts and outlines, STG, May 18, 1959, 1.

[67] Memo, Warren J. North to Administrator, "Background of Project Mercury Schedules," with enclosure, Aug. 14, 1960.

[68] It seems fitting to note here the Air Force viewpoint on this period. Max Rosenberg, Chief, USAF Historical Division Liaison Office, has commented as follows on this section (Oct. 8, 1965): "Within these pages is the story of the major crux of program slippages, which seems not to be recognized. There is detailed listing of each agency's role but no recognition that no one was in charge of *total system* analysis, *total system* design, *total system* engineering, *total system* technical direction. This was one of the features of the Air Force ballistic missile program wherein Ramo-Wooldridge functioned as the *systems* engineering and technical director. The lack of such an agency within the Mercury program was understandable, for NASA was without experience in undertakings of such scope and magnitude, but it should be recognized and recorded historically as an expensive 'lesson learned' that cost NASA (and the United States) perhaps a year or more in meeting the Mercury goals." P. 13.

[69] "Project Mercury Discussions," 22–25. Cf. "Main Results of NASA-McDonnell-

ABMA Conference of 11 February 1959," OR-DAB-DSRW, CAA 59358, Ballistic Missile Agency; and memo, Purser to Gilruth, "Project Mercury Meeting on February 11, 1959, at ABMA," Feb. 17, 1959.

70 See transcript of press conference, "Introduction of the Astronauts," April 9, 1959; NASA news releases 59-111, April 7, and 59-113, April 9, 1959; and memo for the record, Allen O. Gamble, "News Story Concerning Astronaut Selection," Feb. 2, 1962.

71 The "Project Mercury Information Plan," issued in June 1959 at NASA Headquarters, gave overall responsibility for information activities to Walter T. Bonney, Director, Office of Public Information, NASA. The significant decision to divide "official duties" from "personal stories" was made in Washington with the promulgation of "NASA Policy Concerning Mercury Astronauts," May 11, 1959. See also Walter T. Bonney, comments, Dec. 1, 1965.

72 The distinction between senior pilots and professional test pilots took a quantum leap after 1953 with the introduction of "century series" aircraft. Donald K. Slayton, interview, Dec. 16, 1964. Cf. John Dille, ed., We Seven, by the Astronauts Themselves (New York, York, 1962), 70.

73 For criteria, see p. 131. For the best overview of selection philosophy and program arrangements see Ms., Robert B. Voas, "Preliminary Draft of Astronaut Selection Section, Mercury Technical History," Aug. 28, 1963. Cf. Stanley C. White, interview, San Antonio, Aug. 20, 1965, and Donlan, comments, Sept. 3, 1965.

74 Low, "Status Report No. 7—Project Mercury," Feb. 17, 1959. Cf. Low, "Status Report No. 6," Feb. 3, 1959.

75 See David H. Beyer and Saul B. Sells, "Selection and Training of Personnel for Space Flight," Journal of Aviation Medicine, XXVIII (Feb. 1957), 1-6. On the Lovelace Clinic as a parallel institution to Mayo Clinic, see brochure, "Lovelace Foundation for Medical Education and Research" (Albuquerque, undated [about 1958]).

76 Letter, A. H. Schwichtenberg, Head, Aerospace Medical Dept., Lovelace Foundation, to Charles J. Donlan, Nov. 5, 1959.

77 Voas, "Astronaut Selection," 26. See also Mae M. Link, Space Medicine in Project Mercury, NASA SP-4003 (Washington, 1965), Chapter V, "Medical Aspects of Astronaut Selection and Training," 44-59.

78 Charles L. Wilson, ed., "Project Mercury Candidate Evaluation Program," Technical Report 59-505, Wright Air Development Center, Dec. 1959. Cf. letters, Donlan to David K. Trites, Sept. 22, 1959; and Trites to Donlan, "Summary of Psychological Testing of Candidates for Project Mercury," undated.

79 Quoted in letter, Donlan to NASA Hq., Dec. 16, 1960.

80 George E. Ruff, "Medical Criteria in Space Crew Selection," 108th annual meeting, American Medical Assn., Atlantic City, June 9, 1959. Donlan, interview, Langley Field, Va., Jan. 7, 1964, and comments, Sept. 3, 1965. Stanley White vigorously disagreed with this assessment, saying that medical and psychological interviews "were equally important." White interview.

81 NASA/MSC news release, "Biography of John A. Powers," Jan. 1963. Cf. memo, Powers to Project Director, "Project Mercury Public Affairs Officer," June 9, 1959, which encloses the initial public relations plan for STG.

82 House Committee on Science and Astronautics, 86 Cong., 1 sess. (1959), Meeting with the Astronauts (Project Mercury-Man-in-Space Program), May 28, 1959, passim. See also "How to Get a Man Up into Space and Back Again," and "Space Voyagers Rarin' to Orbit," Life, XLVI, April 20, 1959.

83 Quoted but unidentified in George E. Ruff and Edwin Z. Levy, "Psychiatric Evaluation of Candidates for Space Flight," American Journal of Psychiatry, CXVI (Nov. 1959), 391. For the philosophers, see The Basic Writings of Bertrand Russell, 1903-1959, edited by Robert E. Egner and Lester E. Denoun (New York, 1961), 15, 565-576; Teilhard de Chardin, The Phenomenon of Man (New York, 1959), 250, 286, and passim; Walter Kaufmann, Critique of Religion and Philosophy (Garden City, N.Y., 1961), 429.

84 This ends an interesting prose poem by David Greenfield entitled "Which Way Is Heaven?" that appeared in Saturday Review, XLII (July 4, 1959), 39, reflecting a significant popular shift in perspective related to the announcement of the astronauts' selection. Greenfield wrote, "Heaven has always existed in the mind of man as the abode of spiritual beings and the ultimate destination of believers. Its location has always been 'up'. . . . And now at last man is about to ascend physically into this heaven. . . . Will his spiritual outlook be changed by a shock of disillusion? . . ."

Chapter VII

[1] In considering how both technology and techniques began to evolve through the planning and tooling stages and into manufacturing and production, this chapter and the next make the conventional yet conceptually useful distinction between mechanical and human (factors) engineering endeavors. Another important distinction, that which rated pilot safety first and mission success second, was implicit from the start, but became explicit in the production programs only after many technical arguments and much rethinking. The process of man-rating the machines is meant to suggest all the efforts made to perfect a completely automatic system for Earth-orbital flight. The reciprocal process of machine-rating men is meant to focus on the ambiguities in the idea of perfecting a completely automated system for such purposes. Chronologically this division coincides with the major, but by no means singular, concern of those responsible for the execution of Project Mercury during the year of development between the summers of 1959 and 1960.

[2] House Select Committee on Astronautics and Space Exploration, 86 Cong., 1 sess. (1959), *The Next Ten Years in Space, 1959–1969*, report by T. Keith Glennan, Hugh L. Dryden, Abe Silverstein, John P. Hagen, and Homer E. Newell, Jr., 120.

[3] Obituary for Paul D. Taylor, *Airscoop*, Langley Research Center, May 15, 1959. Regarding overtime, see Ms., Paul E. Purser, "Discussion of Project Mercury History and Schedules," Aug. 1960.

[4] "Complement Analysis," STG, Appendix C of confidential staff study, July 10, 1959, C–10.

[5] See James M. Grimwood, *Project Mercury: A Chronology*, NASA SP–4001 (Washington, 1963), 215. Cf. memos, Robert R. Gilruth to staff, "Appointment of Associate Directors," Sept. 15, 1959; and "Organization of Space Task Group," Aug. 10, 1959.

[6] For most of the preliminary operational planning, see the appendices and annexes to Ms., *"Overall Plan:* Department of Defense Support for Project Mercury," undated [ca. Sept. 1959]. See also DOD Representative for Project Mercury Support Operations, *Final Report to the Secretary of Defense on Department of Defense Support of Project Mercury: For the Period 1 July 1959 through 13 June 1963;* approved by Leighton I. Davis, Maj. Gen., USAF, 11 Sept. 1963. The major ex-

ceptions to Maj. Gen. Donald N. Yates' responsibility for military support activities for Mercury were in the areas of man-rating the Atlas and bioastronautical research and training.

[7] Maxime A. Faget recalls Walter C. Williams' being adamantly opposed to vertical manned rocket launches in 1957, but by mid-1958 Williams was supporting the Langley plans on the joint NACA-Advanced Research Projects Agency panel. Faget, interview, Houston, Aug. 4, 1964, and Williams, Aug. 23, 1965. See also memo, Gilruth for staff, "Appointment of Associate Directors," Sept. 15, 1959.

[8] Joachim P. Kuettner, "Manrating Space Carrier Vehicles," in Ernst Stuhlinger et al., eds., *From Peenemünde to Outer Space: Commemorating the Fiftieth Birthday of Wernher von Braun* (Huntsville, Ala., 1962), 629–630. See also "Biographic Sketch: Dr. Joachim P. Kuettner," Marshall Space Flight Center, May 1, 1963; Kuettner, interview, Huntsville, April 28, 1964.

[9] Memo, Kuettner to "all labs," Development Operations Division, Army Ballistic Missile Agency, "Mercury-Adam Project," Jan. 14, 1959; Kuettner, "Mercury Project," draft status report, May 21, 1959. Cf. typescript prospectus, Kuettner, "ABMA's Participation in the Mercury Project," undated [about Aug. 1959]. See also memo, A. Richard Felix to Dir., Aeroballistics Lab., "Visit to NASA, Langley Concerning Future Wind Tunnel Tests of the Jupiter-C Boosted Manned Space Capsule," Jan. 15, 1959; and Mack W. Shettles, "Status Report—Project Mercury," ABMA report No. DFE–IN–09–59, Feb. 13, 1959. Cf. memo, Dieter Grau to "M–G&C–DIR," "Unsatisfactory Condition on MR Abort Sensing System," Oct. 11, 1960.

[10] F. W. Brandner, "Proposal for Mercury-Redstone Automatic Inflight Abort Sensing System," Army Ballistic Missile Agency report No. DG–TR–7–59, Redstone Arsenal, June 5, 1959, 1.

[11] See, for example, letter, James D. Sams to CO, ABMA, "Project Mercury-Redstone Delineation of Responsibility," Oct. 8, 1959; memo, C. J. Kronauer, to Capt (?) Hombaker, "Project Mercury Schedule Notification," Oct. 12, 1959; Debus to Kuettner, "NASA-ABMA–AFMTC Project Mercury Operating Agreement," Nov. 9, 1959; letter, Gen. John B. Medaris to Yates, Dec. 10, 1959; Yates to Medaris, Dec. 21, 1959.

[12] Brig. Gen. Homer A. Boushey in *The*

Next Ten Years in Space, 30.

[13] John R. Pierce quoted sympathetically by Carl Dreher, "Pie in the Sky: Scramble for the Space Dollar," *The Nation,* CXC (Feb. 13, 1960), 133. Such extreme positions were denounced by at least one independent engineer, viewing the man-in-space program in the October issue of the trade journal *Automatic Control.* For reprint, see George K. Arthur, "Why Man in Space?—An Engineer's View," in Richard M. Skinner and William Leavitt, eds., *Speaking of Space: The Best from Space Digest* (Boston, 1962), 142.

[14] Bernhard A. Hohmann, interviews, El Segundo, Calif., Aug. 25, 1964, and Houston, Sept. 16, 1965; E. B. Doll, telephonic interview, El Segundo, Aug. 25, 1964; D. R. White, interview, Houston, Aug. 10, 1964. For an overview of the business evolution from Thompson Ramo Wooldridge into Space Technology Laboratories and Aerospace Corporation see Robert Sheehan, "Thompson Ramo Wooldridge: Two Wings in Space," *Fortune,* LXVII (Feb. 1963), 95–99, 139–146. See also House Committee on Government Operations, 87 Cong., 1 sess., *Air Force Ballistic Missile Management (Formation of Aerospace Corporation),* report No. 324, May 1, 1961.

[15] See [Henry B. Kucheman, Jr.] "Reference File, AFBMD Support, Project Mercury," bound folder of documents, Air Force Space Systems Div., El Segundo, Calif., Jan. 4, 1961; Frank Wendzel and R. W. Keehn, interviews, San Diego, Calif., Aug. 28, 1964. For a description of advances in manufacturing techniques, see Richard Sweeny, "Atlas Generates Fabrication Advances," *Aviation Week,* LXXII (Jan. 4, 1960), 38–49. For an overview of the actors within the BMD–STL–GD/A complex, see transcript, "Proceedings of the Mercury-Atlas Booster Reliability Workshop," GD/A, San Diego, Calif., July 12, 1963, passim.

[16] White interview; Philip E. Culbertson, comments, Aug. 16, 1965. Cf. Convair/Astronautics Report No. AZM–27–321, "Test Equipment for Abort Sensing and Implementation System for Mercury Atlas Flight," July 17, 1959.

[17] Donald K. Slayton, speech, annual meeting, Soc. of Experimental Test Pilots, Los Angeles, Oct. 9, 1959.

[18] Christopher C. Kraft, Jr., "A Review of Knowledge Acquired from the first Manned Satellite Program," MSC fact sheet No. 206, 1.

[19] John P. Mayer and Carl R. Huss, "Trajectory Analysis," in *Mercury Project Summary, Including Results of the Fourth Manned Orbital Flight, May 15 and 16, 1963,* NASA SP–45 (Washington, 1963), 119; John M. Eggleston, "Some Abort Techniques and Procedures for Manned Spacecraft," *Aerospace Engineering,* XXI (Nov. 1962), 17.

[20] Paul A. Campbell, "Man in Space—Where We Stand," *Air Force and Space Digest,* (July 1959), reprinted as Part 3 of Appendix B in Senate Committee on Aeronautical and Space Sciences, 86 Cong., 1 sess. (1959), report No. 1014, *Project Mercury: Man-in-Space Program of the National Aeronautics and Space Administration.* Cf. Siegfried J. Gerathewohl and George R. Steinkamp, "Human Factors Requirements for Putting a Man in Space," paper, ninth International Astronautical Congress, Amsterdam, Aug. 1958.

[21] Perhaps the classic basic text for the modern revival of efficiency expertise was dedicated, both formally and in a limited sense financially, to Glennan by the authors, all professors in the operations research group at Case Institute of Technology since 1952: C. West Churchman, Russell L. Ackoff, and E. Leonard Arnoff, *Introduction to Operations Research* (New York, 1957). See also Maurice Sasieni, Arthur Yaspan, and Lawrence Friedman, *Operations Research—Methods and Problems* (New York, 1957); James H. Batchelor, *Operations Research: An Annotated Bibliography* (2 ed., St. Louis, 1959–1963), Vols. I, II, III, and IV.

[22] S. E. Skinner, Executive Vice Pres., General Motors Corp., "Quality and Reliability Control," speech, first General Motors-wide orientation program, July 23, 1959. For a description of the Atlas reliability problem, see Robert De Roos, "Perspective '64," booklet (General Dynamics/Astronautics, 1964).

[23] See Joan R. Rosenblatt, "On Prediction of System Performance from Information on Component Performance," *Proceedings of the Western Joint Computer Conference,* Los Angeles, Feb. 1957. Cf. Nicholas E. Golovin, "An Approach to Reliability Prediction Program," American Society for Quality Control, *Transactions of 1960 Convention,* San Francisco, May 25, 1960.

[24] Thomas C. Reeves, "Reliability Prediction—Its Validity and Application as a Design Tool," paper No. 60–MD–1, American Soc. of Mechanical Engineers, Feb. 10, 1960, 8.

[25] George M. Low, in comments, Oct. 5, 1965, notes that these discussions "occurred not between Washington and the Field but between the organization responsible for manned space flight both in Washington and the Field and the Reliability people."

[24] Harry R. Powell, "The Impact of Reliability on Design," paper No. 60 MD 2, American Soc. of Mechanical Engineers, April 5, 1960.

[25] See Wernher von Braun, "The Redstone, Jupiter, and Juno," in Eugene M. Emme, ed., *The History of Rocket Technology: Essays on Research, Development, and Utility* (Detroit, 1964), 107-121; Kuettner interview. On the little known Redstone booster recovery system development efforts, see R. I. Johnson et al., "The Mercury-Redstone Project," MSFC Saturn/Apollo Systems Office, TMX 53107, June 1964, 6-22, 6-29; letter, Gilruth to von Braun, with enclosures, Dec. 9, 1959; memo, R. M. Barraza for M-DEP-R&D, MSFC, "Summary of Mercury-Redstone Recovery Program," Aug. 1, 1960.

[28] For details of Redstone and Jupiter flight failures, see three reports prepared by Chrysler Missile Division for MSFC, "Overall Study and Flight Evaluation of the Redstone Missile Propulsion and Associated Systems," MSFC report No. RP-TR 61-11, April 7, 1961; G. G. McDonald, P. R. Brown, and J. L. Montgomery, Jr., "Jupiter Missile and Juno II Vehicle Malfunction Study," MSFC report No. MTP M-P&VE-P-2 62, April 26, 1962; and P. S. Sorce, L. Van Camp, R. E. Stevens, et al., "Redstone Vehicle Malfunction Study (Mercury-Redstone Program)," MSFC report No. DSD-TM-12-60, Original Issue, June 15, 1960; Rev. A, Oct. 31, 1960, Rev. B, May 1, 1961.

[29] Joachim P. Kuettner and Emil Bertram, "Mercury-Redstone Launch Vehicle Development and Performance," in *Mercury Project Summary*, 69. See also Brandner, "Proposal for Abort Sensing System," 4, 5. For STG's first reliability meeting with ABMA, see Purser, log for Gilruth, July 27, 1959. On Chrysler's role, see two brochures, "Redstone," AB 106, Chrysler Missile Division [ca. April 1961], and "Presentation to Manned Spacecraft Center," Chrysler Defense and Space Group, June 20, 1962.

[30] "Project Mercury Indoctrination," report No. 6821, McDonnell Aircraft Corp., May 21, 1959, 160.

[31] "Reliability Program Status for Project Mercury," report No. 7007, McDonnell Aircraft Corp., Aug. 17, 1959, 1, 11, 12.

[32] Tecwyn Roberts, "Minutes of Meeting: Presentation by AFBMD/STL on Safety and Reliability," Nov. 13, 1959, with enclosures. Powell's chart is enclosure 2. Cf. John C. French and Frederick J. Bailey, Jr., "Reliability and Flight Safety," *Mercury Project Summary*, 105-116, for a static view of the results of these discussions.

[33] Ms., F. J. Bailey, Jr., "Reliability and Flight Safety Problems of Manned Spacecraft Flight," April 4, 1962, 5. The crux of the reliability dispute between "statistics," represented by Golovin and NASA Headquarters, and "techniques," represented by STG, McDonnell, and ABMA, was illustrated by the basic commitment among STG engineers to deny the existence of any such thing as "a random failure." Gilruth later expressed this particular attitude toward man-rating machines: "We must regard every malfunction and, in fact, every observed peculiarity in the behavior of a system as an important warning of potential disaster. Only when the cause is thoroughly understood, and a change to eliminate it has been made, can we proceed with the flight program." See Gilruth, "MSC Viewpoints on Reliability and Quality Control," MSC fact sheet No. 93, 1963.

[34] See Purser, log for Gilruth, Aug. 5, 1959.

[35] Charles W. Mathews, interview, Houston, Feb. 24, 1964. Cf. memo, William M. Bland, Jr., and Kraft to Project Dir., "Meeting with Range Safety People at AFMTC, March 31, 1959," April 3, 1959.

[36] Ms., Mathews, "Mercury Abort Sensing and Implementation Systems: History of Development," outline for Project Mercury Technical History Program, July 1, 1963; Kuettner and Bertram, "Mercury-Redstone Launch Vehicle," 72; Kuettner, "Manrating Space Carrier Vehicles," 636.

[37] Compare the detail and progress evidenced in "Status Report No. 3 for Period Ending July 31, 1959," Langley/STG, with that shown in "Status Report No. 4 for Period Ending Oct. 31, 1959," Langley/STG.

[38] Letter, Gilruth to Commanding Officer, Army Ballistic Missile Agency, "Mercury-Redstone Launch Schedule," Aug. 25, 1959. Cf. memo, Purser to Project Dir., "Project Mercury Meeting on 11 February, 1959, at ABMA," with enclosed bar chart. See C. Northcote Parkinson, *Parkinson's Law* (New York, 1959).

[39] Perhaps the most eloquent defense Wernher von Braun ever made against the inevitable shallow cynicism of critics who could not forget the Second World War was a widely printed article entitled "The Acid Test," which first appeared in *Space Journal of the Astro-Sciences*, Vol. 1, No. 3 (Summer 1958), 31-36. For background on the following discussion of

the von Braun team's cohesive esprit, see Walter R. Dornberger, *V-2* (New York, 1954); and Dieter K. Huzel, *Peenemünde to Canaveral* (Englewood Cliffs, N.J., 1962).

[40] For part of the controversy generated by the Mercury-Jupiter cancellation, see letter, John G. Zierdt to NASA Administrator, June 26, 1959; memos, Low to Silverstein, "Cancellation of Mercury-Jupiter Program," July 8 and July 13, 1959; message, Zierdt to Silverstein, July 16, 1959; letters, Silverstein to Medaris, Commanding Officer, Army Ordnance Missile Command, July 21 and July 28, 1959; letter, Herbert F. York to Glennan, Aug. 4, 1959; letter, David H. Newby to Low, Aug. 19, 1959. See also letters, Gilruth to Low, July 1, 1959; Silverstein to Gilruth, July 1, 1959; and Gilruth to Silverstein, July 8, 1959. Memo for files, John A. Powers, "Response to Query on the Subject of Cancellation of Jupiter," Aug. 31, 1959.

[41] George Savignac and E. G. Leever, "Project Mercury Engineering Status Report," McDonnell Aircraft Corp., Aug. 1, 1959, 31; Savignac and Leever, "Bi-Monthly Engineering Status Report," McDonnell Aircraft Corp., Oct. 1, 1959, 39.

[42] Minutes, "Mercury Panel 3 Meeting, 18–19 August, 1959, at Missile Firing Laboratory, Cape Canaveral, Florida." These minutes record numerous bilateral agreements on flight testing, range safety, etc., concurred in by NASA, McDonnell, and Army Ballistic Missile Agency representatives. See especially Part IV, an appendix on operational checkout procedures. Kuettner, "Minutes and Major Results of Project Mercury Coordination Meeting at ABMA," Nov. 20, 1959. Cf. minutes, Jerome B. Hammack, Redstone systems engineer, STG, "Mercury-Redstone Panel II Meeting: Booster and Capsule Checkout Procedures, at ABMA, Nov. 19, 1959," Dec. 8, 1959; message, M. L. Raines to Commanding General, AOMC, Nov. 3, 1959; reply, PR–092200Z, Nov. 9, 1959.

[43] See House Committee on Science and Astronautics, 86 Cong., 2 sess. (1960), *Transfer of the Development Operations Division of the Army Ballistic Missile Agency to the National Aeronautics and Space Administration, Hearings*, Feb. 3, 1960; Robert L. Rosholt, *An Administrative History of NASA, 1950 to 1963;* David S. Akens, Paul K. Freiwirth, and Helen T. Wells, *History of the George C. Marshall Space Flight Center* (Huntsville, Ala., 1960–1962), I, ix.

[44] White, "Development of the Mercury-Atlas Pilot Safety Program," Space Technology Laboratories, June 12, 1961, 4. Cf. Hohmann, "General Aspects of the Pilot Safety Program for Project Mercury Atlas Boosters," Space Technology Laboratories, Feb. 8, 1960, passim. Cf. "System Description—Abort Sensing and Implementation System for Project Mercury," Convair/Astronautics report No. AE60-0576, June 6, 1960.

[45] See C. L. Gandy and I. B. Hanson, "Mercury-Atlas Launch Vehicle Development and Performance," in *Mercury Project Summary*, 94. James R. Dempsey, a vice president of General Dynamics and the manager of its Convair division, later called attention to the 25 percent design safety factor commonly used in the ballistic missile business versus the 1.5 safety margin used in the design of aircraft. See his paper "Launch-Vehicle Considerations for Manned Space Flight," in *Proceedings of First National Conference on the Peaceful Uses of Space*, Tulsa, Oklahoma, May 26–27, 1961 (Washington, 1961), 118.

[46] P. E. Culbertson, "Man-Rating the Atlas as a Mercury Booster," American Institute of Aeronautics and Astronautics, paper No. 65-252, presented at Dayton, Ohio, April 21–23, 1965, 2, 7.

[47] Hohmann interviews and article, "Pilot Safety and Mercury/Atlas," *Astronautics and Aerospace Engineering* (Feb. 1963), 40–42.

[48] Minutes, "Mock-Up Review," 12 through 14 May, 1959, with enclosure addressed to C. H. Zimmerman and Low, June 23, 1959.

[49] Faget interviews; John F. Yardley, interview, St. Louis, Aug. 31, 1964; and MAC "Biographical Information" on Yardley, June 10, 1964. Until the redesignation of STG as MSC on Nov. 1, 1961, and the reorganization of MSC into the Mercury, Gemini, and Apollo Project Offices on Jan. 15, 1962, systems engineering in STG was shared by the Flight Systems Division and the Engineering Division under Faget and James A. Chamberlin, respectively. See Grimwood, *Mercury Chronology*, 219–220.

[50] McDonnell Aircraft Corporation, "Twentieth Annual Report," June 30, 1959, foreword. Cf. "McDonnell Aircraft Corporation, Nineteenth Annual Report, 1958." "Achievements, 1939–1956," "Orientation Manual, 1960–61," 7, and "McDonnell: The First Twenty-Five Years, 1939–1964," 18–28, brochures, McDonnell Aircraft Corp.

[51] Memo, Logan T. MacMillan to D. S. Lewis, "Project Mercury Daily Report, 18 July 1959—Coordination Committee Results,"

McDonnell Aircraft Corp. inter-office memo No. 344; memo, E. M. Flesh to E. Akeroyd, "Capsule Coordination Committee," McDonnell Aircraft Corp. inter-office memo No. 3606, July 2, 1959. See also message, MacMillan to STG, Sept. 16, 1959. Cf. MacMillan, interview, St. Louis, Aug. 31, 1964.

[52] Kendall Perkins, interview, St. Louis, Aug. 31, 1964.

[53] William Dubusker, interview, St. Louis, Sept. 1, 1964; Flesh, interview, St. Louis, Sept. 2, 1964. For a more detailed description of fabricating technique and fusion welding, see David S. Anderton, "How Mercury Capsule Design Evolved," *Aviation Week*, LXXIV (May 22, 1961).

[54] Regarding the Slayton-Carpenter dispute over the best kind of pilot control system, see John Dille, ed., *We Seven, by the Astronauts Themselves* (New York, 1962), 15. Memo, D. P. Murray, MAC Manager of Contracts, to Project Mercury, Engineering and Contract Administration Division, "Mercury Capsule Contract NAS5–59, Contract Change Proposals Nos. 58–1, 61–2, 73 and 76," Sept. 23, 1959.

[55] Edward R. Jones, interview, St. Louis, Sept. 2, 1964. Jones had earned his doctorate in experimental psychology from Washington University in St. Louis, in 1954, and since the first of the decade he had worked in flight safety research.

[56] Minutes, "MAC Project Mercury—Human Factors; Phase A2, Mission Analysis and Preliminary Cockpit Layout," manuscript minutes of oral report by Minneapolis-Honeywell human factors group to McDonnell, March 2, 1959, 3.

[57] Memo, Jones to Yardley, "Failure Analysis," with enclosure, David T. Grober and Jones, "Human Engineering Implications of Failures in the Mercury Capsule," Aug. 10, 1959. These two quotations are from pp. 2, 4, and 5.

[58] Jones, "Man's Integration into the Mercury Capsule," paper, 14th annual meeting, American Rocket Soc., Washington, Nov. 16–19, 1959, 1, 2.

[59] The input of sense data into the ASCS and its output of nervous commands suggests the classic cybernetic approach to understanding the Mercury attitude control system. Consider the machine as if it were an organism in which sensors (like small rate gyros, larger position gyros, and infrared sensitive horizon scanners) provide the brain (ASCS) with the data it needs to compute through its amplifier-calibrators and logic boards the actions required by the muscles (RCS motors) in order to maintain a certain position. Sense organs, a brain, and muscles are necessary black boxes to the performance of any self-regulating system, but Mercury design engineers seldom bothered at first to produce "glass boxes" for operating engineers to determine how to build, work, and improve them. For a helpful introduction to the intricacies of modern gyroscopes, accelerometers, and inertial guidance systems, see "Inertial Guidance Primer," pamphlet, Minneapolis-Honeywell Regulator Company, 1963.

[60] Robert Chilton, interview, Houston, June 2, 1964; Paul F. Horsman, interview, Houston, Feb. 12, 1964; Thomas V. Chambers and Richard R. Carley, comments, Sept. 25, 1965. See also Horsman draft Ms., "Manned Spacecraft Stabilization and Control System," for Mercury Technical History, June 19, 1963.

[61] Memo for files, Chilton, "Alternate Attitude Control System for the Mercury Capsule," July 8, 1959, 3. Cf. memo, Chilton to Project Dir., "Alternate Attitude Control System for the Mercury Capsule," July 1, 1959. See also Chilton, "Attitude Control Systems," progress report, Oct. 21, 1959.

[62] Kurt P. Wagenknecht, McDonnell Aircraft Corp. procurement officer, interview, St. Louis, Sept. 2, 1964.

[63] Roger J. Pierce, "Mercury Capsule Communications," *Astronautics*, IV (Dec. 1959), 24–27, 86–88. Another constant problem was the discovery of toxic byproducts from electrical insulation, which required much equipment redesign.

[64] Minutes, "Special Coordination Meeting at McDonnell," Norman F. Smith, secretary, Oct. 1 and 2, 1959, sec. 2a.0.1, 5.

[65] Letter, Gilruth to Ira H. Abbott, "Required Basic Research on Parachute to Support Manned Space Flight," July 6, 1959, 2. See also memos, G. A. White, J. B. Lee, and Alan B. Kehlet to Chief, Flight Systems Div., "Drogue parachute," Oct. 15, 1959.

[66] Letter, Henry J. E. Reid to NASA, "Required Basic Research on Parachute to Support Manned Space Flight," Sept. 22, 1959; cf. Joe W. Dodson, transcript of taped discussion, "Mercury Parachute History," Sept. 1962, and Russell E. Clickner, comments, Nov. 5, 1965.

[67] Letter, Charles J. Donlan to Low, "Langley Support for Project Mercury," Dec. 9, 1959. The addition of the better "mousetrap" is best described in Aleck C. Bond and

Kehlet, "Review, Scope, and Recent Results of Project Mercury Research and Development Program," paper, 28 annual meeting, Inst. of Aeronautical Sciences, New York City, Jan. 25, 1960.

[68] Purser, log for Gilruth, Dec. 21, 1959. Parachute systems and technology are well described in Ms., Bond and Faget, "Technologies of Manned Space Systems," Chap. 14, "The Role of Ground Testing in Manned Spacecraft Programs," 166–177.

[69] When they become available, see the following classified historical monographs written by Air Force historians: Lee Bowen, *The Threshold of Space: The Air Force National Space Program, 1945–1959*, Sept. 1960; Max Rosenberg, *The Air Force in Space 1959–60*, June 1962; Clarence J. Geiger, *History of the X-20A: Dyna-Soar*, Air Force Systems Command Hist. Pub. Series, 63–50–I, Oct. 1963; Robert L. Perry, *Origins of the USAF Space Program, 1945–1956*, Air Force Systems Command Hist. Pub. Series, 62–24–10, 1961; Ethel M. DeHaven, *Aerospace—The Evolution of USAF Weapons Acquisition Policy, 1945–1961*, Aug. 1962; *Comparisons of NASA Manned Space Program and USAF Manned Military Space Proposal*, Feb. 25, 1960.

[70] George Alexander, "Atlas Accuracy Improves as Test Program Is Completed," *Aviation Week*, LXXVIII (Feb. 25, 1963), 69–75.

[71] Mark Morton, "Progress in Reentry-Recovery Vehicle Development," pamphlet, Missile and Space Vehicle Dept., General Electric Co., Philadelphia, Jan. 2, 1961, 14.

[72] Kehlet and Bruce G. Jackson, STG aerodynamicists responsible for the aerodynamic stability of the Big Joe capsule on entry, wanted this to be a free flight (with the ACS nonoperative from turnaround to max q), but shortly before the launch day "somebody blew the whistle" and changed the plan to full operation of the ACS throughout the flight. As it turned out, Kehlet and Jackson got their wish after all: interviews, Downey, Calif., Aug. 27, 1964, and Houston, Sept. 13, 1965.

[73] "Project Mercury Status Report No. 4," 1, 15–18, 36. Cf. "Project Mercury Status Report No. 3," Ms., Bond, for Project Mercury Tech. Hist. Program, "Big Joe," June 27, 1963. According to Jack A. Kinzler, Langley shop foreman, the Big Joe capsule culminated an intensive manufacturing development that fed directly into STG's relations with McDonnell; see Kinzler draft Ms., "Manufacturing by NASA for Project Mercury," for Mercury Technical History, Aug. 30, 1963.

[74] Memo, Bond to Project Dir., "Visit to Lewis Laboratory with Regard to Instrumentation and Construction of Big Joe Capsule," April 28, 1959. Cf. Ms., Norman Farmer et al., "Instrumentation," for Project Mercury Tech. Hist. Program, June 27, 1963, 12. Ms., Harold Gold, "Attitude Control System for Project HS–24," June 9, 1959; Warren Plohr, interview, Cleveland, May 1, 1964.

[75] Bond, interview, Houston, March 13, 1964; B. Porter Brown, interview, Cape Kennedy, April 30, 1964; Scott H. Simpkinson, interview, Houston, June 2, 1964. See also memo [Simpkinson], NASA–(MTQD) to all concerned, "Personnel Assignments for First Mercury FRF and Launch," Aug. 31, 1959.

[76] The industrial society at the Cape is well described by Richard A. Smith, "Industry's Trial by Fire at Canaveral," in Editors of *Fortune, The Space Industry: America's Newest Giant* (Englewood Cliffs, N.J., 1962), 65 et seq.

[77] For the first STG countdown procedures, see four-page ditto, "HS–24 Countdown of Major Events," in Simpkinson's papers; STG, "Test No. HS–24 General Information for Recovery Forces," NASA Project Mercury working paper No. 101, Aug. 14, 1959.

[78] The following description of the Big Joe flight is based on the documents cited below and on Simpkinson's eyewitness account and vivid recall in interview; "Preliminary Flight Test Results of Big Joe," NASA Project Mercury working paper No. 107, Oct. 12, 1959; "Qualification Tests on the Big Joe Recovery System," NASA Project Mercury working paper No. 108, Oct. 27, 1959. Cf. memo, Warren J. North to T. E. Jenkins, "Flight Mission Data for Project Mercury," Jan. 14, 1960, and John P. Mayer, comments, Sept. 8, 1965.

[79] Memo, Low to Administrator, "Big Joe Shot," Sept. 9, 1959. Carl R. Huss, in comments, Oct. 5, 1965, called attention to the fact that "the reliability of Atlas staging was about as high as it could be" until Big Joe.

[80] Letter, "Big Joe team" to Gilruth, Sept. 6, 1959. This artifact is one of Gilruth's mementos, now sealed in plastic and framed in a plaque on the wall of the office of the director, Manned Spacecraft Center. See also Huss comments.

[81] Memo, Leonard Rabb to Chief, Flight Systems Div., "Heat Shield Performance," Oct. 7, 1959. Bond, interview, Houston, Sept. 22, 1965. See also "Results of Studies Made to Determine Required Retrorocket Capability,"

NASA Project Mercury working paper No. 102, Sept. 22, 1959. In addition, Alan B. Kehlet directed Dennis F. Hasson to investigate an inflatable sphere to accomplish the decrease in decay time for a retrofire failure and to stabilize the capsule in the event of a control system failure. This study was published as NASA Project Mercury working paper No. 113, "Preliminary Study Using Inflatable Spheres for Aerodynamic Stabilization During Reentry," Nov. 18, 1959.

[62] Bond, "Big Joe," 23, 24, 25. The last paragraph of this quotation is somewhat anachronistic in that it disregards the last-minute debates among aerodynamicists over the dynamic stability issue: see ante footnote 72. Regarding afterbody heat protection, other evidence from wind tunnels and from the Navy's Ordnance Aerophysics Laboratory at Daingerfield, Texas, was accumulating also, pointing toward the need for beryllium or a like material to act as heat sink shingles around the antenna canister.

[63] Alexander, "Atlas Accuracy Improves."

[64] Abraham D. Spinak et al., "Special Accident Investigating Committee Report of the Little Joe No. One Misfire on Aug. 21, 1959, Wallops Station," Sept. 18, 1959, 6.

[65] Memo, W. S. Blanchard, Jr., to Assoc. Dir., "Tentative Changes in the Langley Little Joe Support Program," Sept. 3, 1959; "Little Joe Project Progress Report," North American Aviation, Sept. 31, 1959, 6; letter, Gerathewohl to Jerome Hammack, Dec. 30, 1959; letter, Donlan to Gerathewohl, Jan. 22, 1960.

[56] Memo, Low to Administrator, "First Little Joe Launching," Oct. 5, 1959. Cf. memo, Low to Administrator, "Follow-up Report, Little Joe Firing of 11/4/59," Nov. 6, 1959. See "Flight Test Report LJ-6," NASA Project Mercury working paper No. 133, April 22, 1960. See also memo, John F. Royall, Jr., to STG Assoc. Dir., "Preliminary Data from the Flight Test . . . of Little Joe No. 6, Nov. 4, 1959."

[57] "Countdown for the Little Joe 1-A," STG, Nov. 4, 1959. Cf. memo, Silverstein to Dir., Office of Public Information, "Project Mercury Information Plan," July 7, 1959.

[58] Letter, Donlan to Cdr., DesFlotFour, Dec. 29, 1959; "Research and Development Flight Test Program . . . Abort at High Dynamic Pressure, LJ-1A," NASA Project Mercury working paper No. 134, July 25, 1960. George Low has commented (Oct. 5, 1965) that this hangfire on LJ-1A "probably in itself made the entire Little Joe program worthwhile.

Early identification of this problem certainly saved us time and avoided many headaches later."

[60] "Minutes of Meeting, Bio-Paks for Little Joe Flights 2, 3, and 4, June 8, 1959, at STG," June 18, 1959. Cf. memo, Jack C. Heberlig to Gilruth, "Visit of [School of Aviation Medicine personnel, 25 men] to Discuss Bio-Paks [for Little Joe 2, 3, and 4]," April 1, 1959. Ronald Kolenkiewicz, "Minutes of Meeting Concerning Mercury Qualification Test for Little Joe No. 5, June 30, 1959, at NASA-STG, Langley Field, Va.," July 16, 1959. The preliminary operations plan for the aeromedical aspects of LJ-5 was drawn up by Richard S. Johnston on Nov. 26, 1959.

[90] The possibility of flying a manned Little Joe was seriously if secretly considered during this time, but the idea was quickly discarded as technically not feasible because the dynamic pressures were too great: Walter C. Williams, interview, Houston, Aug. 23, 1965.

[91] "Little Joe II," operations plan, STG, Dec. 2, 1959; memo, Low to Administrator, "Little Joe Test No. 3," Dec. 5, 1959. Cf. "Flight Test Report, LJ-2," NASA Project Mercury working paper No. 169, April 1961. "Recovery Operations for Little Joe Test No. Two," NASA Project Mercury working paper No. 122, Jan. 18, 1960. See also letter, Dryden to Gilruth, Dec. 8, 1959; letter, Otis O. Benson, Jr., to Dryden, Dec. 30, 1959.

[92] Memo, George D. Smith to NASA Administrator, "Biological Experiment on Little Joe No. 2," Dec. 31, 1959. Cf. letter, Reid to STG, "In support of Project Mercury—Transmittal of Preliminary Data . . . of Little Joe 2," Dec. 31, 1959; John A. Powers and E. Harry Kolcum, "Information Plan—Little Joe Flight 1-B," Jan. 5, 1960, 2.

[93] Gilruth, "Addendum to Information Plan for Firing of Little Joe 1-B," Jan. 5, 1960, 2.

[94] Memo, Low to NASA Administrator, "Little Joe 1-B (Test No. 4)," Jan. 22, 1960. Cf. "Flight Test Report, LJ-1B," NASA Project Mercury working paper No. 173, March 3, 1961. "Recovery Operations for LJ Test No. One-B," NASA Project Mercury working paper No. 105, Feb. 1960.

[95] Memo, Heberlig to Chief, Flight Systems Div., "Preliminary Reports of the SAM Bio-Pak Experiment in Little Joe 1-B," Feb. 3, 1960. See also letter, Gilruth to Cloid D. Green, School of Aviation Medicine, Brooks AFB, re LJ-1B biophysical aspects, April 27, 1960.

[96] Memo, Harvey H. Hubbard to Assoc.

Dir., STG, "Noise Measurements of Big Joe and Little Joe Mercury Vehicles," Feb. 17, 1960. Cf. letter, Donlan to McDonnell Aircraft Corp., re preliminary results of LJ–1B and LJ–2 compiled for use in production redesign, May 3, 1960. See also booklet, "Project Mercury Photographs of Press Tour, Little Joe 1–B," Jan. 20–21, 1960.

[97] Minutes, Lewis R. Fisher, "Little Joe No. 5," meeting on Jan. 28, 1960.

[98] See, e.g., *Newsweek*, LIV (Oct. 26, 1959), for story and pictures of three Russian cosmonauts, Aleksei Gracher, Aleksei Belokonev, and Ivan Kachur. See also Ari Shternfeld, *Soviet Space Medicine* (2 rev. ed., New York, 1959).

[99] Purser, logs for Gilruth, Dec. 15 and 21, 1959.

[100] Memo, M. Scott Carpenter et al., to Project Dir., "Exchange of Visits with Russian Astronauts," Oct. 21, 1959; T. Keith Glennan, "Opportunities for International Cooperation in Space," *Dept. of State Bulletin* (Jan. 11, 1960), 62. Cf. Vernon Van Dyke, *Pride and Power* (Urbana, Ill., 1964), 244–246; Eugene M. Emme, *Aeronautics and Astronautics: An American Chronology of Science and Technology in the Exploration of Space, 1915–1960* (Washington, 1961), 115. See also Philip C. Jessup and Howard J. Taubenfeld, *Controls for Outer Space and the Antarctic Analogy* (New York, 1959), 251–282; Purser, "Review of Information Relating to Soviet Manned Space Flight Activity," a scrapbook and summary report, Jan. 22, 1960.

[101] Howard C. Kyle, interview, Houston, Oct. 19, 1963; Hartley A. Soulé, interview, Hampton, Va., Jan. 7, 1964. Perhaps the best overview of the complexity of the Mercury network can be gained from the manual "Introduction to Project Mercury and Site Handbook," Western Electric Company, Inc., MG–101, Sept. 1960. This is the first in a series of some 50 volumes of operations and maintenance manuals.

[102] Kraft, "Some Operational Aspects of Project Mercury," speech, annual meeting, Soc. of Experimental Test Pilots, Los Angeles, Oct. 9, 1959, 5, 6, 10. See also Kraft, interview, Houston, Oct. 20, 1964, and "A Study of the Control and Landing Areas for Post Staging Abort Trajectories," NASA Project Mercury working paper No. 100, Aug. 3, 1959.

[103] Gerald M. Truszynski, "Space Communications," NASA pamphlet, 1963, 11; Mayer, interview, Houston, Oct. 19, 1964.

Cf. Mayer, "The Motion of a Space Vehicle within the Earth-Moon System," in *Notes on Space Technology* (Langley, Va., May 1958). Memo, Mayer to Chief, Operations Div., "Trip Report of Visits to STL, Convair/Astronautics, Lockheed, and Stromberg-Carlson on Nov. 30, Dec. 1, through Dec. 4, 1959."

[104] John D. Hodge, interview, Houston, Aug. 11, 1964; David G. Simons, interview, San Antonio, April 24, 1964; Col. George M. Knauf was shortly to undertake the team training of Air Force medical monitors in the areas assigned to him at Patrick Air Force Base and at the Cape. See memo, Stanley C. White to Chief, Flight Systems Div., "Trip to USAF Surgeon General's Office . . . to discuss daily training of medical monitors with Colonel Knauf," Feb. 8, 1960. The STG also conducted medical monitor training at Langley.

[105] Sensitive security matters may be traced backward from various editions of NASA's "Mercury Program Security Classification Guide," SCG–9, the second and final revision of which was dated Dec. 15, 1964. The first of these guides, issued on Aug. 3, 1959, had only the particular command control code used for a specific flight designated at the highest level of security.

[106] The first network specifications, numbered S–45 dated May 21, 1959, were superseded by two revisions until S–45B of Oct. 30, 1959. Memo, Reid to all concerned, "Designation of Organization, Membership, and Operating Procedures for the Source-Selection Panel and the Technical Evaluation Board—Tracking and Ground Instrumentation, Project Mercury," June 12, 1959; memo, North to NASA Administrator, "Background of Project Mercury Schedules," with enclosure, Aug. 14, 1960, 4. The definitive contract with Western Electric, NAS 1–430, was not executed until Jan. 11, 1960, after which some 500 changes were processed before completion in June 1961. See the series of monthly "Progress Report to NASA: Project Mercury," Western Electric Company, Inc., Aug. 1959 to June 1961.

[107] Letter, Reid to Edmond C. Buckley, "Arrangements for Site Survey Teams in Connection with Tracking and Ground Instrumentation Systems for Project Mercury," July 16, 1959. For some indications of the extent of these difficulties, see (for Mexico) Purser, log for Gilruth, Aug. 17, 1959; and (for Africa) Ray W. Hooker, memo for files, "Tracking and Ground Instrumentation Systems for Project

Mercury, Special Report on African Sites," Oct. 20, 1959. See also "Report for the Cisler Committee on Tracking and Ground Instrumentation Systems for Project Mercury," NASA, Nov. 25, 1959.

[107] Arnold W. Frutkin, interview, Washington, Sept. 2, 1965; and Chaps. 1 and 2 of his book, *International Cooperation in Space* (Englewood Cliffs, N.J., 1965). For texts of all executive agreements, memoranda of understanding, and other international arrangements after 1959, see Senate Committee on Aeronautical and Space Sciences, 89 Cong., 1 sess., *United States International Space Programs*, July 30, 1965. Dwight D. Eisenhower, *The White House Years: Waging Peace, 1956–1961* (Garden City, N.Y., 1965), 344.

[108] Alfred Rosenthal, *The Early Years: Goddard Space Flight Center Historical Origins and Activities through December 1962* (Washington, 1964), 53, 57. Cf. "Fifth Anniversary, International Tracking of Space Vehicles," pamphlet, Goddard Space Flight Center, Greenbelt, Md., Jan. 31, 1963. Soulé interview.

[110] See anon., "The Manned Space Flight Tracking Network," pamphlet, NASA Goddard Space Flight Center, Greenbelt, Md., 1965. See also Loyd S. Swenson, Jr., "The Telecommunications Revolution in the Nineteenth Century," paper, American Studies Assn., Claremont, Calif., Nov. 1962.

[111] See Wilfred J. Mayo-Wells, "The Origins of Space Telemetry," in Emme, ed., *The History of Rocket Technology*, 253, 268. See also Harry L. Stiltz, ed., *Aerospace Telemetry* (Englewood Cliffs, N.J., 1961) and Mayer comments.

[112] John T. Mengel, comments, Sept. 14, 1965. Mengel (for the Navy), Edmond Buckley (for NACA), and Gerald De Bey (for the Army) had supported the Air Force studies for "Man-in-Space-Soonest" tracking requirements in 1958. See also Mengel, "Satellite Ground Data Networks," Appendix B in Alfred Rosenthal, *Goddard '63: A Year in Review at Goddard Space Flight Center* (Greenbelt, Md., 1964), B-1, B-9.

[113] M. S. Buist and G. M. Weinberg, "Real-Time Multi-Programming in Project Mercury," in Donald P. Le Galley, ed., *Ballistic Missile and Space Technology* (4 vols., New York, 1960), I, 436. See also J. Painter and E. Chicoine, eds., "Reference Notes on Communication Systems," NASA Manned Spacecraft Center, November 1962.

[114] The Burroughs and IBM computer systems at the Cape sent orbital insertion data by wire to the Goddard prediction computers, which then returned display data to the Mercury Control Center in milliseconds. For more adequate treatments, see Michael Chriss, "Establishment of NASA's Manned Tracking Network," NASA Historical Note HHN-54; Shirley Thomas, *Satellite Tracking Facilities: Their History and Operations* (New York, 1963); P. V. H. Weems et al., *Space Navigation Handbook*, NAVPERS 92988 (Washington, 1961). See also anon., "Mercury History: An Unclassified Documentation of the Contributions of Radio Command Guidance to Project Mercury," mimeographed 24-page document prepared by Information Services, General Electric, Radio Guidance Operation, Syracuse, N.Y., ca. June 1963.

[115] Powers, memo for file, "Points of Emphasis in Promoting the Public Picture of the Space Task Group," undated [ca. Dec. 1959].

Chapter VIII

[1] Jacques Piccard, "Man's Deepest Dive," *National Geographic*, CXVIII (July 1960), 235; Edward L. Beach, "Triton Follows Magellan's Wake," *National Geographic*, CXVIII (Aug. 1960), 585–615; House Committee on Science and Astronautics, 86 Cong., 2 sess. (1960), *Ocean Sciences and National Security*, July 1, 1960; Norris and Ross McWhirter, eds., *Guinness Book of World Records* (paperback ed., New York, 1964), 205, 207; Bern Dibner, *The Victoria and the Triton* (Norwalk, Conn., 1962). On Jan. 23, 1960, a Pacific Fleet task element floated above the Marianas Trench, an abyssal canyon north of Guam, also known as the Challenger Deep, while Jacques Piccard, the son of Auguste who had designed the *Trieste*, and Donald Walsh, a Navy lieutenant, squeezed themselves into the bathyspherical gondola beneath their hydrostatic balloon. In this third of a series of dives, Piccard and Walsh sank down 7000 fathoms, or eight miles, where their vehicle endured 1085 tons of pressure per square foot and where they saw life on the bottom of the ocean. For all mankind, Piccard and Walsh figuratively "took possession of the abyss, the last extreme on our Earth that remained unconquered." Three months later, on April 25, 1960, the nuclear-powered submarine *Triton*, with 183 Americans captained by Edward L. Beach, completed the world's first undersea circumnavigation, following for two months submerged the wake of Magellan's ship, the *Victoria*, at an average speed of 18 knots for 41,519 miles. The inertial guidance

navigation system that made the trip of the *Triton* possible had grown out of the same research and development program, Project Navaho, that had provided the prototype rocket engine for the Redstone, Jupiter/Polaris, Thor, Atlas, and Titan.

[2] House Committee on Science and Astronautics, 86 Cong., 2 sess. (1960), *Hearings, Review of the Space Program* (Part 1, No. 3), testimony of T. Keith Glennan, 170, and *Project Mercury, First Interim Report*, Jan. 27, 1960; John W. Finney, "Soviet Space Man Held Pacific Aim," *New York Times*, Jan. 9, 1960; Finney, "U.S. Steps up Effort in Outer Space Race," *New York Times*, Jan. 19, 1960; Craig Lewis, "NASA's $802 Million Request May Grow," *Aviation Week*, LXXII (Jan. 25, 1960).

[3] Abe Silverstein, quoted in Albert Sehlstedt, Jr., "No Space Man Urgency Seen," *Baltimore Sun*, Jan. 26, 1960; William Hines, "Scientist Urges Use of Space for Humanity," *Washington Evening Star*, Jan. 25, 1960; Ralph E. Lapp, *Man and Space: The Next Decade* (New York, 1961), 55-67; Donald W. Cox, *The Space Race: From Sputnik to Apollo— and Beyond* (Philadelphia, 1962), 88-93; David Wise and Thomas B. Ross, *The U-2 Affair* (New York, 1962).

[4] See Frank H. Samonski, Jr., "Project Mercury Environmental Control System Technical History," MSC, Crew Systems Division report No. 63-34, Nov. 14, 1963, for a most thorough topical overview of this subject.

[5] Seymour Chapin, "The Pressurized Flight Industry in the Southwest Since 1930," paper, Pacific Coast Branch meeting, American Hist. Assn., Los Angeles, Aug. 26, 1964. See also Irwin Stambler, "Environmental System for Mercury Capsule is Simple, Rugged," *Space/Aeronautics*, XXXII (July 1959), 42-45.

[6] A. D. Catterson, interview, Houston, Oct. 23, 1964; memo, Stanley C. White, "Present Status—Major Systems: Environmental Systems," Feb. 1959; memo, Gerard J. Pesman to Tech. Assessment Committee, "Meeting with McDonnell Aircraft Corporation to Discuss Environmental Control System for the Manned Spacecraft Capsule," Jan. 23, 1959. Although STG decided this question in favor of the latter alternative in 1958, the possibility of a change existed throughout 1959. See also William K. Douglas comments, Aug. 17, 1965.

[7] Ms., Maxime A. Faget and Aleck C. Bond, "Technologies of Manned Space Systems," 55. For an excellent view of the controversy about mixed gas versus 100 percent oxygen systems,

see Eugene B. Konecci, "Soviet Bioastronautics—1964," paper, National Space Club, Washington, D.C., Dec. 15, 1964. The Soviet choice of a near-sea-level environment was wise for several reasons, explained Konecci, but he added that the danger of decompression sickness may retard extravehicular operations and therefore "may prove to be the Achilles heel in their program."

[8] Edward H. Olling, interview, Houston, Sept. 14, 1965. See also Olling's Ms. paper, "Design Solutions and Test Results for the Life Support System for Project Mercury," Sept. 1960. Control of atmospheric dust and debris at the micron level was apparently first applied in the aerospace industry at the AiResearch factory in Los Angeles a few weeks before similar arrangements were made at the McDonnell plant in St. Louis.

[9] A. B. Thompson, "Physiological and Psychological Considerations for Manned Space Flight," Report E9R-12349, Rev., Chance Vought Aircraft Inc., Dallas, July 7, 1959, 165.

[10] Ms., John R. Barton, "Systems Engineering Considerations in Designing and Testing the Life Support System for Project Mercury," Oct. 14, 1960, 4.

[11] Minutes, Jack A. Prizzi, "Meeting with McDonnell—Environmental Control System—July 30, 1959, at Space Task Group," Aug. 17, 1959. Cf. memo, White to Chief, Flight Systems Div., "Approval of Specification Control Drawing No. 45-83700, Revision S," Aug. 7, 1959. Eventually capsule No. 7 was standardized on the ECS assumptions of 500 cc./min. oxygen consumption rate, 300 cc./min. cabin leakage rate, and 500 B.t.u./hr. body heating rate.

[12] Memos, Richard S. Johnston to Chief, Flight Systems Div., "Test Program—Environmental System Trainer," July 27, 1959; and "Report on Trip to ACEL to Discuss Installation of ECS Trainer in Altitude Chamber," Sept. 21, 1959; letter, Robert R. Gilruth to Chief, Bureau of Aeronautics, Dept. of the Navy, "Test Program for Environmental System Test Vessel," Sept. 28, 1959; memo, Charles D. Wheelwright to Chief, Flight Systems Div., "Trip Report," Sept. 29, 1959; Johnston, "Mercury Life Support Systems," paper, 28th annual meeting, Institute of Aeronautical Sciences, New York City, Jan. 25-27, 1960, 15.

[13] Memos, Samonski to Chief, Flight Systems Div., "Developments in the Environmental Control System Testing Program at McDonnell," June 13, 1960; and "Progress of Manned ECS Tests at MAC," July 25, 1960;

Ms., Johnston, "The Control and Measurement of the Mercury Capsule Environment," paper, Fifth National Symposium on Space Electronics and Telemetry, Washington, Sept. 19–21, 1960; J. A. Maloney and F. G. Richardson, "Test of a Life Support System under Simulated Operating Conditions," McDonnell Aircraft Corp., March 1, 1961, 21–23.

[11] Memo, White to Chief, Engineering and Contract Administration Div., "Project Mercury Full Pressure Suit Selection," Feb. 27, 1959. See also Frederick R. Ritzinger, Jr., and Ellis G. Aboud, "Pressure Suits—Their Evolution and Development," *Air University Review*, XVI (Jan.–Feb. 1965), 23–32.

[15] Edwin G. Vail and Charles C. Lutz, "Project Mercury Pressure Suit Evaluation," Wright Air Development Center, June 1959; Lee N. McMillion, interview, Houston, Nov. 1, 1963; "Agenda and Conclusion, Pressure Suit Evaluation Conference," STG, July 15, 1959. Cf. "Status Report No. 3 for Period Ending July 21, 1959," STG.

[16] William S. Augerson and McMillion, "Conclusions and Recommendations Concerning the Mercury Pressure Suit," Aug. 29, 1959; letter, STG to Langley Research Center, Attention Procurement Officer, "Project Mercury Pressure Suit Procurement," with enclosure, "Specification—Suit, Full Pressure, Project Mercury," Oct. 2, 1959. Cf. "Status Report No. 3."

[17] W. J. Berus, "Space Suits—Past, Present and Future," paper, spring meeting, Akron Rubber Group, April 4, 1963, 15. See also "Status Report No. 3." Ventilation oxygen entered the suit through a hose connection at the waist, was channeled through suit distribution ducts to body extremities, and flowed freely over the body back to the helmet.

[18] Memo, McMillion to Chief, Flight Systems Div., "Pressure Suit Status Report," Dec. 24, 1959.

[19] D. D. Ewing, "Sizing Problem on Project Mercury Pressure Suit," notes on proposed revision of Contract No. AS 60–8011C, Jan. 25, 1960; memo, McMillion, "Trip Report," March 1, 1960; memo, McMillion to Chief, Flight Systems Div., "Trip Report," June 3, 1960, with enclosure re decisions made in meeting at Goodrich plant, Akron, March 14, 1960. Cf. letter, Ewing to Carl F. Effler, "Report of Mercury Suit Meeting on June 1 and 2, 1960," June 7, 1960. "The complexity and difficulty of donning the full pressure suit was noted with covert satisfaction by the writer, 'an old-partial pressure suit man,' " said

James P. Henry of STG in memo to Chief, Flight Systems Div., "Trip Report," May 6, 1960. Memo, McMillion to Faget, "Astronaut Comment on Pressure Suit," with enclosures, (1) agreements and (2) comments by astronauts, June 27, 1960.

[20] Certainly the most delicate of all such interfaces for the first few leaps into space was that between the biosensors and human skins. The issue of the rectal thermometer designed into the suit was accepted for the moment as a necessary intrusion. See memo, Wheelwright to Chief, Flight Systems Div., "Trip Report," March 1, 1960; letter, Warren J. North to Harold I. Johnson, "Comments on Johnsville Centrifuge Program," Nov. 23, 1960.

[21] Suit pressure was maintained by a demand regulator that metered the oxygen into the system. If cabin pressure failed, the demand regulator sensed the pressure loss, sealed the suit, and maintained it at 4.6 pounds. Should both systems fail—suit and cabin—there was an emergency oxygen valve that fed directly into the inlet hose at the waist junction. Before May 1961, the pressure suit had received 514 hours of manned testing.

Oxygen was metered into the cabin by a regulator to maintain a minimum limit of 5.1 pounds. In designed operation, the cabin system remained at ambient pressure on the pad and up to 27,000 feet. At that altitude it sealed off at 5.5 pounds. If there were a fire or a buildup of toxic gases, the astronaut could decompress the cabin manually, exhaust the toxic odors, and repressurize it. This system received 135 manned test hours at the Navy's Aviation Medical Acceleration Laboratory before May 3, 1961.

[22] Thompson, "Physiological and Psychological Considerations for Manned Space Flight," 4, 24, 47–49, 164. See also White, "Progress in Space Medicine," paper, Second World and Fourth European Congress for Aviation and Space Medicine," Rome, Oct. 27–31, 1959.

[23] D. G. Starkey, "Isolation," in "Physiological and Psychological Considerations for Manned Space Flight," 140–145. See also Philip Solomon, et al., "Sensory Deprivation, a Review," *American Journal of Psychology*, CXIV (Oct. 1957), 4.

[24] See, for example, Johnston, "Mercury Life Support System"; Faget and Robert O. Piland, "Mercury Capsule and Its Flight Systems"; and Bond and Alan B. Kehlet, "Review, Scope and Recent Results of Project Mercury Research and Development Program," papers,

28th annual meeting, Institute of the Aeronautical Sciences, New York City, Jan. 25, 1960.

[25] Charles W. Mathews, "Review of the Operational Plans for Mercury Orbital Mission," paper, 28th annual meeting, Institute of the Aeronautical Sciences, New York City, Jan. 25, 1960.

[26] Edward R. Jones, "Prediction of Man's Vision in and from the Mercury Capsule," paper, 31st annual meeting, Aerospace Medical Assn., Miami Beach, May 9, 1960.

[27] Jones, "Man's Performance in an Orbital Space Vehicle," paper, Iowa Academy of Science, University of Iowa, Iowa City, April 22, 1960, 7, 10.

[28] "Tentative Schedule of Activities for First Months of Training Program," STG, April Oct., 1959.

[29] Project Mercury: First Interim Report, 54–59; "Astronauts: Symposium," Life, XLVII, Sept. 14, 1959; "Seven Brave Women Behind the Astronauts," Life, XLVII, Sept. 21, 1959; "Astronauts Get Their Prodigious Chariot," Life, XLVII, Dec. 14, 1959.

[30] Donald K. Slayton, "Like Seeing My Own Future," Life, XLVII, Feb. 29, 1960; M. Scott Carpenter, "Eerie World of Zero G," Life, XLVII, Mar. 21, 1960; Walter M. Schirra, Jr., "Suit Tailor-Made for Space," Life, XLIX, Aug. 1, 1960; L. Gordon Cooper, Jr., "First Rocket We Will Ride: Redstone's Role in Project Mercury," Life, XLIX, Oct. 3, 1960.

[31] Letters, Lila J. Phillips to Mercury Astronauts, July 21, 1959. Enclosed questionnaires were answered in part by each astronaut.

[32] Hugh L. Dryden, in interview, Washington, Aug. 31, 1965. Walter T. Bonney, in interview with Eugene M. Emme and William Putnam, Washington, Oct. 15, 1965, stressed the administrative need for one rather than seven such contracts, since NASA's modest public information staff was already deluged.

[33] Memo, North to Dir. of Space Flight Development, "Interim Status Report for Project Mercury," Aug. 7, 1959, 2; John A. Powers, interview, Houston, Nov. 12, 1965; Donald Slayton, interview, Houston, Dec. 16, 1964. For the contract made by DeOrsey on May 28, 1959, see House Committee on Science and Astronautics, 87 Cong., 1 sess. (1961), 1962 NASA Authorization, Part I, 147–148. Cf. William Hines, "Astronauts Face 'Exclusivity' Crisis," Washington Evening Star, Dec. 9, 1965. See also John Troan, "NASA Will Police Spacemen," Washington

Daily News, April 4, 1962, for one account of another highly controversial issue, the offer of free homes in Houston.

[34] On NASA public information policy and the division of labor regarding public relations for Mercury between Headquarters and STG, see Walter Bonney's remarks before United Press International Editors' Conference, Washington, NASA release, Sept. 9, 1960. Bonney recalls the day "all hell broke loose!" (p. 4) and how astronaut information policy evolved. Many NASA officials still vigorously defend the propriety and the wisdom of the "personal stories" contracts, but others disagree. See also Walter T. Bonney, comments, Dec. 1, 1965.

[35] Memo, George C. Guthrie to Training Office, "Second Bimonthly Report," Aug. 10, 1959; memos, Stanley Faber to Project Dir., "Outline of the January Program on the Aviation Medical Acceleration Laboratory Centrifuge," Dec. 3, 1959; and "Additional Information on January Centrifuge Program," Dec. 15, 1959. Memo for files, Robert B. Voas, "Astronaut Activities During Missile Preparation, Launch and Flight, Preliminary Outline," Nov. 5, 1959.

[36] Letter, John H. Glenn, Jr., to James B Stockdale, Dec. 17, 1959. See also "Summary of Mercury-Johnsville Centrifuge Program of August 1959," NASA Project Mercury working paper No. 127, June 22, 1960.

[37] For a review article on the resonant frequencies of various bodily organs, see David E. Goldman, M.D., and Henning E. von Gierke, "The Effects of Shock and Vibration on Man," paper, Naval Medical Research Institute, Lecture and Review Series No. 60–3, Bethesda, Md., Jan. 8, 1960.

[38] Memo, William Douglas to Assoc. Dir., "Training, Static Firing of Jupiter with Mercury Capsule," Feb. 10, 1960; William H. Mayes and David A. Hilton, "External and Internal Noise of Capsules," paper, STG Research Dept. meeting, Feb. 1, 1960; letter, Charles J. Donlan to R. W. Costin, July 29, 1960. Even Congressional attention was invited to these problems by the publication of House Committee on Science and Astronautics, 86 Cong., 2 sess. (1960), Noise: Its Effect on Man and Machine, Oct. 13, 1960, 33–35.

[39] Memos, Alan B. Shepard, Jr., for files, "Report on Astronaut Training—Capsule Egress and Water Survival, Pensacola, Florida, Mar. 28–Apr. 1, 1960," April 5, 1960; and "Astronauts' Comments on Mercury Capsule Survival Kit and Equipment," April 28, 1960.

[40] Memo, Shepard to Project Dir., "Personal Parachute Application to Mercury," June 27, 1960. The results of these studies were summarized in memo, William C. Mosely, Jr., for Aleck Bond, "Procedure for Personal Parachute Usage During Mercury-Redstone Missions," April 18, 1961. On Project Excelsior, see Eugene M. Emme, *Aeronautics and Astronautics: An American Chronology of Science and Technology in the Exploration of Space, 1915–1960* (Washington, 1961), 114, 116, 120; Joseph W. Kittinger, "The Long, Lonely Leap," *National Geographic,* CXVIII (Dec. 1960), 854.

[41] "Highlights of the First Year of the Astronaut Training Program," with charts and tables for oral presentation, STG, May 1, 1960.

[42] See, e.g., "Briefing Given to NASA Astronauts," Rocketdyne BC1–59–12, Rocketdyne Div., North American Aviation, Inc., Canoga Park, Calif., Sept. 18, 1959.

[43] Johnson, "Pilots' Training Aids," briefing, Wright Air Development Center, Feb. 3, 1960, 2; letter, the astronauts to Dir., Project Mercury, Feb. 4, 1960.

[44] Robert R. Miller, interview (telephonic), Cleveland, Jan. 26, 1965. For an illustrated catalog of most United States training simulations of this nature, see H. E. von Gierke and E. Steinmetz, eds., *Motion Devices for Linear and Angular Oscillation and for Abrupt Acceleration Studies (Impact),* NAS/NRC Publication 903 (Washington, 1961).

[45] James W. Useller, interview, Cleveland, May 1, 1964. See Useller and Joseph S. Algranti, "Pilot Reactions to High-Speed Rotations," *Aerospace* Magazine, XXXIV (June 1963), 501–504. Test subjects were brought up to speed in about 10–15 seconds, and then were expected to damp out all three axial rotations in the next 30 seconds or so.

[46] Useller interview. Meanwhile the Lewis altitude wind tunnel was being used as a space vacuum chamber and was needed for some important separation tests of the spacecraft from an Atlas adapter. R. R. Miller and Robert B. Nunemaker also ran tests of pyrotechnics, monitored by John B. Lee and Charles Yodzis of STG, that uncovered a host of anomalies in the design and performance of explosive bolts, retrograde and posigrade rockets, and the alignment of the escape rocket. See also souvenir picture booklet, "Astronaut Press Meeting, Lewis Research Center, March 4, 1960."

[47] "Status Report, Crew Training," April 1960, 3; see also memo, Brent Y. Creer and Rodney C. Wingrove to Dir., Ames Research Center, "Preliminary Results of Pilot's Sidearm Controller Tests Conducted on the AMAL–NADC Centrifuge . . .," Feb. 26, 1960.

[48] "Astronauts' Handbook—Project Mercury," preliminary edition, McDonnell Aircraft Corp., Jan. 25, 1960.

[49] "Project Mercury General Systems Document," NASA Project Mercury working paper No. 118, March 10, 1960, rev. Oct. 24, 1960, and March 23, 1961.

[50] Voas, "Human Factors Aspects of the Man-In-Space Program," paper, Air Force Scientific Advisory Board, Psychology and Social Science Panel, Jan. 26, 1961, 24, 7.

[51] Jones, "Analytical Techniques for Defining the Astronaut's Task," and "Astronauts' and Ground Station Failure Reference," papers, ninth annual Human Engineering Conference, Office of Naval Research, St. Louis, June 2, 1961.

[52] Voas, "Human Factors Aspects," 14; Jones, interview, St. Louis, Sept. 2, 1964; "The Failure Task Analysis," McDonnell Aircraft Corp., June 15, 1961, rev. June 21, 1962. Voas, for instance, believed, in spite of considerable opposition, that: "A rough estimate of the priority that should be given to each subsystem in the training program can be expressed as the reliability of the automatic component plus the estimated reliability for the human. Tasks associated with subsystems for where this sum is low should be assigned the highest priority in the training program. This procedure is similar to traditional task analysis procedures, but permits a more qualitative approach to the evaluation of design tradeoffs and the construction of training program."

[53] House Committee on Science and Astronautics, 86 Cong., 2 sess. (1960), *Hearings, Review of the Space Program,* testimony of George M. Low, Feb. 16, 1960, Part II, 761. See also Parts I and III for the overall presentation of a response to NASA's 10-year plan as discussed between Jan. 20 and Mar. 7, 1960. Cf. NASA, *Major Activities in the Programs of the National Aeronautics and Space Administration, October 1, 1959–March 31, 1960* [Third Semiannual Report to Congress], (Washington, 1960).

[54] Letter, Gilruth to Comdr., Air Force Ballistic Missile Div., Oct. 12, 1959; "Project Mercury Quarterly Report No. 5 for Period Ending Jan. 31, 1960," STG, Jan. 31, 1960. See also Leighton I. Davis, Maj. Gen., USAF, Operations Plan 60-1: *Department of Defense Support for Project Mercury,* AFMTC, May 31, 1960; cf. "Overall Plan Department

of Defense Support for Project Mercury Operations," AMR, Jan. 15, 1960.

[55] Sherwood L. Butler, "Monthly Status Report—Project Mercury," Oct. 2, 1959; "Monthly Status Report—Project Mercury," Nov. 3, 1959.

[56] J. E. Miller, "M–133 Elect. Coor. Tie-In Record," McDonnell Aircraft Corp., Jan. 6, 1960.

[57] Frank G. Morgan, Jr., "Summary of Capsule Coordination Meetings," McDonnell Aircraft Corp., Jan. 11, 12, 1960; message, Paul E. Purser to Logan T. MacMillan, Jan. 25, 1960.

[58] T. Keith Glennan, in House Committee on Appropriations, Special Subcommittee on Deficiencies, 86 Cong., 2 sess., Hearings, Feb. 1, 1960, *Supplemental National Aeronautics and Space Administration Appropriations 1960*, 2; cf. pp. 27 and 55.

[59] "Status Report No. 5," STG, 2. This status report continued on the next page with these significant remarks:

"It has also been found possible to make the configuration of the capsules for MR–2 . . . and MR–3 identical. The missions of these capsules remain unchanged. However, in order for the basic capsules to be identical, the quantities to be recorded for the primate carried in MR–2 must remain the same as those to be recorded for the man in MR–3. The advantage of making these capsules identical is that otherwise the first manned flight would have been in a capsule that differed in several respects from those that had been fired previously. Now there will be at least one firing of an identical capsule before inserting a man.

"The operations required for preparation and launch of the capsule have received very careful study, and it has been concluded that these operations will require much more time than was previously estimated. The resultant program with the delayed capsule deliveries was, however, felt to be unacceptable. For this reason, new, rather optimistic target times have been set for the checkout and launch period, and a study has been instituted to see whether these schedules can be met by careful planning of the work and facility utilization and by extra work shifts. The effects of all these factors are being considered in formulating a new schedule."

[60] Memo, Gilruth to staff, "Prospective Move of the Space Task Group to Goddard Space Flight Center, Beltsville, Maryland," Feb. 25, 1960; memo for files, William A.

Herrnstein, Jr., "Work and Travel Performed by Langley Research Center Personnel in Support of Project Mercury," Oct. 6, 1960.

[61] "Anticipated Total Program Cost for Mercury Capsule," McDonnell Aircraft Corp., Jan. 14, 1960. Cf. "Contract NAS 5–59, Mercury Capsule Program—Financial Status Summary," with enclosures, McDonnell Aircraft Corp., May 31, 1960. C. F. Picard, McDonnell Aircraft Corp., Asst. Contract Manager, "Monthly Financial Report," Jan. 22, 1960, 2.

[62] R. O. Piland, interview, Houston, Nov. 5, 1964; memo, Gilruth to staff, "Advanced Vehicle Team," May 25, 1960; Joseph V. Piland, interview, Houston, Oct. 21, 1964.

[63] Memo, Gilruth to staff, "Changes in Organization of the Space Task Group," Jan. 11, 1960. See also Ms., Robert Merrifield and C. F. Bingman, "Organization: Technical History of Project Mercury," June 3, 1963.

[64] Memo for files, anon., "Outline of Off-Range Remote Site Training Program for Flight Control Personnel, " Jan. 14, 1960. Cf. "Aeromedical Flight Controller Briefing," NASA/STG, May 23–27, 1960. "Operation and Maintenance: Flight Controller Remote Sites: Operation Manual, MO–118R," Western Electric Co., June 1960.

[65] Letter, Walter C. Williams to Kurt H. Debus, "Proposal for Mercury-Redstone Coordination Committee," Jan. 18, 1960; letter, Williams to Donald N. Yates, "Mercury-Atlas Flight Test Working Group," Jan. 18, 1960; Howard Gibbons, "Ostrander's Job at NASA Not Related to Space Rift," Newport News *Daily Press*, Dec. 10, 1959. See also proposed memo of understanding, "Relationships Between OSFP and OLVP Groups at AMR," submitted to Ostrander and Silverstein April 29, 1960.

[66] Memos, Williams to staff, "Responsibilities of Mercury Launch Coordination Office," Feb. 11, 1960; "Organization for Mercury Field Operations," Feb. 12, 1960; letter, Williams to Yates, "Position Titles for Operation of Project Mercury," March 9, 1960; letter, Williams to Cdr., DesFlotFour, "Test Objectives and Recovery Requirements for the Project Mercury Atlas Test One," March 15, 1960, with enclosure. The aborted "Launch Operation Manual for Project Mercury," compiled by Dugald O. Black, A. M. Busch, A. M. Eiband, John Janokaitis, Jr., and approved by Scott H. Simpkinson, B. Porter Brown, and G. Merritt Preston at the Cape in March 1960 is a rare but invaluable guide to its

subject at this time.

[67] Memo, William M. Bland, Jr., to Chief, Flight Systems Div., "Division Participation in Project Mercury," March 4, 1960. For an overview of the increasing tempo of Mercury operations at the Cape, see memo, Martin A. Byrnes for Assoc. Director, "Administrative Support for the STG Facilities at Cape Canaveral," March 4, 1960; and C. Frederick Matthews for staff, "Administrative Staff for Mercury Field Operation Organization," May 9, 1960.

[68] Minutes, "Mercury Network Meeting," NASA/STG, Feb. 9, 1960; memo, Gilruth to Div. Chiefs, "Designation of Flight Controllers for Mercury Flight Operations," Feb. 8, 1960; memo, C. F. Matthews to all concerned, "Mercury Flight Controller Personnel Indoctrination and Training Plan Presentation," Feb. 25, 1960; Williams, interview, Houston, Aug. 23, 1965. See also Jim W. McCommis, draft Ms., "Flight Control Operations," for Mercury Technical History, Nov. 19, 1963.

[69] Memo, William W. Petynia to Chief, Flight Systems Div., "Summary Report of the Duties and Responsibilities of the STG Project Engineer During Capsule No. 1 CST," March 16, 1960. For the best overview of the status of the program as seen by the STG managers at the end of this period, see memo for files, Purser, "Additional Background Material on Project Mercury," May 11, 1960; cf. Purser's similar memo, "General Background Material on Project Mercury," March 23, 1959.

[70] See R. I. Johnson, et al., "The Mercury-Redstone Project," TMX53107, MSFC Saturn/Apollo Systems Office, June 1964, 5–39, 41; Ms., "Proceedings of the Mercury-Atlas Booster Reliability Workshop," Convair/Astronautics, San Diego, July 12, 1963, passim. See also ABMA/AOMC instructions, N. I. Reiter, Jr., "Mercury Project Symbol," Oct. 7, 1959, Code AP 940–13, ORDAB–DY.

[71] Bernhard A. Hohmann, "Pilot Safety and Quality Assurance for Project Mercury," report No. STL–TR–60–0000–69047, Feb. 8, 1960; [Kucheman, Henry B.], "Reference File, AFBMD Support, Project Mercury," bound folder of documents, Air Force Space Systems Div., El Segundo, Calif., Jan. 4, 1961, Sect. 5, Table 11; Osmond J. Ritland, interview, Andrews Air Force Base, Md., Dec. 30, 1964.

[72] Hohmann interviews; see p. 189. See also Simpkinson, interview, Houston, Oct. 4, 1965, and papers from the period between

June 1961 and May 1962 when he was assigned to San Diego as Gilruth's special assistant. For more technical details, see R. J. Smith, "Flight Proofing Test Report for Abort Sensing and Control Unit—Mercury—Missileborne," Convair/Astronautics report No. 27A515 R, Aug. 5, 1960.

[73] "Reliability Program Review—Project Mercury," McDonnell Aircraft Corp., Feb. 27, 1960; John C. French, interview, Houston, Aug. 3, 1964. For a retrospective view of reliability in all of the Mercury program, see Walter C. Williams, "On Murphy's Law," in Paul Horowitz, ed., *Manned Space Reliability Symposium,* Vol. I, American Astronautical Society Science and Technology Series (New York, 1964), 1–11.

[74] Purser, log for Gilruth, Jan. 6, 1960; Richard M. Mansfield, "Project Mercury Revisited," *Virginian-Pilot and Portsmouth Star,* March 27, 1960; House Committee on Science and Astronautics, 86 Cong., 2 sess. (1960), *Life Sciences and Space,* Aug. 15, 1960, 13; Senate Committee on Aeronautical and Space Sciences, 86 Cong., 2 sess. (1960), *Space Research in the Life Sciences.* At this juncture, Astronauts Shepard and Grissom were asking for permission to ride the next Little Joe shot into space. Virgil I. Grissom, interview, Houston, March 29, 1965.

[75] Purser, log for Gilruth, Feb. 9, 1960. See also Robert L. Seat, interview, St. Louis, Sept. 1, 1964; Seat and Waldram, "Project Mercury Test Plan," McDonnell Aircraft Corp., Feb. 19, 1959.

[76] Purser, log for Gilruth with enclosures, agenda for conferences on reliability test program, March 9, 1960. Two other Chrysler Corp. engineering executives responsible for factory management of man-rating the Redstone were Robert P. Erickson and Edward J. Dofter: H. D. Lowrey, interview, Washington, Nov. 17, 1965. For details of the factory test programs see R. M. Torigian, "Reliability Test of the Redstone A-7-1 Rocket Engine, RE 7112a," Chrysler Corp. Missile Division Technical Memorandum ML–M125, April 14, 1960; and G. S. Upton, "Mercury-Redstone Aft Section Test Report," CCMD Technical Report GLC–R5, Oct. 1960.

[77] Walter F. Burke, interview, Aug. 31, 1964; MacMillan, interview, St. Louis, Sept. 1, 1964. See also minutes, Jerome B. Hammack and Jack C. Heberlig, "ABMA–MAC–NASA Panel No. 1 Meeting," March 22, 1960; memo, Curtis L. Ferrell to Emil P. Bertram, MFL, "Mercury-Redstone [capsule-booster documen-

tation problem]," May 18, 1960.

[78] James A. Chamberlin, interview, Houston, June 1, 1964; and comments, Sept. 9, 1965. See also memo, Gilruth for all organizational units, "Organization of NASA Participation in CST at MAC," May 12, 1960.

[79] Memo, Silverstein to Dir., Marshall Space Flight Center, "Mercury Capsule Prelaunch Operations at Huntsville," March 29, 1960. A recent revision of ABMA's checkout plans had not shown much effort to save time. See "Mercury Checkout at Systems Analysis and Reliability Laboratory," ABMA–DOD Report No. DRT–TM–5–59, Aug. 13, 1959, Rev. A, March 5, 1960.

[80] Memo, Silverstein to Dir., Marshall Space Flight Center, "Review of Mercury Capsule Prelaunch Operations at Huntsville," April 5, 1960; House Committee on Science and Astronautics, 87 Cong., 1 sess. (1961), *Defense Space Interests, Hearings,* statement and documents, General Thomas D. White, USAF, 91–97.

[81] Purser, "Notes on Manned Space Flight Management Meeting, June 27–28, 1961," 1, 2. See also Gilruth memo, "Organization of NASA Participation in CST."

[82] Memo, Robert E. McKann to Chief, Flight Systems Div., "Visit to STL, CV/A, and Rocketdyne (NAA) Feb. 15–18, 1960," Feb. 29, 1960. See also P. I. Harr, "Results of Reliability Evaluation Test Program for Mercury-Atlas Abort Sensing and Implementation System," Convair/Astronautics report No. AX62–0008, April 24, 1962.

[83] Memo, Edison M. Fields to Chief, Flight Systems Div., "Visit to BMD/STL at Los Angeles," Jan. 19, 1960; letter, Hohmann to Gilruth, March 25, 1960; letter, Williams to Hohmann, April 18, 1960; *Convariety,* Feb. 17, 1960. See also transcript, "Proceedings of the Mercury-Atlas Booster Reliability Workshop," San Diego, July 12, 1963, passim. The reliability team at Convair/Astronautics consisted of factory manager J. P. Hopman, reliability chief H. F. Eppenstein, and quality control manager D. R. Archibald. For similar concerns on the Redstone, see memos, Debus to Earl M. Butler, "Weight and Balance Measurements on Project Mercury," Dec. 23, 1959; and H. R. Palaoro to Butler, "Weight and Balance Measurement Requirements for Project Mercury-Redstone," Feb. 16, 1960.

[84] "Status Report No. 6 for Period Ending April 30, 1960," STG; "MA–1 Report No. 3 for Period Ending Jan. 27, 1960," STG; "MA–1 Report No. 4 for Period Ending Feb. 3, 1960," STG; "MA–1 Report No. 5 for Period Ending Feb. 4, 1960," STG; "MA–1 Report No. 10 for Period Ending April 15, 1960," STG; memo, Bond to Chief, Engineering Div., "MA–1 Test Flight," Feb. 1, 1960.

[85] Memo, North to Dir., Space Flight Programs, "Request for Approval of Mercury Funding," June 24, 1960. See also Evert Clark, "NASA Centralizes Launch Management," *Aviation Week,* LXXII (May 30, 1960), 28, 29.

[86] See Robert L. Rosholt, *An Administrative History of NASA, 1958–1963,* NASA SP–4101 (Washington, 1966), 154–160; memo, T. Keith Glennan to Dir., "Appraisal of NASA's Contractor Policy and Industrial Relations," Feb. 29, 1960. For an excellent overview of NASA policies in general at this time, see the typescript, "Questions and Answers proposed for Congressional Testimony," by Hugh L. Dryden's staff, ca. May 1960.

[87] "Information Requested by McKinsey and Co., Inc.," STG, April 9, 1960; letter, Gilruth to Harry J. Goett, Dir., Goddard Space Flight Center, May 3, 1960.

[88] Rosholt, *Administrative History of NASA,* 154, 101, 124; Rosholt has paraphrased the McKinsey report as follows (pp. 157–158):

"The report revealed that NASA's record in supervising its out-of-house efforts was spotty. Difficulties had arisen because NASA neglected certain basic prerequisites to effective contractor supervision, such as adequate statements of work, sufficient and flexible funding, and properly focused technical responsibility. (A basic problem in connection with the last named prerequisite was NASA's tendency to establish two channels of supervision—one from headquarters, the other from the field center.)

"NASA's supervisory job was difficult in that it could neither use the 'trust the contractor' approach (high reliability was too crucial to be left to the contractor alone) nor the 'tight control' approach (which would 'discourage contractor creativity and initiative'). . . . Therefore NASA had to follow a middle course, which combined contractor operating freedom with close NASA guidance. To achieve this balance it would be essential that there be a constant flow of information back and forth between NASA and the contractor. This flow could be promoted by periodic progress review meetings between NASA and the contractor, the placement of a NASA representative in the contractor's plant (to permit continuous face to face communication), and the use of a progress reporting system."

563

⁵⁹ "Pretest Report for Off-the-Pad Escape System Qualification Test," NASA Project Mercury working paper No. 112, March 1, 1960.

⁶⁰ See "Determination of Net Thrust of Project Mercury Tower Jettison Rocket and Escape Tower Assembly," NASA Project Mercury working paper No. 202, July 3, 1961; "Review of Mercury Launch Abort System Experience . . . .," NASA general working paper No. 10,007, July 15, 1963.

⁶¹ Memo, Bland for Flight System Division files, "Program Objectives," Sept. 30, 1959, 2.

⁶² House Committee on Science and Astronautics, 87 Cong., 1 sess. (1961), *A Chronology of Missile and Astronautic Events*, March 8, 1961, 114, 115. See also Charles S. Sheldon II, "The Challenge of International Competition," paper, third American Inst. of Aeronautics and Astronautics/NASA Manned Space Flight Meeting, Houston, Nov. 6, 1964, 10–11, reprinted and revised as Appendix A in Senate Committee on Aeronautical and Space Sciences, 89 Cong., 1 sess. (1965), *International Cooperation and Organization for Outer Space*, 427–477.

Chapter IX

¹ Memos, George M. Low to Abe Silverstein, "Information for Program Management Plan Meeting," Oct. 6, 1960; T. Keith Glennan to Silverstein, July 11, 1960; Silverstein to Glennan, "MR–3 Launch Date," July 16, 1960; Silverstein to Robert R. Gilruth, "MR–3 Launch Schedule," July 25, 1960; Walter C. Williams to NASA Hq., International Programs Office, "Monthly Summary of Project Mercury Activities," Aug. 8, 1960; Warren J. North, "History of Mercury Schedules: Earliest Possible Manned Flights," chart, Aug. 13, 1960. See also Abe Silverstein, "Progress in Space Flight," *Astronautics*, V (Nov. 1960), 24–25, 140–142.

² For the Report of the President's Commission on National Goals, see Henry M. Wriston, et al., *Goals for Americans* (Englewood Cliffs, N.J., 1960). Note especially the section by Warren Weaver, pp. 101–124, on "A Great Age for Science." Cf. J. L. Penick, Jr., et al., eds., *The Politics of American Science: 1939 to the Present* (Chicago, 1965), 221.

³ House Subcommittee of the Committee on Appropriations, 86 Cong., 1 sess. (1959), *National Aeronautics and Space Administration Appropriations*, testimony of Hugh L. Dryden, 15; House Committee on Science and Astronautics, 86 Cong., 2 sess. (1960), *Review of the Space Program*, Part II, testimony of George M. Low, Feb. 16, 1960, 761. For an excellent analysis of political positions and public opinion on American space policy (1957–1963) as a whole, see Vernon Van Dyke, *Pride and Power: The Rationale of the Space Program* (Urbana, Ill., 1964). Eisenhower's position is described on pp. 82–83.

⁴ Glennan's introspection on the role of international competition was best expressed in an address at a Yale University symposium on Oct. 7, 1960. See also letter, Glennan to Eugene M. Emme, Oct. 19, 1965. For an overview of Air Force programs, see Ernest G. Schwiebert, "USAF's Ballistic Missiles—1954–1964: A Concise History," *Air Force and Space Digest*, XLVII (May 1964), 51–166, later published as *A History of the U.S. Air Force Ballistic Missiles* (New York, 1965).

⁵ The best open monograph comparing Soviet and American space accomplishments is Charles S. Sheldon II, "The Challenge of International Competition," paper, third American Inst. of Aeronautics and Astronautics/NASA Manned Space Flight Meeting, Houston, Nov. 6, 1964, revised and reprinted in Senate Committee on Aeronautical and Space Sciences, 89 Cong., 1 sess. (1965), *International Cooperation and Organization for Outer Space*, Appendix A, 427–477.

⁶ "Project Mercury Discussion," brochure, STG, June 20, 1960. See also memo, Dieter Grau to Dir., Guidance and Control Div., Marshall Space Flight Center, "Unsatisfactory Condition on MR Abort Sensing System," Oct. 11, 1960; minutes, "Resume of Mercury-Redstone Panel 2 Meeting," LOD–MSFC, Aug. 24, 1960.

⁷ "Project Mercury Discussion," B–276, B–187, B–258, B–204; comments, William Underwood, Executive Sec. of CMLC, to Eugene M. Emme, Nov. 1, 1965; draft Ms., B. Leon Hodge, et al., "Recovery Operations Portion," for Mercury Technical History, Aug. 1963.

⁸ NASA Contract No. NAS–190, "Reliability Study of Mercury Capsule System," June 9, 1960, was signed by William P. Kelly, Jr., for the government and by D. P. Murray for McDonnell Aircraft Corp.

⁹ Nicholas E. Golovin, "An Approach to a Reliability Prediction Program," American Society for Quality Control. *Transactions of 1960 Convention*, San Francisco, May 25,

1960, 173. See also, memos, Silverstein to Deputy Assoc. Administrator, "Project Mercury Reliability Analysis," June 21, 1960; Golovin to Dir., Office of Space Flight Programs, "Project Mercury Reliability," June 23, 1960. "Old data and wrong ground rules gave bad figures from our standpoint," said Walter Williams in interview, Houston, Aug. 23, 1965. Silverstein and Low tended to side with the working levels on this issue: see Low, comments, Oct. 5, 1965.

[10] Letter, Glennan to James S. McDonnell, Jr., June 30, 1960, with enclosure [from which next quotation is taken], "Proposed Work Statements for McDonnell on Mercury Capsule System Reliability," June 30, 1960, 2.

[11] Letter, McDonnell to Glennan, July 13, 1960, NASA Central Files, Washington. Apparently Mr. McDonnell was unaware of the NASA–MAC reliability contract NAS–190.

[12] Paul E. Purser, log for Gilruth, July 21, 1960; "Informal Reliability Discussion for STG by AAR Staff," July 21, 1960; Ms. notes on reliability meeting, Purser, July 21, 1960; F. John Bailey, Jr., interview, Houston, July 16, 1964. For a later statement of Headquarters' policy see Landis S. Gephart, "NASA Requirements for Reliability and Quality Assurance," in *Western Space Age Industries and Engineering Exposition and Conference: NASA Day, April 27, 1962*, NASA SP-4 (Washington, 1962), 49–56.

[13] John C. French, interview, Houston, Aug. 3, 1964; memo, Gephart to Everett W. Quintrell, "Background Information on Astronaut's Task Description and Performance Evaluation," Aug. 31, 1960. Cf. letter, J. Y. Brown, Contract Manager, McDonnell Aircraft Corp., to W. P. Kelly, Jr., NASA Contracting Officer, Aug. 24, 1960.

[14] See Low, comments, Oct. 5, 1965; Aleck C. Bond and Maxime A. Faget, Ms., "Technologies of Manned Space Systems," Chap. 14, "The Role of Ground Testing in Manned Spacecraft Programs," 167–177.

[15] Mercury operations were governed by the agreement "Overall Plan—Department of Defense Support for Project Mercury Operations," Jan. 15, 1960, but some of the difficulties in working out specific operational procedures at the Cape may be found in Francis E. Jarrett, Jr., and Robert A. Lindemann, "Historical Origins of NASA's Launch Operations Center," Kennedy Space Center, Historical Monograph No. 1, Cocoa Beach, Fla., Oct. 1964, 69–76. See also letters, Henry N. Moore to distribution, AFMTC, "NASA Organizational Changes

at AMR and PMR," June 27, 1960; and Kurt H. Debus to G. J. Weber, MAC, July 28, 1960; and Ms. paper, anonymous, "Responsibilities and Procedures for AMR Support of Project Mercury," ca. Aug. 1, 1960.

[16] J. F. Shields, personnel study chart, MSC Florida Operations, Jan. 4, 1964; G. Merritt Preston, interview, Cape Kennedy, April 29, 1964; George F. Killmer, Jr., interview, Houston, Sept. 14, 1965. See also Ms. paper, Gilbert B. North, "Development and Checkout of the NASA Mercury Capsule," McDonnell Aircraft Corp. [ca. Sept. 1960].

[17] John F. Yardley, William Dubusker, interviews, St. Louis, Aug. 31, Sept. 1, 1964. See also Ms. paper, H. H. Leutjen, "Ground Checkout and Launch Procedures for Man-in-Space Operations," McDonnell Aircraft Corp. [ca. Aug. 1961]; McDonnell Aircraft Corp. interoffice memo, J. T. Dale to W. F. Burke, "Mercury-Redstone Panel I Meeting at MSFC on 11 August 1960," Aug. 16, 1960. Field procurement was standardized to some extent by memo, Harold G. Collins to all Mercury Hangar S personnel, "Procurement Procedures on Contract NAS 5–59," Sept. 8, 1960.

[18] Project Orbit is not to be confused with Project Orbiter; see p. 29. Yardley, Robert L. Seat, interviews, St. Louis, Sept. 1, 1964; memo, Lewis R. Fisher for Project Director, "Proposal for Environmental Qualification Test of Mercury Capsule," June 21, 1960; A. E. Wilkes, "Proposal for Full Scale Simulated Mission Test, Orbit Phase; Immediate Capabilities," McDonnell Aircraft Corp. report No. 7730, Aug. 29, 1960; memo, Floyd W. Fults to distribution, "Project Orbit Team Member's Responsibilities," McDonnell Aircraft Corp. memo No. PO-650-3, Feb. 2, 1961. For an overview of Project Orbit, see A. M. Paolini, "Evaluation of a Mercury Spacecraft in a Simulated Orbit Environment," McDonnell Aircraft Corp. preliminary report, May 29, 1962.

[19] Gilruth quoted by John J. Williams and Donald M. Corcoran, "Mercury Spacecraft Pre-Launch Preparations at the Launch Site," paper, American Institute of Aeronautics and Astronautics, Space Flight Testing Conference, Cocoa Beach, Fla., March 18–20, 1963, 18. Cf. p. 28. See also draft Ms., Frank M. Crichton, "Quality Control and Inspection," for Project Mercury Technical History, July 3, 1963.

[20] Bond and Faget, "Technologies of Manned Space Systems"; *Development Engineering Inspection Data Book*, SEDR 183, Mc-

Donnell Aircraft Corp., Aug. 16, 1960. For Project Orbit, see F. W. Fultz, A. E. Wilkis, J. J. Mazzoni, et al., informal McDonnell Aircraft Corp. memos, Sept. through Dec. 1960, including preliminary McDonnell report 7869-9 [no title], June 7, 1961: all included in file by Robert A. Hermann and Joe W. Dodson, "Project Orbit notes."

[21] Bailey interview; Mss., "Briefings, NASA-Industry Apollo Technical Conference," July 18, 1961; "Reliability and Flight Safety Problems," April 4, 1962, 8; "Reliability and Crew Safety in Manned Space Flight," Feb. 20, 1963; Bailey, "Review of Lessons Learned in the Mercury Program Relative to Spacecraft Design and Operations," paper, American Institute of Aeronautics and Astronautics Space Flight Testing Conference, Cocoa Beach, Fla., March 18, 1963.

[22] Abe Silverstein, interview, Cleveland, May 1, 1964; House Committee on Science and Astronautics, 87 Cong., 1 sess. (1961), *Fourth Semiannual Report of the National Aeronautics and Space Administration*, 208–209.

[23] Ms., Karl F. Greil, for Mercury Tech. History, "History of the Reaction Control System," July 1962, 160–161. Cf. 145, 67–68 [English trans. by L. S. S.]. See also another draft Ms. by Norman B. Farmer, "Instrumentation," June 27, 1963, for some discussion of equally acute problems.

[24] See R. D. Korando, "Mercury Capsule No. 7: Configuration Specification (Mercury-Redstone No. 3)," Report 603–7, McDonnell Aircraft Corp., Aug. 1, 1960, revised Nov. 10, 1960; R. F. Mackey, "General Flight Plan: Atlas Boosters for Project Mercury," Aerospace Corp. report AS–60–0000–0036, Sept. 1960.

[25] Memo, Faget to Flight Systems Div., "Mercury-Atlas Meeting on Feb. 26, 1960 at Space Technology Laboratories," March 4, 1960, 3.

[26] NASA News Release 60–233, "MA–1 Capsule Instrumentation," undated; memo, Charles J. Donlan to Langley Research Center, attention Clyde Thiele, "Inspection of MA–1 Capsule," March 18, 1960; memo, R. E. McKann to Chief, Flight Systems Div., "Trip to Mercury Project Office at Patrick Air Force Base," April 14, 1960. The basic preflight documentation for MA–1 is found in the following NASA Project Mercury working papers: "MA–1 Mission Directive," No. 132, April 11, 1960; "General Information for MA–1 Recovery Force," No. 142, July 8, 1960;

"Landing Area Prediction MA–1," No. 143, July 13, 1960; "Summary of Calculated Preflight Trajectory Data for MA–1," No. 144, July 25, 1960. See also "Data Acquisition Plan, MA–1," undated; and "Project Mercury Description of Plans for MA–1," prelaunch report, June 24, 1960.

[27] Letter, Walter Williams to Cdr., DesFlot-Four, March 15, 1960, with enclosure, "Test Objectives and Recovery Requirements for the Project Mercury Atlas Test One."

[28] Detailed descriptions of preflight operations for all Mercury launches are summarized in Ms., George F. Killmer, Jr., et al., "Mercury Technical History—Preflight Operations," MSC Florida Operations, Dec. 30, 1963. For MA–1, see pp. 68–71. For an overview of the coordination and cooperation mechanics among the Mercury-Atlas team, see letters, Silverstein to Courtland D. Perkins, Asst. Secy. of the Air Force (R and D), Aug. 26, 1960, and Gilruth to Silverstein, "Project Mercury Coordination between NASA–MAC and BMD-STL Convair," Aug. 26, 1960, with enclosures.

[29] Memo, Low to Administrator, "Mercury-Atlas Test No. 1," July 26, 1960. For the more general "man-rating" procedures for the Atlas Booster about this time, see STL report TR–60–0000–69079, "Atlas Booster Flight Safety Review General Operating Procedures and Organization," June 6, 1960.

[30] Memo, Low to Administrator, "Mercury-Atlas 1, Post-Launch Information," July 29, 1960; see also Ms., "MA–1 Operation, 7/29/60," launch diary, anon. This same day George Low delivered a paper before the first NASA-Industry Conference that officially and publicly named for the first time "Project Apollo" as a manned lunar circumnavigation program for the future: see *NASA-Industry Program Plans Conference*, Washington, D.C., July 28–29, 1960, 80.

[31] Memo, North to Administrator, "Analysis of MA–1 Malfunction," Aug. 22, 1960. See also Sally Anderson, ed., *Final Report Mercury/Atlas Launch Vehicle Program*, Aerospace Corp. report No. TDR–269 (4101)–3, El Segundo, Calif., Nov. 1963, VIII–14.

[32] Joseph A. Kies, Naval Research Laboratory, Washington, "Atlas-Mercury Failure: Examination of Failed Parts," report, Aug. 30, 1960, 3; Andre J. Meyer, Jr., "Trip Report," Aug. 30, 1960.

[33] "Flight Test Report for Mercury-Atlas Mission No. 1 (capsule No. 4)," NASA Project Mercury working paper No. 159, Nov. 4,

1960, 12–1. Some idea of the complexity of data reduction procedures for Mercury in general and of the impact of MA–1 on data coordination procedures in particular may be gleaned from the draft Ms. by Richard G. Arbic and Robert C. Shirley, "Data Coordination," for Mercury Technical History, Part III, M., July 10, 1963.

[31] Minutes, "Mercury-Atlas Coordination Panel, Sept. 14, 1960," Sigurd A. Sjoberg, secretary, with enclosures, Sept. 29, 1960.

[35] Transcript, "Press Group Interview with Gilruth, Williams," Oct. 26, 1960, 2. Leading questions were asked by Douglas Dederer of the *Cocoa* (Fla.) *Tribune*. Gilruth also was reported to have said that he would not be surprised "to wake up any morning" to find the Soviets had accomplished manned orbital flight. Alvin B. Webb, Jr., *Washington Post*, Oct. 30, 1960. Webb also editorialized to say, "Mercury—named for a winged-footed Roman God—appears to have both feet in a molasses vat." House Committee on Science and Astronautics, 87 Cong., 1 sess. (1961), *A Chronology of Missile and Astronautic Events*, 123, 124, 132; Sheldon, "The Challenge of International Competition," passim.

[36] For an overview of the parallel development of this rocket research aircraft see Thomas A. Toll and Jack Fischel, "The X–15 Project: Results and Research," *Astronautics and Aeronautics*, II (March 1960), 20–28.

[37] Eugene M. Emme, *Aeronautics and Astronautics: An American Chronology of Science and Technology in the Exploration of Space, 1915–1960* (Washington, 1961), 126–130.

[38] *Public Papers of the Presidents of the United States: Dwight D. Eisenhower, 1960–61* (Washington, 1961), 630; *A Chronology of Missile and Astronautic Events*, 121, 123. See also Senate Committee on Aeronautical and Space Sciences, 88 Cong., 1 sess. (1963), *Documents on International Aspects of the Exploration and Use of Outer Space, 1954–1962*, May 9, 1963, 181. Eisenhower listed *Pioneer V, Tiros I, Transit 1, Echo 1* and the X–15 flight in the "impressive array of successful experiments" during the year preceding Aug. 17, 1960. He omitted mention of the first successful Polaris launches from the submerged nuclear submarine *George Washington*, on July 20, for flights of over 1000 miles down the Atlantic Missile Range, and he also avoided publicizing the solid-fueled Minuteman missile and the SAMOS and MIDAS satellite programs.

[39] *Washington Post*, Sept. 27, 1960. Chapman Pincher reported in the *Washington Daily News*, Dec. 1, 1960, that Victor Jaanimets, a sailor who deserted the Russian ship that brought Khrushchev to New York, had told U.S. intelligence services that the ship, the *Baltika*, was equipped with mockups and demonstration equipment to advertise the Soviet feat in case they succeeded in an early attempt to put a cosmonaut in orbit.

[40] *A Chronology of Missile and Astronautic Events*, 129. See also Nancy T. Gamarra, "International Aeronautical Federation (FAI)," section in Senate Committee on Aeronautical and Space Sciences, 89 Cong., 1 sess. (1965), *International Cooperation and Organization for Outer Space*, 419–426.

[41] Silverstein quoted in news story in Newport News *Times-Herald*, Aug. 8, 1960. See also Brig. Gen. Thomas R. Phillips, "U.S. Out of Man-in-Space Race Until Saturn Is Ready in 1965," and "Criticism of Mercury Space Program Said to Lack Validity," *St. Louis Post-Dispatch*, Sept. 1 and 2, 1960; "Astronauts Hope for '61 Flight," *New York Times*, Sept. 19, 1960; "NASA's Chief Expects Red Space Shows," Baltimore *Sun*, Sept. 20, 1960; Warren Rogers, Jr., "Man-in-Space Effort by U.S. Rolls Again," *New York Herald Tribune*, Sept. 25, 1960.

[42] *Newsweek*, LIV (Oct. 19, 1959), 73–76. This magazine continued with blanket criticisms in LIV (Nov. 2, 1959), 26; LV (Feb. 8, 1960), 67–68; LV (Feb. 15, 1960), 35; but a special report on the manned space race in *Newsweek*, LVI (July 11, 1960), 55–59, was entitled "The Dawn," symbolizing better understanding of STG's efforts.

[43] Hanson W. Baldwin, "Neglected Factor in the Space Race," *New York Times Magazine*, Jan. 17, 1960, 77; Arthur C. Clarke, "Rocket to the Renaissance," *Playboy*, VII (July 1960), 34, 84.

[44] James Barr, "Is Mercury Program Headed for Disaster?" *Missiles and Rockets*, VII (Aug. 15, 1960), 12–14. See also Carl R. Huss, comments, Oct. 5, 1965.

[45] Memo, Gilruth to staff, "Favorable Press Comments (for a change)," with two enclosures, Sept. 16, 1960: Marvin Miles' article described the "recent splurge of sniping at the Mercury program," and Glennan's letter of August 26 commended the article "as a shot of adrenalin" for all the workers on Mercury.

[46] Memo, North to Administrator, "Background of Project Mercury Schedules," with

enclosures, including a chronology, Aug. 14, 1960. Significant excerpts from this memo illustrated other features of Headquarters concerns:

"A major factor in the compressed Mercury schedule is concurrent effort in the areas of research and development, design, and manufacturing. As a result of this concurrent effort, many of the capsule subcontractors underestimated their costs and delivery dates. As early as October 1959, McDonnell anticipated cost increases ranging from 200% to 450% from some of their major subcontractors, such as Bell Aircraft, AiResearch, Collins Radio, and Grand Central Rocket.

"Because of different flight test objectives, it is possible to fly some of the early capsules with incomplete and unqualified systems.

"From the standpoint of project urgency, it was consistent policy to set . . . classified target schedules as tight as possible. . . . However, since problem areas cannot be pinpointed in advance, it was felt that the project objectives could be most rapidly achieved by purposely setting optimistic target schedules and keeping everyone working to meet these dates. . . .

"One is tempted to extrapolate . . . thereby obtaining May 1961 and November 1961, as the actual launch dates for the manned Redstone and manned orbital flights. It is hoped, however, that based on past experience, subsequent capsules can be more accurately scheduled through capsule systems checkout. Conversely, it must also be remembered that as yet none of the production capsules have been qualified during the maximum Q abort and reentry missions."

[47] Low, "Project Mercury Progress," an address before UPI Editors Conference, Washington, Sept. 9, 1960, NASA News Release 60-275; Low, comments, Oct. 5, 1965.

[48] For the significance of the AACB, see Robert L. Rosholt, *An Administrative History of NASA, 1958 to 1963*, NASA SP-4101 (Washington, 1966), 172-173; see also NASA News Release 60-260, Sept. 13, 1960.

[49] Richard M. Mansfield, "Project Mercury: Race or Pure Science?" *Virginian-Pilot and Portsmouth Star*, Sept. 11, 1960.

[50] "An Open Letter to Richard Nixon and John Kennedy," *Missiles and Rockets*, VII (Oct. 3, 1960), 10-11; John F. Kennedy, "If the Soviets Control Space They Can Control Earth," *Missiles and Rockets*, VII (Oct. 10, 1960), 12-13; "Nixon 'Declines' to Join De-

fense/Space Debate," *Missiles and Rockets*, VII (Oct. 24, 1960), 13; Richard M. Nixon, "Military has Mission to 'Defend' Space," *Missiles and Rockets*, VII (Oct. 31, 1960), 10-11. Cf. a similar set of questions and answers in *Western Aviation, Missile and Space Industries* (Nov. 1960). See also Edward C. Welsh, interview, Washington, Sept. 1, 1965.

[51] See Robert Hotz, editorial, "The Gathering Storm Over Space," *Aviation Week*, LXXIII (Nov. 7, 1960), 21; and "Sharp Defense/Space Changes Expected," *Aviation Week*, LXXIII (Nov. 14, 1960), 30.

[52] Hans W. Gatzke, *The Present in Perspective: A Look at the World Since 1945* (2 ed., Chicago, 1961), 188. See also Philip C. Jessup and Howard J. Taubenfeld, *Controls for Outer Space and the Antarctic Analogy* (New York, 1959), 200, 282.

[53] House Committee on Science and Astronautics, 86 Cong., 2 sess. (1960), *The Practical Values of Space Exploration*, Report No. 2091, July 5, 1960, 1. Cf. revision as House Report No. 1276, Oct. 2, 1961, 20-22.

[54] *Ibid.*, 54. Aside from the better illustrations and the updated figures on space costs and accomplishments, the August 1961 revision of this report contained one significant addition, namely a two-page (20-22) discussion in the national security section entitled "Interpreting The Race," which said in part:

"The fact that we are racing the Russians to the moon and the planets should not be allowed to obscure certain facets of the precise situation we are in.

"To begin with, it is essential to realize that sending men beyond earth's environment requires rockets of very high thrust—big boosters. The Soviets, who have about a 5-year jump on the United States in this field, have such rockets in operation. Our biggest ones are still in the development stage, although they are showing considerable promise. So we begin this particular phase of 'the race' under a marked handicap and doubtless will be in second place for some time to come.

"It is equally important, however, to recognize that 'getting there first' is only one part of the race. Two other parts are just as crucial:

1. What will we learn from our effort to explore beyond the Earth?

2. How will we use this knowledge after it is acquired?

"The Vikings had the technique to get to

the New World 'first,' but England, France, and Spain won the prizes. . . . With no intent to deprecate the notable achievements of the Soviet Union in space research, it can nonetheless be said that the broad scope of the American effort has—thus far at least—been outstanding in its scientific results. And, as subsequent parts of this report suggest, our free enterprise system has been quick to take advantage of the technological fall out.

"In summary, our international prestige and stature, so far as they are influenced by our space activities, depend on all three elements of 'the race'—not on one or two."

[55] Memo, Benjamine J. Garland to Project Director, "Possible Meteoroid Damage to Mercury," with enclosure, June 2, 1960, 3.

[56] Letter, Smith J. DeFrance to Alan B. Kehlet, "Information Requested by STG on Pressure Transducers and an Auxiliary Drag Device for Mercury," with enclosures, Sept. 16, 1960; memo, Caldwell C. Johnson to Faget, "Auxiliary Drag Device—Mercury," Nov. 2, 1960; John P. Mayer, comments, Sept. 8, 1965. Back in 1957 Avco had proposed a metallic drag chute shuttlecock configuration for the same purpose for the Air Force Man-in-Space studies. See also "Summary of Several Short Studies Pertaining to the Retro-Rocket System Capabilities for the Mercury Mission," NASA Project Mercury working paper No. 160, Nov. 9, 1960.

[57] The reinstatement of development work on the pneumatic impact bag followed after Gerard J. Pesman learned the details of more experiments on human impact at Wright-Patterson late in 1960. For a resume of this work see J. W. Brinkley, R. A. Headley, and K. K. Kaiser, "Abrupt Acceleration of Human Subjects in the Semi-Supine Position," paper, Symposium on Bio-Mechanics of Body Restraint and Head Protection, Naval Air Materiels Center, Philadelphia, Pa., June 14–15, 1961.

[58] Memo, Peter J. Armitage and E. N. Harrin to Chief, Operations Div., "Mercury Capsule Water Stability," Oct. 31, 1960.

[59] Memo, Harrin to Chief, Operations Div., "Static Water Stability Tests of Personal Egress Capsule," Jan. 10, 1961.

[60] "Project Mercury Status Report No. 8 for Period Ending October 31, 1960," STG, 17–18; "Astronaut Preparation and Activities Manual for Mercury-Redstone No. 3," NASA Project Mercury working paper No. 174, Feb. 6, 1961.

[61] Memo, Yardley and G. M. Preston to

Silverstein, et al., "Summary of Conclusions Reached Regarding the CST Plans and Cape Checkout Plans for Capsules 5 (MR–2) and 7 (MR–3)," Sept. 9, 1960, 3. For MAC's home factory response to the field workers' difficulties with electrical, piping, sequencing, inspection, and cleanliness problems, see draft memo by H. Earle Moore and Walter F. Burke, "Quality Assurance—Project Mercury," Sept. 12, 1960.

[62] Memo, Richard Sachen and James T. Rose to W. H. Gray, "General Summary of Capsule Systems Tests on Capsule No. 7," Dec. 1, 1960, with enclosures. Convair/Astronautics had encountered the skin-cracking problem in 1955 during the Atlas development program. At that time no solution had been discovered.

[63] Memo, Jerome B. Hammack and Rose to W. H. Gray, "General Summary of Capsule Systems Tests on Capsule No. 7," Dec. 1, 1960, 5, 6. This memo, with enclosures 1–17, gives a detailed engineering history of the problems encountered during the systems testing of the first manned Mercury capsule. Although STG inspectors found 189 electrical and mechanical discrepancies in their final acceptance test, MAC's own inspectors had listed some 370 such discrepancies before their final cleanup prior to delivery.

[64] See Leutjen, "Ground Checkout and Launch Procedures," 3. Revised procedures for expediting checkout "squawk sheets" and discrepancy reports were issued shortly thereafter; see memo, Yardley and Preston to Hangar S Supervisors, "Cape Inspection Policy Clarification," Oct. 20, 1960.

[65] Letter, Williams to Commanding Officer, Air Force Missile Test Center, attention Lt. Col. R. D. Stephens, Sept. 6, 1960; "T-605 Operation, MR Mission," STG, Sept. 8, 1960; "MR-1 Mission Rules," STG, Nov. 2, 1960; letter, Williams to Kurt H. Debus, "Flight Safety Review for MR Missions," Sept. 22, 1960, with enclosure, "Flight Safety Review Plan"; letter, Williams to Cdr. DesFlotFour, "NASA Personnel Assignment for MR-1 Test," Sept. 28, 1960, with enclosures; memos, Low to Administrator, "Tests of Mercury Redstone 1 and Little Joe 5," Nov. 2, 1960; and "LJ-5 and MR-1 launchings," Nov. 4, 1960; Williams, Management Memorandum, No. 13, "Working Hours, Launch Operations Branch," Oct. 5, 1960.

[66] Letter, James P. Gleason to Kenneth E. BeLieu, Nov. 7, 1960. For one source of this concern, see Drew Pearson, "Space Shot

Moved to Election Eve," *Washington Post,* Nov. 2, 1960.

[67] Project Mercury Status Report No. 8"; "Project Mercury Discussion," briefing charts, Oct. 31, 1960.

[68] "Project Mercury Flight Test Report for Little Joe Mission No. 5 (capsule No. 3)," NASA Project Mercury working paper No. 166, Dec. 23, 1960; letter, Williams to R/A F. V. H. Hilles, Dec. 14, 1960; memo, Low for Administrator, "Report on Little Joe No. 5 and Mercury Redstone No. 1," Nov. 10, 1960. See also Fisher, comments, Sept. 15, 1965.

[69] Memo, North to Dir., Space Flight Programs, "Project Mercury PMP Charts," Sept. 21, 1960, explains why the chimp was eliminated from LJ-5. John C. Palmer, "Test Directive for Little Joe V," approved countdown procedures, undated. See also minutes, "Little Joe V AeroMedical Operations Review Meeting," Richard S. Johnston, secretary, July 12, 1960; "Mission Document for Little Joe No. 5 (Capsule No. 3)," NASA Project Mercury working paper No. 121, May 25, 1960.

[70] Low memo, Nov. 10, 1960; memo, Low to Asst. Administrator for Congressional Relations, "Mercury Redstone and Little Joe 5 Launchings," Nov. 16, 1960. The additional Little Joe airframe was suggested by Silverstein. Memos, William M. Bland, Jr., to Faget, "Visit of representatives of NAA–MD to STG," Feb. 1, 1960, and "Further Development of Little Joe Booster," Feb. 8, 1960; North to Silverstein, "Request for Approval Project Mercury Funding," June 27, 1960; Silverstein to Budget Office, "Budget on Approval of Project Mercury Funding," June 29, 1960. Cf. memo, C. J. Donlan to LRC Procurement Officer, "Contract NAS 9-59, Refurbished Little Joe Static Booster, Expedited Delivery," Nov. 16, 1960.

[71] Memo, Johnson to Faget, "Mercury Weight Growth—Effect upon Orbit Insertion Probability, Retrograde Maneuver, Parachute Loads, and Flotation," Nov. 22, 1960, 1–3. Johnson speculated on possibilities:

"The really interesting scheme requires starting all over. Consider six (6) Pioneer or Explorer second stage motors clustered together as a posigrade-retrograde power pack. . . .

"On the subject of parachutes and weights: it is quite likely that the impact skirt system and its associated 100 pounds of weight could be eliminated if the capsule impact attitude could be restricted to 'pilot feet first' and

without much swing. The main difficulty now is the pilot's low tolerance to lateral acceleration. . . . This is not a proposal but it's worth thinking of."

See also Huss comments.

[72] Letter, Gleason to BeLieu, Nov. 3, 1960. For the description of events following, see memos, Low to Administrator, "MR-1 Launching," Nov. 7, 1960; Low to Dir., Space Flight Programs, "Mercury-Redstone 1 Launching," Nov. 14, 1960; Low to Administrator, "MR-1 Launching," Nov. 18, 1960.

[73] For news criticism in the wake of MR–1, see William Hines, "Mercury Failure Puts Early Flight in Doubt," Washington *Evening Star,* Nov. 21, 1960; "Astronaut Flight Still Slated in '61," *New York Times,* Nov. 26, 1960; Louis Kraar, "Man in Space Tests Far Behind Schedule," *Wall Street Journal,* Nov. 28, 1960; and "Space Experts Sniping at Mercury," *Space Age News,* Nov. 21, 1960.

[74] Memo, Low to Administrator, "Attempted Launching of MR–1," Nov. 21, 1960; Hammack, interview, Houston, Feb. 13, 1964; and memo report, Hammack for Proj. Dir., "Attempted Launch of Mercury-Redstone No. 1 Mission on November 21, 1960," Nov. 23, 1960.

[75] Memo, Low to Administrator, "Explanation of MR-1 Failure," Nov. 23, 1960; Joachim P. Kuettner, interview, Huntsville, April 28, 1964.

[76] Memo, Low to Dir., Space Flight Programs, "PMP Briefing on December 2, 1960, Project Mercury," Nov. 28, 1960; and Low comments.

[77] Memo, Low to Administrator, "MR-1 Launch Information," Dec. 15, 1960. For retest preparations, see "Mercury-Redstone, NASA, LOD–LOB, Master Operational Schedule," rev. Nov. 15, 1960, for MR-1, Report No. M-LOD-G-TR-49.4-60; rev. Dec. 2, 1960, for MR-1A, Marshall Space Flight Center. Ms., "MR-1A Review," STG, Dec. 17, 1960.

[78] Memo, Low to Administrator, "Mercury-Redstone 1 Launching," Dec. 20, 1960. See also Jerome B. Hammack and Jack C. Heberlig, "The Mercury Redstone Program," paper, American Rocket Society, Space Flight Report to the Nation, New York City, Oct. 9–15, 1961, 16–17.

[79] Memos, Howard C. Kyle to Mercury Flight Dir., "MR-1 Launch on December 19, 1960—observations"; Tecwyn Roberts to Flight Dir., "Report on Test No. 5111," Dec. 20, 1960; and Stanley C. White to Flight Dir.,

FOOTNOTES

"MR–1A Test No. 5111," Dec. 20, 1960. For the later post-flight inspection of MR–1A, see letter, Purser to Burke, "Contract NAS 5–59; Post-Flight Evaluation of Capsule Number Two," Jan. 31, 1961, with two enclosures. See also Chap. X, footnote 26.

[50] Memo, North to Dir., Space Flight Programs, "Mercury Capsule Changes and Flight Schedule," Dec. 6, 1960:

"Open loop operation of the Abort Sensing and Implementation System (ASIS) is a change which does not detract from the effectivity of the system. This change, in fact, makes the system more reliable and effective because a pilot who is placed in the control loop has the ability to assess whether a true abort situation exists. In this concept, the pilot would get a red light indication that an abort is called for but would manually activate the escape sequence. The inherent aerodynamic stability and high structural strength of the Redstone should provide a sufficient time constant between capsule abort light indication and time for abort decision. The pilot, after observing the abort light, can either immediately abort, if he is in a critical flight regime, or he can rely on secondary cues such as changes in acceleration, changes in attitude, and radio voice transmissions from visual observers or telemeter monitors. Although it is reasonably clear that the Redstone should be flown with an open loop ASIS, the Atlas operational procedure is not yet resolved because allowable pilot reaction time will be somewhat less. I feel, however, that experience with the manned Redstone will convince us that the manned Atlas should also be flown open loop. Incidentally, three Atlas ASIS systems have been flown open loop to date; two would have caused inadvertent aborts."

Warren North was himself a test-pilot engineer, and this viewpoint became even stronger over the next year; see North and Walter Williams, "The NASA Astronaut Program," *Aerospace Engineering*, XX (Jan. 1962), 13–15.

[51] For an overview of the meetings and conferences on the MA–1 failure, see James M. Grimwood, *Project Mercury: A Chronology*, NASA SP–4001 (Washington, 1963), 111, 112. On the MA–1 review of Nov. 16, 1960, see "Mercury-Atlas Program," briefing brochure Nos. AD–60–0000–02356 and AT–60–0829–00415, undated. Minutes, "Summary of Test Programs and Recommendations for MA–2 Launch," Sjoberg, secretary, Nov. 16, 1960; Ms. notes, Purser, "STG Position on MA–1," Dec. 20, 1960; draft letters, Purser to Donlan, Faget, and James A. Chamberlin, Dec. 31, 1960, and Jan. 1, 1961; memo, Low to Dir. Space Flight Programs, "Project Mercury Status," Dec. 29, 1960; and Richard V. Rhode, interview, Washington, Jan. 18, 1966.

[52] *A Chronology of Missile and Astronautics Events*, 135; Sheldon, "The Challenge of International Competition," 11, 26, and comments, Aug. 12, 1965.

[53] G. Pokrovsky, "We Give Space to the Russians," *Washington Daily News*, Dec. 5, 1960; "Lead-Footed Mercury," *Time*, Dec. 5, 1960; "Man in Space," editorial, *New York Times*, Dec. 2, 1960.

Chapter X

[1] *NASA Fifth Semiannual Report to Congress, October 1, 1960, through June 30, 1961*, 153. This report, not published until July 11, 1962, is highly anachronistic (see pp. 5, 6) and should be used with caution. See also memo, Aaron Rosenthal to Dir., Office of Space Flight Programs, "Temporary Reassignment of Manpower Spaces," with enclosures on STG complement requirement for fiscal 1962, Dec. 5, 1960.

[2] Eugene M. Emme, *Aeronautics and Astronautics: An American Chronology of Science and Technology in the Exploration of Space, 1915–1960* (Washington, 1961), 134, 139–151; *STL Space Log* (Jan. 1961), 24, 3–8. Charles S. Sheldon II has corrected the poundage figures in terms of lifting capacity to 100 nautical mile altitude. Official comparisons sometimes unfairly counted the weights of U.S. rocket casings and not those of U.S.S.R. casings.

[3] Senate Committee on Aeronautical and Space Sciences, 88 Cong., 1 sess. (1963), *Documents on International Aspects of the Exploration and Use of Outer Space, 1954–1962*, May 9, 1963, 186.

[4] The informant was Lt. Col. Paul D. Hickman, of the Armed Forces Industrial College. See House Committee on Science and Astronautics, 87 Cong., 1 sess. (1961), *A Chronology of Missile and Astronautics Events*, 139–140; House Committee on Science and Astronautics, 87 Cong., 2 sess. (1962), *Aeronautical and Astronautical Events of 1961*, 1–2; and "U.S. Officer Says 2 Reds Died in Space," Newport News *Daily Press*, Jan. 15, 1961. Soviet spokesmen later denied this report, of course, and most informed American opinion credits the Soviet denial. Two

U.S.S.R. attempted launchings of Mars probes on October 10 and 14, 1960, may have confused this issue. For an important demurrer, see the letter by Julius Epstein, a research associate of the Hoover Institute of Stanford University, reprinted in the *Congressional Record* on Aug. 6, 1965: "Open Versus Secret Procedures in Space Programs," pp. 18813-18814.

[5] *Documents on International Aspects of . . . Outer Space,* 188. For some perspective on the larger interregnum and the search for a national space program between 1958 and 1962, see House Committee on Government Operations, 89 Cong., 1 sess. (1965), *Government Operations in Space* (Analysis of Civil-Military Roles and Relationships), 49–71.

[6] Ms., "Report to the President-Elect of the Ad Hoc Committee on Space," Jerome B. Wiesner, chairman (unclassified version), Jan. 12, 1961, 11, 12.

[7] Ms., "Report to the President-Elect of the Ad Hoc Committee on Space," Wiesner, chairman (classified version), Jan. 10, 1961, 17. The other members of this committee were Kenneth BeLieu, Trevor Gardner, Donald F. Hornig, Edwin H. Land, Max Lehrer, Edward M. Purcell, Bruno B. Rossi, and Harry J. Watters.

[8] At a press conference on Oct. 26, 1960, Robert R. Gilruth was asked about the possibility of using the Titan rather than the Atlas for orbital flight. Gilruth said he preferred the Atlas, pointing out that the technical problems connected with it were being solved, whereas those associated with the Titan were nowhere near solution. The fact that the second stage of the two-stage Titan ignited in flight presented additional problems to orbital flight, he said. In contrast all three Atlas engines ignited at liftoff. Gilruth actually drafted a letter intended for Maj. Gen. Osmond J. Ritland, commander of the Air Force Ballistic Missile Division, asking for a briefing on the possible application of the Titan to the Mercury program. The letter (Gilruth to Ritland, Jan. 18, 1961) was never mailed, primarily because the conceptual development of the follow-on program after Mercury was beginning to take shape. In May 1961 Robert C. Seamans was sold on the Titan II as a launch vehicle for Mercury Mark II, and thereafter NASA and DOD agreed to support each other's use of Titan II and III respectively; Seamans, interview, Washington, Sept. 1, 1965.

[9] House Committee on Science and Astronautics, 87 Cong., 1 sess. (1961), *Third Annual Report in the Fields of Aeronautics and Space,* Jan. 18, 1961, XVI, 8–9; Paul E. Purser, interview, Houston, March 15, 1965; George M. Low, interview, Houston, March 19, 1964.

[10] *Washington Post,* Jan. 12, 1961; "Washington Roundup," *Aviation Week,* LXXIV (Feb. 6, 1961), 5; Washington *Evening Star,* Jan. 12, 1961; Newport News *Daily Press,* Jan. 27, 1961. The Wiesner Report admitted that the committee's review of the nation's space program had been made hastily.

[11] *Public Papers of the Presidents of the United States: Dwight D. Eisenhower, 1960–61* (Washington, 1961), Item 421, 1038, "Farewell Radio and Television Address to the American People," Jan. 17, 1961. Eisenhower had warned: "In the councils of government, we must guard against the acquisition of unwarranted influence, whether sought or unsought, by the military-industrial complex. The potential for the disastrous rise of misplaced power exists and will persist. . . . We must never let the weight of this combination endanger our liberties or democratic processes. . . ."

[12] On the "military-industrial complex" problem, see George T. Hayes, ed., *The Industry-Government Aerospace Relationship,* 2 vols. (Menlo Park, Calif., May 1963), Stanford Research Institute Project No. IS–4216; Robert Hotz, "Gathering Storm Over Space," *Aviation Week,* LXXIII (Nov. 7, 1960), 21; Hotz, "Sharp Defense/Space Changes Expected," *Aviation Week,* LXXIII (Nov. 14, 1960), 30–31. See other articles in *Aviation Week,* LXXIV (Jan. 16, 1961), 21; (Jan. 30, 1961), 21, 34; Robert L. Rosholt, *An Administrative History of NASA, 1958–1963,* NASA SP–4101 (Washington, 1966), 184; House Committee on Science and Astronautics, 87 Cong., 1 sess. (1961), *Military Astronautics (Preliminary Report),* Staff report No. 360, May 4, 1961.

[13] For some of the scientists' criticism of Mercury, see Jay Holmes, *America on the Moon: The Enterprise of the Sixties* (New York, 1961), 72–82. The most prevalent scientific objection to Mercury was expressed by the question "Why put the sensitive stomach and heart of a man out in space when his other senses can be sent out there with man staying on the ground but in the loop?" Douglas R. Lord, interview, Washington, Sept. 3, 1965.

[14] House Committee on Science and Astronautics, 87 Cong., 1 sess. (1961), *NASA Authorization, Hearings,* Part I, March 13–April 17, 1961, 4, 192, 195, 199, 213. Cf. Rosholt, *Administrative History of NASA,* 136–137, 184, 190–195 for more details on the extremely complex financial history of NASA during this period. See also Merton J. Peck and Frederic M. Scherer, *The Weapons Acquisition Process: An Economic Analysis* (Boston, 1962), 100. It is perhaps significant that what purports to be a House Committee on Science and Astronautics manuscript, entitled "Project Mercury: A Preliminary Progress Report," dated October 1960, accurately estimated (at last) a completion cost for Project Mercury at $393 million, of which approximately $110 million would be spent on the McDonnell contract for the spacecraft.

[15] "Interim Report," Joint Air Force/NASA Ad Hoc Committee on Atlas Boosted Space Systems, Jan. 19, 1961. Richard V. Rhode, interview, Washington, Dec. 30, 1964; Bernhard A. Hohmann, interview, Houston, Sept. 16, 1965. Richard V. Rhode pursued the method with which the Atlas contractor would fit the "belly band" to the booster's top sections, since there were small metal appendages that would have to be ground flush to the booster's surface. He was particularly interested in how they would prevent the metal from being undercut and thereby weakening the structural strength even more. General Dynamics responded that they had a technician with capability to prevent undercutting. Rhode asked to be shown. After seeing the proof, he directed that this individual be sent to the Cape to perform this part of the "fix." Rhode, interview, Washington, Jan. 18, 1965.

[16] Letter, Purser to Rhode, Jan. 10, 1961; Ms. notes, Purser, "STG–773, 67–D Instrumentation," Jan. 3, 1961; Ms., "Agenda—Abort Parameters," Jan. 4, 1961. Seamans and Abe Silverstein of NASA Headquarters; James R. Dempsey of Convair/Astronautics, and the Secretaries of the Air Force and the Department of Defense were all involved in telephonic conferences behind the scenes on the MA–2 decisions. For the final decision to go with the "horse collar," see Ms., Purser, "Notes for Rhode Committee: Status of MA–2," Feb. 13, 1961.

[17] Rhode, "The First Hundred Seconds," paper, American Rocket Society Conference on Launch Vehicle Structures and Materials, April 3, 1962. Rhode here applied his experience with the Electra and the Atlas to Saturn problems of fuel slosh, acoustics, panel flutter, buffeting, and wind effects during the first 100 seconds. "In a structural sense there is really no such thing as a 'launch vehicle,' " he said.

[18] Holmes, *America on the Moon,* 189–190; Hotz, "New Vigor for Space Program," *Aviation Week,* LXXIV (Jan 16, 1961), 21.

[19] James E. Webb, interview, Washington, Sept. 3, 1965; Webb, address before Science Convocation at Brandeis University, Waltham, Mass., Nov. 7, 1965, NASA News Release. See also "Washington Roundup," *Aviation Week,* LXXIV (Jan. 30, 1961), 21.

[20] Holmes, *America on the Moon,* 190–192; Senate Committee on Astronautical and Space Sciences, 88 Cong., 1 sess. (1963), *NASA Authorization for Fiscal Year 1964, Hearings,* Part I, 5–6; NASA biography of James E. Webb, Jan. 27, 1964. For details of Webb's background, see Senate Committee on Aeronautical and Space Sciences, 87 Cong., 1 sess. (1961), *Nomination of James Edwin Webb to be Administrator of the National Aeronautics and Space Administration.*

[21] "Washington Roundup," *Aviation Week,* LXXIV (Jan. 30, 1961), 21; "Kennedy Appoints Webb to Direct NASA," *Aviation Week,* LXXIV (Feb. 6, 1961), 29; Hotz, "Success and Disappointment in Space," *Aviation Week,* LXXIV (Feb. 6, 1961), 21; Newport News *Daily Press,* Feb. 5, 1961; Holmes, *America on the Moon,* 192. Webb's appointment was confirmed by the Senate on Feb. 9, and he was sworn in on Feb. 15, 1961.

[22] Letter, Overton Brooks to John F. Kennedy, March 9, 1961; Kennedy to Brooks, March 23, 1961; see also "Washington Roundup," *Aviation Week,* LXXIV (Jan. 16, 1961), 25; "Cooperation Theme is Stressed by NASA and Defense Officials," *Aviation Week,* LXXIV (Jan. 30, 1961), 34; and "Washington Roundup," *Aviation Week,* LXXIV (Feb. 6, 1961), 25.

[23] Excerpts from messages compiled by Purser, special assistant to director, STG, re status of spacecraft No. 5. During one of the McDonnell tests, when the air leakage rate was being checked, the inspectors found that gas seepage was too great. The best seal they could obtain left a leakage rate of 1725 cc./min. at 4.9 p.s.i. for 45 minutes, as against the specified maximum rate of 650 cc. The defect causing this was found at the umbilical connector and traced to warpage of the capsule frame. McDonnell reworked the struts and stringers to make a better fit. This is but

one sample from daily reports to STG about the rework status of one selected component. Afterward, on July 5, 1960, STG approved a spacecraft leak rate of 1000 cc per minute. Memo, Richard S. Johnston, Asst. Head, Life Systems Branch, to Chief, Flight Systems Div., "Capsule Leakage Rates," July 5, 1960.

[23] Message, John J. Williams, Launch Operations, Marshall Space Flight Center, to G. Merritt Preston, STG Cape Operations, Oct. 4, 1960; "Postlaunch Report for Mercury-Redstone No. 2 (MR-2)," NASA/STG, Feb. 13, 1961; NASA News Release 61-14-1, "Project Mercury Background," Jan. 28, 1961. For the MR-2 mission directive, see NASA Project Mercury working paper No. 138, dated Apr. 15, 1960, rev. Nov. 29, 1960, and Jan. 27, 1961.

[24] David S. Akens, Paul K. Freiwirth, and Helen T. Wells, *History of the George C. Marshall Space Flight Center* (Huntsville, Ala., May 1961), Vol. I. Appendix B, "Mercury-Redstone Chronology," 28, 32; Francis E. Jarrett, Jr., and Robert A. Lindemann, "Historical Origins of NASA's Launch Operations Center to July 1, 1962," Kennedy Space Center Historical Monograph No. 1, Cocoa Beach, Fla., Oct. 1964, B-26.

[26] Akens, Freiwirth, and Wells, *History of Marshall Space Flight Center,* Vol. I, 32; memo, E. D. Geissler, Aeroballistics Div., Marshall Space Flight Center, to STG, "Project Mercury-Redstone: Trajectory Data for MR-2," Jan. 23, 1961; memo, Walter C. Williams, Operations Dir., STG, to Marshall Space Flight Center, "Launch Trajectories for MR-2 and Subsequent Flight," Dec. 20, 1960; "Technical Information Summary of Mercury-Redstone Mission MR-2," Marshall Space Flight Center, Jan. 20, 1961. Williams' 12-g nominal reentry decelerations were not connected with the 12-g emergency maximum advocated by the Air Force in 1958 for the "man-in-space" study program. The 12-g maximum desired for the MR-2 mission was set for two reasons: (1) It represented the midway point between a normal Mercury-Atlas reentry (about 8 g) and the worst Mercury-Atlas reentry (about 16 g); and (2) normal reentry for the Mercury-Redstone was about 11 to 12 g. STG felt it was necessary to study the g-load effects on the chimpanzee in this range. The fact that both acceleration and deceleration g loads surpassed 12 served to prove the supine couch concept.

[27] "Project Mercury Technical Information Summary of Mercury-Redstone Mission No. 2 (Capsule No. 5)," NASA/STG, Jan. 24, 1961; "Technical Information Summary Concerning Mercury-Redstone Mission MR-2," MSFC report TPR-M-60-1; NASA News Release 61-14-2, "MR-2 Flight Profile," Jan. 28, 1961; "Project Mercury Background."

[28] NASA News Release 61-14-3, "Animal Flight Program," Jan. 28, 1961; "Information Guide for Animal Launching," July 23, 1959; "Countdown and Procedures (Animal Subject) for Project Mercury Flight MR-2," USAF Aeromedical Field Laboratory, Holloman Air Force Base, N. Mex., Dec. 1960.

[29] Norman E. Stingely, John D. Mosely, and Charles D. Wheelwright, "MR-2 Operations," in *Results of the Project Mercury Ballistic and Orbital Chimpanzee Flights,* NASA SP-39 (Washington, 1963), 7.

[30] "Recovery Operations Requirements for Mercury-Redstone Test No. 2," STG, undated [about Jan. 12, 1961]; "Mercury Recovery Forces," NASA fact sheet, undated; Message, Cdr., DesFlotFour, to STG, "Public Information for MR-2," Jan. 5, 1961. The helicopters were from Marine Aircraft Group 26, the Mercury project officer of which was 1st Lt. Wayne E. Koons, USMCR.

[31] Letter, Walter Williams, STG, to Cdr., DesFlotFour, re NASA personnel assignment for MR-2 test, Jan. 6, 1961.

[32] "Master Operational Schedule, MR-2," Marshall Space Flight Center, Jan. 20, 1961, 5-26, 27-30, 32-47, 48-77; *Final Report: Mercury-Redstone Project Launch Operations,* Marshall Space Flight Center, May 28, 1962, 121, Appendix L, "MR-2 Daily Log Summary," 1-4.

[33] "MR-2 Flight Test Profile—Operations Directive No. 1904, Mercury-Redstone Launch," Air Force Missile Test Center, Jan. 5, 1961, 4-10.

[34] *Ibid.* Ham's depth of respiration was measured by a pneumograph consisting of a rubber tube filled with copper sulfate solution. Electrical resistance of the solution varied as the tube was stretched. At one point during the testing of sensors for measuring the primate's respiration, technicians discovered that when the pneumograph was attached high on the thorax, the chimp breathed low and vice versa. One solution was to use two pneumograph straps in conjunction. *Results of the Project Mercury Ballistic and Orbital Chimpanzee Flights;* A. D. Catterson, MSC Medical Support Operations, interview, Houston, Oct. 23, 1964.

[35] "Countdown and Procedures (Animal Subject) for MR-2"; "Animal Flight Pro-

gram"; *Marshall Star*, Feb. 1, 1961; Stingely, Mosely, and Wheelwright, "MR-2 Operations," 9–11. Each animal received 15 commercial food pellets and a fourth of an orange at a feeding. One 12-ounce serving was given at about T minus 20 hours and another at T minus 15 hours. Water intake was limited to 800 cc. from T minus one day through recovery. The name "Ham" also honored the commander of Holloman Aeromedical Laboratory, Lt. Col. Hamilton Blackshear.

[36] "MR-2 Flight Test Profile—Directive 1904." Staff members under the operations director had a variety of duties and responsibilities. For example, the launch director, located in the blockhouse, reported on the readiness of the launch vehicle; the launch conductor, also in the blockhouse, was responsible for detailed supervision of launch operations; the capsule test conductor had a similar duty on the countdown; and the flight director, located in the Mercury Control Center, had detailed flight-control responsibility from liftoff to touchdown.

[37] Memo, Tecwyn Roberts, Flight Dynamics Officer, to Flight Director, "Report on Test 3805," Feb. 2, 1961; penciled notes on the countdown of MR-2, anon., Jan. 31, 1961. The origin of the popular space term "A.OK" is a matter of widespread public interest. In reporting the *Freedom 7* flight, the press attributed the term to Astronaut Shepard, and indeed NASA News Release 1–61–99, May 5, 1961, has Shepard report "A.OK" shortly after impact. A replay of the flight voice communications tape disclosed that Shepard himself did not use the term. It was Col. John A. "Shorty" Powers who reported Shepard's condition as "A.OK" in a description of the flight. Tecwyn Roberts of STG and Capt. Henry E. Clements of the Air Force had used "A.OK" frequently in reports written more than four months before the Shepard flight. Roberts attributed coinage of the term to Paul Lein, of the Western Electric Co., while the tracking network was being constructed. Lein, however, said that "A.OK" was a communal development among communications engineers while circuits were first being established downrange from Cape Canaveral. The voice circuits at first gave poor quality. The bands were narrow, and the systems operated on 1500 cycles. There was much static and background noise. Words got lost in voice circuit systems checks. To make transmissions clearer, the communicators started using "A.OK" because the letter "A" has a brilliant

sound. Other sources claim that oldtime railroad telegraphers used "A–OK" as one of several terms to report the status of their equipment. Be that as it may, Powers, "the voice of Mercury Control," by his public use of "A.OK," made those three letters a universal symbol meaning "in perfect working order."

[38] Penciled notes on MR-2 countdown; memo, William S. Augerson, Life Systems Group, to Christopher C. Kraft, Mercury Control Center Flight Dir., "Blockhouse Medical Monitoring of MR-2," Feb. 6, 1961; W. J. Kapryan, "Postlaunch Report for MR-2," Feb. 2, 1961. Some flight notes on MR-2, author unknown, dated Feb. 1961, indicated that the inverter had operated at temperatures as high as 200 degrees F.

[39] "Postlaunch Report for MR-2," 9; NASA News Release, Cape Canaveral, Jan. 30, 1961; Roberts memo; memo, Warren J. North, Head, Manned Satellites, NASA Hq., to Franklyn W. Phillips, NASA Hq., "MR-2 Flight Results," Feb. 1, 1961; tape of press conference following MR-2 launch, Cape Canaveral, Jan. 31, 1961. Cf. Carl R. Huss comments, Oct. 5, 1965.

[40] "Postlaunch Report for MR-2," 9; memo, North to STG, "Retrocontrollers Comments," Feb. 9, 1961. Brief accounts of Ham's flight may be found in Kenneth F. Weaver, "Countdown for Space," *National Geographic*, CXIX (May 1961), 725–734; and in Judith Viorst, *Projects: Space* (New York, 1962), 37–38.

[41] Memo, Morton Schler, capsule environment monitor, to Kraft, "MR-2 ECS Flight and Postflight Summary," Feb. 6, 1961.

[42] "Mercury-Redstone II Flight Parameters," chart, Feb. 7, 1961; "Calculated Preflight Trajectory Data for MR-2," Project Mercury working paper No. 168, Jan. 19, 1961. See also North memo.

[43] *NASA Fifth Semiannual Report to Congress.* See also NASA films, *MR-2 Launch*, March 1961, and *Sixth Quarterly Report*, April 1961.

[44] "Postlaunch Report for MR-2," 10; MR-2 flight parameter chart; tape of press conference following MR-2 flight; some flight notes on MR-2, anon., dated Feb. 1961; House Committee on Science and Astronautics, 87 Cong., 1 sess. (1961), *Project Mercury, Second Interim Report*, 34–37; Wayne E. Koons and James L. Lewis, interviews, Houston, Sept. 16, 1965. Robert F. Wallace, an STG information officer on the scene, reported that Ham was excited when returned to Hangar S after

his flight. Being unable to debrief his handlers, Ham alone knew at this time how grueling his flight had been. Flashbulbs and crowding newsmen made him highly agitated, and he snapped at several people. Back in his trailer, his suit was not removed until he became calm, and at that time a famous "grin" photograph was made. Later, when his handler led him back toward a capsule for pictures requested by the TV crews, Ham again became highly perturbed. It took three men to calm the "astrochimp" for the next round of pictures. On April 2, 1963, Ham was given to the National Zoological Park, Smithsonian Institution, Washington, D.C., where for the past several years he has been in good health and has thrilled many children.

[45] The amount of water in the spacecraft caused great concern to members of STG's Life Systems Group when they found the heatshield had punctured holes in the lower pressure bulkhead. Life Systems renewed studying alternatives, making either optional or impossible the deployment of the landing bag. More drop tests were undertaken by the Aeromedical Biophysics Group of the Wright Air Development Division. Simulating the Mercury drop rate of about 30 feet per second, the Wright group found that human test subjects could sustain impacts of about 35 g and recover from "a confused state" in about five seconds. STG considered this within fairly safe limits for an interim measure, but the margin of safety was too small to accept for the routine operation of a Mercury mission. Memo, Gerard J. Pesman to Assoc. Dir., "Use of Impact Bag for Water Landings," Feb. 13, 1961. In all of the manned missions the impact bag was deployed.

[46] See R. I. Johnson, et al., "The Mercury-Redstone Project," Saturn/Apollo Systems Office, Marshall Space Flight Center, June 1964, 8-9. Cf. Huss comments. Regarding the impact bag problems at this time, see memo, Rodney G. Rose to Chief, STG Engineering Div., "Summary of Air Drop and Fatigue Program with Production Capsule No. 5," May 4, 1961, and Ms. paper, "Project Mercury Water Landing Problems," presented to 30th annual AIAA meeting, New York City, Jan. 24, 1962.

[47] Purser, "Notes on Capsule Review Board Meeting," Jan. 20, 1961. The conception of Mercury Mark II (or what was named Project Gemini almost a year later) was taking place at this time. See memo, Purser to STG Dir., "Atlas Modifications, Cost, and Scheduling,"

Jan. 17, 1961. Message, Hohmann and Robert H. Brundin to Philip E. Culbertson, re tests of the restraining band to reduce the discontinuity stresses in the M/A station 502 area, Jan. 16, 1961.

[48] Seamans interview; "MA-2 Mission Directive," NASA Project Mercury working paper No. 140, June 24, 1960, rev. Aug. 11, 1960, Jan. 29, 1961, and Feb. 9, 1961; Donald T. Gregory, "Technical Information Summary of Mercury-Atlas Mission No. 2 (Capsule No. 6)," Feb. 10, 1961.

[49] Rhode interview. Owing to airline engineers' strike, Rhode flew to the Cape via a routine Air Force logistics flight, arriving just in time to climb the gantry and personally inspect the "fix."

[50] Webb interview; memo, George M. Low to Administrator, "Mercury-Atlas 2 Launch," Feb. 18, 1961; "Calculated Trajectory Data for MA-2," NASA Project Mercury working paper No. 163, Dec. 7, 1960.

[51] "Proceedings of the Mercury-Atlas Booster Reliability Workshop," San Diego, July 12, 1963, passim.

[52] Low, interview, Houston, Sept. 15, 1965; Ritland, interview, Andrews AFB, Dec. 30, 1964; Gilruth, interview, Houston, Mar. 18, 1964; P. E. Culbertson, comments, Aug. 16, 1965; Paul P. Haney, comments, Sept. 15, 1965; Purser, notes on MA-2 launch as relayed from Mercury Control Center, Feb. 21, 1961.

[53] "Post Launch Report for Mercury-Atlas No. 2 (MA-2)," STG, March 13, 1961, 161. An unidentified ship, a tanker flying a hammer-and-sickle flag, but apparently without any unusual radar antennas, also was able to see the unusual reentry. Memo, Donald C. Cheatham to Assoc. Dir., "Russian Ship in MA-2 Primary Landing Area," March 8, 1961.

[54] Memo, North to Administrator, "Preliminary MA-2 Flight Results," Feb. 23, 1961. Many NASA engineers and managers think of MA-2 as being "the day Mercury won its spurs" from the Air Force because in retrospect it represented the only potentially serious difference of opinion with the military services throughout the program; see Low comments.

[55] "Press Conference; Mercury-Atlas No. 2," Cape Canaveral, Feb. 21, 1961. See also John H. Glenn, Jr., "We're Going Places No One Has Ever Traveled in a Craft No One's Flown," Life, L (Jan. 27, 1961); Loudon Wainwright, "Chosen Three for First Space Ride," Life, L (March 3, 1961). For the Atlas manufacturer's postflight analysis, see

A. F. Leondis, "Project Mercury Structural Dynamic Analysis (Atlas 67D; MA–2)," Convair/Astronautics report No. AE 61–0743, Aug. 10, 1961.

[56] "The Mercury-Redstone Project," 5–37.

[57] *Ibid.*, 8–15. Before a press conference on February 8, 1961, President Kennedy had cautioned against a premature effort to "put a man in space in order to gain some prestige and have the man take a disproportionate risk." On February 28, Webb announced the President's order for a thorough review of the nation's space programs, and on March 2 a group from the President's Science Advisory Committee was already on tour and at the Atlantic Missile Range for a briefing on Project Mercury. See *Aeronautical and Astronautical Events of 1961*, 5, 8, 9.

[58] Joachim P. Kuettner, note for Dr. von Braun, Feb. 7, 1961; memo, Kuettner to von Braun and others, Marshall Space Flight Center, "Recommendation to Space Task Group on Manned Mercury-Redstone Flight," Feb. 7, 1961; "Daily Journal," Launch Operations Directorate—Marshall Space Flight Center, Feb. 6, 1961.

[59] Memo, Emil P. Bertram to Kurt H. Debus, "MSFC Meeting on MR–3 Manned Flight," Feb. 10, 1961; message, Debus to Kuettner, undated [about Feb. 12, 1961] re Launch Operations Directorate reply to Kuettner's memo of Feb. 7, 1961. See table 8–3 in Johnson et al., "The Mercury-Redstone Project," 8–15. The first priority list of weak "components" included the thrust controller, vibrations, cutoff arming timer, abort sensors, peroxide tank pressure regulator, peroxide system cleanliness, and a liquid oxygen manhole leak.

[60] Memos, North to Dir., Space Flight Programs, "Mercury Status as of March 2, 1961," Mar. 3, 1961, 2, 3; Wernher von Braun to Marshall Space Flight Center, "Sensitivity of Mercury Launching Dates," March 3, 1961.

[61] Message, Marshall Space Flight Center to STG, March 15, 1961; "Project Mercury Status Report No. 10 for Period Ending April 30, 1961," NASA/STG, 31; memo, Jerome B. Hammack, STG Cape Operations, to Project Dir., "Mercury-Redstone Booster Development Flight (MR–BD)," March 26, 1961.

[62] Letters, Brooks to Kennedy, March 9, 1961; Kennedy to Brooks, March 23, 1961. See also Air Force replies to these and other charges in House Committee on Science and Astronautics, 87 Cong., 1 sess. (1961), *Defense*

Space Interests, Hearings, March 17–23, 1961. Purser in his log for Gilruth, March 7, 1961, reported ushering the Hornig panel around Mercury sites from March 1 through 4: "All the comments I overheard were favorable. I also received very favorable direct comments from Dr. Hornig and the various panel members."

[63] Lloyd V. Berkner and Hugh Odishaw, eds., *Science in Space* (New York, 1961). See Holmes, *America on the Moon,* 193–195. See also the special issue devoted to "Space Exploration in the Service of Science" of *Bulletin of the Atomic Scientists,* XVII (May–June 1961), 169–240.

[64] House Committee on Science and Astronautics, 87 Cong., 1 sess. (1961), *Hearings, 1962 NASA Authorization,* Part I, testimony of Abe Silverstein, March 14, 1961, 77, 94, 99.

[65] Luncheon talk by James E. Webb, NASA Administrator, to the American Astronautical Symposium, Washington, D.C., March 17, 1961.

[66] The steps leading to the decision for an accelerated U.S. space program to include landing an American on the moon before 1970, as presented to the Congress on May 25, 1961, are to be detailed in subsequent NASA histories.

[67] Senate Subcommittee of the Committee on Appropriations, 87 Cong., 1 sess. (1961), *Independent Offices Appropriations, 1962, Hearings,* testimony of Hugh L. Dryden, 642–643, 656.

[68] See "The Expanded Space Program," *Historical Sketch of NASA* (EP–29), 27–35.

[69] "Technical Information Summary of Little Joe 5–A (Capsule No. 14)," STG, March 6, 1961, 1–3; "Recovery Operations Requirement for Little Joe Test No. 5–A," undated; and Low comments. See pp. 291–293.

[70] Table adapted from memo, Low to Administrator, "Little Joe 5A Test," March 16, 1961. See also "Mission Directive for Little Joe No. 5A," NASA Project Mercury working paper No. 177, March 7, 1961, 3–1.

[71] Memo, North to Administrator, "Preliminary Flight Results, Little Joe 5–A," March 20, 1961. See also memo, Low to Dir., Space Flight Programs, "Little Joe 5–B Preparation Schedule," March 24, 1961. The fact that both primary and secondary main parachutes deployed immediately after the escape tower jettisoned complicated "quick-look" observations: see transcript, "Press Conference, Little Joe VI [LJ–5A], March 18, 1961," with Robert

L. Krieger and William M. Bland, Jr., at Wallops Island.

[72] Norman F. Smith and Chauvin, "Post-launch Report for Mercury Little Joe No. 5A (LJ-5A)," STG, April 11, 1961, 1. Lewis Fisher, in comments, Sept. 15, 1965, has said that "Little Joe 5A was anything but unedifying. . . . This type of failure may have easily occurred on a Mercury-Atlas flight with very severe program impact had not the Little Joe 5 series pinpointed and fixed a marginal design condition."

[73] Memo, unsigned, "Publicity Releases on Mercury," Marshall Space Flight Center, Feb. 8, 1961.

[74] "Information Plan: Redstone Development Test: MR-BD," NASA, March 21, 1961, 2. For an example of this policy, see NASA News Release 61-57, "Mercury Redstone Booster Development Test," March 22, 1961. One of the most famous of publicity fact sheets, issued by STG from Langley Field on April 10, 1961, was entitled simply "'IF': A Study of Contingency Planning for the Project Mercury Mission."

[75] "The Mercury-Redstone Project," 8–16; "Final Report: Mercury Redstone Project Launch Operations," Appendix O, 2; memo, Geissler, "Project Mercury-Redstone: Trajectory Data for MR-BD," March 20, 1961; "Master Operational Schedule for MR-BD," Marshall Space Flight Center, March 6, 1961; memo, S. Snyder to NASA Technical Personnel, "Mercury-Redstone (MR-BD) Launch," March 23, 1961.

[76] Hammack memo. Mercury working paper 178 was by J. W. Maynard, T. J. Skopinski, and P. S. Leatherman, "Calculated Pre-flight Trajectory Data for Redstone Booster Test (MR-BD)," March 17, 1961.

[77] Memo, Low to Administrator, "Mercury Redstone Booster Development Test," March 27, 1961. See also note, Eugene F. Horton to Powers on MR-BD publicity and point of test in "wriggling" Redstone; message, Powers to Paul Haney, date missing.

[78] Of a total of 71 Redstone booster flights (including 4 Mercury-Redstone) through March 24, 1961, only 10, or 14.1 percent, were classed as failures by the latest revision of a composite document prepared under W. A. Mrazek, Director, Structures and Mechanics Division: "Redstone Vehicle Malfunction Study (Mercury-Redstone Program)," MSFC report No. DSD-TM-12-60, Rev. B, May 1, 1960, 8.

[79] See "Final Report: Mercury-Redstone

Project Launch Operations," Appendix M; Ms., George F. Killmer, Jr., et al., "Mercury Technical History—Preflight Operations," Dec. 30, 1963, 85–90, Fig. 11; James M. Grimwood, Project Mercury: A Chronology, NASA SP-4001 (Washington, 1963), 131, 207, 218.

[80] Purser, log for Gilruth, April 10, 1961; Purser, interview, Houston, Feb. 12, 1964; Gilruth interview; Silverstein, interview, Cleveland, May 1, 1964; Aeronautical and Astronautical Events of 1961, 15. See also "Rumors Fly as Moscow Alerts Press," Washington Post, Apr. 11, 1961.

[81] Donald F. Hornig, chairman, "Report of the Ad Hoc Mercury Panel," Apr. 12, 1961, 18, passim. The membership of this panel included, in addition to Hornig, Paul Beeson, W. John Beil, Milton V. Clauser, Edward H. Heinemann, Lawrence S. Hyland, Donald P. Ling, Robert B. Livingston, Harrison A. Storms, and Cornelius Tobias. The two technical assistants were Douglas R. Lord and James B. Hartgering, and two special consultants were Alfred P. Fishman and Paul Wickham.

[82] Ibid. See also "Debate Reported Over Space Shot: Kerr Asserts Kennedy Aides Disputed Flight's Wisdom," New York Times, May 10, 1961; Lord interview. Mae Mills Link, Space Medicine in Project Mercury, NASA SP-4003 (Washington, 1965), treats at greater length some of these problems in her chapter VIII, entitled "The Season of Crisis: 1961," 112–125.

[83] For an overview of these issues, see chapter on "Gagarin" in Holmes, America on the Moon, 83–92; Thomas A. Reedy, "Britons Say Reds' Timing May Indicate 'Lie in Sky,'" Newport News Daily Press, April 13, 1961. Some question was also raised in Congress and the press whether Gagarin's flight was in fact a complete orbit, since it apparently fell short of its starting point by a few miles.

[84] Memo, Powers to Gilruth, "Pre-planned Comment for Possible Russian Space Shot," Sept. 27, 1960. All quotations are taken from House Committee on Science and Astronautics, 87 Cong., 1 sess. (1961), Discussion of Soviet Man-in-Space Shot, 7, 11, 16, 18, 27, 33.

[85] It is widely believed that Yuri A. Gagarin rode all the way down to impact inside his capsule and that his flight was made fail-safe by the choice of a rather steep reentry trajectory. For pictorial comparisons of the Soviet spacecraft and booster systems, see the series of articles in Aviation Week, LXXXII (May 10, 1965), "Russia Displays Vostok with Spheri-

cal Cabin," 28–29; (May 17, 1965), "Soviets Unveil 3-Stage ICBM," 26–31; (May 24, 1965), "Photos of Vostok Display Reveal New Details of Spacecraft," 76–78; (May 31, 1965), "Photos Show Details of Cabin, Suit," 58–60; (June 7, 1965), "Gazenko Discusses Soviet Space Medicine," 40–45. Cf. memo, M. Scott Carpenter to Gilruth et al., "Cosmonaut Training," Nov. 24, 1964.

[84] These parameters are based on a 28-page typewritten translation by Joseph L. Zygielbaum from *Pravda*, April 25, 1961, entitled "The First Flight of Man into Cosmic Space," and circulated around STG as the best data then available. For comparative information, see Senate Committee on Aeronautical and Space Sciences, 87 Cong., 2 sess. (1962), *Soviet Space Programs: Organization, Plans, Goals, and International Implications*, Table I, 106–107, 108; and Charles S. Sheldon II, "The Challenge of International Competition," paper, the Third American Inst. of Aeronautics and Astronautics/NASA Manned Space Flight Meeting, Houston, Nov. 4–6, 1964, Table V, 26. See also Fédération Aéronautique Internationale, record claim.

[87] *Soviet Man in Space* (Moscow, [1961]), 93. See also Joseph L. Zygielbaum, "The Soviet Space Program," in the World Book Science Annual, *1965 Science Year* (Chicago, 1965), 64–75.

[88] Statement by Yuri A. Gagarin at the Soviet Scientist's Club reported April 16, 1961, in *The First Man in Space: The Record of Yuri Gagarin's Historic First Venture into Cosmic Space: A Collection of Translations from Soviet Press Reports* (New York, 1961), 41; the first quotation is taken from Y. Maksaryov, ed., *Technical Progress in the U.S.S.R., 1959–1965*, trans. David Skvirsky (Moscow, [1963]), 10.

[89] Newport News *Times-Herald*, April 13, 1961; statements of Glenn, Virgil I. Grissom, and Alan B. Shepard, Jr., April 12, 1961; statement of Gilruth, April 12, 1961; NASA News Release 61–80, April 20, 1961.

[90] House Committee on Science and Astronautics, 87 Cong., 1 sess. (1961), Report No. 391, to accompany H.R. 6874, *Authorizing Appropriations to the National Aeronautics and Space Administration*, testimony of Seamans, 360–382; *Aeronautical and Astronautical Events of 1961*, 11, 15; and Seamans, interview, Washington, Sept. 1, 1965. See also "Ups and Downs in Space as U.S. Gets Set to Launch Man," *Life*, L (May 5, 1961).

[91] Memos, North to Dir., Space Flight Programs, "Operational Considerations for MA-3," April 10, 1961; "Mission Change for MA-3," April 17, 1961; Williams, interview, Houston, Aug. 23, 1965; John P. Mayer, comments, Sept. 8, 1965.

[92] Memos, Silverstein to Assoc. Administrator, "Mission Change for Mercury-Atlas 3," April 18, 1961; Snyder to NASA Technical Personnel, Technical Information Center, "Mercury-Atlas 3 (MA-3) Launch," April 24, 1961; "R. J. W." for record, "MA-3 Flight Particulars," April 24, 1961; "Technical Information Summary of Mercury-Atlas Mission No. 3 (Capsule No. 8)," STG, April 17, 1961; "Mission Directive for MA-3," Project Mercury, Oct. 18, 1960, rev. March 31, 1961; "Calculated Pre-Flight Trajectory Data," NASA Project Mercury working paper No. 184, April 14, 1961; "Mercury Control Center Countdown Flight Control and Overall Operations MA-3," March 16, 1961; rev. April 20, 1961; "MA-3 Mission Rules—Correction Copy," undated. See also Huss comments.

[93] Memo, Low to Administrator, "Mercury Atlas 3 Launching," April 24, 1961; John H. Disher to Administrator, "Mercury-Atlas Flight No. 3," April 26, 1961; "Mercury-Atlas No. 3 (MA-3) Memorandum Report for the Project Director," STG, April 28, 1961. This realistic exercise for the launch site recovery team, as well as the beautiful performance of the escape tower, increased confidence in spite of the mission failure.

[94] Memo, Low to Dir., Space Flight Programs, "Atlas 100-D Programmer," June 12, 1961; Hohmann, "Atlas 100-D Investigation Board Status Report," June 14, 1961.

[95] "Mission Directive for Little Joe No. 5-B (Capsule No. 14)," NASA Project Mercury working paper No. 183, April 7, 1961; "Technical Information Summary of Little Joe No. 5-B," April 12, 1961; Alfred I. Alibrando and Horton, "Information Plan: Project Mercury Little Joe Seven," April 7, 1961; NASA News Release 61–82, "Project Mercury Escape System Test: Little Joe Seven," April 20, 1961. Low has commented that "if Little Joe 5B had failed, it might have put a constraint on MR-3 that would have prevented its launching."

[96] "Post-Launch Report for Mercury Little Joe Mission 5B (LJ-5B)," NASA Project Mercury working paper No. 195, June 12, 1961, 1–1, 2–1, passim. So far above the design limits for max-q on Little Joe was the performance of LJ-5B that this production capsule might have carried a man safely

after all if all other provisions had been developed: Williams interview.

[97] "Status Report No. 10 for Period Ending April 30, 1961," STG, was the tenth quarterly review of Project Mercury by the 700 or so members of STG for NASA Headquarters. Of six flights since January, only two (MA-3 and LJ-5A) were admitted failures. Of 10 qualification flight tests with production McDonnell capsules to date (the 4-inch flight of MR-1 was excluded), 6 (including MR-BD) were counted as "successful," although a historical accounting should, on the basis of intent, make that record read 5 out of 10 "unsuccessful" at least. Capsule orbit weight was calculated at 2836 pounds and expected to be 2874 pounds by July, still within Atlas capabilities. "Project Orbit," the simulated orbital test program using Capsule No. 10 in McDonnell's altitude chamber, was well underway; the tracking network and ground instrumentation system was reported 95 percent complete; while ground qualifications testing and reliability testing were said to be 95 and 90 percent complete, respectively. Readiness for the first manned sub-orbital test flight, including the lately renewed studies to "quick-fix" the impact protection, landing system, and reaction control system, and to test more animals in centrifuges, was asserted to be clear if the flight safety review board meetings at the Cape on April 28-29, 1961, should certify both capsule and booster.

Chapter XI

[1] Letter, Larry Stoddard, Rating Section, National Broadcasting Company, Inc., to Sigman Byrd, Hist. and Library Services Br., MSC, March 15, 1965; "Postlaunch Report for Mercury Redstone No. 3 (MR-3)," NASA Project Mercury working paper No. 192, June 16, 1961, 73; James M. Grimwood, Project Mercury: A Chronology, NASA SP-4001 (Washington, 1963), 35, 124; "Postlaunch Trajectory Report for Mercury-Redstone Mission 3 (MR-3, Capsule 7)," NASA Project Mercury working paper No. 210, Oct. 12, 1961, 1-2.

[2] Tape of press conference, Mercury astronauts, Cape Canaveral, Feb. 22, 1961. At the conference Robert R. Gilruth pointed out that the four remaining astronauts were not eliminated, since there would be other flights. He said it was simply that at this point in the program a few had to be selected to participate in a particular mission, and that it was only practical to select those best prepared. The

others would continue training. Nancy Lowe, secretary to the Mercury astronauts for more than four years, said in an interview with the authors on Feb. 27, 1964, that STG had been besieged for interviews only after the announcement that Shepard, Glenn, and Grissom had been selected to train for the first flight.

[3] Memo, George M. Low to Dir., Space Flight Programs, "Project Mercury Status," Jan. 6, 1961; memo, Warren J. North to Dir. of Space Flight Programs, "Mercury Status as of Jan. 13, 1961," Jan. 16, 1961; "Project Mercury Status Report No. 9 for Period Ending Jan. 31, 1961," 3.

[4] Alan B. Shepard, Jr., interview, Houston, Aug. 6, 1964.

[5] House Committee on Science and Astronautics, 87 Cong., 2 sess. (1962), Aeronautical and Astronautical Events of 1961, 7; "Individual Astronaut Monthly Training Schedules, Sept. 1960-Feb. 1961," undated; Donald K. Slayton, "Pilot Training and Preflight Preparation," in Conference on Medical Results of the First U.S. Manned Suborbital Space Flight: A Compilation of Papers, NASA in Cooperation with National Institutes of Health and National Academy of Sciences (Washington, 1961), 95.

[6] "Pilot Preparation for MR-3 Mission," undated; Carmault B. Jackson and Richard S. Johnston, "Astronaut Preparation and Activities Manual for MR-3," NASA/STG, Dec. 1, 1960.

[7] Memo, Sigurd A. Sjoberg, et al., Flight Operations Div., STG, to Assoc. Dir., "Astronaut Briefing and Debriefing for MR-3 Mission," April 4, 1961; letter, Walter C. Williams to Comdr., Air Force Missile Test Center, re personnel at Grand Bahama debriefing, April 26, 1961.

[8] NASA News Release 61-99, "Mercury-Redstone 3 Press Conference, Cape Canaveral," May 5, 1961; memo for files, Martin A. Byrnes, STG, "Recovery MR-3," May 11, 1961; "MR-3 Recovery Operations," anon., undated. R/A G. P. Koch directed recovery operations in the impact area. His supporting ships and their commanders were: carrier, Champlain, Capt. R. Weymouth; destroyers, Decatur, Cdr. A. W. McLane; Wadleigh, Lt. Cdr. D. W. Kelly; Rooks, Cdr. W. H. Patillo; Sullivans, Cdr. F. H. S. Hall; and Abbott, Cdr. R. J. Norman; and radar ship (DDR) N. K. Perry, Cdr. A. O. Roberts. The recovery force again included the P2V aircraft under Cdr. R. H. Casey, Jr.

[9] Letter, Williams to R/A F. V. H. Hilles, March 14, 1961; letter, Cdr., Air Force Missile Test Center, to Hilles, "Mercury Air-Ground Voice Relay and Real-Time Display in AMR Telemetry Aircraft," March 21, 1961.

[10] Message, [Cdr. DesFlotFour] to STG et al., April 19, 1961; memo, Sjoberg et al., to NASA Assoc. Dir., "MR-3 Postflight Debriefing of Alan B. Shepard," Aug. 22, 1961. As it turned out, the same helicopter pilot team (Marine Lts. Wayne E. Koons and George F. Cox) that practiced with the three astronauts in the special training team effected the water recovery of the first suborbital spaceman. Wayne E. Koons and James L. Lewis, interview, Houston, Sept. 16, 1965.

[11] Letter, F. W. Reichelderfer to T. Keith Glennan, June 9, 1960; memo, Williams to Maj. Gen. Leighton I. Davis, "Meteorological Support of Project Mercury," Aug. 31, 1960; Reichelderfer to Gilruth, April 18, 1961, with enclosure, "Status of Weather Support for Project Mercury, April 1961."

[12] "Operations Requirements No. 1904, Mercury-Redstone Launch," Feb. 15, 1961.

[13] Byrnes memo.

[14] Based on a series of interviews. Also see Mae M. Link, Space Medicine in Project Mercury, NASA SP-4003 (Washington, 1965), 112–125. See also p. 331 of this work.

[15] A. Duane Catterson, interview, Houston, April 10, 1964.

[16] Stanley C. White, Richard S. Johnston, and Gerard J. Pesman, "Review of Biomedical Systems Prior to the MR-3 Ballistic Flight," undated. Another criticism leveled by members of the PSAC panel in March 1961 was that the fire hazard in a pure oxygen atmosphere had not been sufficiently dealt with through tests. The subject had been considered by STG; the conclusion was that depressurization would serve as an excellent fire extinguisher. Robert B. Voas, interview, Houston, April 15, 1964. See also p. 287.

[17] Newport News Times-Herald, March 25, 1961; Shreveport Times, April 2, 1961. Howard I. Gibbons, then associated with the Newport News Daily Press, later of the Public Affairs Office, MSC, interviewed the seven astronauts on July 7, 1959, at a NASA Press Day event. The following Sunday, Gibbons predicted in the Daily Press that Alan Shepard would be the first astronaut in space. As far as can be determined, this was the first speculation in the matter. "It was just a good guess," said Gibbons.

[18] Voas interview.

[19] Shepard interview; Gilruth, interview, Houston, March 18, 1964.

[20] Memo, Public Affairs Officer, MSC, to Chief, Hist. and Library Services Br., March 11, 1964. There was some resistance to the publicity buildup. The painful experience of Dec. 6, 1957, when the public witnessed the spectacular launchpad failure of the Vanguard booster, America's first attempt to launch an artificial satellite, had not been forgotten. Wall Street Journal, May 2, 1961.

[21] Washington Post, May 3, 1961; New York Times, May 5, 1961; memos, John H. Disher, Head, Advanced Manned Systems, NASA, to Administrator, "Mercury-Redstone Launching," May 1, 1961, and May 4, 1961.

[22] Chicago Tribune, April 29 and 30, 1961; Washington Daily News, April 29, 1961; Washington Evening Star, April 29, 1961; Washington Post, May 1, 1961; Baltimore Sun, April 30, 1961; New York Times, May 2 and 3, 1961; Newport News Times-Herald, May 2, 1961; "Mercury Astronauts Work as a Team on MR-3," undated. A statement by Gilruth on the mode of pilot selection for MR-3 is contained in NASA Fifth Semiannual Report to Congress, Oct. 1, 1960, through June 30, 1961 (Washington, 1962), 15, 17, 18.

[23] "NASA Note to Editors," April 24, 1961; New York Times, May 2, 1961.

[24] Conference on Medical Results of the First U.S. Manned Sub-orbital Space Flight, 7, 8; "Pilot Preparation for MR-3 Mission," anon., undated. Safety measures, including appropriate actions, covering each time segment of the second half of the split countdown were published just before the MR-3 mission in "Emergency Handbook for Pad Area Rescue, Mercury-Redstone, Capsule 7," May 2, 1961. This document later was revised and reissued on June 29, 1961, to cover Capsule 11 and the MR-4 flight.

[25] Ibid.; Sjoberg, April 4 memo; "Postlaunch Report for MR-3," 43–45. During the early part of the countdown on May 5, John Glenn, the backup pilot, spent considerable time in the spacecraft assisting in systems checkouts. To help relieve any tension Shepard might have built up, Glenn pasted a little sign on the spacecraft panel, reading "No handball playing here." This bit of levity hearkened back to their training days. Later he went to Mercury Control Center and stood behind Donald K. Slayton, spacecraft communicator, helping to gather data to feed to Shepard during the flight.

[26] "Postlaunch Report for MR-3," 45–46;

581

Conference on Medical Results, 8; memo, Henry E. Clements to Christopher C. Kraft, Jr., "Test 108, 4–5 May, 1961, Network Status Monitor Report," May 8, 1961; "Mercury Redstone 3 Press Conference"; memo, Disher to Administrator, "Mercury-Redstone Mission," undated. After four hours without relief and with only a primitive urine collection system, his underwear got wet, but the suit air regenerating system worked very well. Sjoberg, Aug. 22 memo; Lee McMillion, interview, Houston, Oct. 30, 1963; memo, Carl R. Huss to Flight Dir., "Record and Comments on Activities and Observations Made at Retrofire Controller's P o s i t i o n During Test 108 (MR–3)," May 5, 1961.

[27] "Postlaunch Report for MR–3"; *Conference on Medical Results of the First U.S. Manned Suborbital Space Flight,* 74; Shepard, speech, Society of Experimental Test Pilots, Los Angeles, Sept. 30, 1961; letter, John A. Powers to W. J. Phillippi, Aug. 4, 1961. As for the other astronauts, Carpenter and Grissom observed from the Mercury Control Center.

[28] Later, during postlaunch debriefings, Shepard stated that the decision to carry or eliminate the personal parachute on subsequent flights should be left for the prime pilot. An unidentified astronaut at the debriefing (probably Schirra) exclaimed, "Please!"

[29] The "Kennedy call" was to become a standing event in all manned Mercury flights.

[30] Shepard gave a most lucid account of his mission from liftoff to water impact, following his preliminary medical examination aboard the *Champlain.* Shepard's dictated report is contained in "Postlaunch Report for MR–3," and in the Sjoberg debriefing memo of Aug. 22. The latter document also gives questions by the debriefers and answers by the astronaut covering every aspect of the flight. Also see "Shepard and USA Feel A. OK," *Life,* L (May 12, 1961); Alan B. Shepard, Jr., "Astronaut's Story of the Thrust into Space," *Life,* L (May 19, 1961).

[31] "Postlaunch Report for MR–3"; memo, Morton Schler to Kraft, "Postlaunch Summary Report of MR–3 Mission," May 5, 1961; Byrnes memo; Sjoberg, Aug. 22 memo.

[32] *Ibid.;* memo, Slayton to Flight Dir., "MR–3 Mission Report," May 15, 1961. The ships did have a communications problem during spacecraft descent, however, because of background interference from Latin-American broadcasting stations.

[33] Memo, Gilruth to staff, "Congratulatory Messages in Regard to MR–3 Flight," June 17, 1961.

[34] "Documentation of the First Manned Space Flight without Earth Orbit by the United States of America," National Aeronautic Assn., United States Representative, Fédération Aéronautique Internationale, Washington, 1961. Shepard submitted certification of his flight on May 15, 1961. Regarding contrasts between reports of the Shepard and Gagarin flights, cf. *The First Man in Space: The Record of Yuri Gagarin's Historic First Venture into Cosmic Space,* trans. from Soviet press reports (New York, 1961). A large portion of the text is political propaganda. A photograph of the launch is obscured in clouds of smoke—much as the whole program was. The Shepard flight was reported in words and pictures without allusion to political ideology. The report of the Turkish journalists was extracted from *Aeronautical and Astronautical Events of 1961,* 24.

[35] White House News Release, "John F. Kennedy, President of the United States, Special Message to Congress, May 25, 1961." *Freedom 7* was displayed publicly at Cape Canaveral beginning on May 20, 1961, the day the launch area was first opened to the public.

[36] For fiscal data on the fiscal year 1962 program, see House Committee on Science and Astronautics, 87 Cong., 1 sess. (1961), *1962 NASA Authorization, Hearings;* Senate Subcommittee of the Committee on Appropriations, 87 Cong., 1 sess. (1961), *Independent Offices Appropriations, 1962, Hearings;* House Committee on Science and Astronautics, 87 Cong., 1 sess. (1961), *Authorizing Appropriations to the National Aeronautics and Space Administration,* 28–38.

[37] *Mercury Project Summary, Including Results of the Fourth Manned Orbital Flight, May 15 and 16, 1963,* NASA SP–45 (Washington, 1963), 1. This report says more than 2,000,000 people from government, industry, and institutions were involved in Project Mercury. For the components alone there were some 10,000 contractors, subcontractors, and suppliers. The Public Affairs Office of the Manned Spacecraft Center said that the Apollo program had about 40,000 contractors and suppliers as of May 1964. See also Tom Alexander, *Project Apollo: Man to the Moon* (New York, 1964), 8.

[38] Memos, H. Kurt Strass to Chief, Flight Systems, STG, "Activation of Study Program Pertaining to Advanced Manned Space Projects," June 22, 1959; "First Meeting of New

Project Panel, Wednesday, Aug. 12, 1959," Aug. 17, 1959; and "Third Meeting of New Projects Panel, Monday, Sept. 28, 1959," Oct. 1, 1959; memos, Gilruth to staff, "Advanced Vehicle Team," May 25, 1960; "Change in Organization of the Space Task Group," Sept. 1, 1960; and "President's Request for Additional Budget Action," May 26, 1961. A NASA-sponsored "Conference on the Peaceful Uses of Space" was also meeting at this time in Tulsa.

[39] "Manned Spacecraft Development Center, Organizational Concepts and Staffing Requirements," May 1, 1961. Some 13 days before the Presidential pronouncement, a House appropriations authorization document foresaw an increased personnel requirement for STG, estimating the need at about 300 additional people. Moreover, it was noted that the organization would be carried as a separate research center for financial allocation purposes, beginning with fiscal 1962, although STG's work was then domiciled at the Langley Research Center and divided between Langley, Goddard, and the Cape. STG's personnel strength reached 1152 by the end of 1961, and it had proposed some 3000 personnel spaces in the May study for a Manned Spacecraft Development Center. *Authorizing Appropriations to NASA*, 6.

[40] Newport News *Times-Herald*, May 30, 1961; Newport News *Daily Press*, May 30, 1961; *Aeronautical and Astronautical Events of 1961*; memo, Paul E. Purser to Gilruth, "Log for Week of Aug. 7, 1961," Aug. 15, 1961. Besides speculating about the move, the press now began acquainting the public with the new manned space projects. What later became Project Gemini was described, and the lunar program was discussed. The estimated cost of these activities was mentioned frequently. (See *Washington Post*, May 24 and 26, 1961; *New York Times*, May 24 and 26, 1961; Baltimore *Sun*, May 26, 1961.) A cartoon by Herblock, of the *Washington Post*, pictured a launch vehicle and a spacecraft waiting on the pad while the pilot (President Kennedy) walked toward a service station and ordered an attendant (Congress) standing by a fuel pump, "Fill 'er up—I'm in a race."

[41] Virgil I. Grissom, interview, Houston, April 12, 1965; "Postlaunch Memorandum Report for Mercury-Redstone No. 4(MR-4)," Aug. 6, 1961. During his debriefing Grissom complained about having to travel so much for training missions. He suggested that an ALFA trainer be installed at Cape Canaveral.

[42] Excerpts from messages compiled by Purser; Morton J. Stoller, "Some Results of NASA Space Flight Programs in 1960-61," paper, Third International Symposium on Rockets and Astronautics, Tokyo, 1961.

[43] *Results of the Second U.S. Manned Suborbital Space Flight, July 21, 1961* (Washington, 1961), 4; "Postlaunch Memorandum Report for MR-4"; "Astronaut Recovery Handbook (Capsules No. 11 and 15)," McDonnell Aircraft Corp., St. Louis, June 1, 1961.

[44] "MR-4 Press Kit," June 29, 1961; *Results of the Second U.S. Manned Suborbital Flight*, 3, 4. The window measured 19 inches high, 11 inches across the base, and 7½ inches across the top. NASA News Release 61-152, "MR-4 Design Changes," July 16, 1961. The contract change proposal providing for the observation window was submitted in October, 1959. Memo, Purser to Langley Research Center, "Contract NAS 5-59; Contract Change Proposal No. 73, Astronaut Observation Window Installation," Oct. 1, 1959.

[45] "Postlaunch Memorandum Report for MR-4"; memo, Future Projects Br., Aeroballistics Div., Marshall Space Flight Center, "Project Mercury-Redstone: Additional Trajectory Data for MR-4," June 3, 1961.

[46] Newport News *Daily Press*, July 16, 1961. Someone had done Grissom the favor of painting a likeness of the crack in the original Liberty Bell on spacecraft No. 11. Other astronaut assignments for the MR-4 mission put Shepard and Schirra in the Mercury Control Center, the former as "Cap Com," the latter as observer; Slayton and Carpenter in the blockhouse; and Cooper flying the chase plane.

[47] "Postlaunch Memorandum Report for MR-4"; memo, Sjoberg to Assoc. Dir., "MR-4 Postflight Debriefing of Virgil I. Grissom," undated. Grissom became chilled while waiting in the spacecraft for launch on Wednesday, July 19. His suit inlet temperature was about 61 degrees F. On the day of the flight, the suit inlet temperature (55 degrees F) was more comfortable because the astronaut's underclothing remained essentially dry. Reception of medical data from Grissom's flight was better than that from Shepard's.

[48] "MR-4 Design Changes," 61-152.

[49] Grimwood, *Mercury Chronology*, 214; "Postlaunch Memorandum Report for MR-4"; "MR-4 Press Kit"; memo, Low to NASA Administrator, "Mercury-Redstone-4 Launching," July 17, 1961. The recovery forces were deployed in the same manner as for

583

Ham and Shepard. Under direction of R/A J. L. Chew, stationed in Mercury Control Center as an advisor to Williams, the main forces consisted of an aircraft carrier, three destroyers, and two destroyer escorts. Five P2V aircraft, supplemented by Air Rescue Service planes, provided contingency recovery support. Carrier and shore-based helicopters were assigned to pick up the spacecraft, while just off Cape Canaveral a rescue salvage vessel stood by for action in the event of a mission abort. And, once again, land vehicles were deployed around the launch site for duty in case of a catastrophe.

[50] Memo for news media representatives, July 16, 1961; Virgil I. Grissom, "The Trouble with Liberty Bell," in John Dille, ed., *We Seven, by the Astronauts Themselves* (New York, 1962), 216–219.

[51] "Postlaunch Memorandum Report for MR–4."

[52] Dille, ed., *We Seven*, 217–218.

[53] The count was resumed, but after another 15 minutes a 9-minute hold was called for turning off pad-area searchlights—which in the past had caused telemetry interference.

Next came a 41-minute hold because cloudy skies had reduced light conditions to below par for camera coverage. During this hold, the main inverter began to overheat, reaching 190 degrees F, and so Grissom switched to the standby unit to allow the main component to cool. When the count resumed at 15 minutes before launch, he switched back to the main inverter. Significantly, during the 80 extra minutes from astronaut insertion to lift-off, not one of the holds was chargeable to the booster. Sjoberg undated memo; "Postlaunch Memorandum Report for MR–4."

In an interview with Grissom on April 12, 1965, the pilot stated that the misaligned bolt had nothing to do with the premature explosion of the hatch. In fact, if a number of bolts were misaligned it would be unlikely that the hatch would blow off at all. Grissom now has the misaligned bolt as a souvenir.

[54] The following detailed account of Grissom's flight is based, like that for Shepard, on the evidence of the motion picture camera, the tape transcript of communications, the confidential postflight report, the debriefing records, telemetry transcripts, and personal interviews.

[55] The rate control system consumed about 3½ pounds of hydrogen peroxide in 2 minutes. Based on this usage, if that system were used exclusively during an orbital mission, all of

the control fuel would be expended in 20 minutes. Grissom's automatic stabilization and control system worked so slowly during turnaround because, as a later review team discovered, the one-pound rate thrusters contained some decomposed material.

[56] "Postlaunch Memorandum Report for MR–4"; Sjoberg undated memo; *Results of the Second U.S. Manned Suborbital Flight;* "Project Mercury Status Report No. 11 for Period Ending July 31, 1961," NASA/STG, 7–9, 26, 30, 31; memo, Richard J. Wisniewski to NASA Administrator, "Mercury-Redstone-4 Mission," July 24, 1961; memo, John H. Dabbs, to Chief, Flight Operations Div., STG, "Mercury-Redstone-Four High Frequency Air/Ground Communications Test," Aug. 23, 1961; tape of press conference, Cocoa Beach, Fla., July 22, 1961. Participating with Grissom were James E. Webb, who awarded the astronaut the NASA Distinguished Service Medal; Leighton I. Davis; Eberhard F. W. Rees; Robert R. Gilruth; Walter C. Williams; William K. Douglas; Alan B. Shepard, Jr., and John H. Glenn, Jr. For Grissom's personal account of the mission, see Dille, ed., *We Seven*, 205–231. Most of the reports attribute Grissom's sinking lower in the water during the recovery period to the open suit inlet valve. The astronaut felt that the loss of buoyancy was caused by the neck dam. He based his belief on the fact that the dam had been in a rolled position for some five days; tests conducted later disclosed that the rolled rubber sets in two days' time, causing a loss of airtight integrity. Virgil I. Grissom, interview, Houston, April 12, 1965. Also see Virgil I. Grissom, "It was a Good Flight and a Great Float," *Life*, LI (July 28, 1961), and Grissom, "Hero Admits He Was Scared," *Life*, LI (July 28, 1961).

[57] Memo, North to Assoc. Administrator, "Status of MR 4 Hatch Investigation," Aug. 30, 1961; "Postlaunch Memorandum Report for MR–4." Carpenter, after the second orbital flight, was retrieved from his raft, being the only other Mercury astronaut to ride a helicopter to a ship. He, too, was dunked by swells before he was airborne. Grissom expressed his opinion in an interview on April 12, 1965, that he believed the premature hatch explosion was caused by the exterior lanyard being loose. At that time it was held in place by only one screw. Subsequently a better method of securing the lanyard was effected.

[58] Gherman Titov, *700,000 Kilometres Through Space: Notes by Soviet Cosmonaut No. 2* (Moscow [1962]); Titov and Martin

Caidin, *I Am Eagle!* (Indianapolis, 1962), based on interviews with Wilfred Burchett and Anthony Purdy.

[59] For three final reports on the Mercury-Redstone program, see "Final Report Mercury Redstone Project Launch Operation," Marshall Space Flight Center, May 28, 1962; "The Mercury-Redstone Project," MSFC Saturn/ Apollo Systems Office, June 1964; and Jerome B. Hammack and Jack C. Heberlig, "The Mercury-Redstone Program," paper No. 2238-61, read before American Rocket Society, Oct. 9-15, 1961. See also memo, North to Deputy Dir., Space Flight Programs, NASA Hq., "Mercury Status Items for Project Review Meeting, June 27, 1961," June 22, 1961.

[60] Purser, Aug. 15 memo; memo, Gilruth to Silverstein, "Recommendations on MR-5 Flight," undated; *Aeronautical and Astronautical Events of 1961*, 40; memo, Joachim P. Kuettner to Eberhard Rees et al., "Final Disposition of Mercury-Redstone Project," Aug. 24, 1961; David S. Akens, Paul K. Freiwirth, and Helen T. Wells, *History of the George C. Marshall Space Flight Center* (Huntsville, Ala., 1960-1962), 7, 19. In an interview on April 12, 1965, Grissom stated that some of the astronauts wanted to proceed with MR-5 because the launch vehicle and spacecraft were about ready.

[61] Titov, *700,000 Kilometres Through Space*, 60-79, 91-124; Titov and Caidin, *I Am Eagle!* 166-200; Pavel Barashev and Yuri Dokuchayev, *Gherman Titov: First Man to Spend a Day in Space* (New York, 1962), 93-102; Newport News *Daily Press*, Aug. 9, 1961.

[62] Stuart Symington, "Why We Lag in Space," speech, U.S. Senate, June 26, 1961; John W. Finney, "Capital Worried by Lags in Plans on Race to Moon," *New York Times*, Aug. 13, 1961; Vern Haugland, "NASA Hopes to Put Mercury Astronaut in Orbit by Next December or January," Newport News *Times-Herald*, Aug. 7, 1961.

Chapter XII

[1] Message, Walter C. Williams to Cdr., DesFlotFour, Dec. 8, 1960; "Project Mercury Status Report No. 9 for Period Ending Jan. 31, 1961," 40, 41, 43; Paul E. Purser, log for Robert R. Gilruth, April 17, 1961; "Project Mercury Status Report No. 10 for Period Ending April 30, 1961," 33. For a complete discussion of the MA-3 mission, see pp. 335-337.

Counting MA-4 as the fifth Mercury-Atlas combination launched includes Big Joe.

[2] "Status Report No. 10," 33; James M. Grimwood, *Project Mercury, A Chronology*, NASA SP-4001 (Washington, 1963), 214; "Project Mercury Postlaunch Report for Mercury-Atlas Mission 4 (MA-4, Capsule 8A)," NASA Project Mercury working paper No. 213, Nov. 10, 1961.

[3] *Ibid.;* message, NASA Hq. to STG, Aug. 25, 1961; memo, Morton Schler to Flight Dir., "Report on Test 1254," Oct. 3, 1961; Walter C. Williams, interview, Houston, Aug. 23, 1965; Bernhard A. Hohmann, interview, Houston, Sept. 16, 1965; memo, P. I. Harr, GD/A, to Members of Astronautics Reliability Policy Committee, "Minutes of Special 28 August 1961 Meeting on Transistors," Aug. 29, 1961.

[4] "Project Mercury Status Report No. 11 for Period Ending July 31, 1961," 11, 12. As finally configured, Atlas No. 88-D had modifications in the sustainer engine liquid oxygen duct to improve performance, and the first four panels of the upper liquid oxygen tank area were of "thick-skin" materials designed to support high aerodynamic loads. "Postlaunch Report for MA-4." Moreover, a three-second hold-down was programmed for MA-4. Tests conducted by the Rocketdyne Division, North American Aviation, indicated that a two-second hold-down was adequate for Mercury-modified Atlas engines. So for flights beginning with MA-5, STG officials planned to institute the two-second procedure.

[5] NASA News Release 61-182, "Mercury-Atlas 4," Aug. 20, 1961; "Project Mercury Technical Information Summary of Mercury-Atlas Mission No. 4/8A (Capsule No. 8A)," NASA/STG, July 21, 1961. The Mercury ground tracking communications network at this time had 140,000 actual circuit miles, consisting of 100,000 miles of the teletype circuits, 35,000 of telephone circuits, and 5000 of high-speed telemetry circuits.

[6] "Pre-release Draft on Launch Vehicle (MA-4)," STG, undated; "Mercury-Atlas 4"; "Project Mercury Calculated Preflight Trajectory Data for Mercury-Atlas Mission No. 4 (MA-4) (Capsule No. 8A, Atlas No. 88-D)," NASA Project Mercury working paper No. 204, Aug. 2, 1961. The nominal launch trajectory was computed by the Aerospace Corp. and Space Technology Labs. under the technical direction of the Space Task Group. The abort sensing and implementation system continued monitoring during the entire powered phase. If trouble developed,

the clamp-ring released and posigrade rockets fired to separate the spacecraft, and the recovery gear was ready for action. Provided the powered flight phase went well, by about five minutes after launch the radio-inertial guidance system would be measuring speed, altitude, and flight course. If those factors anticipated a successful orbital insertion, the ground guidance computer, in operation shortly after booster engine cutoff, would initiate the shut-down command to the sustainer engine.

[7] "Project Mercury Mission Directive for Mercury-Atlas No. 4 (Capsule No. 8A)," NASA Project Mercury working paper No. 203, July 28, 1961; "Project Mercury Addendum Data Report for Mercury-Atlas Mission 4 (MA-4, Capsule 8A)," NASA Project Mercury working paper No. 218, Nov. 29, 1961.

[8] "Preflight Trajectory Data for MA-4."

[9] Letter, Williams, STG, to Cdr., DesFlot-Four, June 8, 1961, with enclosure, "Project Mercury, Mercury-Atlas No. 4 Recovery Requirements." The recovery forces consisted of 8 destroyers, 12 aircraft, a landing ship dock, and a utility vessel. Williams also stipulated secondary-zone recovery requirements and called for a nine-hour watch. In plotting contingency recovery areas, STG's planners had to allow for trajectory alteration resulting from the added thrust of escape rockets or retrofire in an abort.

[10] Williams letter; "Mission Directive for MA-4." William T. Lauten, Jr., said of the sofar bombs that during the program they jokingly referred to one as the sofar bomb and to the other, which was set to detonate several thousand feet beneath the waves, as the "so-long bomb."

[11] "Storms Hit 2 Mercury Trackers," Newport News Times-Herald, Sept. 12, 1961; "Postlaunch Report for MA-4"; Williams, interview.

[12] Memo, Carl R. Huss to Flight Dir., "Postlaunch Report on Test 1254," Sept. 15, 1961; Purser, penciled notes on MA-4 countdown and flight, Sept. 13, 1961; memo, Walter J. Kapryan, Capsule Systems Monitor, to Flight Dir., "Report on Test 1254," Sept. 29, 1961; memo, Tecwyn Roberts to Flight Dir., "Report on Test 1254," Sept. 25, 1961. Countdown procedures for MA-4 resembled those of the Mercury-Redstone missions. They were conducted in a 500-minute split-count with a 12- to 14-hour hold at T minus 300 for peroxide and pyrotechnics servicing. When the MA-4 count began Sept. 12 the operations

crew feared that hurricane "Debbie" might adversely affect the recovery area, but the count proceeded to T minus 300. At 4 p.m. a weather review found conditions improving, so hydrogen peroxide servicing was begun. The count resumed at 2 a.m., Sept. 13. Weather reviews and a peroxide check, plus the problems described in the text, accounted for holds totaling 2 hours and 4 minutes during countdown.

[13] "Postlaunch Report for MA-4"; Kapryan memo.

[14] Memo, unsigned, to Flight Dir., "Verbal Debriefing at End of Flight—Test 1254," Sept. 13, 1961; Purser notes; Schler memo. The crewman simulator was a gray box, 24 by 12 by 8 inches, which took oxygen out of the environmental control system, emitted carbon dioxide, simulated minor suit leakage of oxygen, and initiated dumping. NASA News Release 61-206, "News Conference, Mercury-Atlas No. 4," Sept. 13, 1961.

[15] Purser notes; "Project Mercury Status Report No. 12 for Period Ending October 31, 1961," undated; Roberts memo; memo, Network Control Group to Flight Dir., "Network Control Group (NCG) Report on Test 1254," undated; memo, Alan B. Shepard to Flight Dir., "Report on Test 1254," undated; "Postlaunch Report for MA-4." During the mission several Mercury astronauts deployed to some of the remote tracking stations; Carpenter to Muchea, Australia; Cooper to Point Arguello, Calif.; Schirra to Guaymas, Mexico; Slayton to Bermuda. Glenn, Grissom, and Shepard were in the control center at Cape Canaveral, with Shepard serving as Capsule Communicator. (Message, STG to NASA Hq., Sept. 9, 1961.) This was the first time that the automatic stabilization and control system, the reaction control system, and the horizon scanner subsystem could be fully evaluated for orbital missions. The mission proved that the attitude control system was adequate for reentry.

[16] Kapryan memo; Purser notes; memo, George M. Low to NASA Administrator, "Preliminary Results of MA-4 Flight," Sept. 15, 1961. R/A John L. Chew, commanding Destroyer Flotilla Four, said at the Cape press conference following the flight that the seas were running only about a foot high in the recovery area—which meant that hurricane Debbie was ineffective in those waters. During the spacecraft's descent, a C-54 aircraft sighted its reentry contrails, shortly thereafter noted deployment of the main parachute, and

finally observed water impact. Pickup by the destroyer *Decatur* was effected at 12:15 p.m. The main chute and the antenna fairing were retrieved about 1000 yards from the spacecraft. All spacecraft recovery aids performed well with the exception of the radar chaff. "Postlaunch Report for MA-4."

[17] "Status Report No. 12."

[18] Kapryan memo; Purser notes; Low memo.

[19] "News Conference, Mercury-Atlas No. 4." The principals at the news conference included Gilruth, Williams, R/A Chew, Col. R. S. Maloney, Col. Paul R. Wignall, Astronaut Virgil I. Grissom, and John A. Powers.

[20] Grimwood, *Mercury Chronology*, 147; NASA News Release 61-207, "Manned Space Flight Laboratory Location," undated; memo, Gilruth to staff, "Location of New Site for Space Task Group," Sept. 19, 1961. The team had surveyed sites in Tampa and Jacksonville, Fla.; New Orleans, Baton Rouge, Bogalusa, and Shreveport, La.; Houston, Beaumont, Corpus Christi, Victoria, Liberty, and Harlingen, Tex.; St. Louis, Mo.; Los Angeles, Berkeley, San Diego, Richmond, Moffett Field, and San Francisco, Calif.; and Boston, Mass. I. Edward Campagna, interview, Houston, June 16, 1963; "Manned Spacecraft Center," NASA/MSC brochure, June 1964. The Humble Oil and Refining Co. detached two tracts from acreage formerly operated as the Clear Lake Ranch and donated them to Rice University. Tract No. 1, consisting of 600 acres, was bought by the Government for $1,400,000. Tract No. 2, of 1020 acres, was donated to the Government, the tracts being transferred simultaneously. J. Wallace Ould, Chief Legal Counsel, MSC, interview, Houston, Sept. 24, 1964.

[21] "Manned Space Flight Laboratory Location"; Robert L. Rosholt, *An Administrative History of NASA, 1958-1963*, NASA SP-4101 (Washington, 1966); Stephen B. Oates, "NASA's Manned Spacecraft Center at Houston, Texas," *Southwestern Historical Quarterly*, LXVII (Jan. 1964). An editorial, "A Long View of What We Lost," in the Newport News *Daily Press*, of Oct. 3, 1961, reflects the public sentiment on the Virginia peninsula on the announced departure of the Space Task Group.

[22] *Houston Chronicle*, Oct. 11, 1961.

[23] *Houston Chronicle, Houston Post, Houston Press*, Sept. 21, 1961; "Manned Spacecraft Center Has Moved to Houston," NASA/MSC brochure, Aug. 1962. Activities of the new spacecraft center were housed in temporary facilities: Farnsworth and Chambers Building, Site 2, headquarters; Rich Building, Site 3, Spacecraft Research Division and Systems Evaluation and Development Division; Lane-Wells Building, Site 4, Life Systems Division; Houston Petroleum Center and Stahl and Meyers Building, Site 5, Project Mercury, Gemini, Apollo, and Flight Operations Division; East End State Bank Building, Site 6, Personnel and Security Divisions; Office City, Site 7, Flight Crew Operations Division; Ellington Air Force Base, Site 8, Procurement, Financial Management, Photographic Services and Supply; Minneapolis-Honeywell Building, Site 9, Public Affairs Office; Canada Dry Building, Site 10, Technical Services Division; KHOU–TV Building, Site 11, Data Computation and Reduction Division; Peachy Building, Site 12, Facilities Division. Later on, the center occupied additional temporary quarters in the Franklin Development Center and in a building formerly occupied by the Veterans Administration, and these became sites 13 and 14. The designation Site 1 was given to the Clear Lake site. "Manned Spacecraft Center Interim Facilities," NASA/MSC brochure, Aug. 15, 1963.

[24] "Houston Relocation Office Opens," Newport News *Times-Herald*, Sept. 27, 1961; memos, Wesley L. Hjornevik to staff, "Relocation Information Center," Oct. 5, 1961, and "Procedure for a Permanent Change of Duty Station," Nov. 1, 1961; memo, W. Kemble Johnson (Relocation Supervisor), to staff, "Relocation Plans," Oct. 18, 1961; memo, Purser to staff, "Designation of STG as 'Manned Spacecraft Center,'" Nov. 1, 1961; memo, unsigned, "Manned Spacecraft Center Building Facilities Requirements," Oct. 13, 1961.

[25] Purser, log for Gilruth, May 15, 1961; Grimwood, *Mercury Chronology*, 129.

[26] Memo, G. Barry Graves to those concerned, "May 16, 1961, Discussion of Proposed Scout Orbital Launch from Cape Canaveral," May 17, 1961. James T. Rose, interview, St. Louis, April 13, 1966.

[27] Memo, Purser to Gilruth, "Meeting on Proposed Scout Range Test," May 18, 1961. Those attending the meeting, held May 17, decided the flight should be scheduled for August.

[28] Purser, log for Gilruth, June 1, 1961; memo, Abe Silverstein to Robert C. Seamans, Jr., "Use of Blue Scout for Checkout of Mercury Network," May 24, 1961. Because of technical difficulties, the Mercury-Scout cost was about three times the $130,000 estimated

by Silverstein. William M. Bland, Jr., interview, Houston, Sept. 3, 1964.

[29] Memo, Purser to Warren J. North, "Details of the Mercury-Scout Instrumentation and Communication System," June 13, 1961; memo, Low to Gilruth and Williams, "Mercury Scout Test," June 22, 1961; memo, North to Deputy Dir., Space Flight Programs, NASA, "Mercury Status Items for Project Review Meeting—June 27, 1961," June 27, 1961.

[30] "Project Mercury, Summary of Calculated Preflight Trajectory Data for the Mercury Network Test Vehicle, MNTV–1," NASA Project Mercury working paper No. 200, July 12, 1961; "Project Mercury Mission Directive for Mercury-Scout Mission No. 1 (MS–1)," NASA Project Mercury working paper No. 201, July 21, 1961. The formal objectives of the Mercury-Scout mission were: (1) test realtime orbital computing capability at Goddard; (2) check out radar digital system and flow of digital data to the computer; (3) tailor the computation to the quality of data received by radar; (4) determine any interference that might exist between communications and data traffic; (5) determine the extent of system errors at radar sites, e.g., antenna misalignment, possible errors of surveyed position; (6) evaluate the updated radar procedures and revise as necessary; and (7) evaluate telemetry signal reception and operation of acquisition aids. "Status Report No. 11," 20.

[31] "Preflight Trajectory Data for the Mercury Test Vehicle, MNTV–1"; "Mission Directive for Mercury-Scout Mission No. 1."

[32] "Status Report No. 12," 21–22; "Status Report No. 11," 21; memo, Williams to Low, "Qualification Tests on Mercury-Scout Payload," July 24, 1961; memo, Low to D. Brainerd Holmes, "Dynamic Checkout of the Mercury Ground Network with Mercury-Scout," Nov. 8, 1961.

[33] "Project Mercury Status Report No. 13 for Period Ending Jan. 31, 1962," NASA/STG. According to the agreement with the Air Force, a launch team from that service was to be used. Letter, Williams to Air Force Systems Command, "Mercury Network Test Vehicle," July 7, 1961; Williams interview.

[34] Low memo. Some nine days after the failure of the Mercury-Scout-1, a one-and-a-half-pound squirrel monkey named Goliath was lost in an Air Force Atlas launching mishap. Thirty-five seconds after the rocket roared skyward, an explosion destroyed the tiny occupant of a small aluminum cylinder in the nose cone. Some newsmen, questioning

the wisdom of the upcoming Mercury-Atlas chimpanzee launch, felt that this was a bad augury. But the Air Force Atlas had been an advanced E model, with modifications whose reliability was unproved, while the D model used in Project Mercury had been through its reliability program. So, Goliath notwithstanding, there was no change of plans. *Baytown* (Texas) *Sun,* Nov. 10, 1961; *Houston Chronicle,* Nov. 17, 1961.

[35] *Washington Post,* Nov. 19, 1961; *Houston Chronicle,* Nov. 12, 1961. Even members of Congress began publicly speculating on the date of the manned flight. Rep. Olin E. Teague told an audience at Texas Agricultural and Mechanical College that he understood the tentative date was Dec. 6. Rep. Victor L. Anfuso predicted the flight would go on Dec. 20. Newport News *Daily Press,* Oct. 25, 1961; *Washington Post,* Dec. 3, 1961.

[36] Purser, log for Gilruth, Sept. 13, 1961; Washington *Evening Star,* Nov. 19 and 28, 1961.

[37] David S. Akens et al., *History of the George C. Marshall Space Flight Center* (Huntsville, Ala., 1960–1962), I, 25–26; *Houston Post,* Oct. 22, 1961.

[38] "Status Report No. 9"; memo, Low to Assoc. Administrator, "MA–5 Launch Schedule," Oct. 18, 1961.

[39] "Status Report No. 11"; Low memo.

[40] "Postlaunch Memorandum Report for Mercury-Atlas No. 5 (MA–5)," NASA/MSC, Dec. 6, 1961; "Project Mercury Mission Directive for Mercury-Atlas 5 (Capsule 9)," Project Mercury working paper No. 208, Oct. 20, 1961.

[41] *Ibid.;* "Project Mercury, Mercury-Atlas No. 5 Recovery Requirements," NASA/STG, Oct. 5, 1961; "Detailed Test Objectives for NASA Mission MA–5," Aerospace Corp., Aug. 31, 1961. Objectives of MA–5 were (1) demonstrate spacecraft structural integrity, including that of ablation shield and afterbody shingles, (2) evaluate spacecraft systems performance during flight, (3) determine reentry motion, (4) determine vibration levels, (5) demonstrate launch vehicle and spacecraft compatibility, (6) demonstrate life-support capability in a three-orbit mission, (7) evaluate abort sensing and implementation system, (8) demonstrate capability of ground command control equipment, (9) evaluate network acquisition aids, and (10) evaluate telemetry performance. "Mission Directive for MA–5."

[42] "Mercury-Atlas No. 5 Recovery Requirements."

[43] "Status Report No. 11"; Low memo; "Detailed Test Objectives for MA-5."

[44] "Project Mercury Calculated Preflight Trajectory Data for Mercury-Atlas Mission 5 (MA-5) (Capsule 9—Atlas 93-D)," Project Mercury working paper No. 207, Oct. 19, 1961. The Atlas rocket was tracked through five orbits. On the fourth the perigee was 93 miles and the apogee 118 miles. "Postlaunch Memorandum Report for Mercury-Atlas No. 5."

[45] "Mission Directive for MA-5." Before his arrival at the Cape, Enos had received 1263 hours of training over a 16-month period, including 343 hours under restraint. *Results of the Project Mercury Ballistic and Orbital Chimpanzee Flights*, NASA SP-39 (Washington, 1963), 39.

[46] Norman E. Stingely and John D. Mosely, "MA-5 Operations," in *Results of the Mercury Chimpanzee Flights*, 35; Jerry Fineg, interview, Holloman AFB, Sept. 15 and 25, 1964; *Huntsville* (Ala.) *Times*, Nov. 29, 1961; Washington *Evening Star*, Dec. 1, 1961; *New York Times*, Nov. 30, 1961; *Houston Chronicle*, Nov. 12, 1961. The intelligence of these chimpanzees was remarkable. One of their training tasks was to pull a lever exactly 50 times, and for his accuracy the animal received a reward of a banana pellet. More or less than 50 pulls caused the training unit to recycle without giving any reward. Stanley C. White of MSC medical operations told a reporter that the chimps would pull the lever "bangity-bangity-bang" about 45 times, then carefully pull Nos. 46, 47, 48, and 49, and finally make pull No. 50 with one hand cupped under the dispenser to receive the reward. (Washington *Evening Star*, Nov. 28, 1961.) In a training test at Holloman a chimp working on a flashing-light problem pulled levers 7000 times in 70 minutes, making only 28 errors. Kenneth F. Weaver, "School for Space Monkeys," in "Countdown for Space," *National Geographic*, reprinted from the May 1961 magazine, 727. Also see article in *Aerospace*, XXXIV (March 1963).

[47] "Postlaunch Memorandum Report for Mercury-Atlas No. 5."

[48] "MA-5 Data Acquisition Plan," NASA/STG, Oct. 20, 1961.

[49] "Mercury Personnel Man Worldwide Tracking Sites During MA-5 Mission," anon., NASA/STG, undated; "Status Report No. 12"; "MA-5 Plan," anon., undated.

[50] "Postlaunch Memorandum Report for Mercury-Atlas No. 5."

[51] William Hines in the Washington *Eve-ning Star* for Nov. 19, 1961, said it would be virtually impossible for the United States to make a manned orbital flight in 1961. On the other side, presenting an optimistic view, see Edward H. Kolcum, "Chimp Shot Raises Hope that U.S. Can Orbit Man Before Year's End," *Aviation Week*, LXXV (Dec. 4, 1961).

[52] "Postlaunch Memorandum Report for Mercury-Atlas No. 5."

[53] Memo, Roberts to Flight Dir., "Report on Test 1810 (MA-5)," Dec. 5, 1961; memo, Schler to Flight Dir., "Report on Test 1810 (MA-5)," Dec. 4, 1961.

[54] "Postlaunch Memorandum Report for Mercury-Atlas No. 5." Communications with the tracking stations were very good during countdown, and there was little interference. Curiously, however, there was a brief period of interference from Radio Moscow just before liftoff. "Debriefing—Test 1810," anon., Nov. 29, 1961.

[55] Roberts memo.

[56] Memo, Christopher C. Kraft, Jr., "Flight Director's Report on Test 1810 (MA-5)," Nov. 30, 1961; "Postlaunch Memorandum Report for Mercury-Atlas No. 5"; "Debriefing—Test 1810." At his press conference in Washington, President Kennedy got a round of laughter when he said, "This chimpanzee who is flying in space took off at 10:08. He reports that everything is perfect and working well." Baltimore *Sun*, Nov. 30, 1961.

[57] *Ibid.*; NASA News Release, "MA-5 News Conference," Nov. 29, 1961. Williams, in interview Aug. 23, 1965, recalled that communications with California had been disrupted momentarily by a tractor somewhere in Arizona that plowed up a telephone cable.

[58] Stingely and Mosely, "MA-5 Operations," 41-50; "Postlaunch Memorandum Report for Mercury-Atlas No. 5." On the continuous-avoidance, discrete-avoidance problem, Enos received his first shock of the first sessions about 15 minutes from launch and the second at the 201-minute point (after he had been weightless for 3 hours). He then pulled the lever correctly for the last 3 presentations before the psychomotor device turned off 207 minutes after launch.

During the first orbit, in the range of the Zanzibar tracking site, Mercury surgeon White noted that Enos' ventricular contractions had become more rapid. This White believed to be normal for the postacceleration period. The chimpanzee's respiration rate had risen with the onset of flight and the increase in his activity. His respiration rate was 21 and his pulse 122 during this phase, as compared with preflight rates of 14 and 94.

[59] "Debriefing—Test 1810"; memo, Donald D. Arabian to Flight Dir., "Report on Test 1810 (MA–5)," Dec. 6, 1961; Kraft memo.

[60] *Ibid.;* "Postlaunch Memorandum Report for Mercury-Atlas No. 5."

[61] *Ibid.;* Schler memo.

[62] Kraft memo; Arabian memo; "MA–5 News Conference." The spacecraft used 14.5 pounds of control fuel from retrofire to fuel jettison. Thirty pounds of fuel were dumped when the main parachute deployed.

[63] Kraft memo; "Postlaunch Memorandum Report for Mercury-Atlas No. 5"; "Unofficial Record of Events—MA–5, November 28 [sic], 1961," anon. On Nov. 2, 1961, Low remarked to Purser that MA–5 should be announced as a one-orbit mission that might be allowed to go three orbits. (Purser, log for Gilruth, Nov. 7, 1961.) MA–5's total recovery force, for the support of aborts, primary, and contingency landing areas consisted of 17 ships and 13 airplanes.

[64] "Postlaunch Memorandum Report for Mercury-Atlas No. 5." The drogue and main parachutes were not recovered, but the Earth-sky camera confirmed that they had functioned without damage. The drogue deployed at 21,000 feet and the main chute at 10,000.

[65] "MA–5 News Conference."

[66] Washington *Evening Star,* Dec. 1, 1961; *New York Times,* Dec. 1, 1961; *Chicago Tribune,* Dec. 1, 1961; *Results of the Mercury Chimpanzee Flights,* 38, 54. A little less than a year later, on Nov. 4, 1962, Enos died of dysentery caused by shigellosis, which resists antibiotics. He had been under night-and-day observation for two months before his death. Pathologists at Holloman reported that they found no symptom that could be attributed or related to his space flight a year before.

[67] *New York Times,* Dec. 1, 1961; Kolcum, "Chimp Shot Raises Hope that U.S. Can Orbit Man Before Year's End"; Washington *Evening Star,* Dec. 6, 1961. The fact that Christmas leaves of absence for thousands of naval personnel in the recovery forces might have to be canceled without assurance that the flight schedule would be kept also entered into the decision to postpone MA–6, Williams said in interview.

[68] House Committee on Science and Astronautics, 87 Cong., 2 sess. (1962), *Aeronautical and Astronautical Events of 1961,* 71; Baltimore *Sun,* Dec. 7, 1961; Low memo.

Chapter XIII

[1] *Washington Post,* Jan. 4 and Feb. 3, 1962; Walter C. Williams, interview, Houston, Aug. 23, 1965; House Committee on Science and Astronautics, 88 Cong., 1 sess. (1963), *Astronautical and Aeronautical Events of 1962,* 15–16.

[2] Washington *Evening Star,* Feb. 4, 1962; *New York Times,* Feb. 4, 1962; *Washington Post,* Feb. 6 and 19, 1962; Shirley Thomas, *Men of Space* (Philadelphia, 1962), V, 29–30; "MA–6 Advisory," 5 p.m., Feb. 15, 1962.

[3] *Space News Roundup,* MSC, I (Feb. 7, 1962); "Project Mercury Status Report No. 4 for Period Ending Oct. 31, 1959," STG, 41; "Project Mercury Status Report No. 6 for Period Ending April 30, 1960," STG, 37; "Project Mercury Status Report No. 8 for Period Ending Oct. 31, 1960," STG, 41; Project Mercury Status Report No. 10 for Period Ending April 30, 1961," STG, 37; "Project Mercury Status Report No. 11 for Period Ending July 31, 1961," STG, 37; "Project Mercury Status Report No. 12 for Period Ending Oct. 31, 1961," STG, 34. The flight schedule chart in October 1961 showed an MA–6 alternate mission. This meant that if the Enos (MA–5) flight had not succeeded another chimpanzee mission, designated MA–6, would have been flown.

[4] Paul E. Purser, compilation of excerpts from messages regarding spacecraft No. 13; Ms., George F. Killmer et al., "Project Mercury Technical History—Preflight Operations," MSC Florida Operations, Dec. 30, 1963, 107–111.

[5] Memo, Robert B. Voas to Mercury astronauts, "Suggested Activities for O r b i t a l Flights," Sept. 18, 1961.

[6] *Ibid.*

[7] Interview, Jocelyn R. Gill, Houston, Oct. 11, 1965.

[8] NASA, "Summary Minutes: Astronomy Subcommittee of the NASA Space Sciences Steering Committee (Meeting No. 8)," Dec. 5, 1961, and App. I, "Suggested Astronomical Tasks for the Mercury Astronauts," Nov. 3, 1961.

[9] Memo, Voas to Williams, "Astronauts' Preparation for Orbital Flight," Sept. 25, 1961; "Project Mercury Astronaut Preparation for Orbital Flight," NASA Project Mercury working paper No. 206, Oct. 13, 1961.

[10] *Ibid.*

[11] *Ibid.* In the event of slow pitch up-thrust, the astronaut was to assume manual

control of pitch. In retrosequence failure, he was to use manual override. If the main electric power supply failed, he was to select a standby source and determine whether reentry was possible at the end of the first orbit or whether earlier entry was necessary.

[12] "Project Mercury Astronaut Preparation and Activities Manual for Mercury-Atlas Mission 6 (MA–6, Spacecraft 13)," NASA Project Mercury working paper No. 215, Dec. 1, 1961.

[13] NASA, "Summary Minutes: Ad Hoc Committee on Astronomical Tasks for the Mercury Astronauts," Jan. 11, 1962.

[14] NASA, "Summary Minutes: Ad Hoc Committee on Astronomical Tasks for the Mercury Astronaut (Meeting No. 2)," Dec. 20, 1961.

[15] "Astronaut Preparation and Activities Manual for MA–6."

[16] "Project Mercury Status Report No. 13 for Period Ending Jan. 31, 1962," STG, 15, 23; "Postlaunch Memorandum Report for Mercury-Atlas No. 6 (MA–6), Part I, Mission Analysis," March 5, 1962; memo, Richard M. Dunham to Voas, "Personnel Survival Equipment Exercise for 2/7/62," Feb. 8, 1962. The life vest was fabricated as a solution for Grissom's swimming problem at the end of the MR–4 mission. The inflated vest had a bulk of less than 20 cubic inches and weighed less than a pound. *Results of the First United States Manned Orbital Space Flight, February 20, 1962* (Washington, 1962), 39. Also John H. Glenn, Jr., "I'll Have to Hit a Keyhole in the Sky," *Life*, LI (Dec. 8, 1961).

[17] "Status Report No. 13," 24; James M. Grimwood, *Project Mercury: A Chronology*, NASA SP–4001 (Washington, 1963), 157; memo, Eugene F. Kranz to Christopher C. Kraft, Jr., "Report on Test 5460 (MA–6)," Feb. 20, 1962. The flotation collar mentioned in the swimmer-training program resulted partly from the loss of Grissom's spacecraft. It was also the product of two years' work, and credit for its design must go to Donald E. Stullken of the Pensacola Naval Air Station. Early in the Mercury program the engineers realized that their hope of adapting a 20-man life raft to keep a spacecraft afloat was not feasible. The "Stullken collar" passed its final test on Jan. 3, 1962. At that time 50 collars had been made at Pensacola and delivered to the recovery forces. In an earlier test, off Wallops Island, one of the collars had kept the MR–2 capsule afloat for 70 hours in waves up to 7 feet high. The collar was made of five-ply life-raft fabric, was attached to the spacecraft by cables around the impact skirt, and was inflated after attachment. Stullken later became an employee of the Manned Spacecraft Center. *Space News Roundup*, MSC, I (Jan. 10, 1962), 23.

[18] "Project Mercury Mission Directive for Mercury-Atlas Mission 6 (MA–6, Spacecraft 13)," NASA Project Mercury working paper No. 216, Dec. 15, 1961; "Project Mercury, Mercury-Atlas No. 6 Recovery Requirements," Dec. 2, 1961. The latter document said that reentry (.05 g) would start about 60 miles west of Florida's Atlantic coast. Recovery forces were told that as a safety measure the ground track was set to continue 1000 miles beyond the third orbit landing area and that the explosive egress hatch had been modified to keep the cover from traveling more than two feet. Several ships had their cranes or davits fitted with a "shepherd's crook," consisting of a 16-foot aluminum pole with a hardened stainless-steel hook at the cable end which was capable of lifting 10,000 pounds. ("Technical Information Summary for Mercury-Atlas Mission 6 (MA–6, Spacecraft 13)," NASA/MSC, Dec. 19, 1961; "Detailed Test Objectives, NASA Mission No. MA–6, Project Mercury, Contract No. AF 04(647)–930," Aerospace Corp., Nov. 10, 1961.) A planning document for the MA–4 mission had indicated that the Atlas hold-down time would be three seconds, to assure that combustion would smooth out; thereafter, beginning with MA–5, the time would be reduced to two seconds. For MA–6 the hold-down time still was listed for three seconds duration.

[19] "NASA Note to Editors," Dec. 5, 1961.

[20] "Public Information Operating Plan, Project Mercury MA–6," NASA, undated; NASA News Release 62–8, "Mercury-Atlas 6 at a Glance," Jan. 21, 1962. For a descriptive impression of the MA–6 mission, see Ralph O. Shankle, *The Twins of Space* (Philadelphia, 1964), 77–100. During that mission, Shankle was a member of the MSC Public Affairs Office. In an interview, John A. "Shorty" Powers on Nov. 12, 1965, said that in his opinion the delays preceding the Glenn flight produced some helpful effects in the way of news reporting. Stories about the "type of hats that Annie [Glenn's wife] was wearing" began to play out. The reporters were forced to become more technically conversant if they were to file stories that would keep their editors happy as well as justify the Florida expense accounts.

[21] Williams interview.

[22] "Postlaunch Memorandum Report for MA-6"; "NASA News Briefing at the Starlite Paladium," Feb. 13, 1962; *Results of the First United States Manned Orbital Space Flight;* NASA News Release 62, "Mercury Recovery Force," undated; *Space News Roundup,* I (Feb. 7, 1962). On the morning of Jan. 27, Glenn's military service boss, Gen. David M. Shoup, the Marine Corps Commandant, joined him for breakfast. The name Glenn chose for his spacecraft, *Friendship 7,* was painted on No. 13 by artist Cecilia Bibby. See DOD Representative for Project Mercury Support Operations, *Final Report to the Secretary of Defense on Department of Defense Support of Project Mercury: For the Period 1 July 1959 through 13 June 1963,* approved by Leighton I. Davis, Maj. Gen., USAF, 11 Sept. 1963, Chart 6, 15. Also see "Man Marked to Do Great Things," *Life,* LII (Feb. 2, 1962).

[23] Washington *Evening Star,* Jan. 31, Feb. 4, 1962; *Washington Post,* Feb. 6, 1962; *National Observer,* Feb. 4, 1962; *New York Times,* Feb. 6, 1962; *Los Angeles Times,* Jan. 31, 1962; *New York Herald Tribune,* Feb. 4, 1962; *Washington Daily News,* Feb. 7, 1962.

[24] "NASA News Briefing at the Starlite Paladium."

[25] "MA-6 Advisory," NASA, 5 p.m., Feb. 15, 1962; "MA-6 Advisory," 5 p.m., Feb. 19, 1962; "Postlaunch Memorandum Report for MA-6."

[26] "MA-6 Advisory," Feb. 19, 1962; Richard Dunham, John J. Van Bockel, and Paul W. Backer, "Continuation of MA-6 Debriefing," March 7, 1962.

[27] "Postlaunch Memorandum Report for MA-6"; "Procedures Log," Mercury Control Center, Feb. 20, 1962; *Space News Roundup,* I (Feb. 21, 1962).

[28] *Ibid.*; Kranz memo; memo, Stanley C. White to Kraft, "Summary Report on Test 5460 (MA-6)," Feb. 22, 1962.

[29] "Procedures Log"; White memo.

[30] On launch day cloud masses continued to hover over the launch area, causing many of the newsmen present to bet "no liftoff today." A little after 7 a.m. one of the Cape weather men, Harlan G. Higgins, noticed that the wind was shifting to drive the clouds away and that the temperature was becoming cooler. He quickly phoned Ernest A. Amman, the weather support man in Mercury Control, and told him that the chances for launch now looked promising.

[31] "Procedures Log"; White memo; "Postlaunch Memorandum Report for MA-6."

[32] *Ibid.*; "Transcript of Public Address Announcements by Col. John Powers Beginning at T Minus 22 Minutes, Describing MA-6 Launch," Feb. 20, 1962. For the story of the people on the beaches, see *New York Times,* Feb. 20, 1962. The impatience of some of the news personnel was understandable. A *New York Times* correspondent reported in mid-February that the often-postponed Glenn flight had already cost the broadcasters $2 million and that each day of delay cost them another $50,000. Newspaper and magazine costs were estimated at about a third of those figures. *New York Times,* Feb. 17, 1962. Also see "Liftoff! for John Glenn and His Family," *Life,* LII (March 2, 1962); "Liftoff and Uplift for the U.S.," *Life,* LII (March 2, 1962); "He Hit That Keyhole in the Sky," *Life,* LII (March 2, 1962); "At School All Systems Are Go," *Life,* LII (March 9, 1962); D. J. Hamblin, "Applause, Tears and Laughter and the Emotions of a Long-Ago Fourth of July," *Life,* LII (March 9, 1962); "Hero's Words to Cherish," *Life,* LII (March 9, 1962); John Glenn, Jr., "If You're Shook Up You Shouldn't Be There," *Life,* LII (March 9, 1962).

[33] White memo; "Postlaunch Memorandum Report for MA-6." The General Electric-Burroughs booster-guidance system performed an interesting operation. Aboard the Atlas were three small black boxes, two of them similar to two-way radios. A radar on the ground automatically tracked signals emanating from these boxes, determining range and position. The operation for the MA-6 mission progressed along the following pattern: A few minutes before launch time Michael Michela, the GE rate console operator, flipped a switch that pointed the rate antennas in the same directions as the precise tracking radar. This was to obtain velocity data. Thomas Waid, the track console operator, pushed a button to place the guidance system in automatic operation. Guidance system signals were aimed on a "cube in space" several hundred feet above the booster. It was simply a matter of waiting until the booster passed through this area, when the signals locked onto a radio transponder and the system began steering the launch vehicle after staging. This condition was maintained until orbital conditions were attained. The system had operated some 8000 hours before MA-6, and some members of the guidance team, consisting of Rodney Borum, John Savarie, Donald Wood, Waid, Robert

Stanton, and Michela, had participated in as many as 121 launches. (News release, "Radio Guidance Functions of Mercury-Atlas 6," Defense Electronics Div., General Electric Co., undated; News release, no title, Defense Electronics Div., General Electric Co., undated.) During the powered phase of the flight, Kraft was notified that signals from a foreign C-band radar transmitter had been intercepted, but the operations team was unable to identify the source. ("Procedures Log.") The guidance equations were developed by C. L. Pitman, Robert Page, and Duncan McPherson of the Space Technology Laboratories. John P. Mayer, comments, Sept. 8, 1965.

[31] "Postlaunch Memorandum Report for MA-6"; "Procedures Log." At sustainer cutoff Glenn was not only aware of weightlessness but felt as though he were tumbling. Shepard and Grissom reported the same sensation. The apogee of Glenn's flight was 162 miles; the perigee, 100 miles.

[33] "Postlaunch Memorandum Report for MA-6"; "Continuation of MA-6 Debriefing." Glenn felt no angular acceleration during turnaround.

[36] *Ibid.*

[37] "Test 5460, Composite Message Summary," Mercury Control Center, Feb. 20, 1962. Over the Kano area on the first pass, Glenn opened his faceplate and ate a xylose (sugar) pill and his tube of applesauce without difficulty. (*Results of the First United States Manned Orbital Space Flight,* 153.) In the Zanzibar area Glenn worked out briefly with his exerciser, and the tracking station noted a temporary increase in his pulse rate to 140.

[38] The engineers later stated that these disagreements were inherent and would crop up whenever major yaw or roll attitudes deviated from zero degrees for an extended period of time. In other words, the gyro "readouts" on the panel, which were reporting an attitude change of about four degrees per minute, were considerably behind Glenn's quickly slewing yaw maneuver. Consequently the best procedure when executing such an operation was to stop the revolving gyroscopes, an action called "caging."

[39] "Postlaunch Memorandum Report for MA-6"; "Test 5460, Composite Message Summary"; "Transcript of Announcements by John Powers"; "Continuation of MA-6 Debriefing." Upon meeting the mayor of Perth later, Glenn remarked facetiously that he had half-expected the mayor to hand him an electric bill. An attempt to observe the airport lights at Woomera had failed because of cloudiness. As for the height of the haze layer, Jocelyn R. Gill of NASA Headquarters said this distance was later measured and found to be about $2\frac{1}{2}$ degrees above the horizon. For other comments on Glenn's observations while in orbit see "National Aeronautics and Space Administration," *Astronomical Journal,* 67, No. 9, Nov. 1962, 655.

[40] "Procedures Log"; "Continuation of MA-6 Debriefing." The particles appeared to be about $\frac{1}{16}$ inch in diameter and to be traveling at about the same speed as the spacecraft.

[41] "Postlaunch Memorandum Report for MA-6." On Feb. 26, 1962, postflight inspectors disassembled the thrust chamber systems and found some loose particles upstream of the fuel-metering orifices. These were found to be pieces of the dutch-weave fuel-distribution screens. Fuel consumption during the first orbit was 4.2 pounds from the automatic tanks and .6 pound from the manual tanks. Those figures were nominal; control trouble did not develop until the flight had been in progress for an hour and 29 minutes.

[42] *Ibid.; Space News Roundup,* I (Feb. 21, 1962); William Hines, "Segment 51," Washington *Evening Star,* March 16, 1962; Maxime A. Faget, interview, Houston, April 19, 1962.

[43] Postflight inspectors were unable to explain the secondary oxygen supply drop. For a report on Glenn's observational efforts, see John H. Glenn, Jr., "Summary Results of the First United States Manned Orbital Space Fight," in *Life Sciences and Space Research,* "A Session of the Third International Space Science Symposium," Washington, D.C., April 30–May 9, 1962 (North Holland Publishing Company, Amsterdam, Netherlands, 1962), 173–183.

[44] "Procedures Log."

[45] *Ibid.;* "Postlaunch Memorandum Report for MA-6"; "Test 5460, Composite Message Summary"; *Results of the First United States Manned Orbital Space Flight,* 190; "Continuation of MA-6 Debriefing."

[46] *Ibid.*

[47] "Postlaunch Memorandum Report for MA-6."

[48] "Postlaunch Memorandum Report for MA-6." At the moment of Glenn's splashdown, the Post Office issued a special 4-cent stamp commemorating the MA-6 mission ("Transcript of Announcements by John Powers"). For a popular account of the MA-6 mission, with excellent illustrations, see Robert B. Voas, "John Glenn's Three Orbits in *Friend-*

ship 7," National Geographic, reprinted from the June 1962 magazine.

⁴⁹ *Ibid.; Astronautics,* VII (May 1962). In a debriefing session a few days after the MA–6 flight, Glenn said he wished he had known of the supposed heatshield and landing bag problem, so that he could have been listening for sound clues. He seemed to be making the point that the pilot, as the thinking part of the man-machine team, should be allowed to participate in decision making. Scott Crossfield, one of the X–15 pilots, expressed this view well in the immediate post-MA–6 period: "Where else would you get a non-linear computer weighing only 160 pounds, having a billion binary decision elements, that can be mass-produced by unskilled labor?" "Continuation of MA–6 Debriefing"; *Aviation Week,* LXXVI (March 5, 1962).

⁵⁰ *Astronautical and Aeronautical Events of 1962,* 18. See Senate Committee on Aeronautical and Space Sciences, 87 Cong., 2 sess. (1962), *Orbital Flight of John H. Glenn, Jr.,* for testimony of astronauts and NASA officials, Feb. 28, 1962.

⁵¹ "Free World Media Treatment of First U.S. Orbital Flight," a file of reports assembled at NASA Hq., March 5, 1962.

⁵² *Aviation Week,* LXXVI (Feb. 26, 1962). Robert R. Gilruth also was the cover subject for *Missiles and Rockets,* X (March 19, 1962). The same issue of the magazine said in an editorial: "It is always a pleasure to sing about an unsung hero. . . . While Astronaut John Glenn was swinging around the earth in *Friendship 7* . . . Robert Gilruth had his feet planted firmly on the ground in Mercury Control." Gilruth had just been awarded the Robert H. Goddard Memorial Trophy on March 16, 1962, by the National Rocket Club.

⁵³ *Astronautical and Aeronautical Events of 1962,* 22, 27; *Friendship 7* tour files, MSC Hist. Archives; Grimwood, *Mercury Chronology,* 184. The text of Glenn's address to the joint session of Congress may be found in the *Washington Post* for Feb. 27, 1962.

⁵⁴ Reports and photographs concerning the "Fourth Orbit of *Friendship 7*" are filed in the MSC Hist. Archives.

⁵⁵ *Washington Post,* Jan. 10, 1962; Washington *Evening Star,* Jan. 6, 1962; David S. Akens, Paul K. Freiwirth, and Helen T. Wells, *History of the George C. Marshall Space Flight Center* (Huntsville, Ala., 1960–1962), I, 21; "Saturn Illustrated Chronology: April 1957–June 1964," NASA/MSFC, Aug. 10, 1964,

52–53; Newport News *Daily Press,* Jan. 4, 1962.

⁵⁶ See Chap. X. House Committee on Science and Astronautics, 87 Cong., 2 sess. (1962), *1963 NASA Authorization, Hearings,* 1, 2.

⁵⁷ *Ibid.,* 3–33; Senate Subcommittee of the Committee on Appropriations, 87 Cong., 2 sess. (1962), *Independent Offices Appropriations, 1963, Hearings,* II, 1503; Washington *Evening Star,* Jan. 7, 1962.

⁵⁸ MSC announcement No. 9, Ref. 2–2, "Establishment of the Mercury Project Office," Jan. 15, 1962.

⁵⁹ MSC announcement No. 12, Ref. 2–2, "Personnel Assignments for Mercury and Gemini Program Offices," Jan. 31, 1962; Maggie Taylor, Apollo Spacecraft Program Office, MSC, interview, Houston, Jan. 12, 1965; Grimwood, *Mercury Chronology,* 220.

⁶⁰ Memo, Dir. of Personnel, MSC, to Philip H. Whitbeck, "Status Report for the Personnel Office," Jan. 26, 1962. At the time of the personnel survey about 400 to 500 could have been termed "old guard." The remainder, being essentialy "new hires," did not really care whether they settled in Hampton or Houston. The 84 who chose not to go were mainly of the "old guard."

⁶¹ MSC announcement No. 21, Ref. 2–1, "Relocation of Manned Spacecraft Center Headquarters," Feb. 26, 1962. In reality the Mercury Project Office moved into the Farnsworth-Chambers Building in Houston on April 16, 1962, a move that preceded the MA–7 flight by a little over a month.

⁶² *Astronautical and Aeronautical Events of 1962,* 36; Donald K. Slayton, interview, Houston, Dec. 16, 1964; letter, William Douglas to L. S. S., Jr., Aug. 17, 1965.

⁶³ During the December 1964 interview Slayton demurred at naming the civilian panel, but newsmen had been less reticent. See *Washington Post,* March 16, 1962; *New York Times,* March 16, 1962. For other material on the Slayton case, see Mae M. Link, *Space Medicine in Project Mercury,* NASA SP–4003 (Washington, 1965). Slayton was not examined personally by Paul Dudley White until June 15, 1962. At that time speculation was revived about Slayton's possible selection for a space flight. Washington *Evening Star,* June 15, 1962.

⁶⁴ Washington *Evening Star,* March 21, 1962; Slayton interview; Paul E. Purser, interview, Houston, Jan. 4, 1965.

[65] Slayton, interview, Houston, Jan. 14, 1965; "Postlaunch Memorandum Report for Mercury-Atlas No. 7 (MA–7), Part I, Mission Analysis," NASA/MSC, June 15, 1962. After MA–7 each backup pilot became the flight astronaut of the succeeding mission in Project Mercury. Also see Loudon Wainwright, "Comes a Quiet Man to Ride Aurora," *Life*, LII (May 18, 1962).

[66] "Technical Information Summary for Mercury-Atlas Mission 7 (MA–7, Spacecraft 18)," MSC, undated.

[67] Gill interview; NASA, "Summary Minutes: Ad Hoc Committee on Scientific Tasks and Training for Man-in-Space (Meeting Nos. 1, 2, 3)," March 16, 26, and April 18, 1962.

[68] NASA News Release 62–113, "MA–7 Press Kit," May 13, 1962.

[69] "Project Mercury Mission Directive for Mercury-Atlas Mission 7 (MA–7, Spacecraft 18)," NASA Project Mercury working paper No. 222, April 9, 1962; "Postlaunch Memorandum Report for MA–7"; *Results of the Second United States Manned Orbital Space Flight, May 24, 1962*, NASA SP–6 (Washington, 1962), 11–13. In the order listed in the text, the experiments were proposed by the Langley Research Center, Lewis Research Center, Massachusetts Institute of Technology Instrumentation Laboratory, the Weather Bureau, and Goddard Space Flight Center.

[70] *Ibid.* Airglow is an emission of light resulting from chemical reactions in the upper atmosphere. Various reactions produce light of different colors. In many cases, molecules of atmospheric gas are split by ultraviolet rays of sunshine. Then, when darkness comes, the gas molecules recombine, emitting light. The illumination of the sky at night usually comes from airglow instead of starlight. *New York Times*, June 3, 1962. Lawrence Dunkelman of Goddard provided Carpenter with the airglow device to make observations. Jocelyn Gill said this was the filter that had been planned for MA–6, but time did not permit Glenn to use it.

[71] *Ibid.*; "Project Mercury Quarterly Status Report No. 14 for Period Ending April 30, 1962," NASA/MSC, May 25, 1962. John Mayer of MSC commented in September 1965, "that photos of the Russian spacecraft indicated that they had an almost identical earth-path indicator." Mayer went on to say that the indicator "was deleted from Mercury flights because it was of little use in the missions."

[72] "Project Mercury Mission Directive for Mercury-Atlas Mission 7"; message, G. Merritt Preston to Gilruth, May 21, 1962; "Weekly Activity Report to the Office of the Director for Manned Space Flight," MSC, May 5, 1962.

[73] "Project Mercury Quarterly Status Report No. 14"; "Weekly Activity Report," MSC/Mercury Project Office, March 17, 1962; "Postlaunch Memorandum Report for MA–7."

[74] Memo, Kraft to Williams et al., "MA–7 Test Flight Reports," June 12, 1962; "Project Mercury Mission Directive for Mercury-Atlas Mission 7"; *Final Report to the Secretary of Defense on Support of Project Mercury*, Chart 6, 15. The Indian Ocean picket ship *Coastal Sentry* (call name "Coastal Sentry Quebec") was stationed at the entrance to the Mozambique Channel off the southeastern coast of Africa for MA–7. "MA–7 Press Kit."

[75] "Project Mercury Quarterly Status Report No. 14." The decision to add a barostat in the recovery arming circuit was a primary reason for delaying the MA–7 launch. After a review meeting on May 16, the engineers had decided that this action was necessary. Late that night the newsmen already at the Cape were advised.

[76] Kraft memo; memo, Harold I. Johnson et al., to those concerned, "MA–7 Remote Site Operations Debriefing," June 1, 1962; "Postlaunch Memorandum Report for MA–7."

[77] Johnson memo.

[78] "Postlaunch Memorandum Report for MA–7." The *New York Times* for May 26, 1962, reported the estimated number of television viewers. Cecilia Bibby was again selected as the artist to paint the name chosen by the astronaut. *New York Times*, May 28, 1962.

[79] Kraft memo; "Postlaunch Memorandum Report for MA–7."

[80] Orbital insertion of *Aurora 7* was almost ideal, the flight path angle and velocity being only .004 degree and 2 feet per second low, respectively. This provided an orbital trajectory of 89.96 miles (perigee) and 144.4 miles (apogee). There was only one anomaly during the powered phase of the flight. The primary auxiliary cutoff signal for the sustainer engine was transmitted by the General Electric-Burroughs guidance system simultaneously with sustainer engine cutoff. The backup auxiliary sustainer cutoff signal had preceded this transmission by .44 second. But the abort enabling switch in the Control Center was in the normal position; since both signals did not lock, an improper signal was prevented. If the launch

vehicle had accepted the erroneous signal, a velocity decrement of about 110 feet per second might have resulted, causing marginal conditions in the go-for-mission decision. ("Postlaunch Memorandum Report for MA-7"; "Project Mercury Quarterly Status Report No. 15 for Period Ending July 31, 1962," NASA/ MSC.) Carpenter said the sensations of weightlessness were similar to those of skindiving.

[51] Kraft memo; "Postlaunch Memorandum Report for MA-7"; *Results of the Second United States Manned Orbital Space Flight*, 78–79. Postflight inspection convinced several engineers that the malfunction of the horizon scanner circuit was a random component failure. Plans were made to try to recover the antenna canister on the next flight for postflight analysis of the scanner unit located in that component. ("Project Mercury Quarterly Status Report No. 15.") Concerning the undesirable suit temperatures, Frank H. Samonski, Jr., capsule environmental monitor, believed a partial freezing in the suit circuit caused an obstruction in the heat exchanger. Carpenter was comfortable once again by the end of the first orbit; he was hot again during the second; and he finally got the suit temperature down to a comfortable level on the third. Suit inlet temperatures ranged between 62 degrees to about 86 degrees during the flight. In all, Carpenter made 13 attempts to adjust the setting to a comfortable range.

[52] *Ibid.*; Washington *Sunday Star*, March 27, 1962. Carpenter later said that the periscope was not worth the weight and space it occupied in the spacecraft. This certainly would be true, he felt, when longer Mercury missions required more oxygen, water, and control fuel. On other aspects of the flight, Carpenter reported that he even saw a dirt road so clearly that he had the impression that if a vehicle had come along he could have seen it, too. In general, he found the daylight view from orbit similar to a view from a high-flying aircraft. He said that navigation at night might be accomplished by using a known star on the horizon.

[83] "Postlaunch Memorandum Report for MA-7."

[84] *Ibid.*

[85] *Ibid.*; Kraft memo.

[86] *Ibid.*; Newport News *Times-Herald*, June 7, 1962; Johnson memo. Carpenter also consumed a xylose tablet without difficulty. At about midway of the second orbit, the flight controller recommended that the pilot drink

water freely to compensate for sweating. Carpenter drank about 1213 cc of water—60 percent while in flight and the remainder while on the life raft awaiting recovery. During the postflight debriefings, Carpenter suggested that henceforth food bags should be transparent and that something should be done about the chocolate items, which had melted in the fluctuating warmth of the cabin.

[87] "Postlaunch Memorandum Report for MA-7." Shortly after retrofire the balloon disappeared, and about seven minutes later, Carpenter lost sight of the tether.

[88] *Ibid.*; Johnson memo; Grimwood, *Mercury Chronology*, 164–165.

[89] "Postlaunch Memorandum Report for MA-7." Also see Winifred Sawtell Cameron, Lt. Col. John H. Glenn, Lt. Cdr. M. Scott Carpenter, and John A. O'Keefe, "Effect of Refraction on the Setting Sun as Seen from Space in Theory and Observation," in the *Astronomical Journal*, 68, No. 5, June 1962, 348–351.

[90] *Results of the Second United States Manned Orbital Space Flight*, 92, 102–103; *New York Times*, June 3, 1962. Later, Lawrence Dunkelman at Goddard, using Carpenter's "Voasmeter" readings, judged the airglow layer to be about two degrees in width. Also, after the Carpenter mission, the Naval Research Laboratory began a study of the night airglow from pictures taken during rocket flights. For the findings of this study see M. J. Koomen, Irene S. Gulledge, D. M. Packer, and R. Tousey, "Night Airglow Observations from Orbiting Spacecraft Compared with Measurements from Rockets," *Science*, Vol. 140, No. 3571, June 7, 1963, 1087–1089.

[91] "Postlaunch Memorandum Report for MA-7." Out of 19 exposed frames, Carpenter was able to get two pictures of the "fireflies." Evidence appeared in other photographs, but these pictures were not in focus.

[92] Kraft memo.

[93] *Ibid.*; Johnson memo; "Postlaunch Memorandum Report for MA-7." Joe Dodson, in an interview, reported that about 18½ pounds of fuel were depleted during the first 10 minutes of reentry. Newport News *Daily Press*, June 6, 1962. When Carpenter switched on the ASCS, the spacecraft had a tendency to pitch down. Fuel conservation during the third orbit had prevented an adequate checkout of the ASCS before retrofire.

[94] Kraft memo; Johnson memo. The interior smoke resulted not from the retrorockets

themselves, but from two fuses that had blown because of the retros' kick.

[95] Memo, Carl R. Huss, et al., to Chief, Flight Operations Div., "Postflight Analysis of MA–7 Trajectory Data to Determine Cause of the Erroneous Landing Point," June 13, 1962; *New York Times,* June 6, 1962. Almost immediately the tracking crews across the nation, beginning in California, confirmed that there would be about a 250-mile overshoot.

[96] Johnson memo.

[97] *Ibid.;* "Postlaunch Memorandum Report for MA–7."

[98] Johnson memo. After the MA–6 flight the Life Systems Division had conducted a manned test to investigate the reentry heating that had occurred. Results showed that closing the helmet visor before reentry and letting the suit circuit operate separately provided a more comfortable environment. At the same time it was decided to lengthen the suit inlet hose. ("Activity Report, Life Systems Division," MSC, April 30, 1962.) After .05 g had been passed on Carpenter's flight, the liquid in the capillary tube began to drain. Thus the results tended to confirm capillary action theory. The ability to maintain a stable fluid position during angular acceleration imposed by the reaction control system indicated that this method of ullage control was valid. The results obtained during MA–7 could be extrapolated for propellants in accordance with laws governing each, namely, surface tension, fluid temperature, and known capillary tube diameter. "Postlaunch Memorandum Report for MA–7."

[99] "Postlaunch Memorandum Report for MA–7."

[100] "Postlaunch Memorandum Report for MA–7"; Kraft memo. During the MA–6 ionization period an erroneous command signal had been received. Engineers believed that this was caused by a mixing of radio-frequency signals, which generated sufficient strength to energize one relay in the command system. This anomaly had been corrected by exchanging the low-frequency telemetry components for others operating on a higher frequency. ("Weekly Activities Report," March 17, 1962; "Highlights, Activities Report, MSC," April 30, 1962.) Ionization during MA–7 was 40 seconds late, furnishing another clue to the overshoot. The behavior of the drogue and main chutes remained unexplained. Tests in early May 1962, at El Centro, Calif., using the exact MA–7 weight had all been successful.

Memo, Aleck C. Bond to Faget, "Weekly Activity Report," May 4, 1962.

[101] "Postlaunch Memorandum Report for MA–7"; Kraft memo.

[102] *Ibid.;* Washington *Sunday Star,* May 27, 1962; "Project Mercury Quarterly Status Report No. 15."

[103] Johnson memo; *New York Times,* May 26, 1962. Carpenter later learned that the Apache pilot's film was confiscated when he returned to Puerto Rico. The pilot had violated the airway zones.

[104] "Postlaunch Memorandum Report for MA–7"; Johnson memo; *New York Times,* May 26, 1962; Washington *Sunday Star,* May 27, 1962. Sergeant Ray McClure, a veteran of 137 jumps, had received the Air Medal for his part in the first successful recovery of a Discoverer capsule in the Pacific north of Hawaii.

[105] Johnson memo.

[106] Kraft memo. A rather complete discussion of the Carpenter recovery matter is contained in Senate Committee on Aeronautical and Space Sciences, 87 Cong., 2 sess. (1962), *NASA Authorization for Fiscal Year 1963: Hearings,* 495–504. Senator Spessard L. Holland (D. Fla.) and D. Brainerd Holmes of NASA, the latter having been present in the Mercury Control Center during the complete recovery, were the principals in this discussion. Holmes stated that he was with R/A John L. Chew and that it did not seem to make a particle of difference to the admiral which service recovered the astronaut. The NASA official interpreted that Chew based his decision on past experiences; Holmes added that he could detect no feeling of interservice rivalry.

[107] "Postlaunch Memorandum Report for MA–7"; Johnson memo; Washington *Evening Star,* May 26, 1962; *Astronautical and Aeronautical Events of 1962,* 86. See also Rene Carpenter, "Scott Carpenter and His Son and His Wife Living Through the Time That Grew Too Long," *Life,* LII (June 1, 1962); and M. Scott Carpenter, "I Got Let in on the Great Secret," *Life,* LII (June 8, 1962).

[108] "Postlaunch Memorandum Report for MA–7."

[109] *New York Times,* May 28, 1962; *Astronautical and Aeronautical Events of 1962,* 89; *Washington Post,* May 30, 1962; Washington *Evening Star,* May 31, 1962. Carpenter, his family, and the Williams family paid a visit to the White House on June 5, 1962. *Washington Post,* June 5, 1962.

[110] Kraft memo; Johnson memo; "Postlaunch Memorandum Report for MA–7"; John

W. Finney, "Astronaut Says His Errors Will Benefit Space Project," *New York Times,* May 28, 1962. Carpenter's contentions were borne out by the changes that were effected. For one thing a drive was made to have a flight plan specifying fewer activities ready well before the next flight. Also, a switch was integrated in the spacecraft by which the pilot could switch off and switch on the high thrusters. If the pilot forgot to reactivate the thrusters, an automatic override ensured their availability just before retrofire. "Project Mercury Quarterly Status Report No. 15"; *Results of the Second United States Manned Orbital Space Flight,* 6.

[111] Newport News *Daily Press,* June 6 and 8, 1962; *New York Times,* June 14, 1962; *Washington Post,* June 28, 1962; Washington *Evening Star,* June 14, 1962. On the subject of pilot selection, the month of June was another milestone in the manned space flight program. On June 1 the deadline closed for applications by astronaut candidates for the second increment to be added to the Mercury seven for the Gemini and Apollo missions. *Astronautical and Aeronautical Events of 1962,* 93.

Chapter XIV

[1] Memo, Richard E. Day, to Management Analysis Office, "Monthly Activity Report, Flight Crew Operations Division," July 30, 1962; memo, Warren J. North [to Management Analysis Division], "Activity Report, Flight Crew Operations Division," Aug. 28, 1962; "Flight Plan for MA–8/16," NASA/MSC, Aug. 7, 1962; "Postlaunch Memorandum Report for Mercury-Atlas No. 8 (MA–8)," NASA/MSC, Oct. 23, 1962, Part I, "Mercury Scientific Experiment Panel: Abstract of the Proceedings at the MA–8 Meeting," MSC, July 19, 1962.

[2] House Committee on Science and Astronautics, 88 Cong., 1 sess. (1963), *Astronautical and Aeronautical Events of 1962* (Washington, 1963), 148, 153; "A Space Gap? And How!" *Washington Daily News,* Aug. 13, 1962; "Orbiting Reds Nearing Each Other, Western Ground Observers Report," *Washington Post,* Aug. 14, 1962; "Soviet Prestige in Space," Washington *Evening Star,* Aug. 19, 1962; Seymour Topping, "Russian Astronauts Only 3 Miles Apart on Closest Paths," *New York Times,* Aug. 22, 1962.

[3] "Minutes of the Senior Staff Meeting," MSC, Aug. 24, 1962; memo, North [to Man-

agement Analysis Division], "Activity Report, Flight Crew Operations Division," Sept. 23, 1962. A rather complete series of proposals for the maneuvering Mercury spacecraft, including pictures of possible configurations, is contained in "Mercury Maneuvering Proposal," NASA/MSC, Aug. 29, 1962.

[4] Kenneth S. Kleinknecht, interview, Houston, May 3, 1965; "Mercury Seven-Orbit Mission Capability," memorandum report, Mercury Project Office, March 5, 1962.

[5] "Mercury Seven-Orbit Mission Capability."

[6] "MA–8 Mission Rules—Preliminary," Aug. 3, 1962; Revision A, Aug. 20, 1962; Revision B, Sept. 24, 1962; "MA–8 Data Acquisition Plan," Aug. 21, 1962; "MA–8 Technical Information Summary" [Aug. 20, 1962]; "Flight Plan for MA–8/16, Revision A," Sept. 10, 1962; "Mission Directive for Mercury-Atlas Mission No. 8 (MA–8—Spacecraft 16)," NASA Project Mercury working paper No. 228, Aug. 31, 1962; "Calculated Preflight Trajectory Data for Mercury-Atlas Mission 8 (MA–8) (Spacecraft No. 16—Atlas 113–D)," NASA Project Mercury working paper No. 229, Sept. 7, 1962; "MA–8 Recovery Requirements," Aug. 15, 1962; "MA–8 Recovery Procedures," Aug. 30, 1962.

[7] Ms., George F. Killmer, Jr., et al., "Mercury Technical History—Preflight Operations," MSC Florida Operations, Dec. 30, 1963, Chart 126; "Weekly Activities Report," Mercury Project Office, April 20, 1962; "Weekly Activities Report," Mercury Project Office, April 13, 1962; "Project Mercury Quarterly Status Report No. 14 for the Period Ending April 30, 1962," NASA/MSC, May 25, 1962; "Weekly Activity Report to the Office of the Director for Manned Space Flight," MSC, May 5, 1962; memo, G. Merritt Preston to Dir., MSC, "Monthly Activities Report No. 6," April 26, 1962.

[8] Memo, James P. Henry to Asst. Dir. for Research and Development, MSC, "Weekly Activity Report for the Life Systems Division," April 20, 1962; "Monthly Activities Report," Life Systems Div., April 30, 1962; memo, Richard S. Johnston to Asst. Dir. for Research and Development, MSC, "Weekly Activities Report," June 15, 1962; memo, Edward L. Hays to Asst. Dir. for Research and Development, "Weekly Activity Report," May 18, 1962; "Activities Report to the Office of the Director for Manned Space Flight," MSC, May 19, 1962.

[9] "Activity Report to the Office of the Di-

rector for Manned Space Flight," MSC, May 12, 1962; "Activity Report to Director for Manned Space Flight," MSC, June 2, 1962.

[10] Robert T. Everline, interview, Houston, April 15, 1965; "Minutes of the Senior Staff Meeting," MSC, Aug. 3, 1962.

[11] "Weekly Activities Report for the Director of Manned Space Flight," MSC, Aug. 11, 1962; "Weekly Activities Report for the Director of Manned Space Flight," MSC, Sept. 1, 1962; Kenneth J. Vogel, interview, Houston, May 6, 1965; Fred T. Pearce, interview, Houston, Feb. 12, 1964.

[12] "Postlaunch Memorandum Report for Mercury-Atlas No. 7 (MA–7)," NASA/MSC, June 15, 1962; "Postlaunch Memorandum Report for Mercury-Atlas No. 8 (MA–8)."

[13] Ibid.; "Project Mercury Quarterly Status Report No. 15 for Period Ending July 31, 1962," NASA/MSC.

[14] "Postlaunch Memorandum Report for MA–8," Part I.

[15] "Minutes of the Senior Staff Meeting," MSC, July 13, 20, Aug. 3, 1962.

[16] Astronautical and Aeronautical Events of 1962, 158; "Project Mercury Quarterly Status Report No. 16 for Period Ending October 31, 1962," NASA/MSC; "Minutes of the Senior Staff Meeting," MSC, Aug. 31, 1962.

[17] "Activity Report," MSC Preflight Operations Div., July 27, 1962; James M. Grimwood, Project Mercury: A Chronology, NASA SP–4001 (Washington, 1963), 214; "Minutes of the Senior Staff Meeting," MSC, Aug. 17, 1962; "Project Mercury Minutes of Meeting of Mercury Atlas Launch Operations Committee," NASA/MSC, Sept. 6, 1962; "Minutes of the Senior Staff Meeting," MSC, Sept. 28, 1962. J. F. Wambolt on July 26, 1962, prepared a "Missile 113–D History" that provides excellent details on the steps taken to man-rate a missile into a Mercury launch vehicle.

[18] Letter, Maj. Gen. Leighton I. Davis, Hq., Air Force Missile Test Center, to Secretary of Defense Robert S. McNamara, "Status of DOD Support of Project Mercury for July 1962," with enclosure, Aug. 13, 1962; memo, North to Management Analysis Div., "Weekly Activity Report, Flight Crew Operations Division," July 2, 1962.

[19] DOD Representative for Project Mercury Support Operations, Final Report to the Secretary of Defense on Department of Defense Support of Project Mercury: For the Period 1 July 1959 through 13 June 1963, approved by Leighton I. Davis, Maj. Gen., USAF, 11 Sept. 1963, 15, 28; "Status Report

No. 15"; "Status Report No. 16"; memo, Christopher C. Kraft, Jr. [to Management Analysis Div.], "Activities Report, Flight Operations Division," Aug. 27, 1962; "Minutes of the Senior Staff Meeting," July 27 and Aug. 10, 1962; Department of Defense press kit for MA–8.

[20] Final Report to the Secretary of Defense, 28; letter, Davis to McNamara, "Postlaunch Memorandum Report for MA–8."

[21] Text, "Address by President John F. Kennedy," Rice University Stadium, Sept. 12, 1962.

[22] "Astronaut's Flight Report," in "Postlaunch Memorandum Report for MA–8," Part I, 7–49.

[23] Robert Young, "Squalls Give Schirra Orbit 50–50 Chance," Chicago Tribune, Oct. 2, 1962; "Schirra Ready for Countdown," Washington Post, Oct. 3, 1962; NASA News Release, "MA–8 Advisory," 5 p.m., Oct. 2, 1962.

[24] "Postlaunch Memorandum Report for MA–8," Part I; Alvin B. Webb, United Press International, "Hangar S Pool Copy," Oct. 3, 1962. Also see "High Dreams for a Man and His Son," Life, LII (June 8, 1962).

[25] The description and all quotations in the following account of the MA–8 flight are taken directly from the extensive "Postlaunch Memorandum Report for Mercury-Atlas No. 8 (MA–8): Part I, Mission Analysis; Part II, Data; Part III, Air-Ground Voice and Debriefing," MSC, Oct. 23, 1962.

[26] Results of the Third United States Manned Orbital Space Flight October 3, 1962, NASA SP–12 (Washington, 1962), 49. The contents of the ditty bag included a camera, two film magazines, an exposure meter, a camera strap, a photometer, a dosimeter, food containers, and an emergency container for motion sickness. See also Grimwood, Mercury Chronology, 172.

[27] "Flight Operations Debriefing of MA–8 Mission [aboard the carrier Kearsarge]," MSC, transcribed Oct. 23, 1962. Like Glenn and Carpenter before him, Schirra said he definitely sensed deceleration at BECO. On the other hand, he did not sense the acceleration tailoff that they had reported when the sustainer engine died. Max-q proved to be considerably noisier than Schirra had been led to expect. During the launch phase he heard many audible clues telling him what was taking place. These he described onomatopoeically, speaking of the jettisoning tower as "a rocket zapping off," of the clamp ring's release of the

spacecraft with a "pung" sound, and of the posigrades' separating spacecraft from booster with a noise that sounded like "khuee."

[28] Fuel usage for the turnaround was only about a tenth of the amount required in previous flights.

[29] For the public dialogue, see "Postlaunch Memorandum Report for MA-8," Part III, Air-Ground Voice and Debriefing, 2–129, 2–130.

[30] Cf. "Postlaunch Memorandum Report for Mercury-Atlas No. 8 (MA-8)," Part I, 7–1–49; Part III. pp. 3–1–18; and "Flight Operations Debriefing of MA-8 Mission," 1–38. See also *Results of the Third United States Manned Orbital Flight*; and messages filed by news pool aboard the *Kearsarge*, Oct. 3, 1962. The fact that Schirra had landed so close to the carrier prompted the engineer who had calculated the retrofiring so precisely to quip that "the carrier must have been 4.5 miles off course."

[31] Notes, John Barbour, Associated Press, "Mercury Control Center Postflight News Conference," Oct. 3, 1962.

[32] "Schirra Flying to Houston after 3-Hour Honolulu Visit," Washington *Evening Star*, Oct. 7, 1962; "MA-8 Press Conference, Houston, Texas," transcript, Oct. 7, 1962; *New York Herald Tribune*, Oct. 9, 1962. Also see John Dille, "At the End of a Great Flight, Big Bull's-Eye," *Life*, LIII (Oct. 12, 1962); and "Bull's Eye from a Front-Row Seat," *Life*, LIII (Oct. 26, 1962); and the special issue of *Newsweek*, LX (Oct. 8, 1962), "The Space Age," passim.

[33] James M. Grimwood, who came to work for STG/MSC in August 1962, remembers clearly this contrast in attitudes.

[34] Letter, A. H. Smith, McDonnell Aircraft Corp., to NASA Procurement and Supply Office, "Mercury Capsule Contract NAS 5–59, Contract Change Proposal No. 340, Eighteen-Orbit Mark I Spacecraft," Sept. 29, 1961; "Project Development Plan for Research Development Utilizing the Mark II Manned Spacecraft," MSC, Langley Air Force Base, Va., Dec. 8, 1961; "Operational Plan for 18-Orbit Manned Mission," STG, Oct. 5, 1961.

[35] On "newspeak," cf. "Project Mercury Status Report No. 12 for Period Ending Jan. 31, 1962," STG. On reorganization, see Grimwood, *Mercury Chronology*, 152, 219; and *NASA Sixth Semiannual Report to Congress, July 1 through December 21, 1961* (Washington, 1962), 137, 139. On the state of the art of physiological research before

MA-9, see J. C. Simons and W. N. Kama, "A Review of the Effects of Weightlessness on Selected Human Motions and Sensations," AMRL memorandum P-36, Wright-Patterson Air Force Base, Ohio, May 1963; James P. Henry, "Physiological and Performance Aspects of Weightlessness," MSC fact sheet No. 73, 1962.

[36] For 1961 feasibility studies, see "Mercury Spacecraft Advanced Versions," AD 61, 224B, control No. C-57978, McDonnell Aircraft Corp., 1961; NASA briefing charts, undated, A-28358, Ames Research Center, 1–31. For MODM evolution, see Robert T. Everline, Edward B. Hamblett, Jr., and William R. Humphrey, "Preliminary Mercury 18-Orbit Spacecraft Information Document," MSC memorandum report, Jan. 11, 1962; Lewis R. Fisher, "Mercury 18-Orbit Information Document (Minimum Weight Spacecraft)," MSC memo report, Jan. 19, 1962. For the basic specification for MODM, see Everline et al., "Manned One-Day Mission Mercury Spacecraft Specification Document," NASA Project Mercury working paper No. 223, April 23, 1962. On concurrent progress with Gemini, see *Astronautical and Aeronautical Events of 1962*, 43, 199.

[37] "Project Mercury Quarterly Status Report No. 16," 1; "Minutes of the Senior Staff Meeting," MSC, Nov. 9, 1962. MSC learned of NASA's formal approval of a 22-orbit flight five weeks later. "Minutes of the Senior Staff Meeting," MSC, Dec. 14, 1962. Orbit 21 would duplicate orbit 6, but MSC decided on 22 orbits to optimize the recovery location near Midway Island again and the margins for error in spacecraft systems and supplies.

[38] Letter, J. Y. Brown, McDonnell Aircraft Corp., to NASA/MSC Mercury Procurement Office, with enclosure, "Financial Status Summary, Mercury One-Day Mission Contract NAS 5–59," Oct. 11, 1962. The major mission-planning meeting for MA-9 was held at Patrick Air Force Base on Dec. 3 and 4, 1962. See Davis, "Minutes of Pre-Operational Conference for Project Mercury One-Day Mission (MA-9)," Dec. 18, 1962.

[39] Mss. for Project Mercury Tech. Hist. Program, Robert B. Merrifield, "Organization," July 1963, Part I, B, 14; and Marvin F. Matthews, "Patents," Oct. 22, 1963, Part I, H. See also Grimwood, *Mercury Chronology*, 178. Two of the "Mercury inventors" were no longer with MSC: Alan B. Kehlet had left government service to work on Apollo for North American Aviation, and Willard S. Blanchard had remained at Langley, saying

FOOTNOTES

"It was hot enough for me right here." Kehlet, interview, Downey, Calif., Aug. 27, 1964; Blanchard, interview, Langley Field, Va., Jan. 6, 1964. Problems in the sociology of invention, particularly that of simultaneity in discovery or innovation, were compounded many times by the teamwork developmental approach in Mercury. Simplistic views of these matters were embodied in the Mercury capsule contract as well as in certain NASA presentations to Congress which tended to become policy. Some indication of the extent to which credit for innovations ought to be diffused may be gained from the letter, Glenn F. Bailey to J. M. Carson, Jr., "Contract NAS 5-59 Inventions," Sept. 8, 1961.

[40] Jocelyn R. Gill, interview, Houston, Oct. 11, 1965; letter, Gill to members of POISE, Jan. 7, 1963. For a critique of Mercury experimental planning, see letter, Edward P. Ney, Professor of Physics, University of Minnesota, to Gill, Aug. 27, 1962.

[41] "Minutes of the Senior Staff Meeting," MSC, Jan. 4, 1963; "Mercury/Atlas (MA-9) Launch Information and Notebook," General Dynamics/Astronautics, San Diego, undated; C. L. Gandy, Jr., and I. B. Hanson, "Mercury-Atlas Launch Vehicle Development and Performance," in *Mercury Project Summary Including Results of the Fourth Manned Orbital Flight May 15 and 16, 1963*, SP-45 (Washington, 1963), 102.

[42] "Gordon Cooper Press Conference," transcript, MSC, Feb. 8, 1963, 1, 3, 11; Charles M. Vaughn, "Differences Between Spacecraft 16 (MA-8) and Spacecraft 20 (MA-9) as of January 11, 1963," McDonnell Aircraft Corp. Cooper himself had been fully briefed on the MA-9 experiments only four days earlier. See memo, Vaughn to Mercury Project Office, "Minutes . . . of the Mercury Experiments Briefing, MA-9/20," Feb. 13, 1963.

[43] "Manned One-Day Mission—Mission Directive for Mercury/Atlas Mission 9 (MA-9) (Spacecraft No. 20—Atlas 130-D)," NASA Project Mercury working paper No. 232, Feb. 12, 1963, rev. April 25, 1963; Boynton, Edison M. Fields, and Donald F. Hughes, "Spacecraft Systems Development and Performance," in *Mercury Project Summary*, 52. For daily diaries of the technical modifications to each MODM spacecraft at the Cape, see Wilbur Allaback's series of weekly reports to Vogel, of MSC Atlantic Missile Range Engineering Operations, Oct. 1962 to May 1963. For an interesting sidelight on the ECS instrumentation, see William H. Bush, Jr., "CO_2 Partial Pressure Measuring System Development," for Mercury Technical History Program, July 23, 1963.

[44] Norman B. Foster, collected documents for Mercury Technical History, "Experiments" folder, Part III, F, May 27, 1963, passim; and Gill interview.

[45] See "Consolidated Activity Report for the Director of Manned Space Flight," MSC, Feb. 23, 1963; Grimwood, *Mercury Chronology*, 158, 167, 180, 183; Ms., Karl F. Greil for Project Mercury Technical History Program, "History of Reaction Control System," July 1963, 12-27; Joe W. Dodson, interview, Houston, March 2, 1965. See also Minutes, "Inflight Scientific Experiments Coordination Panel," Robert B. Voas, secretary, Dec. 17, 1962; Jan. 29, Feb. 25, and March 26, 1963.

[46] "Proceedings of the Mercury-Atlas Booster Reliability Workshop," San Diego, July 12, 1963, 1-56; News release, "Important Mercury-Atlas Refinements," Aerospace Corp., May 6, 1963; "MODM Project Quarterly Status Report No. 18 for Period Ending April 30, 1963," MSC.

[47] "Flight Plan for MA-9/20," March 4, 1963, Rev. A, April 15, 1963; Rev. B, May 10, 1963; "Preparation and Activities Plan for MA-9—Postlaunch Memorandum Report," April 1963; "Public Information Directive," NASA, May 1963; "MA-9 Experiments," SEDR 236, McDonnell Aircraft Corp., April 1, 1963; *Final Report to the Secretary of Defense*, 37, 70, 75. Cf. William K. Douglas, comments, Aug. 17, 1965.

[48] See Philip H. Abelson's editorials in *Science*, CXXXIX (Feb. 1, 1963) and CXL (April 19, 1963). See also John W. Finney, "Astronauts' Camera to Provide TV View of Earth from Space," *New York Times*, April 2, 1963; Howard Simons, "Webb Defends U.S. Men-on-Moon Plan," *Washington Post*, April 21, 1963; Joseph Kraft, "Professors 'Boycott' of Space," Washington *Evening Star*, May 10, 1963; Senate Committee on Aeronautical and Space Sciences, 88 Cong., 1 sess., *Scientists' Testimony on Space Goals*, June 10 and 11, 1963, passim.

[49] "Atlas Repair May Delay Cooper's 22-Orbit Flight," *Washington Post*, April 19, 1963. A Navy physician and NASA official, Frank B. Voris, gave the usual preflight warning for the record: "We can't guarantee 100 percent success, and eventually the odds will catch up with us." Quoted in Allen J. Morrison, "NASA Official Warns of Inevitable Space Tragedy," *Salem* (Oreg.) *Statesman*, April 25, 1963.

[50] The new contingent of astronauts introduced in a televised press conference on Sept. 17, 1962, were assigned specialty areas on Jan. 26, 1963, as follows: Neil A. Armstrong, trainers; Frank Borman, boosters; Charles Conrad, Jr., cockpit; James A. Lovell, Jr., recovery; James A. McDivitt, guidance; Elliot M. See, Jr., electronics; Thomas P. Stafford, communications; Edward H. White II, flight controls; and John W. Young, environmental control. For more details on other allusions in this paragraph, see *Astronautics and Aeronautics, 1963: Chronology on Science, Technology, and Policy*, NASA SP–4004 (Washington, 1964), 28, 69, 184, 190, 192.

[51] Quoted in William Hines, "Cooper to be Out of Contact for Most of 22-Orbit Flight," Washington *Sunday Star*, May 12, 1963. "3-Day Mercury Flight Considered by NASA," *Washington Post*, April 4, 1963. An historical novel based on the plot of what might have happened to MA–10 was written by Martin Caidin, dedicated to Tom Heinsheimer, and published by E. P. Dutton and Co., Inc., in February 1964 under the title *Marooned*. Much authentic flavor of Mercury flight operations may be gleaned from this fictional drama.

[52] See "Astronaut Insured for $100,000," *New York Herald Tribune*, May 9, 1963; S. Oliver Goodman, "Aetna Writes First Astronaut Policies," *Washington Post*, May 9, 1963; "DeOrsey Has Son Write Astronauts' Insurance," Washington *Evening Star*, May 13, 1963; "Cooper Prepares for 22-Orbit Trip," *New York Times*, May 10, 1963; Howard Simons, "Cooper Ready to Take Off; Weather Remains Problem," *Washington Post*, May 14, 1963. Simons also published in the *Post* an excellent series of three articles analyzing the late debate over manned space flight: "Moon Madness? Scientists Divided on Apollo," May 12; "Scientists Now on Sidelines Discontented with Project," May 13; "President Backs Lunar Race Opposed by Some Scientists," May 14, 1963.

[53] Richard Witkin, "Astronaut Flight is Set for Today," *New York Times*, May 15, 1963; Earl Ubell, "The Long and Tense Wait for Astronaut Cooper," *New York Herald Tribune*, May 15, 1963.

[54] Marvin Miles, "Cooper Well on Way to 22 Orbits," *Los Angeles Times*, May 16, 1963; Simons, "Launching Definitely Scheduled: Cooper Set for Another Try," *Washington Post*, May 15, 1963; Hines, "Atlas Boosts Faith-7 Flight As Planned," Washington *Evening Star*, May 15, 1963.

[55] The description and all quotations in the following account of the MA–9 flight are taken directly from the elaborate "Postlaunch Memorandum Report for Mercury-Atlas No. 9 (MA–9): Part I, Mission Analysis; Part II, Data; Part III, Mission Transcripts," MSC, June 24, 1963. For color parallel to the voice transcript, the unedited Mercury Control transcript of John A. Powers' broadcast commentary, "MA–9 Transcript," May 15, 1963, has been followed.

[56] The text of the prayer (taped at time 21:49:38) is as follows:

"I would like to take this time to say a little prayer for all the people, including myself, involved in this launch and this operation. Father, thank You for the success we have had flying this flight. Thank You for the privilege of being able to be in this position, to be up in this wondrous place, seeing all these many startling, wondrous things that You've created. Help guide and direct all of us, that we may shape our lives to be good, that we may be much better Christians, learn to help one another, to work with one another, rather than to fight. Help us to complete this mission successfully. Help us in our future space endeavors, that we may show the world that a democracy really can compete, and still are able to do things in a big way, are able to do research, development, and can conduct various scientific, very technical programs in a completely peaceful environment. Be with all our families. Give them guidance and encouragement, and let them know that everything will be okay. We ask in Thy name. Amen."

[57] See L. Gordon Cooper, Jr., "Everyone Was in a Sweat, I Was Secretly Pleased," *Life*, LIV (June 7, 1963); see also other contract articles: "His Mission Is the Longest U.S. Orbit," *Life*, LIV (May 17, 1963); "He Brings It Right in on the Old Gazoo," *Life*, LIV (May 24, 1963); and "Gordo Gets a Great Hello from the Kids and Kin," *Life*, LIV (May 31, 1963).

[58] "Status Report on Postlaunch Evaluation of Mercury-Atlas Mission No. 9," MSC, May 28, 1963. Quotations are from "MA–9 Press Conference," transcript, May 19, 1963, 7a, 10, 10b.

[59] "MA–9 Scientific Debriefing," transcript, June 26, 1963, 47. Cf. 15. On the skepticism regarding Cooper's vision, see *Aviation Week*, LXXIX (June 17, 1963), 34; (July 1, 1963), 31; and (July 15, 1963), 98. For one of the more important comparative studies of the

astronautical experiences of Glenn, Carpenter, Schirra, and Cooper, see A. Goldberg, L. Hromes, C. E. McLain, and J. Menkes, compilers, "Observations of the Near Wake Reentry Phenomena by the Mercury Astronauts," ARPA TN–64–2, Feb. 1965.

[50] J. C. Jackson, "Manned Space Flight Network Performance Analysis for MA–9," Goddard Space Flight Center publication X–551–63–108, Greenbelt, Md., June 6, 1963, 44. For other details on the results of the fourth manned orbital flight, see *Mercury Project Summary*, 231, 242, and passim.

[61] Webb, interview, Washington, Sept. 3, 1965; Seamans, interview, Washington, Sept. 1, 1965; Senate Committee on Aeronautical and Space Sciences, 88 Cong., 1 sess. (1963), *NASA Authorization for Fiscal Year 1964, Hearings,* Part 2, 772. See also *Scientists' Testimony on Space Goals;* and "Mercury Flights Off, Gemini Comes Next: Astronauts Overruled by NASA," *Houston Chronicle,* June 12, 1963.

Epilogue

[1] McDonnell Aircraft Corp., *NASA Project Gemini Familiarization Manual* (preliminary), SEDR 300, June 1, 1962, passim. See also Ralph O. Shankle, *The Twins of Space* (Philadelphia, 1964) ; and Charles W. Mathews, "Project Gemini—Status and Plans," paper, 25th annual Aerospace Writers' Assn. Convention, Dallas, Tex., May 24, 1963.

[2] E.g., North American Aviation, Inc., *The Apollo Spacecraft,* Space and Information Systems Division, May 15, 1964; NASA Project Apollo working paper No. 1015, *Project Apollo: Space Task Group Study Report,* February 15, 1961, edited by H. Kurt Strass; NASA MSC fact sheet No. 292, "Apollo Program," June 1965; Walter Sullivan, ed., *America's Race for the Moon: The New York Times Story of Project Apollo* (New York, 1962).

[3] Robert C. Seamans, Jr., Hugh L. Dryden, and James E. Webb, interviews, Washington, D.C., Aug. 31, Sept. 3, 1965.

[4] See *Astronautics and Aeronautics, 1963: Chronology on Science, Technology, and Policy,* NASA SP–4004 (Washington, 1964), 241, 244, 376, 417, 505, 506; and *Astronautics and Aeronautics, 1964: Chronology on Science, Technology, and Policy,* NASA SP–4005 (Washington, 1965), 209, 248.

[5] *Ibid.,* 348, 458; Oscar Theodore Barck, Jr., and Nelson Manfred Blake, *Since 1900: A History of the United States in Our Times*

(4th ed., New York, 1965), 877; NASA Office of Educational Programs and Services, pamphlet, "Gemini 4 Extravehicular Activity: A Walk in Space," July 1965.

[6] *Mercury Project Summary, Including Results of the Fourth Manned Orbital Flight, May 15 and 16, 1963,* NASA SP–45 (Washington, 1963).

[7] *Ibid.,* 247–249, part of the paper by J. C. Moser, G. M. Preston, J. J. Williams, and A. E. Morse, Jr.

[8] *Ibid.,* 248. For a similar discussion of quality control for the launch vehicle, see "Manufacturing and Process Controls" in *Proceedings of the Mercury-Atlas Booster Reliability Workshops,* General Dynamics/Astronautics, San Diego, July 12, 1963, 1–56.

[9] See House Committee on Science and Astronautics, 88 Cong., 1 sess. (1963), *Briefing on NASA Reorganization: Project Mercury Summary,* 18–36. See also John W. Finney, "Contractors Cited for an Average of 10 Failures on Each Space Trip," *New York Times,* Oct. 4, 1963; and Edwin Diamond, *The Rise and Fall of the Space Age* (Garden City, N.Y., 1964), 32–46.

[10] Warren Burkett, "NASA Brass Pays Tribute to Industry," *Houston Chronicle,* Oct. 4, 1963; and *New York Times, Washington Post,* and Washington *Evening Star,* Oct. 5, 1963.

[11] See William M. Bland, Jr., and Lewis R. Fisher, "Project Mercury Experience," paper, Aerospace Writers' Assn., Dallas, May 24, 1963; Walter C. Williams, "The Mercury Textbook," paper, American Institute of Aeronautics and Astronautics, Los Angeles, June 17, 1963, MSC fact sheet No. 197; Christopher C. Kraft, Jr., "A Review of Knowledge Acquired from the First Manned Satellite Program," MSC fact sheet No. 206; and Wesley L. Hjornevik, "NASA Programs and Their Management," paper, Harvard Business School Club of Houston, Jan. 28, 1964, MSC fact sheet No. 235.

[12] See *Mercury Project Summary,* 24–26; cf. MSC, "Briefing Materials," prepared for Dr. Robert C. Seamans and Dr. George E. Mueller, Sept. 20–21, 1963 (2 vols., conf.).

[13] *Ibid.,* See also Senate Committee on Aeronautical and Space Sciences, 87 Cong., 2 sess. (1962), Staff Report, *Manned Space Flight Program of the National Aeronautics and Space Administration: Project Mercury, Gemini, and Apollo,* 7.

[14] "Briefing Materials"; Bland and Fisher, and Hjornevik papers.

[15] Fact sheet No. 206, 9. Cf. Robert B. Voas, "The Case History of a Spacecraft (Mercury Project)," MSC fact sheet No. 117, Feb. 5, 1963.

[16] For a few intimations of these questions, see "Our Gamble in Space," special issue of *The Atlantic*, CCXII (August 1963); Lewis Mumford, "Authoritarian and Democratic Technics," *Technology and Culture*, V (Winter 1964), 1–8; Melvin Kranzberg, "The Inner Challenge of Outer Space," paper, University of Houston Lecture-Artist Series, March 3, 1965.

[17] See Alvin M. Weinberg, quoted in James L. Penick, et al., eds., *The Politics of American Science: 1939 to the Present* (Chicago, 1965), 221. See also Weinberg, "Criteria for Scientific Choice," *Minerva* (Winter, 1963), 159–171.

[18] See, for example, Joseph Wood Krutch, "Why I Am Not Going to the Moon," *Saturday Review*, XLVIII (Nov. 20, 1965), 29–31; and Philip H. Abelson, *Saturday Review*, idem.

[19] Hugh L. Dryden, "The Nation's Manned Space Flight," address, Governor's Conference on Oceanography and Astronautics, Kauai, Hawaii, Oct. 1, 1965, 3–4.

Note on Sources
and
Selected Bibliography

LATE IN 1962 AND EARLY IN 1963, while Project Mercury was phasing into the Manned One-Day Mission and evolving also toward Projects Gemini and Apollo, the managers of Mercury conceived the need for a monumental technical history to preserve the engineering "experience gained through the development of the Mercury spacecraft, its systems and components." The Director of the Manned Spacecraft Center, Robert R. Gilruth, expressed the hope that an elaborate, topically organized record in 10 or 12 volumes might "provide a ready reference and guide for present and future MSC space programs and to that end [should] increase the economy and effectiveness of MSC operations." Established in February 1963 as the Project Mercury Technical History Program (PMTHP), this effort produced about 40 retrospective manuscripts prepared by participants in Project Mercury. Although more than 130 authors were assigned sections to prepare and only one third of these ever completed their first drafts before reassignment, these manuscripts, located in the archives of the MSC Historian, furnished much of the basis for this technological history of Mercury.

Concurrently in 1963, Eugene M. Emme, the NASA Historian, was prompting the preservation and collection of documentary materials and encouraging all NASA centers and especially the Mercury Project Office of MSC to proceed with the writing of the historical accounts of the technological, managerial, and administrative development of NASA's major programs. Documentary archives for manned space flight, therefore, began first in Washington and then in Houston while Mercury was still alive. The papers and correspondence of Robert R. Gilruth, George M. Low, Paul E. Purser, John A. Powers, and the astronauts' files constitute the bulk of the material presently contained in these two essentially duplicated archives, but innumerable smaller collections on specific technical and operational matters complement and amplify their usefulness.

In May 1963 a contract was arranged between the Manned Spacecraft Center and the University of Houston to provide for professional help to assimilate and synthesize the massive documentary remains from Mercury in several forms suitable for wide distribution as historical literature. The two academic authors of this volume began full-time work immediately after the termination of Mercury, helping the MSC Historian to complete his *Project Mercury: A Chronology,* NASA SP–4001 (Washington, 1963). Shortly thereafter, an abbreviated and considerably sterilized "PMTHP" was published in one volume as *Mercury Project Summary: Including Results of the Fourth Manned Orbital Flight, May 15 and 16, 1963,* NASA SP–45 (Washington, 1963). These two works are basic reference tools; they are essential to, but not representative of, historical handicraft.

The authors studied Congressional documents; periodicals; secondary literature on space science, technology, and public policy; unclassified governmental, industrial, and military reports; and the artifacts, including audio tapes and photographic records of the program. To orient themselves, they watched sequentially a major portion of more than one million feet of motion picture film, which preserved virtually every significant event and flight operation in Project Mercury.

To maintain some historiographical balance, they sought to subject the widest variety of documents to external (or contextual) and internal scrutiny. Competitive industrial and governmental claims to priorities were weighed. Wherever possible the people who made up the Mercury team were interviewed and each location of Mercury activities visited. Finally the authors concluded that research could proceed most profitably by writing. Concurrent writing and research went on for more than a year, before a "comment edition" was distributed to some 200 critical readers, most of whom found time to offer indispensable suggestions for its improvement.

Footnote readers will have noticed the somewhat different documentary bases of the three parts of this work. Part One rests largely on open (but little used for historical purposes) channels of scientific communication. Part Two is hewn out of a jungle of unpublished technical letters, messages, memoranda, telecon notes, informal reports, and working papers. Part Three is based progressively more on official project documentation, which had improved considerably by that relatively late date.

Unless otherwise specified, all these materials, in original or facsimile form, have been gathered together in the MSC archives. Very few items among those cited in the footnotes are still classified; the vast majority are no longer sensitive and may be examined by students of the early history of manned space flight.

More than 200 personal interviews, 134 Project Mercury working papers, and most of the 4500 typical control and report documents listed in Appendix A of the *Mercury Project Summary* have served as the foundation for this history. The superstructure, however, is selective, as the bibliographical listing also must be. There are many other true tales that need to be placed in survivable form about the technology, administration, public relations, and human side of Project Mercury and the men who worked its wonders. But we authors hope that *This New Ocean* will map the temporal shoreline from which the United States of America cast off on its voyage into space.

606

Persons Interviewed*

1. Aldrich, Arnold D.
2. Algranti, Joseph S.
3. Allaback, Wilbur
4. Allen, H. Julian
5. Armstrong, Stephen A.
6. Atcheson, Kenneth L.
7. Bailey, F. John, Jr.
8. Bailey, Glenn F.
9. Battey, Robert V.
10. Berry, Charles A.
11. Billingham, John
12. Bingman, Charles F.
13. Blanchard, Willard S., Jr.
14. Bland, William M., Jr.
15. Bond, Aleck C.
16. Bost, James E.
17. Bothmer, Clyde B.
18. Boyer, William J.
19. Boynton, John H.
20. Briggs, Thomas
21. Brown, B. Porter
22. Burke, Walter F.
23. Butler, Earl
24. Byrnes, Martin A., Jr.
25. Callanan, R. J.
26. Campagna, I. Edward
27. Canning, Thomas N.
28. Canter, Louis
29. Carley, Richard R.
30. Carpenter, M. Scott
31. Catterson, A. Duane
32. Chamberlin, James A.
33. Chambers, Thomas V.
34. Chauvin, Leo T.
35. Chilton, Robert G.
36. Chop, Albert M.
37. Clements, Henry E.
38. Colchagoff, George
39. Coler, Charles
40. Coston, Charles L.
41. Critzos, O. Constance
42. Day, Richard E.
43. Dembling, Paul C.
44. DeVore, Phoncille
45. Dietlein, Lawrence F.
46. Disher, John H.
47. Dodson, Joe W.
48. Donegan, James J., Jr.
49. Donlan, Charles J.
50. Dryden, Hugh L.
51. Dubusker, William
52. Dunham, Richard M.
53. Eppley, Charles V.
54. Erb, R. Bryan
55. Ertel, Ivan
56. Everline, Robert T.
57. Faget, Maxime A.
58. Fields, Edison M.
59. Fineg, Jerry
60. Fisher, Lewis R.
61. Flesh, E. M.
62. Foster, Norman G.
63. Freitag, Robert
64. French, John C.
65. Frutkin, Arnold W.
66. Garland, Benjamine J.
67. Gates, Sally D.
68. Gibbons, Howard I.
69. Gill, Jocelyn R.
70. Gillespie, Ben M.
71. Gilruth, Robert R.
72. Glenn, John H., Jr.
73. Glennan, T. Keith
74. Goldenbaum, David M.
75. Golovin, Nicholas E.
76. Graves, G. Barry

* All are cited in text or footnotes.

77. Gregory, Don T.
78. Gregory, E. M.
79. Grissom, Virgil I.
80. Guice, Mildred L.
81. Hammack, Jerome B.
82. Haney, Paul P.
83. Harris, Gordon
84. Havenstein, Paul L.
85. Heberlig, Jack C.
86. Hicks, Claiborne R., Jr.
87. Hjornevik, Wesley L.
88. Hodge, John D.
89. Hoffman, Sherwood
90. Hohmann, Bernard A.
91. Holmes, Jay
92. Hopko, Russell N.
93. Horsman, Paul F.
94. Hughes, Donald F.
95. Huss, Carl R.
96. Jackson, Bruce G.
97. Johnson, Caldwell C.
98. Johnson, Harold I.
99. Johnson, W. Kemble
100. Jones, Edward R.
101. Keehn, R. W.
102. Kehlet, Alan B.
103. Killmer, George F., Jr.
104. Kleinknecht, Kenneth S.
105. Knauf, George M.
106. Koons, Wayne E.
107. Kraft, Christopher C., Jr.
108. Kuettner, Joachim P.
109. Kyle, Howard C.
110. Lauten, William T., Jr.
111. Lee, John B.
112. Lein, Paul
113. Letsch, Ernst R.
114. Lewis, James L.
115. Link, Mae M.
116. Lord, Douglas R.
117. Low, George M.
118. Lowe, Nancy
119. MacDougall, George F., Jr.

120. MacMillan, Logan T.
121. Manley, Lynn
122. Mardel, A. D.
123. Mathews, Charles W.
124. Mattson, Axel T.
125. Mayer, John P.
126. Maynard, Owen E.
127. McBarron, James W., II
128. McKann, Robert E.
129. McLeaish, John E.
130. McMillion, Lee W.
131. Mercer, Robert D.
132. Meson, John K.
133. Meyer, Andre J., Jr.
134. Miller, Robert R.
135. Minners, Howard A.
136. Morgan, Frank
137. Moseley, W. C., Jr.
138. Muhley, William C.
139. Nagy, Alex P.
140. Niven, John
141. North, Warren J.
142. Oakley, R. B.
143. Olling, Edward H.
144. Ould, J. Wallace
145. Patterson, Herbert G.
146. Pearce, Fred T.
147. Pearson, Albin O.
148. Pepping, Raymond A.
149. Perkins, Kendall
150. Pesman, Gerard J.
151. Peterson, John J.
152. Petynia, William W.
153. Piland, Joseph V.
154. Piland, Robert O.
155. Plohr, H. Warren
156. Powers, John A.
157. Preston, G. Merritt
158. Purser, Paul E.
159. Putnam, William
160. Rashis, Bernard
161. Reitter, L. M.
162. Rhode, Richard V.

163. Ritland, Osmond J.
164. Roberts, Tecwyn
165. Rose, James T.
166. Rose, Rodney G.
167. Rosholt, Robert
168. Samonski, Frank H., Jr.
169. Sandahl, Carl A.
170. Sanderson, Alan H.
171. Seamans, Robert C., Jr.
172. Seat, Robert L.
173. Seiff, Alvin
174. Shankle, Ralph O.
175. Sheldon, Charles S., II
176. Shepard, Alan B., Jr.
177. Shortal, Joseph
178. Siesal, Henry S.
179. Silverstein, Abe
180. Simons, David G.
181. Simpkinson, Scott H.
182. Sjoberg, Sigurd A.
183. Skinner, Francis J.
184. Slayton, Donald K.
185. Soulé, Hartley A.
186. Stapp, John P.
187. Stonesifer, John C.
188. Stoney, William E.

189. Strughold, Hubertus
190. Stuhlinger, Ernst
191. Stullken, D. E.
192. Syverston, C. A.
193. Taylor, Maggie S.
194. Thompson, Robert F.
195. Transue, J. R.
196. Tsitsera, Voula
197. Useller, James W.
198. Vale, Robert E.
199. Van Bockel, John J.
200. Voas, Robert B.
201. Vogel, Kenneth
202. Wagenknecht, Kurt P.
203. Webb, Dalton
204. Webb, James E.
205. Welsh, Edward C.
206. Wendzel, Frank
207. White, D. R.
208. Williams, Walter C.
209. Witunski, Michael
210. Wood, Clotaire
211. Woodling, C. H.
212. Wyatt, DeMarquis D.
213. Yardley, John F.
214. Zoller, Charles E.

Selected Bibliography

BASIC REPORTS ON PROJECT MERCURY

Air Force Space Systems Division TDR-63-381, Sally Anderson, ed., *Final Report: Mercury/Atlas Launch Vehicle Program* (Inglewood, Calif., Nov. 1963)

Air Force Space Systems Division, General Dynamics/Astronautics, and NASA, *Proceedings of the Mercury-Atlas Booster Reliability Workshop* (San Diego, Calif., July 12, 1963)

American Rocket Society, *Space Flight Report to the Nation*, "The Mercury-Redstone Program," paper by Jerome B. Hammack and Jack C. Heberlig (New York, Oct. 9-15, 1961)

Department of Defense Project Mercury Support Operations, *Final Report to the Secretary of Defense on Department of Defense Support of Project Mercury: For the Period 1 July 1959 through 13 June 1963*, Sept. 11, 1963

Fairchild Publications, Inc., *Manned Spacecraft: Engineering, Design, and Operation*, Paul E. Purser, Maxime A. Faget, and Norman F. Smith, eds. (New York, 1964)

International Business Machines Corporation and Western Electric Company, Inc., *Final Report, Project Mercury*, prepared for NASA, March 1, 1962

NASA, *Project Mercury: A Chronology*, by James M. Grimwood, NASA SP–4001 (Washington, 1963)

NASA, *Results of the Project Mercury Ballistic and Orbital Chimpanzee Flights*, James P. Henry and John D. Mosely, eds., NASA SP–39 (Washington, 1963)

NASA, *Space Medicine in Project Mercury*, by Mae Mills Link, NASA SP–4003 (Washington, 1965)

NASA, *Ninth Semiannual Report to Congress, January 1–June 30, 1963*, "Project Mercury in Review" (Washington, 1964)

NASA, *Mercury Project Summary, Including Results of the Fourth Manned Orbital Flight May 15–16, 1963*, NASA SP–45 (Washington, 1963)

*NASA Manned Spacecraft Center, "Postlaunch Memorandum Report for Mercury-Atlas No. 5 (MA–5)," 1961

*NASA Manned Spacecraft Center, "Postlaunch Memorandum Report for Mercury-Atlas No. 6: Part I, Mission Analysis," 1962

*NASA Manned Spacecraft Center, "Postlaunch Memorandum Report for Mercury-Atlas No. 7 (MA–7), Part I, Mission Analysis," 1962

*NASA Manned Spacecraft Center, "Postlaunch Memorandum Report for Mercury-Atlas No. 8: Part I, Mission Analysis," 1962

*NASA Manned Spacecraft Center, "Postlaunch Memorandum Report for MA–8: Part III, Air-Ground Voice and Debriefing," 1962

*NASA Manned Spacecraft Center, "Postlaunch Memorandum Report for Mercury-Atlas No. 9 (MA–9): Part I, Mission Analysis," 1963

*NASA Manned Spacecraft Center, "Postlaunch Memorandum Report for Mercury-Atlas No. 9 (MA–9): Part II, Data," 1963

*NASA Manned Spacecraft Center, "Postlaunch Memorandum Report for Mercury-Atlas No. 9 (MA–9): Part III, Mission Transcripts," 1963

*NASA Manned Spacecraft Center, "Manned One-Day Mission Quarterly Status Report," numbered 17 and 18, 1962–1963

NASA Marshall Space Flight Center, *Final Report, Mercury-Redstone Project–Launch Operations* by Emil P. Bertram and Richard E. Dutton, MSFC–LOD–62–5 (Cape Canaveral, Fla., May 28, 1962)

NASA Marshall Space Flight Center, Saturn-Apollo Systems Office, *The Mercury-Redstone Project*, R. I. Johnson, et al., eds., TMX–53107 (Huntsville, Ala., June 1964)

*NASA Space Task Group/Manned Spacecraft Center, "Project Mercury Quarterly Status Reports," Nos. 1 through 16, 1959–1962

*NASA Space Task Group, "Postlaunch Memorandum Report for Mercury-Redstone No. 4 (MR–4)," 1961

NASA PROJECT MERCURY WORKING PAPERS

WORKING
PAPER NO.

100 Lunney, Glynn S., "A Study of the Control of Landing Areas for Post Staging Abort Trajectories," August 3, 1959.

101 "Test No. HS–24 [Big Joe] General Information for Recovery Forces," August 14, 1959.

* Flight and status reports not listed as Project Mercury working papers.

WORKING
PAPEF NO.

102 Huss, Carl R., and Lunney, G. S., "Results of Studies Made to Determine Required Retrorocket Capability," September 22, 1959.

103 Hicks, Claiborne R., Jr., and Skopinski, Ted H., "Pre-Stage Abort Studies from the Nominal 105 Nautical Mile Orbital Insertion Trajectory," September 15, 1959.

104 Behuncik, John A., Ferrando, James A., Jr., and Skopinski, T. H., "Preliminary Standard 11-g Type Trajectory—Data for the Early Flights of Mercury-Redstone," September 25, 1959.

105 Graham, John B., Jr., "Recovery Operations for Little Joe Test Number 1-B," February 10, 1960.

106 "Three Degree of Freedom Dynamic Trajectories for 80° and 90° Launch-Pad Abort Conditions with Various Wind Conditions," September 30, 1959.

107 "Preliminary Flight Test Results of the 'Big Joe' Mercury R and D Capsule," October 12, 1959.

108 Hall, John B., Jr., "Qualification Tests on the Big Joe Recovery System," October 27, 1959.

109 Strass, H. Kurt, and Robert, Frank C., "Proposal for a Recoverable Radiation Experiment," November 5, 1959.

110 "Project Mercury Test # HS-24 (XSM-65-10D), Summary of Calculated Preflight Trajectory and Radar Analysis Data," August 31, 1959.

111 Ferrando, J. A., Behuncik, J. A., and Skopinski, T. H., "Mercury-Redstone Separation Distance for Preliminary 11-g Type Trajectory," November 6, 1959.

112 Petynia, William W., and Hasson, Dennis F., "Pretest Report for Off-The-Pad Escape System Qualification Test," March 1, 1960.

113 Hasson, D. F., "Preliminary Study Using Inflatible Spheres for Aerodynamic Stabilization of the Mercury Capsule During Reentry," November 18, 1959.

114 Moseley, William C., Jr., "Summary of the Longitudinal Stability Characteristics of the Little Joe Configurations M=0.05 to M=6.83," December 1, 1959.

115 Windler, Milton L., "Results of Recovery Beacon Test Number 3," December 11, 1959.

116 Skopinski, T. H., Behuncik, J. A., and Ferrando, J. A., Jr., "Mercury-Redstone Abort Study for Preliminary 11-g Type Trajectory," December 15, 1959.

117 Kapryan, Walter J., and Sjoberg, Sigurd A., "Mission Directive for Mercury-Redstone No. 1 [MR-1]," December 15, 1959, Rev. May 20, 1960.

118 Fisher, Lewis R., and Arabian, Donald D., "General Systems Information Document," March 10, 1960.

119 Kyle, Howard C., "Mercury Radio and Command Control System," December 21, 1959.

120 Ferrando, J. A., Behuncik, J. A., and Skopinski, T. H., "Mercury-Redstone Capsule Dispersion Study for Preliminary 11-g Type Trajectory," December 30, 1959.

121 Fisher, L. R., and Chauvin, Leo T., "Mission Document for Little Joe No. 5 (Capsule No. 3)," May 25, 1960.

122 Graham, J. B., Jr., "Recovery Operations for Little Joe Test No. Two," January 18, 1960.

123 Berger, J., "Preliminary Evaluation of Surface Winds at Cape Canaveral," February 19, 1960. [Not released]

124 Moseley, W. C., Jr., "Static Longitudinal Stability Characteristics of the Mercury Capsule Configurations M=0.05 to 20 (Basic Configuration)," March 18, 1960.

125 Windler, M. L., "Results of the Project Mercury HF Recovery Beacon Test No. 1," March 23, 1960.

WORKING
PAPER NO.

126 Henry, J. P., "Status of the Animal Test Program," March 31, 1960. [Not released]

127 "Summary of Mercury-Johnsville Centrifuge Program of August 1959," June 22, 1960.

128 Dunseith, Lynwood, and Lunney, G. S., "Methods and Pertinent Data for Project Mercury Flight Computing Requirements," April 6, 1960. [Superseded by working paper 146]

129 Cheatham, Donald C., and Tynan, Charles I., Jr., "General Information for Launch Site Recovery Forces," March 29, 1960.

130 Smith, Robert P., "Static Longitudinal Stability Characteristics of the Mercury Capsule in Combination with the Mercury-Atlas and Mercury-Redstone Boosters $M = 0.60$ to $M = 3.00$," March 28, 1960.

131 Erb, R. Bryan, "Preliminary Study of Heating Aspects of a Radiation Foil Modification to Extend Mercury Heat-Shield Capability to a Natural Decay Entry," April 8, 1960.

132 Arabian, D. D., and Sjoberg, S. A., "Mercury-Atlas (MA-1) Mission Directive (Capsule No. 4)," April 11, 1960.

133 Rose, James T., and Rose, Rodney G., "Research and Development Flight Test Program Using the Little Joe Booster—Booster Qualification Flight Test (Little Joe No. 6)," April 22, 1960.

134 Enderson, Laurence W., Jr., and Rose, R. G., "Research and Development Flight Test Program Using the Little Joe Booster—Abort at High Dynamic Pressure (Little Joe No. 1A)," July 25, 1960.

135 Rose, J. T., and Rose, R. G., "A Method of Estimating Launch Setting to Correct for the Effects of Wind on the Trajectory of a Little Joe Type Vehicle," April 29, 1960. [See TM-X-492]

136 Brumberg, Paul G., "Special Trajectory Parameters for NASA Mercury Missions," April 22, 1960.

137 Jackson, Bruce G., and Williams, Walter E., "Aerodynamic Results of the Little Joe 1-A Flight," May 16, 1960.

138 Kapryan, W. J., and Sjoberg, S. A., "Mission Directive for Mercury-Redstone Mission No. 2 (Capsule No. 5)," April 16, 1960

139 Jones, Enoch M., "General Discussion of Contingency Recovery," May 17, 1960.

140 Arabian, D. D., Fisher, L. R., Sjoberg, S. A., and Hodge, John D., "Mercury-Atlas (MA-2) Mission Directive (Capsule No. 6)," May 27, 1960. [Supplementary to working paper 118]

141 Ferrando, J. A., Jr., and Skopinski, T. H., "Dispersion Study of Separation Distance after Apogee for Mercury-Redstone Preliminary 11-g Type Trajectory," June 8, 1960.

142 Graham, J. B., Jr., and Hodge, B. Leon, "Test No. MA-1: General Information for Recovery Force," July 8, 1960.

143 Hicks, C. R., Jr., and Hunt, Shirley A., "Information for use in Landing Area Prediction for Mercury-Atlas Mission MA-1 (50-D)," July 13, 1960.

144 Huss, C. R., Allen, Charlie, and Hicks, C. R., Jr., "Summary of Calculated Pre-Flight Trajectory Data for MA-1 (Capsule No. 4, Atlas No. 50-D)," July 25, 1960.

145 Hall, J. B., Jr., "Qualification Tests on the MA-1 Terminal System," July 26, 1960.

146 Dunseith, L. C., Lunney, G. S., and Dalby, James F., "Methods and Pertinent Data for Project Mercury Flight Computing Requirements," July 22, 1960. [Supersedes working paper 128, and was superseded by working paper 191]

147 Lewis, John H., Jr., and Mayo, Alfred P., "A Qualitative Description of the Mercury-Atlas Guidance Equations," October 24, 1960.

148 Morse, Archibald E., Jr., and Kranz, Eugene F., "Mission Directive for Mercury-Redstone Mission No. 3 (Capsule No. 7)," September 6, 1960, Rev. March 20, 1961.

WORKING
PAPER NO.

149 McKann, Robert E., and Sjoberg, S. A., "Mission Directive for Mercury-Atlas No. 3 (Capsule No. 8)," October 18, 1960, Rev. March 31, 1961.

150 Weston, Kenneth C., and Swanson, Joanna E., "A Summary of Wind-Tunnel Heat-Transfer Measurements on the Afterbody of the Project Mercury Capsule Reentry Configuration," August 17, 1960. [See TM–X–495, August 1961, for this report]

151 Wheelwright, Charles D., "Animal Ground Support Facilities," August 17, 1960.

152 Patterson, Herbert G., Ewart, David D., and Hamby, William H., "Determination of Mercury Escape Rocket Thrust Eccentricity from Probability Studies of Miss Distance and Lateral Loads During Pre-Staging Abort from Mercury-Atlas Booster," August 19, 1960.

153 Dodson, Joe W., and Kincaide, William C., "Cleveland Window Abrasion Test," August 18, 1960.

154 Maynard, Owen E., "Reconstruction Investigation of Recovered Components from Mercury-Atlas No. 1 After Mission Failure," August 31, 1960.

155 Windler, M. L., "Evaluation of an S-Band Tracking Beacon as a Recovery Location Aid, Test No. 1," September 26, 1960.

156 Skopinski, T. H., Behuncik, J. A., and Ferrando, J. A., Jr., "Calculated Pre-Flight Trajectory Data for Mercury-Redstone Mission No. 1 (MR–1) (Capsule No. 2)," October 10, 1960.

157 Tynan, C. I., Jr., "Test No. MR–1, General Information for Recovery Forces," October 11, 1960.

158 Henry, J. P., "Status of the Animal Test Program," October 20, 1960.

159 Fields, Edison M., and Bond, Aleck C., "Flight Test Report for Mercury-Atlas Mission No. 1 (Capsule No. 4)," November 4, 1960.

160 Huss, C. R., Hartung, Jack B., Hicks, C. R., Jr., and Allen, C. C., "Summary of Several Short Studies Pertaining to the Retro-Rocket System Capability for the Mercury Mission," November 9, 1960.

161 Johnston, Richard S., "Medical Operation Plan," November 4, 1960.

162 Morris, D. P., Jr., "Medical Recovery Operations," October 10, 1960.

163 Hicks, C. R., Jr., O'Loughlin, John C., Allen, C. C., and Huss, C. R., "Summary of Calculated Pre-Flight Trajectory Data for Mercury-Atlas Mission No. 2 (MA–2) (Capsule No. 6, Atlas No. 67–D)," December 7, 1960.

164 Laughlin, C. Patrick, "Bio-Science Data Plan," December 1, 1960.

165 Morris, D. P., Jr., "Medical Recovery Operations (Animal Flights)," October 10, 1960.

166 Chauvin, L. T., and Fisher, L. R., "Flight Test Report for Little Joe Mission No. 5," December 23, 1960.

167 Skopinski, T. H., Maynard, John W., Jr., and Osgood, C. T., "Wind Influence Coefficients for the Mercury-Redstone Missions," January 6, 1961.

168 Skopinski, T. H., Maynard, J. W., Jr., Behuncik, J. A., and Ferrando, J. A., "Calculated Preflight Trajectory Data for Mercury-Redstone Mission No. 2 (MR–2, Capsule No. 5)," January 19, 1961.

169 Kolenkiewicz, Ronald, and Rose, R. G., "Research and Development Flight Test Program Using the Little Joe Booster-High Altitude Abort (Little Joe No. 2)," April 10, 1961.

170 [Enderson, L. W., and Kapryan, W. J., "Post Launch Report for Mercury-Redstone No. 1A (MR–1A)," ca. January 1961; never published]

171 Jackson, C. B., Dr., "Medical Evaluation Program," January 26, 1961.

172 Hermann, Robert A., "Mission Directive for Simulated Orbital Flight Test Program (Capsule No. 10)," February 15, 1961.

WORKING
PAPER NO.

173   Rose, R. G., and Enderson, L. W., "Research and Development Flight Test Program Using the Little Joe Booster, Abort at High Dynamic Pressure (Little Joe No. 1B)," March 3, 1961.

174   Jackson, C. B., McMillion, L. N., and Johnston, R. S., "Astronaut Preparation and Activities Manual for Mercury-Redstone No. 3," February 6, 1961.

175   Mayo, A. P., and Lewis, J. H., Jr., "Mathematical Procedures for Determination of Capsule Range, Azimuth, Elevation, and Radar Look Angles for Pad-Centered and Earth-Centered Inertial Coordinate System," February 15, 1961.

176   Skopinski, T. H., Behuncik, J. A., and Leatherman, P. S., "Preliminary Probability Study of Mercury-Atlas Post-Stage Separation Velocity and Separation Distance After Retrofiring," March 3, 1961.

177   Fisher, L. R., and Chauvin, L. T., "Mission Directive for Little Joe No. 5A (Capsule No. 14)," March 7, 1961.

178   Maynard, J. W., Skopinski, T. H., and Leatherman, P. S., "Calculated Pre-flight Trajectory Data for Redstone Booster Test (MR–BD)," March 17, 1961.

179   Kuehnel, H. A., "Outline for the Astronaut Acceleration Training Program IV," February 24, 1961.

180   Karakulko, Witalij, "Effects of Propellant and Hardware Temperature on the Starting Response Time of H_2O_2 Reaction Control Thrust Chambers of the Mercury Capsule," March 9, 1961.

181   Llewellyn, John S., Jr., "Heating Characteristics for Three Mercury Exit Models," March 20, 1961.

182   Samonski, F. H., Jr., and Bush, W. H., Jr., "Environmental Control System Test and Astronaut Training Program," March 3, 1961.

183   Chauvin, L. T., and Fisher, L. R., "Mission Directive for Little Joe No. 5B (Capsule No. 14)," April 7, 1961.

184   "Summary of Calculated Preflight Trajectory Data for Mercury-Atlas Mission No. 3 (MA–3) (Capsule No. 8, Atlas No. 100–D)," April 14, 1961.

185   "Calculated Preflight Trajectory Data for Mercury-Redstone Mission No. 3 (MR–3, Capsule No. 7)," April 20, 1961.

186   Ewart, D. D., and Brown, S. W., "Summary of Dynamic Stability Data for the Mercury Capsule and Escape System," March 22, 1961.

187   "Life Systems Aspects of Third Mercury-Aviation Medical Acceleration Laboratory Centrifuge Program," April 20, 1961.

188   Thompson, W. E., and Pesman, G. J., "Preliminary Appraisal of the Project Mercury Acceleration Hazard," May 15, 1961.

189   Kuehnel, H. A., and Glover, Kenneth E., "Program Description and Discussion for the Astronaut Acceleration Training Program III (Mercury-Redstone Mission Training)," May 8, 1961.

190   Maynard, J. W., Jr., Ferrando, J. A., and Leatherman, P. S., "A Probability Study for Determining Escape-Rocket Thrust Eccentricity for the Mercury-Redstone Missions," May 17, 1961.

191   Dalby, J. F., "Methods and Pertinent Data for Project Mercury Flight Computing Requirements," June 1, 1961. [Supersedes working paper 146]

WORKING
PAPER NO.

192 Hammack, J. B., et al., "Post Launch Report for Mercury-Redstone No. 3 (MR-3)," June 16, 1961.

193 Erb, R. B., and Stephens, E. W., "An Analysis of Mercury Heat-Shield Performance During Entry," June 21, 1961.

194 Allen, C. C., and Ferrando, J. A., "Preflight Calculated Tracking Data for the Mercury Network Test Vehicle MNTV-1," June 26, 1961.

195 Fisher, L. R., Chauvin, L. T., and Smith, N. F., "Postlaunch Report for Mercury-Little Joe 5B (LJ-5B)," June 12, 1961.

196 Maynard, J. W., Jr., Behuncik, J. A., and Leatherman, P. S., "Calculated Preflight Trajectory Data for Mercury-Redstone Mission No. 4 (Capsule No. 11)," June 29, 1961.

197 Christopher, Kenneth W., and Kranz, E. F., "Mission Directive for Mercury-Redstone No. 4 (Capsule No. 11)," July 7, 1961.

198 Smith, Norman F., ed., "A Feasibility Study of a Vehicle for 14-Day Orbital Experiments with Animals," July 7, 1961.

199 Hicks, C. R., Jr., O'Loughlin, J. C., and Hunt, S. A., "Tracking and Sighting Data for Stations and Recovery Forces Supporting Mercury-Atlas Mission No. 4," July 7, 1961.

200 Allen, C. C., and Ferrando, J. A., "Summary of Calculated Preflight Trajectory Data for the Mercury Network Test Vehicle MNTV-1," July 12, 1961.

201 Fisher, L. R., "Mission Directive for Mercury-Scout Mission No. 1 (MS-1)," July 21, 1961.

202 Winterhalter, David L., "Determination of Net Thrust of Project Mercury Tower Jettison Rocket and Escape Tower Assembly," July 3, 1961.

203 Gergory, D. T., and Kranz, E. F., "Mission Directive for Mercury-Atlas No. 4 (Capsule No. 8A)," July 28, 1961.

204 Hicks, C. R., Jr., O'Loughlin, J. C., and Hunt, S. A., "Calculated Preflight Trajectory Data for Mercury-Atlas Mission No. 4 (Capsule No. 8A, Atlas No. 88-D)," August 2, 1961.

205 Hartung, Jack B., and Wetmore, Warren C., "A Composite Model Atmosphere for Use in Project Mercury Calculations," September 29, 1961.

206 Zedekar, Raymond G., "Astronaut Preparation for Orbital Flight," October 13, 1961.

207 Hicks, C. R., Jr., and Allen, C. C., "Calculated Preflight Trajectory Data for Mercury-Atlas Mission 5 (MA-5) (Capsule 9—Atlas 93-D)," October 19, 1961.

208 Gregory, D. T., and von Ehrenfried, M. H., "Mission Directive for Mercury-Atlas Mission No. 5 (Capsule No. 9)," October 20, 1961.

209 Hammack, J. B., et al., "Postlaunch Report for Mercury-Redstone No. 4 (MR-4) (Capsule 11)," September 22, 1961.

210 Skopinski, T. H., Ferrando, J. A., and Osgood, C. T., "Postlaunch Trajectory Report for Mercury-Redstone Mission 3 (MR-3, Capsule 7)," October 12, 1961.

211 Skopinski, T. H., Behuncik, J. A., and Leatherman, P. S., "Postlaunch Trajectory Report for Mercury-Redstone Mission 4 (MR-4, Capsule 11)," October 16, 1961.

212 Hicks, C. R., Jr., Allen, C. C., and O'Loughlin, J. C., "Calculated Preflight Abort Trajectory Data and Nominal Trajectory Display Data for MA Mission 5 (MA-5) (Capsule 9, Atlas 93-D)," November 6, 1961.

213 Fields, Edison M., et al., "Postlaunch Report for Mercury-Atlas Mission 4 (MA-4, Capsule 8A)," November 10, 1961.

214 O'Loughlin, J. C., and Leonard, Pauline O., "Tracking and Sighting Data for Stations

WORKING
PAPER NO.

and Recovery Forces Supporting Mercury-Atlas Mission No. 6 (MA-6—Spacecraft 13)," December 13, 1961.

215 McCutcheon, Ernest P., Morris, D. P., McBarron, James W., II, and McMillion, L. N., "Astronaut Preparation and Activities Manual for Mercury-Atlas Mission 6 (MA-6—Spacecraft 13)," December 1, 1961.

216 Christopher, K. W., and Kranz, E. F., "Mission Directive for Mercury-Atlas Mission 6 (MA-6—Spacecraft 13)," December 15, 1961.

217 Hicks, C. R., Jr., and O'Loughlin, J. C., "Calculated Preflight Trajectory Data for Mercury-Atlas Mission 6 (MA-6) (Atlas 109-D—Spacecraft 13)" (Addendum To W. P. Nos. 207 and 212), December 28, 1961.

218 "Addendum Data Report for Mercury-Atlas Mission 4 (MA-4—Spacecraft 8A)," November 29, 1961.

219 Hartung, J. B., "Analysis of Conditions Determining the Transition Regime Between Ballistic and Orbital Flight for Project Mercury," January 9, 1962.

220 Fields, E. M., Everline, Robert T., Jr., Arbic, R. G., Donnelly, Paul C., Sjoberg, S. A., Smith, N. F., and White, S. C., "Postlaunch Report for Mercury-Atlas Mission 5 (MA-5—Spacecraft 9) Part I—Mission Analysis," March 9, 1962.

221 Everline, R. T., Jr., "Postlaunch Report for Mercury-Atlas Mission 5 (MA-5—Spacecraft 9) Part II—Data," March 9, 1962.

222 Boynton, John H., von Ehrenfried, M., "Mission Directive for Mercury-Atlas Mission 7 (MA-7—Spacecraft 18)," April 9, 1962.

223 Everline, R. T., Jr., Fisher, L. R., Bost, James E., Piland, Joseph V., Bland, William M., and Kleinknecht, K. S., "Manned One-Day Mission Mercury Spacecraft Specification Document," April 23, 1962, Rev. 1963.

224 Hicks, C. R., Jr., and Allen, C. C., "Calculated Preflight Trajectory Data for Mercury-Atlas Mission 7 (MA-7) (Spacecraft 18—Atlas 107-D)," May 4, 1962.

225 Hicks, C. R., Jr., Allen, C. C., and O'Loughlin, J. C., "Calculated Preflight Abort Trajectory Display Data and Nominal Trajectory Display Data for Mercury-Atlas Mission 7 (MA-7) (Spacecraft 18—Atlas 107-D)," May 4, 1962.

226 McCutcheon, E. P., Morris, D. P., and McBarron, J. W., II, "Astronaut Preparation and Activities Manual for Orbital Flight," April 10, 1962.

227 Jacobs, Stanley, and Stephens, E. W., "Experimental Results and Analysis of Ablation Tests Performed on Project Mercury Heat Shield Segments in a Langley Research Center Structures Division ARC Facility," May 23, 1962.

228 Boynton, J. H., and Kranz, E. F., "Mission Directive for Mercury-Atlas Mission No. 8 (MA-8—Spacecraft 16)," August 31, 1962.

229 Allen, C. C., Hicks, C. R., Jr., and Bostick, Jerry C., "Calculated Preflight Trajectory Data for Mercury-Atlas Mission 8 (MA-8) (Spacecraft No. 16—Atlas 113-D)," September 7, 1962.

230 Incerto, Donald J., McCreary, Ben F., and Osgood, C. T., "Postlaunch Trajectory Report for Mercury-Atlas Mission No. 4 (MA-4) (Spacecraft No. 8A—Atlas 88-D) and for Mercury-Atlas Mission No. 5 (MA-5) (Spacecraft No. 9—Atlas 93-D)," October, 1962.

231 St. Leger, Leslie G., "Design Study of a Meteoroid Experiment Using an Unmanned Mercury Spacecraft," December 27, 1962.

232 Boynton, J. H., and Kranz, E. F., "Manned One-Day Mission—Mission Directive for Mercury-Atlas Mission 9 (MA-9—Spacecraft 20)," February 12, 1963, Rev. April 25, 1963.

233 Bostick, J. C., and Carter, Thomas F., Jr., "Calculated Preflight Trajectory Data for

616

WORKING
PAPER NO.

the Manned One-Day Mercury-Atlas Mission (MA–9) (Spacecraft No. 20—Atlas 130–D)," March 15, 1963.

234 Bostick, J. C., and Carter, T. F., Jr., "Calculated Preflight Abort Trajectory Data and Flight Dynamics Display Data for the Manned One-Day Mercury-Atlas Mission (MA–9) (Spacecraft No. 20—Atlas 130–D)," April 16, 1963.

235 Geier, Douglas J., Slight, John B., Marak, Ralph J., and Turner, Thomas, "The Development and Qualification Testing of a Lightweight Net Couch and Restraint System for Use in the Mercury Spacecraft" [Never published].

BIBLIOGRAPHICAL AIDS

American Institute of Aeronautics and Astronautics (AIAA), *International Aerospace Abstracts* (Phillipsburg, N.J., 1961—).

Catoe, Lynn E., compiler, *Space Science and Technology Books 1957–1961: A Bibliography with Contents Noted* (Washington, Library of Congress, 1962).

Estep, Raymond, *An Aerospace Bibliography*, Documentary Research Division, Research Studies Institute, Air University (Maxwell Air Force Base, Alabama, 1962—).

Gamble, William B., compiler, *History of Aeronautics: A Selected List of References to Material in the New York Public Library* (New York, 1938).

Gibbs-Smith, Charles H., *The History of Flying*, Reader's Guides, Second Series 9 (Cambridge, England, National Book League, 1957).

Ley, Willy, *Rockets, Missiles, and Space Travel*, revised and enlarged edition (New York, 1957), Bibliography, 489–520.

Moore, Patrick, *Space Exploration*, Reader's Guides, Third Series (Cambridge, England, National Book League, 1958).

National Aerospace Education Council, *Aeronautics and Space Bibliography of Adult Aerospace Books and Materials* (2 ed., Washington, 1964).

National Aeronautics and Space Administration, *Historical Sketch of NASA*, NASA EP–29 (Washington, 1965), Select Historical References, 51–56.

National Aeronautics and Space Administration, *List of Selected References on NASA Programs*, NASA SP–3 (Washington, Library of Congress, 1962).

National Aeronautics and Space Administration, *Scientific and Technical Aerospace Reports (STAR): A Semimonthly Abstract Journal with Indexes* (Washington, 1963—).

National Aeronautics and Space Administration, *Space Scientists and Engineers: Selected Biographical and Bibliographical Listing, 1957–1961*, NASA SP–5 (Washington, 1962).

Renstrom, Arthur G., "Bibliographical Note," in E. M. Emme, ed., *The History of Rocket Technology* (Detroit, 1964), 285–308.

OFFICIAL REPORTS AND DOCUMENTS

Army Air Forces Scientific Advisory Group, *Toward New Horizons: A Report to General of the Army H. H. Arnold* (14 vols., Washington, 1945).

Congress, House, Committee on Appropriations, Subcommittee on Independent Offices, *Hearings* and *Reports* (Washington, 1959–1963).

————, Committee on Government Operations, *Hearings* and *Reports* (Washington, 1959–1963).

————, Committee on Science and Astronautics (née Select Committee), *Hearings* and *Reports* (1959–1965).

Congress, Senate, Committee on Aeronautical and Space Sciences (née Special Committee), *Hearings* and *Reports* (Washington, 1958–1965).

————, Committee on Armed Services, Preparedness Subcommittee (85 Cong., 1 and 2 sess.), *Hearings: Inquiry into Satellite and Missile Programs* (Washington, 1957–1958).

————, Committee on Appropriations, *Hearings* and *Reports* (Washington, 1959–1963).

Department of State, *Documents on International Aspects of the Exploration and Use of Outer Space 1954–1962* (Washington, Senate Doc. No. 18, May 9, 1963).

————, *International Cooperation and Organization for Outer Space* (Washington, Senate Doc. No. 56, Aug. 12, 1965).

National Academy of Sciences—National Research Council, *I.G.Y. Bulletin* (Washington, 1957–1963).

————, Space Science Board, *A Review of Space Research* (Washington, Pub. 1079, 1962).

National Advisory Committee for Aeronautics, *Annual Reports, 1923–1958* (Washington, 1924–1959).

National Aeronautics and Space Administration, *Aeronautical and Astronautical Events of 1961* (Washington, House Committee on Science and Astronautics, 1962).

————, *Astronautical and Aeronautical Events of 1962* (Washington, House Committee on Science and Astronautics, 1963).

————, *Astronautics and Aeronautics: Chronology on Science, Technology, and Policy, 1963, 1964, 1965* (Washington, 1964–1966).

————, *Proceedings of NASA-Industry Program Plans Conferences* (Washington, 1960, 1963).

————, *Proceedings of National Conferences on Peaceful Uses of Space*, 1961–1965 (Washington, 1961–1966).

————, *Semiannual Reports, 1959–1964* (Washington, 1960–1965).

————, Manned Spacecraft Center, *Results of the Second U.S. Manned Suborbital Space Flight, July 21, 1961* (Washington, 1961).

————, Manned Spacecraft Center, *Results of the First U.S. Manned Orbital Space Flight, February 20, 1962* (Washington, 1962).

————, Manned Spacecraft Center, *Results of the Second United States Manned Orbital Space Flight, May 24, 1962*, NASA SP-6 (Washington, 1962).

————, Manned Spacecraft Center, *Results of the Third United States Manned Orbital Space Flight, October 3, 1962*, NASA SP-12 (Washington, 1962).

National Aeronautics and Space Administration, National Institutes of Health, and National Academy of Sciences, *Conference on Medical Results of the First U.S. Manned Suborbital Space Flight: A Compilation of Papers Presented* (Washington, 1961).

Smithsonian Institution, *Annual Reports, 1955–1962* (Washington, 1956–1963).

White House, *U.S. Aeronautical and Space Activities*, annual report with message of the President (Washington, 1959–1966).

BOOKS

Adams, Carsbie C., *Space Flight: Satellites, Spaceships, Space Stations, and Space Travel Explained* (New York, 1958).

Advances in Astronautical Sciences: Proceedings of Third Annual Meeting, American Astronautical Society (New York, 1957).

Akens, David S., *Historical Origins of the George C. Marshall Space Flight Center* (Huntsville, Ala., 1960).

———, Paul K. Freiwirth, and Helen T. Wells, *History of the George C. Marshall Space Flight Center* (Huntsville, Ala., 1960-1962).

Alexander, Tom, *Project Apollo: Man to the Moon* (New York, 1964).

Allen, John E., *Aerodynamics: A Space-Age Survey* (New York, 1963).

Allen, William H., ed., *Dictionary of Technical Terms for Aerospace Use*, NASA SP-7 (Washington, 1965).

Alperin, Morton, M. Stern, and H. Wooster, eds., *Vistas in Astronautics: First Annual Astronautics Symposium* (London, 1958).

Armstrong, Harry G., *Principles and Practices of Aviation Medicine* (3 ed., Baltimore, 1952).

Army Ordnance Corps/General Electric Co., *Hermes Guided Missile Research and Development Project, 1944-1954* (1959).

Bailey, James O., *Pilgrims Through Space and Time: Trends and Patterns in Scientific and Utopian Fiction* (New York, 1957).

Baker, Robert M. L., and Maud W. Makemson, *An Introduction to Astrodynamics* (New York, 1960).

Barashev, Pavel, and Yuri Dokuchayev, *Gherman Titov: First Man to Spend a Day in Space* (New York, 1962).

Bates, D. R., *The Earth and Its Atmosphere* (New York, 1957).

Baxter, James P., *Scientists Against Time* (Boston, 1946).

Bell, Joseph N., *Seven into Space: The Story of the Mercury Astronauts* (Chicago, 1960).

Benecke, Theodore, and A. W. Quick, eds., *History of German Guided Missile Development* (Brunswick, Germany, 1957).

Benson, Otis O., and Hubertus Strughold, eds., *Physics and Medicine of the Atmosphere and Space* (New York, 1960).

Bergaust, Erik, *First Men in Space* (New York, 1960).

———, *Rocket City, U.S.A.: From Huntsville, Ala., to the Moon* (New York, 1963).

———, and Seabrook Hull, *Rocket to the Moon* (Princeton, N.J., 1958).

Bergman, Jules, *Ninety Seconds to Space: The Story of the X-15* (New York, 1960).

Berkner, Lloyd V., *The Scientific Age* (New Haven, 1964).

———, and Hugh Odishaw, eds., *Science in Space* (New York, 1961).

Besserer, C. W., and Hazel C., eds., *Guide to the Space Age* (Englewood Cliffs, N.J., 1959).

Blagonravov, A. H., ed., *Collected Works of K. E. Tsiolkovsky: II, Reactive Flying Machines*, NASA TT F-237 (Washington, 1965).

Blasingame, Benjamin P., *Astronautics* (New York, 1964).

Bloomfield, Lincoln P., ed., *Outer Space: Prospects for Man and Society* (Englewood Cliffs, N.J., 1962).

Bonney, Walter T., *Heritage of Kitty Hawk* (New York, 1962).

Branley, Franklyn M., *Exploring by Astronaut: The Story of Project Mercury* (New York, 1961).

Bridgeman, William, and Jacqueline Hazard, *The Lonely Sky* (New York, 1955).

Bunker, George M., et al., *The Missile Industry—In Defense and the Exploration of Space* (Baltimore, 1961).

Bush, Vannevar, *Modern Arms and Free Men* (New York, 1949).

Caidin, Martin, *The Astronauts: The Story of Project Mercury, America's Man-in-Space Program* (New York, 1960).

———, *Rendezvous in Space* (New York, 1962).

———, *The Man-in-Space Dictionary: A Modern Glossary* (New York, 1963).

———, and Grace Caidin, *Aviation and Space Medicine: Man Conquers the Vertical Frontier* (New York, 1962).

Cameron, A. G. W., ed., *Interstellar Communication: A Collection of Reprints and Original Contributions* (New York, 1963).

Carter, L. J., ed., *Realities of Space Travel: Selected Papers of the British Interplanetary Society* (New York, 1957).

Chapman, John L., *Atlas: The Story of a Missile* (New York, 1960).

Clarke, Arthur C., *The Exploration of Space* (New York, 1959).

———, et al., *Man and Space* (New York, 1964).

Cleator, P. E., *Rockets Through Space* (London, 1936).

Collected Papers on Aviation Medicine, Presented at Aeromedical Panel Meetings of the Advisory Group for Aeronautical Research and Development, North Atlantic Treaty Organization (London, 1955).

Committee on Extension the Standard Atmosphere, *U.S. Standard Atmosphere, 1962* (Washington, 1962).

Cooke, David C., *Flights that Made History* (New York, 1960).

Coombs, Charles I., *Project Mercury* (New York, 1960).

Cov, Donald W., *The Space Race: From Sputnik to Apollo and Beyond* (Philadelphia, 1962).

———, and Michael Stoiko, *Spacepower: What It Means to You* (Philadelphia, 1958).

Craven, Wesley F., and James L. Cate, eds., *History of the Army Air Forces in World War II* (7 vols., Chicago, 1948–1955).

Crossfield, A. Scott, and Clay Blair, *Always Another Dawn: The Story of a Rocket Test Pilot* (Cleveland, 1960).

Davis, Clive E., *Man and Space* (New York, 1960).

Davy, M. J. B., *Interpretative History of Flight* (London, 1948).

De Leeuw, Henrik, *Conquest of the Air: The History and Future of Aviation* (New York, 1960).

Department of the Air Force, *German Aviation Medicine, World War II* (2 vols., Washington, 1950).

Diamond, Edwin, *The Rise and Fall of the Space Age* (Garden City, N.Y., 1964).

Dille, John, ed., *We Seven, by the Astronauts Themselves* (New York, 1962).

Dornberger, Walter R., *V–2* (New York, 1954).

Duke, Neville, and Edward Lanchbery, *The Saga of Flight: From Leonardo da Vinci to the Guided Missile: An Anthology* (New York, 1961).

Dupree, A. Hunter, *Science in the Federal Government: A History of Policies and Activities to 1940* (Cambridge, Mass., 1957).

Durand, William F., *Aerodynamic Theory: A General Review of Progress* (2 ed., 6 vols. in 3, New York, 1963).

Ehricke, Krafft, *Space Flight* (3 vols., Princeton, N.J., 1960).

Eisenhower, Dwight D., *The White House Years: Waging Peace, 1956–1961* (Garden City, N.Y., 1965).

Ellul, Jacques, *The Technological Society* (New York, 1964).

Emme, Eugene M., *Aeronautics and Astronautics: An American Chronology of Science and Technology in the Exploration of Space, 1915–1960* (Washington, 1961).

———, ed., *The History of Rocket Technology: Essays on Research, Development, and Utility* (Detroit, 1964).

———, *A History of Space Flight* (New York, 1965).

———, ed., *The Impact of Air Power: National Security and World Politics* (Princeton, N.J., 1959).

Eppley, Charles V., *The Rocket Research Aircraft Program, 1946–1962* (Edwards Air Force Base, Calif., 1962).

Esnault-Pelterie, Robert, *L'Astronautique* (Paris, 1930).

Etzioni, Amitai, *The Moon-Doggle: Domestic and International Implication of the Space Race* (Garden City, N.Y., 1964).

Faget, Maxime A., *Manned Space Flight* (New York, 1965).

Feodosiev, V. I., and G. B. Siniarev, *Introduction to Rocket Technology*, trans. S. N. Samburoff (New York, 1959).

The First Man In Space: The Record of Yuri Gagarin's Historic First Venture Into Cosmic Space: A Collection of Translations from Soviet Press Reports (New York, 1961).

Flaherty, Bernard E., ed., *Psychophysiological Aspects of Space Flight* (New York, 1961).

Fortune, editors of, *The Space Industry: America's Newest Giant* (Englewood Cliffs, N.J., 1962).

Freudenthal, Elsbeth E., *The Aviation Business: From Kitty Hawk to Wall Street* (New York, 1940).

————, *Flight into History: The Wright Brothers and the Air Age* (Norman, Okla., 1949).

Frutkin, Arnold W., *International Cooperation in Space* (Englewood Cliffs, N.J., 1965).

Gantz, Kenneth F., ed., *Man in Space: The United States Air Force Program for Developing the Spacecraft Crew* (New York, 1959).

————, ed., *The United States Air Force Report on the Ballistic Missile* (New York, 1958).

Gartmann, Heinz, *The Men Behind the Space Rockets* (New York, 1956).

Gatland, Kenneth W., *Development of the Guided Missile* (2 ed., London, 1954).

————, *Spacecraft and Boosters: The First Comprehensive Analysis of More than 70 United States and Soviet Union Launchings to 1961* (London, 1964).

Gavin, James M., *War and Peace in the Space Age* (New York, 1958).

Gaynor, Frank, *Aerospace Dictionary* (New York, 1960).

Gerathewohl, Siegfried J., *Principles of Bioastronautics* (Englewood Cliffs, N.J., 1963).

Gibbs-Smith, Charles H., *The Aeroplane* (London, 1960).

————, *The History of Flying* (New York, 1954).

Gibney, Frank, ed., *The Penkovsky Papers*, trans. Peter Deriabin (Garden City, N.Y., 1965).

———— and George F. Feldman, *The Reluctant Spacefarers: A Study in the Discovery of Politics* (New York, 1965).

Glasstone, Samuel, *Sourcebook on the Space Sciences* (Princeton, N.J., 1965).

Goddard, Robert H., *Rocket Development: Liquid Fuel Rocket Research, 1921–1941*, ed., E. C. Goddard and G. Edward Pendray (Englewood Cliffs, N.J., 1948).

————, *Rockets: Comprising "A Method of Reaching Extreme Altitudes" and "Liquid-Propellant Rocket Development"* (New York, 1946).

Godwin, Felix, *The Exploration of the Solar System* (New York, 1960).

Goodwin, Harold L., *Image of Space* (New York, 1965).

Gordon, Theodore I., and Julian Scheer, *First in Outer Space* (New York, 1959).

Gove, Philip B., *The Imaginary Voyage in Prose and Fiction: A History of Its Criticism and a Guide to Its Study . . .* (New York, 1961).

Gray, George W., *Frontiers of Flight: The Story of NACA Research* (New York, 1948).

Green, Roger L., *Into Other Worlds: Space-Flight from Lucian to Lewis* (New York, 1958).

Grey, Jerry and Vivian, eds., *Space Flight Report to the Nation* (New York, 1962).

Griffith, Alison E., *The National Aeronautics and Space Act: A Study of the Development of Public Policy* (Washington, 1962).

Grimminger, George, *Analysis of Temperature, Pressure, and Density of the Atmosphere Extending to Extreme Altitudes* (Santa Monica, Calif., 1948).

Gubitz, Myron B., *Rocketship X–15* (New York, 1962).

Gurney, Gene, *Americans Into Orbit: The Story of Project Mercury* (New York, 1962).

Haber, Heinz, *Man in Space* (New York, 1953).

Hale, Edward Everett, *The Brick Moon and Other Stories* (Boston, 1899).

Haley, Andrew G., *Rocketry and Space Exploration* (Princeton, N.J., 1958).

Hall, A. R., *The Scientific Revolution, 1500–1800: The Foundation of the Modern Scientific Attitude* (Boston, 1954).

Hanrahan, James H., and David Bushnell, *Space Biology: The Human Factors in Space Travel* (New York, 1960).

Hartt, Julian, *The Mighty Thor: Missile in Readiness* (New York, 1961).

Henry, James P., *Biomedical Aspects of Space Flight* (New York, 1965).

Hewlett, Richard G., and Oscar E. Anderson, Jr., *The New World: 1939–1946: A History of the Atomic Energy Commission* (1 vol. to date, University Park, Pa., 1962 —).

Hoff, Nicholas J., and Walter G. Vincenti, eds., *Aeronautics and Astronautics: Proceedings of the*

Durand Centennial Conference Held at Stanford University 5–8 August 1959 (New York, 1960).

Holley, I. B., Jr., *Ideas and Weapons: Exploitation of the Aerial Weapon by the U.S. During World War I* (New Haven, 1953).

————, *Buying Aircraft: Materiel Procurement for the Army Air Forces* (Washington, 1964).

Holmes, Jay, *America on the Moon: The Enterprise of the Sixties* (Philadelphia, 1962).

Horowitz, Paul, ed., *Manned Space Reliability Symposium*, Vol. 1 of American Astronautical Society Science and Technology Series (New York, 1964).

Howard-White, F. B., *Nickel: An Historical Review* (New York, 1963).

Hunsaker, Jerome C., *Aeronautics at Mid-Century* (New Haven, 1952).

Huzel, Dieter K., *Peenemünde to Canaveral* (Englewood Cliffs, N.J., 1962).

Jastrow, Robert, ed., *The Exploration of Space* (New York, 1960).

Jensen, Jorgen, et al., *Design Guide to Orbital Flight* (New York, 1962).

Jessup, Philip C., and Howard J. Taubenfeld, *Controls for Outer Space and the Antarctic Analogy* (New York, 1959).

Jones, Bessie Z., *Lighthouse in the Sky: History of the Smithsonian Astrophysical Observatory* (Washington, 1965).

Kast, Freemont E., and James E. Rosenzweig, eds., *Science, Technology, and Management* (New York, 1963).

Keyhoe, Donald E., *Flying Saucers in Outer Space* (New York, 1954).

Korol, Alexander G., *Soviet Research and Development: Its Organization, Personnel and Funds* (Cambridge, Mass., 1965).

Kosmodemyansky, A., *Konstantin Tsiolkovsky, His Life and Work*, trans. X. Danko (Moscow, 1956).

Koyré, Alexander, *From the Closed World to the Infinite Universe* (paperback ed., New York, 1958).

Krieger, F. J., ed., *A Casebook on Soviet Astronautics* (2 vols., Santa Monica, Calif., 1956–1957)

————, ed., *The Men Behind the Sputniks* (Washington, 1958).

Lapp, Ralph E., *Man and Space: The Next Decade* (New York, 1961).

Le Galley, Donald P., ed., *Ballistic Missile and Space Technology* (4 vols., New York, 1960).

Lear, John, *Kepler's Dream* (Berkeley, Calif., 1965).

Lees, Sidney, ed., *Air, Space, and Instruments: Draper Anniversary Volume* (New York, 1963).

Lehman, Milton, *This High Man: The Life of Robert H. Goddard* (New York, 1963).

Lerner, Max, *The Age of Overkill: A Preface to World Politics* (New York, 1962).

Levy, Lillian, ed., *Space: Its Impact on Man and Society* (New York, 1965).

Ley, Willy, *Rockets, Missiles, and Space Travel* (3 rev. ed., New York, 1961).

Lindbergh, Charles A., *The Spirit of St. Louis* (New York, 1955).

————, *We: The Famous Flyer's Own Story of His Life and His Transatlantic Flight, Together with His Views on the Future of Aviation* (New York, 1927).

Link, Mae Mills, *Space Medicine in Project Mercury*, NASA SP-4003 (Washington, 1965).

———— and Hubert A. Coleman, *Medical Support of the Army Air Forces in World War II* (Washington, 1955).

Loosbrock, John F., ed., *Space Weapons: A Handbook of Military Astronautics* (New York, 1959).

McCormick, Ernest J., *Human Factors Engineering* (2 ed., New York, 1964).

McFarland, Marvin W., ed., *The Papers of Wilbur and Orville Wright* (2 vols., New York, 1953).

Mallan, Lloyd, *Men, Rockets and Space Rats* (rev. ed., New York, 1962).

————, *Man into Space* (New York, 1960).

Medaris, John B., *Countdown for Decision* (New York, 1960).

Menzel, Donald H., *Flying Saucers* (Cambridge, Mass., 1953).

Michael, Donald N., et al., *Proposed Studies on the Implications of Peaceful Space Activities for Human Affairs* (Washington, 1961).

Morris, Lloyd, and Kendall Smith, *Ceiling Unlimited: The Story of American Aviation from Kitty Hawk to Supersonics* (New York, 1953).

Murchie, Guy, *Music of the Spheres* (Boston, 1961).

Myrus, Don, *The Astronauts* (New York, 1960).

———, *Keeping Up with the Astronauts: The Story of Man's Greatest Adventures in Outer Space* (New York, 1962).

Neal, Roy, *Ace in the Hole: The Story of the Minuteman Missile* (Garden City, N.Y., 1962).

Newell, Homer E., *High Altitude Rocket Research* (New York, 1953).

———, *Sounding Rockets* (New York, 1959).

Nicolson, Marjorie Hope, *Science and Imagination* (Ithaca, N.Y., 1956).

———, *Voyages to the Moon* (paperback ed., New York, 1960).

Niven, John, Courtlandt Canby, and Vernon Welsh, eds., *Dynamic America: A History of General Dynamics Corporation and Its Predecessor Companies* (Garden City, N.Y., 1960).

Oberth, Hermann, *Man into Space: New Projects for Rocket and Space Travel*, trans. G. P. H. De Freville (New York, 1957).

Odishaw, Hugh, ed., *The Challenges of Space* (Chicago, 1962).

Ordway, Frederick I., III, James P. Gardner, and Mitchell R. Sharpe, Jr., *Basic Astronautics: An Introduction to Space Science, Engineering and Medicine* (Englewood Cliffs, N.J., 1962).

———, James P. Gardner, Mitchell R. Sharpe, Jr., and Ronald Wakeford, *Applied Astronautics: An Introduction to Space Flight* (Englewood Cliffs, N.J., 1963).

Ossenbeck, Frederick I., and Patricia C. Kroeck, *Open Space and Peace: A Symposium on Effects of Observation* (Stanford, Calif., 1964).

Ostlin, Melvin T., *Thinking Out Loud About the Space Age: Is the Christian Faith Adequate for a Space Age?* (Philadelphia, 1962).

Parry, Albert, *Russia's Rockets and Missiles* (Garden City, N.Y., 1960).

Parson, Nels A., Jr., *Guided Missiles in War and Peace* (Cambridge, Mass., 1956).

———, *Missiles and the Revolution in Warfare* (Cambridge, Mass., 1962).

Peck, Merton J., and Frederic M. Scherer, *The Weapons Acquisition Process: An Economic Analysis* (Boston, 1962).

Pendray, G. Edward, *The Coming Age of Rocket Power* (New York, 1945).

Penick, J. L., Jr., and C. W. Pursell, Jr., M. B. Sherwood, and Donald C. Swain, eds., *The Politics of American Science: 1939 to the Present* (Chicago, 1965).

Petrov, V., *Artificial Satellites of the Earth*, trans. B. S. Sharma (Delhi, 1960).

Piccard, Auguste, *Between Earth and Sky*, trans. Claude Apcher (London, 1950).

———, *Earth, Sky and Sea*, trans. Christine Stead (New York, 1956).

Pierce, Philip N., and Karl Schuon, *John H. Glenn, Astronaut* (New York, 1962).

Poole, Lynn, and Gray Poole, *Scientists Who Work with Astronauts* (New York, 1964).

Pope, Alan, *Wind-Tunnel Testing* (2 ed., New York, 1954).

Price, Derek J., de Solla, *Little Science, Big Science* (New York, 1963).

Price, Don K., *Government and Science: Their Dynamic Relation in American Democracy* (New York, 1962).

Ramo, Simon, ed., *Peacetime Uses of Outer Space* (New York, 1961).

Randers-Pehrson, N. H., *History of Aviation* (New York, 1944).

Rechtschaffen, Oscar H., ed., *Reflections on Space: Its Implications for Domestic and International Affairs* (Colorado Springs, Colo., 1964).

Ritner, Peter, *The Society of Space* (New York, 1961).

Rosen, Milton W., *The Viking Rocket Story* (New York, 1955).

Rosenthal, Alfred, *The Early Years: Goddard Space Flight Center Historical Origins and Activities Through December 1962* (Washington, 1964).

Rosholt, Robert L., *An Administrative History of NASA, 1958–1963*, NASA SP-4101 (Washington, 1966).

Sänger, Eugen, *Rocket Flight Engineering* (Munich, 1933), NASA Tech. Trans. F-223 (Washington, 1965).

———, *Space Flight: Countdown for the Future*, trans. Karl Frucht (New York, 1965).

Schlaifer, Robert, and S. D. Heron, *Development of Aircraft Engines and Development of Aviation*

623

Fuels: Two Studies of Relations between Government and Business (Boston, 1950).

Schwiebert, Ernest G., *A History of the U.S. Air Force Ballistic Missiles* (New York, 1965).

Seifert, Howard S., ed., *Space Technology* (New York, 1959).

Shankle, Ralph O., *The Twins of Space* (Philadelphia, 1964).

Shelton, William R., *Countdown: The Story of Cape Canaveral* (Boston, 1960).

Shternfeld, Ari, *Soviet Space Science* (2nd rev. ed., New York, 1959).

Simon, Leslie G., *German Research in World War II: An Analysis of the Conduct of Research* (New York, 1947).

Simons, S. Fred, ed., *Progress in the Astronautical Sciences* (Amsterdam, 1962).

Skinner, Richard M., and William Leavitt, eds., *Speaking of Space: The Best From Space Digest* (Boston, 1962).

Slager, Ursula T., *Space Medicine* (Englewood Cliffs, N.J., 1962).

Smith, R. W., and J. W. Altman, *Space Psychology: Some Considerations in the Study of Astronauts' Behavior* (Pittsburgh, 1961).

Stehling, Kurt, *Project Vanguard* (Garden City, N.Y., 1961).

Stillwell, Wendell H., *X–15 Research Results with Selected Bibliography*, NASA SP–60 (Washington, 1965).

Stiltz, Harry L., ed., *Aerospace Telemetry* (Englewood Cliffs, N.J., 1961).

Stover, Carl F., ed., *The Technological Order: Proceedings of the Encyclopedia Britannica Conference* (Detroit, 1963).

Strughold, Hubertus, *The Green and Red Planet: A Physiological Study of the Possibility of Life on Mars* (Albuquerque, 1953).

Struve, Otto, and Velta Zeergs, *Astronomy of the 20th Century* (New York, 1962).

Stuhlinger, Ernst, Frederick I. Ordway, III, Jerry C. McCall, and George C. Bucher, eds., *From Peenemünde to Outer Space: Commemorating the Fiftieth Birthday of Wernher von Braun* (Huntsville, Ala., 1962).

Sullivan, Walter, *Assault on the Unknown: The International Geophysical Year* (New York, 1961).

——, ed., *America's Race for the Moon: The New York Times Story of Project Apollo* (New York, 1962).

Taubenfeld, Howard J., ed., *Space and Society: Studies for the Seminar on Problems of Outer Space* sponsored by the Carnegie Endowment for International Peace (Dobbs Ferry, N.Y., 1964).

Thomas, Shirley, *Men of Space* (7 vols., Philadelphia, 1960–1965).

——, *Satellite Tracking Facilities: Their History and Operation* (New York, 1963).

Titov, Gherman, *700,000 Kilometres Through Space* (Moscow, 1962).

—— and Martin Caidin, *I Am Eagle!* (Indianapolis, 1962).

Vaeth, J. Gordon, *200 Miles Up: The Conquest of the Upper Air* (2 ed., New York, 1956).

Van Dyke, Vernon, *Pride and Power: The Rationale of the Space Program* (Urbana, 1964).

Von Kármán, Theodore, *Aerodynamics: Selected Topics in the Light of Their Historical Development* (Ithaca, N.Y., 1954).

Von Mises, Richard, *Theory of Flight* (2 ed., New York, 1959).

Wainwright, Loudon, and the seven astronauts, *The Astronauts* (New York, 1961).

Waters, Frank, *Robert Gilruth: Engineering Space Exploration* (Chicago, 1963).

White, Clayton S., and Otis O. Benson, eds., *Physics and Medicine of the Upper Atmosphere: A Study of the Aeropause* (Albuquerque, 1952).

White, William J., *A History of the Centrifuge in Aerospace Medicine* (Santa Monica, Calif., 1964).

Wilks, Willard E., *The New Wilderness: What We Know About Space* (New York, 1963).

Williams, Beryl, and Samuel Epstein, *The Rocket Pioneers on the Road to Space* (New York, 1955).

Wise, David, and Thomas B. Ross, *The U–2 Affair* (New York, 1962).

Witkin, Richard, ed., *The Challenge of the Sputniks* (Garden City, N.Y., 1958).

Zaehringer, Alfred J., *Soviet Space Technology* (New York, 1961).

Zarem, Lewis, *New Dimensions of Flight* (New York, 1959).

JOURNAL ARTICLES

Abbot, Charles G., "The Relations Between the Smithsonian Institution and the Wright Brothers," *Smithsonian Miscellaneous Collections*, LXXXI (Sept. 29, 1928).

Alexander, George, "Atlas Accuracy Improves as Test Program is Completed," *Aviation Week*, LXXVIII (Feb. 25, 1963).

Allen, H. Julian, "Hypersonic Flight and the Reentry Problem," *Journal of the Aeronautical Sciences*, XXV (April 1958).

Anderton, David S., "How Mercury Capsule Design Evolved," *Aviation Week*, LXXIV (May 22, 1961).

Andrews, W. H., "Contributions from the X-15 Flight Test Program," *Society of Experimental Test Pilots' Quarterly Review*, V (Sept. 29, 1961).

Armstrong, Harry G., Heinz Haber, and Hubertus Strughold, "Aero Medical Problems of Space Travel, Panel Meeting, School of Aviation Medicine," *Journal of Aviation Medicine*, XX (Dec. 1949).

Baker, Normal L., "Air Force Won't Support Project Adam," *Missiles and Rockets*, III (June 1958).

Ballinger, E. R., "Human Experiments in Subgravity and Prolonged Acceleration," *Journal of Aviation Medicine*, XXIII (Aug. 1952).

Beach, Edward L., "Triton Follows Magellan's Wake," *National Geographic*, CXVIII (Aug. 1960).

Becker, John V., "The X-15 Project: Part I: Origins and Research Background," *Astronautics and Aeronautics*, II (Feb. 1964).

Berry, Charles A., "The Environment of Space in Human Flight," *Aeronautical Engineering Review*, XVII (March 1958).

Beyer, David H., and Saul B. Sells, "Selection and Training of Personnel for Space Flight," *Journal of Aviation Medicine*, XXVIII (Feb. 1957).

Bonney, Walter T., "High-Speed Research Airplanes," *Scientific American*, CLXXXIX (Oct. 1953).

Clark, B., and Ashton Graybiel, "The Break-Off Phenomenon," *Journal of Aviation Medicine*, XXVII (April 1957).

Clark, Carl C., and James D. Hardy, "Preparing Man for Space Flight," *Astronautics*, IV (Feb. 1959).

Clark, Evert, "NASA Centralizes Launch Management," *Aviation Week*, LXXII, (May 30, 1960).

Clarke, Arthur C., "Rocket to the Renaissance," *Playboy*, VII (July 1960).

———, "Space Travel in Fact and Fiction," *British Interplanetary Society Journal*, IX (Sept. 1960).

Colchagoff, George D., "Outline of History of USAF Man-In-Space Research and Development Program," Air Force information policy letter supplement No. 109, Aug. 1962, *Missiles and Rockets*, X (March 26, 1962).

Dixon, Thomas F., "Development Problems of Rocket Engines for Ballistic Missiles," *Interavia*, LXXI (1959).

Donlan, Charles J., and Jack C. Heberlig, "Progress Report on Project Mercury," *Astronautics*, V (Aug. 1960).

Drake, F. D., "Project OZMA," *Physics Today*, XIV (April 1961).

Dryden, Hugh L., "Fact-Finding for Tomorrow's Planes," *National Geographic*, CIV (Dec. 1953).

———, "NACA: What It's Doing and Where It's Going," *Missiles and Rockets*, I (Oct. 1956).

———, "Space Technology and the NACA," *Aeronautical Engineering Review*, XVII (March 1958).

————, "Future Exploration and Utilization of Outer Space," *Technology and Culture* (Spring 1961).

————, "Toward The New Horizons of Tomorrow: First Annual ARS von Kármán Lecture," *Astronautics*, VIII (Jan. 1963).

————, "Footprints on the Moon," *National Geographic*, CXXV (March 1964).

"Dyna-Soar's History Full of Re-Examinations," *Aviation Week*, LXXXVII (July 22, 1963).

Eggers, Alfred J., Jr., "Performance of Long Range Hypervelocity Vehicles," *Jet Propulsion*, XXVII (Nov. 1957).

Eggleston, John M., "Some Abort Techniques and Procedures for Manned Spacecraft," *Aerospace Engineering*, XXI (Nov. 1962).

Emme, Eugene M., "The Impact of Air Power Upon History," *Air University Quarterly Review*, II (Winter 1948).

————, "Yesterday's Dream, Today's Reality," *Airpower Historian*, VII (Oct. 1960).

Faget, Maxime, and Robert O. Piland, "Mercury Capsule and Its Flight Systems," *Aerospace Engineering*, XIX (April 1960).

Ferri, Antonio, Lewis Feldman, and Walter Daskin, "The Use of Lift for Reentry from Satellite Trajectories," *Jet Propulsion*, XXVII (Nov. 1957).

Fisher, Allen C., Jr., "Aviation Medicine on the Threshold of Space," *National Geographic*, CVI (Aug. 1955).

————, "Cape Canaveral's 6000-Mile Shooting Gallery," *National Geographic*, CXVI (Oct. 1959).

————, "Exploring Tomorrow with the Space Agency," *National Geographic*, CXVII (July 1960).

"Flight of the MR-3," *Missiles and Rockets*, VIII (May 15, 1961).

Gatland, Kenneth W., "The Vanguard Project," *Spaceflight*, I (Oct. 1956).

Gerathewohl, Siegfried J., "Physics and Psychophysics of Weightlessness and Visual Perception," *Journal of Aviation Medicine*, XXV (1954).

————, "Weightlessness: The Problem and the Air Force Research Program," *Air University Quarterly Review*, XIV (Oct. 1950).

————, and G. R. Steinkamp, "Human Factors Requirements for Putting a Man into Orbit," *Astronautica Acta*, V (1959).

Gibbs-Smith, Charles H., "The Wright Brothers and Their Invention of the Practical Airplane," *Nature*, CXCVII (June 1, 1963).

Glennan, T. Keith, "Opportunities for International Cooperation in Space Exploration," *U.S. Dept. of State Bulletin* (Jan. 11, 1960).

————, "Space Exploration," *Vital Speeches* (April 16, 1960).

Graybiel, Ashton, et al., "An Account of Experiments in Which Two Monkeys Were Recovered Unharmed After Ballistic Space Flight," *Aerospace Medicine*, XXX (Dec. 1959).

Grether, Walter F., "Psychology and the Space Frontier," *American Psychologist*, XVII (Feb. 1962).

Grimminger, George, "Probability That a Meteorite Will Hit or Penetrate a Body Situated in the Vicinity of the Earth." *Journal of Applied Physics*, XIX (Oct. 1948).

Haber, Fritz, and Heinz Haber, "Possible Methods of Producing the Gravity-Free State for Medical Research," *Journal of Aviation Medicine*, XXI (Oct. 1950).

Hagemann, E. R., "Goddard and His Early Rockets, 1882–1930," *Journal of the Astronautical Sciences*, VII (Summer 1961).

Hall, R. Cargill, "Origins and Development of the Vanguard and Explorer Satellite Programs," *Airpower Historian*, XI (Oct. 1964).

Hanson, C. Frederick, "The Characteristics of the Upper Atmosphere Pertaining to Hypervelocity Flight," *Jet Propulsion*, XXVII (Nov. 1957).

Henry, James P., et al., "Animal Studies of the Subgravity State During Rocket Flight," *Journal of Aviation Medicine*, XXIII (Oct. 1952).

"How Mercury Capsule Design Evolved," *Aviation Week*, LXX (Sept. 21, 1959).

Kennedy, John F., "If the Soviets Control Space They Can Control Earth," *Missiles and Rockets*, VII (Oct. 10, 1960).

Kittinger, Joseph W., "The Long, Lonely Leap," *National Geographic*, CXVIII (Dec. 1960).

Kousnetzov, Andrei G., "Some Results of Biological Experiments in Rockets and Sputnik II," *Journal of Aviation Medicine*, XXIX (Nov. 1958).

Krause, Ernst, "High Altitude Research with V-2 Rockets," *Proceedings of the American Philosophical Society*, XCI (1947).

Lear, John, "The Moon That Refused to be Eclipsed," *Saturday Review*, XLIII (March 5, 1960).

Leavitt, William, "The Weird World of Weightlessness," *Air Force*, XLII (April 1959).

Lees, Lester, "Laminar Heat Transfer Over Blunt-Nosed Bodies at Hypersonic Flight Speeds," *Jet Propulsion*, XXVI (April 1956).

———, "Recent Developments in Hypersonic Flow," *Jet Propulsion*, XXVII (Nov. 1957).

Martin, James A., "The Record-Setting Research Airplanes," *Aeronautical Engineering Review*, XXI (Dec. 1962).

Maxwell, W. R., "Some Aspects of the Origin and Early Development of Astronautics," *Journal of British Interplanetary Society*, XVIII (Sept. 1962).

Means, P., "Mercury Instrumentation: Pilot's Fate Depends on Seven Miles of Wiring," *Missiles and Rockets*, VI (June 13, 1960).

Mohler, Stanley R., "Wiley Post's Aerospace Achievements," *Airpower Historian*, XI (July 1964).

North, Gilbert B., "Development and Checkout of the NASA Mercury Capsule," *Canadian Aeronautical Journal*, VII (Feb. 1961).

Oates, Stephen B., "NASA's Manned Spacecraft Center at Houston, Texas," *Southwestern Historical Quarterly*, LXVII (Jan. 1964).

Oberth, Hermann, "From My Life," *Astronautics*, IV (June 1959).

Pendray, G. Edward, "The First Quarter Century of the American Rocket Society," *Jet Propulsion*, XXV (Nov. 1955).

Piccard, Jacques, "Man's Deepest Dive," *National Geographic*, CXVIII (July 1960).

Pierce, Roger J., "Mercury Capsule Communications," *Astronautics*, IV (Dec. 1959).

Rae, John B., "Financial Problems of the American Aircraft Industry," *Business History Review*, XXXIX (Spring 1965).

———, "Science and Engineering in the History of Aviation," *Technology and Culture*, II (Fall 1961).

Ritland, Osmond J., "Concurrency," *Air University Quarterly Review*, XII (Winter-Spring 1960-61).

Ritzinger, Frederick R., Jr., and Ellis G. Aboud, "Pressure Suits—Their Evolution and Development," *Air University Quarterly Review*, XVI (Jan.-Feb. 1965).

Schiff, L. I., "A Report on the NASA Conference on Experimental Test of Theories of Relativity," *Physics Today*, XIV (Nov. 1961).

Sheehan, Robert, "Thompson Ramo Wooldridge: Two Wings in Space," *Fortune*, LXVII (Feb. 1963).

Simons, David G., "The 1954 Aeromedical Field Laboratory Balloon Flights: Physiological and Radiobiological Aspects," *Journal of Aviation Medicine*, XXVII (April 1956).

———, "Psychophysiological Aspects of Manhigh," *Astronautics*, IV (Feb. 1959).

———, "Review of Biological Effects of Subgravity and Weightlessness," *Jet Propulsion*, XXV (May 1955).

———, "Space Medicine—The Human Body in Space," *Journal of the Franklin Institute Series*, monograph No. 6 (Dec. 1958).

———, and C. H. Steinmetz, "Physiological and Radiobiological Aspects of 1954 Aeromedical Field Laboratory Balloon Flight," *Journal of Aviation Medicine*, XXVI (1955).

627

Singer, S. Fred, "The Use and Uselessness of Outer Space," *Reporter*, XX (June 11, 1959).

Solomon, Philip, et al., "Sensory Deprivation, A Review," *Americal Journal of Psychology*, CXIV (Oct. 1957).

Spiegel, F. S., "Changing Concepts in Physical Standards for Flying," *Aerospace Medicine*, XXXI (Nov. 1960).

Stalder, Jackson R., "A Survey of Heat Transfer Problems Encountered by Hypersonic Aircraft," *Jet Propulsion*, XXVII (Nov. 1957).

Stapp, John P., "Acceleration: How Great a Problem?" *Astronautics*, IV (Feb. 1959).

Strughold, Hubertus, "Atmospheric Space Equivalence," *Journal of Aviation Medicine*, XXV (Aug. 1954).

———, "An Introduction to Astrobiology," *Astronautics*, V (Dec. 1960).

——— "The Medical Problems of Space Flight," *International Record of Medicine*, CLXVIII (1955).

———, "A Simple Classification of the Present and Future Stages of Manned Flight," *Journal of Aviation Medicine*, XXVII (Aug. 1956).

———, "Space Equivalent Conditions," *Astronautica Acta*, I (1955).

———, "The U.S. Air Force Experimental Sealed Cabin," *Journal of Aviation Medicine*, XXVII (Feb. 1956).

———, Heinz Haber, Konrad Buettner, and Fritz Haber, "Where Does Space Begin? Functional Concept of the Boundaries Between Atmosphere and Space," *Aviation Medicine*, XXII (Oct. 1951).

Sweeney, Robert, "Atlas Generates Fabrication Advances," *Aviation Week*, LXXII (Jan. 4, 1960).

———, "Manufacturing the Atlas at Convair," *Interavia*, LXXI (1959).

Thompson, G. V. E., "Oberth—Doyen of Spaceflight Today," *Spaceflight*, I (Oct. 1957).

Toll, Thomas A., and Jack Fischel, "The X-15 Project: Results and New Research," *Astronautics and Aeronautics*, II (March 1964).

Tsiolkovsky, Konstantin E., "An Autobiography," trans. A. N. Petroff, *Astronautics*, IV (May 1959).

Useller, James W., and Joseph S. Algranti, "Pilot Reaction to High Speed Rotation," *Aerospace Medicine*, XXXIV (June 1963).

"USAF School Simulates Living in Space," *Aviation Week*, LXVIII (Jan. 27, 1958).

Van der Wal, F. L., and W. D. Young, "Project MIA (Mouse-in-Able), Experiments on Psychological Response to Space Flight," *Jet Propulsion*, XXXI (Oct. 1959).

Victory, J. F., "The NACA: Cradle of Research," *Flying*, LX (March 1957).

Voas, Robert B., "A Description of the Astronaut's Task in Project Mercury," *Human Factors*, III (Sept. 1961).

Von Beckh, Harald J., "Human Reactions During Flight to Acceleration, Preceded by or Followed by Weightlessness," *Aerospace Medicine*, XXX (June 1959).

———, "Multidirectional G-Protection in Space Vehicles," *Journal of the British Interplanetary Society*, XVI (Sept.–Oct. 1958).

Walker, Joseph A., "I Fly the X-15," *National Geographic*, CXXII (Sept. 1962).

Ward, Julian E., Willard R. Hawkins, and Herbert D. Stallings, "Physiologic Response to Subgravity, I: Mechanics of Nourishment and Deglutination of Solids and Liquids," *Journal of Aviation Medicine*, XXX (March 1959).

———, Willard R. Hawkins, and Herbert D. Stallings, "Physiologic Response to Subgravity, II: Initiation of Micturition," *Aerospace Medicine*, XXX (Aug. 1959).

Weaver, Kenneth F., "Countdown for Space," *National Geographic*, CXIX (May 1961).

Webb, James E., "International Relations and Space," *Vital Speeches* (Oct. 1, 1961).

———, "New Age of Discovery," *Airpower Historian*, XI (July 1964).

Westbrook, C. B., "The Pilot's Role in Space Flight," *Aerospace Engineering*, XVIII (Nov. 1959).

Weyl, A. R., "Gravity and the Prospects for Astronautics," *Aeronautics*, XXXIX (Feb. 1959).
Williams, Walter C., and Hubert M. Drake, "The Research Airplane: Past, Present, and Future," *Aeronautical Engineering Review*, XVII (Jan. 1958).

UNPUBLISHED WORKS

Ambrose, Mary Stone, "The National Space Program," M.A. thesis, 2 vols., American University, 1961.
[Blount, Earl E., Jr.], Special Communications Staff, North American Aviation, Inc., "Comment on the National Space Program: 'Pro and Con'," Vol. III, No. 1, Sept. 1, 1964 [Vol. I—July 1, 1963; Vol. II—Sept. 1, 1963].
Bullard, John A., "History of the Redstone Missile System," AMC 23M, Army Missile Command, 1965.
Bushnell, David, "History of Research in Subgravity and Zero-G at the Air Force Missile Development Center, 1948–1959," Air Force Missile Development Center, 1959.
———, "Major Achievements in Biodynamics: Escape Physiology at the Air Force Missile Development Center, 1953–1958," Air Force Missile Development Center, 1959.
———, "Major Achievements in Space Biology at the Air Force Missile Development Center, 1953–1957," Air Force Missile Development Center [1958].
———, "The Sacramento Peak Observatory, 1947–1962," Air Force Office of Aerospace Research, 1962.
"Chronology of Early USAF Man-in-Space Activity, 1945–1958," Air Force Systems Command [1965].
"Chronology of Early Air Force Man-in-Space Activity, 1955–1960," Air Force Systems Command [1965].
Lasby, Clarence G., "German Scientists in America: Their Importation, Exploitation, and Assimilation, 1945–1952," Ph.D. dissertation, University of California at Los Angeles, 1962.
Levine, Arthur S., "United States Aeronautical Research Policy, 1915–1958: A Study of the Major Policy Decisions of the National Advisory Committee for Aeronautics," Ph.D. dissertation, Columbia University, 1963.
Peyton, Green, and Jean Evans, "History, Aerospace Medical Division, Air Force Systems Command: Reorganization, 1 November 1951–30 June 1962," Brooks Air Force Base, Tex., 1962.
Whipple, Marven R., "History of the Air Force Missile Test Center," Patrick Air Force Base, Fla., 1957.

POSTFLIGHT REPORTS

Proceedings of a Conference on Results of the First U.S. Manned Suborbital Space Flight, United States National Aeronautics and Space Administration in Cooperation with National Institutes of Health and National Academy of Sciences (Washington, 1961).
Results of the Second U.S. Manned Suborbital Space Flight, July 21, 1961, Manned Spacecraft Center, National Aeronautics and Space Administration (Washington, 1961).
Results of the First United States Manned Orbital Space Flight, February 20, 1962, Manned Spacecraft Center, National Aeronautics and Space Administration (Washington, 1962).
Results of the Second United States Manned Orbital Space Flight, May 24, 1962, National Aeronautics and Space Administration, Manned Spacecraft Center, Project Mercury, NASA SP-6 (Washington, 1962).
Results of the Third United States Manned Orbital Space Flight, October 3, 1962, National Aeronautics and Space Administration, Manned Spacecraft Center, Project Mercury, NASA SP-12 (Washington, 1962).

Mercury Project Summary Including Results of the Fourth Manned Orbital Flight, May 15 and 16, 1963, National Aeronautics and Space Administration, Manned Spacecraft Center, Project Mercury, NASA SP–45 (Washington, 1963).

*"Postlaunch Memorandum Report for Mercury-Redstone No. 4 (MR–4)," (NASA Space Task Group, 1961).

*"Postlaunch Memorandum Report for Mercury-Atlas No. 5 (MA–5)," (NASA Manned Spacecraft Center, 1961).

*"Postlaunch Memorandum Report for Mercury-Atlas No. 6: Part I, Mission Analysis," (NASA Manned Spacecraft Center, 1962).

*"Postlaunch Memorandum Report for Mercury-Atlas No. 7 (MA–7), Part I, Mission Analysis," (NASA Manned Spacecraft Center, 1962).

*"Postlaunch Memorandum Report for Mercury-Atlas No. 8: Part I, Mission Analysis," (NASA Manned Spacecraft Center, 1962).

*"Postlaunch Memorandum Report for MA–8: Part III, Air-Ground Voice and Debriefing," (NASA Manned Spacecraft Center, 1962).

*"Postlaunch Memorandum Report for Mercury-Atlas No. 9 (MA–9): Part I, Mission Analysis," (NASA Manned Spacecraft Center, 1963).

*"Postlaunch Memorandum Report for Mercury-Atlas No. 9 (MA–9): Part II, Data," (NASA Manned Spacecraft Center, 1963).

*"Postlaunch Memorandum Report for Mercury-Atlas No. 9 (MA–9: Part III, Mission Transcripts," (NASA Manned Spacecraft Center, 1963).

*Classified flight reports not listed as Project Mercury Working Papers.

Appendix A: Functional Organization of Mercury

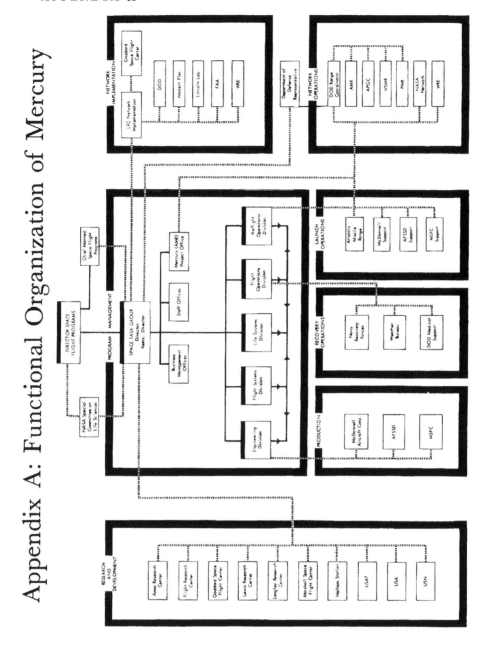

Appendix B
Workflow Organization of Mercury

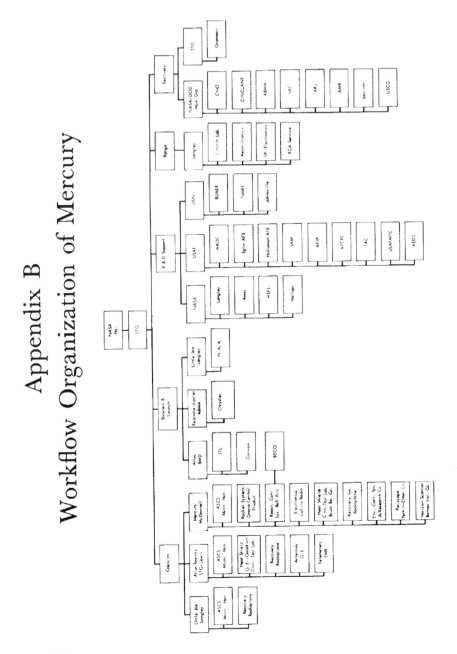

Appendix C
Organization Charts

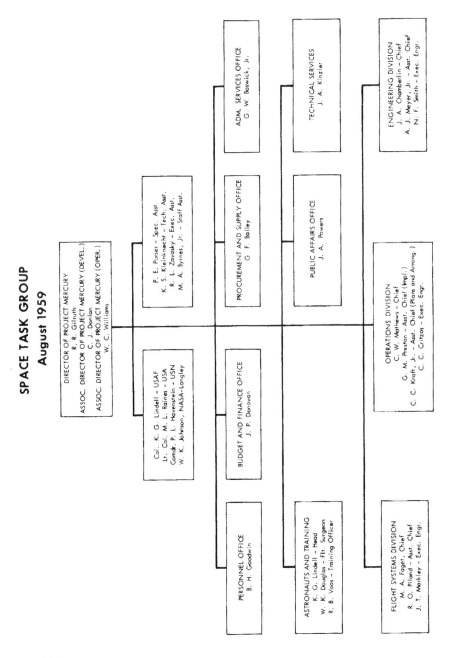

SPACE TASK GROUP
August 1959

DIRECTOR OF PROJECT MERCURY
R. R. Gilruth
ASSOC. DIRECTOR OF PROJECT MERCURY (DEVEL.)
C. J. Donlan
ASSOC. DIRECTOR OF PROJECT MERCURY (OPER.)
W. C. Williams

Col. K. G. Lindell – USAF
Lt. Col. M. L. Raines – USA
Comdr. P. L. Havenstein – USN
W. K. Johnson, NASA-Langley

P. E. Purser – Spec. Asst.
K. S. Kleinknecht – Tech. Asst.
R. L. Zavasky – Exec. Asst.
M. A. Byrnes, Jr. – Staff Asst.

PERSONNEL OFFICE
B. H. Goodwin

BUDGET AND FINANCE OFFICE
J. P. Donovan

ADM. SERVICES OFFICE
G. W. Boswick, Jr.

PROCUREMENT AND SUPPLY OFFICE
G. F. Bailey

TECHNICAL SERVICES
J. A. Kinzler

PUBLIC AFFAIRS OFFICE
J. A. Powers

ASTRONAUTS AND TRAINING
K. G. Lindell – Head
W. K. Douglas – Flt. Surgeon
R. B. Voas – Training Officer

FLIGHT SYSTEMS DIVISION
M. A. Faget, Chief
R. O. Piland – Asst. Chief
J. T. Markley – Exec. Engr.

OPERATIONS DIVISION
C. W. Mathews – Chief
G. M. Preston – Asst. Chief (Impl.)
C. C. Kraft, Jr. – Asst. Chief (Plans and Arrang.)
C. C. Critzos – Exec. Engr.

ENGINEERING DIVISION
J. A. Chamberlin – Chief
A. J. Meyer, Jr. – Asst. Chief
N. F. Smith – Exec. Engr.

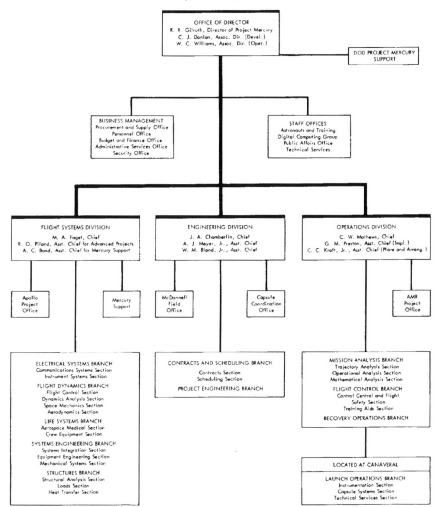

SPACE TASK GROUP
September 26, 1960

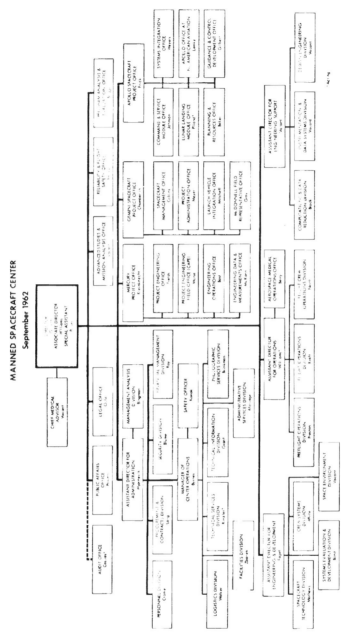

MANNED SPACECRAFT CENTER
September 1962

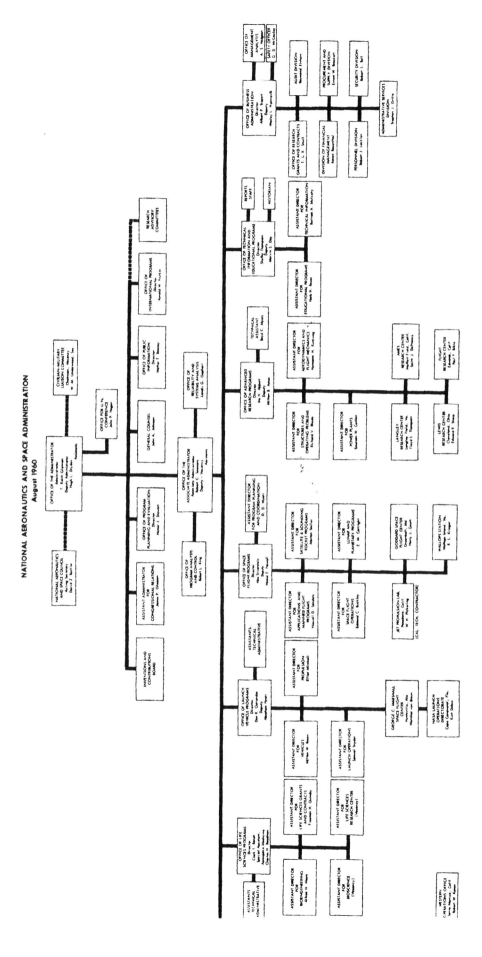

National Aeronautics and Space Administration

August 1960

NATIONAL AERONAUTICS AND SPACE ADMINISTRATION
November 1, 1961

Appendix D
Flight Data Summary

Flight Data Summary

The information in this revised flight data summary is taken from various sources according to the authors' best estimate of reliability. The basic format was made by Jack C. Heberlig for the NASA–MSC newspaper issue of "Mercury Program Summary," October 3–4, 1963, then republished as MSC Fact Sheet

Mission	Pilot	Date	S/C No.	L/V No.	"Orig." scheduled in January 1959	Orbits/period, min:sec	Weightless time, hr:min:sec
LJ–1		8/21/59	BP		7/59		
Big Joe		9/ 9/59	BP	10–D	8/59		
LJ–6		10/ 4/59	BP		Insert		
LJ–1A		11/ 4/59	BP		Insert		
LJ–2	"Sam" monkey	12/ 4/59	BP		9/59		3:13
LJ–1B	"Miss Sam"	1/21/60	BP		11/59		0:28
Beach abort		5/ 9/60	1		Insert		
MA–1		7/29/60	4	50–D	11/59		
LJ–5		11/ 8/60	3		12/59		
MR–1		11/21/60	2	MR–1	10/59		
MR–1A		12/19/60	2A	MR–3	Insert		5:30
MR–2	"Ham" chimp.	1/31/61	5	MR–2	12/59		6:40
MA–2		2/21/61	6	67–D	1/60		
LJ–5A		3/18/61	14		Insert		
MR–BD		3/24/61	BP	MR–5	Insert		
MA–3	Robot	4/25/61	8	100–D	2/60		

No. 201 and in *Mercury Project Summary*, NASA SP 45, pages 50–51. But in expanding this chart, converting it to commonly understood units, and judging each mission's success or failure in the light of the overall program objectives, the authors have returned to the primary classified postlaunch memorandum reports for most of the figures herein.

The sixth column of the table shows the originally scheduled (January 1959) launch date. This early schedule represented optimistic planning in that it assumed a trouble-free preparation and flight program. As the program progressed, some flights were eliminated, others added, and objectives expanded, based on experience gained.

Flight duration, hr : min : sec	Apogee/ perigee, st. miles	Range, max., st. miles	Velocity max.- spa., fix. mph	Max. q, psf	Max. g	Primary objective	Results SC/LV
0:00:20	0. 4	0. 5	. . . .	. . . . . .	. . . . .	Max. q abort and escape	F
0:13:00	95	1, 496	14, 857	675	12	Ablation heatshield	S/F
0:05:10	37	79	3, 075	3, 400	5. 9	Capsule aerodynamics and integrity	P
0:08:11	9	11	2, 022	168	16. 9	Max. q abort and escape	P
0:11:06	53	194	4, 466	2, 150	14. 8	Primate escape at high altitude	S
0:08:35	9	12	2, 022	1, 070	4. 5	Max. q abort and escape	S
0:01:16	. 5	1	976	. . . .	. . . . .	Off-the-pad escape	S
0:03:18	8. 1	6	1, 701	. . . .	. . . . .	Qualify S/C—Atlas combination	F
0:02:22	10. 1	14	1, 785	1, 420	6	Qualify MAC S/C at max. q	F
0:00:02	0	. . . .	. . . .	. . . . . .	. . . . .	Qualify S/C—Redstone combination	F
0:15:45	130. 7	235	4, 909	560	12. 4	Qualify systems for suborbital	S
0:16:39	157	422	5, 857	575	14. 7	Primate suborbital and auto abort	S/P
0:17:56	114	1, 432	13, 227	991	15. 9	Qualify MA interface	S
0:23:48	7. 7	18	1, 783	1, 580	8	Max. q escape and impact	P
0:08:23	113. 5	307	5, 123	580	11	Perfect MR booster	S
0:07:19	4. 5	0	1, 177	880	11	Quick test of S/C— Atlas orbit	F

Mission	Pilot	Date	S/C No.	L/V No.	"Orig." schedules in January 1959	Orbits/period, min:sec.	Weightless time, hr:min:sec.
LJ–5B........	....	4/28/61	14A	....	Insert	....	....
MR–3........	Shepard: *Freedom 7*...	5/ 5/61	7	MR–7	1/60	....	5:16
MR–4........	Grissom: *Liberty Bell 7*.	7/21/61	11	MR–8	2/60	....	5:18
MA–4........	Robot........	9/13/61	8A	88–D	3/60	1/88:19	1:32:28
MS–1........	....	11/ 1/61	NA	....	Insert	....	....
MA–5........	"Enos" chimp.	11/29/61	9	93–D	3/60	2/88:26	3:04:38
MA–6........	Glenn: *Friendship 7*..	2/20/62	13	109–D	4/60	3/88:29	4:48:27
MA–7........	Carpenter: *Aurora 7*....	5/24/62	18	107–D	5/60	3/88:32	4:39:32
MA–8........	Schirra: *Sigma 7*.....	10/ 3/62	16	113–D	6/60	6/88:55	8:56:22
MA–9........	Cooper: *Faith 7*.....	5/15/63	20	130–D	8/60	22. 5/88:45	34:03:30

LJ = Little Joe
MA = Mercury-Atlas
MR = Mercury-Redstone
MS = Mercury-Scout

Beach Abort = Capsule escape rocket test
Big Joe = MA development flight
MR–BD = MR booster development

APPENDIX D

Flight duration, hr: min: sec	Apogee/ perigee, st. miles	Range, max., st. miles	Velocity max.- spa., fix. mph	Max. q, psf	Max. g	Primary objective	Re- sults SC/LV
0:05:25	2. 8	9	1, 780	1, 920	10	Max. q escape and sequence	S/P
0:15:28	116. 5	303	5, 134	580	11	Evaluate man-in- space	S
0:15:37	118. 3	302	5, 168	610	11. 1	Corroborate man-in- space	P/S
1:49:20	142. 1/98. 9	26, 047	17, 526	975	7. 7	S/C environmental control in orbit	P
0:00:43	. . . .	. . . .	. . . . . .	. . .	. . .	. . . .	F
3:20:59	147. 4/99. 5	50, 892	17, 530	1, 012	7. 7	Primate test of ECS in orbit	P/S
4:55:23	162. 2/100	75, 679	17, 544	982	7. 7	Evaluate man-in- orbit	S
4:56:05	166. 8/99. 9	76, 021	17, 549	967	7. 8	Corroborate man-in- orbit	S
9:13:11	175. 8/100	143, 983	17, 558	964	8. 1	Man-machine in orbit for 9 hours	S
34:19:49	165. 9/100. 3	546, 167	17, 547	974	7. 6	Manned 1-day mis- sion in orbit	S

S = Success
P = Partial
F = Failure

Appendix E
Personnel Growth

Date	Scientists and engineers [a]	Total
October 1958...	35	45
December 1958..	(175)	200
June 1959..	(225)	(370)
December 1959..	266	508
June 1960..	(300)	(580)
December 1960..	329	668
June 1961..	354	794
December 1961..	470	1152
June 1962..	799	1786
December 1962..	1254	2392
June 1963..	1514	3345

[a] Based on figures supplied by Mary K. Wood of NASA Headquarters Manpower Analysis Division.
( ) Interpolated figures.

Date	Mercury Program (NASA personnel) [a]
Space Task Group:	
January 1959...	150
July 1959...	350
January 1960..	500
July 1960...	550
January 1961..	680
July 1961...	770
Manned Spacecraft Center:	
January 1962..	850
July 1962...	670
January 1963..	500
July 1963...	400

[a] Based on figures supplied by Robert B. Merrifield of NASA–MSC Office of Long-Range Planning.

Appendix F
Project Mercury Cost Summaries

Precise costs directly attributable to any research and development program are very difficult to determine, and Project Mercury is no exception in this regard. Overhead and support costs accrued for several projects must be allocated and thus estimates rather than specifics are required. The total summary costs are official agency estimates as of February 28, 1966. Costs within the spacecraft manufacturer's contract are broken down in a second table, and a third details costs incurred by the Department of Defense in support of Project Mercury.

Summary Estimates of Costs
Project Mercury
[As of Feb. 28, 1966]

Mercury/1-Day Mission Projects:	
Spacecraft..	$143,413,000
Launch vehicle procurement...................................	82,847,000
Operations and support.......................................	49,298,000
Total project costs..	$275,558,000
Tracking and Data Acquisition:	
Operations and equipment.....................................	$71,900,000
Facilities..	53,200,000
Total TDA costs..	$125,100,000
Grand total costs..	$400,658,000

Contract NAS 5–59 With McDonnell Aircraft Corp.
Mercury Cost Breakdown
[As of Oct. 14, 1965]

Structure and Systems:	
Nonrecurring development	$40,219,000
Recurring cost (20 units)	49,354,000
Models and mockups	1,489,000
Ground-test program	887,000
Trainers	3,088,000
Thermal balance test program	5,712,000
Publications, specifications, and data	345,000
Launch support:	
St. Louis	1,187,000
Cape Kennedy	14,750,000
Spare parts	5,432,000
Aerospace ground equipment	9,951,000
Repairs and modification	1,049,000
1-day mission changes	9,337,000
Total	$142,800,000

Summary of DOD Support of Project Mercury
[through June 1963]

[Extracted from: "Final Report to the Secretary of Defense on Department of Defense Support of Project Mercury," approved by Maj. Gen. L. I. Davis, USAF, Sept. 11, 1963]

Agency	Type/level of support [a]	Actual costs (in thousand dollars)		
		NASA reimbursed	DOD absorbed	Total
AIR FORCE:				
Space Systems Division (SSD).	Atlas boosters, launch crews and facilities, engineering, aircraft support. 23 people plus contractors. 216 aircraft-hours.	73,862	1,351	75,213
AF Missile Test Center (AFMTC).	Operation of 3 network stations, launch support, assist in recovery. 173 people, 2,722 aircraft-hours.	6,569	5,652	12,221

[a] Average number of full-time people.

644

*Summary of DOD Support of Project Mercury—*Continued

(through June 1963)

Agency	Type/level of support [a]	Actual costs (in thousand dollars)		
		NASA reim- bursed	DOD absorbed	Total
Air Proving Ground Center (APGC).	Operation of 1 network station, assist in network training. 21 people, 551 aircraft-hours.	22	956	978
Air Force Communications Service (AFCS).	Communications engineering and installation; communicator deployment to contingency cites. 8 people.	140	201	341
Military Air Transport Service (MATS).	Airlift people and cargo.	1,040	69	1,109
Air Rescue Service (ARS).	Aircraft support to theater commanders; deploy forces for contingency recovery. 6,426 aircraft-hours.	1,063	260	1,323
Aeronautical Chart and Information Center (ACIC).	Cartographic Service. 10 people.	5	190	195
Tactical Air Command (TAC).	Aircraft support for contingency recovery. 546 aircraft-hours.	42	87	129
Air Defense Command (ADC).	Radar aircraft support. 245 aircraft-hours.	3	271	274
U.S. Air Force Europe (USAFE).	Deployment to remote sites for contingency recovery. 2,091 aircraft-hours.	720	279	999
Pacific Air Force (PACAF).	Deployment to remote sites for contingency recovery. 331 aircraft-hours.	362	189	551
Other.	Air Weather Service: weather surveillance and forecasting. AEDC and AFFTC: test facilities.	8	911	919
Total Air Force costs.		83,836	10,416	94,252
NAVY:				
Fleet Operations.	Astronaut and capsule recovery in planned areas. 1,441 ship-days, 4,044 aircraft-hours.	8,934	15,110	24,044
Pacific Missile Range (PMR).	Operation of 3 network stations; aircraft and tracking ship support. 144 people, 347 aircraft-hours, 170 ship-days.	3,321	4,720	8,041
Total Navy costs.		12,255	19,830	32,085

645

Agency	Type/level of support [a]	Actual costs (in thousand dollars)		
		NASA reim-bursed	DOD absorbed	Total
ARMY:				
White Sands Missile Range (WSMR).	Operate 2 network stations, 39 people.	962	247	1, 209
U.S. Army Europe (USAREUR).	Helicopter and pararescuemen support for contingency recovery. 107 Helo-hours.	117	78	195
Other.	LARC support, communications, test facilities, tracking-ship support.	1, 221	405	1, 626
Total Army costs.		2, 300	730	3, 030
BIOASTRONAUTICS (Army, Navy, Air Force):				
Operational.	Aeromedical monitors, recovery medical specialists, medical supplies, hospitals. 159 people average per mission.	497	1, 070	1, 567
Research and development.	Astronaut selection and training; laboratories.	981	1, 320	2, 301
Total bioastronautic costs.		1, 478	2, 390	3, 868
Air Force........................	....	83, 836	10, 416	94, 252
Navy............................	....	12, 255	19, 830	32, 085
Army...........................	....	2, 300	730	3, 030
Bioastronautics.................	....	1, 478	2, 390	3, 868
Total.		99, 869	33, 366	133, 235

Appendix G: Project Mercury Tracking Net

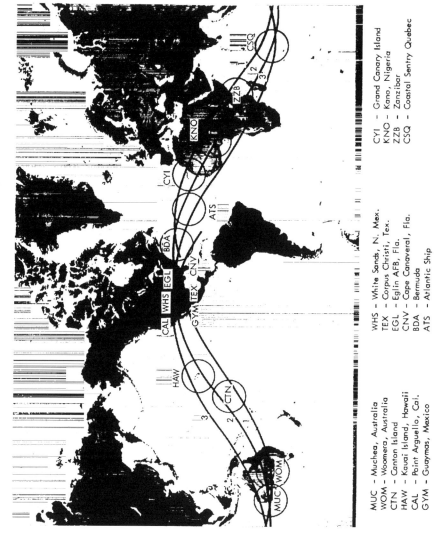

MUC – Muchea, Australia
WOM – Woomera, Australia
CTN – Canton Island
HAW – Kauai Island, Hawaii
CAL – Point Arguello, Cal.
GYM – Guaymas, Mexico

WHS – White Sands, N. Mex.
TEX – Corpus Christi, Tex.
EGL – Eglin AFB, Fla.
CNV – Cape Canaveral, Fla.
BDA – Bermuda
ATS – Atlantic Ship

CYI – Grand Canary Island
KNO – Kano, Nigeria
ZZB – Zanzibar
CSQ – Coastal Sentry Quebec

Ground Instrumentation Plan for Project Mercury

[For 3-orbit missions]

Station name	Coverage, passes	Radar S	Radar C	Telemetry reception	Communication (capsule)	Command control	Acquisition FA	Acquisition SA	Acquisition M	Voice	TTY	SSB radio	Timing
Canaveral	1, 2, 3	(X)	X	X	X	X	X	(X)		X	X		X
Grand Bahama	1, 2, 3		(X)	X	X				X	X	X		AMR
Grand Turk	1, 2, 3		X	X	X				X	X	X		AMR
Bermuda	1, 2, 3	X		X	X	X	X			X	X		X
Atlantic ship	1, 2, 3			X	X		X				X	X	X
Grand Canary Island	1, 2	X		X	X		X				X	X	X
Kano, Nigeria	1, 2			X	X						X	X	X
Zanzibar	1, 2			X	X			X			X	X	X
Indian Ocean ship	1, 2, 3	X		X	X		X	X			X	X	X
Muchea, Australia	1, 2, 3			X	X	X	X				X	X	X
Woomera, Australia	1, 2		X	X	X		X			X	X		X
Canton Island	1, 2			X	X		X	X			X		X
Kauai Island, Hawaii	2, 3	X	X	X	X	X	X			X	X		X
Point Arguello, Calif.	2, 3	X	X	X	X	X	X			X	X		X
Guaymas, Mexico	1, 2, 3	X		X	X	X	X			X	X		X
White Sands, N. Mex.	1, 2, 3		X				X			X	X		X
Corpus Christi, Tex.	1, 2, 3	X					X			X	X		X
Eglin, Fla.	1, 2, 3	(*)	X	X	X		X			X	X		X
Goddard SFC						Ground communications							

FA = Fully automatic.
M = Manual.
*MPQ–31.

SA = Semiautomatic.
SSB = Single side band.
TTY = Telemetry.

Index

A–4, 16, 17, 519 fn 45
A–7, 181, 294
A–9, 519 fn 45
AASCS. *See under* Alternate Attitude Spacecraft Control System
AASS. *See under* Automatic Abort Sensing System
Abbott, Ira H. A., 81, 90, 114
Abbot Committee, 99
Abelson, Philip H., 491
Ablating materials, 63, 64, 87, 126, 127, 461
Ablation (*see also* Heating, aerodynamic), 63–66, 80, 93, 95, 127, 128, 139, 140, 157, 204, 322, 324, 389, 407
Able (monkey) (*see also* Animals in space program), 156
ABMA. *See under* U.S. Army Ballistic Missile Agency
Abort, 92
Abort Sensing and Implementation System (ASIS), 176, 188, 189, 265, 320, 321, 331, 384
Abort systems (*see also under* Spacecraft), 338
Acceleration stress (*see also under* Centrifuges), 36–46 passim, 80, 81, 96, 97, 120, 143, 168, 204, 231, 253, 369, 378, 404, 405
Air Force "ground rule," 97, 120
Acceptance checkout equipment (ACE), 508
ACS. *See under* Attitude control system
Adam, Project, 100, 101, 105, 123, 171, 172, 177, 263, 537 fn 82
Advanced Research Projects Agency (ARPA), 79, 82, 90–93, 97–100, 106, 111, 116, 117, 120, 122, 126, 136, 148, 156, 265, 542 fn 49, 548 fn 7
Advisory Committee on Government Organization, 82, 89
Aerobee, 19, 20, 29, 37–40, 49
Aerobee-Hi, 20
Aerodynamic heating. *See under* Heating, aerodynamic
Aerodynamic stresses, 60
Aerojet-General Corp., 395
Aeromedical Field Laboratory. *See under* U.S. Air Force
Aeromedical Laboratory, Wright Air Development Center. *See under* U.S. Air Force
"Aeronauts," 160
Aeronautics and Astronautics Coordinating Board, 284
Aeronutronic Division. *See under* Ford Motor Co.
Aerospace Corp., 255, 272, 278, 299, 300, 491, 539 fn 18, 585 fn 6, 588 fn 41, 591 fn 18

Aerospace Medical Laboratory, Wright Air Development Center. *See under* U.S. Air Force
Aerospace medicine (*see also* U.S. Air Force: Aeromedical Field Laboratory, Air Force School of Aviation Medicine, Wright Air Development Center: Aeromedical Laboratory, Aerospace Medical Laboratory; U.S. Navy: Aviation Medical Acceleration Laboratory, Naval School of Aviation Medicine), 34, 41, 524 fn 4
acceleration stress, 37–43 passim, 46, 315, 316, 369, 378, 447
aeroembolism, 351
aeropause concept, 34, 116
anoxia, 35
"bends," 231, 351
bioinstrumentation, 416
blackout, 39, 40, 46
bladder function, 38, 39
blood pressure, 39, 416, 434, 484, 496
coordination loss, 39
dehydration, 433
disorientation, 37, 38, 39, 357, 414, 443, 478
dysbarism, 228, 231
eating and drinking in flight, 38, 39, 449, 478, 500
exercise in flight, 480
fatigue, 484
hyperventilation, 228
hypoxia, 228, 231
impact forces, 40
isolation studies, 48
medical monitoring, 80, 216, 449, 469
medication in flight, 418
noise, 231
nausea, 39, 378, 414, 427, 433
oculo-agravic illusion, 38
orthostatic hypotension, 501, 508
postflight examinations, 484
reaction to space flight, 39, 427
redout, 39, 40
research rockets, 19, 29
temperature, 47, 433, 434, 449, 496
timed urine collection, 433
vibration, 231, 447
water immersion research, 42, 43
weightlessness, 36–42 passim, 52, 315, 316, 414, 448, 478
Africa, 220, 331, 335, 339, 399, 426, 435, 445, 474, 480, 495, 497
African, 499
Agena, 79, 462

INDEX

Checkout operations. *See under* Spacecraft Checkout Operations *and* Preflight Checkout Operations

Chenoweth, J. Edgar, 332

Chernushka (dog), 325

"Cherry Picker," 330

Chesapeake Bay, 85, 105

Chew, John L., 420, 457, 583 fn 49, 586 fn 16, 587 fn 19, 597 fn 106

Chicago, Ill., 47

"Chicken switch," 473

Chilton, Robert G., 116, 195, 196, 197, 237, 552 fn 60, 607

Chimpanzees *(see also under names of each)*, 40, 42, 177, 210, 292, 306, 310–318 passim, 331, 335, 346, 381, 390, 393, 397, 399–408 passim

Chinese, 13

Chop, Albert M., xv, 607

Christman, H. T., 398

Chrysler Corp., 21, 123, 255, 257

Chute. *See under* Parachute

Cincinnati Testing and Research Laboratory (CTL), 139, 140

Civil Aeronautics Board, 268

Civilian-Military Liaison Committee (CMLC), 98, 135

Clamann, Hans-Georg, 34, 524 fn 5, 526 fn 44

Clark, David, Co., 228

Clark, J. E., 375

Clark University, 14

Clarke, Arthur C., 281

Clarke, Stuart H., 440

Clauser, Milton V., 578 fn 81

Clear Lake, Tex., 390, 391

Clements, Henry E., 297, 575 fn 37, 607

Cleveland, O., 9, 39, 66, 98, 99, 113, 125, 139, 140, 201, 244, 245

Clifton, Robert G., 489

Clocks *(see also under* Spacecraft), 265

Coastal Sentry Quebec, 595 fn 74

Cobra, 520 fn 52

Cocoa Beach, Fla., 204, 334, 420, 421, 501

Code Sportif, 281

Cohen, Jack, 184, 546 fn 56

Cohn, Stanley H., 184

Colchagoff, George D., 70, 531 fn 42, 533 fn 13, 536 fn 75, 537 fn 89, 607

Coler, Charles J., 607

Colley, Russell M., 230, 231

Collins, Carter C., 43, 46, 96, 120, 148, 526 fn 39

Collins Radio Co., 157, 197, 260, 568 fn 46

Colorado, 332

Columbus, O., 288

Committee on Aerodynamics. *See under* National Advisory Committee for Aeronautics

Committee on Scientific Tasks and Training for Man-in-Space, Ad Hoc (MSC), 443

Committee on Scientific Tasks and Training for Man-in-Space, Ad Hoc (NASA), 466, 489

Communications *(see also under* Spacecraft), 65, 102, 111, 168

Compressibility Research Division. *See under* Langley Memorial Aeronautical Laboratory

Computers *(see also under* Spacecraft), 60, 61, 218, 220, 315, 337, 387, 402, 403, 404, 426

Concurrency, 25

Conference on High-Speed Aerodynamics, 86, 87, 89, 95, 102

Congress of the United States, v, 6, 8, 10, 18, 19, 34, 52, 53, 77, 82, 83, 85, 89, 90, 93, 97, 98, 101, 102, 109, 134, 154, 168, 178, 224, 264, 279, 285, 304, 320, 325, 335, 349, 362–363, 364, 377, 378, 390, 437 illus, 438, 460, 501, 502 illus, 507, 582 fn 35, 583 fn 40, 600 fn 39

Conrad, Charles, Jr., 601 fn 50

Consolidated Vultee Aircraft Corp., 22 designs Atlas, 22

Control and stabilization *(see also under* Spacecraft), 56, 57, 58, 59

Control Center. *See under* Mercury Control Center

Control systems *(see also under* Spacecraft), 66

Convair/Astronautics Division (CV/A) *(see also under* General Dynamics Corp.), 22, 23, 25, 26, 60, 61, 73, 90, 91, 92, 93, 100, 118, 121, 123, 126, 157, 159, 175, 180, 187, 188, 189, 200, 208, 235, 237, 241, 255, 257, 272, 276, 278, 299, 300, 307, 318, 321, 383, 402, 408, 446, 467, 521 fn 67, 551 fn 45, 563 fn 83

Atlas reentry problem, 60, 61, 259

awarded ICBM contract, 23

develops pressurized airframe, 25

Minimum Space Vehicle (with Avco), 91, 92

preferred "Atlas-Mercury," 272

Cook, James, 400

Cooper, L. Gordon, Jr. *(see also under* Astronaut), 160, 164, 164 illus, 173 illus, 229 illus, 235, 236 illus, 237, 289, 345, 351, 377, 402, 406, 414, 428, 460, 485 illus, 489–503 passim, 498 illus, 502 illus, 508, 583 fn 46, 586 fn 15

Cooper, Trudy, 502 illus

Copernican theory, 511

Copernicus, Nicolaus, 5

Corcoran, Donald M., 565 fn 19

Cornell University, vi, 538 fn 9

Corning Glass Works, 367

Corning, N.Y., 367

Corpas, Louis L., 244

Corpus Christi, Tex., 217, 386, 401, 432, 587 fn 20

Cosmic radiation, 49, 50, 51, 52

Cosmic rays, 49, 50, 51, 52, 128, 168

Cosmic Ship No. 1, 300

Cosmic Ship No. 4 *(Korabl Sputnik IV)*, 325

Cosmic Ship No. 5 *(Korabl Sputnik V)*, 331

Cosmic Ship No. 6 *(Korabl Sputnik VI)*. *See Vostok I*

Cosmonaut *(see also under name of each)*, 333

Coston, Charles L., 607

Costs of space programs, 77

Couch *(see also under* Spacecraft), 42, 43, 46, 80, 96, 97, 143, 273, 288, 348, 351, 359, 367, 370, 526 fn 39

Covinsky, N. E., 269

INDEX

INDEX

Made in the USA
San Bernardino, CA
11 December 2015